The Oxford Colour Portuguese Dictionary

The Oxford Colour Portuguese Dictionary

PORTUGUESE–ENGLISH
Compiled by John Whitlam

ENGLISH–PORTUGUESE
Compiled by Lia Correia Raitt

OXFORD
UNIVERSITY PRESS

OXFORD
UNIVERSITY PRESS

Great Clarendon Street, Oxford OX2 6DP

Oxford University Press is a department of the University of Oxford.
It furthers the University's objective of excellence in research, scholarship,
and education by publishing worldwide in

Oxford New York
Auckland Cape Town Dar es Salaam Hong Kong Karachi Kuala Lumpur
Madrid Melbourne Mexico City Nairobi New Delhi Shanghai Taipei Toronto

With offices in
Argentina Austria Brazil Chile Czech Republic France Greece
Guatemala Hungary Italy Japan South Korea Poland Portugal
Singapore Switzerland Thailand Turkey Ukraine Vietnam

Oxford is a registered trade mark of Oxford University Press
in the UK and in certain other countries

Published in the United States
by Oxford University Press

First published as the Portuguese Minidictionary, 1996
First published under the title The Oxford Paperback Portuguese Dictionary, 1996
First published under the title The Oxford Colour Portuguese Dictionary, 1999

British Library Cataloguing in Publication Data

Data available

Library of Congress Cataloging in Publication Data

Data available

ISBN-13: 978-0-19-860386-3

10 9 8

Typeset in Nimrod and Arial
by Pure Tech India Ltd
Printed in China

Contents/Indice

Preface/Prefácio   vi–vii

Introduction/Introdução   viii–ix

Proprietary terms/Nomes comerciais   x

Pronunciation/Pronúncia

   Portuguese/Português   xi–xv

   English/Inglês   xvi–xvii

European Portuguese   xviii–xix

Abbreviations/Abreviaturas   xx–xxii

Portuguese-English   **1–180**
Português-Inglês

English-Portuguese   **181–430**
Inglês-Português

Portuguese verbs/Verbos portugueses   431–436

Preface

The Oxford Colour Portuguese Dictionary has been written for speakers of both Portuguese and English and contains the most useful words and expressions in use today.

The dictionary provides a handy and comprehensive reference work for tourists, students, and business people who require quick and reliable answers to their translation needs.

Thanks are due to: Dr John Sykes, Prof. A. W. Raitt, Commander Virgílio Correia, Marcelo Affonso, Eng. Pedro Carvalho, Eng. Vasco Carvalho, Dr Iva Correia, Dr Ida Reis de Carvalho, Eng. J. Reis de Carvalho, Prof. A. Falcão, Bishop Manuel Falcão, Dr M. Luísa Falcão, Prof. J. Ferraz, Prof. M. de Lourdes Ferraz, Drs Ana and Jorge Fonseca, Mr Robert Howes, Irene Lakhani, Eng. Hugo Pires, Prof. M. Kaura Pires, Dr M. Alexandre Pires, Ambassador L. Pazos Alonso, Dr Teresa Pinto Pereira, Dr Isabel Tully, Carlos Wallenstein, Ligia Xavier, and Dr H. Martins and the members of his Mesa Lusófona at St Antony's College, Oxford.

Prefácio

O *Oxford Colour Portuguese Dictionary* foi escrito por pessoas de língua portuguesa e inglesa, e contém as palavras e expressões mais úteis em uso atualmente.

O dicionário constitui uma obra de referência prática e abrangente para turistas, estudantes e pessoas de negócios que necessitam de respostas rápidas e confiáveis para as suas traduções.

Agradecimentos a: Dr John Sykes, Prof. A. W. Raitt, Comandante Virgílio Correia, Marcelo Affonso, Eng. Pedro Carvalho, Eng. Vasco Carvalho, Dr Iva Correia, Dr Ida Reis de Carvalho, Eng. J. Reis de Carvalho, Prof. A. Falcão, Bispo Manuel Falcão, Dr M. Luísa Falcão, Prof. J. Ferraz, Prof. M. de Lourdes Ferraz, Drs Ana e Jorge Fonseca, Mr Robert Howes, Eng. Hugo Pires, Prof. M. Laura Pires, Dr M. Alexandre Pires, Embaixador L. Pazos Alonso, Dr Teresa Pinto Pereira, Dr Isabel Tully, Carlos Wallenstein, e Dr H. Martins e os membros de sua Mesa Lusófona do St Antony's College, em Oxford.

Introduction

The swung dash (~) is used to replace a headword, or that part of a headword preceding the vertical bar (|).

In both English and Portuguese, only irregular plural forms are given. Plural forms of Portuguese nouns and adjectives ending in a single vowel are formed by adding an *s* (e.g. *livro, livros*). Those ending in *n, r, s* where the stress falls on the final syllable, and *z*, add *es* (e.g. *mulher, mulheres, falaz, falazes*). Nouns and adjectives ending in *m* change the final *m* to *ns* (e.g. *homem, homens, bom, bons*). Most of those ending in *ão* change their ending to *ões* (e.g. *estação, estações*).

Portuguese nouns and adjectives ending in an unstressed *o* form the feminine by changing the *o* to *a* (e.g. *belo, bela*). Those ending in *or* become *ora* (e.g. *trabalhador, trabalhadora*). All other masculine–feminine changes are shown at the main headword.

English and Portuguese pronunciation is given by means of the International Phonetic Alphabet. It is shown for all headwords, and for those derived words whose pronunciation is not easily deduced from that of a headword.

Portuguese verb tables will be found in the appendix.

Introdução

O sinal (∼) é usado para substituir o verbete, ou parte deste precedendo a barra vertical (|).

Tanto em inglês como em português, somente as formas irregulares do plural são dadas. As formas regulares do plural dos substantivos ingleses recebem um *s* (ex. *teacher, teachers*), ou *es* quando terminarem em *ch, sh, s, ss, us, x* ou *z* (ex. *sash, sashes*). Os substantivos terminados em *y* e precedidos por uma consoante, mudam no plural para *ies* (ex. *baby, babies*).

O passado e o particípio passado dos verbos regulares ingleses são formados pelo acréscimo de *ed* á forma infinitiva (ex. *last, lasted*). Os verbos terminados em *e* recebem *d* (ex. *move, moved*). Aqueles terminados em *y* têm o *y* substituído por *ied* (*carry, carried*). As formas irregulares dos verbos aparecem no dicionário em ordem alfabética, remetidas à forma infinitiva, e também, na lista de verbos no apêndice.

As pronúncias inglesa e portuguesa são dadas em acordo com o Alfabeto Fonético Internacional. A pronúncia é dada para todos os verbetes, assim como para aquelas palavras derivadas cuja pronúncia não seja facilmente deduzida a partir do verbete.

Proprietary terms

This dictionary includes some words which are, or are asserted to be, proprietary names or trade marks. Their inclusion does not imply that they have acquired for legal purposes a non-proprietary or general significance, nor is any other judgement implied concerning their legal status. In cases where the editor has some evidence that a word is used as a proprietary name or trade mark this is indicated by the label *propr*, but no judgement concerning the legal status of such words is made or implied thereby.

Nomes comerciais

Este dicionário inclui algumas palavras que são, ou acredita-se ser, nomes comerciais ou marcas registradas. A sua inclusão no dicionário não implica que elas tenham adquirido para fins legais um significado geral ou não-comercial, assim como não afeta em nenhum dos conceitos implícitos o seu status legal.

Nos casos em que o editor tenha prova suficiente de que uma palavra seja usada como um nome comercial ou marca registrada, este emprego é indicado pela etiqueta *propr*, mas nenhuma apreciação relativa ao status legal de tais palavras é feita ou sugerida por esta indicação.

Portuguese pronunciation

Vowels and Diphthongs

a, à, á, â	/ã/	cham*am*, *a*mbos, *a*ntes	1) before *m* at the end of a word, or before *m* or *n* and another consonant, is nasalized
	/a/	*a*b*a*, *à*, *a*col*á*, des*â*nimo	2) in other positions is like *a* in English r*a*ther
ã	/ã/	irm*ã*	is nasalized
e	/ẽ/	s*e*m, v*e*nda	1) before *m* at the end of a word, or before *m* or *n* and another consonant, is nasalized
	/i/	art*e*	2) at the end of a word is like *y* in English happ*y*
	/e/	m*e*nas	3) in other positions is like *e* in English th*e*y
é	/ɛ/	art*é*ria	is like *e* in English g*e*t
ê	/e/	f*ê*mur	is like *e* in English th*e*y
i	/ĩ/	s*i*m, v*i*ndo	1) before *m* at the end of a word, or before *m* or *n* and another consonant, is nasalized
	/i/	f*i*la	2) in other positions is like *ee* in English s*ee*
o	/õ/	c*o*m, s*o*mbra, *o*nda	1) before *m* at the end of a word, or before *m* or *n* and another consonant, is nasalized
	/u/	muit*o*	2) at the end of a word, unstressed, is like *u* in English r*u*le

	/o/	com*o*ver	3) in other positions, unstressed, is like *o* in English p*o*le
	/o/	bob*o*	4) stressed, is like *o* in English p*o*le or *o* in sh*o*p
	/ɔ/	l*o*ja	
ó	/ɔ/	*ó*pera	is like *o* in English p*o*le
ô	/o/	t*ô*nica	is like *o* in English p*o*le
u, ú		g*u*erra, g*u*isado, q*u*e, q*u*ilo	1) is silent in *gue*, and *gui*, *que*, *qui*
	/u/	m*u*la, p*ú*rp*u*ra	2) in other positions is like *u* in English r*u*le
ü gü	/gw/	ung*ü*ento	in the combinations *güe* and *güi* is like *g* in English *g*ot, followed by English *w*
	/kw/	tranq*ü*ilo	in the combinations *qüe* and *qüi* is like *qu* in English *qu*een
ãe	/ãj/	m*ãe*, p*ãe*s, alem*ãe*s	is like *y* in English b*y*, but nasalized
ai	/aj/	v*ai*, p*ai*, s*ai*, c*ai*ta	is like *y* in English b*y*
ao, au	/aw/	*ao*s, *au*todefesa	is like *ow* in English h*ow*
ão	/ãw/	n*ão*	is like *ow* in English h*ow*, but nasalized
ei	/ej/	l*ei*	is like *ey* in English th*ey*
eu	/ew/	d*eu*s, fl*eu*gma	both vowels pronounced separately
oẽ	/õj/	eleiç*õe*s	is like *oi* in English c*oi*n, but nasalized
oi	/oj/	n*oi*te	is like *oi* in English c*oi*n
ou	/o/	p*ou*co	is like *o* in English p*o*le

Consonants

b	/b/	*b*anho	is like *b* in English *b*all
c	/s/	*c*inza, *c*em	1) before *e* or *i* is like *s* in English *s*it
	/k/	*c*asa	2) in other positions is like *c* in English *c*at
ç	/s/	estaçã*o*	is like *s* in English *s*it
ch	/ʃ/	*ch*á	is like *sh* in English *sh*out
d	/dʒ/	*d*izer, don*d*e	1) before *i* or final unstressed *e* is like *j* in English *j*oin
	/d/	*d*ar	2) in other positions is like *d* in English *d*og
f	/f/	*f*alar	is like *f* in English *f*all
g	/ʒ/	a*g*ente, *g*iro	1) before *e* or *i* is like *s* in English vi*s*ion
	/g/	*g*ato	2) in other positions is like *g* in English *g*et
h		*h*aver	is silent in Portuguese, but see *ch*, *lh*, *nh*
j	/ʒ/	*j*unta	is like *s* in English vi*s*ion
k	/k/	*k*it	is like English *k* in *k*ey
l	/w/	fa*l*ta	1) between a vowel and a consonant, or following a vowel at the end of a word, is like *w* in English *w*ater
	/l/	*l*ata	2) in other positions is like *l* in English *l*ike
l	/ʎ/	ca*l*har	is like *ll*i in English mi*lli*on
m		a*m*bas/ãbuʃ/ co*m* /kõ/	1) between a vowel and a consonant, or after a vowel at the end of a word, *m* nasalizes the preceding vowel

	/m/	*m*ato, *m*ão	2) in other positions is like *m* in English *m*other
n		ci*n*ʒa /'sĩza/	1) between a vowel and a consonant, *n* nasalizes the preceding vowel
	/n/	be*n*igno	2) in other positions is like *n* in English *n*ear
nh	/ɲ/	ba*nh*o	is like *ni* in English opi*ni*on
p	/p/	*p*az	is like *p* in English *p*oor
q	/k/	*q*ue, in*q*uieto	1) *qu* before *e* or *i* is like English *k*
	/kw/	*q*uase, *q*uórum	2) *qu* before *a* or *o*, or *qü* before *e* or *i*, is like *qu* in English *qu*een
r	/r/	apa*r*ato, go*r*do	1) between two vowels, or between a vowel and a consonant, is trilled
	/x/	*r*ato, ga*rr*a, mel*r*o, gen*r*o, Is*r*ael	2) at the beginning of a word, or in *rr*, or after *l*, *n*, or *s*, is like *ch* in Scottish lo*ch*
s	/ʃ/	depoi*s*	at the end of a word is like *sh* in English *sh*oot
	/z/	a*s*a, de*s*de, abi*s*mo, I*s*rael	2) between two vowels, or before *b, d, g, l, m, n, r, v,* is like *z* in English *z*ebra
	/s/	*s*uave	3) in other positions is like *s* in English *s*it
t	/tʃ/	*t*io, an*t*es	1) before *i* or final unstressed *e* is like *ch* in English *ch*eese
	/tʃi/	ki*t*	2) at the end of a word is like *chy* in English it*chy*

	/t/	a*t*ar	3) in other positions is like *t* in English *t*ap
v	/v/	lu*v*a	is like *v* in English *v*ain
w	/u/	*w*att	is shorter than English *w*
x	/z/	e*x*ato, e*x*emplo	1) in the prefix *ex* before a vowel, is pronounced like *z* in *z*ero
	/ʃ/	*x*ícara, bai*x*o, pei*x*e, frou*x*o	2) at the beginning of a word or after *ai*, *ei* or *ou*, is pronounced like *sh* in *sh*ow
	/s/	e*x*plodir,	3) is like *s* in English au*x*iliar*s*it
	/ks/	a*x*ila, fi*x*o	4) is like *x* in English e*x*it
			5) in the combination *xce*, *xci*, *x* is not pronounced in Portuguese e.g. exce-lente, e*x*citar
z	/s/	fala*z*	1) at the end of a word, is like *s* in English *s*it
	/z/	di*z*er	2) in other positions, is like English *z*

Pronuncia Inglesa

Vogals e Ditongos

/iː/	*see*, t*ea*	como *i* em g*i*ro
/ɪ/	s*i*t, happ*y*	é um som mais breve do que *i* em l*i*
/e/	s*e*t	como *e* em t*é*pido
/æ/	h*a*t	é um som mais breve do que *a* em *a*mor
/ɑː/	*a*rm, c*a*lm	como *a* em c*a*rtaz
/ɒ/	g*o*t	como *o* em ex*ó*tico
/ɔː/	s*a*w, m*o*re	como *o* em c*o*rte
/ʊ/	p*u*t, l*oo*k	como *u* em m*u*rro
/uː/	t*oo*, d*ue*	como *u* em d*u*ro
/ʌ/	c*u*p, s*o*me	como *a* em p*a*no
/ɜː/	f*i*rm, f*u*r	como *e* em *e*nxerto
/ə/	*a*go, weath*er*	como *e* no português europeu part*e*
/eɪ/	p*a*ge, p*ai*n, p*ay*	como *ei* em l*ei*te
/əʊ/	h*o*me, r*oa*m	é um som mais longo do que *o* em c*o*ma
/aɪ/	f*i*ne, b*y*, g*uy*	como *ai* em s*ai*
/aɪə/	f*i*re, t*y*re	como *ai* em s*ai* seguido por /ə/
/aʊ/	n*ow*, sh*ou*t	como *au* em *au*la
/aʊə/	h*ou*r, fl*ow*er	como *au* em *au*la seguido por /ə/
/ɔɪ/	j*oi*n, b*oy*	como *oi* em d*ói*
/ɪə/	d*ear*, h*ere*, b*eer*	como *ia* em d*ia*
/eə/	h*air*, c*are*, b*ear*, th*ere*	como *e* em et*é*reo
/ʊə/	p*oor*, d*uring*	como *ua* em s*ua*

Consoantes

/p/	sna*p*	como *p* em *p*ato
/b/	*b*ath	como *b* em *b*ala
/t/	*t*ap	como *t* em *t*ela
/d/	*d*ip	como *d* em *d*ar
/k/	*c*at, *k*ite, stoma*ch*, pi*que*	como *c* em *c*asa
/ks/	e*x*ercise	como *x* em a*x*ila
/g/	*g*ot	como *g* em *g*ato
/tʃ/	*ch*in	como *t* em *t*io
/dʒ/	*J*une, *g*eneral, ju*dg*e	como *d* em *d*izer
/f/	*f*all	como *f* em *f*aca
/v/	*v*ine, o*f*	como *v* em *v*aca
/θ/	*th*in, mo*th*	não tem equivalente, soa como um *s* entre os dentes
/ð/	*th*is	não tem equivalente, soa como um *z* entre os dentes
/s/	*s*o, voi*c*e	como *s* em *s*uave
/z/	*z*oo, ro*s*e	como *z* em fa*z*er
/ʃ/	*sh*e, lun*ch*	como *ch* em *ch*egar
/ʒ/	mea*s*ure, vi*s*ion	como *j* em *j*amais
/h/	*h*ow	*h* aspirado
/m/	*m*an	como *m* em *m*ala
/n/	*n*one	como *n* em *n*ada
/ŋ/	si*ng*	como *n* em ci*n*to
/l/	*l*eg	como *l* em *l*uva
/r/	*r*ed, *w*rite	como *r* em ca*r*a
/j/	*y*es, *y*oke	como *i* em *i*oga
/w/	*w*eather, s*w*itch	como *u* ég*u*a

European Portuguese

Brazilian Portuguese, which is used in this dictionary, differs in a number of respects from that used in Portugal and the rest of the Portuguese-speaking world. These differences affect both spelling and pronunciation. Spelling variations appear on the Portuguese–English side. In so far as they affect pronunciation, the main variants are:

Brazilian Portuguese often omits the letters *b*, *c*, *m*, and *p*, which are retained by European Portuguese:

	Brazilian	**European**
b	su*b*til	su*b*til
c	a*c*ção	a*c*ção
	ato	a*c*to
	elétrico	elé*c*trico
m	inde*m*nizar	inde*m*nizar
p	ba*p*tismo	ba*p*tismo
	exce*p*ção	exce*p*ção

Letters *c* and *p* in such variant forms are usually silent, hence acto /'atu/,ba'ptismo /bati3mu/. However, *c* is pronounced in the combination *ect*, hence eléctrico /i'lektriku/.

The combinations *gü* and *qü* become *gu* and *qu*:

	Brazilian	**European**
	un*gü*ento	un*gu*ento
	tran*qü*ilo	tran*qu*ilo

However, they are still pronounced /gw/ and /kw/ respectively.

The other main differences in pronunciation are:

| d | /d/ | *d*ar, *d*izer, bal*d*e, *d*onde | 1) at the beginning of a word, or after *l*, or *n*, is like *d* in English *d*og |

/ð/	ci*d*a*d*e, me*d*roso		2) in other positions is a sound between *d* in English *d*og and *th* in English *th*is
e	/ə/	art*e*	at the end of a word, is like *e* in English quarr*e*l
r	/rr/	*r*ato, ga*rr*a, mel*r*o, gen*r*o, Is*r*ael, guel*r*a, ten*r*o, is*r*aelense	at the beginning of a word, or in *rr*, or after *l*, *n*, or *s*, is strongly trilled
s	/ʃ/	depoi*s*, a*s*co, ra*s*par, co*s*tura	1) at the end of a word, or before *c*, *f*, *p*, *qu*, or *t*, is like English *sh*
	/ʒ/	de*s*de, Islã abi*s*mo, I*s*rael	2) before *b*, *d*, *g*, *l*, *m*, *n*, *r*, or *v* is like *s* in English vi*s*ion
t	/t/	a*t*ar, an*t*es, *t*io	is like *t* in English *t*ap
z	/ʃ/	fala*z*	at the end of a word, is like *sh* in English *sh*ake

Abbreviations/Abreviaturas

adjective	a	adjetivo
abbreviation	abbr/abr	abreviatura
something	aco	alguma coisa
adverb	adv	advérbio
somebody, someone	alg	algúem
article	art	artigo
American (English)	Amer	(inglês) americano
anatomy	anat	anatomia
architecture	arquit	arquitetura
astrology	astr/astrol	astrologia
motoring	auto	automobilismo
aviation	aviat	aviação
Brazilian Portuguese	B	português do Brasil
biology	biol	biologia
botany	bot	botânica
Brazilian Portuguese	Bras	português do Brasil
cinema	cine	cinema
colloquial	colloq	coloquial
commerce	comm/com	comércio
computing	comput	computação
conjunction	conj	conjunção
cookery	culin	cozinha
electricity	electr/eletr	eletricidade
feminine	f	feminina
familiar	fam	familiar
figurative	fig	figurativo
geography	geog	geografia

grammar	gramm/gram	gramática
infinitive	inf	infinitivo
interjection	int	interjeição
interrogative	interr	interrogativo
invariable	invar	invariável
legal, law	jur/jurid	jurídico
language	lang	linguagem
literal	lit	literal
masculine	m	masculino
mathematics	mat	matemática
mechanics	mech	mecânica
medicine	med	medicina
military	mil	militar
music	mus	música
noun	n	substantivo
nautical	naut	náutico
negative	neg	negativo
oneself	o.s.	se, si mesmo
European Portuguese	P	português de Portugal
pejorative	pej	pejorativo
philosophy	phil	filosofia
plural	pl	plural
politics	pol	política
European Portuguese	Port	português de Portugal
past participle	pp	particípio passado
prefix	pref	prefixo
preposition	prep	preposição
present	pres	presente
present participle	pres p	particípio presente
pronoun	pron	pronome

psychology	psych/psic	psicologia
past tense	pt	pretérito
relative	rel	relativo
religion	relig	religião
somebody	sb	alguém
singular	sing	singular
slang	sl	gíria
someone	s.o.	alguém
something	sth	alguma coisa
subjunctive	subj	subjuntivo
technology	techn/tecn	tecnologia
theatre	theat/teat	teatro
television	TV	televisão
university	univ	universidade
auxiliary verb	v aux	verbo auxiliar
intransitive verb	vi	verbo intransitivo
pronominal verb	vpr	verbo pronominal
transitive verb	vt	verbo transitivo
transitive & intransitive verb	vt/i	verbo transitivo e intransitivo

PORTUGUÊS-INGLÊS
PORTUGUESE-ENGLISH

A

a¹ /a/ *artigo* the □ *pron* (*mulher*) her; (*coisa*) it; (*você*) you

a² /a/ *prep* (*para*) to; (*em*) at; **às 3 horas** at 3 o'clock; **à noite** at night; **a lápis** in pencil; **a mão** by hand

à /a/ = a² + a¹

aba /'aba/ *f* (*de chapéu*) brim; (*de camisa*) tail; (*de mesa*) flap

abacate /aba'katʃi/ *m* avocado (pear)

abacaxi /abaka'ʃi/ *m* pineapple; (*fam: problema*) pain, headache

aba|de /a'badʒi/ *m* abbot; ~dia *f* abbey

aba|fado /aba'fadu/ *a* (*tempo*) humid, close; (*quarto*) stuffy; ~far *vt* (*asfixiar*) stifle; muffle <*som*>; smother <*fogo*>; suppress <*informação*>; cover up <*escândalo, assunto*>

abagunçar /abagu'sar/ *vt* mess up

abai|xar /aba'ʃar/ *vt* lower; turn down <*som, rádio*>□ *vi* ~se-bend down

abaixo /a'baʃu/ *adv* down; ~ de below; mais ~ further down; ~-assinado *m* petition

abajur /aba'ʒur/ *m* (*quebra-luz*) lampshade; (*lâmpada*) (table) lamp

aba|lar /aba'lar/ *vt* shake; (*fig*) shock; ~lar-se *vpr* be shocked, be shaken; ~lo *m* shock

abanar /aba'nar/ *vt* shake, wave; wag <*rabo*>; (*com leque*) fan

abando|nar /abãdo'nar/ *vt* abandon; (*deixar*) leave; ~no /o/ *m* abandonment; (*estado*) neglect

abarcar /abar'kar/ *vt* comprise, cover

abarro|tado /abaxo'tadu/ *a* crammed full; (*lotado*) crowded, packed; ~tar *vt* cram full, stuff

abastado /abas'tadu/ *a* wealthy

abaste|cer /abaste'ser/ *vt* supply; fuel <*motor*>; fill up (with petrol) <*carro*>; refuel <*avião*>; ~cimento *m* supply; (*de carro, avião*) refuelling

aba|ter /aba'ter/ *vt* knock down; cut down, fell <*árvore*>; shoot down <*avião, ave*>; slaughter <*gado*>; knock down, cut <*preço*>; ~ter alg <*trabalho*> get s.o. down, wear s.o. out; <*má notícia*> sadden s.o.; <*doença*> lay s.o. low, knock the stuffing out of s.o.; ~tido *a* dispirited, dejected; <*cara*> haggard, worn;

~timento *m* dejection; (*de preço*) reduction

abaulado /abaw'ladu/ *a* convex; <*estrada*> cambered

abcesso /ab'sɛsu/ *m* (*Port*) *veja* abscesso

abdi|cação /abidʒika'sãw/ *f* abdication; ~car *vt/i* abdicate

abdômen /abi'dome/ *m* abdomen

abecedário /abese'dariu/ *m* alphabet, ABC

abeirar-se /abe'rarsi/ *vr* draw near

abe|lha /a'beʎa/ *f* bee; ~lhudo *a* inquisitive, nosy

abençoar /abẽso'ar/ *vt* bless

aber|to /a'bɛrtu/ *pp de* abrir □ *a* open; <*céu*> clear; <*gás, torneira*> on; <*sinal*> green; ~tura *f* opening; (*foto*) aperture; (*pol*) liberalization

abeto /a'betu/ *m* fir (tree)

abis|mado /abiz'madu/ *a* astonished; ~mo *m* abyss

abjeto /abi'ʒɛtu/ *a* abject

abóbada /a'bɔbada/ *f* vault

abobalhado /aboba'ʎadu/ *a* silly

abóbora /a'bɔbora/ *f* pumpkin

abobrinha /abo'briɲa/ *f* courgette, (*Amer*) zucchini

aboli|ção /aboli'sãw/ *f* abolition; ~lir *vt* abolish

abomi|nação /abomina'sãw/ *f* abomination; ~nável (*pl* ~náveis) *a* abominable

abo|nar /abo'nar/ *vt* guarantee <*dívida*>; give a bonus to <*empregado*>; ~no /o/ *m* guarantee; (*no salário*) bonus; (*subsídio*) allowance, benefit; (*reforço*) endorsement

abordar /abor'dar/ *vt* approach <*pessoa*>; broach, tackle <*assunto*>; (*naut*) board

aborre|cer /aboxe'ser/ *vt* (*irritar*) annoy; (*entediar*) bore; ~cer-se *vpr* get annoyed; get bored; ~cido *a* annoyed; bored; ~cimento *m* annoyance; boredom

abor|tar /abor'tar/ *vi* miscarry, have a miscarriage □ *vt* abort; ~to /o/ *m* abortion; (*natural*) miscarriage

aboto|adura /abota'dura/ *f* cufflink; ~ar *vt* button (up) □ *vi* bud

abra|çar /abra'sar/ *vt* hug, embrace;

embrace <*causa*>; **∼ço** *m* hug, embrace

abrandar /abrã'dar/ *vt* ease <*dor*>; temper <*calor, frio*>; mollify, appease, placate <*povo*>; tone down, smooth over <*escândalo*> □ *vi* <*dor*> ease; <*calor, frio*> become less extreme; <*tempestade*> die down

abranger /abrã'ʒer/ *vt* cover; (*entender*) take in, grasp; **∼ a** extend to

abrasileirar /abrazile'rar/ *vt* Brazilianize

abre-|garrafas /abriga'ʃafaʃ/ *m invar* (*Port*) bottle-opener; **∼latas** *m invar* (*Port*) can-opener

abreugrafia /abrewgra'fia/ *f* X-ray

abrevi|ar /abrevi'ar/ *vt* abbreviate <*palavra*>; abridge <*livro*>; **∼atura** *f* abbreviation

abridor /abri'dor/ *m* **∼ (de lata)** can-opener; **∼ de garrafa** bottle-opener

abri|gar /abri'gar/ *vt* shelter; house <*sem-teto*>; **∼gar-se** *vpr* (take) shelter; **∼go** *m* shelter

abril /a'briw/ *m* April

abrir /a'brir/ *vt* open; (*a chave*) unlock; turn on <*gás, torneira*>; make <*buraco, exceção*> □ *vi* open; <*céu, tempo*> clear (up); <*sinal*> turn green; **∼-se** *vpr* open; (*desabafar*) open up

abrupto /a'bruptu/ *a* abrupt

abrutalhado /abruta'ʎadu/ *a* <*sapato*> heavy; <*pessoa*> coarse

abscesso /abi'sesu/ *m* abscess

absolu|tamente /abisoluta'mẽtʃi/ *adv* absolutely; (*não*) not at all; **∼to** *a* absolute; **em ∼to** not at all, absolutely not

absol|ver /abisow'ver/ *vt* absolve; (*jurid*) acquit; **∼vição** *f* absolution; (*jurid*) acquittal

absor|ção /abisor'sãw/ *f* absorption; **∼to** *a* absorbed; <*livro*> absorbing; **∼vente** *a* <*tecido*> absorbent; <*livro*> absorbing; **∼ver** *vt* absorb; **∼ver-se** *vpr* get absorbed

abs|têmio /abis'temiu/ *a* abstemious; (*de álcool*) teetotal □ *m* teetotaller; **∼tenção** *f* abstention; **∼tencionista** *a* abstaining □ *m/f* abstainer; **∼ter-se** *vpr* abstain; **∼ter-se de** refrain from; **∼tinência** *f* abstinence

abstra|ção /abistra'sãw/ *f* abstraction; (*mental*) distraction; **∼ir** *vt* separate; **∼to** *a* abstract

absurdo /abi'surdu/ *a* absurd □ *m* nonsense

abun|dância /abū'dãsia/ *f* abundance; **∼dante** *a* abundant; **∼dar** *vi* abound

abu|sar /abu'zar/ *vi* go too far; **∼sar de** abuse; (*aproveitar-se*) take advantage of; **∼so** *m* abuse.

abutre /a'butri/ *m* vulture

aca|bado /aka'badu/ *a* finished; (*exausto*) exhausted; (*velho*) decrepit; **∼bamento** *m* finish; **∼bar** *vt* finish □ *vi* finish, end; (*esgotar-se*) run out; **∼bar-se** *vpr* end, be over; (*esgotar-se*) run out; **∼bar com** put an end to, end; (*abolir, matar*) do away with; split up with <*namorado*>; wipe out <*adversário*>; **∼bou de chegar** he has just arrived; **∼bar fazendo** *or* **por fazer** end up doing

acabrunhado /akabru'ɲadu/ *a* dejected

aca|demia /akade'mia/ *f* academy; (*de ginástica etc*) gym; **∼dêmico** *a & m* academic

açafrão /asa'frãw/ *m* saffron

acalentar /akalẽ'tar/ *vt* lull to sleep <*bebê*>; cherish <*esperanças*>; have in mind <*planos*>

acalmar /akaw'mar/ *vt* calm (down) □ *vi* <*vento*> drop; <*mar*> grow calm; **∼-se** *vpr* calm down

acam|pamento /akãpa'mẽtu/ *m* camp; (*ato*) camping; **∼par** *vi* camp

aca|nhado /aka'ɲadu/ *a* shy; **∼nhamento** *m* shyness; **∼nhar-se** *vpr* be shy

ação /a'sãw/ *f* action; (*jurid*) lawsuit; (*com*) share

acariciar /akarisi'ar/ *vt* (*com a mão*) caress, stroke; (*adular*) make a fuss of; cherish <*esperanças*>

acarretar /akaxe'tar/ *vt* bring, cause

acasalar /akaza'lar/ *vt* mate; **∼-se** *vpr* mate

acaso /a'kazu/ *m* chance; **ao ∼** at random; **por ∼** by chance

aca|tamento /akata'mẽtu/ *m* respect, deference; **∼tar** *vt* respect, defer to <*pessoa, opinião*>; obey, abide by <*leis, ordens*>; take in <*criança*>

acc-, acç- (*Port*) *veja* **ac-, aç-**

acautelar-se /akawte'larsi/ *vpr* be cautious

acei|tação /asejta'sãw/ *f* acceptance; **∼tar** *vt* accept; **∼tável** (*pl* **∼táveis**) *a* acceptable

acele|ração /aselera'sãw/ *f* acceleration; **∼rador** *m* accelerator; **∼rar** *vi* accelerate □ *vt* speed up

acenar /ase'nar/ *vi* signal; (*saudando*) wave; **∼ com** promise, offer

acender /asẽ'der/ *vt* light <*cigarro, fogo, vela*>; switch on <*luz*>; heat up <*debate*>

aceno /a'senu/ *m* signal; (*de saudação*) wave

acen|to /a'sẽtu/ *m* accent; **∼tuar** *vt* accentuate; accent <*letra*>

acepção /asep'sãw/ *f* sense

acepipes /ase'pipʃ/ *m pl* (*Port*) cocktail snacks

acerca /a'serka/ **∼ de** *prep* about, concerning

acercar-se /aser'karsi/ *vpr* ~ de approach

acertar /aser'tar/ *vt* find <*com o caminho*, (*a*) *casa*>; put right, set <*relógio*>; get right <*pergunta*>; guess (correctly) <*solução*>; hit <*alvo*>; make <*acordo, negócio*>; fix, arrange <*encontro*> □ *vi* (*ter razão*) be right; (*atingir o alvo*) hit the mark; ~ **com** find, happen upon; ~ **em** hit

acervo /a'servu/ *m* collection; (*jurid*) estate

aceso /a'sezu/ *pp de* **acender** □ *a* <*luz*> on; <*fogo*> alight

aces|sar /ase'sar/ *vt* access; ~**sível** (*pl* ~**síveis**) *a* accessible; affordable <*preço*>; ~**so** /ɛ/ *m* access; (*de raiva, tosse*) fit; (*de febre*) attack; ~**sório** *a & m* accessory

acetona /ase'tona/ *f* (*para unhas*) nail varnish remover

achado /a'ʃadu/ *m* find

achaque /a'ʃaki/ *m* ailment

achar /a'ʃar/ *vt* find; (*pensar*) think; ~**-se** *vpr* (*estar*) be; (*considerar-se*) think that one is; **acho que sim/não** I think so/I don't think so

achatar /aʃa'tar/ *vt* flatten; cut <*salário*>

aciden|tado /asidẽ'tadu/ *a* rough <*terreno*>; bumpy <*estrada*>; eventful <*viagem, vida*>; injured <*pessoa*>; ~**tal** (*pl* ~**tais**) *a* accidental; ~**te** *m* accident

acidez /asi'des/ *f* acidity

ácido /'asidu/ *a & m* acid

acima /a'sima/ *adv* above; ~ **de** above; **mais** ~ higher up

acio|nar /asio'nar/ *vt* operate; (*jurid*) sue; ~**nista** *m/f* shareholder

acirrado /asi'xadu/ *a* stiff, tough

acla|mação /aklama'sãw/ *f* acclaim; (*de rei*) acclamation; ~**mar** *vt* acclaim

aclarar /akla'rar/ *vt* clarify, clear up □ *vi* clear up; ~**-se** *vpr* become clear

aclimatar /aklima'tar/ *vt* acclimatize, (*Amer*) acclimate; ~**-se** *vpr* get acclimatized, (*Amer*) get acclimated

aço /'asu/ *m* steel; ~ **inoxidável** stainless steel

acocorar-se /akoko'rarsi/ *vpr* squat (down)

acolá /ako'la/ *adv* over there

acolcho|ado /akowʃo'adu/ *m* quilt; ~**ar** *vt* quilt; upholster <*móveis*>

aco|lhedor /akoʎe'dor/ *a* welcoming; ~**lher** *vt* welcome <*hóspede*>; take in <*criança, refugiado*>; accept <*decisão, convite*>; respond to <*pedido*>; ~**lhida** *f*, ~**lhimento** *m* welcome; (*abrigo*) refuge

acomodar /akomo'dar/ *vt* accommodate; (*ordenar*) arrange; (*tornar cômo*

modo) make comfortable; ~**-se** *vpr* make o.s. comfortable

acompa|nhamento /akõpaɲa'mẽtu/ *m* (*mus*) accompaniment; (*prato*) side dish; (*comitiva*) escort; ~**nhante** *m/f* companion; (*mus*) accompanist; ~**nhar** *vt* accompany, go with; watch <*jogo, progresso*>; keep up with <*eventos, caso*>; keep up with, follow <*aula, conversa*>; share <*política, opinião*>; (*mus*) accompany; **a estrada ~nha o rio** the road runs alongside the river

aconche|gante /akõʃe'gãtʃi/ *a* cosy, (*Amer*) cozy; ~**gar** *vt* (*chegar a si*) cuddle; (*agasalhar*) wrap up; (*na cama*) tuck up; (*tornar cômodo*) make comfortable; ~**gar-se** *vpr* ensconce o.s.; ~**gar-se com** snuggle up to; ~**go** /e/ *m* cosiness, (*Amer*) coziness; (*abraço*) cuddle

acondicionar /akõdʒisio'nar/ *vt* condition; pack, package <*mercadoria*>

aconse|lhar /akõse'ʎar/ *vt* advise; ~**lhar-se** *vpr* consult; ~**lhar alg a** advise s.o. to; ~**lhar aco a alg** recommend sth to s.o.; ~**lhável** (*pl* ~**lháveis**) *a* advisable

aconte|cer /akõte'ser/ *vi* happen; ~**cimento** *m* event

acordar /akor'dar/ *vt/i* wake up

acorde /a'kɔrdʒi/ *m* chord

acordeão /akordʒi'ãw/ *m* accordion

acordo /a'kordu/ *m* agreement; **de ~ com** in agreement with <*pessoa*>; in accordance with <*lei etc*>; **estar de ~** agree

Açores /a'soris/ *m pl* Azores

açoriano /asori'ano/ *a & m* Azorean

acorrentar /akoxẽ'tar/ *vt* chain (up)

acossar /ako'sar/ *vt* hound, badger

acos|tamento /akosta'mẽtu/ *m* hard shoulder, (*Amer*) berm; ~**tar-se** *vpr* lean back

acostu|mado /akostu'madu/ *a* usual, customary; **estar ~mado a** be used to; ~**mar** *vt* accustom; ~**mar-se a** get used to

acotovelar /akotove'lar/ *vt* (*empurrar*) jostle; (*para avisar*) nudge

açou|gue /a'sogi/ *m* butcher's (shop); ~**gueiro** *m* butcher

acovardar /akovar'dar/ *vt* cow, intimidate

acre /'akri/ *a* <*gosto*> bitter; <*aroma*> acrid, pungent; <*tom*> harsh

acredi|tar /akredʒi'tar/ *vt* believe; accredit <*representante*>; ~**tar em** believe <*pessoa, história*>; believe in <*Deus, fantasmas*>; (*ter confiança*) have faith in; ~**tável** (*pl* ~**táveis**) *a* believable

acre-doce /akri'dosi/ *a* sweet and sour

acrescentar /akresẽ'tar/ vt add

acres|cer /akre'ser/ vt (juntar) add; (aumentar) increase □ vi increase; ~cido de with the addition of; ~ce que add to that the fact that

acréscimo /a'krɛsimu/ m addition; (aumento) increase

acriançado /akriã'sadu/ a childish

acrílico /a'kriliku/ a acrylic

acroba|cia /akroba'sia/ f acrobatics; ~ta m/f acrobat

act- (Port) veja at-

acuar /aku'ar/ vt corner

açúcar /a'sukar/ m sugar

açuca|rar /asuka'rar/ vt sweeten; sugar <café, chá>; ~reiro m sugar bowl

açude /a'sudʒi/ m dam

acudir /aku'dʒir/ vt/i ~ (a) come to the rescue (of)

acumular /akumu'lar/ vt accumulate; combine <cargos>

acupuntura /akupũ'tura/ f acupuncture

acu|sação /akuza'sãw/ f accusation; ~sar vt accuse; (jurid) charge; (revelar) reveal, show up; acknowledge <recebimento>

acústi|ca /a'kustʃika/ f acoustics; ~co a acoustic

adap|tação /adapta'sãw/ f adaptation; ~tado a <criança> well-adjusted; ~tar vt adapt; (para encaixar) tailor; ~tar-se vpr adapt; ~tável (pl ~táveis) a adaptable

adega /a'dɛga/ f wine cellar

adentro /a'dẽtru/ adv inside; selva ~ into the jungle

adepto /a'dɛptu/ m follower; (Port: de equipa) supporter

ade|quado /ade'kwadu/ a appropriate, suitable; ~quar vt adapt, tailor

adereços /ade'resus/ m pl props

ade|rente /ade'rẽtʃi/ m/f follower; ~rir vi (colar) stick; join <a partido, causa>; follow <a moda>; ~são f adhesion; (apoio) support; ~sivo a sticky, adhesive □ m sticker

ades|trado /ades'tradu/ a skilled; ~trador m trainer; ~trar vt train; break in <cavalo>

adeus /a'dews/ int goodbye □ m goodbye, farewell

adian|tado /adʒiã'tadu/ a advanced; <relógio> fast; chegar ~tado be early; ~tamento m progress; (pagamento) advance; ~tar vt advance <dinheiro>; put forward <relógio>; bring forward <data, reunião>; get ahead with <trabalho> □ vi <relógio> gain; (ter efeito) be of use; ~tar-se vpr progress, get ahead; não ~ta (fazer) it's no use (doing); ~te adv ahead

adia|r /adʒi'ar/ vt postpone; adjourn <sessão>; ~mento m postponement, adjournment

adi|ção /adʒi'sãw/ f addition; ~cionar vt add; ~do m attaché

adivi|nhação /adʒiviɲa'sãw/ f guesswork; (por adivinho) fortune-telling; ~nhar vt guess; tell <futuro, sorte>; read <pensamento>; ~nho m fortune-teller

adjetivo /adʒe'tʃivu/ m adjective

adminis|tração /adʒiministra'sãw/ f administration; (de empresas) management; ~trador m administrator; manager; ~trar vt administer; manage <empresa>

admi|ração /adʒimira'sãw/ f admiration; (assombro) wonder(ment); ~rado a admired; (surpreso) amazed, surprised; ~rador m admirer □ a admiring; ~rar vt admire; (assombrar) amaze; ~rar-se vpr be amazed; (assombroso) amazing; ~rável (pl ~ráveis) a admirable; (assombroso) amazing

admis|são /adʒimi'sãw/ f admission; (de escola) intake; ~sível (pl ~síveis) a admissible

admitir /adʒimi'tʃir/ vt admit; (permitir) permit, allow; (contratar) take on

adoção /ado'sãw/ f adoption

ado|çar /ado'sar/ vt sweeten; ~cicado a slightly sweet

adoecer /adoe'ser/ vi fall ill □ vt make ill

adoles|cência /adole'sẽsia/ f adolescence; ~cente a & m adolescent

adopt- (Port) veja adot-

adorar /ado'rar/ vt (amar) adore; worship <deus>; (fam: gostar de) love

adorme|cer /adorme'ser/ vi fall asleep; <perna> go to sleep, go numb; ~cido a sleeping; <perna> numb

ador|nar /ador'nar/ vt adorn; ~no /o/ m adornment

ado|tar /ado'tar/ vt adopt; ~tivo a adopted

adquirir /adʒiki'rir/ vt acquire

adu|bar /adu'bar/ vt fertilize; ~bo m fertilizer

adu|lação /adula'sãw/ f flattery; (do público) adulation; ~lar vt make a fuss of; (com palavras) flatter

adulterar /aduwte'rar/ vt adulterate; cook, doctor <contas> □ vi commit adultery

adúltero /a'duwteru/ m adulterer (f -ess) □ a adulterous

adul|tério /aduw'tɛriu/ m adultery; ~to a & m adult

advento /adʒi'vẽtu/ m advent

advérbio /adʒi'vɛrbiu/ m adverb

adver|sário /adʒiver'sariu/ m opponent; (inimigo) adversary; ~sidade f adversity; (adversário) opposed

adver|tência /adʒiver'tẽsia/ f warning; ~tir vt warn

advo|cacia /adʒivoka'sia/ f legal practice; ~gado m lawyer; ~gar vt advocate; (jurid) plead □ vi practise law

aéreo /a'ɛriu/ a air

aero|dinâmica /aerodʒi'namika/ f aerodynamics; ~dinâmico a aerodynamic; ~dromo m airfield; ~moça /o/ f air hostess; ~nauta m airman (f-woman); ~náutica f (força) air force; (ciência) aeronautics; ~nave f aircraft; ~porto /o/ m airport

aeros|sol /aero'sɔw/ (pl ~sóis) m aerosol

afabilidade /afabili'dadʒi/ f friendliness, kindness

afagar /afa'gar/ vt stroke

afamado /afa'madu/ a renowned, famed

afas|tado /afas'tadu/ a remote; <parente> distant; ~tado de (far) away from; ~tamento m removal; (distância) distance; (de candidato) rejection; ~tar vt move away; (tirar) remove; ward off <perigo, ameaça>; put out of one's mind <idéia>; ~tar-se vpr move away; (distanciar-se) distance o.s.; (de cargo) step down

afá|vel /a'favew/ (pl ~veis) a friendly, genial

afazeres /afa'zeris/ m pl business; ~ domésticos (household) chores

afect- (Port) veja afet-

Afeganistão /afeganis'tãw/ m Afghanistan

afe|gão /afe'gãw/ a & m (f ~gã) Afghan

afeição /afej'sãw/ f affection, fondness

afeiçoado /afejsu'adu/ a (devoto) devoted; (amoroso) fond

afeminado /afemi'nadu/ a effeminate

aferir /afe'rir/ vt check, inspect <pesos, medidas>; (avaliar) assess; (cotejar) compare

aferrar /afe'xar/ vt grasp; ~se a cling to

afe|tação /afeta'sãw/ f affectation; ~tado a affected; ~tar vt affect; ~tivo a (carinhoso) affectionate; (sentimental) emotional; ~to /ɛ/ m affection; ~tuoso /o/ a affectionate

afi|ado /afi'adu/ a sharp; skilled <pessoa>; ~ar vt sharpen

aficionado /afisio'nadu/ m enthusiast

afilhado /afi'ʎadu/ m godson (f -daughter)

afili|ação /afilia'sãw/ f affiliation; ~ada f affiliate; ~ar vt affiliate

afim /a'fĩ/ a related, similar

afinado /afi'nadu/ a in tune

afinal /afi'naw/ adv ~ (de contas) (por fim) in the end; (pensando bem) after all

afinar /afi'nar/ vt tune □ vi taper

afinco /a'fĩku/ m perseverance, determination

afinidade /afini'dadʒi/ f affinity

afir|mação /afirma'sãw/ f assertion; ~mar vt claim, assert; ~mativo a affirmative

afivelar /afive'lar/ vt buckle

afixar /afik'sar/ vt stick, post

afli|ção /afli'sãw/ f (física) affliction; (cuidado) anxiety; ~gir vt <doença> afflict; (inquietar) trouble; ~gir-se vpr worry; ~to a troubled, worried

afluente /aflu'ẽtʃi/ m tributary

afo|bação /afoba'sãw/ f fluster, flap; ~bado a in a flap, flustered; ~bar vt fluster; ~bar-se vpr get flustered, get in a flap

afo|gado /afo'gadu/ a drowned; morrer ~gado drown; ~gador m choke; ~gar vt/i drown; (auto) flood; ~garse (matar-se) drown o.s.

afoito /a'fojtu/ a bold, daring

afora /a'fora/ adv pelo mundo ~ throughout the world

afortunado /afortu'nadu/ a fortunate

afresco /a'fresku/ m fresco

África /'afrika/ f Africa; ~ do Sul South Africa

africano /afri'kanu/ a & m African

afrodisíaco /afrodʒi'ziaku/ a & m aphrodisiac

afron|ta /a'frõta/ f affront, insult; ~tar vt affront, insult

afrouxar /afro'ʃar/ vt/i loosen; (de rapidez) slow down; (de disciplina) relax

afta /'afta/ f (mouth) ulcer

afugentar /afuʒẽ'tar/ vt drive away; rout <inimigo>

afundar /afũ'dar/ vt sink; ~se vpr sink

agachar /aga'ʃar/ vi ~se vpr bend down

agarrar /aga'xar/ vt grab, snatch; ~se vpr ~se a cling to, hold on to

agasa|lhar /agaza'ʎar/ vt ~lhar-se vpr wrap up (warmly); ~lho m (casaco) coat; (suéter) sweater

agência /a'ʒẽsia/ f agency; ~ de correio post office; ~ de viagens travel agency

agenda /a'ʒẽda/ f diary

agente /a'ʒẽtʃi/ m/f agent

ágil /'aʒiw/ (pl ágeis) a <pessoa> agile; <serviço> quick, efficient

agili|dade /aʒili'dadʒi/ f agility; (rapidez) speed; ~zar vt speed up, streamline

ágio /'aʒiu/ m premium

agiota /aʒiˈɔta/ m/f loan shark

agir /aˈʒir/ vi act

agi|tado /aʒiˈtadu/ a agitated; <mar> rough; **~tar** vt wave <braços>; wag <rabo>; shake <garrafa>; (perturbar) agitate; **~tar-se** vpr get agitated; <mar> get rough

aglome|ração /aglomeraˈsãw/ f collection; (de pessoas) crowd; **~rar** collect; **~rar-se** vpr gather

agonia /agoˈnia/ f anguish; (da morte) death throes

agora /aˈgɔra/ adv now; (há pouco) just now; **~ mesmo** right now; **de ~ em diante** from now on; **até ~** so far, up till now

agosto /aˈgostu/ m August

agouro /aˈgoru/ m omen

agraciar /agrasiˈar/ vt decorate

agra|dar /agraˈdar/ vt please; (fazer agrados) be nice to, fuss over □ vi be pleasing, please; (cair no gosto) go down well; **~dável** (pl **~dáveis**) a pleasant

agrade|cer /agradeˈser/ vt **~cer aco a alg, ~cer a alg por aco** thank s.o. for sth □ vi say thank you; **~cido** a grateful; **~cimento** m gratitude; pl thanks

agrado /aˈgradu/ m **fazer ~s** a be nice to, make a fuss of

agrafa|r /agraˈfar/ vt (Port) staple; **~dor** m stapler

agrário /aˈgrariu/ a land, agrarian

agra|vante /agraˈvãtʃi/ a aggravating □ f aggravating circumstance; **~var** vt aggravate, make worse; **~var-se** vpr get worse

agredir /agreˈdʒir/ vt attack

agregado /agreˈgadu/ m (em casa) lodger

agres|são /agreˈsãw/ f aggression; (ataque) assault; **~sivo** a aggressive; **~sor** m aggressor

agreste /aˈgrɛstʃi/ a rural

agrião /agriˈãw/ m watercress

agrícola /aˈgrikola/ a agricultural

agricul|tor /agrikuwˈtor/ m farmer; **~tura** f agriculture, farming

agridoce /agriˈdosi/ a bittersweet

agropecuá|ria /agropekuˈaria/ f farming; **~rio** a rural

agru|pamento /agrupaˈmẽtu/ m grouping; **~par** vt group; **~par-se** vpr group (together)

água /ˈagwa/ f water; **dar ~ na boca** be mouthwatering; **ir por ~ abaixo** go down the drain; **~ benta** holy water; **~ doce** fresh water; **~ mineral** mineral water; **~ salgada** salt water; **~ sanitária** household bleach

aguaceiro /agwaˈseru/ m downpour

água-de-|coco /agwadʒiˈkoku/ f coconut water; **~colônia** f eau de cologne

aguado /aˈgwadu/ a watery

aguardar /agwarˈdar/ vt wait for, await □ vi wait

aguardente /agwarˈdẽtʃi/ f spirit

aguarrás /agwaˈxas/ m turpentine

água-viva /agwaˈviva/ f jellyfish

agu|çado /aguˈsadu/ a pointed; <sentidos> acute; **~çar** vt sharpen; **~deza** f sharpness; (mental) perceptiveness; **~do** a sharp; <som> shrill; (fig) acute

agüentar /agwẽˈtar/ vt stand, put up with; hold <peso> □ vi <pessoa> hold out; <suporte> hold

águia /ˈagia/ f eagle

agulha /aˈguʎa/ f needle

ai /aj/ m sigh; (de dor) groan □ int ah!; (de dor) ouch!

aí /aˈi/ adv there; (então) then

aidético /ajˈdɛtʃiku/ a suffering from Aids □ m Aids sufferer

AIDS /ˈajdʒis/ f Aids

ainda /aˈĩda/ adv still; **melhor ~** even better; **não ... ~** not ... yet; **~ assim** even so; **~ bem** just as well; **~ por cima** moreover, in addition; **~ que** even if

aipim /ajˈpĩ/ m cassava

aipo /ˈajpu/ m celery

ajeitar /aʒejˈtar/ vt (arrumar) sort out; (arranjar) arrange; (ajustar) adjust; **~-se** vpr adapt; (dar certo) turn out right, sort o.s. out

ajoe|lhado /aʒoeˈʎadu/ a kneeling (down); **~lhar** vi, **~lhar-se** vpr kneel (down)

aju|da /aˈʒuda/ f help; **~dante** m/f helper; **~dar** vt help

ajuizado /aʒuiˈzadu/ a sensible

ajus|tar /aʒusˈtar/ vt adjust; settle <disputa>; take in <roupa>; **~tar-se** vpr conform; **~tável** (pl **~táveis**) a adjustable; **~te** m adjustment; (acordo) settlement

ala /ˈala/ f wing

ala|gação /alagaˈsãw/ f flooding; **~gadiço** a marshy □ m marsh; **~gar** vt flood

alameda /alaˈmeda/ f avenue

álamo /ˈalamu/ m poplar (tree)

alarde /aˈlardʒi/ m **fazer ~ de** flaunt; make a big thing of <notícia>; **~ar** vt/i flaunt

alargar /alarˈgar/ vt widen; (fig) broaden; let out <roupa>

alarido /alaˈridu/ m outcry

alar|ma /aˈlarma/ m alarm; **~mante** a alarming; **~mar** vt alarm; **~me** m alarm; **~mista** a & m alarmist

alastrar /alasˈtrar/ vt scatter; (disseminar) spread □ vi spread

alavanca /ala'vãka/ f lever; ~ de mudanças gear lever

alban|ês /awba'nes/ a & m (f ~esa) Albanian

Albânia /aw'bania/ f Albania

albergue /aw'bɛrgi/ m hostel

álbum /'awbŭ/ m album

alça /'awsa/ f handle; (de roupa) strap; (de fusil) sight

alcachofra /awka'ʃofra/ f artichoke

alçada /aw'sada/ f competence, power

álcali /'awkali/ m alkali

alcan|çar /awkã'sar/ vt reach; (conseguir) attain; (compreender) understand □ vi reach; (compreender) understanding; ~çável (pl ~çáveis) a reachable; attainable; ~ce m reach; (de tiro) range; (importância) consequence; (compreensão) understanding

alcaparra /awka'paxa/ f caper

alcatra /aw'katra/ f rump steak

alcatrão /awka'trãw/ m tar

álcool /'awkɔw/ m alcohol

alcoó|latra /awkɔ'ɔlatra/ m/f alcoholic; ~lico a & m alcoholic

alcunha /aw'kuɲa/ f nickname

aldeia /aw'deja/ f village

aleatório /alia'tɔriu/ a random, arbitrary

alecrim /ale'krĩ/ m rosemary

ale|gação /alega'sãw/ f allegation; ~gar vt allege

ale|goria /alego'ria/ f allegory; ~górico a allegorical

ale|grar /ale'grar/ vt cheer up; brighten up <casa>; ~grar-se vpr cheer up; ~gre /ɛ/ a cheerful; <cores> bright; ~gria f joy

alei|jado /ale'ʒadu/ a crippled □ m cripple; ~jar vt cripple

alei|tamento /alejta'mẽtu/ m breastfeeding; ~tar vt breast-feed

além /a'lẽj/ adv beyond; ~ de (ao lado de lá de) beyond; (mais de) over; (ademais de) apart from

Alemanha /ale'maɲa/ f Germany

alemão /ale'mãw/ (pl ~mães) a & m (f ~mã) German

alen|tador /alẽta'dor/ a encouraging; ~tar vt encourage; ~tar-se vpr cheer up; ~to m courage; (fôlego) breath

alergia /aler'ʒia/ f allergy

alérgico /a'lɛrʒiku/ a allergic (a to)

aler|ta /a'lɛrta/ a & m alert □ adv on the alert; ~tar vt alert

alfa|bético /awfa'bɛtʃiku/ a alphabetical; ~betização f literacy; ~betizar vt teach to read and write; ~beto m alphabet

alface /aw'fasi/ f lettuce

alfaiate /awfai'atʃi/ m tailor

al|fândega /aw'fãdʒiga/ f customs; ~fandegário a customs □ m customs officer

alfine|tada /awfine'tada/ f prick; (dor) stabbing pain; (fig) dig; ~te /e/ m pin; ~te de segurança safety pin

alforreca /alfo'xeka/ f (Port) jellyfish

alga /'awga/ f seaweed

algarismo /awga'rizmu/ m numeral

algazarra /awga'zaxa/ f uproar, racket

alge|mar /awʒe'mar/ vt handcuff; ~mas /e/ f pl handcuffs

algibeira /alʒi'bejra/ f (Port) pocket

algo /'awgu/ pron something; (numa pergunta) anything □ adv somewhat

algodão /awgo'dãw/ m cotton; ~(-doce) candy floss, (Amer) cotton candy; ~ (hidrófilo) cotton wool, (Amer) absorbent cotton

alguém /aw'gẽj/ pron somebody, someone; (numa pergunta) anybody, anyone

al|gum /aw'gũ/ (f ~guma) a some; (numa pergunta) any; (nenhum) no, not one □ pron pl some; ~guma coisa something

algures /aw'guris/ adv somewhere

alheio /a'ʎeju/ a (de outra pessoa) someone else's; (de outras pessoas) other people's; ~ a foreign to; (impróprio) irrelevant to; (desatento) unaware of; ~ de removed from

alho /'aʎu/ m garlic; ~-poró m leek

ali /a'li/ adv (over) there

ali|ado /ali'adu/ a allied □ m ally; ~ança f alliance; (anel) wedding ring; ~ar vt, ~ar-se vpr ally

aliás /a'ljaʃ/ adv (além disso) what's more, furthermore; (no entanto) however; (diga-se de passagem) by the way, incidentally; (senão) otherwise

álibi /'alibi/ m alibi

alicate /ali'katʃi/ m pliers; ~ de unhas nail clippers

alicerce /ali'sɛrsi/ m foundation; (fig) basis

alie|nado /alie'nadu/ a alienated; (demente) insane; ~nar vt alienate; transfer <bens>; ~nígena a & m/f alien

alimen|tação /alimẽta'sãw/ f (ato) feeding; (comida) food; (tecn) supply; ~tar a food; <hábitos> eating □ vt feed; (fig) nurture; ~tar-se de live on; ~tício a gêneros ~tícios foodstuffs; ~to m food

ali|nhado /ali'ɲadu/ a aligned; <pessoa> smart, (Amer) sharp; ~nhar vt align

alíquota /a'likwota/ f (de imposto) bracket

alisar /ali'zar/ vt smooth (out); straighten <cabelo>

alistar /alis'tar/ *vt* recruit; ∼**-se** *vpr* enlist

aliviar /alivi'ar/ *vt* relieve

alívio /a'liviu/ *m* relief

alma /'awma/ *f* soul

almanaque /awma'naki/ *m* yearbook

almejar /awme'ʒar/ *vt* long for

almirante /awmi'rãtʃi/ *m* admiral

almo|çar /awmo'sar/ *vi* have lunch □ *vt* have lunch for; ∼**ço** /o/ *m* lunch

almofada /awmo'fada/ *f* cushion; (*Port: de cama*) pillow

almôndega /aw'mõdʒiga/ *f* meatball

almoxarifado /awmoʃari'fadu/ *m* storeroom

alô /a'lo/ *int* hallo

alocar /alo'kar/ *vt* allocate

alo|jamento /aloʒa'mẽtu/ *m* accommodation, (*Amer*) accommodations; (*habitação*) housing; ∼**jar** *vt* accommodate; house <*sem-teto*>; ∼**jar-se** *vpr* stay

alongar /alõ'gar/ *vt* lengthen; extend, stretch out <*braço*>

alpendre /aw'pẽdri/ *m* shed; (*pórtico*) porch

Alpes /'awpis/ *m pl* Alps

alpinis|mo /awpi'nizmu/ *m* mountaineering; ∼**ta** *m/f* mountaineer

alqueire /aw'keri/ *m = 4.84 hectares*, (*in São Paulo = 2.42 hectares*)

alquimi|a /awki'mia/ *f* alchemy; ∼**sta** *mf* alchemist

alta /'awta/ *f* rise; **dar** ∼ **a** discharge; **ter** ∼ **be** discharged

altar /aw'tar/ *m* altar

alterar /awte'rar/ *vt* alter; (*falsificar*) falsify; ∼**-se** *vpr* change; (*zangar-se*) get angry

alter|nado /awter'nadu/ *a* alternate; ∼**nar** *vt/i*, ∼**nar-se** *vpr* alternate; ∼**nativa** *f* alternative; ∼**nativo** *a* alternative; <*corrente*> alternating

al|teza /aw'teza/ *f* highness; ∼**titude** *f* altitude

alti|vez /awtʃi'ves/ *f* arrogance; ∼**vo** *a* arrogant; (*elevado*) majestic

alto /'awtu/ *a* high; <*pessoa*> tall; <*barulho*> loud □ *adv* high; <*falar*> loud(ly); <*ler*> aloud □ *m* top; **os** ∼**s e baixos** the ups and downs □ *int* halt!; ∼**-falante** *m* loudspeaker

altura /aw'tura/ *f* height; (*momento*) moment; **ser à** ∼ **de** be up to

aluci|nação /alusina'sãw/ *f* hallucination; ∼**nante** *a* mind-boggling, crazy

aludir /alu'dʒir/ *vi* allude (**a** to)

alu|gar /alu'gar/ *vt* rent <*casa*>; hire, rent <*carro*>; <*locador*> let, rent out, hire out; ∼**guel** (Port), ∼**guer** /ɛ/ *m* rent; (*ato*) renting

alumiar /alumi'ar/ *vt* light (up)

alumínio /alu'miniu/ *m* aluminium, (*Amer*) aluminum

aluno /a'lunu/ *m* pupil

alusão /alu'zãw/ *f* allusion (**a** to)

alvará /awva'ra/ *m* permit, licence

alve|jante /awve'ʒãtʃi/ *m* bleach; ∼**jar** *vt* bleach; (*visar*) aim at

alvenaria /awvena'ria/ *f* masonry

alvo /'awvu/ *m* target

alvorada /awvo'rada/ *f* dawn

alvoro|çar /awvoro'sar/ *vt* stir up, agitate; (*entusiasmar*) excite; ∼**ço** /o/ *m* (*tumulto*) uproar; (*entusiasmo*) excitement

amabilidade /amabili'dadʒi/ *f* kindness

amaci|ante /amasi'ãtʃi/ *m* (*de roupa*) (fabric) conditioner; ∼**ar** *vt* soften; run in <*carro*>

amador /ama'dor/ *a & m* amateur; ∼**ismo** *m* amateurism; ∼**ístico** *a* amateurish

amadurecer /amadure'ser/ *vt/i* <*fruta*> ripen; (*fig*) mature

âmago /'amagu/ *m* heart, core; (*da questão*) crux

amaldiçoar /amawdʒiso'ar/ *vt* curse

amamentar /amamẽ'tar/ *vt* breastfeed

amanhã /ama'ɲã/ *m & adv* tomorrow; **depois de** ∼ the day after tomorrow

amanhecer /amaɲe'ser/ *vi & m* dawn

amansar /amã'sar/ *vt* tame; (*fig*) placate <*pessoa*>

a|mante /a'mãtʃi/ *m/f* lover; ∼**mar** *vt/i* love

amarelo /ama'rɛlu/ *a & m* yellow

amar|go /a'margu/ *a* bitter; ∼**gura** *f* bitterness; ∼**gurar** *vt* embitter; (*sofrer*) endure

amarrar /ama'xar/ *vt* tie (up); (*naut*) moor; ∼ **a cara** frown, scowl

amarrotar /amaxo'tar/ *vt* crease

amassar /ama'sar/ *vt* crush, squash; screw up <*papel*>; crease <*roupa*>; dent <*carro*>; knead <*pão*>; mash <*batatas*>

amá|vel /a'mavew/ (*pl* ∼**veis**) *a* kind

Ama|zonas /ama'zonas/ *m* Amazon; ∼**zônia** *f* Amazonia

âmbar /'ãbar/ *m* amber

ambi|ção /ãbi'sãw/ *f* ambition; ∼**cionar** *vt* aspire to; ∼**cioso** /o/ *a* ambitious

ambien|tal /ãbiẽ'taw/ (*pl* ∼**tais**) *a* environmental; ∼**tar** *vt* set <*filme*, *livro*>; set up <*casa*>; ∼**tar-se** *vpr* settle in; ∼**te** *m* environment; (*atmosfera*) atmosphere

am|biguidade /ãbigwi'dadʒi/ *f* ambiguity; ∼**bíguo** *a* ambiguous

âmbito /'ãbitu/ *m* scope, range

ambos /'ãbus/ *a & pron* both

ambu|lância /ãbu'lãsia/ f ambulance; **~lante** a (que anda) walking; <músico> wandering; <venda> mobile; **~latório** m out-patient clinic

amea|ça /ami'asa/ f threat; **~çador** a threatening; **~çar** vt threaten

ameba /a'mɛba/ f amoeba

amedrontar /amedrõ'tar/ vt scare; **~se** vpr get scared

ameixa /a'meʃa/ f plum; (passa) prune

amém /a'mẽj/ int amen □ m agreement; **dizer ~ a** go along with

amêndoa /a'mẽdoa/ f almond

amendoim /amẽdo'ĩ/ m peanut

ame|nidade /ameni'dadʒi/ f pleasantness; pl pleasantries, small talk; **~nizar** vt ease; calm <ânimos>; settle <disputa>; tone down <repreensão>; **~no** /e/ a pleasant; mild <clima>

América /a'mɛrika/ f America; **~ do Norte/Sul** North/South America

america|nizar /amerikani'zar/ vt Americanize; **~no** a & m American

amestrar /ames'trar/ vt train

ametista /ame'tʃista/ f amethyst

amianto /ami'ãtu/ m asbestos

ami|gar-se /ami'garsi/ vpr make friends; **~gável** (pl **~gáveis**) a amicable

amígdala /a'migdala/ f tonsil

amigdalite /amigda'litʃi/ f tonsillitis

amigo /a'migu/ a friendly □ m friend; **~ da onça** false friend

amistoso /amis'tozu/ a & m friendly

amiúde /ami'udʒi/ adv often

amizade /ami'zadʒi/ f friendship

amnésia /ami'nɛzia/ f amnesia

amnistia /amnis'tia/ f (Port) veja anistia

amo|lação /amola'sãw/ f annoyance; **~lante** a annoying; **~lar** vt annoy, bother; sharpen <faca>; **~lar-se** vpr get annoyed

amolecer /amole'ser/ vt/i soften

amol|gadura /amowga'dura/ f dent; **~gar** vt dent

amoníaco /amo'niaku/ m ammonia

amontoar /amõto'ar/ vt pile up; amass <riquezas>; **~se** vpr pile up

amor /a'mor/ m love; **~ próprio** self-esteem

amora /a'mɔra/ f **~ preta**, (Port) **~ silvestre** blackberry

amordaçar /amorda'sar/ vt gag

amoroso /amo'rozu/ adj loving

amor-perfeito /amorper'fejtu/ m pansy

amorte|cedor /amortese'dor/ m shock absorber; **~cer** vt deaden; absorb <impacto>; break <queda> □ vi fade

amostra /a'mɔstra/ f sample

ampa|rar /ãpa'rar/ vt support; (fig) protect; **~rar-se** lean; **~ro** m (apoio) support; (proteção) protection; (ajuda) aid

ampère /ã'pɛri/ m amp(ere)

ampli|ação /ãplia'sãw/ f (de foto) enlargement; (de casa) extension; **~ar** vt enlarge <foto>; extend <casa>; broaden <conhecimentos>

amplifi|cador /ãplifika'dor/ m amplifier; **~car** vt amplify

amplo /'ãplu/ a <sala> spacious; <roupa> full; <sentido, conhecimento> broad

ampola /ã'pola/ f ampoule

amputar /ãpu'tar/ vt amputate

Amsterdã /amister'dã/, (Port) **Amsterdão** /amiʃter'dãw/ f Amsterdam

amu|ado /amu'adu/ a in a sulk, sulky; **~ar** vi sulk

amuleto /amu'leto/ m charm

amuo /a'muu/ m sulk

ana|crônico /ana'kroniku/ a anachronistic; **~cronismo** m anachronism

anais /a'najs/ m pl annals

analfabeto /anawfa'bɛtu/ a & m illiterate

analisar /anali'zar/ vt analyse

análise /a'nalizi/ f analysis

ana|lista /ana'lista/ m/f analyst; **~lítico** a analytical

analogia /analo'ʒia/ f analogy

análogo /a'nalogu/ a analogous

ananás /ana'naʃ/ m invar (Port) pineapple

anão /a'nãw/ a & m (f **anã**) dwarf

anarquia /anar'kia/ f anarchy; (fig) chaos

anárquico /a'narkiku/ a anarchic

anarquista /anar'kista/ m/f anarchist

ana|tomia /anato'mia/ f anatomy; **~tômico** a anatomical

anca /'ãka/ f (de pessoa) hip; (de animal) rump

anchova /ã'ʃova/ f anchovy

ancinho /ã'siɲu/ m rake

âncora /'ãkora/ f anchor

anco|radouro /ãkora'doru/ m anchorage; **~rar** vt/i anchor

andaime /ã'dajmi/ m scaffolding

an|damento /ãda'mẽtu/ m (progresso) progress; (rumo) course; **dar ~damento a** set in motion; **~dar** m (jeito de andar) gait, walk; (de prédio) floor; (Port: apartamento) flat, (Amer) apartment □ vi (ir a pé) walk; (de trem, ônibus) travel; (a cavalo, de bicicleta) ride; (funcionar, progredir) go; **ele anda deprimido** he's been depressed lately

Andes /'ãdʒis/ *m pl* Andes
andorinha /ãdo'riɲa/ *f* swallow
anedota /ane'dɔta/ *f* anecdote
anel /a'nɛw/ (*pl* **anéis**) *m* ring; (*no cabelo*) curl; ~ **viário** ringroad
anelado /ane'ladu/ *a* curly
anemia /ane'mia/ *f* anaemia
anêmico /a'nemiku/ *a* anaemic
anes|tesia /aneste'zia/ *f* anaesthesia; (*droga*) anaesthetic; ~ **tesiar** *vt* anaesthetize; ~ **tésico** *a* & *m* anaesthetic; ~ **tesista** *m/f* anaesthetist
ane|xar /anek'sar/ *vt* annex < *terras*>; (*em carta*) enclose; (*juntar*) attach; ~ **xo** /ɛ/ *a* attached; (*em carta*) enclosed □ *m* annexe; (*em carta*) enclosure
anfíbio /ã'fibiu/ *a* amphibious □ *m* amphibian
anfiteatro /ãfitʃi'atru/ *m* amphitheatre; (*no teatro*) dress circle
anfi|trião /ãfitri'ãw/ *m* (*f* ~ **triã**) host (*f* -ess)
angariar /ãgari'ar/ *vt* raise < *fundos*>; canvass for < *votos*>; win < *adeptos, simpatia*>
angli|cano /ãgli'kanu/ *a* & *m* Anglican; ~ **cismo** *m* Anglicism
anglo-saxônico /ãglusak'soniku/ *a* Anglo-Saxon
Angola /ã'gɔla/ *f* Angola
angolano /ãgo'lanu/ *a* & *m* Angolan
angra /'ãgra/ *f* inlet, cove
angular /ãgu'lar/ *a* angular
ângulo /'ãgulu/ *m* angle
angústia /ã'gustʃia/ *f* anguish, anxiety
angustiante /ãgustʃi'ãtʃi/ *a* distressing; < *momento*> anxious
ani|mado /ani'madu/ *a* (*vivo*) lively; (*alegre*) cheerful; (*entusiasmado*) enthusiastic; ~ **mador** *a* encouraging □ *m* presenter; (*pl* ~ **mais**) *a* & *m* animal; ~ **mar** *vt* encourage; liven up < *festa*>; ~ **mar-se** *vpr* cheer up; < *festa*> liven up
ânimo /'animu/ *m* courage, spirit; *pl* tempers
animosidade /animozi'dadʒi/ *f* animosity
aniquilar /aniki'lar/ *vt* destroy; (*prostrar*) shatter
anis /a'nis/ *m* aniseed
anistia /anis'tʃia/ *f* amnesty
aniver|sariante /aniversari'ãtʃi/ *m/f* birthday boy (*f* girl); ~ **sário** *m* birthday; (*de casamento etc*) anniversary
anjo /'ãʒu/ *m* angel
ano /'anu/ *m* year; **fazer** ~ **s** have a birthday; ~ **bissexto** leap year; ~ **letivo** academic year; ~ **-bom** *m* New Year

anoi|tecer /anojte'ser/ *m* nightfall □ *vi* ~ **ceu** night fell
anomalia /anoma'lia/ *f* anomaly
anonimato /anoni'matu/ *m* anonymity
anônimo /a'nonimu/ *a* anonymous
anor|mal /anor'maw/ (*pl* ~ **mais**) *a* abnormal
ano|tação /anota'sãw/ *f* note; ~ **tar** *vt* note down, write down
ânsia /'ãsia/ *f* anxiety; (*desejo*) longing; ~ **s de vômito** nausea
ansi|ar /ãsi'ar/ *vi* ~ **por** long for; ~ **edade** *f* anxiety; (*desejo*) eagerness; ~ **oso** /o/ *a* anxious
antártico /ã'tartʃiku/ *a* & *m* Antarctic
antebraço /ãtʃi'brasu/ *m* forearm
antece|dência /ãtese'dẽsia/ *f* **com** ~ **dência** in advance; ~ **dente** *a* preceding; ~ **dentes** *m pl* record, past
antecessor /ãtese'sor/ *m* (*f* ~ **a**) predecessor
anteci|pação /ãtʃisipa'sãw/ *f* anticipation; **com** ~ **pação** in advance; ~ **padamente** *adv* in advance; ~ **pado** *a* advance; ~ **par** *vt* anticipate, forestall; (*adiantar*) bring forward; ~ **par-se** *vpr* be previous
antena /ã'tena/ *f* aerial, (*Amer*) antenna; (*de inseto*) feeler
anteontem /ãtʃi'õtẽ/ *adv* the day before yesterday
antepassado /ãtʃipa'sadu/ *m* ancestor
anterior /ãteri'or/ *a* previous; (*dianteiro*) front
antes /'ãtʃis/ *adv* before; (*ao contrário*) rather; ~ **de/que** before
ante-sala /ãtʃi'sala/ *f* ante-room
anti|biótico /ãtʃibi'ɔtʃiku/ *a* & *m* antibiotic; ~ **caspa** *a* anti-dandruff; ~ **concepcional** (*pl* ~ **concepcionais**) *a* & *m* contraceptive; ~ **congelante** *m* antifreeze; ~ **corpo** *m* antibody
antídoto /ã'tʃidotu/ *m* antidote
antiético /ãtʃi'ɛtʃiku/ *a* unethical
antigamente /ãtʃiga'mẽtʃi/ *adv* formerly
anti|go /ã'tʃigu/ *a* old; (*da antiguidade*) ancient; < *móveis etc*> antique; (*anterior*) former; ~ **guidade** *f* antiquity; (*numa firma*) seniority; *pl* (*monumentos*) antiquities; (*móveis etc*) antiques
anti-|higiênico /ãtʃiʒi'eniku/ *a* unhygienic; ~ **histamínico** *a* & *m* antihistamine; ~ **horário** *a* anticlockwise
antilhano /ãtʃi'ʎanu/ *a* & *m* West Indian
Antilhas /ã'tʃiʎas/ *f pl* West Indies
anti|patia /ãtʃipa'tʃia/ *f* dislike; ~ **pático** *a* unpleasant, unfriendly

antiquado /ãtʃi'kwadu/ a antiquated, out-dated

anti-|semitismo /ãtʃisemi'tʃizmu/ m anti-Semitism; **~séptico** a & m antiseptic; **~social** (pl **~sociais**) a antisocial

antítese /ã'tʃitezi/ f antithesis

antologia /ãtolo'ʒia/ f anthology

antônimo /ã'tonimu/ m antonym

antro /'ãtru/ m cavern; (de animal) lair; (de ladrões) den

antro|pófago /ãtro'pɔfagu/ a man-eating; **~pologia** f anthropology; **~pólogo** m anthropologist

anu|al /anu'aw/ (pl **~ais**) a annual, yearly

anu|lação /anula'sãw/ f cancellation; **~lar** vt cancel; annul <casamento>; (compensar) cancel out □ m ring finger

anunciar /anũsi'ar/ vt announce; advertise <produto>

anúncio /a'nũsiu/ m announcement; (propaganda, classificado) advert(isement); (cartaz) notice

ânus /'anus/ m invar anus

an|zol /ã'zɔw/ (pl **~zóis**) m fish-hook

aonde /a'õdʒi/ adv where

apadrinhar /apadri'ɲar/ vt be godfather to <afilhado>; be best man for <noivo>; (proteger) protect; (patrocinar) support

apa|gado /apa'gadu/ a <fogo> out; <luz, TV> off; (indistinto) faint; (pessoa) dull; **~gar** vt put out <cigarro, fogo>; blow out <vela>; switch off <luz, TV>; rub out <erro>; clean <quadro-negro>; **~gar-se** vpr <fogo, luz> go out; <lembrança> fade; (desmaiar) pass out; (fam: dormir) nod off

apaixo|nado /apaʃo'nadu/ a in love (por with); **~nante** a captivating; **~nar-se** vpr fall in love (por with)

apalpar /apaw'par/ vt touch, feel; <médico> examine

apanhar /apa'ɲar/ vt catch; (do chão) pick up; pick <flores, frutas>; (ir buscar) pick up; (alcançar) catch up □ vi be beaten

aparafusar /aparafu'zar/ vt screw

apa|ra-lápis /apara'lapiʃ/ m invar (Port) pencil sharpener; **~rar** vt catch <bola>; parry <golpe>; trim <cabelo>; sharpen <lápis>

aparato /apa'ratu/ m pomp, ceremony

apare|cer /apare'ser/ vi appear; **~ça!** do drop in!; **~cimento** m appearance

apare|lhagem /apare'ʎaʒẽ/ f equipment; **~lhar** vt equip; **~lho** /e/ m apparatus; (máquina) machine; (de chá) set, service; (fone) phone

aparência /apa'rẽsia/ f appearance; **na ~** apparently

aparen|tado /aparẽ'tadu/ a related; **~tar** vt show; (fingir) feign; **~te** a apparent

apar|tamento /aparta'mẽtu/ m flat, (Amer) apartment; **~tar** vt, **~tar-se** vpr separate; (de briga) part; **~te** m aside

apatia /apa'tʃia/ f apathy

apático /a'patʃiku/ a apathetic

apavo|rante /apavo'rãtʃi/ a terrifying; **~rar** vt terrify; **~rar-se** vpr be terrified

apaziguar /apazi'gwar/ vt appease

apear-se /api'arsi/ vpr (de cavalo) dismount; (de ônibus) alight

ape|gar-se /ape'garsi/ vpr become attached (a to); **~go** /e/ m attachment

ape|lação /apela'sãw/ f appeal; (fig) exhibitionism; **~lar** vi appeal (de against); **~lar para** appeal to; (fig) resort to

apeli|dar /apeli'dar/ vt nickname; **~do** m nickname

apelo /a'pelu/ m appeal

apenas /a'penas/ adv only

apêndice /a'pẽdʒisi/ m appendix

apendicite /apẽdʒi'sitʃi/ f appendicitis

apercebe-se /aperse'bersi/ vpr **~** (de) notice, realize

aperfeiçoar /aperfejso'ar/ vt perfect

aperitivo /aperi'tʃivu/ m aperitif

aper|tado /aper'tadu/ a tight; (sem dinheiro) hard-up; **~tar** vt (segurar) hold tight; tighten <cinto>; press <botão>; squeeze <esponja>; take in <vestido>; fasten <cinto de segurança>; step up <vigilância>; cut down on <despesas> □ break <coração>; (fig) pressurize <pessoa> □ vi <sapato> pinch; <chuva, frio> get worse; <estrada> narrow; **~tar-se** vpr (gastar menos) tighten one's belt; (não ter dinheiro) feel the pinch; **~tar a mão de** alg shake hands with s.o.; **~to** /e/ m pressure; (de botão) press; (dificuldade) tight spot, jàm; **~to de mãos** handshake

apesar /ape'zar/ **~ de** prep in spite of

apeti|te /ape'tʃitʃi/ m appetite; **~toso** /o/ a appetizing

apetrechos /ape'treʃus/ m pl gear; (de pesca) tackle

apimentado /apimẽ'tadu/ a spicy, hot

apinhar /api'ɲar/ vt crowd, pack; **~se** vpr crowd

api|tar /api'tar/ vi whistle □ vt referee <jogo>; **~to** m whistle

aplanar /apla'nar/ vt level <terreno>; (fig) smooth <caminho>; smooth over <problema>

aplau|dir /aplaw'dʒir/ vt applaud; **~so(s)** m (pl) applause

apli|cação /aplika'sãw/ f application; (de dinheiro) investment; (de lei) enforcement; ~**car** *vt* apply; invest <*dinheiro*>; enforce <*lei*>; ~**car-se** *vpr* apply (**a** to); (*ao estudo etc*) apply o.s. (**a** to); ~**que** *m* hairpiece

apoderar-se /apode'rarsi/ *vpr* ~ **de** take possession of; (*de raiva*) take hold of

apodrecer /apodre'ser/ *vt/i* rot

apoi|ar /apoj'ar/ *vt* lean; (*fig*) support; (*basear*) base; ~**ar-se** *vpr* ~**ar-se em** lean on; (*fig*) be based on, rest on; ~**o** *m* support

apólice /a'polisi/ *f* policy; (*ação*) bond

apon|tador /apõta'dor/ *m* pencil sharpener; ~**tar** *vt* (*com o dedo*) point at, point to; point out <*erro, caso interessante*>; aim <*arma*>; name <*nomes*>; put forward <*razão*> □ *vi* <*sol, planta*> come up; (*com o dedo*) point (**para** to)

apoquentar /apokẽ'tar/ *vt* annoy

aporrinhar /apoxi'ɲar/ *vt* annoy

após /a'pɔs/ *adv* after; **loção** ~-**barba** after-shave (lotion)

aposen|tado /apozẽ'tadu/ *a* retired □ *m* pensioner; ~**tadoria** *f* retirement; (*pensão*) pension; ~**tar** *vt*, ~**tar-se** *vpr* retire; ~**to** *m* room

após-guerra /apɔz'gɛxa/ *m* post-war period

apos|ta /a'pɔsta/ *f* bet; ~**tar** *vt* bet (**em** on); (*fig*) have faith (**em** in)

apostila /apos't∫ila/ *f* revision aid, book of key facts

apóstolo /a'pɔstolu/ *m* apostle

apóstrofo /a'pɔstrofu/ *m* apostrophe

apre|ciação /apresia'sãw/ *f* appreciation; ~**ciar** *vt* appreciate; think highly of <*pessoa*>; ~**ciativo** *a* appreciative; ~**ciável** (*pl* ~**ciáveis**) *a* appreciable; ~**ço** /e/ *m* regard

apreen|der /apriẽ'der/ *vt* seize <*contrabando*>; apprehend <*criminoso*>; grasp <*sentido*>; ~**são** *f* apprehension; (*de contrabando*) seizure; ~**sivo** *a* apprehensive

apregoar /aprego'ar/ *vt* proclaim; cry <*mercadoria*>

apren|der /aprẽ'der/ *vt/i* learn; ~**diz** *m/f* (*de ofício*) apprentice; (*de direção*) learner; ~**dizado** *m*, ~**dizagem** *f* (*de ofício*) apprenticeship; (*de profissão*) training; (*escolar*) learning

apresen|tação /aprezẽta'sãw/ *f* presentation; (*teatral etc*) performance; (*de pessoas*) introduction; ~**tador** *m* presenter; ~**tar** *vt* present; introduce <*pessoa*>; ~**tar-se** *vpr* (*identificar-se*) introduce o.s.; <*ocasião, problema*> present o.s., arise; ~**tar-se a** report to <*polícia etc*>; go in for <*exame*>; stand for <*eleição*>; ~**tável** (*pl* ~**táveis**) *a* presentable

apres|sado /apre'sadu/ *a* hurried; ~**sar** *vt* hurry; ~**sar-se** *vpr* hurry (up)

aprimorar /aprimo'rar/ *vt* perfect, refine

aprofundar /aprofũ'dar/ *vt* deepen; study carefully <*questão*>; ~**se** *vpr* get deeper; <*se em* go deeper into

apron|tar /aprõ'tar/ *vt* get ready; pick <*briga*> □ *vi* act up; ~**se** *vpr* get ready

apropriado /apropri'adu/ *a* appropriate, suitable

apro|vação /aprova'sãw/ *f* approval; (*num exame*) pass; ~**var** *vt* approve of; approve <*lei*> □ *vi* make the grade; **ser** ~**vado** (*num exame*) pass

aprovei|tador /aprovejta'dor/ *m* opportunist; ~**tamento** *m* utilization; ~**tar** *vt* take advantage of; take <*ocasião*>; (*utilizar*) use □ *vi* make the most of it; (*Port: adiantar*) be of use; ~**tar-se** *vpr* take advantage (**de** of); ~**te!** (*divirta-se*) have a good time!

aproxi|mação /aprosima'sãw/ *f* (*chegada*) approach; (*estimativa*) approximation; (*chegar*) ~**mado a** <*valor*> approximate; ~**mar** *vt* move nearer; (*aliar*) bring together; ~**mar-se** *vpr* approach, get nearer (**de** to)

ap|tidão /apt∫i'dãw/ *f* aptitude, suitability; ~**to a** suitable

apunhalar /apuɲa'lar/ *vt* stab

apu|rado /apu'radu/ *a* refined; ~**rar** *vt* (*aprimorar*) refine; (*descobrir*) ascertain; investigate <*caso*>; collect <*dinheiro*>; count <*votos*>; ~**rar-se** *vpr* (*com a roupa*) dress smartly; ~**ro** *m* refinement; (*no vestir*) elegance; (*dificuldade*) difficulty; *pl* trouble

aquarela /akwa'rɛla/ *f* watercolour

aquariano /akwari'anu/ *a & m* Aquarian

aquário /a'kwariu/ *m* aquarium; **Aquário** Aquarius

aquartelar /akwarte'lar/ *vt* billet

aquático /a'kwat∫iku/ *a* aquatic, water

aque|cedor /akese'dor/ *m* heater; ~**cer** *vt* heat □ *vi*, ~**cer-se** *vpr* heat up; ~**cimento** *m* heating

aqueduto /ake'dutu/ *m* aqueduct

aquele /a'keli/ *a* that; *pl* those □ *pron* that one; *pl* those; ~ **que** the one that

àquele = a² + aquele

aqui /a'ki/ *adv* here

aquilo /a'kilu/ *pron* that

àquilo = a² + aquilo

aquisi|ção /akizi'sãw/ *f* acquisition; ~**tivo** *a* **poder** ~**tivo** purchasing power

ar /ar/ *m* air; (*aspecto*) look, air; (*Port: no carro*) choke; **ao** ~ **livre** in the

open air; no ~ (*fig*) up in the air;
(*TV*) on air; ~ **condicionado** air
conditioning
árabe /'arabi/ *a & m* Arab; (*ling*) Ar-
abic
Arábia /a'rabia/ *f* Arabia; ~ **Saudita**
Saudi Arabia
arado /a'radu/ *m* plough, (*Amer*) plow
aragem /a'raʒẽ/ *f* breeze
arame /a'rami/ *m* wire; ~ **farpado**
barbed wire
aranha /a'raɲa/ *f* spider
arar /a'rar/ *vt* plough, (*Amer*) plow
arara /a'rara/ *f* parrot
arbi|trar /arbi'trar/ *vt/i* referee
<*jogo*>; arbitrate <*disputa*>; ~**trá-
rio** *a* arbitrary
arbítrio /ar'bitriu/ *m* judgement;
livre ~ free will
árbitro /'arbitru/ *m* arbiter <*da
moda etc*>; (*jurid*) arbitrator; (*de futebol*) referee; (*de tênis*) umpire
arborizado /arbori'zadu/ *a* wooded,
green; <*rua*> tree-lined
arbusto /ar'bustu/ *m* shrub
ar|ca /'arka/ *f* ~**ca de Noé** Noah's
Ark; ~**cada** *f* (*galeria*) arcade; (*arco*)
arch
arcaico /ar'kajku/ *a* archaic
arcar /ar'kar/ *vt* ~ **com** deal with
arcebispo /arse'bispu/ *m* archbishop
arco /'arku/ *m* (*arquit*) arch; (*arma,
mus*) bow; (*eletr, mat*) arc; ~**-da-
velha** *m* coisa do ~**-da-velha** amazing thing; ~**-íris** *m invar* rainbow
ar|dente /ar'dẽtʃi/ *a* burning; (*fig*)
ardent; ~**der** *vi* burn; <*olhos, ferida*>
sting
ar|dil /ar'dʒiw/ (*pl* ~**dis**) *m* trick,
ruse
ardor /ar'dor/ *m* heat; (*fig*) ardour;
com ~ ardently
árduo /'arduu/ *a* strenuous, arduous
área /'aria/ *f* area; (*grande*) ~ penalty area; ~ (**de serviço**) yard
arear /ari'ar/ *vt* scour <*panela*>
areia /a'reja/ *f* sand
arejar /are'ʒar/ *vt* air □ *vi*, ~**-se** *vpr*
get some air; (*descansar*) have a
breather
are|na /a'rena/ *f* arena; ~**noso** /o/ *a*
sandy
arenque /a'rẽki/ *m* herring
argamassa /arga'masa/ *f* mortar
Argélia /ar'ʒɛlia/ *f* Algeria
argelino /arʒe'linu/ *a & m* Algerian
Argentina /arʒẽ'tʃina/ *f* Argentina
argentino /arʒẽ'tʃinu/ *a & m* Argen-
tinian
argila /ar'ʒila/ *f* clay
argola /ar'gola/ *f* ring
argumen|tar /argumẽ'tar/ *vt/i*
argue; ~**to** *m* argument; (*de filme
etc*) subject-matter

ariano /ari'anu/ *a & m* (*do signo
Aries*) Arian
árido /'aridu/ *a* arid; barren
<*deserto*>; (*fig*) dull, dry
Aries /'aris/ *f* Aries
arisco /a'risku/ *a* timid
aristo|cracia /aristokra'sia/ *f*
aristocracy; ~**crata** *m/f* aristocrat;
~**crático** *a* aristocratic
aritmética /aritʃ'mɛtʃika/ *f* arithmetic
arma /'arma/ *f* weapon; *pl* arms; ~ **de
fogo** firearm
ar|mação /arma'sãw/ *f* frame; (*de
óculos*) frames; (*naut*) rigging;
~**madilha** *f* trap; ~**madura** *f* suit
of armour; (*armação*) framework;
~**mar** *vt* (*dar armas a*) arm; (*montar*)
set up, assemble; set up <*máquina*>;
set, lay <*armadilha*>; fit out
<*navio*>;hatch <*plano, complô*>;
cause <*briga*>; ~**mar-se** *vpr* arm o.s.
armarinho /arma'riɲu/ *m* haberdashery, (*Amer*) notions
armário /ar'mariu/ *m* cupboard; (*de
roupa*) wardrobe
arma|zém /arma'zẽj/ *m* warehouse;
(*loja*) general store; (*depósito*) storeroom; ~**zenagem** *f*, ~**zenamento** *m*
storage; ~**zenar** *vt* store
Armênia /ar'menia/ *f* Armenia
armênio /ar'meniu/ *a & m* Armenian
aro /'aru/ *m* (*de roda, óculos*) rim; (*de
porta*) frame
aro|ma /a'roma/ *f* aroma; (*perfume*)
fragrance; ~**mático** *a* aromatic; fra-
grant
ar|pão /ar'pãw/ *m* harpoon; ~**poar** *vt*
harpoon
arquear /arki'ar/ *vt* arch; ~**-se** *vpr*
bend, bow
arque|ologia /arkiolo'ʒia/ *f* archae-
ology; ~**ológico** *a* archaeological;
~**ólogo** *m* archaeologist
arquétipo /ar'kɛtʃipu/ *m* archetype
arquibancada /arkibã'kada/ *f* ter-
races, (*Amer*) bleachers
arquipélago /arki'pɛlagu/ *m* archipe-
lago
arquite|tar /arkite'tar/ *vt* think up;
~**to** /ɛ/ *m* architect; ~**tônico** *a*
architectural; ~**tura** *f* architecture
arqui|var /arki'var/ *vt* file <*papéis*>;
shelve <*plano, processo*>; ~**vista** *m/
f* archivist; ~**vo** *m* file; (*conjunto*)
files; (*móvel*) filing cabinet; *pl* (*do Estado etc*) archives
arran|cada /axã'kada/ *f* lurch; (*de
atleta, fig*) spurt; ~**car** *vt* pull out
<*cabelo etc*>; pull off <*botão etc*>; pull
up <*erva daninha etc*>; take out
<*dente*>; (*das mãos de alg*) wrench,
snatch; extract <*confissão, dinheiro*>
□ *vi* <*carro*> roar off; <*pessoa*> take

off; (*dar solavanco*) lurch forward; ~car-se *vpr* take off; ~co *m* pull, tug; *veja* ~**cada**

arra|nha-céu /axaɲaˈsɛw/ *m* sky-scraper

arra|nhadura /axaɲaˈdura/ *f* scratch; ~**nhão** *m* scratch; ~**nhar** *vt* scratch; have a smattering of <*língua*>

arran|jar /axãˈʒar/ *vt* arrange; (*achar*) get, find; (*resolver*) settle, sort out; ~**jar-se** *vpr* manage; ~**jo** *m* arrangement

arrasar /axaˈzar/ *vt* devastate; raze, flatten <*casa, cidade*>; ~-**se** *vpr* be devastated

arrastar /axasˈtar/ *vt* drag; <*corrente, avalancha*> sweep away; (*atrair*) draw □ *vi* trail; ~-**se** *vpr* crawl; <*tempo*> drag; <*processo*> drag out

arreba|tador /axebataˈdor/ *a* entrancing, shocking <*notícia*>; ~**tar** *vt* (*elevar*) entrance, send; (*chocar*) shock

arreben|tação /axebẽtaˈsãw/ *f* surf; ~**tar** *vi* (*de bomba*) explode; <*corda*> snap, break; <*balão, pessoa*> burst; <*onda*> break; <*guerra, incêndio*> break out □ *vt* snap, break <*corda*>; burst <*balão*>; break down <*porta*>

arrebitar /axebiˈtar/ *vt* turn up <*nariz*>; prick up <*orelhas*>

arreca|dação /axekadaˈsãw/ *f* (*dinheiro*) tax revenue; ~**dar** *vt* collect

arredar /axeˈdar/ *vt* **não** ~ **pé** stand one's ground

arredio /axeˈdʒiu/ *a* withdrawn

arredondar /axedõˈdar/ *vt* round up <*quantia*>; round off <*ângulo*>

arredores /axeˈdɔris/ *m pl* surroundings; (*de cidade*) outskirts

arrefecer /axefeˈser/ *vt/i* cool

arregaçar /axegaˈsar/ *vt* roll up

arrega|lado /axegaˈladu/ *a* <*olhos*> wide; ~**lar** *vt* ~**lar os olhos** be wide-eyed with amazement

arreganhar /axegaˈɲar/ *vt* bare <*dentes*>; ~-**se** *vpr* grin

arrema|tar /axemaˈtar/ *vt* finish off; (*no tricô*) cast off; ~**te** *m* conclusion; (*na costura*) finishing off; (*no futebol*) finishing

arremes|sar /axemeˈsar/ *vt* hurl; ~**so** /e/ *m* throw

arrepen|der-se /axepẽˈdersi/ *vpr* be sorry; <*pecador*> repent; ~**der-se de regret** (*dido* a sorry; <*pecador*> repentant; ~**dimento** *m* regret; (*de pecado, crime*) repentance

arrepi|ado /axepiˈadu/ *a* <*cabelo*> standing on end; <*pele, pessoa*> covered in goose pimples; ~**ar** *vt* (*dar calafrios*) make shudder; make stand on end <*cabelo*>; **me** ~**a** (**a pele**) **it** gives me goose pimples; ~**ar-se** *vpr* (*estremecer*) shudder; <*cabelo*> stand on end; (*na pele*) get goose pimples; ~**o** *m* shudder; **me dá** ~**os** it makes me shudder

arris|cado /axisˈkadu/ *a* risky; ~**car** *vt* risk; ~**car-se** *vpr* take a risk, risk it; ~**car-se a fazer** risk doing

arro|char /axoˈʃar/ *vt* tighten up □ *vi* be tough; ~**cho** /o/ *m* squeeze

arro|gância /axoˈgãsia/ *f* arrogance; ~**gante** *a* arrogant

arro|jado /axoˈʒadu/ *a* bold; ~**jar** *vt* throw

arrombar /axõˈbar/ *vt* break down <*porta*>; break into <*casa*>; crack <*cofre*>

arro|tar /axoˈtar/ *vi* burp, belch; ~**to** /o/ *m* burp

arroz /aˈxoz/ *m* rice; ~ **doce** rice pudding; ~**al** (*pl* ~**ais**) *m* rice field

arrua|ça /axuˈasa/ *f* riot; ~**ceiro** *m* rioter

arruela /axuˈɛla/ *f* washer

arruinar /axuiˈnar/ *vt* ruin; ~-**se** *vpr* be ruined

arru|madeira /axumaˈdera/ *f* (*de hotel*) chambermaid; ~**mar** *vt* tidy (up) <*casa*>; sort out <*papéis, vida*>; pack <*mala*>; (*achar*) find, get; make up <*desculpa*>; (*vestir*) dress up; ~**mar-se** *vpr* (*aprontar-se*) get ready; (*na vida*) sort o.s. out

arse|nal /arseˈnaw/ (*pl* ~**nais**) *m* arsenal

arsênio /arˈseniu/ *m* arsenic

arte /ˈartʃi/ *f* art; **fazer** ~ <*criança*> get up to mischief; ~**fato** *m* product, article

arteiro /arˈteru/ *a* mischievous

artéria /arˈtɛria/ *f* artery

artesa|nal /artezaˈnaw/ (*pl* ~**nais**) *a* craft; ~**nato** *m* craftwork

arte|são /arteˈzãw/ (*pl* ~**s**) *m* (*f* ~**sã**) artisan, craftsman (*f* -woman)

ártico /ˈartʃiku/ *a & m* arctic

articu|lação /artʃikulaˈsãw/ *f* articulation; (*anat, tecn*) joint; ~**lar** *vt* articulate

arti|ficial /artʃifisiˈaw/ (*pl* ~**ficiais**) *a* artificial; ~**fício** *m* trick

artigo /arˈtʃigu/ *m* article; (*com*) item

artilharia /artʃiʎaˈria/ *f* artillery; ~**lheiro** *m* (*mil*) gunner; (*no futebol*) striker

artimanha /artʃiˈmaɲa/ *f* trick; (*método*) clever way

ar|tista /arˈtʃista/ *m/f* artist; ~**tístico** *a* artistic

artrite /arˈtritʃi/ *f* arthritis

árvore /ˈarvori/ *f* tree

arvoredo /arvoˈredu/ *m* grove

as /as/ *artigo & pron veja* **a**¹

ás /as/ *m* ace

às = a² + as

asa /'aza/ f wing; (de xícara) handle; ~-delta f hang-glider

ascen|dência /asē'dēsia/ f ancestry; (superioridade) ascendancy; ~dente a rising; ~der vi rise; ascend <ao trono>; ~são f rise; (relig) Ascension; em ~são rising; (fig) up and coming; ~sor m lift, (Amer) elevator; ~sorista m/f lift operator

asco /'asku/ m revulsion, disgust; dar ~ be revolting

asfalto /as'fawtu/ m asphalt

asfixiar /asfiksi'ar/ vt/i asphyxiate

Ásia /'azia/ f Asia

asiático /azi'atʃiku/ a & m Asian

asilo /a'zilu/ m (refúgio) asylum; (de velhos, crianças) home

as|ma /'azma/ f asthma; ~mático a & m asthmatic

asneira /az'nera/ f stupidity; (uma) stupid thing

aspas /'aspas/ f pl inverted commas

aspargo /as'pargu/ m asparagus

aspecto /as'pεktu/ m appearance, look; (de um problema) aspect

aspereza /aspe'reza/ f roughness; (do clima, de um som) harshness; (fig) rudeness

áspero /'asperu/ a rough; <clima, som> harsh; (fig) rude

aspi|ração /aspira'sãw/ f aspiration; (med) inhalation; ~rador m vacuum cleaner; ~rar vt inhale, breathe in <ar, fumaça>; suck up <líquido>; ~rar a aspire to

aspirina /aspi'rina/ f aspirin

asqueroso /aske'rozu/ a revolting, disgusting

assa|do /a'sadu/ a & m roast; ~dura f (na pele) sore patch

assalariado /asalari'adu/ a salaried □ m salaried worker

assal|tante /asaw'tãtʃi/ m robber; (na rua) mugger; (de casa) burglar; ~tar vt rob; burgle, (Amer) burglarize <casa>; ~to m (roubo) robbery; (a uma casa) burglary; (ataque) assault; (no boxe) round

assanhado /asa'ɲadu/ a worked up; <criança> excitable; (erótico) amorous

assar /a'sar/ vt roast

assassi|nar /asasi'nar/ vt murder; (pol) assassinate; ~nato m murder; (pol) assassination; ~no m murderer; (pol) assassin

asseado /asi'adu/ a well-groomed

as|sediar /asedʒi'ar/ vt besiege <cidade>; (fig) pester; ~sédio m siege; (fig) pestering

assegurar /asegu'rar/ vt (tornar seguro) secure; (afirmar) guarantee; ~ a alg aco/que assure s.o. of sth/ that; ~-se de/que make sure of/that

assembléia /asē'blεja/ f (pol) assembly; (com) meeting

assemelhar /aseme'ʎar/ vt liken; ~-se a be alike; ~-se a resemble, be like

assen|tar /asē'tar/ vt (estabelecer) establish, define; settle <povo>; lay <tijolo> □ vi <pó> settle; ~tar-se vpr settle down; ~tar com go with; ~tar a <roupa> suit; ~to m seat; (fig) basis; tomar ~to take a seat; <pó> settle

assen|tir /asē'tʃir/ vi agree; ~timento m agreement

assessor /ase'sor/ m adviser; ~ar vt advise

assexuado /aseksu'adu/ a asexual

assidui|dade /asidui'dadʒi/ f (à escola) regular attendance; (diligência) diligence

assíduo /a'siduu/ a (que freqüenta) regular; (diligente) assiduous

assim /a'sī/ adv like this, like that; (portanto) therefore; e ~ por diante and so on; ~ como as well as; ~ que as soon as

assimétrico /asi'mεtriku/ a asymmetrical

assimilar /asimi'lar/ vt assimilate; ~-se vpr be assimilated

assinalar /asina'lar/ vt (marcar) mark; (distinguir) distinguish; (apontar) point out

assi|nante /asi'nãtʃi/ m/f subscriber; ~nar vt/i sign; ~natura f (nome) signature; (de revista) subscription

assis|tência /asis'tēsia/ f assistance; (presença) attendance; (público) audience; ~tente a assistant □ m/f assistant; ~tente social social worker; ~tir (a) vt/i (ver) watch; (presenciar) attend; assist <doente>

assoalho /aso'aʎu/ m floor

assoar /aso'ar/ vt ~ o nariz, (Port) ~-se blow one's nose

assobi|ar /asobi'ar/ vt/i whistle; ~o m whistle

associ|ação /asosia'sãw/ f association; ~ado a & m associate; ~ar vt associate (a with); ~ar-se vpr associate; (com) go into partnership (a with)

assolar /aso'lar/ vt devastate

assom|bração /asõbra'sãw/ f ghost; ~brar vt astonish, amaze; ~brar-se vpr be amazed; ~bro m amazement, astonishment; (coisa) marvel; ~broso/o/ a astonishing, amazing

assoprar /aso'prar/ vi blow □ vt blow; blow out <vela>

assovi-veja assobi-

assu|mido /asu'midu/ a (confesso) confirmed, self-confessed; ~mir vt

assume, take on; accept, admit
<*defeito*> □ *vi* take office

assunto /a'sũtu/ *m* subject; (*negócio*) matter

assus|tador /asusta'dor/ *a* frightening; ~**tar** *vt* frighten, scare; ~**tar-se** *vpr* get frightened, get scared

asterisco /aste'risku/ *m* asterisk

as|tral /as'traw/ (*pl* ~**trais**) *m* (*fam*) state of mind; ~**tro** *m* star; ~**trologia** *f* astrology; ~**trólogo** *m* astrologer; ~**tronauta** *m/f* astronaut; ~**tronave** *f* spaceship; ~**tronomia** *f* astronomy; ~**tronômico** *a* astronomical; ~**trônomo** *m* astronomer

as|túcia /as'tusia/ *f* cunning; ~**tuto** *a* cunning; <*comerciante*> astute

ata /'ata/ *f* minutes

ata|ca|dista /ataka'dʒista/ *m/f* wholesaler; ~**do** *m* por ~**do** wholesale

ata|cante /ata'kãtʃi/ *a* attacking □ *m/f* attacker; ~**car** *vt* attack; tackle <*problema*>

atadura /ata'dura/ *f* bandage

ata|lhar /ata'ʎar/ *vi* take a shortcut; ~**lho** *m* shortcut

ataque /a'taki/ *m* attack; (*de raiva, riso*) fit

atar /a'tar/ *vt* tie

atarantado /atarã'tadu/ *a* flustered, in a flap

atarefado /atare'fadu/ *a* busy

atarracado /ataxa'kadu/ *a* stocky

atarraxar /ataxa'ʃar/ *vt* screw

até /a'tɛ/ *prep* (up) to, as far as; (*tempo*) until □ *adv* even; ~ **logo** goodbye; ~ **que** until

atéia /a'tɛja/ *a & f veja* ateu

ateliê /ateli'e/ *m* studio

atemorizar /atemori'zar/ *vt* frighten

Atenas /a'tenas/ *f* Athens

aten|ção /atẽ'sãw/ *f* attention; *pl* (*bondade*) thoughtfulness; com ~**ção** attentively; ~**cioso** *a* thoughtful, considerate

aten|der /atẽ'der/ ~**der** (**a**) *vt/i* answer <*telefone, porta*>; answer to <*nome*>; serve <*freguês*>; see <*paciente, visitante*>; grant, meet <*pedido*>; heed <*conselho*>; ~**dimento** *m* service; (*de médico etc*) consultation

aten|tado /atẽ'tadu/ *m* murder attempt; (*pol*) assassination attempt; (*ataque*) attack (contra on); ~**tar** *vi* ~**tar contra** make an attempt on

atento /a'tẽtu/ *a* attentive; ~ **a** mindful of

aterrador /atexa'dor/ *a* terrifying

ater|ragem /ate'xaʒẽ/ *f* (*Port*) landing; ~**rar** *vi* (*Port*) land

aterris|sagem /atexi'saʒẽ/ *f* landing; ~**sar** *vi* land

ater-se /a'tersi/ *vpr* ~ **a** keep to, go by

ates|tado /ates'tadu/ *m* certificate; ~**tar** *vt* attest (to)

ateu /a'tew/ *a & m* (*f* atéia) atheist

atiçar /atʃi'sar/ *vt* poke <*fogo*>; stir up <*ódio, discórdia*>; arouse <*pessoa*>

atinar /atʃi'nar/ *vt* work out, guess; ~ **com** find; ~ **em** notice

atingir /atʃĩ'ʒir/ *vt* reach; hit <*alvo*>; (*conseguir*) attain; (*afetar*) affect

atirar /atʃi'rar/ *vt* throw □ *vi* shoot; ~ **em** fire at

atitude /atʃi'tudʒi/ *f* attitude; tomar uma ~ take action

ati|va /a'tʃiva/ *f* active service; ~**var** *vt* activate; ~**vidade** *f* activity; ~**vo** *a* active □ *m* (*com*) assets

Atlântico /at'lãtʃiku/ *m* Atlantic

atlas /'atlas/ *m* atlas

at|leta /at'lɛta/ *m/f* athlete; ~**lético** *a* athletic; ~**letismo** *m* athletics

atmosfera /atʃimos'fɛra/ *f* atmosphere

ato /'atu/ *m* act; (*ação*) action; no ~ on the spot

ato|lar /ato'lar/ *vt* bog down; ~**lar-se** *vpr* get bogged down; ~**leiro** *m* bog; (*fig*) fix, spot of trouble

atômico /a'tomiku/ *a* atomic

atomizador /atomiza'dor/ *m* atomizer spray

átomo /'atomu/ *m* atom

atônito /a'tonitu/ *a* astonished, stunned

ator /a'tor/ *m* actor

atordoar /atordo'ar/ *vt* <*golpe, notícia*> stun; <*som*> deafen; (*alucinar*) bewilder

atormentar /atormẽ'tar/ *vt* plague, torment

atração /atra'sãw/ *f* attraction

atracar /atra'kar/ *vt/i* (*naut*) moor; ~**se** *vpr* grapple; (*fam*) neck

atractivo (*Port*) *veja* atrativo

atraente /atra'ẽtʃi/ *a* attractive

atraiçoar /atrajso'ar/ *vt* betray

atrair /atra'ir/ *vt* attract

atrapalhar /atrapa'ʎar/ *vt/i* (*confundir*) confuse; (*estorvar*) hinder; (*perturbar*) disturb; ~**-se** *vpr* get mixed up

atrás /a'traʃ/ *adv* behind; (*no fundo*) at the back; ~ **de** behind; (*depois de, no encalço de*) after; um mês ~ a month ago; ficar ~ be left behind

atra|sado /atra'zadu/ *a* late; <*país, criança*> backward; <*relógio*> slow; <*pagamento*> overdue; <*idéias*> old-fashioned; ~**sar** *vt* delay; put back <*relógio*> □ *vi* be late; <*relógio*> lose; ~**sar-se** *vpr* be late; (*num trabalho*) get behind; (*no pagar*) get into arrears; ~**so** *m* delay; (*de país etc*) backwardness; *pl* (*com*) arrears; com ~**so** late

atrativo /atra'tʃivu/ *m* attraction

através /atra'vɛs/ ∼ **de** *prep* through; *(de um lado ao outro)* across

atravessado /atrave'sadu/ *a* <*espinha*> stuck; **estar com alg** ∼ **na garganta** be fed up with s.o.

atravessar /atrave'sar/ *vt* go through; cross <*rua, rio*>

atre|ver-se /atre'versi/ *vpr* dare; ∼**ver-se a** dare to; ∼**vido** *a* daring; *(insolente)* impudent; ∼**vimento** *m* daring, boldness; *(insolência)* impudence

atribu|ir /atribu'ir/ *vt* attribute (**a** to); confer <*prêmio, poderes*> (**a** on); attach <*importância*> (**a** to); ∼**to** *m* attribute

atrito /a'tritu/ *m* friction; *(desavença)* disagreement

atriz /a'tris/ *f* actress

atrocidade /atrosi'dadʒi/ *f* atrocity

atrope|lar /atrope'lar/ *vt* run over, knock down <*pedestre*>; *(empurrar)* jostle; mix up <*palavras*>; ∼**lamento** *m* *(de pedestre)* running over; ∼**lo** /e/ *m* scramble

atroz /a'tros/ *a* awful, terrible; heinous <*crime*>; cruel <*pessoa*>

atuação /atua'sãw/ *f* *(ação)* action; *(desempenho)* performance

atu|al /atu'aw/ *(pl* ∼**ais)** *a* current, present; <*assunto, interesse*> topical; <*pessoa, carro*> up-to-date; ∼**alidade** *f* *(presente)* present (time); *(de um livro)* topicality; *pl* current affairs; ∼**alizado** *a* up-to-date; ∼**alizar** *vt* update; ∼**alizar-se** *vpr* bring o.s. up to date; ∼**almente** *adv* at present, currently

atum /a'tũ/ *m* tuna

aturdir /atur'dʒir/ *vt veja* **atordoar**

audácia /aw'dasia/ *f* boldness; *(insolência)* audacity

audi|ção /awdʒi'sãw/ *f* hearing; *(concerto)* recital; ∼**ência** *f* audience; *(jurid)* hearing

audiovisu|al /awdʒioviziu'aw/ *(pl* ∼**ais)** *a* audiovisual

auditório /awdʒi'tɔriu/ *m* auditorium; **programa de** ∼ variety show

auge /'awʒi/ *m* peak, height

aula /'awla/ *f* class, lesson; **dar** ∼ teach

aumen|tar /awmẽ'tar/ *vt* increase; raise <*preço, salário*>; extend <*casa*>; *(com lente)* magnify; *(acrescentar)* add □ *vi* increase; <*preço, salário*> go up; ∼**to** *m* increase; *(de salário)* rise, *(Amer)* raise

au|sência /aw'zẽsia/ *f* absence; ∼**sente** *a* absent □ *m/f* absentee

aus|pícios /aws'pisius/ *m pl* auspices; ∼**picioso** /o/ *a* auspicious

auste|ridade /awsteri'dadʒi/ *f* austerity; ∼**ro** /ɛ/ *a* austere

Austrália /aws'tralia/ *f* Australia

australiano /awstrali'anu/ *a & m* Australian

Áustria /'awstria/ *f* Austria

austríaco /aws'triaku/ *a & m* Austrian

autarquia /awtar'kia/ *f* public authority

autêntico /aw'tẽtʃiku/ *a* authentic; genuine <*pessoa*>; true <*fato*>

autobio|grafia /awtobiogra'fia/ *f* autobiography; ∼**gráfico** *a* autobiographical

autocarro /awto'kaxu/ *m* *(Port)* bus

autocrata /awto'krata/ *a* autocratic

autodefesa /awtode'feza/ *f* self-defence

autodidata /awtodʒi'data/ *a & m/f* self-taught (person)

autódromo /aw'tɔdromu/ *m* race track

auto-escola /awtois'kɔla/ *f* driving school

auto-estrada /awtois'trada/ *f* motorway, *(Amer)* expressway

autógrafo /aw'tɔgrafu/ *m* autograph

auto|mação /awtoma'sãw/ *f* automation; ∼**mático** *a* automatic; ∼**matizar** *vt* automate

auto|mobilismo /awtomobi'lizmu/ *m* motoring; *(esporte)* motor racing; ∼**móvel** /ɔ/ *(pl* ∼**móveis)** *m* motor car, *(Amer)* automobile

au|tonomia /awtono'mia/ *f* autonomy; ∼**tônomo** *a* autonomous; <*trabalhador*> selfemployed

autopeça /awto'pesa/ *f* car spare

autópsia /aw'tɔpsia/ *f* autopsy

autor /aw'tor/ *m* *(f* ∼**a)** author; *(de crime)* perpetrator; *(jurid)* plaintiff

auto-retrato /awtoxe'tratu/ *m* self-portrait

autoria /awto'ria/ *f* authorship; *(de crime)* responsibility (**de** for)

autori|dade /awtori'dadʒi/ *f* authority; ∼**zação** *f* authorization; ∼**zar** *vt* authorize

autuar /awtu'ar/ *vt* sue

au|xiliar /awsili'ar/ *a* auxiliary □ *m/f* assistant □ *vt* assist; ∼**xílio** *m* assistance, aid

aval /a'vaw/ *(pl* **avais)** *m* endorsement; *(com)* guarantee

avali|ação /avalia'sãw/ *f* *(de preço)* valuation; *(fig)* evaluation; ∼**ar** *vt* value <*quadro etc*> (**em** at); assess <*danos, riscos*>; *(fig)* evaluate

avan|çar /avã'sar/ *vt* move forward □ *vi* move forward; *(mil, fig)* advance; ∼**çar a** *(montar)* amount to; ∼**ço** *m* advance

avare|za /ava'reza/ *f* meanness; ∼**ento** *a* mean

ava|ria /ava'ria/ f damage; (de máquina) breakdown; ~**riado** a damaged; <máquina> out of order; <carro> broken down; ~**riar** vt damage □ vi be damaged; <máquina> break down

ave /'avi/ f bird; ~ **de rapina** bird of prey

aveia /a'veja/ f oats

avelã /ave'lã/ f hazelnut

avenida /ave'nida/ f avenue

aven|tal /avẽ'taw/ (pl ~**tais**) m apron

aventu|ra /avẽ'tura/ f adventure; (amorosa) fling; ~**rar** vt venture; ~**rar-se** vpr venture (a to); ~**reiro** a adventurous □ m adventurer

averiguar /averi'gwar/ vt check (out)

avermelhado /averme'ʎadu/ a reddish

aver|são /aver'sãw/ f aversion; ~**so** a averse (a to)

aves|sas /a'vɛsas/ **às ~sas** the wrong way round; (de cabeça para baixo) upside down; ~**so** /e/ m **ao ~so** inside out

avestruz /aves'trus/ m ostrich

avi|ação /avia'sãw/ f aviation; ~**ão** m (aero)plane, (Amer) (air)plane; ~**ão a jato** jet

avi|dez /avi'des/ f (cobiça) greediness; ~**do** a greedy

avi|sar /avi'zar/ vt (informar) tell, let know; (advertir) warn; ~**so** m notice; (advertência) warning

avistar /avis'tar/ vt catch sight of

avo /'avu/ m **um doze ~s** one twelfth

avó /a'vɔ/ f grandmother; ~**s** m pl grandparents

avô /a'vo/ m grandfather

avoado /avo'adu/ a dizzy, scatterbrained

avulso /a'vuwsu/ a loose, odd

avultado /avuw'tadu/ a bulky

axila /ak'sila/ f armpit

azaléia /aza'lɛja/ f azalea

azar /a'zar/ m bad luck; **ter** ~ **be** unlucky; ~**ado**, ~**ento** a unlucky

aze|dar /aze'dar/ vt sour □ vi go sour; ~**do** /e/ a sour

azei|te /a'zejtʃi/ m oil; ~**tona** /o/ f olive

azevinho /aze'viɲu/ m holly

azia /a'zia/ f heartburn

azucrinar /azukri'nar/ vt annoy

azul /a'zuw/ (pl azuis) a blue

azulejo /azu'leʒu/ m (ceramic) tile

azul-marinho /azuwma'riɲu/ a invar navy blue

B

babá /ba'ba/ f nanny; ~ **eletrônica** baby alarm

ba|bado /ba'badu/ m frill; ~**bador** m

bib; ~**bar** vt/i, ~**bar-se** vpr drool (por over); <bebê> dribble; ~**beiro** (Port) m bib

baby-sitter /bejbi'siter/ (pl ~**s**) m/f babysitter

bacalhau /baka'ʎaw/ m cod

bacana /ba'kana/ (fam) a great

bacha|rel /baʃa'rɛw/ (pl ~**réis**) bachelor; ~**relado** m bachelor's degree; ~**relar-se** vpr graduate

bacia /ba'sia/ f basin; (da privada) bowl; (anat) pelvis

baço /'basu/ m spleen

bacon /'bejkõ/ m bacon

bactéria /bak'tɛria/ f bacterium; pl bacteria

bada|lado /bada'ladu/ a (fam) talked about; ~**lar** vt ring <sino> □ vi ring; (fam) go out and about; ~**lativo** (fam) a fun-loving, gadabout

badejo /ba'deʒu/ m sea bass

baderna /ba'dɛrna/ f (tumulto) commotion; (desordem) mess

badulaque /badu'laki/ m trinket

bafafá /bafa'fa/ (fam) m to-do, kerfuffle

ba|fo /'bafu/ m bad breath; ~**fômetro** m Breathalyser; ~**forada** f puff

bagaço /ba'gasu/ m pulp; (Port: aguardente) brandy

baga|geiro /baga'ʒeru/ m (de carro) roofrack; (Port: homem) porter; ~**gem** f luggage; (cultural etc) baggage

bagatela /baga'tɛla/ f trifle

Bagdá /bagi'da/ f Baghdad

bago /'bagu/ m berry; (de chumbo) pellet

bagulho /ba'guʎu/ m piece of junk; pl junk; **ele é um** ~ he's as ugly as sin

bagun|ça /ba'gũsa/ f mess; ~**çar** vt mess up; ~**ceiro** a messy □ m messer

baía /ba'ia/ f bay

baiano /ba'janu/ a & m Bahian

baila /'bajla/ f **trazer/vir à** ~ bring/come up

bai|lar /baj'lar/ vt/i dance; ~**larino** m ballet dancer; ~**le** m dance; (de gala) ball

bainha /ba'iɲa/ f (de vestido) hem; (de arma) sheath

baioneta /bajo'neta/ f bayonet

bairro /'bajʃu/ m neighbourhood, area

baixa /'baʃa/ f drop, fall; (de guerra) casualty; (dispensa) discharge; ~**mar** f low tide

baixar /ba'ʃar/ vt lower; issue <ordem>; pass <lei> □ vi drop, fall; (fam: pintar) turn up

baixaria /baʃa'ria/ f sordidness; (uma) sordid thing

baixela /ba'ʃɛla/ f set of cutlery

baixeza /ba'ʃeza/ f baseness

baixo /'baʃu/ a low; <pessoa> short; <som, voz> quiet, soft; <cabeça, olhos> lowered; (vil) sordid □ adv low; <falar> softly, quietly □ m bass; em ~ underneath; (em casa) downstairs; em ~ de under; para ~ down; (em casa) downstairs; por ~ de under(neath)

baju|lador /baʒula'dor/ a obsequious □ m sycophant; ~lar vt fawn on

bala /'bala/ f (de revólver) bullet; (doce) sweet

balada /ba'lada/ f ballad

balaio /ba'laju/ m linen basket

balan|ça /ba'lãsa/ f scales; Balança (signo) Libra; ~ça de pagamentos balance of payments; ~çar vt/i (no ar) swing; (numa cadeira etc) rock; <carro, avião> shake; <navio> roll; ~çar-se vpr swing; ~cete /e/ m trial balance; ~ço m (com) balance sheet; (brinquedo) swing; (movimento no ar) swinging; (de carro, avião) shaking; (de navio) rolling; (de cadeira) rocking; fazer um ~ço de (fig) take stock of

balangandã /balãgã'dã/ m bauble

balão /ba'lãw/ m balloon; soltar um ~-de-ensaio (fig) put out feelers

balar /ba'lar/ vi bleat

balbu|ciar /bawbusi'ar/ vt/i babble; ~cio m babble, babbling

balbúrdia /baw'burdʒia/ f hubbub

bal|cão /baw'kãw/ m (em loja) counter; (de informações, bilhetes) desk; (de cozinha) worktop, (Amer) counter; (no teatro) circle; ~conista m/f shop assistant

balde /'bawdʒi/ m bucket

baldeação /bawdʒia'sãw/ f fazer ~ change (trains)

baldio /baw'dʒiu/ a fallow; terreno ~ (piece of) waste ground

balé /ba'le/ m ballet

balear /bali'ar/ vt shoot

baleia /ba'leja/ f whale

balido /ba'lidu/ m bleat, bleating

balísti|ca /ba'listʃika/ f ballistics; ~co a ballistic

bali|za /ba'liza/ f marker; (luminosa) beacon; ~zar vt mark out

balneário /bawni'ariu/ m seaside resort

balofo /ba'lofu/ a fat, tubby

baloiço, balouço /ba'lojsu, ba'losu/ (Port) m (de criança) swing

balsa /'bawsa/ f (de madeira etc) raft; (que vai e vem) ferry

bálsamo /'bawsamu/ m balm

báltico /'bawtʃiku/ a & m Baltic

baluarte /balu'artʃi/ m bulwark

bambo /'bãbu/ a loose, slack; <pernas> limp; <mesa> wobbly

bambo|lê /bãbo'le/ m hula hoop; ~lear vi <pessoa> sway, totter; <coisa> wobble

bambu /bã'bu/ m bamboo

ba|nal /ba'naw/ (pl ~nais) a banal; ~nalidade f banality

bana|na /ba'nana/ f banana □ (fam) m/f wimp; ~nada f banana fudge; ~neira f banana tree; plantar ~neira do a handstand

banca /'bãka/ f (de trabalho) bench; (de jornais) newsstand; ~ examinadora examining board; ~da f (pol) bench

bancar /bã'kar/ vt (custear) finance; (fazer papel de) play; (fingir) pretend

bancário /bã'kariu/ a bank □ m bank employee

bancarrota /bãka'xota/ f bankruptcy; ir à ~ go bankrupt

banco /'bãku/ m (com) bank; (no parque) bench; (na cozinha, num bar) stool; (de bicicleta) saddle; (de carro) seat; ~ de areia sandbank; ~ de dados database

banda /'bãda/ f band; (lado) side; de ~ sideways on; nestas ~s in these parts; ~ desenhada (Port) cartoon

bandei|ra /bã'dera/ f flag; (divisa) banner; dar ~ra (fam) give o.s. away; ~rante m/f pioneer □ f girl guide; ~rinha m/f linesman

bandeja /bã'deʒa/ f tray

bandido /bã'dʒidu/ m bandit

bando /'bãdu/ m (de pessoas) band; (de pássaros) flock

bandolim /bãdo'lĩ/ m mandolin

bangalô /bãga'lo/ m bungalow

Bangcoc /bã'koki/ f Bangkok

bangue-bangue /bãgi'bãgi/ (fam) m western

banguela /bã'gɛla/ a toothless

banha /'baɲa/ f lard; pl (no corpo) flab

banhar /ba'ɲar/ vt (molhar) bathe; (lavar) bath; ~-se vpr bathe

banhei|ra /ba'ɲera/ f bath, (Amer) bathtub; ~ro m bathroom; (Port) lifeguard

banhista /ba'ɲista/ m/f bather

banho /'baɲu/ m bath; (no mar) bathe, dip; tomar ~ have a bath; (no chuveiro) have a shower; tomar um ~ de loja/cultura go on a shopping/cultural spree; ~ de espuma bubble bath; ~ de sol sunbathing; ~-maria (pl ~s-maria) m bain marie

ba|nimento /bani'mẽtu/ m banishment; ~nir vt banish

banjo /'bãʒu/ m banjo

banqueiro /bã'keru/ m banker

banqueta /bã'keta/ f foot-stool

banque|te /bã'ketʃi/ m banquet; ~teiro m caterer

banzé /bã'zɛ/ (fam) m commotion, uproar

bapt- (*Port*) *veja* **bat-**
baque /'baki/ *m* thud, crash; (*revés*) blow; ~**ar** *vi* topple over □ *vt* hit hard, knock for six
bar /bar/ *m* bar
barafunda /bara'fũda/ *f* jumble; (*barulho*) racket
bara|lhada /bara'ʎada/ *f* jumble; ~**lho** *m* pack of cards, (*Amer*) deck of cards
barão /ba'rãw/ *m* baron
barata /ba'rata/ *f* cockroach
bara|tear /barat∫i'ar/ *vt* cheapen; ~**teiro** *a* cheap
baratinar /barat∫i'nar/ *vt* fluster; (*transtornar*) rattle, shake up
barato /ba'ratu/ *a* cheap □ *adv* cheaply □ (*fam*) *m* **um** ~ great; **que** ~! that's brilliant!
barba /'barba/ *f* beard; *pl* (*de gato etc*) whiskers; **fazer a** ~ shave; ~**da** *f* walkover; (*cavalo*) favourite; ~**do** *a* bearded
barbante /bar'bãt∫i/ *m* string
bar|baridade /barbari'dadʒi/ *f* barbarity; (*fam: muito dinheiro*) fortune; ~**bárie** *f*, ~**barismo** *m* barbarism
bárbaro /'barbaru/ *m* barbarian □ *a* barbaric; (*fam: forte, bom*) terrific
barbatana /barba'tana/ *f* fin
bar|beador /barbia'dor/ *m* shaver; ~**bear** *vt* shave; ~**bear-se** *vpr* shave; ~**bearia** *f* barber's shop; ~**beiragem** (*fam*) *f* bit of bad driving; ~**beiro** *m* barber; (*fam: motorista*) bad driver
bar|ca /'barka/ *f* barge; (*balsa*) ferry; ~**caça** *f* barge; ~**co** *m* boat; ~**co a motor** motorboat; ~**co a remo/vela** rowing/sailing boat, (*Amer*) rowboat/sailboat
barga|nha /bar'gaɲa/ *f* bargain; ~**nhar** *vt/i* bargain
barítono /ba'ritonu/ *m* baritone
barômetro /baro'rometru/ *m* barometer
baronesa /baro'neza/ *f* baroness
barra /'baxa/ *f* bar; (*sinal gráfico*) slash, stroke; (*fam: situação*) situation; **segurar a** ~ hold out; **forçar a** ~ force the issue
barra|ca /ba'xaka/ *f* (*de acampar*) tent; (*na feira*) stall; (*casinha*) hut; (*guarda-sol*) sunshade; ~**cão** *m* shed; ~**co** *m* shack, shanty
barragem /ba'xaʒẽ/ *f* (*represa*) dam
barra-pesada /baxape'zada/ (*fam*) *a invar* <*bairro*> rough; <*pessoa*> shady; (*difícil*) tough
bar|rar /ba'xar/ *vt* bar; ~**reira** *f* barrier; (*em corrida*) hurdle; (*em futebol*) wall
barrento /ba'xẽtu/ *a* muddy

barricada /baxi'kada/ *f* barricade
barri|ga /ba'xiga/ *f* stomach, (*Amer*) belly; ~**ga da perna** calf; ~**gudo** *a* pot-bellied
bar|ril /ba'xiw/ (*pl* ~**ris**) *m* barrel
barro /'baxu/ *m* (*argila*) clay; (*lama*) mud
barroco /ba'xoku/ *a* & *m* baroque
barrote /ba'xɔt∫i/ *m* beam, joist
baru|lheira /baru'ʎera/ *f* racket, din; ~**lhento** *a* noisy; ~**lho** *m* noise
base /'bazi/ *f* base; (*fig: fundamento*) basis; **com** ~ **em** on the basis of; **na** ~ **de** based on; ~**ado** *a* based; (*firme*) well-founded □ (*fam*) *m* joint; ~**ar** *vt* base; ~**ar-se em** be based on
básico /'baziku/ *a* basic
basquete /bas'ket∫i/ *m*, **basquetebol** /basket∫i'bɔw/ *m* basketball
bas|ta /'basta/ *m* **dar um** ~**ta em** call a halt to; ~**tante** *a* (*muito*) quite a lot of; (*suficiente*) enough □ *adv* (*com adjetivo, advérbio*) quite; (*com verbo*) quite a lot; (*suficientemente*) enough
bastão /bas'tãw/ *m* stick; (*num revezamento, de comando*) baton
bastar /bas'tar/ *vi* be enough
bastidores /bast∫i'doris/ *m pl* (*no teatro*) wings; **nos** ~ (*fig*) behind the scenes
bata /'bata/ *f* (*de mulher*) smock; (*de médico etc*) overall
bata|lha /ba'taʎa/ *f* battle; ~**lhador** *a* plucky, feisty □ *m* fighter; ~**lhão** *m* battalion; ~**lhar** *vi* battle; (*esforçar-se*) fight hard □ *vt* fight hard to get
batata /ba'tata/ *f* potato; ~ **doce** sweet potato; ~ **frita** chips, (*Amer*) French fries; (*salgadinhos*) crisps, (*Amer*) potato chips
bate-boca /bat∫i'boka/ *m* row, argument
bate|deira /bate'dera/ *f* whisk; (*de manteiga*) churn; ~**dor** *m* (*policial etc*) outrider; (*no criquete*) batsman; (*no beisebol*) batter; (*de caça*) beater; ~**dor de carteiras** pickpocket
batelada /bate'lada/ *f* batch; ~**s de** heaps of
batente /ba'tẽt∫i/ *m* (*de porta*) doorway; **para o/no** ~ (*fam: ao trabalho*) to/at work
bate-papo /bat∫i'papu/ *m* chat.
bater /ba'ter/ *vt* beat; stamp <*pé*>; slam <*porta*>; strike <*horas*>; take <*foto*>; flap <*asas*>; (*datilografar*) type; (*lavar*) wash; (*usar muito*) wear a lot <*roupa*>; (*fam*) pinch <*carteira*> □ *vi* <*coração*> beat; <*porta*> slam; <*janela*> bang; <*horas*> strike; <*sino*> ring; (*à porta*) knock; (*com o carro*) crash; ~**-se** *vpr* (*lutar*) fight; ~ **à máquina** type; ~ **a**

ou na porta knock at the door; ~ em hit; harp on <*assunto*>; <*luz, sol*> shine on; ~ com o carro crash one's car, have a crash; ~ com a cabeça bang one's head; ele batia os dentes de frio his teeth were chattering with cold; ele não bate bem (*fam*) he's not all there

bate|ria /bate'ria/ *f* (*eletr*) battery; (*mus*) drums; ~ria de cozinha kitchen utensils; ~rista *m/f* drummer

bati|da /ba'tʃida/ *f* beat; (*à porta*) knock; (*no carro*) crash; (*policial*) raid; (*bebida*) cocktail of rum, sugar and fruit juice; ~do *a* beaten; <*roupa*> well worn; <*assunto*> hackneyed □ *m* ~do de leite (*Port*) milkshake

batina /ba'tʃina/ *f* cassock

ba|tismo /ba'tʃizmu/ *m* baptism; ~tizado *m* christening; ~tizar *vt* baptize; (*pôr nome*) christen

batom /ba'tõ/ *m* lipstick

batu|cada /batu'kada/ *f* samba percussion group; ~car *vt/i* drum in a samba rhythm; ~que *m* samba rhythm

batuta /ba'tuta/ *f* baton; sob a ~ de under the direction of

baú /ba'u/ *m* trunk

baunilha /baw'niʎa/ *f* vanilla

bazar /ba'zar/ *m* bazaar; (*loja*) stationery and haberdashery shop

bê-a-bá /bea'ba/ *m* ABC

bea|titude /beatʃi'tudʒi/ *f* (*felicidade*) bliss; (*devoção*) piety, devoutness; ~to *a* (*devoto*) pious, devout; (*feliz*) blissful

bêbado /'bebadu/ *a & m* drunk

bebê /be'be/ *m* baby; ~ de proveta test-tube baby

bebe|deira /bebe'dera/ *f* (*estado*) drunkenness; (*ato*) drinking bout; ~dor *m* drinker; ~douro *m* drinking fountain

beber /be'ber/ *vt/i* drink

bebericar /beberi'kar/ *vt/i* sip

bebida /be'bida/ *f* drink

beca /'beka/ *f* gown

beça /'bɛsa/ *f* à ~ (*fam*) (*com substantivo*) loads of; (*com adjetivo*) really; (*com verbo*) a lot

beco /'beku/ *m* alley; ~ sem saída dead end

bedelho /be'deʎu/ *m* meter o ~ (em) stick one's oar in(to)

bege /'bɛʒi/ *a invar* beige

bei|cinho /bej'siɲu/ *m* fazer ~cinho pout; ~ço *m* lip; ~çudo *a* thick-lipped

beija-flor /bejʒa'flor/ *m* humming-bird

bei|jar /be'ʒar/ *vt* kiss; ~jo *m* kiss; ~joca /ɔ/ *f* peck

bei|ra /'bera/ *f* edge, (*fig. do desastre*

etc) verge, brink; à ~ra de at the edge of; (*fig*) on the verge of; ~rada *f* edge; ~ra-mar *f* seaside; ~rar *vt* (*ficar*) border (on); (*andar*) skirt; (*fig*) border on, verge on; ele está ~rando os 30 anos he's nearing thirty

beisebol /bejsi'bɔw/ *m* baseball

belas-artes /bɛlaʃ'artʃiʃ/ *f pl* fine arts

beldade /bew'dadʒi/ *f*, beleza /be'leza/ *f* beauty

belga /'bɛwga/ *a & m* Belgian

Bélgica /'bɛwʒika/ *f* Belgium

beliche /be'liʃi/ *m* bunk

bélico /'bɛliku/ *a* war

belicoso /beli'kozu/ *a* warlike

belis|cão /belis'kãw/ *m* pinch; ~car *vt* pinch; nibble <*comida*>

Belize /be'lizi/ *m* Belize

belo /'bɛlu/ *a* beautiful

beltrano /bew'tranu/ *m* such-and-such

bem /bẽj/ *adv* well; (*bastante*) quite; (*muito*) very □ *m* good; *pl* goods, property; está ~ (it's) fine, OK; fazer ~ a be good for; tudo ~? (*fam*) how's things?; se ~ que even though; ~ feito (por você) (*fam*) it serves you right; muito ~! well done!; de ~ com alg on good terms with s.o.; ~ como as well as

bem-apessoado /bẽjapeso'adu/ *a* nice-looking; ~-comportado *a* well-behaved; ~-disposto *a* keen, willing; ~-estar *m* well-being; ~-humorado *a* good-humoured; ~-intencionado *a* well-intentioned; ~-passado *a* <*carne*> well-done; ~-sucedido *a* successful; ~-vindo *a* welcome; ~-visto *a* well thought of

bênção /'bẽsãw/ (*pl* ~s) *f* blessing

bendito /bẽ'dʒitu/ *a* blessed

benefi|cência /benefi'sẽsia/ *f* (*bondade*) goodness, kindness; (*caridade*) charity; ~cente *a* <*associação*> charitable; <*concerto, feira*> charity; ~ciado *m* beneficiary; ~ciar *vt* benefit; ~ciar-se *vpr* benefit (de from)

benefício /bene'fisiu/ *m* benefit; em ~ de in aid of

benéfico /be'nɛfiku/ *a* beneficial (a to)

benevolência /benevo'lẽsia/ *f* benevolence

benévolo /be'nɛvolu/ *a* benevolent

benfeitor /bẽfej'tor/ *m* benefactor

bengala /bẽ'gala/ *f* walking stick; (*pão*) French stick

benigno /be'niginu/ *a* benign

ben|to /'bẽtu/ *a* blessed; <*água*> holy; ~zer *vt* bless; ~zer-se *vpr* cross o.s.

berço /'bersu/ *m* (*de embalar*) cradle; (*caminha*) cot; (*fig*) birthplace; ter ~ be from a good family

berimbau /beri'baw/ *m Brazilian percussion instrument shaped like a bow*

berinjela /beri'ʒɛla/ *f* aubergine, (*Amer*) eggplant

Berlim /ber'lĩ/ *f* Berlin

berma /'bɛrma/ (*Port*) *f* hard shoulder, (*Amer*) berm

bermuda /ber'muda/ *f* Bermuda shorts

Berna /'bɛrna/ *f* Berne

ber|rante /be'xãtʃi/ *a* loud, flashy; ~rar *vi* <*pessoa*> shout; <*criança*> bawl; <*boi*> bellow; ~reiro *m* (*gritaria*) yelling, shouting; (*choro*) crying, bawling; ~ro /ɛ/ *m* yell, shout; (*de boi*) bellow; aos ~ros shouting

besouro /be'zoru/ *m* beetle

bes|ta /'besta/ *a* (*idiota*) stupid; (*cheio de si*) full of o.s.; (*pedante*) pretentious □ *f* (*pessoa*) dimwit, numbskull; ficar ~ta (*fam*) be taken aback; ~teira *f* stupidity; (*uma*) stupid thing; falar ~teira talk rubbish; ~tial (*pl* ~tiais) *a* bestial; ~tificar *vt* astound, dumbfound

besuntar /bezũ'tar/ *vt* coat; (*sujar*) smear

betão /be'tãw/ (*Port*) *m* concrete

beterraba /bete'xaba/ *f* beetroot

betoneira /beto'nera/ *f* cement mixer

bexiga /be'ʃiga/ *f* bladder

bezerro /be'zeru/ *m* calf

bibelô /bibe'lo/ *m* ornament

Bíblia /'biblia/ *f* Bible

bíblico /'bibliku/ *a* biblical

biblio|grafia /bibliogra'fia/ *f* bibliography; ~teca /ɛ/ *f* library; ~tecário *m* librarian □ *a* library

bica /'bika/ *f* tap; (*Port: cafezinho*) espresso; suar em ~s drip with sweat

bicama /bi'kama/ *f* truckle bed

bicar /bi'kar/ *vt* peck

bíceps /'biseps/ *m invar* biceps

bicha /'biʃa/ *f* (*Port: fila*) queue; (*Bras: fam*) queer, fairy

bicheiro /bi'ʃeru/ *m* organizer of illegal numbers game, racketeer

bicho /'biʃu/ *m* animal; (*inseto*) insect, (*Amer*) bug; que ~ te mordeu? what's got into you?; ~-da-seda (*pl* ~s-da-seda) *m* silkworm; ~-de-sete-cabeças (*fam*) *m* big deal, big thing; ~-do-mato (*pl* ~s-do-mato) *m* very shy person

bicicleta /bisi'klɛta/ *f* bicycle, bike

bico /'biku/ *m* (*de ave*) beak; (*de faca*) point; (*de sapato*) toe; (*de bule*) spout; (*de caneta*) nib; (*do seio*) nipple; (*de gás*) jet; (*fam*) (*emprego*) odd job, sideline; (*boca*) mouth

bidê /bi'de/ *m* bidet

bidimensio|nal /bidʒimẽsio'naw/ (*pl* ~nais) *a* two-dimensional

biela /bi'ɛla/ *f* connecting rod

Bielo-Rússia /bielo'xusia/ *f* Byelorussia

bielo-russo /bielo'xusu/ *a & m* Byelorussian

bie|nal /bie'naw/ (*pl* ~nais) *a* biennial □ *f* biennial art exhibition

bife /'bifi/ *m* steak

bifo|cal /bifo'kaw/ (*pl* ~cais) *a* bifocal

bifur|cação /bifurka'sãw/ *f* fork; ~car-se *vpr* fork

bigamia /biga'mia/ *f* bigamy

bígamo /'bigamu/ *a* bigamous □ *m* bigamist

bigo|de /bi'gɔdʒi/ *m* moustache; ~dudo *a* with a big moustache

bigorna /bi'gɔrna/ *f* anvil

bijuteria /biʒute'ria/ *f* costume jewellery

bilate|ral /bilate'raw/ (*pl* ~rais) *a* bilateral

bilhão /bi'ʎãw/ *m* thousand million, (*Amer*) billion

bilhar /bi'ʎar/ *m* pool, billiards

bilhe|te /bi'ʎetʃi/ *m* ticket; (*recado*) note; ~te de ida e volta return ticket, (*Amer*) round-trip ticket; o ~te azul (*fam*) the sack; ~teria *f*, (*Port*) ~teira *f* (*no cinema, teatro*) box office; (*na estação*) ticket office

bilíngue /bi'lĩgwi/ *a* bilingual

bilionário /bilio'nariu/ *a & m* billionaire

bílis /'bilis/ *f* bile

binário /bi'nariu/ *a* binary

bingo /'bĩgu/ *m* bingo

binóculo /bi'nɔkulu/ *m* binoculars

biodegradá|vel /biodegra'davew/ (*pl* ~veis) *a* biodegradable

bio|grafia /biogra'fia/ *f* biography; ~gráfico *a* biographical

biógrafo /bi'ɔgrafu/ *m* biographer

bio|logia /biolo'ʒia/ *f* biology; ~lógico *a* biological

biólogo /bi'ɔlogu/ *m* biologist

biombo /bi'õbu/ *m* screen

biônico /bi'oniku/ *a* bionic; (*pol*) unelected

biópsia /bi'ɔpsia/ *f* biopsy

bioquími|ca /bio'kimika/ *f* biochemistry; ~co *a* biochemical □ *m* biochemist

biquíni /bi'kini/ *m* bikini

birma|nês /birma'nes/ *a & m* (*f* ~nesa) Burmese

Birmânia /bir'mania/ *f* Burma

birô /bi'ro/ *m* bureau

bir|ra /'bixa/ *f* wilfulness; fazer ~ra have a tantrum; ~rento *a* wilful

biruta /bi'ruta/ (*fam*) *a* crazy □ *f* windsock

bis /bis/ *int* encore!, more! □ *m invar* encore

bisa|vó /biza'vɔ/ f great-grandmother; **~vós** m pl great-grandparents; **~vô** m great-grandfather

bisbilho|tar /bizbiʎo'tar/ vt pry into □ vi pry; **~teiro** a prying □ m busybody; **~tice** f prying

bisca|te /bis'katʃi/ m odd job; **~teiro** m odd-job man

biscoito /bis'kojtu/ m biscuit, (Amer) cookie

bisnaga /biz'naga/ f (pão) bridge roll; (tubo) tube

bisne|ta /biz'nɛta/ f great-granddaughter; **~to** /ɛ/ m great-grandson; pl great-grandchildren

bis|pado /bis'padu/ m bishopric; **~po** m bishop

bissexto /bi'sestu/ a occasional; ano **~** leap year

bissexu|al /biseksu'aw/ (pl **~ais**) a & m/f bisexual

bisturi /bistu'ri/ m scalpel

bito|la /bi'tɔla/ f gauge; **~lado** a narrow-minded

bizarro /bi'zaxu/ a bizarre

blablablá /blabla'bla/ (fam) m chit-chat

black /'blɛki/ m black market; **~-tie** m evening dress

blas|femar /blasfe'mar/ vi blaspheme; **~fêmia** f blasphemy; **~femo** /e/ a blasphemous □ m blasphemer

blecaute /ble'kawtʃi/ m power cut

ble|far /ble'far/ vi bluff; **~fe** /ɛ/ m bluff

blin|dado /bli'dadu/ a armoured; **~dagem** f armour-plating

blitz /blits/ f invar police spot-check (on vehicles)

blo|co /'blɔku/ m block; (pol) bloc; (de papel) pad; (no carnaval) section; **~quear** vt block; (mil) blockade; **~queio** m blockage; (psic) mental block; (mil) blockade

blusa /'bluza/ f shirt; (de mulher) blouse; (de lã) sweater

boa /'boa/ f de bom; **numa ~** (fam) well; (sem problemas) easily; **estar numa ~** (fam) be doing fine; **~-gente** (fam) a invar nice; **~-pinta** (pl **~s-pintas**) (fam) a nice-looking; **~-praça** (pl **~s-praças**) (fam) a friendly, sociable

boate /bo'atʃi/ f nightclub

boato /bo'atu/ m rumour

boa|-nova /boa'nɔva/ (pl **~s-novas**) f good news; **~-vida** (pl **~s-vidas**) m/f good-for-nothing, waster; **~zinha** a sweet, kind

bo|bagem /bo'baʒẽ/ f silliness; (uma) silly thing; **~beada** f slip-up; **~bear** vi slip up; **~beira** f veja bobagem

bobe /'bɔbi/ m curler, roller

bobina /bo'bina/ f reel; (eletr) coil

bobo /'bobu/ a silly □ m fool; (da corte) jester; **~ca** /ɔ/ (fam) a stupid □ m/f twit

bo|ca /'boka/ f mouth; (no fogão) ring; **~ca da noite** nightfall; **~cado** m (na boca) mouthful; (pedaço) piece, bit; **~cal** (pl **~cais**) m mouthpiece

boce|jar /bose'ʒar/ vi yawn; **~jo** /e/ m yawn

boche|cha /bo'ʃeʃa/ f cheek; **~char** vi rinse one's mouth; **~cho** /e/ m mouthwash; **~chudo** a with puffy cheeks

bodas /'bodas/ f pl wedding anniversary; **~ de prata/ouro** silver/golden wedding

bode /'bɔdʒi/ m (billy) goat; **~ expiatório** scapegoat

bodega /bo'dega/ f (de bebidas) off-licence, (Amer) liquor store; (de secos e molhados) grocer's shop, corner shop

boêmio /bo'emiu/ a & m Bohemian

bofe|tada /bofe'tada/ f, **bofetão** /bofe'tãw/ m slap; **~tear** vt slap

boi /boj/ m bullock, (Amer) steer

bói /boj/ m office boy

bóia /'bɔja/ f (de balizamento) buoy; (de cortiça, isopor etc) float; (câmara de borracha) rubber ring; (de braço) armband, water wing; (na caixa-d'água) ballcock; (fam: comida) grub; **~ salva-vidas** lifebelt; **~-fria** (pl **~s-frias**) m/f itinerant farm labourer

boiar /bo'jar/ vt/i float; (fam) be lost

boico|tar /bojko'tar/ vt boycott; **~te** /ɔ/ m boycott

boiler /'bojler/ (pl **~s**) m boiler

boina /'bojna/ f beret

bo|jo /'boʒu/ m bulge; **~judo** a (cheio) bulging; (arredondado) bulbous

bola /'bɔla/ f ball; **dar ~ para** (fam) give attention to <pessoa>; care about <coisa>; **~ de gude** marble; **~ de neve** snowball

bolacha /bo'laʃa/ f (biscoito) biscuit, (Amer) cookie; (descanso) beermat; (fam: tapa) slap

bo|lada /bo'lada/ f large sum of money; **~lar** vt think up, devise

boléia /bo'lɛja/ f cab; (Port: carona) lift

boletim /bole'tʃĩ/ m bulletin; (escolar) report

bolha /'boʎa/ f bubble; (na pele) blister □ (fam) m/f pain

boliche /bo'liʃi/ m skittles

Bolívia /bo'livia/ f Bolivia

boliviano /bolivi'anu/ a & m Bolivian

bolo /'bolu/ m cake

bo|lor /bo'lor/ m mould, mildew; **~lorento** a mouldy

bolota /bo'lɔta/ *f* (*glande*) acorn; (*bolinha*) little ball

bol|sa /'bowsa/ *f* bag; ~**sa (de estudo)** scholarship; ~**sa (de valores)** stock exchange; ~**sista** *m/f*, (*Port*) ~**seiro** *m* scholarship student; ~**so** /o/ *m* pocket

bom /bõ/ *a* (*f* **boa**) good; (*de saúde*) well; <*comida*> nice; **está** ~ that's fine

bomba[1] /'bõba/ *f* (*explosiva*) bomb; (*doce*) eclair; (*fig*) bombshell; **levar** ~ (*fam*) fail

bomba[2] /'bõba/ *f* (*de bombear*) pump

Bombaim /bõba'ĩ/ *f* Bombay

bombar|dear /bõbardʒi'ar/ *vt* bombard; (*do ar*) bomb; ~**deio** *m* bombardment; (*do ar*) bombing

bomba-relógio /bõbaxe'lɔʒiu/ (*pl* ~**s-relógio**) *f* time bomb

bom|beiro /bõbi'ar/ *m* pump; ~**beiro** *m* fireman; (*encanador*) plumber

bombom /bõ'bõ/ *m* chocolate

bombordo /bõ'bɔrdu/ *m* port

bondade /bõ'dadʒi/ *f* goodness

bonde /'bõdʒi/ *m* tram; (*teleférico*) cable car

bondoso /bõ'dozu/ *a* good(-hearted)

boné /bo'nε/ *m* cap

bone|ca /bo'nεka/ *f* doll; ~**co** /ε/ *m* dummy

bonificação /bonifika'sãw/ *f* bonus

bonito /bo'nitu/ *a* <*mulher*> pretty; <*homem*> handsome; <*tempo, casa etc*> lovely

bônus /'bonus/ *m invar* bonus

boqui|aberto /bokia'bεrtu/ *a* openmouthed, flabbergasted; ~**nha** *f* snack

borboleta /borbo'leta/ *f* butterfly; (*roleta*) turnstile

borbotão /borbo'tãw/ *m* spurt

borbu|lha /bor'buʎa/ *f* bubble; ~**lhar** *vi* bubble

borda /'bɔrda/ *f* edge; ~**do** *a* edged; (*à linha*) embroidered □ *m* embroidery

bordão /bor'dãw/ *m* (*frase*) catchphrase

bordar /bor'dar/ *vt* (*à linha*) embroider

bor|del /bor'dεw/ (*pl* ~**déis**) *m* brothel

bordo /'bɔrdu/ *m* **a** ~ aboard

borra /'bɔxa/ *f* dregs; (*de café*) grounds

borra|cha /bo'xaʃa/ *f* rubber; ~**cheiro** *m* tyre fitter

bor|rão /bo'xãw/ *m* (*de tinta*) blot; (*rascunho*) rough draft; ~**rar** *vt* (*sujar*) blot; (*riscar*) cross out; (*pintar*) daub

borrasca /bo'xaska/ *f* squall

borri|far /boxi'far/ *vt* sprinkle; ~**fo** *m* sprinkling

bosque /'bɔski/ *m* wood

bosta /'bɔsta/ *f* (*de animal*) dung; (*chulo*) crap

bota /'bɔta/ *f* boot

botâni|ca /bo'tanika/ *f* botany; ~**co** *a* botanical □ *m* botanist

bo|tão /bo'tãw/ *m* button; (*de flor*) bud; **falar com os seus** ~**tões** say to o.s.

botar /bo'tar/ *vt* put; put on <*roupa*>; set <*mesa, despertador*>; lay <*ovo*>; find <*defeito*>

bote[1] /'bɔtʃi/ *m* (*barco*) dinghy; ~ **salva-vidas** lifeboat; (*de borracha*) liferaft

bote[2] /'bɔtʃi/ *m* (*de animal etc*) lunge

botequim /butʃi'ki/ *m* bar

botoeira /boto'era/ *f* buttonhole

boxe /'bɔksi/ *m* boxing; ~**ador** *m* boxer

brabo /'brabu/ *a* <*animal*> ferocious; <*calor, sol*> fierce; <*doença*> bad; <*prova, experiência*> tough; (*zangado*) angry

bra|çada /bra'sada/ *f* armful; (*em natação*) stroke; ~**cadeira** (*faixa*) armband; (*ferragem*) bracket; (*de atleta*) sweatband; ~**çal** (*pl* ~**çais**) *a* manual; ~**celete** /e/ *m* bracelet; ~**ço** *m* arm; ~**ço direito** (*fig: pessoa*) right-hand man

bra|dar /bra'dar/ *vt/i* shout; ~**do** *m* shout

braguilha /bra'giʎa/ *f* fly, flies

braile /'brajli/ *m* Braille

bra|mido /bra'midu/ *m* roar; ~**mir** *vi* roar

branco /'brãku/ *a* white □ *m* (*homem*) white man; (*espaço*) blank; **em** ~ <*cheque etc*> blank; **noite em** ~ sleepless night

bran|do /'brãdu/ *a* gentle; <*doença*> mild; (*indulgente*) lenient, soft; ~**dura** *f* gentleness; (*indulgência*) softness, leniency

brasa /'braza/ *f* **em** ~ red-hot; **mandar** ~ (*fam*) go to town

brasão /bra'zãw/ *m* coat of arms

braseiro /bra'zeru/ *m* brasier

Brasil /bra'ziw/ *m* Brazil

brasi|leiro /brazi'leru/ *a* & *m* Brazilian; ~**liense** *a* & *m/f* (*person*) from Brasília

bra|vata /bra'vata/ *f* bravado; ~**vio** *a* wild; <*mar*> rough; ~**vo** *a* (*corajoso*) brave; (*zangado*) angry; <*mar*> rough; ~**vura** *f* bravery

breca /'brεka/ *f* **levado da** ~ very naughty

brecar /bre'kar/ *vt* stop <*carro*>; (*fig*) curb □ *vi* brake

brecha /'brεʃa/ *f* gap; (*na lei*) loophole

bre|ga /'brega/ *a* (*fam*) tacky, naff; ~**guice** (*fam*) *f* tack, tackiness

brejo /'brɛʒu/ *m* marsh; **ir para o ~** (*fig*) go down the drain

brenha /'brɛɲa/ *f* thicket

breque /'brɛki/ *m* brake

breu /brew/ *m* tar, pitch

bre|ve /'brɛvi/ *a* short, brief; **em ~ve** soon, shortly; **~vidade** *f* shortness, brevity

briga /'briga/ *f* fight; (*bate-boca*) argument

briga|da /bri'gada/ *f* brigade; **~deiro** *m* brigadier; (*doce*) chocolate truffle

bri|gão /bri'gãw/ *a* (*f* **~gona**) belligerent; (*na fala*) argumentative □ *m* (*f* **~gona**) troublemaker; **~gar** *vi* fight; (*com palavras*) argue; <*cores*> clash

bri|lhante /bri'ʎãtʃi/ *a* (*reluzente*) shiny; (*fig*) brilliant; **~lhar** *vi* shine; **~lho** *m* (*de sapatos etc*) shine; (*dos olhos, de metais*) gleam; (*das estrelas*) brightness; (*de uma cor*) brilliance; (*fig: esplendor*) splendour

brin|cadeira /brĩka'dera/ *f* (*piada*) joke; (*brinquedo, jogo*) game; **de ~cadeira** for fun; **~calhão** (*f* **~calhona**) *a* playful □ *m* joker; **~car** *vi* (*divertir-se*) play; (*gracejar*) joke

brinco /'brĩku/ *m* earring

brin|dar /brĩ'dar/ *vt* (*saudar*) toast, drink to; (*presentear*) give a gift to; **~dar alg com aco** afford s.o. sth; (*de presente*) give s.o. sth as a gift; **~de** *m* (*saudação*) toast; (*presente*) free gift

brinquedo /brĩ'kedu/ *m* toy

brio /'briu/ *m* self-esteem, character; **~so** /o/ *a* self-confident

brisa /'briza/ *f* breeze

britadeira /brita'dera/ *f* pneumatic drill

britânico /bri'taniku/ *a* British □ *m* Briton; **os ~s** the British

broca /'brɔka/ *f* drill

broche /'brɔʃi/ *m* brooch

brochura /bro'ʃura/ *f* **livro de ~** paperback

brócolis /'brɔkulis/ *m pl*, (*Port*) **brócolos** /'brɔkuluʃ/ *m pl* broccoli

bron|ca /'brõka/ (*fam*) *f* telling-off; **dar uma ~ca em alg** tell s.o. off; **~co** *a* coarse, rough

bronquite /brõ'kitʃi/ *f* bronchitis

bronze /'brõzi/ *m* bronze; **~ado** *a* tanned, brown □ *m* (sun)tan; **~ador** *a* tanning □ *m* suntan lotion; **~amento** *m* tanning; **~ar** *vt* tan; **~ar-se** *vpr* go brown, tan

bro|tar /bro'tar/ *vt* sprout <*folhas, flores*>; spout <*lágrimas, palavras*> □ *vi* <*planta*> sprout; <*água*> spout; <*idéias*> pop up; **~tinho** (*fam*) *m* youngster; **~to** /o/ *m* shoot; (*fam*) youngster

broxa /'brɔʃa/ *f* (large) paint brush □ (*fam*) *a* impotent

bruços /'brusu/ **de ~** face down

bru|ma /'bruma/ *f* mist; **~moso** /o/ *a* misty

brusco /'brusku/ *a* brusque, abrupt

bru|tal /bru'taw/ *a* (*pl* **~tais**) *a* brutal; **~talidade** *f* brutality; **~to** *a* <*feições*> coarse; <*homem*> brutish; <*tom, comentário*> aggressive; <*petróleo*> crude; <*peso, lucro, salário*> gross □ *m* brute

bruxa /'bruʃa/ *f* witch; (*feia*) hag; **~ria** *f* witchcraft

Bruxelas /bru'ʃɛlas/ *f* Brussels

bruxo /'bruʃu/ *m* wizard

bruxulear /bruʃuli'ar/ *vi* flicker

bucha /'buʃa/ *f* (*tampão*) bung; (*para paredes*) rawlplug (R); **acertar na ~** (*fam*) hit the nail on the head

bucho /'buʃu/ *m* gut; **~ de boi** tripe

budis|mo /bu'dʒizmu/ *m* Buddhism; **~ta** *a & m/f* Buddhist

bueiro /bu'eru/ *m* storm drain

búfalo /'bufalu/ *m* buffalo

bu|fante /bu'fãtʃi/ *a* full, puffed; **~far** *vi* snort; (*reclamar*) grumble, moan

bufê /bu'fe/ *m* (*refeição*) buffet; (*serviço*) catering service; (*móvel*) sideboard

buginganga /buʒĩ'gãga/ *f* knickknack

bujão /bu'ʒãw/ *m* **~ de gás** gas cylinder

bula /'bula/ *f* (*de remédio*) directions; (*do Papa*) bull

bulbo /'buwbu/ *m* bulb

bule /'buli/ *m* (*de chá*) teapot; (*de café etc*) pot

Bulgária /buw'garia/ *f* Bulgaria

búlgaro /'buwgaru/ *a & m* Bulgarian

bulhufas /bu'ʎufas/ (*fam*) *pron* nothing

bulício /bu'lisiu/ *m* bustle

bumbum /bũ'bũ/ (*fam*) *m* bottom, bum

bunda /'bũda/ *f* bottom

buquê /bu'ke/ *m* bouquet

buraco /bu'raku/ *m* hole; (*de agulha*) eye; (*jogo de cartas*) rummy; **~ da fechadura** keyhole

burburinho /burbu'riɲu/ *m* (*de vozes*) hubbub

bur|guês /bur'ges/ *a & m* (*f* **~guesa**) bourgeois; **~guesia** *f* bourgeoisie

burlar /bur'lar/ *vt* get round <*lei*>; get past <*defesas, vigilância*>

buro|cracia /burokra'sia/ *f* bureaucracy; **~crata** *m/f* bureaucrat; **~crático** *a* bureaucratic; **~cratizar** *vt* make bureaucratic

bur|rice /bu'xisi/ *f* stupidity; (*uma*) stupid thing; **~ro** *a* stupid; (*ignorante*) dim □ *m* (*animal*) donkey; (*pessoa*) halfwit, dunce; **~ro de carga** (*fig*) workhorse

bus|ca /'buska/ *f* search; **dar ~ca em** search; **~ca-pé** *m* banger; **~car** *vt* fetch; (*de carro*) pick up; **mandar ~car** send for

bússola /'busola/ *f* compass; (*fig*) guide

busto /'bustu/ *m* bust

butique /bu'tʃiki/ *f* boutique

buzi|na /bu'zina/ *f* horn; **~nada** *f* toot (of the horn); **~nar** *vi* sound the horn, toot the horn

C

cá /ka/ *adv* here; **o lado de ~** this side; **para ~** here; **de ~ para lá** back and forth; **de lá para ~** since then; **~ entre nós** between you and me

ca|bal /ka'baw/ (*pl* **~bais**) *a* complete, full; <*prova*> conclusive

cabana /ka'bana/ *f* hut; (*casinha no campo*) cottage

cabeça /ka'besa/ *f* head; (*de lista*) top; (*pessoa inteligente*) mind □ *m/f* (*chefe*) ringleader; (*integrante mais inteligente*) brains; **de ~** <*saber*> off the top of one's head; <*calcular*> in one's head; **de ~ para baixo** upside down; **deu-lhe na ~ de** he took it into his head to; **esquentar a ~** (*fam*) get worked up; **fazer a ~ de alg** convince s.o.; **quebrar a ~** rack one's brains; **subir à ~** go to s.o.'s head; **ter a ~ no lugar** have one's head screwed on; **~da** *f* (*no futebol*) header; (*pancada*) head butt; **dar uma ~da no teto** bang one's head on the ceiling; **~de-porco** (*pl* **~s-de-porco**) *f* tenement; **~de-vento** (*pl* **~s-de-vento**) *m/f* scatterbrain, airhead; **~lho** *m* heading

cabe|cear /kabesi'ar/ *vt* head <*bola*>; **~ceira** *f* head; **~çudo** *a* pigheaded

cabe|dal /kabe'daw/ (*pl* **~dais**) *m* wealth

cabelei|ra /kabe'lera/ *f* head of hair; (*peruca*) wig; **~reiro** *m* hairdresser

cabe|lo /ka'belu/ *m* hair; **cortar o ~lo** have one's hair cut; **~ludo** *a* hairy; (*difícil*) complicated; <*palavra, piada*> dirty

caber /ka'ber/ *vi* fit; (*ter cabimento*) be fitting; **~ a** <*mérito, parte*> be due to; <*tarefa*> fall to; **cabe a você ir** it is up to you to go; **~ em alg** <*roupa*> fit s.o.

cabide /ka'bidʒi/ *m* (*peça de madeira, arame etc*) hanger; (*móvel*) hat stand; (*na parede*) coat rack

cabimento /kabi'mẽtu/ *m* **ter ~** be fitting, be appropriate; **não ter ~** be out of the question

cabine /ka'bini/ *f* cabin; (*de avião*)

cockpit; (*de loja*) changing room; **~ telefônica** phone box, (*Amer*) phone booth

cabisbaixo /kabiz'baʃu/ *a* crestfallen

cabí|vel /ka'bivew/ (*pl* **~veis**) *a* appropriate, fitting

cabo[1] /'kabu/ *m* (*militar*) corporal; **ao ~ de** after; **levar a ~** carry out; **~ eleitoral** campaign worker

cabo[2] /'kabu/ *m* (*fio*) cable; (*de panela etc*) handle; **TV por ~** cable TV; **~ de extensão** extension lead; **~ de força** tug of war

caboclo /ka'boklu/ *a* & *m* mestizo

ca|bra /'kabra/ *f* goat; **~brito** *m* kid

ca|ça /'kasa/ *f* (*atividade*) hunting; (*caçada*) hunt; (*animais*) game □ *m* (*avião*) fighter; **à ~ça de** in pursuit of; **~ça das bruxas** (*fig*) witch hunt; **~çador** *m* hunter; **~ça-minas** *m* invar minesweeper; **~ça-níqueis** *m invar* slot machine; **~çar** *vt* hunt <*animais, criminoso etc*>; (*procurar*) hunt for □ *vi* hunt

cacareco /kaka'rɛku/ *m* piece of junk; *pl* junk

cacare|jar /kakare'ʒar/ *vi* cluck; **~jo** /e/ *m* clucking

caçarola /kasa'rɔla/ *f* saucepan

cacau /ka'kaw/ *m* cocoa

cace|tada /kase'tada/ *f* blow with a club; (*fig*) annoyance; **~te** /e/ *m* club □ (*fam*) *int* damn

cachaça /ka'ʃasa/ *f* white rum

cachê /ka'ʃe/ *m* fee

cache|col /kaʃe'kɔw/ (*pl* **~cóis**) *m* scarf

cachimbo /ka'ʃĩbu/ *m* pipe

cacho /'kaʃu/ *m* (*de banana, uva*) bunch; (*de cabelo*) lock; (*fam: caso*) affair

cachoeira /kaʃo'era/ *f* waterfall

cachor|rinho /kaʃo'xiɲu/ *m* (*nado*) doggy paddle; **~ro** /o/ *m* dog; (*Port*) puppy; (*pessoa*) scoundrel; **~roquente** (*pl* **~ros-quentes**) *m* hot dog

cacife /ka'sifi/ *m* (*fig*) pull

caci|que /ka'siki/ *m* (*índio*) chief; (*político*) boss; **~quia** *f* leadership

caco /'kaku/ *m* shard; (*pessoa*) old crock

cacto /'kaktu/ *m* cactus

caçula /ka'sula/ *m/f* youngest child □ *a* youngest

cada /'kada/ *a* each; **~ duas horas** every two hours; **custam £5 ~ (um)** they cost £5 each; **~ vez mais** more and more; **~ vez mais fácil** easier and easier; **ele fala ~ coisa** (*fam*) he says the most amazing things

cadafalso /kada'fawsu/ *m* gallows

cadarço /ka'darsu/ *m* shoelace

cadas|trar /kadas'trar/ *vt* register; **~tro** *m* register; (*ato*) registration (*policial, bancário*) records, files; (*imobiliário*) land register

cadáver /ka'daver/ *m* (dead) body, corpse; ~**daverico** *a* cadaverous, corpse-like/ <*exame*> post-mortem

cadê /ka'de/ (*fam*) *adv* where is/ are...?

cadeado /kadʒi'adu/ *m* padlock

cadeia /ka'deja/ *f* (*de eventos, lojas etc*) chain; (*prisão*) prison; (*rádio, TV*) network

cadeira /ka'dera/ *f* (*móvel*) chair; (*no teatro*) stall; (*de politico*) seat; (*função de professor*) chair; (*matéria*) subject; *pl* (*anat*) hips; ~ **de balanço** rocking chair; ~ **de rodas** wheelchair; ~ **elétrica** electric chair

ca|dência /ka'dẽsia/ *f* (*mus, da voz*) cadence; (*compasso*) rhythm; ~**denciado** *a* rhythmic; <*passos*> measured

cader|neta /kader'neta/ *f* notebook; (*de professor*) register; (*de banco*) passbook; ~**neta de poupança** savings account; ~**no** /ɛ/ *m* exercise book; (*pequeno*) notebook; (*no jornal*) section

cadete /ka'detʃi/ *m* cadet

cadu|car /kadu'kar/ *vi* <*pessoa*> become senile; <*contrato*> lapse; ~**co** *a* <*pessoa*> senile; <*contrato*> lapsed; ~**quice** *f* senility

cafajeste /kafa'ʒestʃi/ *m* swine

ca|fé /ka'fɛ/ *m* coffee; (*botequim*) café; ~**fé da manhã** breakfast; **tomar** ~**fé** have breakfast; ~**fé-com-leite** *a invar* coffee-coloured, light brown □ *m* white coffee; ~**feeiro** *a* coffee □ *m* coffee plant; ~**feicultura** *f* coffee-growing; ~**feína** *f* caffein(e)

cafetã /kafe'tã/ *m* caftan

cafetão /kafe'tãw/ *m* pimp

cafe|teira /kafe'tera/ *f* coffee pot; ~**zal** (*pl* ~**zais**) *m* coffee plantation; ~**zinho** *m* small black coffee

cafo|na /ka'fona/ (*fam*) *a* naff, tacky; ~**nice** *f* tackiness; (*coisa*) tacky thing

cágado /'kagadu/ *m* turtle

caiar /kaj'ar/ *vt* whitewash

cãibra /'kãjbra/ *f* cramp

cai|da /ka'ida/ *f* fall; *veja* **queda**; ~**do** *a* <*árvore etc*> fallen; <*beiços etc*> drooping; (*deprimido*) dejected; (*apaixonado*) smitten

caimento /kaj'mẽtu/ *m* fall

caipi|ra /kaj'pira/ *a* <*pessoa*> countrified; <*festa, música*> country; <*sotaque*> rural □ *m/f* country person; (*depreciativo*) country bumpkin; ~**rinha** *f* cachaça with limes, sugar and ice

cair /ka'ir/ *vi* fall; <*dente, cabelo*> fall out; <*botão etc*> fall off; <*comércio, trânsito etc*> fall off; <*tecido, cortina*>

hang; ~ **bem/mal** <*roupa*> go well/ badly; <*ato, dito*> go down well/ badly; **estou caindo de sono** I'm really sleepy

cais /kajs/ *m* quay; (*Port: na estação*) platform

caixa /'kaʃa/ *f* box; (*de loja etc*) cash-desk □ *m/f* cashier; ~ **de correio** letter box; ~ **de mudanças** (*Port*) ~ **de velocidades** gear box; ~ **postal** post office box, PO Box; ~**-d'água** (*pl* ~**s-d'água**) *f* water tank; ~**-forte** (*pl* ~**s-fortes**) *f* vault

cai|xão /ka'ʃãw/ *m* coffin; ~**xeiro** *m* (*em loja*) assistant; salesman; ~**xilho** *m* frame; ~**xote** /ɔ/ *m* crate

caju /ka'ʒu/ *m* cashew fruit; ~**eiro** *m* cashew tree

cal /kaw/ *f* lime

calado /ka'ladu/ *a* quiet

calafrio /kala'friu/ *m* shudder, shiver

calami|dade /kalami'dadʒi/ *f* calamity; ~**toso** /o/ *a* calamitous

calar /ka'lar/ *vi* be quiet □ *vt* keep quiet about <*segredo, sentimento*>; silence <*pessoa*>; ~**-se** *vpr* go quiet

calça /'kawsa/; ~ *f* trousers, (*Amer*) pants

calça|da /kaw'sada/ *f* pavement, (*Amer*) sidewalk; (*Port: rua*) roadway; ~**dão** *m* pedestrian precinct; ~**deira** *f* shoe-horn; ~**do** *a* paved □ *m* shoe; *pl* footwear

calcanhar /kawka'ɲar/ *m* heel

calção /kaw'sãw/ *m* shorts; ~ **de banho** swimming trunks

calcar /kaw'kar/ *vt* (*pisar*) trample; (*comprimir*) press; ~ **aco em** (*fig*) base sth on, model sth on

calçar /kaw'sar/ *vt* put on <*sapatos, luvas*>; take <*número*>; pave <*rua*>; (*com calço*) wedge □ *vi* <*sapato*> fit; ~**-se** *vpr* put one's shoes on

calcário /kaw'kariu/ *m* limestone □ *a* <*água*> hard

calças /'kawsas/ *f pl veja* **calça**

calcinha /kaw'siɲa/ *f* knickers, (*Amer*) panties

cálcio /'kawsiu/ *m* calcium

calço /'kawsu/ *m* wedge

calcu|ladora /kawkula'dora/ *f* calculator; ~**lar** *vt/i* calculate; ~**lista** *a* calculating □ *m/f* opportunist

cálculo /'kawkulu/ *m* calculation; (*diferencial*) calculus; (*med*) stone

cal|da /'kawda/ *f* syrup; *pl* hot springs; ~**deira** *f* boiler; ~**deirão** *m* cauldron; ~**do** *m* (*sopa*) broth; (*suco*) juice; ~**do de carne/galinha** beef/ chicken stock

calefação /kalefa'sãw/ *f* heating

caleidoscópio /kalejdos'kɔpiu/ *m* kaleidoscope

calejado /kaleˈʒadu/ *a <mãos>* calloused; *<pessoa>* experienced

calendário /kalẽˈdariu/ *m* calendar

calha /ˈkaʎa/ *f (no telhado)* gutter; *(sulco)* gulley

calhamaço /kaʎaˈmasu/ *m* tome

calhambeque /kaʎãˈbɛki/ *(fam) m* banger

calhar /kaˈʎar/ *vi* **calhou que** it so happened that; **calhou pegar em o mesmo trem** they happened to get the same train; **~ de** happen to; **vir a ~** come at the right time

cali|brado /kaliˈbradu/ *a (bêbado)* tipsy; **~brar** *vt* calibrate; check (the pressure of) *<pneu>*; **~bre** *m* calibre; **coisas desse ~bre** things of this order

cálice /ˈkalisi/ *m (copo)* liqueur glass; *(na missa)* chalice

caligrafia /kaligraˈfia/ *f (letra)* handwriting; *(arte)* calligraphy

calista /kaˈlista/ *m/f* chiropodist, *(Amer)* podiatrist

cal|ma /ˈkawma/ *f* calm; **com ~ma** calmly □ *int* calm down; **~mante** *m* tranquilizer; **~mo** *a* calm

calo /ˈkalu/ *m (na mão)* callus; *(no pé)* corn

calombo /kaˈlõbu/ *m* bump

calor /kaˈlor/ *m* heat; *(agradável, fig)* warmth; **estar com ~** be hot

calo|rento /kaloˈrẽtu/ *a <pessoa>* sensitive to heat; *<lugar>* hot; **~ria** *f* calorie; **~roso** /o/ *a* warm; *<protesto>* lively

calota /kaˈlɔta/ *f* hubcap

calo|te /kaˈlɔtʃi/ *m* bad debt; **~teiro** *m* bad risk

calouro /kaˈloru/ *m (na faculdade)* freshman; *(em outros ramos)* novice

ca|lúnia /kaˈlunia/ *f* slander; **~luniar** *vt* slander; **~lunioso** /o/ *a* slanderous

cal|vície /kawˈvisi/ *f* baldness; **~vo** *a* bald

cama /ˈkama/ *f* bed; **~ de casal/solteiro** double/single bed; **~-beliche** *(pl ~s-beliches) f* bunk bed

camada /kaˈmada/ *f* layer; *(de tinta)* coat

câmara /ˈkamara/ *f* chamber; *(fotográfica)* camera; **em ~ lenta** in slow motion; **~ municipal** town council; *(Port)* town hall

camarada /kamaˈrada/ *a* friendly □ *m/f* comrade; **~gem** *f* comradeship; *(convivência agradável)* camaraderie

câmara-de-ar /kamaradʒiˈar/ *(pl câmaras-de-ar) f* inner tube

camarão /kamaˈrãw/ *m* shrimp; *(maior)* prawn

cama|reira /kamaˈrera/ *f* chambermaid; **~rim** *m* dressing room;

~rote /ɔ/ *m (no teatro)* box; *(num navio)* cabin

cambada /kãˈbada/ *f* gang, horde

cambalacho /kãbaˈlaʃu/ *m* scam

camba|lear /kãbaliˈar/ *vi* stagger; **~lhota** *f* somersault

cambi|al /kãbiˈaw/ *(pl ~ais) a* exchange; **~ante** *m* shade; **~ar** *vt* change

câmbio /ˈkãbiu/ *m* exchange; *(taxa)* rate of exchange; **~ oficial/paralelo** official/black market exchange rate

cambista /kãˈbista/ *m/f (de entradas)* ticket-tout, *(Amer)* scalper; *(de dinheiro)* money changer

Camboja /kãˈbɔʒa/ *m* Cambodia

cambojano /kãboˈʒanu/ *a & m* Cambodian

camburão /kãbuˈrãw/ *m* police van

camélia /kaˈmɛlia/ *f* camelia

camelo /kaˈmelu/ *m* camel

camelô /kameˈlo/ *m* street vendor

camião /kamiˈãw/ *(Port) m veja* **caminhão**

caminhada /kamiˈɲada/ *f* walk

caminhão /kaɾ̃iˈɲãw/ *m* lorry, *(Amer)* truck

cami|nhar /kamiˈɲar/ *vi* walk; *(fig)* advance, progress; **~nho** *m* way; *(estrada)* road; *(trilho)* path; **a ~nho** on the way; **a meio ~nho** halfway; **~nho de ferro** *(Port)* railway, *(Amer)* railroad

caminho|neiro /kamiɲoˈneru/ *m* lorry driver, *(Amer)* truck driver; **~nete** /ɛ/ *m* van

camio|neta /kamioˈneta/ *f* van; **~nista** *(Port) m/f veja* **caminhoneiro**

cami|sa /kaˈmiza/ *f* shirt; **~sa-deforça** *(pl ~sas-de-força) f* straitjacket; **~sa-de-vênus** *(pl ~sas-de-vênus) f* condom; **~seta** /e/ *f* T-shirt; *(de baixo)* vest; **~sinha** *(fam) f* condom; **~sola** /ɔ/ *f* nightdress; *(Port)* sweater

camomila /kamoˈmila/ *f* camomile

campainha /kãpaˈiɲa/ *f* bell; *(da porta)* doorbell

campanário /kãpaˈnariu/ *m* belfry

campanha /kãˈpaɲa/ *f* campaign

campe|ão /kãpiˈãw/ *m (f ~ã)* champion; **~onato** *m* championship

cam|pestre /kãˈpɛstri/ *a* rural; **~pina** *f* grassland

cam|ping /ˈkãpĩ/ *m* camping, *(lugar)* campsite; **~pismo** *(Port) m* camping

campo /ˈkãpu/ *m* field; *(interior)* country; *(de futebol)* pitch; *(de golfe)* course; **~ de concentração** concentration camp; **~nês** *m (f ~nesa)* peasant

camu|flagem /kamuˈflaʒẽ/ *f* camouflage; **~flar** *vt* camouflage

camundongo /kamũˈdõgu/ *m* mouse

cana /'kana/ f cane; ~ **de açúcar** sugar cane

Canadá /kana'da/ m Canada

canadense /kana'dẽsi/ a & m Canadian

ca|nal /ka'naw/ (pl ~**nais**) m channel; (hidrovia) canal

canalha /ka'naʎa/ m/f scoundrel

canali|zação /kanaliza'sãw/ f piping; ~**zador** (Port) m plumber; ~**zar** vt channel < líquido, esforço, recursos >; canalize < rio >; pipe for water and drainage < cidade >

canário /ka'nariu/ m canary

canastra /ka'nastra/ f (~**trona**) ham actor (f actress)

canavi|al /kanavi'aw/ (pl ~**ais**) m cane field; ~**eiro** a sugar cane

canção /kã'sãw/ f song

cance|lamento /kãsela'mẽtu/ m cancellation; ~**lar** vt cancel; (riscar) cross out

câncer /'kãser/ m cancer; **Câncer** (signo) Cancer

cance|riano /kãseri'anu/ a & m Cancerian; ~**rígeno** a carcinogenic; ~**roso** /o/ a cancerous □ m person with cancer

cancro /'kãkru/ m (Port: cáncer) cancer; (fig) canker

candango /kã'dãgu/ m person from Brasília

cande|eiro /kãdʒi'eru/ m (oil-)lamp; ~**labro** m candelabra

candida|tar-se /kãdʒida'tarsi/ vpr (a vaga) apply (a for); (à presidência etc) stand, (Amer) run (a for); ~**to** m candidate (a for); (a vaga) applicant (a for); ~**tura** f candidature; (a vaga) application (a for)

cândido /'kãdʒidu/ a innocent

candomblé /kãdõ'blɛ/ m Afro-Brazilian cult; (reunião) candomble meeting

candura /kã'dura/ f innocence

cane|ca /ka'nɛka/ f mug; ~**co** /ɛ/ m tankard

canela[1] /ka'nɛla/ f (condimento) cinnamon

canela[2] /ka'nɛla/ f (da perna) shin; ~**da** f dar uma ~**da em alg** kick s.o. in the shins; **dar uma ~da em aco** hit one's shins on sth

cane|ta /ka'neta/ f pen; ~ **esferográfica** ball-point pen; ~**ta-tinteiro** (pl ~**tas-tinteiro**) f fountain pen

cangote /kã'gɔtʃi/ m nape of the neck

canguru /kãgu'ru/ m kangaroo

canhão /ka'ɲãw/ m (arma) cannon; (vale) canyon

canhoto /ka'ɲotu/ a left-handed □ m (talão) stub

cani|bal /kani'baw/ (pl ~**bais**) m/f cannibal; ~**balismo** m cannibalism

caniço /ka'nisu/ m reed; (pessoa) skinny person

canícula /ka'nikula/ f heat wave

ca|nil /ka'niw/ (pl ~**nis**) m kennel

canivete /kani'vɛtʃi/ m penknife

canja /'kãʒa/ f chicken soup; (fam) piece of cake

canjica /kã'ʒika/ f corn porridge

cano /'kanu/ m pipe; (de bota) top; (de arma de fogo) barrel

cano|a /ka'noa/ f canoe; ~**agem** f canoeing; ~**ista** m/f canoeist

canonizar /kanoni'zar/ vt canonize

can|saço /kã'sasu/ m tiredness; ~**sado** a tired; ~**sar** vt tire; (aborrecer) bore □ vi, ~**sar-se** vpr get tired; ~**sativo** a tiring; (aborrecido) boring; ~**seira** f tiredness; (lida) toil

can|tada /kã'tada/ f (fam) chat-up; ~**tar** vt/i sing; (fam) chat up

cântaro /'kãtaru/ m **chover a ~s** pour down, bucket down

cantarolar /kãtaro'lar/ vt/i hum

cantei|ra /kã'tera/ f quarry; ~**ro** m (de flores) flowerbed; (artífice) stonemason; ~**ro de obras** site office

cantiga /kã'tʃiga/ f ballad

can|til /kã'tʃiw/ (pl ~**tis**) m canteen; ~**tina** f canteen

canto[1] /'kãtu/ m (ângulo) corner

canto[2] /'kãtu/ m (cantar) singing; ~**tor** m singer; ~**toria** f singing

canudo /ka'nudu/ m (de beber) straw; (tubo) tube; (fam: diploma) diploma

cão /kãw/ (pl **cães**) m dog

caolho /ka'oʎu/ a one-eyed

ca|os /kaws/ m chaos; ~**ótico** a chaotic

capa /'kapa/ f (de livro, revista) cover; (roupa sem mangas) cape; ~ **de chuva** raincoat

capacete /kapa'setʃi/ m helmet

capacho /ka'paʃu/ m doormat

capaci|dade /kapasi'dadʒi/ f capacity; (aptidão) ability; ~**tar** vt enable; (convencer) convince

capataz /kapa'tas/ m foreman

capaz /ka'pas/ a capable (**de** of); **ser ~ de** (poder) be able to; (ser provável) be likely to

cape|la /ka'pɛla/ f chapel; ~**lão** (pl ~**lães**) m chaplain

capen|ga /ka'pẽga/ a doddery; ~**gar** vi dodder

capeta /ka'peta/ m (diabo) devil; (criança) little devil

capilar /kapi'lar/ a hair

ca|pim /ka'pĩ/ m grass; ~**pinar** vt/i weed

capi|tal /kapi'taw/ (pl ~**tais**) a & m/f capital; ~**talismo** m capitalism; ~**talista** a & m/f capitalist; ~**talizar** vt (com) capitalize; (aproveitar) capitalize on

capi|tanear /kapitani'ar/ *vt* captain <*navio*>; (*fig*) lead; **~tania** *f* captaincy; **~tania do porto** port authority; **~tão** (*pl* **~tães**) *m* captain

capitulação /kapitula'sãw/ *f* capitulation, surrender

capítulo /ka'pitulu/ *m* chapter; (*de telenovela*) episode

capô /ka'po/ *m* bonnet, (*Amer*) hood

capoeira /kapo'era/ *f* Brazilian kick-boxing

capo|ta /ka'pɔta/ *f* roof; **~tar** *vi* overturn

capote /ka'pɔtʃi/ *m* overcoat

capri|char /kapri'ʃar/ *vi* excel o.s.; **~cho** *m* (*esmero*) care; (*desejo*) whim; (*teimosia*) contrariness; **~choso** /o/ *a* (*cheio de caprichos*) capricious; (*com esmero*) painstaking, meticulous

Capricórnio /kapri'kɔrniu/ *m* Capricorn

capricorniano /kaprikorni'anu/ *a* & *m* Capricorn

cápsula /'kapsula/ *f* capsule

cap|tar /kap'tar/ *vt* pick up <*emissão, sinais*>; tap <*água*>; catch, grasp <*sentido*>; win <*simpatia, admiração*>; **~tura** *f* capture; **~turar** *vt* capture

capuz /ka'pus/ *m* hood

caquético /ka'kɛtʃiku/ *a* broken-down, on one's last legs

caqui /ka'ki/ *m* persimmon

cáqui /'kaki/ *a invar* & *m* khaki

cara /'kara/ *f* face; (*aparência*) look; (*ousadia*) cheek □ (*fam*) *m* guy; **~ a ~** face to face; **de ~** straightaway; **dar de ~ com** run into; **está na ~** it's obvious; **fechar a ~** frown; **~ de pau** cheek; **~ de tacho** (*fam*) sheepish look

cara|col /kara'kɔw/ (*pl* **~cóis**) *m* snail **caracte|re** /karak'tɛri/ *m* character; **~rística** *f* characteristic, feature; **~rístico** *a* characteristic; **~rizar** *vt* characterize; **~rizar-se** *vpr* be characterized

cara-de-pau /karadʒi'paw/ (*pl* **caras-de-pau**) *a* cheeky, brazen

caramba /ka'rãba/ *int* (*de espanto*) wow; (*de desagrado*) damn

caramelo /kara'mɛlu/ *m* caramel; (*bala*) toffee

caramujo /kara'muʒu/ *m* water snail

caranguejo /karã'geʒu/ *m* crab

caratê /kara'te/ *m* karate

caráter /ka'rater/ *m* character

caravana /kara'vana/ *f* caravan

car|boidrato /karboi'dratu/ *m* carbohydrate; **~bono** /o/ *m* carbon

carbu|rador /karbura'dor/ *m* carburettor, (*Amer*) carburator; **~rante** *m* fuel

carcaça /kar'kasa/ *f* carcass; (*de navio etc*) frame

cárcere /'karseri/ *m* jail

carcereiro /karse'reru/ *m* jailer, warder

carcomido /karko'midu/ *a* worm-eaten; <*rosto*> pock-marked

cardápio /kar'dapiu/ *m* menu

carde|al /kardʒi'aw/ (*pl* **~ais**) *a* cardinal

cardíaco /kar'dʒiaku/ *a* cardiac; **ataque ~** heart attack

cardio|lógico /kardʒio'lɔʒiku/ *a* heart; **~logista** *m/f* heart specialist, cardiologist

cardume /kar'dumi/ *m* shoal

careca /ka'rɛka/ *a* bald □ *f* bald patch

ca|recer /kare'ser/ **~recer de** *vt* lack; **~rência** *f* lack; (*social*) deprivation; (*afetiva*) lack of affection; **~rente** *a* lacking; (*socialmente*) deprived; (*afetivamente*) in need of affection

carestia /kares'tʃia/ *f* high cost; (*geral*) high cost of living; (*escassez*) shortage

careta /ka'reta/ *f* grimace □ *a* (*fam*) straight, square

car|ga /'karga/ *f* load; (*mercadorias*) cargo; (*elétrica*) charge; (*de cavalaria*) charge; (*de caneta*) refill; (*fig*) burden; **~ga horária** workload; **~go** *m* (*função*) post, job; **a ~go de** in the charge of; **~gueiro** *m* (*navio*) cargo ship, freighter

cariar /kari'ar/ *vi* decay

Caribe /ka'ribi/ *m* Caribbean

caricatu|ra /karika'tura/ *f* caricature; **~rar** *vt* caricature; **~rista** *m/f* caricaturist

carícia /ka'risia/ *f* (*com a mão*) stroke, caress; (*carinho*) affection

cari|dade /kari'dadʒi/ *f* charity; **obra de ~dade** charity; **~doso** /o/ *a* charitable

cárie /'kari/ *f* tooth decay

carim|bar /karĩ'bar/ *vt* stamp; post-mark <*carta*>; **~bo** *m* stamp; (*do correio*) postmark

cari|nho /ka'riɲu/ *m* affection; (*um*) caress; **~nhoso** /o/ *a* affectionate

carioca /kari'ɔka/ *a* from Rio de Janeiro □ *m/f* person from Rio de Janeiro □ (*Port*) *m* weak coffee

caris|ma /ka'rizma/ *m* charisma; **~mático** *a* charismatic

carna|val /karna'vaw/ (*pl* **~vais**) *m* carnival; **~valesco** /e/ *a* carnival; <*roupa*> over the top, overdone □ *m* carnival organizer

car|ne /'karni/ *f* (*humana etc*) flesh; (*comida*) meat; **~neiro** *m* sheep; (*macho*) ram; (*como comida*) mutton; **~niça** *f* carrion; **~nificina** *f* slaughter; ~nívoro *a* carnivorous □ *m* carnivore; ~nudo *a* fleshy

caro /ˈkaru/ *a* expensive; *(querido)* dear □ *adv* *<custar, cobrar>* a lot; *<comprar, vender>* at a high price; pagar ~ pay a high price (for)

caroço /kaˈrosu/ *m (de pêssego etc)* stone; *(de maçã)* core; *(em sopa, molho etc)* lump

carona /kaˈrona/ *f* lift

carpete /karˈpetʃi/ *m* fitted carpet

carpin|taria /karpĩtaˈria/ *f* carpentry; ~teiro *m* carpenter

carran|ca /kaˈxãka/ *f* scowl; ~cudo *a* *<cara>* scowling; *<pessoa>* sullen

carrapato /kaxaˈpatu/ *m (animal)* tick; *(fig)* hanger-on

carrasco /kaˈxasku/ *m* executioner; *(fig)* butcher

carre|gado /kaxeˈgadu/ *a* *<céu>* dark, black; *<cor>* dark; *<ambiente>* tense; ~gador *m* porter; ~gamento *m* loading; *(carga)* load; ~gar *vt* load *<navio, arma, máquina fotográfica>*; *(levar)* carry; charge *<bateria, pilha>*; *(pôr em overdo)* pronounce strongly *<letra>*; *(Port)* press

carreira /kaˈxera/ *f* career

carre|tel /kaxeˈtɛw/ *(pl* ~téis*)* *m* reel

car|ril /kaˈxiw/ *(pl* ~ris*)* *(Port) m* rail

carrinho /kaˈxiɲu/ *m (para bagagem, compras)* trolley; *(de criança)* pram; ~ de mão wheel-barrow

carro /ˈkaxu/ *m* car; *(de bois)* cart; ~ alegórico float; ~ esporte sports car; ~ fúnebre hearse; ~ça /ɔ/ *f* cart; ~ceria *f* bodywork; ~chefe *(pl* ~s-chefes*)* *m (no carnaval)* main float; *(fig)* centrepiece; ~forte *(pl* ~s-fortes*)* *m* security van

carros|sel /kaxoˈsɛw/ *(pl* ~séis*)* *m* merry-go-round

carruagem /kaxuˈaʒẽ/ *f* carriage, coach

carta /ˈkarta/ *f* letter; *(mapa)* chart; *(do baralho)* card; ~ branca *(fig)* carte blanche; ~ de condução *(Port)* driving licence, *(Amer)* driver's license; ~-bomba *(pl* ~s-bomba*)* *f* letter bomb; ~da *f (fig)* move

cartão /karˈtãw/ *m* card; *(Port: papelão)* cardboard; ~ de crédito credit card; ~ de visita visiting card; ~postal *(pl* cartões-postais*)* *m* postcard

car|taz /karˈtas/ *m* poster, *(Amer)* bill; em ~ showing, *(Amer)* playing; ~teira *f (para dinheiro)* wallet; *(cartão)* card; *(mesa)* desk; ~teira de identidade identity card; ~teira de motorista driving licence, *(Amer)* driver's license; ~teiro *m* postman

car|tel /karˈtɛw/ *(pl* ~téis*)* *m* cartel

cárter /ˈkarter/ *m* sump

carto|la /karˈtɔla/ *f* top hat □ *m* director; ~lina *f* card; ~mante *m/f* tarot reader, fortune-teller

cartório /karˈtɔriu/ *m* registry office

cartucho /karˈtuʃu/ *m* cartridge; *(de dinamite)* stick; *(de amendoim etc)* bag

car|tum /karˈtũ/ *m* cartoon; ~tunista *m/f* cartoonist

caruncho /kaˈrũʃu/ *m* woodcorm

carvalho /karˈvaʎu/ *m* oak

car|vão /karˈvãw/ *m* coal; *(de desenho)* charcoal; ~voeiro *a* coal

casa /ˈkaza/ *f* house; *(comercial)* firm; *(de tabuleiro)* square; *(de botão)* hole; em ~ at home; para ~ home; na ~ dos 30 anos in one's thirties; ~ da moeda mint; ~ de banho *(Port)* bathroom; ~ de campo country house; ~ de saúde private hospital; ~ decimal decimal place; ~ popular council house

casaco /kaˈzaku/ *m (sobretudo)* coat; *(paletó)* jacket; *(de lã)* pullover

ca|sal /kaˈzaw/ *(pl* ~sais*)* *m* couple; ~samento *m* marriage; *(cerimônia)* wedding; ~sar *vt* marry; *(fig)* combine □ *vi* get married; *(fig)* go together; ~sar-se *vpr* get married; *(fig)* combine; ~sar-se com marry

casarão /kazaˈrãw/ *m* mansion

casca /ˈkaska/ *f (de árvore)* bark; *(de laranja, limão)* peel; *(de banana)* skin; *(de noz, ovo)* shell; *(de milho)* husk; *(de pão)* crust; *(de ferida)* scab

cascalho /kasˈkaʎu/ *m* gravel

cascata /kasˈkata/ *f* waterfall; *(fam)* fib

casca|vel /kaskaˈvɛw/ *(pl* ~véis*)* *m (cobra)* rattlesnake □ *f (mulher)* shrew

casco /ˈkasku/ *m (de cavalo etc)* hoof; *(de navio)* hull; *(garrafa vazia)* empty

ca|sebre /kaˈzɛbri/ *m* hovel, shack; ~seiro *a* *<comida>* home-made; *<pessoa>* home-loving; *<vida>* home □ *m* housekeeper

caserna /kaˈzɛrna/ *f* barracks

casmurro /kazˈmuxu/ *a* sullen

caso /ˈkazu/ *m* case; *(amoroso)* affair; *(conto)* story □ *conj* in case; em todo ou qualquer ~ in any case; fazer ~ de take notice of; vir ao ~ be relevant; ~ contrário otherwise

casório /kaˈzɔriu/ *(fam) m* wedding

caspa /ˈkaspa/ *f* dandruff

casquinha /kasˈkiɲa/ *f (de sorvete)* cone, cornet

cassar /kaˈsar/ *vt* revoke, withdraw *<direitos, autorização>*; ban *<político>*

cassete /kaˈsɛtʃi/ *m* cassette

cassetete /kaseˈtɛtʃi/ *m* truncheon, *(Amer)* nightstick

cassino /kaˈsinu/ *m* casino; ~ de oficiais officers' mess casta|nha /kas'taɲa/ f chestnut; ~nha de caju cashew nut; ~nha-do-pará (pl ~nhas-do-pará) f Brazil nut; ~nheiro m chestnut tree; ~nho a chestnut(-coloured); ~nholas /ɔ/ f pl castanets

castelhano /kaste'ʎanu/ a & m Castilian

castelo /kas'tɛlu/ m castle

casti|çal /kastʃi'saw/ (pl ~çais) f candlestick

cas|tidade /kastʃi'dadʒi/ f chastity; ~tigar vt punish; ~tigo m punishment; ~to a chaste

castor /kas'tor/ m beaver

castrar /kas'trar/ vt castrate

casu|al /kazu'aw/ (pl ~ais) a chance; (fortuito) fortuitous; ~alidade f chance

casulo /ka'zulu/ m (de larva) cocoon

cata /'kata/ f à ~ de in search of

cata|lão /kata'lãw/ (pl ~lães) a & m (f ~lã) Catalan

catalisador /kataliza'dor/ m catalyst; (de carro) catalytic convertor

catalogar /katalo'gar/ vt catalogue

catálogo /ka'talogu/ m catalogue; (de telefones) phone book

Catalunha /kata'luɲa/ f Catalonia

catapora /kata'pora/ f chicken pox

catar /ka'tar/ vt (procurar) search for; (recolher) gather; (do chão) pick up; sort <arroz, café>

catarata /kata'rata/ f waterfall; (no olho) cataract

catarro /ka'taxu/ m catarrh

catástrofe /ka'tastrofi/ f catastrophe

catastrófico /katas'trɔfiku/ a catastrophic

catecismo /kate'sizmu/ m catechism

cátedra /'katedra/ f chair

cate|dral /kate'draw/ (pl ~drais) f cathedral; ~drático m professor

cate|goria /katego'ria/ f category; (social) class; (qualidade) quality; ~górico a categorical; ~gorizar vt categorize

catinga /ka'tʃĩga/ f body odour, stink

cati|vante /katʃi'vãtʃi/ a captivating; ~var vt captivate; ~veiro m captivity; ~vo a & m captive

catolicismo /katoli'sizmu/ m Catholicism

católico /ka'tɔliku/ a & m Catholic

catorze /ka'torzi/ a & m fourteen

cau|da /'kawda/ f tail; ~dal (pl ~dais) m torrent

caule /'kawli/ m stem

cau|sa /'kawza/ f cause; (jurid) case; por ~sa de because of; ~sar vt cause

caute|la /kaw'tɛla/ f caution; (documento) ticket; ~loso /o/ a cautious, careful

cava /'kava/ f armhole

cava|do /ka'vadu/ a <vestido> low-cut; <olhos> deep-set; ~dor a hard-working □ m hard worker

cava|laria /kavala'ria/ f cavalry; ~lariça f stable; ~leiro m horse-man; (na Idade Média) knight

cavalete /kava'letʃi/ m easel

caval|gadura /kavawga'dura/ f mount; ~gar vt/i ride; sit astride <muro, banco>; (saltar) jump

cavalhei|resco /kavaʎe'resku/ a gallant, gentlemanly; ~ro m gentleman □ a gallant, gentlemanly

cavalo /ka'valu/ m horse; a ~ on horseback; ~-vapor (pl ~s-vapor) m horsepower

cavanhaque /kava'ɲaki/ m goatee

cavaquinho /kava'kiɲu/ m ukulele

cavar /ka'var/ vt dig; (fig) go all out for □ vi dig; (fig) go all out; ~ em (vasculhar) delve into; ~ a vida make a living

caveira /ka'vera/ f skull

caverna /ka'vɛrna/ f cavern

caviar /kavi'ar/ m caviar

cavidade /kavi'dadʒi/ f cavity

cavilha /ka'viʎa/ f peg

cavo /'kavu/ a hollow

cavoucar /kavo'kar/ vt excavate

caxemira /kaʃe'mira/ f cashmere

caxumba /ka'ʃũba/ f mumps

cear /si'ar/ vt have for supper □ vi have supper

cebo|la /se'bola/ f onion; ~linha f spring onion

ceder /se'der/ vt give up; (dar) give; (emprestar) lend □ vi (não resistir) give way; ~ a yield to

cedilha /se'dʒiʎa/ f cedilla

cedo /'sedu/ adv early; mais ~ ou mais tarde sooner or later

cedro /'sɛdru/ m cedar

cédula /'sedula/ f (de banco) note, (Amer) bill; (eleitoral) ballot paper

ce|gar /se'gar/ vt blind; blunt <faca>; ~go /ɛ/ a blind; <faca> blunt □ m blind man; às ~gas blindly

cegonha /se'goɲa/ f stork

cegueira /se'gera/ f blindness

ceia /'seja/ f supper

cei|fa /'sejfa/ f harvest; (massacre) slaughter; ~far vt reap; claim <vidas>; (matar) mow down

cela /'sɛla/ f cell

cele|bração /selebra'sãw/ f celebration; ~brar vt celebrate

célebre /'sɛlebri/ a celebrated

celebridade /selebri'dadʒi/ f celebrity

celeiro /se'leru/ m granary

célere /'sɛleri/ a swift, fast

celeste /se'lɛstʃi/ a celestial

celeuma /se'lewma/ f pandemonium

celibato /seli'batu/ *m* celibacy

celofane /selo'fani/ *m* cellophane

celta /'sɛwta/ *a* Celtic □ *m/f* Celt □ *m* (*língua*) Celtic

célula /'sɛlula/ *f* cell

celu|lar /selu'lar/ *a* cellular; ~**lite** *f* cellulite; ~**lose** /ɔ/ *f* cellulose

cem /sẽj/ *a* & *m* hundred

cemitério /semi'tɛriu/ *m* cemetery; (*fig*) graveyard

cena /'sena/ *f* scene; (*palco*) stage; **em** ~ on stage

cenário /se'nariu/ *m* scenery; (*de crime etc*) scene

cênico /'seniku/ *a* stage

cenoura /se'nora/ *f* carrot

cen|so /'sẽsu/ *m* census; ~**sor** *m* censor; ~**sura** *f* (*de jornais etc*) censorship; (*órgão*) censor(s); (*condenação*) censure; ~**surar** *vt* censor <*jornal, filme etc*>; (*condenar*) censure

centavo /sẽ'tavu/ *m* cent

centeio /sẽ'teju/ *m* rye

centelha /sẽ'teʎa/ *f* spark; (*fig: de gênio etc*) flash

cente|na /sẽ'tena/ *f* hundred; **uma** ~**na de** about a hundred; **às** ~**nas** in their hundreds; ~**nário** *m* centenary

centésimo /sẽ'tɛzimu/ *a* hundredth

centi|grado /sẽtʃi'gradu/ *m* centigrade; ~**litro** *m* centilitre; ~**metro** *m* centimetre

cento /'sẽtu/ *a* & *m* hundred; **por** ~ per cent

cen|tral /sẽ'traw/ (*pl* ~**trais**) *a* central; ~**tralizar** *vt* centralize; ~**trar** *vt* centre; ~**tro** *m* centre

cepti- (*Port*) *veja* **ceti-**

cera /'sera/ *f* wax; **fazer** ~ waste time, faff about

cerâmi|ca /se'ramika/ *f* ceramics, pottery; ~**co** *a* ceramic

cer|ca /'serka/ *f* fence; ~**ca viva** hedge □ *adv* ~**ca de** around, about; ~**cado** *m* enclosure; (*para criança*) playpen; ~**car** *vt* surround; (*com muro, cerca*) enclose; (*assediar*) besiege

cercear /sersi'ar/ *vt* (*fig*) curtail, restrict

cerco /'serku/ *m* (*mil*) siege; (*policial*) dragnet

cere|al /seri'aw/ (*pl* ~**ais**) *m* cereal

cere|bral /sere'braw/ (*pl* ~**brais**) *a* cerebral

cérebro /'sɛrebru/ *m* brain; (*inteligência*) intellect

cere|ja /se'reʒa/ *f* cherry; ~**jeira** *f* cherry tree

cerimônia /seri'monia/ *f* ceremony; **sem** ~ unceremoniously; **fazer** ~ stand on ceremony

cerimoni|al /serimoni'aw/ (*pl* ~**ais**) *a* & *m* ceremonial; ~**oso** /o/ *a* ceremonious

cer|rado /se'xadu/ *a* <*barba, mata*> thick; <*punho, dentes*> clenched □ *m* scrubland; ~**rar** *vt* close; ~**rar-se** *vpr* close; <*noites, trevas*> close in

certeiro /ser'teru/ *a* well-aimed, accurate

certeza /ser'teza/ *f* certainty; **com** ~ certainly; **ter** ~ be sure (**de** of; **de que** that)

certidão /sertʃi'dãw/ *f* certificate; ~ **de nascimento** birth certificate

certifi|cado /sertʃifi'kadu/ *m* certificate; ~**car** *vt* certify; ~**car-se** make sure of

certo /'sɛrtu/ *a* (*correto*) right; (*seguro*) certain; (*algum*) a certain □ *adv* right; **dar** ~ work

cerveja /ser'veʒa/ *f* beer; ~**ria** *f* brewery; (*bar*) pub

cervo /'sɛrvu/ *m* deer

cer|zidura /serzi'dura/ *f* darning; ~**zir** *vt* darn

cesariana /sezari'ana/ *f* Caesarian

césio /'sɛziu/ *m* caesium

cessar /se'sar/ *vt/i* cease

ces|ta /'sesta/ *f* basket; (*de comida*) hamper; ~**to** /e/ *m* basket; ~**to de lixo** wastepaper basket

ceticismo /setʃi'sizmu/ *m* scepticism

cético /'sɛtʃiku/ *a* sceptical □ *m* sceptic

cetim /se'tʃĩ/ *m* satin

céu /sɛw/ *m* sky; (*na religião*) heaven; ~ **da boca** roof of the mouth

cevada /se'vada/ *f* barley

chá /ʃa/ *m* tea

chacal /ʃa'kaw/ (*pl* ~**cais**) *m* jackal

chácara /'ʃakara/ *f* smallholding; (*casa*) country cottage

chaci|na /ʃa'sina/ *f* slaughter; ~**nar** *vt* slaughter

chá-de-bar /ʃadʒi'bar/ (*pl* ~**s-de-bar**) *m* bachelor party; ~**de-panela** (*pl* ~**s-de-panela**) *m* hen night, (*Amer*) wedding shower

chafariz /ʃafa'ris/ *m* fountain

chaga /'ʃaga/ *f* sore

chaleira /ʃa'lera/ *f* kettle

chama /'ʃama/ *f* flame

cha|mada /ʃa'mada/ *f* call; (*dos presentes*) roll call; (*dos alunos*) register; ~**mado** *m* call □ *a* (*depois do substantivo*) called; (*antes do substantivo*) so-called; ~**mar** *vt* call; (*para sair etc*) ask, invite; attract <*atenção*>; □ *vi* call; <*telefone*> ring; ~**mar-se** *vpr* be called; ~**mariz** *m* decoy; ~**mativo** *a* showy, flashy

chamejar /ʃame'ʒar/ *vi* flare

chaminé /ʃami'ne/ *f* (*de casa, fábrica*) chimney; (*de navio, trem*) funnel

champanhe /ʃãˈpaɲi/ *m* champagne
champu /ʃãˈpu/ (*Port*) *m* shampoo
chamuscar /ʃamusˈkar/ *vt* singe, scorch
chance /ˈʃãsi/ *f* chance
chanceler /ʃãseˈler/ *m* chancellor
chanchada /ʃãˈʃada/ *f* (*peça*) second-rate play; (*filme*) B movie
chanta|gear /ʃãtaʒiˈar/ *vt* blackmail; ~gem *f* blackmail; ~gista *m/f* blackmailer
chão /ˈʃãw/ (*pl* ~s) *m* ground; (*dentro de casa etc*) floor
chapa /ˈʃapa/ *f* sheet; (*foto*) plate; ~ eleitoral electoral list; ~ de matrícula (*Port*) number plate, (*Amer*) license plate □ *a* (*fam*) *m* mate
chapéu /ʃaˈpɛw/ *m* hat
charada /ʃaˈrada/ *f* riddle
char|ge /ˈʃarʒi/ *f* (political) cartoon; ~gista *m/f* cartoonist
charla|tanismo /ʃarlataˈnizmu/ charlatanism; ~tão (*pl* ~tães) *m* (*f* ~tona) charlatan
charme /ˈʃarmi/ *m* charm; fazer ~me turn on the charm; ~moso /o/ *a* charming
charneca /ʃarˈnɛka/ *f* moor
charuto /ʃaˈrutu/ *m* cigar
chassi /ʃaˈsi/ *m* chassis
chata /ˈʃata/ *f* (*barca*) barge
chate|ação /ʃatʃiaˈsãw/ *f* annoyance; ~ar *vt* annoy; ~ar-se *vpr* get annoyed
cha|tice /ʃaˈtʃisi/ *f* nuisance; ~to *a* (*tedioso*) boring; (*irritante*) annoying; (*mal-educado*) rude; (*plano*) flat
chauvin|ismo /ʃoviˈnizmu/ *m* chauvinism; ~ta *m/f* chauvinist □ *a* chauvinistic
cha|vão /ʃaˈvãw/ *m* cliché; ~ve *f* key; (*ferramenta*) spanner; ~ve de fenda screwdriver; ~ve inglesa wrench; ~veiro *m* (*aro*) keyring; (*pessoa*) locksmith
chávena /ˈʃavena/ *f* soup bowl; (*Port: xícara*) cup
checar /ʃeˈkar/ *vt* check
che|fe /ˈʃefi/ *m/f* (*patrão*) boss; (*gerente*) manager; (*dirigente*) leader; ~fia *f* leadership; (*de empresa*) management; (*sede*) headquarters; ~fiar *vt* lead; be in charge of *<trabalho>*
che|gada /ʃeˈgada/ *f* arrival; ~gado *a* *<amigo, relação>* close; ~gar *vi* arrive; (*deslocar-se*) move up; (*ser suficiente*) be enough □ *vt* bring up *<prato, cadeira>*; ~gar a fazer go as far as doing; aonde você quer ~gar? what are you driving at?; ~gar lá (*fig*) make it
cheia /ˈʃeja/ *f* flood
cheio /ˈʃeju/ *a* full; (*fam: farto*) fed up

chei|rar /ʃeˈrar/ *vt/i* smell (a of); ~roso /o/ *a* scented
cheque /ˈʃeki/ *m* cheque, (*Amer*) check; ~ de viagem traveller's cheque; ~ em branco blank cheque
chi|ado /ʃiˈadu/ *m* (*de pneus, freios*) screech; (*de porta*) squeak; (*de vapor, numa fita*) hiss; ~ar *vi* <*porta*> squeak; <*pneus, freios*> screech; <*vapor, fita*> hiss; <*fritura*> sizzle; (*fam: reclamar*) grumble, moan
chiclete /ʃiˈkletʃi/ *m* chewing gum; ~ de bola bubble gum
chico|tada /ʃikoˈtada/ *f* lash; ~te /ɔ/ *m* whip; ~tear *vt* whip
chi|frar /ʃiˈfrar/ (*fam*) *vt* cheat on *<marido, esposa>*; two-time *<namorado, namorada>*; ~fre *m* horn; ~frudo *a* horned; (*fam*) cuckolded □ *m* cuckold
Chile /ˈʃili/ *m* Chile
chileno /ʃiˈlenu/ *a & m* Chilean
chilique /ʃiˈliki/ (*fam*) *m* funny turn
chil|rear /ʃiwxiˈar/ *vi* chirp, twitter; ~reio *m* chirping, twittering
chimarrão /ʃimaˈʃãw/ *m* unsweetened maté tea
chimpanzé /ʃĩpãˈze/ *m* chimpanzee
China /ˈʃina/ *f* China
chinelo /ʃiˈnelu/ *m* slipper
chi|nês /ʃiˈnes/ *a & m* (*f* ~nesa) Chinese
chinfrim /ʃĩˈfrĩ/ *a* tatty, shoddy
chio /ˈʃiu/ *m* squeak; (*de pneus*) screech; (*de vapor*) hiss
chique /ˈʃiki/ *a* <*pessoa, aparência, roupa*> smart, (*Amer*) sharp; <*hotel, bairro, loja etc*> smart, up-market, posh
chiqueiro /ʃiˈkeru/ *m* pigsty
chis|pa /ˈʃispa/ *f* flash; ~pada *f* dash; ~par *vi* (*soltar chispas*) flash; (*correr*) dash
choca|lhar /ʃokaˈʎar/ *vt/i* rattle; ~lho *m* rattle
cho|cante /ʃoˈkãtʃi/ *a* shocking; (*fam*) incredible; ~car *vt/i* hatch *<ovos>*; (*ultrajar*) shock; ~car-se *vpr* <*carros etc*> crash; <*teorias etc*> clash
chocho /ˈʃoʃu/ *a* dull, insipid
chocolate /ʃokoˈlatʃi/ *m* chocolate
chofer /ʃoˈfɛr/ *m* chauffeur
chope /ˈʃopi/ *m* draught lager
choque /ˈʃɔki/ *m* shock; (*colisão*) collision; (*conflito*) clash
cho|radeira /ʃoraˈdera/ *f* fit of crying; ~ramingar *vi* whine; ~ramingas *m/f* inviar whiner; ~rão *m* (*salgueiro*) weeping willow □ *a* (~rona) tearful; ~rar *vi* cry; ~ro /o/ *m* crying; ~roso /o/ *a* tearful
chouriço /ʃoˈrisu/ *m* black pudding; (*Port*) sausage

chover /ʃo'ver/ *vi* rain

chuchu /ʃu'ʃu/ *m* chayote

chucrute /ʃu'krutʃi/ *m* sauerkraut

chumaço /ʃu'masu/ *m* wad

chum|bado /ʃũ'badu/ (*fam*) *a* knocked out; ~**bar** (*Port*) *vt* fill <*dente*>; fail <*aluno*> □ *vi* <*aluno*> fail; ~**bo** *m* lead; (*Port: obturação*) filling

chu|par /ʃu'par/ *vt* suck; <*esponja*> suck up; ~**peta** /e/ *f* dummy, (*Amer*) pacifier

churras|caria /ʃuxaska'ria/ *f* barbecue restaurant; ~**co** *m* barbecue; ~**queira** *f* barbecue; ~**quinho** *m* kebab

chu|tar /ʃu'tar/ *vt/i* kick; (*fam: adivinhar*) guess; ~**te** *m* kick; ~**teira** *f* football boot

chu|va /'ʃuva/ *f* rain; ~**va de pedra** hail; ~**varada** *f* torrential rainstorm; ~**veiro** *m* shower; ~**viscar** *vi* drizzle; ~**visco** *m* drizzle; ~**voso** /o/ *a* rainy

cica|triz /sika'tris/ *f* scar; ~**trizar** *vt* scar □ *vi* <*ferida*> heal

cic|lismo /si'klizmu/ *m* cycling; ~**lista** *m/f* cyclist; ~**lo** *m* cycle; ~**lone** /o/ *m* cyclone; ~**lovia** *f* cycle lane

cida|dania /sidada'nia/ *f* citizenship; ~**dão** (*pl* ~**dãos**) *m* (*f* ~**dã**) citizen; ~**def** town; (*grande*) city; ~**dela** /ɛ/ *f* citadel

ciência /si'ēsia/ *f* science

cien|te /si'ētʃi/ *a* aware; ~**tífico** *a* scientific; ~**tista** *m/f* scientist

ci|fra /'sifra/ *f* figure; (*código*) cipher; ~**frão** *m* dollar sign; ~**frar** *vt* encode

cigano /si'ganu/ *a & m* gypsy

cigarra /si'gaxa/ *f* cicada; (*dispositivo*) buzzer

cigar|reira /siga'xera/ *f* cigarette case; ~**ro** *m* cigarette

cilada /si'lada/ *f* trap; (*estratagema*) trick

cilindrada /silĩ'drada/ *f* (engine) capacity

cilíndrico /si'lĩdriku/ *a* cylindrical

cilindro /si'lĩdru/ *m* cylinder; (*rolo*) roller

cílio /'siliu/ *m* eyelash

cima /'sima/ *f* em ~ on top; (*na casa*) upstairs; em ~ de on, on top of; para ~ up; (*na casa*) upstairs; por ~ over the top; por ~ de over; de ~ from above; ainda por ~ moreover

cimbalo /'sĩbalu/ *m* cymbal

cimeira /si'mera/ *f* crest; (*Port: cúpula*) summit

cimen|tar /simē'tar/ *vt* cement; ~**to** *m* cement

cinco /'sĩku/ *a & m* five

cine|asta /sini'asta/ *m/f* film-maker; ~**ma** /e/ *m* cinema

Cingapura /sĩga'pura/ *f* Singapore

cínico /'siniku/ *a* cynical □ *m* cynic

cinismo /si'nizmu/ *m* cynicism

cinqüen|ta /sĩ'kwẽta/ *a & m* fifty; ~**tão** *a & m* (*f* ~**tona**) fifty-year-old

cinti|lante /sĩtʃi'lãtʃi/ *a* glittering; ~**lar** *vi* glitter

cin|to /'sĩtu/ *m* belt; ~**to de segurança** seatbelt; ~**tura** *f* waist; ~**turão** *m* belt

cin|za /'sĩza/ *f* ash □ *a invar* grey; ~**zeiro** *m* ashtray

cin|zel /sĩ'zɛw/ (*pl* ~**zéis**) *m* chisel; ~**zelar** *vt* carve

cinzento /sĩ'zẽtu/ *a* grey

cipó /si'pɔ/ *m* vine, liana; ~**poal** (*pl* ~**poais**) *m* jungle

cipreste /si'prɛstʃi/ *m* cypress

cipriota /sipri'ɔta/ *a & m* Cypriot

ciranda /si'rãda/ *f* (*fig*) merry-go-round

cir|cense /sir'sēsi/ *a* circus; ~**co** *m* circus

circu|íto /sir'kuitu/ *m* circuit; ~**lação** *f* circulation; ~**lar** *a & f* circular □ *vt* circulate □ *vi* <*dinheiro, sangue*> circulate; <*carro*> drive; <*ônibus*> run; <*trânsito*> move; <*pessoa*> go round

círculo /'sirkulu/ *m* circle

circunci|dar /sirkũsi'dar/ *vt* circumcise; ~**ção** *f* circumcision

circun|dar /sirkũ'dar/ *vt* surround; ~**ferência** *f* circumference; ~**flexo** /ɛks/ *a & m* circumflex; ~**scrição** *f* district; ~**scrição eleitoral** constituency; ~**specto** /ɛ/ *a* circumspect; ~**stância** *f* circumstance; ~**stanciado** *a* detailed; ~**stancial** (*pl* ~**stanciais**) *a* circumstantial; ~**stante** *m/f* bystander

cirrose /si'xɔzi/ *f* cirrhosis

cirur|gia /sirur'ʒia/ *f* surgery; ~**gião** *m* (*f* ~**giã**) surgeon

cirúrgico /si'rurʒiku/ *a* surgical

cisão /si'zãw/ *f* split, division

cisco /'sisku/ *m* speck

cisma[1] /'sizma/ *m* schism

cis|ma[2] /'sizma/ *f* (*mania*) fixation; (*devaneio*) imagining, daydream; (*prevenção*) irrational dislike; (*de criança*) whim; ~**mar** *vt/i* be lost in thought; <*criança*> be insistent; ~**mar** *m* brood over; ~**mar de ou em fazer** insist on doing; ~**mar que** insist on thinking that; ~**mar com alg** take a dislike to s.o.

cisne /'sizni/ *m* swan

cistite /sis'tʃitʃi/ *f* cystitis

ci|tação /sita'sãw/ *f* quotation; (*jurid*) summons; ~**tar** *vt* quote; (*jurid*) summon

ciúme /si'umi/ *m* jealousy; **ter ~s de** be jealous of

ciu|meira /siu'mera/ *f* fit of jealousy; **~mento** *a* jealous

cívico /'siviku/ *a* civic

ci|vil /si'viw/ (*pl* **~vis**) *a* civil □ *m* civilian; **~vilidade** *f* civility

civili|zação /siviliza'sãw/ *f* civilization; **~zado** *a* civilized; **~zar** *vt* civilize

civismo /si'vizmu/ *m* public spirit

cla|mar /kla'mar/ *vt/i* cry out, clamour (**por** for); **~mor** *m* outcry; **~moroso** /o/ *a* <*protesto*> loud, noisy; <*erro, injustiça*> blatant

clandestino /klãdes'tʃinu/ *a* clandestine

cla|ra /'klara/ *f* egg white; **~rabóia** *f* skylight; **~rão** *m* flash; **~rear** *vt* brighten, clarify <*questão*> □ *vi* brighten up; (*fazer-se dia*) become light; **~reira** *f* clearing; **~reza** /e/ *f* clarity; **~ridade** *f* brightness; (*do dia*) daylight

cla|rim /kla'rĩ/ *m* bugle; **~rinete** /e/ *m* clarinet

clarividente /klarivi'dẽtʃi/ *m/f* clairvoyant

claro /'klaru/ *a* clear; <*luz*> bright; <*cor*> light □ *adv* clearly □ *int* of course; **~ que sim/não** of course/of course not; **às claras** openly; **noite em ~** sleepless night; **já é dia ~** it's already daylight

classe /'klasi/ *f* class; **~ média** middle class

clássico /'klasiku/ *a* classical; (*famoso, exemplar*) classic □ *m* classic

classifi|cação /klasifika'sãw/ *f* classification; (*numa competição esportiva*) placing, place; **~cado** *a* classified; <*candidato*> successful; <*esportista, time*> qualified; **~car** *vt* classify; (*considerar*) describe (**de** as); **~car-se** *vpr* <*candidato, esportista*> qualify; (*chamar-se*) describe o.s. (**de** as); **~catório** *a* qualifying

classudo /kla'sudu/ (*fam*) *a* classy

claustro|fobia /klawstrofo'bia/ *f* claustrophobia; **~fóbico** *a* claustrophobic

cláusula /'klawzula/ *f* clause

cla|ve /'klavi/ *f* clef; **~vícula** *f* collar bone

cle|mência /kle'mẽsia/ *f* clemency; **~mente** *a* <*pessoa*> lenient; <*tempo*> clement

cleptomaníaco /kleptoma'niaku/ *m* kleptomaniac

clérigo /'klɛrigu/ *m* cleric, clergyman

clero /'klɛru/ *m* clergy

clien|te /kli'ẽtʃi/ *m/f* (*de loja*) customer; (*de advogado, empresa*) client;

~tela /ɛ/ *f* (*de loja*) customers; (*de restaurante, empresa*) clientele

cli|ma /'klima/ *m* climate; **~mático** *a* climatic

clímax /'klimaks/ *m invar* climax

clíni|ca /'klinika/ *f* clinic; **~ca geral** general practice; **~co** *a* clinical □ *m* **~co geral** general practitioner, GP

clipe /'klipi/ *m* clip; (*para papéis*) paper clip

clone /'kloni/ *m* clone

cloro /'kloru/ *m* chlorine

close /'klozi/ *m* close-up

clube /'klubi/ *m* club

coação /koa'sãw/ *f* coercion

coadjuvante /koadʒu'vãtʃi/ *a* <*ator*> supporting □ *m/f* (*em peça, filme*) co-star; (*em crime*) accomplice

coador /koa'dor/ *m* strainer; (*de legumes*) colander; (*de café*) filter bag

coadunar /koadu'nar/ *vt* combine

coagir /koa'ʒir/ *vt* compel

coagu|lar /koagu'lar/ *vt/i* clot; **~-se** *vpr* clot

coágulo /ko'agulu/ *m* clot

coalhar /koa'ʎar/ *vt/i* curdle; **~-se** *vpr* curdle

coalizão /koali'zãw/ *f* coalition

coar /ko'ar/ *vt* strain

coaxar /koa'ʃar/ *vi* croak □ *m* croaking

cobaia /ko'baja/ *f* guinea pig

cober|ta /ko'bɛrta/ *f* (*de cama*) bedcover; (*de navio*) deck; **~to** /ɛ/ *a* covered □ *pp de* **cobrir**; **~tor** *m* blanket; **~tura** *f* (*revestimento*) covering; (*reportagem*) coverage; (*seguro*) cover; (*apartamento*) penthouse

cobi|ça /ko'bisa/ *f* greed, covetousness; **~çar** *vt* covet; **~çoso** /o/ *a* covetous

cobra /'kobra/ *f* snake

co|brador /kobra'dor/ *m* (*no ônibus*) conductor; **~brança** *f* (*de dívida*) collection; (*de preço*) charging; (*de atitudes*) asking for something in return (**de** for); **~brança de penalti/falta** penalty (kick)/free kick; **~brar** *vt* collect <*dívida*>; ask for <*coisa prometida*>; take <*pênalti*>; **~brar aco a alg** <*em dinheiro*> charge s.o. for sth; (*fig*) make s.o. pay for sth; **~brar uma falta** (*no futebol*) take a free kick

cobre /'kobri/ *m* copper

cobrir /ko'brir/ *vt* cover; **~-se** *vpr* <*pessoa*> cover o.s. up; <*coisa*> be covered

cocaína /koka'ina/ *f* cocaine

co|çar /ko'sar/ *vt* scratch □ *vi* (*esfregar-se*) scratch; (*comichar*) itch; **~-se** *vpr* scratch o.s.

cócegas /'kɔsegas/ *f pl* **fazer ~ em** tickle; **sentir ~** be ticklish

coceira /ko'sera/ f itch
cochi|char /koʃi'ʃar/ vt/i whisper; **~cho** m whisper
cochi|lada /koʃi'lada/ f doze; **~lar** vi doze; **~lo** m snooze
coco /'koku/ m coconut
cócoras /'kɔkoras/ f pl de ~ squatting; ficar de ~ squat
codificar /kodʒifi'kar/ vt encode <mensagem>; codify <leis>
código /'kɔdʒigu/ m code; ~ de barras bar code
codinome /kodʒi'nomi/ m codename
coeficiente /koefisi'ẽtʃi/ m coefficient; (fig: fator) factor
coelho /ko'eʎu/ m rabbit
coentro /ko'ẽtru/ m coriander
coerção /koer'sãw/ f coercion
coe|rência /koe'rẽsia/ f (lógica) coherence; (consequência) consistency; **~rente** a (lógico) coherent; (consequente) consistent
coexis|tência /koezis'tẽsia/ f coexistence; **~tir** vi coexist
cofre /'kɔfri/ m safe; (de dinheiro público) coffer
cogi|tação /koʒita'sãw/ f contemplation; fora de ~tação out of the question; **~tar** vt/i contemplate
cogumelo /kogu'mɛlu/ m mushroom
coibir /koi'bir/ vt restrict; **~-se de** keep o.s. from
coice /'kojsi/ m kick
coinci|dência /koĩsi'dẽsia/ f coincidence; **~dir** vi coincide
coisa /'kojza/ f thing
coitado /koj'tadu/ m poor thing; ~ do pai poor father
cola /'kɔla/ f glue; (cópia) crib
colabo|ração /kolabora'sãw/ f collaboration; (de escritor etc) contribution; **~rador** m collaborator; (em jornal, livro) contributor; **~rar** vi collaborate; (em jornal, livro) contribute (em to)
colagem /ko'laʒẽ/ f collage
colágeno /ko'laʒenu/ m collagen
colapso /ko'lapsu/ m collapse
colar[1] /ko'lar/ m necklace
colar[2] /ko'lar/ vt (grudar) stick; (copiar) crib □ vi stick; (copiar) crib; <desculpa etc> stand up, stick
colarinho /kola'riɲu/ m collar; (de cerveja) head
colate|ral /kolate'raw/ (pl **~rais**) a efeito **~ral** side effect
col|cha /'kowʃa/ f bedspread; **~chão** m mattress
colchete /kow'ʃetʃi/ m fastener; (sinal de pontuação) square bracket; ~ de pressão press stud, popper
colchonete /kowʃo'nɛtʃi/ m (foldaway) mattress

coldre /'kowdri/ m holster
cole|ção /kole'sãw/ f collection; **~cionador** m collector; **~cionar** vt collect
colega /ko'lɛga/ m/f (amigo) friend; (de trabalho) colleague
colegi|al /koleʒi'aw/ (pl **~ais**) a school □ m/f schoolboy (f -girl)
colégio /ko'lɛʒiu/ m secondary school, (Amer) high school
coleira /ko'lera/ f collar
cólera /'kɔlera/ f (doença) cholera; (raiva) fury
colérico /ko'lɛriku/ a (furioso) furious □ m (doente) cholera victim
colesterol /koleste'rɔw/ m cholesterol
cole|ta /ko'lɛta/ f collection; **~tânea** f collection; **~tar** vt collect
colete /ko'letʃi/ m waistcoat, (Amer) vest; ~ salva-vidas life-jacket, (Amer) life-preserver
coletivo /kole'tʃivu/ a collective; <transporte> public □ m bus
colheita /ko'ʎejta/ f harvest; (produtos colhidos) crop
colher[1] /ko'ʎer/ f spoon
colher[2] /ko'ʎer/ vt pick <flores, frutos>; gather <informações>
colherada /koʎe'rada/ f spoonful
colibri /koli'bri/ m hummingbird
cólica /'kɔlika/ f colic
colidir /koli'dʒir/ vi collide
coli|gação /koliga'sãw/ f (pol) coalition; **~gado** m (pol) coalition partner; **~gar** vt bring together; **~gar-se** vpr join forces; (pol) form a coalition
colina /ko'lina/ f hill
colírio /ko'liriu/ m eyewash
colisão /koli'zãw/ f collision
collant /ko'lã/ (pl **~s**) m body; (de ginástica) leotard
colmeia /kow'meja/ f beehive
colo /'kɔlu/ f (regaço) lap; (pescoço) neck
colo|cação /koloka'sãw/ f placing; (emprego) position; (exposição de fatos) statement; (de aparelho, pneus, carpete etc) fitting; **~cado** a placed; o primeiro **~cado** (em ranking) person in first place; **~cador** m fitter; **~car** vt put; fit <aparelho, pneus, carpete etc>; put forward, state <opinião, idéias>; (empregar) get a job for
Colômbia /ko'lõbia/ f Colombia
colombiano /kolõbi'anu/ a & m Colombian
cólon /'kɔlõ/ m colon
colônia[1] /ko'lonia/ f (colonos) colony
colônia[2] /ko'lonia/ f (perfume) cologne
coloni|al /koloni'aw/ (pl **~ais**) a colonial; **~alismo** m colonialism;

~alista *a* & *m/f* colonialist; ~zar *vt* colonize

colono /ko'lonu/ *m* settler, colonist; (*lavrador*) tenant farmer

coloqui|al /koloki'aw/ (*pl* ~ais) *a* colloquial

colóquio /ko'lɔkiu/ *m* (*conversa*) conversation; (*congresso*) conference

colo|rido /kolo'ridu/ *a* colourful □ *m* colouring; ~rir *vt* colour

colu|na /ko'luna/ *f* column; (*vertebral*) spine; ~nável (*pl* ~náveis) *a* famous □ *m/f* celebrity; ~nista *m/f* columnist

com /kõ/ *prep* with; o comentário foi comigo the comment was meant for me; você está ~ a chave? have you got the key?; ~ seis anos de idade at six years of age

coma /'koma/ *f* coma

comadre /ko'madri/ *f* (*madrinha*) godmother of one's child; (*mãe do afilhado*) mother of one's godchild; (*urinol*) bedpan

coman|dante /komã'dãtʃi/ *m* commander; ~dar *vt* lead; (*ordenar*) command; (*elevar-se acima de*) dominate; ~do *m* command; (*grupo*) commando group

comba|te /kõ'batʃi/ *m* combat; (*a drogas, doença etc*) fight (a against); ~ter *vt/i* fight; ~ter-se *vpr* fight

combi|nação /kõbina'sãw/ *f* combination; (*acordo*) arrangement; (*plano*) scheme; (*roupa*) petticoat; ~nar *vt* (*juntar*) combine; (*ajustar*) arrange □ *vi* go together, match; ~nar com go with, match; ~nar de sair arrange to go out; ~nar-se *vpr* (*juntar-se*) combine; (*harmonizar-se*) go together, match

comboio /kõ'boju/ *m* convoy; (*Port: trem*) train

combustí|vel /kõbus'tʃivew/ (*pl* ~veis) *m* fuel

come|çar /kome'sar/ *vt/i* start, begin; ~ço /e/ *m* beginning, start

comédia /ko'mɛdʒia/ *f* comedy

comediante /komedʒi'ãtʃi/ *m/f* comedian (*f* comedienne)

comemo|ração /komemora'sãw/ *f* (*celebração*) celebration; (*lembrança*) commemoration; ~rar *vt* (*festejar*) celebrate; (*lembrar*) commemorate; ~rativo *a* commemorative

comen|tar /komẽ'tar/ *vt* comment on; (*falar mal de*) make comments about; ~tário *m* comment; (*de texto, na TV etc*) commentary; sem ~tários no comment; ~tarista *m/f* commentator

comer /ko'mer/ *vt* eat; <*ferrugem etc*> eat away; take <*peça de xadrez*> □ *vi* eat; ~-se *vpr* (*de raiva etc*) be

consumed (de with); dar de ~ a feed

comerci|al /komersi'aw/ (*pl* ~ais) *a* & *m* commercial; ~alizar *vt* market; ~ante *m/f* trader; ~ar *vi* do business, trade; ~ário *m* shopworker

comércio /ko'mɛrsiu/ *m* (*atividade*) trade; (*loja etc*) business; (*lojas*) shops

comes /'komis/ *m pl* ~ e bebes (*fam*) food and drink; ~tíveis *m pl* foods, food; ~tível (*pl* ~tíveis) *a* edible

cometa /ko'meta/ *m* comet

cometer /kome'ter/ *vt* commit <*crime*>; make <*erro*>

comichão /komi'ʃãw/ *f* itch

comício /ko'misiu/ *m* rally

cômico /'komiku/ *a* (*de comédia*) comic; (*engraçado*) comical

comida /ko'mida/ *f* food; (*uma*) meal

comigo = com + mim

comi|lão /komi'lãw/ *a* (*f* ~lona) greedy □ *m* (*f* ~lona) glutton

cominho /ko'miɲu/ *m* cummin

comiserar-se /komize'rarsi/ *vpr* commiserate (de with)

comis|são /komi'sãw/ *f* commission; ~sário *m* commissioner; ~sário de bordo (*aéreo*) steward; (*de navio*) purser; ~sionar *vt* commission

comi|tê /komi'te/ *m* committee; ~tiva *f* group; (*de uma pessoa*) retinue

como /'komu/ *adv* (*na condição de*) as; (*da mesma forma que*) like; (*de que maneira*) how □ *conj* as; ~? (*pedindo repetição*) pardon?; ~ se as if; assim ~ as well as

cômoda /'komoda/ *f* chest of drawers, (*Amer*) bureau

como|didade /komodʒi'dadʒi/ *f* comfort; (*conveniência*) convenience; ~dismo *m* complacency; ~dista *a* complacent

cômodo /'komodu/ *a* comfortable; (*conveniente*) convenient □ *m* (*aposento*) room

como|vente /komo'vẽtʃi/ *a* moving; ~ver *vt* move □ *vi* be moving; ~ver-se *vpr* be moved

compacto /kõ'paktu/ *a* compact □ *m* single

compadecer-se /kõpade'sersi/ *vpr* feel pity (de for)

compadre /kõ'padri/ *m* (*padrinho*) godfather of one's child; (*pai do afilhado*) father of one's godchild

compaixão /kõpaj'ʃãw/ *f* compassion

companhei|rismo /kõpaɲe'rizmu/ *m* companionship; ~ro *m* (*de viagem etc*) companion; (*amigo*) friend, mate

companhia /kõpa'ɲia/ *f* company; fazer ~ a alg keep so. company

compa|ração /kõpara'sãw/ *f* comparison; ~rar *vt* compare; ~rativo *a* comparative; ~**rável** (*pl* ~**ráveis**) *a* comparable

compare|cer /kõpare'ser/ *vi* appear; ~**cer a** attend; ~**cimento** *m* attendance

comparsa /kõ'parsa/ *m/f* (*ator*) bit player; (*cúmplice*) sidekick

comparti|lhar /kõpartʃi'ʎar/ *vt/i* share (**de** in); ~**mento** *m* compartment

compassado /kõpa'sadu/ *a* (*medido*) measured; (*ritmado*) regular

compassivo /kõpa'sivu/ *a* compassionate

compasso /kõ'pasu/ *m* (*mus*) beat, time; (*instrumento*) compass, pair of compasses

compatí|vel /kõpa'tʃivew/ (*pl* ~**veis**) *a* compatible

compatriota /kõpatri'ɔta/ *m/f* compatriot, fellow countryman (*f* -woman)

compelir /kõpe'lir/ *vt* compel

compene|tração /kõpenetra'sãw/ *f* conviction; ~**trar** *vt* convince; ~**trar-se** *vpr* convince o.s.

compen|sação /kõpẽsa'sãw/ *f* compensation; (*de cheques*) clearing; ~**sar** *vt* make up for <*defeitos, danos*>; offset <*peso, gastos*>; clear <*cheques*> □ *vi* <*crime*> pay

compe|tência /kõpe'tẽsia/ *f* competence; ~**tente** *a* competent

compe|tição /kõpetʃi'sãw/ *f* competition; ~**tidor** *m* competitor; ~**tir** *vi* compete; ~**tir a** be up to; ~**tividade** *f* competitiveness; ~**titivo** *a* competitive

compla|cência /kõpla'sẽsia/ *f* complaisance; ~**cente** *a* obliging

complemen|tar /kõplemẽ'tar/ *vt* complement □ *a* complementary; ~**to** *m* complement

comple|tar /kõple'tar/ *vt* complete; top up <*copo, tanque etc*>; ~**tar 20 anos** turn 20; ~**to** /ε/ *a* complete; (*cheio*) full up; **por** ~**to** completely; **escrever por** ~**to** write out in full

comple|xado /kõplek'sadu/ *a* with a complex; ~**xidade** *f* complexity; ~**xo** /ε/ *a & m* complex

compli|cação /kõplika'sãw/ *f* complication; ~**cado** *a* complicated; ~**car** *vt* complicate; ~**car-se** *vpr* get complicated

complô /kõ'plo/ *m* conspiracy, plot

com|ponente /kõpo'nẽtʃi/ *a & m* component; ~**por** *vt/i* compose; ~**por-se** *vpr* (*controlar-se*) compose o.s.; ~**por-se de** be composed of

compor|tamento /kõporta'mẽtu/ *m* behaviour; ~**tar** *vt* hold; bear <*dor, prejuízo*>; ~**tar-se** *vpr* behave

composi|ção /kõpozi'sãw/ *f* composi-

tion; (*acordo*) conciliation; ~**tor** *m* (*de música*) composer; (*gráfico*) compositor

compos|to /kõ'postu/ *pp de* **compor** □ *a* compound; <*pessoa*> level-headed □ *m* compound; ~**to de** made up of; ~**tura** *f* composure

compota /kõ'pɔta/ *f* fruit in syrup

com|pra /'kõpra/ *f* purchase; *pl* shopping; **fazer** ~**pras** go shopping; ~**prador** *m* buyer; ~**prar** *vt* buy; bribe <*oficial, juiz*>; pick <*briga*>

compreen|der /kõpriẽ'der/ *vt* (*conter em si*) contain; (*estender-se a*) cover, take in; (*entender*) understand; ~**são** *f* understanding; ~**sível** (*pl* ~**síveis**) *a* understandable; ~**sivo** *a* understanding

compres|sa /kõ'prεsa/ *f* compress; ~**são** *f* compression; ~**sor** *m* compressor; **rolo** ~**sor** steamroller

compri|do /kõ'pridu/ *a* long; ~**mento** *m* length

compri|mido /kõpri'midu/ *m* pill, tablet □ *a* <*ar*> compressed; ~**mir** *vt* (*apertar*) press; (*reduzir o volume de*) compress

compromete|dor /kõpromete'dor/ *a* compromising; ~**ter** *vt* (*envolver*) involve; (*prejudicar*) compromise; ~**ter alg a fazer** commit s.o. to doing; ~**ter-se** *vpr* (*obrigar-se*) commit o.s.; (*prejudicar-se*) compromise o.s.; ~**tido** *a* (*ocupado*) busy; (*noivo*) spoken for

compromisso /kõpro'misu/ *m* commitment; (*encontro marcado*) appointment; **sem** ~ without obligation

compro|vação /kõprova'sãw/ *f* proof; ~**vante** *m* receipt; ~**var** *vt* prove

compul|são /kõpuw'sãw/ *f* compulsion; ~**sivo** *a* compulsive; ~**sório** *a* compulsory

compu|tação /kõputa'sãw/ *f* computation; (*matéria, ramo*) computing; ~**tador** *m* computer; ~**tadorizar** *vt* computerize; ~**tar** *vt* compute

comum /ko'mũ/ *a* common; (*não especial*) ordinary; **fora do** ~ out of the ordinary; **em** ~ <*trabalho*> joint; <*atuar*> jointly; **ter muito em** ~ have a lot in common

comungar /komũ'gar/ *vi* take communion

comunhão /komu'ɲãw/ *f* communion; (*relig*) (Holy) Communion

comuni|cação /komunika'sãw/ *f* communication; ~**cação social/visual** media studies/ graphic design; ~**cado** *m* notice; (*pol*) communiqué; ~**car** *vt* communicate; (*unir*) connect □ *vi*, ~**car-se** *vpr* communicate; ~**cativo** *a* communicative

comu|nidade /komuni'dadʒi/ f community; **~nismo** m communism; **~nista** a & m/f communist; **~nitário** a (da comunidade) community; (para todos juntos) communal

côncavo /'kõkavu/ a concave

conce|ber /kõse'ber/ vt conceive; (imaginar) conceive of □ vi conceive; **~bível** (pl **~bíveis**) a conceivable

conceder /kõse'der/ vt grant; **~ em** accede to

concei|to /kõ'sejtu/ m concept; (opinião) opinion; (fama) reputation; **~tuado** a highly thought of; **~tuar** vt (imaginar) conceptualize; (avaliar) assess

concen|tração /kõsẽtra'sãw/ f concentration; (de jogadores) training camp; **~trar** vt concentrate; **~trar-se** vpr concentrate

concepção /kõsep'sãw/ f conception; (opinião) view

concernir /kõser'nir/ vt **~ a** concern

concerto /kõ'sertu/ m concert

conces|são /kõse'sãw/ f concession; **~sionária** f dealership; **~sionário** m dealer

concha /'kõʃa/ f (de molusco) shell; (colher) ladle

concili|ação /kõsilia'sãw/ f conciliation; **~ador** a conciliatory; **~ar** vt reconcile

concílio /kõ'siliu/ m council

conci|são /kõsi'zãw/ f conciseness; **~so** a concise

conclamar /kõkla'mar/ vt call <eleição, greve>; call upon <pessoa>

conclu|dente /kõklu'dẽtʃi/ a conclusive; **~ir** vt/i conclude; **~são** f conclusion; **~sivo** a concluding

concor|dância /kõkor'dãsia/ f agreement; **~dante** a consistent; **~dar** vi agree (em to) □ vt bring into line; **~data** f abrir **~data** go into liquidation

concórdia /kõ'kɔrdʒia/ f concord

concor|rência /kõko'xẽsia/ f competition (a for); **~rente** a competing; **~rer** vi compete (a for); **~rer para** contribute to; **~rido** a popular

concre|tizar /kõkretʃi'zar/ vt realize; **~tizar-se** vpr be realized; **~to** /ɛ/ a & m concrete

concurso /kõ'kursu/ m contest; (prova) competition

con|dado /kõ'dadu/ m county; **~de** m count

condeco|ração /kõdekora'sãw/ f decoration; **~rar** vt decorate

conde|nação /kõdena'sãw/ f condemnation; (jurid) conviction; **~nar** vt condemn; (jurid) convict

conden|sação /kõdẽsa'sãw/ f condensation; **~sar** vt condense; **~sar-se** vpr condense

condescen|dência /kõdesẽ'dẽsia/ f acquiescence; **~dente** a acquiescent; **~der** vi acquiesce; **~der a** comply with <pedido, desejo>; **~der a ir** condescend to go

condessa /kõ'desa/ f countess

condi|ção /kõdʒi'sãw/ f condition; (qualidade) capacity; **ter ~ção** ou **~ções para** be able to; **em boas ~ções** in good condition; **~cionado** a conditioned; **~cional** (pl **~cionais**) a conditional; **~cionamento** m conditioning

condimen|tar /kõdʒimẽ'tar/ vt season; **~to** m seasoning

condoer-se /kõdo'ersi/ vpr **~ de** feel sorry for

condolência /kõdo'lẽsia/ f sympathy; pl condolences

condomínio /kõdo'miniu/ m (taxa) service charge

condu|ção /kõdu'sãw/ f (de carro etc) driving; (transporte) transport; **~cente** a conducive (a to); **~ta** f conduct; **~to** m conduit; **~tor** m (de carro) driver; (eletr) conductor; **~zir** vt lead; drive <carro>; (eletr) conduct □ vi (de carro) drive; (levar) lead (a to)

cone /'koni/ m cone

conectar /konek'tar/ vt connect

cone|xão /konek'sãw/ f connection; **~xo** /ɛ/ a connected

confec|ção /kõfek'sãw/ f (roupa) off-the-peg outfit; (loja) clothes shop, boutique; (fábrica) clothes manufacturer; **~cionar** vt make

confederação /kõfedera'sãw/ f confederation

confei|tar /kõfej'tar/ vt ice; **~taria** f cake shop; **~teiro** m confectioner

confe|rência /kõfe'rẽsia/ f conference; (palestra) lecture; **~rencista** m/f speaker

conferir /kõfe'rir/ vt check (com against); (conceder) confer (a on) □ vi (controlar) check; (estar exato) tally

confes|sar /kõfe'sar/ vt/i confess; **~sar-se** vpr confess; **~sionário** m confessional; **~sor** m confessor

confete /kõ'fetʃi/ m confetti

confi|ança /kõfi'ãsa/ f (convicção) confidence; (fé) trust; **~ante** a confident (em of); **~ar** vt (dar) entrust; **~ar em** trust; **~ável** (pl **~áveis**) a reliable; **~dência** f confidence; **~dencial** (pl **~denciais**) a confidential; **~denciar** vt tell in confidence; **~dente** m/f confidant (f confidante)

configu|ração /kõfigura'sãw/ f configuration; **~rar** vt (representar) represent; (formar) shape; (comput) configure

con|finar /kõfi'nar/ vi ~finar com border on; ~fins m pl borders
confir|mação /kõfirma'sãw/ f confirmation; ~mar vt confirm; ~mar-se vpr be confirmed
confis|car /kõfis'kar/ vt confiscate; ~co m confiscation
confissão /kõfi'sãw/ f confession
confla|gração /kõflagra'sãw/ f conflagration; ~grar vt set alight; (fig) throw into turmoil
confli|tante /kõfli'tãtʃi/ a conflicting; ~to m conflict
confor|mação /kõforma'sãw/ f resignation; ~mado a resigned (com to); ~mar vt adapt (a to); ~mar-se com conform to <regra, política>; resign o.s. to, come to terms with <destino, evento>; ~me /ɔ/ prep according to □ conj depending on; ~me it depends; ~midade f conformity; ~mismo m conformism; ~mista a & m/f conformist
confor|tar /kõfor'tar/ vt comfort; ~tável (pl ~táveis) a comfortable; ~to /o/ m comfort
confraternizar /kõfraterni'zar/ vi fraternize
confron|tação /kõfrõta'sãw/ f confrontation; ~tar vt confront; (comparar) compare; ~to m confrontation; (comparação) comparison
con|fundir /kõfũ'dʒir/ vt confuse; ~fundir-se vpr get confused; ~fusão f confusion; (desordem) mess; (tumulto) commotion; ~fuso a (que confunde) confusing; (confundido) confused; (que confunde) confusing
conge|lador /kõʒela'dor/ m freezer; ~lamento m (de preços etc) freeze; ~lar vt freeze; ~lar-se vpr freeze
congênito /kõ'ʒenitu/ a congenital
congestão /kõʒes'tãw/ f congestion
congestio|nado /kõʒestʃio'nadu/ a <rua, cidade> congested; <pessoa, rosto> flushed; <olhos> bloodshot; ~namento m (de trânsito) traffic jam; ~nar vt congest; ~nar-se vpr <rua> get congested; <rosto> flush
conglomerado /kõglome'radu/ m conglomerate
congratular /kõgratu'lar/ vt congratulate (por on)
congre|gação /kõgrega'sãw/ f (na igreja) congregation; (reunião) gathering; ~gar vt bring together; ~gar-se vpr congregate
congresso /kõ'grɛsu/ m congress
conhaque /ko'ɲaki/ m brandy
conhe|cedor /koɲese'dor/ a knowing □ m connoisseur; ~cer vt know; (ser apresentado a) get to know; (visitar) go to, visit; ~cido a known; (famoso) well-known □ m acquaintance;

~cimento m knowledge; tomar ~cimento de learn of; travar ~cimento com alg make s.o.'s acquaintance, become acquainted with s.o.
cônico /'koniku/ a conical
coni|vência /koni'vẽsia/ f connivance; ~vente a conniving (em in)
conjetu|ra /kõʒe'tura/ f conjecture; ~rar vt/i conjecture
conju|gação /kõʒuga'sãw/ f (ling) conjugation; ~gar vt conjugate <verbo>
cônjuge /'kõʒuʒi/ m/f spouse
conjun|ção /kõʒũ'sãw/ f conjunction; ~tivo a & m subjunctive □ m set; (roupa) outfit; (musical) group; o ~to de the body of; em ~to jointly; ~tura f state of affairs; (económica) state of the economy
conosco = com + nós
cono|tação /konota'sãw/ f connotation; ~tar vt connote
conquanto /kõ'kwãtu/ conj although, even though
conquis|ta /kõ'kista/ f conquest; (proeza) achievement; ~tador m conqueror □ a conquering; ~tar vt conquer <terra, país>; win <riqueza, independência>; win over <pessoa>
consa|gração /kõsagra'sãw/ f (de uma igreja) consecration; (dedicação) dedication; ~grado a <artista, expressão> established; ~grar vt consecrate <igreja>; establish <artista, estilo>; (dedicar) dedicate (a to); ~grar-se a dedicate o.s. to
consci|ência /kõsi'ẽsia/ f (moralidade) conscience; (sentidos) consciousness; (no trabalho) conscientiousness; (de um fato etc) awareness; ~encioso /o/ a conscientious; ~ente a conscious; ~entizar vt make aware (de of); ~entizar-se vpr become aware (de of)
consecutivo /kõseku'tʃivu/ a consecutive
conse|guinte /kõse'gĩtʃi/ a por ~guinte consequently; ~guir vt get; ~guir fazer manage to do □ vi succeed
conse|lheiro /kõse'ʎeru/ m counsellor, adviser; ~lho /e/ m piece of advice; pl advice; (órgão) council
consen|so /kõ'sẽsu/ m consensus; ~timento m consent; ~tir vt allow □ vi consent (em to)
conse|qüência /kõse'kwẽsia/ f consequence; por ~qüência consequently; ~qüente a consequent; (coerente) consistent
conser|tar /kõser'tar/ vt repair; ~to /e/ m repair

conser|va /kõ'sɛrva/ f (em vidro) preserve; (em lata) tinned food; ~vação f preservation; ~vador a & m conservative; ~vadorismo m conservatism; ~vante a & m preservative; ~var vt preserve; (manter, guardar) keep; ~var-se vpr keep; ~vatório m conservatory

conside|ração /kõsidera'sãw/ f consideration; (estima) esteem; levar em ~ração take into consideration; ~rar vt consider; (estimar) think highly of □ vi consider; ~rar-se vpr consider o.s.; ~rável (pl ~ráveis) a considerable

consig|nação /kõsigna'sãw/ f consignment; ~nar vt consign

consigo = com + si

consis|tência /kõsis'tẽsia/ f consistency; ~tente a firm; ~tir vi consist (em in)

consoante /kõso'ãtʃi/ f consonant

conso|lação /kõsola'sãw/ f consolation; ~lador a consoling; ~lar vt console; ~lar-se vpr console o.s.

consolidar /kõsoli'dar/ vt consolidate; mend <fratura>

consolo /kõ'solu/ m consolation

consórcio /kõ'sɔrsiu/ m consortium

consorte /kõ'sɔrtʃi/ m/f consort

conspícuo /kõs'pikuu/ a conspicuous

conspi|ração /kõspira'sãw/ f conspiracy; ~rador m conspirator; ~rar vi conspire

cons|tância /kõs'tãsia/ f constancy; ~tante a & f constant; ~tar vi (em lista etc) appear; não me ~ta I am not aware; ~ta que it is said that; ~tar de consist of

consta|tação /kõstata'sãw/ f observation; ~tar vt note, notice; certify <óbito>

conste|lação /kõstela'sãw/ f constellation; ~lado a star-studded

conster|nação /kõsterna'sãw/ f consternation; ~nar vt dismay

consti|pação /kõstʃipa'sãw/ f (Port: resfriado) cold; ~pado a (resfriado) with a cold; (no intestino) constipated; ~par-se vpr (Port: resfriarse) get a cold

constitu|cional /kõstʃitusio'naw/ (pl ~cionais) a constitutional; ~ição f constitution; ~inte a constituent □ f Constituinte Constituent Assembly; ~ir vt form <governo, sociedade>; (representar) constitute; (nomear) appoint

constran|gedor /kõstrãʒe'dor/ a embarrassing; ~ger vt embarrass; (coagir) constrain; ~ger-se vpr get embarrassed; ~gimento m (embaraço) embarrassment; (coação) constraint

constru|ção /kõstru'sãw/ f construction; (terreno) building site; ~ir vt build <casa, prédio>; (fig) construct; ~tivo a constructive; ~tor m builder; ~tora f building firm

cônsul /'kõsuw/ (pl ~es) m consul

consulado /kõsu'ladu/ m consulate

consul|ta /kõ'suwta/ f consultation; ~tar vt consult; ~tor m consultant; ~toria f consultancy; ~tório m (médico) surgery; (Amer) office

consu|mação /kõsuma'sãw/ f (taxa) minimum charge; ~mado a fato ~mado fait accompli; ~mar vt accomplish <projeto>; carry out <crime, sacrifício>; consummate <casamento>

consu|midor /kõsumi'dor/ a & m consumer; ~mir vt consume; take up <tempo>; ~mismo m consumerism; ~mista a m/f consumerist; ~mo m consumption

conta /'kõta/ f (a pagar) bill; (bancária) account; (contagem) count; (de vidro etc) bead; pl (com) accounts; em ~ economical; por ~ de on account of; por ~ própria on one's own account; ajustar ~s settle up; dar ~ de (fig) be up to; dar ~ do recado (fam) deliver the goods; dar-se ~ de realize; fazer ~ de pretend; ficar por ~ de be left to; levar ou ter em ~ take into account; prestar ~s de account for; tomar ~ de take care of; ~ bancária bank account; ~ corrente current account

contabi|lidade /kõtabili'dadʒi/ f accountancy; (contas) accounts; (seção) accounts department; ~lista (Port) m/f accountant; ~lizar vt write up <quantia>; (fig) notch up

contact- (Port) veja contat-

conta|dor /kõta'dor/ m (pessoa) accountant; (de luz etc) meter; ~gem f counting; (de pontos num jogo) scoring; ~gem regressiva countdown

contagi|ante /kõtaʒi'ãtʃi/ a infectious; ~ar vt infect; ~ar-se vpr become infected

contágio /kõ'taʒiu/ m infection

contagioso /kõtaʒi'ozu/ a contagious

contami|nação /kõtamina'sãw/ f contamination; ~nar vt contaminate

contanto /kõ'tãtu/ adv ~ que provided that

contar /kõ'tar/ vt/i count; (narrar) tell; ~ com count on

conta|tar /kõta'tar/ vt contact; ~to m contact; entrar em ~to com get in touch with; tomar ~to com come into contact with

contem|plação /kõtẽpla'sãw/ f contemplation; ~plar vt (considerar) contemplate; (*dizer respeito a*) concern; ~**plar alg com** treat s.o. to □ *vi* ponder; ~**plativo** *a* contemplative

contemporâneo /kõtẽpoˈraniu/ *a & m* contemporary

contenção /kõtẽˈsãw/ *f* containment

conten|cioso /kõtẽsiˈozu/ *a* contentious; ~**da** *f* dispute

conten|tamento /kõtẽtaˈmẽtu/ *m* contentment; ~**tar** *vt* satisfy; ~**tar-se** *vpr* be content; ~**te** *a* (*feliz*) happy; (*satisfeito*) content; ~**to** **m a** ~**to** satisfactorily

conter /kõˈter/ *vt* contain; ~**-se** *vpr* contain o.s.

conterrâneo /kõteˈxaniu/ *m* fellow countryman (*f* -woman)

contestar /kõtesˈtar/ *vt* question; (*jurid*) dispute

conteúdo /kõteˈudu/ *m* (*de recipiente*) contents; (*fig: de carta etc*) content

contexto /kõˈtestu/ *m* context

contigo = **com** + **ti**

continência /kõtʃiˈnẽsia/ *f* (*mil*) salute

continen|tal /kõtʃinẽˈtaw/ (*pl* ~**tais**) *a* continental; ~**te** *m* continent

contin|gência /kõtʃĩˈʒẽsia/ *f* contingency; ~**gente** *a* (*eventual*) possible; (*incerto*) contingent □ *m* contingent

continu|ação /kõtʃinuaˈsãw/ *f* continuation; ~**ar** *vt/i* continue; **eles** ~**am ricos** they are still rich; ~**idade** *f* continuity

contínuo /kõˈtʃinuu/ *a* continuous □ *m* office junior

con|tista /kõˈtʃista/ *m/f* (short) story writer; ~**to** *m* (short) story; ~**to de fadas** fairy tale; ~**to-do-vigário** (*pl* ~**tos-do-vigário**) *m* confidence trick, swindle

contorcer /kõtorˈser/ *vt* twist; ~**-se** *vpr* (*de dor*) writhe

contor|nar /kõtorˈnar/ *vt* go round; (*fig*) get round <*obstáculo, problema*>; (*cercar*) surround; (*delinear*) outline; ~**no** /o/ *m* outline; (*da paisagem*) contour

contra /ˈkõtra/ *prep* against

contra-atacar /kõtrataˈkar/ *vt* counterattack; ~**-ataque** *m* counterattack

contrabaixo /kõtraˈbaʃu/ *m* double bass

contrabalançar /kõtrabalãˈsar/ *vt* counterbalance

contraban|dear /kõtrabãdʒiˈar/ *vt* smuggle; ~**dista** *m/f* smuggler; ~**do** *m* (*ato*) smuggling; (*artigos*) contraband

contração /kõtraˈsãw/ *f* contraction

contracenar /kõtraseˈnar/ *vi* ~ **com** play up to

contraceptivo /kõtrasepˈtʃivu/ *a & m* contraceptive

contracheque /kõtraˈʃɛki/ *m* pay slip

contradi|ção /kõtradʒiˈsãw/ *f* contradiction; ~**tório** *a* contradictory; ~**zer** *vt* contradict; ~**zer-se** *vpr* <*pessoa*> contradict o.s.; <*idéias etc*> be contradictory

contragosto /kõtraˈgostu/ *m* **a** ~ reluctantly

contrair /kõtraˈir/ *vt* contract; pick up <*hábito, vício*>; ~**-se** *vpr* contract

contramão /kõtraˈmãw/ *f* opposite direction □ *a invar* one way

contramestre /kõtraˈmɛstri/ *m* supervisor; (*em navio*) bosun

contra-ofensiva /kõtraofẽˈsiva/ *f* counter-offensive

contrapar|tida /kõtraparˈtʃida/ *f* (*fig*) compensation; **em** ~ on the other hand

contraproducente /kõtraprodu-ˈsẽtʃi/ *a* counter-productive

contrari|ar /kõtrariˈar/ *vt* go against, run counter to; (*aborrecer*) annoy; ~**edade** *f* adversity; (*aborrecimento*) annoyance

contrário /kõˈtrariu/ *a* opposite; (*desfavorável*) adverse; ~ *a* contrary to; <*pessoa*> opposed to □ *m* opposite; **pelo** *ou* **ao** ~ on the contrary; **ao** ~ **de** contrary to; **em** ~ to the contrary

contras|tante /kõtrasˈtãtʃi/ *a* contrasting; ~**tar** *vt/i* contrast; ~**te** *m* contrast

contra|tante /kõtraˈtãtʃi/ *m/f* contractor; ~**tar** *vt* employ, take on <*operários*>

contratempo /kõtraˈtẽpu/ *m* hitch

contra|to /kõˈtratu/ *m* contract; ~**tual** (*pl* ~**tuais**) *a* contractual

contraven|ção /kõtravẽˈsãw/ *f* contravention; ~**tor** *m* offender

contribu|ição /kõtribuiˈsãw/ *f* contribution; ~**inte** *m/f* contributor; (*pagador de impostos*) taxpayer; ~**ir** *vt* contribute □ *vi* contribute; (*pagar impostos*) pay tax

contrição /kõtriˈsãw/ *f* contrition

contro|lar /kõtroˈlar/ *vt* control; (*fiscalizar*) check; ~**le** /o/, (*Port*) ~**lo** /o/ *m* control; (*fiscalização*) check

contro|vérsia /kõtroˈvɛrsia/ *f* controversy; ~**verso** /ɛ/ *a* controversial

contudo /kõˈtudu/ *conj* nevertheless

contundir /kõtũˈdʒir/ *vt* (*dar hematoma em*) bruise; injure <*jogador*>; ~**se** *vpr* bruise o.s.; <*jogador*> get injured

conturbado /kõturˈbadu/ *a* troubled

contu|são /kõtuˈzãw/ *f* bruise; (*de jogador*) injury; ~**so** *a* bruised; <*jogador*> injured

convales|cença /kõvale'sẽsa/ f convalescence; ∼**cer** vi convalesce

convenção /kõvẽ'sãw/ f convention

conven|cer /kõvẽ'ser/ vt convince; ∼**cido** a (convicto) convinced; (metido) conceited; ∼**cimento** m (convicção) conviction; (imodéstia) conceitedness

convencio|nal /kõvẽsio'naw/ (pl ∼**nais**) a conventional

conveni|ência /kõveni'ẽsia/ f convenience; ∼**ente** a convenient; (cabível) appropriate

convênio /kõ'veniu/ m agreement

convento /kõ'vẽtu/ m convent

convergir /kõver'ʒir/ vi converge

conver|sa /kõ'vɛrsa/ f conversation; a ∼**sa dele** the things he says; ∼**sa fiada** idle talk; ∼**sação** f conversation; ∼**sado** a <pessoa> talkative; <assunto> talked about; ∼**sador** a talkative

conversão /kõver'sãw/ f conversion

conversar /kõver'sar/ vi talk

conver|sível /kõver'sivew/ (pl ∼**síveis**) a & m convertible; ∼**ter** vt convert; ∼**ter-se** vpr be converted; ∼**tido** m convert

con|vés /kõ'vɛs/ (pl ∼**veses**) m deck

convexo /kõ'vɛksu/ a convex

convic|ção /kõvik'sãw/ f conviction; ∼**to** a 'convinced; (ferrenho) confirmed; <criminoso> convicted

convi|dado /kõvi'dadu/ m guest; ∼**dar** vt invite; ∼**dativo** a inviting

convincente /kõvĩ'sẽtʃi/ a convincing

convir /kõ'vir/ vi (ficar bem) be appropriate; (concordar) agree (em on); ∼ **a suit**, be convenient for; **convém notar que** one should note that

convite /kõ'vitʃi/ m invitation

convi|vência /kõvi'vẽsia/ f coexistence; (relação) close contact; ∼**ver** vi coexist; (ter relações) associate (com with)

convívio /kõ'viviu/ m association (com with)

convocar /kõvo'kar/ vt call <eleições, greve>; call upon <pessoa> (a to); (ao serviço militar) call up

convosco = **com** + **vós**

convul|são /kõvuw'sãw/ f (do corpo) convulsion; (da sociedade etc) upheaval; ∼**sionar** vt convulse <corpo>; (fig) churn up; ∼**sivo** a convulsive

cooper /'kuper/ m jogging; **fazer** ∼ go jogging

coope|ração /koopera'sãw/ f cooperation; ∼**rar** vi cooperate; ∼**rativa** f cooperative; ∼**rativo** a cooperative

coorde|nação /koordena'sãw/ f coordination; ∼**nada** f coordinate; ∼**nar** vt coordinate

copa /'kɔpa/ f (de árvore) top; (aposento) breakfast room; (torneio) cup; pl (naipe) hearts; **a Copa (do Mundo)** the World Cup; ∼**-cozinha** (pl ∼**s-cozinhas**) f kitchen-diner

cópia /'kɔpia/ f copy

copiar /kopi'ar/ vt copy

co-piloto /kopi'lotu/ m co-pilot

copioso /kopi'ozu/ a ample; <refeição> substantial

copo /'kɔpu/ m glass

coque /'kɔki/ m (penteado) bun

coqueiro /ko'keru/ m coconut palm

coqueluche /koke'luʃi/ f (doença) whooping cough; (mania) fad

coque|tel /koke'tɛw/ (pl ∼**téis**) m cocktail; (reunião) cocktail party

cor[1] /kor/ m **de** ∼ by heart

cor[2] /kor/ f colour; **TV a** ∼**es** colour TV; **pessoa de** ∼ coloured person

coração /kora'sãw/ m heart

cora|gem /ko'raʒẽ/ f courage; ∼**joso** /o/ a courageous

co|ral[1] /ko'raw/ (pl ∼**rais**) m (animal) coral

co|ral[2] /ko'raw/ (pl ∼**rais**) m (de cantores) choir □ a choral

co|rante /ko'rãtʃi/ a & m colouring; ∼**rar** vt colour □ vi blush

cor|da /'kɔrda/ f rope; (mus) string; (para roupa lavada) clothes line; **dar** ∼ **a em** wind <relógio>; ∼**da bamba** tightrope; ∼**das vocais** vocal chords; ∼**dão** m cord; (de sapatos) lace; (policial) cordon

cordeiro /kor'deru/ m lamb

cor|del /kor'dɛw/ (de ∼**déis**) (Port) m string; **literatura de** ∼**del** trash

cor-de-rosa /kordʒi'rɔza/ a invar pink

cordi|al /kordʒi'aw/ (pl ∼**ais**) a & m cordial; ∼**alidade** f cordiality

cordilheira /kordʒi'ʎera/ f chain of mountains

coreano /kori'anu/ a & m Korean

Coréia /ko'rɛja/ f Korea

core|ografia /koriogra'fia/ f choreography; ∼**ógrafo** m choreographer

coreto /ko'retu/ m bandstand

coriza /ko'riza/ f runny nose

corja /'kɔrʒa/ f pack; (de pessoas) rabble

córner /'kɔrner/ m corner

coro /'koru/ m chorus

coro|a /ko'roa/ f crown; (de flores etc) wreath □ (fam) m/f old man (f woman); ∼**ação** f coronation; ∼**ar** vt crown

coro|nel /koro'nɛw/ (pl ∼**néis**) m colonel

coronha /ko'roɲa/ f butt

corpete /kor'petʃi/ m bodice

corpo /'kɔrpu/ m body; (físico de mulher) figure; (físico de homem) physique; ~ de bombeiros fire brigade; ~ diplomático diplomatic corps; ~ docente teaching staff, (*Amer*) faculty; ~-a-~ *m invar* pitched battle; ~ral (*pl* ~rais) *a* physical; <*pena*> corporal

corpulência /korpu'lẽsia/ *f* stoutness; ~lento *a* stout

correção /koxe'sãw/ *f* correction

corre-corre /kɔxi'kɔxi/ *m* (*debandada*) stampede; (*correria*) rush

correct- (*Port*) *veja* corret-

corre|diço /koxe'dʒisu/ *a* <*porta*> sliding; ~dor *m* (*atleta*) runner; (*passagem*) corridor

correia /ko'xeja/ *f* strap; (*peça de máquina*) belt; (*para cachorro*) lead, (*Amer*) leash

correio /ko'xeju/ *m* post, mail; (*repartição*) post office; **pôr no ~** post, (*Amer*) mail; ~ **aéreo** air mail

correlação /koxela'sãw/ *f* correlation

correligionário /koxeliʒio'nariu/ *m* party colleague

corrente /ko'xẽtʃi/ *a* <*água*> running; <*mês, conta*> current; <*estilo*> fluid; (*usual*) common □ *f* (*de água, eletricidade*) current; (*cadeia*) chain; ~ **de ar** draught; ~**za** /e/ *f* current; (*de ar*) draught

cor|rer /ko'xer/ *vi* (*à pé*) run; (*de carro*) drive fast, speed; (*fazer rápido*) rush; <*água, sangue*> flow; <*tempo*> elapse; <*boato*> go round □ *vt* draw <*cortina*>; run <*risco*>; ~**reria** *f* rush

correspon|dência /koxespõ'dẽsia/ *f* correspondence; ~**dente** *a* corresponding □ *m/f* correspondent; (*equivalente*) equivalent; ~**der** *vi* ~**der a** correspond to; (*retribuir*) return; ~**der-se** *vpr* correspond (com with)

corre|tivo /koxe'tʃivu/ *a* corrective □ *m* punishment; ~**to** /ɛ/ *a* correct

corretor /koxe'tor/ *m* broker; ~ **de imóveis** estate agent, (*Amer*) realtor

corrida /ko'xida/ *f* (*prova*) race; (*ação de correr*) run; (*de táxi*) ride

corrigir /koxi'ʒir/ *vt* correct

corrimão /koxi'mãw/ (*pl* ~s) *m* handrail; (*de escada*) banister

corriqueiro /koxi'keru/ *a* ordinary, run-of-the-mill

corroborar /koxobo'rar/ *vt* corroborate

corroer /koxo'er/ *vt* corrode <*metal*>; (*fig*) erode; ~**se** *vpr* corrode; (*fig*) erode

corromper /koxõ'per/ *vt* corrupt; ~**se** *vpr* be corrupted

corro|são /koxo'zãw/ *f* (*de metal*) corrosion; (*fig*) erosion; ~**sivo** *a* corrosive

corrup|ção /koxup'sãw/ *f* corruption; ~**to a** corrupt

cor|tada /kor'tada/ *f* (*em tênis*) smash; (*em pessoa*) put-down; ~**tante** *a* cutting; ~**tar** *vt* cut; cut off <*luz, telefone, perna etc*>; cut down <*árvore*>; cut out <*efeito, vício*>; take away <*prazer*>; (*com o carro*) cut up; (*desprezar*) cut dead □ *vi* cut; ~**tar o cabelo** (*no cabeleireiro*) get one's hair cut; ~**te**[1] /ɔ/ *m* cut; (*gume*) blade; (*desenho*) cross-section; **sem** ~**te** <*faca*> blunt; ~**te de cabelo** haircut

cor|te[2] /'kortʃi/ *f* court; ~**tejar** *vt* court; ~**tejo** /e/ *m* (*séquito*) retinue; (*fúnebre*) cortège; ~**tês** *a* (*f* ~**tesa**) courteous, polite; ~**tesão** (*pl* ~**tesãos**) *m* courtier; ~**tesia** *f* courtesy

corti|ça /kor'tʃisa/ *f* cork; ~**ço** *m* (*casa popular*) slum tenement

cortina /kor'tʃina/ *f* curtain

cortisona /kortʃi'zona/ *f* cortisone

coruja /ko'ruʒa/ *f* owl □ *a* <*pai, mãe*> proud, doting

coruscar /korus'kar/ *vi* flash

corvo /'korvu/ *m* crow

cós /kɔs/ *m invar* waistband

coser /ko'zer/ *vt/i* sew

cosmético /koz'mɛtʃiku/ *a* & *m* cosmetic

cósmico /'kɔzmiku/ *a* cosmic

cosmo /'kɔzmu/ *m* cosmos; ~**nauta** *m/f* cosmonaut; ~**polita** *a* cosmopolitan □ *m/f* globetrotter

costa /'kɔsta/ *f* coast; *pl* (*dorso*) back; **Costa do Marfim** Ivory Coast; **Costa Rica** Costa Rica

costarriquenho /kostaxi'keɲu/ *a* & *m* Costa Rican

cos|teiro /kos'teru/ *a* coastal; ~**tela** /ɛ/ *f* rib; ~**teleta** /e/ *f* chop; *pl* (*suíças*) sideburns; ~**telinha** *f* (*de porco*) spare rib

costu|mar /kostu'mar/ *vt* ~**ma fazer** he usually does; ~**mava fazer** he used to do; ~**me** *m* (*uso*) custom; (*traje*) costume; **de** ~**me** usually; **como de** ~**me** as usual; **ter o** ~**me de** have a habit of; ~**meiro** *a* customary

costu|ra /kos'tura/ *f* sewing; ~**rar** *vt/i* sew; ~**reira** *f* (*mulher*) dressmaker; (*caixa*) needlework box

co|ta /'kɔta/ *f* quota; ~**tação** *f* (*preço*) rate; (*apreço*) rating; ~**tado** *a* <*ação*> quoted; (*conceituado*) highly rated; ~**tar** *vt* rate; quote <*ações*>

cotejar /kote'ʒar/ *vt* compare; ~**jo** /e/ *m* comparison

cotidiano /kotʃidʒi'anu/ *a* everyday □ *m* everyday life

cotonete /koto'nɛtʃi/ *m* cotton bud

cotove|lada /kotove'lada/ f (*para abrir caminho*) shove; (*para chamar atenção*) nudge; ~lo /e/ m elbow

coura|ça /ko'rasa/ f (*armadura*) breastplate; (*de navio, animal*) armour; ~çado (Port) m battleship

couro /'koru/ m leather; ~ cabeludo scalp

couve /'kovi/ f spring greens; ~-de-bruxelas (pl ~s-de-bruxelas) f Brussels sprout; ~-flor (pl ~s-flores) f cauliflower

couvert /ku'vɛr/ (pl ~s) m cover charge

cova /'kɔva/ f (*buraco*) pit; (*sepultura*) grave

covar|de /ko'vardʒi/ m/f coward □ a cowardly; ~dia f cowardice

coveiro /ko'veru/ m gravedigger

covil /ko'viw/ (pl ~vis) m den, lair

covinha /ko'viɲa/ f dimple

co|xa /'koʃa/ f thigh; ~xear vi hobble

coxia /ko'ʃia/ f aisle

coxo /'koʃu/ a hobbling; ser ~ hobble

co|zer /ko'zer/ vt/i cook; ~zido m stew, casserole

cozi|nha /ko'ziɲa/ f (*aposento*) kitchen; (*comida, ação*) cooking; (*arte*) cookery; ~nhar vt/i cook; ~nheiro m cook

crachá /kra'ʃa/ m badge, (Amer) button

crânio /'kraniu/ m skull; (*pessoa*) genius

crápula /'krapula/ m/f scoundrel

craque /'kraki/ m (*de futebol*) soccer star; (*fam*) expert

crase /'krazi/ f contraction; a com ~ a grave (à)

crasso /'krasu/ a crass

cratera /kra'tɛra/ f crater

cravar /kra'var/ vt drive in <*prego*>; dig <*unha*>; stick <*estaca*>; ~ com os olhos stare at; ~-se vpr stick

cravejar /krave'ʒar/ vt nail; (*com balas*) spray, riddle

cravo¹ /'kravu/ m (*flor*) carnation; (*condimento*) clove

cravo² /'kravu/ m (*na pele*) blackhead; (*prego*) nail

cravo³ /'kravu/ m (*instrumento*) harpsichord

creche /'krɛʃi/ f crèche

credenci|ais /kredẽsi'ajs/ f pl credentials; ~ar vt qualify

credi|ário /kredʒi'ariu/ m hire purchase agreement, credit plan; ~bilidade f credibility; ~tar vt credit

crédito /'krɛdʒitu/ m credit; a ~ on credit

cre|do /'krɛdu/ m creed □ int heavens; ~dor m creditor □ a <*saldo*> credit

crédulo /'krɛdulu/ a gullible

cre|mação /krema'sãw/ f cremation; ~mar vt cremate; ~matório m crematorium

cre|me /'krɛmi/ a invar & m cream; ~me Chantilly whipped cream; ~me de leite (sterilized) cream; ~moso /o/ a creamy

cren|ça /'krẽsa/ f belief; (*superstição*) superstition; ~te m believer; (*protestante*) Protestant □ a religious; (*protestante*) Protestant; estar ~te que believe that

crepe /'krɛpi/ m crepe

crepitar /krepi'tar/ vi crackle

crepom /kre'põ/ m crepe; papel ~ tissue paper

crepúsculo /kre'puskulu/ m twilight

crer /krer/ vt/i believe (em in); creio que I think (that); ~-se vpr believe o.s. to be

cres|cendo /kre'sẽdu/ m crescendo; ~cente a growing □ m crescent; ~cer vi grow; <*bolo*> rise; ~cido a grown; ~cimento m growth

crespo /'krespu/ a <*cabelo*> frizzy; <*mar*> choppy

cretino /kre'tʃinu/ m cretin

cria /'kria/ f baby; pl young

criação /kria'sãw/ f creation; (*educação*) upbringing; (*de animais*) raising; (*gado*) livestock

criado /kri'adu/ m servant; ~-mudo (pl ~s-mudos) m bedside table

criador /kria'dor/ m creator; (*de animais*) farmer, breeder

crian|ça /kri'ãsa/ f child □ a childish; ~çada f kids; ~ice f childishness; (*uma*) childish thing

criar /kri'ar/ vt (*fazer*) create; bring up <*filhos*>; rear <*animais*>; grow <*planta*>; pluck up <*coragem*>; ~-se vpr be brought up, grow up

criati|vidade /kriatʃivi'dadʒi/ f creativity; ~vo a creative

criatura /kria'tura/ f creature

crime /'krimi/ m crime

crimi|nal /krimi'naw/ (pl ~nais) a criminal; ~nalidade f crime; ~noso m criminal

crina /'krina/ f mane

crioulo /kri'olu/ a & m creole; (*negro*) black

cripta /'kripta/ f crypt

crisálida /kri'zalida/ f chrysalis

crisântemo /kri'zãtemu/ m chrysanthemum

crise /'krizi/ f crisis

cris|ma /'krizma/ f confirmation; ~mar vt confirm; ~mar-se vpr get confirmed

crista /'krista/ f crest

cris|tal /kris'taw/ (pl ~tais) m crystal; (*vidro*) glass; ~talino a crystal-clear; ~talizar vt/i crystallize cris|tandade /kristã'dadʒi/ f Christendom; ~tão (pl ~tãos) a & m (f ~tã) Christian; ~tianismo m Christianity

Cristo /'kristu/ m Christ

cri|tério /kri'tεriu/ m discretion; (norma) criterion; ~terioso a perceptive, discerning

crítica /'kritʃika/ f criticism; (análise) critique; (de filme, livro) review; (críticos) critics

criticar /kritʃi'kar/ vt criticize; review <filme, livro>

crítico /'kritʃiku/ a critical □ m critic

crivar /kri'var/ vt (furar) riddle

cri|vel /'krivew/ (pl ~veis) a credible

crivo /'krivu/ m sieve; (fig) scrutiny

crocante /kro'kãtʃi/ a crunchy

croché /kro'ʒε/ m crochet

crocodilo /kroko'dʒilu/ m crocodile

cromo /'kromu/ m chrome

cromossomo /kromo'somu/ m chromosome

crôni|ca /'kronika/ f (histórica) chronicle; (no jornal) feature; (conto) short story; ~co a chronic

cronista /kro'nista/ m/f (de jornal) feature writer; (contista) short story writer; (historiador) chronicler

crono|grama /krono'grama/ m schedule; ~logia f chronology; ~lógico a chronological; ~metrar vt time

cronômetro /kro'nometru/ m stopwatch

croquete /kro'kεtʃi/ m savoury meatball in breadcrumbs

croqui /kro'ki/ m sketch

crosta /'krosta/ f crust; (em ferida) scab

cru /kru/ a (f ~a) raw; <luz, tom, palavra> harsh; crude; <verdade> unvarnished, plain

cruci|al /krusi'aw/ (pl ~ais) a crucial

crucifi|cação /krusifika'sãw/ f crucifixion; ~car vt crucify; ~xo /ks/ m crucifix

cru|el /kru'εw/ (pl ~éis) a cruel; ~eldade f cruelty; ~ento a bloody

crupe /'krupi/ m croup

crustáceos /krus'tasius/ m pl shellfish

cruz /krus/ f cross

cruza|da /kru'zada/ f crusade; ~do[1] m (soldado) crusader

cru|zado[2] /kru'zadu/ m (moeda) cruzado; ~zador m cruiser; ~zamento m (de ruas) crossroads, junction, (Amer) intersection; (de raças) cross; ~zar vt cross □ vi <navio> cruise; ~zar com pass; ~zar-se vpr cross; <pessoas> pass each other;

~zeiro m (moeda) cruzeiro; (viagem) cruise; (cruz) cross

cu /ku/ m (chulo) arse, (Amer) ass

Cuba /'kuba/ f Cuba

cubano /ku'banu/ a & m Cuban

cúbico /'kubiku/ a cubic

cubículo /ku'bikulu/ m cubicle

cubis|mo /ku'bizmu/ m cubism; ~ta a & m/f cubist

cubo /'kubu/ m cube; (de roda) hub

cuca /'kuka/ (fam) f head

cuco /'kuku/ m cuckoo; (relógio) cuckoo clock

cu|-de-ferro /kudʒi'fεxu/ (pl ~s-de-ferro) (fam) m swot

cueca /ku'εka/ f underpants; pl (Port: de mulher) knickers

cueiro /ku'eru/ m baby wrap

cuia /'kuia/ f gourd

cuidado /kui'dadu/ m care; com ~ carefully; ter ou tomar ~ be careful; ~so /o/ a careful

cuidar /kui'dar/ vi ~ de take care of; ~-se vpr look after o.s.

cujo /'kuʒu/ pron whose

culatra /ku'latra/ f breech; sair pela ~ (fig) backfire

culiná|ria /kuli'naria/ f cookery; ~rio a culinary

culmi|nância /kuwmi'nãsia/ f culmination; ~nante a culminating; ~nar vi culminate (em in)

cul|pa /'kuwpa/ f guilt; foi ~pa minha it was my fault; ter ~pa de be to blame for; ~pabilidade f guilt; ~pado a guilty □ m culprit; ~par vt blame (de for); (na justiça) find guilty (de of); ~par-se vpr take the blame (de for); ~pável (pl ~páveis) a culpable, guilty

culti|var /kuwtʃi'var/ vt cultivate; grow <plantas>; ~vo m cultivation; (de plantas) growing

cul|to /'kuwtu/ a cultured □ m cult; ~tura f culture; (de terra) cultivation; ~tural (pl ~turais) a cultural

cumbuca /kũ'buka/ f bowl

cume /'kumi/ m peak

cúmplice /'kũplisi/ m/f accomplice

cumplicidade /kũplisi'dadʒi/ f complicity

cumprimen|tar /kũprimẽ'tar/ vt/i (saudar) greet; (parabenizar) compliment; ~to m (saudação) greeting; (elogio) compliment; (de lei, ordem) compliance (de with); (de promessa, palavra) fulfilment

cumprir /kũ'prir/ vt keep <promessa, palavra>; comply with <lei, ordem>; do <dever>; carry out <obrigações>; serve <pena>; ~ com keep to □ vi cumpre-nos ir we should go; ~-se vpr be fulfilled

cúmulo /'kumulu/ *m* height; é o ∼! that's the limit!

cunha /'kuɲa/ *f* wedge

cunha|da /ku'ɲada/ *f* sister-in-law; ∼**do** *m* brother-in-law

cunhar /ku'ɲar/ *vt* coin <*palavra, expressão*>; mint <*moedas*>

cunho /'kuɲu/ *m* hallmark

cupim /ku'pĩ/ *m* termite

cupom /ku'põ/ *m* coupon

cúpula /'kupula/ *f* (*de abóbada*) dome; (*de abajur*) shade; (*chefia*) leadership; (*reunião de*) ∼ summit (meeting)

cura /'kura/ *f* cure □ *m* curate, priest

curandeiro /kurã'deru/ *m* (*religioso*) faith-healer; (*índio*) medicine man; (*charlatão*) quack

curar /ku'rar/ *vt* cure; dress <*ferida*>; ∼**-se** *vpr* be cured

curativo /kura'tʃivu/ *m* dressing

curá|vel /ku'ravew/ (*pl* ∼**veis**) *a* curable

curin|ga /ku'rĩga/ *m* wild card; ∼**gão** *m* joker

curio|sidade /kuriozi'dadʒi/ *f* curiosity; ∼**so** /o/ *a* curious □ *m* (*espectador*) onlooker

cur|ral /ku'xaw/ (*pl* ∼**rais**) *m* pen

currículo /ku'xikulu/ *m* curriculum; (*resumo*) curriculum vitae, CV

cur|sar /kur'sar/ *vt* attend <*escola, aula*>; study <*matéria*>; ∼**so** *m* course; ∼**sor** *m* cursor

curta-metragem /kurtame'traʒẽ/ (*pl* ∼**s-metragens**) *m* short (film)

cur|tição /kurtʃi'sãw/ (*fam*) *f* enjoyment; ∼**tir** *vt* (*fam*) enjoy; tan <*couro*>

curto /'kurtu/ *a* short; <*conhecimento, inteligência*> limited; ∼**-circuito** (*pl* ∼**s-circuitos**) *m* short circuit

cur|va /'kurva/ *f* curve; (*de estrada, rio*) bend; ∼**va fechada** hairpin bend; ∼**var** *vt* bend; ∼**var-se** *vpr* bend; (*fig*) bow (a to); ∼**vo** *a* curved; <*estrada*> winding

cus|parada /kuspa'rada/ *f* spit; ∼**pe** *m* spit, spittle; ∼**pir** *vt/i* spit

cus|ta /'kusta/ *f* à ∼**ta de** at the expense of; ∼**tar** *vt* cost □ *vi* (*ser difícil*) be hard; ∼**tar a fazer** (*ter dificuldade*) find it hard to do; (*demorar*) take a long time to do; ∼**tear** *vt* finance, fund; ∼**teio** *m* funding; (*relação de despesas*) costing; ∼**to** *m* cost; a ∼**to** with difficulty

custódia /kus'tɔdʒia/ *f* custody

cutelo /ku'telu/ *m* cleaver

cutícula /ku'tʃikula/ *f* cuticle

cútis /'kutʃis/ *f* invar complexion

cutucar /kutu'kar/ *vt* (*com o cotovelo, joelho*) nudge; (*com o dedo*) poke; (*com instrumento*) prod

czar /zar/ *m* tsar

D

da = de + a

dádiva /'dadʒiva/ *f* gift; (*donativo*) donation

dado /'dadu/ *m* (*de jogar*) die, dice; (*informação*) fact, piece of information; *pl* data

daí /da'i/ *adv* (*no espaço*) from there; (*no tempo*) then; ∼ **por diante** from then on; e ∼? (*fam*) so what?

dali /da'li/ *adv* from over there

dália /'dalia/ *f* dahlia

dal|tónico /daw'toniku/ *a* colour-blind; ∼**tonismo** *m* colour-blindness

dama /'dama/ *f* lady; (*em jogos*) queen; *pl* (*jogo*) draughts, (*Amer*) checkers; ∼ **de honra** bridesmaid

da|nado /da'nadu/ *a* damned; (*zangado*) angry; (*travesso*) naughty; ∼**nar-se** *vpr* get angry; ∼**ne-se!** (*fam*) who cares?

dan|ça /'dãsa/ *f* dance; ∼**çar** *vt* dance □ *vi* dance; (*fam*) miss out; <*coisa*> go by the board; <*crimonoso*> get caught; ∼**çarino** *m* dancer; ∼**ceteria** *f* discotheque

da|nificar /danifi'kar/ *vt* damage; ∼**ninho** *a* undesirable; ∼**no** *m* (*pl*) damage; ∼**noso** /o/ *a* damaging

dantes /'dãtʃis/ *adv* formerly

daquela(s), daquele(s) = de + aquela(s), aquele(s)

daqui /da'ki/ *adv* from here; ∼ **a 2 dias** in 2 days(' time); ∼ **a pouco** in a minute; ∼ **em diante** from now on

daquilo = de + aquilo

dar /dar/ *vt* give; have <*dormida, lida etc*>; do <*pulo, cambalhota etc*>; cause <*problemas*>; produce <*frutas, leite*>; deal <*cartas*>; (*lecionar*) teach □ *vi* (*ser possível*) be possible; (*ser suficiente*) be enough; ∼ **com** come across; ∼ **em** lead to; ele dá para ator he'd make a good actor; ∼ **por** (*considerar como*) consider to be; (*reparar em*) notice; ∼**-se** *vpr* <*coisa*> happen; <*pessoa*> get on

dardo /'dardu/ *m* dart; (*no atletismo*) javelin

das = de + as

da|ta /'data/ *f* date; **de longa** ∼ long since; ∼**tar** *vt/i* date

dati|lografar /datʃilogra'far/ *vt/i* type; ∼**lografia** *f* typing; ∼**lógrafo** *m* typist

de /dʒi/ *prep* of; (*procedência*) from; ∼ **carro** by car; **trabalho** ∼ **repórter** I work as a reporter

debaixo /dʒi'baʃu/ *adv* below; ~ de under

debalde /dʒi'bawdʒi/ *adv* in vain

debandada /debã'dada/ *f* stampede

deba|te /de'batʃi/ *m* debate; ~**ter** *vt* debate; ~**ter-se** *vpr* grapple

debelar /debe'lar/ *vt* overcome

dé|bil /'dɛbiw/ (*pl* ~**beis**) *a* feeble; ~**bil mental** retarded (person)

debili|dade /debili'dadʒi/ *f* debility; ~**tar** *vt* debilitate; ~**tar-se** *vpr* become debilitated

debitar /debi'tar/ *vt* debit

débito /'dɛbitu/ *m* debit

debo|chado /debo'ʃadu/ *a* sardonic; ~**char** *vt* mock; ~**che** /ɔ/ *m* jibe

debruar /debru'ar/ *vt/i* edge

debruçar-se /debru'sarsi/ *vpr* bend over; ~ **sobre** study

debrum /de'brũ/ *m* edging

debulhar /debu'ʎar/ *vt* thresh

debu|tante /debu'tãtʃi/ *f* debutante; ~**tar** *vi* debut, make one's debut

década /'dɛkada/ *f* decade; a ~ **dos 60** the sixties

deca|dência /deka'dẽsia/ *f* decadence; ~**dente** *a* decadent

decair /deka'ir/ *vi* decline; (*degringolar*) go downhill; <*planta*> wilt

decal|car /dekaw'kar/ *vt* trace; ~**que** *m* tracing

decapitar /dekapi'tar/ *vt* decapitate

decatlo /de'katlu/ *m* decathlon

de|cência /de'sẽsia/ *f* decency; ~**cente** *a* decent

decepar /dese'par/ *vt* cut off

decep|ção /desep'sãw/ *f* disappointment; ~**cionar** *vt* disappoint; ~**cionar-se** *vpr* be disappointed

decerto /dʒi'sɛrtu/ *adv* certainly

deci|dido /desi'dʒidu/ *a* <*pessoa*> determined; ~**dir** *vt/i* decide; ~**dir-se** *vpr* make up one's mind; ~**dir-se por** decide on

decíduo /de'siduu/ *a* deciduous

decifrar /desi'frar/ *vt* decipher

deci|mal /desi'maw/ (*pl* ~**mais**) *a* & *m* decimal

décimo /'dɛsimu/ *a* & *m* tenth; ~ **primeiro** eleventh; ~ **segundo** twelfth; ~ **terceiro** thirteenth; ~ **quarto** fourteenth; ~ **quinto** fifteenth; ~ **sexto** sixteenth; ~ **sétimo** seventeenth; ~ **oitavo** eighteenth; ~ **nono** nineteenth

deci|são /desi'zãw/ *f* decision; ~**sivo** *a* decisive

decla|ração /deklara'sãw/ *f* declaration; ~**rado** *a* <*inimigo*> sworn; <*crente*> avowed; <*ladrão*> self-confessed; ~**rar** *vt* declare

decli|nação /deklina'sãw/ *f* declension; ~**nar** *vt* ~**nar (de)** de-

cline □ *vi* decline; <*sol*> go down; <*chão*> slope down

declínio /de'kliniu/ *m* decline

declive /de'klivi/ *m* (downward) slope, incline

decodificar /dekodʒifi'kar/ *vt* decode

deco|lagem /deko'laʒẽ/ *f* take-off; ~**lar** *vi* take off; (*fig*) get off the ground

decom|por /dekõ'por/ *vt* break down; contort <*feições*>; ~**por-se** *vpr* break down; <*cadáver*> decompose; ~**posição** *f* (*de cadáver*) decomposition

deco|ração /dekora'sãw/ *f* decoration; (*aprendizagem*) learning by heart; ~**rar** *vt* (*adornar*) decorate; (*aprender*) learn by heart, memorize; ~**rativo** *a* decorative; ~**reba** /ɛ/ (*fam*) *f* rote-learning; ~**ro** /o/ *m* decorum; ~**roso** /o/ *a* decorous

decor|rência /deko'xẽsia/ *f* consequence; ~**rente** *a* resulting (de from); ~**rer** *vi* <*tempo*> elapse; <*acontecimento*> pass off; (*resultar*) result (de from) □ *m* no ~**rer de** in the course of; com o ~**rer do tempo** in time, with the passing of time

deco|tado /deko'tadu/ *a* low-cut; ~**te** /ɔ/ *m* neckline

decrépito /de'krɛpitu/ *a* decrepit

decres|cente /dekre'sẽtʃi/ *a* decreasing; ~**cer** *vi* decrease

decre|tar /dekre'tar/ *vt* decree; declare <*estado de sítio*>; ~**to** /ɛ/ *m* decree; ~**to-lei** (*pl* ~**tos-leis**) *m* act

decurso /de'kursu/ *m* course

de|dal /de'daw/ (*pl* ~**dais**) *m* thimble; ~**dão** *m* (*da mão*) thumb; (*do pé*) big toe

dedetizar /dedetʃi'zar/ *vt* spray with insecticide

dedi|cação /dedʒika'sãw/ *f* dedication; ~**car** *vt* dedicate; devote <*tempo*>; ~**car-se** *vpr* dedicate o.s. (a to); ~**catória** *f* dedication

dedilhar /dedʒi'ʎar/ *vt* pluck

dedo /'dedu/ *m* finger; (*do pé*) toe; cheio de ~**s** all fingers and thumbs; (*sem graça*) awkward; ~-**duro** (*pl* ~**s-duros**) *m* sneak; (*político, criminoso*) informer

dedução /dedu'sãw/ *f* deduction

dedurar /dedu'rar/ *vt* sneak on; (*à policia*) inform on

dedu|tivo /dedu'tʃivu/ *a* deductive; ~**zir** *vt* (*descontar*) deduct; (*concluir*) deduce

defa|sado /defa'zadu/ *a* out of step; ~**sagem** *f* gap, lag

defecar /defe'kar/ *vi* defecate

defei|to /de'fejtu/ *m* defect; botar ~**to em** find fault with; ~**tuoso** /o/ *a* defective

defen|der /defĕ'der/ vt defend; **~der-se** vpr (virar-se) fend for o.s.; (contra-atacar) defend o.s. (de against); **~siva** f na **~siva** on the defensive; **~sor** m defender; (advogado) defence counsel

defe|rência /defe'rēsia/ f deference; **~rente** a deferential

defesa /de'feza/ f defence □ m defender

defici|ência /defisi'ēsia/ f deficiency; **~ente** a deficient; (física ou mentalmente) handicapped □ m/f handicapped person

déficit /'defisitfi/ (pl **~s**) m deficit

deficitário /defisitfi'ariu/ a in deficit; <empresa> loss-making

definhar /defi'nar/ vi waste away; <planta> wither

defi|nição /defini'sãw/ f definition; **~nir** vt define; **~nir-se** vpr (descrever-se) define o.s.; (decidir-se) come to a decision; (explicar-se) make one's position clear; **~nitivo** a definitive; **~nível** (pl **~níveis**) a definable

defla|ção /defla'sãw/ f deflation; **~cionário** a deflationary

deflagrar /defla'grar/ vt set off □ vi break out

defor|mar /defor'mar/ vt misshape; deform <corpo>; distort <imagem>; **~midade** f deformity

defraudar /defraw'dar/ vt defraud (de of)

defron|tar /defrõ'tar/ vt **~tar com** face; **~te** adv opposite; **~te de** opposite

defumar /defu'mar/ vt smoke

defunto /de'fũtu/ a & m deceased

dege|lar /deʒe'lar/ vt/i thaw; **~lo** /e/ m thaw

degeneração /deʒenera'sãw/ f degeneration

degenerar /deʒene'rar/ vi degenerate (em into)

degolar /dego'lar/ vt cut the throat of

degra|dação /degrada'sãw/ f degradation; **~dante** a degrading; **~dar** vt degrade

degrau /de'graw/ m step

degringolar /degrĩgo'lar/ vi deteriorate, go downhill

degustar /degus'tar/ vt taste

dei|tada /dej'tada/ f lie-down; **~tado** a lying down; (dormindo) in bed; (fam: preguiçoso) idle; **~tar** vt lay down; (na cama) put to bed; (pôr) put; (Port: jogar) throw □ vi, **~tar-se** vpr lie down; (ir para cama) go to bed

dei|xa /'deʃa/ f cue; **~xar** vt leave; (permitir) let; **~xar de** (parar) stop; (omitir) fail; não pôde **~xar de rir** he couldn't help laughing; **~xar alg**

nervoso make s.o. annoyed; **~xar cair** drop; **~xar a desejar** leave a lot to be desired; **~xa (para lá)** (fam) never mind, forget it

dela(s) = de + ela(s)

delatar /dela'tar/ vt report

délavé /dela've/ a invar faded

dele(s) = de + ele(s)

dele|gação /delega'sãw/ f delegation; **~gacia** f police station; **~gado** m delegate; **~gado de polícia** police chief; **~gar** vt delegate

delei|tar /delej'tar/ vt delight; **~tar-se** vpr delight (com in); **~te** m delight; **~toso** /o/ a delightful

delgado /dew'gadu/ a slender

delibe|ração /delibera'sãw/ f deliberation; **~rar** vt/i deliberate

delica|deza /delika'deza/ f delicacy; (cortesia) politeness; **~do** a delicate; (cortês) polite

delícia /de'lisia/ f delight; **ser uma ~** <comida> be delicious; <sol etc> be lovely

delici|ar /delisi'ar/ vt delight; **~ar-se** delight (com in); **~oso** /o/ a delightful, lovely; <comida> delicious

deline|ador /delinia'dor/ m eye-liner; **~ar** vt outline

delin|qüência /delĩ'kwẽsia/ f delinquency; **~qüente** a & m delinquent

deli|rante /deli'rãtʃi/ a rapturous; (med) delirious; **~rar** vi go into raptures; <doente> be delirious

delírio /de'liriu/ m (febre) delirium; (excitação) raptures

delito /de'litu/ m crime

delonga /de'lõga/ f delay

delta /'dewta/ f delta

dema|gogia /demago'ʒia/ f demagogy; **~gógico** a demagogic; **~gogo** /o/ m demagogue

demais /dʒi'majs/ a & adv (muito) very much; (em demasia) too much; **os ~** the rest, the others; **é ~!** (fam) it's great!

deman|da /de'mãda/ f demand; (jurid) action; **~dar** vt sue

demão /de'mãw/ f coat

demar|car /demar'kar/ vt demarcate; **~catório** a demarcation

demasia /dema'zia/ f excess; **em ~** too much, (many)

de|mência /de'mēsia/ f insanity; (med) dementia; **~mente** a insane; (med) demented

demissão /demi'sãw/ f sacking, dismissal; **pedir ~** resign

demitir /demi'tʃir/ vt sack, dismiss; **~-se** vpr resign

demo|cracia /demokra'sia/ f democracy; **~crata** m/f democrat; **~crático** a democratic; **~cratizar**

vt democratize; ~grafia *f* demography; ~gráfico *a* demographic

demolição /demoli'sãw/ *f* demolition; ~lir *vt* demolish

demônio /de'moniu/ *m* demon

demonstração /demõstra'sãw/ *f* demonstration; ~trar *vt* demonstrate; ~trativo *a* demonstrative

demora /de'mɔra/ *f* delay; ~rado *a* lengthy; ~rar *vi* (*levar*) take; (*tardar a voltar, terminar etc*) be long; (*levar muito tempo*) take a long time □ *vt* delay

dendê /dẽ'de/ *m* (*óleo*) palm oil

denegrir /dene'grir/ *vt* denigrate

dengoso /dẽ'gozu/ *a* coy

dengue /'dẽgi/ *m* dengue

denominação /denomina'sãw/ *f* denomination; ~nar *vt* name

denotar /deno'tar/ *vt* denote

densidade /dẽsi'dadʒi/ *f* density; ~so *a* dense

dentado /dẽ'tadu/ *a* serrated; ~tadura *f* (set of) teeth; (*postiça*) dentures, false teeth; ~tal (*pl* ~tais) *a* dental; ~tário *a* dental; ~te *m* tooth; (*de alho*) clove; ~te do siso wisdom tooth; (*dentadura*) teeth; ~tição *f* teething; ~tifrico *m* toothpaste; ~tista *m/f* dentist

dentre = de + entre

dentro /'dẽtru/ *adv* inside; lá ~ in there; por ~ on the inside; ~ de inside; (*tempo*) within

dentuça /dẽ'tusa/ *f* buck teeth; ~ço *a* with buck teeth

denúncia /de'nũsia/ *f* (*à polícia etc*) report; (*na imprensa etc*) disclosure

denunciar /denũsi'ar/ *vt* (*à polícia etc*) report; (*na imprensa etc*) denounce

deparar /depa'rar/ *vi* ~ com come across

departamento /departa'mẽtu/ *m* department

depauperar /depawpe'rar/ *vt* impoverish

depenar /depe'nar/ *vt* pluck <*aves*>; (*roubar*) fleece

dependência /depẽ'dẽsia/ *f* dependence; *pl* premises; ~dente *a* dependent (de on) □ *m/f* dependant; ~der *vi* depend (de on)

depilação /depila'sãw/ *f* depilation; ~lar *vt* depilate; ~latório *m* depilatory cream

deplorar /deplo'rar/ *vt* deplore; ~rável (*pl* ~ráveis) *a* deplorable

depoente /depo'ẽtʃi/ *m/f* witness; ~poimento *m* (*à polícia*) statement; (*na justiça, fig*) testimony

depois /de'pojs/ *adv* after(wards); ~ de after; ~ que after

depor /de'por/ *vi* (*na polícia*) make a statement; (*na justiça*) give evidence, testify □ *vt* lay down <*armas*>; depose < *rei, presidente*>

deportação /deporta'sãw/ *f* deportation; ~tar *vt* deport

depositante /depozi'tãtʃi/ *m/f* depositor; ~tar *vt* deposit; cast <*voto*>; place <*confiança*>

depósito /de'pɔzitu/ *m* deposit; (*armazém*) warehouse

depravação /deprava'sãw/ *f* depravity; ~vado *a* depraved; ~var *vt* deprave

depreciação /depresia'sãw/ *f* (*perda de valor*) depreciation; (*menosprezo*) deprecation; ~ciar *vt* (*desvalorizar*) devalue; (*menosprezar*) deprecate; ~ciar-se *vpr* <*bens*> depreciate; <*pessoa*> deprecate o.s.; ~ciativo *a* deprecatory

depredação /depreda'sãw/ *f* depredation; ~dar *vt* wreck

depressa /dʒi'prɛsa/ *adv* fast, quickly

depressão /depre'sãw/ *f* depression; ~sivo *a* depressive

deprimente /depri'mẽtʃi/ *a* depressing; ~mido *a* depressed; ~mir *vt* depress; ~mir-se *vpr* get depressed

depurar /depu'rar/ *vt* purify

deputação /deputa'sãw/ *f* deputation; ~tado *m* deputy, MP, (*Amer*) congressman (*f* -woman); ~tar *vt* delegate

deque /'dɛki/ *m* (sun)deck

deriva /de'riva/ *f* à ~va adrift; andar à ~va drift; ~vação *f* derivation; ~var *vt* derive; (*desviar*) divert □ *vi*, ~var-se *vpr* derive, be derived (de from); <*navio*> drift

dermatologia /dermatolo'ʒia/ *f* dermatology; ~gista *m/f* dermatologist

derradeiro /dexa'deru/ *a* last, final

derramamento /dexama'mẽtu/ *m* spill, spillage; ~mamento de sangue bloodshed; ~mar *vt* spill; shed <*lágrimas*>; ~mar-se *vpr* spill; ~mem spill, spillage; ~me cerebral stroke

derrapagem /dexa'paʒẽ/ *f* skidding; (*uma*) skid; ~par *vi* skid

derreter /dexe'ter/ *vt* melt; ~-se *vpr* melt

derrota /de'xɔta/ *f* defeat; ~tar *vt* defeat; ~tismo *m* defeatism; ~tista *a & m/f* defeatist

derrubar /dexu'bar/ *vt* knock down; bring down <*governo*>

desabafar /dʒizaba'far/ *vi* speak one's mind; ~fo *m* outburst

desabamento /dʒizaba'mẽtu/ *m* collapse; ~bar *vi* collapse; <*chuva*> pour down

desabotoar /dʒiaboto'ar/ *vt* unbutton

desabri|gado /dʒiabri'gadu/ *a* homeless; ~**gar** *vt* make homeless

desabrochar /dʒiabro'ʃar/ *vi* blossom, bloom

desaça|tar /dʒiaka'tar/ *vt* defy; ~**to** *m* (*de pessoa*) disrespect; (*da lei etc*) disregard

desacerto /dʒia'sertu/ *m* mistake

desacompanhado /dʒiakõpa-'nadu/ *a* unaccompanied

desaconse|lhar /dʒiakõse'ʎar/ *vt* advise against; ~**lhável** (*pl* ~**lháveis**) *a* inadvisable

desacor|dado /dʒiakor'dadu/ *a* unconscious; ~**do** /o/ *m* disagreement

desacostu|mado /dʒiakostu'madu/ *a* unaccustomed; ~**mar** *vt* ~**mar alg de** break s.o. of the habit of; ~**mar-se de** get out of the habit of

desacreditar /dʒiakredʒi'tar/ *vt* discredit

desafeto /dʒia'fɛtu/ *m* disaffection

desafi|ador /dʒiafia'dor/ *a* <*tarefa*> challenging; <*pessoa*> defiant; ~**ar** *vt* challenge; (*fazer face a*) defy <*perigo, morte*>

desafi|nado /dʒiafi'nadu/ *a* out of tune; ~**nar** *vi* (*cantando*) sing out of tune; (*tocando*) play out of tune □ *vt* put out of tune

desafio /dʒia'fiu/ *m* challenge

desafivelar /dʒiafive'lar/ *vt* unbuckle

desafo|gar /dʒiafo'gar/ *vt* vent; (*despertar*) relieve; ~**gar-se** *vpr* give vent to one's feelings; ~**go** /o/ *m* (*alívio*) relief

desafo|rado /dʒiafo'radu/ *a* cheeky; ~**ro** /o/ *m* cheek; (*um*) liberty

desafortunado /dʒiafortu'nadu/ *a* unfortunate

desagra|dar /dʒiagra'dar/ *vt* displease; ~**dável** (*pl* ~**dáveis**) *a* unpleasant; ~**do** *m* displeasure

desagravo *m* redress, amends

desagregar /dʒiagre'gar/ *vt* split up; ~**se** *vpr* split up

desaguar /dʒia'gwar/ *vt* drain □ *vi* <*rio*> flow (em into)

desajeitado /dʒiaʒej'tadu/ *a* clumsy

desajuizado /dʒiaʒui'zadu/ *a* foolish

desajus|tado /dʒiaʒus'tadu/ *a* (*psic*) maladjusted; ~**te** *m* (*psic*) maladjustment

desalen|tar /dʒialē'tar/ *vt* dishearten; ~**tar-se** *vpr* get disheartened; ~**to** *m* discouragement

desali|nhado /dʒiali'nadu/ *a* untidy; ~**nho** *m* untidiness

desalojar /dʒialo'ʒar/ *vt* turn out <*inquilino*>; flush out <*inimigo, ladrões*>

desamarrar /dʒiama'xar/ *vt* untie □ *vi* cast off

desamarrotar /dʒiamaxo'tar/ *vt* smooth out

desamassar /dʒiama'sar/ *vt* smooth out

desambientado /dʒiãbiē'tadu/ *a* unsettled

desampa|rar /dʒizãpa'rar/ *vt* abandon; ~**ro** *m* abandonment

desandar /dʒizã'dar/ *vi* <*molho*> separate; ~ **a** start to

de|sanimar /dʒizani'mar/ *vt* discourage □ *vi* <*pessoa*> lose heart; <*fato*> be discouraging; ~**sânimo** *m* discouragement

desapaixonado /dʒizapaʃo'nadu/ *a* dispassionate

desaparafusar /dʒizaparafu'zar/ *vt* unscrew

desapare|cer /dʒizapare'ser/ *vi* disappear; ~**cimento** *m* disappearance

desapego /dʒiza'pegu/ *m* detachment; (*indiferença*) indifference

desapercebido /dʒizaperse'bidu/ *a* unnoticed

desapertar /dʒizaper'tar/ *vt* loosen

desapon|tamento /dʒizapõta'mētu/ *m* disappointment; ~**tar** *vt* disappoint

desapropriar /dʒizapropri'ar/ *vt* expropriate

desapro|vação /dʒizaprova'sãw/ *f* disapproval; ~**var** *vt* disapprove of

desaproveitado /dʒizaprovej'tadu/ *a* wasted

desar|mamento /dʒizarma'mētu/ *m* disarmament; ~**mar** *vt* disarm; take down <*barraca*>

desarran|jar /dʒizaxã'ʒar/ *vt* mess up; upset <*estômago*>; ~**jo** *m* mess; (*do estômago*) upset

desarregaçar /dʒizaxega'sar/ *vt* roll down

desarru|mado /dʒizaxu'madu/ *a* untidy; ~**mar** *vt* untidy; unpack <*mala*>

desarticular /dʒizartʃiku'lar/ *vt* dislocate

desarvorado /dʒizarvo'radu/ *a* disoriented, at a loss

desassociar /dʒizasosi'ar/ *vt* disassociate; ~**se** *vpr* disassociate o.s.

desas|trado /dʒizas'tradu/ *a* accident-prone; ~**tre** *m* disaster; ~**troso** /o/ *a* disastrous

desatar /dʒiza'tar/ *vt* untie; ~ **a chorar** dissolve in tears

desatarraxar /dʒizataxa'ʃar/ *vt* unscrew

desaten|cioso /dʒizatēsi'ozu/ *a* inattentive; ~**to** *a* oblivious (a to)

desati|nar /dʒizatʃi'nar/ *vt* bewilder □ *vi* not think straight; ~**no** *m* mental aberration, bewilderment; (*um*) folly

desativar /dʒizatʃi'var/ vt deactivate; shut down <*fábrica*>

desatrelar /dʒizatre'lar/ vt unhitch

desatualizado /dʒizatuali'zadu/ a out-of-date

desavença /dʒiza'vẽsa/ f disagreement

desavergonhado /dʒizavergo'ɲadu/ a shameless

desbancar /dʒizbã'kar/ vt outdo

desbaratar /dʒizbara'tar/ vt (*desperdiçar*) waste

desbocado /dʒizbo'kadu/ a outspoken

desbotar /dʒizbo'tar/ vt/i fade

desbra|vador /dʒizbrava'dor/ m explorer; ~var vt explore

desbun|dante /dʒizbũ'dãtʃi/ (*fam*) a mind-blowing; ~dar (*fam*) vt blow the mind of □ vi flip, freak out; ~de (*fam*) m knockout

descabido /dʒiska'bidu/ a inappropriate

descalabro /dʒiska'labru/ m débâcle

descalço /dʒis'kawsu/ a barefoot

descambar /dʒiskã'bar/ vi deteriorate, degenerate

descan|sar /dʒiskã'sar/ vt/i rest; ~so m rest; (*de prato, copo*) mat

desca|rado /dʒiska'radu/ a blatant; ~ramento m cheek

descarga /dʒis'karga/ f (*eletr*) discharge; (*da privada*) flush; dar ~ flush (the toilet)

descarregar /dʒiskaxe'gar/ vt unload <*mercadorias*>; discharge <*poluentes*>; vent <*raiva*> □ vi <*bateria*> go flat; ~ em cima de alg take it out on s.o.

descarrilhar /dʒiskaxi'ʎar/ vt/i derail

descar|tar /dʒiskar'tar/ vt discard; ~tável (*pl* ~táveis) a disposable

descascar /dʒiskas'kar/ vt peel <*frutas, batatas*>; shell <*nozes*> □ vi <*pessoa, pele*> peel

descaso /dʒis'kazu/ m indifference

descen|dência /dʒisẽ'dẽsia/ f descent; ~dente a descended □ m/f descendant; ~der vi descend (from)

descentralizar /dʒisẽtrali'zar/ vt decentralize

des|cer /de'ser/ vi go down; <*avião*> descend; (*do ônibus, trem*) get off; (*do carro*) get out □ vt go down <*escada, ladeira*>; ~cida f descent

desclassificar /dʒisklasifi'kar/ vt disqualify

desco|berta /dʒisko'bɛrta/ f discovery; ~berto /ɛ/ a uncovered; <*conta*> overdrawn; a ~berto overdrawn; ~bridor m discoverer; ~brimento m discovery; ~brir vt discover; (*expor*) uncover

descolar /dʒisko'lar/ vt unstick; (*fam*) (*dar*) give; (*arranjar*) get hold of, rustle up; (*Port*) <*avião*> take off

descom|por /dʒiskõ'por/ vt (*censurar*) scold; ~-se vpr <*pessoa*> lose one's composure; ~postura f (*estado*) loss of composure; (*censura*) talking-to

descomprometido /dʒiskõprome'tʃidu/ a free

descomu|nal /dʒiskomu'naw/ (*pl* ~nais) a extraordinary; (*grande*) huge

desconcentrar /dʒiskõsẽ'trar/ vt distract

desconcer|tante /dʒiskõser'tãtʃi/ a disconcerting; ~tar vt disconcert

desconexo /dʒisko'nɛksu/ a incoherent

desconfi|ado /dʒiskõfi'adu/ a suspicious; ~ança f mistrust; ~ar vi suspect

desconfor|tável /dʒiskõfor'tavew/ (*pl* ~táveis) a uncomfortable; ~to /o/ m discomfort

descongelar /dʒiskõʒe'lar/ vt defrost <*geladeira*>; thaw <*comida*>

descongestio|nante /dʒiskõʒestʃio'nãtʃi/ a & m decongestant; ~nar vt decongest

desconhe|cer /dʒiskoɲe'ser/ vt not know; ~cido a unknown □ m stranger

desconsiderar /dʒiskõside'rar/ vt ignore

desconsolado /dʒiskõso'ladu/ a disconsolate

descontar /dʒiskõ'tar/ vt deduct; (*não levar em conta*) discount

desconten|tamento /dʒiskõtẽta'mẽtu/ m discontent; ~te a discontent

desconto /dʒis'kõtu/ m discount; dar um ~ (*fig*) make allowances

descontra|ção /dʒiskõtra'sãw/ f informality; ~ído a informal, casual; ~ir vt relax; ~ir-se vpr relax

descontro|lar-se /dʒiskõtro'larsi/ vpr <*pessoa*> lose control; <*coisa*> go out of control; ~le /o/ m lack of control

desconversar /dʒiskõver'sar/ vi change the subject

descortesia /dʒiskorte'zia/ f rudeness

descostu|rar /dʒiskostu'rar/ vt unrip; ~rar-se vpr come undone

descrédito /dʒis'krɛdʒitu/ m discredit

descren|ça /dʒis'krẽsa/ f disbelief; ~te a sceptical, disbelieving

des|crever /dʒis'krever/ vt describe; ~crição f description; ~critivo a descriptive

descui|dado /dʒiskui'dadu/ a careless; ~dar vt neglect; ~do m carelessness; (*um*) oversight

descul|pa /dʒis'kuwpa/ f excuse; pe-
dir ∼pas apologize; ∼par vt excuse;
∼pe! sorry!; ∼par-se vpr apologize;
∼pável (pl ∼páveis) a excusable

desde /'dezdʒi/ prep since; ∼ que
since

des|dém /dez'dēj/ m disdain;
∼denhar vt disdain; ∼nhoso /o/ a
disdainful

desdentado /dʒizdē'tadu/ a toothless

desdita /dʒiz'dʒita/ f unhappiness

desdizer /dʒizdʒi'zer/ vt take back,
withdraw □ vi take back what one
said

desdo|bramento /dʒizdobra'mētu/ m
implication; (de abrir) unfold;
break down <dados, contas>; ∼brar vt (abrir) unfold;
∼brar-se vpr unfold; (empenhar-se) go to a
lot of trouble, bend over backwards

dese|jar /deze'ʒar/ vt want; (apaixo-
nadamente) desire; ∼jar aco a alg
wish s.o. sth; ∼jável (pl ∼jáveis) a
desirable; ∼jo /e/ m wish; (forte)
desire; ∼joso /o/ a desirous

deselegante /dʒizele'gātʃi/ a inel-
egant

desemaranhar /dʒizemara'ɲar/ vt
untangle

desembara|çado /dʒizībara'sadu/ a
<pessoa> confident, nonchalant;
∼çar-se vpr rid o.s. (de of); ∼ço m
confidence, ease

desembar|car /dʒizībar'kar/ vt/i
disembark; ∼que m disembarkation;
(seção do aeroporto) arrivals

desembocar /dʒizībo'kar/ vi flow

desembol|sar /dʒizībow'sar/ vt
spend, pay out; ∼so /o/ m expenditure

desembrulhar /dʒizībru'ʎar/ vt unwrap

desembuchar /dʒizību'ʃar/ (fam) vi
(desabafar) get things off one's chest;
(falar logo) spit it out

desempacotar /dʒizīpako'tar/ vt unpack

desempatar /dʒizīpa'tar/ vt decide
<jogo>

desempe|nhar /dʒizīpe'ɲar/ vt per-
form; play <papel>; ∼nho m performance

desempre|gado /dʒizīpre'gadu/ a un-
employed; ∼go /e/ m unemployment

desencadear /dʒizīkadʒi'ar/ vt set
off, trigger

desencaminhar /dʒizīkami'ɲar/ vt
lead astray; embezzle <dinheiro>

desencantar /dʒizīkã'tar/ vt disenchant

desencon|trar-se /dʒizīkõ'trarsi/ vpr
miss each other, fail to meet; ∼tro m
failure to meet

desencorajar /dʒizīkora'ʒar/ vt discourage

desenferrujar /dʒizīfexu'ʒar/ vt de-
rust <metal>; stretch <pernas>; brush
up <lingua>

desenfreado /dʒizīfri'adu/ a unbridled

desenganar /dʒizīga'nar/ vt dis-
abuse; declare incurable <doente>

desengonçado /dʒizīgõ'sadu/ a
<pessoa> ungainly

desengre|nado /dʒizīgre'nadu/ a
<carro> in neutral; ∼nar vt put in
neutral <carro>; (tec) disengage

dese|nhar /deze'ɲar/ vt draw;
∼nhista m/f drawer; (industrial)
designer; ∼nho /e/ m drawing

desenlace /dʒizī'lasi/ m dénouement,
outcome

desenredar /dʒizīxe'dar/ vt unravel

desenrolar /dʒizīxo'lar/ vt unroll
<rolo>

desenten|der /dʒizītē'der/ vt mis-
understand; ∼der-se vpr (não se dar
bem) not get on; ∼dimento m misunderstanding

desenterrar /dʒizīte'xar/ vt dig up
<cadáver>; unearth <informação>

desentortar /dʒizītor'tar/ vt
straighten out

desentupir /dʒizītu'pir/ vt unblock

desenvol|to /dʒizī'vowtu/ a casual,
nonchalant; ∼tura f casualness, non-
chalance; com ∼tura nonchal-
antly; ∼ver vt develop; ∼ver-se
vpr develop; ∼vimento m develop-
ment

desequi|librado a unbalanced;
∼librar vt unbalance; ∼librar-se
vpr become unbalanced; ∼líbrio m
imbalance

deser|ção /dezer'sãw/ f desertion;
∼tar vt/i desert; ∼to /ɛ/ a deserted;
ilha ∼ta desert island □ m desert;
∼tor m deserter

desespe|rado /dʒizispe'radu/ a
desperate; ∼rador a hopeless; ∼rar
vt (desesperançar) make despair □ vi,
∼rar-se vpr despair; ∼ro /e/ m despair

desestabilizar /dʒizistabili'zar/ vt
destabilize

desestimular /dʒizistʃimu'lar/ vt discourage

desfal|car /dʒisfaw'kar/ vt embezzle;
∼que m embezzlement

desfal|ecer /dʒisfale'ser/ vt (des-
maiar) faint; ∼ecimento m faint

desfavor /dʒisfa'vor/ m disfavour

desfavo|rável /dʒisfavo'ravew/ (pl
∼ráveis) a unfavourable; ∼recer vt
be unfavourable to; treat less favour-
ably <minorias etc>

desfazer /dʒisfa'zer/ vt undo; unpack
<mala>; strip <cama>; break
<contrato>; clear up <mistério>; ∼-se

vpr come undone; <*casamento*> break up; <*sonhos*> crumble; ~-**se em lá- grimas** dissolve into tears

desfe|char /dʒiʃeˈʃar/ *vt* throw <*murro, olhar*>; ~**cho** /e/ *m* outcome, dénouement

desfeita /dʒiʃˈfejta/ *f* slight, insult

desferir /dʒiʃfeˈrir/ *vt* give <*pontapé*>; launch <*ataque*>; fire <*flecha*>

desfiar /dʒiʃfiˈar/ *vt* pick the meat off <*frango*>; ~-**se** *vpr* <*tecido*> fray

desfigurar /dʒiʃfiguˈrar/ *vt* disfigure; (*fig*) distort

desfi|ladeiro /dʒiʃfilaˈderu/ *m* pass; ~**lar** *vi* parade; ~**le** *m* parade; ~**le de modas** fashion show

desflorestamento /dʒiʃfloreʃtaˈmẽtu/ *m* deforestation

desforra /dʒiʃˈfoxa/ *f* revenge

desfraldar /dʒiʃfrawˈdar/ *vt* unfurl

desfrutar /dʒiʃfruˈtar/ *vt* enjoy

desgas|tante /dʒizgaʃˈtãtʃi/ *a* wearing, stressful; ~**tar** *vt* wear out; ~-**se** *vpr* (*de máquina etc*) wear and tear; (*de pessoa*) stress and strain

desgosto /dʒizˈgoʃtu/ *m* sorrow

desgovernar-se /dʒizgoverˈnarsi/ *vpr* go out of control

desgraça /dʒizˈgrasa/ *f* misfortune; ~**do** *a* wretched □ *m* wretch

desgravar /dʒizgraˈvar/ *vt* erase

desgrenhado /dʒizgreˈɲadu/ *a* unkempt

desgrudar /dʒizgruˈdar/ *vt* unstick; ~-**se** *vpr* <*pessoa*> tear o.s. away

desidra|tação /dʒizidrataˈsãw/ *f* dehydration; ~**tar** *vt* dehydrate

design|nação /dezignaˈsãw/ *f* designation; ~**nar** *vt* designate

desi|gual /dʒiziˈgwaw/ (*pl* ~**guais**) *a* unequal; <*terreno*> uneven; ~**gualdade** *f* inequality; (*de terreno*) unevenness

desilu|dir /dʒiziluˈdʒir/ *vt* disillusion; ~**são** *f* disillusionment

desinfe|tante /dʒizĩfeˈtãtʃi/ *a & m* disinfectant; ~**tar** *vt* disinfect

desinibido /dʒizĩniˈbidu/ *a* uninhibited

desintegrar-se /dʒizĩteˈgrarsi/ *vpr* disintegrate

desinteres|sado /dʒizĩtereˈsadu/ *a* uninterested; ~**sante** *a* uninteresting; ~**sar-se** *vpr* lose interest (de in); ~**se** /e/ *m* disinterest

desis|tência /dezisˈtẽsia/ *f* giving up; ~**tir** *vt*/*i* ~**tir (de)** give up

desle|al /dʒizleˈaw/ (*pl* ~**ais**) *a* disloyal; ~**aldade** *f* disloyalty

deslei|xado /dʒizleˈʃadu/ *a* sloppy; (*no vestir*) scruffy; ~**xo** *m* carelessness; (*no vestir*) scruffiness

desli|gado /dʒizliˈgadu/ *a* <*luz, TV*> off; <*pessoa*> absent-minded; ~**gar** *vt*

turn off <*luz, TV, motor*>; hang up, put down <*telefone*> □ *vi* (*ao telefonar*) hang up, put the phone down

deslindar /dʒizlĩˈdar/ *vt* clear up, solve

desli|zante /dʒizliˈzãtʃi/ *a* slippery; <*inflação*> creeping; ~**zar** *vi* slip; ~**zar-se** *vpr* creep; ~**ze** *m* slip; (*fig: erro*) slip-up

deslo|cado /dʒizloˈkadu/ *a* <*membro*> dislocated; (*fig*) out of place; ~**car** *vt* move; (*med*) dislocate; ~**car-se** *vpr* move

deslum|brado /dʒizlũˈbradu/ *a* (*fig*) starry-eyed; ~**bramento** *m* (*fig*) wonderment; ~**brante** *a* dazzling; ~**brar** *vt* dazzle; ~**brar-se** *vpr* (*fig*) be dazzled

desmai|ado /dʒizmajˈadu/ *a* unconscious; ~**ar** *vi* faint; ~**o** *m* faint

desman|cha-prazeres /dʒizmã- ʃapraˈzeris/ *m/f invar* spoilsport; ~**char** *vt* break up; break off <*noivado*>; shatter <*sonhos*>; ~**char-se** *vpr* break up; (*no ar, na água, em lágrimas*) dissolve

desmantelar /dʒizmãteˈlar/ *vt* dismantle

desmarcar /dʒizmarˈkar/ *vt* cancel <*encontro*>

desmascarar /dʒizmaskeˈrar/ *vt* unmask

desma|tamento /dʒizmataˈmẽtu/ *m* deforestation; ~**tar** *vt* clear (of forest)

desmedido /dʒizmeˈdidu/ *a* excessive

desmemoriado /dʒizmemoriˈadu/ *a* forgetful

desmen|tido /dʒizmẽˈtʃidu/ *m* denial; ~**tir** *vt* deny

desmiolado /dʒizmioˈladu/ *a* brainless

desmontar /dʒizmõˈtar/ *vt* dismantle

desmorali|zante /dʒizmoraliˈzãtʃi/ *a* demoralizing; ~**zar** *vt* demoralize

desmoro|namento /dʒizmorona- ˈmẽtu/ *m* collapse; ~**nar** *vt* destroy; ~**nar-se** *vpr* collapse

desnatar /dʒiznaˈtar/ *vi* skim <*leite*>

desnecessário /dʒizneseˈsariu/ *a* unnecessary

desni|vel /dʒizˈnivew/ (*pl* ~**veis**) *m* difference in height

desnortear /dʒiznortʃiˈar/ *vt* disorientate, (*Amer*) disorient

desnutrição /dʒiznutriˈsãw/ *f* malnutrition

desobe|decer /dʒizobedeˈser/ *vt*/*i* ~**decer (a)** disobey; ~**diência** *f* disobedience; ~**diente** *a* disobedient

desobrigar /dʒizobriˈgar/ *vt* release (de from)

desobstruir /dʒizobistruˈir/ *vt* unblock; empty <*casa*>

desocupado /dʒizoku'padu/ a unoc-cupied

desodorante /dʒizodo'rãtʃi/ m, (Port) **desodorizante** /dʒizoduri'zãtʃi/ m deodorant

deso|lação /dezola'sãw/ f desolation; ~**lado** a <lugar> desolate; <pessoa> desolated; ~**lar** vt desolate

desones|tidade /dʒizonestʃi'dadʒi/ f dishonesty; ~**to** /ɛ/ a dishonest

deson|ra /dʒi'zõxa/ f dishonour; ~**rar** vt dishonour; ~**roso** /o/ a dishonourable

desor|deiro /dʒizor'deru/ a trouble-making □ m troublemaker; ~**dem** f disorder; ~**denado** a disorganized; <vida> disordered; ~**denar** vt disorganize

desorgani|zação /dʒizorganiza'sãw/ f disorganization; ~**zar** vt disorganize; ~**zar-se** vpr get disorganized

desorientar /dʒizoriẽ'tar/ vt disorientate, (Amer) disorient

desossar /dʒizo'sar/ vt bone

deso|va /dʒi'zɔva/ f roe; ~**var** vi spawn

despa|chado /dʒispa'ʃadu/ a efficient; ~**chante** m/f (de mercadorias) shipping agent; (de documentos) documentation agent; ~**char** vt deal with; dispatch, forward <mercadorias>; ~**cho** m dispatch

desparafusar /dʒisparafu'zar/ vt unscrew

despeda|çar /dʒispeda'sar/ vt (rasgar) tear to pieces; (quebrar) smash; ~**se** vpr <vidro, vaso> smash; <papel, tecido> tear

despe|dida /dʒispe'dʒida/ f farewell; ~**dida de solteiro** stag night, (Amer) bachelor party; ~**dir** vt dismiss; sack <empregado>; ~**dir-se** vpr say goodbye (de to)

despei|tado /dʒispej'tadu/ a spiteful; ~**to** m spite; a ~**to de** despite, in spite of

despe|jar /dʒispe'ʒar/ vt pour out <líquido>; empty <recipiente>; evict <inquilino>; ~**jo** /e/ m (de inquilino) eviction

despencar /dʒispẽ'kar/ vi plummet

despender /dʒispẽ'der/ vt spend <dinheiro>

despensa /dʒis'pẽsa/ f pantry, larder

despentear /dʒispẽtʃi'ar/ vt mess up <cabelo>; mess up the hair of <pessoa>

despercebido /dʒisperse'bidu/ a unnoticed

desper|diçar /dʒisperdʒi'sar/ vt waste; ~**dício** m waste

desper|tador /dʒisperta'dor/ m alarm clock; ~**tar** vt rouse <pessoa>;

(fig) arouse <interesse, suspeitas etc> □ vi awake

despesa /dʒis'peza/ f expense

des|pido /des'pidu/ a bare, stripped (de of); ~**pir** vt strip (de of); strip off <roupa>; ~**pir-se** vpr strip (off), get undressed

despo|jar /dʒispo'ʒar/ vt strip (de of); ~**jar-se** vpr divest o.s. (de of); ~**jo** /o/ m spoils, booty; ~**jos mortais** mortal remains

despontar /dʒispõ'tar/ vi emerge

despor|tista /diʃpur'tiʃta/ (Port) m/f sportsman (f-woman); ~**tivo** (Port) a sporting; ~**to** /o/ (Port) m sport; **carro de** ~**to** sports car

déspota /'dɛspota/ m/f despot

despótico /des'pɔtʃiku/ a despotic

despovoar /dʒispovo'ar/ vt depopulate

desprender /dʒisprẽ'der/ vt detach; (da parede) take down; ~**se** vpr come off; (fig) detach o.s.

despreocupado /dʒisprioku'padu/ a unconcerned

despreparado /dʒisprepa'radu/ a unprepared

despretensioso /dʒispretẽsi'ozu/ a unpretentious

desprestigiar /dʒisprestʃiʒi'ar/ vt discredit

desprevenido /dʒispreve'nidu/ a off one's guard, unprepared; **apanhar** ~ catch unawares

despre|zar /dʒispre'zar/ vt despise; (ignorar) ignore; ~**zível** (pl ~**zíveis**) a despicable; ~**zo** /e/ m contempt

desproporção /dʒispropor'sãw/ f disproportion

desproporcio|nado /dʒisproporsio'nadu/ a disproportionate; ~**nal** (pl ~**nais**) a disproportional

despropositado /dʒispropozi'tadu/ a (absurdo) preposterous

desprovido /dʒispro'vidu/ a ~ **de** without

desqualificar /dʒiskwalifi'kar/ vt disqualify

desqui|tar-se /dʒiski'tarsi/ vpr (legally) separate; ~**te** m (legal) separation

desrespei|tar /dʒizxespej'tar/ vt not respect; (ignorar) disregard; ~**to** m disrespect; ~**toso** /o/ a disrespectful

dessa(s), desse(s) = de + essa(s), esse(s)

desta = de + esta

desta|camento /dʒistaka'mẽtu/ m detachment; ~**car** vt detach; (ressaltar) bring out, make stand out; ~**carse** vpr (desprender-se) come off; <corredor> break away; (sobressair) stand out (sobre against); ~**cável** (pl

~cáveis/ *a* detachable; <*caderno*> pull-out

destam|pado /dʒistã'padu/ *a* (*panela*) uncovered; ~**par** *vt* remove the lid of

destapar /dʒista'par/ *vt* uncover

destaque /dʒis'taki/ *m* prominence; (*coisa, pessoa*) highlight; (*do noticiário*) headline

destas, deste = de + estas, este

destemido /dʒiste'midu/ *a* intrepid, courageous

desterrar /dʒiste'xar/ *vt* (*exilar*) exile

destes = de + estes

destilar /dʒisti'lar/ *vt* distil; ~**ia** *f* distillery

desti|nado /destʃi'nadu/ *a* (*fadado*) destined; ~**nar** *vt* intend, mean (para for); ~**natário** *m* addressee; ~**no** *m* (*de viagem*) destination; (*sorte*) fate

destituir /destʃitu'ir/ *vt* remove

desto|ante /dʒisto'ãtʃi/ *a* <*sons*> discordant; <*cores*> clashing; ~**ar** *vi* ~**ar de** clash with

destrancar /dʒistrã'kar/ *vt* unlock

destreza /des'treza/ *f* skill

destrinchar /dʒistrĩ'ʃar/ *vt* (*expor*) dissect; (*resolver*) sort out

destro /'destru/ *a* skilful

destro|çar /dʒistro'sar/ *vt* wreck; ~**ços** *m pl* wreckage

destronar /dʒistro'nar/ *vt* depose

destroncar /dʒistrõ'kar/ *vt* rick

destru|ição /dʒistrui'sãw/ *f* destruction; ~**idor** *a* destructive □ *m* destroyer; ~**ir** *vt* destroy

desumano /dʒizu'manu/ *a* inhuman; (*cruel*) inhumane

desunião /dʒizuni'ãw/ *f* disunity

desu|sado /dʒizu'zadu/ *a* disused; ~**so** *m* disuse

desvairado /dʒizvaj'radu/ *a* delirious, raving

desvalori|zação /dʒizvaloriza'sãw/ *f* devaluation; ~**zar** *vt* devalue

desvanta|gem /dʒizvã'taʒe/ *f* disadvantage; ~**joso** /o/ *a* disadvantageous

desve|lar /dʒizve'lar/ *vt* unveil; uncover <*segredo*>; ~**lar-se** *vpr* go to a lot of trouble; ~**lo** /e/ *m* great care

desvencilhar /dʒizvẽsi'ʎar/ *vt* extricate, free

desvendar /dʒizvẽ'dar/ *vt* reveal <*segredo*>; solve <*mistério*>

desventura /dʒizvẽ'tura/ *f* misfortune; (*infelicidade*) unhappiness

desviar /dʒizvi'ar/ *vt* divert <*trânsito, rio, atenção, dinheiro*>; avert <*golpe, suspeitas, olhos*>; ~**se** *vpr* deviate; <*do tema*> digress

desvincular /dʒizvĩku'lar/ *vt* free

desvio /dʒiz'viu/ *m* diversion; (*do trânsito*) diversion, (*Amer*) detour; (*linha ferroviária*) siding

desvirtuar /dʒizvirtu'ar/ *vt* misrepresent <*verdade*>

deta|lhado /deta'ʎadu/ *a* detailed; ~**lhar** *vt* detail; ~**lhe** *m* detail

detec|tar /detek'tar/ *vt* detect; ~**tive** (*Port*) *m veja* **detetive**; ~**tor** *m* detector

de|tenção /detẽ'sãw/ *f* (*prisão*) detention; ~**tentor** *m* holder; ~**ter** *vt* (*ter*) hold; (*prender*) detain

detergente /deter'ʒẽtʃi/ *m* detergent

deterio|ração /deteriora'sãw/ *f* deterioration; ~**rar** *vt* damage; ~**rar-se** *vpr* deteriorate

determi|nação /determina'sãw/ *f* determination; ~**nado** *a* (*certo*) certain; (*resoluto*) determined; ~**nar** *vt* determine

detestar /detes'tar/ *vt* hate

detetive /dete'tʃivi/ *m* detective

detido /de'tʃidu/ *pp de* **deter** □ *a* thorough □ *m* detainee

detonar /deto'nar/ *vt* detonate; (*fam: criticar*) pull to pieces □ *vi* detonate

detrás /de'traʃ/ *adv* behind ~ *prep* ~ de behind

detrito /de'tritu/ *m* detritus

deturpar /detur'par/ *vt* misrepresent, distort

deus /dews/ *m* (*f* **deusa**) god (*f* goddess); ~**dará** *m* ao ~**dará** at the mercy of chance

devagar /dʒiva'gar/ *adv* slowly

deva|near /devani'ar/ *vi* daydream; ~**neio** *m* daydream

devas|sar /deva'sar/ *vt* expose; ~**sidão** *f* debauchery; ~**so** *a* debauched

devastar /devas'tar/ *vt* devastate

de|vedor /deve'dor/ *a* debit □ *m* debtor; ~**ver** *vt* owe □ *vaux* ~**ve** fazer (*obrigação*) he has to do; ~**ve** chegar (*probabilidade*) he should arrive; ~**ve ser** (*suposição*) he must be; ~**ve ter ido** he must have gone; ~**v(e)ria fazer** he ought to do; ~**v(e)ria ter feito** he ought to have done; ~**vidamente** *adv* duly; ~**vido** *a* due (**a** to)

devoção /devo'sãw/ *f* devotion

de|volução /devolu'sãw/ *f* return; ~**volver** *vt* return

devorar /devo'rar/ *vt* devour

devo|tar /devo'tar/ *vt* devote; ~**tar-se** *vpr* devote o.s. (**a** to); ~**to** /ɔ/ *a* devout

dez /dɛs/ *a & m* ten

dezanove /dza'nɔv/ (*Port*) *a & m* nineteen

dezas|seis /dza'sejʃ/ (*Port*) *a & m* sixteen; ~**sete** /ɛ/ (*Port*) *a & m* seventeen

dezembro /de'zẽbru/ *m* December

deze|na /de'zena/ f ten; **uma ~ (de)** about ten; **~nove** /ɔ/ a & m nineteen

dezes|seis /dʒize'sejs/ a & m sixteen; **~sete** /ɛ/ a & m seventeen

dezoito /dʒi'zojtu/ a & m eighteen

dia /'dʒia/ m day; **de ~** by day; **(no) ~ 20 de julho** (on) July 20th; **~ de folga** day off; **~ útil** working day; **~-a-~** m everyday life

dia|bete /dʒia'bɛtʃi/ f diabetes; **~bético** a & m diabetic

dia|bo /dʒi'abu/ m devil; **~bólico** a diabolical, devilish; **~brete** /e/ m little devil; **~brura** f (de criança) bit of mischief; pl mischief

diadema /dʒia'dema/ m tiara

diafragma /dʒia'fragima/ m diaphragm

dia|gnosticar /dʒiagnostʃi'kar/ vt diagnose; **~gnóstico** m diagnosis □ a diagnostic

diago|nal /dʒiago'naw/ (pl **~nais**) a & f diagonal

diagra|ma /dʒia'grama/ m diagram; **~mação** f design; **~mador** m designer; **~mar** vt design <livro, revista>

dialect- (Port) veja **dialet-**

dia|lética /dʒia'lɛtʃika/ f dialectics; **~leto** /ɛ/ m dialect

dialogar /dʒialo'gar/ vi talk; (pol) hold talks

diálogo /dʒi'alogu/ m dialogue

diamante /dʒia'mãtʃi/ m diamond

diâmetro /dʒi'ametru/ m diameter

dian|te /dʒi'ãtʃi/ adv **de ... em ~te** from ... on(wards); **~te de** (enfrentando) faced with; (perante) before; **~teira** f lead; **~teiro** a front

diapasão /dʒiapa'zãw/ m tuning-fork

diapositivo /dʒiapozi'tʃivu/ m transparency

diá|ria /dʒi'aria/ f daily rate; **~rio** a daily

diarista /dʒia'rista/ m/f day labourer; (faxineira) daily (help)

diarréia /dʒia'xeja/ f diarrhoea

dica /'dʒika/ f tip, hint

dicção /dʒik'sãw/ f diction

dicionário /dʒisio'nariu/ m dictionary

didáti|ca /dʒi'datʃika/ f teaching methodology; **~co** a teaching; <livro> educational; <estilo> didactic

die|ta /dʒi'ɛta/ f diet; **de ~ta** on a diet; **~tista** m/f dietician

difa|mação /dʒifama'sãw/ f defamation; **~mar** vt defame; **~matório** a defamatory

diferen|ça /dʒife'rẽsa/ f difference; **~cial** (pl **~ciais**) a & f differential; **~ciar** vt differentiate; **~ciar-se** vpr differ; **~te** a different

dife|rimento /dʒiferi'mẽtu/ m deferment; **~rir** vt defer □ vi differ

difí|cil /dʒi'fisiw/ (pl **~ceis**) a difficult; (improvável) unlikely

dificilmente /dʒifisiw'mẽtʃi/ adv **~ poderá fazê-lo** he's unlikely to be able to do it

dificul|dade /dʒifikuw'dadʒi/ f difficulty; **~tar** vt make difficult

difteria /dʒifte'ria/ f diphtheria

difun|dir /dʒifũ'dʒir/ vt spread; (pela rádio) broadcast; diffuse <luz, calor>; **~dir-se** vpr spread

difu|são /dʒifu'zãw/ f diffusion; **~so** a diffuse

dige|rir /dʒiʒe'rir/ vt digest; **~rível** (pl **~ríveis**) a digestible

diges|tão /dʒiʒes'tãw/ f digestion; **~tivo** a digestive

digi|tal /dʒiʒi'taw/ (pl **~tais**) a digital; **impressão ~tal** fingerprint; **~tar** vt key

dígito /'dʒiʒitu/ m digit

digladiar /dʒigladʒi'ar/ vi do battle

dig|nar-se /dʒig'narsi/ vpr deign (**de** to); **~nidade** f dignity; **~nificar** vt dignify; **~no** a worthy (**de** of); (decoroso) dignified

dilace|rante /dʒilase'rãtʃi/ a <dor> excruciating; **~rar** vt tear to pieces

dilapidar /dʒilapi'dar/ vt squander

dilatar /dʒila'tar/ vt expand; (med) dilate; **~-se** vpr expand; (med) dilate

dilema /dʒi'lema/ m dilemma

diletante /dʒile'tãtʃi/ a & m/f dilettante

dili|gência /dʒili'ʒẽsia/ f diligence; (carruagem) stagecoach; **~gente** a diligent, hard-working

diluir /dʒilu'ir/ vt dilute

dilúvio /dʒi'luviu/ m deluge

dimen|são /dʒimẽ'sãw/ f dimension; **~sionar** vt size up

diminu|ição /dʒiminui'sãw/ f reduction; **~ir** vt reduce □ vi lessen; <carro, motorista> slow down; **~tivo** a & m diminutive; **~to** a minute

Dinamarca /dʒina'marka/ f Denmark

dinamar|quês /dʒinamar'kes/ (**~quesa**) a Danish □ m Dane

dinâmi|ca /dʒi'namika/ f dynamics; **~co** a dynamic

dina|mismo /dʒina'mizmu/ m dynamism; **~mite** f dynamite

dínamo /'dʒinamu/ m dynamo

dinastia /dʒinas'tʃia/ f dynasty

dinda /'dʒida/ (fam) f godmother

dinheiro /dʒi'ɲeru/ m money

dinossauro /dʒino'sawru/ m dinosaur

diocese /dʒio'sɛzi/ f diocese

dióxido /dʒi'ɔksidu/ m dioxide; **~ de carbono** carbon dioxide

diplo|ma /dʒi'ploma/ m diploma; **~macia** f diplomacy; **~mar-se** vpr take one's diploma; ~**mata** *m/f* diplomat □ *a* diplomatic; ~**mático** *a* diplomatic

direção /dʒire'sãw/ *f* (*sentido*) direction; (*de empresa*) management; (*condução de carro*) driving; (*manuseio do volante*) steering

direct-(*Port*) *veja* **diret-**

direi|**ta** /dʒi'rejta/ *f* right; ~**tinho** *adv* exactly right; ~**tista** *a* rightwing □ *m/f* rightwinger, rightist; ~**to** *a* right; (*ereto*) straight □ *adv* properly □ *m* right

direi|**tas** /dʒi'rɛtas/ *f pl* direct (presidential) elections; ~**to** *a* direct □ *adv* directly; ~**tor** *m* director; (*de escola*) headteacher; (*de jornal*) editor; ~**torgerente** managing director; ~**toria** (*diretores*) board of directors; (*sala*) boardroom; ~**tório** *m* directory; ~**triz** *f* directive

diri|**gente** /dʒiri'ʒẽtʃi/ *a* leading □ *m/f* leader; ~**gir** *vt* direct; manage <*empresa*>; drive <*carro*>; ~**gir-se** *vpr* (*ir*) make one's way; ~**gir-se a** (*falar com*) address

dis|**cagem** /dʒis'kaʒẽ/ *f* dialling; ~**car** *vt/i* dial

discente /dʒi'sẽtʃi/ *a* **corpo** ~ student body

discer|**nimento** /dʒiserni'mẽtu/ *m* discernment; ~**nir** *vt* discern

discipli|**na** /dʒisi'plina/ *f* discipline; ~**nador** *a* disciplinary; ~**nar** *vt* discipline

discipulo /dʒi'sipulu/ *m* disciple

disc-jóquei /dʒisk'ʒɔkej/ *m* disc-jockey

disco /'dʒisku/ *m* disc; (*de música*) record; (*no atletismo*) discus □ (*fam*) *f* disco; ~ **flexível/rígido** floppy/ hard disk; ~ **laser** CD, compact disc; ~ **voador** flying saucer

discor|**dante** /dʒiskor'dãtʃi/ *a* conflicting; ~**dar** *vi* disagree (**de** with)

discote|**ca** /dʒisko'tɛka/ *f* discotheque; ~**cário** *m* DJ

discre|**pância** /dʒiskre'pãsia/ *f* discrepancy; ~**pante** *a* inconsistent; ~**par** *vi* diverge (**de** from)

dis|**creto** /dʒis'krɛtu/ *a* discreet; ~**crição** *f* discretion

discrimi|**nação** /dʒiskrimina'sãw/ *f* discrimination; (*descrição*) description; ~**nar** *vt* discriminate; ~**natório** *a* discriminatory

discur|**sar** /dʒiskur'sar/ *vi* speak; ~**so** *m* speech

discussão /dʒisku'sãw/ *f* discussion; (*briga*) argument

discu|**tir** /dʒisku'tʃir/ *vt/i* discuss; (*brigar*) argue; ~**tível** (*pl* ~**tíveis**) *a* debatable

disenteria /dʒizẽte'ria/ *f* dysentery

disfar|**çar** /dʒisfar'sar/ *vt* disguise; ~**çar-se** *vpr* disguise o.s.; ~**ce** *m* disguise

dis|**lético** /dʒiz'lɛtʃiku/ *a* & *m* dyslexic; ~**lexia** *f* dyslexia; ~**léxico** *a* & *m* dyslexic

dispa|**rada** /dʒispa'rada/ *f* bolt; ~**rado** *adv* **o melhor** ~**rado** the best by a long way; ~**rar** *vt* fire <*arma*> □ *vi* (*com arma*) fire; <*preços, inflação*> shoot up; <*corredor*> surge ahead

disparate /dʒispa'ratʃi/ *m* piece of nonsense; *pl* nonsense

dis|**pêndio** /dʒis'pẽdʒiu/ *m* expenditure; ~**pendioso** /o/ *a* costly

dispen|**sa** /dʒis'pẽsa/ *f* exemption; ~**sar** *vt* (*distribuir*) dispense; (*isentar*) exempt (**de** from); (*prescindir de*) dispense with; ~**sável** (*pl* ~**sáveis**) *a* dispensable

dispersar /dʒisper'sar/ *vt* disperse; waste <*energias*> □ *vi*, ~**-se** *vpr* disperse

disperso /dʒis'pɛrsu/ *adj* scattered

dispo|**nibilidade** /dʒisponibili-'dadʒi/ *f* availability; ~**nível** (*pl* ~**níveis**) *a* available

dis|**por** /dʒis'por/ *vt* arrange □ *vi* ~**por de** have at one's disposal; ~**por-se** *vpr* form up □ *m* **ao seu** ~**por** at your disposal; ~**posição** *f* (*vontade*) willingness; (*arranjo*) arrangement; (*de espírito*) frame of mind; (*de testamento etc*) provision; **à** ~**posição de alg at** s.o.'s disposal; ~**positivo** *m* device; ~**posto** *a* prepared, willing (**a** to)

dispu|**ta** /dʒis'puta/ *f* dispute; ~**tar** *vt* dispute; (*tentar ganhar*) compete for

disquete /dʒis'ketʃi/ *m* diskette, floppy (disk)

dissabores /dʒisa'boris/ *m pl* troubles

disseminar /dʒisemi'nar/ *vt* disseminate

dissertação /dʒiserta'sãw/ *f* dissertation, lecture

dissi|**dência** /dʒisi'dẽsia/ *f* dissidence; ~**dente** *a* & *m* dissident

dissídio /dʒi'sidʒiu/ *m* dispute

dissimular /dʒisimu'lar/ *vt* hide □ *vi* dissimulate

disso = **de** + **isso**

dissi|**par** /dʒisi'par/ *vt* clear <*nevoeiro*>; dispel <*dúvidas, suspeitas, ilusões*>; dissipate <*fortuna*>; ~**-se** *vpr* <*nevoeiro*> clear; <*dúvidas etc*> be dispelled

dissolu|**ção** /dʒisolu'sãw/ *f* dissolution; ~**to** *a* dissolute

dissolver /dʒisow'ver/ *vt* dissolve; ~**-se** *vpr* dissolve

dissuadir /dʒisua'dʒir/ *vt* dissuade (**de** from)

distância /dʒis'tãsia/ f distance

distan|ciar /dʒistãsi'ar/ vt distance; ~ciar-se vpr distance o.s.; ~te a distant

disten|der /dʒistẽ'der/ vt stretch <pernas>; relax <músculo>; ~der-se vpr relax; ~são f (med) pull; ~são muscular pulled muscle

distin|ção /dʒistʃĩ'sãw/ f distinction; ~guir vt distinguish (de from); ~guir-se vpr distinguish o.s.; ~tivo a distinctive □ m badge; ~to a distinct; <senhor> distinguished

disto = de + isto

distor|ção /dʒistor'sãw/ f distortion; ~cer vt distort

distra|ção /dʒistra'sãw/ f distraction; ~ido a absent-minded; ~ir vt distract; (divertir) amuse; ~ir-se vpr be distracted; (divertir-se) amuse o.s.

distribu|ição /dʒistribui'sãw/ f distribution; ~idor m distributor; ~idora f distributor, distribution company; ~ir vt distribute

distrito /dʒis'tritu/ m district

distúrbio /dʒis'turbiu/ m trouble

di|tado /dʒi'tadu/ m dictation; (provérbio) saying; ~tador m dictator; ~tadura f dictatorship; ~tame m dictate; ~tar vt dictate; ~tatorial (pl ~tatoriais) a dictatorial

dito /'dʒitu/ a ~ e feito no sooner said than done □ m remark

ditongo /dʒi'tõgu/ m diphthong

DIU /'dʒiu/ m IUD, coil

diurno /dʒi'urnu/ a day

divã /dʒi'vã/ m couch

divagar /dʒiva'gar/ vi digress

diver|gência /dʒiver'ʒẽsia/ a divergence; ~gente a divergent; ~gir vi diverge (de from); ~são f diversion; (divertimento) amusement; ~sidade f diversity; ~sificar vt/i diversify; ~so /ɛ/ a (diferente) diverse; pl (vários) several; ~tido a (engraçado) funny; (que se curte) enjoyable; ~timento m enjoyment, fun; (um) amusement; ~tir vt amuse; ~tir-se vpr enjoy o.s., have fun

dívida /'dʒivida/ f debt; ~ externa foreign debt

divi|dendo /dʒivi'dẽdu/ m dividend; ~dido a <pessoa> torn; ~dir vt divide; (compartilhar) share; ~dir-se vpr be divided

divindade /dʒivĩ'dadʒi/ f divinity

divino /dʒi'vinu/ a divine

divi|sa /dʒi'viza/ f (lema) motto; (galão) stripes; (fronteira) border; pl foreign currency; ~são f division; ~sória f partition; ~sório a dividing

divorci|ado /dʒivorsi'adu/ a divorced □ m divorcé (f divorcée); ~ar vt

divorce; ~ar-se vpr get divorced; ~ar-se de divorce

divórcio /dʒi'vorsiu/ m divorce

divul|gado /dʒivuw'gadu/ a widespread; ~gar vt spread; publish <notícia>; divulge <segredo>; ~gar-se vpr be spread

dizer /dʒi'zer/ vt say; ~ a alg que tell sb that; ~ para alg fazer tell s.o. to do □ vi ~ com go with; ~-se vpr claim to be □ m saying

dizimar /dʒizi'mar/ vt decimate

do = de +o

dó /dɔ/ m pity; dar ~ be pitiful; ter ~ de feel sorry for

do|ação /doa'sãw/ f donation; ~ador m donor; ~ar vt donate

do|bra /'dɔbra/ f fold; (de calça) turn-up, (Amer) cuff; ~bradiça f hinge; ~bradiço a pliable; ~brado a (duplo) double; ~brar vt (duplicar) double; (fazer dobra em) fold; (curvar) bend; go round <esquina>; ring <sinos> (Port) dub <filme> □ vi double; <sinos> ring; ~brar-se vpr bend; ~bro m double

doca /'dɔka/ f dock

doce /'dosi/ a sweet; <água> fresh □ m sweet; ~ de leite fudge

docente /do'sẽtʃi/ a teaching; corpo ~ teaching staff, (Amer) faculty

dócil /'dɔsiw/ (pl ~ceis) a docile

documen|tação /dokumẽta'sãw/ f documentation; ~tar vt document; ~tário a & m documentary; ~to m document

doçura /do'sura/ f sweetness

dodói /do'dɔj/ (fam) m ter ~ have a pain □ a poorly, ill

doen|ça /do'ẽsa/ f illness; (infecciosa, fig) disease; ~te a ill; ~tio a <criança, aspecto> sickly; <interesse, curiosidade> morbid

doer /do'er/ vi hurt; <cabeça, músculo> ache

dog|ma /'dɔgima/ m dogma; ~mático a dogmatic

doido /'dojdu/ a crazy

dois /dojs/ a & m (f duas) two

dólar /'dɔlar/ m dollar

dolo|rido /dolo'ridu/ a sore; ~roso /o/ a painful

dom /dõ/ m gift

do|mador /doma'dor/ m tamer; ~mar vt tame

doméstica /do'mɛstʃika/ f housemaid

domesticar /domestʃi'kar/ vt domesticate

doméstico /do'mɛstʃiku/ a domestic

domi|ciliar /domisili'ar/ a home; ~cílio m home

domi|nação /domina'sãw/ f domination; ~nador a domineering; ~nante a dominant; ~nar vt dom-

inate; have a command of <*língua*>;
~nar-se *vpr* control o.s.
domin|go /do'mĩgu/ *m* Sunday;
~gueiro *a* Sunday
domini|cal /domini'kaw/ (*pl* ~cais)
a Sunday; ~cano *a & m* Dominican
domínio /do'miniu/ *m* command
dona /'dona/ *f* owner; Dona (*com
nome*) Miss; ~ de casa *f* housewife
donativo /dona'tʃivu/ *m* donation
donde /'dõdʒi/ *adv* from where; (*motivo*) from whence
dono /'donu/ *m* owner
donzela /dõ'zɛla/ *f* maiden
dopar /do'par/ *vt* drug
dor /dor/ *f* pain; (*menos aguda*) ache;
~ de cabeça headache
dor|mente /dor'mẽtʃi/ *a* numb □ *m*
sleeper; ~mida *f* sleep; ~minhoco
/o/ *m* sleepyhead; ~mir *vi* sleep;
~mitar *vi* doze; ~mitório *m* bedroom; (*comunitário*) dormitory
dorso /'dorsu/ *m* back; (*de livro*) spine
dos = de + os
do|sagem /do'zaʒẽ/ *f* dosage; ~sar *vt*
moderate; ~se /ɔ/ *f* dose; (*de uisque
etc*) shot, measure
dossiê /dosi'e/ *m* file
do|tação /dota'sãw/ *f* endowment;
~tado *a* gifted; ~tado de endowed
with; ~tar *vt* endow (de with); ~te
/ɔ/ *m* (*de noiva*) dowry; (*dom*) endow-
ment
dou|rado /do'radu/ *a* (*de cor*) golden;
(*revestido de ouro*) gilded, gilt □ *m* gilt;
~rar *vt* gild
dou|to /'dotu/ *a* learned; ~tor *m*
doctor; ~torado *m* doctorate, PhD;
~trina *f* doctrine; ~trinar *vt* indoc-
trinate
doze /'dozi/ *a & m* twelve
dragão /dra'gãw/ *m* dragon
dragar /dra'gar/ *vt* dredge
drágea /'draʒia/ *f* lozenge
dra|ma /'drama/ *m* drama; ~malhão
m melodrama; ~mático *a* dramatic;
~matizar *vt* dramatize; ~maturgo
m dramatist, playwright
drapeado /drapi'adu/ *a* draped
drástico /'drastʃiku/ *a* drastic
dre|nagem /dre'naʒẽ/ *f* drainage;
~nar *vt* drain; ~no /ɛ/ *m* drain
driblar /dri'blar/ *vt* (*em futebol*)
dribble round, beat; (*fig*) get round
drinque /'drĩki/ *m* drink
drive /'drajvi/ *m* disk drive
dro|ga /'drɔga/ *f* drug; (*fam*) (*coisa
sem valor*) dead loss; (*coisa chata*)
drag □ *int* damn; ~gado *a* on drugs
□ *m* drug addict; ~gar *vt* drug;
~gar-se *vpr* take drugs; ~garia *f*
dispensing chemist's, pharmacy
duas /'duas/ *veja* dois
dúbio /'dubiu/ *a* dubious

dub|lagem /du'blaʒẽ/ *f* dubbing;
~lar *vt* dub <*filme*>; mime
<*música*>; ~lê *m* double
ducentésimo /dusẽ'tɛzimu/ *a* two-
hundredth
ducha /'duʃa/ *f* shower
ducto /'duktu/ *m* duct
duelo /du'ɛlu/ *m* duel
duende /du'ẽdʒi/ *m* elf
dueto /du'etu/ *m* duet
duna /'duna/ *f* dune
duodécimo /duo'dɛsimu/ *a* twelfth
duodeno /duo'dɛnu/ *m* duodenum
dupla /'dupla/ *f* pair, duo; <*no tênis*>
doubles
duplex /du'plɛks/ *a invar* two-floor □
m invar two-floor apartment, (*Amer*)
duplex
dupli|car /dupli'kar/ *vt/i* double;
~cidade *f* duplicity; ~cata *f* duplicate
duplo /'duplu/ *a* double
duque /'duki/ duke; ~sa /e/ *f* duchess
du|ração /dura'sãw/ *f* duration;
~radouro *a* lasting; ~rante *prep*
during; ~rar *vi* last; ~rável (*pl*
~ráveis) *a* durable
durex /du'rɛks/ *m invar* sellotape
du|reza /du'reza/ *f* hardness; ~ro *a*
hard; (*fam: sem dinheiro*) hard up,
broke
dúvida /'duvida/ *f* doubt; (*pergunta*)
query
duvi|dar /duvi'dar/ *vt/i* doubt;
~doso *a* doubtful
duzentos /du'zẽtus/ *a & m* two hundred
dúzia /'duzia/ *f* dozen

E

e /i/ *conj* and
ébano /'ɛbanu/ *m* ebony
ébrio /'ɛbriu/ *a* drunk □ *m* drunkard
ebulição /ebuli'sãw/ *f* boiling
eclesiástico /eklezi'astʃiku/ *a* ecclesiastical
eclético /e'klɛtʃiku/ *a* eclectic
eclip|sar /eklip'sar/ *vt* eclipse; ~se *m*
eclipse
eclodir /eklo'dʒir/ *vi* emerge; (*esto-
urar*) break out; open
eco /'ɛku/ *m* echo; ter ~ have
repercussions; ~ar *vt/i* echo
eco|logia /ekolo'ʒia/ *f* ecology;
~lógico *a* ecological; ~logista *m/f*
ecologist
eco|nomia /ekono'mia/ *f* economy;
(*ciência*) economics; *pl* (*dinheiro poupado*) savings; ~nômico *a* economic;
(*rentável, barato*) economical; ~no-
mista *m/f* economist; ~nomizar *vt*
save □ *vi* economize

écran /ɛˈkrã/ (Port) m screen

eczema /ekˈzɛma/ m eczema

edição /edʒiˈsãw/ f edition; (de filmes) editing

edificante /edʒifiˈkãtʃi/ a edifying

edifício /edʒiˈfisiu/ m building

Edimburgo /edʒĩˈburgu/ f Edinburgh

edi|tal /edʒiˈtaw/ (pl ~tais) m announcement; ~tar vt publish; (comput) edit; ~to m edict; ~tor m publisher; ~tora f publishing company; ~torial (pl ~toriais) a publishing □ m editorial

edredom /edreˈdõ/ m, (Port) **edredão** /edreˈdãw/ m quilt

educa|ção /edukaˈsãw/ f (ensino) education; (polidez) good manners; é falta de ~ção it's rude; ~cional (pl ~cionais) a education

edu|cado /eduˈkadu/ a polite; ~car vt educate; ~cativo a educational

efeito /eˈfejtu/ m effect; fazer ~ have an effect; para todos os ~s to all intents and purposes; ~ colateral side effect; ~ estufa greenhouse effect

efêmero /eˈfẽmeru/ a ephemeral

efeminado /efemiˈnadu/ a effeminate

efervescente /eferveˈstʃi/ a effervescent

efe|tivar /efeˈtʃivar/ vt bring into effect; (contratar) make a permanent member of staff; ~tivo a real, effective; <cargo, emprego> permanent; ~tuar vt carry out, effect

efi|cácia /efiˈkasia/ f effectiveness; ~caz a effective

efici|ência /efisiˈẽsia/ f efficiency; ~ente a efficient

efígie /eˈfiʒi/ f effigy

efusivo /efuˈzivu/ a effusive

Egeu /eˈʒew/ a & m Aegean

égide /ˈɛʒidʒi/ f aegis

egípcio /eˈʒipsiu/ a & m Egyptian

Egito /eˈʒitu/ m Egypt

ego /ˈɛgu/ m ego; ~cêntrico a self-centred, egocentric; ~ismo m selfishness; ~ista a selfish □ m/f egoist □ m (de rádio etc) earplug

égua /ˈɛgwa/ f mare

eis /ejs/ adv (aqui está) here is/are; (isso é) that is

eixo /ˈejʃu/ m axle; (mat, entre cidades) axis; pôr nos ~s set straight

ela /ˈɛla/ pron she; (coisa) it; (com preposição) her; (coisa) it

elaborar /elaboˈrar/ vt (fazer) make, produce; (desenvolver) work out

elasticidade /elastʃisiˈdadʒi/ f (de coisa) elasticity; (de pessoa) suppleness

elástico /eˈlastʃiku/ a elastic □ m (de borracha) elastic band; (de calcinha etc) elastic

ele /ˈeli/ pron he; (coisa) it; (com preposição) him; (coisa) it

electr- (Port) veja eletr-

eléctrico /iˈlɛktriku/ (Port) m tram, (Amer) streetcar □ a veja elétrico

elefante /eleˈfãtʃi/ m elephant

ele|gância /eleˈgãsia/ f elegance; ~gante a elegant

eleger /eleˈʒer/ vt elect; ~-se vpr get elected

elegia /eleˈʒia/ f elegy

elei|ção /elejˈsãw/ f election; ~to a elected, elect; <povo> chosen; ~tor m voter; ~torado m electorate; ~toral (pl ~torais) a electoral

elemen|tar /elemẽˈtar/ a elementary; ~to m element

elenco /eˈlẽku/ m (de filme, peça) cast

eletri|cidade /eletrisiˈdadʒi/ f electricity; ~cista m/f electrician

elétrico /eˈlɛtriku/ a electric

eletri|ficar /eletrifiˈkar/ vt electrify; ~zar vt electrify

eletro /eˈletru/ m ECG; ~cutar vt electrocute; ~do m /ˈɛ/ m electrode; ~domésticos m pl electrical appliances

eletrôni|ca /eleˈtronika/ f electronics; ~co a electronic

ele|vação /eleˈvasãw/ f elevation; (aumento) rise; ~vado a high; <sentimento, estilo> elevated; ~vador m lift, (Amer) elevator; ~var vt raise; (promover) elevate; ~var-se vpr rise

elimi|nar /elimiˈnar/ vt eliminate; ~natória f heat; ~natório a eliminatory

elipse /eˈlipsi/ f ellipse

elíptico /eˈliptʃiku/ a elliptical

eli|te /eˈlitʃi/ f elite; ~tismo m elitism; ~tista a & m/f elitist

elmo /ˈɛwmu/ m helmet

elo /ˈɛlu/ m link

elo|giar /eloʒiˈar/ vt praise; ~giar alg por compliment s.o. on; ~gio m (louvor) praise; (um) compliment; ~gioso /o/ a complimentary

elo|qüência /eloˈkwẽsia/ f eloquence; ~qüente a eloquent

eluci|dar /elusiˈdar/ vt elucidate; ~dativo a elucidatory

em /j/ prep in; (sobre) on; ela está no Eduardo she's at Eduardo's (house); de casa ~ casa from house to house; aumentar ~ 10% increase by 10%

emagre|cer /emagreˈser/ vi lose weight, get thinner □ vt make thinner; ~cimento m slimming

emanar /emaˈnar/ vi emanate (de from)

emanci|pação /emãsipaˈsãw/ f emancipation; ~par vt emancipate; ~par-se vpr become emancipated

emara|nhado /emaraˈnadu/ a tangled □ m tangle; ~nhar vt tangle; (envolver) entangle; ~nhar-se vpr get tangled up; (*envolver-se*) become entangled (**em** in)

embaçar /ība'sar/, (*Port*) **embaciar** /ibasi'ar/ *vt* steam up <*vidro*> □ *vi* <*vidro*> steam up; <*olhos*> grow misty

embainhar /ībaj'nar/ *vt* hem <*vestido, calça*>

embaixa|da /ība'ʃada/ *f* embassy; ~**dor** *m* ambassador; ~**triz** *f* ambassador; (*esposa*) ambassador's wife

embaixo /ī'baʃu/ *adv* underneath; (*em casa*) downstairs; ~ **de** under

emba|lagem /ība'laʒē/ *f* packaging; ~**lar**[1] *vt* pack

emba|lar[2] /ība'lar/ *vt* rock <*criança*>; ~**lo** *m* (*fig*) excitement, thrill

embalsamar /ībawsa'mar/ *vt* embalm

embara|çar /ībara'sar/ *vt* embarrass; ~**çar-se** *vpr* get embarrassed (**com** by); ~**ço** *m* embarrassment; ~**çoso** /o/ *a* embarrassing

embaralhar /ībara'ʎar/ *vt* muddle up; shuffle <*cartas*>; ~**-se** *vpr* get muddled up

embar|cação /ībarka'sãw/ *f* vessel; ~**cadouro** *m* wharf; ~**car** *vt/i* board, embark

embar|gado /ībar'gadu/ *a* <*voz*> faltering; ~**go** *m* embargo

embarque /ī'barki/ *m* boarding; (*seção do aeroporto*) departures

embasba|cado /ībazba'kadu/ *a* open-mouthed; ~**car-se** *vpr* be left open-mouthed

embate /ī'batʃi/ *m* (*de carros etc*) crash; (*fig*) clash

embebedar /ībebe'dar/ *vt* make drunk; ~**-se** *vpr* get drunk

embeber /ībe'ber/ *vt* soak; ~**-se em** soak up; ~**-se em** get absorbed in

embele|zador /ībeleza'dor/ *a* <*cirurgia*> cosmetic; ~**zar** *vt* embellish; spruce up <*casa*>; ~**zar-se** *vpr* make o.s. beautiful

embevecer /ībeve'ser/ *vt* captivate, engross; ~**-se** *vpr* get engrossed, be captivated

emblema /ē'blema/ *m* emblem

embocadura /īboka'dura/ *f* (*de instrumento*) mouthpiece; (*de freio*) bit; (*de rio*) mouth; (*de rua*) entrance

êmbolo /'ēbulu/ *m* piston

embolsar /ībow'sar/ *vt* pocket; (*reembolsar*) reimburse

embora /ī'bora/ *adv* away □ *conj* although

emborcar /ībor'kar/ *vi* overturn; <*barco*> capsize

emboscada /ībos'kada/ *f* ambush

embrai|agem /ēbraj'aʒē/ (*Port*) *f* veja **embreagem** ~**ar** (*Port*) *vi* veja **embrear**

embre|agem /ēbri'aʒē/ *f* clutch; ~**ar** *vi* let in the clutch

embria|gar /ēbria'gar/ *vt* intoxicate; ~**gar-se** *vpr* get drunk, become intoxicated; ~**guez** /e/ *f* drunkenness; ~**guez no volante** drunken driving

embri|ão /ēbri'ãw/ *m* embryo; ~**onário** *a* embryonic

embro|mação /ībroma'sãw/ *f* flannel; ~**mar** *vt* flannel, string along; (*enganar*) con □ *vi* stall, drag one's feet

embru|lhada /ībru'ʎada/ *f* muddle; ~**lhar** *vt* wrap up <*pacote*>; upset <*estômago*>; (*confundir*) muddle up; ~**lhar-se** *vpr* <*pessoa*> get muddled up; ~**lho** *m* parcel; (*fig*) mix-up

embur|rado /ību'xadu/ *a* sulky; ~**rar** *vi* sulk

embuste /ī'bustʃi/ *m* hoax, put-up job

embu|tido /ību'tʃidu/ *a* built-in, fitted; ~**tir** *vt* build in, fit

emen|da /e'mēda/ *f* correction, improvement; (*de lei*) amendment; ~**dar** *vt* correct; amend <*lei*>; ~**dar-se** *vpr* mend one's ways

ementa /i'mēta/ (*Port*) *f* menu

emer|gência /emer'ʒēsia/ *f* emergency; ~**gente** *a* emergent; ~**gir** *vi* surface

emi|gração /emigra'sãw/ *f* emigration; (*de aves etc*) migration; ~**grado** *a* & *m* émigré; ~**grante** *a* & *m/f* emigrant; ~**grar** *vi* emigrate; <*aves, animais*> migrate

emi|nência /emi'nēsia/ *f* eminence; ~**nente** *a* eminent

emis|são /emi'sãw/ *f* (*de ações etc*) issue; (*na rádio, TV*) transmission, broadcast; (*de som, gases*) emission; ~**sário** *m* emissary; ~**sor** *m* transmitter; ~**sora** *f* (*de rádio*) radio station; (*de TV*) TV station

emitir /emi'tʃir/ *vt* issue <*ações, selos etc*>; emit <*sons*>; (*pela rádio, TV*) transmit, broadcast

emoção /emo'sãw/ *f* emotion; (*excitação*) excitement

emocio|nal /emosio'naw/ (*pl* ~**nais**) *a* emotional; ~**nante** *a* (*excitante*) exciting; (*comovente etc*) touching, emotional; ~**nar** *vt* (*excitar*) excite; (*comover*) move, touch; ~**nar-se** *vpr* get emotional

emoldurar /emowdu'rar/ *vt* frame

emotivo /emo'tʃivu/ *a* emotional

empacar /īpa'kar/ *vi* <*cavalo*> baulk; <*negociações etc*> grind to a halt; <*orador*> dry up

empacotar /īpako'tar/ *vt* pack up; (*pôr em pacotes*) packet

empa|da /ē'pada/ *f* pie; ~**dão** *m* (large) pie

empalhar /īpa'ʎar/ *vt* stuff

empalidecer /īpalide'ser/ *vi* turn pale

empanar¹ /ẽpa'nar/ vt tarnish, dull

empanar² /ẽpa'nar/ vt cook in batter <carne etc>

empanturrar /ĩpãtu'xar/ vt stuff; ~-se vpr stuff o.s. (de with)

empapar /ĩpa'par/ vt soak

empa|tar /ẽpa'tar/ vt draw <jogo> □ vi <times> draw; <corredores> tie; ~te m (em jogo) draw; (em corrida, votação) tie; (em xadrez, fig) stalemate

empatia /ẽpa'tʃia/ f empathy

empecilho /ẽpe'siʎu/ m hindrance

empenar /ẽpe'nar/ vt/i warp

empe|nhar /ẽpe'ɲar/ vt (penhorar) pawn; (prometer) pledge; ~nhar-se vpr do one's utmost (em to); ~nho /e/ m (compromisso) pledge; (diligência) effort, commitment

emperrar /ẽpe'xar/ vt make stick □ vi stick

emperti|gado /ĩpertʃi'gadu/ a upright; ~gar-se vpr stand up straight

empilhar /ĩpi'ʎar/ vt pile up

empi|nado /ĩpi'nadu/ a erect; (ingreme) sheer, steep; <nariz> turned-up; (fig) stuck-up; ~nar vt stand upright; fly <pipa>; tip up <copo>

empírico /ẽ'piriku/ a empirical

emplacar /ĩpla'kar/ vt notch up <pontos, sucessos, anos>; license <carro>

emplastro /ĩ'plastru/ m surgical plaster; ~ de nicotina nicotine patch

empobre|cer /ĩpobre'ser/ vt impoverish; ~cimento m impoverishment

empoleirar /ĩpole'rar/ vt perch; ~-se vpr perch

empol|gação /ĩpowga'sãw/ f fascination; ~gante a fascinating; ~gar vt fascinate

empossar /ĩpo'sar/ vt swear in

empreen|dedor /ĩpriẽde'dor/ a enterprising □ m entrepreneur; ~der vt undertake; ~dimento m undertaking

empre|gada /ĩpre'gada/ f (doméstica) maid; ~gado m employee; ~gador m employer; ~gar vt employ; ~gar-se vpr get a job; ~gatício a vínculo ~gatício contract of employment; ~go /e/ m (trabalho) job; (uso) use; ~guismo m patronage

emprei|tada /ĩprej'tada/ f commission, contract; (empreendimento) venture; ~teira f contractor, firm of contractors; ~teiro m contractor

empre|sa /ĩ'preza/ f company, ~sariado m business community; ~sarial (pl ~sariais) a business; ~sário m businessman; (de cantor etc) manager

empres|tado /ĩpres'tadu/ a on loan; pedir ~tado (ask to) borrow; tomar ~tado borrow; ~tar vt lend

empréstimo /ĩ'prestʃimu/ m loan

empur|rão /ĩpu'xãw/ m push; ~rar vt push

emular /emu'lar/ vt emulate

enamorado /enamo'radu/ a (apaixonado) in love

encabeçar /ĩkabe'sar/ vt head

encabu|lado /ĩkabu'ladu/ a shy; ~lar vt embarrass; ~lar-se vpr be shy

encadear /ĩkade'ar/ vt chain ou link together

encader|nação /ĩkaderna'sãw/ f binding; ~nado a bound; (com capa dura) hardback; ~nar vt bind

encai|xar /ĩka'ʃar/ vt/i fit; ~xe m (cavidade) socket; (juntura) joint

encalço /ĩ'kawsu/ m pursuit; no ~ de in pursuit of

encalhar /ĩka'ʎar/ vi <barco> run aground; (fig) get bogged down; <mercadoria> not sell; (fam: ficar solteiro) be left on the shelf

encaminhar /ĩkami'ɲar/ vt (dirigir) steer, direct; (remeter) pass on; set in motion <processo>; ~-se vpr set out

encana|dor /ĩkana'dor/ m plumber; ~mento m plumbing

encan|tador /ĩkãta'dor/ a enchanting; ~tamento m enchantment; ~tar vt enchant; ~to m charm

encaraco|lado /ĩkarako'ladu/ a curly; ~lar vt curl; ~lar-se vpr curl up

encarar /ĩka'rar/ vt confront, face

encarcerar /ĩkarse'rar/ vt imprison

encardido /ĩkar'dʒidu/ a grimy

encarecidamente /ĩkaresida'mẽtʃi/ adv insistently

encargo /ĩ'kargu/ m task, responsibility

encar|nação /ĩkarna'sãw/ f (do espírito) incarnation; (de um personagem) embodiment; ~nar vt embody; play <papel>

encarre|gado /ĩkaxe'gadu/ a in charge (de of) □ m person in charge; (de operários) foreman; ~gado de negócios chargé d'affaires; ~gar vt ~gar alg de put s.o. in charge of; ~gar-se de undertake to

encarte /ĩ'kartʃi/ m insert

ence|nação /ĩsena'sãw/ f (de peça) production; (fingimento) playacting; ~nar vt put on □ vi put it on

ence|radeira /ĩsera'dera/ f floor polisher; ~rar vt wax

encer|rado /ĩse'xadu/ a <assunto> closed; ~ramento m close; ~rar vt close; ~rar-se vpr close

encharcar /ĩʃar'kar/ vt soak

en|chente /ẽ'ʃẽtʃi/ f flood; ~cher vt fill; (fam) annoy □ (fam) vi be annoying; ~cher-se vpr fill up; (fam: fartar-se) get fed up (de with)

enciclopédia /ẽsiklo'pɛdʒia/ *f* encyclopaedia

enco|berto /ĩko'bɛrtu/ *a* <*céu, tempo*> overcast; ~**brir** *vt* cover up □ *vi* <*tempo*> become overcast

encolher /ĩko'ʎer/ *vt* shrug <*ombros*>; pull up <*pernas*>; shrink <*roupa*> □ *vi* <*roupa*> shrink; ~**se** *vpr* (*de medo*) shrink; (*de frio*) huddle; (*espremer-se*) squeeze up

encomen|da /ĩko'mẽda/ *f* order; **de ou sob** ~**da** to order; ~**dar** *vt* order (a from)

encon|trão /ĩkõ'trãw/ *m* bump; (*empurrão*) shove; ~**trar** *vt* (*achar*) find; (*ver*) meet; ~**trar com** meet; ~**trar-se** *vpr* (*ver-se*) meet; (*estar*) be; ~**tro** *m* meeting; (*mil*) encounter; **ir ao** ~**tro de** go to meet; (*fig*) meet; **ir de** ~**tro a** run into; (*fig*) go against

encorajar /ĩkora'ʒar/ *vt* encourage

encor|pado /ĩkor'padu/ *a* stocky; <*vinho*> full-bodied; ~**par** *vt/i* fill out

encos|ta /ĩ'kɔsta/ *f* slope; ~**tar** (*apoiar*) lean; park <*carro*>; leave on the latch <*porta*>; (*pôr de lado*) put aside □ *vi* <*carro*> pull in; ~**tar-se** *vpr* lean; ~**to** /o/ *m* back

encravado /ĩkra'vadu/ *a* <*unha, pêlo*> ingrowing; ~**var** *vt* stick

encren|ca /ĩ'krẽka/ *f* fix, jam; *pl* trouble; ~**car** *vt* get into trouble <*pessoa*>; complicate <*situação*> □ *vi* <*situação*> get complicated; <*carro*> break down; ~**car-se** *vpr* <*pessoa*> get into trouble; ~**queiro** *m* troublemaker

encres|pado /ĩkres'padu/ *a* <*mar*> choppy; ~**par** *vt* frizz <*cabelo*>; ~**par-se** *vpr* <*cabelo*> go frizzy; <*mar*> get choppy

encruzilhada /ĩkruzi'ʎada/ *f* crossroads

encurralar /ĩkuxa'lar/ *vt* hem in, pen in

encurtar /ĩkur'tar/ *vt* shorten

endere|çar /ĩdere'sar/ *vt* address; ~**ço** /e/ *m* address

endinheirado /ĩdʒiɲe'radu/ *a* well-off

endireitar /ĩdʒirej'tar/ *vt* straighten; ~**se** *vpr* straighten up

endivi|dado /ĩdʒivi'dadu/ *a* in debt; ~**dar** *vt* put into debt; ~**dar-se** *vpr* get into debt

endoidecer /ĩdojde'ser/ *vi* get mad

endos|sar /ĩdo'sar/ *vt* endorse; ~**so** /o/ *m* endorsement

endurecer /ĩdure'ser/ *vt/i* harden

ener|gético /ener'ʒɛtʃiku/ *a* energy; ~**gia** *f* energy

enérgico /e'nɛrʒiku/ *a* vigorous; <*remédio, discurso*> powerful

enevoado /enevu'adu/ *a* (*com névoa*) misty; (*com nuvens*) cloudy

enfarte /ĩ'fartʃi/ *m* heart attack

ênfase /'ẽfazi/ *f* emphasis; **dar** ~ **a** emphasize

enfático /ẽ'fatʃiku/ *a* emphatic

enfatizar /ẽfatʃi'zar/ *vt* emphasize

enfei|tar /ĩfej'tar/ *vt* decorate; ~**tar-se** *vpr* dress up; ~**te** *m* decoration

enfeitiçar /ĩfejtʃi'sar/ *vt* bewitch

enfer|magem /ĩfer'maʒẽ/ *f* nursing; ~**maria** *f* ward; ~**meira** *f* nurse; ~**meiro** *m* male nurse; ~**midade** *f* illness; ~**mo** *a* sick □ *m* patient

enferru|jado /ĩfexu'ʒadu/ *a* rusty; ~**jar** *vt/i* rust

enfezado /ĩfe'zadu/ *a* bad-tempered

enfiar /ĩfi'ar/ *vt* put; slip on <*roupa*>; thread <*agulha*>; string <*pérolas*>

enfileirar /ĩfilej'rar/ *vt* line up; ~**se** *vpr* line up

enfim /ẽ'fĩ/ *adv* (*finalmente*) finally; (*resumindo*) anyway

enfo|car /ĩfo'kar/ *vt* tackle; ~**que** *m* approach

enfor|camento /ĩforka'mẽtu/ *m* hanging; ~**car** *vt* hang; ~**car-se** *vpr* hang o.s.

enfraquecer /ĩfrake'ser/ *vt/i* weaken

enfrentar /ĩfrẽ'tar/ *vt* face

enfumaçado /ĩfuma'sadu/ *a* smoky

enfurecer /ĩfure'ser/ *vt* infuriate; ~**se** *vpr* get furious

enga|jamento /ĩgaʒa'mẽtu/ *m* commitment; ~**jado** *a* committed; ~**jar-se** *vpr* get involved (**em** in)

engalfinhar-se /ĩgawfi'ɲarsi/ *vpr* grapple

enga|nado /ĩga'nadu/ *a* (*errado*) mistaken; ~**nar** *vt* deceive; cheat on <*marido, esposa*>; stave off <*fome*>; ~**nar-se** *vpr* be mistaken; ~**no** *m* (*erro*) mistake; (*desonestidade*) deception

engarra|famento /ĩgaxafa'mẽtu/ *m* traffic jam; ~**far** *vt* bottle <*vinho etc*>; block <*trânsito*>

engas|gar /ĩgaz'gar/ *vt* choke □ *vi* choke; <*motor*> backfire; ~**go** *m* choking

engastar /ĩgaʃ'tar/ *vt* set <*jóias*>

engatar /ĩga'tar/ *vt* hitch <*reboque etc*> (a to); engage <*marcha*>

engatinhar /ĩgatʃi'ɲar/ *vi* crawl; (*fig*) start out

engave|tamento /ĩgaveta'mẽtu/ *m* pile-up; ~**tar** *vt* shelve

engelhar /ĩʒe'ʎar/ *vt* (*na pele*) wrinkle

enge|nharia /ĩʒeɲa'ria/ *f* engineering; ~**nheiro** *m* engineer; ~**nho** /e/ *m* (*de pessoa*) ingenuity; (*de açúcar*) sugar mill; (*máquina*) device; ~**nhoca** /ɔ/ *f* gadget; ~**nhoso** *a* ingenious

engessar /ĩʒe'sar/ *vt* put in plaster

engodo /ĩ'godu/ *m* lure

engolir /ĩgo'lir/ *vt/i* swallow; ~ **em seco** gulp

engomar /ĩgo'mar/ *vt* press; (*com goma*) starch

engordar /ĩgor'dar/ *vt* make fat; fatten <*animais*> □ *vi* <*pessoa*> put on weight; <*comida*> be fattening

engraçado /ĩgra'sadu/ *a* funny

engradado /ĩgra'dadu/ *m* crate

engravidar /ĩgravi'dar/ *vt* make pregnant □ *vi* get pregnant

engraxar /ĩgra'ʃar/ *vt* polish

engre|nado /ĩgre'nadu/ *a* <*carro*> in gear; ~**nagem** *f* gear; (*fig*) mechanism; ~**nar** *vt* put into gear <*carro*>; strike up <*conversa*>; ~**nar-se** *vpr* mesh; (*fig*) <*pessoas*> get on

engrossar /ĩgro'sar/ *vt* thicken; raise <*voz*> □ *vi* thicken; <*pessoa*> turn nasty

enguia /ẽ'gia/ *f* eel

engui|çar /ẽgi'sar/ *vi* break down; ~**ço** *m* breakdown

enig|ma /e'nigma/ *m* enigma; ~**mático** *a* enigmatic

enjaular /ĩʒaw'lar/ *vt* cage

enjo|ar /ĩʒo'ar/ *vt* sicken □ *vi*, ~**ar-se** *vpr* get sick (**de** of); ~**ativo** *a* <*comida*> sickly; <*livro etc*> boring

enjôo /ĩ'ʒou/ *m* sickness

enlameado /ĩlami'adu/ *a* muddy

enlatado /ĩla'tadu/ *a* tinned, canned; ~**s** *m pl* tinned foods

enle|var /ẽle'var/ *vt* enthral; ~**vo**/e/ *m* rapture

enlouquecer /ĩloke'ser/ *vt* drive mad □ *vi* go mad

enluarado /ĩlua'radu/ *a* moonlit

enor|me /e'nɔrmi/ *a* enormous; ~**midade** *f* enormity

enquadrar /ĩkwa'drar/ *vt* fit □ *vi*, ~**se** *vpr* fit in

enquanto /ĩ'kwãtu/ *conj* while; ~ **isso** meanwhile; **por** ~ for the time being

enquête /ã'kɛtʃi/ *f* survey

enraivecer /ĩxajve'ser/ *vt* enrage

enredo /ẽ'xedu/ *m* plot

enrijecer /ĩxiʒe'ser/ *vt* stiffen; ~**se** *vpr* stiffen

enrique|cer /ĩxike'ser/ *vt* (*dar dinheiro a*) make rich; (*fig*) enrich □ *vi* get rich; ~**cimento** *m* enrichment

enro|lado /ĩxo'ladu/ *a* complicated; ~**lar** *vt* (*envolver*) roll up; (*complicar*) complicate; (*enganar*) cheat; ~**lar-se** *vpr* (*envolver-se*) roll up; (*confundir-se*) get mixed up

enroscar /ĩxos'kar/ *vt* twist

enrouquecer /ĩxoke'ser/ *vi* go hoarse

enrugar /ĩxu'gar/ *vt* wrinkle <*pele, tecido*>; furrow <*testa*>

enrustido /ĩxus'tʃidu/ *a* repressed

ensaboar /ĩsabo'ar/ *vt* soap

ensai|ar /ĩsaj'ar/ *vt* (*provar*) try out; (*repetir*) rehearse; ~**o** *m* (*prova*) test; (*repetição*) rehearsal; (*escrito*) essay

ensangüentado /ĩsãgwẽ'tadu/ *a* bloody, bloodstained

enseada /ĩsi'ada/ *f* inlet

ensebado /ĩse'badu/ *a* greasy

ensimesmado /ĩsimez'madu/ *a* lost in thought

ensi|nar /ẽsi'nar/ *vt/i* teach (**aco a alg** s.o. sth); ~**nar alg a nadar** teach s.o. to swim; ~**no** *m* teaching; (*em geral*) education

ensolarado /ĩsola'radu/ *a* sunny

enso|pado /ĩso'padu/ *a* soaked □ *m* stew; ~**par** *vt* soak

ensurde|cedor /ĩsurdese'dor/ *a* deafening; ~**cer** *vt* deafen □ *vi* go deaf

entabular /ĩtabu'lar/ *vt* open, start

entalar /ĩta'lar/ *vt* wedge, jam; (*em apertos*) get; ~**se** *vpr* get wedged, get jammed; (*em apertos*) get caught up

entalhar /ĩta'ʎar/ *vt* carve

entanto /ĩ'tãtu/ *m* **no** ~ however

então /ĩ'tãw/ *adv* then; (*nesse caso*) so

entardecer /ĩtarde'ser/ *m* sunset

ente /'ẽtʃi/ *m* being

entea|da /ẽtʃi'ada/ *f* stepdaughter; ~**do** *m* stepson

entedi|ante /ĩtedʒi'ãtʃi/ *a* boring; ~**ar** *vt* bore; ~**ar-se** *vpr* get bored

enten|der /ĩtẽ'der/ *vt* understand; ~**der-se** *vpr* (*dar-se bem*) get on (**com** with); **dar a** ~**der** give to understand; ~**der de futebol** know about football; ~**dimento** *m* understanding

enternecedor /ĩternese'dor/ *a* touching

enter|rar /ĩte'xar/ *vt* bury; ~**ro**/e/ *m* burial; (*cerimônia*) funeral

entidade /ẽtʃi'dadʒi/ *f* entity; (*órgão*) body

entornar /ĩtor'nar/ *vt* tip over, spill

entorpe|cente /ĩtorpe'sẽtʃi/ *m* drug, narcotic; ~**cer** *vt* numb

entortar /ĩtor'tar/ *vt* make crooked

entrada /ẽ'trada/ *f* entry; (*onde se entra*) entrance; (*bilhete*) ticket; (*prato*) starter; (*pagamento*) deposit; *pl* (*no cabelo*) receding hairline; **dar** ~ **a** enter; ~ **proibida** no entry

entranhas /ĩ'traɲas/ *f pl* entrails

entrar /ẽ'trar/ *vi* go/come in; ~ **com** enter <*dados*>; put in <*dinheiro*>; ~ **em detalhes** go into details; ~ **em vigor** come into force

entravar /ẽtra'var/ *vt* hamper

entre /'ẽtri/ *prep* between; (*em meio a*) among

entreaberto /ẽtria'bɛrtu/ *a* half-open

entrecortar /ētrikor'tar/ vt intersperse; (*cruzar*) intersect

entre|ga /ĩ'trɛga/ f delivery; (*rendição*) surrender; ~ga a domicílio home delivery; ~gar vt hand over; deliver <*mercadorias, cartas*>; hand in <*caderno, trabalho escolar*>; ~gar-se vpr give o.s. up (a to); ~gue pp de entregar

entrelaçar /ētrela'sar/ vt intertwine; clasp <*mãos*>

entrelinhas /ētri'liɲas/ f pl ler nas ~ read between the lines

entremear /ētrimi'ar/ vt intersperse

entreolhar-se /ētrio'ʎarsi/ vpr look at one another

entretanto /ētre'tãtu/ conj however

entre|tenimento /ētreteni'mētu/ m entertainment; ~ter vt entertain

entrever /ētre'ver/ vt glimpse

entrevis|ta /ētre'vista/ f interview; ~tador m interviewer; ~tar vt interview

entristecer /ĩtriste'ser/ vt sadden □ vi be saddened (com by)

entroncamento /ĩtrõka'mētu/ m junction

entrosar /ĩtro'zar/ vt/i integrate

entu|lhar /ĩtu'ʎar/ vt cram (de with); ~lho m rubble

entupir /ĩtu'pir/ vt block; ~pir-se vpr get blocked; (*de comida*) stuff o.s. (de with)

enturmar-se /ĩtur'marsi/ vpr mix in, fit in

entusias|mar /ĩtuziaz'mar/ vt fill with enthusiasm; ~mar-se vpr get enthusiastic (com about); ~mo m enthusiasm; ~ta m/f enthusiast □ a enthusiastic

entusiástico /ĩtuzi'astʃiku/ a enthusiastic

enumerar /enume'rar/ vt enumerate

envelope /ẽve'lɔpi/ m envelope

envelhecer /ĩveʎe'ser/ vt/i age

envenenar /ĩvene'nar/ vt poison; (*fam*) soup up <*carro*>

envergadura /ĩverga'dura/ f wingspan; (*fig*) scale

envergo|nhado /ĩvergo'ɲadu/ a ashamed; (*constrangido*) embarrassed; ~nhar vt disgrace; (*constranger*) embarrass; ~nhar-se vpr be ashamed; (*acanhar-se*) get embarrassed

envernizar /ĩverni'zar/ vt varnish

en|viado /ĩvi'adu/ m envoy; ~viar vt send; ~vio m (*ato*) sending; (*remessa*) consignment

envidraçar /ĩvidra'sar/ vt glaze

enviesado /ĩvie'zadu/ a (*não vertical*) slanting; (*torto*) crooked

envol|vente /ĩvow'vētʃi/ a compelling, gripping; ~ver vt (*embrulhar*) wrap; (*enredar*) involve; ~ver-se vpr (*enrolar-se*) wrap o.s.; (*enredar-se*) get involved; ~vimento m involvement

enxada /ẽ'ʃada/ f hoe

enxaguar /ẽʃa'gwar/ vt rinse

enxame /ẽ'ʃami/ m swarm

enxaqueca /ẽʃa'keka/ f migraine

enxergar /ĩʃer'gar/ vt/i see

enxer|tar /ĩʃer'tar/ vt graft; ~to /e/ m graft

enxotar /ĩʃo'tar/ vt drive away

enxofre /ẽ'ʃofri/ m sulphur

enxo|val /ẽʃo'vaw/ (pl ~vais) m (*de noiva*) trousseau; (*de bebê*) layette

enxugar /ĩʃu'gar/ vt dry; ~se vpr dry o.s.

enxurrada /ĩʃu'xada/ f torrent; (*fig*) flood

enxuto /ĩ'ʃutu/ a dry; <*corpo*> shapely

enzima /ẽ'zima/ f enzyme

epicentro /epi'sẽtru/ m epicentre

épico /'ɛpiku/ a epic

epidemia /epide'mia/ f epidemic

epi|lepsia /epilep'sia/ f epilepsy; ~léptico a & m epileptic

epílogo /e'pilogu/ m epilogue

episódio /epi'zɔdʒiu/ m episode

epitáfio /epi'tafiu/ m epitaph

época /'ɛpoka/ f time; (*da história*) age, period; fazer ~ make history; móveis da ~ period furniture

epopéia /epo'pɛja/ f epic

equação /ekwa'sãw/ f equation

equador /ekwa'dor/ m equator; o Equador Ecuador

equatori|al /ekwatori'aw/ (pl ~ais) a equatorial; ~ano a & m Ecuadorian

equilibrar /ekili'brar/ vt balance; ~se vpr balance

equilíbrio /eki'libriu/ m balance

equipa /e'kipa/ (Port) f team

equi|pamento /ekipa'mētu/ m equipment; ~par vt equip

equiparar /ekipa'rar/ vt equate (com with); ~se vpr compare (a with)

equipe /e'kipi/ f team

equitação /ekita'sãw/ f riding

equiva|lência /ekiva'lẽsia/ f equivalence; ~lente a equivalent; ~ler vi be equivalent (a to)

equivo|cado /ekivo'kadu/ a mistaken; ~car-se vpr make a mistake

equívoco /e'kivoku/ a equivocal □ m mistake

era /'ɛra/ f era

erário /e'rariu/ m exchequer

ereção /ere'sãw/ f erection

eremita /ere'mita/ m/f hermit

ereto /e'rɛtu/ a erect

erguer /er'ger/ vt raise; erect <*monumento* etc>; ~se vpr rise

eri|çado /eri'sadu/ a bristling; ~çar-se vpr bristle

ermo /'ermu/ a deserted □ m wilderness

erosão /ero'zãw/ f erosion

erótico /e'rɔtʃiku/ a erotic

erotismo /ero'tʃizmu/ m eroticism

er|rado /e'xadu/ a wrong; ~**rante** a wandering; ~**rar** vt (não fazer certo) get wrong; miss <alvo> □ vi (enganar-se) be wrong; (vaguear) wander; ~**ro** /e/ m mistake; **fazer um** ~**ro** make a mistake; ~**rôneo** a erroneous

erudi|ção /erudʒi'sãw/ f learning; ~**to** a learned; <música> classical □ m scholar

erupção /erup'sãw/ f (vulcânica) eruption; (cutânea) rash

erva /'ɛrva/ f herb; ~ **daninha** weed; ~**-doce** f aniseed

ervilha /er'viʎa/ f pea

esban|jador /izbãʒa'dor/ a extravagant □ m spendthrift; ~**jar** vt squander; burst with <saúde, imaginação, energia etc>

esbar|rão /izba'xãw/ m bump; ~**rar** vi ~**rar com** ou **em** bump into <pessoa>; come up against <problema>

esbelto /iz'bɛwtu/ a svelte

esbo|çar /izbo'sar/ vt sketch <desenho etc>; outline <plano etc>; ~**çar um sorriso** give a hint of a smile; ~**ço** /o/ m (desenho) sketch; (plano) outline; (de um sorriso) hint

esbofetear /izbofetʃi'ar/ vt slap

esborrachar /izboxa'ʃar/ vt squash; ~**-se** vpr crash

esbravejar /izbrave'ʒar/ vi rant, rail

esbura|cado /izbura'kadu/ a full of holes; ~**car** vt make holes in

esbuga|lhado /izbuga'ʎadu/ a <olhos> bulging; ~**lhar-se** vpr <olhos> pop out

escabroso /iska'brozu/ a (fig) difficult, tough

escada /is'kada/ f (dentro de casa) stairs; (na rua) steps; (de mão) ladder; ~ **de incêndio** fire escape; ~ **rolante** escalator; ~**ria** f staircase

escafan|drista /iskafã'drista/ m/f diver; ~**dro** m diving suit

escala /is'kala/ f scale; (de navio) port of call; (de avião) stopover; **fazer** ~ stop over; **sem** ~ <vôo> non-stop

esca|lada /iska'lada/ f (fig) escalation; ~**lão** m echelon, level; ~**lar** vt (subir a) scale; (designar) select

escaldar /iskaw'dar/ vt scald; blanch <vegetais>

escalfar /iskaw'far/ vt poach

escalonar /iskalo'nar/ vt schedule <pagamento>

escama /is'kama/ f scale

escanca|rado /iskãka'radu/ a wide open; ~**rar** vt open wide

escandalizar /iskãdali'zar/ vt scandalize; ~**-se** vpr be scandalized

escândalo /is'kãdalu/ m (vexame) scandal; (tumulto) fuss, uproar; **fazer um** ~ make a scene

escandaloso /iskãda'lozu/ a (chocante) scandalous; (espalhafatoso) outrageous, loud

Escandinávia /iskãdʒi'navia/ f Scandinavia

escandinavo /iskãdʒi'navu/ a & m Scandinavian

escanga|lhado /iskãga'ʎadu/ a broken; ~**lhar** vt break up; ~**lhar-se** vpr fall to pieces; ~**lhar-se de rir** split one's sides laughing

escaninho /iska'niɲu/ m pigeonhole

escanteio /iskã'teju/ m corner

esca|pada /iska'pada/ f (fuga) escape; (aventura) escapade; ~**pamento** m exhaust; ~**par** vi ~**par a** ou **de** (livrar-se) escape from; (evitar) escape; ~**pou-lhe a palavra** the word slipped out; **o copo** ~**pou-me das mãos** the glass slipped out of my hands; **o nome me** ~**pa** the name escapes me; ~**par de boa** have a narrow escape; ~**patória** f way out; (desculpa) pretext; ~**pe** m escape; (de carro etc) exhaust; ~**pulir** vi escape (de from)

escaramuça /iskara'musa/ f skirmish

escaravelho /iskara'vɛʎu/ m beetle

escarcéu /iskar'sɛw/ m uproar, fuss

escarlate /iskar'latʃi/ a scarlet

escarnecer /iskarne'ser/ vt mock

escárnio /is'karniu/ m derision

escarpado /iskar'padu/ a steep

escarrado /iska'xadu/ m **ele é o pai** ~ he's the spitting image of his father

escarro /is'kaxu/ m phlegm

escas|sear /iskasi'ar/ vi run short; ~**sez** f shortage; ~**so** a (raro) scarce; (ralo) sparse

esca|vadeira /iskava'dera/ f digger; ~**var** vt excavate

esclare|cer /isklare'ser/ vt explain <fatos>; enlighten <pessoa>; ~**cer-se** vpr <fato> be explained; <pessoa> find out; ~**cimento** m (de pessoas) enlightenment; (de fatos) explanation

esclerosado /isklero'zadu/ a senile

escoar /isko'ar/ vt/i drain

esco|cês /isko'ses/ a (f ~**cesa**) Scottish □ m (f ~**cesa**) Scot

Escócia /is'kɔsia/ f Scotland

esco|la /is'kɔla/ f school; ~**la de samba** samba school; ~**lar** a school □ m/f schoolchild; ~**laridade** f schooling

esco|lha /is'koʎa/ f choice; ~**lher** vt choose

escol|ta /is'kɔwta/ f escort; ~tar vt escort

escombros /is'kõbruʃ/ m pl debris

escon|de-esconde /iskõdʒis'kõdʒi/ m hide-and-seek; ~der vt hide; ~der-se vpr hide; ~derijo m hiding place; (de bandidos) hideout; ~didas f pl às ~didas secretly

esco|ra /is'kɔra/ f prop; ~rar vt prop up; ~rar-se vpr <argumento etc> be based (em on)

escore /is'kɔri/ m score

escória /is'kɔria/ f scum, dross

escori|ação /iskoria'sãw/ f graze, abrasion; ~ar vt graze

escorpião /iskorpi'ãw/ m scorpion; Escorpião Scorpio

escorredor /iskoxe'dor/ m drainer

escorrega /isko'xega/ m slide

escorre|gador /iskoxega'dor/ m slide; ~gão m slip; ~gar vi slip

escor|rer /isko'xer/ vt drain □ vi trickle; ~rido a <cabelo> straight

escoteiro /isko'teru/ m boy scout

escotilha /isko'tʃiʎa/ f hatch

esco|va /is'kova/ f brush; fazer ~va no cabelo blow-dry one's hair; ~va de dentes toothbrush; ~var vt brush; ~vinha f cabelo à ~vinha crew-cut

escra|chado /iskra'ʃadu/ a (fam) a outspoken; ~char (fam) vt tell off

escra|vatura /iskrava'tura/ f slavery; ~vidão f slavery; ~vizar vt enslave; ~vo m slave

escre|vente /iskre'vẽtʃi/ m/f clerk; ~ver vt/i write

escri|ta /is'krita/ f writing; ~to pp de escrever □ a written; por ~to in writing; ~tor m writer; ~tório m office; (numa casa) study

escritu|ra /iskri'tura/ f (a Bíblia) scripture; (contrato) deed; ~ração f bookkeeping; ~rar vt keep, write up <contas>; draw up <documento>

escri|vaninha /iskriva'niɲa/ f bureau, writing desk; ~vão m (f ~vã) registrar

escrúpulo /is'krupulu/ m scruple

escrupuloso /iskrupu'lozu/ a scrupulous

escrutínio /iskru'tʃiniu/ m ballot

escu|dar /isku'dar/ vt shield; ~deria f team; ~do m shield; (moeda) escudo

escula|chado /iskula'ʃadu/ (fam) a sloppy; ~char (fam) vt mess up <coisa>; tell off <pessoa>; ~cho (fam) m (bagunça) mess; (bronca) telling-off

escul|pir /iskuw'pir/ vt sculpt; ~tor m sculptor; ~tura f sculpture; ~tural (pl ~turais) a statuesque

escuma /is'kuma/ f scum; ~deira f skimmer

escuna /is'kuna/ f schooner

escu|ras /is'kuraʃ/ f pl às ~ras in the dark; ~recer vt darken □ vi get dark; ~ridão f darkness; ~ro a & m dark

escuso /is'kuzu/ a shady

escu|ta /is'kuta/ f listening; estar à ~ta be listening; ~ta telefônica phone tapping; ~tar vt (perceber) hear; (prestar atenção a) listen to □ vi (poder ouvir) hear; (prestar atenção) listen

esdrúxulo /iz'druʃulu/ a weird

esfacelar /isfase'lar/ vt wreck

esfalfar /isfaw'far/ vt wear out; ~se vpr get worn out

esfaquear /isfaki'ar/ vt stab

esfarelar /isfare'lar/ vt crumble; ~se vpr crumble

esfarrapado /isfaxa'padu/ a ragged; <desculpa> lame

es|fera /is'fɛra/ f sphere; ~férico a spherical

esferográfi|co /isfero'grafiku/ a caneta ~ca ball-point pen

esfiapar /isfia'par/ vt fray; ~se vpr fray

esfinge /is'fĩʒi/ f sphinx

esfolar /isfo'lar/ vt skin; (fig) overcharge

esfomeado /isfomi'adu/ a starving, famished

esfor|çar-se /isfor'sarsi/ vpr make an effort; ~ço /o/ m effort; fazer ~ço make an effort

esfre|gaço /isfre'gasu/ m smear; ~gar vt rub; (para limpar) scrub

esfriar /isfri'ar/ vt cool □ vi cool (down); (sentir frio) get cold

esfumaçado /isfuma'sadu/ a smoky

esfuziante /isfuzi'ãtʃi/ a irrepressible, exuberant

esganar /izga'nar/ vt throttle

esganiçado /izgani'sadu/ a shrill

esgarçar /izgar'sar/ vt/i fray

esgo|tado /izgo'tadu/ a exhausted; <estoque, lotação> sold out; ~tamento m exhaustion; ~tamento nervoso nervous breakdown; ~tar vt exhaust; (gastar) use up; ~tar-se vpr <pessoa> become exhausted; <estoque, lotação> sell out; <recursos, provisões> run out; ~to /o/ m drain; (de detritos) sewer

esgri|ma /iz'grima/ f fencing; ~mir vt brandish □ vi fence; ~mista m/f fencer

esgrouvinhado /izgrovi'ɲadu/ a tousled, dishevelled

esgueirar-se /izge'rarsi/ vpr slip, sneak

esguelha /iz'geʎa/ f de ~ askew; <olhar> askance

esgui|char /izgi'ʃar/ vt/i spurt, squirt; ~cho m jet, spurt

esguio /iz'giɔ/ a slender

eslavo /iz'lavu/ a Slavic □ m Slav

esmaecer /izmaj'ser/ vi fade

esma|gador /izmaga'dor/ a <vitória, maioria> overwhelming; <provas> incontrovertible; ~gar vt crush

esmalte /iz'mawtʃi/ m enamel; ~ de unhas nail varnish

esmeralda /izme'rawda/ f emerald

esme|rar-se /izme'rarsi/ vpr take great care (em over); ~ro /e/ m great care

esmigalhar /izmiga'ʎar/ vt crumble <pão etc>; shatter <vidro, copo>; ~se <pão etc> crumble; <vidro, copo> shatter

esmiuçar /izmiu'sar/ vt examine in detail

esmo /'ezmu/ m a ~ <escolher> at random; <andar> aimlessly; <falar> nonsense

esmola /iz'mɔla/ f donation; pl charity

esmorecer /izmore'ser/ vi flag

esmurrar /izmu'xar/ vt punch

esno|bar /izno'bar/ vt snub □ vi be snobbish; ~be /iz'nɔbi/ a snobbish □ m/f snob; ~bismo m snobbishness

esotérico /ezo'tɛriku/ a esoteric

espa|çar /ispa'sar/ vt space out; make less frequent <visitas, consultas etc>; ~cial /p ~ciais/ a space; ~ço m space; (cultural etc) venue; ~çoso /o/ a spacious

espada /is'pada/ f sword; pl (naipe) spades; ~chim m swordsman

espádua /is'padua/ f shoulder blade

espaguete /ispa'getʃi/ m spaghetti

espaire|cer /ispajre'ser/ vi amuse □ vi relax; (dar uma volta) go for a walk; ~cimento m recreation

espaldar /ispaw'dar/ m back

espalhafato /ispaʎa'fatu/ m (barulho) fuss, uproar; (de roupa etc) extravagance; ~so /o/ a (barulhento) noisy, rowdy; (ostentoso) extravagant

espalhar /ispa'ʎar/ vt scatter; spread <notícia, terror etc>; shed <luz>; ~se vpr spread; <pessoas> spread out

espa|nador /ispana'dor/ m feather duster; ~nar vt dust

Espanha /is'paɲa/ f Spain

espa|nhol /ispa'ɲɔw/ (pl ~nhóis) a (f ~nhola) Spanish □ m (f ~nhola) Spaniard; (língua) Spanish; os ~nhóis the Spanish

espan|talho /ispã'taʎu/ m scarecrow; ~tar vt (admirar) amaze; (assustar) scare; (afugentar) drive away; ~tar-se vpr (admirar-se) be amazed; (assustar-se) get scared; ~to m (susto) fright; (admiração) amazement; ~toso /o/ a amazing

esparadrapo /ispara'drapu/ m sticking plaster

espargo /is'pargu/ (Port) m asparagus

esparramar /ispaxa'mar/ vt scatter; ~se vpr be scattered, spread

espartano /ispar'tanu/ a spartan

espartilho /ispar'tʃiʎu/ m corset

espas|mo /is'pazmu/ m spasm; ~módico a spasmodic

espatifar /ispatʃi'far/ vt smash; ~se vpr smash; <carro, avião> crash

especi|al /ispesi'aw/ (pl ~ais) a special; ~alidade f speciality; ~alista m/f specialist

especiali|zado /ispesiali'zadu/ a specialized; <mão-de-obra> skilled; ~zar-se vpr specialize (em in)

especiaria /ispesia'ria/ f spice

espécie /is'pɛsi/ f sort, kind; (de animais) species

especifi|cação /ispesifika'sãw/ f specification; ~car vt specify

específico /ispe'sifiku/ a specific

espécime /is'pesimi/ m specimen

espectador /ispekta'dor/ m (de TV) viewer; (de jogo, espetáculo) spectator; (de acidente etc) onlooker

espectro /is'pɛktru/ m (fantasma) spectre; (de cores) spectrum

especu|lação /ispekula'sãw/ f speculation; ~lador m speculator; ~lar vi speculate (sobre on); ~lativo a speculative

espe|lhar /ispe'ʎar/ vt mirror; ~lhar-se vpr be mirrored; ~lho /e/ m mirror; ~lho retrovisor rearview mirror

espelunca /ispe'lũka/ (fam) f dive

espera /is'pɛra/ f wait; à ~ de waiting for

esperan|ça /ispe'rãsa/ f hope; ~çoso /o/ a hopeful

esperar /ispe'rar/ vt (aguardar) wait for; (desejar) hope for; (contar com) expect □ vi wait (por for); fazer alg ~ keep s.o. waiting; espero que ele venha I hope (that) he comes; espero que sim/não I hope so/not

esperma /is'pɛrma/ m sperm

espernear /isperni'ar/ vi kick; (fig: reclamar) kick up

esper|talhão /isperta'ʎãw/ m (f ~talhona) wise guy; ~teza /e/ f cleverness; (uma) clever move; ~to /e/ a clever

espes|so /is'pesu/ a thick; ~sura f thickness

espe|tacular /ispetaku'lar/ a spectacular; ~táculo m (no teatro etc) show; (cena impressionante) spectacle; ~taculoso /o/ a spectacular

espe|tar /ispe'tar/ vt (cravar) stick; (furar) skewer; ~tar-se vpr (cravar-se) stick; (ferir-se) prick o.s.; ~tinho _m_ skewer; (_de carne etc_) kebab; ∼to /e/ _m_ spit

espevitado /ispevi'tadu/ _a_ cheeky

espezinhar /ispezi'ɲar/ _vt_ walk all over

espi|a /is'pia/ _m/f_ spy; ∼ão _m_ (_f_ ∼ã) spy; ∼ada _f_ peep; ∼ar _vt_ (_observar_) spy on; (_aguardar_) watch for □ _vi_ peer, peep

espicaçar /ispika'sar/ _vt_ goad <_pessoa_>; excite <_imaginação, curiosidade_>

espichar /ispi'ʃar/ _vt_ stretch □ _vi_ shoot up; ∼-se _vpr_ stretch out

espiga /is'piga/ _f_ (_de trigo etc_) ear; (_de milho_) cob

espina|fração /ispinafra'sãw/ (_fam_) _f_ telling-off; ∼frar (_fam_) _vt_ tell off; ∼fre _m_ spinach

espingarda /ispĩ'garda/ _f_ rifle, shotgun

espinha /is'piɲa/ _f_ (_de peixe_) bone; (_na pele_) spot; ∼ dorsal spine

espinho /is'piɲu/ _m_ thorn; ∼so /o/ _a_ thorny; (_fig_) difficult, tough

espio|nagem /ispio'naʒẽ/ _f_ espionage, spying; ∼nar _vt_ spy on □ _vi_ spy

espi|ral /ispi'raw/ (_pl_ ∼rais) _a_ & _f_ spiral

espírita /is'pirita/ _a_ & _m/f_ spiritualist

espiritismo /ispiri'tʃizmu/ _m_ spiritualism

espírito /is'piritu/ _m_ spirit; (_graça_) wit

espiritu|al /ispiritu'aw/ (_pl_ ∼ais) _a_ spiritual; ∼oso /o/ _a_ witty

espir|rar /ispi'xar/ _vt_ spurt □ _vi_ <_pessoa_> sneeze; <_lama, tinta etc_> spatter; <_fogo, lenha, fritura etc_> spit; ∼ro _m_ sneeze

esplêndido /is'plẽʒidu/ _a_ splendid

esplendor /isplẽ'dor/ _m_ splendour

espoleta /ispo'leta/ _f_ fuse

espoliar /ispoli'ar/ _vt_ plunder, pillage

espólio /is'poliu/ _m_ (_herdado_) estate; (_roubado_) spoils

espon|ja /is'pôʒa/ _f_ sponge; ∼joso /o/ _a_ spongy

espon|taneidade /ispôtanej'dadʒi/ _f_ spontaneity; ∼tâneo _a_ spontaneous

espora /is'pɔra/ _f_ spur

esporádico /ispo'radʒiku/ _a_ sporadic

esporear /ispori'ar/ _vt_ spur on

espor|te /is'pɔrtʃi/ _m_ sport □ _a invar_ <_roupa_> casual; _carro_ ∼te sports car; ∼tista _m/f_ sportsman (_f_ -woman); ∼tiva _f_ sense of humour; ∼tivo _a_ sporting

espo|sa /is'poza/ _f_ wife; ∼so _m_ husband

espregui|çadeira /ispregiza'dera/ _f_ (_tipo cadeira_) deckchair; (_tipo cama_) sun lounger; ∼çar-se _vpr_ stretch

esprei|ta /is'prejta/ _f_ ficar à ∼ta lie in wait; ∼tar _vt_ stalk <_caça, vítima_>; spy on <_vizinhos, inimigos etc_>; look out for <_ocasião_> □ _vi_ peep, spy

espre|medor /ispreme'dor/ _m_ squeezer; ∼mer _vt_ squeeze; wring out <_roupa_>; squash <_pessoa_>; ∼mer-se _vpr_ squeeze up

espu|ma /is'puma/ _f_ foam; ∼ma de borracha foam rubber; ∼mante _a_ <_vinho_> sparkling; ∼mar _vi_ foam, froth

espúrio /is'puriu/ _a_ spurious

esqua|dra /is'kwadra/ _f_ squad; ∼dra de polícia (_Port_) police station; ∼drão _m_ squadron; ∼dria _f_ doors and windows; ∼drinhar _vt_ explore; ∼dro _m_ set square

esqualidez /iskwali'des/ _f_ squalor

esquálido /is'kwalidu/ _a_ squalid

esquartejar /iskwarte'ʒar/ _vt_ chop up

esque|cer /iske'ser/ _vt/i_ forget; ∼cer-se de forget; ∼cido _a_ forgotten; (_com memória fraca_) forgetful; ∼cimento _m_ oblivion; (_memória fraca_) forgetfulness

esque|lético /iske'letʃiku/ _a_ skinny, skeleton-like; ∼leto /e/ _m_ skeleton

esque|ma /is'kema/ _m_ outline, draft; (_operação_) scheme; ∼ma de segurança security operation; ∼mático _a_ schematic

esquentar /iskẽ'tar/ _vt_ warm up □ _vi_ warm up; <_roupa_> be warm; ∼-se _vpr_ get annoyed; ∼ a cabeça (_fam_) get worked up

esquer|da /is'kerda/ _f_ left; à ∼da (_posição_) on the left; (_direção_) to the left; ∼dista _a_ left-wing □ _m/f_ left-winger; ∼do /e/ _a_ left

esqui /is'ki/ _m_ ski; (_esporte_) skiing; ∼ aquático water skiing; ∼ador _m_ skier; ∼ar _vi_ ski

esquilo /is'kilu/ _m_ squirrel

esquina /is'kina/ _f_ corner

esquisi|tice /iskizi'tʃisi/ _f_ strangeness; (_uma_) strange thing; ∼to _a_ strange

esqui|var-se /iski'varsi/ _vpr_ dodge out of the way; ∼var-se de dodge; ∼vo _a_ elusive; <_pessoa_> aloof, antisocial

esquizo|frenia /iskizofre'nia/ _f_ schizophrenia; ∼frênico _a_ & _m_ schizophrenic

es|sa /'ɛsa/ _pron_ that (one); ∼sa é boa that's a good one; ∼sa não come off it; por ∼sas e outras for these and other reasons; ∼se /e/ _a_ that; _pl_ those; (_fam: este_) this; _pl_ these □ _pron_ that one; _pl_ those; (_fam: este_) this one; _pl_ these

essência /e'sẽsia/ _f_ essence

essenci|al /eseˈsiaw/ (pl ~ais) a essential; o ~al what is essential

estabele|cer /estabeleˈser/ vt establish; ~cer-se vpr establish o.s.; ~cimento m establishment

estabili|dade /istabiliˈdadʒi/ f stability; ~zar vt stabilize; ~zar-se vpr stabilize

estábulo /isˈtabulu/ m cowshed

estaca /isˈtaka/ f stake; (de barraca) peg; voltar à ~ zero go back to square one

estação /istaˈsãw/ f (do ano) season; (ferroviária etc) station; ~ balneária seaside resort

estacar /istaˈkar/ vi stop short

estaciona|mento /istasionaˈmẽtu/ m (ação) parking; (lugar) car park, (Amer) parking lot; ~r vt/i park

estada /isˈtada/ f, estadia /istaˈdʒia/ f stay

estádio /isˈtadʒiu/ m stadium

esta|dista /istaˈdʒista/ m/f statesman (f -woman); ~do m state; ~do civil marital status; ~do de espírito state of mind; Estados Unidos da América United States of America; Estado-Maior m Staff; ~dual (pl ~duais) a state

esta|fa /isˈtafa/ f exhaustion; ~fante a exhausting; ~far vt tire out; ~far-se vpr get tired out

estagi|ar /istaʒiˈar/ vi do a traineeship; ~ário m trainee

estágio /isˈtaʒiu/ m traineeship

estag|nado /istagiˈnadu/ a stagnant; ~nar vi stagnate

estalagem /istaˈlaʒẽ/ f inn

estalar /istaˈlar/ vt (quebrar) crack; (fazer barulho com) click □ vi crack

estaleiro /istaˈleru/ m shipyard

estalo /isˈtalu/ m crack; (de dedos, língua) click; me deu um ~ it clicked (in my mind)

estam|pa /isˈtãpa/ f print; ~pado a (tecido) patterned □ m (desenho) pattern; (tecido) print; ~par vt print

estampido /istãˈpidu/ m bang

estancar /istãˈkar/ vt staunch; ~-se vpr dry up

estância /isˈtãsia/ f ~ hidromineral spa

estandarte /istãˈdartʃi/ m banner

estanho /isˈtaɲu/ m tin

estanque /isˈtãki/ a watertight

estante /isˈtãtʃi/ f bookcase

estapafúrdio /istapaˈfurdʒiu/ a weird, odd

estar /isˈtar/ vi be;(~ em casa) be in; está chovendo, (Port) está a chover it's raining; ~ com have; ~ com calor/sono be hot/sleepy; ~ para terminar be about to finish; ele não está para ninguém he's not avail-

able to see anyone; o trabalho está por terminar the work is yet to be finished

estardalhaço /istardaˈʎasu/ m (barulho) fuss; (ostentação) extravagance

estarre|cedor /istaxeseˈdor/ a horrifying; ~cer vt horrify; ~cer-se vpr be horrified

esta|tal /istaˈtaw/ (pl ~tais) a state-owned □ f state company

estate|lado /istateˈladu/ a sprawling; ~lar vt knock down; ~lar-se vpr go sprawling

estático /isˈtatʃiku/ a static

estatísti|ca /istaˈtʃistʃika/ f statistics; ~co a statistical

estati|zação /istatʃizaˈsãw/ f nationalization; ~zar vt nationalize

estátua /isˈtatua/ f statue

estatueta /istatuˈeta/ f statuette

estatura /istaˈtura/ f stature

estatuto /istaˈtutu/ m statute

está|vel /isˈtavew/ (pl ~veis) a stable

este¹ /ˈestʃi/ m a invar & m east

este² /ˈestʃi/ a this; pl these □ pron this one; pl these; (mencionado por último) the latter

esteio /isˈteju/ m prop, (fig) mainstay

esteira /isˈtera/ f (tapete) mat; (rastro) wake

estelionato /istelioˈnatu/ m fraud

estender /istẽˈder/ vt (desdobrar) spread out; (alongar) stretch; (ampliar) extend; hold out <mão>; hang out <roupa>; roll out <massa>; draw out <conversa>; ~-se vpr (deitar-se) stretch out; (ir longe) stretch, extend; ~-se sobre dwell on

esteno|datilógrafo /istenodatʃiˈlɔgrafu/ m shorthand typist; ~grafia f shorthand

estepe /isˈtɛpi/ m spare wheel

esterco /isˈterku/ m dung

estéreo /isˈteriu/ a invar stereo

estere|otipado /isteriotʃiˈpadu/ a stereotypical; ~ótipo m stereotype

esté|ril /isˈtɛriw/ (pl ~reis) a sterile

esterili|dade /isteriliˈdadʒi/ f sterility; ~zar vt sterilize

esterli|no /isterˈlino/ a libra ~na pound sterling

esteróide /isteˈrɔjdʒi/ m steroid

estética /isˈtɛtʃika/ f aesthetics

esteticista /istetʃiˈsista/ m/f beautician

estético /isˈtɛtʃiku/ a aesthetic

estetoscópio /istetosˈkɔpiu/ m stethoscope

estiagem /istʃiˈaʒẽ/ f dry spell

estibordo /istʃiˈbordu/ m starboard

esti|cada /istʃiˈkada/ f dar uma ~cada go on; ~car vt stretch □ (fam) vi go on; ~car-se vpr stretch out estigma /iʃˈtʃigima/ m stigma; ~tizar vt brand (de as)

estilhaçar /iʃtʃiʎaˈsar/ vt shatter; ~çar-se vpr shatter; ~ço m shard, fragment

estilingue /iʃtʃiˈlĩgi/ m catapult

estilismo /iʃtʃiˈlizmu/ m fashion design; ~ta m/f fashion designer

estilístico /iʃtʃiˈliʃtʃiku/ a stylistic; ~lizar vt stylize; ~lo m style; ~lo de vida lifestyle

estima /eʃˈtʃima/ f esteem; ~mação f estimation; cachorro de ~mação pet dog; ~mado a esteemed; Estimado Senhor Dear Sir; ~mar vt value <bens, jóias etc> (em at); estimate <valor, preço etc> (em at); think highly of <pessoa>; ~mativa f estimate

estimulante /iʃtʃimuˈlãtʃi/ a stimulating □ m stimulant; ~lar vt stimulate; (incentivar) encourage

estímulo /iʃˈtʃimulu/ m stimulus; (incentivo) incentive

estio /iʃˈtʃiu/ m summer

estipulação /iʃtʃipulaˈsãw/ f stipulation; ~lar vt stipulate

estirar /iʃtʃiˈrar/ vt stretch; ~se vpr stretch

estirpe /iʃˈtʃirpi/ f stock, line

estivador /iʃtʃivaˈdor/ m docker

estocada /iʃtʃoˈkada/ f thrust

estocar /iʃtoˈkar/ vt stock □ vi stock up

Estocolmo /iʃtoˈkɔwmu/ f Stockholm

estofar /iʃtoˈfar/ vt upholster <móveis>; ~fo /o/ m upholstery

estóico /iʃˈtɔjku/ a & m stoic

estojo /iʃˈtoʒu/ m case

estômago /iʃˈtomagu/ m stomach

Estônia /iʃˈtonia/ f Estonia

estonteante /iʃtõtʃiˈãtʃi/ a stunning, mind-boggling; ~ar vt stun

estopim /iʃtoˈpĩ/ m fuse; (fig) flashpoint

estoque /iʃˈtɔki/ m stock

estore /iʃˈtɔri/ m blind

estória /iʃˈtɔria/ f story

estorvar /iʃtorˈvar/ vt hinder; obstruct <entrada, trânsito>; ~vo /o/ m hindrance

estourado /iʃtoˈradu/ a <pessoa> explosive; ~rar vi <bomba, escândalo, pessoa> blow up; <pneu> burst; <guerra> break out; <moda, cantor etc> make it big; ~ro m (de bomba, moda etc) explosion; (de pessoa) outburst; (de pneu) blowout; (de guerra) outbreak

estrábico /iʃˈtrabiku/ a <olhos> squinty; <pessoa> squint-eyed

estrabismo /iʃtraˈbizmu/ m squint

estraçalhar /iʃtrasaˈʎar/ vt tear to pieces

estrada /iʃˈtrada/ f road; ~ de ferro railway, (Amer) railroad; ~ de rodagem highway; ~ de terra dirt road

estrado /iʃˈtradu/ m podium; (de cama) base

estraga-prazeres /iʃtragapraˈzeris/ m/f invar spoilsport

estragão /iʃtraˈgãw/ m tarragon

estragar /iʃtraˈgar/ vt (tornar desagradável) spoil; (acabar com) ruin □ vi (quebrar) break; (apodrecer) go off; ~go m damage; pl damage; (da guerra, do tempo) ravages

estrangeiro /iʃtrãˈʒeru/ a foreign □ m foreigner; do ~ from abroad; para o/no ~ abroad

estrangular /iʃtrãguˈlar/ vt strangle

estranhar /iʃtraˈɲar/ vt (achar estranho) find strange; (não se adaptar a) find it hard to get used to; (não se sentir à vontade com) be shy with; ~nhar que find it strange that; estou te ~nhando that's not like you; não é de se ~nhar it's not surprising; ~nheza /e/ f (esquisitice) strangeness; (surpresa) surprise; ~nho a strange □ m stranger

estratagema /iʃtrataˈʒema/ m stratagem

estratégia /iʃtraˈtɛʒia/ f strategy; ~gico a strategic

estrato /iʃˈtratu/ m (camada) stratum; (nuvem) stratus; ~sfera f stratosphere

estreante /iʃtriˈãtʃi/ a new □ m/f newcomer; ~ar vt premiere <peça, filme>; embark on <carreira>; wear for the first time <roupa> □ vi <pessoa> make one's début; <filme, peça> open

estrebaria /iʃtrebaˈria/ f stable

estréia /iʃˈtreja/ f (de pessoa) début; (de filme, peça) première

estreitar /iʃtrejˈtar/ vt narrow; take in <vestido>; make closer <relações, laços> □ vi narrow; ~tar-se vpr <relações> become closer; ~to a narrow; <relações, laços> close; <saia> straight □ m strait

estrela /iʃˈtrela/ f star; ~lado a <céu> starry; <ovo> fried; ~lado por <filme etc> starring; ~la-do-mar (pl ~las-do-mar) f starfish; ~lar vt fry <ovo>; star in <filme, peça>; ~lato m stardom; ~lismo m star quality

estremecer /iʃtremeˈser/ vt shake; strain <relações, amizade> □ vi shudder; <relações, amizade> become strained; ~cimento m shudder; (de relações, amizade) strain

estrepar-se /iʃtreˈparsi/ (fam) vpr come a cropper

estrépito /is'trɛpitu/ m noise; com ~ noisily

estrepitoso /istrepi'tozu/ a noisy; <*sucesso etc*> resounding

estres|sante /istre'sãtʃi/ a stressful; ~**sar** vt stress; ~**se** /ɛ/ m stress

estria /is'tria/ f streak; (*no corpo*) stretch mark

estribeira /istri'bera/ f stirrup; **perder as ~s** lose control

estribilho /istri'biʎu/ m chorus

estribo /is'tribu/ m stirrup

estridente /istri'dẽtʃi/ a strident

estripulia /istripu'lia/ f antic

estrito /is'tritu/ a strict

estrofe /is'trɔfi/ f stanza, verse

estrogonofe /istrogo'nɔfi/ m stroganoff

estrógeno /is'trɔʒenu/ m oestrogen

estron|do /is'trõdu/ m crash; ~**doso** /o/ a loud; <*aplausos*> thunderous; <*sucesso, fracasso*> resounding

estropiar /istropi'ar/ vt cripple <*pessoa*>; mangle <*palavras*>

estrume /is'trumi/ m manure

estrutu|ra /istru'tura/ f structure; ~**ral** (pl ~**rais**) a structural; ~**rar** vt structure

estuário /istu'ariu/ m estuary

estudan|te /istu'dãtʃi/ m/f student; ~**til** (pl ~**tis**) a student

estudar /istu'dar/ vt/i study

estúdio /is'tudʒiu/ m studio

estu|dioso /istudʒi'ozu/ a studious □ m scholar; ~**do** /u/ m study

estufa /is'tufa/ f (*para plantas*) greenhouse; (*de aquecimento*) stove; ~**do** m stew

estupefato /istupe'fatu/ a dumbfounded

estupendo /istu'pẽdu/ a stupendous

estupidez /istupi'des/ f (*grosseria*) rudeness; (*uma*) rude thing; (*burrice*) stupidity; (*uma*) stupid thing

estúpido /is'tupidu/ a (*grosso*) rude, coarse; (*burro*) stupid □ m lout

estupor /istu'por/ m stupor

estu|prador /istupra'dor/ m rapist; ~**prar** vt rape; ~**pro** m rape

esturricar /istuxi'kar/ vt parch

esvair-se /izva'irsi/ vpr fade; ~ **em sangue** bleed to death

esvaziar /izvazi'ar/ vt empty; ~**se** vpr empty

esverdeado /izverdʒi'adu/ a greenish

esvoa|çante /izvoa'sãtʃi/ a <*cabelo*> fly-away; ~**çar** vi flutter

eta /'eta/ int what a

etapa /e'tapa/ f stage; (*de corrida, turnê etc*) leg

etário /e'tariu/ a age

éter /'ɛter/ m ether

etéreo /e'tɛriu/ a ethereal

eter|nidade /eterni'dadʒi/ f eternity; ~**no** /ɛ/ a eternal

éti|ca /'ɛtʃika/ f ethics; ~**co** a ethical

etimo|logia /etʃimolo'ʒia/ f etymology; ~**lógico** a etymological

etíope /e'tʃiopi/ a & m/f Ethiopian

Etiópia /etʃi'ɔpia/ f Ethiopia

etique|ta /etʃi'keta/ f (*rótulo*) label; (*bons modos*) etiquette; ~**tar** vt label

étnico /'ɛtʃiniku/ a ethnic

eu /ew/ pron I □ m self; **mais alto do que ~** taller than me; **sou ~** it's me

EUA m pl USA

eucalipto /ewka'liptu/ m eucalyptus

eufemismo /ewfe'mizmu/ m euphemism

euforia /ewfo'ria/ f euphoria

Europa /ew'rɔpa/ f Europe

euro|peu /ewro'pew/ a & m (f ~**péia**) European

eutanásia /ewta'nazia/ f euthanasia

evacu|ação /evakua'sãw/ f evacuation; ~**ar** vt evacuate

evadir /eva'dʒir/ vt evade; ~**se** vpr escape (*de* from)

evan|gelho /evã'ʒɛʎu/ m gospel; ~**gélico** a evangelical

evaporar /evapo'rar/ vt evaporate; ~**se** vpr evaporate

eva|são /eva'zãw/ f escape; (*fiscal etc*) evasion; ~**são escolar** truancy; ~**siva** f excuse; ~**sivo** a evasive

even|to /e'vẽtu/ m event; ~**tual** (pl ~**tuais**) a possible; ~**tualidade** f eventuality

evidência /evi'dẽsia/ f evidence

eviden|ciar /evidẽsi'ar/ vt show up; ~**ciar-se** vpr show up; ~**te** a obvious, evident

evi|tar /evi'tar/ vt avoid; ~**tar de beber** avoid drinking; ~**tável** (pl ~**táveis**) a avoidable

evocar /evo'kar/ vt call to mind, evoke <*passado etc*>; call up <*espíritos etc*>

evolu|ção /evolu'sãw/ f evolution; ~**ir** vi evolve

exacerbar /ezaser'bar/ vt exacerbate

exage|rado /ezaʒe'radu/ a over the top; ~**rar** vt (*atribuir proporções irreais a*) exaggerate; (*fazer em excesso*) overdo □ vi (*ao falar*) exaggerate; (*exceder-se*) overdo it; ~**ro** /e/ m exaggeration

exa|lação /ezala'sãw/ f fume; (*agradável*) scent; ~**lar** vt give off <*perfume etc*>

exal|tação /ezawta'sãw/ f (*excitação*) agitation; (*engrandecimento*) exaltation; ~**tar** vt (*excitar*) agitate; (*enfurecer*) infuriate; (*louvar*) exalt; ~**tar-se** vpr (*excitar-se*) get agitated; (*enfurecer-se*) get furious

exa|me /e'zami/ m examination; (*na escola*) exam(ination); ~**me de**

sangue blood test; ~minar *vt* examine

exaspe|ração /ezaspera'sãw/ *f* exasperation; ~rar *vt* exasperate; ~rar-se *vpr* get exasperated

exa|tidão /ezatʃi'dãw/ *f* exactness; ~to *a* exact

exaurir /ezaw'rir/ *vt* exhaust; ~-se *vpr* become exhausted

exaus|tivo /ezaws'tʃivu/ *a* exhaustive; <*trabalho*> exhausting; ~to *a* exhausted

exceção /ese'sãw/ *f* exception; abrir ~ make an exception; com ~ de with the exception of

exce|dente /ese'dẽtʃi/ *a & m* excess, surplus; ~der *vt* exceed; ~der-se *vpr* overdo it

exce|lência /ese'lẽsia/ *f* excellence; (*tratamento*) excellency; ~lente *a* excellent

excentricidade /esẽtrisi'dadʒi/ *f* eccentricity

excêntrico /e'sẽtriku/ *a & m* eccentric

excep|ção /iʃse'sãw/ (*Port*) *f* veja exceção; ~cional (*pl* ~cionais) *a* exceptional; (*deficiente*) handicapped

exces|sivo /ese'sivu/ *a* excessive; ~so /ɛ/ *m* excess; ~so de bagagem excess baggage; ~so de velocidade speeding

exce|to /e'sɛtu/ *prep* except; ~tuar *vt* except

exci|tação /esita'sãw/ *f* excitement; ~tante *a* exciting; ~tar *vt* excite; ~tar-se *vpr* get excited

excla|mação /isklama'sãw/ *f* exclamation; ~mar *vt/i* exclaim

exclu|ir /isklu'ir/ *vt* exclude; ~são *f* exclusion; com ~são de with the exclusion of; ~sividade *f* exclusive rights; com ~sividade exclusively; ~sivo *a* exclusive; ~so *a* excluded

excomungar /iskomũ'gar/ *vt* excommunicate

excremento /iskre'mẽtu/ *m* excrement

excur|são /iskur'sãw/ *f* excursion; (*a pé*) hike, walk; ~sionista *m/f* day-tripper; (*a pé*) hiker, walker

execu|ção /ezeku'sãw/ *f* execution; ~tante *m/f* performer; ~tar *vt* carry out <*ordem, plano etc*>; perform <*papel, música*>; execute <*preso, criminoso etc*>; ~tivo *a & m* executive

exem|plar /ezẽ'plar/ *a* exemplary □ *m* (*de espécie*) example; (*de livro, jornal etc*) copy; ~plificar *vt* exemplify

exemplo /e'zẽplu/ *m* example; a ~ de following the example of; por ~ for example; dar o ~ set an example

exequível /eze'kwivew/ *a* (*pl* ~veis) *a* feasible

exer|cer /ezer'ser/ *vt* exercise; exert <*pressão, influência*>; carry on <*profissão*>; ~cício *m* exercise; (*mil*) drill; (*de profissão*) practice; (*financeiro*) financial year; ~citar *vt* exercise; practise <*ofício*>; ~citar-se *vpr* train

exército /e'zɛrsitu/ *m* army

exibição /ezibi'sãw/ *f* (*de filme, passaporte etc*) showing; (*de talento, força, ostentação*) show

exibicionis|mo /ezibisio'nizmu/ *m* exhibitionism; ~ta *a & m/f* exhibitionist

exi|bido /ezi'bidu/ <*pessoa*> pretentious □ *m* show-off; ~bir *vt* show; (*ostentar*) show off; ~bir-se *vpr* (*ostentar-se*) show off

exi|gência /ezi'ʒẽsia/ *f* demand; ~gente *a* demanding; ~gir *vt* demand

exíguo /e'zigwu/ *a* (*muito pequeno*) tiny; (*escasso*) minimal

exi|lado /ezi'lado/ *a* exiled □ *m* exile; ~lar *vt* exile; ~lar-se *vpr* go into exile

exílio /e'ziliu/ *m* exile

exímio /e'zimiu/ *a* distinguished

eximir /ezi'mir/ *vt* exempt (de from); ~-se de get out of

exis|tência /ezis'tẽsia/ *f* existence; ~tencial (*pl* ~tenciais) *a* existential; ~tente *a* existing; ~tir *vi* exist

êxito /'ezitu/ *m* success; (*música, filme etc*) hit; ter ~ succeed

êxodo /'ezodu/ *m* exodus

exonerar /ezone'rar/ *vt* (*de cargo*) dismiss, sack; ~-se *vpr* resign

exorbitante /ezorbi'tãtʃi/ *a* exorbitant

exor|cismo /ezor'sizmu/ *m* exorcism; ~cista *m/f* exorcist; ~cizar *vt* exorcize

exótico /e'zɔtʃiku/ *a* exotic

expan|dir /ispã'dʒir/ *vt* spread; ~dir-se *vpr* spread; <*pessoa*> open up; ~dir-se sobre expand upon; ~são *f* expansion; ~sivo *a* expansive, open

expatri|ado /ispatri'ado/ *a & m* expatriate; ~ar-se *vpr* leave one's country

expectativa /ispekta'tʃiva/ *f* expectation; na ~ de expecting; estar na ~ wait to see what happens; ~ de vida life expectancy

expedição /espedʒi'sãw/ *f* (*de encomendas, cartas*) dispatch; (*de passaporte, diploma etc*) issue; (*viagem*) expedition

expediente /ispedʒi'ẽtʃi/ *a* <*pessoa*> resourceful □ *m* (*horário*) working hours; (*meios*) expedient; meio ~ part-time

expe|dir /ispe'dʒir/ *vt* dispatch <*encomendas, cartas*>; issue <*passaporte, diploma*>; ~**dito** *a* prompt, quick

expelir /ispe'lir/ *vt* expel

experi|ência /isperi'ẽsia/ *f* experience; (*teste, tentativa*) experiment; ~**ente** *a* experienced

experimen|tação /isperimẽta'sãw/ *f* experimentation; ~**tado** *a* experienced; ~**tar** *vt* (*provar*) try out; try on <*roupa*>; try <*comida*>; (*sentir, viver*) experience; ~**to** *m* experiment

expi|ração /espira'sãw/ *f* (*vencimento*) expiry; (*de ar*) exhalation; ~**rar** *vt* exhale □ *vi* (*morrer, vencer*) expire; (*expelir ar*) breath out, exhale

expli|cação /isplika'sãw/ *f* explanation; ~**car** *vt* explain; ~**car-se** *vpr* explain o.s.; ~**cável** (*pl* ~**cáveis**) *a* explainable

explicitar /isplisi'tar/ *vt* set out

explícito /is'plisitu/ *a* explicit

explodir /isplo'dʒir/ *vt* explode □ *vi* explode; <*ator etc*> make it big

explo|ração /isplora'sãw/ *f* (*uso, abuso*) exploitation; (*pesquisa*) exploration; ~**rar** *vt* (*tirar proveito de*) exploit; (*esquadrinhar*) explore

explo|são /isplo'zãw/ *f* explosion; ~**sivo** *a & m* explosive

expor /es'por/ *vt* (*sujeitar, arriscar*) expose (**a** to); display <*mercadorias*>; exhibit <*obras de arte*>; (*explicar*) expound; ~ **a vida** risk one's life; ~**se** *vpr* expose o.s. (**a** to)

expor|tação /isporta'sãw/ *f* export; ~**tador** *a* exporting □ *m* exporter; ~**tadora** *f* export company; ~**tar** *vt* export

exposi|ção /ispozi'sãw/ *f* (*de arte etc*) exhibition; (*de mercadorias*) display; (*de filme fotográfico*) exposure; (*explicação*) exposition; ~**tor** *m* exhibitor

exposto /is'postu/ *a* (*exposto*) on show; <*mercadoria, obra de arte*> on display

expres|são /ispre'sãw/ *f* expression; ~**sar** *vt* express; ~**sar-se** *vpr* express o.s.; ~**sivo** *a* expressive; <*número, quantia*> significant; ~**so** /ɛ/ *a & m* express

exprimir /ispri'mir/ *vt* express; ~**se** *vpr* express o.s.

expropriar /ispropri'ar/ *vt* expropriate

expul|são /ispuw'sãw/ *f* expulsion; (*de jogador*) sending off; ~**sar** *vt* (*de escola, partido, país etc*) expel; (*de clube, bar, festa etc*) throw out; (*de jogo*) send off; ~**so** *pp de* **expulsar**

expur|gar /ispur'gar/ *vt* purge; expurgate <*livro*>; ~**go** *m* purge

êxtase /'estazi/ *f* ecstasy

extasiado /istazi'adu/ *a* ecstatic

exten|são /istẽ'sãw/ *f* extension; (*tamanho, alcance, duração*) extent; (*de terreno*) expanse; ~**sivo** *a* extensive; ~**so** *a* extensive; **por** ~**so** in full

extenu|ante /istenu'ãtʃi/ *a* wearing, tiring; ~**ar** *vt* tire out; ~**ar-se** *vpr* tire o.s. out

exterior /isteri'or/ *a* outside, exterior; <*aparência*> outward; <*relações, comércio etc*> foreign □ *m* outside, exterior; (*de pessoa*) exterior; **o** ~ (*outros países*) abroad; **para o/no** ~ abroad

exter|minar /istermi'nar/ *vt* exterminate; ~**mínio** *m* extermination

exter|nar /ister'nar/ *vt* show; ~**na** /ɛ/ *f* location shot; ~**no** /ɛ/ *a* external; <*dívida etc*> foreign □ *m* day-pupil

extin|ção /istʃĩ'sãw/ *f* extinction; ~**guir** *vt* extinguish <*fogo*>; wipe out <*dívida, animal, povo*>; ~**guir-se** *vpr* <*fogo, luz*> go out; <*animal, planta*> become extinct; ~**to** *a* extinct; <*organização, pessoa*> defunct; ~**tor** *m* fire extinguisher

extirpar /istʃir'par/ *vt* remove <*tumor etc*>; uproot <*ervas daninhas*>; eradicate <*abusos*>

extor|quir /istor'kir/ *vt* extort; ~**são** *f* extortion

extra /'estra/ *a & m/f* extra; **horas** ~**s** overtime

extração /istra'sãw/ *f* extraction; (*da loteria*) draw

extraconju|gal /estrakõʒu'gaw/ (*pl* ~**gais**) *a* extramarital

extracurricular /estrakuriku'lar/ *a* extracurricular

extradi|ção /istradʒi'sãw/ *f* extradition; ~**tar** *vt* extradite

extrair /istra'ir/ *vt* extract; draw <*números da loteria*>

extrajudici|al /estraʒudʒisi'aw/ (*pl* ~**ais**) *a* out-of-court; ~**almente** *adv* out of court

extraordinário /istraordʒi'nariu/ *a* extraordinary

extrapolar /istrapo'lar/ *vt* (*exceder*) overstep; (*calcular*) extrapolate □ *vi* overstep the mark, go too far

extra-sensori|al /estrasẽsori'aw/ (*pl* ~**ais**) *a* extra-sensory

extraterrestre /estrate'xestri/ *a & m* extraterrestrial

extrato /is'tratu/ *m* extract; (*de conta*) statement

extrava|gância /istrava'gãsia/ *f* extravagance; ~**gante** *a* extravagant

extravasar /istrava'zar/ *vt* release, let out <*emoções, sentimentos*> □ *vi* overflow

extra|viado /istravi'adu/ *a* lost; ~**viar** *vt* lose, mislay <*papéis, car-*

ta>; lead astray <*pessoa*>; embezzle <*dinheiro*>; ∼**viar-se** *vpr* go astray; <*carta*> get lost; ∼**vio** *m* (*perda*) misplacement; (*de dinheiro*) embezzlement

extre|midade /estremi'dadʒi/ *f* end; (*do corpo*) extremity; ∼**mismo** *m* extremism; ∼**mista** *a & m/f* extremist; ∼**mo** /e/ *a & m* extreme; **o Extremo Oriente** the Far East; ∼**moso** /o/ *a* doting

extrovertido /istrover'tʃido/ *a & m* extrovert

exube|rância /ezube'rãsia/ *f* exuberance; ∼**rante** *a* exuberant

exultar /ezuw'tar/ *vi* exult

exumar /ezu'mar/ *vt* exhume <*cadáver*>; dig up <*documentos etc*>

F

fã /fã/ *m/f* fan

fábrica /'fabrika/ *f* factory

fabri|cação /fabrika'sãw/ *f* manufacture; ∼**cante** *m/f* manufacturer; ∼**car** *vt* manufacture; (*inventar*) fabricate

fábula /'fabula/ *f* fable; (*fam: dinheirão*) fortune

fabuloso /fabu'lozu/ *a* fabulous

faca /'faka/ *f* knife; ∼**da** *f* knife blow; **dar uma** ∼**da em** (*fig*) get some money off

façanha /fa'saɲa/ *f* feat

facção /fak'sãw/ *f* faction

face /'fasi/ *f* face; (*do rosto*) cheek; ∼**ta** /e/ *f* facet

fachada /fa'ʃada/ *f* façade

facho /'faʃu/ *m* beam

faci|al /fasi'aw/ (*pl* ∼**ais**) *a* facial

fá|cil /'fasiw/ (*pl* ∼**ceis**) *a* easy; <*pessoa*> easy-going

facili|dade /fasili'dadʒi/ *f* ease; (*talento*) facility; ∼**tar** *vt* facilitate

fã-clube /fã'klubi/ *m* fan club

fac-símile /fak'simili/ *m* facsimile, (*fax*) fax

fact- (*Port*) *veja* **fat-**

facul|dade /fakuw'dadʒi/ *f* (*mental etc*) faculty; (*escola*) university, (*Amer*) college; **fazer** ∼**dade** go to university; ∼**tativo** *a* optional

fada /'fada/ *f* fairy; ∼**do** *a* destined, doomed; ∼**madrinha** (*pl* ∼**s-madrinhas**) *f* fairy godmother

fadiga /fa'dʒiga/ *f* fatigue

fa|dista /fa'dʒista/ *m/f* fado singer; ∼**do** *m* fado

fagote /fa'gɔtʃi/ *m* bassoon

fagulha /fa'guʎa/ *f* spark

faia /'faja/ *f* beech

faisão /faj'zãw/ *m* pheasant

faísca /fa'iska/ *f* spark

fais|cante /fajs'kãtʃi/ *a* sparkling; ∼**car** *vi* spark; (*cintilar*) sparkle

faixa /'faʃa/ *f* strip; (*cinto*) sash; (*em karatê, judô*) belt; (*da estrada*) lane; (*para pedestres*) zebra crossing, (*Amer*) crosswalk; (*atadura*) bandage; (*de disco*) track; ∼ **etária** age group

fajuto /fa'ʒutu/ (*fam*) *a* fake

fala /'fala/ *f* speech

falácia /fa'lasia/ *f* fallacy

fa|lado /fa'ladu/ *a* <*língua*> spoken; <*caso, pessoa*> talked about; ∼**lante** *a* talkative; ∼**lar** *vt/i* speak; (*dizer*) say; ∼**lar com** talk to; ∼**lar de** *ou* **em** talk about; **por** ∼**lar em** speaking of; **sem** ∼**lar em** not to mention; ∼**lou!** (*fam*) OK!; ∼**latório** *m* (*boatos*) talk; (*som de vozes*) talking

falaz /fa'las/ *a* fallacious

falcão /faw'kãw/ *m* falcon

falcatrua /fawka'trua/ *f* swindle

fale|cer /fale'ser/ *vi* die, pass away; ∼**cido** *a & m* deceased; ∼**cimento** *m* death

falência /fa'lêsia/ *f* bankruptcy; **ir à** ∼ go bankrupt

falésia /fa'lezia/ *f* cliff

fa|lha /'faʎa/ *f* fault; (*omissão*) failure; ∼**lhar** *vi* fail; ∼**lho** *a* faulty

fálico /'faliku/ *a* phallic

fa|lido /fa'lidu/ *a & m* bankrupt; ∼**lir** *vi* go bankrupt; ∼**lível** (*pl* ∼**líveis**) *a* fallible

falo /'falu/ *m* phallus

fal|sário /faw'sariu/ *m* forger; ∼**sear** *vt* falsify; ∼**sete** *m* falsetto; ∼**sidade** *f* falseness; (*mentira*) falsehood

falsifi|cação /fawsifika'sãw/ *f* forgery; ∼**cador** *m* forger; ∼**car** *vt* falsify; forge <*documentos, notas*>

falso /'fawsu/ *a* false

fal|ta /'fawta/ *f* lack; (*em futebol*) foul; **em** ∼**ta** at fault; **por** ∼**ta de** for lack of; **sem** ∼**ta** without fail; **fazer** ∼**ta** be needed; **sentir a** ∼**ta de** miss; ∼**tar** *vi* be missing; <*aluno*> be absent; ∼**tam dois dias para** it's two days until; **me** ∼**ta ...** I don't have ...; ∼**tar a** miss <*aula etc*>; break <*palavra, promessa*>; ∼**to** *a* short (**de** of)

fa|ma /'fama/ *f* reputation; (*celebridade*) fame; ∼**migerado** *a* notorious

família /fa'milia/ *f* family

famili|ar /famili'ar/ *a* familiar; (*de família*) family; ∼**aridade** *f* familiarity; ∼**arizar** *vt* familiarize; ∼**arizar-se** *vpr* familiarize o.s.

faminto /fa'mĩtu/ *a* starving

famoso /fa'mozu/ *a* famous

fanático /fa'natʃiku/ *a* fanatical □ *m* fanatic

fanatismo /fana'tʃizmu/ *m* fanaticism

fanfarrão /fãfaˈxãw/ m braggart

fanhoso /faˈɲozu/ a nasal; ser ~ talk through one's nose

fanta|sia /fãtaˈzia/ f (faculdade) imagination; (devaneio) fantasy; (roupa) fancy dress; ~siar vt dream up □ vi fantasize; ~siar-se upr dress up (de as); ~sioso /o/ a fanciful; <pessoa> imaginative; ~sista a imaginative

fantasma /fãˈtazma/ m ghost; ~górico a ghostly

fantástico /fãˈtastʃiku/ a fantastic

fantoche /fãˈtɔʃi/ m puppet

faqueiro /faˈkeru/ m canteen of cutlery

fara|ó /faraˈɔ/ m pharaoh; ~ônico a (fig) of epic proportions

farda /ˈfarda/ f uniform; ~do a uniformed

fardo /ˈfardu/ m (fig) burden

fare|jador /fareʒaˈdor/ a cão ~jador sniffer dog; ~jar vt sniff out □ vi sniff

farelo /faˈrelu/ m bran; (de pão) crumb; (de madeira) sawdust

farfalhar /farfaˈʎar/ vi rustle

farináceo /fariˈnasiu/ a starchy; ~s m pl starchy foods

farin|ge /faˈrĩʒi/ f pharynx; ~gite f pharyngitis

farinha /faˈriɲa/ f flour; ~ de rosca breadcrumbs

far|macêutico /farmaˈsewtʃiku/ a pharmaceutical □ m (pessoa) pharmacist; ~mácia f (loja) chemist's, (Amer) pharmacy; (ciência) pharmacy

faro /ˈfaru/ m sense of smell; (fig) nose

faroeste /faroˈɛstʃi/ m (filme) western; (região) wild west

faro|fa /faˈrɔfa/ f fried manioc flour; ~feiro (fam) m day-tripper

fa|rol /faˈrɔw/ m (pl ~róis) m (de carro) headlight; (de trânsito) traffic light; (à beira-mar) lighthouse; ~rol alto full beam; ~rol baixo dipped beam; ~roleiro a boastful □ m bighead; ~rolete /e/ m, (Port) ~rolim m side-light; (traseiro) tail-light

farpa /ˈfarpa/ f splinter; (de metal, fig) barb; ~do a arame ~do barbed wire

farra /ˈfaxa/ (fam) f partying; cair na ~ go out and party

farrapo /faˈxapu/ m rag

far|rear /faxiˈar/ (fam) vi party; ~rista (fam) m/f raver

far|sa /ˈfarsa/ f (peça) farce; (fingimento) pretence; ~sante m/f (brincalhão) joker; (pessoa sem seriedade) unreliable character

far|tar /farˈtar/ vt satiate; ~tar-se upr (saciar-se) gorge o.s. (de with); (cansar) tire (de of); ~to a (abundante) plentiful; (cansado) fed up (de with); ~tura f abundance

fascículo /faˈsikulu/ m instalment

fasci|nação /fasinaˈsãw/ f fascination; ~nante a fascinating; ~nar vt fascinate

fascínio /faˈsiniu/ m fascination

fas|cismo /faˈsizmu/ m fascism; ~cista a & m/f fascist

fase /ˈfazi/ f phase

fa|tal /faˈtaw/ (pl ~tais) a fatal; ~talismo m fatalism; ~talista a fatalistic □ m/f fatalist; ~talmente adv inevitably

fatia /faˈtʃia/ f slice

fatídico /faˈtʃidʒiku/ a fateful

fati|gante /fatʃiˈgãtʃi/ a tiring; ~gar vt tire, fatigue

fato¹ /ˈfatu/ m fact; de ~ as a matter of fact, in fact; ~ consumado fait accompli

fato² /ˈfatu/ (Port) m suit

fator /faˈtor/ m factor

fátuo /ˈfatu/ a fatuous

fatu|ra /faˈtura/ f invoice; ~ramento m turnover; ~rar vt invoice for <encomenda>; make <dinheiro>; (fig: emplacar) notch up □ vi (fam) rake it in

fauna /ˈfawna/ f fauna

fava /ˈfava/ f broad bean; mandar alg às ~s tell s.o. where to get off

favela /faˈvɛla/ f shanty town; ~do m shanty-dweller

favo /ˈfavu/ m honeycomb

favor /faˈvor/ m favour; a ~ de in favour of; por ~ please; faça ~ please

favo|rável /favoˈravew/ (pl ~ráveis) a favourable; ~recer vt favour; ~ritismo m favouritism; ~rito a & m favourite

faxi|na /faˈʃina/ f clean-up; ~neiro m cleaner

fazen|da /faˈzẽda/ f (de café, gado etc) farm; (tecido) fabric, material; (pública) treasury; ~deiro m farmer

fazer /faˈzer/ vt do; (produzir) make; ask <pergunta>; ~-se upr (tornar-se) become; ~-se de make o.s. out to be; ~ anos have a birthday; ~ 20 anos be twenty; faz dois dias que ele está aqui he's been here for two days; faz dez anos que ele morreu it's ten years since he died; tanto faz it doesn't matter

faz-tudo /fasˈtudu/ m/f invar jack of all trades

fé /fɛ/ f faith

fe|bre /ˈfɛbri/ f fever; ~bre amarela yellow fever; ~bre do feno hay fever; ~bril (pl ~bris) a feverish

fe|chado /feˈʃadu/ a closed; <curva> sharp; <sinal> red; <torneira> off; <tempo> overcast; <cara> stern; <pessoa> reserved; ~chadura f lock; ~**chamento** *m* closure; ~**char** *vt* close, shut; turn off <*torneira*>; do up <*calça, casaco*>; close <*negócio*> □ *vi* close, shut; <*sinal*> go red; <*tempo*> cloud over; ~**char à chave** lock; ~**char a cara** frown; ~**cho** /e/ *m* fastener; ~**cho ecler** zip

fécula /'fɛkula/ *f* starch

fecun|dar /fekũ'dar/ *vt* fertilize; ~**do** *a* fertile

feder /fe'der/ *vi* stink

fede|ração /federa'sãw/ *f* federation; ~**ral** (*pl* ~**rais**) *a* federal; (*fam*) huge; ~**rativo** *a* federal

fedor /fe'dor/ *m* stink, stench; ~**ento** *a* stinking

feérico /fee'riku/ *a* magical

feições /fej'sõjs/ *f pl* features

feijão /fe'ʒãw/ *m* bean; (*coletivo*) beans; ~**joada** *f* bean stew; ~**joeiro** *m* bean plant

feio /'feju/ *a* ugly; <*palavra, situação, tempo*> nasty; <*olhar*> dirty; ~**so** /o/ *a* plain

fei|ra /'fera/ *f* market; (*industrial*) trade fair; ~**rante** *m/f* market trader

feiti|caria /fejtʃi'sera/ *f* magic; ~**ceira** *f* witch; ~**ceiro** *m* wizard □ *a* bewitching; ~**ço** *m* spell

feitio /fej'tʃiu/ *m* (*de pessoa*) make-up; ~**to** *pp de* **fazer** □ *m* (*ato*) deed; (*proeza*) feat □ *conj* like; **bem** ~**to** **por ele** (it) serves him right; ~**tura** *f* making

feiura /fej'ura/ *f* ugliness

feixe /'fejʃi/ *m* bundle

fel /fɛw/ *f* gall; (*fig*) bitterness

felicidade /felisi'dadʒi/ *f* happiness

felici|tações /felisita'sõjs/ *f pl* congratulations; ~**tar** *vt* congratulate (por on)

felino /fe'linu/ *a* feline

feliz /fe'lis/ *a* happy; ~**ardo** *a* lucky; ~**mente** *adv* fortunately

fel|pa /'fewpa/ *f* (*de pano*) nap; (*penugem*) down, fluff; ~**pudo** *a* fluffy

feltro /'fewtru/ *m* felt

fêmea /'femia/ *a & f* female

femi|nil /femi'niw/ (*pl* ~**nis**) *a* feminine; ~**nilidade** *f* femininity; ~**nino** *a* female; <*palavra*> feminine; ~**nismo** *m* feminism; ~**nista** *a & m/f* feminist

fêmur /'femur/ *m* femur

fen|da /'fẽda/ *f* crack; ~**der** *vt/i* split, crack

feno /'fenu/ *m* hay

fenome|nal /fenome'naw/ (*pl* ~**nais**) *a* phenomenal

fenômeno /fe'nomenu/ *m* phenomenon

fera /'fera/ *f* wild beast; **ficar uma** ~ get really angry; **ser** ~ **em** (*fam*) be brilliant at

féretro /'fɛretru/ *m* coffin

feriado /feri'adu/ *m* public holiday

férias /'fɛrias/ *f pl* holiday(s), (*Amer*) vacation; **de** ~ on holiday; **tirar** ~ take a holiday

feri|da /fe'rida/ *f* injury; (*com arma*) wound; ~**do** *a* injured; (*mil*) wounded □ *m* injured person; **os** ~**dos** the injured; (*mil*) the wounded; ~**r** *vt* injure; (*com arma*) wound; (*magoar*) hurt

fermen|tar /fermẽ'tar/ *vt/i* ferment; ~**to** *m* yeast; (*fig*) ferment; ~**to em pó** baking powder

fe|rocidade /ferosi'dadʒi/ *f* ferocity; ~**roz** *a* ferocious

fer|rado /fe'xadu/ *a* **estou** ~**rado** (*fam*) I've had it; ~**rado no sono** fast asleep; ~**radura** *f* horseshoe; ~**ragem** *f* ironwork; *pl* hardware; ~**ramenta** *f* tool; (*coletivo*) tools; ~**rão** *m* (*de abelha*) sting; ~**rar** *vt* brand <*gado*>; shoe <*cavalo*>; ~**rar-se** (*fam*) *vpr* come a cropper; ~**reiro** *m* blacksmith; ~**renho** *a* <*partidário etc*> staunch; <*vontade*> iron

férreo /'fɛxiu/ *a* iron

ferro /'fɛxu/ *m* iron; ~**lho** /o/ *m* bolt; ~**velho** (*pl* ~**s-velhos**) *m* (*pessoa*) scrap-metal dealer; (*lugar*) scrap-metal yard; ~**via** *f* railway, (*Amer*) railroad; ~**viário** *a* railway □ *m* railway worker

ferrugem /fe'xuʒẽ/ *f* rust

fér|til /'fɛrtʃiw/ (*pl* ~**teis**) *a* fertile

fertili|dade /fertʃili'dadʒi/ *f* fertility; ~**zante** *m* fertilizer; ~**zar** *vt* fertilize

fer|vente /fer'vẽtʃi/ *a* boiling; ~**ver** *vi* boil; (*de raiva*) seethe; ~**vilhar** *vi* bubble; ~**vilhar de** swarm with; ~**vor** *m* fervour; ~**vura** *f* boiling

fes|ta /'festa/ *f* party; (*religiosa*) festival; ~**tejar** *vt/i* celebrate; (*acolher*) fete; ~**tejo** /e/ *m* celebration; ~**tim** *m* feast; ~**tival** (*pl* ~**tivais**) *m* festival; ~**tividade** *f* festivity; ~**tivo** *a* festive

feti|che /fe'tʃiʃi/ *m* fetish; ~**chismo** *m* fetishism; ~**chista** *m/f* fetishist □ *a* fetishistic

fétido /'fɛtʃidu/ *a* fetid

feto[1] /'fɛtu/ *m* (*no útero*) foetus

feto[2] /'fɛtu/ (*Port*) *m* (*planta*) fern

feu|dal /few'daw/ (*pl* ~**dais**) *a* feudal; ~**dalismo** *m* feudalism

fevereiro /feve'reru/ *m* February

fezes /'fɛzis/ *f pl* faeces

fiação /fia'sãw/ *f* (*eletr*) wiring; (*fábrica*) mill

fia|do /fi'adu/ *a* <*conversa*> idle □ *adv* <*comprar*> on credit; ~**dor** *m* guarantor

fiambre /fi'ãbri/ *m* cooked ham

fiança /fiˈãsa/ f surety; (*jurid*) bail

fiapo /fiˈapu/ m thread

fiar /fiˈar/ vt spin <*lã etc*>

fiasco /fiˈasku/ m fiasco

fibra /ˈfibra/ f fibre

ficar /fiˈkar/ vi (*tornar-se*) become; (*estar, ser*) be; (*manter-se*) stay; ~ **fazendo** keep (on) doing; ~ **com** keep; get <*impressão, vontade*>; ~ **com medo** get scared; ~ **de fazer** arrange to do; ~ **para** be left for; ~ **bom** turn out well; (*recuperar-se*) get better; ~ **bem** look good

fic|ção /fikˈsãw/ f fiction; ~**ção científica** science fiction; ~**cionista** m/f fiction writer

fi|cha /ˈfiʃa/ f (*de telefone*) token; (*de jogo*) chip; (*da caixa*) ticket; (*de fichário*) file card; (*na polícia*) record; (*Port: tomada*) plug; ~**chário** m, (*Port*) ~**cheiro** m file; (*móvel*) filing cabinet

fictício /fikˈtʃisiu/ a fictitious

fidalgo /fiˈdalgu/ m nobleman

fide|digno /fideˈdʒignu/ a trustworthy; ~**lidade** f fidelity

fiduciário /fidusiˈariu/ a fiduciary □ m trustee

fi|el /fiˈεw/ (*pl* ~**éis**) a faithful □ m **os** ~**éis** (*na igreja*) the congregation

figa /ˈfiga/ f talisman

fígado /ˈfigadu/ f liver

fi|go /ˈfigu/ m fig; ~**gueira** f fig tree

figu|ra /fiˈgura/ f figure; (*carta de jogo*) face card; (*fam: pessoa*) character; **fazer (má)** ~**ra** make a (bad) impression; ~**rado** a figurative; ~**rante** m/f extra; ~**rão** m big shot; ~**rar** vi appear, figure; ~**rativo** a figurative; ~**rinha** f sticker; ~**rino** m fashion plate; (*de filme, peça*) costume design; (*fig*) model; **como manda o** ~**rino** as it should be

fila /ˈfila/ f line; (*de espera*) queue, (*Amer*) line; (*fileira*) row; **fazer** ~ queue up, (*Amer*) stand in line; ~ **indiana** single file

filamento /filaˈmẽtu/ m filament

filante /fiˈlãtʃi/ (*fam*) m/f sponger

filan|tropia /filãtroˈpia/ f philanthropy; ~**trópico** a philanthropic; ~**tropo** /o/ m philanthropist

filão /fiˈlãw/ m (*de ouro*) seam; (*fig*) money-spinner

filar /fiˈlar/ (*fam*) vt sponge, cadge

filar|mônica /filarˈmonika/ f philharmonic (orchestra); ~**mônico** a philharmonic

filate|lia /filateˈlia/ f philately; ~**lista** m/f philatelist

filé /fiˈlε/ m fillet

fileira /fiˈlera/ f row

filete /fiˈletʃi/ m fillet

fi|lha /ˈfiʎa/ f daughter; ~**lho** m son; *pl* (*crianças*) children; ~**lho da puta** (*chulo*) bastard, (*Amer*) son of a bitch; ~**lho de criação** foster child; ~**lho único** only child; ~**lhote** m (*de cão*) pup; (*de lobo etc*) cub; *pl* young

fili|ação /filiaˈsãw/ f affiliation; ~**al** (*pl* ~**ais**) a filial □ f branch

Filipinas /filiˈpinas/ f pl Philippines

filipino /filiˈpinu/ a & m Filipino

fil|madora /fiwmaˈdora/ f camcorder; ~**magem** f filming; ~**mar** vt/i film; ~**me** m film

fi|lologia /filoloˈʒia/ f philology; ~**lólogo** m philologist

filo|sofar /filozoˈfar/ vi philosophize; ~**sofia** f philosophy; ~**sófico** a philosophical

filósofo /fiˈlozofu/ m philosopher

fil|trar /fiwˈtrar/ vt filter; ~**tro** m filter

fim /fĩ/ m end; **a** ~ **de** (*para*) in order to; **estar a** ~ **de** fancy; **por** ~ finally; **sem** ~ endless; **ter** ~ come to an end; ~ **de semana** weekend

fi|nado /fiˈnadu/ a & m deceased, departed; ~**nal** (*pl* ~**nais**) a final □ m end □ f final; ~**nalista** m/f finalist; ~**nalizar** vt/i finish

finan|ças /fiˈnãsas/ f pl finances; ~**ceiro** a financial □ m financier; ~**ciamento** m financing; (*um*) loan; ~**ciar** vt finance; ~**cista** m/f financier

fincar /fĩˈkar/ vt plant; ~ **o pé** (*fig*) dig one's heels in

findar /fĩˈdar/ vt/i end

fineza /fiˈneza/ f finesse; (*favor*) kindness

fin|gido /fĩˈʒidu/ a feigned; <*pessoa*> insincere; ~**gimento** m pretence; ~**gir** vt pretend; feign <*doença etc*> □ vi pretend; ~**gir-se de** pretend to be

finito /fiˈnitu/ a finite

finlan|dês /fĩlãˈdes/ a (*f* ~**desa**) Finnish □ m (*f* ~**desa**) Finn; (*língua*) Finnish

Finlândia /fĩˈlãdʒia/ f Finland

fi|ninho /fiˈniɲu/ adv **sair de** ~**ninho** slip away; ~**no** a (*não grosso*) thin; <*areia, pó etc*> fine; (*refinado*) refined; ~**nório** a crafty; ~**nura** f thinness; fineness

fio /ˈfiu/ m thread; (*elétrico*) wire; (*de sangue, água*) trickle; (*de luz, esperança*) glimmer; (*de navalha etc*) edge; **horas a** ~ hours on end

fir|ma /ˈfirma/ f firm; (*assinatura*) signature; ~**mamento** m firmament; ~**mar** vt fix; (*basear*) base □ vi settle; ~**mar-se** upr be based (**em** on); ~**me** a firm; <*tempo*> settled □ adv firmly; ~**meza** f firmness

fis|cal /fisˈkaw/ (*pl* ~**cais**) m inspector; ~**calização** f inspection;

~**calizar** *vt* inspect; ~**co** *m* inland revenue, (*Amer*) internal revenue service

fis|gada /fiz'gada/ *f* stabbing pain; ~**gar** *vt* hook

físi|ca /'fizika/ *f* physics; ~**co** *a* physical □ *m* (*pessoa*) physicist; (*corpo*) physique

fisio|nomia /fiziono'mia/ *f* face; ~**nomista** *m/f* ser ~**nomista** have a good memory for faces; ~**terapeuta** *m/f* physiotherapist; ~**terapia** *f* physiotherapy

fissura /fi'sura/ *f* fissure; (*fam*) craving; ~**do** *a* ~**do em** (*fam*) mad about

fita /'fita/ *f* tape; (*fam: encenação*) playacting; **fazer** ~ (*fam*) put on an act; ~ **adesiva** (*Port*) adhesive tape; ~ **métrica** tape measure

fitar /fi'tar/ *vt* stare at

fivela /fi'vɛla/ *f* buckle

fi|xador /fiksa'dor/ *m* (*de cabelo*) setting lotion; (*de fotos*) fixative; ~**xar** *vt* fix; stick up <*cartaz*>; ~**xo** *a* fixed

flácido /'flasidu/ *a* flabby

flagelo /fla'ʒɛlu/ *m* scourge

fla|grante /fla'grãtʃi/ *a* flagrant; **apanhar em** ~**grante (delito)** catch in the act; ~**grar** *vt* catch

flame|jante /flame'ʒãtʃi/ *a* blazing; ~**jar** *vi* blaze

flamengo /fla'mẽgu/ *a* Flemish □ *m* Fleming; (*língua*) Flemish

flamingo /fla'mĩgu/ *m* flamingo

flâmula /'flamula/ *f* pennant

flanco /'flãku/ *m* flank

flanela /fla'nɛla/ *f* flannel

flanquear /flãki'ar/ *vt* flank

flash /flɛʃ/ *m invar* flash

flau|ta /'flawta/ *f* flute; ~**tista** *m/f* flautist

flecha /'flɛʃa/ *f* arrow

fler|tar /fler'tar/ *vi* flirt; ~**te** *m* flirtation

fleuma /'flewma/ *f* phlegm

fle|xão /flek'sãw/ *f* press-up, (*Amer*) push-up; (*ling*) inflection; ~**xibilidade** *f* flexibility; ~**xionar** *vt/i* flex <*perna, braço*>; (*ling*) inflect; ~**xível** (*pl* ~**xiveis**) *a* flexible

fliperama /flipe'rama/ *f* pinball machine

floco /'flɔku/ *m* flake

flor /flor/ *f* flower; **a fina** ~ the cream; **à** ~ **da pele** (*fig*) on edge

flo|ra /'flɔra/ *f* flora; ~**reado** *a* full of flowers; (*fig*) florid; ~**reio** *m* clever turn of phrase; ~**rescer** *vi* flower; ~**resta** /ɛ/ *f* forest; ~**restal** (*pl* ~**restais**) *a* forest; ~**rido** *a* in flower; (*fig*) florid; ~**rir** *vi* flower

flotilha /flo'tʃiʎa/ *f* flotilla

flu|ência /flu'ẽsia/ *f* fluency; ~**ente** *a* fluent

flui|dez /flui'des/ *f* fluidity; ~**do** *a* & *m* fluid

fluir /flu'ir/ *vi* flow

fluminense /flumi'nẽsi/ *a* & *m* (person) from Rio de Janeiro state

fluorescente /fluore'sẽtʃi/ *a* fluorescent

flutu|ação /flutua'sãw/ *f* fluctuation; ~**ante** *a* floating; ~**ar** *vi* float; <*bandeira*> flutter; (*hesitar*) waver

fluvi|al /fluvi'aw/ (*pl* ~**ais**) *a* river

fluxo /'fluksu/ *m* flow; ~**grama** *m* flowchart

fobia /fo'bia/ *f* phobia

foca /'fɔka/ *f* seal

focalizar /fokali'zar/ *vt* focus on

focinho /fo'siɲu/ *m* snout

foco /'fɔku/ *m* focus; (*fig*) centre

fofo /'fofu/ *a* soft; <*pessoa*> cuddly

fofo|ca /fo'fɔka/ *f* piece of gossip; *pl* gossip; ~**car** *vi* gossip; ~**queiro** *m* gossip □ *a* gossipy

fo|gão /fo'gãw/ *m* stove; (*de cozinhar*) cooker; ~**go** /o/ *m* fire; **tem** ~**go?** have you got a light?; **ser** ~**go** (*fam*) (*ser chato*) be a pain in the neck; (*ser incrível*) be amazing; ~**gos de artifício** fireworks; ~**goso** /o/ *a* fiery; ~**gueira** *f* bonfire; ~**guete** /e/ *m* rocket

foice /'fojsi/ *f* scythe

fol|clore /fow'klɔri/ *m* folklore; ~**clórico** *a* folk

fole /'fɔli/ *m* bellows

fôlego /'folegu/ *m* breath; (*fig*) stamina

fol|ga /'fɔwga/ *f* rest, break; (*fam: cara-de-pau*) cheek; ~**gado** *a* <*roupa*> full, loose; <*vida*> leisurely; (*fam: atrevido*) cheeky; ~**gar** *vt* loosen □ *vi* have time off

fo|lha /'foʎa/ *f* leaf; (*de papel*) sheet; **novo em** ~**lha** brand new; ~**lha de pagamento** payroll; ~**lhagem** *f* foliage; ~**lhear** *vt* leaf through; ~**lheto** /e/ *m* pamphlet; ~**lhinha** *f* tear-off calendar; ~**lhudo** *a* leafy

foli|a /fo'lia/ *f* revelry; ~**ão** *m* (*f* ~**ona**) reveller

folículo /fo'likulu/ *m* follicle

fome /'fɔmi/ *f* hunger; **estar com** ~ be hungry

fomentar /fomẽ'tar/ *vt* foment

fone /'foni/ *m* (*de telefone*) receiver; (*de rádio etc*) headphones

fonema /fo'nema/ *m* phoneme

fonéti|ca /fo'nɛtʃika/ *f* phonetics; ~**co** *a* phonetic

fonologia /fonolo'ʒia/ *f* phonology

fonte /'fõtʃi/ *f* (*de água*) spring; (*fig*) source

fora /'fɔra/ *adv* outside; (*não em casa*) out; (*viajando*) away □ *prep* except; **dar um** ~ drop a clanger; **dar um**

~ em alg cut s.o. dead; chuck <*namorado*>; por ~ on the outside; ~-de-lei *m/f invar* outlaw

foragido /fora'ʒidu/ *a* at large, on the run □ *m* fugitive

forasteiro /foras'teru/ *m* outsider

forca /'forka/ *f* gallows

for|ça /'forsa/ *f* (*vigor*) strength; (*violência*) force; (*elétrica*) power; dar uma ~ça a alg help s.o. out; fazer ~ça make an effort; ~ças armadas armed forces; ~çar *vt* force; ~ça-tarefa (*pl* ~ças-tarefa) *f* task force

fórceps /'forseps/ *m invar* forceps

forçoso /for'sozu/ *a* forced

for|ja /'forʒa/ *f* forge; ~jar *vt* forge

forma /'forma/ *f* (*contorno*) shape; (*maneira*) way; de qualquer ~ anyway; manter a ~ keep fit

fôrma /'forma/ *f* (*mould*); (*de cozinha*) baking tin

for|mação /forma'sãw/ *f* formation; (*educação*) education; (*profissionalizante*) training; ~mado *m* graduate; ~mal (*pl* ~mais) *a* formal; ~malidade *f* formality; ~malizar *vt* formalize; ~mar *vt* form; (*educar*) educate; ~mar-se *vpr* be formed; <*estudante*> graduate; ~mato *m* format; ~matura *f* graduation

formidá|vel /formi'davew/ (*pl* ~veis) *a* formidable; (*muito bom*) tremendous

formi|ga /for'miga/ *f* ant; ~gamento *m* pins and needles; ~gar *vi* swarm (de with); <*perna, mão etc*> tingle; ~gueiro *m* ants' nest

formosura /formo'zura/ *f* beauty

fórmula /'formula/ *f* formula

formu|lação /formula'sãw/ *f* formulation; ~lar *vt* formulate; ~lário *m* form

fornalha /for'naʎa/ *f* furnace

forne|cedor /fornese'dor/ *m* supplier; ~cer *vt* supply; ~cer aco a alg supply s.o. with sth; ~cimento *m* supply

forno /'fornu/ *m* oven; (*para louça etc*) kiln

foro /'foru/ *m* forum

forra /'fɔxa/ *f* ir à ~ get one's own back

for|ragem /fo'xaʒẽ/ *f* fodder; ~rar *vt* line <*roupa, caixa etc*>; cover <*sofá etc*>; carpet <*assoalho, sala etc*>; ~ro /o/ *m* (*de roupa, caixa etc*) lining; (*de sofá etc*) cover; (*carpete*) (fitted) carpet

forró /fo'xɔ/ *m* type of Brazilian dance

fortale|cer /fortale'ser/ *vt* strengthen; ~cimento *m* strengthening; ~za /e/ *f* fort·ress

for|te /'fortʃi/ *a* strong; <*golpe*> hard; <*chuva*> heavy; <*físico*> muscular □ *adv* strongly; <*bater, chover*> hard □

m (*militar*) fort; (*habilidade*) strong point, forte; ~tificação *f* fortification; ~tificar *vt* fortify

fortu|ito /for'tuitu/ *a* chance; ~na *f* fortune

fosco /'fosku/ *a* dull; <*vidro*> frosted

fosfato /fos'fatu/ *m* phosphate

fósforo /'fɔsforu/ *m* match; (*elemento químico*) phosphor

fossa /'fosa/ *f* pit; na ~ (*fig*) miserable, depressed

fós|sil /'fɔsiw/ (*pl* ~seis) *m* fossil

fosso /'fosu/ *m* ditch; (*de castelo*) moat

foto /'fotu/ *f* photo; ~cópia *f* photocopy; ~copiadora *f* photocopier; ~copiar *vt* photocopy; ~gênico *a* photogenic; ~grafar *vt* photograph; ~grafia *f* photography; ~gráfico *a* photographic

fotógrafo /fo'tɔgrafu/ *m* photographer

foz /fos/ *f* mouth

fração /fra'sãw/ *f* fraction

fracas|sado /fraka'sadu/ *a* failed □ *m* failure; ~sar *vi* fail; ~so *m* failure

fracionar /frasio'nar/ *vt* break up

fraco /'fraku/ *a* weak; <*luz, som*> faint; <*mediocre*> poor □ *m* weakness, weak spot

fract- (*Port*) *veja* frat-

frade /'fradʒi/ *m* friar

fragata /fra'gata/ *f* frigate

frá|gil /'fraʒiw/ (*pl* ~geis) *a* fragile; <*pessoa*> frail

fragilidade /fraʒili'dadʒi/ *f* fragility; (*de pessoa*) frailty

fragmen|tar /fragmẽ'tar/ *vt* fragment; ~tar-se *vpr* fragment; ~to *m* fragment

fra|grância /fra'grãsia/ *f* fragrance; ~grante *a* fragrant

fralda /'frawda/ *f* nappy, (*Amer*) diaper

framboesa /frãbo'eza/ *f* raspberry

França /'frãsa/ *f* France

fran|cês /frã'ses/ *a* (*f* ~cesa) French □ *m* (*f* ~cesa) Frenchman (*f* -woman); (*língua*) French; os ~ceses the French

franco /'frãku/ *a* (*honesto*) frank; (*óbvio*) clear; (*gratuito*) free □ *m* franc; ~-atirador (*pl* ~-atiradores) *m* sniper; (*fig*) maverick

frangalho /frã'gaʎu/ *m* tatter

frango /'frãgu/ *m* chicken

franja /'frãʒa/ *f* fringe; (*do cabelo*) fringe, (*Amer*) bangs

fran|quear /frãki'ar/ *vt* frank <*carta*>; ~queza /e/ *f* frankness; ~quia *f* (*de cartas*) franking; (*jur*) franchise

fran|zino /frã'zinu/ *a* skinny; ~zir *vt* gather <*tecido*>; wrinkle <*testa*>

fraque /'fraki/ *m* morning suit

fraqueza /fra'keza/ f weakness; (de luz, som) faintness

frasco /'frasku/ m bottle

frase /'frazi/ f (oração) sentence; (locução) phrase; ~ado m phrasing

frasqueira /fras'kera/ f vanity case

frater|nal /frater'naw/ (pl ~nais) a fraternal; ~nidade f fraternity; ~nizar vi fraternize; ~no a fraternal

fratu|ra /fra'tura/ f fracture; ~rar vt fracture; ~rar-se vpr fracture

frau|dar /fraw'dar/ vt defraud; ~de f fraud; ~dulento a fraudulent

frear /fri'ar/ vt/i brake

freezer /'frizer/ m freezer

fre|guês /fre'ges/ m (f ~guesa) customer; ~guesia f (de loja etc) clientele; (paróquia) parish

frei /frej/ m brother

freio /'freju/ m brake; (de cavalo) bit

freira /'frera/ f nun

freixo /'freʃu/ m ash

fremir /fre'mir/ vi shake

frêmito /'fremitu/ m wave

frenesi /frene'zi/ m frenzy

frenético /fre'netʃiku/ a frantic

frente /'frētʃi/ f front; em ~ a ou de in front of; para a ~ forward; pela ~ ahead; fazer ~ a face

freqüência /fre'kwēsia/ f frequency; (assiduidade) attendance; com muita ~ often

freqüen|tador /frekwēta'dor/ m regular visitor (de to); ~tar vt frequent; (cursar) attend; ~te a frequent

fres|cão /fres'kāw/ m air-conditioned coach; ~co /e/ a <comida etc> fresh; <vento, água, quarto> cool; (fam) (afetado) affected; (exigente) fussy; ~cobol m kind of racquetball; ~cor m freshness; ~cura f (fam) (afetação) affectation; (ser exigente) fussiness; (coisa sem importância) trifle

fresta /'fresta/ f slit

fre|tar /fre'tar/ vt charter <avião>; hire <caminhão>; ~te /ɛ/ m freight; (aluguel de avião) charter; (de caminhão) hire

frevo /'frevu/ m type of Brazilian dance

fria /'fria/ (fam) f difficult situation, spot; ~gem f chill

fric|ção /frik'sāw/ f friction; ~cionar vt rub

fri|eira /fri'era/ f chilblain; ~eza /e/ f coldness

frigideira /friʒi'dera/ f frying pan

frígido /'friʒidu/ a frigid

frigorífico /frigo'rifiku/ m cold store, refrigerator, fridge

frincha /'friʃa/ f chink

frio /'friu/ a & m cold; estar com ~ be cold; ~rento a sensitive to the cold

frisar /fri'zar/ vt (enfatizar) stress; crimp <cabelo>

friso /'frizu/ m frieze

fri|tada /fri'tada/ f fry-up; ~tar vt fry; ~tas f pl chips, (Amer) French fries; ~to a fried; está ~to (fam) he's had it; ~tura f fried food

frivolidade /frivoli'dadʒi/ f frivolity; frívolo a frivolous

fronha /'froɲa/ f pillowcase

fronte /'frõtʃi/ f forehead, brow

frontei|ra /frõ'tera/ f border; ~riço a border

frota /'frota/ f fleet

frou|xidão /froʃi'dāw/ f looseness; (moral) laxity; ~xo a loose; <regulamento> lax; <pessoa> lackadaisical

fru|gal /fru'gaw/ (pl ~gais) a frugal; ~galidade f frugality

frus|tração /frustra'sāw/ f frustration; ~trante a frustrating; ~trar vt frustrate

fru|ta /'fruta/ f fruit; ~ta-do-conde (pl ~tas-do-conde) f sweetsop; ~ta-pão (pl ~tas-pão) f breadfruit; ~teira f fruitbowl; ~tífero a (fig) fruitful; ~to m fruit

fubá /fu'ba/ m maize flour

fu|çar /fu'sar/ vi nose around; ~ças (fam) f pl face, chops

fu|ga /'fuga/ f escape; ~gaz a fleeting; ~gida f escape; ~gir vi run away; (soltar-se) escape; ~gir a avoid; ~gitivo a & m fugitive

fulano /fu'lanu/ m whatever his name is

fuleiro /fu'leru/ a down-market, cheap and cheerful

fulgor /fuw'gor/ m brightness; (fig) splendour

fuligem /fu'liʒē/ f soot

fulmi|nante /fuwmi'nātʃi/ a devastating; ~nar vt strike down; (fig) devastate; ~nado por um raio struck by lightning □ vi (criticar) rail

fu|maça /fu'masa/ f smoke; ~maceira f cloud of smoke; ~mante. (Port) ~mador m smoker; ~mar vt/i smoke; ~mê a invar smoked; ~megar vi smoke; ~mo m (tabaco) tobacco; (Port: fumaça) smoke; (fumar) smoking

função /fū'sāw/ f function; em ~ de as a result of; fazer as funções de function as

funcho /'fūʃu/ m fennel

funcio|nal /fūsio'naw/ (pl ~nais) a functional; ~nalismo m civil service; ~namento m working; ~nar vi work; ~nário m employee; ~nário público civil servant

fun|dação /fūda'sāw/ f foundation; ~dador m founder □ a founding

fundamen|tal /fũdamẽ'taw/ (*pl*
　~tais) *a* fundamental; **~tar** *vt* (*base-*
　ar) base; (*justificar*) substantiate;
　~to *m* foundation
fun|dar /fũ'dar/ *vt* (*criar*) found;
　(*basear*) base; **~dar-se** *vpr* be based
　(**em** on); **~dear** *vi* drop anchor,
　anchor; **~dilho** *m* seat
fundir /fũ'dʒir/ *vt* melt <*ouro, ferro*>;
　cast <*sino, estátua*>; (*juntar*) merge;
　~se *vpr* <*ouro, ferro*> melt; (*juntar-
　se*) merge
fundo /'fũdu/ *a* deep □ *m* (*parte de
　baixo*) bottom; (*parte de trás*) back;
　(*de quadro, foto*) background; (*de di-
　nheiro*) fund; **no ~** basically; **~s** *m pl*
　(*da casa etc*) back; (*recursos*) funds
fúnebre /'funebri/ *a* funereal
funerário /fune'rariu/ *a* funeral
funesto /fu'nɛstu/ *a* fatal
fungar /fũ'gar/ *vt/i* sniff
fungo /'fũgu/ *m* fungus
fu|nil /fu'niw/ (*pl* **~nis**) *m* funnel;
　~nilaria *f* panel-beating; (*oficina*)
　bodyshop
furacão /fura'kãw/ *m* hurricane
furado /fu'radu/ *a* **papo ~** (*fam*) hot
　air
furão /fu'rãw/ *m* (*animal*) ferret
furar /fu'rar/ *vt* pierce <*orelha etc*>;
　puncture <*pneu*>; make a hole in
　<*roupa etc*>; jump <*fila*>; break
　<*greve*> □ *vi* <*roupa etc*> go into a
　hole; <*pneu*> puncture; (*fam*) <*pro-
　grama*> fall through
fur|gão /fur'gãw/ *m* van; **~goneta** /e/
　(*Port*) *f* van
fúria /'furia/ *f* fury
furioso /furi'ozu/ *a* furious
furo /'furu/ *m* hole; (*de pneu*) punc-
　ture; (*jornalístico*) scoop; (*fam*: *gafe*)
　blunder, faux pas; **dar um ~** put
　one's foot in it
furor /fu'ror/ *m* furore
fur|ta-cor /furta'kor/ *a invar* iri-
　descent; **~tar** *vt* steal; **~tivo** *a*
　furtive; **~to** *m* theft
furúnculo /fu'rũkulu/ *m* boil
fusão /fu'zãw/ *f* fusion; (*de empresas*)
　merger
fusca /'fuska/ *f* VW beetle
fuselagem /fuze'laʒẽ/ *f* fuselage
fusí|vel /fu'zivew/ (*pl* **~veis**) *m* fuse
fuso /'fuzu/ *m* spindle; **~ horário**
　time zone
fustigar /fustʃi'gar/ *vt* lash; (*fig*: *com
　palavras*) lash out at
futebol /futʃi'bɔw/ *m* football;
　~ístico *a* football
fú|til /'futʃiw/ (*pl* **~teis**) *a* frivolous,
　inane
futilidade /futʃili'dadʒi/ *f* frivolity,
　inanity; (*uma*) frivolous thing
futu|rismo /futu'rizmu/ *m* futurism;

~rista *a & m* futurist; **~rístico** *a*
futuristic; **~ro** *a & m* future
fu|zil /fu'ziw/ (*pl* **~zis**) *m* rifle;
　~zilamento *m* shooting; **~zilar** *vt*
　shoot □ *vi* flash; **~zileiro** *m*
　rifleman; **~zileiro naval** marine
fuzuê /fuzu'e/ *m* commotion

G

gabar-se /ga'barsi/ *vpr* boast (**de** of)
gabarito /gaba'ritu/ *m* calibre
gabinete /gabi'netʃi/ *m* (*em casa*)
　study; (*escritório*) office; (*ministros*)
　cabinet
gado /'gadu/ *m* livestock; (*bovino*)
　cattle
gaélico /ga'ɛliku/ *a & m* Gaelic
gafanhoto /gafa'ɲotu/ *m* (*pequeno*)
　grasshopper; (*grande*) locust
gafe /'gafi/ *f* faux pas, gaffe
gafieira /gafi'era/ *f* dance; (*salão*)
　dance hall
gagá /ga'ga/ *a* (*fam*) senile
ga|go /'gagu/ *a* stuttering □ *m* stut-
　terer; **~gueira** *f* stutter; **~guejar** *vi*
　stutter
gaiato /gaj'atu/ *a* funny
gaiola /gaj'ola/ *f* cage
gaita /'gajta/ *f* **~ de foles** bagpipes
gaivota /gaj'vota/ *f* seagull
gajo /'gaʒu/ *m* (*Port*) guy, bloke
gala /'gala/ *f* **festa de ~** gala; **roupa
　de ~** formal dress
galã /ga'lã/ *m* leading man
galan|tear /galãtʃi'ar/ *vt* woo; **~teio**
　m wooing; (*um*) courtesy
galão /ga'lãw/ *m* (*enfeite*) braid; (*mil*)
　stripe; (*medida*) gallon; (*Port*: *café*)
　white coffee
galáxia /ga'laksia/ *f* galaxy
galé /ga'lɛ/ *f* galley
galego /ga'legu/ *a & m* Galician
galera /ga'lɛra/ *f* (*fam*) crowd
galeria /gale'ria/ *f* gallery
Gales /'galis/ *m* **País de ~** Wales
ga|lês /ga'les/ *a* (*f* **~lesa**) Welsh □ *m*
　(*f* **~lesa**) Welshman (*f* -woman);
　(*língua*) Welsh
galeto /ga'letu/ *m* spring chicken
galgar /gaw'gar/ *vt* (*transpor*) jump
　over; climb <*escada*>
galgo /'gawgu/ *m* greyhound
galheteiro /gaʎe'teru/ *m* cruet stand
galho /'gaʎu/ *m* branch; **quebrar um
　~** (*fam*) help out
galináceos /gali'nasius/ *m pl* poultry
gali|nha /ga'liɲa/ *f* chicken; **~-
　nheiro** *m* chicken coop
galo /'galu/ *m* cock; (*inchação*) bump
galocha /ga'lɔʃa/ *f* Wellington boot
galo|pante /galo'pãtʃi/ *a* galloping;
　~par *vi* gallop; **~pe** /ɔ/ *m* gallop

galpão /gaw'pãw/ *m* shed

galvanizar /gawvani'zar/ *vt* galvanize

gama /'gama/ *f* (*musical*) scale; (*fig*) range

gamado /ga'madu/ *a* besotted (*por* with)

gamão /ga'mãw/ *m* backgammon

gamar /ga'mar/ *vi* fall in love (*por* with)

gana /'gana/ *f* desire

ganância /ga'nãsia/ *f* greed

ganancioso /ganãsi'ozu/ *a* greedy

gancho /'gãʃu/ *m* hook

gangorra /gã'goxa/ *f* seesaw

gangrena /gã'grena/ *f* gangrene

gangue /'gãgi/ *m* gang

ga|nhador /gaɲa'dor/ *m* winner □ *a* winning; **~nhar** *vt* win <*corrida, prêmio*>; earn <*salário*>; get <*presente*>; gain <*vantagem, tempo, amigo*> □ *vi* win; **~nhar a vida** earn a living; **~nha-pão** *m* livelihood; **~nho** *m* gain; *pl* (*no jogo*) winnings □ *pp de* **ganhar**

ga|nido /ga'nidu/ *m* squeal; (*de cachorro*) yelp; **~nir** *vi* squeal; <*cachorro*> yelp

ganso /'gãsu/ *m* goose

gara|gem /ga'raʒẽ/ *f* garage; **~gista** *m/f* garage attendant

garanhão /gara'ɲãw/ *m* stallion

garan|tia /garã'tʃia/ *f* guarantee; **~tir** *vt* guarantee

garatujar /garatu'ʒar/ *vt* scribble

gar|bo /'garbu/ *m* grace; **~boso** *a* graceful

garça /'garsa/ *f* heron

gar|com /gar'sõ/ *m* waiter; **~conete** /ɛ/ *f* waitress

gar|fada /gar'fada/ *f* forkful; **~fo** *m* fork

gargalhada /garga'ʎada/ *f* gale of laughter; **rir às ~s** roar with laughter

gargalo /gar'galu/ *m* bottleneck; **tomar no ~** drink out of the bottle

garganta /gar'gãta/ *f* throat

gargare|jar /gargare'ʒar/ *vi* gargle; **~jo** /e/ *m* gargle

gari /ga'ri/ *m/f* (*lixeiro*) dustman, (*Amer*) garbage collector; (*varredor de rua*) roadsweeper, (*Amer*) street-sweeper

garim|par /garĩ'par/ *vi* prospect; **~peiro** *m* prospector; **~po** *m* mine

garo|a /ga'roa/ *f* drizzle; **~ar** *vi* drizzle

garo|ta /ga'rota/ *f* girl; **~to** /o/ *m* boy; (*Port: café*) coffee with milk

garoupa /ga'ropa/ *f* grouper

garra /'gaxa/ *f* claw; (*fig*) drive, determination; *pl* (*poder*) clutches

garra|fa /ga'xafa/ *f* bottle; **~fada** *f* blow with a bottle; **~fão** *m* flagon

garrancho /ga'xãʃu/ *m* scrawl

garrido /ga'xidu/ *a* (*alegre*) lively

garupa /ga'rupa/ *f* (*de animal*) rump; (*de moto*) pillion seat

gás /gas/ *m* gas; *pl* (*intestinais*) wind, (*Amer*) gas; **~ lacrimogéneo** tear gas

gasóleo /ga'zɔliu/ *m* diesel oil

gasolina /gazo'lina/ *f* petrol

gaso|sa /ga'zɔza/ *f* fizzy lemonade, (*Amer*) soda; **~so** *a* gaseous; <*bebida*> fizzy

gáspea /'gaspia/ *f* upper

gas|tador /gasta'dor/ *a* & *m* spendthrift; **~tar** *vt* spend <*dinheiro, tempo*>; use up <*energia*>; wear out <*roupa, sapatos*>; **~to** *m* expense; *pl* spending, expenditure; **dar para o ~to** do

gastrenterite /gastrẽte'ritʃi/ *f* gastroenteritis

gástrico /'gastriku/ *a* gastric

gastrite /gas'tritʃi/ *f* gastritis

gastronomia /gastrono'mia/ *f* gastronomy

ga|ta /'gata/ *f* cat; (*fam*) sexy woman; **~tão** *m* (*fam*) hunk

gatilho /ga'tʃiʎu/ *m* trigger

ga|tinha /ga'tʃiɲa/ *f* (*fam*) sexy woman; **~to** *m* cat; (*fam*) hunk; **fazer alg de ~to-sapato** treat s.o. like a doormat

gatuno /ga'tunu/ *m* crook □ *a* crooked

gaúcho /ga'uʃu/ *a* & *m* (person) from Rio Grande do Sul

gaveta /ga'veta/ *f* drawer

gavião /gavi'ãw/ *m* hawk

gaze /'gazi/ *f* gauze

gazela /ga'zɛla/ *f* gazelle

gazeta /ga'zeta/ *f* gazette

geada /ʒi'ada/ *f* frost

ge|ladeira /ʒela'dera/ *f* fridge; **~lado** *a* frozen; (*muito frio*) freezing □ *m* (*Port*) ice cream; **~lar** *vt/i* freeze

gelati|na /ʒela'tʃina/ *f* (*sobremesa*) jelly; (*pó*) gelatine; **~noso** /o/ *a* gooey

geléia /ʒe'lɛja/ *f* jam

ge|leira /ʒe'lera/ *f* glacier; **~lo** /e/ *m* ice

gema /'ʒema/ *f* (*de ovo*) yolk; (*pedra*) gem; **carioca da ~** carioca born and bred; **~da** *f* egg yolk whisked with sugar

gêmeo /'ʒemiu/ *a* & *m* twin; **Gêmeos** (*signo*) Gemini

ge|mer /ʒe'mer/ *vi* moan, groan; **~mido** *m* moan, groan

gene /'ʒɛni/ *m* gene; **~alogia** *f* genealogy; **~alógico** *a* genealogical; **árvore ~alógica** family tree

Genebra /ʒe'nɛbra/ *f* Geneva

gene|ral /ʒene'raw/ (*pl* **~rais**) *m* general; **~ralidade** *f* generality; **~ralização** *f* generalization;

~ralizar *vt/i* generalize; ~ralizar-se *upr* become generalized

genérico /ʒe'nɛriku/ *a* generic

género /'ʒeneru/ *m* type, kind; (*gramatical*) gender; (*literário*) genre; *pl* goods; ~s alimentícios foodstuffs; ela não faz o meu ~ she's not my type

gene|rosidade /ʒenerozi'dadʒi/ *f* generosity; ~roso /o/ *a* generous

genéti|ca /ʒe'nɛtʃika/ *f* genetics; ~co *a* genetic

gengibre /ʒẽ'ʒibri/ *m* ginger

gengiva /ʒẽ'ʒiva/ *f* gum

geni|al /ʒeni'aw/ (*pl* ~ais) *a* brilliant

gênio /'ʒeniu/ *m* genius; (*temperamento*) temperament

genioso /ʒeni'ozu/ *a* temperamental

geni|tal /ʒeni'taw/ (*pl* ~tais) *a* genital

genitivo /ʒeni'tʃivu/ *a* & *m* genitive

genocídio /ʒeno'sidʒiu/ *m* genocide

genro /'ʒẽxu/ *m* son-in-law

gente /'ʒẽtʃi/ *f* people; (*fam*) folks; a ~ (*sujeito*) we; (*objeto*) us □ *interj* (*fam*) gosh

gen|til /ʒẽ'tʃiw/ (*pl* ~tis) *a* kind; ~tileza /e/ *f* kindness

genuíno /ʒenu'inu/ *a* genuine

geo|grafia /ʒeogra'fia/ *f* geography; ~gráfico *a* geographical

geógrafo /ʒe'ɔgrafu/ *m* geographer

geo|logia /ʒeolo'ʒia/ *f* geology; ~lógico *a* geological

geólogo /ʒe'ɔlogu/ *m* geologist

geo|metria /ʒeome'tria/ *f* geometry; ~métrico *a* geometrical; ~político *a* geopolitical

Geórgia /ʒi'ɔrʒia/ *f* Georgia

georgiano /ʒiorʒi'anu/ *a* & *m* Georgian

gera|ção /ʒera'sãw/ *f* generation; ~dor *m* generator

ge|ral /ʒe'raw/ (*pl* ~rais) *a* general □ *f* (*limpeza*) spring-clean; em ~ral in general

gerânio /ʒe'raniu/ *m* geranium

gerar /ʒe'rar/ *vt* create; generate <*eletricidade*>

gerência /ʒe'rẽsia/ *f* management

gerenci|ador /ʒerẽsia'dor/ *m* manager; ~al (*pl* ~ais) *a* management; ~ar *vt* manage

gerente /ʒe'rẽtʃi/ *m* manager □ *a* managing

gergelim /ʒerʒe'lĩ/ *m* sesame

geri|atria /ʒeria'tria/ *f* geriatrics; ~átrico *a* geriatric

geringonça /ʒerĩ'gõsa/ *f* contraption

gerir /ʒe'rir/ *vt* manage

germâni|co /ʒer'maniku/ *a* Germanic

ger|me /'ʒɛrmi/ *m* germ; ~me de trigo wheatgerm; ~minar *vi* germinate

gerúndio /ʒe'rũdʒiu/ *m* gerund

gesso /'ʒesu/ *m* plaster

ges|tação /ʒesta'sãw/ *f* gestation; ~tante *f* pregnant woman

gestão /ʒes'tãw/ *f* management

ges|ticular /ʒestʃiku'lar/ *vi* gesticulate; ~to /'ʒɛstu/ *m* gesture

gibi /ʒi'bi/ *m* (*fam*) comic

Gibraltar /ʒibraw'tar/ *f* Gibraltar

gigan|te /ʒi'gãtʃi/ *a* & *m* giant; ~tesco /e/ *a* gigantic

gilete /ʒi'lɛtʃi/ *f* razor blade □ *a* & *m/f* (*fam*) bisexual

gim /ʒĩ/ *m* gin

ginásio /ʒi'naziu/ *m* (*escola*) secondary school; (*de ginástica*) gymnasium

ginasta /ʒi'nasta/ *m/f* gymnast

ginásti|ca /ʒi'nastʃika/ *f* gymnastics; (*aeróbica*) aerobics; ~co *a* gymnastic

gineco|logia /ʒinekolo'ʒia/ *f* gynaecology; ~gista *m/f* gynaecologist

gingar /ʒĩ'gar/ *vi* sway

gira-discos /ʒira'dʒiʃkuʃ/ *m invar* (*Port*) record player

girafa /ʒi'rafa/ *f* giraffe

gi|rar /ʒi'rar/ *vt/i* spin, revolve; ~rassol (*pl* ~rassóis) *m* sunflower; ~ratório *a* revolving

gíria /'ʒiria/ *f* slang; (*uma* ~) slang expression

giro /'ʒiru/ *m* spin, turn □ *a* (*Port fam*) great

giz /ʒis/ *m* chalk

gla|cê /gla'se/ *m* icing; ~cial (*pl* ~ciais) *a* icy

glamour /gla'mur/ *m* glamour; ~oso /o/ *a* glamorous

glândula /'glãdula/ *f* gland

glandular /glãdu'lar/ *a* glandular

glicerina /glise'rina/ *f* glycerine

glicose /gli'kɔzi/ *f* glucose

glo|bal /glo'baw/ (*pl* ~bais) *a* (*mundial*) global; <*preço etc*> overall; ~bo /o/ *m* globe; ~bo ocular eyeball

glóbulo /'glɔbulu/ *m* globule; (*do sangue*) corpuscle

glória /'glɔria/ *f* glory

glori|ficar /glorifi'kar/ *vt* glorify; ~oso /o/ *a* glorious

glossário /glo'sariu/ *m* glossary

glu|tão /glu'tãw/ *m* (*f* ~tona) glutton □ *a* (*f* ~tona) greedy

gnomo /ʒi'nomu/ *m* gnome

godê /go'de/ *a* flared

goela /go'ɛla/ *f* gullet

gogó /go'gɔ/ *m* (*fam*) Adam's apple

goia|ba /goj'aba/ *f* guava; ~bada *f* guava jelly; ~beira *f* guava tree

gol /'gow/ (*pl* ~s) *m* goal

gola /'gɔla/ *f* collar

gole /'gɔli/ *m* mouthful

go|lear /goli'ar/ *vt* thrash; ~leiro *m* goalkeeper

golfe /'gowfi/ *m* golf

golfinho /gow'fiɲu/ *m* dolphin

golfista /gow'fista/ *m/f* golfer

golo /'golu/ *m* (*Port*) goal

golpe /'gɔwpi/ *m* blow; (*manobra*) trick; ~ (*de estado*) coup (d'état); ~ de mestre masterstroke; ~ de vento gust of wind; ~ de vista glance; ~ar *vt* hit

goma /'goma/ *f* gum; (*para roupa*) starch

gomo /'gomu/ *m* segment

gôndola /'gõdola/ *f* rack

gongo /'gõgu/ *m* gong

gonorréia /gono'xeja/ *f* gonorrhea

gonzo /'gõzu/ *m* hinge

gorar /go'rar/ *vi* go wrong, fail

gor|do /'gordu/ *a* fat; ~ducho *a* plump

gordu|ra /gor'dura/ *f* fat; ~rento *a* greasy; ~roso /u/ *a* fatty; <*pele*> greasy, oily

gorgolejar /gorgole'ʒar/ *vi* gurgle

gorila /go'rila/ *m* gorilla

gor|jear /gorʒi'ar/ *vi* twitter; ~jeio *m* twittering

gorjeta /gor'ʒeta/ *f* tip

gorro /'goxu/ *m* hat

gos|ma /'gɔzma/ *f* slime; ~mento *a* slimy

gos|tar /gos'tar/ *vi* ~tar de like; ~to /o/ *m* taste; (*prazer*) pleasure; para o meu ~ to for my taste; ter ~to de taste of; ~toso *a* nice; <*comida*> nice, tasty; (*fam*) <*pessoa*> gorgeous

go|ta /'gota/ *f* drop; (*que cai*) drip; (*doença*) gout; foi a ~ta d'água (*fig*) it was the last straw; ~teira *f* (*buraco*) leak; (*cano*) gutter; ~tejar *vi* drip; <*telhado*> leak □ *vt* drip

gótico /'gɔtʃiku/ *a* Gothic

gotícula /go'tʃikula/ *f* droplet

gover|nador /governa'dor/ *m* governor; ~namental (*pl* ~namentais) *a* government; ~nanta *f* housekeeper; ~nante *a* ruling □ *m/f* ruler; ~nar *vt* govern; ~nista *a* government □ *m/f* government supporter; ~no /e/ *m* government

go|zação /goza'sãw/ *f* joking; (*uma*) send-up; ~zado *a* funny; ~zar *vt* ~zar (de) enjoy; (*fam: zombar de*) make fun of □ *vi* (*ter orgasmo*) come; ~zo *m* (*prazer*) enjoyment; (*posse*) possession; (*orgasmo*) orgasm; ser um ~zo be funny

Grã-Bretanha /grãbre'taɲa/ *f* Great Britain

graça /'grasa/ *f* grace; (*piada*) joke; (*humor*) humour, funny side; (*jur*) pardon; de ~ for nothing; sem ~ (*enfadonho*) dull; (*não engraçado*) unfunny; (*envergonhado*) embarrassed; ser uma ~ be lovely; ter ~ be funny; não tem ~ sair sozinho it's no fun to go out alone; ~s a thanks to

grace|jar /grase'ʒar/ *vi* joke; ~jo /e/ *m* joke

graci|nha /gra'siɲa/ *f* ser uma ~nha be sweet; ~oso /o/ *a* gracious

grada|ção /grada'sãw/ *f* gradation; ~tivo *a* gradual

grade /'gradʒi/ *f* grille, grating; (*cerca*) railings; atrás das ~s behind bars; ~ado *a* <*janela*> barred

grado /'gradu/ *m* de bom/mau ~ willingly/unwillingly

gradu|ação /gradua'sãw/ *f* graduation; (*mil*) rank; (*variação*) gradation; ~ado *a* <*escala*> graduated; <*estudante*> graduate; <*militar*> high-ranking; (*eminente*) respected; ~al (*pl* ~ais) *a* gradual; ~ar *vt* graduate <*escala*>; (*ordenar*) grade; (*regular*) regulate; ~ar-se *vpr* <*estudante*> graduate

grafia /gra'fia/ *f* spelling

gráfi|ca /'grafika/ *f* (*arte*) graphics; (*oficina*) print shop; ~co *a* graphic □ *m* (*pessoa*) printer; (*diagrama*) graph; *pl* (*de computador*) graphics

grã-fino /grã'finu/ (*fam*) *a* posh, upper-class □ *m* posh person

grafite /gra'fitʃi/ *f* (*mineral*) graphite; (*de lápis*) lead; (*pichação*) piece of graffiti

grafologia /grafolo'ʒia/ *f* graphology; ~fólogo *m* graphologist

grama[1] /'grama/ *f* gramme

grama[2] /'grama/ *f* grass; ~do *m* lawn; (*campo de futebol*) field

gramática /gra'matʃika/ *f* grammar

gramati|cal /gramatʃi'kaw/ (*pl* ~cais) *a* grammatical

gram|peador /grãpia'dor/ *m* stapler; ~pear *vt* staple <*papéis etc*>; tap <*telefone*>; ~po *m* (*de cabelo*) hairclip; (*para papéis etc*) staple; (*ferramenta*) clamp

grana /'grana/ *f* (*fam*) cash

granada /gra'nada/ *f* (*projétil*) grenade; (*pedra*) garnet

gran|dalhão /grãda'ʎãw/ *a* (*f* ~dalhona*) enormous; ~dão *a* (*f* ~dona*) huge; ~de *a* big; (*fig*) <*escritor, amor etc*> great; ~deza /e/ *f* greatness; (*tamanho*) magnitude; ~dioso /o/ *a* grand

granel /gra'nɛw/ *m* a ~ in bulk

granito /gra'nitu/ *m* granite

granizo /gra'nizu/ *m* hail

gran|ja /'grãʒa/ *f* farm; ~jear *vt* win, gain

granulado /granu'ladu/ *a* granulated

grânulo /'granulu/ *m* granule

grão /grãw/ (*pl* ~s) *m* grain; (*de café*) bean; ~-de-bico (*pl* ~s-de-bico) *m* chickpea

grasnar /graz'nar/ *vi* <*pato*> quack; <*rã*> croak; <*corvo*> caw

grati|dão /grati'dãw/ f gratitude; ~**ficação** f (dinheiro a mais) gratuity; (recompensa) gratification; ~**ficante** a gratifying; ~**ficar** vt (dar dinheiro a) give a gratuity to; (recompensar) gratify

gratinado /grati'nadu/ a & m gratin

grátis /'gratfis/ adv free

grato /'gratu/ a grateful

gratuito /gra'tuitu/ a (de graça) free; (sem motivo) gratuitous

grau /graw/ m degree; **escola de 1º/2º** ~ primary/secondary school

graúdo /gra'udu/ a big; (importante) important

gra|vação /grava'sãw/ f (de som) recording; (de desenhos etc) engraving; ~**vador** m (pessoa) engraver; (máquina) tape recorder; ~**vadora** f record company; ~**var** vt record <música, disco>; (fixar na memória) memorize; (estampar) engrave

gravata /gra'vata/ f tie; (golpe) stranglehold; ~ **borboleta** bowtie

grave /'gravi/ a serious; <voz, som> deep; <acento> grave

grávida /'gravida/ f pregnant

gravidade /gravi'dadʒi/ f gravity

gravidez /gravi'des/ f pregnancy

gravura /gra'vura/ f engraving; (em livro) illustration

graxa /'graʃa/ f (de sapatos) polish; (de lubrificar) grease

Grécia /'grɛsia/ f Greece

grego /'gregu/ a & m Greek

grei /grej/ f flock

gre|lha /'grɛʎa/ f grill; ~**lhado** a grilled □ m grill; ~**lhar** vt grill

grêmio /'gremiu/ m guild, association

grená /gre'na/ a & m dark red

gre|ta /'greta/ f crack; ~**tar** vt/i crack

gre|ve /'grɛvi/ f strike; **entrar em** ~ **ve** go on strike; ~**ve de fome** hunger strike; ~**vista** m/f striker

gri|fado /gri'fadu/ a in italics; ~**far** vt italicize

griffe /'grifi/ f label, line

gri|lado /gri'ladu/ a (fam) hung-up; ~**lar** (fam) vt bug; ~**lar-se** vpr get hung-up (com about)

grilhão /gri'ʎãw/ m fetter

grilo /'grilu/ m (bicho) cricket; (fam) (preocupação) hang-up; (problema) hassle; (barulho) squeak

grinalda /gri'nawda/ f garland

gringo /'grĩgu/ (fam) a foreign □ m foreigner

gri|pado /gri'padu/ a **estar/ficar** ~**pado** have/get the flu; ~**par-se** vpr get the flu; ~**pe** f flu, influenza

grisalho /gri'zaʎu/ a grey

gri|tante /gri'tãtʃi/ a <erro> glaring, gross; <cor> loud, garish; ~**tar** vt/i shout; (de medo) scream; ~**taria** f

shouting; ~**to** m shout; (de medo) scream; **aos** ~**tos** in a loud voice; **no** ~**to** (fam) by force

grogue /'grɔgi/ a groggy

grosa /'grɔza/ f gross

groselha /gro'zɛʎa/ f (vermelha) redcurrant; (espinhosa) gooseberry; ~ **negra** blackcurrant

gros|seiro /gro'seru/ a rude; (tosco, malfeito) rough; ~**seria** f rudeness; (uma) rude thing; ~**so** /o/ a thick; <voz> deep; (fam) <pessoa, atitude> rude; ~**sura** f thickness; (fam: grosseria) rudeness

grotesco /gro'tesku/ a grotesque

grua /'grua/ f crane

gru|dado /gru'dadu/ a stuck; (fig) very attached (em to); ~**dar** vt/i stick; ~**de** m glue; ~**dento** a sticky

gru|nhido /gru'ɲidu/ m grunt; ~**nhir** vi grunt

grupo /'grupu/ m group

gruta /'gruta/ f cave

guaraná /gwara'na/ m guarana

guarani /gwara'ni/ a & m/f Guarani

guarda /'gwarda/ f guard □ m/f guard; (policial) policeman (f -woman); ~ **costeira** coastguard; ~**chuva** m umbrella; ~**costas** m invar bodyguard; ~**dor** m parking attendant; ~**florestal** (pl ~**s-florestais**) m/f forest ranger; ~**louça** m china cupboard; ~**napo** m napkin, serviette; ~**noturno** (pl ~**s-noturnos**) m night watchman

guardar /gwar'dar/ vt (pôr no lugar) put away; (conservar) keep; (vigiar) guard; (não esquecer) remember; ~**se de** guard against

guarda|-redes /gwarda'xedʃ/ m invar (Port) goalkeeper; ~**roupa** m wardrobe; ~**sol** (pl ~**sóis**) m sunshade

guardi|ão /gwardʒi'ãw/ (pl ~**ães** ou ~**ões**) m (f ~**ã**) guardian

guarita /gwa'rita/ f sentry box

guar|necer /gwarne'ser/ vt (fortificar) garrison; (munir) equip; (enfeitar) garnish; ~**nição** f (mil) garrison; (enfeite) garnish

Guatemala /gwate'mala/ f Guatemala

guatemalteco /gwatemal'tɛku/ a & m Guatemalan

gude /'gudʒi/ m **bola de** ~ marble

guelra /'gɛwxa/ f gill

guer|ra /'gɛxa/ f war; ~**reiro** m warrior □ a warlike; ~**rilha** f guerrilla war; ~**rilheiro** a & m guerrilla

gueto /'getu/ m ghetto

guia /'gia/ m/f guide □ m guide(book) □ f delivery note

Guiana /gi'ana/ f Guyana

guianense /gia'nɛsi/ a & m/f Guyanan

guiar /gi'ar/ vt guide; drive <veículo> □ vi drive; ~-se vpr be guided

guichê /gi'ʃe/ m window

guidom /gi'dõ/, (Port) guidão /gi'dãw/ m handlebars

guilhotina /giʎo'tʃina/ f guillotine

guimba /'gĩba/ f butt

guinada /gi'nada/ f change of direction; dar uma ~ change direction

guinchar¹ /gĩ'ʃar/ vi squeal; <freios> screech

guinchar² /gĩ'ʃar/ vt tow <carro> (içar) winch

guincho¹ /'gĩʃu/ m squeal; (de freios) screech

guincho² /'gĩʃu/ m (máquina) winch; (veículo) tow truck

guin|dar /gĩ'dar/ vt hoist; ~daste m crane

Guiné /gi'nɛ/ f Guinea

gui|sado /gi'zadu/ m stew; ~sar vt stew

guitar|ra /gi'taxa/ f (electric) guitar; ~rista m/f guitarist

guizo /'gizu/ m bell

gu|la /'gula/ f greed; ~lodice f greed; ~loseima f delicacy; ~loso /o/ a greedy

gume /'gumi/ m cutting edge

guri /gu'ri/ m boy; ~a f girl

guru /gu'ru/ m guru

gutu|ral /gutu'raw/ (pl ~rais) a guttural

H

há|bil /'abiw/ (pl ~beis) a clever, skilful

habili|dade /abili'dadʒi/ f skill; ter ~dade com be good with; ~doso /o/ a skilful; ~tação f qualification; ~tar vt qualify

habi|tação /abita'sãw/ f housing; (casa) dwelling; ~tacional (pl ~tacionais) a housing; ~tante m/f inhabitant; ~tar vt inhabit □ vi live; ~tável (pl ~táveis) a habitable

hábito /'abitu/ m habit

habitu|al /abitu'aw/ (pl ~ais) a habitual; ~ar vt accustom (a to); ~ar-se vpr get accustomed (a to)

hadoque /a'dɔki/ m haddock

Haia /'aja/ f the Hague

Haiti /aj'tʃi/ m Haiti

haitiano /ajtʃi'anu/ a & m Haitian

hálito /'alitu/ m breath

halitose /ali'tɔzi/ f halitosis

hall /xɔw/ (pl ~s) m hall; (de hotel) foyer

halte|re /aw'tɛri/ m dumbbell; ~rofilismo m weight lifting; ~rofilista m/f weight lifter

hambúrguer /ã'burger/ m hamburger

hangar /ã'gar/ m hangar

haras /'aras/ m invar stud farm

hardware /'xarduer/ m hardware

harmo|nia /armo'nia/ f harmony; ~nioso /o/ a harmonious; ~nizar vt harmonize; (conciliar) reconcile; ~nizar-se vpr (combinar) tone in; (concordar) coincide

har|pa /'arpa/ f harp; ~pista m/f harpist

haste /'astʃi/ m pole; (de planta) stem, stalk; ~ar vt hoist, raise

Havaí /ava'i/ m Hawaii

havaiano /avaj'anu/ a & m Hawaiian

haver /a'ver/ m credit; pl possessions □ vt (auxiliar) havia sido it had been; (impessoal) há there is/are; ele trabalha aqui há anos he's been working here for years; ela morreu há vinte anos (atrás) she died twenty years ago

haxixe /a'ʃiʃi/ m hashish

he|braico /e'brajku/ a & m Hebrew; ~breu a & m (f ~bréia) Hebrew

hectare /ek'tari/ m hectare

hediondo /edʒi'õdu/ a hideous

hein /ẽj/ int eh

hélice /'ɛlisi/ f propeller

helicóptero /eli'kɔpteru/ m helicopter

hélio /'ɛliu/ m helium

heliporto /eli'portu/ m heliport

hem /ẽj/ int eh

hematoma /ema'toma/ m bruise

hemisfério /emis'fɛriu/ m hemisphere; Hemisfério Norte/Sul Northern/Southern Hemisphere

hemo|filia /emofi'lia/ f haemophilia; ~fílico a & m haemophiliac; ~globina f haemoglobin; ~grama m blood count

hemor|ragia /emoxa'ʒia/ f haemorrhage; ~róidas f pl haemorrhoids

henê /e'ne/ m henna

hepatite /epa'tʃitʃi/ f hepatitis

hera /'ɛra/ f ivy

herál|dica /e'rawdʒika/ f heraldry; ~co a heraldic

herança /e'rãsa/ f inheritance; (de um povo etc) heritage

her|bicida /erbi'sida/ m weedkiller; ~bívoro a herbivorous □ m herbivore

her|dar /er'dar/ vt inherit; ~deiro m heir

hereditário /eredʒi'tariu/ a hereditary

here|ge /e'rɛʒi/ m/f heretic; ~sia f heresy

herético /e'rɛtʃiku/ a heretical

hermético /er'mɛtʃiku/ a airtight; (fig) obscure

hérnia /'ɛrnia/ f hernia

herói /e'rɔj/ m hero; ~co a heroic

hero|ína /ero'ina/ f (*mulher*) heroine; (*droga*) heroin; ~ismo m heroism

herpes /'ɛrpis/ m invar herpes; ~-zoster m shingles

hesi|tação /ezita'sãw/ f hesitation; ~tante a hesitant; ~tar vi hesitate

hetero|doxo /etero'dɔksu/ a unorthodox; ~geneo a heterogeneous

heterossexu|al /eteroseksu'aw/ (*pl* ~ais) a & m heterosexual

hexago|nal /eksago'naw/ (*pl* ~nais) a hexagonal

hexágono /ek'sagonu/ m hexagon

hiato /i'atu/ m hiatus

hiber|nação /iberna'sãw/ f hibernation; ~nar vi hibernate

híbrido /'ibridu/ a & m hybrid

hidrante /i'drãtʃi/ m fire hydrant

hidra|tante /idra'tãtʃi/ f moisturising □ m moisturizer; ~tar vt moisturize □to m ~to de carbono carbohydrate

hidráuli|ca /i'drawlika/ f hydraulics; ~co a hydraulic

hidrelétri|ca /idre'lɛtrika/ f hydroelectric power station; ~co a hydroelectric

hidro|avião /idroavi'ãw/ m seaplane; ~carboneto e/ m hydrocarbon

hidrófilo /i'drɔfilu/ a absorbent; algodão ~ cotton wool, (*Amer*) absorbent cotton

hidrofobia /idrofo'bia/ f rabies

hidro|gênio /idro'ʒeniu/ m hydrogen; ~massagem f banheira de ~massagem jacuzzi; ~via f waterway

hiena /i'ena/ f hyena

hierarquia /ierar'kia/ f hierarchy

hieróglifo /ie'rɔglifu/ m hieroglyphic

hifen /'ifẽ/ m hyphen

higi|ene /iʒi'eni/ f hygiene; ~ênico a hygienic

hilari|ante /ilari'ãtʃi/ a hilarious; ~dade f hilarity

Himalaia /ima'laja/ m Himalayas

hin|di /ĩ'dʒi/ m Hindi; ~du a & m/f Hindu; ~duísmo m Hinduism; ~duista a m/f Hindu

hino /'inu/ m hymn; ~ nacional national anthem

hipermercado /ipermer'kadu/ m hypermarket

hipersensí|vel /ipersẽ'sivew/ (*pl* ~veis) a hypersensitive

hipertensão /ipertẽ'sãw/ f hypertension

hípico /'ipiku/ a horseriding

hipismo /i'pizmu/ m horseriding; (*corridas*) horseracing

hip|nose /ipi'nɔzi/ f hypnosis; ~nótico a hypnotic; ~notismo m hypnotism; ~notizador m hypnotist; ~notizar vt hypnotize

hipocondríaco /ipokõ'driaku/ a & m hypochondriac

hipocrisia /ipokri'zia/ f hypocrisy

hipócrita /i'pɔkrita/ m/f hypocrite □ a hypocritical

hipódromo /i'pɔdromu/ m race course, (*Amer*) race track

hipopótamo /ipo'pɔtamu/ m hippopotamus

hipote|ca /ipo'tɛka/ f mortgage; ~car vt mortgage; ~cário a mortgage

hipotermia /ipoter'mia/ f hypothermia

hipótese /i'pɔtezi/ f hypothesis; na ~ de in the event of; na pior das ~s at worst

hipotético /ipo'tɛtʃiku/ a hypothetical

hirto /'irtu/ adj rigid, stiff

hispânico /is'paniku/ a Hispanic

histamina /ista'mina/ f histamine

his|terectomia /isterekto'mia/ f hysterectomy; ~teria f hysteria; ~térico a hysterical; ~terismo m hysteria

his|tória /is'tɔria/ f (*do passado*) history; (*conto*) story; pl (*amolação*) trouble; ~toriador m historian; ~tórico a historical; (*marcante*) historic □ m history

hoje /'oʒi/ adv today; ~ em dia nowadays; ~ de manhã this morning; ~ à noite tonight

Holanda /o'lãda/ f Holland

holan|dês /olã'des/ a (f ~desa) Dutch □ m (f ~desa) Dutchman (f -woman); (*língua*) Dutch; os ~deses the Dutch

holding /'xɔwdʒĩ/ (*pl* ~s) f holding company

holerite /ole'ritʃi/ m pay slip

holo|causto /olo'kawstu/ m holocaust; ~fote /ɔ/ m spotlight; ~grama m hologram

homem /'omẽ/ m man; ~ de negócios businessman; ~-rã (*pl* homens-rã) m frogman

homena|gear /omenaʒi'ar/ vt pay tribute to; ~gem f tribute; em ~gem a in honour of

homeo|pata /omio'pata/ m/f homoeopath; ~patia f homoeopathy; ~pático a homoeopathic

homérico /o'mɛriku/ a (*estrondoso*) booming; (*extraordinário*) phenomenal

homi|cida /omi'sida/ a homicidal □ m/f murderer; ~cídio m homicide; ~cídio involuntário manslaughter

homo|geneizado /omoʒenej'zadu/ a <*leite*> homogenized; ~gêneo a homogeneous

homologar /omolo'gar/ vt ratify

homólogo /o'mɔlogu/ *m* opposite number □ *a* equivalent

homónimo /o'monimu/ *m* (*xará*) namesake; (*vocábulo*) homonym

homossexu|al /omoseksu'aw/ (*pl* ~ais) *a* & *m* homosexual; ~alismo *m* homosexuality

Honduras /õ'duras/ *f* Honduras

hondurenho /õdu'reɲu/ *a* & *m* Honduran

hones|tidade /onestʃi'dadʒi/ *f* honesty; ~to /ɛ/ *a* honest

hono|rário /ono'rariu/ *a* honorary; ~rários *m pl* fees; ~rífico *a* honorific

hon|ra /'õxa/ *f* honour; ~radez *f* honesty, integrity; ~rado *a* honourable; ~rar *vt* honour; ~roso /o/ *a* honourable

hóquei /'ɔkej/ *m* (field) hockey; ~ sobre gelo ice hockey; ~ sobre patins roller hockey

hora /'ɔra/ *f* (*unidade de tempo*) hour; (*ocasião*) time; que ~s são? what's the time?; a que ~s? at what time?; às três ~s at three o'clock; dizer as ~s tell the time; tem ~s? do you have the time?; de ~ em ~ every hour; em cima da ~ at the last minute; na ~ (*naquele momento*) at the time; (*no ato*) on the spot; (*a tempo*) on time; está na ~ de ir it's time to go; na ~ H (*no momento certo*) at just the right moment; (*no momento crítico*) at the crucial moment; meia ~ half an hour; toda a ~ all the time; fazer ~ kill time; marcar ~ make an appointment; perder a ~ lose track of time; não tenho ~ my time is my own; não vejo a ~ de ir I can't wait to go; ~s extras overtime; ~s vagas spare time

horário /o'rariu/ *a* hourly; km ~s km per hour □ *m* (*hora*) time; (*tabela*) timetable; (*de trabalho etc*) hours; ~ nobre prime time

horda /'ɔrda/ *f* horde

horista /o'rista/ *a* paid by the hour □ *m/f* worker paid by the hour

horizon|tal /orizõ'taw/ (*pl* ~tais) *a* & *f* horizontal; ~te *m* horizon

hor|monal /ormo'naw/ (*pl* ~monais) *a* hormonal; ~mónio *m* hormone

horóscopo /o'rɔskopu/ *m* horoscope

horrendo /o'xẽdu/ *a* horrid

horripi|lante /oxipi'lãtʃi/ *a* horrifying; ~lar *vt* horrify

horrí|vel /o'xivew/ (*pl* ~veis) *a* horrible, awful

horror /o'xor/ *m* horror (a of); (*coisa horrorosa*) horrible thing; ser um ~ be awful; que ~! how awful!

horro|rizar /oxori'zar/ *vt/i* horrify; ~rizar-se *vpr* be horrified; ~roso /o/ *a* horrible

horta /'ɔrta/ *f* vegetable plot; ~ comercial market garden, (*Amer*) truck farm; ~liça *f* vegetable

hortelã /orte'lã/ *f* mint; ~-pimenta peppermint

horti|cultor /ortʃikuw'tor/ *m* horticulturalist; ~cultura *f* horticulture; ~frutigranjeiros *m pl* fruit and vegetables; ~granjeiros *m pl* vegetables

horto /'ɔrtu/ *m* market garden; (*viveiro*) nursery

hospe|dagem /ospe'daʒẽ/ *f* accommodation; ~dar *vt* put up; ~dar-se *vpr* stay

hóspede /'ɔspedʒi/ *m/f* guest

hospedei|ra /ospe'dera/ *f* landlady; ~ra de bordo (*Port*) stewardess; ~ro *m* landlord

hospício /os'pisiu/ *m* (*de loucos*) asylum

hospi|tal /ospi'taw/ (*pl* ~tais) *m* hospital; ~talar *a* hospital; ~taleiro *a* hospitable; ~talidade *f* hospitality; ~talizar *vt* hospitalize

hóstia /'ɔstʃia/ *f* Host, Communion wafer

hos|til /os'tʃiw/ (*pl* ~tis) *a* hostile; ~tilidade *f* hostility; ~tilizar *vt* antagonize

ho|tel /o'tɛw/ (*pl* ~téis) *m* hotel; ~teleiro *a* hotel □ *m* hotelier

huma|nidade /umani'dadʒi/ *f* humanity; ~nismo *m* humanism; ~nista *a* & *m/f* humanist; ~nitário *a* & *m* humanitarian; ~nizar *vt* humanize; ~no *a* human; (*compassivo*) humane; ~nos *m pl* humans

húmido /'umidu/ *adj* (*Port*) humid

humil|dade /umiw'dadʒi/ *f* humility; ~de *a* humble

humi|lhação /umiʎa'sãw/ *f* humiliation; ~lhante *a* humiliating; ~lhar *vt* humiliate

humor /u'mor/ *m* humour; (*disposição do espírito*) mood; de bom/mau ~ in a good/bad mood

humo|rismo /umo'rizmu/ *m* humour; ~rista *m/f* (*no palco*) comedian; (*escritor*) humorist; ~rístico *a* humorous

húngaro /'ũgaru/ *a* & *m* Hungarian

Hungria /ũ'gria/ *f* Hungary

hurra /'uxa/ *int* hurrah □ *m* cheer

I

ia|te /i'atʃi/ *m* yacht; ~tismo *m* yachting; ~tista *m/f* yachtsman (*f* -woman)

ibérico /i'bɛriku/ *a* & *m* Iberian

ibope /i'bɔpi/ *m* **dar ~** (*fam*) be popular

içar /i'sar/ *vt* hoist

iceberg /ajs'bɛrgi/ (*pl* ~s) *m* iceberg

icone /i'koni/ *m* icon

iconoclasta /ikono'klasta/ *m/f* iconoclast □ *a* iconoclastic

icterícia /ikte'risia/ *f* jaundice

ida /'ida/ *f* going; **na ~** on the way there; **~ e volta** return, (*Amer*) round trip

idade /i'dadʒi/ *f* age; **meia ~** middle age; **homem de meia ~** middle-aged man; **senhor de ~** elderly man; **Idade Média** Middle Ages

ideal /ide'aw/ (*pl* ~ais) *a* & *m* ideal; **~alismo** *m* idealism; **~alista** *m/f* idealist □ *a* idealistic; **~alizar** *vt* (*criar*) devise; (*sublimar*) idealize; **~ar** *vt* devise; **~ário** *m* ideas

idéia /i'dɛja/ *f* idea; **mudar de ~** change one's mind

idem /'idẽ/ *adv* ditto

idêntico /i'dẽtʃiku/ *a* identical

identidade /idẽtʃi'dadʒi/ *f* identity; **~ficar** *vt* identify; **~ficar-se** *vpr* identify (**com** with)

ideologia /ideolo'ʒia/ *f* ideology; **~lógico** *a* ideological

idílico /i'dʒiliku/ *a* idyllic

idílio /i'dʒiliu/ *m* idyll

idioma /idʒi'oma/ *m* language; **~mático** *a* idiomatic

idiota /idʒi'ɔta/ *m/f* idiot □ *a* idiotic; **~tice** /i/ stupidity; (*uma*) stupid thing

idolatrar /idola'trar/ *vt* idolize; **~tria** /i/ idolatry

ídolo /'idulu/ *m* idol

idôneo /i'doniu/ *a* suitable

idoso /i'dozu/ *a* elderly

Iêmen /i'emẽ/ *m* Yemen

iemenita /ieme'nita/ *a* & *m/f* Yemeni

iene /i'ɛni/ *m* yen

iglu /i'glu/ *m* igloo

ignição /igni'sãw/ *f* ignition

ignomínia /igno'minia/ *f* ignominy

ignorância /igno'rãsia/ *f* ignorance; **~rante** *a* ignorant; **~rar** (*desconsiderar*) ignore; (*desconhecer*) not know

igreja /i'greʒa/ *f* church

igual /i'gwaw/ (*pl* ~ais) *a* equal; (*em aparência*) identical; (*liso*) even □ *m/f* equal; **por ~** equally; **~ a** equal to; **level** <*terreno*>; **~alar(-se) a** be equal to; **~aldade** *f* equality; **~alitário** *a* egalitarian; **~almente** *adv* equally; (*como resposta*) the same to you; **~alzinho** *a* exactly the same (**a** as)

iguaria /igwa'ria/ *f* delicacy

iídiche /i'idifi/ *m* Yiddish

ilegal /ile'gaw/ (*pl* ~gais) *a* illegal; **~galidade** *f* illegality

ilegítimo /ile'ʒitʃimu/ *a* illegitimate

ilegível /ile'ʒivew/ (*pl* ~veis) *a* illegible

ileso /i'lɛzu/ *a* unhurt

iletrado /ile'tradu/ *adj* & *m* illiterate

ilha /'iʎa/ *f* island

ilharga /i'ʎarga/ *f* side

ilhéu /i'ʎɛw/ *m* (*f* **ilhoa**) islander

ilhós /i'ʎɔs/ *m invar* eyelet

ilhota /i'ʎɔta/ *f* small island

ilícito /i'lisitu/ *a* illicit

ilimitado /ilimi'tadu/ *a* unlimited

ilógico /i'lɔʒiku/ *a* illogical

iludir /ilu'dʒir/ *vt* delude; **~-se** *vpr* delude o.s.

iluminação /ilumina'sãw/ *f* lighting; (*inspiração*) enlightenment; **~nar** *vt* light up, illuminate; (*inspirar*) enlighten

ilusão /ilu'zãw/ *f* illusion; (*sonho*) delusion; **~sionista** *m/f* illusionist; **~sório** *a* illusory

ilustração /ilustra'sãw/ *f* illustration; (*erudição*) learning; **~trador** *m* illustrator; **~trar** *vt* illustrate; **~trativo** *a* illustrative; **~tre** *a* illustrious; **~tríssimo senhor** Dear Sir

imã /'imã/ *m* magnet

imaculado /imaku'ladu/ *a* immaculate

imagem /i'maʒẽ/ *f* image; (*da TV*) picture

imaginação /imaʒina'sãw/ *f* imagination; **~nar** *vt* imagine; **~nário** *a* imaginary; **~nativo** *a* imaginative; **~nável** (*pl* ~náveis) *a* imaginable; **~noso** /o/ *a* imaginative

imaturidade /imaturi'dadʒi/ *f* immaturity; **~ro** *a* immature

imbatível /ĩba'tʃivew/ (*pl* ~veis) *a* unbeatable

imbecil /ĩbe'siw/ (*pl* ~cis) *a* stupid □ *m/f* imbecile

imberbe /ĩ'bɛrbi/ *adj* (*sem barba*) beardless

imbricar /ĩbri'kar/ *vt* overlap; **~-se** *vpr* overlap

imediações /imedʒia'sõjs/ *f pl* vicinity; **~tamente** *adv* immediately; **~to** *a* immediate

imemorial /imemori'aw/ (*pl* ~ais) *a* immemorial

imensidão /imẽsi'dãw/ *f* vastness; **~so** *a* immense

imergir /imer'ʒir/ *vt* immerse

imigração /imigra'sãw/ *f* immigration; **~grante** *a* & *m/f* immigrant; **~grar** *vi* immigrate

iminência /imi'nẽsia/ *f* imminence; **~nente** *a* imminent

imiscuir-se /imisku'irsi/ *vpr* interfere

imitação /imita'sãw/ *f* imitation; **~tador** *m* imitator; **~tar** *vt* imitate imobili|ária /imobili'aria/ f estate agent's, (*Amer*) realtor; ~ário *a* property; ~dade *f* immobility; ~zar *vt* immobilize

imo|ral /imo'raw/ (*pl* ~rais) *a* immoral; ~ralidade *f* immorality

imor|tal /imor'taw/ (*pl* ~tais) *a* immortal □ *m/f* member of the Brazilian Academy of Letters; ~talidade *f* immortality; ~talizar *vt* immortalize

imó|vel /i'mɔvew/ (*pl* ~veis) *a* motionless, immobile □ *m* building, property; *pl* property, real estate

impaci|ência /impasi'ĕsia/ *f* impatience; ~entar-se *vpr* get impatient; ~ente *a* impatient

impacto /ī'paktu/, (*Port*) impacte /ī'paktʃi/ *m* impact

impagá|vel /ipa'gavew/ (*pl* ~veis) *a* priceless

ímpar /'īpar/ *a* unique; <*número*> odd

imparci|al /iparsi'aw/ (*pl* ~ais) *a* impartial; ~alidade *f* impartiality

impasse /ī'pasi/ *m* impasse

impassí|vel /ipa'sivew/ (*pl* ~veis) *a* impassive

impecá|vel /ipe'kavew/ (*pl* ~veis) *a* impeccable

impe|dido /ipe'dʒidu/ *a* <*rua*> blocked; (*Port*: *ocupado*) engaged, (*Amer*) busy; (*no futebol*) offside; ~dimento *m* prevention; (*estorvo*) obstruction; (*no futebol*) offside position; ~dir *vt* stop; (*estorvar*) hinder; block <*rua*>; ~dir alg de ir *ou* que alg vá stop s.o. going

impelir /ipe'lir/ *vt* drive

impenetrá|vel /ipene'travew/ (*pl* ~veis) *a* impenetrable

impensá|vel /ipẽ'savew/ (*pl* ~veis) *a* unthinkable

impe|rador /ipera'dor/ *m* emperor; ~rar *vi* reign, rule; ~rativo *a* & *m* imperative; ~ratriz *f* empress

impercepti|vel /ipersep'tʃivew/ (*pl* ~veis) *a* imperceptible

imperdí|vel /iper'dʒivew/ (*pl* ~veis) *a* unmissable

imperdoá|vel /iperdo'avew/ (*pl* ~veis) *a* unforgivable

imperfei|ção /iperfej'sãw/ *f* imperfection; ~to *a* & *m* imperfect

imperi|al /iperi'aw/ (*pl* ~ais) *a* imperial; ~alismo *m* imperialism; ~alista *a* & *m/f* imperialist

império /i'periu/ *m* empire

imperioso /iperi'ozu/ *a* imperious; <*necessidade*> pressing

imperme|abilizar /ipermiabili'zar/ *vt* waterproof; ~ável (*pl* ~áveis) *a* waterproof; (*fig*) impervious (a to) □ *m* raincoat

imperti|nência /ipertʃi'nẽsia/ *f* impertinence; ~nente *a* impertinent

impesso|al /ipeso'aw/ (*pl* ~ais) *a* impersonal

ímpeto /'īpetu/ *m* (*vontade*) urge, impulse; (*de emoção*) surge; (*movimento*) start; (*na física*) impetus

impetuo|sidade /ipetuozi'dadʒi/ *f* impetuosity; ~so /o/ *a* impetuous

impiedoso /ipie'dozu/ *a* merciless

impingir /ipī'ʒir/ *vt* foist (a on)

implacá|vel /ipla'kavew/ (*pl* ~veis) *a* implacable

implan|tar /iplã'tar/ *vt* introduce; (*no corpo*) implant; ~te *m* implant

implemen|tar /iplemẽ'tar/ *vt* implement; ~to *m* implement

impli|cação /iplika'sãw/ *f* implication; ~cância *f* (*ato*) harassment; (*antipatia*) grudge; estar de ~cância com have it in for; ~cante *a* troublesome □ *m/f* troublemaker; ~car *vt* (*comprometer*) implicate; ~car (em) (*dar a entender*) imply; (*acarretar, exigir*) involve; ~car com (*provocar*) pick on; (*antipatizar*) not get on with

implícito /i'plisitu/ *a* implicit

implorar /iplo'rar/ *vt* plead for (a from)

imponente /ipo'nẽtʃi/ *a* imposing

impopular /ipopu'lar/ *a* unpopular

impor /ī'por/ *vt* impose (a on); command <*respeito*>; ~-se *vpr* assert o.s.

impor|tação /iporta'sãw/ *f* import; ~tador *m* importer; ~tadora *f* import company; ~tados *m pl* imported goods; ~tância *f* importance; (*quantia*) amount; ter ~tância be important; ~tante *a* important; ~tar *vt* import <*mercadorias*> □ *vi* matter; ~tar em (*montar a*) amount to; (*resultar em*) lead to; ~tar-se (com) mind

importu|nar /iportu'nar/ *vt* bother; ~no *a* annoying

imposição /ipozi'sãw/ *f* imposition

impossibili|dade /iposibili'dadʒi/ *f* impossibility; ~tar *vt* make impossible; ~tar alg de ir, ~tar a alg ir prevent s.o. from going, make it impossible for s.o. to go

impossí|vel /ipo'sivew/ (*pl* ~veis) *a* impossible

impos|to /ī'postu/ *m* tax; ~to de renda income tax; ~to sobre o valor acrescentado (*Port*) VAT; ~tor *m* impostor; ~tura *f* deception

impo|tência /ipo'tẽsia/ *f* impotence; ~tente *a* impotent

impreci|são /ipresi'zãw/ *f* imprecision; ~so *a* imprecise

impregnar /ipreg'nar/ *vt* impregnate

imprensa /ī'prẽsa/ *f* press; ~ marrom gutter press

imprescindí|vel /ĩpresĩ'dʒivew/ (*pl* ~veis) *a* essential

impres|são /ĩpre'sãw/ *f* impression; (*no prelo*) printing; ~**são** digital fingerprint; ~**sionante** *a* (*imponente*) impressive; (*comovente*) striking; ~**sionar** *vt* (*causar admiração*) impress; (*comover*) make an impression on; ~**sionar-se** *vpr* be impressed (com by); ~**sionável** (*pl* ~**sioná-veis**) *a* impressionable; ~**sionismo** *m* impressionism; ~**sionista** *a & m/f* impressionist; ~**so** *a* printed □ *m* printed sheet; *pl* printed matter; ~**sor** *m* printer; ~**sora** *f* printer

imprestá|vel /ĩpres'tavew/ (*pl* ~veis) *a* useless

impre|visível /ĩprevi'zivew/ (*pl* ~**visíveis**) *a* unpredictable; ~**visto** *a* unforeseen □ *m* unforeseen circumstance

imprimir /ĩpri'mir/ *vt* print

impropério /ĩpro'pɛriu/ *m* term of abuse; *pl* abuse

impróprio /ĩ'prɔpriu/ *a* improper; (*inadequado*) unsuitable (para for)

imprová|vel /ĩpro'vavew/ (*pl* ~veis) *a* unlikely

improvi|sação /ĩproviza'sãw/ *f* improvisation; ~**sar** *vt/i* improvise; ~**so** *m* de ~**so** on the spur of the moment

impru|dência /ĩpru'dẽsia/ *f* recklessness; ~**dente** *a* reckless

impul|sionar /ĩpuwsio'nar/ *vt* drive; ~**sivo** *a* impulsive; ~**so** *m* impulse

impu|ne /ĩ'puni/ *a* unpunished; ~**nidade** *f* impunity

impu|reza /ĩpu'reza/ *f* impurity; ~**ro** *a* impure

imun|dície /ĩmũ'dʒisi/ *f* filth; ~**do** *a* filthy

imu|ne /i'muni/ *a* immune (a to); ~**nidade** *f* immunity; ~**nizar** *vt* immunize

inabalá|vel /inaba'lavew/ (*pl* ~veis) *a* unshakeable

iná|bil /i'nabiw/ (*pl* ~bis) *a* (*desafeitado*) clumsy

inabitado /inabi'tadu/ *a* uninhabited

inacabado /inaka'badu/ *a* unfinished

inaceitá|vel /inasej'tavew/ (*pl* ~veis) *a* unacceptable

inacessí|vel /inase'sivew/ (*pl* ~veis) *a* inaccessible

inacreditá|vel /inakredʒi'tavew/ (*pl* ~veis) *a* unbelievable

inadequado /inade'kwadu/ *a* unsuitable

inadmissí|vel /inadʒimi'sivew/ (*pl* ~veis) *a* inadmissible

inadvertência /inadʒiver'tẽsia/ *f* oversight

inalar /ina'lar/ *vt* inhale

inalcançá|vel /inawkã'savew/ (*pl* ~veis) *a* unattainable

inalterá|vel /inawte'ravew/ (*pl* ~veis) *a* unchangeable

inanição /inani'sãw/ *f* starvation

inanimado /inani'madu/ *a* inanimate

inapto /i'naptu/ *a* (*incapaz*) unfit

inati|vidade /inatʃivi'dadʒi/ *f* inactivity; ~**vo** *a* inactive

inato /i'natu/ *a* innate

inaudito /inaw'dʒitu/ *a* unheard of

inaugu|ração /inawgura'sãw/ *f* inauguration; ~**ral** (*pl* ~**rais**) *a* inaugural; ~**rar** *vt* inaugurate

incabí|vel /ĩka'bivew/ (*pl* ~veis) *a* inappropriate

incalculá|vel /ĩkawku'lavew/ (*pl* ~veis) *a* incalculable

incandescente /ĩkãde'sẽtʃi/ *a* red-hot

incansá|vel /ĩkã'savew/ (*pl* ~veis) *a* tireless

incapaci|tado /ĩkapasi'tadu/ *a* <pessoa> disabled; ~**tar** *vt* incapacitate

incauto /ĩ'kawtu/ *a* reckless

incendi|ar /ĩsẽdʒi'ar/ *vt* set alight; ~**ar-se** *vpr* catch fire; ~**ário** *a* incendiary; (*fig*) <discurso> inflammatory □ *m* arsonist; (*fig*) agitator

incêndio /ĩ'sẽdʒiu/ *m* fire

incenso /ĩ'sẽsu/ *m* incense

incenti|var /ĩsẽtʃi'var/ *vt* encourage; ~**vo** *m* incentive

incer|teza /ĩser'teza/ *f* uncertainty; ~**to** /ɛ/ *a* uncertain

inces|to /ĩ'sɛstu/ *m* incest; ~**tuoso** /o/ *a* incestuous

in|chação /ĩʃa'sãw/ *f* swelling; ~**char** *vt/i* swell

inci|dência /ĩsi'dẽsia/ *f* incidence; ~**dente** *m* incident; ~**dir** *vi* ~**dir em** <luz> shine on; <imposto> be payable on

incinerar /ĩsine'rar/ *vt* incinerate

inci|são /ĩsi'zãw/ *f* incision; ~**sivo** *a* incisive

incitar /ĩsi'tar/ *vt* incite

incli|nação /ĩklina'sãw/ *f* (*do chão*) incline; (*da cabeça*) nod; (*propensão*) inclination; ~**nado** *a* <chão> sloping; <edifício> leaning; (*propenso*) inclined (a to); ~**nar** *vt* tilt; nod <cabeça> □ *vi* <chão> slope; <edifício> lean; (*tender*) incline (para towards); ~**nar-se** *vpr* lean

inclu|ir /ĩklu'ir/ *vt* include; ~**são** *f* inclusion; ~**sive** *prep* including □ *adv* inclusive; (*até*) even; ~**so** *a* included

incoe|rência /ĩkoe'rẽsia/ *f* (*falta de nexo*) incoherence; (*inconseqüência*) inconsistency; ~**rente** *a* (*sem nexo*) incoherent; (*inconseqüente*) inconsistent incógni|ta /ĩ'kɔgnita/ f unknown; ~to adv incognito

incolor /ĩko'lor/ a colourless

incólume /ĩ'kɔlumi/ a unscathed

incomodar /ĩkomo'dar/ vt bother □ vi be a nuisance; ~-se vpr (dar-se ao trabalho) bother (em to); ~-se (com) be bothered (by), mind

incómodo /ĩ'komodu/ a (desagradável) tiresome; (sem conforto) uncomfortable □ m nuisance

incompa|rável /ĩkõpa'ravew/ (pl ~ráveis) a incomparable; ~tível (pl ~tíveis) a incompatible

incompe|tência /ĩkõpe'tēsia/ f incompetence; ~tente a incompetent

incompleto /ĩkõ'pletu/ a incomplete

incompreensí|vel /ĩkõprĩë'sivew/ (pl ~veis) a incomprehensible

inconcebí|vel /ĩkõse'bivew/ (pl ~veis) a inconceivable

incondicio|nal /ĩkõdʒisio'naw/ (pl ~nais) a unconditional; <fã, partidário> firm

inconformado /ĩkõfor'madu/ a unreconciled (com to)

inconfundí|vel /ĩkõfũ'dʒivew/ (pl ~veis) a unmistakeable

inconsciente /ĩkõsi'ẽtʃi/ a & m unconscious

inconseqüente /ĩkõse'kwẽtʃi/ a inconsistent

incons|tância /ĩkõs'tãsia/ f changeability; ~tante a changeable

inconstitucio|nal /ĩkõstʃitusio-'naw/ (pl ~nais) a unconstitutional

incontestá|vel /ĩkõtes'tavew/ (pl ~veis) a indisputable

inconveni|ente /ĩkõveni'ẽtʃi/ a (difícil) inconvenient; (desagradável) annoying, tiresome; (indecente) unseemly □ m drawback

incorporar /ĩkorpo'rar/ vt incorporate

incorrer /ĩko'xer/ vi ~ em <multa etc> incur

incorrigí|vel /ĩkoxi'ʒivew/ (pl ~veis) a incorrigible

incrédulo /ĩ'krɛdulu/ a incredulous

incremen|tado /ĩkremẽ'tadu/ a (fam) stylish; ~tar vt build up; (fam) jazz up; ~to m development, growth

incriminar /ĩkrimi'nar/ vt incriminate

incrí|vel /ĩ'krivew/ (pl ~veis) a incredible

incu|bação /ĩkuba'sãw/ f incubation; ~badora f incubator; ~bar vt/i incubate

inculto /ĩ'kuwtu/ a <pessoa> uneducated; <terreno> uncultivated

incum|bência /ĩkũ'bẽsia/ f task; ~bir vt ~bir alg de aco/de ir assign s.o. sth/to go □ vi ~bir a be up to; ~bir-se de take on

incurá|vel /ĩku'ravew/ (pl ~veis) a incurable

incursão /ĩkur'sãw/ f incursion

incutir /ĩku'tʃir/ vt instil (em in)

indagar /ĩda'gar/ vt inquire (into)

inde|cência /ĩde'sẽsia/ f indecency; ~cente a indecent

indecifrá|vel /ĩdesi'fravew/ (pl ~veis) a indecipherable

indeciso /ĩde'sizu/ a undecided

indecoroso /ĩdeko'rozu/ a indecorous

indefi|nido /ĩdefi'nidu/ a indefinite; ~nível (pl ~níveis) a indefinable

indelé|vel /ĩde'lɛvew/ (pl ~veis) a indelible

indelica|deza /ĩdelika'deza/ f impoliteness; (uma) impolite thing; ~do a impolite

indeni|zação /ĩdeniza'sãw/ f compensation; ~zar vt compensate

indepen|dência /ĩdepẽ'dẽsia/ f independence; ~dente a independent

indescriti|vel /ĩdʒiskri'tʃivew/ (pl ~veis) a indescribable

indesculpá|vel /ĩdʒiskuw'pavew/ (pl ~veis) a inexcusable

indesejá|vel /ĩdeze'ʒavew/ (pl ~veis) a undesirable

indestruti|vel /ĩdʒistru'tʃivew/ (pl ~veis) a indestructible

indeterminado /ĩdetermi'nadu/ a indeterminate

indevido /ĩde'vidu/ a undue

indexar /ĩdek'sar/ vt index; index-link <salário, preços>

Índia /'ĩdʒia/ f India

indiano /ĩdʒi'anu/ a & m Indian

indi|cação /ĩdʒika'sãw/ f indication; (do caminho) directions; (nomeação) nomination; (recomendação) recommendation; ~cador m indicator; (dedo) index finger □ a indicative (de of); ~car vt indicate; (para cargo, prêmio) nominate (para for); (recomendar) recommend; ~cativo a & m indicative

índice /'ĩdʒisi/ m (taxa) rate; (em livro etc) index; ~ de audiência ratings

indiciar /ĩdʒisi'ar/ vt charge

indício /ĩ'dʒisiu/ m sign, indication; (de crime) clue

indife|rença /ĩdʒife'rẽsa/ f indifference; ~rente a indifferent

indígena /ĩ'dʒiʒena/ a indigenous, native □ m/f native

indiges|tão /ĩdʒiʒes'tãw/ f indigestion; ~to a indigestible; (fig) heavygoing

indig|nação /ĩdʒigna'sãw/ f indignation; ~nado a indignant; ~nar vt make indignant; **~nar-se** *vpr* get indignant (**com** about)

indig|nidade /ĩdʒigni'dadʒi/ *f* indignity; **~no** *a* <*pessoa*> unworthy; <*ato*> despicable

índio /'ĩdʒiu/ *a* & *m* Indian

indire|ta /ĩdʒi'rɛta/ *f* hint; **~to** /ɛ/ *a* indirect

indis|creto /ĩdʒis'krɛtu/ *a* indiscreet; **~crição** *f* indiscretion

indiscriminado /ĩdʒiskrimi'nadu/ *a* indiscriminate

indiscutí|vel /ĩdʒisku'tʃivew/ (*pl* **~veis**) *a* unquestionable

indispensá|vel /ĩdʒispẽ'savew/ (*pl* **~veis**) *a* indispensable

indisponí|vel /ĩdʒispo'nivew/ (*pl* **~veis**) *a* unavailable

indis|por /ĩdʒis'por/ *vt* upset; **~por alg contra** turn s.o. against; **~por-se** *vpr* fall out (**com** with); **~posição** *f* indisposition; **~posto** *a* (*doente*) indisposed

indistinto /ĩdʒis'tʃĩtu/ *a* indistinct

individu|al /ĩdʒividu'aw/ (*pl* **~ais**) *a* individual; **~alidade** *f* individuality; **~alismo** *m* individualism; **~alista** *a* & *m/f* individualist

indivíduo /ĩdʒi'viduu/ *m* individual

indizí|vel /ĩdʒi'zivew/ (*pl* **~veis**) *a* unspeakable

índole /'ĩdoli/ *f* nature

indo|lência /ĩdo'lẽsia/ *f* indolence; **~lente** *a* indolent

indolor /ĩdo'lor/ *a* painless

Indonésia /ĩdo'nɛzia/ *f* Indonesia

indonésio /ĩdo'nɛziu/ *a* & *m* Indonesian

indubitá|vel /ĩdubi'tavew/ (*pl* **~veis**) *a* undoubted

indul|gência /ĩduw'ʒẽsia/ *f* indulgence; **~gente** *a* indulgent

indulto /ĩ'duwtu/ *m* pardon

indumentária /ĩdumẽ'taria/ *f* outfit

indústria /ĩ'dustria/ *f* industry

industri|al /ĩdustri'aw/ (*pl* **~ais**) *a* industrial □ *m/f* industrialist; **~alizado** *a* <*país*> industrialized; <*mercadoria*> manufactured; <*comida*> processed; **~alizar** *vt* industrialize <*país, agricultura etc*>; process <*comida, lixo etc*>; **~oso** /o/ *a* industrious

induzir /ĩdu'zir/ *vt* (*persuadir*) induce; (*inferir*) infer (**de** from); **~ em erro** lead astray, mislead s.o.

inebriante /inebri'ãtʃi/ *a* intoxicating

inédito /i'nɛdʒitu/ *a* unheard-of, unprecedented; (*não publicado*) unpublished

ineficaz /inefi'kas/ *a* ineffective

inefici|ência /inefisi'ẽsia/ *f* inefficiency; **~ente** *a* inefficient

inegá|vel /ine'gavew/ (*pl* **~veis**) *a* undeniable

inépcia /i'nɛpsia/ *f* ineptitude

inepto /i'nɛptu/ *a* inept

inequívoco /ine'kivoku/ *a* unmistakeable

inércia /i'nɛrsia/ *f* inertia

inerente /ine'rẽtʃi/ *a* inherent (**a** in)

inerte /i'nɛrtʃi/ *a* inert

inesgotá|vel /inezgo'tavew/ (*pl* **~veis**) *a* inexhaustible

inesperado /inespe'radu/ *a* unexpected

inesquecí|vel /ineske'sivew/ (*pl* **~veis**) *a* unforgettable

inevitá|vel /inevi'tavew/ (*pl* **~veis**) *a* inevitable

inexato /ine'zatu/ *a* inaccurate

inexis|tência /inezis'tẽsia/ *f* lack; **~tente** *a* non-existent

inexperi|ência /inisperi'ẽsia/ *f* inexperience; **~ente** *a* inexperienced

inexpressivo /inespre'sivu/ *a* expressionless

infalí|vel /ĩfa'livew/ (*pl* **~veis**) *a* infallible

infame /ĩ'fami/ *a* despicable; (*péssimo*) dreadful

infâmia /ĩ'famia/ *f* disgrace

infância /ĩ'fãsia/ *f* childhood

infantaria /ĩfãta'ria/ *f* infantry

infan|til /ĩfã'tʃiw/ *a* <*roupa, livro*> children's; (*bobo*) childish; **~tilidade** *f* childishness; (*uma*) childish thing

infarto /ĩ'fartu/ *m* heart attack

infec|ção /ĩfek'sãw/ *f* infection; **~cionar** *vt* infect; **~cioso** *a* infectious

infeliz /ĩfe'lis/ *a* (*não contente*) unhappy; (*inconveniente*) unfortunate; (*desgraçado*) wretched □ *m* (*desgraçado*) wretch; **~mente** *adv* unfortunately

inferi|or /ĩferi'or/ *a* lower; (*em qualidade*) inferior (**a** to); **~oridade** *f* inferiority

inferir /ĩfe'rir/ *vt* infer

infer|nal /ĩfer'naw/ (*pl* **~nais**) *a* infernal; **~nizar** *vt* **~nizar a vida dele** make his life hell; **~no** /ɛ/ *m* hell

infér|til /ĩ'fɛrtʃiw/ (*pl* **~teis**) *a* infertile

infertilidade /ĩfertʃili'dadʒi/ *f* infertility

infestar /ĩfes'tar/ *vt* infest

infetar /ĩfe'tar/ *vt* infect

infidelidade /ĩfideli'dadʒi/ *f* infidelity

infi|el /ĩfi'ew/ (*pl* **~éis**) *a* unfaithful

infiltrar /ĩfiw'trar/ *vt* infiltrate; **~-se em** infiltrate

ínfimo /'ĩfimu/ *a* lowest; (*muito pequeno*) tiny

infindá|vel /ĩfĩ'davew/ (*pl* **~veis**) *a* unending

infinidade /ĩfini'dadʒi/ f infinity; uma ~ de an infinite number of

infini|tesimal /ĩfinitezi'maw/ (pl ~tesimais) a infinitesimal; ~tivo a & m infinitive; ~to a infinite □ m infinity

infla|ção /ĩfla'sãw/ f inflation; ~cionar vt inflate; ~cionário a inflationary; ~cionista a & m/f inflationist

infla|mação /ĩflama'sãw/ f inflammation; ~mar vt inflame; ~mar-se vpr become inflamed; ~matório a inflammatory; ~mável (pl ~máveis) a inflammable

in|flar vt inflate; ~flar-se vpr inflate; ~flável (pl ~fláveis) a inflatable

infle|xibilidade /ĩfleksibili'dadʒi/ f inflexibility; ~xível (pl ~xíveis) a inflexible

infligir /ĩfli'ʒir/ vt inflict (a on)

influência /ĩflu'ẽsia/ f influence

influen|ciar /ĩfluẽsi'ar/ vt ~ciar (em) influence; ~ciar-se vpr be influenced; ~ciável (pl ~ciáveis) a open to influence; ~te a influential

influir /ĩflu'ir/ vi ~ em ou sobre influence

informação /ĩforma'sãw/ f information; (uma) a piece of information; (mil) intelligence; pl information

infor|mal /ĩfor'maw/ (pl ~mais) a informal; ~malidade f informality

infor|mar /ĩfor'mar/ vt inform; ~mar-se vpr find out (de about); ~mática f information technology; ~mativo a informative; ~matizar vt computerize; ~me m (mil) piece of intelligence

infortúnio /ĩfor'tuniu/ m misfortune

infração /ĩfra'sãw/ f infringement

infra-estrutura /ĩfraistru'tura/ f infrastructure

infrator /ĩfra'tor/ m offender

infravermelho /ĩfraver'meʎu/ a infrared

infringir /ĩfrĩ'ʒir/ vt infringe

infrutífero /ĩfru'tʃiferu/ a fruitless

infundado /ĩfũ'dadu/ a unfounded

infundir /ĩfũ'dʒir/ vt (insuflar) infuse; (incutir) instil

infusão /ĩfu'zãw/ f infusion

ingenuidade /ĩʒenui'dadʒi/ f naivety

ingênuo /ĩ'ʒenuu/ a naive

Inglaterra /ĩgla'tɛra/ f England

ingerir /ĩʒe'rir/ vt ingest; (engolir) swallow

in|glês /ĩ'gles/ a (f ~glesa) English □ m (f ~glesa) Englishman (f -woman); (língua) English; os ~gleses the English

ingra|tidão /ĩgratʃi'dãw/ f ingratitude; ~to a ungrateful

ingrediente /ĩgredʒi'ẽtʃi/ m ingredient

ingreme /'ĩgrimi/ a steep

ingres|sar /ĩgre'sar/ vi ~sar em join; ~so m entry; (bilhete) ticket

inhame /i'ɲami/ m yam

ini|bição /inibi'sãw/ f inhibition; ~bir vt inhibit

inici|ado /inisi'adu/ m initiate; ~al (pl ~ais) a & f initial; ~ar vt (começar) begin; (em ciência, seita etc) initiate (em into) □ vi begin; ~ativa f initiative

início /i'nisiu/ m beginning

iguala|vel /inigwa'lavew/ (pl ~veis) a unparalleled

inimaginável /inimaʒi'navew/ (pl ~veis) a unimaginable

inimi|go /ini'migu/ a & m enemy; ~zade f enmity

ininterrupto /inĩte'xuptu/ a continuous

inje|ção /ĩʒe'sãw/ f injection; ~tado a <olhos> bloodshot; ~tar vt inject; ~tável (pl ~táveis) a <droga> intravenous

injúria /ĩ'ʒuria/ f insult

injuriar /ĩʒuri'ar/ vt insult

injus|tiça /ĩʒus'tʃisa/ f injustice; ~tiçado a wronged; ~to a unfair, unjust

ino|cência /ino'sẽsia/ f innocence; ~centar vt clear (de of); ~cente a innocent

inocular /inoku'lar/ vt inoculate

inócuo /i'nɔkuu/ a harmless

inodoro /ino'dɔru/ a odourless

inofensivo /inofẽ'sivu/ a harmless

inoportuno /inopor'tunu/ a inopportune

inorgânico /inor'ganiku/ a inorganic

inóspito /i'nɔspitu/ a inhospitable

ino|vação /inova'sãw/ f innovation; ~var vt/i innovate

inoxidá|vel /inoksi'davew/ (pl ~veis) a <aço> stainless

inquérito /ĩ'kɛritu/ m inquiry

inquie|tação /ĩkieta'sãw/ f concern; ~tador, ~tante a worrying; ~tar vt worry; ~tar-se vpr worry; ~to /ɛ/ a uneasy

inquili|nato /ĩkili'natu/ m tenancy; ~no m tenant

inquirir /ĩki'rir/ vt cross-examine <testemunha>

Inquisição /ĩkizi'sãw/ f a ~ the Inquisition

insaciá|vel /ĩsasi'avew/ (pl ~veis) a insatiable

insalubre /ĩsa'lubri/ a unhealthy

insatis|fação /ĩsatʃisfa'sãw/ f dissatisfaction; ~fatório a unsatisfactory; ~feito a dissatisfied

ins|crever /iskre'ver/ vt (registrar) register; (gravar) inscribe; ~crever-se vpr register; (em escola etc) enrol; ~crição f (registro) registration; (em clube, escola) enrolment; (em monumento etc) inscription

insegu|rança /isegu'rãsa/ f insecurity; ~ro a insecure

insemi|nação /isemina'sãw/ f insemination; ~nar vt inseminate

insen|satez /isẽsa'tes/ f folly; ~sato a foolish; ~sibilidade f insensitivity; ~sível (pl ~síveis) a insensitive

insepa|rável /isepa'ravew/ (pl ~veis) a inseparable

inserção /iser'sãw/ f insertion

inserir /ise'rir/ vt insert; enter <dados>

inse|ticida /iseti'sida/ m insecticide; ~to /ɛ/ m insect

insígnia /i'signia/ f insignia

insignifi|cância /isignifi'kãsia/ f insignificance; ~cante a insignificant

insincero /isĩ'sɛru/ a insincere

insinu|ante /isinu'ãtʃi/ a suggestive; ~ar vt/i insinuate

insípido /i'sipidu/ a insipid

insis|tência /isis'tẽsia/ f insistence; ~tente a insistent; ~tir vt/i insist (em on)

insolação /isola'sãw/ f sunstroke

inso|lência /iso'lẽsia/ f insolence; ~lente a insolent

insólito /i'sɔlitu/ a unusual

insolú|vel /iso'luvew/ (pl ~veis) a insoluble

insone /i'soni/ a <noite> sleepless; <pessoa> insomniac □ m/f insomniac

insônia /i'sonia/ f insomnia

insosso /i'sosu/ a bland; (sem sabor) tasteless; (sem sal) unsalted

inspe|ção /ispe'sãw/ f inspection; ~cionar vt inspect; ~tor m inspector

inspi|ração /ispira'sãw/ f inspiration; ~rar vt inspire; ~rar-se vpr take inspiration (em from)

instabilidade /istabili'dadʒi/ f instability

insta|lação /istala'sãw/ f installation; ~lar vt install; ~lar-se vpr install o.s.

instan|tâneo /istã'taniu/ a instant; ~te m instant

instaurar /istaw'rar/ vt set up

instá|vel /i'stavew/ (pl ~veis) a unstable; <tempo> unsettled

insti|gação /istʃiga'sãw/ f instigation; ~gante a stimulating; ~gar vt incite

instin|tivo /istʃĩ'tʃivu/ a instinctive; ~to m instinct

institu|cional /istʃitusio'naw/ (pl ~cionais) a institutional; ~ição f institution; ~ir vt set up; set <prazo>; ~to m institute

instru|ção /istru'sãw/ f instruction; ~ir vt instruct; train <recrutas>; (informar) advise (sobre of)

instrumen|tal /istrumẽ'taw/ (pl ~tais) a instrumental; ~tista m/f instrumentalist; ~to m instrument

instru|tivo /istru'tʃivu/ a instructive; ~tor m instructor

insubstituí|vel /isubistʃitu'ivew/ (pl ~veis) a irreplaceable

insucesso /isu'sesu/ m failure

insufici|ência /isufisi'ẽsia/ f insufficiency; (dos órgãos) failure; ~ente a insufficient

insulina /isu'lina/ f insulin

insul|tar /isuw'tar/ vt insult; ~to m insult

insuperá|vel /isupe'ravew/ (pl ~veis) a <problema> insurmountable; <qualidade> unsurpassed

insuportá|vel /isupor'tavew/ (pl ~veis) a unbearable

insur|gente /isur'ʒẽtʃi/ a & m/f insurgent; ~gir-se vpr rise up, revolt; ~reição f insurrection

intato /ĩ'tatu/ a intact

integra /'ĩtegra/ f full text; na ~ in full

inte|gração /ĩtegra'sãw/ f integration; ~gral (pl ~grais) a whole; arroz/pão ~gral brown rice/bread; ~grante a integral □ m/f member; ~grar vt make up, form; ~grar-se em become a part of; ~gridade f integrity

integro /'ĩtegru/ a honest

intei|ramente /ĩtera'mẽtʃi/ adv completely; ~rar vt (informar) fill in, inform (de about); ~rar-se vpr find out (de about); ~riço a in one piece; ~ro a whole

intelec|to /ĩte'lɛktu/ m intellect; ~tual (pl ~tuais) a & m/f intellectual

inteli|gência /ĩteli'ʒẽsia/ f intelligence; ~gente a clever, intelligent; ~gível (pl ~gíveis) a intelligible

intem|périe /ĩtẽ'pɛri/ f bad weather; ~pestivo a ill-timed

inten|ção /ĩtẽ'sãw/ f intention; segundas ~ções ulterior motives

intencio|nado /ĩtẽsio'nadu/ a bem ~nado well-meaning; ~nal (pl ~nais) a intentional; ~nar vt intend

inten|sidade /ĩtẽsi'dadʒi/ f intensity; ~sificar vt intensify; ~sificar-se vpr intensify; ~sivo a intensive; ~so a intense

intento /ĩ'tẽtu/ m intention

intera|ção /ĩtera'sãw/ f interaction; ~gir vi interact; ~tivo a interactive inter|calar /ĩterka'lar/ vt insert; ~câmbio m exchange; ~ceptar vt intercept

intercontinen|tal /ĩterkõtʃinẽ'taw/ (pl ~tais) a intercontinental

interdepen|dência /ĩterdepẽ'dẽsia/ f interdependence; ~dente a interdependent

interdi|ção /ĩterdʒi'sãw/ f closure; (jurid) injunction; ~tar vt close <rua etc>; (proibir) ban

interes|sante /ĩtere'sãtʃi/ a interesting; ~sar vt interest □ vi be relevant; ~sar-se vpr be interested (em ou por in); ~se /e/ m interest; (próprio) self-interest; ~seiro a self-seeking

interestadu|al /ĩteristadu'aw/ (pl ~ais) a interstate

interface /ĩter'fasi/ f interface

interfe|rência /ĩterfe'rẽsia/ f interference; ~rir vi interfere

interfone /ĩter'fɔni/ m intercom

ínterim /'ĩterĩ/ m interim; nesse ~ in the interim

interino /ĩteri'nu/ a temporary

interior /ĩteri'or/ a inner; (dentro do país) internal, domestic □ m inside; (do país) country, interior

inter|jeição /ĩterʒej'sãw/ f interjection; ~ligar vt interconnect; ~locutor m interlocutor; ~mediário a & m intermediary

intermédio /ĩter'mɛdʒiu/ m por ~ de through

interminá|vel /ĩtermi'navew/ (pl ~veis) a interminable

intermitente /ĩtermi'tẽtʃi/ a intermittent

internacio|nal /ĩternasio'naw/ (pl ~nais) a international

inter|nar vt intern <preso>; admit to hospital <doente>; ~nato m boarding school; ~no a internal

interpelar /ĩterpe'lar/ vt question

interpor /ĩter'por/ vt interpose; ~-se vpr intervene

interpre|tação /ĩterpreta'sãw/ f interpretation; ~tar vt interpret; perform <papel, música>; intérprete m/f (de línguas) interpreter; (de teatro etc) performer

interro|gação /ĩteroga'sãw/ f interrogation; ~gar vt interrogate, question; ~gativo a interrogative; ~gatório m interrogation

inter|romper /ĩtexõ'per/ vt interrupt; ~rupção f interruption; ~ruptor m switch

interurbano /ĩterur'banu/ a long-distance □ m trunk call

intervalo /ĩter'valu/ m interval

inter|venção /ĩtervẽ'sãw/ f intervention; ~vir vi intervene

intesti|nal /ĩtestʃi'naw/ (pl ~nais) a intestinal; ~no m intestine

inti|mação /ĩtʃima'sãw/ f (da justiça) summons; ~mar vt order; (à justiça) summon

intimidade /ĩtʃimi'dadʒi/ f intimacy; (entre amigos) closeness; (vida intima) private life; ter ~ com be close to

intimidar /ĩtʃimi'dar/ vt intimidate; ~-se vpr be intimidated

íntimo /'ĩtʃimu/ a intimate; <amigo> close; <vida> private □ m close friend

intitular /ĩtʃitu'lar/ vt entitle

intocá|vel /ĩto'kavew/ (pl ~veis) a untouchable

intole|rância /ĩtole'rãsia/ f intolerance; ~rante a intolerant; ~rável (pl ~ráveis) a intolerable

intoxi|cação /ĩtoksika'sãw/ f poisoning; ~cação alimentar food poisoning; ~car vt poison

intragá|vel /ĩtra'gavew/ (pl ~veis) a <comida> inedible; <pessoa> unbearable

intransigente /ĩtrãzi'ʒẽtʃi/ a uncompromising

intransi|tável /ĩtrãzi'tavew/ (pl ~táveis) a impassable; ~tivo a intransitive

intratá|vel /ĩtra'tavew/ (pl ~veis) a <pessoa> difficult

intra-uterino /ĩtrauteri'nu/ a dispositivo ~ intra-uterine device, IUD

intrépido /ĩ'trepidu/ a intrepid

intri|ga /ĩ'triga/ f intrigue; (enredo) plot; ~gante a intriguing; ~gar vt intrigue

intrincado /ĩtrĩ'kadu/ a intricate

intrínseco /ĩ'trĩsiku/ a intrinsic

introdu|ção /ĩtrodu'sãw/ f introduction; ~tório a introductory; ~zir vt introduce

introme|ter-se /ĩtrome'tersi/ vpr interfere; ~tido a interfering □ m busybody

introspec|ção /ĩtrospek'sãw/ f introspection; ~tivo a introspective

introvertido /ĩtrover'tʃidu/ a introverted □ m introvert

intruso /ĩ'truzu/ a intrusive □ m intruder

intu|ição /ĩtui'sãw/ f intuition; ~ir vt intuit; ~itivo a intuitive; ~to m purpose

inumano /inu'manu/ a inhuman

inumerá|vel /inume'ravew/ (pl ~veis) a innumerable

inúmero /i'numeru/ a countless

inun|dação /inũda'sãw/ f flood; ~dar vt/i flood

inusitado /inuzi'tadu/ a unusual

inú|til /i'nutʃiw/ (pl ~teis) a useless

inutilmente /inutʃiw'mẽtʃi/ *adv* in vain

inutilizar /inutʃili'zar/ *vt* render useless; damage <*aparelho*>; thwart <*esforços*>

invadir /iva'dʒir/ *vt* invade

invali|dar /ivali'dar/ *vt* invalidate; disable <*pessoa*>; ~**dez** /e/ *f* disability

inválido /i'validu/ *a* & *m* invalid

invariá|vel /ivari'avew/ (*pl* ~**veis**) *a* invariable

inva|são /iva'zãw/ *f* invasion; ~**sor** *m* invader □ *a* invading

inve|ja /ĩ'vɛʒa/ *f* envy; ~**jar** *vt* envy; ~**jável** (*pl* ~**jáveis**) *a* enviable; ~**joso** /o/ *a* envious

inven|ção /ĩvẽ'sãw/ *f* invention; ~**tar** *vt* invent; ~**tário** *m* inventory; ~**tivo** *a* inventive; ~**tor** *m* inventor

inver|nar /iver'nar/ *vi* winter, spend the winter; ~**no** /ɛ/ *m* winter

inverossí|mil /ĩvero'simiw/ (*pl* ~**meis**) *a* improbable

inver|são /ĩver'sãw/ *f* inversion; ~**so** *a* inverse; <*ordem*> reverse □ *m* reverse; ~**ter** *vt* reverse; (*colocar de cabeça para baixo*) invert

invertebrado /ĩverte'bradu/ *a* & *m* invertebrate

invés /ĩ'vɛs/ *m* **ao** ~ **de** instead of

investida /ĩves'tʃida/ *f* attack

investidura /ĩvestʃi'dura/ *f* investiture

investi|gação /ĩvestʃiga'sãw/ *f* investigation; ~**gar** *vt* investigate

inves|timento /ĩvestʃi'mẽtu/ *m* investment; ~**tir** *vt/i* invest; ~**tir contra** attack

inveterado /ĩvete'radu/ *a* inveterate

inviá|vel /ĩvi'avew/ (*pl* ~**veis**) *a* impracticable

invicto /ĩ'viktu/ *a* unbeaten

invisí|vel /ĩvi'zivew/ (*pl* ~**veis**) *a* invisible

invocar /ĩvo'kar/ *vt* invoke; (*fam*) pester

invólucro /ĩ'vɔlukru/ *m* covering

involuntário /ĩvolũ'tariu/ *a* involuntary

invulnerá|vel /ĩvuwne'ravew/ (*pl* ~**veis**) *a* invulnerable

iodo /i'odu/ *m* iodine

ioga /i'ɔga/ *f* yoga

iogurte /io'gurtʃi/ *m* yoghurt

ir /ir/ *vi* go; ~**-se** *vpr* go away; **vou voltar** I will come back; **vou melhorando** I am (gradually) getting better

ira /'ira/ *f* wrath

Irã /i'rã/ *m* Iran

iraniano /irani'anu/ *a* & *m* Iranian

Irão /i'rãw/ *m* (*Port*) Iran

Iraque /i'raki/ *m* Iraq

iraquiano /iraki'anu/ *a* & *m* Iraqui

Irlanda /ir'lãda/ *f* Ireland

irlan|dês /irlã'des/ *a* (*f* ~**desa**) Irish □ *m* (*f* ~**desa**) Irishman (*f* -woman); (*língua*) Irish; **os** ~**deses** the Irish

irmã /ir'mã/ *f* sister

irmandade /irmã'dadʒi/ *f* (*associação*) brotherhood

irmão /ir'mãw/ (*pl* ~**s**) *m* brother

ironia /iro'nia/ *f* irony

irônico /i'roniku/ *a* ironic

irracio|nal /ixasio'naw/ (*pl* ~**nais**) *a* irrational

irradiar /ixadʒi'ar/ *vt* radiate; (*pelo rádio*) broadcast □ *vi* shine; ~**-se** *vpr* spread, radiate

irre|al /ixe'aw/ (*pl* ~**ais**) *a* unreal

irreconhecí|vel /ixekoɲe'sivew/ (*pl* ~**veis**) *a* unrecognizable

irrecuperá|vel /ixekupe'ravew/ (*pl* ~**veis**) *a* irretrievable

irrefletido /ixefle'tʃidu/ *a* rash

irregu|lar /ixegu'lar/ *a* irregular; (*inconstante*) erratic; ~**laridade** *f* irregularity

irrelevante /ixele'vãtʃi/ *a* irrelevant

irrepará|vel /ixepa'ravew/ (*pl* ~**veis**) *a* irreparable

irrepreensí|vel /ixepriẽ'sivew/ (*pl* ~**veis**) *a* irreproachable

irrequieto /ixeki'ɛtu/ *a* restless

irresistí|vel /ixezis'tʃivew/ (*pl* ~**veis**) *a* irresistible

irresoluto /ixezo'lutu/ *a* <*questão*> unresolved; <*pessoa*> indecisive

irresponsá|vel /ixespõ'savew/ (*pl* ~**veis**) *a* irresponsible

irreverente /ixeve'rẽtʃi/ *a* irreverent

irri|gação /ixiga'sãw/ *f* irrigation; ~**gar** *vt* irrigate

irrisório /ixi'zɔriu/ *a* derisory

irri|tação /ixita'sãw/ *f* irritation; ~**tadiço** *a* irritable; ~**tante** *a* irritating; ~**tar** *vt* irritate; ~**tar-se** *vpr* get irritated

irromper /ixõ'per/ *vi* ~ **em** burst into

isca /'iska/ *f* bait

isen|ção /izẽ'sãw/ *f* exemption; ~**tar** *vt* exempt; ~**to** *a* exempt

Islã /iz'lã/ *m* Islam

islâmico /iz'lamiku/ *a* Islamic

isla|mismo /izla'mizmu/ *m* Islam; ~**mita** *a* & *m/f* Muslim

islan|dês /izlã'des/ *a* (*f* ~**desa**) Icelandic □ *m* (*f* ~**desa**) Icelander; (*língua*) Icelandic

Islândia /iz'lãdʒia/ *f* Iceland

iso|lamento /izola'mẽtu/ *m* isolation; (*eletr*) insulation; ~**lante** *a* insulating; ~**lar** *vt* isolate; (*eletr*) insulate □ *vi* (*contra azar*) touch wood, (*Amer*) knock on wood

isopor /izo'por/ *m* polystyrene

isqueiro /is'keru/ *m* lighter

Israel /izxa'ɛw/ m Israel
israe|lense /izraj'lēsi/ a & m/f Israeli; **~lita** a & m/f Israelite
isso /'isu/ pron that; **por ~** therefore
isto /'istu/ pron this; **~ é** that is
Itália /i'talia/ f Italy
italiano /itali'anu/ a & m Italian
itálico /i'taliku/ a & m italic
item /'itē/ m item
itine|rante /itʃine'rātʃi/ a itinerant; **~rário** m itinerary
Iugoslávia /iugoz'lavia/ f Yugoslavia
iugoslavo /iugoz'lavu/ a & m Yugoslavian

J

já /ʒa/ adv already; (agora) right away □ conj on the other hand; **desde ~** from now on; **~ não** no longer; **~ que** since; **~ ~** in no time
jabuticaba /ʒabutʃi'kaba/ f jaboticaba
jaca /'ʒaka/ f jack fruit
jacaré /ʒaka'rɛ/ m alligator
jacinto /ʒa'situ/ m hyacinth
jactância /ʒak'tãsia/ f boasting
jade /'ʒadʒi/ m jade
jaguar /ʒagu'ar/ m jaguar
jagunço /ʒa'gũsu/ m hired gunman
jamais /ʒa'majs/ adv never
Jamaica /ʒa'majka/ f Jamaica
jamaicano /ʒamaj'kanu/ a & m Jamaican
jamanta /ʒa'mãta/ f juggernaut
janeiro /ʒa'neru/ m January
janela /ʒa'nɛla/ f window
jangada /ʒã'gada/ f (fishing) raft
janta /'ʒãta/ f (fam) dinner
jantar /ʒã'tar/ m dinner □ vi have dinner □ vt have for dinner
Japão /ʒa'pãw/ m Japan
japo|na /ʒa'pona/ f pea jacket □ m/f (fam) Japanese; **~nês** a & m (f **~nesa**) Japanese
jaqueira /ʒa'kera/ f jack-fruit tree
jaqueta /ʒa'keta/ f jacket
jarda /'ʒarda/ f yard
jar|dim /ʒar'dʒĩ/ m garden; **~dim-de-infância** (pl **~dins-de-infância**) kindergarten
jardi|nagem /ʒardʒi'naʒē/ f gardening; **~nar** vi garden; **~neira** f (calça) dungarees; (vestido) pinafore dress, (Amer) jumper; (ónibus) open-sided bus; (para flores) flower stand; **~neiro** m gardener
jargão /ʒar'gãw/ m jargon
jar|ra /'ʒaxa/ f pot; **~ro** m jug
jasmim /ʒaz'mĩ/ m jasmine
jato /'ʒatu/ m jet
jaula /'ʒawla/ f cage

ja|zer /ʒa'zer/ vi lie; **~zida** f deposit; **~zigo** m grave
jazz /dʒaz/ m jazz; **~ista** m/f jazz artist; **~ístico** a jazzy
jeca /'ʒɛka/ m/f country bumpkin □ a countrified; (cafona) tacky; **~tatu** m/f country bumpkin
jei|tão /ʒej'tãw/ m (fam) individual style; **~tinho** m knack; **~to** m way; (de pessoa) manner; (habilidade) skill; **de qualquer ~to** anyway; **de ~to nenhum** no way; **pelo ~to** by the looks of things; **sem ~to** awkward; **dar um ~to** find a way; **dar um ~to em** (arrumar) tidy up; (consertar) fix; (torcer) twist <pé etc>; **ter ~to de** look like; **ter ou levar ~to para** be good at; **tomar ~to** pull one's socks up; **~toso** /o/ a skilful; (de aparência) elegant
je|juar /ʒeʒu'ar/ vi fast; **~jum** m fast
Jeová /ʒio'va/ m **testemunha de ~** Jehovah's witness
jérsei /'ʒersej/ m jersey
jesuíta /ʒezu'ita/ a & m/f Jesuit
Jesus /ʒe'zus/ m Jesus
jibóia /ʒi'bɔja/ f boa constrictor
jiboiar /ʒiboj'ar/ vi have a rest to let one's dinner go down
jiló /ʒi'lɔ/ m okra
jipe /'ʒipi/ m jeep
jiu-jitsu /ʒiu'ʒitsu/ m jiu-jitsu
joa|lheiro /ʒoa'ʎeru/ m jeweller; **~lheria** f jeweller's (shop)
joaninha /ʒoa'niɲa/ f ladybird, (Amer) ladybug; (alfinete) safety pin
João-ninguém /ʒoãwnĩ'gēj/ (pl **joões-ninguém**) m nobody
jocoso /ʒo'kozu/ a jocular
joe|lhada /ʒoe'ʎada/ f blow with the knee; **~lheira** f kneepad; **~lho** /e/ m knee; **de ~lhos** kneeling
jo|gada /ʒo'gada/ f move; **~gado** a <pessoa> flat out; <papéis, roupa etc> lying around; **~gador** m player; (no cassino etc) gambler; **~gar** vt play; (atirar) throw; (arriscar no jogo) gamble □ vi play; (no cassino etc) gamble; (balançar) toss; **~gar fora** throw away; **~gatina** f gambling
jogging /'ʒɔgĩ/ m (cooper) jogging; (roupa) track suit
jogo /'ʒogu/ m (partida) game; (ação de jogar) play; (jogatina) gambling; (conjunto) set; **em ~** at stake; **~ de cintura** (fig) flexibility, room to manoeuvre; **~ de luz** lighting effects; **~ do bicho** illegal numbers game; **Jogos Olímpicos** Olympic Games; **~da-velha** m noughts and crosses
joguete /ʒo'getʃi/ m plaything
jóia /'ʒɔja/ f jewel; (propina) entry fee □ a (fam) great

joio /ˈʒoju/ m chaff; separar o ∼ do trigo separate the wheat from the chaff

jóquei /ˈʒɔkej/ m (pessoa) jockey; (lugar) race course

Jordânia /ʒorˈdɐniɐ/ f Jordan

jordaniano /ʒordaniˈanu/ a & m Jordanian

jor|nada /ʒorˈnada/ f (viagem) journey; ∼nada de trabalho working day; ∼nal (pl ∼nais) m newspaper; (na TV) news

jorna|leco /ʒornaˈlɛku/ m rag, scandal sheet; ∼leiro m (vendedor) newsagent, (Amer) newsdealer; (entregador) paperboy; ∼lismo m journalism; ∼lista m/f journalist; ∼lístico a journalistic

jor|rar /ʒoˈxar/ vi gush, spurt; ∼ro /ˈʒoxu/ m spurt

jota /ˈʒɔta/ m letter J

jovem /ˈʒɔvẽ/ a young; (criado por jovens) youth □ m/f young man (f -woman); pl young people

jovi|al /ʒoviˈaw/ (pl ∼ais) a jovial

juba /ˈʒuba/ f mane

jubileu /ʒubiˈlew/ m jubilee

júbilo /ˈʒubilu/ m joy

ju|daico /ʒuˈdajku/ a Jewish; ∼daísmo m Judaism; ∼deu a (f ∼dia) Jewish □ m (f ∼dia) Jew; ∼diação f ill-treatment; (uma) terrible thing; ∼diar vi ∼diar de ill-treat

judici|al /ʒudʒisiˈaw/ (pl ∼ais) a judicial; ∼ário a judicial □ m judiciary; ∼oso /o/ a judicious

judô /ʒuˈdo/ m judo

judoca /ʒuˈdɔka/ m/f judo player

jugo /ˈʒugu/ m yoke

juiz /ʒuˈis/ m (f juíza) judge; (em jogos) referee

juizado /ʒuiˈzadu/ m court

juízo /ʒuˈizu/ m judgement; (tino) sense; (tribunal) court; perder o ∼ lose one's head; ter ∼ be sensible; tomar ou criar ∼ come to one's senses

jujuba /ʒuˈʒuba/ f (bala) fruit jelly

jul|gamento /ʒuwgaˈmẽtu/ m judgement; ∼gar vt judge; pass judgement on <réu>; (imaginar) think; ∼gar-se vpr consider o.s.

julho /ˈʒuʎu/ m July

jumento /ʒuˈmẽtu/ m donkey

junção /ʒũˈsãw/ f join; (ação) joining

junco /ˈʒũku/ m reed

junho /ˈʒuɲu/ m June

juni|no /ʒuˈninu/ a festa ∼na St John's Day festival

júnior /ˈʒunior/ a & m junior

jun|ta /ˈʒũta/ f board; (pol) junta; ∼tar vt (acrescentar) add; (uma coisa a outra) join; (uma coisa com outra)

combine; save up <dinheiro>; gather up <papéis, lixo etc> □ vi gather; ∼tar-se vpr join together; <multidão> gather; <casal> live together; ∼tar-se a join; ∼to a together; ∼to □ adv together; ∼to a next to; ∼to com together with

ju|ra /ˈʒura/ f vow; ∼rado m juror; ∼ramentado a accredited; ∼ramento m oath; ∼rar vt/i swear; ∼ra? (fam) really?

júri /ˈʒuri/ m jury

jurídico /ʒuˈridʒiku/ a legal

juris|consulto /ʒuriskõˈsuwtu/ m legal advisor; ∼dição f jurisdiction; ∼prudência f jurisprudence; ∼ta m/f jurist

juros /ˈʒurus/ m pl interest

jus /ˈʒus/ m fazer ∼ a live up to

jusante /ʒuˈzãtʃi/ f a ∼ downstream

justamente /ʒustaˈmẽtʃi/ adv exactly; (com justiça) fairly

justapor /ʒustaˈpor/ vt juxtapose

justi|ça /ʒusˈtʃisa/ f (perante a lei) justice; (para com outros) fairness; (tribunal) court; ∼ceiro a fair-minded □ m vigilante

justifi|cação /ʒustʃifikaˈsãw/ f justification; ∼car vt justify; ∼cativa f justification; ∼cável (pl ∼cáveis) a justifiable

justo /ˈʒustu/ a fair; (apertado) tight □ adv just

juve|nil /ʒuveˈniw/ (pl ∼nis) a youthful; (para jovens) for young people; <time, torneio> junior □ m junior championship

juventude /ʒuvẽˈtudʒi/ f youth

K

karaokê /karaoˈke/ m karaoke

kart /ˈkartʃi/ (pl ∼s) m go-kart

ketchup /keˈtʃupi/ m ketchup

kit /ˈkitʃi/ (pl ∼s) m kit

kitchenette /kitʃeˈnetʃi/ f bedsitter

Kuwait /kuˈwajtʃi/ m Kuwait

kuwaitiano /kuwajtʃiˈanu/ a & m Kuwaiti

L

lá /la/ adv there; até ∼ <ir> there; <esperar etc> until then; por ∼ (naquela direção) that way; (naquele lugar) around there; ∼ fora outside; sei ∼ how should I know?

lã /lã/ f wool

labareda /labaˈreda/ f flame

lábia /labia/ f flannel; ter ∼ have the gift of the gab

lábio /ˈlabio/ m lip

labirinto /labi'rïtu/ *m* labyrinth

laboratório /labora'tɔriu/ *m* laboratory

laborioso /labori'ozu/ *a* hard-working

labu|ta /la'buta/ *f* drudgery; ~tar *vi* slog

laca /'laka/ *f* lacquer

laçada /la'sada/ *f* slipknot

lacaio /la'kaju/ *m* lackey

la|çar /la'sar/ *vt* lasso <*boi*>; ~ço *m* bow; (*de vaqueiro*) lasso; (*vínculo*) tie

lacônico /la'koniku/ *a* laconic

lacraia /la'kraja/ *f* centipede

la|crar /la'krar/ *vt* seal; ~cre *m* (*substância*) sealing wax; (*fechamento*) seal

lacri|mejar /lakrime'ʒar/ *vi* water; ~mogêneo *a* <*gás*> tear; <*filme*> tearjerking; ~moso /o/ *a* tearful

lácteo /'laktʃiu/ *a* milk; Via Láctea Milky Way

lacticínio /laktʃi'siniu/ *m veja* laticínio

lacuna /la'kuna/ *f* gap

ladainha /lada'iɲa/ *f* litany

la|dear /ladʒi'ar/ *vt* flank; sidestep <*dificuldade*>; ~deira *f* slope

lado /'ladu/ *m* side; o ~ de cá/lá this/that side; ao ~ de beside; ~ a ~ side by side; para este ~ this way; por outro ~ on the other hand

la|drão /la'drãw/ *m* (*f* ~dra) thief; (*tubo*) overflow pipe □ *a* thieving

ladrar /la'drar/ *vi* bark

ladri|lhar /ladri'ʎar/ *vt* tile; ~lho *m* tile

ladroagem /ladro'aʒẽ/ *f* stealing

lagar|ta /la'garta/ *f* caterpillar; (*numa roda*) caterpillar track; ~tear *vi* bask in the sun; ~tixa *f* gecko; ~to *m* lizard

lago /'lagu/ *m* lake

lagoa /la'goa/ *f* lagoon

lagos|ta /la'gosta/ *f* lobster; ~tim *m* crayfish, (*Amer*) crawfish

lágrima /'lagrima/ *f* tear

laia /'laja/ *f* kind

laico /'lajku/ *adj* <*pessoa*> lay; <*ensino*> secular

laivos /'lajvus/ *m pl* traces

laje /'laʒi/ *m* flagstone; ~ar *vt* pave

lajota /la'ʒota/ *f* small paving stone

lama /'lama/ *f* mud; ~çal (*pl* ~çais) *m* bog; ~cento *a* muddy

lamba|da /lã'bada/ *f* lambada; ~teria *f* lambada club

lam|ber /lã'ber/ *vt* lick; ~bida *f* lick

lambreta /lã'breta/ *f* moped

lambris /lã'bris/ *m pl* panelling

lambuzar /lãbu'zar/ *vt* smear; ~-se *vpr* get sticky

lamen|tar /lamē'tar/ *vt* (*lastimar*) lament; (*sentir*) be sorry; ~tar-se de lament; ~tável (*pl* ~táveis) *a* lamentable; ~to *m* lament

lâmina /'lamina/ *f* blade; (*de persiana*) slat

laminar /lami'nar/ *vt* laminate

lâmpada /'lãpada/ *f* light bulb; (*abajur*) lamp

lampe|jar /lãpe'ʒar/ *vi* flash; ~jo /e/ *m* flash

lampião /lãpi'ãw/ *m* lantern

lamúria /la'muria/ *f* moaning

lamuriar-se /lamuri'arsi/ *vpr* moan (de about)

lan|ça /'lãsa/ *f* spear; ~çamento *m* (*de navio, foguete, produto*) launch; (*de filme, disco*) release; (*novo produto*) new line; (*novo filme, disco*) release; (*novo livro*) new title; (*em livro comercial*) entry; ~çar *vt* (*atirar*) throw; launch <*navio, foguete, novo produto, livro*>; release <*filme, disco*>; (*em livro comercial*) enter; (*em leilão*) bid; ~çar mão de make use of; ~ce *m* (*num filme, jogo*) bit, moment; (*episódio*) episode; (*questão*) matter; (*jogada*) move; (*em leilão*) bid; (*de escada*) flight; (*de casas*) row

lancha /'lãʃa/ *f* launch

lan|char /lã'ʃar/ *vi* have a snack □ *vt* have a snack of; ~che *m* snack; ~chonete /ɛ/ *f* snack bar

lancinante /lãsi'nãtʃi/ *a* <*dor*> shooting; <*grito*> piercing

lânguido /'lãgidu/ *a* languid

lantejoula /lãte'ʒola/ *f* sequin

lanter|na /lã'terna/ *f* lantern; (*de bolso*) torch, (*Amer*) flashlight; ~nagem *f* panel-beating; (*oficina*) body-shop; ~ninha *m/f* usher (*f* usherette)

lanugem /la'nuʒẽ/ *f* down

lapela /la'pɛla/ *f* lapel

lapi|dar /lapi'dar/ *vt* cut <*pedra preciosa*>; (*fig*) polish

lápide /'lapidʒi/ *f* tombstone

lápis /'lapis/ *m invar* pencil

lapiseira /lapi'zera/ *f* propelling pencil; (*caixa*) pencil box

Lapônia /la'ponia/ *f* Lappland

lapso /'lapsu/ *m* lapse

la|qué /la'ke/ *m* lacquer; ~quear *vt* lacquer

lar /lar/ *m* home

laran|ja /la'rãʒa/ *f* orange □ *a invar* orange; ~jada *f* orangeade; ~jeira *f* orange tree

lareira /la'rera/ *f* hearth, fireplace

lar|gada /lar'gada/ *f* start; dar a ~gada start off; ~gar *vt* (*soltar*) let go of; give up <*estudos, emprego etc*>; ~gar de fumar give up smoking; ~go *a* wide; <*roupa*> loose □ *m* (*praça*) square; ao ~go (*no alto-mar*) out at sea; ~gura *f* width

larin|ge /la'riʒi/ *f* larynx; ~gite *f* laryngitis

larva /'larva/ *f* larva

lasanha /la'zaɲa/ f lasagna
las|ca /'laska/ f chip; **~car** vt/i chip; **de ~car** (fam) awful
lástima /'lastʃima/ f shame
lastro /'lastru/ m ballast
la|ta /'lata/ f (material) tin; (recipiente) tin, (Amer) can; **~ta de lixo** dustbin, (Amer) trash can; **~tão** m brass
late|jante /late'ʒãtʃi/ a throbbing; **~jar** vi throb
latente /la'tẽtʃi/ a latent
late|ral /late'raw/ (pl **~rais**) a side, lateral
laticínio /latʃi'siniu/ m dairy product
latido /la'tʃidu/ m bark
lati|fundiário /latʃifũdʒi'ariu/ a landowning □ m landowner; **~fúndio** m estate
latim /la'tʃĩ/ m Latin
latino /la'tʃinu/ a & m Latin; **~americano** a & m Latin American
latir /la'tʃir/ vi bark
latitude /latʃi'tudʒi/ f latitude
lauda /'lawda/ f side
laudo /'lawdu/ m report, findings
lava /'lava/ f lava
lava|bo /la'vabu/ m toilet; **~dora** f washing machine; **~gem** f washing; **~gem a seco** dry cleaning; **~gem cerebral** brainwashing
lavanda /la'vãda/ f lavender
lavanderia /lavãde'ria/ f laundry
lavar /la'var/ vt wash; **~ a seco** dry-clean; **~-se** vpr wash
lavatório /lava'tɔriu/ m (Port) wash-basin
lavoura /la'vora/ f (agricultura) farming; (terreno) field
lav|rador /lavra'dor/ m farmhand; **~rar** vt work; draw up <documento>
laxante /la'ʃãtʃi/ a & m laxative
lazer /la'zer/ m leisure
le|al /le'aw/ (pl **~ais**) a loyal; **~aldade** f loyalty
leão /le'ãw/ m lion; **Leão** (signo) Leo; **~-de-chácara** (pl **leões-de-chácara**) m bouncer
lebre /'lɛbri/ f hare
lecionar /lesio'nar/ vt/i teach
le|gação /lega'sãw/ f legation; **~gado** m (pessoa) legate; (herança) legacy
le|gal /le'gaw/ (pl **~gais**) a legal; (fam) good; <pessoa> nice; **tá ~gal** OK; **~galidade** f legality; **~galizar** vt legalize
legar /le'gar/ vt bequeath
legenda /le'ʒẽda/ f (de quadro) caption; (de filme) subtitle; (inscrição) inscription
legi|ão /leʒi'ãw/ f legion; **~onário** m (romano) legionary; (da legião estrangeira) legionnaire
legis|lação /leʒizla'sãw/ f legislation; **~lador** m legislator; **~lar** vi

legislate; **~lativo** a legislative □ m legislature; **~latura** f legislature; **~ta** m/f legal expert
legiti|mar /leʒitʃi'mar/ vt legitimize; **~midade** f legitimacy
legítimo /le'ʒitʃimu/ a legitimate
legí|vel /le'ʒivew/ (pl **~veis**) a legible
légua /'lɛgwa/ f league
legume /le'gumi/ m vegetable
lei /lej/ f law
leigo /'lejgu/ a lay □ m layman
lei|lão /lej'lãw/ m auction; **~loar** vt auction; **~loeiro** m auctioneer
leitão /lej'tãw/ m sucking pig
lei|te /'lejtʃi/ m milk; **~te condensado/desnatado** condensed/skimmed milk; **~teira** f (jarro) milk jug; (panela) milk saucepan; **~teiro** m milkman □ a <vaca> dairy
leito /'lejtu/ m bed
leitor /lej'tor/ m reader
leitoso /lej'tozu/ a milky
leitura /lej'tura/ f (ação) reading; (material) reading matter
lema /'lema/ m motto
lem|brança /lẽ'brãsa/ f memory; (presente) souvenir; **~brar** vt/i remember; **~brar-se** remember; **~brar aco a alg** remind s.o. of sth; **~brete** /e/ m reminder
leme /'lemi/ m rudder
len|ço /'lẽsu/ m (para o nariz) hand-kerchief; (para vestir) scarf; **~çol** /ɔ/ (pl **~çóis**) m sheet
len|da /'lẽda/ f legend; **~dário** a legendary
lenha /'leɲa/ f firewood; (uma) log; **~dor** m woodcutter
lente /'lẽtʃi/ f lens; **~ de contato** contact lens
lentidão /lẽtʃi'dãw/ f slowness
lentilha /lẽ'tʃiʎa/ f lentil
lento /'lẽtu/ a slow
leoa /le'oa/ f lioness
leopardo /lio'pardu/ m leopard
le|pra /'lɛpra/ f leprosy; **~proso** /o/ a leprous □ m leper
leque /'lɛki/ m fan; (fig) array
ler /ler/ vt/i read
ler|deza /ler'deza/ f sluggishness; **~do** /ɛ/ a sluggish
le|são /le'zãw/ f lesion, injury; **~sar** vt damage
lésbi|ca /'lɛzbika/ f lesbian; **~co** a lesbian
lesionar /lezio'nar/ vt injure
lesma /'lezma/ f slug
leste /'lestʃi/ m east
le|tal /le'taw/ (pl **~tais**) a lethal
le|tão /le'tãw/ a & m (f **~tã**) Latvian
letargia /letar'ʒia/ f lethargy
letivo /le'tʃivu/ a **ano ~** academic year

Letônia /le'tonia/ *f* Latvia
letra /'letra/ *f* letter; (*de música*) lyrics, words; (*caligrafia*) writing; **Letras** Modern Languages; **ao pé da ~** literally; **com todas as ~s** in no uncertain terms; **tirar de ~** take in one's stride; **~ de fôrma** block letter
letreiro /le'treru/ *m* sign
leucemia /lewse'mia/ *f* leukaemia
leva /ɛ/ *f* batch
levado /le'vadu/ *a* naughty
levan|tamento /levãta'mẽtu/ *m* (*enquete*) survey; (*rebelião*) uprising; **~tamento de pesos** weightlifting; **~tar** *vt* raise; lift <*peso*> □ *vi* get up; **~tar-se** *vpr* get up; (*revoltar-se*) rise up
levante /le'vãtʃi/ *m* east
levar /le'var/ *vt* take; lead <*vida*>; get <*tapa, susto etc*> □ *vi* lead (**a** to)
leve /'levi/ *a* light; (*não grave*) slight; **de ~** lightly
levedura /leve'dura/ *f* yeast
leveza /le'veza/ *f* lightness
levi|andade /leviã'dadʒi/ *f* frivolity; **~ano** *a* frivolous
levitar /levi'tar/ *vi* levitate
lexi|cal /leksi'kaw/ (*pl* **~cais**) *a* lexical
léxico /'leksiku/ *m* lexicon
lexicografia /leksikogra'fia/ *f* lexicography
lhe /ʎi/ *pron* (*a ele*) to him; (*a ela*) to her; (*a você*) to you; **~s** *pron* to them; (*a vocês*) to you
liba|nês /liba'nes/ *a & m* (*f* **~nesa**) Lebanese
Líbano /'libanu/ *m* Lebanon
libélula /li'bɛlula/ *f* dragonfly
libe|ração /libera'sãw/ *f* release; **~ral** (*pl* **~rais**) *a & m* liberal; **~ralismo** *m* liberalism; **~ralizar** *vt* liberalize; **~rar** *vt* release
liberdade /liber'dadʒi/ *f* freedom; **pôr em ~** set free; **~ condicional** probation
libero /'liberu/ *m* sweeper
liber|tação /liberta'sãw/ *f* liberation; **~tar** *vt* free
Líbia /'libia/ *f* Libya
líbio /'libiu/ *a & m* Libyan
libi|dinoso /libidʒi'nozu/ *a* lecherous; **~do** *f* libido
li|bra /'libra/ *f* pound; **Libra** (*signo*) Libra; **~briano** *a & m* Libran
lição /li'sãw/ *f* lesson
licen|ça /li'sẽsa/ *f* leave; (*documento*) licence; **com ~ça** excuse me; **de ~ça** on leave; **sob ~ça** under licence; **~ciar** *vt* (*autorizar*) license; (*dar férias a*) give leave to; **~ciar-se** *vpr* (*tirar férias*) take leave; (*formar-se*) graduate; **~ciatura** *f* degree; **~cioso** /o/ *a* licentious

liceu /li'sew/ *m* (*Port*) secondary school, (*Amer*) high school
licor /li'kor/ *m* liqueur
lida /'lida/ *f* slog, grind; (*leitura*) read
lidar /li'dar/ *vt/i* **~ com** deal with
lide /'lidʒi/ *f* (*trabalho*) work
líder /'lider/ *m/f* leader
lide|rança /lide'rãsa/ *f* (*de partido etc*) leadership; (*em corrida, jogo etc*) lead; **~rar** *vt* lead
lido /'lidu/ *a* well-read
liga /'liga/ *f* (*aliança*) league; (*tira*) garter; (*presilha*) suspender; (*de metais*) alloy
li|gação /liga'sãw/ *f* connection; (*telefônica*) call; (*amorosa*) liaison; **~gada** *f* call, ring; **~gado** *a* <*luz, TV*> on; **~gado em** attached to <*pessoa*>; hooked on <*droga*>; **~gamento** *m* ligament; **~gar** *vt* join, connect; switch on <*luz, TV etc*>; start up <*carro*>; bind <*amigos*> □ *vi* ring up, call; **~gar para** (*telefonar*) ring, call; (*dar importância*) care about; (*dar atenção*) pay attention to; **~gar-se** *vpr* join
ligeiro /li'ʒeru/ *a* light; <*ferida, melhora*> slight; (*ágil*) nimble
lilás /li'las/ *m* lilac □ *a invar* mauve
lima[1] /'lima/ *f* (*ferramenta*) file
lima[2] /'lima/ *f* (*fruta*) sweet orange
limão /li'mãw/ *m* lime; (*amarelo*) lemon
limar /li'mar/ *vt* file
limeira /li'mera/ *f* sweet orange tree
limiar /limi'ar/ *m* threshold
limi|tação /limita'sãw/ *f* limitation; **~tar** *vt* limit; **~tar-se** *vpr* limit o.s.; **~tar(-se) com** border on; **~te** *m* limit; (*de terreno*) boundary; **passar dos ~tes** go too far; **~te de velocidade** speed limit
limo|eiro /limo'eru/ *m* lime tree; **~nada** *f* lemonade
lim|pador /lĩpa'dor/ *m* **~pador de pára-brisas** windscreen wiper; **~par** *vt* clean; wipe <*lágrimas, suor*>; (*fig*) clean up <*cidade, organização*>; **~peza** /e/ *f* (*ato*) cleaning; (*qualidade*) cleanness; (*fig*) clean-up; **~peza pública** sanitation; **~po** *a* clean; <*céu, consciência*> clear; <*lucro*> net, clear; (*fig*) pure; **passar a ~po** write up <*trabalho*>; (*fig*) sort out <*vida*>; **tirar a ~po** get to the bottom of <*caso*>
limusine /limu'zini/ *f* limousine
lince /'lĩsi/ *m* lynx
lindo /'lĩdu/ *a* beautiful
linear /lini'ar/ *a* linear
lingote /lĩ'gɔtʃi/ *m* ingot
língua /'lĩgwa/ *f* (*na boca*) tongue; (*idioma*) language; **~ materna** mother tongue

linguado /lĩ'gwadu/ m sole

lingua|gem /lĩ'gwaʒẽ/ f language; ~jar m speech, dialect

lingüeta /lĩ'gweta/ f bolt

lingüiça /lĩ'gwisa/ f pork sausage

lin|güista /lĩ'gwiʃta/ m/f linguist; ~güística f linguistics; ~güístico a linguistic

linha /'liɲa/ f line; (fio) thread; perder a ~ lose one's cool; ~ aérea airline; ~ de fogo firing line; ~ de montagem assembly line; ~gem f lineage

linho /'liɲu/ m linen; (planta) flax

linóleo /li'nɔliu/ m lino(leum)

lipoaspiração /lipoaspira'sãw/ f liposuction

liqui|dação /likida'sãw/ f liquidation; (de loja) clearance sale; (de conta) settlement; ~dar vt liquidate; settle <conta>; pay off <dívida>; sell off, clear <mercadorias>

liqüidificador /likwidʒifika'dor/ m liquidizer

líqüido /'likidu/ a liquid; <lucro, salário> net □ m liquid

liri|ca /'lirika/ f (mus) lyrics; (poesia) lyric poetry; ~co a lyrical; < poesia> lyric

lírio /'liriu/ m lily

Lisboa /liz'boa/ f Lisbon

lisboeta /lizbo'eta/ a & m/f (person) from Lisbon

liso /'lizu/ a smooth, (sem desenho) plain; <cabelo> straight; (fam: duro) broke

lison|ja /li'zõʒa/ f flattery; ~jear vt flatter

lista /'lista/ f list; (listra) stripe; ~ telefônica telephone directory

listra /'listra/ f stripe; ~do a striped, stripey

lite|ral /lite'raw/ (pl ~rais) a literal; ~rário a literary; ~ratura f literature

litígio /li'tʃiʒiu/ m dispute; (jurid) lawsuit

lito|ral /lito'raw/ (pl ~rais) m coastline; ~râneo a coastal

litro /'litru/ m litre

Lituânia /litu'ania/ f Lithuania

lituano /litu'anu/ a & m Lithuanian

living /'livĩ/ (pl ~s) m living room

livrar /li'vrar/ vt free; (salvar) save; ~-se vpr escape; ~-se de get rid of

livraria /livra'ria/ f bookshop

livre /'livri/ a free; ~ de impostos tax-free; ~-arbítrio m free will

liv|reiro /li'vreru/ m bookseller; ~ro m book; ~ro de consulta reference book; ~ro de cozinha cookery book; ~ro de texto text book

li|xa /'liʃa/ f (de unhas) emery board; (para madeira etc) sandpaper; ~xar

vt sand <madeira>; file <unhas>; estou me ~xando (fam) I couldn't care less

li|xeira /li'ʃera/ f dustbin, (Amer) garbage can; ~xeiro m dustman, (Amer) garbage collector; ~xo m rubbish, (Amer) garbage; (atômico) waste

lobisomem /lobi'zomẽ/ m werewolf

lobo /'lobu/ m wolf; ~-marinho (pl ~s-marinhos) m sea lion

lóbulo /'lɔbulu/ m lobe

lo|cação /loka'sãw/ f (de imóvel) lease; (de carro) rental; ~cador m (de casa) landlord; ~cadora f rental company; (de videos) video shop

lo|cal /lo'kaw/ (pl ~cais) a local □ m site; (de um acidente etc) scene; ~calidade f locality; ~calização f location; ~calizar vt locate; ~calizar-se vpr (orientar-se) get one's bearings

loção /lo'sãw/ f lotion; ~ após-barba aftershave lotion

locatário /loka'tariu/ m (de imóvel) tenant; (de carro etc) hirer

locomo|tiva /lokomo'tʃiva/ f locomotive; ~ver-se vpr get around

locu|ção /loku'sãw/ f phrase; ~tor m announcer

lodo /'lodu/ m mud; ~so /o/ a muddy

logaritmo /loga'ritʃimu/ m logarithm

lógi|ca /'lɔʒika/ f logic; ~co a logical

logo /'lɔgu/ adv (em seguida) straightaway; (em breve) soon; (justamente) just; ~ mais later; ~ antes/depois just before/straight after; ~ que as soon as; até ~ goodbye

logotipo /logo'tʃipu/ m logo

logradouro /logra'doru/ m public place

loiro /'lojru/ a veja louro

lo|ja /'lɔʒa/ f shop, (Amer) store; ~ja de departamentos department store; ~ja maçônica masonic lodge; ~jista m/f shopkeeper

lom|bada /lõ'bada/ f (de livro) spine; (na rua) speed bump; ~binho m tenderloin; ~bo m back; (carne) loin

lona /'lona/ f canvas

Londres /'lõdris/ f London

londrino /lõ'drinu/ a London □ m Londoner

longa-metragem /lõgame'traʒẽ/ (pl longas-metragens) m feature film

longe /'lõʒi/ adv far, a long way; de ~ from a distance; (por muito) by far; ~ disso far from it

longevidade /lõʒevi'dadʒi/ f longevity

longínquo /lõ'ʒĩkwu/ a distant

longitude /lõʒi'tudʒi/ f longitude

longo /'lõgu/ a long □ m long dress; ao ~ de along; (durante) through, over

lontra /'lõtra/ f otter
lorde /'lɔrdʒi/ m lord
lorota /lo'rɔta/ (fam) f fib
losango /lo'zãgu/ m diamond
lo|tação /lota'sãw/ f capacity; (ônibus) bus; ~**tação esgotada** full house; <teatro, ônibus> full; ~**tar** vt fill □ vi fill up
lote /'lɔtʃi/ m (quinhão) portion; (de terreno) plot, (Amer) lot; (em leilão) lot; (porção de coisas) batch
loteria /lote'ria/ f lottery
louça /'losa/ f china; (pratos etc) crockery; **lavar a ~** wash up, (Amer) do the dishes
lou|co /'loku/ a mad, crazy □ m madman; **estou ~co para ir** (fam) I'm dying to go; ~**cura** f madness; (uma) crazy thing
louro /'loru/ a blond □ m laurel; (condimento) bayleaf
lou|var /lo'var/ vt praise; ~**vável** (pl ~**váveis**) a praiseworthy; ~**vor** /o/ m praise
lua /'lua/ f moon; ~-**de-mel** f honeymoon
lu|ar /lu'ar/ m moonlight; ~**arento** a moonlit
lubrifi|cação /lubrifika'sãw/ f lubrication; ~**cante** a lubricating □ m lubricant; ~**car** vt lubricate
lucidez /lusi'des/ f lucidity
lúcido /'lusidu/ a lucid
lu|crar /lu'krar/ vi profit (**com** by); ~**cratividade** f profitability; ~**crativo** a profitable, lucrative; ~**cro** m profit
ludibriar /ludʒibri'ar/ vt cheat
lúdico /'ludʒiku/ a playful
lugar /lu'gar/ m place; (espaço) room; **em ~ de** in place of; **em primeiro ~** in the first place; **em algum ~** somewhere; **em todo ~** everywhere; **dar ~ a** give rise to; **ter ~** take place
lugarejo /luga'reʒu/ m village
lúgubre /'lugubri/ a gloomy, dismal
lula /'lula/ f squid
lume /'lumi/ m fire
luminária /lumi'naria/ f light, lamp; pl illuminations
luminoso /lumi'nozu/ a luminous; <idéia> brilliant
lunar /lu'nar/ a lunar □ m mole
lupa /'lupa/ f magnifying glass
lusco-fusco /lusku'fusku/ m twilight
lusitano /luzi'tanu/, **luso** /'luzu/ a & m Portuguese
lus|trar /lus'trar/ vt shine, polish; ~**tre** m shine; (fig) lustre; (luminária) light, lamp; ~**troso** /o/ a shiny
lu|ta /'luta/ f fight, struggle; ~**ta livre** wrestling; ~**tador** m fighter; (de luta livre) wrestler; ~**tar** vi fight □ vt do <judô etc>

luto /'lutu/ m mourning
luva /'luva/ f glove
luxação /luʃa'sãw/ f dislocation
Luxemburgo /luʃẽ'burgu/ m Luxembourg
luxembur|guês /luʃẽbur'ges/ a (f ~**guesa**) Luxemburg □ m (f ~**guesa**) Luxemburger; (língua) Luxemburgish
luxo /'luʃu/ m luxury; **hotel de ~** luxury hotel; **cheio de ~** (fam) fussy
luxuoso /luʃu'ozu/ a luxurious
luxúria /lu'ʃuria/ f lust
luxuriante /luʃuri'ãtʃi/ a lush
luz /lus/ f light; **à ~ de** by the light of <velas etc>; in the light of <fatos etc>; **dar à ~** give birth to
luzidio /luzi'dʒio/ a shiny
luzir /lu'zir/ vi shine

M

maca /'maka/ f stretcher
maçã /ma'sã/ f apple
macabro /ma'kabru/ a macabre
maca|cão /maka'kãw/ m (de trabalho) overalls, (Amer) coveralls; (tipo de calça) dungarees; (roupa inteiriça) jumpsuit; (para bebê) romper suit; ~**co** m monkey; (aparelho) jack
maçada /ma'sada/ f bore
maçaneta /masa'neta/ f doorknob
maçante /ma'sãtʃi/ a boring
macar|rão /maka'xãw/ m pasta; (espaguete) spaghetti; ~**ronada** f pasta with tomato sauce and cheese
macarrônico /maka'xoniku/ a broken
macete /ma'setʃi/ m trick
machado /ma'ʃadu/ m axe
ma|chão /ma'ʃãw/ a tough □ m tough guy; ~**chismo** m machismo; ~**chista** a chauvinistic □ m male chauvinist; ~**cho** a male; <homem> macho □ m male
machu|cado /maʃu'kadu/ m injury; (na pele) sore patch; ~**car** vt/i hurt; ~**car-se** vpr hurt o.s.
maciço /ma'sisu/ a solid; <dose etc> massive □ m massif
macieira /masi'era/ f apple tree
maciez /masi'es/ f softness
macilento /masi'lẽtu/ a haggard
macio /ma'siu/ a soft; <carne> tender
maço /'masu/ m (de cigarros) packet; (de notas) bundle
ma|çom /ma'sõ/ m freemason; ~**çonaria** f freemasonry
maconha /ma'koɲa/ f marijuana
maçônico /ma'soniku/ a masonic
má-criação /makria'sãw/ f rudeness
macrobiótico /makrobi'ɔtʃiku/ a macrobiotic

macum|ba /ma'kũba/ f Afro-Brazilian cult; (*uma*) spell; ~**beiro** *m* follower of macumba (= *a* macumba)
madame /ma'dami/ f lady
Madeira /ma'dera/ f Madeira
madeira /ma'dera/ f wood □ *m* (*vinho*) Madeira; ~ **de lei** hardwood
madeirense /made'rẽsi/ *a* & *m* Madeiran
madeixa /ma'defa/ f lock
madrasta /ma'drasta/ f stepmother
madrepérola /madre'pɛrola/ f mother of pearl
madressilva /madre'siwva/ f honeysuckle
Madri /ma'dri/ f Madrid
madrinha /ma'driɲa/ f (*de batismo*) godmother; (*de casamento*) bridesmaid
madru|gada /madru'gada/ f early morning; ~**gador** *m* early riser; ~**gar** *vi* get up early
maduro /ma'duru/ *a* <*fruta*> ripe; <*pessoa*> mature
mãe /mãj/ f mother; ~**-de-santo** (*pl* ~**s-de-santo**) f macumba priestess
maes|tria /majs'tria/ f expertise; ~**tro** *m* conductor
máfia /'mafia/ f mafia
magazine /maga'zini/ *m* department store
magia /ma'ʒia/ f magic
mági|ca /'maʒika/ f magic; (*uma*) magic trick; ~**co** *a* magic □ *m* magician
magis|tério /maʒis'tɛriu/ *m* teaching; (*professores*) teachers; ~**trado** *m* magistrate
magnânimo /mag'nanimu/ *a* magnanimous
magnata /mag'nata/ *m* magnate
magnésio /mag'nɛziu/ *m* magnesium
mag|nético /mag'nɛtʃiku/ *a* magnetic; ~**netismo** *m* magnetism; ~**netizar** *vt* magnetize; (*fig*) mesmerize
mag|nificência /magnifi'sẽsia/ f magnificence; ~**nífico** *a* magnificent
magnitude /magni'tudʒi/ f magnitude
mago /'magu/ *m* magician; **os reis** ~**s** the Three Wise Men
mágoa /'magoa/ f sorrow
magoar /mago'ar/ *vt/i* hurt; ~**-se** *vpr* be hurt
ma|gricela /magri'sɛla/ *a* skinny; ~**gro** *a* thin; <*leite*> skimmed; <*carne*> lean; (*fig*) meagre
maio /'maju/ *m* May
maiô /ma'jo/ *m* swimsuit
maionese /majo'nɛzi/ f mayonnaise
maior /ma'jɔr/ *a* bigger; <*escritor, amor etc*> greater; **o** ~ **carro** the biggest car; **o** ~ **escritor** the greatest writer; ~ **de idade** of age

Maiorca /ma'jɔrka/ f Majorca
maio|ria /majo'ria/ f majority; **a** ~**ria dos brasileiros** most Brazilians; ~**ridade** f majority, adulthood
mais /majs/ *adv* & *pron* more; ~ **dois** two more; **dois dias a** ~ two more days; **não trabalho** ~ I don't work any more; ~ **ou menos** more or less
maisena /maj'zena/ f cornflour, (*Amer*) cornstarch
maitre /mɛtr/ *m* head waiter
maiúscula /ma'juskula/ f capital letter
majes|tade /maʒes'tadʒi/ f majesty; ~**toso** *a* majestic
major /ma'ʒɔr/ *m* major
majoritário /maʒori'tariu/ *a* majority
mal /maw/ *adv* badly; (*quase não*) hardly □ *conj* hardly □ *m* evil; (*doença*) sickness; **não faz** ~ never mind; **levar a** ~ take offence at; **passar** ~ be sick
mala /'mala/ f suitcase; (*do carro*) boot, (*Amer*) trunk; ~ **aérea** air courier
malabaris|mo /malaba'rizmu/ *m* juggling act; ~**ta** *m/f* juggler
malagradecido /malagrade'sidu/ *a* ungrateful
malagueta /mala'geta/ f chilli pepper
malaio /ma'laju/ *a* & *m* Malay
Malaísia /mala'izia/ f Malaysia
malaísio /mala'iziu/ *a* & *m* Malaysian
malan|dragem /malã'draʒẽ/ f hustling; (*uma*) clever trick; ~**dro** *a* cunning □ *m* hustler
malária /ma'laria/ f malaria
mal-assombrado /malasõ'bradu/ *a* haunted
Malavi /mala'vi/ *m* Malawi
malcriado /mawkri'adu/ *a* rude
mal|dade /maw'dadʒi/ f wickedness; (*uma*) wicked thing; **por** ~**dade** out of spite; ~**dição** f curse; ~**dito** *a* cursed, damned; ~**doso** /o/ *a* wicked
malea|vel /mali'avew/ (*pl* ~**veis**) *a* malleable
maledicência /maledi'sẽsia/ f malicious gossip
maléfico /ma'lɛfiku/ *a* evil; (*prejudicial*) harmful
mal-encarado /malĩka'radu/ *a* shady, dubious □ *m* shady character
mal-entendido /malĩtẽ'dʒidu/ *m* misunderstanding
mal-estar /malis'tar/ *m* (*doença*) ailment; (*constrangimento*) discomfort
maleta /ma'leta/ f overnight bag
malévolo /ma'lɛvolu/ *a* malevolent
malfei|to /maw'fejtu/ *a* (*roupa etc*) badly made; (*fig*) wrongful; ~**tor** *m* wrongdoer; ~**toria** f wrongdoing

ma|lha /'maʎa/ f (*ponto*) stitch; (*tricô*) knitting; (*tecido*) jersey; (*casaco*) jumper, (*Amer*) sweater; (*para ginástica*) leotard; (*de rede*) mesh; fazer ~**lha** knit; ~**lhado** a <*animal*> dappled; ~**lhar** vt beat; thresh <*trigo etc*> □ vi (*fam*) work out

mal-humorado /malumo'radu/ a in a bad mood, grumpy

malícia /ma'lisia/ f (*má índole*) malice; (*astúcia*) guile; (*humor*) innuendo

malicioso /malisi'ozu/ a (*mau*) malicious; (*astuto*) crafty; (*que põe malícia*) dirty-minded

maligno /ma'liginu/ a malignant

malmequer /mawme'ker/ m marigold

maloca /ma'lɔka/ f Indian village

malo|grar-se /malo'grarsi/ vpr go wrong, fail; ~**gro** /o/ m failure

mal-passado /mawpa'sadu/ a <*carne*> rare

Malta /'mawta/ f Malta

malte /'mawtʃi/ m malt

maltrapilho /mawtra'piʎu/ a scruffy

maltratar /mawtra'tar/ vt ill-treat, mistreat

malu|co /ma'luku/ a mad, crazy □ m madman; ~**quice** f madness; (*uma*) crazy thing

malvado /maw'vadu/ a wicked

malver|sação /mawversa'sãw/ f mismanagement; (*de fundos*) misappropriation; ~**sar** vt mismanage; misappropriate <*dinheiro*>

Malvinas /maw'vinas/ f pl Falklands

mamadeira /mama'dera/ f (baby's) bottle

mamãe /ma'mãj/ f mum

mamão /ma'mãw/ m papaya

ma|mar /ma'mar/ vi suckle; ~**mata** f (*fam*) fiddle

mamífero /ma'miferu/ m mammal

mamilo /ma'milu/ m nipple

mamoeiro /mamo'eru/ m papaya tree

manada /ma'nada/ f herd

manan|ci|al /manãsi'aw/ (*pl* ~**ais**) m spring; (*fig*) rich source

man|cada /mã'kada/ f blunder; ~**car** vi limp; ~**car-se** vpr (*fam*) take the hint, get the message

Mancha /'mãʃa/ f o canal da ~ the English Channel

man|cha /'mãʃa/ f stain; (*na pele*) mark; ~**char** vt stain

manchete /mã'ʃɛtʃi/ f headline

manco /'mãku/ a lame □ m cripple

mandachuva /mãda'ʃuva/ m (*fam*) bigwig; (*chefe*) boss

man|dado /mã'dadu/ m order; ~**dado de busca** search warrant; ~**dado de prisão** arrest warrant; ~**damento** m commandment; ~**dante** m/f person

in charge; ~**dão** a (f ~**dona**) bossy; ~**dar** vt (*pedir*) order; (*enviar*) send □ vi be in charge; ~**dar-se** vpr (*fam*) take off; ~**dar buscar** fetch; ~**dar dizer** send word; ~**dar alg ir** tell s.o. to go; ~**dar ver** (*fam*) go to town; ~**dar em alg** order s.o. about; ~**dato** m mandate

mandíbula /mã'dʒibula/ f (lower) jaw

mandioca /mãdʒi'ɔka/ f manioc

maneira /ma'nera/ f way; *pl* (*boas*) manners; **desta** ~ in this way; **de qualquer** ~ anyway

mane|jar /mane'ʒar/ vt handle; operate <*máquina*>; ~**jável** (*pl* ~**jáveis**) a manageable; ~**jo** /e/ m handling

manequim /mane'ki/ m (*boneco*) dummy; (*medida*) size □ m/f mannequin, model

maneta /ma'neta/ a one-armed □ m/f person with one arm

manga¹ /'mãga/ f (*de roupa*) sleeve

manga² /'mãga/ f (*fruta*) mango

manganês /mãga'nes/ m manganese

mangue /'mãgi/ m mangrove swamp

mangueira¹ /mã'gera/ f (*tubo*) hose

mangueira² /mã'gera/ f (*árvore*) mango tree

manha /'maɲa/ f tantrum

manhã /ma'ɲã/ f morning; **de** ~ in the morning

manhoso /ma'ɲozu/ a wilful

mania /ma'nia/ f (*moda*) craze; (*doença*) mania

maníaco /ma'niaku/ a manic □ m maniac; ~**-depressivo** a & m manic depressive

manicômio /mani'komiu/ m lunatic asylum

manicura /mani'kura/ f manicure; (*pessoa*) manicurist

manifes|tação /manifesta'sãw/ f manifestation; (*passeata*) demonstration; ~**tante** m/f demonstrator; ~**tar** vt manifest, demonstrate; ~**tar-se** vpr (*revelar-se*) manifest o.s.; (*exprimir-se*) express an opinion; ~**to** /ɛ/ a manifest, clear □ m manifesto

manipular /manipu'lar/ vt manipulate

manjedoura /mãʒe'dora/ f manger

manjericão /mãʒeri'kãw/ m basil

mano|bra /ma'nɔbra/ f manoeuvre; ~**brar** vt manoeuvre; ~**brista** m/f parking valet

mansão /mã'sãw/ f mansion

man|sidão /mãsi'dãw/ f gentleness; (*do mar*) calm; ~**sinho** adv **de** ~**sinho** (*devagar*) slowly; (*de leve*) gently; (*de fininho*) stealthily; ~**so** a gentle; <*mar*> calm; <*animal*> tame

manta /'mãta/ f blanket; (*casaco*) cloak

mantei|ga /mã'tejga/ f butter; ~**gueira** f butter dish

manter /mã'ter/ vt keep; ~-**se** vpr keep; (sustentar-se) keep o.s.

mantimentos /mãtʃi'mẽtus/ m pl provisions

manto /'mãtu/ m mantle

manu|al /manu'aw/ (pl ~**ais**) a & m manual; ~**fatura** f manufacture; (fábrica) factory; ~**faturar** vt manufacture

manuscrito /manus'kritu/ a handwritten □ m manuscript

manu|sear /manuzi'ar/ vt handle; ~**seio** m handling

manutenção /manutẽ'sãw/ f maintenance; (de prédio) upkeep

mão /mãw/ (pl ~**s**) f hand; (do trânsito) direction; (de tinta) coat; **abrir** ~ **de** give up; **agüentar** a ~ hang on; **dar a** ~ **a alg** hold s.o.'s hand; (cumprimentando) shake s.o.'s hand; **deixar alg na** ~ let s.o. down; **enfiar ou meter a** ~ **em** hit, slap; **lançar** ~ **de** make use of; **escrito à** ~ written by hand; **ter à** ~ have to hand; **de** ~**s dadas** hand in hand; **em segunda** ~ second-hand; **fora de** ~ out of the way; ~ **única** one way; ~-**de-obra** f labour

mapa /'mapa/ m map

maquete /ma'ketʃi/ f model

maqui|agem /maki'aʒẽ/ f make-up; ~**ar** vt make up; ~**ar-se** vpr put on make-up

maquiavélico /makia'vɛliku/ a Machiavellian

maqui|lagem, ~**lar**, (Port) ~**lhagem**, ~**lhar** veja **maqui|agem**, ~**ar**

máquina /'makina/ f machine; (ferroviária) engine; **escrever à** ~ type; ~ **de costura** sewing machine; ~ **de escrever** typewriter; ~ **de lavar** (roupa) washing machine; ~ **de lavar pratos** dishwasher; ~ **fotográfica** camera

maqui|nação /makina'sãw/ f machination; ~**nal** (pl ~**nais**) a mechanical; ~**nar** vt/i plot; ~**naria** f machinery; ~**nista** m/f (ferroviário) engine driver; (de navio) engineer

mar /mar/ m sea

maracujá /maraku'ʒa/ m passion fruit; ~**jazeiro** m passion-fruit plant

marasmo /ma'razmu/ f stagnation

marato|na /mara'tona/ f marathon; ~**nista** m/f marathon runner

maravi|lha /mara'viʎa/ f marvel; **às mil** ~**lhas** wonderfully; ~**lhar** vt amaze; ~**lhar-se** vpr marvel (**de** at); ~**lhoso** /o/ a marvellous

mar|ca /'marka/ f mark; (de carro, máquina) make; (de cigarro, sabão etc) brand; ~**ca registrada** registered trademark; ~**cação** f marking; (Port: discagem) dialling; ~**cador** m marker; (em livro) bookmark; (placar) scoreboard; (jogador) scorer; ~**cante** a outstanding; ~**capasso** m pacemaker; ~**car** vt mark; arrange <hora, encontro, jantar etc>; score <gol, ponto>; (Port: discar) dial; <relógio, termómetro> show; brand <gado>; (observar) keep a close eye on; (impressionar) leave one's mark on □ vi make one's mark; ~**car época** make history; ~**car hora** make an appointment; ~**car o compasso** beat time; ~**car os pontos** keep the score

marce|naria /marsena'ria/ f cabinet-making; (oficina) cabinet maker's workshop; ~**neiro** m cabinet maker

mar|cha /'marʃa/ f march; (de carro) gear; **pôr-se em** ~**cha** get going; ~**cha à ré**, (Port) ~**cha atrás** reverse; ~**char** vi march

marci|al /marsi'aw/ (pl ~**ais**) a martial; ~**ano** a & m Martian

marco[1] /'marku/ m (sinal) landmark

marco[2] /'marku/ m (moeda) mark

março /'marsu/ m March

maré /ma'rɛ/ f tide

mare|chal /mare'ʃaw/ (pl ~**chais**) m marshal

maresia /mare'zia/ f smell of the sea

marfim /mar'fi/ m ivory

margarida /marga'rida/ f daisy; (para impressora) daisywheel

margarina /marga'rina/ f margarine

mar|gem /'marʒẽ/ f (de rio) bank; (de lago) shore; (parte em branco, fig) margin; ~**ginal** (pl ~**ginais**) a marginal; (delinqüente) delinquent □ m/f delinquent □ f (rua) riverside road; ~**ginalidade** f delinquency; ~**ginalizar** vt marginalize

marido /ma'ridu/ m husband

marimbondo /marĩ'bõdu/ m hornet

marina /ma'rina/ f marina

mari|nha /ma'riɲa/ f navy; ~**nha mercante** merchant navy; ~**nheiro** m sailor; ~**nho** a marine

marionete /mario'netʃi/ f puppet

mariposa /mari'poza/ f moth

mariscos /ma'riskus/ m seafood

mari|tal /mari'taw/ (pl ~**tais**) a marital

marítimo /ma'ritʃimu/ a sea; <cidade> seaside

marmanjo /mar'mãʒu/ m grown-up

marme|lada /marme'lada/ f (fam) fix; ~**lo** /ɛ/ m quince

marmita /mar'mita/ f (de soldado) mess tin; (de trabalhador) lunchbox

mármore /'marmori/ m marble

marmóreo /mar'mɔriu/ a marble

marquise /mar'kizi/ f awning

marreco /ma'xɛku/ m wild duck

Marrocos /maˈxɔkus/ m Morocco
marrom /maˈxõ/ a & m brown
marroquino /maxoˈkinu/ a & m Moroccan
Marte /ˈmartʃi/ m Mars
marte|lada /marteˈlada/ f hammer blow; ~**lar** vt/i hammer; ~**lar em** (fig) go on and on about; ~**lo** /ɛ/ m hammer
mártir /ˈmartʃir/ m/f martyr
mar|tírio /marˈtʃiriu/ m martyrdom; (fig) torture; ~**tirizar** vt martyr; (fig) torture
marujo /maˈruʒu/ m sailor
mar|xismo /markˈsizmu/ m Marxism; ~**xista** a & m/f Marxist
mas /mas/ conj but
mascar /masˈkar/ vt chew
máscara /ˈmaskara/ f mask; (tratamento facial) face-pack
mascarar /maskaˈrar/ vt mask
mascate /masˈkatʃi/ m street vendor
mascavo /masˈkavu/ a açúcar ~ brown sugar
mascote /masˈkɔtʃi/ f mascot
masculi|no /maskuˈlinu/ a male; (para homens) men's; <palavra> masculine □ m masculine
másculo /ˈmaskulu/ a masculine
masmorra /mazˈmoxa/ f dungeon
masoquis|mo /mazoˈkizmu/ m masochism; ~**ta** m/f masochist □ a masochistic
massa /ˈmasa/ f mass; (de pão) dough; (de torta, empada) pastry; (macarrão etc) pasta; **cultura de** ~ mass culture; **em** ~ en masse; **as** ~**s** the masses
massa|crante /masaˈkrãtʃi/ a gruelling; ~**crar** vt massacre, (fig. maçar) wear out; ~**cre** m massacre
massa|gear /masaʒiˈar/ vt massage; ~**gem** f massage; ~**gista** m/f masseur (f masseuse)
mastigar /mastʃiˈgar/ vt chew; (ponderar) chew over
mastro /ˈmastru/ m mast; (de bandeira) flagpole
mastur|bação /masturbaˈsãw/ f masturbation; ~**bar-se** vpr masturbate
mata /ˈmata/ f forest
mata-borrão /mataboˈxãw/ m blotting paper
matadouro /mataˈdoru/ m slaughterhouse
mata|gal /mataˈgaw/ (pl ~**gais**) m thicket
mata-moscas /mataˈmoskas/ m invar fly spray
ma|tança /maˈtãsa/ f slaughter; ~**tar** vt kill; satisfy <fome>; quench <sede>; guess <charada>; (fazer nas coxas) dash off; (fam) skive off <aula, serviço> □ vi kill

mata-ratos /mataˈxatus/ m invar rat poison
mate[1] /ˈmatʃi/ m (chá) maté
mate[2] /ˈmatʃi/ a invar matt
matemáti|ca /mateˈmatʃika/ f mathematics; ~**co** a mathematical □ m mathematician
matéria /maˈtɛria/ f (assunto, disciplina) subject; (no jornal) article; (substância) matter; (usada para fazer algo) material; **em** ~ **de** in the way of
materi|al /materiˈaw/ (pl ~**ais**) m materials □ a material; ~**alismo** m materialism; ~**alista** a materialistic □ m/f materialist; ~**alizar-se** vpr materialize
matéria-prima /maˈtɛriaˈprima/ (pl **matérias-primas**) f raw material
mater|nal /materˈnaw/ (pl ~**nais**) a maternal; ~**nidade** f maternity; (clínica) maternity hospital; ~**no** /ɛ/ a maternal; **língua** ~**na** mother tongue
mati|nal /matʃiˈnaw/ (pl ~**nais**) a morning; ~**nê** f matinée
matiz /maˈtʃis/ m shade; (político) colouring; (pontinha: de ironia etc) tinge
matizar /matʃiˈzar/ vt tinge (de with)
mato /ˈmatu/ m scrubland, bush
matraca /maˈtraka/ f rattle; (tagarela) chatterbox
matreiro /maˈtreru/ a cunning
matriar|ca /matriˈarka/ f matriarch; ~**cal** (pl ~**cais**) a matriarchal
matrícula /maˈtrikula/ f enrolment; (taxa) enrolment fee; (Port: de carro) number plate, (Amer) license plate
matricular /matrikuˈlar/ vt enrol; ~**-se** vpr enrol
matri|monial /matrimoniˈaw/ (pl ~**moniais**) a marriage; ~**mônio** m marriage
matriz /maˈtris/ f matrix; (útero) womb; (sede) head office
maturidade /maturiˈdadʒi/ f maturity
matutino /matuˈtʃinu/ a morning □ m morning paper
matuto /maˈtutu/ a countrified □ m country bumpkin
mau /maw/ a (f **má**) bad; ~**-caráter** m invar bad lot □ a invar no-good; ~**-olhado** m evil eye
mausoléu /mawzoˈlɛw/ m mausoleum
maus-tratos /mawsˈtratus/ m pl ill-treatment
maxilar /maksiˈlar/ m jaw
máxima /ˈmasima/ f maxim
maximizar /masimiˈzar/ vt maximize; (exagerar) play up
máximo /ˈmasimu/ a (antes do substantivo) utmost, greatest; (depois do substantivo) maximum □ m

maximum; o ∼ (*fam: o melhor*) really something; **ao** ∼ to the maximum; **no** ∼ at most

maxixe /ma'ʃiʃi/ *m* gherkin

me /mi/ *pron* me; (*indireto*) (to) me; (*reflexivo*) myself

meada /mi'ada/ *f* skein; **perder o fio da** ∼ lose one's thread

meados /mi'adus/ *m pl* ∼ **de maio** mid-May

meandro /mi'ãdru/ *f* meander; *pl* (*fig*) twists and turns

mecâni|ca /me'kanika/ *f* mechanics; ∼**co** *a* mechanical □ *m* mechanic

meca|nismo /meka'nizmu/ *m* mechanism; ∼**nizar** *vt* mechanize

mecenas /me'sɛnas/ *m invar* patron

mecha /'mɛʃa/ *f* (*de vela*) wick; (*de bomba*) fuse; (*porção de cabelos*) lock; (*cabelo tingido*) highlight; ∼**do** *a* highlighted

meda|lha /me'daʎa/ *f* medal; ∼**lhão** *m* medallion; (*jóia*) locket

média /'mɛdʒia/ *f* average; (*café*) white coffee; **em** ∼ on average

medi|ação /medʒia'sãw/ *f* mediation; ∼**ador** *m* mediator; ∼**ante** *prep* through, by; ∼**ar** *vi* mediate

medica|ção /medʒika'sãw/ *f* medication; ∼**mento** *m* medicine

medição /medʒi'sãw/ *f* measurement

medicar /medʒi'kar/ *vt* treat □ *vi* practise medicine; ∼**-se** *vpr* dose o.s. up

medici|na /medʒi'sina/ *f* medicine; ∼**na legal** forensic medicine; ∼**nal** (*pl* ∼**nais**) *a* medicinal

médico /'mɛdʒiku/ *m* doctor □ *a* medical; ∼**-legal** (*pl* ∼**-legais**) *a* forensic; ∼**-legista** (*pl* ∼**s-legistas**) *m/f* forensic scientist

medi|da /me'dʒida/ *f* measure; (*dimensão*) measurement; **à** ∼ **da que** as; **sob** ∼**da** made to measure; **tirar as** ∼**das de alg** take s.o.'s measurements; ∼**dor** *m* meter

medie|val /medʒie'vaw/ (*pl* ∼**vais**) *a* medieval

médio /'mɛdʒiu/ *a* (*típico*) average; <*tamanho, prazo*> medium; <*classe, dedo*> middle

medíocre /me'dʒiokri/ *a* mediocre

mediocridade /medʒiokri'dadʒi/ *f* mediocrity

medir /me'dʒir/ *vt* measure; weigh <*palavras*> □ *vi* measure; ∼**-se** *vpr* measure o.s.; **quanto você mede?** how tall are you?

medi|tação /medʒita'sãw/ *f* meditation; ∼**tar** *vi* meditate

mediterrâneo /medʒite'xaniu/ *a* Mediterranean □ *m* **o Mediterrâneo** the Mediterranean

médium /'mɛdʒiũ/ *m/f* medium

medo /'medu/ *m* fear; **ter** ∼ **de** be

afraid of; **com** ∼ afraid; ∼**nho** /o/ *a* frightful

medroso /me'drozu/ *a* fearful, timid

medula /me'dula/ *f* marrow

megalomania /megaloma'nia/ *f* megalomania

meia /'meja/ *f* (*comprida*) stocking; (*curta*) sock; (*seis*) six; ∼**-calça** (*pl* ∼**s-calças**) *f* tights, (*Amer*) pantihose; ∼**-idade** *f* middle age; ∼**-noite** *f* midnight; ∼**-volta** (*pl* ∼**s-voltas**) *f* about-turn

mei|go /'mejgu/ *a* sweet; ∼**guice** *f* sweetness

meio /'meju/ *a* half □ *adv* rather □ *m* (*centro*) middle; (*ambiente*) environment; (*recurso*) means; ∼ **litro** half a litre; **dois meses e** ∼ two and a half months; **em** ∼ **a** amid; **por** ∼ **de** through; **o** ∼ **ambiente** the environment; **os** ∼**s de comunicação** the media; ∼**-dia** *m* midday; ∼**-fio** *m* kerb; ∼**-termo** *m* (*acordo*) compromise

mel /mɛw/ *m* honey

mela|ço /me'lasu/ *m* molasses; ∼**do** *a* sticky □ *m* treacle

melancia /melã'sia/ *f* watermelon

melan|colia /melãko'lia/ *f* melancholy; ∼**cólico** *a* melancholy

melão /me'lãw/ *m* melon

melar /me'lar/ *vt* make sticky

melhor /me'ʎɔr/ *a & adv* better; **o** ∼ the best

melho|ra /me'ʎɔra/ *f* improvement; ∼**ras!** get well soon!; ∼**ramento** *m* improvement; ∼**rar** *vt* improve □ *vi* improve; <*doente*> get better

melin|drar /melĩ'drar/ *vt* hurt; ∼**drar-se** *vpr* be hurt; ∼**droso** /o/ *a* delicate; <*pessoa*> sensitive

melodi|a /melo'dʒia/ *f* melody; ∼**oso** /o/ *a* melodious

melodra|ma /melo'drama/ *m* melodrama; ∼**mático** *a* melodramatic

meloso /me'lozu/ *a* sickly sweet

melro /'mɛwxu/ *m* blackbird

membrana /mẽ'brana/ *f* membrane

membro /'mẽbru/ *m* member; (*braço, perna*) limb

memo|rando /memo'rãdu/ *m* memo; ∼**rável** (*pl* ∼**ráveis**) *a* memorable

memória /me'mɔria/ *f* memory; *pl* (*autobiografia*) memoirs

men|ção /mẽ'sãw/ *f* mention; **fazer** ∼**ção de** mention; ∼**cionar** *vt* mention

mendi|cância /mẽdʒi'kãsia/ *f* begging; ∼**gar** *vi* beg; ∼**go** *m* beggar

menina /me'nina/ *f* girl; **a** ∼ **dos olhos de alg** the apple of s.o.'s eye

meningite /menĩ'ʒitʃi/ *f* meningitis

meni|nice /meni'nisi/ *f* (*idade*) childhood; ∼**no** *m* boy

menopausa /meno'pawza/ f menopause

menor /me'nɔr/ a smaller □ m/f minor; o/a ~ the smallest; (mínimo) the slightest; (menos) the least

menos /'menos/ adv & pron less □ prep except; **dois dias a** ~ two days less; **a** ~ **que** unless; **ao ou pelo** ~ at least; **o** ~ **bonito** the least pretty; ~**prezar** vt look down upon; ~**prezo** /e/ m disdain

mensa|geiro /mēsa'ʒeru/ m messenger; ~**gem** f message

men|sal /mē'saw/ (pl ~**sais**) a monthly; ~**salidade** f monthly payment; ~**salmente** adv monthly

menstru|ação /mēstrua'sãw/ f menstruation; ~**ada a estar** ~**ada** be having one's period; ~**al** (pl ~**ais**) a menstrual; ~**ar** vi menstruate

menta /'mēta/ f mint

men|tal /mē'taw/ (pl ~**tais**) a mental; ~**talidade** f mentality; ~**te** f mind

men|tir /mē'tʃir/ vi lie; ~**tira** f lie; ~**tiroso** /o/ a lying □ m liar

mentor /mē'tor/ m mentor

mercado /mer'kadu/ m market; ~**ria** f commodity; pl goods

mercan|te /mer'kãtʃi/ a merchant; ~**til** (pl ~**tis**) a mercantile; ~**tilismo** m commercialism

mercê /mer'se/ f à ~ **de** at the mercy of

merce|aria /mersia'ria/ f grocer's; ~**eiro** /e/ m grocer

mercenário /merse'nariu/ a & m mercenary

mercúrio /mer'kuriu/ m mercury; **Mercúrio** Mercury

merda /'mɛrda/ f (chulo) shit

mere|cedor /merese'dor/ a deserving; ~**cer** vt deserve □ vi be deserving; ~**cimento** m merit

merenda /me'rēda/ f packed lunch; ~**escolar** school dinner

mere|trício /mere'trisiu/ m prostitution; ~**triz** f prostitute

mergu|lhador /merguʎa'dor/ m diver; ~**lhar** vt dip (em into) □ vi (na água) dive; (no trabalho) bury o.s.; ~**lho** m dive; (esporte) diving; (banho de mar) dip

meridi|ano /meridʒi'anu/ m meridian; ~**onal** (pl ~**onais**) a southern

mérito /'mɛritu/ m merit

merluza /mer'luza/ f hake

mero /'mɛru/ a mere

mês /mes/ (pl **meses**) m month

mesa /'meza/ f table; (de trabalho) desk; ~ **de centro** coffee table; ~ **de jantar** dining table; ~ **telefônica** switchboard

mesada /me'zada/ f monthly allowance

mescla /'mɛskla/ f mixture, blend

mesmice /mez'misi/ f sameness

mesmo /'mezmu/ a same □ adv (até) even; (justamente) right; (de verdade) really; **você** ~ you yourself; **hoje** ~ this very day; ~ **assim** even so; ~ **que** even if; **dá no** ~ it comes to the same thing; **fiquei na mesma** I'm none the wiser

mesqui|nharia /meskiɲa'ria/ f meanness; (uma) mean thing; ~**nho** a mean

mesquita /mes'kita/ f mosque

Messias /me'sias/ m Messiah

mesti|çagem /mestʃi'saʒē/ f interbreeding; ~**ço** a <pessoa> of mixed race; <animal> crossbred □ m (pessoa) person of mixed race; (animal) mongrel

mes|trado /mes'tradu/ m master's degree; ~**tre** /ɛ/ m (f ~**tra**) master (f mistress); (de escola) teacher □ a main; <chave> master; ~**tre-de-obras** (pl ~**tres-de-obras**) m foreman; ~**tre-sala** (pl ~**tres-salas**) m master of ceremonies (in carnival procession); ~**tria** f expertise

meta /'mɛta/ f (de corrida) finishing post; (gol, fig) goal

meta|bólico /meta'bɔliku/ a metabolic; ~**bolismo** m metabolism

metade /me'tadʒi/ f half; **pela** ~ halfway

metafísi|ca /meta'fizika/ f metaphysics; ~**co** a metaphysical

metáfora /me'tafora/ f metaphor

metafórico /meta'fɔriku/ a metaphorical

me|tal /me'taw/ (pl ~**tais**) m metal; pl (numa orquestra) brass; ~**tálico** a metallic

meta|lurgia /metalur'ʒia/ f metallurgy; ~**lúrgica** f metal works; ~**lúrgico** a metallurgical □ m metalworker

metamorfose /metamor'fɔzi/ f metamorphosis

metano /me'tanu/ m methane

meteórico /mete'ɔriku/ a meteoric

meteoro /mete'oru/ m meteor; ~**logia** f meteorology; ~**lógico** a meteorological; ~**logista** m/f (cientista) meteorologist; (na TV) weather forecaster

meter /me'ter/ vt put; ~-**se** vpr (envolver-se) get (em into); (intrometer-se) meddle (em in); ~ **medo** be frightening

meticuloso /metʃiku'lozu/ a meticulous

metido /me'tʃidu/ a snobbish; **ele é** ~ **a perito** he thinks he's an expert

metódico /me'tɔdʒiku/ a methodical

metodista /meto'dʒista/ a & m/f Methodist

método /'mɛtodu/ *m* method

metra|lhadora /metraʎa'dora/ *f* machine gun; **~lhar** *vt* machine-gun

métri|co /'mɛtriku/ *a* metric; **fita ~ca** tape measure

metro[1] /'mɛtru/ *m* metre

metro[2] /'mɛtru/ *m* (*Port: metropolitano*) underground, (*Amer*) subway

metrô /me'tro/ *m* underground, (*Amer*) subway

metrópole /me'trɔpoli/ *f* metropolis

metropolitano /metropoli'tanu/ *a* metropolitan □ *m* (*Port*) underground, (*Amer*) subway

meu /mew/ *a* (*f* **minha**) □ *pron* (*f* **minha**) mine; **um amigo ~** a friend of mine; **fico na minha** (*fam*) I keep myself to myself

mexer /me'ʃer/ *vt* move; (*com colher etc*) stir □ *vi* move; **~-se** *vpr* move; (*apressar-se*) get a move on; **~ com** (*comover*) affect, get to; (*brincar com*) tease; (*trabalhar com*) work with; **~ em** touch

mexeri|ca /meʃe'rika/ *f* tangerine; **~car** *vi* gossip; **~co** *m* piece of gossip; *pl* gossip; **~queiro** a gossiping □ *m* gossip

mexicano /meʃi'kanu/ *a & m* Mexican

México /'mɛʃiku/ *m* Mexico

mexido /me'ʃidu/ *a* **ovos ~s** scrambled eggs

mexilhão /meʃi'ʎãw/ *m* mussel

mi|ado /mi'adu/ *m* miaow; **~ar** *vi* miaow

micróbio /mi'krɔbiu/ *m* microbe

micro|cosmo /mikro'kɔzmu/ *m* microcosm; **~empresa** /e/ *f* small business; **~empresário** *m* small businessman; **~filme** *m* microfilm; **~fone** *m* microphone; **~onda** /e/ *f* microwave; (**forno de**) **~s** *m* microwave (oven); **~ônibus** *m* invar minibus; **~processador** *m* microprocessor

microrganismo /mikrorga'nizmu/ *m* microorganism

microscó|pico /mikros'kɔpiku/ *a* microscopic; **~pio** *m* microscope

mídia /'midʒia/ *f* media

migalha /mi'gaʎa/ *f* crumb

mi|gração /migra'sãw/ *f* migration; **~grar** *vi* migrate; **~gratório** a migratory

mijar /mi'ʒar/ *vi* (*fam*) pee; **~jar-se** *vpr* wet o.s.; **~jo** *m* (*fam*) pee

mil /miw/ *a & m* invar thousand; **estar a ~** be on top form

mila|gre /mi'lagri/ *m* miracle; **~groso** /o/ a miraculous

milênio /mi'leniu/ *m* millennium

milésimo /mi'lɛzimu/ a thousandth

milha /'miʎa/ *f* mile

milhão /mi'ʎãw/ *m* million; **um ~ de dólares** a million dollars

milhar /mi'ʎar/ *m* thousand; **~es de vezes** thousands of times; **aos ~es** in their thousands

milho /'miʎo/ *m* maize, (*Amer*) corn

milico /mi'liku/ *m* (*fam*) military man; **os ~s** the military

mili|grama /mili'grama/ *m* milligram; **~litro** *m* millilitre; **~metro** /e/ *m* millimetre

milionário /milio'nariu/ *a & m* millionaire

mili|tante /mili'tãtʃi/ *a & m* militant; **~tar** a military □ *m* soldier

mim /mĩ/ *pron* me

mimar /mi'mar/ *vt* spoil

mímica /'mimika/ *f* mime; (*brincadeira*) charades

mi|na /'mina/ *f* mine; **~nar** *vt* mine; (*fig: prejudicar*) undermine

mindinho /mĩ'dʒiɲu/ *m* little finger, (*Amer*) pinkie

minei|ro /mi'neru/ *a* mining; (*de MG*) from Minas Gerais □ *m* miner; (*de MG*) person from Minas Gerais

mine|ração /minera'sãw/ *f* mining; **~ral** (*pl* **~rais**) *a & m* mineral; **~rar** *vt/i* mine

minério /mi'nɛriu/ *m* ore

mingau /mĩ'gaw/ *m* porridge

mingua /'mĩgwa/ *f* lack

minguante /mĩ'gwãtʃi/ *a* **quarto ~** last quarter

minguar /mĩ'gwar/ *vi* dwindle

minha /'miɲa/ *a & pron veja* **meu**

minhoca /mi'ɲɔka/ *f* worm

miniatura /minia'tura/ *f* miniature

mini|malista /minima'lista/ *a & m/f* minimalist; **~mizar** *vt* minimize; (*subestimar*) play down

mínimo /'minimu/ *a* (*muito pequeno*) tiny; (*mais baixo*) minimum □ *m* minimum; **a mínima idéia** the slightest idea; **no ~** at least

minissaia /mini'saja/ *f* miniskirt

minis|terial /ministeri'aw/ (*pl* **~teriais**) *a* ministerial; **~tério** *m* ministry; **Ministério do Interior** Home Office, (*Amer*) Department of the Interior

minis|trar /minis'trar/ *vt* administer; **~tro** *m* minister; **primeiro ~tro** prime minister

Minorca /mi'nɔrka/ *f* Menorca

mino|ritário /minori'tariu/ *a* minority; **~ria** *f* minority

minúcia /mi'nusia/ *f* detail

minucioso /minusi'ozu/ *a* thorough

minúscu|la /mi'nuskula/ *f* small letter; **~lo** *a* <*letra*> small; (*muito pequeno*) minuscule

minuta /mi'nuta/ *f* (*rascunho*) rough draft

minuto /mi'nutu/ *m* minute

miolo /mi'olu/ *f* (*de fruta*) flesh; (*de pão*) crumb; *pl* brains

míope /'miopi/ *a* short-sighted

miopia /mio'pia/ *f* myopia

mira /'mira/ *f* sight; **ter em** ~ have one's sights on

mirabolante /mirabo'lãt∫i/ *a* amazing; <*idéias, plano*> grandiose

mi|ragem /mi'raʒẽ/ ~rante *m* lookout; ~rar *vt* look at; ~rar-se *vpr* look at o.s.

mirim /mi'rĩ/ *a* little

miscelânea /mise'lania/ *f* miscellany

miscigenação /misiʒena'sãw/ *f* interbreeding

mise-en-plis /mizã'pli/ *m* shampoo and set

mise|rá|vel /mize'ravew/ (*pl* ~veis) *a* miserable

miséria /mi'zɛria/ *f* misery; (*pobreza*) poverty; **uma** ~ (*pouco dinheiro*) a pittance; **chorar** ~ claim poverty

miseri|córdia /mizeri'kɔrdʒia/ *f* mercy; ~cordioso *a* merciful

misógino /mi'zɔʒinu/ *m* misogynist □ *a* misogynistic

miss /'misi/ *f* beauty queen

missa /'misa/ *f* mass

missão /mi'sãw/ *f* mission

mis|sil /'misiw/ (*pl* ~seis) *m* missile; ~sil de longo alcance long-range missile

missionário /misio'nariu/ *m* missionary

missiva /mi'siva/ *f* missive

mis|tério /mis'teriu/ *m* mystery; ~terioso /o/ *a* mysterious; ~ticismo *m* mysticism

místico /'mist∫iku/ *m* mystic □ *a* mystical

misto /'mistu/ *a* mixed □ *m* mix; ~ quente toasted ham and cheese sandwich

mistu|ra /mis'tura/ *f* mixture; ~rar *vt* mix; (*confundir*) mix up; ~rar-se *vpr* mix (*com* with)

mítico /'mit∫iku/ *a* mythical

mito /'mitu/ *m* myth; ~logia *f* mythology; ~lógico *a* mythological

miudezas /miu'dezas/ *f pl* odds and ends

miúdo /mi'udu/ *a* tiny, minute; <*chuva*> fine; <*despesas*> minor □ *m* (*criança*) child, little one; *pl* (*de galinha*) giblets; **trocar em** ~s go into detail

mixaria /mi∫a'ria/ *f* (*fam*) (*soma irrisória*) pittance

mixórdia /mi'∫ɔrdʒia/ *f* muddle

mnemônico /ne'moniku/ *a* mnemonic

mobíliar /mobi'lar/ *vt* (*Port*) furnish

mobília /mo'bilia/ *f* furniture

mobili|ar /mobili'ar/ *vt* furnish; ~ário *m* furniture

mobili|dade /mobili'dadʒi/ *f* mobility; ~zar *vt* mobilize

moça /'mosa/ *f* girl

moçambicano /mosãbi'kanu/ *a & m* Mozambican

Moçambique /mosã'biki/ *m* Mozambique

moção /mo'sãw/ *f* motion

mochila /mo'∫ila/ *f* rucksack

moço /'mosu/ *a* young □ *m* boy, lad

moda /'mɔda/ *f* fashion; **na** ~ fashionable

modalidade /modali'dadʒi/ *f* (*esporte*) event

mode|lagem /mode'laʒẽ/ *f* modelling; ~lar *vt* model (*a on*); ~lar-se *vpr* model o.s. (*a on*) □ *a* model; ~lo /e/ *m* model

mode|ração /modera'sãw/ *f* moderation; ~rado *a* moderate; ~rar *vt* moderate; reduce <*velocidade, despesas*>; ~rar-se *vpr* restrain oneself

moder|nidade /moderni'dadʒi/ *f* modernity; ~nismo *m* modernism; ~nista *a & m/f* modernist; ~nizar *vt* modernize; ~no /ɛ/ *a* modern

modess /mo'dʒis/ *m invar* sanitary towel

modéstia /mo'dɛst∫ia/ *f* modesty

modesto /mo'dɛstu/ *a* modest

módico /'mɔdʒiku/ *a* modest

modifi|cação /modʒifika'sãw/ *f* modification; ~car *vt* modify

mo|dismo /mo'dʒizmu/ *m* idiom; ~dista *f* dressmaker

modo /'mɔdu/ *m* way; (*ling*) mood; *pl* (*maneiras*) manners

modular /modu'lar/ *vt* modulate □ *a* modular

módulo /'mɔdulu/ *m* module

moeda /mo'ɛda/ *f* (*peça de metal*) coin; (*dinheiro*) currency

mo|edor /moe'dor/ *m* ~edor de café coffee-grinder; ~edor de carne mincer; ~er *vt* grind <*café, trigo*>; squeeze <*cana*>; mince <*carne*>; (*bater*) beat

mo|fado /mo'fadu/ *a* mouldy; ~far *vi* moulder; ~fo /o/ *m* mould

mogno /'mɔgnu/ *m* mahogany

moinho /mo'iɲu/ *m* mill; ~ de vento windmill

moisés /moj'zɛs/ *m invar* carry-cot

moita /'mojta/ *f* bush

mola /'mɔla/ *f* spring

mol|dar /mow'dar/ *vt* mould; cast <*metal*>; ~de /ɔ/ *m* mould; (*para costura etc*) pattern

moldu|ra /mow'dura/ *f* frame; ~rar *vt* frame

mole /'mɔli/ *a* soft; <*pessoa*> listless; (*fam*) (*fácil*) easy □ *adv* easily; **é ~?** (*fam*) can you believe it?

molécula /mo'lɛkula/ *f* molecule

moleque /mo'lɛki/ *m* (*menino*) lad; (*de rua*) urchin; (*homem*) scoundrel

molestar /moles'tar/ *vt* bother

moléstia /mo'lɛstʃia/ *f* disease

moletom /mole'tõ/ *m* (*tecido*) knitted cotton; (*blusa*) sweatshirt

moleza /mo'leza/ *f* softness; (*de pessoa*) laziness; **viver na ~** lead a cushy life; **ser ~** be easy

mo|lhado /mo'ʎadu/ *a* wet; **~lhar** *vt* wet; **~lhar-se** *vpr* get wet

molho[1] /'mɔʎu/ *m* (*de chaves*) bunch; (*de palha*) sheaf

molho[2] /'moʎu/ *m* sauce; (*para salada*) dressing; **deixar de ~** leave in soak <*roupa*>; **~ inglês** Worcester sauce

molusco /mo'lusku/ *m* mollusc

momen|tâneo /momẽ'taniu/ *a* momentary; **~to** *m* moment; (*força*) momentum

Mônaco /'monaku/ *m* Monaco

monar|ca /mo'narka/ *m/f* monarch; **~quia** *f* monarchy; **~quista** *a* & *m/f* monarchist

monástico /mo'nastʃiku/ *a* monastic

monção /mõ'sãw/ *f* monsoon

mone|tário /mone'tariu/ *a* monetary; **~tarismo** *m* monetarism; **~tarista** *a* & *m/f* monetarist

monge /'mõʒi/ *m* monk

monitor /moni'tor/ *m* monitor; **~ de vídeo** VDU

monitorar /monito'rar/ *vt* monitor

mono|cromo /mono'krɔmu/ *a* monochrome; **~gamia** *f* monogamy

monógamo /mo'nɔgamu/ *a* monogamous

monograma /mono'grama/ *m* monogram

monólogo /mo'nɔlogu/ *m* monologue

mononucleose /mononukli'ɔzi/ *f* glandular fever

mono|pólio /mono'pɔliu/ *m* monopoly; **~polizar** *vt* monopolize

monossílabo /mono'silabu/ *a* monosyllabic □ *m* monosyllable

monotonia /monoto'nia/ *f* monotony

monótono /mo'nɔtonu/ *a* monotonous

monóxido /mo'nɔksidu/ *m* **~ de carbono** carbon monoxide

mons|tro /'mõstru/ *m* monster; **~truosidade** *f* monstrosity; **~truoso** /o/ *a* monstrous

monta|dor /mõta'dor/ *m* (*de cinema*) editor; **~dora** *f* assembly company; **~gem** *f* assembly; (*de filme*) editing; (*de peça teatral*) production

monta|nha /mõ'taɲa/ *f* mountain; **~nha-russa** (*pl* **~nhas-russas**) *f* roller coaster; **~nhismo** *m* mountaineering; **~nhoso** /o/ *a* mountainous

mon|tante /mõ'tãtʃi/ *m* amount □ *a* rising; **a ~tante** upstream; **~tão** *m* heap; **~tar** *vt* ride <*cavalo, bicicleta*>; assemble <*peças, máquina*>; put up <*barraca*>; set up <*empresa, escritório*>; mount <*guarda, diamante*>; put on <*espetáculo, peça*>; edit <*filme*> □ *vi* ride; **~tar a** <*dívidas etc*> amount to; **~tar em** (*subir em*) mount; **~taria** *f* mount; **~te** *m* heap; **um ~te de coisas** (*fam*) loads of things; **o Monte Branco** Mont Blanc

Montevidéu /mõtʃivi'dɛw/ *f* Montevideo

montra /'mõtra/ *f* (*Port*) shop window

monumen|tal /monumẽ'taw/ (*pl* **~tais**) *a* monumental; **~to** *m* monument

mora|da /mo'rada/ *f* dwelling; (*Port*) address; **~dia** *f* dwelling; **~dor** *m* resident

mo|ral /mo'raw/ (*pl* **~rais**) *a* moral □ *f* (*ética*) morals; (*de uma história*) moral □ *m* (*ânimo*) morale; (*de pessoa*) moral sense; **~ralidade** *f* morality; **~ralista** *a* moralistic □ *m/f* moralist; **~ralizar** *vi* moralize

morango /mo'rãgu/ *m* strawberry

morar /mo'rar/ *vi* live

moratória /mora'tɔria/ *f* moratorium

mórbido /'mɔrbidu/ *a* morbid

morcego /mor'segu/ *m* bat

mor|daça /mor'dasa/ *f* gag; (*para cão*) muzzle; **~daz** *a* scathing; **~der** *vt/i* bite; **~dida** *f* bite

mordo|mia /mordo'mia/ *f* (*no emprego*) perk; (*de casa etc*) comfort; **~mo** /o/ *m* butler

more|na /mo'rena/ *f* brunette; **~no** *a* dark; (*bronzeado*) brown □ *m* dark person

morfina /mor'fina/ *f* morphine

moribundo /mori'bũdu/ *a* dying

moringa /mo'rĩga/ *f* water jug

morma|cento /morma'sẽtu/ *a* sultry; **~ço** *m* sultry weather

morno /'mornu/ *a* lukewarm

moro|sidade /morozi'dadʒi/ *f* slowness; **~so** /o/ *a* slow

morrer /mo'xer/ *vi* die; <*luz, dia, ardor, esperança etc*> fade; <*carro*> stall

morro /'moxu/ *m* hill; (*fig: favela*) slum

mortadela /morta'dɛla/ *f* mortadella, salami

mor|tal /mor'taw/ (*pl* **~tais**) *a* & *m* mortal; **~talha** *f* shroud; **~talidade** *f* mortality; **~tandade** *f* slaughter; **~te** /ɔ/ *f* death; **~tífero** *a* deadly; **~tificar** *vt* mortify; **~to** /o/ *a* dead mosaico /mo'zajku/ *m* mosaic

mosca /'moska/ *f* fly

Moscou /mos'ku/, (*Port*) Moscovo /moʃ'kovu/ *f* Moscow

mosquito /mos'kitu/ *m* mosquito

mostarda /mos'tarda/ *f* mustard

mosteiro /mos'teru/ *m* monastery

mos|tra /'mɔstra/ *f* display; dar ~tras de show signs of; pôr à ~tra show up; ~trador *m* face, dial; ~trar *vt* show; ~trar-se *vpr* (*revelar-se*) show o.s. to be; (*exibir-se*) show off; ~truário *m* display case

mo|tel /mo'tɛw/ (*pl* ~téis) *m* motel

motim /mo'tʃĩ/ *m* riot; (*na marinha*) mutiny

moti|vação /motʃiva'sãw/ *f* motivation; ~var *vt* (*incentivar*) motivate; (*provocar*) cause; ~vo *m* (*razão*) reason; (*estímulo*) motive; (*na arte, música*) motif; dar ~vo de give cause for

moto /'mɔtu/ *f* motorbike; ~ca /mo-'tɔka/ *f* (*fam*) motorbike

motoci|cleta /motosi'klɛta/ *f* motorcycle; ~clismo *m* motorcycling; ~clista *m/f* motorcyclist

motoqueiro /moto'keru/ *m* (*fam*) biker

motor /mo'tor/ *m* (*de carro, avião etc*) engine; (*elétrico*) motor □ *a* (*f motriz*) <*força*> driving; (*anat*) motor; ~ de arranque starter motor; ~ de popa outboard motor

moto|rista /moto'rista/ *m/f* driver; ~rizado *a* motorized; ~rizar *vt* motorize

movedi|ço /move'dʒisu/ *a* unstable, moving; areia ~ça quicksand

mó|vel /'mɔvew/ (*pl* ~veis) *a* <*peça, parte*> moving; <*tropas*> mobile; <*festa*> movable □ *m* piece of furniture; *pl* furniture

mo|ver /mo'ver/ *vt* move; (*impulsionar, fig*) drive; ~ver-se *vpr* move; ~vido *a* driven; ~vido a álcool alcohol-powered

movimen|tação /movimẽta'sãw/ *f* bustle; ~tado *a* <*rua, loja*> busy; <*música, sessão*> up-beat, lively; <*pessoa, sessão*> lively; ~tar *vt* liven up; ~tar-se *vpr* move; ~to *m* movement; (*tecn*) motion; (*na rua etc*) activity

muam|ba /mu'ãba/ *f* contraband; ~beiro *m* smuggler

muco /'muku/ *m* mucus

muçulmano /musuw'manu/ *a & m* Muslim

mu|da /'muda/ *f* (*planta*) seedling; ~da de roupa change of clothes; ~dança *f* change; (*de casa*) move; (*de carro*) transmission; ~dar *vt/i* change; ~dar de assunto change the subject; ~dar (de casa) move (house); ~dar de cor change colour;

~dar de idéia change one's mind; ~dar de lugar change places; ~dar de roupa change (clothes); ~dar-se *vpr* move

mu|dez /mu'des/ *f* silence; ~do *a* silent; (*deficiente*) dumb; <*telefone*> dead □ *m* mute

mu|gido /mu'ʒidu/ *m* moo; ~gir *vi* moo

muito /'mũitu/ *a* a lot of; *pl* many □ *pron* a lot □ *adv* (*com adjetivo, advérbio*) very; (*com verbo*) a lot; ~ maior much bigger; ~ tempo a long time

mula /'mula/ *f* mule

mulato /mu'latu/ *a & m* mulatto

muleta /mu'leta/ *f* crutch

mulher /mu'ʎer/ *f* woman; (*esposa*) wife

mulherengo /muʎe'rẽgu/ *a* womanizing □ *m* womanizer, ladies' man

mul|ta /'muwta/ *f* fine; ~tar *vt* fine

multicolor /muwtʃiko'lor/ *a* multi-coloured

multidão /muwtʃi'dãw/ *f* crowd

multinacio|nal /muwtʃinasio-'naw/ (*pl* ~nais) *a & f* multinational

multipli|cação /muwtʃiplika-'sãw/ *f* multiplication; ~car *vt* multiply; ~car-se *vpr* multiply; ~cidade *f* multiplicity

múltiplo /'muwtʃiplu/ *a & m* multiple

multirraci|al /muwtʃixasi'aw/ (*pl* ~ais) *a* multiracial

múmia /'mumia/ *f* mummy

mun|dano /mũ'danu/ *a* <*prazeres etc*> worldly; <*vida, mulher*> society; ~dial (*pl* ~diais) *a* world □ *m* world championship; ~do *m* world; todo (o) ~do everybody

munição /muni'sãw/ *f* ammunition

muni|cipal /munisi'paw/ (*pl* ~cipais) *a* municipal; ~cípio *m* (*lugar*) borough, community; (*prédio*) town hall; (*autoridade*) local authority

munir /mu'nir/ *vt* provide (de with); ~-se *vpr* equip o.s. (de with)

mu|ral /mu'raw/ (*pl* ~rais) *a & m* mural; ~ralha *f* wall

mur|char /mur'ʃar/ *vi* <*planta*> wither, wilt; <*salada*> go limp; <*beleza*> fade □ *vt* wither, wilt <*planta*>; ~cho *a* <*planta*> wilting; <*pessoa*> broken

mur|murar /murmu'rar/ *vi* murmur; (*queixar-se*) mutter □ *vt* murmur; ~múrio *m* murmur

muro /'muru/ *m* wall

murro /'muxu/ *m* punch

musa /'muza/ *f* muse

muscu|lação /muskula'sãw/ *f* weight-training; ~lar *a* muscular; ~latura *f* musculature

músculo /'muskulu/ *m* muscle

musculoso /musku'lozu/ *a* muscular

museu /mu'zew/ *m* museum

musgo /'muzgu/ *m* moss

música /'muzika/ *f* music; (*uma*) song; ~ **de câmara** chamber music; ~ **de fundo** background music; ~ **clássica** *ou* **erudita** classical music

musi|cal /muzi'kaw/ (*pl* ~**cais**) *a* & *m* musical; ~**car** *vt* set to music

músico /'muziku/ *m* musician □ *a* musical

musse /'musi/ *f* mousse

mutilar /mutʃi'lar/ *vt* mutilate; maim <*pessoa*>

mutirão /mutʃi'rãw/ *m* joint effort

mútuo /'mutuu/ *a* mutual

muxoxo /mu'ʃoʃu/ *m* **fazer** ~ tut

N

na = **em** + **a**

nabo /'nabu/ *m* turnip

nação /na'sãw/ *f* nation

nacio|nal /nasio'naw/ (*pl* ~**nais**) *a* national; (*brasileiro*) home-produced; ~**nalidade** *f* nationality; ~**nalismo** *m* nationalism; ~**nalista** *a* & *m/f* nationalist; ~**nalizar** *vt* nationalize

naco /'naku/ *m* chunk

nada /'nada/ *pron* nothing □ *adv* not at all; **de** ~ (*não há de quê*) don't mention it; **que** ~!, ~ **disso!** no way!

na|dadeira /nada'dera/ *f* (*de peixe*) fin; (*de mergulhador*) flipper; ~**dador** *m* swimmer; ~**dar** *vi* swim

nádegas /'nadegas/ *f pl* buttocks

nado /'nadu/ *m* ~ **borboleta** butterfly stroke; ~ **de costas** backstroke; ~ **de peito** breaststroke; **atravessar a** ~ swim across

náilon /'najlõ/ *m* nylon

naipe /'najpi/ *m* (*em jogo de cartas*) suit

namo|rada /namo'rada/ *f* girlfriend; ~**rado** *m* boyfriend; ~**rador** *a* amorous □ *m* ladies' man; ~**rar** *vt* (*ter relação com*) go out with; (*cobiçar*) eye up □ *vi* <*casal*> (*ter relação*) go out together; (*beijar-se etc*) kiss and cuddle; <*homem*> have a girlfriend; <*mulher*> have a boyfriend; ~**ro** /o/ *m* relationship

nanar /na'nar/ *vi* (*col*) sleep

nanico /na'niku/ *a* tiny

não /nãw/ *adv* not; (*resposta*) no □ *m* no; ~**-alinhado** *a* non-aligned; ~**-conformista** *a* & *m/f* non-conformist

naquela, naquele, naquilo = **em** + **aquela, aquele, aquilo**

narci|sismo /narsi'zizmu/ *m* narcissism; ~**sista** *m/f* narcissist □ *a* narcissistic; ~**so** *m* narcissus

narcótico /nar'kɔtʃiku/ *a* & *m* narcotic

nari|gudo /nari'gudu/ *a* with a big nose; **ser** ~**gudo** have a big nose; ~**na** *f* nostril

nariz /na'ris/ *m* nose

nar|ração /naxa'sãw/ *f* narration; ~**rador** *m* narrator; ~**rar** *vt* narrate; ~**rativa** *f* narrative; ~**rativo** *a* narrative

nas = **em** + **as**

na|sal /na'zaw/ (*pl* ~**sais**) *a* nasal; ~**salizar** *vt* nasalize

nas|cença /na'sẽsa/ *f* birth; ~**cente** *a* nascent □ *f* source; ~**cer** *vi* be born; <*dente, espinha*> grow; <*planta*> sprout; <*sol, lua*> rise; <*dia*> dawn; (*fig*) <*empresa, projeto etc*> come into being □ *m* **o** ~**cer do sol** sunrise; ~**cimento** *m* birth

nata /'nata/ *f* cream

natação /nata'sãw/ *f* swimming

Natal /na'taw/ *m* Christmas

na|tal /na'taw/ (*pl* ~**tais**) *a* <*país, terra*> native

nata|lício /nata'lisiu/ *a* & *m* birthday; ~**lidade** *f* índice de ~**lidade** birth rate; ~**lino** *a* Christmas

nati|vidade /natʃivi'dadʒi/ *f* nativity; ~**vo** *a* & *m* native

nato /'natu/ *a* born

natu|ral /natu'raw/ (*pl* ~**rais**) *a* natural; (*oriundo*) originating (**de** from) □ *m* native (**de** of)

natura|lidade /naturali'dadʒi/ *f* naturalness; **com** ~**lidade** matter-of-factly; **de** ~**lidade carioca** born in Rio de Janeiro; ~**lismo** *m* naturalism; ~**lista** *a* & *m/f* naturalist; ~**lizar** *vt* naturalize; ~**lizar-se** *vpr* become naturalized

natureza /natu'reza/ *f* nature; ~ **morta** still life

naturis|mo /natu'rizmu/ *m* naturism; ~**ta** *m/f* naturist

nau|fragar /nawfra'gar/ *vi* <*navio*> be wrecked; <*tripulação*> be shipwrecked; (*fig*) <*plano, casamento etc*> founder; ~**frágio** *m* shipwreck; (*fig*) failure

náufrago /'nawfragu/ *m* castaway

náusea /'nawzia/ *f* nausea

nauseabundo /nawzia'bũdu/ *a* nauseating

náuti|ca /'nawtʃika/ *f* navigation; ~**co** *a* nautical

na|val /na'vaw/ (*pl* ~**vais**) *a* naval; **construção** ~**val** shipbuilding

navalha /na'vaʎa/ *f* razor; ~**da** *f* cut with a razor

nave /'navi/ *f* nave; ~ **espacial** spaceship

nave|gação /navega'sãw/ *f* navigation; (*tráfego*) shipping; ~**gador** *m* navigator; ~**gante** *m/f* seafarer; ~**gar** *vt* navigate; sail <*mar*> □ *vi* sail; (traçar o rumo) navigate; ~gável (pl ~gáveis) a navigable

navio /na'viu/ m ship; ~ cargueiro cargo ship; ~ de guerra warship; ~ petroleiro oil tanker

nazista /na'zista/, (Port) nazi /na'zi/ a & m/f Nazi

neblina /ne'blina/ f mist

nebulosa /nebu'lɔza/ f nebula; ~sidade f cloud; ~so /o/ a cloudy; (fig) obscure

necessaire /nese'sɛr/ m toilet bag; ~sário a necessary; ~sidade f necessity; (que se impõe) need; (pobreza) need; ~sitado a needy □ m person in need; ~sitar vt require; (tornar necessário) necessitate; ~sitar de need

necrológio /nekro'lɔʒiu/ m obituary column; ~tério m mortuary, (Amer) morgue

néctar /'nɛktar/ m nectar

nectarina /nekta'rina/ f nectarine

nefasto /ne'fastu/ a fatal

negação /nega'sãw/ f denial; (ling) negation; ser uma ~gação em be hopeless at; (que se impõe) need; ~gar vt deny; ~gar-se a refuse to; ~gativa f refusal; (ling) negative; ~gativo a & m negative

negligência /negli'ʒesia/ f negligence; ~genciar vt neglect; ~gente a negligent

negociação /negosia'sãw/ f negotiation; ~ador m negotiator; ~ante m/f dealer (de in); ~ar vt/i negotiate; ~ar em deal in; ~ata f shady deal; ~ável (pl ~áveis) a negotiable

negócio /ne'gosiu/ m deal; (fam: coisa) thing; pl business; a ou de ~s <viajar> on business

negocista /nego'sista/ m wheeler-dealer □ a wheeler-dealing

negrito /ne'gritu/ m bold; ~gro /e/ a & m black; (de raça) Negro

nela, nele = em + ela, ele

nem /nẽj/ adv not even □ conj ... ~ ... neither ... nor ...; ~ sempre not always; ~ todos not all; ~ que not even if; que ~ like; ~ eu nor do I

nenê /ne'ne/, neném /ne'nẽj/ m baby

nenhum /ne'nũ/ a (f nenhuma) no □ pron (f nenhuma) not one; ~ dos dois neither of them; ~ erro no mistakes; erro ~ no mistakes at all, not a single mistake; ~ lugar nowhere

nenúfar /ne'nufar/ m waterlily

neologismo /neolo'ʒizmu/ m neologism

néon /'nɛõ/ m neon

neozelandês /neozelã'des/ a (f ~desa) New Zealand □ m (f ~desa) New Zealander

Nepal /ne'paw/ m Nepal

nervo /'nervu/ m nerve; ~sismo m (chateação) annoyance; (medo) nerv-

ousness; ~so /o/ a <sistema, doença> nervous; (chateado) annoyed; (medroso) nervous; deixar alg ~so get on s.o.'s nerves

nessa(s), nesse(s) = em + essa(s), esse(s)

nesta(s), neste(s) = em + esta(s), este(s)

neta /'nɛta/ f granddaughter; ~to /ɛ/ m grandson; pl grandchildren

neurologia /newrolo'ʒia/ f neurology; ~lógico a neurological; ~logista m/f neurologist

neurose /new'rɔzi/ f neurosis; ~rótico a neurotic

neutralidade /newtrali'dadʒi/ f neutrality; ~zar vt neutralize

neutrão /new'trãw/ m (Port) veja nêutron

neutro /'newtru/ a neutral

nêutron /'newtrõ/ m neutron

nevada /ne'vada/ f snowfall; ~vado a snow-covered; ~var vi snow; ~vasca f snowstorm; ~ve /ɛ/ f snow

névoa /'nɛvoa/ f haze

nevoeiro /nevo'eru/ m fog

nexo /'nɛksu/ m connection; sem ~ incoherent

Nicarágua /nika'ragwa/ f Nicaragua

nicaraguense /nikara'gwẽsi/ a & m/f Nicaraguan

nicho /'niʃu/ m niche

nicotina /niko'tʃina/ f nicotine

Níger /'niʒer/ m Niger

Nigéria /ni'ʒɛria/ f Nigeria

nigeriano /niʒeri'anu/ a & m Nigerian

Nilo /'nilu/ m Nile

ninar /ni'nar/ vt lull to sleep

ninfa /'nĩfa/ f nymph

ninguém /nĩ'gẽj/ pron no-one, nobody

ninhada /ni'nada/ f brood

ninharia /nina'ria/ f trifle

ninho /'ninu/ m nest

níquel /'nikew/ m nickel

nisei /ni'sej/ a & m/f Japanese Brazilian

nisso = em + isso

nisto = em + isto

nitidez /nitʃi'des/ f (de imagem etc) sharpness

nítido /'nitʃidu/ a <imagem, foto> sharp; <diferença, melhora> distinct, clear

nitrogênio /nitro'ʒeniu/ m nitrogen

nível /'nivew/ (pl ~veis) m level; a ~ de in terms of

nivelamento /nivela'mẽtu/ m levelling

nivelar /nive'lar/ vt level

no = em + o

nó /nɔ/ m knot; dar um ~ tie a knot; ~ dos dedos knuckle; um ~ na garganta a lump in one's throat

nobre /'nɔbri/ *a* noble; < *bairro*> exclusive ▢ *m/f* noble; ~**za** /e/ *f* nobility

noção /no'sãw/ *f* notion; *pl* (*rudimentos*) elements

nocaute /no'kawtʃi/ *m* knockout; pôr alg ~ knock s.o. out; ~**ar** *vt* knock out

nocivo /no'sivu/ *a* harmful

nódoa /'nodoa/ *f* (*Port*) stain

nogueira /no'gera/ *f* (*árvore*) walnut tree

noi|tada /noj'tada/ *f* night; ~**te** *f* night; (*antes de dormir*) evening; à *ou* de ~**te** at night; (*antes de dormir*) in the evening; hoje à ~**te** tonight; ontem à ~**te** last night; boa ~**te** (*ao chegar*) good evening; (*ao despedir-se*) good night; ~**te** em branco *ou* claro sleepless night

noi|vado /noj'vadu/ *m* engagement; ~**va** *f* fiancée; (*no casamento*) bride; ~**vo** *m* fiancé; (*no casamento*) bridegroom; os ~**vos** the engaged couple; (*no casamento*) the bride and groom; ficar ~**vo** get engaged

no|jento /no'ʒẽtu/ *a* disgusting; ~**jo** /o/ *m* disgust

nômade /'nomadʒi/ *m/f* nomad ▢ *a* nomadic

nome|ação /nomia'sãw/ *f* appointment; ~**ar** *vt* (*para cargo*) appoint; (*chamar pelo nome*) name

nomi|nal /nomi'naw/ (*pl* ~**nais**) *a* nominal

nonagésimo /nona'ʒεzimu/ *a* ninetieth

nono /'nonu/ *a* & *m* ninth

nora /'nɔra/ *f* daughter-in-law

nordes|te /nor'dεstʃi/ *m* northeast; ~**tino** *a* Northeastern ▢ *m* person from the Northeast (*of Brazil*)

nórdico /'nɔrdʒiku/ *a* Nordic

nor|ma /'nɔrma/ *f* norm; ~**mal** (*pl* ~**mais**) *a* normal

normali|dade /normali'dadʒi/ *f* normality; ~**zar** *vt* bring back to normal; normalize < *relações diplomáticas*>; ~**zar-se** *vpr* return to normal

noroeste /noro'εstʃi/ *a* & *m* northwest

norte /'nortʃi/ *a* & *m* north; ~**africano** *a* & *m* North African; ~**americano** *a* & *m* North American; ~**coreano** *a* & *m* North Korean

nortista /nor'tʃista/ *a* Northern ▢ *m/f* Northerner

Noruega /noru'εga/ *f* Norway

norue|guês /norue'ges/ *a* & *m* (*f* ~**guesa**) Norwegian

nos[1] /nus/ = em + os

nos[2] /nus/ *pron* us; (*indireto*) (to) us; (*reflexivo*) ourselves

nós /nɔs/ *pron* we; (*depois de preposição*) us

nos|sa /'nɔsa/ *int* gosh; ~**so** /ɔ/ *a* our ▢ *pron* ours

nos|talgia /nostaw'ʒia/ *f* nostalgia; ~**tálgico** *a* nostalgic

nota /'nɔta/ *f* note; (*na escola etc*) mark; (*conta*) bill; custar uma ~ (preta) (*fam*) cost a bomb; tomar ~ take note (de of); ~ fiscal receipt

no|tação /nota'sãw/ *f* notation; ~**tar** *vt* notice, note; fazer ~**tar** point out; ~**tável** (*pl* ~**táveis**) *a* & *m/f* notable

notícia /no'tʃisia/ *f* piece of news; *pl* news

notici|ar /notʃi'sjar/ *vt* report; ~**ário** *m* (*na TV*) news; (*em jornal*) news section; ~**arista** *m/f* (*na TV*) newsreader; (*em jornal*) news reporter; ~**oso** /o/ *a* agência ~**osa** news agency

notifi|cação /notʃifika'sãw/ *f* notification; ~**car** *vt* notify

notí|vago /no'tʃivagu/ *a* nocturnal ▢ *m* night person

notório /no'tɔriu/ *a* well-known

noturno /no'turnu/ *a* night; < *animal*> nocturnal

nova /'nɔva/ *f* piece of news; ~**mente** *adv* again

novato /no'vatu/ *m* novice

nove /'nɔvi/ *a* & *m* nine; ~**centos** *a* & *m* nine hundred

novela /no'vεla/ *f* (*na TV*) soap opera; (*livro*) novella

novembro /no'vẽbru/ *m* November

noventa /no'vẽta/ *a* & *m* ninety

noviço /no'visu/ *m* novice

novidade /novi'dadʒi/ *f* novelty; (*notícia*) piece of news; *pl* (*notícias*) news

novilho /no'viʎu/ *m* calf

novo /'novu/ *a* new; (*jovem*) young; de ~ again; ~ em folha brand new

noz /nɔs/ *f* walnut; ~ moscada nutmeg

nu /nu/ *a* (*f* ~**a**) < *corpo, pessoa*> naked; < *braço, parede, quarto*> bare ▢ *m* nude; ~ em pêlo stark naked; a verdade ~**a** e crua the plain truth

nuança /nu'ãsa/ *f* nuance

nu|blado /nu'bladu/ *a* cloudy; ~**blar** *vt* cloud; ~**blar-se** *vpr* cloud over

nuca /'nuka/ *f* nape of the neck

nuclear /nukli'ar/ *a* nuclear

núcleo /'nukliu/ *m* nucleus

nu|dez /nu'des/ *f* nakedness; (*na TV etc*) nudity; (*da parede etc*) bareness; ~**dismo** *m* nudism; ~**dista** *m/f* nudist

nulo /'nulu/ *a* void

num, numa(s) = em + um, uma(s)

nume|ral /nume'raw/ (*pl* ~rais) *a & m* numeral; ~rar *vt* number
numérico /nu'mɛriku/ *a* numerical
número /'numeru/ *m* number; (*de jornal, revista*) issue; (*de sapatos*) size; (*espetáculo*) act; fazer ~ make up the numbers
numeroso /nume'rozu/ *a* numerous
nunca /'nũka/ *adv* never; ~ mais never again
nuns = em + uns
nupci|al /nupsi'aw/ (*pl* ~ais) *a* bridal
núpcias /'nupsias/ *f pl* marriage
nu|trição /nutri'sãw/ *f* nutrition; ~trir *vt* nourish; (*fig*) harbour <*ódio, esperança*>; ~tritivo *a* nourishing; <*valor*> nutritional
nuvem /'nuvẽ/ *f* cloud

O

o /u/ *artigo* the □ *pron* (*homem*) him; (*coisa*) it; (*você*) you; ~ que (*a coisa que*) what; (*aquele que*) the one that; ~ quê? what?; meu livro e ~ do João my book and John's (one)
ó /ɔ/ *int* (*fam*) look
ô /o/ *int* oh
oásis /o'azis/ *m invar* oasis
oba /'oba/ *int* great
obcecar /obise'kar/ *vt* obsess
obe|decer /obede'ser/ *vt* ~decer a obey; ~diência *f* obedience; ~diente *a* obedient
obe|sidade /obezi'dadʒi/ *f* obesity; ~so /e/ *a* obese
óbito /'ɔbitu/ *m* death
obituário /obitu'ariu/ *m* obituary
obje|ção /obiʒe'sãw/ *f* objection; ~tar *vt/i* object (a to)
objeti|va /obiʒe'tʃiva/ *f* lens; ~vidade *f* objectivity; ~vo *a & m* objective
objeto /obi'ʒetu/ *m* object
oblíquo /o'blikwu/ *a* oblique; <*olhar*> sidelong
obliterar /oblite'rar/ *vt* obliterate
oblongo /o'blõgu/ *a* oblong
obo|é /obo'ɛ/ *m* oboe; ~ísta *m/f* oboist
obra /'ɔbra/ *f* work; em ~s being renovated; ~ de arte work of art; ~ de caridade charity; ~-prima (*pl* ~s-primas) *f* masterpiece
obri|gação /obriga'sãw/ *f* obligation; (*título*) bond; ~gado *int* thank you; (*não querendo*) no thank you; ~gar *vt* force, oblige (a to); ~gar-se *vpr* undertake (a to); ~gatório *a* obligatory, compulsory
obsce|nidade /obiseni'dadʒi/ *f* obscenity; ~no /e/ *a* obscene

obscu|ridade /obiskuri'dadʒi/ *f* obscurity; ~ro *a* obscure
obséquio /obi'sɛkiu/ *m* favour
obsequioso /obiseki'ozu/ *a* obsequious
obser|vação /obiserva'sãw/ *f* observation; ~vador *a* observant □ *m* observer; ~vância *f* observance; ~var *vt* observe; ~vatório *m* observatory
obses|são /obise'sãw/ *f* obsession; ~sivo *a* obsessive
obsoleto /obiso'letu/ *a* obsolete
obstáculo /obis'takulu/ *m* obstacle
obstar /obis'tar/ *vt* stand in the way (a of)
obs|tetra /obis'tɛtra/ *m/f* obstetrician; ~tetrícia *f* obstetrics; ~tétrico *a* obstetric
obsti|nação /obistina'sãw/ *f* obstinacy; ~nado *a* obstinate; ~nar-se *vpr* insist (em on)
obstru|ção /obistru'sãw/ *f* obstruction; ~ir *vt* obstruct
ob|tenção /obitẽ'sãw/ *f* obtaining; ~ter *vt* obtain
obtu|ração /obitura'sãw/ *f* filling; ~rador *m* shutter; ~rar *vt* fill <*dente*>
obtuso /obi'tuzu/ *a* obtuse
óbvio /'ɔbviu/ *a* obvious
ocasi|ão /okazi'ãw/ *f* occasion; (*oportunidade*) opportunity; (*compra*) bargain; ~onal (*pl* ~onais) *a* chance; ~onar *vt* cause
Oceania /osia'nia/ *f* Oceania
oce|ânico /osi'aniku/ *a* ocean; ~ano *m* ocean
ociden|tal /oside'taw/ (*pl* ~tais) *a* western □ *m/f* Westerner; ~te *m* West
ócio /'ɔsiu/ *m* (*lazer*) leisure; (*falta de trabalho*) idleness
ocioso /osi'ozu/ *a* idle □ *m* idler
oco /'oku/ *a* hollow; <*cabeça*> empty
ocor|rência /okoˈxɛsia/ *f* occurrence; ~rer *vi* occur (a to)
ocu|lar /oku'lar/ *a* testemunha ~lar eye witness; ~lista *m/f* optician
óculos /'ɔkulus/ *m pl* glasses; ~ de sol sunglasses
ocul|tar /okuw'tar/ *vt* conceal; ~to *a* hidden; (*sobrenatural*) occult
ocu|pação /okupa'sãw/ *f* occupation; ~pado <*a pessoa*> busy; <*cadeira*> taken; <*telefone*> engaged, (*Amer*) busy; ~par *vt* occupy; take up <*tempo, espaço*>; hold <*cargo*>; ~par-se *vpr* keep busy; ~par-se com *ou* de be involved with <*política, literatura etc*>; take care of <*cliente, doente, problema*>; occupy one's time with <*leitura, palavras cruzadas etc*>
ode /'ɔdʒi/ *f* ode

odiar /oˈdʒiˈar/ vt hate

ódio /ˈɔdʒiu/ m hatred, hate; (*raiva*) anger

odioso /odʒiˈozu/ a hateful

odontologia /odõtoloˈʒia/ f dentistry

odor /oˈdor/ m odour

oeste /oˈɛstʃi/ a & m west

ofe|gante /ofeˈgãtʃi/ a panting; ~**gar** vi pant

ofen|der /ofeˈder/ vt offend; ~**der-se** vpr take offence; ~**sa** f insult; ~**siva** f offensive; ~**sivo** a offensive

ofere|cer /ofereˈser/ vt offer; ~**cer-se** vpr <*pessoa*> offer o.s. (**como** as); <*ocasião*> arise; ~**cer-se para ajudar** offer to help; ~**cimento** m offer

oferenda /ofeˈrẽda/ f offering

oferta /oˈfɛrta/ f offer; **em ~** on offer; **a ~ e a demanda** supply and demand

ofici|al /ofisiˈaw/ (*pl* ~**ais**) a official □ m officer; ~**alizar** vt make official; ~**ar** vi officiate

oficina /ofiˈsina/ f workshop; (*para carros*) garage, (*Amer*) shop

ofício /oˈfisiu/ m (*profissão*) trade; (*na igreja*) service

oficioso /ofisiˈozu/ a unofficial

ofus|cante /ofusˈkãtʃi/ a dazzling; ~**car** vt dazzle <*pessoa*>; obscure <*sol etc*>; (*fig: eclipsar*) outshine

oi /oj/ int (*cumprimento*) hi; (*resposta*) yes?

oi|tavo /ojˈtavu/ a & m eighth; ~**tenta** a & m eighty; ~**to** a & m eight; ~**tocentos** a & m eight hundred

olá /oˈla/ int hello

olaria /olaˈria/ f pottery

óleo /ˈɔliu/ m oil

oleo|duto /oliuˈdutu/ m oil pipeline; ~**so** /o/ a oily

olfato /owˈfatu/ m sense of smell

olhada /oˈʎada/ f look; **dar uma ~** have a look

olhar /oˈʎar/ vt look at; (*assistir*) watch □ vi look □ m look; ~ **para** look at; ~ **por** look after; **e olhe lá** (*fam*) and that's pushing it

olheiras /oˈʎeras/ f pl dark rings under one's eyes

olho /ˈoʎu/ m eye; **a ~ nu** with the naked eye; **custar os ~s da cara** cost a fortune; **ficar de ~** keep an eye out; **ficar de ~ em** keep an eye on; **pôr alg no ~ da rua** throw s.o. out; **não pregar o ~** not sleep a wink; ~ **gordo** *ou* **grande** envy; ~ **mágico** peephole; ~ **roxo** black eye

Olimpíada /oliˈpiada/ f Olympic Games

olímpico /oˈlĩpiku/ a <*jogos, vila*> Olympic; (*fig*) blithe

oliveira /oliˈvera/ f olive tree

olmo /ˈowmu/ m elm

om|breira /õˈbrera/ f (*para roupa*) shoulder pad; ~**bro** m shoulder; **dar de ~bros** shrug one's shoulders

omelete /omeˈlɛtʃi/, (*Port*) **omeleta** /omeˈleta/ f omelette

omis|são /omiˈsãw/ f omission; ~**so** a negligent, remiss

omitir /omiˈtʃir/ vt omit

omni- (*Port*) *veja* **oni-**

omoplata /omoˈplata/ f shoulder blade

onça¹ /ˈõsa/ f (*peso*) ounce

onça² /ˈõsa/ f (*animal*) jaguar

onda /ˈõda/ f wave; **pegar ~** (*fam*) surf

onde /ˈõdʒi/ adv where; **por ~?** which way?; ~ **quer que** wherever

ondu|lação /õdulaˈsãw/ f undulation; (*do cabelo*) wave; ~**lado** a wavy; ~**lante** a undulating; ~**lar** vt wave <*cabelo*> □ vi undulate

onerar /oneˈrar/ vt burden

ônibus /ˈonibus/ m invar bus; ~ **espacial** space shuttle

onipotente /onipoˈtẽtʃi/ a omnipotent

onírico /oˈniriku/ a dreamlike

onisciente /onisiˈẽtʃi/ a omniscient

onomatopéia /onomatoˈpɛja/ f onomatopoeia

ontem /ˈõtẽ/ adv yesterday

onze /ˈõzi/ a & m eleven

opaco /oˈpaku/ a opaque

opala /oˈpala/ f opal

opção /opiˈsãw/ f option

ópera /ˈɔpera/ f opera

ope|ração /operaˈsãw/ f operation; (*bancária etc*) transaction; ~**rador** m operator; ~**rar** vt operate; operate on <*doente*>; work <*milagre*> □ vi operate; ~**rar-se** vpr (*acontecer*) come about; (*fazer operação*) have an operation; ~**rário** a working □ m worker

opereta /opeˈreta/ f operetta

opinar /opiˈnar/ vt think □ vi express one's opinion

opinião /opiniˈãw/ f opinion; **na minha ~** in my opinion; ~ **pública** public opinion

ópio /ˈɔpiu/ m opium

opor /oˈpor/ vt put up <*resistência, argumento*>; (*pôr em contraste*) contrast (**a** with); ~**-se a** (*não aprovar*) oppose; (*ser diferente*) contrast with

oportu|nidade /oportuniˈdadʒi/ f opportunity; ~**nista** a & m/f opportunist; ~**no** a opportune

oposi|ção /opoziˈsãw/ f opposition (**a** to); ~**cionista** a opposition □ m/f opposition politician

oposto /oˈpostu/ a & m opposite

opres|são /opre'sãw/ f oppression; (*no peito*) tightness; **~sivo** a oppressive; **~sor** m oppressor

oprimir /opri'mir/ vt oppress; (*com trabalho*) weigh down □ vi be oppressive

optar /opi'tar/ vi opt (**por** for); **~ por ir** opt to go

óptica, óptico veja ótica, ótico

opu|lência /opu'lẽsia/ f opulence; **~lento** a opulent

ora /'ɔra/ adv & conj now □ int come; **~ essa!** come now!; **~ ..., ~ ...** first ..., then

oração /ora'sãw/ f (*prece*) prayer; (*discurso*) oration; (*frase*) clause

oráculo /o'rakulu/ m oracle

orador /ora'dor/ m orator

oral /o'raw/ (*pl* **orais**) a & f oral

orar /o'rar/ vi pray

órbita /'ɔrbita/ f orbit; (*do olho*) socket

orçamen|tário /orsamẽ'tariu/ a budgetary; **~to** m (*plano financeiro*) budget; (*previsão dos custos*) estimate

orçar /or'sar/ vt estimate (**em** at)

ordeiro /or'deru/ a orderly

ordem /'ɔrdẽ/ f order; **por ~ alfabética** in alphabetical order; **~ de pagamento** banker's draft; **~ do dia** agenda

orde|nação /ordena'sãw/ f ordering; (*de padre*) ordination; **~nado** a ordered □ m wages; **~nar** vt order; put in order <*papéis, livros etc*>; ordain <*padre*>

ordenhar /orde'ɲar/ vt milk

ordinário /ordʒi'nariu/ a (*normal*) ordinary; (*grosseiro*) vulgar; (*de má qualidade*) inferior; (*sem caráter*) rough

orégano /o'rɛganu/ m oregano

ore|lha /o'reʎa/ f ear; **~lhão** m phone booth; **~lhudo** a with big ears; **ser ~lhudo** have big ears

orfanato /orfa'natu/ m orphanage

ór|fão /'ɔrfãw/ (*pl* **~fãos**) a & m (*f* **~fã**) orphan

orgânico /or'ganiku/ a organic

orga|nismo /orga'nizmu/ m organism; (*do Estado etc*) institution; **~nista** m/f organist

organi|zação /organiza'sãw/ f organization; **~zador** a organizing □ m organizer; **~zar** vt organize

órgão /'ɔrgãw/ (*pl* **~s**) m organ; (*do Estado etc*) body

orgasmo /or'gazmu/ m orgasm

orgia /or'ʒia/ f orgy

orgu|lhar /orgu'ʎar/ vt make proud; **~lhar-se** vpr be proud (**de** of); **~lho** m pride; **~lhoso** /o/ a proud

orien|tação /oriẽta'sãw/ f orientation; (*direção*) direction; (*vocacional etc*) guidance; **~tador** m advisor; **~tal** (*pl* **~tais**) a eastern; (*da Asia*) oriental; **~tar** vt direct; (*aconselhar*) advise; (*situar*) position; **~tar-se** get one's bearings; **~tar-se por** be guided by; **~te** m east; **Oriente Médio** Middle East; **Extremo Oriente** Far East

orifício /ori'fisiu/ m opening; (*no corpo*) orifice

origem /o'riʒẽ/ f origin; **dar ~ a** give rise to; **ter ~** originate

origi|nal /oriʒi'naw/ (*pl* **~nais**) a & m original; **~nalidade** f originality; **~nar** vt give rise to; **~nar-se** vpr originate; **~nário** a <*planta, animal*> native (**de** to); <*pessoa*> originating (**de** from)

oriundo /o'rjũdu/ a originating (**de** from)

orla /'ɔrla/ f border; **~ marítima** seafront

ornamen|tação /ornamẽta'sãw/ f ornamentation; **~tal** (*pl* **~tais**) a ornamental; **~tar** vt decorate; **~to** m ornament

orques|tra /or'kɛstra/ f orchestra; **~tra sinfônica** symphony orchestra; **~tral** (*pl* **~trais**) a orchestral; **~trar** vt orchestrate

orquídea /or'kidʒia/ f orchid

ortodoxo /orto'dɔksu/ a orthodox

orto|grafia /ortogra'fia/ f spelling, orthography; **~gráfico** a orthographic

orto|pedia /ortope'dʒia/ f orthopaedics; **~pédico** a orthopaedic; **~pedista** m/f orthopaedic surgeon

orvalho /or'vaʎu/ m dew

os /us/ artigo & pron veja **o**

oscilar /osi'lar/ vi oscillate

ósseo /'ɔsiu/ a bone

os|so /'osu/ m bone; **~sudo** a bony

ostensivo /ostẽ'sivu/ a ostensible

osten|tação /ostẽta'sãw/ f ostentation; **~tar** vt show off; **~toso** a showy, ostentatious

osteopata /ostʃio'pata/ m/f osteopath

ostra /'ostra/ f oyster

ostracismo /ostra'sizmu/ m ostracism

otário /o'tariu/ m (*fam*) fool

óti|ca /'ɔtʃika/ f (*ciência*) optics; (*loja*) optician's; (*ponto de vista*) viewpoint; **~co** a optical

otimis|mo /otʃi'mizmu/ m optimism; **~ta** m/f optimist □ a optimistic

ótimo /'ɔtʃimu/ a excellent

otorrino /oto'xinu/ m ear, nose and throat specialist

ou /o/ conj or; **~ ... ~ ...** either... or...; **~ seja** in other words

ouriço /o'risu/ m hedgehog; **~-do-mar** (*pl* **~s-do-mar**) m sea urchin

ouri|ves /oˈrivis/ m/f invar jeweller; **~vesaria** f (loja) jeweller's

ouro /ˈoru/ m gold; pl (naipe) diamonds; **de ~** golden

ou|sadia /ozaˈdʒia/ f daring; (uma) daring step; **~sado** a daring; **~sar** vt/i dare

outdoor /ˈawtdor/ (pl ~s) m billboard

outo|nal /otoˈnaw/ (pl ~nais) a autumnal; **~no** /o/ m autumn, (Amer) fall

outorgar /otorˈɡar/ vt grant

ou|trem /oˈtrẽj/ pron (outro) someone else; (outros) others; **~tro** a other □ pron (outro) another (one); pl others; **~tro copo** another glass; **~tra coisa** something else; **~tro dia** the other day; **no ~tro dia** the next day; **~tra vez** again; **~trora** adv once upon a time; **~trossim** adv equally

outubro /oˈtubru/ m October

ou|vido /oˈvidu/ m ear; **de ~vido** by ear; **dar ~vidos a** listen to; **~vinte** m/f listener; **~vir** vt hear; (atentamente) listen to □ vi hear; **~vir dizer que** hear that; **~vir falar de** hear of

ovação /ovaˈsãw/ f ovation

oval /oˈvaw/ (pl ovais) a & f oval

ovário /oˈvariu/ m ovary

ovelha /oˈveʎa/ f sheep

óvni /ˈɔvni/ m UFO

ovo /ˈovu/ m egg; **~ cozido/frito/mexido/pochê** boiled/fried/scrambled/poached egg

oxi|genar /oksiʒeˈnar/ vt bleach <cabelo>; **~gênio** m oxygen

ozônio /oˈzoniu/ m ozone

P

pá /pa/ f spade; (de hélice) blade; (de moinho) sail □ m (Port: fam) mate

pacato /paˈkatu/ a quiet

paci|ência /pasiˈẽsia/ f patience; **~ente** a & m/f patient

pacificar /pasifiˈkar/ vt pacify

pacifico /paˈsifiku/ a peaceful; **Oceano Pacífico** Pacific Ocean; **ponto ~** undisputed point

pacifis|mo /pasiˈfizmu/ m pacifism; **~ta** a & m/f pacifist

paço /ˈpasu/ m palace

pacote /paˈkɔtʃi/ m (de biscoitos etc) packet; (mandado pelo correio) parcel; (econômico, turístico, software) package

pacto /ˈpaktu/ m pact

padaria /padaˈria/ f baker's (shop), bakery

padecer /padeˈser/ vt/i suffer

padeiro /paˈderu/ m baker

padiola /padʒiˈɔla/ f stretcher

padrão /paˈdrãw/ m standard; (desenho) pattern

padrasto /paˈdrastu/ m stepfather

padre /ˈpadri/ m priest

padrinho /paˈdriɲu/ m (de batismo) godfather; (de casamento) best man

padroeiro /padroˈeru/ m patron saint

padronizar /padroniˈzar/ vt standardize

paetê /pajˈte/ m sequin

paga /ˈpaɡa/ f pay; **~mento** m payment

pa|gão /paˈɡãw/ (pl ~gãos) a & m (f ~gã) pagan

pagar /paˈɡar/ vt pay for <compra, erro etc>; pay <dívida, conta, empregado etc>; pay back <empréstimo>; repay <gentileza etc> □ vi pay; **eu pago para ver** I'll believe it when I see it

página /ˈpaʒina/ f page

pago /ˈpaɡu/ a paid □ pp de pagar

pagode /paˈɡɔdʒi/ m (torre) pagoda; (fam) singalong

pai /paj/ m father; pl (pai e mãe) parents; **~-de-santo** (pl ~s-de-santo) m macumba priest

pai|nel /pajˈnɛw/ (pl ~néis) m panel; (de carro) dashboard

paio /ˈpaju/ m pork sausage

pairar /pajˈrar/ vi hover

país /paˈis/ m country; **País de Gales** Wales; **Países Baixos** Netherlands

paisa|gem /pajˈzaʒẽj/ f landscape; **~gista** m/f landscape gardener

paisana /pajˈzana/ f à ~ <policial> in plain clothes; <soldado> in civilian clothes

paixão /pajˈʃãw/ f passion

pala /ˈpala/ f (de boné) peak; (de automóvel) sun visor

palácio /paˈlasiu/ m palace

paladar /palaˈdar/ m palate, taste

palanque /paˈlãki/ m stand

palavra /paˈlavra/ f word; **pedir a ~** ask to speak; **ter ~** be reliable; **tomar a ~** start to speak; **sem ~** <pessoa> unreliable; **~ de ordem** watchword; **~s cruzadas** crossword

palavrão /palaˈvrãw/ m swearword

palco /ˈpawku/ m stage

palestino /palesˈtʃinu/ a & m Palestinian

palestra /paˈlɛstra/ f lecture

paleta /paˈleta/ f palette

paletó /paleˈtɔ/ m jacket

palha /ˈpaʎa/ f straw

palha|çada /paʎaˈsada/ f joke; **~ço** m clown

paliativo /paliaˈtʃivu/ a & m palliative

palidez /paliˈdes/ f paleness

pálido /ˈpalidu/ a pale

pali|tar /pali'tar/ *vt* pick □ *vi* pick one's teeth; **~teiro** *m* toothpick holder; **~to** *m* (*para dentes*) toothpick; (*de fósforo*) matchstick; (*pessoa magra*) beanpole

pal|ma /'pawma/ *f* palm; *pl* (*aplauso*) clapping; **bater ~mas** clap; **~meira** *f* palm tree; **~mito** *m* palm heart; **~mo** *m* span; **~mo a ~mo** inch by inch

palpá|vel /paw'pavew/ (*pl* **~veis**) *a* palpable

pálpebra /'pawpebra/ *f* eyelid

palpi|tação /pawpita'sãw/ *f* palpitation; **~tante** *a* (*fig*) thrilling; **~tar** *vi* <*coração*> flutter; <*pessoa*> tremble; (*dar palpite*) stick one's oar in; **~te** *m* (*pressentimento*) hunch; (*no jogo etc*) tip; **dar ~te** stick one's oar in

panacéia /pana'sɛja/ *f* panacea

Panamá /pana'ma/ *m* Panama

panamenho /pana'meɲu/ *a* & *m* Panamanian

pan-americano /panameri'kanu/ *a* Pan-American

pança /'pãsa/ *f* paunch

pancada /pã'kada/ *f* blow; **~ d'água** downpour; **~ria** *f* fight, punch-up

pâncreas /'pãkrias/ *m invar* pancreas

pançudo /pã'sudu/ *a* paunchy

panda /'pãda/ *f* panda

pandarecos /pãda'rɛkus/ *m pl* **aos** *ou* **em ~** battered

pandeiro /pã'deru/ *m* tambourine

pandemônio /pãde'moniu/ *m* pandemonium

pane /'pani/ *f* breakdown

panela /pa'nɛla/ *f* saucepan; **~ de pressão** pressure cooker

panfleto /pã'fletu/ *m* pamphlet

pânico /'paniku/ *m* panic; **em ~** in a panic; **entrar em ~** panic

panifica|ção /panifika'sãw/ *f* bakery; **~dora** *f* bakery

pano /'panu/ *m* cloth; **~ de fundo** backdrop; **~ de pó** duster; **~ de pratos** tea towel

pano|rama /pano'rama/ *m* panorama; **~râmico** *a* panoramic

panqueca /pã'kɛka/ *f* pancake

panta|nal /pãta'naw/ (*pl* **~nais**) *m* marshland

pântano /'pãtanu/ *m* marsh

pantanoso /pãta'nozu/ *a* marshy

pantera /pã'tɛra/ *f* panther

pão /pãw/ (*pl* **pães**) *m* bread; **~ de fôrma** sliced loaf; **~ integral** brown bread; **~-de-ló** *m* sponge cake; **~-duro** (*pl* **pães-duros**) (*fam*) *a* stingy, tight-fisted □ *m/f* skinflint; **~zinho** *m* bread roll

Papa /'papa/ *m* Pope

papa /'papa/ *f* (*de nenem*) food; (*arroz etc*) mush

papagaio /papa'gaju/ *m* parrot

papai /pa'paj/ *m* dad, daddy; **Papai Noël** Father Christmas

papar /pa'par/ *vt/i* (*fam*) eat

papari|car /papari'kar/ *vt* pamper; **~cos** *m pl* pampering

pa|pel /pa'pɛw/ (*pl* **~péis**) *m* (*de escrever etc*) paper; (*um*) piece of paper; (*numa peça, filme*) part; (*fig: função*) role; **de ~pel passado** officially; **~pel de alumínio** aluminium foil; **~pel higiênico** toilet paper; **~pelada** *f* paperwork; **~pelão** *m* cardboard; **~pelaria** *f* stationer's (shop); **~pelzinho** *m* scrap of paper

papo /'papu/ *f* (*fam: conversa*) talk; (*do rosto*) double chin; **bater um ~** (*fam*) have a chat; **~ furado** idle talk

papoula /pa'pola/ *f* poppy

páprica /'paprika/ *f* paprika

paque|ra /pa'kɛra/ *f* (*fam*) pick-up; **~rador** *a* flirtatious □ *m* flirt; **~rar** *vt* flirt with <*pessoa*>; eye up <*vestido, carro etc*> □ *vi* flirt

paquista|nês /pakista'nes/ *a* & *m* (*f* **~nesa**) Pakistani

Paquistão /pakis'tãw/ *m* Pakistan

par /par/ *a* even □ *m* pair; (*parceiro*) partner; **a ~ de** up to date with <*notícias etc*>; **sem ~** unequalled

para /'para/ *prep* for; (*a*) to; **~ que so that**; **~ quê?** what for?; **~ casa** home; **estar ~ sair** be about to leave; **era ~ eu ir** I was supposed to go

para|benizar /parabeni'zar/ *vt* congratulate (**por** on); **~béns** *m pl* congratulations

parábola /pa'rabola/ *f* (*conto*) parable; (*curva*) parabola

parabóli|co /para'bɔliku/ *a* **antena ~ca** satellite dish

pára|-brisa /para'briza/ *m* windscreen, (*Amer*) windshield; **~choque** *m* bumper

para|da /pa'rada/ *f* stop; (*interrupção*) stoppage; (*militar*) parade; (*fam: coisa difícil*) ordeal, challenge; **~da cardíaca** cardiac arrest; **~deiro** *m* whereabouts

paradisíaco /paradʒi'ziaku/ *a* idyllic

parado /pa'radu/ *a* <*trânsito, carro*> at a standstill, stopped; (*fig*) <*pessoa*> dull; **ficar ~** <*pessoa*> stand still; <*trânsito*> come to a standstill; (*fig: deixar de trabalhar*) stop work

parado|xal /paradok'saw/ (*pl* **~xais**) *a* paradoxical; **~xo** /ɔ/ *m* paradox

parafina /para'fina/ *f* paraffin

paráfrase /pa'rafrazi/ *f* paraphrase

parafrasear /parafrazi'ar/ *vt* paraphrase

parafuso /para'fuzu/ *f* screw; **entrar em** ~ get into a state

para|gem /pa'raʒẽ/ *f* (*Port: parada*) stop; **nestas** ~**gens** in these parts

parágrafo /pa'ragrafu/ *m* paragraph

Paraguai /para'gwaj/ *m* Paraguay

paraguaio /para'gwaju/ *a & m* Paraguayan

paraíso /para'izu/ *m* paradise

pára-lama /para'lama/ *m* (*de carro*) wing, (*Amer*) fender; (*de bicicleta*) mudguard

parale|la /para'lɛla/ *f* parallel; *pl* (*aparelho*) parallel bars; ~**lepípedo** *m* paving stone; ~**lo** /ɛ/ *a & m* parallel

para|lisar /parali'zar/ *vt* paralyse; bring to a halt <*fábrica, produção*>; ~**lisar-se** *vpr* become paralysed; <*fábrica, produção*> grind to a halt; ~**lisia** *f* paralysis; ~**lítico** *a & m* paralytic

paranói|a /para'nɔja/ *f* paranoia; ~**to** *a* paranoid

parapeito /para'pejtu/ *m* (*muro*) parapet; (*da janela*) window-sill

pára-que|das /para'kedas/ *m invar* parachute; ~**dista** *m/f* parachutist; (*militar*) paratrooper

parar /pa'rar/ *vt/i* stop; ~ **de fumar** stop smoking; **ir** ~ end up

pára-raios /para'xajus/ *m invar* lightning conductor

parasita /para'zita/ *a & m/f* parasite

parceiro /par'seru/ *m* partner

parce|la /par'sela/ *f* (*de terreno*) plot; (*prestação*) instalment; ~**lar** *vt* spread <*pagamento*>

parceria /parse'ria/ *f* partnership

parci|al /parsi'aw/ (*pl* ~**ais**) *a* partial; (*partidário*) biased; ~**alidade** *f* bias

parco /'parku/ *a* frugal; <*recursos*> scant

par|dal /par'daw/ (*pl* ~**dais**) *m* sparrow; ~**do** *a* <*papel*> brown; <*pessoa*> mulatto

pare|cer /pare'ser/ *vi* (*ter aparência de*) seem; (*ter semelhança com*) be like; ~**cer-se com** look like, resemble □ *m* opinion; ~**cido** *a* similar (**com** to)

parede /pa'redʒi/ *f* wall

paren|te /pa'rẽtʃi/ *m/f* relative, relation; ~**tesco** /e/ *m* relationship

parêntese /pa'rẽtʃizi/ *f* parenthesis; *pl* (*sinais*) brackets, parentheses

paridade /pari'dadʒi/ *f* parity

parir /pa'rir/ *vt* give birth to □ *vi* give birth

parlamen|tar /parlamẽ'tar/ *a* parliamentary □ *m/f* member of parliament; ~**tarismo** *m* parliamentary system; ~**to** *m* parliament

parmesão /parme'zãw/ *a & m* (*queijo*) ~ Parmesan (cheese)

paródia /pa'rɔdʒia/ *f* parody

parodiar /parodʒi'ar/ *vt* parody

paróquia /pa'rɔkia/ *f* parish

parque /'parki/ *m* park

parte /'partʃi/ *f* part; (*quinhão*) share; (*num litigio, contrato*) party; **a maior** ~ **de** most of; **à** ~ (*de lado*) aside; (*separadamente*) separately; **um erro da sua** ~ a mistake on your part; **em** ~ in part; **em alguma** ~ somewhere; **por toda** ~ everywhere; **por** ~ **do pai** on one's father's side; **fazer** ~ **de** be part of; **tomar** ~ **em** take part in

parteira /par'tera/ *f* midwife

partici|pação /partʃisipa'sãw/ *f* participation; (*numa empresa, nos lucros*) share; ~**pante** *a* participating □ *m/f* participant; ~**par** *vi* take part (**de** *ou* **em** in)

particípio /partʃi'sipiu/ *m* participle

partícula /par'tʃikula/ *f* particle

particu|lar /partʃiku'lar/ *a* private; (*especial*) unusual □ *m* (*pessoa*) private individual; *pl* (*detalhes*) particulars; **em** ~ **lar** (*especialmente*) in particular; (*a sós*) in private; ~**laridade** *f* peculiarity

partida /par'tʃida/ *f* (*saída*) departure; (*de corrida*) start; (*de futebol, xadrez etc*) match; **dar** ~ **em** start up

parti|dário /partʃi'dariu/ *a* partisan □ *m* supporter; ~**tido** *a* broken □ *m* (*político*) party; (*casamento, par*) match; **tirar** ~**tido de** benefit from; **tomar o** ~**tido de** side with; ~**tilha** *f* division; ~**tir** *vi* (*sair*) depart; <*corredor*> start □ *vt* break; ~**tir-se** *vpr* break; **a** ~**tir de** ... from ... onwards; ~**tir para** (*fam*) resort to; ~**tir para outra** do something different, change direction; ~**titura** *f* score

parto /'partu/ *m* birth

parvo /'parvu/ *a* (*Port*) stupid

Páscoa /'paskoa/ *f* Easter

pas|mar /paz'mar/ *vt* amaze; ~**marse** *vpr* be amazed (**com** at); ~**mo** *a* amazed □ *m* amazement

passa /'pasa/ *f* raisin

pas|sada /pa'sada/ *f* **dar uma** ~**sada em** call in at; ~**sadeira** *f* (*mulher*) woman who irons; (*Port: faixa*) zebra crossing, (*Amer*) crosswalk; ~**sado** *a* <*ano, mês, semana*> last; <*tempo, particípio etc*> past; <*fruta, comida*> off □ *m* past; **são duas horas** ~**sadas** it's gone two o'clock; **bem/mal** ~**sado** <*bife*> well done/rare

passa|geiro /pasa'ʒeru/ *m* passenger □ *a* passing; ~**gem** *f* passage; (*bilhete*) ticket; **de** ~**gem** <*dizer etc*> in passing; **estar de** ~**gem** be passing through; ∼gem de ida e volta return ticket, (*Amer*) round trip ticket

passaporte /pasa'pɔrtʃi/ *m* passport

passar /pa'sar/ *vt* pass; spend <*tempo*>; cross <*ponte, rio*>; (*a ferro*) iron <*roupa etc*>; (*aplicar*) put on <*creme, batom etc*> □ *vi* pass; <*dor, medo, chuva etc*> go; (*ser aceitável*) be passable □ *m* passing; ∼-se *vpr* happen; passou a beber muito he started to drink a lot; passei dos 30 anos I'm over thirty; não passa de um boato it's nothing more than a rumour; ∼ por go through; go along <*rua*>; (*ser considerado*) be taken for; fazer-se ∼ por pass o.s. off as; ∼ por cima de (*fig*) overlook; ∼ sem do without

passarela /pasa'rɛla/ *f* (*sobre rua*) footbridge; (*para desfile de moda*) catwalk

pássaro /'pasaru/ *m* bird

passatempo /pasa'tẽpu/ *m* pastime

passe /'pasi/ *m* pass

pas|sear /pasi'ar/ *vi* go out and about; (*viajar*) travel around □ *vt* take for a walk; ∼seata *f* protest march; ∼seio *m* outing; (*volta a pé*) walk; (*volta de carro*) drive; dar um ∼seio (*a pé*) go for a walk; (*de carro*) go for a drive

passio|nal /pasio'naw/ (*pl* ∼nais) *a* crime ∼nal crime of passion

passista /pa'sista/ *m/f* dancer

passí|vel /pa'sivew/ (*pl* ∼veis) *a* ∼vel de subject to

passi|vidade /pasivi'dadʒi/ *f* passivity; ∼vo *a* passive □ *m* (*com*) liabilities; (*ling*) passive

passo /'pasu/ *m* step; (*velocidade*) pace; (*barulho*) footstep; ∼ a ∼ step by step; a dois ∼s de a stone's throw from; dar um ∼ take a step

pasta /'pasta/ *f* (*matéria*) paste; (*bolsa*) briefcase; (*fichário*) folder; ministro sem ∼ minister without portfolio; ∼ de dentes toothpaste

pas|tagem /pas'taʒẽ/ *f* pasture; ∼tar *vi* graze

pas|tel /pas'tɛw/ (*pl* ∼téis) *m* (*para comer*) samosa; (*Port: doce*) pastry; (*para desenhar*) pastel; ∼telão *m* (*comédia*) slapstick; ∼telaria *f* (*loja*) samosa vendor, (*Port*) pastry shop; (*Port: pastéis*) pastries

pasteurizado /pastewri'zadu/ *a* pasteurized

pastilha /pas'tʃiʎa/ *f* pastille

pas|to /'pastu/ *m* (*erva*) fodder, feed; (*lugar*) pasture; ∼tor *m* (*de gado*) shepherd; (*clérigo*) vicar; ∼tor alemão (*cachorro*) Alsatian; ∼toral (*pl* ∼torais) *a* pastoral

pata /'pata/ *f* paw; ∼da *f* kick

patamar /pata'mar/ *m* landing; (*fig*) level

patê /pa'te/ *m* pâté

patente /pa'tẽtʃi/ *a* obvious □ *f* (*mil*) rank; (*de invenção*) patent; ∼ar *vt* patent <*produto, invenção*>

pater|nal /pater'naw/ (*pl* ∼nais) *a* paternal; ∼nidade *f* paternity; ∼no /ɛ/ *a* paternal

pate|ta /pa'tɛta/ *a* daft, silly □ *m/f* fool; ∼tice *f* stupidity; (*uma*) silly thing

patético /pa'tɛtʃiku/ *a* pathetic

patíbulo /pa'tʃibulu/ *m* gallows

pati|faria /patʃifa'ria/ *f* roguishness; (*uma*) dirty trick; ∼fe *m* scoundrel

patim /pa'tʃĩ/ *m* skate; ∼ de rodas roller skate

pati|nação /patʃina'sãw/ *f* skating; (*rinque*) skating rink; ∼nador *m* skater; ∼nar *vi* skate; <*carro*> skid; ∼nete /ɛ/ *m* skateboard

pátio /'patʃiu/ *m* courtyard; (*de escola*) playground

pato /'patu/ *m* duck

pato|logia /patolo'ʒia/ *f* pathology; ∼lógico *a* pathological; ∼logista *m/f* pathologist

patrão /pa'trãw/ *m* boss

pátria /'patria/ *f* homeland

patriar|ca /patri'arka/ *m* patriarch; ∼cal (*pl* ∼cais) *a* patriarchal

patrimônio /patri'moniu/ *m* (*bens*) estate, property; (*fig: herança*) heritage

patri|ota /patri'ɔta/ *m/f* patriot; ∼ótico *a* patriotic; ∼otismo *m* patriotism

patroa /pa'troa/ *f* boss; (*fam: esposa*) missus, wife

patro|cinador /patrosina'dor/ *m* sponsor; ∼cinar *vt* sponsor; ∼cínio *m* sponsorship

patru|lha /pa'truʎa/ *f* patrol; ∼lhar *vt/i* patrol

pau /paw/ *m* stick; (*fam: cruzeiro*) cruzeiro; (*chulo: pênis*) prick; *pl* (*naipe*) clubs; a meio ∼ at half mast; rachar ∼ (*fam: brigar*) row, fight like cat and dog; ∼lada *f* blow with a stick

paulista /paw'lista/ *a & m/f* (*person*) from the state of) São Paulo; ∼no *a & m* (*person*) from the city of) São Paulo

pausa /'pawza/ *f* pause; ∼do *a* slow

pauta /'pawta/ *f* (*em papel*) lines; (*de música*) stave; (*fig: de discussão etc*) agenda; ∼do *a* <*papel*> lined

pavão /pa'vãw/ *m* peacock

pavilhão /pavi'ʎãw/ *m* pavilion; (*no jardim*) summerhouse

pavimen|tar /pavimẽ'tar/ *vt* pave; ∼to *m* floor; (*de rua etc*) surface

pavio /pa'viu/ *m* wick

pavor /pa'vor/ *m* terror; ter ∼ de be terrified of; ∼oso /o/ *a* dreadful

paz /pas/ *f* peace; **fazer as ~es** make up

pé /pε/ *m* foot; (*planta*) plant; (*de móvel*) leg; **a ~** on foot; **ao ~ da letra** literally; **estar de ~** <*festa etc*> be on; **ficar de ~** stand up; **em ~** standing (up); **em ~ de igualdade** on an equal footing

peão /pi'ãw/ *m* (*Port*: *pedestre*) pedestrian; (*no xadrez*) pawn

peça /'pɛsa/ *f* piece; (*de máquina, carro etc*) part; (*teatral*) play; **pregar uma ~ em** play a trick on; **~ de reposição** spare part; **~ de vestuário** item of clothing

pe|cado /pe'kadu/ *m* sin; **~cador** *m* sinner; **~caminoso** /o/ *a* sinful; **~car** *vi* (*contra a religião*) sin; (*fig*) fall down

pechin|cha /pe'ʃĩʃa/ *f* bargain; **~char** *vi* bargain, haggle

peçonhento /peso'ɲẽtu/ *a* **animais ~s** vermin

pecu|ária /peku'aria/ *f* livestock-farming; **~ário** *a* livestock; **~arista** *m/f* livestock farmer

peculi|ar /pekuli'ar/ *a* peculiar; **~aridade** *f* peculiarity

pecúlio /pe'kuliu/ *m* savings

pedaço /pe'dasu/ *m* piece; **aos ~s** in pieces; **cair aos ~s** fall to pieces

pedágio /pe'daʒiu/ *m* toll; (*cabine*) tollbooth

peda|gogia /pedago'ʒia/ *f* education; **~gógico** *a* educational; **~gogo** /o/ *m* educationalist

pe|dal /pe'daw/ (*pl* **~dais**) *m* pedal; **~dalar** *vt/i* pedal

pedante /pe'dãtʃi/ *a* pretentious □ *m/f* pseud

pé|-de-atleta /pɛdʒiat'lɛta/ *m* athlete's foot; **~-de-meia** (*pl* **~s-de-meia**) *m* nest egg; **~-de-pato** (*pl* **~s-de-pato**) *m* flipper

pederneira /peder'nera/ *f* flint

pedes|tal /pedes'taw/ (*pl* **~tais**) *m* pedestal

pedestre /pe'dɛstri/ *a & m/f* pedestrian

pé|-de-vento /pɛdʒi'vẽtu/ (*pl* **~s-de-vento**) *m* gust of wind

pedia|tra /pedʒi'atra/ *m/f* paediatrician; **~tria** *f* paediatrics

pedicuro /pedʒi'kuru/ *m* chiropodist, (*Amer*) podiatrist

pe|dido /pe'dʒidu/ *m* request; (*encomenda*) order; **a ~dido de** at the request of; **~dido de demissão** resignation; **~dido de desculpa** apology; **~dir** *vt* ask for; (*num restaurante etc*) order □ *vi* ask; **~dir a alg para algo ir** ask s.o. for sth; **~dir para alg ir** ask s.o. to go; **~dir desculpa**

apologize; **~dir em casamento** propose to

pedinte /pe'dʒĩtʃi/ *m/f* beggar

pedra /'pedra/ *f* stone; **~ de gelo** ice cube; **chuva de ~** hail; **~ pomes** pumice stone

pedregoso /pedre'gozu/ *a* stony

pedreiro /pe'dreru/ *m* builder

pegada /pe'gada/ *f* footprint; (*de goleiro*) save

pegajoso /pega'ʒozu/ *a* sticky

pegar /pe'gar/ *vt* get; catch <*bola, doença, ladrão, ônibus*>; (*segurar*) get hold of; pick up <*emissora, hábito, mania*> □ *vi* (*aderir*) stick; <*doença*> be catching; <*moda*> catch on; <*carro, motor*> start; <*mentira, desculpa*> stick; **~-se** *vpr* come to blows; **~ bem/mal** go down well/badly; **~ fogo** catch fire; **pega essa rua** take that street; **~ em** grab; **~ no sono** get to sleep

pego /'pɛgu/ *pp de* **pegar**

pei|dar /pej'dar/ *vt* (*chulo*) fart; **~do** *m* (*chulo*) fart

pei|to /'pejtu/ *m* chest; (*seio*) breast; (*fig*: *coragem*) guts; **~toril** (*pl* **~toris**) *m* window-sill; **~tudo** *a* <*mulher*> busty; (*fig*: *corajoso*) gutsy

pei|xaria /pe'ʃaria/ *f* fishmonger's; **~xe** *m* fish; **Peixes** (*signo*) Pisces; **~xeiro** *m* fishmonger

pela = **por** + **a**

pelado /pe'ladu/ *a* (*nu*) naked, in the nude

pelan|ca /pe'lãka/ *f* roll of fat; *pl* flab; **~cudo** *a* flabby

pelar /pe'lar/ *vt* peel <*fruta, batata*>; skin <*animal*>; (*fam*: *tomar dinheiro de*) fleece

pelas = **por** + **as**

pele /'pɛli/ *f* skin; (*como roupa*) fur; **~teiro** *m* furrier; **~teria** *f* furrier's

pelica /pe'lika/ *f* **luvas de ~** kid gloves

pelicano /peli'kanu/ *m* pelican

película /pe'likula/ *f* skin

pelo = **por** + **o**

pêlo /'pelu/ *m* hair; (*de animal*) coat; **nu em ~** stark naked; **montar em ~** ride bareback

pelos = **por** + **os**

pelotão /pelo'tãw/ *m* platoon

pelúcia /pe'lusia/ *f* **bicho de ~** soft toy, fluffy animal

peludo /pe'ludu/ *a* hairy

pena[1] /'pena/ *f* (*de ave*) feather; (*de caneta*) nib

pena[2] /'pena/ *f* (*castigo*) penalty; (*de amor etc*) pang; **é uma ~ que** it's a pity that; **que ~!** what a pity!; **dar ~** be upsetting; **estar com ou ter ~ de** feel sorry for; **(não) vale a ~** it's (not) worth it; **vale a ~ tentar** it's worth trying; ~ **de morte** death penalty

penada /pe'nada/ f stroke of the pen

pe|nal /pe'naw/ (pl ~**nais**) a penal; ~**nalidade** f penalty; ~**nalizar** vt penalize

pênalti /'penawtʃi/ m penalty

penar /pe'nar/ vi suffer

pen|dente /pẽ'dẽtʃi/ a hanging; (fig: causa) pending; ~**der** vi hang; (inclinar-se) slope; (tender) be inclined (a to); ~**dor** m inclination

pêndulo /'pẽdulu/ m pendulum

pendu|rado /pẽdu'radu/ a hanging; (fam: por fazer, pagar) outstanding; ~**rar** vt hang (up); (fam) put on the slate <compra> □ vi (fam) pay later; ~**ricalho** m pendant

penedo /pe'nedu/ m rock

penei|ra /pe'nera/ f sieve; ~**rar** vt sieve, sift □ vi drizzle

pene|tra /pe'nɛtra/ m/f (fam) gatecrasher; ~**tração** f penetration; (fig) perspicacity; ~**trante** a <som, olhar> piercing; <dor> sharp; <ferida> deep; <frio> biting; <análise, espírito> incisive, perceptive; ~**trar** vt penetrate □ vi ~**trar em** enter <casa>; (fig) penetrate

penhasco /pe'ɲasku/ m cliff

penhoar /peɲo'ar/ m dressing gown

penhor /pe'ɲor/ m pledge; **casa de** ~**es** pawnshop

penicilina /penisi'lina/ f penicillin

penico /pe'niku/ m potty

península /pe'nĩsula/ f peninsula

pênis /'penis/ m invar penis

penitência /peni'tẽsia/ f (arrependimento) penitence; (expiação) penance

penitenci|ária /penitẽsi'aria/ f prison; ~**rio** a prison □ m prisoner

penoso /pe'nozu/ a <experiência, tarefa, assunto> painful; <trabalho, viagem> hard, difficult

pensa|dor /pẽsa'dor/ m thinker; ~**mento** m thought

pensão /pẽ'sãw/ f (renda) pension; (hotel) guesthouse; ~ (**alimentícia**) (paga por ex-marido) alimony; ~ **completa** full board

pen|sar /pẽ'sar/ vt/i think (em of ou about); ~**sativo** a thoughtful, pensive

pên|sil /'pẽsiw/ (pl ~**seis**) a **ponte** ~**sil** suspension bridge

penso /'pẽsu/ m (curativo) dressing

pentágono /pẽ'tagonu/ m pentagon

pentatlo /pẽ'tatlu/ m pentathlon

pente /'pẽtʃi/ m comb; ~**adeira** f dressing table; ~**ado** m hairstyle, hairdo; ~**ar** vt comb; ~**ar-se** vpr do one's hair; (com pente) comb one's hair

Pentecostes /pẽte'kɔstʃis/ m Whitsun

pente-fino /pẽtʃi'finu/ m **passar a** ~ go over with a fine-tooth comb

pente|lhar /pẽte'ʎar/ vt (fam) bother; ~**lho** /e/ m pubic hair; (fam: pessoa inconveniente) pain (in the neck)

penugem /pe'nuʒẽ/ f down

penúltimo /pe'nuwtʃimu/ a last but one, penultimate

penumbra /pe'nũbra/ f half-light

penúria /pe'nuria/ f penury, extreme poverty

pepino /pe'pinu/ m cucumber

pepita /pe'pita/ f nugget

peque|nez /peke'nes/ f smallness; (fig) pettiness; ~**ninho** a tiny; ~**no** /e/ a small; (mesquinho) petty

Pequim /pe'ki/ f Peking, Beijing

pequinês /peki'nes/ m Pekinese

pêra /'pera/ f pear

perambular /perãbu'lar/ vi wander

perante /pe'rãtʃi/ prep before

percalço /per'kawsu/ m pitfall

perceber /perse'ber/ vt realize; (Port: entender) understand; (psiqu) perceive

percen|tagem /persẽ'taʒẽ/ f percentage; ~**tual** (pl ~**tuais**) a & m percentage

percep|ção /persep'sãw/ f perception; ~**tível** (pl ~**tíveis**) a perceptible

percevejo /perse'veʒu/ m (bicho) bedbug; (tachinha) drawing pin, (Amer) thumbtack

per|correr /perko'xer/ vt cross; cover <distância>; (viajar por) travel through; ~**curso** m journey

percus|são /perku'sãw/ f percussion; ~**sionista** m/f percussionist

percutir /perku'tʃir/ vt strike

perda /'perda/ f loss; ~ **de tempo** waste of time

perdão /per'dãw/ f pardon

perder /per'der/ vt lose; (não chegar a ver, pegar) miss <ônibus, programa na TV etc>; waste <tempo> □ vi lose; ~-**se** vpr get lost; ~-**se de alg** lose s.o.; ~ **aco de vista** lose sight of sth

perdiz /per'dʒis/ f partridge

perdoar /perdo'ar/ vt forgive (**aco a alg** s.o. for sth)

perdulário /perdu'lariu/ a & m spendthrift

perdurar /perdu'rar/ vi endure; <coisa ruim> persist

pere|cer /pere'ser/ vi perish; ~**cível** (pl ~**cíveis**) a perishable

peregri|nação /peregrina'sãw/ f peregrination; (romaria) pilgrimage; ~**nar** vi roam; (por motivos religiosos) go on a pilgrimage; ~**no** m pilgrim

pereira /pe'rera/ f pear tree

peremptório /perẽp'tɔriu/ a peremptory

perene /pe'reni/ a perennial

pererereca /pere'rɛka/ f tree frog

perfazer /perfa'zer/ vt make up
perfeccionis|mo /perfeksio'nizmu/ m perfectionism; **~ta** a & m/f perfectionist
perfei|ção /perfej'sãw/ f perfection; **~to** a & m perfect
per|fil /per'fiw/ (pl ~fis) m profile; **~filar** vt line up; **~filar-se** vpr line up
perfu|mado /perfu'madu/ a <flor, ar> fragrant; <sabonete etc> scented; <pessoa> with perfume on; **~mar** vt perfume; **~mar-se** vpr put perfume on; **~maria** f perfumery; (fam) trimmings, frills; **~me** m perfume
perfu|rador /perfura'dor/ m punch; **~rar** vt punch <papel, bilhete>; drill through <chão>; perforate <úlcera, pulmão etc>; **~ratriz** f drill
pergaminho /perga'miɲu/ m parchment
pergun|ta /per'gũta/ f question; **fazer uma ~ta** ask a question; **~tar** vt/i ask; **~tar aco a alg** ask s.o. sth; **~tar por** ask after
perícia /pe'risia/ f (mestria) expertise; (inspeção) investigation; (peritos) experts
perici|al /perisi'aw/ (pl ~ais) a expert
pericli|tante /perikli'tãtʃi/ a precarious; **~tar** vi be at risk
peri|feria /perife'ria/ f periphery; (da cidade) outskirts; **~férico** a & m peripheral
perigo /pe'rigu/ m danger; **~so** /o/ a dangerous
perímetro /pe'rimetru/ m perimeter
periódico /peri'ɔdʒiku/ a periodic □ m periodical
período /pe'riodu/ m period; **trabalhar meio ~** work part-time
peripécias /peri'pɛsias/ f pl ups and downs, vicissitudes
periquito /peri'kitu/ m parakeet; (de estimação) budgerigar
periscópio /peris'kɔpiu/ m periscope
perito /pe'ritu/ a & m expert (**em** at)
per|jurar /perʒu'rar/ vi commit perjury; **~júrio** m perjury; **~juro** m perjurer
perma|necer /permane'ser/ vi remain; **~nência** f permanence; (estadia) stay; **~nente** a permanent □ m perm
permeá|vel /permi'avew/ (pl ~veis) a permeable
permis|são /permi'sãw/ f permission; **~sível** (pl ~síveis) a permissible; **~sivo** a permissive
permitir /permi'tʃir/ vt allow, permit; **~ a alg ir** allow s.o. to go
permutar /permu'tar/ vt exchange

perna /'pɛrna/ f leg
pernicioso /pernisi'ozu/ a pernicious
per|nil /per'niw/ (pl ~nis) m leg
pernilongo /perni'lõgu/ m (large) mosquito
pernoi|tar /pernoj'tar/ vi spend the night; **~te** m overnight stay
pérola /'pɛrola/ f pearl
perpendicular /perpẽdʒiku'lar/ a perpendicular
perpetrar /perpe'trar/ vt perpetrate
perpetu|ar /perpetu'ar/ vt perpetuate; **~idade** f perpetuity
perpétu|o /per'pɛtuu/ a perpetual; **prisão ~a** life imprisonment
perple|xidade /perpleksi'dadʒi/ f puzzlement; **~xo** /ɛ/ a puzzled
persa /'pɛrsa/ a & m/f Persian
perse|guição /persegi'sãw/ f pursuit; (de minorias etc) persecution; **~guidor** m pursuer; (de minorias etc) persecutor; **~guir** vt pursue; persecute <minoria, seita etc>
perseve|rança /perseve'rãsa/ f perseverance; **~rante** a persevering; **~rar** vi persevere
persiana /persi'ana/ f blind
pérsico /'pɛrsiku/ a **Golfo Pérsico** Persian Gulf
persignar-se /persig'narsi/ vt cross o.s.
persis|tência /persis'tẽsia/ f persistence; **~tente** a persistent; **~tir** vi persist
perso|nagem /perso'naʒẽ/ m/f (pessoa famosa) personality; (em livro, filme etc) character; **~nalidade** f personality; **~nalizar** vt personalize; **~nificar** vt personify
perspectiva /perspek'tʃiva/ f (na arte, ponto de vista) perspective; (possibilidade) prospect
perspi|cácia /perspi'kasia/ f insight, perceptiveness; **~caz** a perceptive
persua|dir /persua'dʒir/ vt persuade (**alg a** s.o. to); **~são** f persuasion; **~sivo** a persuasive
perten|cente /pertẽ'sẽtʃi/ a belonging (**a** to); (que tem a ver com) pertaining (**a** to); **~cer** vi belong (**a** to); (referir-se) pertain (**a** to); **~ces** m pl belongings
perto /'pɛrtu/ adv near (**de** to); **aqui ~** near here, nearby; **de ~** closely; <ver> close up
pertur|bação /perturba'sãw/ f disturbance; (do espírito) anxiety; **~bado** a <pessoa> unsettled, troubled; **~bar** vt disturb; **~bar-se** vpr get upset, be perturbed
Peru /pe'ru/ m Peru
peru /pe'ru/ m turkey
perua /pe'rua/ f (carro grande) estate car, (Amer) station wagon; (caminho-

nete/ van; (*para escolares etc*) minibus; (*fam: mulher*) brassy woman

peruano /peru'ano/ *a & m* Peruvian

peruca /pe'ruka/ *f* wig

perver|são /perver'sãw/ *f* perversion; ~**so** *a* perverse; ~**ter** *vt* pervert

pesadelo /peza'delu/ *m* nightmare

pesado /pe'zadu/ *a* heavy; <*estilo, livro*> heavy-going □ *adv* heavily

pêsames /'pezamis/ *m pl* condolences

pesar[1] /pe'zar/ *vt* weigh up □ *vi* weigh; (*influir*) carry weight; ~ **sobre** <*ameaça etc*> hang over; ~**-se** *vpr* weigh o.s.

pesar[2] /pe'zar/ *m* sorrow; ~**oso** /o/ *a* sorry, sorrowful

pes|ca /'pɛska/ *f* fishing; **ir à** ~**ca** go fishing; ~**cador** *m* fisherman; ~**car** *vt* catch; (*retirar da água*) fish out □ *vi* fish; (*fam*) (*entender*) understand; (*cochilar*) nod off; ~**car de** (*fam*) know all about

pescoço /pes'kosu/ *m* neck

peseta /pe'zeta/ *f* peseta

peso /'pezu/ *m* weight; **de** ~ (*fig*) <*pessoa*> influential; <*livro, argumento*> authoritative

pesqueiro /pes'keru/ *a* fishing

pesqui|sa /pes'kiza/ *f* research; (*uma*) study; *pl* research; ~**sa de mercado** market research; ~**sador** *m* researcher; ~**sar** *vt/i* research

pêssego /'pesigu/ *m* peach

pessegueiro /pesi'geru/ *m* peach tree

pessimis|mo /pesi'mizmu/ *m* pessimism; ~**ta** *a* pessimistic □ *m/f* pessimist

péssimo /'pɛsimu/ *a* terrible, awful

pesso|a /pe'soa/ *f* person; *pl* people; **em** ~**a** in person; ~**al** (*pl* ~**ais**) *a* personal □ *m* staff; (*fam*) folks

pesta|na /pes'tana/ *f* eyelash; **tirar uma** ~**na** (*fam*) have a nap; ~**nejar** *vi* blink; **sem** ~**nejar** (*fig*) without batting an eyelid

pes|te /'pɛsti/ *f* (*doença*) plague; (*criança etc*) pest; ~**ticida** *m* pesticide

pétala /'pɛtala/ *f* petal

peteca /pe'tɛka/ *f* kind of shuttlecock; (*jogo*) kind of badminton played with the hand

peteleco /pete'lɛku/ *m* flick

petição /petʃi'sãw/ *f* petition

petisco /pe'tʃisku/ *m* savoury, titbit

petrificar /petrifi'kar/ *vt* petrify; (*de surpresa*) stun; ~**-se** *vpr* be petrified; (*de surpresa*) be stunned

petroleiro /petro'leru/ *a* oil □ *m* oil tanker

petróleo /pe'trɔliu/ *m* oil, petroleum; ~ **bruto** crude oil

petrolífero /petro'liferu/ *a* oil-producing

petroquími|ca /petro'kimika/ *f* petrochemicals; ~**co**a petrochemical

petu|lância /petu'lãsia/ *f* cheek; ~**lante** *a* cheeky

peúga /pi'uga/ *f* (*Port*) sock

pevide /pe'vidʒi/ *f* (*Port*) pip

pia /'pia/ *f* (*do banheiro*) washbasin; (*da cozinha*) sink; ~ **batismal** font

piada /pi'ada/ *f* joke

pia|nista /pia'nista/ *m/f* pianist; ~**no** *m* piano; ~**no de cauda** grand piano

piar /pi'ar/ *vi* <*pinto*> cheep; <*coruja*> hoot

picada /pi'kada/ *f* (*de agulha, alfinete etc*) prick; (*de abelha, vespa*) sting; (*de mosquito, cobra*) bite; (*de heroína*) shot; (*de avião*) nosedive; **o fim da** ~ (*fig*) the limit

picadeiro /pika'deru/ *m* ring

picante /pi'kãtʃi/ *a* <*comida*> hot, spicy; <*piada*> risqué; <*filme, livro*> raunchy

pica-pau /pika'paw/ *m* woodpecker

picar /pi'kar/ *vt* (*com agulha, alfinete etc*) prick; <*abelha, vespa, urtiga*> sting; <*mosquito, cobra*> bite; <*pássaro*> peck, chop <*carne, alho etc*>; shred <*papel*> □ *vi* <*peixe*> bite; <*lã, cobertor*> prickle

picareta /pika'reta/ *f* pickaxe

pi|chação /piʃa'sãw/ *f* piece of graffiti; *pl* graffiti; ~**char** *vt* spray with graffiti <*muro, prédio*>; spray <*grafite, desenho*>; ~**che** *m* pitch

picles /'piklis/ *m pl* pickles

pico /'piku/ *m* peak; **20 anos e** ~ (*Port*) just over 20

picolé /piko'lɛ/ *m* ice lolly

pico|tar /piko'tar/ *vt* perforate; ~**te** /ɔ/ *m* perforations

pie|dade /pie'dadʒi/ *f* (*religiosidade*) piety; (*compaixão*) pity; ~**doso** /o/ *a* merciful, compassionate

pie|gas /pi'ɛgas/ *a invar* <*filme, livro*> sentimental, schmaltzy; <*pessoa*> soppy; ~**guice** *f* sentimentality

pifar /pi'far/ *vi* (*fam*) break down, go wrong

pigar|rear /pigaxi'ar/ *vi* clear one's throat; ~**ro** *m* frog in the throat

pigmento /pig'mẽtu/ *m* pigment

pig|meu /pig'mew/ *a & m* (*f* ~**méia**) pygmy

pijama /pi'ʒama/ *m* pyjamas

pilantra /pi'lãtra/ *m/f* (*fam*) crook

pilão /pi'lãw/ *m* (*na cozinha*) pestle; (*na construção*) ram

pilar /pi'lar/ *m* pillar

pilastra /pi'lastra/ *f* pillar

pileque /pi'lɛki/ *m* drinking session; **tomar um** ~ get drunk

pilha /'piʎa/ *f* (*monte*) pile; (*elétrica*) battery

pilhar /pi'ʎar/ *vt* pillage

pilhéria /pi'ʎɛria/ f joke

pilotar /pilo'tar/ vt fly, pilot <avião>; drive <carro>

pilotis /pilo'tʃis/ m pl pillars

piloto /pi'lotu/ m pilot; (de carro) driver; (de gás) pilot light □ a invar pilot

pílula /'pilula/ f pill

pimen|ta /pi'mẽta/ f pepper; ~ta de Caiena cayenne pepper; ~ta-do-reino f black pepper; ~ta-malagueta (pl ~tas-malagueta) f chilli pepper; ~tão m (bell) pepper; ~teira f pepper pot

pinacoteca /pinako'tɛka/ f art gallery

pin|ça /'pĩsa/ (para tirar pêlos) tweezers; (para segurar) tongs; (de siri etc) pincer; ~çar vt pluck <sobrancelhas>

pin|cel /pĩ'sɛw/ (pl ~céis) m brush; ~celada f brush stroke; ~celar vt paint

pin|ga /'pĩga/ f Brazilian rum; ~gado a <café> with a dash of milk; ~gar vi drip; (começar a chover) spit (with rain) □ vt drip; ~gente m pendant; ~go m drop; (no i) dot

pingue-pongue /pĩgi'põgi/ m table tennis

pingüim /pĩ'gwĩ/ m penguin

pi|nha /'piɲa/ f pine cone; ~nheiro f pine tree; ~nho m pine

pino /'pinu/ m pin; (para trancar carro) lock; a ~ upright; bater ~ <carro> knock

pin|ta /'pĩta/ f (sinal) mole; (fam: aparência) look; ~tar vt paint; dye <cabelo>; put make-up on <rosto, olhos> □ vi paint; (fam) <pessoa> show up; <problema, oportunidade> crop up; ~tar-se vpr put on make-up

pintarroxo /pĩta'xoʃu/ m robin

pinto /'pĩtu/ m chick

pin|tor /pĩ'tor/ m painter; ~tura f painting

pio[1] /'piu/ m (de pinto) cheep; (de coruja) hoot

pio[2] /'piu/ a pious

piolho /pi'oʎu/ m louse

pioneiro /pio'neru/ m pioneer □ a pioneering

pior /pi'ɔr/ a & adv worse; o ~ the worst

pio|ra /pi'ɔra/ f worsening; ~rar vt make worse, worsen □ vi get worse, worsen

pipa /'pipa/ f (que voa) kite; (de vinho) cask

pipilar /pipi'lar/ vi chirp

pipo|ca /pi'pɔka/ f popcorn; ~car vi spring up; ~queiro m popcorn seller

pique /'piki/ m (disposição) energy; a ~ vertically; ir a ~ <navio> sink

piquenique /piki'niki/ m picnic

pique|te /pi'ketʃi/ m picket; ~teiro m picket

pirado /pi'radu/ a (fam) crazy

pirâmide /pi'ramidʒi/ f pyramid

piranha /pi'raɲa/ f piranha; (fam: mulher) maneater

pirar /pi'rar/ (fam) vi flip out, go mad

pirata /pi'rata/ a & m/f pirate; ~ria f piracy

pires /'piris/ m invar saucer

pirilampo /piri'lãpu/ m glow-worm

Pireneus /piri'news/ m pl Pyrenees

pirra|ça /pi'xasa/ f spiteful act; fazer ~ça be spiteful; ~cento a spiteful

pirueta /piru'eta/ f pirouette

pirulito /piru'litu/ m lollipop

pi|sada /pi'zada/ f step; (rastro) footprint; ~sar vt tread on; tread <uvas, palco>; (esmagar) trample on □ vi step; ~sar em step on; (entrar) set foot in

pis|cadela /piska'dɛla/ f wink; ~capisca m indicator; ~car vi (com o olho) wink; (pestanejar) blink; <estrela, luz> twinkle; <motorista> indicate □ m num ~car de olhos in a flash

piscicultura /pisikuw'tura/ f fish farming; (lugar) fish farm

piscina /pi'sina/ f swimming pool

piso /'pizu/ m floor

pisotear /pizotʃi'ar/ vt trample

pista /'pista/ f track; (da estrada) carriageway; (para aviões) runway; (de circo) ring; (dica) clue; ~ de dança dancefloor

pistache /pis'taʃi/ m, **pistacho** /pis'taʃu/ m pistachio (nut)

pisto|la /pis'tɔla/ f pistol; (para pintar) spray gun; ~lão m influential contact; ~leiro m gunman

pitada /pi'tada/ f pinch

piteira /pi'tera/ f cigarette-holder

pitoresco /pito'resku/ a picturesque

pitu /pi'tu/ m crayfish

pivete /pi'vɛtʃi/ m/f child thief

pivô /pi'vo/ m pivot

pixaim /piʃa'ĩ/ a frizzy

pizza /'pitsa/ f pizza; ~ria f pizzeria

placa /'plaka/ f plate; (de carro) number plate, (Amer) license plate; (comemorativa) plaque; (em computador) board; ~ de sinalização roadsign

placar /pla'kar/ m scoreboard; (escore) scoreline

plácido /'plasidu/ a placid

plagi|ário /plaʒi'ariu/ m plagiarist; ~ar vt plagiarize

plágio /'plaʒiu/ m plagiarism

plaina /'plajna/ f plane

planador /plana'dor/ m glider

planalto /pla'nawtu/ m plateau

planar /pla'nar/ vi glide

planeamento, planear (Port) veja planeamento, planejar
plane|jamento /planeʒa'mẽtu/ m planning; ~jamento familiar family planning; ~jar vt plan
planeta /pla'neta/ m planet
planície /pla'nisi/ f plain
planificar /planifi'kar/ vt (programar) plan (out)
planilha /pla'niʎa/ f spreadsheet
plano /'planu/ a flat □ m plan; (superfície, nível) plane; primeiro ~ foreground
planta /'plãta/ f plant; (do pé) sole; (de edifício) ground plan; ~ção f (ato) planting; (terreno) plantation; ~do a deixar alg ~do (fam) keep s.o. waiting around
plantão /plã'tãw/ m duty; (noturno) night duty; estar de ~ be on duty
plantar /plã'tar/ vt plant
plas|ma /'plazma/ m plasma; ~mar vt mould, shape
plásti|ca /'plastʃika/ f face-lift; ~co a & m plastic
plataforma /plata'fɔrma/ f platform
plátano /'platanu/ m plane tree
platéia /pla'tɛja/ f audience; (parte do teatro) stalls, (Amer) orchestra
platina /pla'tʃina/ f platinum; ~dos m pl points
platônico /pla'toniku/ a platonic
plausí|vel /plaw'zivew/ (pl ~veis) a plausible
ple|be /'plɛbi/ f common people; ~beu a (f ~béia) plebeian □ m (f ~béia) commoner; ~biscito m plebiscite
plei|tear /plejtʃi'ar/ vt contest; ~to m (litígio) case; (eleitoral) contest
ple|namente /plena'mẽtʃi/ adv fully; ~nário a plenary □ m plenary assembly; ~no /e/ a full; em ~ verão in the middle of summer
plissado /pli'sadu/ a pleated
pluma /'pluma/ f feather; ~gem f plumage
plu|ral /plu'raw/ (pl ~rais) a & m plural
plutônio /plu'toniu/ m plutonium
pluvi|al /pluvi'aw/ (pl ~ais) a rain
pneu /pi'new/ m tyre; ~mático a pneumatic □ m tyre
pneumonia /pineumo'nia/ f pneumonia
pó /pɔ/ f powder; (poeira) dust; leite em ~ powdered milk
pobre /'pɔbri/ a poor □ m/f poor man (f woman); os ~s the poor; ~za /e/ f poverty
poça /'posa/ f pool; (deixada pela chuva) puddle
poção /po'sãw/ f potion

pocilga /po'siwga/ f pigsty
poço /'posu/ f (de água, petróleo) well; (de mina, elevador) shaft
podar /po'dar/ vt prune
pó-de-arroz /pɔdʒia'xoz/ m (face) powder
poder /po'der/ m power □ v aux can, be able; (eventualidade) may; ele pode/podia/poderá vir he can/could/might come; ele pôde vir he was able to come; pode ser que it may be that; ~ com stand up to; em ~ de alg in sb's possession; estar no ~ be in power
pode|rio /pode'riu/ m might; ~roso /o/ a powerful
pódio /'pɔdʒiu/ m podium
podre /'podri/ a rotten; (fam) (cansado) exhausted; (doente) grotty; ~ de rico filthy rich; ~s m pl faults
poei|ra /po'era/ f dust; ~rento a dusty
poe|ma /po'ema/ m poem; ~sia f (arte) poetry; (poema) poem; ~ta m poet
poético /po'ɛtʃiku/ a poetic
poetisa /poe'tʃiza/ f poetess
pois /pojs/ conj as, since; ~ é that's right; ~ não of course; ~ não? can I help you?; ~ sim certainly not
pola|co /pu'laku/ (Port) a Polish □ m Pole; (língua) Polish
polar /po'lar/ a polar
polarizar /polari'zar/ vt polarize; ~-se vpr polarize
pole|gada /pole'gada/ f inch; ~gar m thumb
poleiro /po'leru/ m perch
polêmi|ca /po'lemika/ f controversy, debate; ~co a controversial
pólen /'pɔlẽ/ m pollen
policia /po'lisia/ f police □ m/f policeman (f -woman)
polici|al /polisi'aw/ (pl ~ais) a <carro, inquérito etc> police; <romance, filme> detective □ m/f policeman (f -woman); ~amento m policing; ~ar vt police
poli|dez /poli'des/ f politeness; ~do a polite
poli|gamia /poliga'mia/ f polygamy; ~glota a & m/f polyglot
Polinésia /poli'nɛzia/ f Polynesia
polinésio /poli'nɛziu/ a & m Polynesian
pólio /'pɔliu/ f polio
polir /po'lir/ vt polish
polissílabo /poli'silabu/ m polysyllable
políti|ca /po'litʃika/ f politics; (uma) policy; ~co a political □ m politician
pólo¹ /'pɔlu/ m pole
pólo² /'pɔlu/ m (jogo) polo; ~ aquático water polo

polo|nês /polo'nes/ a (f ~nesa) Polish □ m (f ~nesa) Pole; (língua) Polish

Polônia /po'lonia/ f Poland

polpa /'powpa/ f pulp

poltrona /pow'trona/ f armchair

polu|ente /polu'etʃi/ a & m pollutant; ~ição f pollution; ~ir vt pollute

polvilhar /powvi'ʎar/ vt sprinkle

polvo /'powvu/ m octopus

pólvora /'powvora/ f gunpowder

polvorosa /powvo'rɔza/ f uproar; em ~ in uproar; <pessoa> in a flap

pomada /po'mada/ f ointment

pomar /po'mar/ m orchard

pom|ba /'põba/ f dove; ~bo m pigeon

pomo-de-Adão /pomudʃia'dãw/ m Adam's apple

pom|pa /'põpa/ f pomp; ~poso /o/ a pompous

ponche /'põʃi/ m punch

ponderar /põde'rar/ vt/i ponder

pônei /'ponej/ m pony

ponta /'põta/ f end; (de faca, prego) point; (de nariz, dedo, língua) tip; (de sapato) toe; (Cin, Teat: papel curto) walk-on part; (no campo de futebol) wing; (jogador) winger; **na ~ dos pés** on tip-toe; **uma ~ de** a touch of <ironia etc>; **agüentar as ~s** (fam) hold on; **~-cabeça** /e/ f **de ~-cabeça** upside down

pontada /põ'tada/ f (dor) twinge

pontapé /põta'pɛ/ m kick; ~ **inicial** kick-off

pontaria /põta'ria/ f aim; **fazer ~** take aim

ponte /'põtʃi/ f bridge; ~ **aérea** shuttle; (em tempo de guerra) airlift; ~ **de safena** heart bypass; ~ **pênsil** suspension bridge

ponteiro /põ'teru/ m pointer; (de relógio) hand

pontiagudo /põtʃia'gudu/ a sharp

pontilhado /põtʃi'ʎadu/ a dotted

ponto /'põtu/ m point; (de costura, tricô) stitch; (no final de uma frase) full stop, (Amer) period; (sinalzinho, no i) dot; (de ônibus) stop; (no teatro) prompter; **a ~ de** on the point of; **ao ~** <carne> medium; **até certo ~** to a certain extent; **às duas em ~** at exactly two o'clock; **dormir no ~** (fam) miss the boat; **entregar os ~s** (fam) give up; **fazer ~** (fam) hang out; **dois ~s** colon; ~ **de exclamação/interrogação** exclamation/question mark; ~ **de táxi** taxi rank, (Amer) taxi stand; ~ **de vista** point of view; ~ **morto** neutral; ~**-e-vírgula** m semicolon

pontu|ação /põtua'sãw/ f punctuation; ~**al** (pl ~**ais**) a punctual; ~**alidade** f punctuality; ~**ar** vt punctuate

pontudo /põ'tudu/ a pointed

popa /'popa/ f stern

popu|lação /popula'sãw/ f population; ~**lacional** (pl ~**lacionais**) a population; ~**lar** a popular; ~**laridade** f popularity; ~**larizar** vt popularize; ~**larizar-se** vpr become popular

pôquer /'poker/ m poker

por /por/ prep for; (através de) through; (indicando meio, agente) by; (motivo) out of; ~ **ano/mês/** etc per year/month/etc; ~ **cento** per cent; ~ **aqui** (nesta área) around here; (nesta direção) this way; ~ **dentro/fora** on the inside/outside; ~ **isso** for this reason; ~ **sorte** luckily; ~ **que** why; ~ **mais caro que seja** however expensive it may be; **está ~ acontecer/fazer** it is yet to happen/to be done

pôr /por/ vt put; put on <roupa, chapéu, óculos>; lay <mesa, ovos> □ m o ~ **do sol** sunset; ~**-se** vpr <sol> set; ~**-se a** start to; ~**-se a caminho** set off

porão /po'rãw/ m (de prédio) basement; (de casa) cellar; (de navio) hold

porca /'pɔrka/ f (de parafuso) nut; (animal) sow

porção /por'sãw/ f portion; **uma ~ de** (muitos) a lot of

porcaria /porka'ria/ f (sujeira) filth; (coisa malfeita) piece of trash; pl trash

porcelana /porse'lana/ f china

porcentagem /porsẽ'taʒẽ/ f percentage

porco /'porku/ a filthy □ m (animal, fig) pig; (carne) pork; ~**-espinho** (pl ~**s-espinhos**) m porcupine

porém /po'rẽj/ conj however

pormenor /porme'nɔr/ m detail

por|nô /por'no/ a porn □ m porn film; ~**nografia** f pornography; ~**nográfico** a pornographic

poro /'pɔru/ m pore; ~**so** /o/ a porous

por|quanto /por'kwãtu/ conj since; ~**que** /por'ki/ conj because; (Port: por quê?) why; ~**quê** /por'ke/ adv (Port) why □ m reason why

porquinho|-da-índia /porkiɲuda-'ĩdʒia/ (pl ~**s-da-índia**) m guinea pig

porrada /po'xada/ f (fam) beating

porre /'pɔxi/ m (fam) drinking session, booze-up; **de ~** drunk; **tomar um ~** get drunk

porta /'pɔrta/ f door

porta-aviões /pɔrtavi'õjs/ m invar aircraft carrier

portador /porta'dor/ m bearer

portagem /por'taʒẽ/ f (Port) toll

porta|chaves /pɔrta'ʃavis/ m invar key-holder ou key-ring; ~**-jóias** m in-

var jewellery box; ~-**lápis** *m invar* pencil holder; ~-**luvas** *m invar* glove compartment; ~-**malas** *m invar* boot, (*Amer*) trunk; ~-**niqueis** *m invar* purse

portanto /por'tãtu/ *conj* therefore

portão /por'tãw/ *m* gate

portar /por'tar/ *vt* carry; ~-**se** *vpr* behave

porta|-**retrato** /pɔrtaxe'tratu/ *m* photo frame; ~-**revistas** *m invar* magazine rack

portaria /porta'ria/ *f* (*entrada*) entrance; (*decreto*) decree

portá|**til** (*pl* ~**teis**) *a* portable ~-**toalhas** /pɔrtato'aʎas/ *m invar* towel rail; ~-**voz** *m*/*f* spokesman (*f* -woman)

porte /'pɔrtʃi/ *m* (*frete*) carriage; (*de cartas etc*) postage; (*de pessoa*) bearing; (*dimensão*) scale; **de grande**/**pequeno** ~ large-/small-scale

porteiro /por'teru/ *m* doorman; ~ **eletrónico** entryphone

porto /'portu/ *m* port; **o Porto** Oporto; ~ **de escala** port of call; **Porto Rico** *m* Puerto Rico; ~-**riquenho** /e/ *a* & *m* Puertorican

portuense /portu'ẽsi/ *a* & *m*/*f* (person) from Oporto

Portugal /portu'gaw/ *m* Portugal

portu|**guês** /portu'ges/ *a* & *m* (*f* ~**guesa**) Portuguese

portuário /portu'ariu/ *a* port □ *m* dock worker, docker

po|**sar** /po'zar/ *vi* pose; ~-**se** /o/ *f* pose; (*de filme*) exposure

pós-datar /pɔzda'tar/ *vt* postdate

pós-escrito /pɔzis'kritu/ *m* postscript

pós-gradua|**ção** /pɔzgradua'sãw/ *f* postgraduation; ~**do** *a* & *m* postgraduate

pós-guerra /pɔz'gɛxa/ *m* post-war period; **a Europa do** ~ post-war Europe

posi|**ção** /pozi'sãw/ *f* position; ~**cionar** *vt* position; ~**tivo** *a* & *m* positive

posologia /pozolo'ʒia/ *f* dosage

pos|**sante** /po'sãtʃi/ *a* powerful; ~**se** /ɔ/ *f* (*de casa etc*) possession, ownership; (*do presidente etc*) swearing in; *pl* (*pertences*) possessions; **tomar** ~**se** take office; **tomar** ~**se de** take possession of

posses|**são** /pose'sãw/ *f* possession; ~**sivo** *a* possessive; ~**so** /ɛ/ *a* possessed; (*com raiva*) furious

possibili|**dade** /posibili'dadʒi/ *f* possibility; ~**tar** *vt* make possible

possí|**vel** /po'sivew/ (*pl* ~**veis**) *a* possible; **fazer todo o** ~**vel** do one's best

possuir /posu'ir/ *vt* possess; (*ser dono de*) own

posta /'pɔsta/ *f* (*de peixe*) steak

pos|**tal** /pos'taw/ (*pl* ~**tais**) *a* postal □ *m* postcard

postar /pos'tar/ *vt* place; ~-**se** *vpr* position o.s.

poste /'pɔstʃi/ *m* post

pôster /'poster/ *m* poster

posteri|**dade** /posteri'dadʒi/ *f* posterity; ~**or** *a* (*no tempo*) subsequent, later; (*no espaço*) rear; ~**ormente** *adv* subsequently

postiço /pos'tʃisu/ *a* false

posto /'postu/ *m* post; ~ **de gasolina** petrol station, (*Amer*) gas station; ~ **de saúde** health centre □ *pp de* **pôr**; ~ **que** although

póstumo /'pɔstumu/ *a* posthumous

postura /pos'tura/ *f* posture

potá|**vel** /po'tavew/ (*pl* ~**veis**) *a* **água** ~**vel** drinking water

pote /'pɔtʃi/ *m* pot; (*de vidro*) jar

potência /po'tẽsia/ *f* power

poten|**cial** /potẽsi'aw/ (*pl* ~**ciais**) *a* & *m* potential; ~**te** *a* potent

potro /'potru/ *m* foal

pouco /'poku/ *a* (*largo*) little; *pl* few □ *adv* not much □ *m* **um** ~ a little; ~ **a** ~ little by little; **aos** ~**s** gradually; **daqui a** ~ shortly; **por** ~ almost; ~ **tempo** a short time

pou|**pança** /po'pãsa/ *f* saving; (*conta*) savings account; ~**par** *vt* save; spare < *vida*>

pouquinho /po'kiɲu/ *m* **um** ~ (**de**) a little

pou|**sada** /po'zada/ *f* inn; ~**sar** *vi* land; ~**so** *m* landing

po|**vão** /po'vãw/ *m* common people; ~**vo** /o/ *m* people

povo|**ação** /povoa'sãw/ *f* settlement; ~**ar** *vt* populate

poxa /'poʃa/ *int* gosh

pra /pra/ *prep* (*fam*) *veja* **para**

praça /'prasa/ *f* (*largo*) square; (*mercado*) market □ *m* (*soldado*) private

prado /'pradu/ *m* meadow

pra-frente /pra'frẽtʃi/ *a invar* (*fam*) with it, modern

praga /'praga/ *f* curse; (*inseto, doença, pessoa*) pest

prag|**mático** /prag'matʃiku/ *a* pragmatic; ~**matismo** *m* pragmatism

praguejar /prage'ʒar/ *vt*/*i* curse

praia /'praja/ *f* beach

pran|**cha** /'prãʃa/ *f* plank; (*de surfe*) board; ~**cheta** /e/ *f* drawing board

pranto /'prãtu/ *m* weeping

pra|**ta** /'prata/ *f* silver; ~**taria** *f* (*coisas de prata*) silverware; ~**teado** *a* silver-plated; (*cor*) silver

prateleira /prate'lera/ *f* shelf

prática /'pratʃika/ *f* practice; **na** ~ in practice

prati|cante /pratʃiˈkātʃi/ a practising □ m/f apprentice; (de esporte etc) player; ~car vt practise; (cometer, executar) carry out □ vi practise; ~cável (pl ~cáveis) a practicable

prático /ˈpratʃiku/ a practical

prato /ˈpratu/ m (objeto) plate; (comida) dish; (parte de uma refeição) course; (do toca-discos) turntable; pl (instrumento) cymbals; ~ fundo dish; ~ principal main course

praxe /ˈpraʃi/ f normal practice; de ~ usually

prazer /praˈzer/ m pleasure; muito ~ (em conhecê-lo) pleased to meet you; ~oso /o/ a pleasurable

prazo /ˈprazu/ m term, time; a ~ <compra etc> on credit; a curto/longo ~ in the short/long term; último ~ deadline

preâmbulo /priˈābulu/ m preamble

precário /preˈkariu/ a precarious

precaução /prekawˈsāw/ f precaution

preca|ver-se /prekaˈversi/ vpr take precautions (de against); ~vido a cautious

prece /ˈpresi/ f prayer

prece|dência /preseˈdēsia/ f precedence; ~dente a preceding □ m precedent; ~der vt/i precede

preceito /preˈsejtu/ m precept

precioso /presiˈozu/ a precious

precipício /presiˈpisiu/ m precipice

precipi|tação /presipitaˈsāw/ f haste; (chuva etc) precipitation; ~tado a <fuga> headlong; <decisão, ato> hasty, rash; ~tar vt (lançar) throw; (antecipar) hasten; ~tar-se vpr (lançar-se) throw o.s.; (apressar-se) rush; (agir sem pensar) act rashly

precisão /presiˈzāw/ f precision, accuracy

precisamente /presizaˈmētʃi/ adv precisely

preci|sar /presiˈzar/ vt (necessitar) need; (indicar com exatidão) specify □ vi be necessary; ~sar de need; ~so ir I have to go; ~sa-se wanted; ~so a (exato) precise; (necessário) necessary

preço /ˈpresu/ m price; ~ de custo cost price; ~ fixo set price

precoce /preˈkɔsi/ a <fruto> early; <velhice, calvície etc> premature; <criança> precocious

precon|cebido /prekōseˈbidu/ a preconceived; ~ceito m prejudice; ~ceituoso a prejudiced

preconizar /prekoniˈzar/ vt advocate

precursor /prekurˈsor/ m forerunner

preda|dor /predaˈdor/ m predator; ~tório a predatory

predecessor /predeseˈsor/ m predecessor

predestinar /predestʃiˈnar/ vt predestine

predeterminar /predetermiˈnar/ vt predetermine

predição /predʒiˈsāw/ f prediction

predile|ção /predʒileˈsāw/ f preference; ~to /ɛ/ a favourite

prédio /ˈprɛdʒiu/ m building

predis|por /predʒisˈpor/ vt prepare (para for); (tornar parcial) prejudice (contra against); ~por-se vpr prepare o.s.; ~posto a predisposed; (contra) prejudiced

predizer /predʒiˈzer/ vt predict, foretell

predomi|nância /predomiˈnāsia/ f predominance; ~nante a predominant; ~nar vi predominate

predomínio /predoˈminiu/ m predominance

preencher /priēˈʃer/ vt fill; fill in, (Amer) fill out <formulário>; meet <requisitos>

pré|-escola /prɛisˈkɔla/ f infant school, (Amer) preschool; ~-escolar a pre-school; ~-estréia f preview; ~-fabricado a prefabricated

prefácio /preˈfasiu/ m preface

prefei|to /preˈfejtu/ m mayor; ~tura f prefecture; (prédio) town hall

prefe|rência /prefeˈrēsia/ f preference; (direito no trânsito) right of way; de ~rência preferably; ~rencial (pl ~renciais) a preferential; <rua> main; ~rido a favourite; ~rir vt prefer (a to); ~rível (pl ~ríveis) a preferable

prefixo /preˈfiksu/ m prefix

prega /ˈprɛga/ f pleat

pregador¹ /pregaˈdor/ m (de roupa) peg

pre|gador² /pregaˈdor/ m (quem prega) preacher; ~gão m (de vendedor) cry; ~gão (na bolsa de valores) trading; (em leilão) bidding

pregar¹ /preˈgar/ vt fix; (com prego) nail; sew on <botão>; não ~ olho not sleep a wink; ~ uma peça em play a trick on; ~ um susto em alg give s.o. a fright

pregar² /preˈgar/ vt/i preach

prego /ˈpregu/ m nail

pregui|ça /preˈgisa/ f laziness; (bicho) sloth; estou com ~ça de ir I can't be bothered to go; ~çoso a lazy

pré-histórico /prɛisˈtɔriku/ a prehistoric

preia-mar /prejaˈmar/ f high tide

prejudi|car /preʒudʒiˈkar/ vt harm; damage <saúde>; ~car-se vpr harm o.s.; ~cial (pl ~ciais) a harmful, damaging (a to)

prejuízo /preʒuˈizu/ m damage; (*financeiro*\ loss; em ~ de to the detriment of

prejulgar /preʒuwˈgar/ vt prejudge

preliminar /prelimiˈnar/ a & m/f preliminary

prelo /ˈprɛlu/ m printing press; no ~ being printed

preludio /preˈludʒiu/ m prelude

prematuro /premaˈturu/ a premature

premeditar /premedʒiˈtar/ vt premeditate

premente /preˈmētʃi/ a pressing

premi|ado /premiˈadu/ a <*romance, atleta etc*> prize-winning; <*bilhete, número etc*> winning ◻ m prize-winner; ~ar vt award a prize to <*romance, atleta etc*>; reward <*honestidade, mérito*>

prêmio /ˈpremiu/ m prize; (*de seguro*) premium; **Grande Prêmio** (*de F1*) Grand Prix

premissa /preˈmisa/ f premiss

premonição /premoniˈsãw/ f premonition

pré-na|tal /prɛnaˈtaw/ (pl ~tais) a antenatal, (*Amer*) prenatal

prenda /ˈprēda/ f (*Port*) present; ~s domésticas household chores; ~do a domesticated

pren|dedor /prēdeˈdor/ m clip; ~dedor de roupa clothes peg; ~der vt (*pregar*) fix; (*capturar*) arrest; (*atar*) tie up <*cachorro*>; tie back <*cabelo*>; (*restringir*) restrict; (*ligar afetivamente*) bind; ~der (a atenção de) alg grab s.o.('s attention)

prenhe /ˈprɛɲi/ a pregnant

prenome /preˈnomi/ m first name

pren|sa /ˈprēsa/ f press; ~sar vt press

preocu|pação /preokupaˈsãw/ f concern; ~pante a worrying; ~par vt worry; ~par-se vpr worry (com about)

prepa|ração /preparaˈsãw/ f preparation; ~rado m preparation; ~rar vt prepare; ~rar-se vpr prepare, get ready; ~rativos m pl preparations; ~ro m preparation; (*competência*) knowledge; ~ro físico physical fitness

preponderar /prepõdeˈrar/ vi prevail (sobre over)

preposição /prepoziˈsãw/ f preposition

prerrogativa /prexogaˈtʃiva/ f prerogative

presa /ˈpreza/ f (*de caça*) prey; (*de cobra*) fang; (*de elefante*) tusk; ~ de guerra spoils of war

prescin|dir /presīˈdʒir/ vi ~dir de dispense with; ~divel (pl ~diveis) a dispensable

pres|crever /preskreˈver/ vt prescribe; ~crição f prescription; (*norma*) rule

presen|ça /preˈzēsa/ f presence; ~ça de espírito presence of mind; ~çar vt (*estar presente a*) be present at; (*testemunhar*) witness; ~te a & m present; ~tear ~ tear alg (com aco) give s.o. (sth as) a present

presépio /preˈzɛpiu/ m crib

preser|vação /prezervaˈsãw/ f preservation; ~var vt preserve, protect; ~vativo m (*em comida*) preservative; (*camisinha*) condom

presi|dência /preziˈdēsia/ f presidency; (*de uma reunião*) chair; ~dencial (pl ~denciais) a presidential; ~dencialismo m presidential system; ~dente m (~ denta) president; (*de uma reunião*) chairperson

presidiário /preziˈdʒiariu/ m convict

presídio /preˈzidʒiu/ m prison

presidir /preziˈdʒir/ vi preside (a over)

presilha /preˈziʎa/ f fastener; (*de cabelo*) slide

preso /ˈprezu/ pp de prender ◻ m prisoner; ficar ~ get stuck; <*saia, corda etc*> get caught

pressa /ˈprɛsa/ f hurry; às ~s in a hurry, hurriedly; estar com ou ter ~ be in a hurry

presságio /preˈsaʒiu/ m omen

pressão /preˈsãw/ f pressure; fazer ~ sobre put pressure on; ~ arterial blood pressure

pressen|timento /presētʃiˈmētu/ m premonition, feeling; ~tir vt sense

pressionar /presioˈnar/ vt press <*botão*>; pressure <*pessoa*>

pressupor /presuˈpor/ vt <*pessoa*> presume; <*coisa*> presuppose

pressurizado /presuriˈzadu/ a pressurized

presta|ção /prestaˈsãw/ f repayment, instalment; ~tar vt render <*contas, serviço*> ◻ vi be of use; não ~ta he/it is no good; ~tar atenção pay attention; ~tar juramento take an oath; ~tativo a helpful; ~tável (pl ~táveis) a serviceable

prestes /ˈprɛstʃis/ a invar ~ a about to

prestidigita|ção /prestʃidʒiʒitaˈsãw/ f conjuring; ~dor m conjurer

pres|tigiar /prestʃiʒiˈar/ vt give prestige to; ~tígio m prestige; ~tigioso /o/ a prestigious

préstimo /ˈprɛstʃimu/ m merit

presumir /prezuˈmir/ vt presume

presun|ção /prezūˈsãw/ f presumption; ~çoso /o/ a presumptuous

presunto /preˈzūtu/ m ham

pretendente /pretẽ'dẽtʃi/ *m/f* (*candidato*) candidate, applicant

preten|der /pretẽ'der/ *vt* intend; **∼são** *f* pretension; **∼sioso** /o/ *a* pretentious

preterir /prete'rir/ *vt* disregard

pretérito /pre'tʃritu/ *m* preterite

pretexto /pre'testu/ *m* pretext

preto /'pretu/ *a* & *m* black; **∼e-branco** *a invar* black and white

prevalecer /prevale'ser/ *vi* prevail

prevenção /prevẽ'sãw/ *f* (*impedimento*) prevention; (*parcialidade*) bias

prevenir /preve'nir/ *vt* (*evitar*) prevent; (*avisar*) warn; **∼-se** *vpr* take precautions

preventivo /prevẽ'tʃivu/ *a* preventive

prever /pre'ver/ *vt* foresee, predict

previdência /previ'dẽsia/ *f* foresight; **∼ social** social security

prévio /'prεviu/ *a* prior

previ|são /previ'zãw/ *f* prediction, forecast; **∼são do tempo** weather forecast; **∼sível** (*pl* **∼síveis**) *a* predictable

pre|zado /pre'zadu/ *a* esteemed; **Prezado Senhor** Dear Sir; **∼zar** *vt* think highly of; **∼zar-se** *vpr* have self-respect

prima /'prima/ *f* cousin

primário /pri'mariu/ *a* primary; (*fundamental*) basic

primata /pri'mata/ *m* primate

primave|ra /prima'vεra/ *f* spring; (*flor*) primrose; **∼ril** (*pl* **∼ris**) *a* spring

primazia /prima'zia/ *f* primacy

primei|ra /pri'mera/ *f* (*marcha*) first (gear); **de ∼ra** first-rate; <*carne*> prime; **∼ra-dama** (*pl* **∼ras-damas**) *f* first lady; **∼ranista** *m/f* first-year (student); **∼ro** *a* & *adv* first; **no dia ∼ro de maio** on the first of May; **em ∼ro lugar** (*para começar*) in the first place; (*numa corrida, competição*) in first place; **∼ro de tudo** first of all; **∼ros socorros** first aid; **∼ro-ministro** (*pl* **∼ros-ministros**) *m* (*f* **∼ra-ministra**) prime-minister

primitivo /primi'tʃivu/ *a* primitive

primo /'primu/ *m* cousin □ **a número ∼** prime number; **∼gênito** *a* & *m* first-born

primor /pri'mor/ *m* perfection

primordi|al /primordʒi'aw/ (*pl* **∼ais**) *a* (*primitivo*) primordial; (*fundamental*) fundamental

primoroso /primo'rozu/ *a* exquisite

princesa /pri'seza/ *f* princess

princi|pado /prĩsipi'adu/ *m* principality; **∼pal** (*pl* **∼pais**) *a* main □ *m* principal

príncipe /'prĩsipi/ *m* prince

principiante /prĩsipi'ãtʃi/ *m/f* beginner

princípio /prĩ'sipiu/ *m* (*início*) beginning; (*regra*) principle; **em ∼** in principle; **por ∼** on principle

priori|dade /priori'dadʒi/ *f* priority; **∼tário** *a* priority

prisão /pri'zãw/ *f* (*ato de prender*) arrest; (*cadeia*) prison; (*encarceramento*) imprisonment; **∼ perpétua** life imprisonment; **∼ de ventre** constipation

prisioneiro /prizio'neru/ *m* prisoner

prisma /'prizma/ *m* prism

privação /priva'sãw/ *f* deprivation

privacidade /privasi'dadʒi/ *f* privacy

pri|vada /pri'vada/ *f* toilet; **∼vado** *a* private; **∼vado de** deprived of; **∼var** *vt* deprive (**de** of); **∼var-se** *vpr* deprive o.s. (**de** of)

privati|vo /priva'tʃivu/ *a* private; **∼zar** *vt* privatize

privi|legiado /privileʒi'adu/ *a* privileged; <*tratamento*> preferential; **∼legiar** *vt* favour; **∼légio** *m* privilege

pró (*fam*) = **para + o**

pró /prɔ/ *adv* for □ *m* **os ∼s e os contras** the pros and cons

proa /'proa/ *f* bow, prow

probabilidade /probabili'dadʒi/ *f* probability

proble|ma /pro'blema/ *m* problem; **∼mático** *a* problematic

proce|dência /prose'dẽsia/ *f* origin; **∼dente** *a* logical; **∼dente de** coming from; **∼der** *vi* proceed; (*comportar-se*) behave; (*na justiça*) take legal action; **∼der de** come from; **∼dimento** *m* procedure; (*comportamento*) behaviour; (*na justiça*) proceedings

proces|sador /prosesa'dor/ *m* processor; **∼sador de texto** word processor; **∼samento** *m* processing; (*na justiça*) prosecution; **∼samento de dados** data processing; **∼sar** *vt* process; (*por crime*) prosecute; (*por causa civil*) sue; **∼so** /ε/ *m* process; (*criminal*) trial; (*civil*) lawsuit

procla|mação /proklama'sãw/ *f* proclamation; **∼mar** *vt* proclaim

procri|ação /prokria'sãw/ *f* procreation; **∼ar** *vt/i* procreate

procu|ra /pro'kura/ *f* search; (*de produto*) demand; **à ∼ra de** in search of; **∼ração** *f* power of attorney; **∼rado** *a* sought after, in demand; **∼rado pela polícia** wanted by the police; **∼rador** *m* (*mandatário*) proxy; (*advogado*) public prosecutor; **∼rar** *vt* look for; (*contatar*) get in touch with; (*ir visitar*) lookup; **∼rar saber** try to find out

prodígio /pro'dʒiʒiu/ *m* wonder; (*pessoa*) prodigy

prodigioso /prodʒiʒi'ozu/ a prodigious

pródigo /'prɔdigu/ a lavish, extravagant

produ|ção /produ'sãw/ f production; ~**tividade** f productivity; ~**tivo** a productive; ~**to** m product; (*renda*) proceeds; ~**to nacional bruto** gross national product; ~**tos agrícolas** agricultural produce; ~**tor** m producer □ a **país** ~**tor de trigo** wheat-producing country; ~**zido** a (*fam: arrumado*) done up; ~**zir** vt produce

proeminente /proemi'nẽtʃi/ a prominent

proeza /pro'eza/ f achievement

profa|nar /profa'nar/ vt desecrate; ~**no** a profane

profecia /profe'sia/ f prophecy

proferir /profe'rir/ vt utter; give <*discurso, palestra*>; pass <*sentença*>

profes|sar /profe'sar/ vt profess; ~**so** /ɛ/ a professed; <*político etc*> seasoned; ~**sor** m teacher; ~**sor catedrático** professor

pro|feta /pro'fɛta/ m prophet; ~**fético** a prophetic; ~**fetizar** vt prophesy

profissão /profi'sãw/ f profession

profissio|nal /profisio'naw/ (pl ~**nais**) a & m/f professional; ~**nalismo** m professionalism; ~**nalizante** a vocational; ~**nalizar-se** vpr <*esportista etc*> turn professional

profun|didade /profũdʒi'dadʒi/ f depth; ~**do** a deep; <*sentimento etc*> profound

profusão /profu'zãw/ f profusion

prog|nosticar /prognostʃi'kar/ vt forecast; ~**nóstico** m forecast; (*med*) prognosis

progra|ma /pro'grama/ m programme; (*de computador*) program; (*diversão*) thing to do; ~**mação** f programming; ~**mador** m programmer; ~**mar** vt plan; program <*computador etc*>; ~**mável** (pl ~**máveis**) a programmable

progredir /progre'dʒir/ vi progress

progres|são /progre'sãw/ f progression; ~**sista** a & m/f progressive; ~**sivo** a progressive; ~**so** /ɛ/ m progress

proi|bição /proibi'sãw/ f ban (de on); ~**bido** a forbidden; ~**bir** vt forbid (alg de s.o. to); ban <*livro, importações etc*>; ~**bitivo** a prohibitive

proje|ção /proʒe'sãw/ f projection; ~**tar** vt plan <*viagem, estrada etc*>; design <*casa, carro etc*>; project <*filme, luz*>

projé|til /pro'ʒɛtʃiw/ (pl ~**teis**) m projectile

proje|tista /proʒe'tʃista/ m/f designer; ~**to** /ɛ/ m project; (*de casa, carro*) design; ~**to de lei** bill; ~**tor** m projector

prol /prɔw/ m **em** ~ **de** on behalf of

prole /'prɔli/ f offspring; ~**tariado** m proletariat; ~**tário** a & m proletarian

prolife|ração /prolifera'sãw/ f proliferation; ~**rar** vi proliferate

prolífico /pro'lifiku/ a prolific

prolixo /pro'liksu/ a verbose, long-winded

prólogo /'prɔlogu/ m prologue

prolon|gado /prolõ'gadu/ a prolonged; ~**gar** vt prolong; ~**gar-se** vpr go on

promessa /pro'mɛsa/ f promise

prome|tedor /promete'dor/ a promising; ~**ter** vt promise □ vi (*dar esperança*) show promise; ~**ter voltar** promise to return

promíscuo /pro'miskuu/ a promiscuous

promis|sor /promi'sor/ a promising; ~**sória** f promissory note

promoção /promo'sãw/ f promotion

promontório /promõ'tɔriu/ m promontory

promo|tor /promo'tor/ m promoter; (*advogado*) prosecutor; ~**ver** vt promote

promulgar /promuw'gar/ vt promulgate

prono|me /pro'nomi/ m pronoun; ~**minal** (pl ~**minais**) a pronominal

pron|tidão /prõtʃi'dãw/ f readiness; **com** ~**tidão** promptly; **estar de** ~**tidão** be at the ready; ~**tificar** vt get ready; ~**tificar-se** vpr volunteer (a to; para for); ~**to** a ready; (*rápido*) prompt □ int that's that; ~**to-socorro** (pl ~**tos-socorros**) m casualty department; (*Port: reboque*) towtruck; ~**tuário** m (*manual*) manual, handbook; (*médico*) notes; (*policial*) record, file

pronúncia /pro'nũsia/ f pronunciation

pronunci|ado /pronũsi'adu/ a pronounced; ~**amento** m pronouncement; ~**ar** vt pronounce

propagar /propa'gar/ vt propagate <*espécie*>; spread <*notícia, idéia, fé*>; ~**se** vpr spread; <*espécie*> propagate

propen|são /propẽ'sãw/ f propensity; ~**so** a inclined (a to)

propiciar /propisi'ar/ vt provide; ~**picio** a propitious

propina /pro'pina/ f bribe; (*Port: escolar*) fee

propor /pro'por/ vt propose; ~**se** vpr set o.s. <*objetivo*>; ~**se a estudar** set out to study

proporção /propor'sãw/ *f* proportion
proporcio|nado /proporsio'nadu/ *a*
proportionate (**a** to); **bem ~nado** well
proportioned; **~nal** (*pl* **~nais**) *a*
proportional; **~nar** *vt* provide
proposi|ção /propozi'sãw/ *f* proposi-
tion; **~tado** *a*, **~tal** (*pl* **~tais**) *a* in-
tentional
propósito /pro'pɔzitu/ *m* intention; **a
~** by the way; **a ~ de** on the subject
of; **chegar a ~** arrive at the right
time; **de ~** on purpose
proposta /pro'pɔsta/ *f* proposal
propriamente /propria'mẽtʃi/ *adv*
strictly; **a casa ~ dita** the house
proper
proprie|dade /proprie'dadʒi/ *f* prop-
erty; (*direito sobre bens*) ownership;
~tário *m* owner; (*de casa alugada*)
landlord
próprio /'prɔpriu/ *a* (*de si*) own;
<*sentido*> literal; <*nome*> proper;
meu ~ carro my own car; **um carro
~ a** car of my own; **o ~ rei** the king
himself; **~ a** peculiar to; **~ para**
suited to
prorro|gação /proxoga'sãw/ *f* exten-
sion; (*de dívida*) deferment; (*em futebol etc*) extra time; **~gar** *vt* extend
<*prazo*>; defer <*pagamento*>
pro|sa /'prɔza/ *f* prose; **~sador** *m*
prose writer; **~saico** *a* prosaic
proscrever /proskre'ver/ *vt* proscribe
prospecto /pros'pɛktu/ *m* (*livro*) brochure; (*folheto*) leaflet
prospe|rar /prospe'rar/ *vi* prosper;
~ridade *f* prosperity
próspero /'prɔsperu/ *a* prosperous
prosse|guimento /prosegi'mẽtu/ *m*
continuation; **~guir** *vt* continue □ *vi*
proceed, go on
prostitu|ição /prostʃitui'sãw/ *f*
prostitution; **~ta** *f* prostitute
pros|tração /prostra'sãw/ *f* debility;
~trado *a* prostrate; **~trar** *vt* prostrate; (*enfraquecer*) debilitate; **~trar-
se** *vpr* prostrate o.s.
protago|nista /protago'nista/ *m/f*
protagonist; **~nizar** *vt* be at the centre of <*acontecimento*>; feature in
<*peça, filme*>
prote|ção /prote'sãw/ *f* protection;
~cionismo *m* protectionism;
~cionista *a* & *m/f* protectionist;
~ger *vt* protect; **~gido** *m* protégé
proteína /prote'ina/ *f* protein
protelar /prote'lar/ *vt* put off
protes|tante /protes'tãtʃi/ *a* & *m/f*
Protestant; **~tar** *vt/i* protest; **~to**
/ɛ/ *m* protest
protetor /prote'tor/ *m* protector □ *a*
protective
protocolo /proto'kɔlu/ *m* protocol;
(*registro*) register

protótipo /pro'tɔtʃipu/ *m* prototype
protuberância /protube'rãsia/ *f*
bulge
pro|va /'prɔva/ *f* (*que comprova*) proof;
(*teste*) trial; (*exame*) exam; (*esportiva*)
competition; (*de livro etc*) proof; *pl* (*na
justiça*) evidence; **à ~va de bala** bul-
letproof; **pôr à ~va** put to the test;
~vado *a* proven; **~var** *vt* try <*comida*>; try on <*roupa*>; try out <*carro,
novo sistema etc*>; (*comprovar*) prove
prová|vel /pro'vavew/ (*pl* **~veis**) *a*
probable
proveito /pro'vejtu/ *m* profit,
advantage; **tirar ~ de** (*beneficiar-se*)
profit from; (*explorar*) take advantage
of; **~so** /o/ *a* useful
proveni|ência /proveni'ẽsia/ *f* origin;
~ente *a* originating (**de** from)
proventos /pro'vẽtus/ *m pl* proceeds
prover /pro'ver/ *vt* provide (**de** with)
provérbio /pro'vɛrbiu/ *m* proverb
proveta /pro'veta/ *f* test tube; **bebê de
~** test-tube baby
provi|dência /provi'dẽsia/ *f* (*medida*)
measure, step; (*divina*) providence;
tomar ~dências take steps, take
action; (*enfatizar*) get hold
of, provide; (*resolver*) see to, take care
of □ *vi* take action
província /pro'vĩsia/ *f* province;
(*longe da cidade*) provinces
provinci|al /provĩsi'aw/ *a* (*pl* **~ais**) *a*
provincial; **~ano** *a* & *m* provincial
provir /pro'vir/ *vi* come (**de** from);
(*resultar*) be due (**de** to)
provi|são /provi'zãw/ *f* provision;
~sório *a* provisional
provo|cação /provoka'sãw/ *f* provoca-
tion; **~cador**, **~cante** *a* provocative;
~car *vt* provoke; (*ocasionar*) cause
proximidade /prosimi'dadʒi/ *f* closeness; *pl* (*imediações*) vicinity
próximo /'prɔsimo/ *a* (*no tempo*) next;
(*perto*) near, close (**de** to); <*parente*>
close; <*futuro*> near □ *m* neighbour,
fellow man
pru|dência /pru'dẽsia/ *f* prudence;
~dente *a* prudent
prumo /'prumu/ *m* plumb line; **a ~**
vertically
prurido /pru'ridu/ *m* itch
pseudônimo /psew'donimu/ *m*
pseudonym
psica|nálise /psika'nalizi/ *f* psycho-
analysis; **~nalista** *m/f* psychoana-
lyst
psi|cologia /psikolo'ʒia/ *f* psycho-
logy; **~cológico** *a* psychological;
~cólogo *m* psychologist
psico|pata /psiko'pata/ *m/f* psycho-
path; **~se** /ɔ/ *f* psychosis;
~terapeuta *m/f* psychotherapist;
~terapia *f* psycho-therapy

psicótico /pisiˈkɔtʃiku/ *a* & *m* psychotic

psique /piˈsiki/ *f* psyche

psiqui|atra /pisikiˈatra/ *m/f* psychiatrist; **~atria** *f* psychiatry; **~átrico** *a* psychiatric

psíquico /piˈsikiku/ *a* psychological

pua /ˈpua/ *f* bit

puberdade /puberˈdadʒi/ *f* puberty

publi|cação /publikaˈsãw/ *f* publication; **~car** *vt* publish

publici|dade /publisiˈdadʒi/ *f* publicity; (*reclame*) advertising; **~tário** *a* publicity; (*de reclame*) advertising □ *m* advertising executive

público /ˈpubliku/ *a* public □ *m* public; (*platéia*) audience; **em ~** in public; **o grande ~** the general public

pudera /puˈdɛra/ *int* no wonder!

pudico /puˈdʒiku/ *a* prudish

pudim /puˈdʒĩ/ *m* pudding

pudor /puˈdor/ *m* modesty, shame

pue|ril /pueˈriw/ (*pl* **~ris**) *a* puerile

pugilis|mo /puʒiˈlizmu/ *m* boxing; **~ta** *m* boxer

pu|ído /puˈidu/ *a* worn through; **~ir** *vt* wear through

pujan|ça /puˈʒãsa/ *f* power; **~te** *a* powerful; (*de saúde*) robust

pular /puˈlar/ *vt* jump (over); (*omitir*) skip □ *vi* jump; **~ de contente** jump for joy; **~ carnaval** celebrate Carnival; **~ corda** skip

pulga /ˈpuwɡa/ *f* flea

pulmão /puwˈmãw/ *m* lung

pulo /ˈpulu/ *m* jump; **dar um ~ em** drop by; **dar ~s** jump up and down

pulôver /puˈlover/ *m* pullover

púlpito /ˈpuwpitu/ *m* pulpit

pul|sar /puwˈsar/ *vi* pulsate; **~seira** *f* bracelet; **~so** *m* (*do braço*) wrist; (*batimento arterial*) pulse

pulular /puluˈlar/ *vi* swarm (**de** with)

pulveri|zador /puwverizaˈdor/ *m* spray; **~zar** *vt* spray <*líquido*>; (*reduzir a pó, fig*) pulverize

pun|gente /pũˈʒẽtʃi/ *a* consuming; **~gir** *vt* afflict

pu|nhado /puˈɲadu/ *m* handful; **~nhal** (*pl* **~nhais**) *m* dagger; **~nhalada** *f* stab wound; **~nho** *m* fist; (*de camisa etc*) cuff; (*de espada*) hilt

pu|nição /puniˈsãw/ *f* punishment; **~nir** *vt* punish; **~nitivo** *a* punitive

pupila /puˈpila/ *f* pupil

purê /puˈre/ *m* purée; **~ de batata** mashed potato

pureza /puˈreza/ *f* purity

pur|gante /purˈɡãtʃi/ *a* & *m* purgative; **~gar** *vt* purge; **~gatório** *m* purgatory

purificar /purifiˈkar/ *vt* purify

puritano /puriˈtanu/ *a* & *m* puritan

puro /ˈpuru/ *a* pure; <*aguardente*> neat; **~ e simples** pure and simple; **~-sangue** (*pl* **~s-sangues**) *a* & *m* thoroughbred

púrpura /ˈpurpura/ *f* a purple

purpurina /purpuˈrina/ *f* glitter

purulento /puruˈlẽtu/ *a* festering

pus /pus/ *m* pus

pusilânime /puziˈlanimi/ *a* faint-hearted

pústula /ˈpustula/ *f* pimple

puta /ˈputa/ *f* whore □ *a invar* (*fam*) **um ~ carro** one hell of a car; **filho da ~** (*chulo*) bastard; **~ que (o) pariu!** (*chulo*) fucking hell!

puto /ˈputu/ *a* (*fam*) furious

putrefazer /putrefaˈzer/ *vi* putrefy

puxa /ˈpuʃa/ *int* gosh

pu|xado /puˈʃadu/ *a* (*fam*) <*exame*> tough; <*trabalho*> hard; <*aluguel, preço*> steep; **~xador** *m* handle; **~xão** *m* pull, tug; **~xa-puxa** *m* toffee; **~xar** *vt* pull; strike up <*conversa*>; bring up <*assunto*>; **~xar de uma perna limp;** **~xar para** (*parecer com*) take after; **~xar por** (*exigir muito de*) push (hard); **~xa-saco** *m* (*fam*) creep

Q

QI /ke i/ *m* IQ

quadra /ˈkwadra/ *f* (*de tênis etc*) court; (*quarteirão*) block; **~do** *a* & *m* square

quadragésimo /kwadraˈʒɛzimu/ *a* fortieth

qua|dril /kwaˈdriw/ (*pl* **~dris**) *m* hip

quadrilha /kwaˈdriʎa/ *f* (*bando*) gang; (*dança*) square dance

quadrinho /kwaˈdriɲu/ *m* frame; **história em ~s** comic strip

quadro /ˈkwadru/ *m* picture; (*pintado*) painting; (*tabela*) table; (*pessoal*) staff; (*equipe*) team; (*de uma peça*) scene; **~-negro** (*pl* **~s-negros**) *m* blackboard

quadruplicar /kwadrupliˈkar/ *vt/i* quadruple

quádruplo /ˈkwadruplu/ *a* quadruple; **~s** *m pl* (*crianças*) quads

qual /kwaw/ (*pl* **quais**) *pron* which (one); **o/a ~** (*coisa*) that, which; (*pessoa*) that, who; **~ é o seu nome?** what's your name?; **seja ~ for a decisão** whatever the decision may be

qualidade /kwaliˈdadʒi/ *f* quality; **na ~ de** in one's capacity as, as

qualifi|cação /kwalifikaˈsãw/ *f* qualification; **~car** *vt* qualify; (*descrever*) describe (**de** as); **~car-se** *vpr* qualify

qualitativo /kwalita'tʃivu/ *a* qualitative

qualquer /kwaw'kɛr/ (*pl* **quaisquer**) *a* any; **um livro** ~ any old book; ~ **um** any one

quando /'kwãdu/ *adv & conj* when; ~ **quer que** whenever; ~ **de** at the time of; ~ **muito** at most

quantia /kwã'tʃia/ *f* amount

quanti|dade /kwãtʃi'dadʒi/ *f* quantity; **uma** ~**dade de** a lot of; **em** ~**dade** in large amounts; ~**ficar** *vt* quantify; ~**tativo** *a* quantitative

quanto /'kwãtu/ *adv & pron* how much; (*pl* how many; ~ **tempo?** how long?; ~ **mais barato melhor** the cheaper the better; **tão alto** ~ **eu** as tall as me; ~ **ri!** how I laughed!; ~ **a** as for; ~ **antes** as soon as possible

quaren|ta /kwa'rẽta/ *a & m* (*f* ~**tona**) forty-year-old; ~**tena** /e/ *f* quarantine

quaresma /kwa'rɛzma/ *f* Lent

quarta /'kwarta/ *f* (*dia*) Wednesday; (*marcha*) fourth (gear); ~**-de-final** (*pl* ~**s-de-final**) *f* quarter final; ~**-feira** (*pl* ~**s-feiras**) *f* Wednesday

quartanista /kwarta'nista/ *m/f* fourth-year (student)

quarteirão /kwarte'rãw/ *m* block

quar|tel /kwar'tɛw/ (*pl* ~**téis**) *m* barracks; ~**tel-general** (*pl* ~**téis-generais**) *m* headquarters

quarteto /kwar'tetu/ *m* quartet; ~ **de cordas** string quartet

quarto /'kwartu/ *a* fourth □ *m* (*parte*) quarter; (*aposento*) bedroom; (*guarda*) watch; **são três e/menos um** ~ (*Port*) it's quarter past/to three; ~ **de banho** (*Port*) bathroom; ~ **de hora** quarter of an hour; ~ **de hóspedes** guest room

quartzo /'kwartzu/ *m* quartz

quase /'kwazi/ *adv* almost, nearly; ~ **nada/nunca** hardly anything/ever

quatro /'kwatru/ *a & m* four; **de** ~ (*no chão*) on all fours; ~**centos** *a & m* four hundred

que /ki/ *a* which, what; ~ **dia é hoje?** what's the date today?; ~ **homem!** what a man!; ~ **triste!** how sad! □ *pron* what; ~ **é** ~ **é?** what is it? □ *pron rel* (*coisa*) which, that; (*pessoa*) who, that; (*interrogativo*) what; **o dia em** ~ … the day when/that … □ *conj* that; (*porque*) because; **espero** ~ **sim/não** I hope so/not

quê /ke/ *pron* what □ *m* **um** ~ something; **não tem de** ~ don't mention it

quebra /'kɛbra/ *f* break; (*de empresa, banco*) crash; (*de força*) cut; **de** ~ in addition; ~**-cabeça** *m* jigsaw (puzzle); (*fig*) puzzle; ~**diço** *a* breakable; ~**do** *a* broken; <*carro*> broken down;

~**dos** *m pl* small change; ~**-galho** (*fam*) *m* stopgap; ~**-mar** *m* breakwater; ~**-molas** *m invar* speed bump; ~**-nozes** *m invar* nutcrackers; ~**-pau** (*fam*) *m* row; ~**-quebra** *m* riot

quebrar /ke'brar/ *vt* break □ *vi* break; <*carro etc*> break down; <*banco, empresa etc*> crash, go bust; ~**-se** *vpr* break

queda /'kɛda/ *f* fall; **ter uma** ~ **por** have a soft spot for; ~**-de-braço** *f* arm wrestling

quei|jeira /ke'ʒera/ *f* cheese dish; ~**jo** *m* cheese; ~**jo prato** cheddar; ~**jo-de-minas** *m* Cheshire cheese

queima /'kejma/ *f* burning; ~**da** *f* forest fire; ~**do** *a* burnt; (*bronzeado*) tanned, brown; **cheiro de** ~**do** smell of burning

queimar /kej'mar/ *vt* burn; (*bronzear*) tan □ *vi* burn; <*lâmpada*> go; <*fusível*> blow; ~**-se** *vpr* burn o.s.; (*bronzear-se*) go brown

queima-roupa /kejma'ʃopa/ *f* **à** ~ point-blank

quei|xa /'keʃa/ *f* complaint; ~**xar-se** *vpr* complain (**de** about)

queixo /'keʃu/ *m* chin; **bater o** ~ shiver

queixoso /ke'ʃozu/ *a* plaintive □ *m* plaintiff

quem /kẽj/ *pron* who; (*a pessoa que*) anyone who, he who; **de** ~ **é este livro?** whose is this book?; ~ **quer que** whoever; **seja** ~ **for** whoever it is; ~ **falou isso fui eu** it was me who said that; ~ **me dera (que)** … I wish …, if only

Quênia /'kenia/ *m* Kenya

queniano /keni'anu/ *a & m* Kenyan

quen|tão /kẽ'tãw/ *m* mulled wine; ~**te** *a* hot; (*com calor agradável*) warm; ~**tura** *f* heat

quepe /'kɛpi/ *m* cap

quer /kɛr/ *conj* ~ … ~ … whether … or …

querer /ke'rer/ *vt/i* want; **quero ir** I want to go; **quero que você vá** I want you to go; **eu queria falar com o Sr X** I'd like to speak to Mr X; **vai** ~ **vir amanhã?** do you want to come tomorrow?; **vou** ~ **um cafezinho** I'd like a coffee; **se você quiser** if you want; **queira sentar** do sit down; ~ **dizer** mean; **quer dizer** (*isto é*) that is to say, I mean

querido /ke'ridu/ *a* dear □ *m* darling

quermesse /ker'mɛsi/ *f* fête, fair

querosene /kero'zeni/ *m* kerosene

questão /kes'tãw/ *m* question; (*assunto*) matter; **em** ~ in question; **fazer** ~ **de** really want to; **não faço** ~ **de ir** I don't mind not going

questio|nar /kestʃio'nar/ *vt/i* question; ~**nário** *m* questionnaire; ~**nável** (*pl* ~**náveis**) *a* questionable

quiabo /ki'abu/ *m* okra

quibe /'kibi/ *m* savoury meatball

quicar /ki'kar/ *vt/i* bounce

quiche /'kiʃi/ *f* quiche

quie|to /ki'etu/ *a* (*calado*) quiet; (*imóvel*) still; ~**tude** *f* quiet

quilate /ki'latʃi/ *m* carat; (*fig*) calibre

quilha /'kiʎa/ *f* keel

quilo /'kilo/ *m* kilo; ~**grama** *m* kilogram; ~**metragem** *f* mileage; ~**métrico** *a* mile-long

quilômetro /ki'lometru/ *m* kilometre

quimbanda /kĩ'bãda/ *m* Afro-Brazilian cult

qui|mera /ki'mɛra/ *f* fantasy; ~**mérico** *a* fanciful

quími|ca /'kimika/ *f* chemistry; ~**co** *a* chemical □ *m* chemist

quimioterapia /kimiotera'pia/ *f* chemotherapy

quimono /ki'mɔnu/ *m* kimono

quina /'kina/ *f* de ~ edgeways

quindim /kĩ'dʒĩ/ *m* sweet made of coconut, sugar and egg yolks

quinhão /ki'ɲãw/ *m* share

quinhentos /ki'ɲetus/ *a & m* five hundred

quinina /ki'nina/ *f* quinine

qüinquagésimo /kwĩkwa'ʒɛzimu/ *a* fiftieth

quinquilharias /kĩkiʎa'rias/ *f pl* knick-knacks

quinta¹ /'kĩta/ *f* (*fazenda*) farm

quinta² /'kĩta/ *f* (*dia*) Thursday; ~**-feira** (*pl* ~**s-feiras**) *f* Thursday

quin|tal /kĩ'taw/ (*pl* ~**tais**) *m* back yard

quinteiro /kĩ'tajru/ *m* (*Port*) farmer

quinteto /kĩ'tetu/ *m* quintet

quin|to /'kĩtu/ *a & m* fifth; ~**tuplo** *a* fivefold; ~**tuplos** *m pl* (*crianças*) quins

quinze /'kĩzi/ *a & m* fifteen; às dez e ~ at quarter past ten; são ~ para as dez it's quarter to ten; ~**na** /e/ *f* fortnight; ~**nal** (*pl* ~**nais**) *a* fortnightly; ~**nalmente** *adv* fortnightly

quiosque /ki'ɔski/ *m* (*banca*) kiosk; (*no jardim*) gazebo

quiro|mância /kiro'mãsia/ *f* palmistry; ~**mante** *m/f* palmist

quisto /'kistu/ *m* cyst

quitan|da /ki'tãda/ *f* grocer's (shop); ~**deiro** *m* grocer

qui|tar /ki'tar/ *vt* pay off <*dívida*>; ~**te a estar** ~**te** be quits

quociente /kwosi'etʃi/ *m* quotient

quórum /'kwɔrũ/ *m* quorum

R

rã /xã/ *f* frog

rabanete /xaba'netʃi/ *m* radish

rabear /xabi'ar/ *vi* <*caminhão*> jackknife

rabino /xa'binu/ *m* rabbi

rabis|car /xabis'kar/ *vt* scribble □ *vi* (*escrever mal*) scribble; (*fazer desenhos*) doodle; ~**co** *m* doodle

rabo /'xabu/ *m* (*de animal*) tail; com o ~ do olho out of the corner of one's eye; ~**-de-cavalo** (*pl* ~**s-de-cavalo**) *m* pony tail

rabugento /xabu'ʒetu/ *a* grumpy

raça /'xasa/ *f* (*de homens*) race; (*de animais*) breed

ração /xa'sãw/ *f* (*de comida*) ration; (*para animal*) food

racha /'xaʃa/ *f* crack; ~**dura** *f* crack

rachar /xa'ʃar/ *vt* (*dividir*) split; (*abrir fendas em*) crack; chop <*lenha*>; split <*despesas*> □ *vi* (*dividir-se*) split; (*apresentar fendas*) crack; (*ao pagar*) split the cost

raci|al /xasi'aw/ (*pl* ~**ais**) *a* racial

racio|cinar /xasiosi'nar/ *vi* reason; ~**cínio** *m* reasoning; ~**nal** (*pl* ~**nais**) *a* rational; ~**nalizar** *vt* rationalize

racio|namento /xasiona'metu/ *m* rationing; ~**nar** *vt* ration

racis|mo /xa'sizmu/ *m* racism; ~**ta** *a & m/f* racist

radar /xa'dar/ *m* radar

radia|ção /xadʒia'sãw/ *f* radiation; ~**dor** *m* radiator

radialista /xadʒia'lista/ *m/f* radio announcer

radiante /xadʒi'ãtʃi/ *a* (*de alegria*) overjoyed

radi|cal /xadʒi'kaw/ (*pl* ~**cais**) *a & m* radical; ~**car-se** *vpr* settle

rádio¹ /'xadʒiu/ *m* radio □ *f* radio station

rádio² /'xadʒiu/ *m* (*elemento*) radium

radioati|vidade /xadioatʃivi'dadʒi/ *f* radioactivity; ~**vo** *a* radioactive

radiodifusão /xadʒiodʒifu'zãw/ *f* broadcasting

radiogra|far /xadʒiogra'far/ *vt* X-ray <*pulmões*, *osso etc*>; radio <*mensagem*>; ~**fia** *f* X-ray

radiolo|gia /xadʒiolo'ʒia/ *f* radiology; ~**gista** *m/f* radiologist

radio|novela /xadʒiono'vɛla/ *f* radio serial; ~**patrulha** *f* patrol car; ~**táxi** *m* radio taxi; ~**terapia** *f* radiotherapy, ray treatment

raia /'xaja/ *f* (*em corrida*) lane; (*peixe*) ray

rainha /xa'iɲa/ f queen; ~-mãe f queen mother

raio /'xaju/ m (de luz etc) ray; (de círculo) radius; (de roda) spoke; (relâmpago) bolt of lightning; ~ de ação range

rai|va /'xajva/ f rage; (doença) rabies; estar com ~va be furious (de with); ter ~va de alg have it in for s.o.; ~voso a furious; <cachorro> rabid

raiz /xa'iz/ f root; ~ quadrada/cúbica square/cube root

ra|jada /xa'ʒada/ f (de vento) gust; (de tiros) burst

ra|lador /xala'dor/ m grater; ~lar vt grate

ralé /xa'lɛ/ f rabble

ralhar /xa'ʎar/ vi scold

ralo¹ /'xalu/ m (ralador) grater; (de escoamento) drain

ralo² /'xalu/ a <cabelo> thinning; <sopa, tecido> thin; <vegetação> sparse; <café> weak

ra|mal /xa'maw/ (pl ~mais) m (telefone) extension; (de ferrovia) branch line

ramalhete /xama'ʎetʃi/ m posy, bouquet

ramifi|cação /xamifika'sãw/ f branch; ~car-se vi branch off

ramo /'xamu/ m branch; (profissional etc) field; (buquê) bunch; **Domingo de Ramos** Palm Sunday

rampa /'xãpa/ f ramp

rancor /xã'kor/ m resentment; ~oso /o/ a resentful

rançoso /xã'sozu/ a rancid

ran|ger /xã'ʒer/ vt grind <dentes> □ vi creak; ~gido m creak

ranhura /xa'ɲura/ f groove; (para moedas) slot

rapariga /xapa'riga/ f (Port) girl

rapaz /xa'pas/ m boy

rapé /xa'pɛ/ m snuff

rapidez /xapi'des/ f speed

rápido /'xapidu/ a fast □ adv <fazer> quickly; <andar> fast

rapina /xa'pina/ f ave de ~ bird of prey

rapo|sa /xa'poza/ f vixen; ~so m fox

rapsódia /xap'sɔdʒia/ f rhapsody

rap|tar /xap'tar/ vt abduct, kidnap <criança>; ~to m abduction, kidnapping (de criança)

raquete /xa'kɛtʃi/ f, (Port) **raqueta** /xa'keta/ f racquet

raquítico /xa'kitʃiku/ a puny

ra|ramente /xara'mẽtʃi/ adv rarely; ~ridade f rarity; ~ro a rare □ adv rarely

rascunho /xas'kuɲu/ m rough version, draft

ras|gado /xaz'gadu/ a torn; (fig)

<elogios etc> effusive; ~gão m tear; ~gar vt tear; (em pedaços) tear up □ vi, ~gar-se vpr tear; ~go m tear; (fig) burst

raso /'xazu/ a <água> shallow; <sapato> flat; <colher etc> level

ras|pão /xas'pãw/ m graze; atingir de ~pão graze; ~par vt shave <cabeça, pêlos>; plane <madeira>; (para limpar) scrape; (tocar de leve) graze; ~par em scrape

ras|teiro /xas'teru/ a <planta> creeping; <animal> crawling; ~tejante a crawling; <voz> slurred; ~tejar vi crawl

rasto /'xastu/ m veja **rastro**

ras|trear /xastri'ar/ vt track <satélite etc>; scan <céu, corpo etc>; ~tro m trail

ratear¹ /xatʃi'ar/ vi <motor> miss

ra|tear² /xatʃi'ar/ vt share; ~teio m sharing

ratifi|cação /xatʃifika'sãw/ f ratification; ~car vt ratify

rato /'xatu/ m rat; (camundongo) mouse; ~eira f mousetrap

ravina /xa'vina/ f ravine

razão /xa'zãw/ f reason; (proporção) ratio □ m ledger; à ~ de at the rate of; em ~ de on account of; ter ~ be right; não ter ~ be wrong

razoá|vel /xazo'avew/ (pl ~veis) a reasonable

ré¹ /xɛ/ f (na justiça) defendant

ré² /xɛ/ f (marcha) reverse; dar ~ reverse

reabastecer /xeabaste'ser/ vt/i refuel

reabilitar /xeabili'tar/ vt rehabilitate

rea|ção /xea'sãw/ f reaction; ~ção em cadeia chain reaction; ~cionário a & m reactionary

readmitir /xeadʒimi'tʃir/ vt reinstate <funcionário>

reagir /xea'ʒir/ vi react; <doente> respond

reajus|tar /xeaʒus'tar/ vt readjust; ~te m adjustment

re|al¹ /xe'aw/ (pl ~ais) a (verdadeiro) real; (da realeza) royal

real|çar /xeaw'sar/ vt highlight; ~ce m prominence

realejo /xea'leʒu/ m barrel organ

realeza /xea'leza/ f royalty

realidade /xeali'dadʒi/ f reality

realimentação /xealimẽta'sãw/ f feedback

realis|mo /xea'lizmu/ m realism; ~ta a realistic □ m/f realist

reali|zado /xeali'zadu/ a <pessoa> fulfilled; ~zar vt (fazer) carry out; (tornar real) realize <sonho, capital>; ~zar-se vpr <sonho> come true; <pessoa> fulfil o.s.; <casamento, reunião etc> take place

realmente /xeaw'mẽtʃi/ *adv* really
reaparecer /xeapare'ser/ *vi* reappear
reativar /xeatʃi'var/ *vt* reactivate
reaver /xea'ver/ *vt* get back
reavivar /xeavi'var/ *vt* revive
rebaixar /xebaj'ʃar/ *vt* lower < *preço*>; (*fig*) demean □ *vi* < *preços*> drop; ~se *vpr* demean o.s.
rebanho /xe'baɲu/ *m* herd; (*fiéis*)flock
reba|te /xe'batʃi/ *m* alarm; ~ter *vt* return < *bola*>; refute < *acusação*>; (*à máquina*) retype
rebelar-se /xebe'larsi/ *vpr* rebel
rebel|de /xe'bɛwdʒi/ *a* rebellious □ *m/f* rebel; ~dia *f* rebelliousness
rebelião /xebeli'ãw/ *f* rebellion
reben|tar /xebẽ'tar/ *vt/i* veja **arrebentar**; ~to *m* (*de planta*) shoot; (*descendente*) offspring
rebite /xe'bitʃi/ *m* rivet
rebobinar /xebobi'nar/ *vt* rewind
rebo|cador /xeboka'dor/ *m* tug; ~car *vt* (*tirar*) tow; (*cobrir com reboco*) plaster; ~co /o/ *m* plaster
rebolar /xebo'lar/ *vi* swing one's hips
reboque /xe'bɔki/ *m* towing; (*veículo a* ~) trailer; (*com guindaste*) tow-truck; a ~ on tow
rebuçado /xebu'sadu/ *m* (*Port*) sweet, (*Amer*) candy
rebuliço /xebu'lisu/ *m* commotion
rebuscado /xebus'kadu/ *a* récherché
recado /xe'kadu/ *m* message
reca|ída /xeka'ida/ *f* relapse; ~ir *vi* relapse; < *acento, culpa*> fall
recal|cado /xekaw'kadu/ *a* repressed; ~car *vt* repress
recanto /xe'kãtu/ *m* nook, recess
recapitular /xekapitu'lar/ *vt* review □ *vi* recap
reca|tado /xeka'tadu/ *a* reserved, withdrawn; ~to *m* reserve
recear /xesi'ar/ *vt/i* fear (*por* for)
rece|ber /xese'ber/ *vt* receive; entertain < *convidados*> □ *vi* (~ *ber salário*) get paid; (~ *ber convidados*) entertain; ~bimento *m* receipt
receio /xe'seju/ *m* fear
recei|ta /xe'sejta/ *f* (*de cozinha*) recipe; (*médica*) prescription; (*dinheiro*) revenue; ~tar *vt* prescribe
recém-casados /xesẽjka'zadus/ *m pl* newly-weds; ~-chegado *m* new-comer; ~-nascido *a* newborn □ *m* newborn child, baby
recente /xe'sẽtʃi/ *a* recent; ~mente *adv* recently
receoso /xese'ozu/ *a* (*apreensivo*) afraid
recep|ção /xesep'sãw/ *f* reception; (*Port: de carta*) receipt; ~cionar *vt* receive; ~cionista *m/f* receptionist; ~táculo *m* receptacle; ~tivo *a* receptive; ~tor *m* receiver

reces|são /xese'sãw/ *f* recession; ~so /ɛ/ *m* recess
re|chear /xeʃi'ar/ *vt* stuff < *frango, assado*>; fill < *empada*>; ~cheio *m* (*para frango etc*) stuffing; (*de empada etc*) filling
rechonchudo /xeʃõ'ʃudu/ *a* plump
recibo /xe'sibu/ *m* receipt
reciclar /xesik'lar/ *vt* recycle
recife /xe'sifi/ *m* reef
recinto /xe'sĩtu/ *m* enclosure
recipiente /xesipi'ẽtʃi/ *m* container
reciprocar /xesipro'kar/ *vt* reciprocate
recíproco /xe'siproku/ *a* reciprocal; < *sentimento*> mutual
reci|tal /xesi'taw/ (*pl* ~tais) *m* recital; ~tar *vt* recite
recla|mação /xeklama'sãw/ *f* complaint; (*no seguro*) claim; ~mar *vt* claim □ *vi* complain (**de** about); (*no seguro*) claim; ~me *m*, (*Port*) ~mo *m* advertising
reclinar-se /xekli'narsi/ *vpr* recline
recluso /xe'kluzu/ *a* reclusive □ *m* recluse
recobrar /xeko'brar/ *vt* recover; ~se *vpr* recover
recolher /xeko'ʎer/ *vt* collect; (*retirar*) withdraw; ~se *vpr* retire
recomeçar /xekome'sar/ *vt/i* start again
recomen|dação /xekomẽda'sãw/ *f* recommendation; ~dar *vt* recommend; ~dável (*pl* ~dáveis) *a* advisable
recompen|sa /xekõ'pẽsa/ *f* reward; ~sar *vt* reward
reconcili|ação /xekõsilia'sãw/ *f* reconciliation; ~ar *vt* reconcile; ~ar-se *vpr* be reconciled
reconhe|cer /xekoɲe'ser/ *vt* recognize; (*admitir*) acknowledge; (*mil*) reconnoitre; identify < *corpo*>; ~cimento *m* recognition; (*gratidão*) gratitude; (*mil*) reconnaissance; (*de corpo*) identification; ~cível (*pl* ~cíveis) *a* recognizable
reconsiderar /xekõside'rar/ *vt/i* reconsider
reconstituir /xekõstʃitu'itʃi/ *m* tonic
reconstituir /xekõstʃitu'ir/ *vt* reform; reconstruct < *crime, cena*>
reconstruir /xekõstru'ir/ *vt* rebuild
recor|dação /xekorda'sãw/ *f* recollection; (*objeto*) memento; ~dar *vt* recollect; ~dar-se (**de**) recall
recor|de /xe'kɔrdʒi/ *a invar & m* record; ~dista *a* record-breaking □ *m/f* record-holder
recorrer /xeko'xer/ *vi* ~ a turn to < *médico, amigo*>; resort to < *violência, tática*>; ~ **de** appeal against

recor|tar /xekor'tar/ vt cut out; ~te /ɔ/ m cutting, (*Amer*) clipping

recostar /xekos'tar/ vt lean back; ~se vpr lean back

recreio /xe'kreju/ m recreation; (*na escola*) break

recriar /xekri'ar/ vt recreate

recriminação /xekrimina'sãw/ f recrimination

recrudescer /xekrude'ser/ vi intensify

recru|ta /xe'kruta/ m/f recruit; ~tamento m recruitment; ~tar vt recruit

recu|ar /xeku'ar/ vi move back; <*tropas*> retreat; (*no tempo*) go back; (*ceder*) back down; (*não cumprir*) back out (de of) □ vt move back; ~o m retreat; (*fig: de intento*) climbdown

recupe|ração /xekupera'sãw/ f recovery; ~rar vt recover; make up <*atraso, tempo perdido*>; ~rar-se vpr recover (de from)

recurso /xe'kursu/ m resort; (*coisa útil*) resource; (*na justiça*) appeal; *pl* resources

recu|sa /xe'kuza/ f refusal; ~sar vt refuse; turn down <*convite, oferta*>; ~sar-se vpr refuse (a to)

reda|ção /xeda'sãw/ f (de livro, contrato) draft; (*pessoal*) editorial staff; (*seção*) editorial department; (*na escola*) composition; ~tor m editor

rede /'xedʒi/ f net; (*para deitar*) hammock; (*fig: sistema*) network

rédea /'xedʒia/ f rein

redemoinho /xedemo'iɲu/ m veja rodamoinho

reden|ção /xedẽ'sãw/ f redemption; ~tor a redeeming □ m redeemer

redigir /xedʒi'ʒir/ vt draw up <*contrato*>; write <*artigo*>; edit <*dicionário*>

redimir /xedʒi'mir/ vt redeem

redobrar /xedo'brar/ vt redouble

redon|deza /xedõ'deza/ f roundness; *pl* vicinity; ~do a round

redor /xe'dor/ m ao ou em ~ de around

redução /xedu'sãw/ f reduction

redun|dante /xedũ'dãtʃi/ a redundant; ~dar vi ~dar em develop into

redu|zido /xedu'zidu/ a limited; (*pequeno*) small; ~zir vt reduce; ~zir-se vpr (*ficar reduzido*) be reduced (a to); (*resumir-se*) come down (a to)

reeleger /xeele'ʒer/ vt re-elect; ~se vpr be re-elected

reeleição /xeelej'sãw/ f re-election

reembol|sar /xeẽbow'sar/ vt reimburse <*pessoa*>; refund <*dinheiro*>; ~so /o/ m refund; ~so postal cash on delivery

reencarnação /xeẽkarna'sãw/ f reincarnation

reentrância /xeẽ'trãsia/ f recess

reescalonar /xeeskalo'nar/ vt reschedule

reescrever /xeeskre'ver/ vt rewrite

refastelar-se /xefaste'larsi/ vpr stretch out

refazer /xefa'zer/ vt redo; rebuild <*vida*>; ~se vpr recover (de from)

refei|ção /xefej'sãw/ f meal; ~tório m dining hall

refém /xe'fẽj/ m hostage

referência /xefe'rẽsia/ f reference; com ~ a with reference to

referendum /xefe'rẽdũ/ m referendum

refe|rente /xefe'rẽtʃi/ a ~rente a regarding; ~rir vt report; ~rir-se vpr refer (a to)

refestelar-se /xefeste'larsi/ vpr (*Port*) veja refastelar-se

re|fil /xe'fiw/ (*pl* ~fis) m refill

refi|nado /xefi'nadu/ a refined; ~namento m refinement; ~nar vt refine; ~naria f refinery

refle|tido /xefle'tʃidu/ a <*decisão*> well-thought-out; <*pessoa*> thoughtful; ~tir vt/i reflect; ~tir-se vpr be reflected; ~xão /ks/ f reflection; ~xivo /ks/ a reflexive; ~xo /ɛks/ a <*luz*> reflected; <*ação*> reflex □ m (de luz etc) reflection; (*físico*) reflex; (*no cabelo*) streak

refluxo /xe'fluksu/ m ebb

refo|gado /xefo'gadu/ m lightly fried mixture of onions and garlic; ~gar vt fry lightly

refor|çar /xefor'sar/ vt reinforce; ~ço /o/ m reinforcement

refor|ma /xe'fɔrma/ f (da lei etc) reform; (*na casa etc*) renovation; (de militar) discharge; (*pensão*) pension; ~ma ministerial cabinet reshuffle; ~mado a reformed; (*Port: aposentado*) retired □ m (*Port*) pensioner; ~mar vt reform <*lei, sistema etc*>; renovate <*casa, prédio*>; (*Port: aposentar*) retire; ~mar-se vpr (*Port: aposentar-se*) retire; <*criminoso*> reform; ~matório m reform school; ~mista a & m/f reformist

refratário /xefra'tariu/ a <*tigela etc*> ovenproof, heatproof

refrear /xefri'ar/ vt rein in <*cavalo*>; (*fig*) curb, keep in check <*paixões etc*>; ~se vpr restrain o.s.

refrega /xe'frega/ f clash, fight

refres|cante /xefres'kãtʃi/ a refreshing; ~car vt freshen, cool <*ar*>; refresh <*pessoa, memória etc*> □ vi get cooler; ~car-se vpr refresh o.s.; ~co /e/ m (*bebida*) soft drink; *pl* refreshments refrige|rado /xefriʒe'radu/ a cooled; <casa etc> air-conditioned; (na geladeira) refrigerated; ~rador m refrigerator; ~rante m soft drink; ~rar vt keep cool; (na geladeira) refrigerate

refugi|ado /xefuʒi'adu/ m refugee; ~ar-se vpr take refuge

refúgio /xe'fuʒiu/ m refuge

refugo /xe'fugu/ m waste, refuse

refutar /xefu'tar/ vt refute

regaço /xe'gasu/ m lap

regador /xega'dor/ m watering can

regalia /xega'lia/ f privilege

regar /xe'gar/ vt water

regata /xe'gata/ f regatta

regatear /xegatʃi'ar/ vi bargain, haggle

re|gência /xe'ʒẽsia/ f (de verbo etc) government; ~gente m/f (de orquestra) conductor; ~ger vt govern □ vi rule

região /xeʒi'ãw/ f region; (de cidade etc) area

regi|me /xe'ʒimi/ m regime; (dieta) diet; fazer ~me diet; ~mento m (militar) regiment; (regulamento) regulations

régio /'xeʒiu/ a regal

regio|nal /xeʒio'naw/ (pl ~nais) a regional

regis|trador /xeʒistra'dor/ a caixa ~tradora cash register; ~trar vt register; (anotar) record; ~tro m (lista) register; (de um fato, em banco de dados) record; (ato de ~trar) registration

rego /'xegu/ m (de arado) furrow; (de roda) rut; (para escoamento) ditch

regozi|jar /xegozi'ʒar/ vt delight; ~jar-se vpr be delighted; ~jo m delight

regra /'xɛgra/ f rule; pl (menstruações) periods; em ~ as a rule

regres|sar /xegre'sar/ vi return; ~sivo a regressive; contagem ~siva countdown; ~so /ɛ/ m return

régua /'xɛgwa/ f ruler

regu|lagem /xegu'laʒẽ/ f (de carro) tuning; ~lamento m regulations; ~lar a regular; <estatura, qualidade etc> average □ vt regulate; tune <carro, motor>; set <relógio> □ vi work; ~lar-se por go by, be guided by; ~laridade f regularity; ~larizar vt regularize

regurgitar /xegurʒi'tar/ vt bring up

rei /xej/ m king; ~nado m reign

reincidir /xeĩsi'dʒir/ vi <criminoso> reoffend

reino /'xejnu/ m kingdom; (fig: da fantasia etc) realm; Reino Unido United Kingdom

reiterar /xejte'rar/ vt reiterate

reitor /xej'tor/ m chancellor, (Amer) president

reivindi|cação /xejvĩdʒika'sãw/ f demand; ~car vt claim, demand

rejei|ção /xeʒej'sãw/ f rejection; ~tar vt reject

rejuvenescer /xeʒuvene'ser/ vt rejuvenate □ vi be rejuvenated

rela|ção /xela'sãw/ f relationship; (relatório) account; (lista) list; pl relations; com ou em ~ a in relation to, regarding

relacio|namento /xelasiona'mẽtu/ m relationship; ~nar vt relate (com to); (listar) list; ~nar-se vpr relate (com to)

relações-públicas /xelasõjs'publikas/ m/f invar public-relations person

relâmpago /xe'lãpagu/ m flash of lightning; pl lightning □ a lightning; num ~ in a flash

relampejar /xelãpe'ʒar/ vi flash; relampejou there was a flash of lightning

relance /xe'lãsi/ m glance; olhar de ~ glance (at)

rela|tar /xela'tar/ vt relate; ~tivo a relative; ~to m account; ~tório m report

rela|xado /xela'ʃadu/ a relaxed; <disciplina> lax; <pessoa> lazy, complacent; ~xamento m (físico) relaxation; (de pessoa) complacency; ~xante a relaxing □ m tranquillizer; ~xar vt relax □ vi (descansar) relax; (tornar-se omisso) get complacent; ~xar-se vpr relax; ~xe m relaxation

reles /'xɛlis/ a invar <gente> common; <ação> despicable

rele|vância /xele'vãsia/ f relevance; ~vante a relevant; ~var vt emphasize; ~vo /e/ m relief; (importância) prominence

religi|ão /xeliʒi'ãw/ f religion; ~oso /o/ a religious

relin|char /xelĩ'ʃar/ vi neigh; ~cho m neighing

relíquia /xe'likia/ f relic

relógio /xe'lɔʒiu/ m clock; (de pulso) watch

relu|tância /xelu'tãsia/ f reluctance; ~tante a reluctant; ~tar vi be reluctant (em to)

reluzente /xelu'zẽtʃi/ a shining, gleaming

relva /'xɛwva/ f grass; ~do m lawn

remador /xema'dor/ m rower

remanescente /xemane'sẽtʃi/ a remaining □ m remainder

remar /xe'mar/ vt/i row

rema|tar /xema'tar/ vt finish off; ~te m finish; (adorno) finishing touch; (de piada) punch line

remediar /xemedʒi'ar/ vt remedy

remédio /xe'medʒiu/ m (contra doença) medicine, drug; (a problema etc) remedy

remelento /xeme'lẽtu/ a bleary

remen|dar /xemẽ'dar/ vt mend; (com pedaço de pano) patch; ~**do** m mend; (pedaço de pano) patch

remessa /xe'mɛsa/ f (de mercadorias) shipment; (de dinheiro) remittance

reme|tente /xeme'tẽtʃi/ m/f sender; ~**ter** vt send <mercadorias, dinheiro etc>; refer <leitor> (**a** to)

remexer /xeme'ʃer/ vt shuffle <papéis>; stir up <poeira, lama>; wave <braços> □ vi rummage; ~**-se** vpr move around

reminiscência /xemini'sẽsia/ f reminiscence

remir /xe'mir/ vt redeem; ~**-se** vpr redeem o.s.

remissão /xemi'sãw/ f (de pecados) redemption; (de doença, pena) remission; (num livro) cross-reference

remo /'xemu/ m oar; (esporte) rowing

remoção /xemo'sãw/ f removal

remoinho /xemo'iɲu/ m (Port) veja **rodamoinho**

remontar /xemõ'tar/ vi ~ **a** <coisa> date back to; <pessoa> think back to

remorso /xe'mɔrsu/ m remorse

remo|to /xe'mɔtu/ a remote; ~**ver** vt remove

remune|ração /xemunera'sãw/ f payment; ~**rador** a profitable; ~**rar** vt pay

rena /'xena/ f reindeer

re|nal /xe'naw/ (pl ~**nais**) a renal, kidney

Renascença /xena'sẽsa/ f Renaissance

renas|cer /xena'ser/ vi be reborn; ~**cimento** m rebirth

renda[1] /'xẽda/ f (tecido) lace

ren|da[2] /'xẽda/ f income; (Port: aluguel) rent; ~**der** bring in, yield <lucro>; earn <juros>; fetch <preço>; bring <resultado> □ vi <investimento, trabalho, ação> go a long way; <produto comprado> give value for money; ~**der-se** vpr surrender; ~**dição** f surrender; ~**dimento** m (renda) income; (de investimento, terreno) yield; (de motor etc) output; (de produto comprado) value for money; ~**doso** /o/ a profitable

rene|gado /xene'gadu/ a & m renegade; ~**gar** vt renounce

renhido /xe'ɲidu/ a hard-fought

Reno /'xenu/ m Rhine

reno|mado /xeno'madu/ a renowned; ~**me** /o/ m renown

reno|vação /xenova'sãw/ f renewal; ~**var** vt renew

renque /'xẽki/ m row

ren|tabilidade /xẽtabili'dadʒi/ f profitability; ~**tável** (pl ~**táveis**) a profitable

rente /'xẽtʃi/ adv ~ **a** close to □ a <cabelo> cropped

renúncia /xe'nũsia/ f renunciation (**a** of); (a cargo) resignation (**a** from)

renunciar /xenũsi'ar/ vi <presidente etc> resign; ~ **a** give up; waive <direito>

reorganizar /xeorgani'zar/ vt reorganize

repa|ração /xepara'sãw/ f reparation; (conserto) repair; ~**rar** vt (consertar) repair; make up for <ofensa, injustiça, erro>; make good <danos, prejuízo> □ vi ~**rar (em)** notice; ~**ro** m (conserto) repair

repar|tição /xepartʃi'sãw/ f division; (seção do governo) department; ~**tir** vt divide up

repassar /xepa'sar/ vt revise <matéria, lição>

repatriar /xepatri'ar/ vt repatriate

repe|lente /xepe'lẽtʃi/ a & m repellent; ~**lir** vt repel; reject <ideia, proposta etc>

repensar /xepẽ'sar/ vt/i rethink

repen|te /xe'pẽtʃi/ m **de** ~**te** suddenly; (fam: talvez) maybe; ~**tino** a sudden

reper|cussão /xeperku'sãw/ f repercussion; ~**cutir** vi <som> reverberate; (fig: ter efeito) have repercussions

repertório /xeper'tɔriu/ m (músico etc) repertoire; (lista) list

repe|tição /xepetʃi'sãw/ f repetition; ~**tido** a repeated; ~**tidas vezes** repeatedly; ~**tir** vt repeat □ vi (ao comer) have seconds; ~**tir-se** vpr <pessoa> repeat o.s.; <fato, acontecimento> recur; ~**titivo** a repetitive

repi|car /xepi'kar/ vt/i ring; ~**que** m ring

replay /xe'plej/ (pl ~**s**) m action replay

repleto /xe'plɛtu/ a full up

réplica /'xɛplika/ f reply; (cópia) replica

replicar /xepli'kar/ vt answer □ vi reply

repolho /xe'poʎu/ m cabbage

repor /xe'por/ vt (num lugar) put back; (substituir) replace

reportagem /xepor'taʒẽ/ f (uma) report; (ato) reporting

repórter /xe'pɔrter/ m/f reporter

reposição /xepozi'sãw/ f replacement

repou|sar /xepo'sar/ vt/i rest; ~**so** m rest

repreen|der /xepriẽ'der/ vt rebuke, reprimand; ~**são** f rebuke, reprimand; ~sivel (pl ~siveis) a reprehensible

represa /xe'preza/ f dam

represália /xepre'zalia/ f reprisal

represen|tação /xeprezẽta'sãw/ f representation; (espetáculo) performance; (ofício de ator) acting; ~tante m/f representative; ~tar vt represent; (no teatro) perform <peça>; play <papel, personagem> □ vi <ator> act; ~tativo a representative

repres|são /xepre'sãw/ f repression; ~sivo a repressive

repri|mido /xepri'midu/ a repressed; ~mir vt repress

reprise /xe'prizi/ f (na TV) repeat; (de filme) rerun

reprodu|ção /xeprodu'sãw/ f reproduction; ~zir vt reproduce; ~zir-se vpr (multiplicar-se) reproduce; (repetir-se) recur

repro|vação /xeprova'sãw/ f disapproval; (em exame) failure; ~var vt (rejeitar) disapprove of; (em exame) fail; ser ~vado <aluno> fail

rép|til /'xɛptʃiw/ (pl ~teis) m reptile

república /xe'publika/ f republic; (de estudantes) hall of residence

republicano /xepubli'kanu/ a & m republican

repudiar /xepudʒi'ar/ vt disown; repudiate <esposa>

repug|nância /xepug'nãsia/ f repugnance; ~nante a repugnant

repul|sa /xe'puwsa/ f repulsion; (recusa) rejection; ~sivo a repulsive

reputação /xeputa'sãw/ f reputation

requebrar /xeke'brar/ vt swing; ~se vpr sway

requeijão /xeke'ʒãw/ m cheese spread, cottage cheese

reque|rer /xeke'rer/ vt (pedir) apply for; (exigir) require; ~rimento m application

requin|tado /xeki'tadu/ a refined; ~tar vt refine; ~te m refinement

requisi|ção /xekizi'sãw/ f requisition; ~tar vt requisition; ~to m requirement

rês /xes/ (pl reses) f head of cattle; pl cattle

rescindir /xesi'dʒir/ vt rescind

rés-do-chão /xɛzdu'ʃãw/ m invar (Port) ground floor, (Amer) first floor

rese|nha /xe'zeɲa/ f review; ~nhar vt review

reser|va /xe'zɛrva/ f reserve; (em hotel, avião etc, ressalva) reservation; ~var vt reserve; ~vatório m reservoir; ~vista m/f reservist

resfri|ado /xesfri'adu/ a estar ~ado have a cold □ m cold; ~ar vt cool □ vi get cold; (tornar-se morno) cool down; ~ar-se vpr catch a cold

resga|tar /xezga'tar/ vt (salvar) rescue; (remir) redeem; ~te m (salvamento) rescue; (pago por refém) ransom; (remissão) redemption

resguardar /xezgwar'dar/ vt protect; ~se vpr protect o.s. (de from)

residência /xezi'dẽsia/ f residence

residen|cial /xezidẽsi'aw/ (pl ~ciais) a <bairro> residential; <telefone etc> home; ~te a & m/f resident

residir /xezi'dʒir/ vi reside

resíduo /xe'ziduu/ m residue

resig|nação /xezigna'sãw/ f resignation; ~nado a resigned; ~nar-se vpr resign o.s. (com to)

resina /xe'zina/ f resin

resis|tência /xezis'tẽsia/ f resistance; (de atleta, mental) endurance; (de material, objeto) toughness; ~tente a strong, tough; <tecido, roupa> hardwearing; <planta> hardy; resistant to; ~tir vi (opor ~tência) resist; (aguentar) <pessoa> hold out; <objeto> hold; ~tir a (combater) resist; (aguentar) withstand; ~tir ao tempo stand the test of time

resmun|gar /xezmũ'gar/ vi grumble; ~go m grumbling

resolu|ção /xezolu'sãw/ f resolution; (firmeza) resolve; (de problema) solution; ~to a resolute; ~to a resolved to

resolver /xezow'ver/ vt (esclarecer) sort out; solve <problema, enigma>; (decidir) decide; ~se vpr make up one's mind (a to)

respaldo /xes'pawdu/ m (de cadeira) back; (fig: apoio) backing

respectivo /xespek'tʃivu/ a respective

respei|tabilidade /xespejtabili'dadʒi/ f respectability; ~tador a respectful; ~tar vt respect; ~tável (pl ~táveis) a respectable; ~to m respect (por for); a ~to de about; este ~to in this respect; com ~to a with regard to; dizer ~to a concern; ~toso a respectful

respin|gar /xespĩ'gar/ vt/i splash; ~go m splash

respi|ração /xespira'sãw/ f breathing; ~rador m respirator; ~rar vt/i breathe; ~ratório a respiratory; ~ro m breath; (descanso) break, breather

resplande|cente /xesplãde'sẽtʃi/ a resplendent; ~cer vi shine

resplendor /xesplẽ'dor/ m brilliance; (fig) glory

respon|dão /xespõ'dãw/ a (f ~dona) cheeky; ~der vt/i answer; (com insolência) answer back; ~der a answer; ~der por answer for, take responsibility for

responsabili|dade /xespõsabili-
'dadʒi/ f responsibility; ~**zar** vt hold
responsible (**por** for); ~**zar-se** vpr
take responsibility (**por** for)

responsá|vel /xespõ'savew/ (pl
~**veis**) a responsible (**por** for)

resposta /xes'pɔsta/ f answer

resquício /xes'kisiu/ m vestige, remnant

ressabiado /xesabi'adu/ a wary, suspicious

ressaca /xe'saka/ f (depois de beber)
hangover; (do mar) undertow

ressaltar /xesaw'tar/ vt emphasize □
vi stand out

ressalva /xe'sawva/ f reservation,
proviso; (proteção) safeguard

ressarcir /xesar'sir/ vt refund

resse|cado /xese'kadu/ a <terra>
parched; <pele> dry; ~**car** vt/i dry
up

ressen|tido /xesẽ'tʃidu/ a resentful;
~**timento** m resentment; ~**tir-se de**
(ofender-se) resent; (ser influenciado)
show the effects of

ressequido /xese'kidu/ a veja **ressecado**

resso|ar /xeso'ar/ vi resound; ~**-
nância** f resonance; ~**nante** a
resonant; ~**nar** vi (Port) snore

ressurgimento /xesurʒi'mẽtu/ m resurgence

ressurreição /xesuxej'sãw/ f resur-
rection

ressuscitar /xesusi'tar/ vt revive

restabele|cer /xestabele'ser/ vt re-
store; restore to health <doente>;
~**cer-se** vpr recover; ~**cimento** m
restoration; (de doente) recovery

res|tante /xes'tãtʃi/ a remaining □ m
remainder; ~**tar** vi remain; ~**ta-me
dizer que** ... it remains for me to say
that

restau|ração /xestawra'sãw/ f res-
toration; ~**rante** m restaurant;
~**rar** vt restore

restitu|ição /xestʃitui'sãw/ f return,
restitution; ~**ir** vt (devolver) return;
restore <forma, força etc>; reinstate
<funcionário>

resto /'xɛstu/ m rest; pl (de comida)
left-overs; (de cadáver) remains; **de
~** besides

restrição /xestri'sãw/ f restriction

restringir /xestrĩ'ʒir/ vt restrict

restrito /xes'tritu/ a restricted

resul|tado /xezuw'tadu/ m result;
~**tante** a resulting (de from); ~**tar**
vi result (de from; em in)

resu|mir /xezu'mir/ vt (abreviar)
summarize; (conter em poucas palavras) sum up; ~**mir-se** vpr (ser expresso em poucas palavras) be
summed up; ~**mir-se em** (ser

apenas) come down to; ~**mo** m
summary; **em ~mo** briefly

resvalar /xezva'lar/ vi (sem querer)
slip; (deslizar) slide

reta /'xɛta/ f (linha) straight line; (de
pista etc) straight; ~ **final** home
straight

retaguarda /xeta'gwarda/ f rear-
guard

retalho /xe'taʎu/ m scrap; **a ~** (Port)
retail

retaliação /xetalia'sãw/ f retaliation

retangular /xetãgu'lar/ a rectangu-
lar

retângulo /xe'tãgulu/ m rectangle

retar|dado /xetar'dadu/ a retarded □
m retard; ~**dar** vt delay; ~**datário** m
latecomer

retenção /xetẽ'sãw/ f retention

reter /xe'ter/ vt keep <pessoa>; hold
back <águas, riso, lágrimas>; (na
memória) retain; ~**-se** vpr restrain
o.s.

rete|sado /xete'zadu/ a taut; ~**sar** vt
pull taut

reticência /xetʃi'sẽsia/ f reticence

reti|dão /xetʃi'dãw/ f rectitude;
~**ficar** vt rectify

reti|rada /xetʃi'rada/ f (de tropas) re-
treat; (de dinheiro) withdrawal;
~**rado** a secluded; ~**rar** vt withdraw; (afastar) move away; ~**rar-se**
vpr <tropas> retreat; (afastar-se)
withdraw; (de uma atividade) retire;
~**ro** m retreat

reto /'xɛtu/ a <linha etc> straight;
<pessoa> honest

retocar /xeto'kar/ vt touch up <dese-
nho, maquiagem etc>; alter <texto>

reto|mada /xeto'mada/ f (continua-
ção) resumption; (reconquista) re-
taking; ~**mar** vt (continuar com)
resume; (conquistar de novo) retake

retoque /xe'tɔki/ m finishing touch

retorcer /xetor'ser/ vt twist; ~**-se** vpr
writhe

retóri|ca /xe'tɔrika/ f rhetoric; ~**co** a
rhetorical

retor|nar /xetor'nar/ vi return; ~**no**
m return; (na estrada) turning place;
dar ~no do a U-turn

retrair /xetra'ir/ vt retract, withdraw; ~**-se** vpr (recuar) withdraw;
(encolher-se) retract

retrasa|do /xetra'zadu/ a **a semana
~da** the week before last

retratar[1] /xetra'tar/ vt (desdizer) retract

retra|tar[2] /xetra'tar/ vt (em quadro,
livro) portray, depict; ~**to** m portrait;
(foto) photo; (representação) por-
trayal; ~**to falado** identikit picture

retribuir /xetribu'ir/ vt return
<favor, visita>; repay <gentileza>

retroativo /xetroa'tʃivu/ a retroactive; <pagamento> backdated

retro|ceder /xetrose'der/ vi retreat; (desistir) back down; ~cesso /ɛ/ m retreat; (ao passado) regression

retrógrado /xe'trɔgradu/ a retrógrade

retrospec|tiva /xetrospek'tʃiva/ f retrospective; ~tiva a retrospective; ~to /ɛ/ m look back; em ~to in retrospect

retrovisor /xetrovi'zor/ a & m (espelho) ~ rear-view mirror

retrucar /xetru'kar/ vt/i retort

retum|bante /xetũ'bãtʃi/ a resounding; ~bar vi (re)sound

réu /'xɛw/ m (f ré) r̯é defendant

reumatismo /xewma'tʃizmu/ m rheumatism

reu|nião /xeuni'ãw/ f meeting; (descontraída) get-together; (de família) reunion; ~nião de cúpula summit meeting; ~nir vt bring together <pessoas>; combine <qualidades>; ~nir-se vpr meet; <amigos, familiares> get together; ~nir-se a join

revanche /xe'vãʃi/ f revenge; (jogo) return match

reveillon /xeve'jõ/ (pl ~s) m New Year's Eve

reve|lação /xevela'sãw/ f revelation; (de fotos) developing; (novo talento) promising newcomer; ~lar vt reveal; develop <filme, fotos>; ~lar-se vpr (vir a ser) turn out to be

revelia /xeve'lia/ f à ~ by default; à ~ without the knowledge of

reven|dedor /xevêde'dor/ m dealer; ~der vt resell

rever /xe'ver/ vt (ver de novo) see again; (revisar) revise; (examinar) check

reve|rência /xeve'resia/ f reverence; (movimento do busto) bow; (dobrando os joelhos) curtsey; ~rente a reverent

reverso /xe'vɛrsu/ m reverse; o ~ da medalha the other side of the coin

revés /xe'vɛs/ (pl reveses) m setback

reves|timento /xevestʃi'mẽtu/ m covering; ~tir vt cover

reve|zamento /xeveza'mẽtu/ m alternation; ~zar vt/i alternate; ~zar-se vpr alternate

revi|dar /xevi'dar/ vt return <golpe, insulto>; refute <crítica>; (retrucar) retort □ vi hit back; ~de m response

revigorar /xevigo'rar/ vt strengthen □ vi, ~-se vpr regain one's strength

revi|rar /xevi'rar/ vt turn out <bolsos, gavetas>; turn over <terra>; turn inside out <roupa>; roll <olhos>; ~rar-se vpr toss and turn; ~ravolta /ɔ/ f (na política etc) about-face, about-turn; (da situação) turnabout, dramatic change

revi|são /xevi'zãw/ f (de lições etc) revision; (de máquina, motor) overhaul; (de carro) service; ~são de provas proofreading; ~sar vt revise <provas, lições>; service <carro>; ~sor m (de bilhetes) ticket inspector; ~sor de provas proofreader

revis|ta /xe'vista/ f (para ler) magazine; (teatral) revue; (de tropas etc) review; passar ~ta a review; ~tar vt search

reviver /xevi'ver/ vt relive □ vi revive

revogar /xevo'gar/ vt revoke <lei>; cancel <ordem>

revol|ta /xe'vɔwta/ f (rebelião) revolt; (indignação) disgust; ~tante a disgusting; ~tar vt disgust; ~tar-se vpr (rebelar-se) revolt; (indignar-se) be disgusted; ~to /o/ a <casa, gaveta> upside down; <cabelo> dishevelled; <mar> rough; <mundo, região> troubled; <anos> turbulent

revolu|ção /xevolu'sãw/ f revolution; ~cionar vt revolutionize; ~cionário a & m revolutionary

revolver /xevow'ver/ vt turn over <terra>; roll <olhos>; go through <gavetas, arquivos>

revólver /xe'vowver/ m revolver

re|za /'xɛza/ f prayer; ~zar vi pray □ vt say <missa, oração>; (dizer) state

riacho /xi'aʃu/ m stream

ribalta /xi'bawta/ f footlights

ribanceira /xibã'sera/ f embankment

ribombar /xibõ'bar/ vi rumble

rico /'xiku/ a rich □ m rich man; os ~s the rich

ricochete /xiko'ʃetʃi/ m ricochet; ~ar vi ricochet

ricota /xi'kɔta/ f curd cheese, ricotta

ridicularizar /xidʒikulari'zar/ vt ridicule

ridículo /xi'dʒikulu/ a ridiculous

ri|fa /'xifa/ f raffle; ~far vt raffle

rifão /xi'fãw/ m saying

rifle /'xifli/ m rifle

rigidez /xiʒi'des/ f rigidity

rígido /'xiʒidu/ a rigid

rigor /xi'gor/ m severity; (meticulosidade) rigour; vestido a ~ evening dress; de ~ essential

rigoroso /xigo'rozu/ a strict; <inverno, pena> severe, harsh; <lógica, estudo> rigorous

rijo /'xiʒu/ a stiff; <músculos> firm

rim /xĩ/ m kidney; pl (parte das costas) small of the back

ri|ma /'xima/ f rhyme; ~mar vt/i rhyme

rí|mel /'ximew/ (pl ~meis) m mascara

ringue /'xĩgi/ m ring

rinoceronte /xinose'rõtʃi/ *m* rhinoceros

rinque /'xĩki/ *m* rink

rio /'xio/ *m* river

riqueza /xi'keza/ *f* wealth; *(qualidade)* richness; *pl* riches

rir /xir/ *vi* laugh (**de** at)

risada /xi'zada/ *f* laugh, laughter; **dar ~ laugh**

ris|ca /'xiska/ *f* stroke; *(listra)* stripe; *(do cabelo)* parting; **à ~ca** to the letter; **~car** *vt* (*apagar*) cross out <*erro*>; strike <*fósforo*>; scratch <*mesa, carro etc*>; write off <*amigo etc*>; **~co¹** *m* (*na parede etc*) scratch; *(no papel)* line; *(esboço)* sketch

risco² /'xisku/ *m* risk

riso /'xizu/ *m* laugh; **~nho** /o/ *a* smiling

ríspido /'xispidu/ *a* harsh

rítmico /'xitʃmiku/ *a* rhythmic

ritmo /'xitʃimu/ *m* rhythm

rito /'xitu/ *m* rite

ritu|al /xitu'aw/ (*pl* **~ais**) *a* & *m* ritual

ri|val /xi'vaw/ (*pl* **~vais**) *a* & *m/f* rival; **~validade** *f* rivalry; **~valizar** *vt* rival □ *vi* vie (**com** with)

rixa /'xiʃa/ *f* fight

robô /xo'bo/ *m* robot

robusto /xo'bustu/ *a* robust

roça /'xɔsa/ *f* (*campo*) country

rocambole /xokã'bɔli/ *m* roll

roçar /xo'sar/ *vt* graze; **~ em** brush against

ro|cha /'xɔʃa/ *f* rock; **~chedo** /e/ *m* cliff

roda /'xɔda/ *f* (*de carro etc*) wheel; (*de amigos etc*) circle; **~ da** *f* round; **~do** *a* **saia ~da** full skirt; **~gigante** (*pl* **~s-gigantes**) *f* big wheel, (*Amer*) ferris wheel; **~moinho** *m* (*de vento*) whirlwind; (*na água*) whirlpool; (*fig*) whirl, swirl; **~pé** *m* skirting board, (*Amer*) baseboard

rodar /xo'dar/ *vt* (*fazer girar*) spin; (*viajar por*) go round; do <*quilometragem*>; shoot <*filme*>; run <*programa*> □ *vi* (*girar*) spin; (*de carro*) drive round

rodear /xodʒi'ar/ *vt* (*circundar*) surround; (*andar ao redor de*) go round

rodeio /xo'deju/ *m* (*ao falar*) circumlocution; (*de gado*) round-up; **falar sem ~s** talk straight

rodela /xo'dɛla/ *f* (*de limão etc*) slice; (*peça de metal*) washer

rodízio /xo'dʒiziu/ *m* rota

rodo /'xɔdu/ *m* rake

rodopiar /xodopi'ar/ *vi* spin round

rodovi|a /xodo'via/ *f* highway; **~ária** *f* bus station; **~ário** *a* road; **polícia ~ária** traffic police

ro|edor /xoe'dor/ *m* rodent; **~er** *vt* gnaw; bite <*unhas*>; (*fig*) eat away

rogar /xo'gar/ *vi* request

rojão /xo'ʒãw/ *m* rocket

rol /xɔw/ (*pl* **róis**) *m* roll

rolar /xo'lar/ *vt* roll □ *vi* roll; (*fam*) (*acontecer*) happen

roldana /xow'dana/ *f* pulley

roleta /xo'leta/ *f* (*jogo*) roulette; (*borboleta*) turnstile

rolha /'xoʎa/ *f* cork

roliço /xo'lisu/ *a* <*objeto*> cylindrical; <*pessoa*> plump

rolo /'xolu/ *m* (*de filme, tecido etc*) roll; (*máquina, bobe*) roller; **~ compressor** steamroller; **~ de massa** rolling pin

Roma /'xoma/ *f* Rome

romã /xo'mã/ *f* pomegranate

roman|ce /xo'mãsi/ *m* (*livro*) novel; (*caso*) romance; **~cista** *m/f* novelist

romano /xo'manu/ *a* & *m* Roman

romântico /xo'mãtʃiku/ *a* romantic

romantismo /xomã'tʃizmu/ *m* (*amor*) romance; (*idealismo*) romanticism

romaria /xoma'ria/ *f* pilgrimage

rombo /'xõbu/ *m* hole

Romênia /xo'menia/ *f* Romania

romeno /xo'menu/ *a* & *m* Romanian

rom|per /xõ'per/ *vt* break; break off <*relações*> □ *vi* <*dia*> break; <*sol*> rise; **~per com** break up with; **~pimento** *m* break; (*de relações*) breaking off

ron|car /xõ'kar/ *vi* (*ao dormir*) snore; <*estômago*> rumble; **~co** *m* snoring; (*um*) snore; (*de motor*) roar

ron|da /'xõda/ *f* round, patrol; **~dar** *vt* (*patrulhar*) patrol; (*espreitar*) prowl around □ *vi* <*vigia etc*> patrol; <*animal, ladrão*> prowl around

ronronar /xõxo'nar/ *vi* purr

roque¹ /'xɔki/ *m* (*em xadrez*) rook

ro|que² /'xɔki/ *m* (*música*) rock; **~queiro** *m* rock musician

rosa /'xɔza/ *f* rose □ *a invar* pink; **~do** *a* rosy; <*vinho*> rosé

rosário /xo'zariu/ *m* rosary

rosbife /xoz'bifi/ *m* roast beef

rosca /'xoska/ *f* (*de parafuso*) thread; (*biscoito*) rusk; **farinha de ~** breadcrumbs

roseira /xo'zera/ *f* rosebush

roseta /xo'zeta/ *f* rosette

rosnar /xoz'nar/ *vi* <*cachorro*> growl; <*pessoa*> snarl

rosto /'xostu/ *m* face

rota /'xɔta/ *f* route

rota|ção /xota'sãw/ *f* rotation; **~tividade** *f* turnround; **~tivo** *a* rotating

rotei|rista /xote'rista/ *m/f* scriptwriter; **~ro** *m* (*de viagem*) itinerary;

(*de filme, peça*) script; (*de discussão etc*) outline

roti|na /xoˈtʃina/ *f* routine; ~**neiro** *a* routine

rótula /ˈxɔtula/ *f* kneecap

rotular /xotuˈlar/ *vt* label (**de** as)

rótulo /ˈxɔtulu/ *m* label

rou|bar /xoˈbar/ *vt* steal <*dinheiro, carro etc*>; rob <*pessoa, loja etc*> □ *vi* steal; (*em jogo*) cheat; ~**bo** *m* theft, robbery

rouco /ˈxoku/ *a* hoarse; <*voz*> gravelly

rou|pa /ˈxopa/ *f* clothes; (*uma*) outfit; ~**pa de baixo** underwear; ~**pa de cama** bedclothes; ~**pão** *m* dressing gown

rouquidão /xokiˈdãw/ *f* hoarseness

rouxi|nol /xoʃiˈnɔw/ (*pl* ~**nóis**) *m* nightingale

roxo /ˈxoʃu/ *a* purple

rua /ˈxua/ *f* street

rubéola /xuˈbɛola/ *f* German measles

rubi /xuˈbi/ *m* ruby

rude /ˈxudʒi/ *a* rude

rudimentos /xudʒiˈmẽtus/ *m pl* rudiments, basics

ruela /xuˈɛla/ *f* backstreet

rufar /xuˈfar/ *vi* <*tambor*> roll □ *m* roll

ruga /ˈxuga/ *f* (*na pele*) wrinkle; (*na roupa*) crease

ru|gido /xuˈʒidu/ *m* roar; ~**gir** *vi* roar

ruibarbo /xuiˈbarbu/ *m* rhubarb

ruído /xuˈidu/ *m* noise

ruidoso /xuiˈdozu/ *a* noisy

ruim /xuˈĩ/ *a* bad

ruína /xuˈina/ *f* ruin

ruivo /ˈxuivu/ *a* <*cabelo*> red; <*pessoa*> red-haired □ *m* redhead

rulê /xuˈle/ *a* **gola** ~ roll-neck

rum /xũ/ *m* rum

ru|mar /xuˈmar/ *vi* head (**para** for); ~**mo** *m* course; ~**mo a** heading for; **sem** ~**mo** <*vida*> aimless; <*andar*> aimlessly

rumor /xuˈmor/ *m* (*da rua, de vozes*) hum; (*do trânsito*) rumble; (*boato*) rumour

ru|ral /xuˈraw/ (*pl* ~**rais**) *a* rural

rusga /ˈxuzga/ *f* quarrel, disagreement

rush /xaʃ/ *m* rush hour

Rússia /ˈxusia/ *f* Russia

russo /ˈxusu/ *a & m* Russian

rústico /ˈxustʃiku/ *a* rustic

S

Saará /saaˈra/ *m* Sahara

sábado /ˈsabadu/ *m* Saturday

sabão /saˈbãw/ *m* soap; ~ **em pó** soap powder

sabatina /sabaˈtʃina/ *f* test

sabedoria /sabedoˈria/ *f* wisdom

saber /saˈber/ *vt/i* know (**de** about); (*descobrir*) find out (**de** about) □ *m* knowledge; **eu sei cantar** I know how to sing, I can sing; **sei lá** I've no idea; **que eu saiba** as far as I know

sabiá /sabiˈa/ *m* thrush

sabi|chão /sabiˈʃãw/ *a & m* (*f* ~**chona**) know-it-all

sábio /ˈsabiu/ *a* wise □ *m* wise man

sabone|te /saboˈnetʃi/ *m* bar of soap; ~**teira** *f* soapdish

sabor /saˈbor/ *m* flavour; **ao** ~ **de** at the mercy of

sabo|rear /saboriˈar/ *vt* savour; ~**roso** *a* tasty

sabo|tador /sabotaˈdor/ *m* saboteur; ~**tagem** *f* sabotage; ~**tar** *vt* sabotage

saca /ˈsaka/ *f* sack

sacada /saˈkada/ *f* balcony

sa|cal /saˈkaw/ (*pl* ~**cais**) *a* (*fam*) boring

saca|na /saˈkana/ (*fam*) *a* (*desonesto*) devious; (*lascivo*) dirty-minded, naughty □ *m/f* rogue; ~**nagem** (*fam*) *f* (*esperteza*) trickery; (*sexo*) sex; (*uma*) dirty trick; ~**near** (*fam*) *vt* (*enganar*) do the dirty on; (*amolar*) take the mickey out of

sacar /saˈkar/ *vt/i* withdraw <*dinheiro*>; draw <*arma*>; (*em tênis, vôlei etc*) serve; (*fam*) (*entender*) understand

saçaricar /sasariˈkar/ *vi* play around

sacarina /sakaˈrina/ *f* saccharine

saca-rolhas /sakaˈxoʎas/ *m invar* corkscrew

sacer|dócio /saserˈdɔsiu/ *m* priesthood; ~**dote** /ɔ/ *m* priest; ~**dotisa** *f* priestess

sachê /saˈʃe/ *m* sachet

saciar /sasiˈar/ *vt* satisfy

saco /ˈsaku/ *m* bag; **que** ~! (*fam*) what a pain!; **estar de** ~ **cheio** (**de**) (*fam*) be fed up (with), be sick (of); **encher o** ~ **de alg** (*fam*) get on s.o.'s nerves; **puxar o** ~ **de alg** (*fam*) suck up to s.o.; ~ **de dormir** sleeping bag; ~**la** /ɔ/ *f* bag; ~**lão** *m* wholesale fruit and vegetable market; ~**lejar** *vt* shake

sacramento /sakraˈmẽtu/ *m* sacrament

sacri|ficar /sakrifiˈkar/ *vt* sacrifice; have put down <*cachorro etc*>; ~**fício** *m* sacrifice; ~**légio** *m* sacrilege

sacrílego /saˈkrilegu/ *a* sacrilegious

sacro /ˈsakru/ *a* <*música*> religious

sacrossanto /sakroˈsãtu/ *a* sacrosanct

sacu|dida /sakuˈdʒida/ *f* shake; ~**dir** *vt* shake

sádico /'sadʒiku/ *a* sadistic □ *m* sadist

sadio /sa'dʒiu/ *a* healthy

sadismo /sa'dʒizmu/ *m* sadism

safa|deza /safa'deza/ *f* (*desonestidade*) deviousness; (*libertinagem*) indecency; (*uma*) dirty trick; ~**do** *a* (*desonesto*) devious; (*lascivo*) dirty-minded; (*esperto*) quick; <*criança*> naughty

safena /sa'fɛna/ *f* ponte de ~ heart bypass; ~**do** *m* bypass patient

safira /sa'fira/ *f* sapphire

safra /'safra/ *f* crop

sagitariano /saʒitari'anu/ *a* & *m* Sagittarian

Sagitário /saʒi'tariu/ *m* Sagittarius

sagrado /sa'gradu/ *a* sacred

saguão /sa'gwãw/ *m* (*de teatro, hotel*) foyer, (*Amer*) lobby; (*de estação, aeroporto*) concourse

saia /'saja/ *f* skirt; ~**-calça** (*pl* ~**s-calças**) *f* culottes

saída /sa'ida/ *f* (*partida*) departure; (*porta, fig*) way out; **de** ~ at the outset; **estar de** ~ be on one's way out

sair /sa'ir/ *vi* (*de dentro*) go/come out; (*partir*) leave; (*desprender-se*) come off; <*mancha*> come out; (*resultar*) turn out; ~**-se** *vpr* fare; ~**-se com** (*dizer*) come out with; ~ **mais barato** work out cheaper

sal /saw/ (*pl* **sais**) *m* salt; ~ **de frutas** Epsom salts

sala /'sala/ *f* (*numa casa*) lounge; (*num lugar público*) hall; (*classe*) class; **fazer** ~ **a** entertain; ~ **de aula** classroom; ~ **de embarque** departure lounge; ~ **de espera** waiting room; ~ **de jantar** dining room; ~ **de operação** operating theatre

sala|da /sa'lada/ *f* salad; (*fig*) jumble, mishmash; ~**da de frutas** fruit salad; ~**deira** *f* salad bowl

sala-e-quarto /sali'kwartu/ *m* two-room flat

sala|me /sa'lami/ *m* salami; ~**minho** *m* pepperoni

salão /sa'lãw/ *m* hall; (*de cabeleireiro*) salon; (*de carros*) show; ~ **de beleza** beauty salon

salari|al /salari'aw/ (*pl* ~**ais**) *a* wage

salário /sa'lariu/ *m* salary

sal|dar /saw'dar/ *vt* settle; ~**do** *m* balance

saleiro /sa'leru/ *m* salt cellar

sal|gadinhos /sawga'dʒiɲus/ *m pl* snacks; ~**gado** *a* salty; <*preço*> exorbitant; ~**gar** *vt* salt

salgueiro /saw'geru/ *m* willow; ~ **chorão** weeping willow

saliência /sali'ẽsia/ *f* projection

salien|tar /saliẽ'tar/ *vt* (*deixar claro*) point out; (*acentuar*) highlight; ~**tar-se** *vpr* distinguish o.s.; ~**te** *a* prominent

saliva /sa'liva/ *f* saliva

salmão /saw'mãw/ *m* salmon

salmo /'sawmu/ *m* psalm

salmonela /sawmo'nɛla/ *f* salmonella

salmoura /saw'mora/ *f* brine

salpicar /sawpi'kar/ *vt* sprinkle; (*sem querer*) spatter

salsa /'sawsa/ *f* parsley

salsicha /saw'siʃa/ *f* sausage

saltar /saw'tar/ *vt* (*pular*) jump; (*omitir*) skip □ *vi* jump; ~ **à vista** be obvious; ~ **do ônibus** get off the bus

saltear /sawtʃi'ar/ *vt* sauté <*batatas etc*>

saltitar /sawtʃi'tar/ *vi* hop

salto /'sawtu/ *m* (*pulo*) jump; (*de sapato*) heel; ~ **com vara** pole vault; ~ **em altura** high jump; ~ **em distância** long jump; ~**-mortal** (*pl* ~**s-mortais**) *m* somersault

salu|bre /sa'lubri/ *a* healthy; ~**tar** *a* salutary

salva¹ /'sawva/ *f* (*de canhões*) salvo; (*bandeja*) salver; ~ **de palmas** round of applause

salva² /'sawva/ *f* (*erva*) sage

salva|ção /sawva'sãw/ *f* salvation; ~**dor** *m* saviour

salvaguar|da /sawva'gwarda/ *f* safeguard; ~**dar** *vt* safeguard

sal|vamento /sawva'mẽtu/ *m* rescue; (*de navio*) salvage; ~**var** *vt* save; ~**var-se** *vpr* escape; ~**va-vidas** *m invar* (*bóia*) lifebelt □ *m/f* (*pessoa*) lifeguard □ *a* **barco** ~**va-vidas** lifeboat; ~**vo** *a* safe □ *prep* save; **a** ~**vo** safe

samambaia /samã'baja/ *f* fern

sam|ba /'sãba/ *m* samba; ~**ba-canção** (*pl* ~**bas-canção**) *m* slow samba □ *a invar* **cueca** ~**ba-canção** boxer shorts; ~**ba-enredo** (*pl* ~**bas-enredo**) *m* samba story; ~**bar** *vi* samba; ~**bista** *m/f* (*dançarino*) samba dancer; (*compositor*) composer of sambas; ~**bódromo** *m* Carnival parade ground

samovar /samo'var/ *m* tea urn

sanar /sa'nar/ *vt* cure

san|ção /sã'sãw/ *f* sanction; ~**cionar** *vt* sanction

sandália /sã'dalia/ *f* sandal

sandes /'sãdiʃ/ *f invar* (*Port*) sandwich

sanduíche /sãdu'iʃi/ *m* sandwich

sane|amento /sania'mẽtu/ *m* (*esgotos*) sanitation; (*de finanças*) rehabilitation; ~**ar** *vt* set straight <*finanças*>

sanfona /sã'fona/ *f* (*instrumento*) accordion; (*tricô*) ribbing; ~**do** *a* <*porta*> folding; <*pulôver*> ribbed

san|grar /sã'grar/ *vt/i* bleed; ~**grento** *a* bloody; <*carne*> rare;

~**gria** *f* bloodshed; (*de dinheiro*) extortion

sangue /'sãgi/ *m* blood; ~ **pisado** bruise; ~**frio** *m* cool, coolness

sanguessuga /sãgi'suga/ *f* leech

sanguinário /sãgi'nariu/ *a* bloodthirsty

sanguíneo /sã'giniu/ *a* blood

sanidade /sani'dadʒi/ *f* sanity

sanitário /sani'tariu/ *a* sanitary; ~**s** *mpl* toilets

san|tidade /sãtʃi'dadʒi/ *f* sanctity; ~**tificar** *vt* sanctify; ~**to** a holy □ *m* saint; **todo** ~**to dia** every single day; ~**tuário** *m* sanctuary

São /sãw/ *a* Saint

são /sãw/ (*pl* ~**s**) *a* (*f* **sã**) healthy; (*mentalmente*) sane; <*conselho*> sound

sapata /sa'pata/ *f* shoe; ~**ria** *f* shoe shop

sapate|ado /sapatʃi'adu/ *m* tap dancing; ~**ador** *m* tap dancer; ~**ar** *vi* tap one's feet; (*dançar*) tap-dance

sapa|teiro /sapa'teru/ *m* shoemaker; ~**tilha** *f* pump; ~**tilha de balé** ballet shoe; ~**to** *m* shoe

sapeca /sa'pɛka/ *a* saucy

sa|pinho /sa'piɲu/ *m* thrush; ~**po** *m* toad

saque[1] /'saki/ *m* (*do banco*) withdrawal; (*em tênis, vôlei etc*) serve

saque[2] /'saki/ *m* (*de loja etc*) looting; ~**ar** *vt* loot

saraiva /sa'rajva/ *f* hail; ~**da** *f* hailstorm; **uma** ~**da de** a hail of

sarampo /sa'rãpu/ *m* measles

sarar /sa'rar/ *vt* cure □ *vi* get better; <*ferida*> heal

sar|casmo /sar'kazmu/ *m* sarcasm; ~**cástico** *a* sarcastic

sarda /'sarda/ *f* freckle

Sardenha /sar'deɲa/ *f* Sardinia

sardento /sar'dẽtu/ *a* freckled

sardinha /sar'dʒiɲa/ *f* sardine

sardônico /sar'doniku/ *a* sardonic

sargento /sar'ʒẽtu/ *m* sergeant

sarjeta /sar'ʒeta/ *f* gutter

Satanás /sata'nas/ *m* Satan

satânico /sa'taniku/ *a* satanic

satélite /sa'tɛlitʃi/ *a & m* satellite

sátira /'satʃira/ *f* satire

satírico /sa'tʃiriku/ *a* satirical

satirizar /satʃiri'zar/ *vt* satirize

satisfa|ção /satʃisfa'sãw/ *f* satisfaction; **dar** ~**ções a** answer to; ~**tório** *a* satisfactory; ~**zer** *vt* ~**a** (a) satisfy □ *vi* be satisfactory; ~**zer-se** *vpr* be satisfied

satisfeito /satʃis'fejtu/ *a* satisfied; (*contente*) content; (*de comida*) full

saturar /satu'rar/ *vt* saturate

Saturno /sa'turnu/ *m* Saturn

saudação /sawda'sãw/ *f* greeting

saudade /saw'dadʒi/ *f* longing; (*lembrança*) nostalgia; **estar com** ~**s de** miss; **matar** ~**s** catch up

saudar /saw'dar/ *vt* greet

saudá|vel /saw'davew/ (*pl* ~**veis**) *a* healthy

saúde /sa'udʒi/ *f* health □ *int* (*ao beber*) cheers; (*ao espirrar*) bless you

saudo|sismo /sawdo'zizmu/ *m* nostalgia; ~**so** /o/ *a* longing; **estar** ~**so de** miss; **o nosso** ~**so amigo** our much-missed friend

sauna /'sawna/ *f* sauna

saxofo|ne /sakso'foni/ *m* saxophone; ~**nista** *m/f* saxophonist

sazo|nado /sazo'nadu/ *a* seasoned; ~**nal** (*pl* ~**nais**) *a* seasonal

se[1] /si/ *conj* if; **não sei** ~ ... I don't know if/whether

se[2] /si/ *pron* (*ele mesmo*) himself; (*ela mesma*) herself; (*você mesmo*) yourself; (*eles/elas*) themselves; (*vocês*) yourselves; (*um ao outro*) each other; **dorme-**~ **tarde no Brasil** people go to bed late in Brazil; **aqui** ~ **fala inglês** English is spoken here

sebo /'sebu/ *m* (*sujeira*) grease; (*livraria*) secondhand bookshop; ~**so** /o/ *a* greasy; <*pessoa*> slimy

seca /'seka/ *f* drought; ~**dor** *m* ~**dor de cabelo** hairdryer; ~**dora** *f* tumble dryer

seção /se'sãw/ *f* section; (*de loja*) department

secar /se'kar/ *vt/i* dry

sec|ção /sek'sãw/ *f veja* **seção**; ~**cionar** *vt* split up

seco /'seku/ *a* dry; <*resposta, tom*> curt; <*pessoa, caráter*> cold; <*barulho, pancada*> dull; **estar** ~ **por** I'm dying for

secretaria /sekreta'ria/ *f* (*de empresa*) general office; (*ministério*) department

secretá|ria /sekre'taria/ *f* secretary; ~**ria eletrônica** ansaphone; ~**rio** *m* secretary

secreto /se'krɛtu/ *a* secret

secular /seku'lar/ *a* (*não religioso*) secular; (*antigo*) age-old

século /'sɛkulu/ *m* century; *pl* (*muito tempo*) ages

secundário /sekũ'dariu/ *a* secondary

secura /se'kura/ *f* dryness; **estar com uma** ~ **de** be longing for/to

seda /'seda/ *f* silk

sedativo /seda'tʃivu/ *a & m* sedative

sede[1] /'sɛdʒi/ *f* headquarters; (*local de governo*) seat

sede[2] /'sedʒi/ *f* thirst (**de** for); **estar com** ~ be thirsty

sedentário /sedẽ'tariu/ *a* sedentary

sedento /se'dẽtu/ *a* thirsty (**de** for)

sediar /sedʒi'ar/ *vt* host

sedimen|tar /sedʒimẽ'tar/ *vt* consolidate; **~to** *m* sediment
sedoso /se'dozu/ *a* silky
sedu|ção /sedu'sãw/ *f* seduction; **~tor** *a* seductive; **~zir** *vt* seduce
segmento /seg'mẽtu/ *m* segment
segredo /se'gredu/ *m* secret; (*de cofre etc*) combination
segregar /segre'gar/ *vt* segregate
segui|da /se'gida/ *f* **em ~da** (*imediatamente*) straight away; (*depois*) next; **~do** *a* followed (**de** by); **cinco horas ~das** five hours running; **~dor** *m* follower; **~mento** *m* continuation; **dar ~mento a** go on with
se|guinte /se'gĩtʃi/ *a* following; <*dia, semana etc*> next; **~guir** *vt/i* follow; (*continuar*) continue; **~guir-se** *vpr* follow; **~guir em frente** (*ir embora*) go; (*indicação na rua*) go straight ahead
segun|da /se'gũda/ *f* (*dia*) Monday; (*marcha*) second; **de ~da** second-rate; **~da-feira** (*pl* **~das-feiras**) *f* Monday; **~do** *a & m* second □ *adv* secondly □ *prep* according to □ *conj* according to what; **~das intenções** ulterior motives; **de ~da mão** second-hand
segu|rança /segu'rãsa/ *f* security; (*estado de seguro*) safety; (*certeza*) assurance □ *m/f* security guard; **~rar** *vt* hold; **~rar-se** *vpr* (*controlar-se*) control o.s.; **~rar-se em** hold on to; **~ro** *a* secure; (*fora de perigo*) safe; (*com certeza*) sure □ *m* insurance; **estar no ~ro** <*bens*> be insured; **fazer ~ro de** insure; **~ro-desemprego** *m* unemployment benefit
seio /'seju/ *m* breast, bosom; **no ~ de** within
seis /sejs/ *a & m* six; **~centos** *a & m* six hundred
seita /'sejta/ *f* sect
seixo /'sejʃu/ *m* pebble
sela /'sɛla/ *f* saddle
selar¹ /se'lar/ *vt* saddle <*cavalo*>
selar² /se'lar/ *vt* seal; (*franquear*) stamp
sele|ção /sele'sãw/ *f* selection; (*time*) team; **~cionar** *vt* select; **~to** /ɛ/ *a* select
selim /se'lĩ/ *m* saddle
selo /'selu/ *m* seal; (*postal*) stamp; (*de discos*) label
selva /'sewva/ *f* jungle; **~gem** *a* wild; **~geria** *f* savagery
sem /sẽj/ *prep* without; **~ eu saber** without me knowing; **ficar ~ dinheiro** run out of money
semáforo /se'maforu/ *m* (*na rua*) traffic lights; (*de ferrovia*) signal
sema|na /se'mana/ *f* week; **~nal** (*pl*

~nais) *a* weekly; **~nalmente** *adv* weekly; **~nário** *m* weekly
semear /semi'ar/ *vt* sow
semelhan|ça /seme'ʎãsa/ *f* similarity; **~te** *a* similar; (*tal*) such
sêmen /'semẽ/ *m* semen
semente /se'mẽtʃi/ *f* seed; (*em fruta*) pip
semestre /se'mɛstri/ *m* six months; (*da faculdade etc*) term, (*Amer*) semester
semi|círculo /semi'sirkulu/ *m* semicircle; **~final** (*pl* **~finais**) *f* semifinal
seminário /semi'nariu/ *m* (*aula*) seminar; (*colégio religioso*) seminary
sem-número /sẽ'numeru/ *m* **um ~ de** innumerable
sempre /'sẽpri/ *adv* always; **como ~** as usual; **para ~** for ever; **~ que** whenever
sem-|terra /sẽ'texa/ *m/f invar* landless labourer; **~teto** *a* homeless □ *m/f* homeless person; **~vergonha** *a invar* brazen □ *m/f invar* scoundrel
sena|do /se'nadu/ *m* senate; **~dor** *m* senator
senão /si'nãw/ *conj* otherwise; (*mas antes*) but rather □ *m* snag
senda /'sẽda/ *f* path
senha /'seɲa/ *f* (*palavra*) password; (*número*) code; (*sinal*) signal
senhor /se'ɲor/ *m* gentleman; (*homem idoso*) older man; (*tratamento*) sir □ *a* (*f ~a*) mighty; **Senhor** (*com nome*) Mr; (*Deus*) Lord; **o ~** (*você*) you
senho|ra /se'ɲɔra/ *f* lady; (*mulher idosa*) older woman; (*tratamento*) madam; **Senhora** (*com nome*) Mrs; **a ~ra** (*você*) you; **nossa ~ra!** (*fam*) gosh; **~ria** *f* **Vossa Senhoria** you; **~rita** *f* young lady; (*tratamento*) miss; **Senhorita** (*com nome*) Miss
se|nil (*pl* **~nis**) *a* senile; **~nilidade** *f* senility
sensação /sẽsa'sãw/ *f* sensation
sensacio|nal /sẽsasio'naw/ (*pl* **~nais**) *a* sensational; **~nalismo** *m* sensationalism; **~nalista** *a* sensationalist
sen|sato /sẽ'satu/ *a* sensible; **~sibilidade** *f* sensitivity; **~sível** (*pl* **~síveis**) *a* sensitive; (*que se pode sentir*) noticeable; **~so** *m* sense; **~sual** (*pl* **~suais**) *a* sensual
sen|tado /sẽ'tadu/ *a* sitting; **~tar** *vt/i* sit; **~tar-se** *vpr* sit down
sentença /sẽ'tẽsa/ *f* sentence
sentido /sẽ'tʃidu/ *m* sense; (*direção*) direction □ *a* hurt; **fazer** *ou* **ter ~** make sense
sentimen|tal /sẽtʃimẽ'taw/ (*pl* **~tais**) *a* sentimental; **vida ~tal** love life; **~to** *m* feeling

sentinela /sẽtʃi'nɛla/ f sentry
sentir /sẽ'tʃir/ vt feel; (notar) sense; smell <cheiro>; taste <gosto>; tell <diferença>; (ficar magoado por) be hurt by □ vi feel; ~-se vpr feel; **sinto muito** I'm very sorry
sepa|ração /separa'sãw/ f separation; ~**rado** a separate; <casal> separated; ~**rar** vt separate; ~**rar-se** vpr separate
séptico /'sɛptʃiku/ a septic
sepul|tar /sepuw'tar/ vt bury; ~**tura** f grave
seqüência /se'kwẽsia/ f sequence
sequer /se'kɛr/ adv **nem** ~ not even
seqües|trador /sekwestra'dor/ m kidnapper; (de avião) hijacker; ~**trar** vt kidnap <pessoa>; hijack <avião>; sequestrate <bens>; ~**tro** /ɛ/ m (de pessoa) kidnapping; (de avião) hijack; (de bens) sequestration
ser /ser/ vi **be** □ m being; **é** (como resposta) yes; **você gosta, não é?** you like it, don't you?; **ele foi morto** he was killed; **será que ele volta?** I wonder if he's coming back; **ou seja** in other words; **a não** ~ except; **a não** ~ **que** unless; **não sou de fofocar** I'm not one to gossip
sereia /se'reja/ f mermaid
serenata /sere'nata/ f serenade
sereno /se'renu/ a serene; <tempo> fine
série /'sɛri/ f series; (na escola) grade; **fora de** ~ (fam) incredible
seriedade /serie'dadʒi/ f seriousness
serin|ga /se'rĩga/ f syringe; ~**gueiro** m rubber tapper
sério /'sɛriu/ a serious; (responsável) responsible; ~? really?; **falar** ~ be serious; **levar a** ~ take seriously
sermão /ser'mãw/ m sermon
serpen|te /ser'pẽtʃi/ f serpent; ~**tear** vi wind; ~**tina** f streamer
serra¹ /'sɛxa/ f (montanhas) mountain range
serra² /'sɛxa/ f (de serrar) saw; ~**gem** f sawdust; ~**lheiro** m locksmith
serrano /se'xanu/ a mountain
serrar /se'xar/ vt saw
ser|tanejo /serta'neʒu/ a from the backwoods □ m backwoodsman; ~**tão** m backwoods
servente /ser'vẽtʃi/ m/f labourer
Sérvia /'sɛrvia/ f Serbia
servi|çal /servi'saw/ (pl ~**çais**) a helpful □ m/f servant; ~**ço** m service; (trabalho) work; (tarefa) job; **estar de** ~**ço** be on duty; ~**dor** m servant
ser|vil /ser'viw/ (pl ~**vis**) a servile
sérvio /'sɛrviu/ a & m Serbian
servir /ser'vir/ vt serve □ vi serve; (ser adequado) do; (ser útil) be of use; <roupa, sapato etc> fit; ~-se

vpr (ao comer etc) help o.s. (**de** to); ~-**se de** make use of; ~ **como** ou **de** serve as; **para que serve isso?** what is this (used) for?
sessão /se'sãw/ f session; (no cinema) showing, performance
sessenta /se'sẽta/ a & m sixty
seta /'sɛta/ f arrow; (de carro) indicator
sete /'sɛtʃi/ a & m seven; ~**centos** a & m seven hundred
setembro /se'tẽbru/ m September
setenta /se'tẽta/ a & m seventy
sétimo /'sɛtʃimu/ a seventh
setuagésimo /setua'ʒɛzimu/ a seventieth
setor /se'tor/ m sector
seu /sew/ a (f **sua**) (dele) his; (dela) her; (de coisa) its; (deles) their; (de você, de vocês) your □ pron (dele) his; (dela) hers; (deles) theirs; (de você, de vocês) yours; ~ **idiota!** you idiot!; **seu João** Mr John
seve|ridade /severi'dadʒi/ f severity; ~**ro** /ɛ/ a severe
sexagésimo /seksa'ʒɛzimu/ a sixtieth
sexo /'sɛksu/ m sex; **fazer** ~ have sex
sex|ta /'sesta/ f Friday; ~**ta-feira** (pl ~**tas-feiras**) f Friday; **Sexta-feira Santa** Good Friday; ~**to** /e/ a & m sixth
sexu|al /seksu'aw/ (pl ~**ais**) a sexual; **vida** ~**al** sex life
sexy /'sɛksi/ a invar sexy
shopping /'ʃɔpĩ/ (pl ~**s**) m shopping centre, (Amer) mall
short /'ʃortʃi/ m (pl ~**s**) shorts; **um** ~ a pair of shorts
show /'ʃou/ (pl ~**s**) m show; (de música) concert
si /si/ pron (ele) himself; (ela) herself; (coisa) itself; (você) yourself; (eles) themselves; (vocês) yourselves; (qualquer pessoa) oneself; **em** ~ in itself; **fora de** ~ beside o.s.; **cheio de** ~ full of o.s.; **voltar a** ~ come round
sibilar /sibi'lar/ vi hiss
SIDA /'sida/ f (Port) AIDS
side|ral /side'raw/ (pl ~**rais**) a **espaço** ~**ral** outer space
siderurgia /siderur'ʒia/ f iron and steel industry
siderúrgi|ca /side'rurʒika/ f steelworks; ~**co** a iron and steel □ m steelworker
sifão /si'fãw/ m syphon
sífilis /'sifilis/ f syphilis
sigilo /si'ʒilu/ m secrecy; ~**so** /o/ a secret
sigla /'sigla/ f acronym
signatário /signa'tariu/ m signatory
signifi|cação /signifika'sãw/ f significance; ~**cado** m meaning; ~**car** vt mean; ~**cativo** a significant

signo /ˈsignu/ *m* sign

silaba /ˈsilaba/ *f* syllable

silenciar /silẽsiˈar/ *vt* silence

silêncio /siˈlẽsiu/ *m* silence

silencioso /silẽsiˈozu/ *a* silent □ *m* silencer, (*Amer*) muffler

silhueta /siʎuˈeta/ *f* silhouette

silício /siˈlisiu/ *m* silicon

silicone /siliˈkoni/ *m* silicone

silo /ˈsilu/ *m* silo

silvar /siwˈvar/ *vi* hiss

silvestre /siwˈvɛstri/ *a* wild; ∼**vicultura** *f* forestry

sim /sĩ/ *adv* yes; **acho que** ∼ I think so

simbólico /sĩˈbɔliku/ *a* symbolic

simbolismo /sĩboˈlizmu/ *m* symbolism; ∼**lizar** *vt* symbolize

símbolo /ˈsĩbolu/ *m* symbol

simetria /simeˈtria/ *f* symmetry; ∼**métrico** *a* symmetrical

similar /simiˈlar/ *a* similar

simpatia /sĩpaˈtʃia/ *f* (*qualidade*) pleasantness; (*afeto*) fondness (**por** for); (*compreensão, apoio*) sympathy; *pl* sympathies; **ter** ∼**patia por** be fond of; ∼**pático** *a* nice

simpatizante /sĩpatʃiˈzãtʃi/ *a* sympathetic □ *m/f* sympathizer; ∼**zar** *vi* ∼**zar com** take a liking to <*pessoa*>; sympathize with <*idéias, partido etc*>

simples /ˈsĩplis/ *a invar* simple; (*único*) single □ *f* (*no tênis etc*) singles; ∼**mente** *adv* simply

simplicidade /sĩplisiˈdadʒi/ *f* simplicity; ∼**ficar** *vt* simplify

simplório /sĩˈplɔriu/ *a* simple

simpósio /sĩˈpɔziu/ *m* symposium

simulação /simulaˈsãw/ *f* simulation; ∼**lar** *vt* simulate

simultâneo /simuwˈtaniu/ *a* simultaneous

sina /ˈsina/ *f* fate

sinagoga /sinaˈgɔga/ *f* synagogue

sinal /siˈnaw/ (*pl* ∼**nais**) *m* sign; (*aviso, de rádio etc*) signal; (*de trânsito*) traffic light; (*no telefone*) tone; (*dinheiro*) deposit; (*na pele*) mole; **por** ∼**nal** as a matter of fact; ∼**nal de pontuação** punctuation mark; ∼**naleira** *f* traffic lights; ∼**nalização** *f* (*na rua*) road signs; ∼**nalizar** *vt* signal; signpost <*rua, cidade*>

sinceridade /sĩseriˈdadʒi/ *f* sincerity; ∼**ro** /ɛ/ *a* sincere

sincronia /sĩkroˈnia/ *f* synchronization; ∼**nizar** *vt* synchronize

sindical /sĩdʒiˈkaw/ (*pl* ∼**cais**) *a* trade union; ∼**calismo** *m* trade unionism; ∼**calista** *m/f* trade unionist; ∼**calizar** *vt* unionize; ∼**cato** *m* trade union

síndico /ˈsĩdʒiku/ *m* house manager

síndrome /ˈsĩdromi/ *f* syndrome

sineta /siˈneta/ *f* bell

sinfonia /sĩfoˈnia/ *f* symphony; ∼**fônica** *f* symphony orchestra

singeleza /sĩʒeˈleza/ *f* simplicity; ∼**lo** /ɛ/ *a* simple

singular /sĩguˈlar/ *a* singular; (*estranho*) peculiar; ∼**larizar** *vt* single out

sinistrado /sinisˈtradu/ *a* damaged; ∼**tro** *a* sinister □ *m* accident

sino /ˈsinu/ *m* bell

sinônimo /siˈnonimu/ *a* synonymous □ *m* synonym

sintaxe /sĩˈtaksi/ *f* syntax

síntese /ˈsĩtezi/ *f* synthesis

sintético /sĩˈtɛtʃiku/ *a* (*artificial*) synthetic; (*resumido*) concise; ∼**tetizar** *vt* summarize

sintoma /sĩˈtoma/ *m* symptom; ∼**mático** *a* symptomatic

sintonizador /sĩtonizaˈdor/ *m* tuner; ∼**zar** *vt* tune <*rádio, TV*>; tune in to <*emissora*> □ *vi* be in tune (**com** with)

sinuca /siˈnuka/ *f* snooker

sinuoso /sinuˈozu/ *a* winding

sinusite /sinuˈzitʃi/ *f* sinusitis

sirene /siˈrɛni/ *f* siren

siri /siˈri/ *m* crab

Síria /ˈsiria/ *f* Syria

sírio /ˈsiriu/ *a & m* Syrian

siso /ˈsizu/ *m* good sense

sistema /sisˈtema/ *m* system; ∼**mático** *a* systematic

sisudo /siˈzudu/ *a* serious

sítio /ˈsitʃiu/ *m* (*chácara*) farm; (*Port: local*) place; **estado de** ∼ state of siege

situação /situaˈsãw/ *f* situation; (*no governo*) party in power; ∼**ar** *vt* situate; ∼**ar-se** *vpr* be situated; <*pessoa*> position o.s.

smoking /izˈmokĩ/ (*pl* ∼**s**) *m* dinner jacket, (*Amer*) tuxedo

só /sɔ/ *a* alone; (*sentindo solidão*) lonely □ *adv* only; **um** ∼ **voto** one single vote; ∼ **um carro** only one car; **a** ∼**s** alone; **imagina** ∼ just imagine; ∼ **que** except (that)

soalho /soˈaʎu/ *m* floor

soar /soˈar/ *vt/i* sound

sob /ˈsobi/ *prep* under

soberania /soberaˈnia/ *f* sovereignty; ∼**no** *a & m* sovereign

soberbo /soˈberbu/ *a* <*pessoa*> haughty; (*magnífico*) splendid

sobra /ˈsobra/ *f* surplus; *pl* leftovers; **tempo de** ∼ (*muito*) plenty of time; **ficar de** ∼ be left over; **ter aco de** ∼ (*sobrando*) have sth left over

sobraçar /sobraˈsar/ *vt* carry under one's arm

sobrado /soˈbradu/ *m* (*casa*) house; (*andar*) upper floor

sobrancelha /sobrã'seʎa/ f eyebrow

so|brar /so'brar/ vi be left; **~bram-me dois** I have two left

sobre /'sobri/ prep (em cima de) on; (por cima de, acima de) over; (acerca de) about

sobreaviso /sobria'vizu/ m estar de ~ be on one's guard

sobrecapa /sobri'kapa/ f dust jacket

sobrecarregar /sobrikaxe'gar/ vt overload

sobreloja /sobri'lɔʒa/ f mezzanine

sobremesa /sobri'meza/ f dessert

sobrenatu|ral /sobrinatu'raw/ (pl **~rais**) a supernatural

sobrenome /sobri'nomi/ m surname

sobrepor /sobri'por/ vt superimpose

sobrepujar /sobripu'ʒar/ vt (em altura) tower over; (em valor, número etc) surpass; overwhelm <adversário>; overcome <problemas>

sobrescritar /sobriskri'tar/ vt address

sobressair /sobrisa'ir/ vi stand out; **~-se** vpr stand out

sobressalente /sobrisa'lẽtʃi/ a spare

sobressal|tar /sobrisaw'tar/ vt startle; **~tar-se** vpr be startled; **~to** m (movimento) start; (susto) fright

sobretaxa /sobri'taʃa/ f surcharge

sobretudo /sobri'tudu/ adv above all □ m overcoat

sobrevir /sobri'vir/ vi happen suddenly; (seguir) ensue; **~ a** follow

sobrevi|vência /sobrivi'vẽsia/ f survival; **~vente** a surviving □ m/f survivor; **~ver** vt/i **~ver (a)** survive

sobrevoar /sobrivo'ar/ vt fly over

sobri|nha /so'briɲa/ f niece; **~nho** m nephew

sóbrio /'sɔbriu/ a sober

socar /so'kar/ vt (esmurrar) punch; (amassar) crush

soci|al /sosi'aw/ (pl **~ais**) a social; **camisa ~al** dress shirt; **~alismo** m socialism; **~alista** a & m/f socialist; **~alite** /-a'lajtʃi/ m/f socialite; **~ável** (pl **~áveis**) a sociable

sociedade /sosie'dadʒi/ f society; (parceria) partnership; **~ anônima** limited company

sócio /'sɔsiu/ m (de empresa) partner; (de clube) member

socio-econômico /sosioeko'nomiku/ a socio-economic

soci|ologia /sosiolo'ʒia/ f sociology; **~ológico** a sociological; **~ólogo** m sociologist

soco /'soku/ m punch; **dar um ~ em** punch

socor|rer /soko'xer/ vt help; **~ro** m aid □ int help; **primeiros ~ros** first aid

soda /'sɔda/ f (água) soda water; **~ cáustica** caustic soda

sódio /'sɔdʒiu/ m sodium

sofá /so'fa/ m sofa; **~-cama** (pl **~s-camas**) m sofa-bed

sofisticado /sofistʃi'kadu/ a sophisticated

so|fredor /sofre'dor/ a martyred; **~frer** vt suffer <dor, derrota, danos etc>; have <acidente>; undergo <operação, mudança etc> □ vi suffer; **~frer de** suffer from <doença>; have trouble with <coração etc>; **~frido** a long-suffering; **~frimento** m suffering; **~frível** (pl **~fríveis**) a passable

soft /'sɔftʃi/ (pl **~s**) m software package; **~ware** m software; (um) software package

so|gra /'sɔgra/ f mother-in-law; **~gro** /o/ m father-in-law; **~gros** /ɔ/ m pl in-laws

soja /'sɔʒa/ f soya, (Amer) soy

sol /sɔw/ (pl **sóis**) m sun; **faz ~** it's sunny

sola /'sɔla/ f sole; **~do** a <bolo> flat

solapar /sola'par/ vt undermine

solar[1] /so'lar/ a solar

solar[2] /so'lar/ vt sole <sapato> □ vi <bolo> go flat

solavanco /sola'vãku/ m jolt; **dar ~s** jolt

soldado /sow'dadu/ m soldier

sol|dadura /sowda'dura/ f weld; **~dar** vt weld

soldo /'sowdu/ m pay

soleira /so'lera/ f doorstep

sole|ne /so'leni/ a solemn; **~nidade** f (cerimônia) ceremony; (qualidade) solemnity

soletrar /sole'trar/ vt spell

solici|tação /solisita'sãw/ f request (de for); (por escrito) application (de for); **~tante** m/f applicant; **~tar** vt request; (por escrito) apply for

solícito /so'lisitu/ a helpful

solidão /soli'dãw/ f loneliness

soli|dariedade /solidarie'dadʒi/ f solidarity; **~dário** a supportive (com of)

soli|dez /soli'des/ f solidity; **~dificar** vt solidify; **~dificar-se** vpr solidify

sólido /'sɔlidu/ a & m solid

solista /so'lista/ m/f soloist

solitá|ria /soli'taria/ f (verme) tapeworm; (cela) solitary confinement; **~rio** a solitary

solo[1] /'sɔlu/ m (terra) soil; (chão) ground

solo[2] /'sɔlu/ m solo

soltar /sow'tar/ vt let go <prisioneiros, animal etc>; let loose <cães>; (deixar de segurar) let go of; loosen <gravata, corda etc>; let down

<*cabelo*>; let out <*grito, suspiro etc*>; let off <*foguetes*>; tell <*piada*>; take off <*freio*>; ~**-se** *vpr* <*peça, parafuso*> come loose; <*pessoa*> let o.s. go

soltei|**ra** /sow'tera/ *a* (*livre*) single woman; ~**rão** *m* bachelor; ~**ro** *a* single □ *m* single man; ~**rona** *f* spinster

solto /'sowtu/ *a* (*livre*) free; <*cães*> loose; <*cabelo*> down; <*arroz*> fluffy; (*frouxo*) loose; (*à vontade*) relaxed; (*abandonado*) abandoned; **correr** ~ run wild

solução /solu'sãw/ *f* solution

soluçar /solu'sar/ *vi* (*ao chorar*) sob; (*engasgar*) hiccup

solucionar /solusio'nar/ *vt* solve

soluço /so'lusu/ *m* (*ao chorar*) sob; (*engasgo*) hiccup; **estar com** ~**s** have the hiccups

solú|**vel** /so'luvew/ (*pl* ~**veis**) *a* soluble

solvente /sow'vẽtʃi/ *a & m* solvent

som /sõ/ *m* sound; (*aparelho*) stereo; **um** ~ (*fam*) (*música*) a bit of music

so|**ma** /'soma/ *f* sum; ~**mar** *vt* add up <*números etc*>; (*ter como soma*) add up to

sombra /'sõbra/ *f* shadow; (*área abrigada do sol*) shade; **à** ~ **de** in the shade of; **sem** ~ **de dúvida** without a shadow of a doubt

sombre|**ado** /sõbri'adu/ *a* shady □ *m* shading; ~**ar** *vt* shade

sombrinha /sõ'briɲa/ *f* parasol

sombrio /sõ'briu/ *a* gloomy

somente /so'mẽtʃi/ *adv* only

sonâmbulo /so'nãbulu/ *m* sleepwalker

sonante /so'nãtʃi/ *a* **moeda** ~ hard cash

sonata /so'nata/ *f* sonata

son|**da** /'sõda/ *f* probe; ~**dagem** *f* (*no mar*) sounding; (*de terreno*) survey; ~**dagem de opinião** opinion poll; ~**dar** *vt* probe; sound <*profundeza*>; (*fig*) sound out <*pessoas, opiniões etc*>

soneca /so'nɛka/ *f* nap; **tirar uma** ~ have a nap

sone|**gação** /sonega'sãw/ *f* (*de impostos*) tax evasion; ~**gador** *m* tax dodger; ~**gar** *vt* withhold

soneto /so'netu/ *m* sonnet

so|**nhador** /soɲa'dor/ *a* dreamy □ *m* dreamer; ~**nhar** *vt/i* dream (**com** about); ~**nho** /'soɲu/ *m* dream; (*doce*) doughnut

sono /'sonu/ *m* sleep; **estar com** ~ be sleepy; **pegar no** ~ get to sleep; ~**lento** *a* sleepy

sono|**plastia** /sonoplas'tʃia/ *f* sound effects; ~**ridade** *f* sound quality; ~**ro** /ɔ/ *a* sound; <*voz*> sonorous; <*consoante*> voiced

sonso /'sõsu/ *a* devious

sopa /'sopa/ *f* soup

sopapo /so'papu/ *m* slap; **dar um** ~ **em** slap

sopé /so'pɛ/ *m* foot

sopeira /so'pera/ *f* soup tureen

soprano /so'pranu/ *m/f* soprano

so|**prar** /so'prar/ *vt* blow <*folhas etc*>; blow up <*balão*>; blow out <*vela*> □ *vi* blow; ~**pro** *m* blow; (*de vento*) puff; **instrumento de** ~**pro** wind instrument

soquete[1] /so'kɛtʃi/ *f* ankle sock

soquete[2] /so'kɛtʃi/ *m* socket

sordi|**dez** /sordʒi'des/ *f* sordidness; (*imundície*) squalor

sórdido /'sordʒidu/ *a* (*reles*) sordid; (*imundo*) squalid

soro /'soru/ *m* (*remédio*) serum; (*de leite*) whey

sorrateiro /soxa'teru/ *a* crafty

sor|**ridente** /soxi'dẽtʃi/ *a* smiling; ~**rir** *vi* smile; ~**riso** *m* smile

sorte /'sɔrtʃi/ *f* luck; (*destino*) fate; **pessoa de** ~ lucky person; **por** ~ luckily; **ter ou dar** ~ be lucky; **tive a** ~ **de conhecê-lo** I was lucky enough to meet him; **tirar a** ~ draw lots; **trazer ou dar** ~ bring good luck

sor|**tear** /sortʃi'ar/ *vt* draw for <*prèmio*>; select in a draw <*pessoa*>; ~**teio** *m* draw

sorti|**do** /sor'tʃidu/ *a* assorted; ~**mento** *m* assortment

sorumbático /sorũ'batʃiku/ *a* sombre, gloomy

sorver /sor'ver/ *vt* sip <*bebida*>

sósia /'sɔzia/ *m/f* double

soslaio /soz'laju/ *m* **de** ~ sideways; <*olhar*> askance

sosse|**gado** /sose'gadu/ *a* <*vida*> quiet; **ficar** ~**gado** <*pessoa*> rest assured; ~**gar** *vt* reassure □ *vi* rest; ~**go** /e/ *m* peace

sótão /'sɔtãw/ (*pl* ~**s**) *m* attic, loft

sotaque /so'taki/ *m* accent

soterrar /sote'xar/ *vt* bury

soutien /suti'ã/ (*pl* ~**s**) *m* (*Port*) bra

sova|**co** /so'vaku/ *m* armpit; ~**queira** *f* BO, body odour

soviético /sovi'etʃiku/ *a & m* Soviet

sovi|**na** /so'vina/ *a* stingy, mean, (*Amer*) cheap □ *m/f* cheapskate; ~**nice** *f* stinginess, meanness, (*Amer*) cheapness

sozinho /so'ziɲu/ *a* (*sem ninguém*) alone, on one's own; (*por si próprio*) by o.s.; **falar** ~ talk to o.s.

spray /is'prej/ (*pl* ~**s**) *m* spray

squash /is'kweʃ/ *m* squash

stand /is'tãdʒi/ (*pl* ~**s**) *m* stand

status /is'tatus/ *m* status

stripper /is'triper/ (*pl* ~**s**) *m/f* stripper

strip-tease /istrıpi'tʃizi/ *m* striptease

sua /'sua/ *a & pron veja* seu

su|ado /su'adu/ *a <pessoa, roupa>* sweaty; (*fig*) hard-earned; ~**ar** *vt/i* sweat; ~**ar por/para** (*fig*) work hard for/to; ~**ar frio** come out in a cold sweat

sua|ve /su'avi/ *a <toque, subida>* gentle; *<gosto, cheiro, dor, inverno>* mild; *<música, voz>* soft; *<vinho>* smooth; *<trabalho>* light; *<prestações>* easy; ~**vidade** *f* gentleness; mildness; softness; smoothness; *veja* suave; ~**vizar** *vt* soften; soothe *<dor, pessoa>*

subalterno /subaw'tɛrnu/ *a & m* subordinate

subconsciente /subikõsi'ẽtʃi/ *a & m* subconscious

subdesenvolvido /subidʒizivow'vidu/ *a* underdeveloped

súbdito /'subditu/ *m* (*Port*) *veja* súdito

subdividir /subidʒivi'dʒir/ *vt* subdivide

subemprego /subĩ'pregu/ *m* menial job

subemprei|tar /subĩprej'tar/ *vt* subcontract; ~**teiro** *m* subcontractor

subenten|der /subĩtẽ'der/ *vt* infer; ~**dido** *a* implied □ *m* insinuation

subestimar /subestʃi'mar/ *vt* underestimate

su|bida /su'bida/ *f* (*ação*) ascent; (*ladeira*) incline; (*de preços etc, fig*) rise; ~**bir** *vi* go up; *<rio, águas>* rise □ *vt* go up, climb; ~**bir em** climb *<árvore>*; get up onto *<mesa>*; get on *<ônibus>*

súbito /'subitu/ *a* sudden; (**de**) ~ suddenly

subjacente /subiʒa'sẽtʃi/ *a* underlying

subjeti|vidade /subiʒetʃivi'dadʒi/ *f* subjectivity; ~**vo** *a* subjective

subjugar /subiʒu'gar/ *vt* subjugate

subjuntivo /subiʒũ'tʃivu/ *a & m* subjunctive

sublevar-se /suble'varsi/ *vpr* rise up

sublime /su'blimi/ *a* sublime

subli|nhado /subli'ɲadu/ *m* underlining; ~**nhar** *vt* underline

sublocar /sublo'kar/ *vt/i* sublet

submarino /subima'rinu/ *a* underwater □ *m* submarine

submer|gir /subimer'ʒir/ *vt* submerge; ~**gir-se** *vpr* submerge; ~**so** *a* submerged

submeter /subime'ter/ *vt* subject (a to); put down, subdue *<povo, rebeldes etc>*; submit *<projeto>*; ~**se** *vpr* (*render-se*) submit; ~**se a** (*sofrer*) undergo

submis|são /subimi'sãw/ *f* submission; ~**so** *a* submissive

submundo /subi'mũdu/ *m* underworld

subnutrição /subinutri'sãw/ *f* malnutrition

subordi|nado /subordʒi'nadu/ *a & m* subordinate; ~**nar** *vt* subordinate (a to)

subor|nar /subor'nar/ *vt* bribe; ~**no** /o/ *m* bribe

subproduto /subipro'dutu/ *m* byproduct

subs|crever /subiskre'ver/ *vt* sign *<carta etc>*; subscribe to *<opinião>*; subscribe *<dinheiro>* (**para** to); ~**crever-se** *vpr* sign one's name; ~**crição** *f* subscription; ~**crito** *pp de* ~**crever**

subseqüente /subise'kwẽtʃi/ *a* subsequent

subserviente /subiservi'ẽtʃi/ *a* subservient

subsidiar /subisidʒi'ar/ *vt* subsidize

subsidiá|ria /subisidʒi'aria/ *f* subsidiary; ~**rio** *a* subsidiary

subsídio /subi'sidʒiu/ *m* subsidy

subsistência /subisis'tẽsia/ *f* subsistence

subsolo /subi'sɔlu/ *m* (*porão*) basement

substância /subis'tãsia/ *f* substance

substan|cial /subistãsi'aw/ *a* (*pl* ~**ciais**) *a* substantial; ~**tivo** *m* noun

substitu|ição /subistʃitui'sãw/ *f* replacement; substitution; ~**ir** *vt* (*pôr B no lugar de A*) replace (**A por B** A with B); (*usar B em vez de A*) substitute (**A por B** B for A); ~**to** *a & m* substitute

subterfúgio /subiter'fuʒiu/ *m* subterfuge

subterrâneo /subite'xaniu/ *a* underground

sub|til /sub'til/ (*pl* ~**tis**) *a* (*Port*) *veja* sutil

subtra|ção /subitra'sãw/ *f* subtraction; ~**ir** *vt* subtract *<números>*; (*roubar*) steal

suburbano /subur'banu/ *a* suburban

subúrbio /su'burbiu/ *m* suburbs

subven|ção /subivẽ'sãw/ *f* grant, subsidy; ~**cionar** *vt* subsidize

subver|são /subiver'sãw/ *f* subversion; ~**sivo** *a & m* subversive

sucata /su'kata/ *f* scrap metal; ~**tear** *vt* scrap

succão /suk'sãw/ *f* suction

suce|der /suse'der/ *vi* (*acontecer*) happen □ *vt* ~**der a** succeed *<rei etc>*; (*vir depois*) follow; ~**der-se** *vpr* follow on from one another; ~**dido** *a* **bem** ~**dido** successful

suces|são /suse'sãw/ *f* succession;
~sivo *a* successive; **~so** /ɛ/ *m* success; (*música*) hit; **fazer** *ou* **ter ~so**
be successful; **~sor** *m* successor
sucinto /su'sĩtu/ *a* succinct
suco /'suku/ *m* juice
suculento /suku'lẽtu/ *a* juicy
sucumbir /sukũ'bir/ *vi* succumb (**a** to)
sucur|sal /sukur'saw/ (*pl* **~sais**) *f*
branch
Sudão /su'dãw/ *m* Sudan
sudário /su'dariu/ *m* shroud
sudeste /su'dɛstʃi/ *a & m* southeast; **o**
Sudeste Asiático Southeast Asia
súdito /'sudʒitu/ *m* subject
sudoeste /sudo'ɛstʃi/ *a & m* south-
west
Suécia /su'ɛsia/ *f* Sweden
sueco /su'ɛku/ *a & m* Swedish
suéter /su'ɛter/ *m/f* sweater
sufici|ência /sufisi'ẽsia/ *f* sufficiency;
~ente *a* enough, sufficient; **o ~ente**
enough
sufixo /su'fiksu/ *m* suffix
suflê /su'fle/ *m* soufflé
sufo|cante /sufo'kãtʃi/ *a* stifling;
~car *vt* (*asfixiar*) suffocate; (*fig*)
stifle □ *vi* suffocate; **~co** /o/ *m*
hassle; **estar num ~co** be having a
tough time
sufrágio /su'fraʒiu/ *m* suffrage
sugar /su'gar/ *vt* suck
sugerir /suʒe'rir/ *vt* suggest
suges|tão /suʒes'tãw/ *f* suggestion;
dar uma ~tão make a suggestion;
~tivo *a* suggestive
Suíça /su'isa/ *f* Switzerland
suíças /su'isas/ *f pl* sideburns
sui|cida /sui'sida/ *a* suicidal □ *m/f*
suicide (victim); **~cidar-se** *vpr* commit suicide; **~cídio** *m* suicide
suíço /su'isu/ *a & m* Swiss
suíno /su'inu/ *a & m* pig
suíte /su'itʃi/ *f* suite
su|jar /su'ʒar/ *vt* dirty; (*fig*) sully <*re-
putação etc*> □ *vi*, **~jar-se** *vpr* get
dirty; **~jar-se com alg** queer one's
pitch with s.o.; **~jeira** *f* dirt; (*uma*)
dirty trick
sujei|tar /suʒej'tar/ *vt* subject (**a** to);
~tar-se *vpr* subject o.s. (**a** to); **~to** *a*
subject (**a** to) □ *m* (*de oração*) subject;
(*pessoa*) person
su|jidade /suʒi'dadʒi/ *f* (*Port*) dirt;
~jo *a* dirty
sul /suw/ *a invar & m* south; **~-
africano** *a & m* South African; **~-
americano** *a & m* South American;
~-coreano *a & m* South Korean
sul|car /suw'kar/ *vt* furrow <*testa*>;
~co *m* furrow
sulfúrico /suw'furiku/ *a* sulphuric
sulista /su'lista/ *a* southern □ *m/f*
southerner

sultão /suw'tãw/ *m* sultan
sumário /su'mariu/ *a* <*justiça*> summary; <*roupa*> skimpy, brief
su|miço /su'misu/ *m* disappearance;
dar ~miço em spirit away; **tomar**
chá de ~miço disappear; **~mido**
a <*cor, voz*> faint; **ele anda**
~mido he's disappeared; **~mir** *vi*
disappear
sumo /'sumu/ *m* (*Port*) juice
sumptuoso /sũtu'ozu/ *a* (*Port*) *veja*
suntuoso
sunga /'sũga/ *f* swimming trunks
suntuoso /sũtu'ozu/ *a* sumptuous
suor /su'or/ *m* sweat
superar /supe'rar/ *vt* overcome <*dificuldade etc*>; surpass <*expectativa,
pessoa*>
superá|vel /supe'ravew/ (*pl* **~veis**) *a*
surmountable; **~vit** (*pl* **~vits**) *m*
surplus
superestimar /superestʃi'mar/ *vt*
overestimate
superestrutura /superistru'tura/ *f*
superstructure
superfici|al /superfisi'aw/ (*pl* **~ais**)
a superficial
superfície /super'fisi/ *f* surface; (*medida*) area
supérfluo /su'pɛrfluu/ *a* superfluous
superintendência /superĩtẽ'dẽsia/ *f*
bureau
superi|or /superi'or/ *a* (*de cima*)
upper; <*ensino*> higher; <*número, temperatura etc*> greater (**a** than); (*melhor*)
superior (**a** to) □ *m* superior;
~oridade *f* superiority
superlativo /superla'tʃivu/ *a & m*
superlative
superlota|ção /superlota'sãw/ *f* over-
crowding; **~do** *a* overcrowded
supermercado /supermer'kadu/ *m*
supermarket
superpotência /superpo'tẽsia/ *f*
superpower
superpovoado /superpovo'adu/ *a*
overpopulated
supersecreto /superse'krɛtu/ *a* top
secret
supersensí|vel /supersẽ'sivew/ (*pl*
~veis) *a* oversensitive
supersônico /super'soniku/ *a* supersonic
supersti|ção /superstʃi'sãw/ *f* super-
stition; **~cioso** /o/ *a* superstitious
supervi|são /supervi'zãw/ *f* super-
vision; **~sionar** *vt* supervise; **~sor**
m supervisor
supetão /supe'tãw/ *m* **de ~** all of a
sudden
suplantar /suplã'tar/ *vt* supplant
suplemen|tar /supleme'tar/ *a* supple-
mentary □ *vt* supplement; **~to** *m* supplement

suplente /su'plẽtʃi/ *a & m/f* substitute

supletivo /suple'tʃivu/ *a* supplementary; **ensino ~** adult education

súplica /'suplika/ *f* plea; **tom de ~** pleading tone

suplicar /supli'kar/ *vt* plead for; (*em juízo*) petition for

suplício /su'plisiu/ *m* torture; (*fig: aflição*) torment

supor /su'por/ *vt* suppose

supor|tar /supor'tar/ *vt* (*sustentar*) support; (*tolerar*) stand, bear; **~tável** (*pl* **~táveis**) *a* bearable; **~te** /ɔ/ *m* support

suposição /supozi'sãw/ *f* supposition

supositório /supozi'toriu/ *m* suppository

supos|tamente /suposta'mẽtʃi/ *adv* supposedly; **~to** /o/ *a* supposed; **~to que** supposed that

supre|macia /suprema'sia/ *f* supremacy; **~mo** /e/ *a* supreme

supressão /supre'sãw/ *f* (*de lei, cargo, privilégio*) abolition; (*de jornal, informação, nomes*) suppression; (*de palavras, cláusula*) deletion

suprimento /supri'mẽtu/ *m* supply

suprimir /supri'mir/ *vt* abolish <*lei, cargo, privilégio*>; suppress <*jornal, informação, nomes*>; delete <*palavras, cláusula*>

suprir /su'prir/ *vt* provide for <*família, necessidades*>; make up for <*falta*>; make up <*quantia*>; supply <*o que falta*>; (*substituir*) take the place of; **~ alg de** provide s.o. with; **~ A por B** substitute B for A

supurar /supu'rar/ *vi* turn septic

sur|dez /sur'des/ *f* deafness; **~do** *a* deaf; <*consoante*> voiceless □ *m* deaf person; **os ~dos** the deaf; **~do-mudo** (*pl* **~dos-mudos**) *a* deaf and dumb □ *m* deaf-mute

sur|fe /'surfi/ *m* surfing; **~fista** *m/f* surfer

sur|gimento /surʒi'mẽtu/ *m* appearance; **~gir** *vi* arise; **~gir à mente** spring to mind

Suriname /suri'nami/ *m* Surinam

surpreen|dente /surpriẽ'dẽtʃi/ *a* surprising; **~der** *vt* surprise □ *vi* be surprising; **~der-se** *vpr* be surprised (de at)

surpre|sa /sur'preza/ *f* surprise; **de ~sa** by surprise; **~so** /e/ *a* surprised

sur|ra /'suxa/ *f* thrashing; **~rado** *a* <*roupa*> worn-out; **~rar** *vt* thrash <*pessoa*>; wear out <*roupa*>

surrealis|mo /suxea'lizmu/ *m* surrealism; **~ta** *a & m/f* surrealist

surtir /sur'tʃir/ *vt* produce; **~ efeito** be effective

surto /'surtu/ *m* outbreak

suscept- (*Port*) *veja* **suscet-**

susce|tibilidade /suset∫ibili'dadʒi/ *f* (*de pessoa*) sensitivity; **~tível** (*pl* **~tíveis**) *a* <*pessoa*> touchy, sensitive; **~tível de** open to

suscitar /susi'tar/ *vt* cause; raise <*dúvida, suspeita*>

suspei|ta /sus'pejta/ *f* suspicion; **~tar** *vt/i* **~tar (de)** suspect; **~to** *a* suspicious; (*duvidoso*) suspect □ *m* suspect; **~toso** /o/ *a* suspicious

suspen|der /suspẽ'der/ *vt* suspend; **~são** *f* suspension; **~se** *m* suspense; **~so** *a* suspended; **~sórios** *m pl* braces, (*Amer*) suspenders

suspi|rar /suspi'rar/ *vi* sigh; **~rar por** long for; **~ro** *m* sigh; (*doce*) meringue

sussur|rar /susu'xar/ *vt/i* whisper; **~ro** *m* whisper

sustar /sus'tar/ *vt/i* stop

susten|táculo /suste'takulu/ *m* mainstay; **~tar** *vt* support; (*afirmar*) maintain; **~to** *m* support; (*ganha-pão*) livelihood

susto /'sustu/ *m* fright

sutiã /sutʃi'ã/ *m* bra

su|til /su'tʃiw/ (*pl* **~tis**) *a* subtle; **~tileza** /e/ *f* subtlety

sutu|ra /su'tura/ *f* suture; **~rar** *vt* suture

T

tá /ta/ *int* (*fam*) OK; *veja* **estar**

taba|caria /tabaka'ria/ *f* tobacconist's; **~co** *m* tobacco

tabefe /ta'befi/ *m* slap

tabe|la /ta'bɛla/ *f* table; **~lar** *vt* tabulate

tablado /ta'bladu/ *m* platform

tabu /ta'bu/ *a & m* taboo

tábua /'tabua/ *f* board; **~ de passar roupa** ironing board

tabuleiro /tabu'leru/ *m* (*de xadrez etc*) board

tabuleta /tabu'lɛta/ *f* (*letreiro*) sign

taça /'tasa/ *f* (*prêmio*) cup; (*de champanhe etc*) glass

ta|cada /ta'kada/ *f* shot; **de uma ~cada** in one go; **~car** *vt* hit <*bola*>; (*fam*) throw

tacha /'taʃa/ *f* tack

tachar /ta'ʃar/ *vt* brand (de as)

tachinha /ta'ʃiɲa/ *f* drawing pin, (*Amer*) thumbtack

tácito /'tasitu/ *a* tacit

taciturno /tasi'turnu/ *a* taciturn

taco /'taku/ *m* (*de golfe*) club; (*de bilhar*) cue; (*de hóquei*) stick

tact- (*Port*) *veja* **tat-**

tagare|la /taga'rɛla/ *a* chatty, talkative □ *m/f* chatterbox; **~lar** *vi* chatter

tailan|dês /tajlã'des/ *a & m* (*f* ~**desa**) Thai

Tailândia /taj'lãdʒia/ *f* Thailand

tailleur /ta'jɛr/ (*pl* ~ **s**) *m* suit

Taiti /taj'tʃi/ *m* Tahiti

tal /taw/ (*pl* **tais**) *a* such; **que** ~? what do you think?, (*Port*) how are you?; **que** ~ **uma cerveja?** how about a beer?; ~ **como** such as; ~ **qual** just like; **um** ~ **de João** someone called John; **e** ~ and so on

tala /'tala/ *f* splint

talão /ta'lãw/ *m* stub; ~ **de cheques** chequebook

talco /'tawku/ *m* talc

talen|to /ta'lẽtu/ *m* talent; ~**toso** /o/ *a* talented

talhar /ta'ʎar/ *vt* slice <*dedo, carne*>; carve <*pedra, imagem*>

talharim /taʎa'rĩ/ *m* tagliatelle

talher /ta'ʎɛr/ *m* set of cutlery; *pl* cutlery

talho /'taʎu/ *m* (*Port*) butcher's

talismã /taliz'mã/ *m* charm, talisman

talo /'talu/ *m* stalk

talvez /taw'ves/ *adv* perhaps; ~ **ele venha amanhã** he may come tomorrow

tamanco /ta'mãku/ *m* clog

tamanho /ta'maɲu/ *m* size □ *adj* such

tâmara /'tamara/ *f* date

tamarindo /tama'rĩdu/ *m* tamarind

também /tã'bẽj/ *adv* also; ~ **não not** ... either, neither

tam|bor /tã'bor/ *m* drum; ~**borilar** *vi* <*dedos*> drum; <*chuva*> patter; ~**borim** *m* tambourine

Tâmisa /'tamiza/ *m* Thames

tam|pa /'tãpa/ *f* lid; ~**pão** *m* (*vaginal*) tampon; ~**par** *vt* put the lid on <*recipiente*>; (*tapar*) cover; ~**pinha** *f* top□ *m/f* (*Jam*) shorthouse

tampouco /tã'poku/ *adv* nor, neither

tanga /'tãga/ *f* G-string; (*avental*) loincloth

tangente /tã'ʒẽtʃi/ *f* tangent; **pela** ~ (*fig*) narrowly

tangerina /tãʒe'rina/ *f* tangerine

tango /'tãgu/ *m* tango

tanque /'tãki/ *m* tank; (*para lavar roupa*) sink

tanto /'tãtu/ *a & pron* so much; *pl* so many □ *adv* so much; ~ ... **como** ... both ... and ...; ~ (...) **quanto** as much (...) as; ~ **melhor** so much the better; ~ **tempo** so long; **vinte e** ~**s anos** twenty odd years; **nem** ~ not as much; **um** ~ **difícil** somewhat difficult; ~ **que** to the extent that

Tanzânia /tã'zania/ *f* Tanzania

tão /tãw/ *adv* so; ~ **grande quanto** as big as; ~**somente** *adv* solely

tapa /'tapa/ *m ou f* slap; **dar um** ~ **em** slap

tapar /ta'par/ *vt* (*cobrir*) cover; block <*luz, vista*>; cork <*garrafa*>

tapeçaria /tapesa'ria/ *f* (*pano*) tapestry; (*loja*) carpet shop

tape|tar /tape'tar/ *vt* carpet; ~**te** /e/ *m* carpet

tapioca /tapi'ɔka/ *f* tapioca

tapume /ta'pumi/ *m* fence

taquicardia /takikar'dʒia/ *f* palpitations

taquigra|far /takigra'far/ *vt/i* write in shorthand; ~**fia** *f* shorthand

tara /'tara/ *f* fetish; ~**do** *a* sex-crazed □ *m* sex maniac; **ser** ~**do por** be crazy about

tar|dar /tar'dar/ *vi* (*atrasar*) be late; (*demorar muito*) be long □ *vt* delay; ~**dar a responder** take a long time to answer, be a long time answering; **o mais** ~**dar** at the latest; **sem mais** ~**dar** without further delay; ~**de** *adv* late □ *f* afternoon; **hoje à** ~**de** this afternoon; ~**de da noite** late at night; ~**dinha** *f* late afternoon; ~**dio** *a* late

tarefa /ta'rɛfa/ *f* task, job

tarifa /ta'rifa/ *f* tariff; ~ **de embarque** airport tax

tarimbado /tarĩ'badu/ *a* experienced

tarja /'tarʒa/ *f* strip

ta|rô /ta'ro/ *m* tarot; ~**rólogo** *m* tarot reader

tartamu|dear /tartamudʒi'ar/ *vi* stammer; ~**do** *a* stammering □ *m* stammerer

tártaro /'tartaru/ *m* tartar

tartaruga /tarta'ruga/ *f* (*bicho*) turtle; (*material*) tortoiseshell

tatear /tatʃi'ar/ *vt* feel □ *vi* feel one's way

táti|ca /'tatʃika/ *f* tactics; ~**co** *a* tactical

tá|til /'tatʃiw/ (*pl* ~**teis**) *a* tactile

tato /'tatu/ *m* (*sentido*) touch; (*diplomacia*) tact

tatu /ta'tu/ *m* armadillo

tatu|ador /tatua'dor/ *m* tattooist; ~**agem** *f* tattoo; ~**ar** *vt* tattoo

tauromaquia /tawroma'kia/ *f* bullfighting

taxa /'taʃa/ *f* (*a pagar*) charge; (*índice*) rate; ~ **de câmbio** exchange rate; ~ **de juros** interest rate; ~ **rodoviária** road tax

taxar /ta'ʃar/ *vt* tax

taxativo /taʃa'tʃivu/ *a* firm, categorical

táxi /'taksi/ *m* taxi

taxiar /taksi'ar/ *vi* taxi

taxímetro /tak'simetru/ *m* taxi meter

taxista /tak'sista/ *m/f* taxi driver

tchã /tʃã/ *m* (*fam*) special something

tchau /tʃaw/ *int* goodbye, bye

tcheco /'tʃɛku/ *a & m* Czech

Tchecoslováquia /tʃekoslo'vakia/ f Czechoslovakia

te /tʃi/ pron you; (a ti) to you

tear /tʃi'ar/ m loom

teatral /tʃia'traw/ (pl ~trais) a theatrical; <grupo> theatre; ~tro m theatre; ~trólogo m playwright

tecelagem /tese'laʒẽ/ f (trabalho) weaving; (fábrica) textile factory; ~lão m (f ~lã) weaver

tecer /te'ser/ vt/i weave; ~cido m cloth; (no corpo) tissue

tecla /'tɛkla/ f key; ~cladista m/f (músico) keyboard player; (de computador) keyboard operator; ~clado m keyboard; ~clar vt key (in)

técnica /'tɛknika/ f technique; ~co a technical □ m specialist; (de time) manager; (que mexe com máquinas) technician

tecnocrata /tekno'krata/ m/f technocrat; ~logia f technology; ~lógico a technological

teco-teco /tɛku'tɛku/ m light aircraft

tecto /'tɛtu/ m (Port) veja teto

tédio /'tɛdʒiu/ m boredom

tedioso /tedʒi'ozu/ a boring, tedious

Teerã /tee'rã/ f Teheran

teia /'teja/ f web

teima /'tejma/ f persistence; ~mar vi insist; ~mar em ir insist on going; ~mosia f stubbornness; ~moso /o/ a stubborn; <ruído> insistent

teixo /'tejʃu/ m yew

Tejo /'teʒu/ m Tagus

tela /'tɛla/ f (de cinema, TV etc) screen; (tecido, pintura) canvas

telecomandado /telekomã'dadu/ a remote-controlled; ~do m remote control

telecomunicação /telekomunika-'sãw/ f telecommunication

teleférico /tele'fɛriku/ m cable car

telefonar /telefo'nar/ vi telephone; ~nar para alg phone s.o.; ~ne /o/ m telephone; (número) phone number; ~ne celular cell phone; ~ne sem fio cordless phone; ~nema /e/ m phone call; ~nia f telephone technology

telefônico /tele'foniku/ a telephone; cabine ~ca phone box, (Amer) phone booth; mesa ~ca switchboard

telefonista /telefo'nista/ m/f (da companhia telefônica) operator; (dentro de empresa etc) telephonist

telegrafar /telegra'far/ vt/i telegraph; ~gráfico a telegraphic

telégrafo /te'lɛgrafu/ m telegraph

telegrama /tele'grama/ m telegram; ~guiado a remote- controlled

telejornal /teleʒor'naw/ (pl ~nais) m television news

telenovela /teleno'vɛla/ f TV soap opera; ~objetiva f telephoto lens

telepatia /telepa'tʃia/ f telepathy; ~pático a telepathic

telescópico /teles'kɔpiku/ a telescopic; ~pio m telescope

telespectador /telespekta'dor/ m television viewer □ a viewing

televisão /televi'zãw/ f television; ~são a cabo cable television; ~sionar vt televise; ~sivo a television; ~sor m television set

telex /te'lɛks/ m invar telex

telha /'teʎa/ f tile; ~do m roof

tema /'tema/ m theme; ~mático a thematic

temer /te'mer/ vt fear □ vi be afraid; ~ por fear for

temerário /teme'rariu/ a reckless; ~ridade f recklessness; ~roso /o/ a fearful

temido /te'midu/ a feared; ~mível (pl ~míveis) a fearsome; ~mor m fear

tempão /tẽ'pãw/ m um ~ a long time

temperado /tẽpe'radu/ a <clima> temperate □ pp de temperar

temperamental /tẽperamẽ'taw/ (pl ~tais) a temperamental; ~to m temperament

temperar /tẽpe'rar/ vt season <comida>; temper <aço>

temperatura /tẽpera'tura/ f temperature

tempero /tẽ'peru/ m seasoning

tempestade /tẽpes'tadʒi/ f storm; ~tuoso /o/ a stormy; (fig) tempestuous

templo /'tẽplu/ m temple

tempo /'tẽpu/ m (período) time; (atmosfera) weather; (do verbo) tense; (de jogo) half; ao mesmo ~ at the same time; nesse meio ~ in the meantime; o ~ todo all the time; de todos os ~s of all time; quanto ~ how long; muito/pouco ~ a long/short time; ~ integral full time

têmpora /'tẽpora/ f temple

temporada /tẽpo'rada/ f (sazão) season; (tempo) while; ~ral (pl ~rais) a temporal □ m storm; ~rário a temporary

tenacidade /tenasi'dadʒi/ f tenacity; ~naz a tenacious □ f tongs

tenção /tẽ'sãw/ f intention

tencionar /tẽsio'nar/ vt intend

tenda /'tẽda/ f tent

tendão /tẽ'dãw/ m tendon; ~ de Aquiles Achilles tendon

tendência /tẽ'dẽsia/ f (moda) trend; (propensão) tendency

tendencioso /tẽdẽsi'ozu/ a tendentious

ten|der /tẽ'der/ *vi* tend (para to- wards); ~de a engordar he tends to get fat; o tempo ~de a ficar bom the weather is improving

tenebroso /tene'brozu/ *a* dark; (*fig: terrível*) dreadful

tenente /te'nẽtʃi/ *m/f* lieutenant

tênis /'tenis/ *m invar* (*jogo*) tennis; (*sapato*) trainer; um ~ (*par*) a pair of trainers; ~ de mesa table tennis

tenista /te'nista/ *m/f* tennis player

tenor /te'nor/ *m* tenor

tenro /'tẽxu/ *a* tender

ten|são /tẽ'sãw/ *f* tension; ~são (ar- terial) blood pressure; ~so *a* tense

tentação /tẽta'sãw/ *f* temptation

tentáculo /tẽ'takulu/ *m* tentacle

ten|tador /tẽta'dor/ *a* tempting; ~tar *vt* try; (*seduzir*) tempt □ *vi* try; ~tativa *f* attempt; ~tativo *a* tenta- tive

tênue /'tenui/ *a* faint

teo|logia /teolo'ʒia/ *f* theology; ~lógico *a* theological

teólogo /te'ɔlogu/ *m* theologian

teor /te'or/ *m* (*de gordura etc*) content; (*de carta, discurso*) drift

teo|rema /teo'rema/ *m* theorem; ~ria *f* theory

teórico /te'ɔriku/ *a* theoretical

teorizar /teori'zar/ *vt* theorize

tépido /'tɛpidu/ *a* tepid

ter /ter/ *vt* have; tenho vinte anos I am twenty (years old); ~ medo/sede be afraid/thirsty; tenho que *ou* de ir I have to go; tem (*há*) there is/are; não tem de quê mention it; ~ a ver com have to do with

tera|peuta /tera'pewta/ *m/f* therap- ist; ~pêutico *a* therapeutic; ~pia *f* therapy

terça /'tersa/ *f* Tuesday; ~-feira (*pl* ~s-feiras) *f* Tuesday; Terça-Feira Gorda Shrove Tues- day

tercei|ra /ter'sera/ *f* (*marcha*) third; ~ranista *m/f* third-year; ~ro *a* third □ *m* third party

terço /'tersu/ *m* third

ter|çol /ter'sɔis/ *m* stye

tergal /ter'gaw/ *m* Terylene

térmi|co /'termiku/ *a* thermal; garra- fa ~ca Thermos flask

termi|nal /termi'naw/ (*pl* ~nais) *a* & *m* terminal; ~nal de vídeo VDU; ~nante *a* definite; ~nar *vt* finish □ *vi* <*pessoa, coisa*> finish; <*coisa*> end; ~nar com alg (*cortar relação*) break up with s.o.

ter|minologia /terminolo'ʒia/ *f* ter- minology; ~mo[1] /'termu/ *m* term; pôr ~mo a put an end to; meio ~mo compromise

termo[2] /'termu/ *m* (*Port*) Thermos flask

ter|mômetro /ter'mometru/ *m* ther- mometer; ~mostato *m* thermostat

terno[1] /'ternu/ *m* suit

ter|no[2] /'ternu/ *a* tender; ~nura *f* tenderness

terra /'texa/ *f* land; (*solo, elétrico*) earth; (*chão*) ground; a Terra Earth; por ~ on the ground; ~ natal home- land

terraço /te'xasu/ *m* terrace

terra|cota /texa'kɔta/ *f* terracotta; ~moto /texa'mɔtu/ *m* (*Port*) earth- quake; ~plenagem *f* earth moving

terreiro /te'xeru/ *m* meeting place for Afro-Brazilian cults

terremoto /texe'mɔtu/ *m* earthquake

terreno /te'xenu/ *a* earthly □ *m* ground; (*geog*) terrain; (*um*) piece of land; ~ baldio piece of waste ground

térreo /'texiu/ *a* ground-floor; (an- dar) ~ ground floor, (*Amer*) first floor

terrestre /te'xestri/ *a* <*animal, bata- lha, forças*> land; (*da Terra*) of the Earth, the Earth's; <*alegrias etc*> earthly

terrificante /texifi'kãtʃi/ *a* terrifying

terrina /te'xina/ *f* tureen

territori|al /texitori'aw/ (*pl* ~ais) *a* territorial

território /texi'tɔriu/ *m* territory

terri|vel /te'xivew/ (*pl* ~veis) *a* ter- rible

terror /te'xor/ *m* terror; filme de ~ horror film

terroris|mo /texo'rizmu/ *m* ter- rorism; ~ta *a* & *m/f* terrorist

tese /'tɛzi/ *f* theory; (*escrita*) thesis

teso /'tezu/ *a* (*apertado*) taut; (*rígido*) stiff

tesoura /te'zora/ *f* scissors; uma ~ a pair of scissors

tesou|reiro /tezo'reru/ *m* treasurer; ~ro *m* treasure; (*do Estado*) treas- ury

testa /'tɛsta/ *f* forehead; ~-de-ferro (*pl* ~s-de-ferro) *m* frontman

testamento /testa'mẽtu/ *m* will; (*na Bíblia*) testament

tes|tar /tes'tar/ *vt* test; ~te /ɛ/ *m* test

testemu|nha /teste'muɲa/ *f* witness; ~nha ocular eye witness; ~nhar *vt* bear witness to □ *vi* testify; ~nho *m* evidence, testimony

testículo /tes'tʃikulu/ *m* testicle

teta /'teta/ *f* teat

tétano /'tɛtanu/ *m* tetanus

teto /'tɛtu/ *m* ceiling; ~ solar sun roof

tétrico /'tɛtriku/ *a* (*triste*) dismal; (*me- donho*) horrible

teu /tew/ (*f* tua) *a* your □ *pron* yours

têx|til /'testʃiw/ (*pl* ~teis) *m* textile

tex|to /'testu/ *m* text; ~tura *f* texture

texugo /te'ʃugu/ *m* badger

tez /tes/ *f* complexion

ti /tʃi/ *pron* you

tia /'tʃia/ *f* aunt; ∼-avó (*pl* ∼s-avós) *f* great aunt

tiara /tʃi'ara/ *f* tiara

tíbia /'tʃibia/ *f* shinbone

ticar /tʃi'kar/ *vi* tick

tico /'tʃiku/ *m* um ∼ de a little bit of

tiete /tʃi'ɛtʃi/ *m/f* fan

tifo /'tʃifu/ *m* typhoid

tigela /tʃi'ʒela/ *f* bowl; de meia ∼ smalltime

tigre /'tʃigri/ *m* tiger; ∼sa /e/ *f* tigress

tijolo /tʃi'ʒolu/ *m* brick

til /'tʃiw/ (*pl* tis) *m* tilde

tilintar /tʃilĩ'tar/ *vi* jingle □ *m* jingling

timão /tʃi'mãw/ *m* tiller

timbre /'tʃibri/ *m* (*insígnia*) crest; (*em papel*) heading; (*de som*) tone; (*de vogal*) quality

time /'tʃimi/ *m* team

timidez /tʃimi'des/ *f* shyness

tímido /'tʃimidu/ *a* shy

tímpano /'tʃipanu/ *m* (*tambor*) kettledrum; (*no ouvido*) eardrum

tina /'tʃina/ *f* vat

tingir /tʃi'ʒir/ *vt* dye <*tecido, cabelo*>; (*fig*) tinge

ti|nido /tʃi'nidu/ *m* tinkling; ∼nir *vi* tinkle; <*ouvidos*> ring; (*tremer*) tremble; estar ∼nindo (*fig*) be in peak condition

tino /'tʃinu/ *m* sense, judgement; ter ∼ para have a flair for

tin|ta /'tʃita/ *f* (*para pintar*) paint; (*para escrever*) ink; (*para tingir*) dye; ∼teiro *m* inkwell

tintim /tʃĩ'tʃĩ/ *m* contar ∼ por ∼ give a blow-by-blow account of

tin|to /'tʃitu/ *a* dyed; <*vinho*> red; ∼tura *f* dye; (*fig*) tinge; ∼turaria *f* dry cleaner's

tio /'tʃiu/ *m* uncle; *pl* (∼ e tia) uncle and aunt; ∼-avó (*pl* ∼s-avós) *m* great uncle

típico /'tʃipiku/ *a* typical

tipo /'tʃipu/ *m* type

tipóia /tʃi'pɔja/ *f* sling

tique /'tʃiki/ *m* (*sinal*) tick; (*do rosto etc*) twitch

tíquete /'tʃiketʃi/ *m* ticket

tiquinho /tʃi'kiɲu/ *m* um ∼ de a tiny bit of

tira /'tʃira/ *f* strip □ *m/f* (*fam*) copper, (*Amer*) cop

tiracolo /tʃira'kɔlu/ *m* a ∼ <*bolsa*> over one's shoulder; <*pessoa*> in tow

tiragem /tʃi'raʒẽ/ *f* (*de jornal*) circulation

tira|-gosto /tʃira'gostu/ *m* snack; ∼manchas *m invar* stain remover

ti|rania /tʃira'nia/ *f* tyranny; ∼rânico *a* tyrannical; ∼rano *m* tyrant

tirar /tʃi'rar/ *vt* (*afastar*) take away; (*de dentro*) take out; take off <*roupa, sapato, tampa*>; take <*foto, cópia, férias*>; clear <*mesa*>; get <*nota, diploma, salário*>; get out <*mancha*>

tiritar /tʃiri'tar/ *vi* shiver

tiro /'tʃiru/ *m* shot; ∼ ao alvo shooting; é ∼ e queda (*fam*) it can't fail; ∼teio *m* shoot-out

titânio /tʃi'taniu/ *m* titanium

títere /'tʃiteri/ *m* puppet

ti|tia /tʃi'tʃia/ *f* auntie; ∼tio *m* uncle

titití /tʃitʃi'tʃi/ *m* (*fam*) talk

titubear /tʃitubi'ar/ *vi* stagger, totter; (*fig: hesitar*) waver

titular /tʃitu'lar/ *m/f* title holder; (*de time*) captain □ *vt* title

título /'tʃitulu/ *m* title; (*obrigação*) bond; a ∼ de on the basis of; a ∼ pessoal on a personal basis

toa /'toa/ *f* à ∼ (*sem rumo*) aimlessly; (*ao acaso*) at random; (*sem motivo*) without reason; (*em vão*) for nothing; (*desocupado*) at a loose end; (*de repente*) out of the blue

toada /to'ada/ *f* melody

toalete /toa'lɛtʃi/ *m* toilet

toalha /to'aʎa/ *f* towel; ∼ de mesa tablecloth

tobogã /tobo'gã/ *m* (*rampa*) slide; (*trenó*) toboggan

toca /'tɔka/ *f* burrow

toca|-discos /tɔka'dʒiskus/ *m invar* record player; ∼-fitas *m invar* tape player

tocaia /to'kaja/ *f* ambush

tocante /to'kãtʃi/ *a* (*enternecedor*) moving

tocar /to'kar/ *vt* touch; play <*piano, música, disco etc*>; ring <*campainha*> □ *vi* touch; <*pianista, música, disco etc*> play; <*campainha, telefone, sino*> ring; ∼-se *vpr* touch; (*mancar-se*) take the hint; ∼ a (*dizer respeito*) concern; ∼ em touch; touch on <*assunto*>

tocha /'tɔʃa/ *f* torch

toco /'toku/ *m* (*de árvore*) stump; (*de cigarro*) butt

toda /'toda/ *f* a ∼ at full speed

todavia /toda'via/ *conj* however

todo /'todu/ *a* all; (*cada*) every; *pl* all; ∼ o dinheiro all the money; ∼ dia, ∼s os dias every day; ∼s os alunos all the pupils; o dia ∼ all day; em ∼ lugar everywhere; ∼ mundo, ∼s everyone; ∼s nós all of us; ao ∼ in all; ∼-poderoso *a* almighty

tofe /'tɔfi/ *m* toffee

toga /'tɔga/ *f* gown; (*de romano*) toga

toicinho /toj'siɲu/ *m* bacon

toldo /'towdu/ *m* awning

tole|rância /tole'rãsia/ f tolerance; **~rante** a tolerant; **~rar** vt tolerate; **~rável** (pl **~ráveis**) a tolerable

to|lice /to'lisi/ f foolishness; (uma) foolish thing; **~lo** /o/ a foolish □ m fool

tom /tõ/ m tone

to|mada /to'mada/ f (conquista) capture; (elétrica) plughole; (de filme) shot; **~mar** vt take; (beber) drink; **~mar café** have breakfast

tomara /to'mara/ int I hope so; **~ que** let's hope that; **~-que-caia** a invar <vestido> strapless

tomate /to'matʃi/ m tomato

tom|bar /tõ'bar/ vt (derrubar) knock down; list <edifício> □ vi fall over; **~bo m** fall; **levar um ~bo** have a fall

tomilho /to'miʎu/ m thyme

tomo /'tomu/ m volume

tona /'tona/ f trazer à ~ bring up; vir à ~ emerge

tonalidade /tonali'dadʒi/ f (de música) key; (de cor) shade

to|nel /to'nɛw/ (pl **~néis**) m cask; **~nelada** f tonne

tôni|ca /'tonika/ f tonic; (fig: assunto) keynote; **~co** a & m tonic

tonificar /tonifi'kar/ vt tone up

ton|tear /tõtʃi'ar/ vt **~tear alg** make s.o.'s head spin; **~teira** f dizziness; **~to** a (zonzo) dizzy; (bobo) stupid; (atrapalhado) flustered; **~tura** f dizziness

to|pada /to'pada/ f trip; **dar uma ~pada em** stub one's toe on; **~par** vt agree to, accept; **~par com** bump into <pessoa>; come across <coisa>

topázio /to'paziu/ m topaz

topete /to'petʃi/ m quiff

tópico /'tɔpiku/ a topical □ m topic

topless /topi'lɛs/ a invar & adv topless

topo /'topu/ m top

topografia /topogra'fia/ f topography

topônimo /to'ponimu/ m place name

toque /'tɔki/ m touch; (da campainha, do telefone) ring; (de instrumento) playing; **dar um ~ em** (fam) have a word with

Tóquio /'tɔkiu/ f Tokyo

tora /'tɔra/ f log

toranja /to'rãʒa/ f grapefruit

tórax /'tɔraks/ m invar thorax

tor|ção /tor'sãw/ f (do braço etc) sprain; **~cedor** m supporter; **~cer** vt twist; (machucar) sprain; (espremer) wring <roupa>; (centrifugar) spin <roupa> □ vi (gritar) cheer (por for); (desejar sucesso) keep one's fingers crossed (por for; **para que** that); **~cer-se** vpr twist about;

~cicolo /ɔ/ m stiff neck; **~cida** f (torção) twist; (torcedores) supporters; (gritaria) cheering

tormen|ta /tor'mẽta/ f storm; **~to m** torment; **~toso** /o/ a stormy

tornado /tor'nadu/ m tornado

tornar /tor'nar/ vt make; **~-se** vpr become

torne|ado /torni'adu/ a **bem ~ado** shapely; **~ar** vt turn

torneio /tor'neju/ m tournament

torneira /tor'nera/ f tap, (Amer) faucet

torniquete /torni'ketʃi/ m (para ferido) tourniquet; (Port: de entrada) turnstile

torno /'tornu/ m lathe; (de ceramista) wheel; **em ~ de** around

tornozelo /torno'zelu/ m ankle

toró /to'rɔ/ m downpour

torpe /'torpi/ a dirty

torpe|dear /torpedʒi'ar/ vt torpedo; **~do** /e/ m torpedo

torpor /tor'por/ m torpor

torra|da /to'xada/ f piece of toast; pl toast; **~deira** f toaster

torrão /to'xãw/ m (de terra) turf; (de açúcar) lump

torrar /to'xar/ vt toast <pão>; roast <café>; blow <dinheiro>; sell off <mercadorias>

torre /'toxi/ f tower; (em xadrez) rook; **~ de controle** control tower; **~ão** m turret

torrefação /toxefa'sãw/ f (ação) roasting; (fábrica) coffee-roasting plant

torren|cial /toxẽsi'aw/ (pl **~ciais**) a torrential; **~te** f torrent

torresmo /to'xezmu/ m crackling

tórrido /'tɔxidu/ a torrid

torrone /to'xoni/ m nougat

torso /'torsu/ m torso

torta /'tɔrta/ f pie, tart

tor|to /'tɔrtu/ a crooked; **a ~ e a direito** left, right and centre; **~tuoso** a winding

tortu|ra /tor'tura/ f torture; **~rador** m torturer; **~rar** vt torture

to|sa /'tɔza/ f (de cachorro) clipping; (de ovelhas) shearing; **~são** m fleece; **~sar** vt clip <cachorro>; shear <ovelhas>; crop <cabelo>

tosco /'tosku/ a rough, coarse

tosquiar /toski'ar/ vt shear <ovelha>

tos|se /'tɔsi/ f cough; **~se de cachorro** whooping cough; **~sir** vi cough

tostão /tos'tãw/ m penny

tostar /tos'tar/ vt brown <carne>; tan <pele, pessoa>; **~-se** vpr (ao sol) go brown

to|tal /to'taw/ (pl **~tais**) a & m total

totali|dade /totali'dadʒi/ f entirety; **~tário** a totalitarian; **~zar** vt total touca /'toka/ f bonnet; (de freira) wimple; ~ de banho bathing cap; ~dor m dressing table

toupeira /to'pera/ f mole

tou|rada /to'rada/ f bullfight; ~reiro m bullfighter; ~ro m bull; Touro (signo) Taurus

tóxico /'tɔksiku/ a toxic □ m toxic substance

toxicômano /toksi'komanu/ m drug addict

toxina /tok'sina/ f toxin

traba|lhador /trabaʎa'dor/ a <pessoa> hard-working; <classe> working □ m worker; ~lhar vt work □ vi work; (numa peça, filme) act; ~lheira f big job; ~lhista a labour; ~lho m work; (um) job; (na escola) assignment; dar-se o ~lho de to the trouble of; ~lho de parto labour; ~lhos forçados hard labour; ~lhoso a laborious

traça /'trasa/ f moth

tração /tra'sãw/ f traction

tra|çar /tra'sar/ vt draw; draw up <plano>; set out <ordens>; ~ço m stroke; (entre frases) dash; (vestígio) trace; (característica) trait; pl (do rosto) features

tractor /trat'tor/ m (Port) veja trator

tradi|ção /tradʒi'sãw/ f tradition; ~cional (pl ~cionais) a traditional

tradu|ção /tradu'sãw/ f translation; ~tor m translator; ~zir vt/i translate (de from; para into)

trafe|gar /trafe'gar/ vi run; ~gável (pl ~gáveis) a open to traffic

tráfego /'trafegu/ m traffic

trafi|cância /trafi'kãsia/ f trafficking; ~cante m/f trafficker; ~car vt/i traffic (com in)

tráfico /'trafiku/ m traffic

tra|gada /tra'gada/ f (de bebida) swallow; (de cigarro) drag; ~gar vt swallow; inhale <fumaça>

tragédia /tra'ʒɛdʒia/ f tragedy

trágico /'traʒiku/ a tragic

trago /'tragu/ m (de bebida) swallow; (de cigarro) drag; de um ~ in one go

trai|ção /traj'sãw/ f (ato) betrayal; (deslealdade) treachery; (da pátria) treason; ~coeiro a treacherous; ~dor a treacherous □ m traitor

trailer /'trejler/ (pl ~s) m (de filme etc) trailer; (casa móvel) caravan, (Amer) trailer

traineira /traj'nera/ f trawler

training /'trejnĩ/ (pl ~s) m track suit

trair /tra'ir/ vt betray; be unfaithful to <marido, mulher>; ~-se vpr give o.s. away

tra|jar /tra'ʒar/ vt wear; ~jar-se vpr dress (de in); ~je m outfit; ~je a

rigor evening dress; ~je espacial space suit

traje|to /tra'ʒɛtu/ m (percurso) journey; (caminho) route; ~tória f trajectory; (fig) course

tralha /'traʎa/ f (trastes) junk

tra|ma /'trama/ f plot; ~mar vt/i plot

trambique /trã'biki/ m (fam) m con; ~queiro (fam) m con artist

tramitar /trami'tar/ vi be processed

trâmites /'tramitʃis/ m pl channels

tramóia /tra'mɔja/ f scheme

trampolim /trãpo'lĩ/ m (de ginástica) trampoline; (de piscina, fig) springboard

tranca /'trãka/ f bolt; (em carro) lock

trança /'trãsa/ f (de cabelo) plait

tran|cafiar /trãkafi'ar/ vt lock up; ~car vt lock; cancel <matrícula>

trançar /trã'sar/ vt plait <cabelo>; weave <palha etc>

tranco /'trãku/ m jolt; aos ~s e barrancos in fits and starts

tranqueira /trã'kera/ f junk

tranqüi|lidade /trãkwili'dadʒi/ f tranquillity; ~lizador a reassuring; ~lizante m tranquilliser □ a reassuring; ~lizar vt reassure; ~lizar-se vpr be reassured; ~lo a <bairro, sono> peaceful; <pessoa, voz, mar> calm; <consciência> clear; <sucesso, lucro> sure-fire □ adv with no trouble

transa /'trãza/ f (fam) (negócio) deal; (caso) affair; ~ção f transaction; ~do a (fam) <roupa, pessoa, casa> stylish; <relação> healthy

Transamazônica /trãzama'zonika/ f trans-Amazonian highway

transar /trã'zar/ (fam) vt set up; do <drogas> □ vi (negociar) deal; (fazer sexo) have sex

transatlântico /trãzat'lãtʃiku/ a transatlantic □ m liner

transbordar /trãzbor'dar/ vi overflow

transcen|dental /trãsẽdẽ'taw/ (pl ~dentais) a transcendental; ~der vt/i ~der (a) transcend

trans|crever /trãskre'ver/ vt transcribe; ~crição f transcription; ~crito a transcribed □ m transcript

transe /'trãzi/ m trance

transeunte /trãzi'ũtʃi/ m/f passer-by

transfe|rência /trãsfe'rẽsia/ f transfer; ~ridor m protractor; ~rir vt transfer; ~rir-se vpr transfer

transfor|mação /trãsforma'sãw/ f transformation; ~mador m transformer; ~mar vt transform; ~mar-se vpr be transformed

trânsfuga /'trãsfuga/ m/f deserter; (de um país) defector

transfusão /trãsfu'zãw/ f transfusion

trans|gredir /trãzgre'dʒir/ vt infringe; **~gressão** f infringement

transi|ção /trãzi'sãw/ f transition; **~cional** (pl **~cionais**) a transitional

transi|gente /trãzi'ʒẽtʃi/ a open to compromise; **~gir** vi compromise

transis|tor /trãzis'tor/ m transistor; **~torizado** a transistorized

transi|tar /trãzi'tar/ vi pass; **~tável** (pl **~táveis**) a passable; **~tivo** a transitive

trânsito /'trãzitu/ m traffic; **em ~** in transit

transitório /trãzi'toriu/ a transitory

translúcido /trãz'lusidu/ a translucent

transmis|são /trãzmi'sãw/ f transmission; **~sor** m transmitter

transmitir /trãzmi'tʃir/ vt transmit <programa, calor, doença>; convey <notícia, ordens>; transfer <herança, direito>; **~-se** vpr <doença> be transmitted

transpa|recer /trãspare'ser/ vi be visible; (fig) <emoção, verdade> come out; **~rência** f transparency; **~rente** a transparent

transpi|ração /trãspira'sãw/ f perspiration; **~rar** vt exude □ vi (suar) perspire; <notícia> trickle through; <verdade> come out

transplan|tar /trãsplã'tar/ vt transplant; **~te** m transplant

transpor /trãs'por/ vt cross <rio, fronteira>; get over <obstáculo, dificuldade>; transpose <letras, música>

transpor|tadora /trãsporta'dora/ f transport company; **~tar** vt transport; (em contas) carry forward; **~te** m transport; **~te coletivo** public transport

transposto /trãs'postu/ pp de **transpor**

transtor|nar /trãstor'nar/ vt mess up <papéis, casa>; disrupt <rotina, ambiente>; disturb, upset <pessoa>; **~nar-se** vpr <pessoa> be rattled; **~no** /o/ m (de casa, rotina) disruption; (de pessoa) disturbance; (contratempo) upset

transver|sal /trãzver'saw/ (pl **~sais**) a (rua) **~sal** cross street; **~so** /ɛ/ a transverse

transvi|ado /trãzvi'adu/ a wayward; **~ar** vt lead astray

trapa|ça /tra'pasa/ f swindle; **~cear** vi cheat; **~ceiro** a crooked □ m cheat

trapa|lhada /trapa'ʎada/ f bungle; **~lhão** a (f **~lhona**) bungling □ m (f **~lhona**) bungler

trapézio /tra'pɛziu/ m trapeze

trapezista /trape'zista/ m/f trapeze artist

trapo /'trapu/ m rag

traquéia /tra'keja/ f windpipe, trachea

traquejo /tra'keʒu/ m knack

traquinas /tra'kinas/ a invar mischievous

trás /tras/ adv **de ~** from behind; **a roda de ~** the back wheel; **de ~ para frente** back to front; **para ~** backwards; **deixar para ~** leave behind; **por ~ de** behind

traseiro /tra'zeru/ a rear, back □ m bottom

trasladar /trazla'dar/ vt transport

traspas|sado /traspa'sadu/ a <paletó> double-breasted; **~sar** vt pierce

traste /'trastʃi/ m (pessoa) pain; (coisa) piece of junk

tra|tado /tra'tadu/ m (pacto) treaty; (estudo) treatise; **~tamento** m treatment; (título) title; **~tar** vt treat; negotiate <preço, venda> □ vi (manter relações) have dealings (com with); (combinar) negotiate <preço>; **~tar de** deal with; **~tar alg de** ou **por** address s.o. as; **~tar de voltar** (tentar) seek to return; (resolver) decide to return; **~tar-se de** be a matter of; **~tável** (pl **~táveis**) a <doença> treatable; <pessoa> accommodating; **~tos** m pl **maus ~tos** illtreatment

trator /tra'tor/ m tractor

trauma /'trawma/ m trauma; **~tizante** a traumatic; **~tizar** vt traumatize

tra|vão /tra'vãw/ m (Port) brake; **~var** vt lock <rodas, músculos>; stop <carro>; block <passagem>; strike up <amizade, conversa>; wage <luta, combate> □ vi (Port) brake

trave /'travi/ f beam, joist; (do gol) crossbar

traves|sa /tra'vɛsa/ f (trave) crossbar; (rua) side street; (prato) dish; (pente) slide; **~são** m dash; **~seiro** m pillow; **~sia** f crossing; **~so** /e/ a <criança> naughty; **~sura** f prank; pl mischief

travesti /traves'tʃi/ m transvestite; (artista) drag artist; **~do** a in drag

trazer /tra'zer/ vt bring; bear <nome, ferida>; wear <barba, chapéu, cabelo curto>

trecho /'treʃu/ m (de livro etc) passage; (de rua etc) stretch

treco /'trεku/ m (fam) m (coisa) thing; (ataque) turn

trégua /'trεgwa/ f truce; (fig) respite

trei|nador /trejna'dor/ m trainer; **~namento** m training; **~nar** vt train <atleta, animal>; practise <língua etc> □ vi <atleta> train;

<pianista, principiante> practise;
~no *m* training; (*um*) training
session
trejeito /tre'ʒejtu/ *m* grimace
trela /'trɛla/ *f* lead, (*Amer*) leash
treliça /tre'lisa/ *f* trellis
trem /trẽj/ *m* train; **~ de aterrissagem** undercarriage; **~ de carga**
goods train, (*Amer*) freight train
trema /'trema/ *m* dieresis
treme|deira /treme'dera/ *f* shiver;
~licar *vi* tremble; **~luzir** *vi* glimmer, flicker
tremendo /tre'mẽdu/ *a* tremendous
tre|mer /tre'mer/ *vi* tremble; *<terra>*
shake; **~mor** *m* tremor; (*tremedeira*)
shiver; **~mular** *vi* *<bandeira>* flutter; *<luz, estrela>* glimmer, flicker
trêmulo /'tremulu/ *a* trembling;
<luz> flickering
trena /'trena/ *f* tape measure
trenó /tre'nɔ/ *m* sledge, (*Amer*) sled;
(*puxado a cavalos etc*) sleigh
tre|padeira /trepa'dera/ *f* climbing
plant; **~par** *vt* climb □ *vi* climb; (*chulo*) fuck
três /tres/ *a & m* three
tresloucado /trezlo'kadu/ *a* deranged
trevas /'trevas/ *f pl* darkness
trevo /'trevu/ *m* (*planta*) clover; (*rodoviário*) interchange
treze /'trezi/ *a & m* thirteen
trezentos /tre'zẽtus/ *a & m* three
hundred
triagem /tri'aʒẽ/ *f* (*escolha*) selection;
(*separação*) sorting; **fazer uma ~ de**
sort
tri|angular /triãgu'lar/ *a* triangular;
~ângulo *m* triangle
tri|bal /tri'baw/ (*pl* **~bais**) *a* tribal;
~bo *f* tribe
tribu|na /tri'buna/ *f* rostrum; **~nal**
(*pl* **~nais**) *m* court
tribu|tação /tributa'sãw/ *f* taxation;
~tar *vt* tax; **~tário** *a* tax □ *m*
tributary; **~to** *m* tribute
tri|cô /tri'ko/ *m* knitting; **artigos de
~cô** knitwear; **~cotar** *vt/i* knit
tridimensio|nal /tridʒimẽsio'naw/
(*pl* **~nais**) *a* a three- dimensional
trigêmeo /tri'ʒemiu/ *m* triplet
trigésimo /tri'ʒɛzimu/ *a* thirtieth
tri|go /'trigu/ *m* wheat; **~gueiro** *a*
dark
trilha /'triʎa/ *f* path; (*pista, de disco*)
track; **~ sonora** soundtrack
trilhão /tri'ʎãw/ *m* billion, (*Amer*)
trillion
trilho /'triʎu/ *m* track
trilogia /trilo'ʒia/ *f* trilogy
trimes|tral /trimes'traw/ (*pl* **~-
trais**) *a* quarterly; **~tre** /ɛ/ *m* quarter; (*do ano letivo*) term
trincar /trĩ'kar/ *vt/i* crack

trincheira /trĩ'ʃera/ *f* trench
trinco /'trĩku/ *m* latch
trindade /trĩ'dadʒi/ *f* trinity
trinta /'trĩta/ *a & m* thirty
trio /'triu/ *m* trio; **~ elétrico** music
float
tripa /'tripa/ *f* gut
tripé /tri'pɛ/ *m* tripod
tripli|car /tripli'kar/ *vt/i*, **~car-se**
vpr treble; **~cata** *f* triplicate
triplo /'triplu/ *a & m* triple
tripu|lação /tripula'sãw/ *f* crew;
~lante *m/f* crew member; **~lar** *vt*
man
triste /'tristʃi/ *a* sad; **~za** /e/ *f* sad-
ness; **é uma ~za** (*fam*) it's pathetic
tritu|rador /tritura'dor/ *m* (*de papel*)
shredder; **~rador de lixo** waste dis-
posal unit; **~rar** *vt* shred *<legumes,
papel>*; grind up *<lixo>*
triun|fal /triũ'faw/ (*pl* **~fais**) *a*
triumphal; **~fante** *a* triumphant;
~far *vi* triumph; **~fo** *m* triumph
trivi|al /trivi'aw/ (*pl* **~ais**) *a* trivial;
~alidade *f* triviality; *pl* trivia
triz /tris/ *m* **por um ~** narrowly, by a
hair's breadth; **não foi atropelado
por um ~** he narrowly missed being
knocked down
tro|ca /'trɔka/ *f* exchange; **em ~ca de**
in exchange for; **~cadilho** /i/ *m* pun;
~cado *m* change; **~cador** *m*
conductor; **~car** *vt* (*dar e receber*) exchange (**por** for); change *<dinheiro,
lençóis, lâmpada, lugares etc>*; (*transpor*) change round; (*confundir*) mix
up; **~car-se** *vpr* change; **~car de
roupa/trem/lugar** change clothes/
trains/places; **~ca-troca** *m* swap;
~co /o/ *m* change; **~co de quê?**
what for?; **dar o ~co em alg** pay
s.o. back
troço /'trɔsu/ (*fam*) *m* (*coisa*) thing;
(*ataque*) turn; **me deu um ~** I had a
funny turn
troféu /tro'fɛw/ *m* trophy
trólebus /'trɔlebus/ *m invar* trolley
bus
trom|ba /'trõba/ *f* (*de elefante*) trunk;
(*cara amarrada*) long face; **~bada** *f*
crash; **~ba-d'água** (*pl* **~bas-
d'água**) *f* downpour; **~badinha** *m*
bag snatcher; **~bar** *vi* **~bar com**
crash into *<poste, carro>*; bump into
<pessoa>
trombo|ne /trõ'bɔni/ *m* trombone;
~nista *m/f* trombonist
trompa /'trõpa/ *f* French horn; **~ de
Falópio** fallopian tube
trompe|te /trõ'petʃi/ *m* trumpet;
~tista *m/f* trumpeter
tron|co /'trõku/ *m* trunk; **~cudo** *a*
stocky
trono /'tronu/ *m* throne

tropa /ˈtrɔpa/ f troop; (*exército*) army; *pl* troops;~ **de choque** riot police

trope|ção /tropeˈsãw/ m trip; (*erro*) slip-up;~**çar** vi trip; (*errar*) slip up; ~**ço** /e/ m stumbling block

trópego /ˈtrɔpegu/ a unsteady

tropi|cal /tropiˈkaw/ (*pl* ~**cais**) a tropical

trópico /ˈtrɔpiku/ m tropic

tro|tar /troˈtar/ vi trot;~**te** /ɔ/ m (*de cavalo*) trot; (*de estudantes*) practical joke; (*mentira*) hoax

trouxa /ˈtroʃa/ f (*de roupa etc*) bundle □ m/f (*fam*) sucker □ a (*fam*) gullible

tro|vão /troˈvãw/ m clap of thunder; pl thunder;~**vejar** vi thunder;~**voada** f thunderstorm;~**voar** vi thunder

trucidar /trusiˈdar/ vt slaughter

trucu|lência /trukuˈlẽsia/ f barbarity; ~**lento** a (*cruel*) barbaric; (*brigão*) belligerent

trufa /ˈtrufa/ f truffle

trunfo /ˈtrũfu/ m trump; (*fig*) trump card

truque /ˈtruki/ m trick

truta /ˈtruta/ f trout

tu /tu/ *pron* you

tua /ˈtua/ *veja* **teu**

tuba /ˈtuba/ f tuba

tubarão /tubaˈrãw/ m shark

tubá|rio /tubaˈriu/ a **gravidez** ~**ria** ectopic pregnancy

tuberculose /tuberkuˈlɔzi/ f tuberculosis

tubo /ˈtubu/ m tube; (*no corpo*) duct

tubulação /tubulaˈsãw/ f ducting

tucano /tuˈkanu/ m toucan

tudo /ˈtudu/ *pron* everything;~ **bem?** (*cumprimento*) how are things?;~ **de bom** all the best; **em** ~ **quanto é lugar** all over the place

tufão /tuˈfãw/ m typhoon

tulipa /tuˈlipa/ f tulip

tumba /ˈtũba/ f tomb

tumor /tuˈmor/ m tumour; ~ **cerebral** brain tumour

túmulo /ˈtumulu/ m grave

tumul|to /tuˈmuwtu/ m commotion; (*motim*) riot; ~**tuado** a disorderly, rowdy; ~**tuar** vt disrupt □ vi cause a commotion; ~**tuoso** a tumultuous

tú|nel /ˈtunew/ (*pl* ~**neis**) m tunnel

túnica /ˈtunika/ f tunic

Tunísia /tuˈnizia/ f Tunisia

tupiniquim /tupiniˈkĩ/ a Brazilian

turbante /turˈbãtʃi/ m turban

turbilhão /turbiˈʎãw/ m whirlwind

turbina /turˈbina/ f turbine

turbu|lência /turbuˈlẽsia/ f turbulence; ~**lento** a turbulent

turco /ˈturku/ a & m Turkish

turfa /ˈturfa/ f peat

turfe /ˈturfi/ m horse-racing

turis|mo /tuˈrizmu/ m tourism; **fazer** ~**mo** go sightseeing; ~**ta** m/f tourist

turístico /tuˈristʃiku/ a <*ponto, indústria*> tourist; <*viagem*> sightseeing

turma /ˈturma/ f group; (*na escola*) class

turnê /turˈne/ f tour

turno /ˈturnu/ m (*de trabalho*) shift; (*de competição, eleição*) round

turquesa /turˈkeza/ m/f & a invar turquoise

Turquia /turˈkia/ f Turkey

turra /ˈtuxa/ f **às** ~**s com** at loggerheads with

tur|var /turˈvar/ vt cloud; ~**vo** a cloudy

tutano /tuˈtanu/ m marrow

tutela /tuˈtɛla/ f guardianship

tutor /tuˈtor/ m guardian

tutu /tuˈtu/ m (*vestido*) tutu; (*prato*) beans with bacon and manioc flour

TV /teˈve/ f TV

U

ubíquo /uˈbikwu/ a ubiquitous

Ucrânia /uˈkrania/ f Ukraine

ucraniano /ukraniˈanu/ a & m Ukrainian

ué /uˈɛ/ *int* hang on

ufa /ˈufa/ *int* phew

ufanis|mo /ufaˈnizmu/ m chauvinism; ~**ta** a & m/f chauvinist

Uganda /uˈgãda/ m Uganda

ui /ui/ *int* (*de dor*) ouch; (*de nojo*) ugh; (*de espanto*) oh

uísque /uˈiski/ m whisky

ui|var /uiˈvar/ vi howl;~**vo** m howl

úlcera /ˈuwsera/ f ulcer

ulterior /uwteriˈor/ a further

ulti|mamente /uwtʃimaˈmẽtʃi/ adv recently; ~**mar** vt finalize; ~**mato** m ultimatum

último /ˈuwtʃimu/ a last; <*moda, notícia etc*> latest; **em** ~ **caso** as a last resort; **nos** ~**s anos** in recent years; **por** ~ last

ultra|jante /uwtraˈʒãtʃi/ a offensive; ~**jar** vt offend; ~**je** m outrage

ultraleve /uwtraˈlɛvi/ m microlite

ultra|mar /uwtraˈmar/ m overseas; ~**marino** a overseas

ultrapas|sado /uwtrapaˈsadu/ a outdated; ~**sagem** f overtaking, (*Amer*) passing; ~**sar** vt (*de carro*) overtake, (*Amer*) pass; (*ser superior a*) surpass; (*exceder*) exceed; (*extrapolar*) go beyond □ vi overtake, (*Amer*) pass

ultra-sonografia /uwtrasonograˈfia/ f ultrasound scan

ultravioleta /uwtravioˈleta/ a ultraviolet

ulu|lante /ulu'lãtʃi/ *a* (*fig*) blatant; **∼lar** *vi* wail

um /ũ/ (*f* **uma**; *m pl* **uns**, *f pl* **umas**) *art* a, an; *pl* some □ *a & pron* one; **∼ ao outro** one another; **vieram umas 20 pessoas** about 20 people came

umbanda /ũ'bãda/ *m* Afro-Brazilian cult

umbigo /ũ'bigu/ *m* navel

umbili|cal /ũbili'kaw/ (*pl* **∼cais**) *a* umbilical

umedecer /umede'ser/ *vt* moisten; **∼-se** *vpr* moisten

umidade /umi'dadʒi/ *f* moisture; (*desagradável*) damp; (*do ar*) humidity

úmido /'umidu/ *a* moist; <*parede, roupa etc*> damp; <*ar, clima*> humid

unânime /u'nanimi/ *a* unanimous

unanimidade /unanimi'dadʒi/ *f* unanimity

undécimo /ũ'dɛsimu/ *a* eleventh

ungüento /ũ'gwẽtu/ *m* ointment

unha /'uɲa/ *f* nail; (*de animal, utensílio*) claw

unhar /u'ɲar/ *vt* claw

união /uni'ãw/ *f* union; (*concórdia*) unity; (*ato de unir*) joining

unicamente /unika'mẽtʃi/ *adv* only

único /'uniku/ *a* only; (*ímpar*) unique

uni|dade /uni'dadʒi/ *f* unit; **∼do a** united; <*família*> close

unifi|cação /unifika'sãw/ *f* unification; **∼car** *vt* unify

unifor|me /uni'fɔrmi/ *a* uniform; <*superfície*> even □ *m* uniform; **∼midade** *f* uniformity; **∼mizado** *a* <*policial etc*> uniformed; (*padronizado*) standardized; **∼zar** *vt* (*padronizar*) standardize

unilate|ral /unilate'raw/ (*pl* **∼rais**) *a* unilateral

unir /u'nir/ *vt* unite <*povo, nações, família etc*>; (*ligar, casar*) join; (*combinar*) combine (**a** *ou* **com** with); **∼-se** *vpr* (*aliar-se*) unite (**a** with); (*juntar-se*) join together; (*combinar-se*) combine (**a** *ou* **com** with)

unissex /uni'sɛks/ *a invar* unisex

uníssono /u'nisonu/ *m* **em ∼** in unison

univer|sal /univer'saw/ (*pl* **∼sais**) *a* universal

universi|dade /universi'dadʒi/ *f* university; **∼tário** *a* university □ *m* university student

universo /uni'vɛrsu/ *m* universe

untar /ũ'tar/ *vt* grease <*forma*>; spread <*pão*>; smear <*corpo, rosto etc*>

upa /'upa/ *int* (*incentivando*) upsadaisy; (*ao cair algo etc*) whoops

urânio /u'raniu/ *m* uranium

Urano /u'ranu/ *m* Uranus

urbanis|mo /urba'nizmu/ *m* town

planning; **∼ta** *m/f* town planner

urbani|zado /urbani'zadu/ *a* built-up; **∼zar** *vt* urbanize

urbano /ur'banu/ *a* (*da cidade*) urban; (*refinado*) urbane

urdir /ur'dʒir/ *vt* weave; (*maquinar*) hatch

urdu /ur'du/ *m* Urdu

ur|gência /ur'ʒẽsia/ *f* urgency; **∼gente** *a* urgent; **∼gir** *vi* be urgent; <*tempo*> press; **∼ge irmos** we must go urgently

uri|na /u'rina/ *f* urine; **∼nar** *vt* pass □ *vi* urinate; **∼nol** (*pl* **∼nóis**) *m* (*penico*) chamber pot; (*em banheiro*) urinal

urna /'urna/ *f* (*para cinzas*) urn; (*para votos*) ballot box; *pl* (*fig*) polls

ur|rar /u'xar/ *vt/i* roar; **∼ro** *m* roar

urso /'ursu/ *m* bear; **∼-branco** (*pl* **∼s-brancos**) *m* polar bear

urti|cária /urtʃi'karia/ *f* nettle rash; **∼ga** *f* nettle

urubu /uru'bu/ *m* black vulture

Uruguai /uru'gwaj/ *m* Uruguay

uruguaio /uru'gwaju/ *a & m* Uruguayan

urze /'urzi/ *f* heather

usado /u'zadu/ *a* used; <*roupa*> worn; <*palavra*> common

usar /u'zar/ *vt* wear <*roupa, óculos, barba etc*>; **∼ (de)** (*utilizar*) use

usina /u'zina/ *f* plant; **∼ termonuclear** nuclear power station

uso /'uzu/ *m* use; (*de palavras, linguagem*) usage; (*praxe*) practice

usu|al /uzu'aw/ (*pl* **∼ais**) *a* common; **∼ário** *m* user; **∼fruir** *vt* enjoy <*coisas boas*>; have the use of <*prédio, jardim etc*>; **∼fruto** *m* use

usurário /uzu'rariu/ *a* money-grubbing □ *m* money-lender

usurpar /uzur'par/ *vt* usurp

uten|sílio /utẽ'siliu/ *m* utensil; **∼te** *m/f* (*Port*) user

útero /'uteru/ *m* uterus, womb

UTI /ute'i/ *f* intensive care unit

útil /'utʃiw/ (*pl* **úteis**) *a* useful; **dia ∼** workday

utili|dade /utʃili'dadʒi/ *f* usefulness; (*uma*) utility; **∼tário** *a* utilitarian; **∼zar** *vt* (*empregar*) use; (*tornar útil*) utilize; **∼zável** (*pl* **∼záveis**) *a* usable

utopia /uto'pia/ *f* Utopia

utópico /u'tɔpiku/ *a* Utopian

uva /'uva/ *f* grape

úvula /'uvula/ *f* uvula

V

vaca /'vaka/ *f* cow

vaci|lante /vasi'lãtʃi/ *a* wavering; <*luz*> flickering; **∼lar** *vi* waver;

< *luz* > flicker; (*fam: bobear*) slip up

vaci|na /va'sina/ *f* vaccine; ~**nação** *f* vaccination; ~**nar** *vt* vaccinate

vácuo /'vakuu/ *m* vacuum

va|diar /vadʒi'ar/ *vi* (*viver ocioso*) laze around; (*fazer cera*) mess about; ~**dio** *a* idle □ *m* idler

vaga /'vaga/ *f* (*posto*) vacancy; (*para estacionar*) parking place

vagabun|dear /vagabũdʒi'ar/ *vi* (*perambular*) roam; (*vadiar*) laze around; ~**do** *a* < *pessoa, vida* > idle; < *produto, objeto* > shoddy □ *m* tramp; (*pessoa vadia*) bum

vaga-lume /vaga'lumi/ *m* glow-worm

va|gão /va'gãw/ *m* (*de passageiros*) carriage, (*Amer*) car; (*de carga*) wagon; ~**gão-leito** (*pl* ~**gões-leitos**) *m* sleeping car; ~**gão-restaurante** (*pl* ~**gões-restaurantes**) *m* dining car

vagar[1] /va'gar/ *vi* < *pessoa* > wander about; < *barco* > drift

vagar[2] /va'gar/ *vi* < *cargo, apartamento* > become vacant

vagaroso /vaga'rozu/ *a* slow

vagem /'vaʒẽ/ *f* green bean

vagi|na /va'ʒina/ *f* vagina; ~**nal** (*pl* ~**nais**) *a* vaginal

vago[1] /'vagu/ *a* (*indefinido*) vague

vago[2] /'vagu/ *a* (*desocupado*) vacant; < *tempo* > spare

vaguear /vagi'ar/ *vi* roam

vai|a /'vaja/ *f* boo; ~**ar** *vt/i* boo

vai|dade /vaj'dadʒi/ *f* vanity; ~**doso** *a* vain

vaivém /vaj'vẽj/ *m* comings and goings, toing and froing

vala /'vala/ *f* ditch; ~ **comum** mass grave

vale[1] /'vali/ *m* (*de rio etc*) valley

vale[2] /'vali/ *m* (*ficha*) voucher; ~ **postal** postal order

valen|tão /valẽ'tãw/ *a* (*f* ~**tona**) tough □ *m* tough guy; ~**te** *a* brave; ~**tia** *f* bravery; (*uma*) feat

valer /va'ler/ *vt* be worth □ *vi* be valid; ~ **aco a alg** earn s.o. sth; ~**se de** avail o.s. of; ~ **a pena** be worth it; **vale a pena tentar** it's worth trying; **mais vale desistir** it's better to give up; **vale tudo** anything goes; **fazer** ~ enforce < *lei* >; **stand up for** < *direitos* >; **para** ~ (a *sério*) for real; (*muito*) really

vale|-refeição /valirefej'sãw/ (*pl* ~**s-refeição**) *m* luncheon voucher

valeta /va'leta/ *f* gutter

valete /va'letʃi/ *m* jack

valia /va'lia/ *f* value

validar /vali'dar/ *vt* validate

válido /'validu/ *a* valid

valioso /vali'ozu/ *a* valuable

valise /va'lizi/ *f* travelling bag

valor /va'lor/ *m* value; (*valentia*) valour; *pl* (*títulos*) securities; **no** ~ **de** to the value of; **sem** ~ worthless; **objetos de** ~ valuables; ~ **nominal** face value

valori|zação /valoriza'sãw/ *f* (*apreciação*) valuing; (*aumento no valor*) increase in value; ~**zado** *a* highly valued; ~**zar** *vt* (*apreciar*) value; (*aumentar o valor de*) increase the value of; ~**zar-se** *vt* < *coisa* > increase in value; < *pessoa* > value o.s.

val|sa /'vawsa/ *f* waltz; ~**sar** *vi* waltz

válvula /'vawvula/ *f* valve

vampiro /vã'piru/ *m* vampire

vandalismo /vãda'lizmu/ *m* vandalism

vândalo /'vãdalu/ *m* vandal

vangloriar-se /vãglori'arsi/ *vpr* brag (**de** about)

vanguarda /vã'gwarda/ *f* vanguard; (*de arte*) avant-garde

vanta|gem /vã'taʒẽ/ *f* advantage; **contar** ~**gem** boast; **levar** ~**gem** have the advantage (**a** over); **tirar** ~**gem de** take advantage of; ~**joso** /o/ *a* advantageous

vão /vãw/ (*pl* ~**s**) *a* (*f* **vã**) vain □ *m* gap; **em** ~ in vain

vapor /va'por/ *m* (*fumaça*) steam; (*gás*) vapour; (*barco*) steamer; **máquina a** ~ steam engine; **a todo** ~ at full blast

vaporizar /vapori'zar/ *vt* vaporize; (*com spray*) spray

vaqueiro /va'keru/ *m* cowboy

vaquinha /va'kina/ *f* collection, whip-round

vara /'vara/ *f* rod; ~ **cívil** civil district; ~ **mágica** *ou* **de condão** magic wand

va|ral /va'raw/ (*pl* ~**rais**) *m* washing line

varanda /va'rãda/ *f* veranda

varão /va'rãw/ *m* male

varar /va'rar/ *vt* (*furar*) pierce; (*passar por*) sweep through

varejão /vare'ʒãw/ *m* wholesale store

varejeira /vare'ʒera/ *f* bluebottle

vare|jista /vare'ʒista/ *a* retail □ *m/f* retailer; ~**jo** /e/ *m* retail trade; **vender a** ~**jo** sell retail

vari|ação /varia'sãw/ *f* variation; ~**ado** *a* varied; ~**ante** *a* & *f* variant; ~**ar** *vt/i* vary; **para variar** for a change; ~**ável** (*pl* ~**áveis**) *a* variable; < *tempo* > changeable

varicela /vari'sɛla/ *f* chickenpox

variedade /varie'dadʒi/ *f* variety

vários /'varius/ *a pl* several

varíola /va'riola/ *f* smallpox

variz /va'ris/ *f* varicose vein

varo|nil /varo'niw/ (pl ~**nis**) a manly

var|rer /va'xer/ vt sweep; (fig) sweep away; ~**rido** a um doido ~**rido** a raving lunatic

Varsóvia /var'sɔvia/ f Warsaw

vascular /vasku'ʎar/ vt search through

vasectomia /vazekto'mia/ f vasectomy

vaselina /vaze'lina/ f vaseline

vasilha /va'ziʎa/ f jug

vaso /'vazu/ m pot; (para flores) vase; ~ **sanguíneo** blood vessel

vassoura /va'sora/ f broom

vas|tidão /vastʃi'dãw/ f vastness; ~**to** a vast

vatapá /vata'pa/ m spicy North-Eastern dish

Vaticano /vatʃi'kanu/ m Vatican

vati|cinar /vatʃisi'nar/ vt prophesy; ~**cínio** m prophecy

va|zamento /vaza'mẽtu/ m leak; ~**zante** f ebb tide; ~**zão** m outflow; **dar** ~**zão a** (fig) give vent to; ~**zar** vt/i leak

vazio /va'ziu/ a empty □ m emptiness; (um) void

veado /vi'adu/ m deer

ve|dação /veda'sãw/ f (de casa, janela) insulation; (em motor etc) gasket; ~**dar** vt seal <recipiente, abertura>; stanch <sangue>; seal off <saída, área>; ~**dar aco (a alg)** prohibit sth (for s.o.)

vedete /ve'dɛte/ f star

vee|mência /vee'mẽsia/ f vehemence; ~**mente** a vehement

vege|tação /veʒeta'sãw/ f vegetation; ~**tal** (pl ~**tais**) a & m vegetable; ~**tar** vi vegetate; ~**tariano** a & m vegetarian

veia /'veja/ f vein

veicular /veiku'lar/ vt convey; place <anúncios>

veículo /ve'ikulu/ m vehicle; (de comunicação etc) medium

vela¹ /'vɛla/ f (de barco) sail; (esporte) sailing

vela² /'vɛla/ f candle; (em motor) spark plug; **segurar a** ~ (fam) play gooseberry

velar¹ /ve'lar/ vt (cobrir) veil

velar² /ve'lar/ vt watch over □ vi keep vigil

veleidade /velej'dadʒi/ f whim

ve|leiro /ve'leru/ m sailing boat; ~**lejar** vi sail

velhaco /ve'ʎaku/ a crooked □ m crook

ve|lharia /veʎa'ria/ f old thing; ~**lhice** f old age; ~**lho** /ɛ/ a old □ m old man; ~**lhote** /ɔ/ m old man

velocidade /velosi'dadʒi/ f speed;

(Port: marcha) gear; **a toda** ~ at full speed; ~ **máxima** speed limit

velocímetro /velo'simetru/ m speedometer

velocista /velo'sista/ m/f sprinter

velório /ve'lɔriu/ m wake

veloz /ve'los/ a fast

veludo /ve'ludu/ m velvet; ~ **cotelê** corduroy

ven|cedor /vẽse'dor/ a winning □ m winner; ~**cer** vt win over <adversário etc>; win <partida, corrida, batalha> □ vi (triunfar) win; <prestação, aluguel, dívida> fall due; <contrato, passaporte, prazo> expire; <apólice> mature; ~**cido** a **dar-se por** ~**cido** give in; ~**cimento** m (de dívida, aluguel) due date; (de contrato, prazo) expiry date; (de alimento, remédio etc) best before date; (salário) payment; pl earnings

venda¹ /'vẽda/ f sale; (loja) general store; **à** ~ on sale; **pôr à** ~ put up for sale

ven|da² /'vẽda/ f blindfold; ~**dar** vt blindfold

venda|val /vẽda'vaw/ (pl ~**vais**) m gale, storm

ven|dável /vẽ'davew/ (pl ~**dáveis**) a saleable; ~**dedor** m (de loja) shop assistant; (em geral) seller; ~**der** vt/i sell; **estar** ~**dendo saúde** be bursting with health

vendeta /vẽ'deta/ f vendetta

veneno /ve'nenu/ m poison; (de cobra etc, malignidade) venom; ~**so** /o/ a poisonous; (maldoso) venomous

vene|ração /venera'sãw/ f reverence; (de Deus etc) worship; ~**rar** vt revere; worship <Deus etc>

vené|reo /ve'nɛriu/ a **doença** ~**rea** venereal disease

Veneza /ve'neza/ f Venice

veneziana /venezi'ana/ f shutter

Venezuela /venezu'ɛla/ f Venezuela

venezuelano /venezue'lanu/ a & m Venezuelan

venta /'vẽta/ f nostril

ven|tania /vẽta'nia/ f gale; ~**tar** vi be windy; ~**tarola** /ɔ/ f fan

venti|lação /vẽtʃila'sãw/ f ventilation; ~**lador** m fan; ~**lar** vt ventilate; air <sala, roupa>

ven|to /'vẽtu/ m wind; **de** ~**to em popa** smoothly; ~**toinha** f (cata-vento) weather vane; (Port: ventilador) fan; ~**tosa** /ɔ/ f sucker; ~**toso** /o/ a windy

ven|tre /'vẽtri/ m belly; ~**tríloquo** m ventriloquist

Vênus /'venus/ f Venus

ver /ver/ vt see; watch <televisão>; (resolver) see to □ vi see □ m **a meu** ~ in my view; ~**-se** vpr (no espelho *etc*) see o.s.; (*em estado, condição*) find o.s.; (*um ao outro*) see each other; **ter a ~ com** have to do with; **vai ~ que ela não sabe** (*fam*) I bet she doesn't know; **vê se você não volta tarde** see you don't get back late; **viu?** (*fam*) right?

veracidade /verasi'dadʒi/ *f* truthfulness

vera|near /verani'ar/ *vi* spend the summer; **~neio** *m* summer holiday, (*Amer*) summer vacation; **~nista** *m/f* holidaymaker, (*Amer*) vacationer

verão /ve'rãw/ *m* summer

veraz /ve'ras/ *a* truthful

verbas /'vɛrbas/ *f pl* funds

ver|bal /ver'baw/ (*pl* **~bais**) *a* verbal; **~bete** /e/ *m* entry; **~bo** *m* verb; **~borragia** *f* waffle; **~boso** /o/ *a* verbose

verda|de /ver'dadʒi/ *f* truth; **de ~** <*coisa*> real; <*fazer*> really; **na ~de** actually; **para falar a ~de** to tell the truth; (*real*) <*declaração, pessoa*> truthful; (*real*) true

verde /'verdʒi/ *a & m* green; **jogar ~ para colher maduro** fish for information; **~abacate** *a invar* avocado; **~amarelo** *a* yellow and green; (*brasileiro*) Brazilian; (*nacionalista*) nationalistic; **~esmeralda** *a invar* emerald green; **~jar** *vi* turn green

verdu|ra /ver'dura/ *f* (*para comer*) greens; (*da natureza*) greenery; **~reiro** *m* greengrocer, (*Amer*) produce dealer

vereador /veria'dor/ *m* councillor

vereda /ve'reda/ *f* path

veredito /vere'dʒitu/ *m* verdict

vergar /ver'gar/ *vt/i* bend

vergo|nha /ver'goɲa/ *f* (*pudor*) shame; (*constrangimento*) embarrassment; (*timidez*) shyness; (*uma*) disgrace; **ter ~nha** be ashamed; be embarrassed; be shy; **cria** *ou* **tome ~nha na cara!** you should be ashamed of yourself!; **~nhoso** /o/ *a* shameful

verídico /ve'ridʒiku/ *a* true

verificar /verifi'kar/ *vt* check, verify <*fatos, dados etc*>; **~ que** ascertain that; **~ se** check that; **~-se** *vpr* <*previsão etc*> come true; <*acidente etc*> happen

verme /'vɛrmi/ *m* worm

verme|lhidão /vermeʎi'dãw/ *f* redness; **~lho** /e/ *a & m* red; **no ~lho** (*endividado*) in the red

vernáculo /ver'nakulu/ *a & m* vernacular

verniz /ver'nis/ *f* varnish; (*couro*) patent leather

veros|símil /vero'simiw/ (*pl*

~símeis) *a* plausible; **~similhança** *f* plausibility

verruga /ve'xuga/ *f* wart

ver|sado /ver'sadu/ *a* well-versed (**em** in); **~são** *f* version; **~sar sobre** concern; **~sátil** (*pl* **~sáteis**) *a* versatile; **~satilidade** *f* versatility; **~sículo** *m* (*da Bíblia*) verse; **~so1** /ɛ/ *m* verse

verso2 /ɛ/ *m* (*de página*) reverse, other side; **vide ~** see over

vértebra /'vɛrtebra/ *f* vertebra

verte|brado /verte'bradu/ *a & m* vertebrate; **~bral** (*pl* **~brais**) *a* spinal

ver|tente /ver'tẽtʃi/ *f* slope; **~ter** *vt* (*derramar*) pour; shed <*lágrimas, sangue*>; (*traduzir*) render (**para** into)

verti|cal /vertʃi'kaw/ (*pl* **~cais**) *a & f* vertical; **~gem** *f* dizziness; **~ginoso** /o/ *a* dizzy

vesgo /'vezgu/ *a* cross-eyed

vesícula /ve'zikula/ *f* gall bladder

vespa /'vespa/ *f* wasp

véspera /'vɛspera/ *f* **a ~** the day before; **a ~ de** the eve of; **a ~ de Natal** Christmas Eve; **nas ~s de** on the eve of

vespertino /vesper'tʃinu/ *a* evening

ves|te /'vɛstʃi/ *f* robe; **~tiário** *m* (*para se trocar*) changing room; (*para guardar roupa*) cloakroom

vestibular /vestʃibu'lar/ *m* university entrance exam

vestíbulo /ves'tʃibulu/ *m* hall(way); (*do teatro*) foyer

vestido /ves'tʃidu/ *m* dress □ *a* dressed (**de** in)

vestígio /ves'tʃiʒiu/ *m* trace

ves|timenta /vestʃi'mẽta/ *f* (*de sacerdote*) vestments; **~tir** *vt* (*pôr*) put on; (*usar*) wear; (*pôr roupa em*) dress; (*dar roupa a*) clothe; **~tir-se** *vpr* dress; **~tir-se de branco/de padre** dress in white/as a priest; **~tuário** *m* clothing

vetar /ve'tar/ *vt* veto

veterano /vete'ranu/ *a & m* veteran

veterinário /veteri'nariu/ *a* veterinary □ *m* vet

veto /'vɛtu/ *m* veto

véu /vɛw/ *m* veil

vexa|me /ve'ʃami/ *m* disgrace; **dar um ~me** make a fool of o.s.; **~minoso** /o/ *a* disgraceful

vexar /ve'ʃar/ *vt* shame; **~-se** *vpr* be ashamed (**de** of)

vez /ves/ *f* (*ocasião*) time; (*turno*) turn; **às ~es** sometimes; **cada ~ mais** more and more; **de ~** for good; **desta ~** this time; **de ~ em quando** now and again, from time to time; **de uma ~** (*ao mesmo tempo*) at once; (*de um* *golpe*) in one go; **de uma ~ por todas** once and for all; **duas ~es** twice; **em ~ de** instead of; **fazer as ~es de** take the place of; **mais uma ~, outra ~** again; **muitas ~es** (*com muita frequência*) often; (*repetidamente*) many times; **raras ~es** seldom; **repetidas ~es** repeatedly; **uma ~** once; **uma ~ que** since

via /'via/ *f* (*estrada*) road; (*rumo, meio*) way; (*exemplar*) copy; (*trâmites*) channels □ *prep* via; **em ~s de** on the point of; **por ~ aérea/marítima** by air/sea; **por ~ das dúvidas** just in case; **por ~ de regra** as a rule; **Via Láctea** Milky Way

viabili|dade /viabili'dadʒi/ *f* feasibility; **~zar** *vt* make feasible

viação /via'sãw/ *f* (*transporte*) road transport; (*estradas*) road network; (*companhia*) bus company

viaduto /via'dutu/ *m* viaduct; (*rodoviário*) flyover, (*Amer*) overpass

via|gem /vi'aʒē/ *f* (*uma*) trip, journey; (*em geral*) travelling; *pl* (*de uma pessoa*) travels; (*em geral*) travel; **boa ~gem!** have a good trip!; **~gem de negócios** business trip; **~jado** *a* well-travelled; **~jante** *a* travelling □ *m/f* traveller; **~jar** *vi* travel; **estar a ~jando** (*fam*) (*com o pensamento longe*) be miles away

viário /vi'ariu/ *a* road; **anel ~** ring road

viatura /via'tura/ *f* vehicle

viá|vel /vi'avew/ (*pl* **~veis**) *a* feasible

víbora /'vibora/ *f* viper

vi|bração /vibra'sãw/ *f* vibration; (*fig*) thrill; **~brante** *a* vibrant; **~brar** *vt* shake □ *vi* vibrate; (*fig*) be thrilled (**com** by)

vice /'visi/ *m/f* deputy

vice-cam|peão /visikãpi'ãw/ *m* (*f* **~peã**) runner-up

vicejar /vise'ʒar/ *vi* flourish

vice-presiden|te /visiprezi'dētʃi/ *m* (*f* **~ta**) vice-president

vice-rei /visi'xej/ *m* viceroy

vice-versa /visi'vɛrsa/ *adv* vice-versa

vici|ado /visi'adu/ *a* addicted (**em** to) □ *m* addict; **um ~ado em drogas** a drug addict; **~ar** *vt* (*falsificar*) tamper with; (*estragar*) ruin □ *vi* <*droga*> be addictive; **~ar-se** *vpr* get addicted (**em** to)

vício /'visiu/ *m* vice

vicioso /visi'ozu/ *a* **círculo ~** vicious circle

vicissitudes /visisi'tudʒis/ *f pl* ups and downs

viço /'visu/ *m* (*de plantas*) exuberance; (*de pessoa, pele*) freshness; **~so** /o/ *a* <*planta*> lush; <*pele, pessoa*> fresh

vida /'vida/ *f* life; **sem ~** lifeless; **dar ~ a** liven up

videira /vi'dera/ *f* vine

vidente /vi'dētʃi/ *m/f* clairvoyant

vídeo /'vidʒiu/ *m* video; (*tela*) screen

video|cassete /vidʒiuka'sɛtʃi/ *m* (*fita*) video tape; (*aparelho*) video, (*Amer*) VCR; **~clipe** *m* video; **~clube** *m* video club; **~game** *m* videogame; **~teipe** *m* video tape

vidra|ça /vi'drasa/ *f* window pane; **~çaria** *f* (*fábrica*) glassworks; (*vidraças*) glazing; **~ceiro** *m* glazier

vi|drado /vi'dradu/ *a* glazed; **estar ~drado em** *ou* **por** (*fam*) love; **~drar** *vt* glaze □ *vi* (*fam*) fall in love (**em** *ou* **por** with); **~dro** *m* (*material*) glass; (*pote*) jar; (*janela*) window; **~dro fumê** tinted glass

viela /vi'ɛla/ *f* alley

Viena /vi'ɛna/ *f* Vienna

Vietnã /vietʃi'nã/ *m*, (*Port*) **Vietname** /viet'nam/ *m* Vietnam

vietnamita /vietna'mita/ *a* & *m/f* Vietnamese

viga /'viga/ *f* joist

vigarice /viga'risi/ *f* swindle

vigário /vi'gariu/ *m* vicar

vigarista /viga'rista/ *m/f* swindler, con artist

vi|gência /vi'ʒēsia/ *f* (*qualidade*) force; (*tempo*) period in force; **~gente** *a* in force

vigésimo /vi'ʒɛzimu/ *a* twentieth

vigi|a /vi'ʒia/ *f* (*guarda*) watch; (*em navio*) porthole □ *m* night watchman; **~ar** *vt* (*observar*) watch; (*cuidar de*) watch over; (*como sentinela*) guard □ *vi* keep watch

vigi|lância /viʒi'lãsia/ *f* vigilance; **~lante** *a* vigilant

vigília /vi'ʒilia/ *f* vigil

vigor /vi'gor/ *m* vigour; **em ~** in force

vigo|rar /vigo'rar/ *vi* be in force; **~roso** *a* vigorous

vil /viw/ (*pl* **vis**) *a* base, despicable

vila /'vila/ *f* (*cidadezinha*) small town; (*casa elegante*) villa; (*conjunto de casas*) housing estate; **~ olímpica** Olympic village

vi|lania /vi'lania/ *f* villainy; **~lão** *m* (*f* **~lã**) villain

vilarejo /vila'reʒu/ *m* village

vilipendiar /vilipēdʒi'ar/ *vt* disparage

vime /'vimi/ *m* wicker

vina|gre /vi'nagri/ *m* vinegar; **~grete** /ɛ/ *m* vinaigrette

vin|car /vĩ'kar/ *vt* crease; line <*rosto*>; **~co** *m* crease; (*no rosto*) line

vincular /vĩku'lar/ *vt* bond, tie

vínculo /'vĩkulu/ *m* link, bond; **~ empregatício** contract of employment

vinda /'vĩda/ f coming; **dar as boas ~s a** welcome

vindicar /vĩdʒi'kar/ vt vindicate

vindima /vĩ'dʒima/ f vintage

vin|do /'vĩdu/ pp e pres de **vir**; **~douro** a coming

vin|gança /vĩ'gãsa/ f vengeance, revenge; **~gar** vt revenge □ vi <flores> thrive; <criança> survive; <plano, empreendimento> be successful; **~gar-se** vpr take one's revenge (**de** for; **em** on); **~gativo** a vindictive

vinha /'viɲa/ f vineyard

vinhedo /vi'ɲedu/ m vineyard

vinheta /vi'ɲeta/ f (na TV etc) sequence

vinho /'viɲu/ m wine □ a invar maroon; **~ do Porto** port

vinícola /vi'nikola/ a wine-growing

vinicul|tor /vinikuw'tor/ m wine grower; **~tura** f wine growing

vinil /vi'niw/ m vinyl

vinte /'vĩtʃi/ a & m twenty; **~na** /e/ f score

viola /vi'ɔla/ f viola

violação /viola'sãw/ f violation

violão /vio'lãw/ m guitar

violar /vio'lar/ vt violate

vio|lência /vio'lẽsia/ f violence; (uma) act of violence; **~lentar** vt rape <mulher>; **~lento** a violent

violeta /vio'leta/ f violet □ a invar violet

violi|nista /violi'nista/ m/f violinist; **~no** m violin

violonce|lista /violõse'lista/ m/f cellist; **~lo** /ɛ/ m cello

vir /vir/ vi come; **o ano que vem** next year; **venho lendo os jornais** I have been reading the papers; **vem cá** come here; (fam) listen; **isso não vem ao caso** that's irrelevant; **~ a ser** turn out to be; **~ com** give <argumento etc>

virabrequim /virabre'kĩ/ m crankshaft

viração /vira'sãw/ f breeze

vira-casaca /viraka'zaka/ m/f turncoat

vira|da /vi'rada/ f turn; **~do** a <roupa> inside out; (de cabeça para baixo) upside down; **~do para** facing

vira-lata /vira'lata/ m mongrel

virar /vi'rar/ vt turn; turn over <disco, barco etc>; turn inside out <roupa>; turn out <bolsos>; tip <balde, água etc> □ vi turn; <barco> turn over; (tornar-se) become; **~se** vpr turn round; (na vida) get by, cope; **~se para** turn to; **vira e mexe** every so often

viravolta /vira'vowta/ f about-turn

virgem /'virʒẽ/ a <fita> blank;

<floresta, noiva etc> virgin □ virgin; **Virgem** (signo) Virgo

virgindade /virʒĩ'dadʒi/ f virginity

vírgula /'virgula/ f comma; (decimal) point

vi|ril /vi'riw/ (pl **~ris**) a virile

virilha /vi'riʎa/ f groin

virilidade /virili'dadʒi/ f virility

virtu|al /virtu'aw/ (pl **~ais**) a virtual

virtude /vir'tudʒi/ f virtue

virtuo|sismo /virtuo'zizmu/ m virtuosity; **~so** /o/ a virtuous □ m virtuoso

virulento /viru'lẽtu/ a virulent

vírus /'virus/ m invar virus

visão /vi'zãw/ f vision; (aspecto, ponto de vista) view

visar /vi'zar/ vt aim at <caça, alvo>; **~ (a)** aim for <objetivo>; <medida, ação> be aimed at

vísceras /'viseras/ f pl innards

viscon|de /vis'kõdʒi/ m viscount; **~dessa** /e/ f viscountess

viscoso /vis'kozu/ a viscous

viseira /vi'zera/ f visor

visibilidade /vizibili'dadʒi/ f visibility

visionário /vizio'nariu/ a & m visionary

visi|ta /vi'zita/ f visit; (visitante) visitor; **fazer uma ~ta a alg** pay s.o. a visit; **~tante** a visiting □ m/f visitor; **~tar** vt visit

visí|vel /vi'zivew/ (pl **~veis**) a visible

vislum|brar /vizlũ'brar/ vt (entrever) glimpse; (imaginar) envisage; **~bre** m glimpse

visom /vi'zõ/ m mink

visor /vi'zor/ m viewfinder

vis|ta /'vista/ f sight; (dos olhos) eyesight; (panorama) view; **à ~ta** (visível) in view; (em dinheiro) in cash; **à primeira ~ta** at first sight; **pôr à ~ta** put on show; **de ~ta** <conhecer> by sight; **em ~ta de** in view of; **ter em ~ta** have in view; **dar na ~ta** attract attention; **fazer ~ta** look nice; **fazer ~ta grossa** turn a blind eye (**a** to); **perder de ~ta** lose sight of; **a perder de ~ta** as far as the eye can see; **uma ~ta** a quick look; **~to** a seen □ m visa; **pelo ~to** by the looks of things; **~to que** seeing that

visto|ria /visto'ria/ f inspection; **~riar** vt inspect

vistoso /vis'tozu/ a eye-catching

visu|al /vizu'aw/ (pl **~ais**) a visual □ m look; **~alizar** vt visualize

vi|tal /vi'taw/ (pl **~tais**) a vital; **~talício** a for life; **~talidade** f vitality

vita|mina /vita'mina/ *f* vitamin; (*bebida*) liquidized fruit drink; ~**minado** *a* with added vitamins; ~**mínico** *a* vitamin

vitela /vi'tɛla/ *f* (*carne*) veal

viticultura /vitʃikuw'tura/ *f* viticulture

vítima /'vitʃima/ *f* victim

viti|mar /vitʃi'mar/ *vt* (*matar*) claim the life of; **ser** ~**mado por** fall victim to

vitória /vi'tɔria/ *f* victory

vitorioso /vitori'ozu/ *a* victorious

vi|tral /vi'traw/ (*pl* ~**trais**) *m* stained glass window

vitrine /vi'trini/ *f* shop window

vitrola /vi'trɔla/ *f* jukebox

viú|va /vi'uva/ *f* widow; ~**vo** *a* widowed ▫ *m* widower

viva /'viva/ *f* cheer ▫ *int* hurray; ~ **a rainha** long live the queen

vivacidade /vivasi'dadʒi/ *f* vivacity

vivalma /vi'vawma/ *f* **não há** ~ **lá fora** there's not a soul outside

vivar /vi'var/ *vt/i* cheer

vivaz /vi'vas/ *a* lively, vivacious; <*planta*> hardy

viveiro /vi'veru/ *m* (*de plantas*) nursery; (*de peixes*) fishpond; (*de aves*) aviary; (*fig*) breeding ground

vivência /vi'vẽsia/ *f* experience

vívido /'vividu/ *a* vivid

viver /vi'ver/ *vt/i* live (**de** on) ▫ *m* life; **ele vive reclamando** he's always complaining

víveres /'viveris/ *m pl* provisions

vivissecção /vivisek'sãw/ *f* vivisection

vivo /'vivu/ *a* (*que vive*) living; (*animado*) lively; <*cor*> bright ▫ *m* **os** ~**s** the living; **ao** ~ **live**; **estar** ~ **be** alive; **dinheiro** ~ cash

vizi|nhança /vizi'ɲãsa/ *f* neighbourhood; ~**nho** *a* neighbouring ▫ *m* neighbour

vo|ador /voa'dor/ *a* flying; ~**ar** *vi* fly; (*explodir*) blow up; **sair** ~**ando** rush off

vocabulário /vokabu'lariu/ *m* vocabulary

vocábulo /vo'kabulu/ *m* word

voca|ção /voka'sãw/ *f* vocation; ~**cional** (*pl* ~**cionais**) *a* vocational; **orientação** ~**cional** careers guidance

vo|cal /vo'kaw/ (*pl* ~**cais**) *a* vocal

você /vo'se/ *pron* you; ~**s** *pron* you

vociferar /vosife'rar/ *vi* shout abuse

vodca /'vɔdʒka/ *f* vodka

voga /'vɔga/ *f* (*moda*) vogue

vo|gal /vo'gaw/ (*pl* ~**gais**) *f* vowel

volante /vo'lãtʃi/ *m* (*de carro*) steering wheel

volá|til /vo'latʃiw/ (*pl* ~**teis**) *a* volatile

vôlei /'volej/ *m*, **voleibol** /volej'bɔw/ *m* volleyball

volt /'vɔwtʃi/ (*pl* ~**s**) *m* volt

volta /'vɔwta/ *f* (*retorno*) return; (*da pista*) lap; (*resposta*) response; **às** ~**s com** tied up with; **de** ~ back; **em** ~ **de** around; **na** ~ on the way back; **na** ~ **do correio** by return of post; **por** ~ **de** around; **dar** ~ **ao mundo** go round the world; **dar a** ~ **por cima** make a comeback; **dar meia** ~ turn round; **dar uma** ~ (*a pé*) go for a walk; (*de carro*) go for a drive; **dar uma** ~ **em** turn round; **dar** ~**s** spin round; **ter** ~ get a response; ~ **e meia** every so often; ~**do** *a* ~**do para** geared towards

voltagem /vow'taʒẽ/ *f* voltage

voltar /vow'tar/ *vi* go/come back, return ▫ *vt* rewind <*fita*>; ~-**se** *vpr* turn round; ~-**se para/contra** turn to/against; ~ **a si** come to; ~ **a fazer** do again; ~ **atrás** backtrack

volu|me /vo'lumi/ *m* volume; ~**moso** *a* sizeable; <*som*> loud

voluntário /volũ'tariu/ *a & m* volunteer

volúpia /vo'lupia/ *f* sensuality, lust

voluptuoso /voluptu'ozu/ *a* sensual; <*mulher*> voluptuous

volú|vel /vo'luvew/ (*pl* ~**veis**) *a* fickle

vomitar /vomi'tar/ *vt/i* vomit

vômito /'vomitu/ *m* vomit; *pl* vomiting

vontade /võ'tadʒi/ *f* will; **à** ~ (*bem*) at ease; (*quanto quiser*) as much as one likes; **fique à** ~ make yourself at home; **tem comida à** ~ there's plenty of food; **estar com** ~ **de** feel like; **isso me dá** ~ **de chorar** it makes me feel like crying; **fazer a** ~ **de alg** do what s.o. wants

vôo /'vou/ *m* flight; **levantar** ~ take off; ~ **livre** hang-gliding

voraz /vo'ras/ *a* voracious

vos /vus/ *pron* you; (*a vocês*) to you

vós /vɔs/ *pron* you

vosso /'vɔsu/ *a* your ▫ *pron* yours

vo|tação /vota'sãw/ *f* vote; ~**tante** *m/f* voter; ~**tar** *vt* vote on <*lei etc*>; (*dedicar*) devote; (*prometer*) vow ▫ *vi* vote (**em** for)

voto /'vɔtu/ *m* (*em votação*) vote; (*promessa*) vow; *pl* (*desejos*) wishes

vo|vó /vo'vɔ/ *f* grandma; ~**vô** *m* grandpa

voz /vɔs/ *f* voice; **dar** ~ **de prisão a alg** place s.o. under arrest

vozeirão /voze'rãw/ *m* loud voice

vozerio /voze'riu/ *m* shouting

vul|cânico /vuw'kaniku/ *a* volcanic; ~**cão** *m* volcano

vul|gar /vuw'gar/ a ordinary; (*baixo*) vulgar; **~garizar** vt popularize; (*tornar baixo*) vulgarize; **~go** adv commonly known as

vulne|rabilidade /vuwnerabili'dadʒi/ f vulnerability; **~rável** (*pl* **~ráveis**) a vulnerable

vul|to /'vuwtu/ m (*figura*) figure; (*tamanho*) bulk; (*importância*) importance; **de ~to** important; **~toso** /o/ a bulky; (*importante*) important

W

walkie-talkie /uɔki'tɔki/ (*pl* **~s**) m walkie-talkie

walkman /uɔk'mɛn/ m invar walkman

watt /u'ɔtʃi/ (*pl* **~s**) m watt

windsur|fe /uĩ'surfi/ m windsurfing; **~fista** m/f windsurfer

X

xadrez /ʃa'dres/ m (*jogo*) chess; (*desenho*) check; (*fam: prisão*) prison □ a invar check

xale /'ʃali/ m shawl

xampu /ʃã'pu/ m shampoo

xará /ʃa'ra/ m/f namesake

xarope /ʃa'rɔpi/ m syrup

xaxim /ʃa'ʃĩ/ m plant fibre

xenofobia /ʃenofo'bia/ f xenophobia

xenófobo /ʃe'nɔfobu/ a xenophobic □ m xenophobe

xepa /'ʃepa/ f scraps

xeque¹ /'ʃeki/ m (*árabe*) sheikh

xeque² /'ʃeki/ m (*no xadrez*) check; **~-mate** m checkmate

xere|ta /ʃe'reta/ (*fam*) a nosy □ m/f nosy parker; **~tar** (*fam*) vi nose around

xerez /ʃe'res/ m sherry

xerife /ʃe'rifi/ m sheriff

xerocar /ʃero'kar/ vt photocopy

xerox /ʃe'rɔks/ m invar photocopy

xexelento /ʃeʃe'lẽtu/ (*fam*) a scruffy □ m scruff

xícara /'ʃikara/ f cup

xiita /ʃi'ita/ a & m/f Shiite

xilofone /ʃilo'foni/ m xylophone

xingar /ʃĩ'gar/ vt swear at □ vi swear

xis /ʃis/ m invar letter X; **o ~ do problema** the crux of the problem

xixi /ʃi'ʃi/ (*fam*) m wee; **fazer ~** do a wee

xô /ʃo/ int shoo

xucro /'ʃukru/ a ignorant

Z

zagueiro /za'geru/ m fullback

Zaire /'zajri/ m Zaire

Zâmbia /'zãbia/ f Zambia

zan|gado /zã'gadu/ a cross, annoyed; **~gar** vt annoy; **~garse** vpr get cross, get annoyed (**com** with)

zanzar /zã'zar/ vi wander

zarpar /zar'par/ vi set off; (*de navio*) set sail

zebra /'zebra/ f zebra; (*pessoa*) fool; (*resultado*) upset

ze|lador /zela'dor/ m caretaker, (*Amer*) janitor; **~lar** vt **~lar (por)** take care of; **~lo** /e/ m zeal; **~lo por** devotion to; **~loso** /o/ a zealous

zero /'zɛru/ m zero; (*em escores*) nil; **~-quilômetro** a invar brand new

ziguezague /zigi'zagi/ m zigzag; **~ar** vi zigzag

Zimbábue /zĩ'babui/ m Zimbabwe

zinco /'zĩku/ m zinc

zíper /'ziper/ m zip, zipper

zodíaco /zo'dʒiaku/ m zodiac

zoeira /zo'era/ f din

zom|bador /zõba'dor/ a mocking; **~bar** vi **~bar (de)** mock; **~baria** f mockery

zona /'zona/ f (*área*) zone; (*de cidade*) district; (*desordem*) mess; (*tumulto*) commotion; (*bairro do meretrício*) red-light district

zonzo /'zõzu/ a dizzy

zôo /'zou/ m zoo

zoo|logia /zoolo'ʒia/ f zoology; **~lógico** a zoological

zoólogo /zo'ɔlogu/ m zoologist

zulu /zu'lu/ a & m/f Zulu

zum /zũ/ m zoom lens

zumbi /zũ'bi/ m zombie

zum|bido /zũ'bidu/ m buzz; (*no ouvido*) ringing; **~bir** vi buzz

zu|nido /zu'nidu/ m (*de vento, bala*) whistle; (*de inseto*) buzz; **~nir** vi <*vento, bala*> whistle; <*inseto*> buzz

zunzum /zũ'zũ/ m rumour

Zurique /zu'riki/ f Zurich

zurrar /zu'xar/ vi bray

ENGLISH-PORTUGUESE
INGLÊS-PORTUGUÊS

A

a /ə/; *emphatic* /eɪ/ (*before vowel* **an** /ən/; *emphatic* /æn/) *a* um. **two pounds a metre** duas libras o metro. **sixty miles an hour** sessenta milhas por hora, (*P*) à hora. **once a year** uma vez por ano

aback /ə'bæk/ *adv* **taken ~** desconcertado, (*P*) surpreendido

abandon /ə'bændən/ *vt* abandonar □ *n* abandono *m*. **~ed** *a* abandonado; (*behaviour*) livre, dissoluto. **~ment** *n* abandono *m*

abashed /ə'bæʃt/ *a* confuso, (*P*) atrapalhado

abate /ə'beɪt/ *vt/i* abater, abrandar, diminuir. **~ment** *n* abrandamento *m*, diminuição *f*

abattoir /'æbætwɑ:(r)/ *n* matadouro *m*

abbey /'æbɪ/ *n* abadia *f*, mosteiro *m*

abbreviat|e /ə'bri:vɪeɪt/ *vt* abreviar. **~ion** /-'eɪʃn/ *n* abreviação *f*; (*short form*) abreviatura *f*

abdicat|e /'æbdɪkeɪt/ *vt/i* abdicar. **~ion** /-'keɪʃn/ *n* abdicação *f*

abdom|en /'æbdəmən/ *n* abdómen *m*, (*P*) abdómen *m*. **~inal** /-'dɒmɪnl/ *a* abdominal

abduct /æb'dʌkt/ *vt* raptar. **~ion** /-ʃn/ *n* rapto *m*. **~or** *n* raptor, -a *mf*

aberration /æbə'reɪʃn/ *n* aberração *f*

abet /ə'bet/ *vt* (*pt* **abetted**) (*jur*) instigar; (*aid*) auxiliar

abeyance /ə'beɪəns/ *n* **in ~** (*matter*) em suspenso; (*custom*) em desuso

abhor /əb'hɔ:(r)/ *vt* (*pt* **abhorred**) abominar, ter horror a. **~rence** /-'hɒrəns/ *n* horror *m*. **~rent** /-'hɒrənt/ *a* abominável, execrável

abide /ə'baɪd/ *vt* (*pt* **abided**) suportar, tolerar. **~ by** (*promise*) manter; (*rules*) acatar

abiding /ə'baɪdɪŋ/ *a* eterno, perpétuo

ability /ə'bɪlətɪ/ *n* capacidade *f* (**to do** para or de fazer); (*cleverness*) habilidade *f*, esperteza *f*

abject /'æbdʒekt/ *a* abjeto, (*P*) abjecto

ablaze /ə'bleɪz/ *a* em chamas; (*fig*) aceso, (*P*) excitado

abl|e /'eɪbl/ *a* (**~er**, **~est**) capaz (**to** de). **be ~e to** (*have power, opportunity*) ser capaz de, poder; (*know how*

to) ser capaz de, saber. **~y** *adv* habilmente

ablutions /ə'blu:ʃnz/ *npl* ablução *f*, abluções *fpl*

abnormal /æb'nɔ:ml/ *a* anormal. **~ity** /-'mælətɪ/ *n* anormalidade *f*. **~ly** *adv* (*unusually*) excepcionalmente

aboard /ə'bɔ:d/ *adv* a bordo □ *prep* a bordo de

abode /ə'bəʊd/ *n* (*old use*) habitação *f*. **place of ~** domicílio *m*

aboli|sh /ə'bɒlɪʃ/ *vt* abolir, extinguir. **~tion** /æbə'lɪʃn/ *n* abolição *f*, extinção *f*

abominable /ə'bɒmɪnəbl/ *a* abominável, detestável

abominat|e /ə'bɒmɪneɪt/ *vt* abominar, detestar. **~ion** /-'neɪʃn/ *n* abominação *f*

abort /ə'bɔ:t/ *vt/i* (*fazer*) abortar. **~ive** *a* (*attempt etc*) abortado, malogrado

abortion /ə'bɔ:ʃn/ *n* aborto *m*. **have an ~** fazer um aborto, ter um aborto. **~ist** *n* abortad/or, -eira *mf*

abound /ə'baʊnd/ *vi* abundar (**in** em)

about /ə'baʊt/ *adv* (*approximately*) aproximadamente, cerca de; (*here and there*) aqui e ali; (*all round*) por todos os lados, em roda, em volta; (*in existence*) por aí □ *prep* acerca de, sobre; (*round*) em torno de; (*somewhere in*) em. **~-face**, **~-turn** *ns* reviravolta *f*. **~ here** por aqui. **be ~ to** estar prestes a. **he was ~ to eat** ia comer. **how** *or* **what ~ leaving?** e se nós fôssemos embora? **know/talk ~** saber/falar sobre

above /ə'bʌv/ *adv* acima, por cima □ *prep* sobre. **he's not ~ lying** ele não éde mentir. **~ all** sobretudo. **~-board** *a* franco, honesto □ *adv* com lisura. **~-mentioned** *a* acima, supracitado

abrasion /ə'breɪʒn/ *n* atrito *m*; (*injury*) escoriação *f*, esfoladura *f*

abrasive /ə'breɪsɪv/ *a* abrasivo; (*fig*) agressivo □ *n* abrasivo *m*

abreast /ə'brest/ *adv* lado a lado. **keep ~ of** manter-se a par de

abridge /ə'brɪdʒ/ *vt* abreviar. **~ment**

n abreviação *f*, abreviatura *f*, redução *f*; (*abridged text*) resumo *m*

abroad /əˈbrɔːd/ *adv* no estrangeiro; (*far and wide*) por todo o lado. **go ~** ir para o estrangeiro

abrupt /əˈbrʌpt/ *a* (*sudden, curt*) brusco; (*steep*) abrupto. **~ly** *adv* (*suddenly*) bruscamente; (*curtly*) com brusquidão. **~ness** *n* brusquidão *f*; (*steepness*) declive *m*

abscess /ˈæbsɪs/ *n* abscesso *m*, (P) abcesso *m*

abscond /əbˈskɒnd/ *vi* evadir-se, andar fugido

absen|t[1] /ˈæbsənt/ *a* ausente; (*look etc*) distraído. **~ce** *n* ausência *f*; (*lack*) falta *f*. **~t-minded** *a* distraído. **~t-mindedness** *n* distração *f*, (P) distracção *f*

absent[2] /əbˈsent/ *v refl* **~ o.s.** ausentar-se

absentee /æbsənˈtiː/ *n* ausente *mf*, (P) absentista *mf*. **~ism** *n* absenteísmo *m*, (P) absentismo *m*

absolute /ˈæbsəluːt/ *a* absoluto; (*colloq: coward etc*) autêntico, (P) verdadeiro. **~ly** *adv* absolutamente

absolution /æbsəˈluːʃn/ *n* absolvição *f*

absolve /əbˈzɒlv/ *vt* (*from sin*) absolver (**from** de); (*from vow*) desligar (**from** de)

absor|b /əbˈsɔːb/ *vt* absorver. **~ption** *n* absorção *f*

absorbent /əbˈsɔːbənt/ *a* absorvente. **~ cotton** (*Amer*) algodão hidrófilo *m*

abst|ain /əbˈsteɪn/ *vi* abster-se (**from** de). **~ention** /-ˈstenʃn/ *n* abstenção *f*

abstemious /əbˈstiːmɪəs/ *a* abstémio, sóbrio

abstinen|ce /ˈæbstɪnəns/ *n* abstinência *f*. **~t** *a* abstinente

abstract[1] /ˈæbstrækt/ *a* abstrato, (P) abstracto

abstract[2] /əbˈstrækt/ *vt* (*take out*) extrair; (*separate*) separar. **~ed** *a* distraído. **~ion** /-ʃn/ *n* (*of mind*) distração *f*, (P) distracção *f*; (*idea*) abstração *f*, (P) abstracção *f*

absurd /əbˈsɜːd/ *a* absurdo. **~ity** *n* absurdo *m*

abundan|t /əˈbʌndənt/ *a* abundante. **~ce** *n* abundância *f*

abuse[1] /əˈbjuːz/ *vt* (*misuse*) abusar de; (*ill-treat*) maltratar; (*insult*) injuriar, insultar

abus|e[2] /əˈbjuːs/ *n* (*wrong use*) abuso *m* (**of** de); (*insults*) insultos *m pl*. **~ive** *a* injurioso, ofensivo

abysmal /əˈbɪzməl/ *a* abismal; (*colloq: bad*) abissal

abyss /əˈbɪs/ *n* abismo *m*

academic /ækəˈdemɪk/ *a* académico, (P) académico, universitário; (*schol-*

arly) intelectual; (*pej*) acadêmico, (P) teórico □ *n* universitário

academy /əˈkædəmɪ/ *n* academia *f*

accede /əkˈsiːd/ *vi* **~ to** (*request*) aceder a; (*post*) assumir; (*throne*) ascender a, subir a

accelerat|e /əkˈseləreɪt/ *vt* acelerar □ *vi* acelerar-se; (*auto*) acelerar. **~ion** /-ˈreɪʃn/ *n* aceleração *f*

accelerator /əkˈseləreɪtə(r)/ *n* (*auto*) acelerador *m*

accent[1] /ˈæksənt/ *n* acento *m*; (*local pronunciation*) sotaque *m*

accent[2] /ækˈsent/ *vt* acentuar

accentuate /ækˈsentʃʊeɪt/ *vt* acentuar

accept /əkˈsept/ *vt* aceitar. **~able** *a* aceitável. **~ance** *n* aceitação *f*; (*approval*) aprovação *f*

access /ˈækses/ *n* acesso *m* (**to** a). **~ible** /əkˈsesəbl/ *a* acessível

accessory /əkˈsesərɪ/ *a* acessório □ *n* acessório *m*; (*jur: person*) cúmplice *m*

accident /ˈæksɪdənt/ *n* acidente *m*, desastre *m*; (*chance*) acaso *m*. **~al** /-ˈdentl/ *a* acidental, fortuito, (P) /-ˈdentəlɪ/ *adv* acidentalmente, por acaso

acclaim /əˈkleɪm/ *vt* aclamar □ *n* aplauso *m*, aclamações *fpl*

acclimatiz|e /əˈklaɪmətaɪz/ *vt/i* aclimatar(-se). **~ation** /-ˈzeɪʃn/ *n* aclimatação *f*

accommodat|e /əˈkɒmədeɪt/ *vt* acomodar; (*lodge*) alojar; (*adapt*) adaptar; (*supply*) fornecer; (*oblige*) fazer a vontade de. **~ing** *a* obsequioso, amigo de fazer vontades. **~ion** /-ˈdeɪʃn/ *n* acomodação *f*; (*rooms*) alojamento *m*, quarto *m*

accompan|y /əˈkʌmpənɪ/ *vt* acompanhar. **~iment** *n* acompanhamento *m*. **~ist** *n* (*mus*) acompanhad/or, (B) -eira *mf*

accomplice /əˈkʌmplɪs/ *n* cúmplice *mf*

accomplish /əˈkʌmplɪʃ/ *vt* (*perform*) executar, realizar; (*achieve*) realizar, conseguir fazer. **~ed** *a* acabado. **~ment** *n* realização *f*; (*ability*) talento *m*, dote *m*

accord /əˈkɔːd/ *vi* concordar □ *vt* conceder □ *n* acordo *m*. **of one's own ~** por vontade própria, espontaneamente. **~ance** *n* **in ~ance with** em conformidade com, de acordo com

according /əˈkɔːdɪŋ/ *adv* **~ to** conforme. **~ly** *adv* (*therefore*) por conseguinte, por consequência; (*appropriately*) conformemente

accordion /əˈkɔːdɪən/ *n* acordeão *m*

accost /əˈkɒst/ *vt* abordar, abeirar-se de

account /əˈkaʊnt/ *n* (*comm*) conta *f*; (*description*) relato *m*; (*importance*) importância *f* □ *vt* considerar. ~ **for** dar contas de, explicar. **on** ~ **of** por causa de. **on no** ~ em caso algum. **take into** ~ ter *or* levar em conta. ~**able** /-əbl/ *a* responsável (**for** por). ~**ability** /-ˈbɪlətɪ/ *n* responsabilidade *f*

accountant /əˈkaʊntənt/ *n* contador(a) *m/f*, (*P*) contabilista *mf*

accrue /əˈkruː/ *vi* acumular-se. ~ **to** reverter em favor de

accumulat|e /əˈkjuːmjʊleɪt/ *vt/i* acumular(-se). ~**ion** /-ˈleɪʃn/ *n* acumulação *f*, acréscimo *m*

accumulator /əˈkjuːmjʊleɪtə(r)/ *n* (*electr*) acumulador *m*

accura|te /ˈækjərət/ *a* exato, (*P*) exacto, preciso. ~**cy** *n* exatidão *f*, (*P*) exactidão *f*, precisão *f*. ~**tely** *adv* com exatidão, (*P*) exactidão

accus|e /əˈkjuːz/ *vt* acusar. **the** ~**ed** *o* acusado. ~**ation** /ækjuːˈzeɪʃn/ *n* acusação *f*

accustom /əˈkʌstəm/ *vt* acostumar, habituar. ~**ed** *a* acostumado, habituado. **get** ~**ed to** acostumar-se a, habituar-se a

ace /eɪs/ *n* ás *m*

ache /eɪk/ *n* dor *f* □ *vi* doer. **my leg** ~**s** dói-me a perna, tenho dores na perna

achieve /əˈtʃiːv/ *vt* realizar, efetuar; (*success*) alcançar. ~**ment** *n* realização *f*; (*feat*) feito *m*, façanha *f*, sucesso *m*

acid /ˈæsɪd/ *a* ácido; (*wine*) azedo; (*words*) áspero □ *n* ácido *m*. ~**ity** /əˈsɪdətɪ/ *n* acidez *f*

acknowledge /əkˈnɒlɪdʒ/ *vt* reconhecer. ~ (**receipt of**) acusar a recepção de. ~**ment** *n* reconhecimento *m*; (*letter etc*) acusação *f* de recebimento, (*P*) aviso *m* de recepção

acne /ˈæknɪ/ *n* acne *mf*

acorn /ˈeɪkɔːn/ *n* bolota *f*, glande *f*

acoustic /əˈkuːstɪk/ *a* acústico. ~**s** *npl* acústica *f*

acquaint /əˈkweɪnt/ *vt* ~ **s.o. with sth** pôr alg a par de alg coisa. **be** ~**ed with** (*person, fact*) conhecer. ~**ance** *n* (*knowledge, person*) conhecimento *m*; (*person*) conhecido *m*

acquiesce /ækwɪˈes/ *vi* consentir. ~**nce** /ækwɪˈesns/ *n* aquiescência *f*, consentimento *m*

acquir|e /əˈkwaɪə(r)/ *vt* adquirir. ~**sition** /ækwɪˈzɪʃn/ *n* aquisição *f*

acquit /əˈkwɪt/ *vt* (*pt* **acquitted**) absolver. ~ **o.s. well** sair-se bem. ~**tal** *n* absolvição *f*

acrid /ˈækrɪd/ *a* acre

acrimon|ious /ækrɪˈməʊnɪəs/ *a* acrimonioso. ~**y** /ˈækrɪmənɪ/ *n* acrimónia *f*, (*P*) acrimónia *f*

acrobat /ˈækrəbæt/ *n* acrobata *mf*.

~**ic** /-ˈbætɪk/ *a* acrobático. ~**ics** /-ˈbætɪks/ *npl* acrobacia *f*

acronym /ˈækrənɪm/ *n* sigla *f*

across /əˈkrɒs/ *adv* & *prep* (*side to side*) de lado a lado (de), de um lado para o outro (de); (*on the other side*) do outro lado (de); (*crosswise*) através (de), de través. **go** *or* **walk** ~ atravessar. **swim** ~ atravessar a nado

act /ækt/ *n* (*deed, theatr*) ato *m*, (*P*) acto *m*; (*in variety show*) número *m*; (*decree*) lei *f* □ *vi* agir, atuar, (*P*) actuar; (*theatr*) representar; (*function*) funcionar; (*pretend*) fingir □ *vt* (*part, role*) desempenhar. ~ **as** servir de. ~**ing** *a* interino □ *n* (*theatr*) desempenho *m*

action /ˈækʃn/ *n* ação *f*, (*P*) acção *f*; (*mil*) combate *m*. **out of** ~ fora de combate; (*techn*) avariado. **take** ~ agir, atuar, (*P*) actuar

activ|e /ˈæktɪv/ *a* ativo, (*P*) activo; (*interest*) vivo; (*volcano*) em atividade, (*P*) actividade. ~**ity** /-ˈtɪvətɪ/ *n* atividade *f*, (*P*) actividade *f*

ac|tor /ˈæktə(r)/ *n* ator *m*, (*P*) actor *m*. ~**tress** *n* atriz *f*, (*P*) actriz *f*

actual /ˈæktʃʊəl/ *a* real, verdadeiro; (*example*) concreto. **the** ~ **pen which** a própria caneta que. ~**ity** /-ˈælətɪ/ *n* realidade *f*. ~**ly** *adv* (*in fact*) na realidade

acumen /əˈkjuːmen/ *n* agudeza *f*, perspicácia *f*

acupunctur|e /ˈækjʊpʌŋktʃə(r)/ *n* acupuntura *f*, (*P*) acupunctura *f*. ~**ist** *n* acupunturador *m*, (*P*) acupuncturista *mf*

acu|te /əˈkjuːt/ *a* agudo; (*mind*) perspicaz; (*emotion*) intenso, vivo; (*shortage*) grande. ~**ly** *adv* vivamente.

ad /æd/ *n* (*colloq*) anúncio *m*

AD *abbr* dC

adamant /ˈædəmənt/ *a* inflexível

adapt /əˈdæpt/ *vt/i* adaptar(-se). ~**ation** /ædæpˈteɪʃn/ *n* adaptação *f*. ~**or** (*electr*) *n* adaptador *m*

adaptab|le /əˈdæptəbl/ *a* adaptável. ~**ility** /-ˈbɪlətɪ/ *n* adaptabilidade *f*

add /æd/ *vt/i* acrescentar. ~ (**up**) somar. ~ **up to** (*total*) elevar-se a

adder /ˈædə(r)/ *n* víbora *f*

addict /ˈædɪkt/ *n* viciado *m*. **drug** ~ (*B*) viciado em droga, viciado da droga, (*P*) toxicodependente *mf*

addict|ed /əˈdɪktɪd/ *a* **be** ~**ed to** (*drink, drugs; fig*) ter o vício de. ~**ion** /-ʃn/ *n* (*med*) dependência *f*; (*fig*) vício *m*. ~**ive** *a* que produz dependência

addition /əˈdɪʃn/ *n* adição *f*. **in** ~ além disso. **in** ~ **to** além de. ~**al** /-ʃənl/ *a* adicional, suplementar

address /ə'dres/ n endereço m; (speech) discurso m □ vt endereçar; (speak to) dirigir-se a

adenoids /'ædmɔɪdz/ npl adenóides mpl

adept /'ædept/ a & n especialista (mf), perito (m) (at em)

adequa|te /'ædıkwət/ a adequado; (satisfactory) satisfatório. ~cy n adequação f, (of person) competência f. ~tely adv adequadamente

adhere /əd'hıə(r)/ vi aderir (to a)

adhesive /əd'hi:sɪv/ a & n adesivo (m). ~ plaster esparadrapo m, (P) adesivo m

adjacent /ə'dʒeɪsnt/ a adjacente, contiguo (to a)

adjective /'ædʒektɪv/ n adjetivo m, (P) adjectivo m

adjoin /ə'dʒɔɪn/ vt confinar com, ficar contiguo a

adjourn /ə'dʒɜ:n/ vt adiar □ vi suspender a sessão. ~ to (go) passar a, ir para

adjudicate /ə'dʒu:dıkeıt/ vt/i julgar; (award) adjudicar

adjust /ə'dʒʌst/ vt/i (alter) ajustar, regular; (arrange) arranjar. ~ (o.s.) to adaptar-se a. ~able a regulável. ~ment n (techn) regulação f, afinação f, (of person) adaptação f

ad lib /æd'lɪb/ vi (pt ad libbed) (colloq) improvisar □ adv à vontade

administer /əd'mınıstə(r)/ vt administrar

administrat|e /əd'mınıstreıt/ vt administrar, gerir. ~ion /-'streıʃn/ n administração f. ~or n administrador m

administrative /əd'mınıstrətıv/ a administrativo

admirable /'ædmərəbl/ a admirável

admiral /'ædmərəl/ n almirante m

admir|e /əd'maıə(r)/ vt admirar. ~ation /-mı'reıʃn/ n admiração f. ~er /-'maıərə(r)/ n admirador m

admission /əd'mıʃn/ n admissão f; (to museum, theatre, etc) ingresso m, (P) entrada f; (confession) confissão f

admit /əd'mıt/ vt (pt admitted) (let in) admitir, permitir a entrada a; (acknowledge) reconhecer, admitir. ~ to confessar. ~tance n admissão f

admoni|sh /əd'mɒnıʃ/ vt admoestar. ~tion /-nıʃn/ n admoestação f

adolescen|t /ædə'lesnt/ a & n adolescente (mf). ~ce n adolescência f

adopt /ə'dɒpt/ vt adotar, (P) adoptar. ~ed child filho adotivo, (P) adoptivo. ~ion /-ʃn/ n adoção f, (P) adopção f

ador|e /ə'dɔ:(r)/ vt adorar. ~able a adorável. ~ation /ædə'reıʃn/ n adoração f

adorn /ə'dɔ:n/ vt adornar, enfeitar

adrenalin /ə'drenəlın/ n adrenalina f

adrift /ə'drıft/ a & adv à deriva

adult /'ædʌlt/ a & n adulto (m). ~hood n idade f adulta, (P) maioridade f

adulterat|e /ə'dʌltərət/ vt adulterar. ~ion /'reıʃn/ n adulteração f

adulter|y /ə'dʌltərı/ n adultério m. ~er, ~ess ns adúlter/o, -a mf. ~ous a adúltero

advance /əd'va:ns/ vt/i avançar □ n avanço m; (payment) adiantamento m □ a (payment, booking) adiantado. in ~ com antecedência. ~d a avançado. ~ment n promoção f, ascensão f

advantage /əd'va:ntıdʒ/ n vantagem f. take ~ of aproveitar-se de, tirar partido de; (person) explorar. ~ous /ædvən'teıdʒəs/ a vantajoso

adventur|e /əd'ventʃə(r)/ n aventura f. ~er n aventureiro m, explorador m. ~ous a aventuroso

adverb /'ædvɜ:b/ n advérbio m

adversary /'ædvəsərı/ n adversário m, antagonista mf

advers|e /'ædvɜ:s/ a (contrary) adverso; (unfavourable) desfavorável. ~ity /əd'vɜ:sətı/ n adversidade f

advert /'ædvɜ:t/ n (colloq) anúncio m

advertise /'ædvətaız/ vt/i anunciar, fazer publicidade (de); (sell) pôr um anúncio (para). ~ for procurar; ~r /-ə(r)/ n anunciante mf

advertisement /əd'vɜ:tısmənt/ n anúncio m; (advertising) publicidade f

advice /əd'vaıs/ n conselho(s) mpl; (comm) aviso m

advis|e /əd'vaız/ vt aconselhar; (inform) avisar, informar. ~e against desaconselhar. ~able a aconselhável. ~er n conselheiro m; (in business) consultor m. ~ory a consultivo

advocate¹ /'ædvəkət/ n (jur) advogado m; (supporter) defensor/a m/f

advocate² /'ædvəkeıt/ vt advogar, defender

aerial /'eərıəl/ a aéreo □ n antena f

aerobatics /eərə'bætıks/ npl acrobacia f aérea

aerobics /eə'rəubıks/ n ginástica f aeróbica

aerodynamic /eərəudaı'næmık/ a aerodinâmico

aeroplane /'eərəpleın/ n avião m

aerosol /'eərəsɒl/ n aerossol m

aesthetic /i:s'θetık/ a estético.

affair /ə'feə(r)/ n (business) negócio m; (romance) ligação f, aventura f; (matter) assunto m. love ~ paixão f

affect /ə'fekt/ vt afetar, (P) afectar. ~ation /æfek'teıʃn/ n afetação f, (P) afecção f. **~ed** a afetado, (P) afectado, pretencioso

affection /əˈfekʃn/ n afeição f, afeto m, (P) afecto m

affectionate /əˈfekʃənət/ a afetuoso, (P) afectuoso, carinhoso

affiliat|e /əˈfɪlɪeɪt/ vt afiliar. **~ed company** filial f. **~ion** /-ˈeɪʃn/ n afiliação f

affirm /əˈfɜːm/ vt afirmar. **~ation** /æfəˈmeɪʃn/ n afirmação f

affirmative /əˈfɜːmətɪv/ a afirmativo □ n afirmativa f

afflict /əˈflɪkt/ vt afligir. **~ion** /-ʃn/ n aflição f

affluen|t /ˈæfluənt/ a rico, afluente. **~ce** n riqueza f, afluência f

afford /əˈfɔːd/ vt (have money for) permitir-se, ter meios (para). **can you afford the time?** você teria tempo? **I can't afford a car** eu não posso comprar um carro. **we can't afford to lose** não podemos perder

affront /əˈfrʌnt/ n afronta f □ vt insultar

afield /əˈfiːld/ adv **far ~** longe

afloat /əˈfləʊt/ adv & a à tona, a flutuar; (at sea) no mar; (business) lançado, (P) sem dívidas

afraid /əˈfreɪd/ a **be ~** ter medo (of, to de; that que); (be sorry) lamentar, ter muita pena. **I'm ~ (that)** (regret to say) lamento or tenho muita pena de dizer que

afresh /əˈfreʃ/ adv de novo

Africa /ˈæfrɪkə/ n África f. **~n** a & n africano (m)

after /ˈɑːftə(r)/ adv depois □ prep depois de □ conj depois que. **~ all** afinal de contas. **~ doing**, depois de fazer. **be ~** (seek) querer, pretender. **~-effect** n sequela f, (P) sequela f, efeito m retardado; (of drug) efeito m secundário

aftermath /ˈɑːftəmæθ/ n consequências fpl

afternoon /ɑːftəˈnuːn/ n tarde f

aftershave /ˈɑːftəʃeɪv/ n loção f após-barba, (P) loção f para a barba

afterthought /ˈɑːftəθɔːt/ n reflexão f posterior. **as an ~** pensando melhor

afterwards /ˈɑːftəwədz/ adv depois, mais tarde

again /əˈɡen/ adv de novo, outra vez; (on the other hand) por outro lado. **then ~** além disso

against /əˈɡenst/ prep contra

age /eɪdʒ/ n idade f; (period) época f, idade f □ vt/i (pres p ageing) envelhecer. **~s** (colloq: very long time) há séculos mpl. **of ~** (jur) maior. **ten years of ~** com/de dez anos. **under ~** menor. **~-group** n faixa etária f. **~less** a sempre jovem

aged[1] /eɪdʒd/ a **~ six** de seis anos de idade

aged[2] /ˈeɪdʒɪd/ a idoso, velho

agen|cy /ˈeɪdʒənsɪ/ n agência f; (means) intermédio m. **~t** n agente mf

agenda /əˈdʒendə/ n ordem f do dia

aggravat|e /ˈæɡrəveɪt/ vt agravar; (colloq: annoy) irritar. **~ion** /-ˈveɪʃn/ n (worsening) agravamento m; (exasperation) irritação f; (colloq: trouble) aborrecimentos mpl

aggregate /ˈæɡrɪɡeɪt/ vt/i agregar (-se) □ a /ˈæɡrɪɡət/ total, global □ n (total, mass, materials) agregado m. **in the ~** no todo

aggress|ive /əˈɡresɪv/ a agressivo; (weapons) ofensivo. **~ion** /-ʃn/ n agressão f. **~iveness** n agressividade f. **~or** n agressor m

aggrieved /əˈɡriːvd/ a (having a grievance) lesado

agil|e /ˈædʒaɪl/ a ágil. **~ity** /əˈdʒɪlətɪ/ n agilidade f

agitat|e /ˈædʒɪteɪt/ vt agitar. **~ion** /-ˈteɪʃn/ n agitação f. **~or** n agitador m

agnostic /æɡˈnɒstɪk/ a & n agnóstico (m)

ago /əˈɡəʊ/ adv há. **a month ~** há um mês. **long ~** há muito tempo

agon|y /ˈæɡənɪ/ n agonia f; (mental) angústia f. **~ize** vi atormentar-se, torturar-se. **~izing** a angustiante, (P) doloroso

agree /əˈɡriː/ vt/i concordar; (of figures) acertar. **~ that** reconhecer que. **~ to do** concordar em or aceitar fazer. **~ to sth** concordar com alguma coisa. **seafood doesn't ~ with me** não me dou bem com mariscos. **~d** a (time, place) combinado. **be ~d** estar de acordo

agreeable /əˈɡriːəbl/ a agradável. **be ~ to** estar de acordo com

agreement /əˈɡriːmənt/ n acordo m; (gramm) concordância f; (contract) contrato m. **in ~** de acordo

agricultur|e /ˈæɡrɪkʌltʃə(r)/ n agricultura f. **~al** /-ˈkʌltʃərəl/ a agrícola

aground /əˈɡraʊnd/ adv **run ~** (of ship) encalhar

ahead /əˈhed/ adv à frente, adiante; (in advance) adiantado. **~ of sb** diante de alguém, à frente de alguém. **~ of time** antes da hora, adiantado. **straight ~** sempre em frente

aid /eɪd/ vt ajudar □ n ajuda f. **~ and abet** ser cúmplice de. **in ~ of** em auxílio de, a favor de

AIDS /eɪdz/ n (med) AIDS f, (P) sida f

ail /eɪl/ vt **what ~s you?** o que é que você tem? **~ing** a doente. **~ment** n doença f, achaque m

aim /eɪm/ vt (gun) apontar; (efforts) dirigir; (send) atirar (at para) □ vi visar □ n alvo m. ~ at visar. ~ to aspirar a, tencionar. **take** ~ fazer pontaria. ~**less** a, ~**lessly** adv sem objetivo, (P) objectivo

air /eə(r)/ n ar m □ vt arejar; (views) expor □ a (base etc) aéreo. **in the** ~ (rumour) espalhado; (plans) no ar. **on the** ~ (radio) no ar. ~**-conditioned** a com ar condicionado. ~**-conditioning** n condicionamento m do ar, (P) ar m condicionado. ~**-force** Força f Aérea. ~ **hostess** aeromoça f, (P) hospedeira f de bordo. ~ **raid** ataque m aéreo

airborne /ˈeəbɔːn/ a (aviat: in flight) no ar; (diseases) levado pelo ar; (freight) por transporte aéreo

aircraft /ˈeəkrɑːft/ n (pl invar) avião m. ~**-carrier** n porta-aviões m

airfield /ˈeəfiːld/ n campo m de aviação

airgun /ˈeəɡʌn/ n espingarda f de pressão

airlift /ˈeəlɪft/ n ponte f aérea □ vt transportar em ponte aérea

airline /ˈeəlaɪn/ n linha f aérea

airlock /ˈeəlɒk/ n câmara f de vácuo; (in pipe) bolha f de ar

airmail /ˈeəmeɪl/ n correio m aéreo. **by** ~ por avião

airport /ˈeəpɔːt/ n aeroporto m

airsick /ˈeəsɪk/ a enjoado. ~**ness** /-nɪs/ n enjôo m, (P) enjoo m

airstrip /ˈeəstrɪp/ n pista f de aterrissagem, (P) pista f de aterragem

airtight /ˈeətaɪt/ a hermético

airy /ˈeərɪ/ a (-ier, -iest) arejado; (manner) desenvolto

aisle /aɪl/ n (of church) nave f lateral; (gangway) coxia f

ajar /əˈdʒɑː(r)/ adv & a entreaberto

alabaster /ˈæləbɑːstə(r)/ n alabastro m

à la carte /ɑːlɑːˈkɑːt/ adv & a à la carte, (P) à lista

alarm /əˈlɑːm/ n alarme m; (clock) campainha f □ vt alarmar. ~**-clock** n despertador m. ~**-bell** n campainha f de alarme. ~**ing** a alarmante. ~**ist** n alarmista mf

alas /əˈlæs/ int ai! ai de mim!

albatross /ˈælbətrɒs/ n albatroz m

album /ˈælbəm/ n álbum m

alcohol /ˈælkəhɒl/ n álcool m. ~**ic** /-ˈhɒlɪk/ a (person, drink) alcoólico □ n alcoólico m. ~**ism** n alcoolismo m

alcove /ˈælkəʊv/ n recesso m, alcova f

ale /eɪl/ n cerveja f inglesa

alert /əˈlɜːt/ a (lively) vivo; (watchful) vigilante □ n alerta m □ vt alertar. **be on the** ~ estar alerta

algebra /ˈældʒɪbrə/ n álgebra f. ~**ic** /-ˈbreɪk/ a algébrico

Algeria /ælˈdʒɪərɪə/ n Argélia f. ~**n** a & n argelino (m)

alias /ˈeɪlɪəs/ n (pl -ases) outro nome m, nome falso m, (P) pseudónimo m □ adv aliás

alibi /ˈælɪbaɪ/ n (pl -is) álibi m, (P) alibi m

alien /ˈeɪlɪən/ n & a estrangeiro (m). ~ **to** (contrary) contrário a; (differing) alheio a, estranho a

alienat|e /ˈeɪlɪəneɪt/ vt alienar. ~**ion** /-ˈneɪʃn/ n alienação f

alight[1] /əˈlaɪt/ vi descer; (bird) pousar

alight[2] /əˈlaɪt/ a (on fire) em chamas; (lit up) aceso

align /əˈlaɪn/ vt alinhar. ~**ment** n alinhamento m

alike /əˈlaɪk/ a semelhante, parecido □ adv da mesma maneira. **look** or **be** ~ parecer-se

alimony /ˈælɪmənɪ/ n pensão f alimentar, (P) de alimentos

alive /əˈlaɪv/ a vivo. **be** ~ **to** sensível a. ~ **with** fervilhando de, (P) a fervilhar de

alkali /ˈælkəlaɪ/ n (pl -is) álcali m, (P) alcali m

all /ɔːl/ a & pron todo (f & pl -a, -os, -as) □ pron (everything) tudo □ adv completamente, de todo □ n tudo m. ~ **the better/less/more/worse** etc tanto melhor/menos/mais/pior etc. ~ (the) men todos os homens. ~ **of us** todos nós. ~ **but** quase, todos menos. ~ **in** (colloq: exhausted) estafado. ~**-in** a tudo incluído. ~ **out** a fundo, (P) completamente. ~**-out** a (effort) máximo. ~ **over** (in one's body) todo; (finished) acabado; (in all parts of) por todo. ~ **right** bem; (as a response) está bem. ~ **round** em tudo; (for all) para todos. ~**-round** a geral. ~ **the same** apesar de tudo. **it's** ~ **the same to me** (para mim) tanto faz

allay /əˈleɪ/ vt acalmar

allegation /ælɪˈɡeɪʃn/ n alegação f

allege /əˈledʒ/ vt alegar. ~**dly** /-ɪdlɪ/ adv segundo dizem, alegadamente

allegiance /əˈliːdʒəns/ n fidelidade f, lealdade f

allegor|y /ˈælɪɡərɪ/ n alegoria f. ~**ical** /-ˈɡɒrɪkl/ a alegórico

allerg|y /ˈælədʒɪ/ n alergia f. ~**ic** /əˈlɜːdʒɪk/ a alérgico

alleviate /əˈliːvɪeɪt/ vt aliviar

alley /ˈælɪ/ n (pl -eys) (street) viela f; (for bowling) pista f

alliance /əˈlaɪəns/ n aliança f

allied /ˈælaɪd/ a aliado

alligator /ˈælɪɡeɪtə(r)/ n jacaré m

allocat|e /ˈæləkeɪt/ vt (share out) distribuir; (assign) destinar. ~**ion** /-ˈkeɪʃn/ n atribuição f

allot /ə'lɒt/ *vt* (*pt* **allotted**) atribuir. **~ment** *n* atribuição *f*; (*share*) distribuição *f*; (*land*) horta *f* alugada

allow /ə'laʊ/ *vt* permitir; (*grant*) conceder, dar; (*reckon on*) contar com; (*agree*) admitir, reconhecer. **~ sb to** (+ *inf*) permitir a alg (+ *inf or que* + *subj*). **~ for** levar em conta

allowance /ə'laʊəns/ *n* (*for employees*) ajudas *fpl* de custo; (*monthly, for wife, child*) benefício *m*; (*tax*) desconto *m*. **make ~s for** (*person*) levar em consideração, ser indulgente para com; (*take into account*) atender a, levar em consideração

alloy /ə'lɔɪ/ *n* liga *f*

allude /ə'luːd/ *vi* **~ to** aludir a

allure /ə'lʊə(r)/ *vt* seduzir, atrair

allusion /ə'luːʒn/ *n* alusão *f*

ally[1] /'ælaɪ/ *n* (*pl* **-lies**) aliado *m*

ally[2] /ə'laɪ/ *vt* aliar. **~ oneself with/ to** aliar-se a/com

almanac /'ɔːlmənæk/ *n* almanaque *m*

almighty /ɔːl'maɪtɪ/ *a* todo-poderoso; (*colloq*) grande, formidável

almond /'ɑːmənd/ *n* amêndoa *f*. **~ paste** maçapão *m*

almost /'ɔːlməʊst/ *adv* quase

alone /ə'ləʊn/ *a* & *adv* só. **leave ~** (*abstain from interfering with*) deixar em paz. **let ~** (*without considering*) sem or para não falar de

along /ə'lɒŋ/ *prep* ao longo de □ *adv* (*onward*) para diante. **all ~** durante todo o tempo. **~ with** com. **move ~, please** ande, por favor

alongside /əlɒŋ'saɪd/ *adv* (*naut*) atracado. **come ~** acostar □ *prep* ao lado de

aloof /ə'luːf/ *adv* à parte □ *distante*. **~ness** *n* reserva *f*

aloud /ə'laʊd/ *adv* em voz alta

alphabet /'ælfəbet/ *n* alfabeto *m*. **~ical** /-'betɪkl/ *a* alfabético

alpine /'ælpaɪn/ *a* alpino, alpestre

Alps /ælps/ *npl* **the ~** os Alpes *mpl*

already /ɔːl'redɪ/ *adv* já

also /'ɔːlsəʊ/ *adv* também

altar /'ɔːltə(r)/ *n* altar *m*

alter /'ɔːltə(r)/ *vt/i* alterar(-se), modificar(-se). **~ation** /-'reɪʃn/ *n* alteração *f*; (*to garment*) modificação *f*

alternate[1] /ɔːl'tɜːnət/ *a* alternado. **~ly** *adv* alternadamente

alternate[2] /'ɔːltəneɪt/ *vt/i* alternar (-se). **~ing current** (*elect*) corrente *f* alterna. **~or** *n* (*elect*) alternador *m*

alternative /ɔːl'tɜːnətɪv/ *a* alternativo □ *n* alternativa *f*. **~ly** *adv* em alternativa. **or ~ly** ou então

although /ɔːl'ðəʊ/ *conj* embora, conquanto

altitude /'æltɪtjuːd/ *n* altitude *f*

altogether /ɔːltə'geðə(r)/ *adv* (*completely*) completamente; (*in total*) ao todo; (*on the whole*) de modo geral

aluminium /æljʊ'mɪnɪəm/ (*Amer* **aluminum** /ə'luːmɪnəm/) *n* alumínio *m*

always /'ɔːlweɪz/ *adv* sempre

am /æm/ *see* be

a.m. /eɪ'em/ *adv* da manhã

amalgamate /ə'mælgəmeɪt/ *vt/i* amalgamar(-se); (*comm*) fundir

amass /ə'mæs/ *vt* amontoar, juntar

amateur /'æmətə(r)/ *n* & *a* amador (*m*). **~ish** *a* (*pej*) de amador, (*P*) amadorístico

amaz|e /ə'meɪz/ *vt* assombrar, espantar. **~ed** *a* assombrado. **~ement** *n* assombro *m*. **~ingly** *adv* espantosamente

Amazon /'æməzən/ *n* **the ~** o Amazonas

ambassador /æm'bæsədə(r)/ *n* embaixador *m*

amber /'æmbə(r)/ *n* âmbar *m*; (*traffic light*) luz *f* amarela

ambigu|ous /æm'bɪgjʊəs/ *a* ambíguo. **~ity** /-'gjuːətɪ/ *n* ambiguidade *f*, (*P*) ambiguidade *f*

ambition /æm'bɪʃn/ *n* ambição *f*. **~ous** *a* ambicioso

ambivalen|t /æm'bɪvələnt/ *a* ambivalente. **~ce** *n* ambivalência *f*

amble /'æmbl/ *vi* caminhar sem pressa

ambulance /'æmbjʊləns/ *n* ambulância *f*

ambush /'æmbʊʃ/ *n* emboscada *f* □ *vt* fazer uma emboscada para, (*P*) fazer uma emboscada a

amenable /ə'miːnəbl/ *a* **~ to** (*responsive*) sensível a

amend /ə'mend/ *vt* emendar, corrigir. **~ment** *n* (*to rule*) emenda *f*. **~s** *n* **make ~s for** reparar, compensar

amenities /ə'miːnətɪz/ *npl* (*pleasant features*) atrativos *mpl* (*P*) atractivos *mpl*; (*facilities*) confortos *mpl*, comodidades *fpl*

America /ə'merɪkə/ *n* América *f*. **~n** *a* & *n* americano (*m*). **~nism** /-nɪzəm/ *n* americanismo *m*. **~nize** *vt* americanizar

amiable /'eɪmɪəbl/ *a* amável

amicable /'æmɪkəbl/ *a* amigável, amigo

amid(st) /ə'mɪd(st)/ *prep* entre, no meio de

amiss /ə'mɪs/ *a* & *adv* mal. **sth ~** qq coisa que não está bem. **take sth ~** levar qq coisa a mal

ammonia /ə'məʊnɪə/ *n* amoníaco *m*

ammunition /æmjʊ'nɪʃn/ *n* munições *fpl*

amnesia /æm'niːzɪə/ *n* amnésia *f*

amnesty /'æmnəstɪ/ n anistia f, (P) amnistia f

amok /ə'mɒk/ adv run ~ enlouquecer; (crowd) correr desordenadamente

among(st) /ə'mʌŋ(st)/ prep entre, no meio de. ~ **ourselves** (aqui) entre nós

amoral /eɪ'mɒrəl/ a amoral

amorous /'æmərəs/ a amoroso

amount /ə'maʊnt/ n quantidade f; (total) montante m; (sum of money) quantia f □ vi ~ **to** elevar-se a; (fig) equivaler a

amp /æmp/ n (colloq) ampère m

amphibi|an /æm'fɪbɪən/ n anfíbio m. ~**ous** a anfíbio

ampl|e /'æmpl/ a (-er, -est) (large, roomy) amplo; (enough) suficiente, bastante. ~**y** adv amplamente

amplif|y /'æmplɪfaɪ/ vt ampliar, amplificar. ~**ier** n amplificador m

amputat|e /'æmpjʊteɪt/ vt amputar. ~**ion** /-'teɪʃn/ n amputação f

amus|e /ə'mjuːz/ vt divertir. ~**ement** n divertimento m. ~**ing** a divertido

an /ən, æn/ see **a**

anachronism /ə'nækrənɪzəm/ n anacronismo m

anaem|ia /ə'niːmɪə/ n anemia f. ~**ic** a anêmico, (P) anémico

anaesthetic /ænɪs'θetɪk/ n anestético m, (P) anestésico m. **give an** ~ **to** anestesiar

anaesthetist /ə'niːsθətɪst/ n anestesista mf

anagram /'ænəgræm/ n anagrama m

analog(ue) /'ænəlɒg/ a análogo

analogy /ə'nælədʒɪ/ n analogia f

analys|e /'ænəlaɪz/ vt analisar. ~**t** /-ɪst/ n analista mf

analysis /ə'næləsɪs/ n (pl -yses) /-əsiːz/ análise f

analytic(al) /ænə'lɪtɪk(l)/ a analítico

anarch|y /'ænəkɪ/ n anarquia f. ~**ist** n anarquista mf

anatom|y /ə'nætəmɪ/ n anatomia f. ~**ical** /ænə'tɒmɪkl/ a anatômico, (P) anatómico

ancest|or /'ænsestə(r)/ n antepassado m. ~**ral** /-'sestrəl/ a ancestral (pl -ais)

ancestry /'ænsestrɪ/ n ascendência f, estirpe f

anchor /'æŋkə(r)/ n âncora f □ vt/i ancorar. ~**age** /-rɪdʒ/ n ancoradouro m

anchovy /'æntʃəvɪ/ n enchova f, (P) anchova f

ancient /'eɪnʃənt/ a antigo

ancillary /æn'sɪlərɪ/ a ancilar, (P) subordinado

and /ənd/; emphatic /ænd/ conj e. **go** ~ **see** vá ver. **better** ~ **better**/**less** ~ **less** etc cada vez melhor/menos etc

anecdote /'ænɪkdəʊt/ n anedota f

angel /'eɪndʒl/ n anjo m. ~**ic** /æn'dʒelɪk/ a angélico, angelical

anger /'æŋgə(r)/ n cólera f, zanga f □ vt irritar

angle¹ /'æŋgl/ n ângulo m

angle² /'æŋgl/ vi (fish) pescar (à linha). ~ **for** (fig: compliments, information) andar à procura de. ~**r** /-ə(r)/ n pescador m

anglicism /'æŋglɪsɪzəm/ n anglicismo m

Anglo- /'æŋgləʊ/ pref anglo-

Anglo-Saxon /æŋgləʊ'sæksn/ a & n anglo-saxão (m)

angr|y /'æŋgrɪ/ a (-ier, -iest) zangado. **get** ~**y** zangar-se (with com). ~**ily** adv furiosamente

anguish /'æŋgwɪʃ/ n angústia f

angular /'æŋgjʊlə(r)/ a angular; (features) anguloso

animal /'ænɪml/ a & n animal (m)

animate¹ /'ænɪmət/ a animado

animat|e² /'ænɪmeɪt/ vt animar. ~**ion** /-'meɪʃn/ n animação f. ~**ed cartoon** filme m de bonecos animados, (P) de desenhos animados

animosity /ænɪ'mɒsətɪ/ n animosidade f

aniseed /'ænɪsiːd/ n semente f de anis

ankle /'æŋkl/ n tornozelo m. ~ **sock** meia f soquete

annex /ə'neks/ vt anexar. ~**ation** /ænek'seɪʃn/ n anexação f

annexe /'æneks/ n anexo m

annihilate /ə'naɪəleɪt/ vt aniquilar

anniversary /ænɪ'vɜːsərɪ/ n aniversário m

announce /ə'naʊns/ vt anunciar. ~**ment** n anúncio m. ~**r** /-ə(r)/ n (radio, TV) locutor m

annoy /ə'nɔɪ/ vt irritar, aborrecer. ~**ance** n aborrecimento m. ~**ed** a aborrecido (with com). **get** ~**ed** aborrecer-se. ~**ing** a irritante

annual /'ænjʊəl/ a anual □ n (bot) planta f anual; (book) anuário m. ~**ly** adv anualmente

annuity /ə'njuːətɪ/ n anuidade f

annul /ə'nʌl/ vt (pt annulled) anular. ~**ment** n anulação f

anomal|y /ə'nɒməlɪ/ n anomalia f. ~**ous** a anómalo, (P) anómalo

anonym|ous /ə'nɒnɪməs/ a anônimo, (P) anónimo. ~**ity** /ænə'nɪmətɪ/ n anonimato m

anorak /'ænəræk/ n anoraque m, anorak m

another /ə'nʌðə(r)/ a & pron (um) outro. ~ **ten minutes** mais dez minutos. **to one** ~ um ao outro, uns aos outros

answer /'ɑːnsə(r)/ n resposta f; (solution) solução f □ vt responder a;

(*prayer*) atender a □ *vi* responder. ~ **the door** atender à porta. ~ **back** retrucar, (P) responder torto. ~ **for** responder por. ~**able** *a* responsável (for por; to perante). ~**ing machine** *n* secretária *f* eletrónica

ant /ænt/ *n* formiga *f*

antagonis|m /æn'tægənɪzəm/ *n* antagonismo *m*. ~**t** *n* antagonista *mf.* ~**tic** /-'nɪstɪk/ *a* antagónico, (P) antagónico, hostil

antagonize /æn'tægənaɪz/ *vt* antagonizar, hostilizar

Antarctic /æn'tɑ:ktɪk/ *n* Antártico, (P) Antárctico *m* □ *a* antártico, (P) antárctico

ante- /ænti/ *pref* ante-

antecedent /æntɪ'si:dnt/ *a* & *n* antecedente (*m*)

antelope /ˈæntɪləʊp/ *n* antilope *m*

antenatal /æntɪ'neɪtl/ *a* pré-natal

antenna /æn'tenə/ *n* (*pl* -**ae** /-i:/) antena *f*

anthem /ˈænθəm/ *n* cântico *m.* **national** ~ hino *m* nacional

anthology /æn'θɒlədʒɪ/ *n* antologia *f*

anthropolog|y /ænθrə'pɒlədʒɪ/ *n* antropologia *f.* ~**ist** *n* antropólogo *m*

anti- /æntɪ/ *pref* anti-. ~**aircraft** /-eəkrɑ:ft/ *a* antiaéreo

antibiotic /æntɪbaɪ'ɒtɪk/ *n* antibiótico *m*

antibody /ˈæntɪbɒdɪ/ *n* anticorpo *m*

anticipat|e /æn'tɪsɪpeɪt/ *vt* (*foresee, expect*) prever; (*forestall*) antecipar-se a. ~**ion** /-'peɪʃn/ *n* antecipação *f;* (*expectation*) expectativa *f.* **in** ~**ion of** na previsão or expectativa de

anticlimax /æntɪ'klaɪmæks/ *n* anticlímax *m;* (*let-down*) decepção *f.* **it was an** ~ não correspondeu à expectativa

anticlockwise /æntɪ'klɒkwaɪz/ *adv* & *a* no sentido contrário ao dos ponteiros dum relógio

antics /ˈæntɪks/ *npl* (*of clown*) palhaçadas *fpl;* (*behaviour*) comportamento *m* bizarro

anticyclone /æntɪ'saɪkləʊn/ *n* anticiclone *m*

antidote /ˈæntɪdəʊt/ *n* antidoto *m*

antifreeze /ˈæntɪfri:z/ *n* anticongelante *m*

antihistamine /æntɪ'hɪstəmi:n/ *a* & *n* anti-histamínico (*m*)

antipathy /æn'tɪpəθɪ/ *n* antipatia *f*

antiquated /ˈæntɪkweɪtɪd/ *a* antiquado

antique /æn'ti:k/ *a* antigo □ *n* antiguidade *f.* ~ **dealer** antiquário *m.* ~ **shop** loja *f* de antiguidades, (P) antiquário *m*

antiquity /æn'tɪkwətɪ/ *n* antiguidade *f*

antiseptic /æntɪ'septɪk/ *a* & *n* antisséptico (*m*)

antisocial /æntɪ'səʊʃl/ *a* anti-social; (*unsociable*) insociável

antithesis /æn'tɪθəsɪs/ *n* (*pl* -**eses**) /-si:z/ antitese *f*

antlers /ˈæntləz/ *npl* chifres *mpl*, esgalhos *mpl*

antonym /ˈæntənɪm/ *n* antónimo *m*, (P) antónimo *m*

anus /ˈeɪnəs/ *n* ânus *m*

anvil /ˈænvɪl/ *n* bigorna *f*

anxiety /æŋ'zaɪətɪ/ *n* ansiedade *f;* (*eagerness*) ânsia *f*

anxious /ˈæŋkʃəs/ *a* (*worried, eager*) ansioso (to de, por). ~**ly** *adv* ansiosamente; (*eagerly*) impacientemente

any /ˈenɪ/ *a* & *pron* qualquer, quaisquer; (*in neg and interr sentences*) algum, alguns; (*in neg sentences*) nenhum, nenhuns; (*every*) todo. **at** ~ **moment** a qualquer momento. **at** ~ **rate** de qualquer modo, em todo o caso. **in** ~ **case** em todo o caso. **have you** ~ **money/friends?** você tem (algum) dinheiro/(alguns) amigos? **I don't have** ~ **time** não tenho nenhum tempo or tempo nenhum or tempo algum. **has she** ~? ela tem algum? **she doesn't have** ~ ela não tem nenhum □ *adv* (*at all*) de modo algum or nenhum; (*a little*) um pouco. ~ **less/the worse** *etc* menos/pior *etc*

anybody /ˈenɪbɒdɪ/ *pron* qualquer pessoa; (*somebody*) alguém; (*after negative*) ninguém. **he didn't see** ~ ele não viu ninguém

anyhow /ˈenɪhaʊ/ *adv* (*no matter how*) de qualquer modo; (*badly*) de qualquer maneira, ao acaso, (*in any case*) em todo o caso. **you can try,** ~ em todo o caso, você pode tentar

anyone /ˈenɪwʌn/ *pron* = **anybody**

anything /ˈenɪθɪŋ/ *pron* (*something*) alguma coisa; (*no matter what*) qualquer coisa; (*after negative*) nada. **he didn't say** ~ não disse nada. **it is** ~ **but cheap** é tudo menos barato. ~ **you do** tudo o que você fizer

anyway /ˈenɪweɪ/ *adv* de qualquer modo; (*in any case*) em todo o caso

anywhere /ˈenɪweə(r)/ *adv* (*somewhere*) em qualquer parte; (*after negative*) em parte alguma/nenhuma. ~ **else** em qualquer outro lado. ~ **you go** onde quer que você vá. **he doesn't go** ~ ele não vai a lado nenhum

apart /ə'pɑ:t/ *adv* à parte, (*separated*) separado; (*into pieces*) aos bocados. ~ **from** à parte, além de. **ten metres** ~ a dez metros de distância entre si. **come** ~ desfazer-se. **keep** ~ manter separado. **take** ~ desmontar

apartment /ə'pa:tmənt/ n (Amer) apartamento m. ~s aposentos mpl

apath|y /'æpəθɪ/ n apatia f. ~etic /-'θetɪk/ a apático

ape /eɪp/ n macaco m □ vt macaquear

aperitif /ə'perətɪf/ n aperitivo m

aperture /'æpətʃə(r)/ n abertura f

apex /'eɪpeks/ n ápice m, cume m

apiece /ə'pi:s/ adv cada, por cabeça

apologetic /əpɒlə'dʒetɪk/ a (tone etc) apologético, de desculpas. **be** ~ desculpar-se. ~ally /-əlɪ/ adv desculpando-se

apologize /ə'pɒlədʒaɪz/ vi desculpar-se (**for**, de, por; **to** junto de, perante), pedir desculpa (**for**, por; **to**, a)

apology /ə'pɒlədʒɪ/ n desculpa f; (defence of belief) apologia f

apostle /ə'pɒsl/ n apóstolo m

apostrophe /ə'pɒstrəfɪ/ n apóstrofe f

appal /ə'pɔ:l/ vt (pt **appalled**) estarrecer. ~**ling** a estarrecedor

apparatus /æpə'reɪtəs/ n aparelho m

apparent /ə'pærənt/ a aparente. ~**ly** adv aparentemente

apparition /æpə'rɪʃn/ n aparição f

appeal /ə'pi:l/ vi (jur) apelar (**to** para); (attract) atrair (**to** a); (for funds) angariar □ n apelo m; (attractiveness) atrativo m, (P) atractivo m; (for funds) angariação f. ~ **to sb for sth** pedir uma coisa a alg. ~**ing** a (attractive) atraente

appear /ə'pɪə(r)/ vi aparecer; (seem) parecer; (in court, theatre) apresentar-se. ~**ance** n aparição f; (aspect) aparência f; (in court) comparecimento m, (P) comparência f

appease /ə'pi:z/ vt apaziguar

appendage /ə'pendɪdʒ/ n apêndice m

appendicitis /əpendɪ'saɪtɪs/ n apendicite f

appendix /ə'pendɪks/ n (pl **-ices** /-si:z/) (of book) apêndice m; (pl **-ixes** /-ksɪz/) (anat) apêndice m

appetite /'æpɪtaɪt/ n apetite m

appetizer /'æpɪtaɪzə(r)/ n (snack) tira-gosto m; (drink) aperitivo m

appetizing /'æpɪtaɪzɪŋ/ a apetitoso

applau|d /ə'plɔ:d/ vt/i aplaudir. ~**se** n aplauso(s) m(pl)

apple /'æpl/ n maçã f. ~ **tree** macieira f

appliance /ə'plaɪəns/ n aparelho m, instrumento m, utensílio m. house**hold** ~**s** utensílios mpl domésticos

applicable /'æplɪkəbl/ a aplicável

applicant /'æplɪkənt/ n candidato m (**for** a)

application /æplɪ'keɪʃn/ n aplicação f; (request) pedido m; (form) formulário m; (for job) candidatura f

appl|y /ə'plaɪ/ vt aplicar □ vi ~**y to** (refer) aplicar-se a; (ask) dirigir-se a.

~**y for** (job, grant) candidatar-se a. ~**y o.s. to** aplicar-se a. ~**ied** a aplicado

appoint /ə'pɔɪnt/ vt (to post) nomear; (time, date) marcar. well-~**ed** a bem equipado, bem provido. ~**ment** n nomeação f; (meeting) entrevista f; (with friends) encontro m; (with doctor etc) consulta f, (P) marcação f; (job) posto m

apprais|e /ə'preɪz/ vt avaliar. ~**al** n avaliação f

appreciable /ə'pri:ʃəbl/ a apreciável

appreciat|e /ə'pri:ʃɪeɪt/ vt (value) apreciar; (understand) compreender; (be grateful for) estar/ficar grato por □ vi encarecer. ~**ion** /-'eɪʃn/ n apreciação f; (rise in value) encarecimento m; (gratitude) reconhecimento m. ~**ive** /ə'pri:ʃɪətɪv/ a apreciador; (grateful) reconhecido

apprehen|d /æprɪ'hend/ vt (seize, understand) apreender; (dread) recear. ~**sion** n apreensão f

apprehensive /æprɪ'hensɪv/ a apreensivo

apprentice /ə'prentɪs/ n aprendiz, -a mf □ vt pôr como aprendiz (**to** de). ~**ship** n aprendizagem f

approach /ə'prəʊtʃ/ vt aproximar; (with request or offer) abordar □ vi aproximar-se □ n aproximação f. ~ **to** (problem) abordagem f de; (place) acesso m a; (person) diligência junto de. ~**able** a acessível

appropriate[1] /ə'prəʊprɪət/ a apropriado, próprio. ~**ly** adv apropriadamente, a propósito

appropriate[2] /ə'prəʊprɪeɪt/ vt apropriar-se de

approval /ə'pru:vl/ n aprovação f. **on** ~ (comm) sob condição, à aprovação

approv|e /ə'pru:v/ vt/i aprovar. ~**e of** aprovar. ~**ingly** adv com ar de aprovação

approximate[1] /ə'prɒksɪmət/ a aproximado. ~**ly** adv aproximadamente

approximat|e[2] /ə'prɒksɪmeɪt/ vt/i aproximar(-se) de. ~**ion** /-'meɪʃn/ n aproximação f

apricot /'eɪprɪkɒt/ n damasco m

April /'eɪprəl/ n Abril m. ~ **Fool's Day** o primeiro de Abril, o dia das mentiras. **make an** ~ **fool of** pregar uma mentira em, (P) pregar uma mentira

apron /'eɪprən/ n avental m

apt /æpt/ a apto; (pupil) dotado. **be** ~ **to** ser propenso a. ~**ly** adv apropriadamente

aptitude /'æptɪtju:d/ n aptidão f, (P) aptitude f

aqualung /'ækwəlʌŋ/ n escafandro autónomo, (P) autónomo m

aquarium /ə'kweəriəm/ n (pl -ums) aquário m

Aquarius /ə'kweəriəs/ n (astr) Aquário m

aquatic /ə'kwætik/ a aquático; (sport) náutico, aquático

aqueduct /'ækwidʌkt/ n aqueduto m

Arab /'ærəb/ a & n árabe (mf). ~ic a & n (lang) árabe (m), arábico (m). **a~ic numerals** algarismos mpl árabes or arábicos

Arabian /ə'reibiən/ a árabe

arable /'ærəbl/ a arável

arbitrary /'a:bitrəri/ a arbitrário

arbitrat|e /'a:bitreit/ vi arbitrar. ~**ion** /-'treiʃn/ n arbitragem f. ~**or** n árbitro m

arc /a:k/ n arco m. ~ **lamp** lâmpada f de arco. ~ **welding** soldadura f a arco

arcade /a:'keid/ n (shop) arcada f. **amusement** ~ fliperama m

arch /a:tʃ/ n arco m; (vault) abóbada f □ vt/i arquear(-se)

arch- /a:tʃ/ pref arqui-.

archaeolog|y /a:ki'blədʒi/ n arqueologia f. ~**ical** /-ə'lɒdʒikl/ a arqueológico. ~**ist** n arqueólogo m

archaic /a:'keiik/ a arcaico

archbishop /a:tʃ'biʃəp/ n arcebispo m

arch-enemy /a:tʃ'enəmi/ n inimigo m número um

archer /'a:tʃə(r)/ n arqueiro m. ~**y** n tiro m ao arco

archetype /'a:kitaip/ n arquétipo m

architect /'a:kitekt/ n arquiteto m, (P) arquitecto m

architectur|e /'a:kitektʃə(r)/ n arquitetura f, (P) arquitectura f ~**al** /-'tektʃərəl/ a arquitetónico, (P) arquitectónico

archiv|es /'a:kaivz/ npl arquivo m. ~**ist** /-ivist/ n arquivista mf

archway /'a:tʃwei/ n arcada f

Arctic /'a:ktik/ a ártico m, (P) árctico m □ a ártico, (P) árctico. ~ **weather** tempo m glacial

ardent /'a:dnt/ a ardente. ~**ly** adv ardentemente

ardour /'a:də(r)/ n ardor m

arduous /'a:djuəs/ a árduo

are /a:(r)/; emphatic /a:(r)/ see be

area /'eəriə/ n área f

arena /ə'ri:nə/ n arena f

aren't /a:nt/ = are not

Argentin|a /a:dʒən'ti:nə/ n Argentina f. ~**ian** /-'tiniən/ a & n argentino (m)

argu|e /'a:gju:/ vi discutir; (reason) argumentar, arguir □ vt (debate) discutir. ~**e that** alegar que. ~**able** a alegável. **it's** ~**able that** pode-se sustentar que

argument /'a:gjomənt/ n (dispute) disputa f; (reasoning) argumento m. ~**ative** /-'mentətiv/ a que gosta de discutir, argumentativo

arid /'ærid/ a árido

Aries /'eəri:z/ n (astr) Áries m, Carneiro m

arise /ə'raiz/ vi (pt arose, pp arisen) surgir. ~ **from** resultar de

aristocracy /æri'stɒkrəsi/ n aristocracia f

aristocrat /'æristəkræt/ n aristocrata mf. ~**ic** /-'krætik/ a aristocrático

arithmetic /ə'riθmətik/ n aritmética f

ark /a:k/ n **Noah's** ~ arca f de Noé

arm[1] /a:m/ n braço m. ~ **in** ~ de braço dado

arm[2] /a:m/ vt armar □ n (mil) arma f. ~**ed robbery** assalto m à mão armada

armament /'a:məmənt/ n armamento m

armchair /'a:mtʃeə(r)/ n cadeira f de braços, poltrona f

armistice /'a:mistis/ n armistício m

armour /'a:mə(r)/ n armadura f; (on tanks etc) blindagem f. ~**ed** a blindado

armoury /'a:məri/ n arsenal m

armpit /'a:mpit/ n axila f, sovaco m

arms /a:mz/ npl armas fpl. **coat of** ~ brasão m

army /'a:mi/ n exército m

aroma /ə'rəumə/ n aroma m. ~**tic** /ærə'mætik/ a aromático

arose /ə'rəuz/ see arise

around /ə'raund/ adv em redor, em volta; (here and there) por aí □ prep em redor de, em torno de, em volta de; (approximately) aproximadamente. ~ **here** por aqui

arouse /ə'rauz/ vt despertar; (excite) excitar

arrange /ə'reindʒ/ vt arranjar; (time, date) combinar. ~ **to do sth** combinar fazer alg coisa. ~**ment** n arranjo m; (agreement) acordo m. **make** ~**ments (for)** (plans) tomar disposições (para); (preparations) fazer preparativos (para)

array /ə'rei/ vt revestir □ **an** ~ **of** (display) um leque de, uma série de

arrears /ə'riəz/ npl dividas fpl em atraso, atrasos fpl. **in** ~ em atraso

arrest /ə'rest/ vt (by law) deter, prender; (process, movement) deter □ n captura f. **under** ~ sob prisão

arrival /ə'raivl/ n chegada f. **new** ~ recém-chegado m

arrive /ə'raiv/ vi chegar

arrogan|t /'ærəgənt/ a arrogante. ~**ce** n arrogância f. ~**tly** adv com arrogância

arrow /'ærəʊ/ n flecha f, seta f

arsenal /'a:sənl/ n arsenal m

arsenic /'a:snɪk/ n arsénico m, (P) arsénio m

arson /'a:sn/ n fogo m posto. ~ist n incendiário m

art[1] /a:t/ n arte f. the ~s (univ) letras fpl. fine ~s belas-artes fpl. ~ gallery museu m (de arte); (private) galeria f de arte

artery /'a:təri/ n artéria f

artful /'a:tfl/ a manhoso. ~ness n manha f

arthritis /a:'θraɪtɪs/ n artrite f

artichoke /'a:tɪtʃəʊk/ n alcachofra f. **Jerusalem** ~ topinambo m

article /'a:tɪkl/ n artigo m. ~d a (jur) em estágio, (P) a estagiar

articulate[1] /a:'tɪkjʊlət/ a que se exprime com clareza; (speech) bem articulado

articulat|e[2] /a:'tɪkjʊleɪt/ vt/i articular. ~ed lorry camião m articulado. ~ion /-'leɪʃn/ n articulação f

artifice /'a:tɪfɪs/ n artifício m

artificial /a:tɪ'fɪʃl/ a artificial

artillery /a:'tɪləri/ n artilharia f

artisan /a:tɪ'zæn/ n artífice mf, artesão m, artesã f

artist /'a:tɪst/ n artista mf. ~ic /-'tɪstɪk/ a artístico. ~ry n arte f

artiste /a:'ti:st/ n artista mf

artless /'a:tlɪs/ a ingénuo, (P) ingénuo, simples

as /əz/; emphatic /æz/ adv & conj como; (while) enquanto; (when) quando. ~ a gift de presente. ~ tall as tão alto quanto, (P) tão alto como □ pron que. I ate the same ~ he comi o mesmo que ele. ~ for, ~ to quanto a. ~ from a partir de. ~ if como se. ~ much tanto, tantos. ~ many quanto, quantos. ~ soon as logo que. ~ well (also) também. ~ well as (in addition to) assim como

asbestos /æz'bestəs/ n asbesto m, amianto m

ascend /ə'send/ vt/i subir. ~ the throne ascender or subir ao trono

ascent /ə'sent/ n ascensão f; (slope) subida f, rampa f

ascertain /æsə'teɪn/ vt certificar-se de. ~ that certificar-se de que

ascribe /ə'skraɪb/ vt atribuir

ash[1] /æʃ/ n ~(-tree) freixo m

ash[2] /æʃ/ n cinza f. A~ Wednesday Quarta-feira f de Cinzas. ~en a pálido

ashamed /ə'ʃeɪmd/ a be ~ ter vergonha, ficar envergonhado (of de, por)

ashore /ə'ʃɔ:(r)/ adv em terra. go ~ desembarcar

ashtray /'æʃtreɪ/ n cinzeiro m

Asia /'eɪʃə/ n ásia f. ~n a & n asiático (m)

aside /ə'saɪd/ adv de lado, de parte □ n (theat) aparte m. ~ from (Amer) à parte

ask /a:sk/ vt/i pedir; (a question) perguntar; (invite) convidar. ~ sb sth pedir uma coisa a alguém. ~ about informar-se de. ~ after sb pedir notícias de alg, perguntar por alg. ~ for pedir. ~ sb in mandar entrar alg. ~ sb to do sth pedir alguém para fazer alguma coisa

askew /ə'skju:/ adv & a de través, de esguelha

asleep /ə'sli:p/ adv & a adormecido; (numb) dormente. fall ~ adormecer

asparagus /ə'spærəgəs/ n (plant) aspargo m, (P) espargo m; (culin) aspargos mpl, (P) espargo m

aspect /'æspekt/ n aspecto m; (direction) exposição f

aspersions /ə'spɜ:ʃnz/ npl cast ~ on caluniar

asphalt /'æsfælt/ n asfalto m □ vt asfaltar

asphyxiat|e /əs'fɪksɪeɪt/ vt/i asfixiar. ~ion /-'eɪʃn/ n asfixia f

aspir|e /əs'paɪə(r)/ vi ~e to aspirar a. ~ation /æspə'reɪʃn/ n aspiração f

aspirin /'æsprɪn/ n aspirina f

ass /æs/ n burro m. make an ~ of o.s. fazer papel de palhaço, (P) fazer figura de parvo

assail /ə'seɪl/ vt assaltar, agredir. ~ant n assaltante mf, agressor m

assassin /ə'sæsɪn/ n assassino m

assassinat|e /ə'sæsɪneɪt/ vt assassinar. ~ion /-'eɪʃn/ n assassinato m

assault /ə'sɔ:lt/ n assalto m □ vt assaltar, atacar

assemble /ə'sembl/ vt (people) reunir; (fit together) montar □ vi reunir-se

assembly /ə'semblɪ/ n assembleia f, (P) assembleia f. ~ line linha f de montagem

assent /ə'sent/ n assentimento m □ vi ~ to consentir em

assert /ə'sɜ:t/ vt afirmar; (one's rights) reivindicar. ~ o.s. impor-se. ~ion /-ʃn/ n asserção f. ~ive a dogmático, peremptório. ~iveness n assertividade f, (P) firmeza f

assess /ə'ses/ vt avaliar; (payment) estabelecer o montante de. ~ment n avaliação f. ~or n (valuer) avaliador m

asset /'æset/ n (advantage) vantagem f. ~s (comm) ativo m, (P) activo m; (possessions) bens mpl

assiduous /ə'sɪdjʊəs/ a assíduo

assign /ə'saɪn/ vt atribuir, destinar;

(*jur*) transmitir. ~ **sb to** designar alg para

assignation /æsɪɡˈneɪʃn/ *n* combinação *f* (de hora e local) de encontro

assignment /əˈsaɪnmənt/ *n* tarefa *f*, missão *f*; (*jur*) transmissão *f*

assimilat|e /əˈsɪmɪleɪt/ *vt/i* assimilar(-se). ~**ion** /-ˈeɪʃn/ *n* assimilação *f*

assist /əˈsɪst/ *vt/i* ajudar. ~**ance** *n* ajuda *f*, assistência *f*

assistant /əˈsɪstənt/ *n* (*helper*) assistente *mf*, auxiliar *mf*; (*in shop*) ajudante *mf*, empregado *m* □ *a* adjunto

associat|e[1] /əˈsəʊʃɪeɪt/ *vt* associar □ *vi* ~**e with** conviver com. ~**ion** /-ˈeɪʃn/ *n* associação *f*

associate[2] /əˈsəʊʃɪət/ *a* & *n* associado (*m*)

assort|ed /əˈsɔːtɪd/ *a* variados; (*foods*) sortidos. ~**ment** *n* sortimento *m*, (*P*) sortido *m*

assume /əˈsjuːm/ *vt* assumir; (*presume*) supor, presumir

assumption /əˈsʌmpʃn/ *n* suposição *f*

assurance /əˈʃʊərəns/ *n* certeza *f*, garantia *f*; (*insurance*) seguro *m*; (*self-confidence*) segurança *f*, confiança *f*

assure /əˈʃʊə(r)/ *vt* assegurar. ~**d** *a* certo, garantido. **rest** ~**d that** ficar certo que

asterisk /ˈæstərɪsk/ *n* asterisco *m*

asthma /ˈæsmə/ *n* asma *f*. ~**tic** /-ˈmætɪk/ *a* & *n* asmático (*m*)

astonish /əˈstɒnɪʃ/ *vt* espantar. ~**ingly** *adv* espantosamente. ~**ment** *n* espanto *m*

astound /əˈstaʊnd/ *vt* assombrar

astray /əˈstreɪ/ *adv* & *a* **go** ~ perder-se, extraviar-se. **lead** ~ desencaminhar

astride /əˈstraɪd/ *adv* & *prep* escarranchado (em)

astringent /əˈstrɪndʒənt/ *a* & *n* adstringente (*m*)

astrolog|y /əˈstrɒlədʒɪ/ *n* astrologia *f*. ~**er** *n* astrólogo *m*

astronaut /ˈæstrənɔːt/ *n* astronauta *mf*

astronom|y /əˈstrɒnəmɪ/ *n* astronomia *f*. ~**er** *n* astrónomo *m*, (*P*) astrônomo *m*. ~**ical** /æstrəˈnɒmɪkl/ *a* astronómico, (*P*) astronômico

astute /əˈstjuːt/ *a* astuto, astucioso. ~**ness** *n* astúcia *f*

asylum /əˈsaɪləm/ *n* asilo *m*

at /ət/; *emphatic* /æt/ *prep* a, em. ~ **home** em casa. ~ **night** à noite. ~ **once** imediatamente; (*simultaneously*) ao mesmo tempo. ~ **school** na escola. ~ **sea** no mar. ~ **the door** na porta. ~ **times** às vezes. **angry/surprised** ~ zangado/surpreendido

com. **not** ~ **all** de nada. **no wind** ~ **all** nenhum vento

ate /et/ *see* **eat**

atheis|t /ˈeɪθɪɪst/ *n* ateu *m*. ~**m** /-zəm/ *n* ateísmo *m*

athlet|e /ˈæθliːt/ *n* atleta *mf*. ~**ic** /-ˈletɪk/ *a* atlético. ~**ics** /-ˈletɪks/ *n*(*pl*) atletismo *m*

Atlantic /ətˈlæntɪk/ *a* atlântico □ *n* ~ (**Ocean**) Atlântico *m*

atlas /ˈætləs/ *n* atlas *m*

atmospher|e /ˈætməsfɪə(r)/ *n* atmosfera *f*. ~**ic** /-ˈferɪk/ *a* atmosférico

atom /ˈætəm/ *n* átomo *m*. ~**ic** /əˈtɒmɪk/ *a* atómico, (*P*) atômico. ~**(ic) bomb** bomba *f* atómica, (*P*) atômica

atomize /ˈætəmaɪz/ *vt* atomizar, vaparizar, pulverizar. ~**r** /-ə(r)/ *n* pulverizador *m*, vaporizador *m*

atone /əˈtəʊn/ *vi* ~ **for** expiar. ~**ment** *n* expiação *f*

atrocious /əˈtrəʊʃəs/ *a* atroz

atrocity /əˈtrɒsətɪ/ *n* atrocidade *f*

atrophy /ˈætrəfɪ/ *n* atrofia *f* □ *vt/i* atrofiar(-se)

attach /əˈtætʃ/ *vt/i* (*affix*) ligar(-se), prender(-se); (*join*) juntar(-se). ~**ed** *a* (*document*) junto, anexo. **be** ~**ed to** (*like*) estar apegado a. ~**ment** *n* ligação *f*; (*affection*) apego *m*; (*accessory*) acessório *m*

attaché /əˈtæʃeɪ/ *n* (*pol*) adido *m*. ~ **case** pasta *f*

attack /əˈtæk/ *n* ataque *m* □ *vt/i* atacar. ~**er** *n* atacante *mf*

attain /əˈteɪn/ *vt* atingir. ~**able** *a* atingível. ~**ment** *n* consecução *f*. ~**ments** *npl* conhecimentos *mpl*, talentos *mpl* adquiridos

attempt /əˈtempt/ *vt* tentar □ *n* tentativa *f*

attend /əˈtend/ *vt/i* atender (**to** a); (*escort*) acompanhar; (*look after*) tratar; (*meeting*) comparecer a; (*school*) frequentar, (*P*) frequentar. ~**ance** *n* comparecimento *m*; (*times present*) frequência *f*, (*P*) frequência *f*; (*people*) assistência *f*

attendant /əˈtendənt/ *a* concomitante, que acompanha □ *n* empregado *m*; (*servant*) servidor *m*

attention /əˈtenʃn/ *n* atenção *f*. ~! (*mil*) sentido! **pay** ~ prestar atenção (**to** a)

attentive /əˈtentɪv/ *a* atento; (*considerate*) atencioso

attest /əˈtest/ *vt/i* ~ (**to**) atestar. ~ **a signature** reconhecer uma assinatura. ~**ation** /ætəˈsteɪʃn/ *n* atestação *f*, prova *f*

attic /ˈætɪk/ *n* sótão *m*, águafurtada *f*

attitude /ˈætɪtjuːd/ *n* atitude *f*

attorney /əˈtɜːnɪ/ n (pl **-eys**) procurador m; (Amer) advogado m

attract /əˈtrækt/ vt atrair. **~ion** /-ʃn/ n atração f, (P) atracção f, (charm) atrativo m, (P) atractivo m

attractive /əˈtræktɪv/ a atraente. **~ly** adv atraentemente, agradavelmente

attribute[1] /əˈtrɪbjuːt/ vt **~ to** atribuir a

attribute[2] /ˈætrɪbjuːt/ n atributo m

attrition /əˈtrɪʃn/ n war of **~** guerra f de desgaste

aubergine /ˈəʊbəʒiːn/ n berinjela f

auburn /ˈɔːbən/ a cor de acaju, castanho-avermelhado

auction /ˈɔːkʃn/ n leilão m □ vt leiloar. **~eer** /-əˈnɪə(r)/ n leiloeiro m, (P) pregoeiro m

audacious /ɔːˈdeɪʃəs/ a audacioso, audaz. **~ty** /-æsətɪ/ n audácia f

audible /ˈɔːdəbl/ a audível

audience /ˈɔːdɪəns/ n auditório m; (theat, radio; interview) audiência f

audiovisual /ɔːdɪəʊˈvɪʒʊəl/ a audiovisual

audit /ˈɔːdɪt/ n auditoria f □ vt fazer uma auditoria

audition /ɔːˈdɪʃn/ n audição f □ vt dar/fazer uma audição

auditor /ˈɔːdɪtə(r)/ n perito-contador m, (P) perito-contabilista m

auditorium /ɔːdɪˈtɔːrɪəm/ n auditório m

augment /ɔːgˈment/ vt/i aumentar (-se)

augur /ˈɔːgə(r)/ vi **~ well/ill** ser de bom ou mau agouro

August /ˈɔːgəst/ n Agosto m

aunt /ɑːnt/ n tia f

au pair /əʊˈpeə(r)/ n au pair f

aura /ˈɔːrə/ n aura f, emanação f

auspices /ˈɔːspɪsɪz/ npl **under the ~ of** sob os auspícios or o patrocínio de

auspicious /ɔːˈspɪʃəs/ a auspicioso

auster|e /ɔːˈstɪə(r)/ a austero. **~ity** /-erətɪ/ n austeridade f

Australia /ɒˈstreɪlɪə/ n Austrália f. **~n** a & n australiano (m)

Austria /ˈɒstrɪə/ n Áustria f. **~n** a & n austríaco (m)

authentic /ɔːˈθentɪk/ a autêntico. **~ity** /-ənˈtɪsətɪ/ n autenticidade f

authenticate /ɔːˈθentɪkeɪt/ vt autenticar

author /ˈɔːθə(r)/ n autor m, autora f. **~ship** n (origin) autoria f

authoritarian /ɔːθɒrɪˈteərɪən/ a autoritário

authorit|y /ɔːˈθɒrətɪ/ n autoridade f; (permission) autorização f. **~ative** /-ɪtətɪv/ a (trusted) autorizado; (manner) autoritário

authoriz|e /ˈɔːθəraɪz/ vt autorizar. **~ation** /-ˈzeɪʃn/ n autorização f

autistic /ɔːˈtɪstɪk/ a autista, autístico

autobiography /ɔːtəˈbaɪɒɡrəfɪ/ n autobiografia f

autocrat /ˈɔːtəkræt/ n autocrata mf. **~ic** /-ˈkrætɪk/ a autocrático

autograph /ˈɔːtəɡrɑːf/ n autógrafo m □ vt autografar

automat|e /ˈɔːtəmeɪt/ vt automatizar. **~ion** /-təˈmeɪʃn/ n automação f

automatic /ɔːtəˈmætɪk/ a automático □ n (car) automático m. **~ally** /-klɪ/ adv automaticamente

automobile /ˈɔːtəməbiːl/ n (Amer) automóvel m

autonom|y /ɔːˈtɒnəmɪ/ n autonomia f. **~ous** a autónomo, (P) autónomo

autopsy /ˈɔːtɒpsɪ/ n autópsia f

autumn /ˈɔːtəm/ n outono m. **~al** /-ˈtʌmnəl/ a outonal

auxiliary /ɔːɡˈzɪlɪərɪ/ a & n auxiliar (mf). **~ verb** verbo m auxiliar

avail /əˈveɪl/ vt **~ o.s. of** servir-se de □ vi (be of use) valer □ n **of no ~** inútil. **to no ~** sem resultado, em vão

availab|le /əˈveɪləbl/ a disponível. **~ility** /-ˈbɪlətɪ/ n disponibilidade f

avalanche /ˈævəlɑːnʃ/ n avalanche f

avaric|e /ˈævərɪs/ n avareza f. **~ious** /-ˈrɪʃəs/ a avarento

avenge /əˈvendʒ/ vt vingar

avenue /ˈævənjuː/ n avenida f; (fig: line of approach) via f

average /ˈævərɪdʒ/ n média f □ a médio □ vt tirar a média de; (produce, do) fazer em média □ vi **~ out at** dar de média, dar uma média de. **on ~** em média

avers|e /əˈvɜːs/ a be **~e to** ser avesso a. **~ion** /-ʃn/ n aversão f, repugnância f

avert /əˈvɜːt/ vt (turn away) desviar; (ward off) evitar

aviary /ˈeɪvɪərɪ/ n aviário m

aviation /eɪvɪˈeɪʃn/ n aviação f

avid /ˈævɪd/ a ávido

avocado /ævəˈkɑːdəʊ/ n (pl **-s**) abacate m

avoid /əˈvɔɪd/ vt evitar. **~able** a que se pode evitar, evitável. **~ance** n evitação f

await /əˈweɪt/ vt aguardar

awake /əˈweɪk/ vt/i (pt **awoke**, pp **awoken**) acordar □ a **be ~** estar acordado

awaken /əˈweɪkən/ vt/i despertar. **~ing** n despertar m

award /əˈwɔːd/ vt atribuir, conferir; (jur) adjudicar □ n recompensa f, prémio m, (P) prémio m; (scholarship) bolsa f

aware /əˈweə(r)/ a ciente, cônscio. **be ~ of** estar consciente de or ter consciência de. **become ~ of** tomar consciência de. **make sb ~ of** sensibilizar alg para. **~ness** n consciência f

away /ə'weɪ/ adv (at a distance) longe; (to a distance) para longe; (absent) fora; (persistently) sem parar; (entirely) completamente. **eight miles ~** a oito milhas (de distância). **four days ~** dai a quatro dias □ a & n ~ (match) jogo m fora de casa

awe /ɔː/ n assombro m, admiração f reverente, terror m respeitoso. **~some** a assombroso. **~struck** a assombrado, aterrado

awful /'ɔːfl/ a terrível. **~ly** adv muito, terrivelmente

awhile /ə'waɪl/ adv por algum tempo

awkward /'ɔːkwəd/ a difícil; (clumsy, difficult to use) desajeitado, maljeitoso; (inconvenient) inconveniente; (embarrassing) embaraçoso; (embarrassed) embaraçado. **an ~ customer** (colloq) um preguês perigoso or intratável

awning /'ɔːnɪŋ/ n toldo m

awoke, awoken /ə'wəʊk, ə'wəʊkən/ see **awake**

awry /ə'raɪ/ adv torto. **go ~** dar errado. **be ~** estar torto

axe /æks/ n machado m □ vt (pres p **axing**) (reduce) cortar; (dismiss) despedir

axiom /'æksɪəm/ n axioma m

axis /'æksɪs/ n (pl **axes** /-iːz/) eixo m

axle /'æksl/ n eixo (de roda) m

Azores /ə'zɔːz/ n Açores mpl

B

BA abbr see **Bachelor of Arts**

babble /'bæbl/ vi balbuciar; (baby) palrar; (stream) murmurar □ n balbúcio m; (of baby) palrice f; (of stream) murmúrio m

baboon /bə'buːn/ n babuíno m

baby /'beɪbɪ/ n bebé m, (P) bebê m. **~ carriage** (Amer) carrinho m de bebé, (P) bebê. **~-sit** vi tomar conta de crianças. **~-sitter** n baby-sitter mf, babá f

babyish /'beɪbɪɪʃ/ a infantil

bachelor /'bætʃələ(r)/ n solteiro m. **B~ of Arts/Science** Bacharel m em Letras/Ciências

back /bæk/ n (of person, hand, chair) costas fpl; (of animal) dorso m; (of car, train) parte f traseira; (of house, room) fundo m; (of coin) reverso m; (of page) verso m; (football) beque m; zagueiro m, (P) defesa m □ a traseiro, posterior; (taxes) em atraso □ adv atrás, para trás; (returned) de volta □ vt (support) apoiar; (horse) apos-

tar em; (car) (fazer) recuar □ vi recuar. **at the ~ of beyond** em casa do diabo, no fim do mundo. **~-bencher** n (pol) deputado m sem pasta. **~ down** desistir (**from** de). **~ number** número m atrasado. **~ out** (of an undertaking etc) fugir (ao combinado etc). **~ up** (auto) fazer marcha à ré, (P) atrás; (comput) tirar um back-up de. **~-up** n apoio m; (comput) back-up m; (Amer: traffic-jam) engarrafamento m □ a de reserva; (comput) back-up

backache /'bækeɪk/ n dor f nas costas

backbiting /'bækbaɪtɪŋ/ n maledicência f

backbone /'bækbəʊn/ n espinha f dorsal

backdate /bæk'deɪt/ vt antedatar

backer /'bækə(r)/ n (of horse) apostador m; (of cause) partidário m, apoiante mf; (comm) patrocinador m, financiador m

backfire /bæk'faɪə(r)/ vi (auto) dar explosões no tubo de escape; (fig) sair o tiro pela culatra

background /'bækɡraʊnd/ n (of picture) fundo m, segundo-plano m; (context) contexto m; (environment) meio m; (experience) formação f

backhand /'bækhænd/ n (tennis) esquerda f. **~ed** a com as costas da mão. **~ed compliment** cumprimento m ambíguo. **~er** /-'hændə(r)/ n (sl: bribe) suborno m, (P) luvas fpl (colloq)

backing /'bækɪŋ/ n apoio m; (comm) patrocínio m

backlash /'bæklæʃ/ n (fig) reação f violenta, repercussões fpl

backlog /'bæklɒɡ/ n acúmulo m (de trabalho etc)

backside /'bæksaɪd/ n (colloq: buttocks) traseiro m

backstage /bæk'steɪdʒ/ a & adv por detrás dos bastidores

backstroke /'bækstrəʊk/ n nado m de costas

backtrack /'bæktræk/ vi (fig) voltar atrás

backward /'bækwəd/ a retrógrado; (retarded) atrasado; (step, look, etc) para trás

backwards /'bækwədz/ adv para trás; (walk) para trás; (fall) de costas, para trás; (in reverse order) de trás para diante, às avessas. **go ~ and forwards** ir e vir, andar para trás e para a frente. **know sth ~** saber alg coisa de trás para a frente

backwater /'bækwɔːtə(r)/ n (pej: place) lugar m atrasado

bacon /'beɪkən/ n toucinho m defumado; (in rashers) bacon m

bacteria /bæk'tɪərɪə/ npl bactérias fpl.~l a bacteriano

bad /bæd/ a (worse, worst) mau; (accident) grave; (food) estragado; (ill) doente. **feel** ~ sentir-se mal. ~ **language** palavrões mpl. ~**mannered** a mal educado. ~**tempered** a mal humorado. ~**ly** adv mal; (seriously) gravemente. **want** ~**ly** (desire) desejar imensamente, ter grande vontade de; (need) precisar muito de

badge /bædʒ/ n emblema m; (policeman's) crachá m, (P) distintivo m

badger /bædʒə(r)/ n texugo m □ vt atormentar; (pester) importunar

badminton /'bædmɪntən/ n badminton m

baffle /'bæfl/ vt atrapalhar, desconcertar

bag /bæg/ n saco m; (handbag) bolsa f, carteira f.~**s** (luggage) malas fpl □ vt (pt bagged) ensacar; (colloq: take) embolsar

baggage /'bægɪdʒ/ n bagagem f

baggy /'bægɪ/ a (clothes) muito largo, bufante

bagpipes /'bægpaɪps/ npl gaita f de foles

Bahamas /bə'haːməz/ npl the ~ as Bahamas fpl

bail¹ /beɪl/ n fiança f □ vt pôr em liberdade sob fiança.**be out on** ~ estar solto sob fiança

bail² /beɪl/ vt ~ (**out**) (naut) esgotar, tirar água de

bailiff /'beɪlɪf/ n (officer) oficial m de diligências; (of estate) feitor m

bait /beɪt/ n isca f □ vt pôr isca; (fig) atormentar (com insultos), atazanar

bak|**e** /beɪk/ vt/i cozer (no forno); (bread, cakes, etc) assar; (in the sun) torrar. ~**er** n padeiro m; (of cakes) doceiro m. ~**ing** n cozedura f; (batch) fornada f. ~**ing-powder** n fermento m em pó. ~**ing tin** forma f

bakery /'beɪkərɪ/ n padaria f; (cakes) confeitaria f

balance /'bæləns/ n equilíbrio m; (scales) balança f; (sum) saldo m; (comm) balanço m. ~ **of power** equilíbrio m político. ~ **of trade** balança f comercial. ~**sheet** n balanço m □ vt equilibrar; (weigh up) pesar; (budget) equilibrar □ vi equilibrar-se. ~**d** a equilibrado

balcony /'bælkənɪ/ n balcão m; (in a house) varanda f

bald /bɔːld/ a (-er, -est) calvo, careca; (tyre) careca. ~**ing** a be ~**ing** ficar calvo. ~**ly** adv a nu e cru, (P) secamente. ~**ness** n calvície f

bale¹ /beɪl/ n (of straw) fardo m; (of cotton) balote m □ vt enfardar

bale² /beɪl/ vi ~ **out** saltar em pára-quedas

balk /bɔːk/ vt frustrar, contrariar □ vi ~ **at** assustar-se com, recuar perante

ball¹ /bɔːl/ n bola f. ~**-bearing** n rolamento m de esferas. ~**-cock** n válvula f de depósito de água. ~**-point** n esferográfica f

ball² /bɔːl/ n (dance) baile m

ballad /'bæləd/ n balada f

ballast /'bæləst/ n lastro m

ballerina /bælə'riːnə/ n bailarina f

ballet /'bæleɪ/ n balé m, (P) ballet m, bailado m

balloon /bə'luːn/ n balão m

ballot /'bælət/ n escrutínio m. ~ (-**paper**) n cédula f eleitoral, (P) boletim m de voto. ~**-box** n urna f □ vi (pt balloted) (pol) votar □ vt (members) consultar por voto secreto

ballroom /'bɔːlruːm/ n salão m de baile

balm /baːm/ n bálsamo m. ~**y** a balsâmico; (mild) suave

balustrade /bælə'streɪd/ n balaustrada f

bamboo /bæm'buː/ n bambu m

ban /bæn/ vt (pt banned) banir. ~ **from** proibir de □ n proibição f

banal /bə'naːl/ a banal. ~**ity** /-ælətɪ/ n banalidade f

banana /bə'naːnə/ n banana f

band /bænd/ n (for fastening) cinta f, faixa f; (strip) tira f, banda f; (mil) banda f; (mus: dance, jazz) conjunto m; (group) bando m □ vi ~ **together** juntar-se

bandage /'bændɪdʒ/ n atadura f, (P) ligadura f □ vt ligar

bandit /'bændɪt/ n bandido m

bandstand /'bændstænd/ n coreto m

bandwagon /'bændwægən/ n **climb on the** ~ (fig) apanhar o trem

bandy /'bændɪ/ vt trocar. ~ **a story about** espalhar uma história

bandy-legged /'bændɪlegd/ a cambaio, de pernas tortas

bang /bæŋ/ n (blow) pancada f; (loud noise) estouro m, estrondo m; (of gun) detonação f □ vt/i (hit, shut) bater □ vi explodir □ int pum. ~ **in the middle** jogar no meio. **shut the door with a** ~ bater (com) a porta

banger /'bæŋə(r)/ n (firework) bomba f; (sl: sausage) salsicha f. (**old**) ~ (sl: car) calhambeque m (colloq)

bangle /'bæŋgl/ n pulseira f, bracelete m

banish /'bænɪʃ/ vt banir, desterrar

banisters /'bænɪstəz/ npl corrimão m

banjo /'bændʒəʊ/ pl (~**s**) banjo m

bank¹ /bæŋk/ n (of river) margem f; (of earth) talude m; (of sand) banco m

□ *vt* amontoar □ *vi* (*aviat*) inclinar-se numa curva

bank² /bæŋk/ *n* (*comm*) banco *m* □ *vt* depositar no banco. **~ account** conta *f* bancária. **~ holiday** feriado *m* nacional. **~ on** contar com. **~ rate** taxa *f* bancária. **~ with** ter conta em

bank|er /'bæŋkə(r)/ *n* banqueiro *m*. **~ing** /-ɪŋ/ *n* operações *fpl* bancárias; (*career*) carreira *f* bancária, banca *f*

banknote /'bæŋknəʊt/ *n* nota *f* de banco

bankrupt /'bæŋkrʌpt/ *a* & *n* falido (*m*). **go ~** falir □ *vt* levar à falência. **~cy** *n* falência *f*, bancarrota *f*

banner /'bænə(r)/ *n* bandeira *f*, estandarte *m*

banns /bænz/ *npl* proclamas *mpl*, (*P*) banhos *mpl*

banquet /'bæŋkwɪt/ *n* banquete *m*

banter /'bæntə(r)/ *n* gracejo *m*, brincadeira *f* □ *vi* gracejar, brincar

baptism /'bæptɪzəm/ *n* batismo *m*, (*P*) baptismo *m*

Baptist /'bæptɪst/ *n* batista *mf*, (*P*) baptista *mf*

baptize /bæp'taɪz/ *vt* batizar, (*P*) baptizar

bar /ba:(r)/ *n* (*of chocolate*) tablette *f*, barra *f*; (*of metal, soap, sand etc*) barra *f*; (*of door, window*) tranca *f*; (*in pub*) bar *m*; (*counter*) balcão *m*, bar *m*; (*mus*) barra *f* de compasso; (*fig: obstacle*) barreira *f*; (*in lawcourt*) teia *f*. **the B~** a advocacia *f* □ *vt* (*pt* **barred**) (*obstruct*) barrar; (*prohibit*) proibir (**from** de); (*exclude*) excluir; (*door, window*) trancar □ *prep* salvo, exceto, (*P*) excepto **~ none** sem exceção, (*P*) excepção. **~ code** código *m* de barra. **behind ~s** na cadeia

Barbados /ba:'beɪdɒs/ *n* Barbados *mpl*

barbarian /ba:'beərɪən/ *n* bárbaro *m*

barbaric /ba:'bærɪk/ *a* bárbaro. **~ty** /-ətɪ/ *n* barbaridade *f*

barbarous /'ba:bərəs/ *a* bárbaro

barbecue /'ba:bɪkju:/ *n* (*grill*) churrasqueira *f*; (*occasion, food*) churrasco *m* □ *vt* assar

barbed /ba:bd/ *a* **~ wire** arame *m* farpado

barber /'ba:bə(r)/ *n* barbeiro *m*

barbiturate /ba:'bɪtjʊrət/ *n* barbitúrico *m*

bare /beə(r)/ *a* (**-er, -est**) nu; (*room*) vazio; (*mere*) mero □ *vt* pôr à mostra, pôr a nu, descobrir

bareback /'beəbæk/ *adv* em pêlo

barefaced /'beəfeɪst/ *a* descarado

barefoot /'beə(r)fʊt/ *adv* descalço

barely /'beəlɪ/ *adv* apenas, mal

bargain /'ba:gɪn/ *n* (*deal*) negócio *m*;

(*good buy*) pechincha *f* □ *vi* negociar; (*haggle*) regatear. **~ esperar for**

barge /ba:dʒ/ *n* barcaça *f* □ *vi* **~ in** interromper (desapropositadamente); (*into room*) irromper

bark¹ /ba:k/ *n* (*of tree*) casca *f*

bark² /ba:k/ *n* (*of dog*) latido *m* □ *vi* latir. **his ~ is worse than his bite** cão que ladra não morde

barley /'ba:lɪ/ *n* cevada *f*. **~ sugar** *n* açúcar *m* de cevada. **~ water** *n* água *f* de cevada

barmaid /'ba:meɪd/ *n* empregada *f* de bar

barman /'ba:mən/ *n* (*pl* **-men**) barman *m*, empregado *m* de bar

barmy /'ba:mɪ/ *a* (*sl*) maluco

barn /ba:n/ *n* celeiro *m*

barometer /bə'rɒmɪtə(r)/ *n* barômetro *m*, (*P*) barómetro *m*

baron /'bærən/ *n* barão *m*. **~ess** *n* baronesa *f*

baroque /bə'rɒk/ *a* & *n* barroco (*m*)

barracks /'bærəks/ *n* quartel *m*, caserna *f*

barrage /'bæra:ʒ/ *n* barragem *f*; (*fig*) enxurrada *f*; (*mil*) fogo *m* de barragem

barrel /'bærəl/ *n* (*of oil, wine*) barril *m*; (*of gun*) cano *m*. **~-organ** *n* realejo *m*

barren /'bærən/ *a* estéril; (*soil*) árido, estéril

barricade /bærɪ'keɪd/ *n* barricada *f* □ *vt* barricar

barrier /'bærɪə(r)/ *n* barreira *f*; (*hindrance*) entrave *m*, barreira *f*

barring /'ba:rɪŋ/ *prep* salvo, exceto, (*P*) excepto

barrister /'bærɪstə(r)/ *n* advogado *m*

barrow /'bærəʊ/ *n* carrinho *m* de mão

barter /'ba:tə(r)/ *n* troca *f* □ *vt* trocar

base /beɪs/ *n* base *f* □ *vt* basear (**on** em) □ *a* baixo, ignóbil. **~less** *a* infundado

baseball /'beɪsbɔ:l/ *n* beisebol *m*

basement /'beɪsmənt/ *n* porão *m*, (*P*) cave *f*

bash /bæʃ/ *vt* bater com violência □ *n* pancada *f* forte. **have a ~ at** (*sl*) experimentar

bashful /'bæʃfl/ *a* tímido

basic /'beɪsɪk/ *a* básico, elementar, fundamental. **~ally** *adv* basicamente, no fundo

basil /'bæzl/ *n* mangericão *m*

basin /'beɪsn/ *n* bacia *f*; (*for food*) tigela *f*; (*naut*) ante-doca *f*; (*for washing*) pia *f*

basis /'beɪsɪs/ *n* (*pl* **bases** /-si:z/) base *f*

bask /ba:sk/ *vi* **~ in the sun** apanhar sol

basket /'ba:skɪt/ *n* cesto *m*

basketball /ˈbɑːskɪtbɔːl/ n basquete(-bol) m

Basque /bɑːsk/ a & n basco (m)

bass[1] /bæs/ n (pl **bass**) (fish) perca f

bass[2] /beɪs/ a (mus) grave □ n (pl **basses**) (mus) baixo m

bassoon /bəˈsuːn/ n fagote m

bastard /ˈbɑːstəd/ n (illegitimate child) bastardo m; (sl: pej) safado (sl) m; (colloq: not pej) cara (colloq) m

baste /beɪst/ vt (culin) regar (com molho)

bastion /ˈbæstɪən/ n bastião m, baluarte m

bat[1] /bæt/ n (cricket) pá f; (baseball) bastão m; (table tennis) rafuete f □ vt/i (pt **batted**) bater (em). **without ∼ting an eyelid** sem pestanejar

bat[2] /bæt/ n (zool) morcego m

batch /bætʃ/ n (loaves) fornada f; (people) monte m; (goods) remessa f; (papers, letters etc) batelada f, monte m

bated /ˈbeɪtɪd/ a **with ∼ breath** com a respiração em suspenso, com a respiração suspensa

bath /bɑːθ/ n (pl **-s** /bɑːðz/) banho m; (tub) banheira f. **∼s** (washing) banho m público; (swimming) piscina f □ vt dar banho a □ vi tomar banho

bathe /beɪð/ vt dar banho em; (wound) limpar □ vi tomar banho (de mar) □ n banho m (de mar). **∼r** /-ə(r)/ n banhista mf

bathing /ˈbeɪðɪŋ/ n banho m de mar. **∼-costume/-suit** n traje m de banho, (P) fato m de banho

bathrobe /ˈbɑːθrəʊb/ n (Amer) roupão m

bathroom /ˈbɑːθruːm/ n banheiro m, (P) casa f de banho

baton /ˈbætən/ n (mus) batuta f; (policeman's) cassete m; (mil) bastão m

battalion /bəˈtæliən/ n batalhão m

batter /ˈbætə(r)/ vt bater, espancar, maltratar □ n (culin: for cakes) massa f de bolos; (culin: for frying) massa f de empanar. **∼ed** a (car, pan) amassado; (child, wife) maltratado, espancado. **∼ing** n **take a ∼ing** levar pancada or uma surra

battery /ˈbætərɪ/ n (mil, auto) bateria f; (electr) pilha f

battle /ˈbætl/ n batalha f; (fig) luta f □ vi combater, batalhar, lutar

battlefield /ˈbætlfiːld/ n campo m de batalha

battlements /ˈbætlmənts/ npl ameias fpl

battleship /ˈbætlʃɪp/ n couraçado m

baulk /bɔːlk/ vt/i = **balk**

bawdy /ˈbɔːdɪ/ a (**-ier, -iest**) obsceno, indecente

bawl /bɔːl/ vt/i berrar

bay[1] /beɪ/ n (bot) loureiro m

bay[2] /beɪ/ n (geog) baia f. **∼ window** janela f saliente

bay[3] /beɪ/ n (bark) latido m □ vi latir. **at ∼** (animal; fig) cercado, (P) em apuros. **keep at ∼** manter à distância

bayonet /ˈbeɪənɪt/ n baioneta f

BC abbr (before Christ) a C

be /biː/ vi (pres am, are, is; pt was, were; pp been) (permanent quality/place) ser; (temporary place/state) estar; (become) ficar. **∼ hot/right** etc ter calor/razão etc. **he's 30** (age) ele tem 30 anos. **it's fine/cold** etc (weather) faz bom tempo/frio etc. **how are you?** (health) como está? **I'm a doctor — are you?** eu sou médico — é mesmo? **it's pretty, isn't it?** é bonito, não é? **he is to come** (must) ele deve vir. **how much is it?** (cost) quanto é? **∼ reading eating** etc estar lendo/comendo etc. **the money was found** o dinheiro foi encontrado. **have been to** ter ido a, ter estado em

beach /biːtʃ/ n praia f

beacon /ˈbiːkən/ n farol m; (marker) baliza f

bead /biːd/ n conta f. **∼ of sweat** gota f de suor

beak /biːk/ n bico m

beaker /ˈbiːkə(r)/ n copo m de plástico com bico; (in lab) proveta f

beam /biːm/ n (of wood) trave f, viga f; (of light) raio m; (of torch) feixe m de luz □ vt/i (radiate) irradiar; (fig) sorrir radiante. **∼ing** a radiante

bean /biːn/ n feijão m. **broad ∼** fava f. **coffee ∼s** café m em grão. **runner ∼** feijão m verde

bear[1] /beə(r)/ n urso m

bear[2] /beə(r)/ vt/i (pt **bore**, pp **borne**) sustentar, suportar; (endure) agüentar, (P) aguentar, suportar; (child) dar à luz. **∼ in mind** ter em mente, lembrar. **∼ left** virar à esquerda. **∼ on** relacionar-se com, ter a ver com. **∼ out** confirmar. **∼ up!** coragem! **∼able** a tolerável, suportável. **∼er** n portador m

beard /bɪəd/ n barba f. **∼ed** a barbado, com barba

bearing /ˈbeərɪŋ/ n (manner) porte m; (relevance) relação f; (naut) marcação f. **get one's ∼s** orientar-se

beast /biːst/ n (animal, person) besta f, animal m; (in fables) fera f. **∼ of burden** besta f de carga

beat /biːt/ vt/i (pt **beat**, pp **beaten**) bater □ n (med) batimento m; (mus) compasso m, ritmo m; (of drum) toque m; (of policeman) ronda f, (P) giro m. **∼ about the bush** estar com rodeios. **∼ a retreat** bater em retirada. **∼ it**

(*sl: go away*) pôr-se a andar. **it ∼s me** (*colloq*) não consigo entender. **∼ up** espancar. **∼er** *n* (*culin*) batedeira *f*. **∼ing** *n* sova *f*

beautician /bjuː'tɪʃn/ *n* esteticista *mf*

beautiful /'bjuːtɪfl/ *a* belo, lindo. **∼ly** *adv* lindamente

beautify /'bjuːtɪfaɪ/ *vt* embelezar

beauty /'bjuːtɪ/ *n* beleza *f*. **∼ parlour** instituto *m* de beleza. **∼ spot** sinal *m* no rosto, mosca *f*; (*place*) local *m* pitoresco

beaver /'biːvə(r)/ *n* castor *m*

became /bɪ'keɪm/ *see* **become**

because /bɪ'kɒz/ *conj* porque □ *adv* **∼ of** por causa de

beckon /'bekən/ *vt/i* **∼ (to)** fazer sinal (para)

become /bɪ'kʌm/ *vt/i* (*pt* **became**, *pp* **become**) tornar-se; (*befit*) ficar bem a. **what has ∼ of her?** que é feito dela?

becoming /bɪ'kʌmɪŋ/ *a* que fica bem, apropriado

bed /bed/ *n* cama *f*; (*layer*) camada *f*, (*of sea*) fundo *m*; (*of river*) leito *m*; (*of flowers*) canteiro *m* □ *vt/i* (*pt* **bedded**) **∼ down** ir deitar-se. **∼ in** plantar. **∼ and breakfast** (**b & b**) quarto *m* com café da manhã. **∼-sit(ter)** *n* (*colloq*) misto *m* de quarto e sala. **go to ∼** ir para cama. **in ∼** na cama. **∼ding** *n* roupa *f* de cama

bedclothes /'bedkləʊðz/ *n* roupa *f* de cama

bedlam /'bedləm/ *n* confusão *f*, balbúrdia *f*

bedraggled /bɪ'drægld/ *a* (*wet*) molhado; (*untidy*) desarrumado; (*dishevelled*) desgrenhado

bedridden /'bedrɪdn/ *a* preso ao leito, doente de cama

bedroom /'bedruːm/ *n* quarto *m* de dormir

bedside /'bedsaɪd/ *n* cabeceira *f*. **∼ manner** (*doctor's*) modos *mpl* que inspiram confiança

bedspread /'bedspred/ *n* colcha *f*

bedtime /'bedtaɪm/ *n* hora *f* de deitar, hora *f* de ir para a cama

bee /biː/ *n* abelha *f*. **make a ∼-line for** ir direto a

beech /biːtʃ/ *n* faia *f*

beef /biːf/ *n* carne *f* de vaca

beefburger /'biːfbɜːgə(r)/ *n* hambúrguer *m*

beehive /'biːhaɪv/ *n* colméia *f*

been /biːn/ *see* **be**

beer /bɪə(r)/ *n* cerveja *f*

beet /biːt/ *n* beterraba *f*

beetle /'biːtl/ *n* escaravelho *m*

beetroot /'biːtruːt/ *n* (raiz de) beterraba *f*

before /bɪ'fɔː(r)/ *prep* (*time*) antes de; (*place*) em frente de □ *adv* antes; (*al-*

ready) já □ *conj* antes que. **∼ leaving** antes de partir. **∼ he leaves** antes que ele parta, antes de ele partir

beforehand /bɪ'fɔːhænd/ *adv* de antemão, antecipadamente

befriend /bɪ'frend/ *vt* tornar-se amigo de; (*be helpful to*) auxiliar

beg /beg/ *vt/i* (*pt* **begged**) mendigar; (*entreat*) suplicar. **∼ sb's pardon** pedir desculpa a alg. **∼ the question** fazer uma petição de princípio. **it's going ∼ging** está sobrando

began /bɪ'gæn/ *see* **begin**

beggar /'begə(r)/ *n* mendigo *m*, pedinte *mf*; (*colloq: person*) cara (*colloq*) *m*

begin /bɪ'gɪn/ *vt/i* (*pt* **began**, *pp* **begun**, *pres p* **beginning**) começar, principiar. **∼ner** *n* principiante *mf*. **∼ning** *n* começo *m*, princípio *m*

begrudge /bɪ'grʌdʒ/ *vt* ter inveja de; (*give*) dar de má vontade. **∼ doing** fazer de má vontade *or* a contragosto

beguile /bɪ'gaɪl/ *vt* enganar

begun /bɪ'gʌn/ *see* **begin**

behalf /bɪ'hɑːf/ *n* **on ∼ of** em nome de; (*in the interest of*) em favor de

behave /bɪ'heɪv/ *vi* portar-se. **∼ (o.s.)** portar-se bem

behaviour /bɪ'heɪvjə(r)/ *n* conduta *f*, comportamento *m*

behead /bɪ'hed/ *vt* decapitar

behind /bɪ'haɪnd/ *prep* atrás de □ *adv* atrás; (*late*) com atraso □ *n* (*colloq: buttocks*) traseiro (*colloq*) *m*. **∼ the times** antiquado, retrógrado. **leave ∼** deixar para trás

behold /bɪ'həʊld/ *vt* (*pt* **beheld**) (*old use*) ver

beholden /bɪ'həʊldən/ *a* em dívida (**to** para com)

beige /beɪʒ/ *a & n* bege (*m*), (*P*) beige (*m*)

being /'biːɪŋ/ *n* ser *m*. **bring into ∼** criar. **come into ∼** nascer, originar-se

belated /bɪ'leɪtɪd/ *a* tardio, atrasado

belch /beltʃ/ *vi* arrotar □ *vt* **∼ out** (*smoke*) vomitar, lançar □ *n* arroto *m*

belfry /'belfrɪ/ *n* campanário *m*

Belgium /'beldʒəm/ *n* Bélgica *f*. **∼an** *a & n* belga (*mf*)

belief /bɪ'liːf/ *n* crença *f*; (*trust*) confiança *f*; (*opinion*) convicção *f*

believe /bɪ'liːv/ *vt/i* acreditar. **∼e in** acreditar em. **∼able** *a* crível. **∼er** /-ə(r)/ *n* crente *mf*

belittle /bɪ'lɪtl/ *vt* depreciar

bell /bel/ *n* sino *m*; (*small*) sineta *f*; (*on door, of phone*) campainha *f*; (*on cat, toy*) guizo *m*

belligerent /bɪ'lɪdʒərənt/ *a & n* beligerante (*mf*)

bellow /'beləʊ/ *vt/i* berrar, bramir. ~ **out** rugir

bellows /'beləʊz/ *npl* fole *m*

belly /'belɪ/ *n* barriga *f*, ventre *m*. ~**ache** *n* dor *f* de barriga

bellyful /'belɪfʊl/ *n* **have a ~** estar com a barriga cheia

belong /bɪ'lɒŋ/ *vi* ~ **(to)** pertencer (a); (*club*) ser sócio (de)

belongings /bɪ'lɒŋɪŋz/ *npl* pertences *mpl*. **personal ~** objetos *mpl* de uso pessoal

beloved /bɪ'lʌvɪd/ *a & n* amado (*m*)

below /bɪ'ləʊ/ *prep* abaixo de, debaixo de □ *adv* abaixo, em baixo; (*on page*) abaixo

belt /belt/ *n* cinto *m*; (*techn*) correia *f*. (*fig*) zona *f* □ *vt* (*sl: hit*) zurzir □ *vi* (*sl: rush*) safar-se

bemused /bɪ'mju:zd/ *a* estonteado, confuso; (*thoughtful*) pensativo

bench /bentʃ/ *n* banco *m*; (*seat, working-table*) bancada *f*. **the ~** (*jur*) os magistrados (no tribunal)

bend /bend/ *vt/i* (*pt & pp* **bent**) curvar(-se); (*arm, leg*) dobrar; (*road, river*) fazer uma curva, virar □ *n* curva *f*. ~ **over** debruçar-se *or* inclinar-se sobre

beneath /bɪ'ni:θ/ *prep* abaixo de, debaixo de; (*fig*) abaixo de □ *adv* debaixo, em baixo

benediction /benɪ'dɪkʃn/ *n* bênção *f*

benefactor /'benɪfæktə(r)/ *n* benfeitor *m*

beneficial /benɪ'fɪʃl/ *a* benéfico, proveitoso

benefit /'benɪfɪt/ *n* (*advantage, performance*) benefício *m*; (*profit*) proveito *m*; (*allowance*) subsídio *m* □ *vt/i* (*pt* **benefited**, *pres p* **benefiting**) (*be useful to*) beneficiar (**by** de); (*do good to*) beneficiar, fazer bem a; (*receive benefit*) lucrar, ganhar (**by, from** com)

beneficiary /benɪ'fɪʃərɪ/ *n* beneficiário *m*

benevolen|t /bɪ'nevələnt/ *a* benevolente. ~**ce** *n* benevolência *f*

benign /bɪ'naɪn/ *a* (*incl med*) benigno

bent /bent/ *see* **bend** □ *n* (*skill*) aptidão *f*, jeito *m*; (*liking*) queda *f* □ *a* curvado; (*twisted*) torto; (*sl: dishonest*) desonesto. ~ **on** decidido a

bequeath /bɪ'kwi:ð/ *vt* legar

bequest /bɪ'kwest/ *n* legado *m*

bereave|d /bɪ'ri:vd/ *a* **the ~d wife/** *etc* a esposa/*etc* do falecido. **the ~d family** a família enlutada. ~**ment** *n* luto *m*

bereft /bɪ'reft/ *a* ~ **of** privado de

beret /'bereɪ/ *n* boina *f*

Bermuda /bə'mju:də/ *n* Bermudas *fpl*

berry /'berɪ/ *n* baga *f*

berserk /bə'sɜ:k/ *a* **go ~** ficar louco de raiva, perder a cabeça

berth /bɜ:θ/ *n* (*in ship*) beliche *m*; (*in train*) couchette *f*; (*anchorage*) ancoradouro *m* □ *vi* atracar. **give a wide ~ to** passar ao largo, (*P*) de largo

beside /bɪ'saɪd/ *prep* ao lado de, junto de. ~ **o.s.** fora de si. **be ~ the point** não ter nada a ver com o assunto, não vir ao caso

besides /bɪ'saɪdz/ *prep* além de; (*except*) fora, salvo □ *adv* além disso

besiege /bɪ'si:dʒ/ *vt* sitiar, cercar. ~ **with** assediar

best /best/ *a & n* **(the) ~** (o/a) melhor (*mf*) □ *adv* melhor. ~ **man** padrinho *m* de casamento. **at (the) ~** na melhor das hipóteses. **do one's ~** fazer o (melhor) que se pode. **make the ~ of** tirar o melhor partido de. **the ~ part of** a maior parte de. **to the ~ of my knowledge** que eu saiba

bestow /bɪ'stəʊ/ *vt* conferir. ~ **praise** fazer *or* tecer elogios

best-seller /best'selə(r)/ *n* best-seller *m*

bet /bet/ *n* aposta *f* □ *vt/i* (*pt* **bet** *or* **betted**) apostar (**on** em)

betray /bɪ'treɪ/ *vt* trair. ~**al** *n* traição *f*

better /'betə(r)/ *a & adv* melhor □ *vt* melhorar □ *n* our ~**s** os nossos superiores *mpl*. **all the ~** tanto melhor. ~ **off** (*richer*) mais rico. **he's ~ off at home** é melhor para ele ficar em casa. **I'd ~ go** é melhor ir-me embora. **the ~ part of it** a maior parte disso. **get ~** melhorar. **get the ~ of sb** levar a melhor em relação a alg

betting-shop /'betɪŋʃɒp/ *n* agência *f* de apostas

between /bɪ'twi:n/ *prep* entre □ *adv* **in ~** no meio, no intervalo. ~ **you and me** aqui entre nós

beverage /'bevərɪdʒ/ *n* bebida *f*

beware /bɪ'weə(r)/ *vi* acautelar-se (**of** com), tomar cuidado (**of** com)

bewilder /bɪ'wɪldə(r)/ *vt* desorientar. ~**ment** *n* desorientação *f*, confusão *f*

bewitch /bɪ'wɪtʃ/ *vt* encantar, cativar

beyond /bɪ'jɒnd/ *prep* além de; (*doubt, reach*) fora de □ *adv* além. **it's ~ me** isso ultrapassame. **he lives ~ his means** ele vive acima dos seus meios

bias /'baɪəs/ *n* parcialidade *f*; (*pej: prejudice*) preconceito *m*; (*sewing*) viés *m* □ *vt* (*pt* **biased**) influenciar. ~**ed** *a* parcial. ~**ed against** de prevenção contra, (*P*) de pé atrás contra

bib /bɪb/ *n* babeiro *m*, babette *m*

Bible /'baɪbl/ *n* Bíblia *f*

biblical /'bɪblɪkl/ *a* bíblico

bibliography /bɪblɪˈɒɡrəfɪ/ n bibliografia f

bicarbonate /baɪˈkɑːbənət/ n ~ of soda bicarbonato m de soda

biceps /ˈbaɪseps/ n biceps m

bicker /ˈbɪkə(r)/ vi questionar, discutir

bicycle /ˈbaɪsɪkl/ n bicicleta f □ vi andar de bicicleta

bid /bɪd/ n oferta f, lance m; (attempt) tentativa f □ vt/i (pt **bid**, pres p **bidding**) fazer uma oferta, lançar, oferecer como lance. ~**der** n licitante mf. **the highest** ~**der** quem dá or oferece mais

bide /baɪd/ vt ~ **one's time** esperar pelo bom momento

bidet /ˈbiːdeɪ/ n bidê m, (P) bidé m

biennial /baɪˈenɪəl/ a bienal

bifocals /baɪˈfəʊklz/ npl óculos mpl bifocais

big /bɪɡ/ a (**bigger, biggest**) grande; (sl: generous) generoso □ adv (colloq) em grande. ~-**headed** a pretensioso, convencido. ~ **shot** (sl) manda-chuva m. **talk** ~ gabar-se (colloq). **think** ~ (colloq) ter grandes planos

bigam|y /ˈbɪɡəmɪ/ n bigamia f. ~**ist** n bígamo m. ~**ous** a bígamo

bigot /ˈbɪɡət/ n fanático m, intolerante mf. ~**ed** a fanático, intolerante. ~**ry** n fanatismo m, intolerância f

bigwig /ˈbɪɡwɪɡ/ n (colloq) mandachuva m

bike /baɪk/ n (colloq) bicicleta f

bikini /bɪˈkiːnɪ/ n (pl -**is**) biquíni m

bilberry /ˈbɪlbərɪ/ n arando m

bile /baɪl/ n bílis f

bilingual /baɪˈlɪŋɡwəl/ a bilingue

bilious /ˈbɪlɪəs/ a bilioso

bill[1] /bɪl/ n (invoice) fatura f, (P) factura f; (in restaurant) conta f; (pol) projeto m, (P) projecto m de lei; (Amer: banknote) nota f de banco; (poster) cartaz m □ vt faturar, (P) facturar; (theatre) anunciar, pôr no programa. ~ **of exchange** letra f de câmbio. ~ **sb for** apresentar a alg a conta de

bill[2] /bɪl/ n (of bird) bico m

billiards /ˈbɪlɪədz/ n bilhar m

billion /ˈbɪlɪən/ n (10[9]) mil milhões, (10[12]) um milhão de milhões

bin /bɪn/ n (for storage) caixa f, lata f, (for rubbish) lata f do lixo, (P) caixote m

bind /baɪnd/ vt (pt **bound**) (tie) atar; (book) encadernar; (jur) obrigar; (cover the edge of) debruar □ n (sl: bore) chatice f (sl). **be** ~**ing on** ser obrigatório para

binding /ˈbaɪndɪŋ/ n encadernação f; (braid) debrum m

binge /bɪndʒ/ n (sl) **go on a** ~ cair na farra; (overeat) empanturrar-se

bingo /ˈbɪŋɡəʊ/ n bingo m □ int acertei!

binoculars /bɪˈnɒkjʊləz/ npl binóculo m

biochemistry /baɪəʊˈkemɪstrɪ/ n bioquímica f

biodegradable /baɪəʊdɪˈɡreɪdəbl/ a biodegradável

biograph|y /baɪˈɒɡrəfɪ/ n biografia f. ~**er** n biógrafo m

biolog|y /baɪˈɒlədʒɪ/ n biologia f. ~**ical** /-əˈlɒdʒɪkl/ a biológico. ~**ist** n biólogo m

biopsy /ˈbaɪɒpsɪ/ n biópsia f

birch /bɜːtʃ/ n (tree) bétula f; (whip) vara f de videoiro

bird /bɜːd/ n ave f, pássaro m; (sl: girl) garota f (colloq). ~ **sanctuary** refúgio m ornitológico. ~-**watcher** n ornitófilo m

Biro /ˈbaɪərəʊ/ n (pl -**os**) (caneta) esferográfica f, Bic f

birth /bɜːθ/ n nascimento m. ~ **certificate** certidão f de nascimento. ~ **control/rate** controle m/índice m de natalidade. ~-**place** n lugar m de nascimento. **give** ~ **to** dar à luz

birthday /ˈbɜːθdeɪ/ n aniversário m, (P) dia m de anos. **his** ~ **is on 9 July** ele faz anos no dia 9 de julho

birthmark /ˈbɜːθmɑːk/ n sinal m

biscuit /ˈbɪskɪt/ n biscoito m, bolacha f

bisect /baɪˈsekt/ vt dividir ao meio

bishop /ˈbɪʃəp/ n bispo m

bit[1] /bɪt/ n (small piece, short time) pedaço m, bocado m; (of bridle) freio m; (of tool) broca f. **a** ~ um pouco

bit[2] /bɪt/ see **bite**

bitch /bɪtʃ/ n cadela f; (sl: woman) peste f (fig), cadela f (sl) □ vt/i (colloq: criticize) malhar, (P) cortar (em) (colloq); (colloq: grumble) resmungar. ~**y** a (colloq) maldoso

bite /baɪt/ vt/i (pt **bit**, pp **bitten**) morder; (insect) picar □ n mordida f; (sting) picada f. **have a** ~ (to eat) comer qualquer coisa

biting /ˈbaɪtɪŋ/ a cortante

bitter /ˈbɪtə(r)/ a amargo; (weather) glacial. ~**ly** adv amargamente. **it's** ~**ly cold** está um frio de rachar. ~**ness** n amargura f; (resentment) ressentimento m

bizarre /bɪˈzɑː(r)/ a bizarro

black /blæk/ a (-**er, -est**) negro, preto □ n negro m, preto m. **a B**~ (person) um preto, uma negra □ vt enegrecer; (goods) boicotar. ~ **and blue** coberto de nódoas negras. ~ **coffee** café m (sem leite). ~ **eye** olho m negro. ~ **ice** gelo m negro sobre o asfalto. ~ **market** mercado m negro. ~ **spot** (place) local m perigoso, ponto m negro

blackberry /'blækbərɪ/ n amora f silvestre

blackbird /'blækbɜːd/ n melro m

blackboard /'blækbɔːd/ n quadro m preto

blackcurrant /'blækkʌrənt/ n groselha f negra

blacken /'blækən/ vt/i escurecer. ~ sb's name difamar, denegrir

blackleg /'blækleg/ n fura-greves m

blacklist /'blæklɪst/ n lista f negra □ vt pôr na lista negra

blackmail /'blækmeɪl/ n chantagem f □ vt fazer chantagem. ~er n chantagista mf

blackout /'blækaʊt/ n (wartime) blecaute m; (med) desmaio m; (electr) falta f de corrente; (theatr) apagar m de luzes

blacksmith /'blæksmɪθ/ n ferreiro m

bladder /'blædə(r)/ n bexiga f

blade /bleɪd/ n lâmina f; (of oar, propeller) pá f; (of grass) ervinha f, folhinha f de erva

blame /bleɪm/ vt culpar □ n culpa f. **be to ~** ser o culpado. ~**less** a irrepreensível; (innocent) inocente

bland /blænd/ a (-er, -est) (of manner) suave; (mild) brando; (insipid) insipido

blank /blæŋk/ a (space, cheque) em branco; (look) vago; (wall) nu □ n espaço m em branco; (cartridge) cartucho m sem bala

blanket /'blæŋkɪt/ n cobertor m; (fig) manto m □ vt (pt **blanketed**) cobrir com cobertor; (cover thickly) encobrir, recobrir. **wet ~** desmancha-prazeres mf

blare /bleə(r)/ vt/i ressoar, atroar □ n clangor m; (of horn) buzinar m

blasé /'blɑːzeɪ/ a blasé

blaspheme /blæs'fiːm/ vt/i blasfemar

blasphem|y /'blæsfəmɪ/ n blasfémia f, (P) blasfêmia f. ~**ous** a blasfemo

blast /blɑːst/ n (gust) rajada f; (sound) som m; (explosion) explosão f □ vt dinamitar. ~! droga! ~**ed** a maldito. ~**-furnace** n alto forno m. ~**-off** n (of missile) lançamento m, início m de combustão

blatant /'bleɪtnt/ a flagrante; (shameless) descarado

blaze /bleɪz/ n chamas fpl; (light) clarão m; (outburst) explosão f □ vi arder; (shine) resplandecer, brilhar. **~ a trail** abrir o caminho, ser pioneiro

blazer /'bleɪzə(r)/ n blazer m

bleach /bliːtʃ/ n descolorante, descorante m; (household) água f sanitária □ vt/i branquear; (hair) oxigenar

bleak /bliːk/ a (-er, -est) (place) desolado; (chilly) frio; (fig) desanimador

bleary-eyed /'blɪərɪaɪd/ a com olhos injetados

bleat /bliːt/ n balido m □ vi balir

bleed /bliːd/ vt/i (pt **bled**) sangrar

bleep /bliːp/ n bip m. ~**er** n bip m

blemish /'blemɪʃ/ n defeito m; (on reputation) mancha f □ vt manchar

blend /blend/ vt/i (go well together) combinar-se □ n mistura f. ~**er** n (culin) liquidificador m

bless /bles/ vt abençoar. **be ~ed with** ter a felicidade de ter. ~**ing** n benção f; (thing one is glad of) felicidade f. **it's a ~ing in disguise** há males que vêm para bem

blessed /'blesɪd/ a bem-aventurado; (colloq: cursed) maldito

blew /bluː/ see **blow**

blight /blaɪt/ n doença f de plantas; (fig) influência f maligna □ vt arruinar, frustrar

blind /blaɪnd/ a cego □ vt cegar □ n (on window) persiana f; (deception) ardil m. ~ **alley** (incl fig) beco m sem saida. ~ **man/woman** cego m/cega f. **be ~ to** não ver. **turn a ~ eye to** fingir não ver, fechar os olhos a. ~**ly** adv às cegas. ~**ness** n cegueira f

blindfold /'blaɪndfəʊld/ a & adv de olhos vendados □ n venda f □ vt vendar os olhos a

blink /blɪŋk/ vi piscar

blinkers /'blɪŋkəz/ npl antolhos mpl

bliss /blɪs/ n felicidade f, beatitude f. ~**ful** a felicíssimo. ~**fully** adv maravilhosamente

blister /'blɪstə(r)/ n bolha f, empola f □ vi empolar

blizzard /'blɪzəd/ n tempestade f de neve, nevasca f

bloated /'bləʊtɪd/ a inchado

bloater /'bləʊtə(r)/ n arenque m salgado e defumado

blob /blɒb/ n pingo m grosso; (stain) mancha f

bloc /blɒk/ n bloco m

block /blɒk/ n bloco m; (buildings) quarteirão m; (in pipe) entupimento m. ~ **(of flats)** prédio m (de andares) □ vt bloquear, obstruir; (pipe) entupir. ~ **letters** maiúsculas fpl. ~**age** n obstrução f

blockade /blɒ'keɪd/ n bloqueio m □ vt bloquear

bloke /bləʊk/ n (colloq) sujeito m (colloq), cara m (colloq)

blond /blɒnd/ a & n louro (m)

blonde /blɒnd/ a & n loura (f)

blood /blʌd/ n sangue m □ a (bank, donor, transfusion, etc) de sangue; (poisoning) do sangue; (group, vessel) sangüíneo. ~**-curdling** a horrendo. ~ **pressure** tensão f arterial. ~ **test**

exame *m* de sangue. ~less *a* (*fig*) pacífico

bloodhound /'blʌdhaʊnd/ *n* sabujo *m*

bloodshed /'blʌdʃed/ *n* derramamento *m* de sangue, carnificina *f*

bloodshot /'blʌdʃɒt/ *a* injetado *or* (*P*) injectado de sangue

bloodstream /'blʌdstri:m/ *n* sangue *m*, fluxo *m* sangüíneo

bloodthirsty /'blʌdθɜ:stɪ/ *a* sanguinário

bloody /'blʌdɪ/ *a* (-ier, -iest) ensangüentado, (*with much bloodshed*) sangrento; (*sl*) grande, maldito □ *adv* (*sl*) pra burro. ~-minded *a* (*colloq*) do contra (*colloq*), chato (*sl*)

bloom /blu:m/ *n* flor *f*; (*beauty*) frescura *f*, viço *m* □ *vi* florir; (*fig*) vicejar. in ~ em flor

blossom /'blɒsəm/ *n* flor *f*. in ~ em flor □ *vi* (*flower*) florir, desabrochar; (*develop, flourish*) florescer, desabrochar

blot /blɒt/ *n* mancha *f* □ *vt* (*pt* **blotted**) manchar; (*dry*) secar. ~ out apagar; (*hide*) tapar, toldar. ~ter, ~ting-paper *n* (papel) mata-borrão *m*

blotch /blɒtʃ/ *n* mancha *f*. ~y *a* manchado

blouse /blaʊz/ *n* blusa *f*; (*in uniform*) blusão *m*

blow¹ /bləʊ/ *vt/i* (*pt* **blew**, *pp* **blown**) soprar; (*fuse*) fundir-se, queimar; (*sl: squander*) esbanjar; (*trumpet etc*) tocar. ~ a whistle apitar. ~ away *or* off *vt* levar, soprar □ *vi* roar, ir pelos ares (fora). ~-dry *vt* (*hair*) fazer um *brushing* □ *n brushing m*. ~ one's nose assoar o nariz. ~ out (*candle*) apagar, soprar. ~-out *n* (*colloq*: of tyre) rebentar *m*; (*colloq*: large meal) comilança *f* (*colloq*). ~ over passar. ~ up *vt* (*explode*) explodir; (*tyre*) encher; (*photograph*) ampliar □ *vi* (*explode*) explodir

blow² /bləʊ/ *n* pancada *f*; (*slap*) bofetada *f*; (*punch*) murro *m*; (*fig*) golpe *m*

blowlamp /'bləʊlæmp/ *n* maçarico *m*

blown /bləʊn/ *see* **blow¹**

bludgeon /'blʌdʒən/ *n* moca *f* □ *vt* malhar em. ~ to death matar à pancada

blue /blu:/ *a* (-er, -est) azul; (*indecent*) indecente □ *n* azul *m*. come out of the ~ ser inesperado. ~s *n* (*mus*) blues. have the ~s estar deprimido (*colloq*)

bluebell /'blu:bel/ *n* jacinto *m* dos bosques

bluebottle /'blu:bɒtl/ *n* mosca *f* varejeira

blueprint /'blu:prɪnt/ *n* cópia *f* fotográfica de planta; (*fig*) projeto *m*, (*P*) projecto *m*

bluff /blʌf/ *vi* blefar, (*P*) fazer bluff □ *vt* enganar (fingindo), blefar □ *n* blefe *m*, (*P*) bluff *m*

blunder /'blʌndə(r)/ *vi* cometer um erro crasso; (*move*) avançar às cegas *or* tateando □ *n* erro *m* crasso, (*P*) bronca *f*

blunt /blʌnt/ *a* (-er, -est) embotado; (*person*) direto, (*P*) directo □ *vt* embotar. ~ness *n* franqueza *f* rude. ~ly *adv* sem rodeios.

blur /blɜ:(r)/ *n* mancha *f* □ *vt* (*pt* **blurred**) (*smear*) manchar; (*make indistinct*) toldar

blurb /blɜ:b/ *n* contracapa *f*, sinopse *f* de um livro

blurt /blɜ:t/ *vt* ~ out deixar escapar

blush /blʌʃ/ *vi* corar □ *n* rubor *m*, vermelhidão *f*

bluster /'blʌstə(r)/ *vi* (*wind*) soprar em rajadas; (*swagger*) andar com ar fanfarrão. ~y *a* borrascoso

boar /bɔ:(r)/ *n* varrão *m*. wild ~ javali *m*

board /bɔ:d/ *n* tábua *f*; (*for notices*) quadro *m*, (*P*) placard *m*; (*food*) pensão *f*; (*admin*) conselho *m* □ *vt/i* cobrir com tábuas; (*aircraft, ship, train*) embarcar (em); (*bus, train*) subir (em). full ~ pensão *f* completa. half ~ meia-pensão *f*. on ~ a bordo. ~ up entaipar. ~ with ser pensionista em casa de. ~er *n* pensionista *mf*; (*at school*) interno *m*. ~ing-card *n* cartão *m* de embarque. ~ing-house *n* pensão *f*. ~ing-school *n* internato *m*

boast /bəʊst/ *vi* gabar-se □ *vt* orgulhar-se de □ *n* gabarolice *f*. ~er *n* gabola *mf*. ~ful *a* vaidoso. ~fully *adv* com vaidade, gabando-se

boat /bəʊt/ *n* barco *m*. in the same ~ nas mesmas circunstâncias. ~ing *n* passear de barco

bob /bɒb/ *vt/i* (*pt* **bobbed**) (*curtsy*) inclinar-se; (*hair*) cortar pelos ombros, (*P*) cortar à Joãozinho. ~ (up and down) andar para cima e para baixo

bobbin /'bɒbɪn/ *n* bobina *f*; (*sewing-machine*) canela *f*, bobina *f*

bob-sleigh /'bɒbsleɪ/ *n* trenó *m*

bode /bəʊd/ *vi* ~ well/ill ser de bom/mau agouro

bodice /'bɒdɪs/ *n* corpete *m*

bodily /'bɒdɪlɪ/ *a* corporal, físico. □ *adv* (*in person*) fisicamente, em pessoa; (*lift*) em peso

body /'bɒdɪ/ *n* corpo *m*; (*organization*) organismo *m*. ~(work) *n* (*of car*) carroçaria *f*, (*P*) ~ a *n* em massa. the main ~ of o grosso de. ~-building *n* body building *m*

bodyguard /'bɒdɪgɑːd/ n guarda-costas m; (escort) escolta f

bog /bɒg/ n pântano m □ vt get ~ged down atolar-se; (fig) ficar emperrado

boggle /'bɒgl/ vi the mind ~s não dá para imaginar

bogus /'bəʊgəs/ a falso

boil[1] /bɔɪl/ n (med) furúnculo m

boil[2] /bɔɪl/ vt/i ferver. come to the ~ ferver. ~ down to resumir-se a. ~ over transbordar. ~ing hot fervendo. ~ing point ponto m de ebulição

boiler /'bɔɪlə(r)/ n caldeira f. ~ suit macacão m, (P) fato m de macaco

boisterous /'bɔɪstərəs/ a turbulento; (noisy and cheerful) animado

bold /bəʊld/ a (-er -est) ousado; (of colours) vivo. ~ness n ousadia f

Bolivia /bə'lɪvɪə/ n Bolívia f. ~n a & n boliviano (m)

bollard /'bɒləd/ n (ship) abita f; (road) poste m

bolster /'bəʊlstə(r)/ n travesseiro m □ vt sustentar; ajudar. ~ one's spirits levantar o moral

bolt /bəʊlt/ n (on door etc) ferrolho m; (for nut) parafuso m; (lightning) relâmpago m □ vt aferrolhar; (food) engolir □ vi fugir, disparar. ~ upright teso como um fuso

bomb /bɒm/ n bomba f □ vt bombardear. ~er n (aircraft) bombardeiro m; (person) bombista mf

bombard /bɒm'bɑːd/ vt bombardear. ~ment n bombardeamento m

bombastic /bɒm'bæstɪk/ a bombástico

bombshell /'bɒmʃel/ n granada f; (fig) bomba f

bond /bɒnd/ n (agreement) compromisso m; (link) laço m, vínculo m; (comm) obrigação f. in ~ em depósito na alfândega

bondage /'bɒndɪdʒ/ n escravidão f, servidão f

bone /bəʊn/ n osso m; (of fish) espinha f □ vt desossar. ~-dry a completamente seco, ressecado. ~ idle preguiçoso

bonfire /'bɒnfaɪə(r)/ n fogueira f

bonnet /'bɒnɪt/ n chapéu m; (auto) capô m do motor, (P) capot m

bonus /'bəʊnəs/ n bónus m, (P) bónus m

bony /'bəʊnɪ/ a (-ier -iest) ossudo; (meat, fish) cheio de ossos/de espinhas

boo /buː/ int fora □ vt/i vaiar □ n vaia f

boob /buːb/ n (sl: mistake) asneira f, disparate m □ vi (sl) fazer asneira(s)

booby /'buːbɪ/ n ~ prize prêmio m de consolação. ~ trap bomba f armadilhada

book /bʊk/ n livro m. ~s (comm) contas fpl, escrita f □ vt (enter) averbar, registrar; (comm) escriturar; (reserve) marcar, reservar. ~ of matches carteira f de fósforos. ~ of tickets (bus, tube) caderneta f de módulos. be fully ~ed ter a lotação esgotada. ~ing office bilheteria f, (P) bilheteira f

bookcase /'bʊkkeɪs/ n estante f

bookkeep|**er** /'bʊkiːpə(r)/ n guarda-livros m. ~ing n contabilidade f, escrituração f

booklet /'bʊklɪt/ n brochura f

bookmaker /'bʊkmeɪkə(r)/ n book (maker) m

bookmark /'bʊkmɑːk/ n marca f de livro, marcador m de página

bookseller /'bʊkselə(r)/ n livreiro m

bookshop /'bʊkʃɒp/ n livraria f

bookstall /'bʊkstɔːl/ n quiosque m

boom /buːm/ vi ribombar; (of trade) prosperar □ n (sound) ribombo m; (comm) boom m, prosperidade f

boon /buːn/ n benção f, vantagem f

boost /buːst/ vt desenvolver, promover; (morale) levantar; (price) aumentar □ n força f (colloq). ~er n (med) dose suplementar f; (vaccine) revacinação f, (P) reforço m

boot /buːt/ n bota f; (auto) portamala f □ vt ~ (up) (comput) to ~ (in addition) ainda por cima

booth /buːð/ n barraca f; (telephone, voting) cabine f

booty /'buːtɪ/ n saque m, pilhagem f

booze /buːz/ vi (colloq) embebedar-se (colloq), encharcar-se (colloq) □ n (colloq) pinga f (colloq)

border /'bɔːdə(r)/ n borda f, margem f; (frontier) fronteira f; (garden bed) canteiro m □ vi ~ on confinar com; (be almost the same as) atingir as raias de

borderline /'bɔːdəlaɪn/ n linha f divisória. ~ case caso m limite

bore[1] /bɔː(r)/ see **bear**[2]

bore[2] /bɔː(r)/ vt/i (techn) furar, perfurar □ n (of gun barrel) calibre m

bore[3] /bɔː(r)/ vt aborrecer, entediar □ n maçante m; (thing) chatice f. be ~d aborrecer-se, maçar-se. ~dom n tédio m. boring a tedioso, maçante

born /bɔːn/ a nascido. be ~ nascer

borne /bɔːn/ see **bear**[2]

borough /'bʌrə/ n município m

borrow /'bɒrəʊ/ vt pedir emprestado (from a)

bosom /'bʊzəm/ n peito m; (woman's; fig: midst) seio m. ~ friend amigo m íntimo

boss /bɒs/ n (colloq) patrão m, patroa f, manda-chuva (colloq) m □ vt mandar. ~ sb about (colloq) mandar em alg

bossy /'bɒsɪ/ a mandão, autoritário

botan|y /'bɒtənɪ/ n botânica f. ~**ical** /bə'tænɪkl/ a botânico. ~**ist** /-ɪst/ n botânico m

botch /bɒtʃ/ vt atamancar; (spoil) estragar, escangalhar

both /bəʊθ/ a & pron ambos, os dois □ adv ~ ... and não só ... mas também, tanto ... como. ~ **of us** nós dois. ~ **the books** ambos os livros

bother /'bɒðə(r)/ vt/i incomodar(-se) □ n (inconvenience) incômodo m, (P) incómodo m, trabalho m; (effort) custo m, trabalho m; (worry) preocupação f. **don't** ~ não se incomode. **I can't be** ~**ed** não posso me dar o trabalho

bottle /'bɒtl/ n garrafa f; (small) frasco m; (for baby) mamadeira f, (P) biberão m □ vt engarrafar. ~**opener** n sacarolhas m. ~ **up** reprimir

bottleneck /'bɒtlnek/ n (obstruction) entrave m; (traffic-jam) engarrafamento m

bottom /'bɒtəm/ n fundo m; (of hill) sopé m; (buttocks) traseiro m □ a inferior; (last) último. **from top to** ~ de alto a baixo. ~**less** a sem fundo

bough /baʊ/ n ramo m

bought /bɔːt/ see **buy**

boulder /'bəʊldə(r)/ n pedregulho m

bounce /baʊns/ vi saltar; (of person) pular, dar pulos; (sl: of cheque) ser devolvido □ vt fazer saltar □ n (of ball) salto m, (P) ressalto m

bound[1] /baʊnd/ vi pular; (move by jumping) ir aos pulos □ n pulo m

bound[2] /baʊnd/ see **bind**. **be** ~**ed a** ~ **for** ir com destino a, ir para. **be** ~ **to** (obliged) ser obrigado a; (certain) haver de. **she's** ~ **to like it** ela há de gostar disso

boundary /'baʊndrɪ/ n limite m

bound|s /baʊndz/ npl limites mpl. **out of** ~**s** interdito. ~**ed by** limitado por. ~**less** a sem limites

bouquet /bʊ'keɪ/ n ramo m de flores; (wine) aroma m

bout /baʊt/ n período m; (med) ataque m; (boxing) combate m

boutique /bu:'ti:k/ n boutique f

bow[1] /bəʊ/ n (weapon, mus) arco m; (knot) laço m. ~**legged** a de pernas tortas. ~**tie** n gravata borboleta f, (P) laço m

bow[2] /baʊ/ n vênia f, (P) vénia f □ vt/i inclinar(-se), curvar-se

bow[3] /baʊ/ n (naut) proa f

bowels /'baʊəlz/ npl intestinos mpl; (fig) entranhas fpl

bowl[1] /bəʊl/ n (basin) bacia f; (for food) tigela f; (of pipe) fornilho m

bowl[2] /bəʊl/ n (ball) boliche m, (P) bola f de madeira. ~**s** npl boliche m,

(P) jogo m com bolas de madeira □ vt (cricket) lançar. ~ **over** siderar, varar. ~**ing** n boliche m, (P) bowling m. ~**ing-alley** n pista f

bowler[1] /'bəʊlə(r)/ n (cricket) lançador m

bowler[2] /'bəʊlə(r)/ n ~ (hat) (chapéu de) coco m

box[1] /bɒks/ n caixa f; (theatr) camarote m □ vt pôr dentro duma caixa. ~ **in** fechar. ~ **office** n bilheteira f, (P) bilheteira f. **Boxing Day** feriado m no primeiro dia útil depois do Natal

box[2] /bɒks/ vt/i (sport) lutar boxe. ~ **the ears of** esbofetear. ~**er** n pugilista m, boxeur m. ~**ing** n boxe m, pugilismo m

boy /bɔɪ/ n rapaz m. ~**friend** n namorado m. ~**hood** n infância f. ~**ish** a de menino

boycott /'bɔɪkɒt/ vt boicotar □ n boicote m

bra /brɑː/ n soutien m

brace /breɪs/ n braçadeira f; (dental) aparelho m; (tool) berbequim m; (of birds) par m. ~**s** npl (for trousers) suspensórios mpl □ vt apoiar, firmar. ~ **o.s.** concentrar as energias, fazer força; (for blow) preparar-se

bracelet /'breɪslɪt/ n bracelete m, pulseira f

bracing /'breɪsɪŋ/ a tonificante, estimulante

bracken /'brækən/ n (bot) samambaia f, (P) feto m

bracket /'brækɪt/ n suporte m; (group) grupo m □ vt (pt **bracketed**) pôr entre parênteses; (put together) pôr em pé de igualdade, agrupar. **age/income** ~ faixa f etária/salarial. **round** ~**s** parênteses mpl. **square** ~**s** parênteses mpl, colchetes mpl

brag /bræg/ vi (pt **bragged**) gabar-se (about de)

braid /breɪd/ n galão m; (of hair) trança f

Braille /breɪl/ n braile m

brain /breɪn/ n cérebro m, miolos mpl (colloq); (fig) inteligência f. ~**s** (culin) miolos mpl. ~**child** n invenção f. ~**less** a estúpido

brainwash /'breɪnwɒʃ/ vt fazer uma lavagem cerebral

brainwave /'breɪnweɪv/ n idéia f, (P) ideia f genial

brainy /'breɪnɪ/ a (-ier, -iest) inteligente, esperto

braise /breɪz/ vt (culin) estufar

brake /breɪk/ n travão m □ vt/i travar. ~ **light** farol m do freio

bran /bræn/ n (husks) farelo m

branch /brɑːntʃ/ n ramo m; (of road) ramificação f; (of railway line) ramal *m*; (*comm*) sucursal *f*; (*of bank*) balcão *m* □ *vi* ~ (**off**) bifurcar-se, ramificar-se

brand /brænd/ *n* marca *f* □ *vt* marcar. ~ **name** marca *f* de fábrica. ~**-new** *a* novo em folha. ~ **sb as** tachar alg de, (*P*) rotular alg de

brandish /ˈbrændɪʃ/ *vt* brandir

brandy /ˈbrændɪ/ *n* aguardente *f*, conhaque *m*

brass /brɑːs/ *n* latão *m*. **the** ~ (*mus*) os metais *mpl* □ *a* de cobre, de latão. **get down to** ~ **tacks** tratar das coisas sérias. **top** ~ (*sl*) os chefões (*colloq*)

brassière /ˈbræsɪə(r)/ *n* soutien *m*

brat /bræt/ *n* (*pej*) fedelho *m*

bravado /brəˈvɑːdəʊ/ *n* bravata *f*

brave /breɪv/ *a* (**-er**, **-est**) bravo, valente □ *vt* arrostar. ~**ry** /-ərɪ/ *n* bravura *f*

brawl /brɔːl/ *n* briga *f*, rixa *f*, desordem *f* □ *vi* brigar

brawn /brɔːn/ *n* força *f* muscular, músculo *m*. ~**y** *a* musculoso

bray /breɪ/ *n* zurro *m* □ *vi* zurrar

brazen /ˈbreɪzn/ *a* descarado

brazier /ˈbreɪzɪə(r)/ *n* braseiro *f*

Brazil /brəˈzɪl/ *n* Brasil *m*. ~**ian** *a* & *n* brasileiro (*m*). ~ **nut** castanha *f* do Pará

breach /briːtʃ/ *n* quebra *f*; (*gap*) brecha *f* □ *vt* abrir uma brecha em. ~ **of contract** quebra *f* de contrato. ~ **of the peace** perturbação *f* da ordem pública. ~ **of trust** abuso *m* de confiança

bread /bred/ *n* pão *m*. ~**-winner** *n* ganha-pão *m*

breadcrumbs /ˈbredkrʌmz/ *npl* migalhas *fpl*; (*culin*) farinha *f* de rosca

breadline /ˈbredlaɪn/ *n* **on the** ~ na miséria

breadth /bredθ/ *n* largura *f*; (*of mind, view*) abertura *f*

break /breɪk/ *vt* (*pt* **broke**, *pp* **broken**) partir, quebrar; (*vow, silence, etc*) quebrar; (*law*) transgredir; (*journey*) interromper; (*news*) dar; (*a record*) bater □ *vi* partir-se, quebrar-se; (*voice, weather*) mudar □ *n* quebra *f*, ruptura *f*; (*interval*) intervalo *m*; (*colloq: opportunity*) oportunidade *f*, chance *f*. ~ **one's arm/leg** quebrar o braço/a perna ~ **down** *vt* analisar □ *vi* (*of person*) ir-se abaixo; (*of machine*) avariar-se. ~ **in** forçar uma entrada. ~ **off** *vt* quebrar □ *vi* desligar-se. ~ **out** rebentar. ~ **up** *vt/i* terminar *vi* (*of schools*) entrar em férias. ~**able** *a* quebrável. ~**age** *n* quebra *f*

breakdown /ˈbreɪkdaʊn/ *n* (*techn*) avaria *f*, pane *f*; (*med*) esgotamento *m* nervoso; (*of figures*) análise *f* □ *a*

(*auto*) de pronto-socorro. ~ **van** pronto-socorro *m*

breaker /ˈbreɪkə(r)/ *n* vaga *f* de rebentação

breakfast /ˈbrekfəst/ *n* café *m* da manhã

breakthrough /ˈbreɪkθruː/ *n* descoberta *f* decisiva, avanço *m*

breakwater /ˈbreɪkwɔːtə(r)/ *n* quebra-mar *m*

breast /brest/ *n* peito *m*. ~**-feed** *vt* (*pt* **-fed**) amamentar. ~**-stroke** *n* estilo *m* bruços

breath /breθ/ *n* respiração *f*. **bad** ~ mau hálito *m*. **out of** ~ sem fôlego. **under one's** ~ num murmúrio, baixo. ~**less** *a* ofegante

breathalyser /ˈbreθəlaɪzə(r)/ *n* aparelho *m* para medir o nível de álcool no sangue, bafômetro *m* (*colloq*)

breath|e /briːð/ *vt/i* respirar. ~**e in** inspirar. ~**e out** expirar. ~**ing** *n* respiração *f*. ~**ing-space** *n* pausa *f*

breather /ˈbriːðə(r)/ *n* pausa *f* de descanso, momento *m* para respirar

breathtaking /ˈbreθteɪkɪŋ/ *a* assombroso, arrebatador

bred /bred/ *see* **breed**

breed /briːd/ *vt* (*pt* **bred**) criar □ *vi* reproduzir-se □ *n* raça *f*. ~**er** *n* criador *m*. ~**ing** *n* criação *f*; (*fig*) educação *f*

breeze /briːz/ *n* brisa *f*. ~**y** *a* fresco

brevity /ˈbrevətɪ/ *n* brevidade *f*

brew /bruː/ *vt* (*beer*) fabricar; (*tea*) fazer; (*fig*) armar, tramar □ *vi* fermentar; (*tea*) preparar; (*fig*) armar-se, preparar-se □ *n* decocção *f*; (*tea*) infusão *f*. ~**er** *n* cervejeiro *m*. ~**ery** *n* cervejaria *f*

bribe /braɪb/ *n* suborno *m*, (*P*) peita *f* □ *vt* subornar. ~**ry** /-ərɪ/ *n* suborno *m*, corrupção *f*

brick /brɪk/ *n* tijolo *m*

bricklayer /ˈbrɪkleɪə(r)/ *n* pedreiro *m*

bridal /ˈbraɪdl/ *a* nupcial

bride /braɪd/ *n* noiva *f*

bridegroom /ˈbraɪdɡrʊm/ *n* noivo *m*

bridesmaid /ˈbraɪdzmeɪd/ *n* dama *f* de honra, (*P*) honor

bridge¹ /brɪdʒ/ *n* ponte *f*; (*of nose*) cana *f* □ *vt* ~ **a gap** preencher uma lacuna

bridge² /brɪdʒ/ *n* (*cards*) bridge *m*

bridle /ˈbraɪdl/ *n* cabeçada *f*, freio *m* □ *vt* refrear. ~**-path** *n* atalho *m*, carreiro *m*

brief¹ /briːf/ *a* (**-er**, **-est**) breve. ~**s** *npl* (*men's*) cueca *f*, (*P*) slip *m*; (*women's*) calcinhas *fpl*, (*P*) cuecas *fpl*. ~**ly** *adv* brevemente

brief² /briːf/ *n* (*jur*) sumário *m*; (*case*) causa *f*; (*instructions*) instruções *fpl* □ *vt* dar instruções a briefcase /'bri:fkeɪs/ n pasta f

brigad|e /brɪ'geɪd/ n brigada f. ~ier /-ə'dɪə(r)/ n brigadeiro m

bright /braɪt/ a (-er, -est) brilhante; (of colour) vivo; (of light) forte; (room) claro; (cheerful) alegre; (clever) inteligente. ~ness n (sheen) brilho m; (clarity) claridade f; (intelligence) inteligência f

brighten /'braɪtn/ vt alegrar □ vi (of weather) clarear; (of face) animar-se, iluminar-se

brillian|t /'brɪljənt/ a brilhante. ~ce n brilho m

brim /brɪm/ n borda f; (of hat) aba f □ vi (pt brimmed) ~ over transbordar, cair por fora

brine /braɪn/ n salmoura f

bring /brɪŋ/ vt (pt brought) trazer. ~ about causar. ~ back trazer (de volta); (call to mind) relembrar. ~ down trazer para baixo; (bird, plane) abater; (prices) baixar. ~ forward adiantar, apresentar. ~ it off ser bem sucedido (em alg coisa). ~ out (take out) tirar; (show) revelar; (book) publicar. ~ round or to reanimar, fazer voltar a si. ~ to bear (pressure etc) exercer. ~ up educar; (med) vomitar; (question) levantar

brink /brɪŋk/ n beira f, borda f

brisk /brɪsk/ a (-er, -est) (pace, movement) vivo, rápido; (business, demand) grande

bristl|e /'brɪsl/ n pêlo m. ~y a eriçado

Britain /'brɪtn/ n Grã-Bretanha f

British /'brɪtɪʃ/ a britânico. the ~ n povo m britânico, os britânicos mpl

brittle /'brɪtl/ a frágil

broach /brəʊtʃ/ vt abordar, entabular, encetar

broad /brɔ:d/ a (-er, -est) largo; (daylight) pleno. ~ bean fava f. ~-minded a tolerante, liberal. ~ly adv de modo geral

broadcast /'brɔ:dka:st/ vt/i (pt broadcast) transmitir, fazer uma transmissão; (person) cantar, falar etc na rádio or na TV □ n emissão f. ~ing a & n (de) rádiodifusão (f)

broaden /'brɔ:dn/ vt/i alargar(-se)

broccoli /'brɒkəlɪ/ n inv brócolis mpl, (P) brócolos mpl

brochure /'brəʊʃə(r)/ n brochura f

broke /brəʊk/ see break □ a (sl) depenado (sl), liso (sl), (P) teso (sl)

broken /'brəʊkən/ see break □ a ~ English inglês m estropeado. ~-hearted a com o coração despedaçado

broker /'brəʊkə(r)/ n corretor m, broker m

bronchitis /brɒŋ'kaɪtɪs/ n bronquite f

bronze /brɒnz/ n bronze m

brooch /brəʊtʃ/ n broche m

brood /bru:d/ n ninhada f □ vi chocar; (fig) cismar. ~y a (hen) choca; (fig) sorumbático, melancólico

brook /brʊk/ n regato m, ribeiro m

broom /bru:m/ n vassoura f; (bot) giesta f

broth /brɒθ/ n caldo m

brothel /'brɒθl/ n bordel m

brother /'brʌðə(r)/ n irmão m. ~-in-law n (pl ~s-in-law) cunhado m. ~hood n irmandade f, fraternidade f. ~ly a fraternal

brought /brɔ:t/ see bring

brow /braʊ/ n (forehead) testa f; (of hill) cume m; (eyebrow) sobrancelha f

browbeat /'braʊbi:t/ vt (pt -beat, pp -beaten) intimidar

brown /braʊn/ a (-er, -est) castanho □ n castanho m □ vt/i acastanhar; (in the sun) bronzear, tostar; (meat) alourar

browse /braʊz/ vi (through book) folhear; (of animal) pastar; (in a shop) olhar sem comprar

bruise /bru:z/ n hematoma m, contusão f □ vt causar um hematoma. ~d a coberto de hematomas, contuso; (fruit) machucado

brunette /bru:'net/ n morena f

brunt /brʌnt/ n the ~ of o maior peso de, o pior de

brush /brʌʃ/ n escova f; (painter's) pincel m; (skirmish) escaramuça f. ~ against roçar. ~ aside não fazer caso de. ~ off (colloq: reject) mandar passear (colloq). ~ up (on) aperfeiçoar

brusque /bru:sk/ a brusco

Brussels /'brʌslz/ n Bruxelas f. ~ sprouts couve-de-Bruxelas f

brutal /'bru:tl/ a brutal. ~ity /-'tælətɪ/ n brutalidade f

brute /bru:t/ n & a (animal, person) bruto (m). by ~ force por força bruta

B Sc abbr see Bachelor of Science

bubb|le /'bʌbl/ n bolha f; (of soap) bola f de sabão □ vi borbulhar. ~le gum n chiclete m, (P) pastilha f elástica. ~le over transbordar. ~ly a efervescente

buck[1] /bʌk/ n macho m □ vi dar galões, (P) corcovear. ~ up vt/i (sl) animar(-se); (sl: rush) apressar-se, despachar-se

buck[2] /bʌk/ n (Amer sl) dólar m

buck[3] /bʌk/ n ~ pass the ~ (sl) fazer o jogo do empurra

bucket /'bʌkɪt/ n balde m

buckle /'bʌkl/ n fivela f □ vt/i afivelar(-se); (bend) torcer(-se), vergar. ~ down to empenhar-se

bud /bʌd/ n botão m, rebento m □ vi (pt budded) rebentar. in ~ em botão

Buddhis|t /'budɪst/ a & n budista (mf). **~m** /-zəm/ n budismo m

budding /'bʌdɪŋ/ a nascente, em botão, incipiente

budge /bʌdʒ/ vt/i mexer(-se)

budgerigar /'bʌdʒərɪgɑː(r)/ n periquito m

budget /'bʌdʒɪt/ n orçamento m □ vi (pt budgeted) **~ for** prever no orçamento m

buff /bʌf/ n (colour) côr f de camurça; (colloq) fanático m, entusiasta mf □ vt polir

buffalo /'bʌfələu/ n (pl -oes) búfalo m; (Amer) bisão m

buffer /'bʌfə(r)/ n pára-choque m

buffet¹ /'bufeɪ/ n (meal, counter) bufê m, (P) bufete m

buffet² /'bʌfɪt/ vt (pt buffeted) esbofetear; (by wind, rain; fig) fustigar

buffoon /bə'fuːn/ n palhaço m

bug /bʌg/ n (insect) bicho m, (bed-bug) percevejo m; (sl: germ) vírus m; (sl: device) microfone de escuta; (sl: defect) defeito m □ vt (pt bugged) grampear; (Amer sl: annoy) chatear (sl)

bugbear /'bʌgbeə(r)/ n papão m

buggy /'bʌgɪ/ n (for baby) carrinho m

bugle /'bjuːgl/ n clarim m, corneta f

build /bɪld/ vt/i (pt built) construir, edificar □ n físico m, compleição f. **~ up** vt/i criar; (increase) aumentar; (accumulate) acumular(-se). **~up** n acumulação f; (fig) publicidade f. **~er** n construtor m, empreiteiro m; (workman) operário m

building /'bɪldɪŋ/ n edifício m, prédio m. **~ site** canteiro m de obras. **~ society** sociedade f de investimentos imobiliários

built /bɪlt/ see build. **~-in** a incorporado. **~-in wardrobe** armário m embutido na parede. **~-up** a urbanizado

bulb /bʌlb/ n bolbo m; (electr) lâmpada f. **~ous** a bolboso

Bulgaria /bʌl'geərɪə/ n Bulgária f. **~n** a & n búlgaro (m)

bulg|e /bʌldʒ/ n bojo m, saliência f □ vi inchar; (jut out) fazer uma saliência. **~ing** a inchado; (pocket etc) cheio

bulk /bʌlk/ n quantidade f, volume m. **in ~** por grosso; (loose) a granel. **the ~ of** a maior parte de. **~y** a volumoso

bull /bul/ n touro m. **~'s-eye** n (of target) centro m do alvo, mosca f

bulldog /'buldɒg/ n buldogue m

bulldoze /'buldəuz/ vt terraplanar. **~r** /-ə(r)/ n bulldozer m

bullet /'bulɪt/ n bala f. **~-proof** a à prova de balas; (vehicle) blindado

bulletin /'bulətɪn/ n boletim m

bullfight /'bulfaɪt/ n tourada f, corrida f de touros. **~er** n toureiro m. **~ing** n tauromaquia f

bullring /'bulrɪŋ/ n arena f, (P) praça f de touros

bully /'bulɪ/ n mandão m, pessoa f prepotente; (schol) terror m, o mau □ vt intimidar; (treat badly) atormentar; (coerce) forçar (into a)

bum¹ /bʌm/ n (sl: buttocks) traseiro m, bunda f (sl)

bum² /bʌm/ n (Amer sl) vagabundo m

bump /bʌmp/ n choque m, embate m; (swelling) inchaço m; (on head) galo m □ vt/i bater, chocar. **~ into** bater em, chocar com; (meet) esbarrar com, encontrar. **~y** a (surface) irregular; (ride) aos solavancos

bumper /'bʌmpə(r)/ n pára-choques m inv □ a excepcional

bun /bʌn/ n pãozinho m doce com passas; (hair) coque m

bunch /bʌntʃ/ n (of flowers) ramo m; (of keys) molho m; (of people) grupo m; (of grapes) cacho m

bundle /'bʌndl/ n molho m □ vt atar num molho; (push) despachar

bung /bʌŋ/ n batoque m, rolha f □ vt rolhar; (sl: throw) atirar, deitar. **~ up** entupir

bungalow /'bʌŋgələu/ n chalé m; (outside Europe) bungaló m, (P) bungalow m

bungle /'bʌŋgl/ vt fazer mal feito, estragar

bunion /'bʌnjən/ n (med) joanete m

bunk /bʌŋk/ n (in train) couchette f; (in ship) beliche m. **~-beds** npl beliches mpl

bunker /'bʌŋkə(r)/ n (mil) abrigo m, casamata f, bunker m; (golf) obstáculo m em cova de areia

buoy /bɔɪ/ n bóia f □ vt. **~ up** animar

buoyan|t /'bɔɪənt/ a flutuante; (fig) alegre. **~cy** n (fig) alegria f, exuberância f

burden /'bɜːdn/ n fardo m □ vt collegar, sobrecarregar. **~some** a pesado

bureau /'bjuərəu/ n (pl -eaux) /-əuz/ (desk) secretária f; (office) seção f, (P) secção f

bureaucracy /bjuə'rɒkrəsɪ/ n burocracia f

bureaucrat /'bjuərəkræt/ n burocrata mf. **~ic** /-'krætɪk/ a burocrático

burger /'bɜːgə(r)/ n hambúrguer m

burglar /'bɜːglə(r)/ n ladrão m, assaltante mf. **~ alarm** n alarme m contra ladrões. **~ize** vt (Amer) assaltar. **~y** n assalto m

burgle /'bɜːgl/ vt assaltar

burial /'berɪəl/ n enterro m

burlesque /bɜː'lesk/ n paródia f

burly /'bɜːlɪ/ a (-ier, -iest) robusto e corpulento, forte

Burm|a /'bɜːmə/ n Birmânia f. **~ese**
/-'miːz/ a & n birmanês (m)
burn /bɜːn/ vt (pt burned or burnt)
queimar □ vi queimar(-se), arder □ n
queimadura f. **~ down** reduzir a
cinzas. **~er** n (of stove) bico m de
gás. **~ing** a (thirst, desire) ardente;
(topic) candente
burnish /'bɜːnɪʃ/ vt polir, brunir
burnt /bɜːnt/ see **burn**
burp /bɜːp/ n (colloq) arroto m □ vi
(colloq) arrotar
burrow /'bʌrəʊ/ n toca f □ vi cavar,
fazer uma toca
burst /bɜːst/ vt/i (pt burst) arreben-
tar □ n estouro m, rebentar m; (of
anger, laughter) explosão f; (of firing)
rajada f; (of energy) acesso m. **~ into**
(flames, room, etc) irromper em. **~
into tears** desatar num choro, desfazer-se em lágrimas. **~ out laughing**
desatar a rir
bury /'berɪ/ vt sepultar, enterrar;
(hide) esconder; (engross, thrust) mergulhar
bus /bʌs/ n (pl buses) ônibus m, (P)
autocarro m. **~-stop** n paragem f
bush /bʊʃ/ n arbusto m; (land) mato
m. **~y** a espesso
business /'bɪznɪs/ n (trade, shop,
affair) negócio m; (task) função f;
(occupation) ocupação f. **have no
~ to** não ter o direito de. **it's no ~
of yours** não é da sua conta. **mind
your own ~** cuide da sua vida.
that's my ~ isso é meu problema.
~like a eficiente, sistemático.
~man n homem m de negócios, comerciante m
busker /'bʌskə(r)/ n músico m ambulante
bust[1] /bʌst/ n busto m
bust[2] /bʌst/ vt/i (pt busted or bust)
(sl) = **burst** **break** a falido. **~-up** n
(sl) discussão f, (P) bulha f. **go ~** (sl)
falir
bustl|e /'bʌsl/ vi andar numa azáfa-
ma; (hurry) apressar-se □ n azáfama
f. **~ing** a animado, movimentado
bus|y /'bɪzɪ/ a (-ier -iest) ocupado;
(street) movimentado; (day) atarefado
□ vt **~y o.s. with** ocupar-se com.
~ily adv ativamente, atarefadamente
busybody /'bɪzɪbɒdɪ/ n intrometido
m, pessoa f abelhuda
but /bʌt/ conj mas □ prep exceto, (p)
excepto, senão □ adv apenas, só. **all
~** todos menos; (nearly) quaze, por
pouco não. **~ for** sem, se não fosse.
last ~ one/two penúltimo/antepe-
núltimo. **nobody ~** ninguém a não
ser
butcher /'bʊtʃə(r)/ n açougueiro m,
(P) homem m do talho; (fig) carrasco

m □ vt chacinar. **the ~'s** açougue m,
(P) talho m. **~y** n chacina f
butler /'bʌtlə(r)/ n mordomo m
butt /bʌt/ n (of gun) coronha f; (of
cigarette) ponta f; (target) alvo m de
troça, de ridículo etc; (cask) barril m
□ vt/i dar cabeçada em. **~ in** interromper
butter /'bʌtə(r)/ n manteiga f □ vt pôr
manteiga em. **~-bean** n feijão m
branco
buttercup /'bʌtəkʌp/ n botão-de-ouro m
butterfly /'bʌtəflaɪ/ n borboleta f
buttock /'bʌtək/ n nádega f
button /'bʌtn/ n botão m □ vt/i abo-
toar(-se)
buttonhole /'bʌtnhəʊl/ n casa f de
botão; (in lapel) botoeira f □ vt (fig)
obrigar a ouvir
buttress /'bʌtrɪs/ n contraforte m;
(fig) esteio m □ vt sustentar
buxom /'bʌksəm/ a roliço, rechonchudo
buy /baɪ/ vt (pt bought) comprar
(from a); (sl: believe) engolir (colloq)
□ n compra f. **~er** n comprador m
buzz /bʌz/ n zumbido m □ vi zumbir.
~ off (sl) pôr-se a andar. **~er** n campainha f
by /baɪ/ prep (near) junto de, perto de;
(along, past, means) por; (according
to) conforme; (before) antes de. **~
land/sea/air** por terra/mar/ar. **~
bike/car** etc de bicicleta/carro etc.
~ day/night de dia/noite. **~ the
kilo** por quilo. **~ now** a esta hora.
~ accident/mistake sem querer. **~
oneself** sozinho □ adv (near) perto.
and ~ muito em breve. **~ and large**
no conjunto. **~-election** n eleição f
suplementar. **~-law** n regulamento
m. **~-product** n derivado m
bye(-bye) /'baɪ(baɪ)/ int (colloq) adeus,
adeusinho
bygone /'baɪgɒn/ a passado. **let ~s be
~s** o que passou, passou
bypass /'baɪpɑːs/ n (estrada) secundária f, desvio m; (med) by-pass m,
ponte f de safena □ vt fazer um desvio; (fig) contornar
bystander /'baɪstændə(r)/ n circunstante mf, espectador m
byte /baɪt/ n

C

cab /kæb/ n táxi m; (of lorry, train)
cabina f, cabine f
cabaret /'kæbəreɪ/ n variedades fpl,
cabaré m
cabbage /'kæbɪdʒ/ n couve f, repolho m
cabin /'kæbɪn/ n cabana f; (in plane)
cabina f; (in ship) camarote m

cabinet /'kæbɪnɪt/ n armário m. **C~** (pol) gabinete m

cable /'keɪbl/ n cabo m. **~-car** n funicular m, teleférico m. **~ railway** funicular m. **~ television** televisão f a cabo

cache /kæʃ/ n (esconderijo m de) tesouro m, armas fpl, provisões f pl

cackle /'kækl/ n cacarejo m □ vi cacarejar

cactus /'kæktəs/ n (pl **~es** or **cacti** /-taɪ/) cacto m

caddie /'kædɪ/ n (golf) caddie m

caddy /'kædɪ/ n lata f para o chá

cadet /kə'det/ n cadete m

cadge /kædʒ/ vt/i filar, (P) cravar

Caesarean /sɪ'zeərɪən/ a **~ (section)** cesariana f

café /'kæfeɪ/ n café m

cafeteria /kæfɪ'tɪərɪə/ n cafeteria f, restaurante m self-service

caffeine /'kæfiːn/ n cafeína f

cage /keɪdʒ/ n gaiola f

cagey /'keɪdʒɪ/ a (colloq: secretive) misterioso, reservado

cajole /kə'dʒəʊl/ vt ~ sb into doing sth convencer alguém (com lábia ou lisonjas) a fazer alg coisa

cake /keɪk/ n bolo m. **~d** a empastado. his shoes were **~d** with mud tinha os sapatos cobertos de lama. a piece of **~** (sl) canja f (sl)

calamity /kə'læmətɪ/ n calamidade f

calcium /'kælsɪəm/ n cálcio m

calculat|e /'kælkjʊleɪt/ vt/i calcular; (Amer: suppose) supor. **~ed** a (action) deliberado, calculado. **~ing** a calculista. **~ion** /-'leɪʃn/ n cálculo m. **~or** n calculador m, (P) maquina f de calcular

calendar /'kælɪndə(r)/ n calendário m

calf[1] /kɑːf/ n (pl **calves**) (young cow or bull) vitelo m, bezerro m; (of other animals) cria f

calf[2] /kɑːf/ n (pl **calves**) (of leg) barriga f da perna

calibrat|e /'kælɪbreɪt/ vt calibrar. **~ion** /-breɪʃn/ n calibragem f

calibre /'kælɪbə(r)/ n calibre m

calico /'kælɪkəʊ/ n pano m de algodão; (printed) chita f, algodão m

call /kɔːl/ vt/i chamar; (summon) convocar; (phone) telefonar. **~** (in or round) (visit) passar por casa de □ n chamada f; (bird's cry) canto m; (shout) brado m, grito m. be **~ed** (named) chamar-se. be on **~** estar de serviço. **~ back** (phone) tornar a telefonar; (visit) voltar. **~ for** (demand) pedir, requerer; (fetch) ir buscar. **~ off** cancelar. **~ on** (visit) visitar, fazer uma visita a. **~ out** (to) chamar. **~ up** (mil) mobilizar, recrutar; (phone) telefonar. **~-box** n

cabina f telefónica, (P) telefónica. **~er** n visitante f, visita f, (phone) chamador m, (P) pessoa f que faz a chamada. **~ing** n vocação f

callous /'kæləs/ a insensível. **~ly** adv sem piedade.

callow /'kæləʊ/ a (-er, -est) inexperiente, verde

calm /kɑːm/ a (-er, -est) calmo □ n calma f □ vt/i **~ (down)** acalmar (-se). **~ness** n calma f

calorie /'kælərɪ/ n caloria f

camber /'kæmbə(r)/ n (of road) abaulamento m

camcorder /'kæmkɔːdə(r)/ n câmera f de filmar

came /keɪm/ see come

camel /'kæml/ n camelo m

camera /'kæmərə/ n máquina f fotográfica; (cine, TV) câmera f. **~man** n (pl **-men**) operador m

camouflage /'kæməflɑːʒ/ n camuflagem f □ vt camuflar

camp[1] /kæmp/ n acampamento m □ vi acampar. **~-bed** n cama f de campanha. **~er** n campista mf; (car) auto-caravana f. **~ing** n campismo m

camp[2] /kæmp/ a afetado, efeminado

campaign /kæm'peɪn/ n campanha f □ vi fazer campanha

campsite /'kæmpsaɪt/ n área f de camping, (P) parque m de campismo

campus /'kæmpəs/ n (pl **-puses** /-pəsɪz/) campus m, (P) cidade f universitária

can[1] /kæn/ n vasilha f de lata; (for food) lata f (de conserva) □ vt (pt canned) enlatar. **~ned music** música f em fita para locais públicos. **~-opener** n abridor m de latas, (P) abrelatas m

can[2] /kæn/ v aux (be able to) poder, ser capaz de; (know how to) saber. I **~not/~'t** to não posso ir

Canad|a /'kænədə/ n Canadá m. **~ian** /kə'neɪdɪən/ a & n canadense (mf), (P) canadiano (m)

canal /kə'næl/ n canal m

canary /kə'neərɪ/ n canário m. **C~ Islands** npl as (Ilhas) Canárias

cancel /'kænsl/ vt (pt cancelled) cancelar; (cross out) riscar; (stamps) inutilizar. **~ out** vi (fig) neutralizar-se mutuamente. **~lation** /-'leɪʃn/ n cancelamento m

cancer /'kænsə(r)/ n câncer m, cancro m. **C~** (astrol) Caranguejo m, Câncer m. **~ous** a canceroso

candid /'kændɪd/ a franco. **~ly** adv francamente

candida|te /'kændɪdeɪt/ n candidato m. **~cy** /-əsɪ/ n candidatura f

candle /'kændl/ n vela f; (in church) vela f, cirio m. **~-light** n luz f de velas

candlestick /'kændlstɪk/ n castiçal m

candour /'kændə(r)/ n franqueza f, candura f

candy /'kændɪ/ n bala f, (P) açúcar cándi; (Amer: sweet, sweets) doce(s) m (pl). ~floss n algodão-doce f

cane /keɪn/ n cana f; (walking-stick) bengala f; (for baskets) verga f; (school: for punishment) vergasta f □ vt vergastar

canine /'keɪnaɪn/ a & n canino (m)

canister /'kænɪstə(r)/ n lata f

cannabis /'kænəbɪs/ n cânhamo m, maconha f

cannibal /'kænɪbl/ n canibal mf. ~ism /-zəm/ n canibalismo m

cannon /'kænən/ n inv canhão m. ~ball n bala f de canhão

cannot /'kænət/ = can not

canny /'kænɪ/ a (-ier, -iest) astuto, manhoso

canoe /kə'nu:/ n canoa f □ vi andar de canoa. ~ing n (sport) canoagem f. ~ist n canoeiro m, (P) canoísta mf

canon /'kænən/ n cónego m, (P) cónego m; (rule) cânone m

canonize /'kænənaɪz/ vt canonizar

canopy /'kænəpɪ/ n dossel m; (over doorway) toldo m, marquise f; (fig) abóbada f

can't /ka:nt/ = can not

cantankerous /kæn'tæŋkərəs/ a irascível, intratável

canteen /kæn'ti:n/ n cantina f; (flask) cantil m; (for cutlery) estojo m

canter /'kæntə(r)/ n meio galope m, cánter m □ vi andar a meio galope

canton /'kæntɒn/ n cantão m

canvas /'kænvəs/ n lona f; (for painting or tapestry) tela f

canvass /'kænvəs/ vt/i angariar votos or fregueses

canyon /'kænjən/ n canhão m, (P) desfiladeiro m

cap /kæp/ n (with peak) boné m; (without peak) barrete m; (of nurse) touca f; (of bottle, pen, tube, etc) tampa f; (mech) tampa f, tampão m □ vt (pt capped) (bottle, pen, tube, etc) tapar, tampar; (rates) impor um limite a; (outdo) suplantar; (sport) selecionar, (P) seleccionar. ~ped with encimado de, coroado de

capable /'keɪpəbl/ a (person) capaz (of de); (things, situations) suscetível, (P) susceptível (of de). ~ility /-'bɪlətɪ/ n capacidade f. ~ly adv capazmente

capacity /kə'pæsətɪ/ n capacidade f. in one's ~ as na (sua) qualidade de

cape¹ /keɪp/ n (cloak) capa f

cape² /keɪp/ n (geog) cabo m

caper¹ /'keɪpə(r)/ vi andar aos pinotes

caper² /'keɪpə(r)/ n (culin) alcaparra f

capillary /kə'pɪlərɪ/ n (pl -ies) vaso m capilar

capital /'kæpɪtl/ a capital □ n (town) capital f; (money) capital m. ~ (letter) maiúscula f. ~ punishment pena f de morte

capitalis|t /'kæpɪtəlɪst/ a & n capitalista (mf). ~m /-zəm/ n capitalismo m

capitalize /'kæpɪtəlaɪz/ vi capitalizar; (finance) financiar; (writing) escrever com maiúscula. ~ on tirar partido de

capitulat|e /kə'pɪtʃʊleɪt/ vi capitular. ~ion /-'leɪʃn/ n capitulação f

capricious /kə'prɪʃəs/ a caprichoso

Capricorn /'kæprɪkɔ:n/ n (astrol) Capricórnio m

capsicum /'kæpsɪkəm/ n pimento m

capsize /kæp'saɪz/ vt/i virar(-se)

capsule /'kæpsju:l/ n cápsula f

captain /'kæptɪn/ n capitão m; (navy) capitão-de-mar-e-guerra m □ vt capitanear, comandar

caption /'kæpʃn/ n legenda f; (heading) título m

captivate /'kæptɪveɪt/ vt cativar

captiv|e /'kæptɪv/ a & n cativo (m), prisioneiro (m). ~ity /-'tɪvətɪ/ n cativeiro m

captor /'kæptə(r)/ n captor m

capture /'kæptʃə(r)/ vt capturar; (attention) prender □ n captura f

car /ka:(r)/ n carro m. ~ ferry barca f para carros. ~-park n (parque m de) estacionamento (m). ~ phone telefone m de carro. ~-wash n estação f de lavagem

carafe /kə'ræf/ n garrafa f para água ou vinho

caramel /'kærəmel/ n caramelo m.

carat /'kærət/ n quilate m

caravan /'kærəvæn/ n caravana f, reboque m

caraway /'kærəweɪ/ n ~ seed cariz f

carbohydrate /ka:bəʊ'haɪdreɪt/ n hidrato m de carbono

carbon /'ka:bən/ n carbono m. ~ copy cópia f em papel carbono, (P) químico. ~ monoxide óxido m de carbono. ~ paper papel m carbono, (P) químico

carburettor /ka:bjʊ'retə(r)/ n carburador m

carcass /'ka:kəs/ n carcaça f

card /ka:d/ n cartão m; (postcard) postal m; (playing-card) carta f. ~-game(s) n(pl) jogo(s) m(pl) de cartas. ~ index n fichário m, (P) ficheiro m

cardboard /'ka:dbɔ:d/ n cartão m, papelão m

cardiac /'ka:dɪæk/ a cardíaco

cardigan /'ka:dɪgən/ n casaco m de lã

cardinal /'ka:dɪnl/ a cardeal, principal. ~ **number** numeral m cardinal □ n (relig) cardeal m
care /keə(r)/ n cuidado m; (concern) interesse m □ vi ~ **about** (be interested) estar interessado m; (be worried) estar preocupado com. ~ **for** (like) gostar de; (look after) tomar conta de. **take** ~ tomar cuidado. **take** ~ **of** cuidar de; (deal with) tratar de. **he couldn't** ~ **less** ele está pouco ligando, ele não dá a menor (colloq)
career /kə'rɪə(r)/ n carreira f □ vi ir a toda a velocidade, ir numa carreira
carefree /'keəfri:/ a despreocupado
careful /'keəfl/ a cuidadoso; (cautious) cauteloso. ~! cuidado! ~**ly** adv cuidadosamente; (cautiously) cautelosamente
careless /'keəlɪs/ a descuidado (**about** com). ~**ly** adv descuidadamente. ~**ness** n descuido m, negligência f
caress /kə'res/ n carícia f □ vt acariciar
caretaker /'keəteɪkə(r)/ n zelador m duma casa vizia; (janitor) zelador m, (P) porteiro m
cargo /'ka:gəʊ/ n (pl -oes) carregamento m, carga f
Caribbean /kærɪ'bi:ən/ a caraíba. **the** ~ as Caraíbas fpl
caricature /'kærɪkətjʊə(r)/ n caricatura f □ vt caricaturar
caring /'keərɪŋ/ a carinhoso, afetuoso, (P) afectuoso
carnage /'ka:nɪdʒ/ n carnificina f
carnation /ka:'neɪʃn/ n cravo m
carnival /'ka:nɪvl/ n carnaval m
carol /'kærəl/ n cântico m or canto m de Natal
carp¹ /ka:p/ n inv carpa f
carp² /ka:p/ vi ~ (**at**) criticar
carpenter /'ka:pɪntə(r)/ n carpinteiro m. ~**ry** n carpintaria f
carpet /'ka:pɪt/ n tapete m □ vt (pt **carpeted**) atapetar. **with fitted** ~**s** (estar) atapetado. **be on the** ~ (colloq) ser chamado à ordem. ~-**sweeper** n limpador m de tapetes
carport /'ka:pɔ:t/ n abrigo m, (P) telheiro m para automóveis
carriage /'kærɪdʒ/ n carruagem f; (of goods) frete m, transporte m; (cost, bearing) porte m
carriageway /'kærɪdʒweɪ/ n faixa f de rodagem, pista f
carrier /'kærɪə(r)/ n transportador m; (company) transportadora f; (med) portador m. ~ (**bag**) saco m de plástico
carrot /'kærət/ n cenoura f
carry /'kærɪ/ vt/i levar; (goods) transportar; (involve) acarretar; (have for sale) ter à venda. **be carried away** entusiasmar-se, deixar-se levar. ~-**cot** n moisés m. ~ **off** levar à força; (prize) incluir. ~ **it off** sair-se bem (de). ~ **on** continuar; (colloq: flirt) flertar; (colloq: behave) portar-se (mal). ~ **out** executar; (duty) cumprir. ~ **through** levar a cabo
cart /ka:t/ n carroça f; carro m □ vt acarretar; (colloq) carregar com
cartilage /'ka:tɪlɪdʒ/ n cartilagem f
carton /'ka:tn/ n embalagem f de cartão or de plástico; (of yogurt) embalagem f, pote m; (of milk) pacote m
cartoon /ka:'tu:n/ n desenho m humorístico, caricatura f; (strip) estória f em quadrinhos, (P) banda f desenhada; (film) desenhos mpl animados. ~**ist** n caricaturista mf; (of strip, film) desenhador m
cartridge /'ka:trɪdʒ/ n cartucho m
carv|e /ka:v/ vt esculpir, talhar; (meat) trinchar. ~**ing** n obra f de talha; (on tree-trunk) incisão f. ~**ing knife** faca f de trinchar, trinchante m
cascade /kæs'keɪd/ n cascata f □ vi cair em cascata
case¹ /keɪs/ n caso m; (jur) causa f, processo m; (phil) argumentos mpl. **in any** ~ em todo caso. **in** ~ (**of**) no caso (de). **in that** ~ nesse caso
case² /keɪs/ n caixa f; (crate) caixa f, caixote m; (for camera, jewels, spectacles, etc) estojo m; (suitcase) mala f; (for cigarettes) cigarreira f
cash /kæʃ/ n dinheiro m, numerário m, cash m □ vt (obtain money for) cobrar, receber; (give money for) pagar. **be short of** ~ ter pouco dinheiro. ~ **a cheque** (receive/give) cobrar/descontar um cheque. ~ **in** receber. ~ **in** (**on**) aproveitar-se de. **in** ~ em dinheiro. **pay** ~ pagar em dinheiro. ~ **desk** caixa f. ~ **dispenser** caixa f electrónica. ~-**flow** n cash-flow m. ~ **register** caixa f registadora, (P) registradora f
cashew /kæ'ʃu:/ n caju m
cashier /kæ'ʃɪə(r)/ n caixa mf
cashmere /kæʃ'mɪə(r)/ n caxemira f
casino /kə'si:nəʊ/ n (pl -os) casino m
cask /ka:sk/ n casco m, barril m
casket /'ka:skɪt/ n pequeno cofre m; (Amer: coffin) caixão m
casserole /'kæsərəʊl/ n caçarola f; (stew) estufado m
cassette /kə'set/ n cassette f. ~-**player** n gravador m. ~-**recorder** n
cast /ka:st/ vt (pt **cast**) lançar, arremessar; (shed) despojar-se de; (vote) dar; (metal) fundir; (shadow) projetar, (P) projectar □ n (theatr) elenco m; (mould) molde m; (med) aparelho

m de gesso. ~ **iron** *n* ferro *m* fundido. ~**-iron** *a* de ferro fundido; (*fig*) muito forte. ~**-offs** *npl* roupa *f* velha

castanets /ˈkæstəˈnets/ *npl* castanholas *fpl*

castaway /ˈkaːstəweɪ/ *n* náufrago *m*

caste /kaːst/ *n* casta *f*

castigate /ˈkæstɪgeɪt/ *vt* castigar

castle /ˈkaːsl/ *n* castelo *m*; (*chess*) torre *f*

castor /ˈkaːstə(r)/ *n* roda *f* de pé de móvel. ~ **sugar** açúcar *m* em pó

castrat|e /kæˈstreɪt/ *vt* castrar. ~**ion** /-ʃn/ *n* castração *f*

casual /ˈkæʒʊəl/ *a* (*chance: meeting*) casual; (*careless, unmethodical*) descuidado; (*informal*) informal. ~ **clothes** roupa *f* prática *or* de lazer. ~ **work** trabalho *m* ocasional. ~**ly** *adv* casualmente; (*carelessly*) sem cuidado

casualty /ˈkæʒʊəltɪ/ *n* (*dead*) morto *m*; (*death*) morte *f*; (*injured*) ferido *m*; (*victim*) vítima *f*; (*mil*) baixa *f*

cat /kæt/ *n* gato *m*. ~**'s-eyes** *npl* (*P*) reflectores *mpl*

Catalonia /kætəˈləʊnɪə/ *n* Catalunha *f*

catalogue /ˈkætəlɒg/ *n* catálogo *m* □ *vt* catalogar

catalyst /ˈkætəlɪst/ *n* catalisador *m*

catapult /ˈkætəpʌlt/ *n* (*child's*) atiradeira *f*, (*P*) fisga *f* □ *vt* catapultar

cataract /ˈkætərækt/ *f* (*waterfall & med*) catarata *f*

catarrh /kəˈtaː(r)/ *n* catarro *m*

catastroph|e /kəˈtæstrəfɪ/ *n* catástrofe *f*. ~**ic** /kætəsˈtrɒfɪk/ *a* catastrófico

catch /kætʃ/ *vt* (*pt* **caught**) apanhar; (*grasp*) agarrar; (*hear*) perceber □ *vi* prender-se (**in** em); (*get stuck*) ficar preso □ *n* apanha *f*; (*of fish*) pesca *f*; (*trick*) ratoeira *f*; (*snag*) problema *m*; (*on door*) trinco *m*; (*fastener*) fecho *m*. ~ **fire** pegar fogo, (*P*) incendiar-se. ~ **on** (*colloq*) pegar, tornar-se popular. ~ **sb's eye** atrair a atenção de alg. ~ **sight of** avistar. ~ **up** (**with**) pôr-se a par (**com**); (*work*) pôr em dia. ~**-phrase** *n* clichê *m*

catching /ˈkætʃɪŋ/ *a* contagioso, infeccioso

catchment /ˈkætʃmənt/ *n* ~ **area** (*geog*) bacia *f* de captação; (*fig: of school, hospital*) área *f*

catchy /ˈkætʃɪ/ *a* (*tune*) que pega fácil

categorical /kætɪˈgɒrɪkl/ *a* categórico

category /ˈkætɪgərɪ/ *n* categoria *f*

cater /ˈkeɪtə(r)/ *vi* fornecer comida (para clubes, casamentos, etc). ~ **for** (*pander to*) satisfazer; (*consumers*) dirigir-se a. ~**er** *n* fornecedor *m*. ~**ing** *n* catering *m*

caterpillar /ˈkætəpɪlə(r)/ *n* lagarta *f*

cathedral /kəˈθiːdrəl/ *n* catedral *f*

catholic /ˈkæθəlɪk/ *a* universal; (*eclectic*) eclético, (*P*) ecléctico. **C~** *a* & *n* católico (*m*). **C~ism** /kəˈθɒlɪsɪzəm/ *n* catolicismo *m*

cattle /ˈkætl/ *npl* gado *m*

catty /ˈkætɪ/ *a* (dissimuladamente) maldoso, com perfídia

caught /kɔːt/ *see* **catch**

cauldron /ˈkɔːldrən/ *n* caldeirão *m*

cauliflower /ˈkɒlɪflaʊə(r)/ *n* couve-flor *f*

cause /kɔːz/ *n* causa *f* □ *vt* causar. ~ **sth to grow/move** *etc* fazer crescer/mexer *etc* alg coisa

causeway /ˈkɔːzweɪ/ *n* estrada *f* elevada, caminho *m* elevado

caustic /ˈkɔːstɪk/ *a* cáustico

caut|ion /ˈkɔːʃn/ *n* cautela *f*; (*warning*) aviso *m* □ *vt* avisar. ~**ous** /ˈkɔːʃəs/ *a* cauteloso. ~**ously** *adv* cautelosamente

cavalry /ˈkævəlrɪ/ *n* cavalaria *f*

cave /keɪv/ *n* caverna *f*, gruta *f* □ *vi* ~ **in** desabar, dar de si

caveman /ˈkeɪvmæn/ *n* (*pl* **-men**) troglodita *m*, homem *m* das cavernas, (*fig*) (tipo) primário *m*

cavern /ˈkævən/ *n* caverna *f*. ~**ous** *a* cavernoso

caviare /ˈkævɪɑː(r)/ *n* caviar *m*

caving /ˈkeɪvɪŋ/ *n* espeleologia *f*

cavity /ˈkævətɪ/ *n* cavidade *f*

cavort /kəˈvɔːt/ *vi* curvetear; (*person*) andar aos pinotes

CD /siːˈdiː/ *see* **compact disc**

cease /siːs/ *vt/i* cessar. ~**-fire** *n* cessar-fogo *m*. ~**less** *a* incessante

cedar /ˈsiːdə(r)/ *n* cedro *m*

cedilla /sɪˈdɪlə/ *n* cedilha *f*

ceiling /ˈsiːlɪŋ/ *n* (*lit & fig*) teto *m*, (*P*) tecto *m*

celebrat|e /ˈselɪbreɪt/ *vt/i* celebrar, festejar. ~**ion** /ˈbreɪʃn/ *n* celebração *f*, festejo *m*

celebrated /ˈselɪbreɪtɪd/ *a* célebre

celebrity /sɪˈlebrətɪ/ *n* celebridade *f*

celery /ˈselərɪ/ *n* aipo *m*

celiba|te /ˈselɪbət/ *a* celibatário. ~**cy** *n* celibato *m*

cell /sel/ *n* (*of prison, convent*) cela *f*; (*biol, pol, electr*) célula *f*

cellar /ˈselə(r)/ *n* porão *m*, cave *f*; (*for wine*) adega *f*, cave *f*

cell|o /ˈtʃeləʊ/ *n* (*pl* **-os**) violoncelo *m*. ~**ist** *n* violoncelista *mf*

Cellophane /ˈseləfeɪn/ *n* (*p*) celofane *m*

cellular /ˈseljʊlə(r)/ *a* celular

Celt /kelt/ *n* celta *mf*. ~**ic** *a* celta, céltico

cement /sɪˈment/ *n* cimento *m* □ *vt* cimentar. ~**-mixer** *n* betoneira *f*

cemetery /'semətrɪ/ n cemitério m
censor /'sensə(r)/ n censor m □ vt censurar. ~**ship** n censura f
censure /'senʃə(r)/ n censura f, crítica f □ vt censurar, criticar
census /'sensəs/ n recenseamento m, censo m
cent /sent/ n cêntimo m
centenary /sen'ti:nərɪ/ n centenário m
centigrade /'sentɪɡreɪd/ a centígrado
centilitre /'sentɪliːtə(r)/ n centílitro m
centimetre /'sentɪmiːtə(r)/ n centímetro m
centipede /'sentɪpiːd/ n centopéia f, (P) centopeia f
central /'sentrəl/ a central. ~ **heating** aquecimento m central. ~**ize** vt centralizar. ~**ly** adv no centro
centre /'sentə(r)/ n centro m □ vt (pt **centred**) centrar □ vi ~ **on** concentrar-se em, fixar-se em
centrifugal /sen'trɪfjʊɡl/ a centrífugo
century /'sentʃərɪ/ n século m
ceramic /sɪ'ræmɪk/ a (object) em cerâmica. ~**s** n cerâmica f
cereal /'sɪərɪəl/ n cereal m
cerebral /'serɪbrəl/ a cerebral
ceremonial /serɪ'məʊnɪəl/ a de cerimónia □ n cerimonial m
ceremony /'serɪmənɪ/ n cerimónia f, (P) cerimónia f. ~**ious** /-'məʊnɪəs/ a cerimonioso
certain /'sɜːtn/ a certo. **be** ~ **ter a** certeza. **for** ~ com certeza, ao certo. **make** ~ confirmar, verificar. ~**ly** adv com certeza, certamente. ~**ty** n certeza f
certificate /sə'tɪfɪkət/ n certificado m; (birth, marriage) certidão f; (health) atestado m
certify /'sɜːtɪfaɪ/ vt/i certificar. ~**ied** a (as insane) declarado
cervical /sɜː'vaɪkl/ a cervical; (of cervix) do útero
cesspit, cesspool /'sespɪt, 'sespuːl/ ns fossa f sanitária
chafe /tʃeɪf/ vt/i esfregar; (make/become sore) esfolar/ficar esfolado; (fig) irritar(-se)
chaff /tʃɑːf/ vt brincar com □ n brincadeira f; (husk) casca f
chaffinch /'tʃæfɪntʃ/ n tentilhão m
chagrin /'ʃæɡrɪn/ n decepção f, desgosto m, aborrecimento m
chain /tʃeɪn/ n corrente f, cadeia f; (series) cadeia f □ vt acorrentar. ~ **reaction** reacção f, (P) reacção f em cadeia. ~-**smoke** vi fumar cigarros um atrás do outro. ~ **store** loja f pertencente a uma cadeia
chair /tʃeə(r)/ n cadeira f; (position of chairman) presidência f; (univ) cátedra f □ vt presidir

chairman /'tʃeəmən/ n (pl -men) presidente mf
chalet /'ʃæleɪ/ n chalé m
chalk /tʃɔːk/ n greda f, cal f; (for writing) giz m □ vt traçar com giz
challenge /'tʃælɪndʒ/ n desafio m; (by sentry) interpelação f □ vt desafiar; (question truth of) contestar. ~**er** n (sport) pretendente mf (ao título). ~**ing** a estimulante, que constitui um desafio
chamber /'tʃeɪmbə(r)/ n (old use) aposento m. ~-**maid** n arrumadeira f. ~ **music** música f de câmara. **C**~ **of Commerce** Câmara f de Comércio
chamois /'ʃæmɪ/ n ~(-**leather**) camurça f
champagne /ʃæm'peɪn/ n champanhe m
champion /'tʃæmpɪən/ n campeão m, campeã f □ vt defender. ~**ship** n campeonato m
chance /tʃɑːns/ n acaso m; (luck) sorte f; (opportunity) oportunidade f, chance f; (likelihood) hipótese f, probabilidade f; (risk) risco m □ a casual, fortuito □ vi calhar □ vt arriscar. **by** ~ por acaso
chancellor /'tʃɑːnsələ(r)/ n chanceler m. **C**~ **of the Exchequer** Ministro m das Finanças
chancy /'tʃɑːnsɪ/ a arriscado
chandelier /ʃændə'lɪə(r)/ n lustre m
change /tʃeɪndʒ/ vt mudar; (exchange) trocar (**for** por); (clothes, house, trains, etc) mudar de □ vi mudar; (clothes) mudar-se, mudar de roupa □ n mudança f; (money) troco m. **a** ~ **of clothes** uma muda de roupa. ~ **hands** (ownership) mudar de dono. ~ **into** (a butterfly etc) transformar-se em; (evening dress etc) pôr. ~ **one's mind** mudar de idéia. ~ **over** passar, mudar (**to** para). ~-**over** n mudança f. ~**able** a variável
channel /'tʃænl/ n canal m □ vt (pt **channelled**) canalizar. **the C**~ **Islands** as Ilhas do Canal da Mancha. **the (English) C**~ o Canal da Mancha
chant /tʃɑːnt/ n cântico m; (of crowd etc) vt/i cantar, entoar
chaos /'keɪɒs/ n caos m. ~**tic** /-'ɒtɪk/ a caótico
chap /tʃæp/ n (colloq) sujeito m, (B) cara m, (P) tipo m
chapel /'tʃæpl/ n capela f
chaperon /'ʃæpərəʊn/ n pau-de-cabeleira m, chaperon m □ vt servir de pau-de-cabeleira or de chaperon
chaplain /'tʃæplɪn/ n capelão m. ~**cy** n capelania f
chapter /'tʃæptə(r)/ n capítulo m
char /tʃɑː(r)/ vt (pt **charred**) carbonizar

character /'kærəktə(r)/ *n* caráter *m*, (P) carácter *m*; (*in novel, play*) personagem *m*; (*reputation*) fama *f*; (*eccentric person*) excêntrico *m*; (*letter*) caractere *m*, (P) carácter *m*. ~**ize** *vt* caracterizar

characteristic /kærəktə'rɪstɪk/ *a* característico □ *n* característica *f*. ~**ally** *adv* tipicamente

charade /ʃə'rɑːd/ *n* charada *f*

charcoal /'tʃɑːkəʊl/ *n* carvão *m* de lenha

charge /tʃɑːdʒ/ *n* preço *m*; (*electr, mil*) carga *f*; (*jur*) acusação *f*; (*task, custody*) cargo *m* □ *vt/i* (*price*) cobrar; (*enemy*) atacar; (*jur*) incriminar. **be in ~ of** ter a cargo. **take ~ of** encarregar-se de

chariot /'tʃærɪət/ *n* carro *m* de guerra *or* triunfal

charisma /kə'rɪzmə/ *n* carisma *m*. ~**tic** /kærɪz'mætɪk/ *a* carismático

charit|y /'tʃærətɪ/ *n* caridade *f*; (*society*) instituição *f* de caridade. ~**able** *a* caridoso

charlatan /'ʃɑːlətən/ *n* charlatão *m*

charm /tʃɑːm/ *n* encanto *m*, charme *m*; (*spell*) feitiço *m*; (*talisman*) amuleto *m* □ *vt* encantar. ~**ing** *a* encantador

chart /tʃɑːt/ *n* (*naut*) carta *f*; (*table*) mapa *m*, gráfico *m*, tabela *f* □ *vt* fazer o mapa de

charter /'tʃɑːtə(r)/ *n* carta *f*. ~ (**flight**) (voo) charter *m* □ *vt* fretar. ~**ed accountant** *n* perito *m* contador, (P) perito *m* de contabilidade

charwoman /'tʃɑːwʊmən/ *n* (*pl* -**women**) faxineira *f*, (P) mulher *f* a dias

chase /tʃeɪs/ *vt* perseguir □ *vi* (*colloq*) correr (**after** atrás de) □ *n* caça *f*, perseguição *f*. ~ **away** *or* **off** afugentar, expulsar

chasm /'kæzm/ *n* abismo *m*

chassis /'ʃæsɪ/ *n* chassi *m*

chaste /tʃeɪst/ *a* casto

chastise /tʃæs'taɪz/ *vt* castigar

chastity /'tʃæstətɪ/ *n* castidade *f*

chat /tʃæt/ *n* conversa *f* □ *vi* (*pt* **chatted**) conversar, cavaquear. **have a ~** bater um papo, (P) dar dois dedos de conversa. ~**ty** *a* conversador

chatter /'tʃætə(r)/ *vi* tagarelar. **his teeth are** ~**ing** seus dentes estão tiritando □ *n* tagarelice *f*

chauffeur /'ʃəʊfə(r)/ *n* motorista *m*, chofer (particular) *m*, chauffeur *m*

chauvinis|t /'ʃəʊvɪnɪst/ *n* chauvinista *mf*. **male** ~**t** (*pej*) machista *m*. ~**m** /-zəm/ *n* chauvinismo *m*

cheap /tʃiːp/ *a* (-**er**, -**est**) barato; (*fare, rate*) reduzido. ~(**ly**) *adv* barato. ~**ness** *n* barateza *f*

cheapen /'tʃiːpən/ *vt* depreciar

cheat /tʃiːt/ *vt* enganar, trapacear □ *vi* (*at games*) roubar, (P) fazer batota; (*in exams*) copiar □ *n* intrujão *m*; (*at games*) trapaceiro *m*, (P) batoteiro *m*

check[1] /tʃek/ *vt/i* (*examine*) verificar; (*tickets*) revisar; (*restrain*) controlar, refrear □ *n* verificação *f*; (*tickets*) controle *m*; (*curb*) freio *m*; (*chess*) xeque *m*; (*Amer: bill*) conta *f*; (*Amer: cheque*) cheque *m*. ~ **in** assinar o registro; (*at airport*) fazer o check-in. ~-**in** *n* check-in *m*. ~ **out** pagar a conta. ~-**out** *n* caixa *f*. ~-**up** *n* exame *m* médico, check-up *m*

check[2] /tʃek/ *n* (*pattern*) xadrez *m*. ~**ed** *a* de xadrez

checkmate /'tʃekmeɪt/ *n* xeque-mate *m*

cheek /tʃiːk/ *n* face *f*; (*fig*) descaramento *m*. ~**y** *a* descarado

cheer /tʃɪə(r)/ *n* alegria *f*; (*shout*) viva *m* □ *vt/i* aclamar, aplaudir. ~**s!** à sua, (P) vossa (saúde)!; (*thank you*) obrigadinho. ~ (**up**) animar(-se). ~**ful** *a* bem disposto; alegre

cheerio /tʃɪərɪ'əʊ/ *int* (*colloq*) até logo, (P) adeusinho

cheese /tʃiːz/ *n* queijo *m*

cheetah /'tʃiːtə/ *n* chita *f*, lobo-tigre *m*

chef /ʃef/ *n* cozinheiro-chefe *m*

chemical /'kemɪkl/ *a* químico □ *n* produto *m* químico

chemist /'kemɪst/ *n* farmacêutico *m*; (*scientist*) químico *m*. ~**'s (shop)** *n* farmácia *f*. ~**ry** *n* química *f*

cheque /tʃek/ *n* cheque *m*. ~-**book** *n* talão *m* de cheques. ~-**card** *n* cartão *m* de banco

cherish /'tʃerɪʃ/ *vt* estimar, querer; (*hope*) acalentar

cherry /'tʃerɪ/ *n* cereja *f*. ~-**tree** *n* cerejeira *f*

chess /tʃes/ *n* jogo *m* de xadrez. ~-**board** *n* tabuleiro *m* de xadrez

chest /tʃest/ *n* peito *m*; (*for money, jewels*) cofre *m*. ~ **of drawers** cômoda *f*, (P) cómoda *f*

chestnut /'tʃesnʌt/ *n* castanha *f*. ~-**tree** *n* castanheiro *m*

chew /tʃuː/ *vt* mastigar. ~**ing-gum** *n* chiclete *m*, (P) pastilha *f* elástica

chic /ʃiːk/ *a* chique

chick /tʃɪk/ *n* pinto *m*

chicken /'tʃɪkɪn/ *n* galinha *f* □ *vi* ~ **out** (*sl*) acovardar-se. ~-**pox** *n* catapora *f*, (P) varicela *f*

chicory /'tʃɪkərɪ/ *n* (*for coffee*) chicória *f*; (*for salad*) endívia *f*

chief /tʃiːf/ *n* chefe *m* □ *a* principal. ~**ly** *adv* principalmente

chilblain /'tʃɪlbleɪn/ *n* frieira *f*

child /tʃaɪld/ *n* (*pl* **children** /'tʃɪldrən/) criança *f*; (*son*) filho *m*;

(*daughter*) filha *f*. ~**hood** *n* infância *f*, meninice *f*. ~**ish** *a* infantil; (*immature*) acriançado, pueril. ~**less** *a* sem filhos. ~**like** *a* infantil. ~**minded** *n* babá *f* que cuida de crianças em sua propria casa

childbirth /'tʃaɪldbɜ:θ/ *n* parto *m*

Chile /'tʃɪlɪ/ *n* Chile *m*. ~**an** *a* & *n* chileno (*m*)

chill /tʃɪl/ *n* frio *m*; (*med*) resfriado *m*, (*P*) constipação *f* □ *vt/i* arrefecer; (*culin*) refrigerar. ~**y** *a* frio. **be** *or* **feel** ~**y** ter frio

chilli /'tʃɪlɪ/ *n* (*pl* -**ies**) malagueta *f*

chime /tʃaɪm/ *n* carrilhão *m*; (*sound*) música *f* de carrilhão □ *vt/i* tocar

chimney /'tʃɪmnɪ/ *n* (*pl* -**eys**) chaminé *f*. ~**sweep** *n* limpador *m* de chaminés, (*P*) limpa-chaminés *m*

chimpanzee /tʃɪmpæn'zi:/ *n* chimpanzé *m*

chin /tʃɪn/ *n* queixo *m*

china /'tʃaɪnə/ *n* porcelana *f*; (*crockery*) louça *f*

Chin|a /'tʃaɪnə/ *n* China *f*. ~**ese** /-'ni:z/ *a* & *n* chinês (*m*)

chink¹ /tʃɪŋk/ *n* (*crack*) fenda *f*, fresta *f*

chink² /tʃɪŋk/ *n* tinir *m* □ *vt/i* (fazer) tinir

chip /tʃɪp/ *n* (*broken piece*) bocado *m*; (*culin*) batata *f* frita 'em palitos; (*gambling*) ficha *f*; (*electronic*) chip *m*, circuito *m* integrado □ *vt/i* (*pt* **chipped**) lascar(-se)

chipboard /'tʃɪpbɔ:d/ *n* compensado *m* (de madeira)

chiropodist /kɪ'rɒpədɪst/ *n* calista *mf*

chirp /tʃɜ:p/ *n* pipilar *m*; (*of cricket*) cricri *m* □ *vi* pipilar; (*cricket*) cantar, fazer cricri

chisel /'tʃɪzl/ *n* cinzel *m*, escopro *m* □ *vt* (*pt* **chiselled**) talhar

chivalr|y /'ʃɪvlrɪ/ *n* cavalheirismo *m*. ~**ous** *a* cavalheiresco

chive /tʃaɪv/ *n* cebolinho *m*

chlorine /'klɔ:ri:n/ *n* cloro *m*

chocolate /'tʃɒklɪt/ *n* chocolate *m*

choice /tʃɔɪs/ *n* escolha *f* □ *a* escolhido, seleto, (*P*) seleccionado

choir /'kwaɪə(r)/ *n* coro *m*

choirboy /'kwaɪəbɔɪ/ *n* menino *m* de coro, corista *m*, (*P*) coralista *m*

choke /tʃəʊk/ *vt/i* sufocar; (*on food*) engasgar(-se) □ *n* (*auto*) afogador *m*, (*P*) botão *m* do ar (*colloq*)

cholesterol /kə'lestərɒl/ *n* colesterol *m*

choose /tʃu:z/ *vt/i* (*pt* **chose**, *pp* **chosen**) escolher; (*prefer*) preferir. ~ **to do** decidir fazer

choosy /'tʃu:zɪ/ *a* (*colloq*) exigente, difícil de contentar

chop /tʃɒp/ *vt/i* (*pt* **chopped**) cortar □

n (*wood*) machadada *f*; (*culin*) costeleta *f*. ~ **down** abater. ~**per** *n* cutelo *m*; (*sl: helicopter*) helicóptero *m*

choppy /'tʃɒpɪ/ *a* (*sea*) picado

chopstick /'tʃɒpstɪk/ *n* fachi *m*, pauzinho *m*

choral /'kɔ:rəl/ *a* coral

chord /kɔ:d/ *n* (*mus*) acorde *m*

chore /tʃɔ:(r)/ *n* trabalho *m*; (*unpleasant task*) tarefa *f* maçante. **household** ~**s** afazeres *mpl* domésticos

choreograph|er /kɒrɪ'ɒgrəf(ə)r/ *n* coreógrafo *m*. ~**y** *n* coreografia *f*

chortle /'tʃɔ:tl/ *n* risada *f* □ *vi* rir alto

chorus /'kɔ:rəs/ *n* coro *m*; (*of song*) refrão *m*, estribilho *m*

chose, chosen /tʃəʊz, 'tʃəʊzn/ *see* **choose**

Christ /kraɪst/ *n* Cristo *m*

christen /'krɪsn/ *vt* batizar, (*P*) baptizar. ~**ing** *n* batismo *m*, (*P*) baptismo *m*

Christian /'krɪstʃən/ *a* & *n* cristão (*m*). ~ **name** nome *m* de batismo, (*P*) baptismo. ~**ity** /-strænətɪ/ *n* cristandade *f*

Christmas /'krɪsməs/ *n* Natal *m* □ *a* do Natal. ~ **card** cartão *m* de Boas Festas. ~ **Day**/**Eve** dia *m*/véspera *f* de Natal. ~ **tree** árvore *f* de Natal

chrome /krəʊm/ *n* cromo *m*

chromosome /'krəʊməsəʊm/ *n* cromossoma *m*

chronic /'krɒnɪk/ *a* crônico, (*P*) crónico

chronicle /'krɒnɪkl/ *n* crônica *f*

chronological /krɒnə'lɒdʒɪkl/ *a* cronológico

chrysanthemum /krɪ'sænθəməm/ *n* crisântemo *m*

chubby /'tʃʌbɪ/ *a* (-**ier**, -**iest**) gorducho, rechonchudo

chuck /tʃʌk/ *vt* (*colloq*) deitar, atirar. ~ **out** (*person*) expulsar; (*thing*) jogar fora, (*P*) deitar fora

chuckle /'tʃʌkl/ *n* riso *m* abafado □ *vi* rir sozinho

chum /tʃʌm/ *n* (*colloq*) amigo *m* íntimo, camarada *mf*. ~**my** *a* amigável

chunk /tʃʌŋk/ *n* (grande) bocado *m*, naco *m*

church /tʃɜ:tʃ/ *n* igreja *f*

churchyard /'tʃɜ:tʃjɑ:d/ *n* cemitério *m*

churlish /'tʃɜ:lɪʃ/ *a* grosseiro, indelicado

churn /tʃɜ:n/ *n* batedeira *f*; (*milk-can*) vasilha *f* de leite □ *vt* bater. ~ **out** produzir em série

chute /ʃu:t/ *n* calha *f*; (*for rubbish*) conduta *f* de lixo

chutney /'tʃʌtnɪ/ *n* (*pl*-**eys**) chutney *m*

cider /'saɪdə(r)/ *n* sidra *f*, (*P*) cidra *f*

cigar /sɪ'gɑ:(r)/ *n* charuto *m*

cigarette /sɪgəˈret/ n cigarro m. **~-case** n cigarreira f

cinder /ˈsɪndə(r)/ n brasa f. **burnt to a ~** estorricado

cinema /ˈsɪnəmə/ n cinema m

cinnamon /ˈsɪnəmən/ n canela f

cipher /ˈsaɪfə(r)/ n cifra f

circle /ˈsɜːkl/ n circulo m; (theat) balção m □ vt dar a volta a □ vi descrever circulos, voltear

circuit /ˈsɜːkɪt/ n circuito m

circuitous /sɜːˈkjuːɪtəs/ a indireto, tortuoso

circular /ˈsɜːkjolə(r)/ a circular

circulat|e /ˈsɜːkjoleɪt/ vt/i (fazer) circular. **~ion** /-ˈleɪʃn/ n circulação f; (sales of newspaper) tiragem f

circumcis|e /ˈsɜːkəmsaɪz/ vt circuncidar. **~ion** /-ˈsɪʒn/ n circuncisão f

circumference /səˈkʌmfərəns/ n circunferência f

circumflex /ˈsɜːkəmfleks/ n circunflexo m

circumstance /ˈsɜːkəmstəns/ n circunstância f. **~s** (means) situação f econômica, (P) econômica

circus /ˈsɜːkəs/ n circo m

cistern /ˈsɪstən/ n reservatório m; (of WC) autoclismo m

cit|e /saɪt/ vt citar. **~ation** /-ˈteɪʃn/ n citação f

citizen /ˈsɪtɪzn/ n cidadão m, cidadã f; (of town) habitante mf. **~ship** n cidadania f

citrus /ˈsɪtrəs/ n **~ fruit** citrino m

city /ˈsɪtɪ/ n cidade f

civic /ˈsɪvɪk/ a cívico

civil /ˈsɪvl/ a civil; (rights) cívico; (polite) delicado. **~ servant** funcionário m público. **C~ Service** Administração f Pública. **~ war** guerra f civil. **~ity** /-ˈvɪlətɪ/ n civilidade f, cortesia f

civilian /sɪˈvɪlɪən/ a & n civil (mf), paisano m

civiliz|e /ˈsɪvəlaɪz/ vt civilizar. **~ation** /-ˈzeɪʃn/ n civilização f

claim /kleɪm/ vt reclamar; (assert) pretender □ vi (from insurance) reclamar □ n reivindicação f; (assertion) afirmação f; (right) direito m; (from insurance) reclamação f

clairvoyant /kleəˈvɔɪənt/ n vidente mf □ a clarividente

clam /klæm/ n molusco m

clamber /ˈklæmbə(r)/ vi trepar

clammy /ˈklæmɪ/ a (-ier, -iest) úmido, (P) húmido e pegajoso

clamour /ˈklæmə(r)/ n clamor m, vociferação f □ vi **~ for** exigir aos gritos

clamp /klæmp/ n grampo m; (for car) bloqueador m □ vt prender com grampo; (a car) bloquear. **~ down on**

apertar, suprimir; (colloq) cair em cima de (colloq)

clan /klæn/ n clã m

clandestine /klænˈdestɪn/ a clandestino

clang /klæŋ/ n tinir m

clap /klæp/ vt/i (pt clapped) aplaudir; (put) meter □ n aplauso m; (of thunder) ribombo m. **~ one's hands** bater palmas

claptrap /ˈklæptræp/ n parlapatice f

claret /ˈklærət/ n clarete m

clarif|y /ˈklærɪfaɪ/ vt esclarecer. **~ication** /-ɪˈkeɪʃn/ n esclarecimento m

clarinet /klærɪˈnet/ n clarinete m

clarity /ˈklærətɪ/ n claridade f

clash /klæʃ/ n choque m; (sound) estridor m; (fig) conflito m □ vt/i entrechocar(-se); (of colours) destoar

clasp /klɑːsp/ n (fastener) fecho m; (hold, grip) aperto m de mão □ vt apertar, serrar

class /klɑːs/ n classe f □ vt classificar

classic /ˈklæsɪk/ a & n clássico (m). **~s** npl letras fpl clássicas, (P) estudos mpl clássicos. **~al** a clássico

classif|y /ˈklæsɪfaɪ/ vt classificar. **~ication** /-ɪˈkeɪʃn/ n classificação f. **~ied advertisement** (anúncio m) classificado (m)

classroom /ˈklɑːsruːm/ n sala f de aulas

clatter /ˈklætə(r)/ n estardalhaço m □ vi fazer barulho

clause /klɔːz/ n cláusula f; (gram) oração f

claustrophob|ia /klɔːstrəˈfəʊbɪə/ n claustrofobia f. **~ic** a claustrofóbico

claw /klɔː/ n garra f; (of lobster) tenaz f, pinça f □ vt (seize) agarrar; (scratch) arranhar; (tear) rasgar

clay /kleɪ/ n argila f, barro m

clean /kliːn/ a (-er, -est) limpo □ adv completamente □ vt limpar □ vi **~ up** fazer a limpeza. **~-shaven** a de cara rapada. **~er** n faxineira f, (P) mulher f da limpeza; (of clothes) empregado m da tinturaria. **~ly** adv com limpeza, como deve ser

cleans|e /klenz/ vt limpar; (fig) purificar. **~ing cream** creme m de limpeza

clear /klɪə(r)/ a (-er, -est) claro; (glass) transparente; (without obstacles) livre; (profit) líquido; (sky) limpo □ adv claramente □ vt limpar; (the table) tirar; (jump) transpor; (debt) saldar; (jur) absolver; (through customs) despachar □ vi (of fog) dissipar-se; (sky) limpar. **~ of** (away from) afastado de. **~ off** or **out** (sl) sair andando, zarpar. **~ out** (clean) fazer a limpeza. **~ up** (*tidy*) arrumar; (*mystery*) desvendar; (*of weather*) clarear, limpar. **~ly** *adv* claramente

clearance /'klɪərəns/ *n* autorização *f*; (*for ship*) despacho *m*; (*space*) espaço *m* livre. **~ sale** liquidação *f*, saldos *mpl*

clearing /'klɪərɪŋ/ *n* clareira *f*

clearway /'klɪəweɪ/ *n* rodovia *f* de estacionamento proibido

cleavage /'kliːvɪdʒ/ *n* divisão *f*; (*between breasts*) rego *m* (*of dress*) decote *m*

cleaver /'kliːvə(r)/ *n* cutelo *m*

clef /klef/ *n* (*mus*) clave *f*

cleft /kleft/ *n* fenda *f*

clench /klentʃ/ *vt* (*teeth, fists*) cerrar; (*grasp*) agarrar

clergy /'klɜːdʒɪ/ *n* clero *m*. **~man** *n* (*pl* **-men**) clérigo *m*, sacerdote *m*

cleric /'klerɪk/ *n* clérigo *m*. **~al** *a* (*relig*) clerical; (*of clerks*) do escritório

clerk /klɑːk/ *n* auxiliar *m* de escritório

clever /'klevə(r)/ *a* (**-er, -est**) esperto, inteligente; (*skilful*) hábil, habilidoso. **~ly** *adv* inteligentemente; (*skilfully*) habilmente, habilidosamente. **~ness** *n* esperteza *f*, inteligência *f*

cliché /'kliːʃeɪ/ *n* chavão *m*, lugar-comum *m*, cliché *m*

click /klɪk/ *n* estalido *m*, clique *m* □ *vi* dar um estalido

client /'klaɪənt/ *n* cliente *mf*

clientele /kliːən'tel/ *n* clientela *f*

cliff /klɪf/ *n* penhasco *m*. **~s** *npl* falésia *f*

climat|e /'klaɪmɪt/ *n* clima *m*. **~ic** /'mætɪk/ *a* climático

climax /'klaɪmæks/ *n* clímax *m*, ponto *m* culminante

climb /klaɪm/ *vt* (*stairs*) subir; (*tree, wall*) subir em, trepar em; (*mountain*) escalar □ *vi* subir, trepar □ *n* subida *f*; (*mountain*) escalada *f*. **~ down** descer; (*fig*) dar a mão à palmatória (*fig*). **~er** *n* (*sport*) alpinista *mf*; (*plant*) trepadeira *f*

clinch /klɪntʃ/ *vt* (*deal*) fechar; (*argument*) resolver

cling /klɪŋ/ *vi* (*pt* **clung**) **~ (to)** agarrar-se (a); (*stick*) colar-se (a)

clinic /'klɪnɪk/ *n* clínica *f*

clinical /'klɪnɪkl/ *a* clínico

clink /klɪŋk/ *n* tinido *m* □ *vt/i* (fazer) tilintar

clip[1] /klɪp/ *m* (*for paper*) clipe *m*; (*for hair*) grampo *m*, (P) gancho *m*; (*for tube*) braçadeira *f* □ *vt* (*pt* **clipped**) prender

clip[2] /klɪp/ *vt* (*pt* **clipped**) cortar; (*trim*) aparar □ *n* tosquia *f*; (*colloq: blow*) murro *m*. **~ping** *n* recorte *m*

clique /kliːk/ *n* panelinha *f*, facção *f*, conventículo *m*

cloak /kləʊk/ *n* capa *f*, manto *m*

cloakroom /'kləʊkruːm/ *n* vestiário *m*; (*toilet*) toalete *m*, (P) lavabo *m*

clock /klɒk/ *n* relógio *m* □ *vi* **~in/out** marcar o ponto (à entrada/à saída). **~ up** (*colloq: miles etc*) fazer

clockwise /'klɒkwaɪz/ *a* & *adv* no sentido dos ponteiros do relógio

clockwork /'klɒkwɜːk/ *n* mecanismo *m*. **go like ~** ir às mil maravilhas

clog /klɒg/ *n* tamanco *m*, soco *m* □ *vt/i* (*pt* **clogged**) entupir(-se)

cloister /'klɔɪstə(r)/ *n* claustro *m*

close[1] /kləʊs/ *a* (**-er, -est**) próximo (**to** de); (*link, collaboration*) estreito; (*friend*) íntimo; (*weather*) abafado □ *adv* perto. **~ at hand, ~ by** muito perto. **~ together** (*crowded*) espremido. **have a ~ shave** (*fig*) escapar por um triz. **~up** *n* grande plano *m*. **~ly** *adv* de perto. **~ness** *n* proximidade *f*

close[2] /kləʊz/ *vt/i* fechar(-se); (*end*) terminar; (*of shop etc*) fechar □ *n* fim *m*. **~d shop** organização *f* que só admite trabalhadores sindicalizados

closet /'klɒzɪt/ *n* (*Amer*) armário *m*

closure /'kləʊʒə(r)/ *n* encerramento *m*

clot /klɒt/ *n* coágulo *m* □ *vi* (*pt* **clotted**) coagular

cloth /klɒθ/ *n* pano *m*; (*tablecloth*) toalha *f* de mesa

cloth|e /kləʊð/ *vt* vestir. **~ing** *n* vestuário *m*, roupa *f*

clothes /kləʊðz/ *npl* roupa *f*, vestuário *m*. **~-line** *n* varal *m* para roupa

cloud /klaʊd/ *n* núvem *f* □ *vt/i* toldar (-se). **~y** *a* nublado, toldado; (*liquid*) turvo

clout /klaʊt/ *n* cascudo *m*, (P) carolo *m*; (*colloq: power*) poder *m* efectivo □ *vt* (*colloq*) bater

clove /kləʊv/ *n* cravo *m*. **~ of garlic** dente *m* de alho

clover /'kləʊvə(r)/ *n* trevo *m*

clown /klaʊn/ *n* palhaço *m* □ *vi* fazer palhaçadas

club /klʌb/ *n* clube *m*; (*weapon*) cacete *m*. **~s** (*cards*) paus *mpl* □ *vt/i* (*pt* **clubbed**) dar bordoadas *or* cacetadas (em). **~ together** (*share costs*) cotizar-se

cluck /klʌk/ *vi* cacarejar

clue /kluː/ *n* indício *m*, pista *f*; (*in crossword*) definição *f*. **not have a ~** (*colloq*) não fazer a menor idéia

clump /klʌmp/ *n* maciço *m*, tufo *m*

clumsy /'klʌmzɪ/ *a* (**-ier, -iest**) desajeitado

clung /klʌŋ/ *see* cling

cluster /ˈklʌstə(r)/ n (pequeno) grupo m; (bot) cacho m □ vt/i agrupar(-se)

clutch /klʌtʃ/ vt agarrar (em), apertar □ vi agarrar-se (at a) □ n (auto) embreagem f, (P) embraiagem f. ~es npl garras fpl

clutter /ˈklʌtə(r)/ n barafunda f, desordem f □ vt atravancar

coach /kəʊtʃ/ n ònibus m, (P) camioneta f, (of train) carruagem f; (sport) treinador m □ vt (tutor) dar aulas a; (sport) treinar

coagulate /kəʊˈægjʊleɪt/ vt/i coagular(-se)

coal /kəʊl/ n carvão m

coalfield /ˈkəʊlfiːld/ n região f carbonífera

coalition /kəʊəˈlɪʃn/ n coligação f

coarse /kɔːs/ a (-er, -est) grosseiro

coast /kəʊst/ n costa f □ vi costear; (cycle) descer em roda-livre; (car) ir em ponto morto. ~al a costeiro

coastguard /ˈkəʊstɡɑːd/ n polícia f marítima

coastline /ˈkəʊstlaɪn/ n litoral m

coat /kəʊt/ n casaco m; (of animal) pêlo m; (of paint) camada f, demão f □ vt cobrir. ~ of arms brasão m. ~ing n camada f

coax /kəʊks/ vt levar com afagos ou lisonjas, convencer

cobble /ˈkɒbl/ n ~(-stone) n pedra f de calçada

cobweb /ˈkɒbweb/ n teia f de aranha

cocaine /kəʊˈkeɪn/ n cocaína f

cock /kɒk/ n (male bird) macho m; (rooster) galo m □ vt (gun) engatilhar; (ears) fitar. ~-eyed a (sl: askew) de esguelha

cockerel /ˈkɒkərəl/ n frango m, galo m novo

cockle /ˈkɒkl/ n berbigão m

cockney /ˈkɒknɪ/ n (pl -eys) (person) londrino m; (dialect) dialeto m do leste de Londres

cockpit /ˈkɒkpɪt/ n cabine f

cockroach /ˈkɒkrəʊtʃ/ n barata f

cocktail /ˈkɒkteɪl/ n cocktail m, coquetel m. fruit ~ salada f de fruta

cocky /ˈkɒkɪ/ a (-ier, -iest) convencido (colloq)

cocoa /ˈkəʊkəʊ/ n cacau m

coconut /ˈkəʊkənʌt/ n coco m

cocoon /kəˈkuːn/ n casulo m

cod /kɒd/ n (pl invar) bacalhau m. ~-liver oil óleo m de fígado de bacalhau

code /kəʊd/ n código m □ vt codificar

coeducational /kəʊedʒʊˈkeɪʃənl/ a misto

coerce /kəʊˈɜːs/ vt coagir. ~ion /-ʃn/ n coação f, (P) coacção f

coexist /kəʊɪɡˈzɪst/ vi coexistir. ~ence n coexistência f

coffee /ˈkɒfɪ/ n café m. ~ bar café m.

~-pot n cafeteira f. ~-table n mesa f baixa

coffin /ˈkɒfɪn/ n caixão m

cog /kɒɡ/ n dente m de roda. a ~ in the machine (fig) uma rodinha na engrenagem

cogent /ˈkəʊdʒənt/ a convincente; (relevant) pertinente

cognac /ˈkɒnjæk/ n conhaque m

cohabit /kəʊˈhæbɪt/ vi coabitar

coherent /kəˈhɪərənt/ a coerente

coil /kɔɪl/ vt/i enrolar(-se) □ n rolo m; (electr) bobina f; (one ring) espiral f; (contraceptive) dispositivo m intrauterino, DIU

coin /kɔɪn/ n moeda f □ vt cunhar

coincide /kəʊɪnˈsaɪd/ vi coincidir

coinciden|ce /kəʊˈɪnsɪdəns/ n coincidência f. ~tal /-ˈdentl/ a que acontece por coincidência

colander /ˈkʌləndə(r)/ n peneira f, (P) coador m

cold /kəʊld/ a (-er, -est) frio □ n frio m; (med) resfriado m, constipação f. be or feel ~ estar com frio. it's ~ está frio. ~-blooded a (person) insensível; (deed) a sangue frio. ~-cream creme m para a pele. ~ness n frio m, (of feeling) frieza f

coleslaw /ˈkəʊlslɔː/ n salada f de repolho cru

colic /ˈkɒlɪk/ n cólica(s) f (pl)

collaborat|e /kəˈlæbəreɪt/ vi colaborar. ~ion /-ˈreɪʃn/ n colaboração f. ~or n colaborador m

collapse /kəˈlæps/ vi desabar; (med) ter um colapso □ n colapso m

collapsible /kəˈlæpsəbl/ a desmontável, dobrável

collar /ˈkɒlə(r)/ n gola f; (of shirt) colarinho m; (of dog) coleira f □ vt (colloq) pôr a mão a. ~-bone n clavícula f

colleague /ˈkɒliːɡ/ n colega mf

collect /kəˈlekt/ vt (gather) juntar; (fetch) ir/vir buscar; (money, rent) cobrar; (as hobby) colecionar, (P) coleccionar □ vi juntar-se. call ~ (Amer) chamar a cobrar. ~ion /-ʃn/ n coleção f, (P) colecção f; (in church) coleta f, (P) colecta f; (of mail) tiragem f, coleta f, (P) abertura f. ~or n (as hobby) colecionador m, (P) coleccionador m

collective /kəˈlektɪv/ a coletivo, (P) colectivo

college /ˈkɒlɪdʒ/ n colégio m

collide /kəˈlaɪd/ vi colidir

colliery /ˈkɒliərɪ/ n mina f de carvão

collision /kəˈlɪʒn/ n colisão f, choque m; (fig) conflito m

colloquial /kəˈləʊkwɪəl/ a coloquial. ~ism n expressão f coloquial

collusion /kəˈluːʒn/ n conluio m

colon /ˈkəʊlən/ n (gram) dois pontos mpl; (anat) côlon m

colonel /'kɜːnl/ n coronel m
colonize /'kɒlənaɪz/ vt colonizar
colon|y /'kɒlənɪ/ n colónia f, (P) colónia f. ~ial /kə'ləʊnɪəl/ a & n colonial (mf)
colossal /kə'lɒsl/ a colossal
colour /'kʌlə(r)/ n cor f □ a (photo, TV, etc) a cores; (film) colorido □ vt colorir, dar cor a □ vi (blush) corar. ~-blind a daltónico, (P) daltónico. ~ful a colorido. ~ing n (of skin) cor f; (in food) corante m. ~less a descolorido
coloured /'kʌləd/ a (pencil, person) de cor □ n pessoa f de cor
column /'kɒləm/ n coluna f
columnist /'kɒləmnɪst/ n colunista mf
coma /'kəʊmə/ n coma m
comb /kəʊm/ n pente m □ vt pentear; (search) vasculhar. ~ one's hair pentear-se
combat /'kɒmbæt/ n combate m □ vt (pt combated) combater
combination /kɒmbɪ'neɪʃn/ n combinação f
combine /kəm'baɪn/ vt/i combinar (-se), juntar(-se), reunir(-se)
combustion /kəm'bʌstʃən/ n combustão f
come /kʌm/ vi (pt came, pp come) vir; (arrive) chegar; (occur) suceder. ~ about acontecer. ~ across encontrar, dar com. ~ away or off soltar-se. ~ back voltar. ~-back n regresso m; (retort) réplica f. ~ by obter. ~ down descer; (price) baixar. ~-down n humilhação f. ~ from vir de. ~ in entrar. ~ into (money) herdar. ~ off (succeed) ter êxito; (fare) sair-se. ~ on! vamos! ~ out sair. ~ round (after fainting) voltar a si; (be converted) deixar-se convencer. ~ to (amount to) montar a. ~ up subir; (seeds) despontar; (fig) surgir. ~ up with (idea) vir com, propor. ~-uppance n castigo m merecido
comedian /kə'miːdɪən/ n comediante mf
comedy /'kɒmədɪ/ n comédia f
comet /'kɒmɪt/ n cometa m
comfort /'kʌmfət/ n conforto m □ vt confortar, consolar. ~able a confortável
comic /'kɒmɪk/ a cómico, (P) cómico □ n cómico m; (periodical) estórias fpl em quadrinhos, (P) revista f de banda desenhada. ~ strip estória f em quadrinhos, (p) banda f desenhada. ~al a cómico, (P) cómico
coming /'kʌmɪŋ/ n vinda f □ a próximo. ~s and goings idas e vindas fpl
comma /'kɒmə/ n vírgula f
command /kə'maːnd/ n (mil) coman-

do m; (order) ordem f; (mastery) domínio m □ vt comandar; (respect) inspirar, impor. ~er n comandante m. ~ing a imponente
commandeer /kɒmən'dɪə(r)/ vt requisitar
commandment /kə'maːndmənt/ n mandamento m
commemorat|e /kə'meməreɪt/ vt comemorar. ~ion /-'reɪʃn/ n comemoração f. ~ive a comemorativo
commence /kə'mens/ vt/i começar. ~ment n começo m
commend /kə'mend/ vt louvar; (entrust) confiar. ~able a louvável. ~ation /kɒmen'deɪʃn/ n louvor m
comment /'kɒment/ n comentário m □ vi comentar. ~ on comentar, fazer comentários
commentary /'kɒməntrɪ/ n comentário m; (radio, TV) relato m
commentat|e /'kɒmənteɪt/ vi fazer um relato. ~or n (radio, TV) comentarista mf, (P) comentador m
commerce /'kɒmɜːs/ n comércio m
commercial /kə'mɜːʃl/ a comercial □ n publicidade (comercial) f. ~ize vt comercializar
commiserat|e /kə'mɪzəreɪt/ vi ~ with compadecer-se de. ~ion /-'reɪʃn/ n comiseração f, pesar m
commission /kə'mɪʃn/ n comissão f; (order for work) encomenda f □ vt encomendar; (mil) nomear. ~ to do encarregar de fazer. out of ~ fora de serviço ativo, (P) activo. ~er n comissário m; (police) chefe m
commit /kə'mɪt/ vt (pt committed) cometer; (entrust) confiar. ~ o.s. comprometer-se, empenhar-se. ~ suicide suicidar-se. ~ to memory decorar. ~ment n compromisso m
committee /kə'mɪtɪ/ n comissão f, comitê f, (P) comité m
commodity /kə'mɒdətɪ/ n artigo m, mercadoria f
common /'kɒmən/ a (-er, -est) comum; (usual) usual, corrente; (pej: ill-bred) ordinário □ n prado m público, (P) baldio m. ~ law direito m consuetudinário. C~ Market Mercado m Comum. ~-room n sala f dos professores. ~ sense bom senso m, senso m comum. House of C~s Câmara f dos Comuns. in ~ em comum. ~ly adv mais comum
commoner /'kɒmənə(r)/ n plebeu m
commonplace /'kɒmənpleɪs/ a banal □ n lugar-comum m
commotion /kə'məʊʃn/ n agitação f, confusão f, barulheira f
communal /'kɒmjʊnl/ a (of a commune) comunal; (shared) comum

commune /'kɒmjuːn/ n comuna f

communicat|e /kə'mjuːnɪkeɪt/ vt/i comunicar. ∼ion /-'keɪʃn/ n comunicação f. ∼ion cord sinal m de alarme. ∼ive /-ətɪv/ a comunicativo

communion /kə'mjuːnɪən/ n comunhão f

communis|t /'kɒmjʊnɪst/ n comunista mf □ a comunista. ∼m /-zəm/ n comunismo m

community /kə'mjuːnətɪ/ n comunidade f. ∼ centre centro m comunitário

commute /kə'mjuːt/ vi viajar diariamente para o trabalho. ∼r /-ə(r)/ n pessoa f que viaja diariamente para o trabalho

compact¹ /kəm'pækt/ a compacto. ∼ disc /'kɒmpækt/ cd m

compact² /'kɒmpækt/ n estojo m de pó-de-arroz, (P) caixa f

companion /kəm'pænɪən/ n companheiro m. ∼ship n companhia f, convívio m

company /'kʌmpənɪ/ n companhia f; (guests) visitas fpl. keep sb ∼ fazer companhia a alg

comparable /'kɒmpərəbl/ a comparável

compar|e /kəm'peə(r)/ vt/i comparar(-se) (to, with com). ∼ative /-'pærətɪv/ a comparativo; (comfort etc) relativo

comparison /kəm'pærɪsn/ n comparação f

compartment /kəm'pɑːtmənt/ n compartimento m

compass /'kʌmpəs/ n bússola f. ∼es compasso m

compassion /kəm'pæʃn/ n compaixão f. ∼ate a compassivo

compatib|le /kəm'pætəbl/ a compatível. ∼ility /-'bɪlətɪ/ n compatibilidade f

compel /kəm'pel/ vt (pt compelled) compelir, forçar. ∼ling a irresistível, convincente

compensat|e /'kɒmpənseɪt/ vt/i compensar. ∼ion /-'seɪʃn/ n compensação f; (financial) indenização f, (P) indemnização f

compete /kəm'piːt/ vi competir. ∼ with rivalizar com

competen|t /'kɒmpɪtənt/ a competente. ∼ce n competência f

competition /kɒmpə'tɪʃn/ n competição f; (comm) concorrência f

competitive /kəm'petɪtɪv/ a (sport, prices) competitivo. ∼ examination concurso m

competitor /kəm'petɪtə(r)/ n competidor m, concorrente mf

compile /kəm'paɪl/ vt compilar, coligir. ∼r /-ə(r)/ n compilador m

complacen|t /kəm'pleɪsnt/ a satisfeito consigo mesmo, (P) complacente. ∼cy n (auto-)satisfação f, (P) complacência f

complain /kəm'pleɪn/ vi queixar-se (about, of de)

complaint /kəm'pleɪnt/ n queixa f; (in shop) reclamação f; (med) doença f, achaque m

complement /'kɒmplɪmənt/ n complemento m □ vt completar, complementar. ∼ary /-'mentrɪ/ a complementar

complet|e /kəm'pliːt/ a completo; (finished) acabado; (downright) perfeito □ vt completar; (a form) preencher. ∼ely adv completamente. ∼ion /-ʃn/ n conclusão f, feitura f, realização f

complex /'kɒmpleks/ a complexo □ n complexo m. ∼ity /kəm'pleksətɪ/ n complexidade f

complexion /kəm'plekʃn/ n cor f da tez; (fig) caráter m, (P) carácter m, aspecto m

compliance /kəm'plaɪəns/ n docilidade f; (agreement) conformidade f. in ∼ with em conformidade com

complicat|e /'kɒmplɪkeɪt/ vt complicar. ∼ed a complicado. ∼ion /-'keɪʃn/ n complicação f

compliment /'kɒmplɪmənt/ n cumprimento m □ vt /'kɒmplɪment/ cumprimentar

complimentary /kɒmplɪ'mentrɪ/ a amável, elogioso. ∼ copy oferta f. ∼ ticket bilhete m grátis

comply /kəm'plaɪ/ vi ∼ with agir em conformidade com

component /kəm'pəʊnənt/ n componente m; (of machine) peça f □ a componente, constituinte

compose /kəm'pəʊz/ vt compor. ∼ o.s. acalmar-se, dominar-se. ∼d a calmo, senhor de si. ∼r /-ə(r)/ n positor m

composition /kɒmpə'zɪʃn/ n composição f

compost /'kɒmpɒst/ n húmus m, adubo m

composure /kəm'pəʊʒə(r)/ n calma f, domínio m de si mesmo

compound /'kɒmpaʊnd/ n composto m; (enclosure) cercado m, recinto m □ a composto. ∼ fracture fratura f, (P) fractura f exposta

comprehen|d /kɒmprɪ'hend/ vt compreender. ∼sion n compreensão f

comprehensive /kɒmprɪ'hensɪv/ a compreensivo, vasto; (insurance) contra todos os riscos. ∼ school escola f de ensino secundário técnico e académico, (P) académico

compress /kəm'pres/ vt comprimir. ~ion /-ʃn/ n compressão f

comprise /kəm'praɪz/ vt compreender, abranger

compromise /'kɒmprəmaɪz/ n compromisso m □ vt comprometer □ vi chegar a um meio-termo

compulsion /kəm'pʌlʃn/ n (constraint) coação f; (psych) desejo m irresistível

compulsive /kəm'pʌlsɪv/ a (psych) compulsivo; (liar, smoker etc) inveterado

compulsory /kəm'pʌlsərɪ/ a obrigatório, compulsório

computer /kəm'pju:tə(r)/ n computador m. ~ science informática f. ~ize vt computerizar

comrade /'kɒmreɪd/ n camarada mf. ~ship n camaradagem f

con¹ /kɒn/ vt (pt **conned**) (sl) enganar □ n (sl) intrujice f, vigarice f, burla f. ~ **man** (sl) intrujão m, vigarista m, burlão m

con² /kɒn/ see **pro**

concave /'kɒŋkeɪv/ a côncavo

conceal /kən'si:l/ vt ocultar, esconder. ~ment n encobrimento m

concede /kən'si:d/ vt conceder, admitir; (in a game etc) ceder

conceit /kən'si:t/ n presunção f. ~ed a presunçoso, presumido, cheio de si

conceivabl|e /kən'si:vəbl/ a concebível. ~y adv possivelmente

conceive /kən'si:v/ vt/i conceber

concentrat|e /'kɒnsntreɪt/ vt/i concentrar(-se). ~ion /-'treɪʃn/ n concentração f

concept /'kɒnsept/ n conceito m

conception /kən'sepʃn/ n concepção f

concern /kən'sɜːn/ n (worry) preocupação f; (business) negócio m □ vt dizer respeito a, respeitar. ~ o.s. with, be ~ed with interessar-se por, ocupar-se de; (regard) dizer respeito a. **it's no ~ of mine** não me diz respeito. ~ing prep sobre, respeitante a

concerned /kən'sɜːnd/ a inquieto, preocupado (about com)

concert /'kɒnsət/ n concerto m

concerted /kən'sɜːtɪd/ a concertado

concession /kən'seʃn/ n concessão f

concise /kən'saɪs/ a conciso. ~ly adv concisamente

conclu|de /kən'klu:d/ vt concluir □ vi terminar. ~ding a final. ~sion n conclusão f

conclusive /kən'klu:sɪv/ a conclusivo. ~ly adv de forma conclusiva

concoct /kən'kɒkt/ vt preparar por mistura; (fig: invent) fabricar. ~ion /-ʃn/ n mistura f; (fig) invenção f, mentira f

concrete /'kɒŋkri:t/ n concreto m, (P) cimento m □ a concreto □ vt concretar, (P) cimentar

concur /kən'kɜː(r)/ vi (pt **concurred**) concordar; (of circumstances) concorrer

concussion /kən'kʌʃn/ n comoção f cerebral

condemn /kən'dem/ vt condenar. ~ation /kɒndem'neɪʃn/ n condenação f

condens|e /kən'dens/ vt/i condensar (-se). ~ation /kɒnden'seɪʃn/ n condensação f

condescend /kɒndɪ'send/ vi condescender; (lower o.s.) rebaixar-se

condition /kən'dɪʃn/ n condição f □ vt condicionar. **on ~ that** com a condição de que. ~al a condicional. ~er n (for hair) condicionador m, creme m rinse

condolences /kən'dəʊlənsɪz/ npl condolências fpl, pêsames mpl, sentimentos mpl

condom /'kɒndəm/ n preservativo m

condone /kən'dəʊn/ vt desculpar, fechar os olhos a

conducive /kən'dju:sɪv/ a be ~ to contribuir para, ser propício a

conduct¹ /kən'dʌkt/ vt conduzir, dirigir; (orchestra) reger

conduct² /'kɒndʌkt/ n conduta f

conductor /kən'dʌktə(r)/ n maestro m; (electr; of bus) condutor m. ~ress n (of bus) condutora f

cone /kəʊn/ n cone m; (bot) pinha f; (for ice-cream) casquinha f, (P) cone m

confectioner /kən'fekʃnə(r)/ n confeiteiro m, (P) pasteleiro m. ~y n confeitaria f, (P) pastelaria f

confederation /kənfedə'reɪʃn/ n confederação f

confer /kən'fɜː(r)/ vt (pt **conferred**) vt conferir, outorgar □ vi conferenciar

conference /'kɒnfərəns/ n conferência f. **in ~** em reunião f

confess /kən'fes/ vt/i confessar; (relig) confessar(-se). ~ion /-ʃn/ n confissão f. ~ional n confessionário m. ~or n confessor m

confetti /kən'fetɪ/ n confetes mpl, (P) confeti mpl

confide /kən'faɪd/ vt confiar □ vi ~ in confiar em

confiden|t /'kɒnfɪdənt/ a confiante, confiado. ~ce n confiança f; (boldness) confiança f em al. s; (secret) confidência f. ~ce trick vigarice f. **in ~ce** em confidência

confidential /kɒnfɪ'denʃl/ a confidencial

confine /kən'faɪn/ vt fechar; (limit) limitar (to a). ~ment n detenção f; (med) parto m

confirm /kən'fɜːm/ vt confirmar. ~**ation** /kɒnfə'meɪʃn/ n confirmação f. ~**ed** a (*bachelor*) inveterado

confiscat|**e** /'kɒnfɪskeɪt/ vt confiscar. ~**ion** /-'keɪʃn/ n confiscação f

conflict[1] /'kɒnflɪkt/ n conflito m

conflict[2] /kən'flɪkt/ vi estar em contradição. ~**ing** a contraditório

conform /kən'fɔːm/ vt/i conformar (-se)

confound /kən'faʊnd/ vt confundir. ~**ed** a (*colloq*) maldito

confront /kən'frʌnt/ vt confrontar, defrontar, enfrentar. ~ **with** confrontar-se com. ~**ation** /kɒnfrʌn'teɪʃn/ n confrontação f

confus|**e** /kən'fjuːz/ vt confundir. ~**ed** a confuso. ~**ing** a que faz confusão. ~**ion** /-ʒn/ n confusão f

congeal /kən'dʒiːl/ vt/i congelar, solidificar

congenial /kən'dʒiːnɪəl/ a (*agreeable*) simpático

congenital /kən'dʒenɪtl/ a congénito, (P) congênito

congest|**ed** /kən'dʒestɪd/ a congestionado. ~**ion** /-tʃn/ n (*traffic*) congestionamento m; (*med*) congestão f

congratulat|**e** /kən'grætjʊleɪt/ vt felicitar, dar os parabéns (on por). ~**ions** /-'leɪʃnz/ npl felicitações fpl, parabéns mpl

congregat|**e** /'kɒŋgrɪgeɪt/ vi reunir-se. ~**ion** /-'geɪʃn/ n (in church) congregação f, fiéis mpl

congress /'kɒŋgres/ n congresso m. C~ (*Amer*) Congresso m

conjecture /kən'dʒektʃə(r)/ n conjectura f, (P) conjetura f □ vt/i conjeturar, (P) conjecturar

conjugal /'kɒndʒʊɡl/ a conjugal

conjugat|**e** /'kɒndʒʊgeɪt/ vt conjugar. ~**ion** /-'geɪʃn/ n conjugação f

conjunction /kən'dʒʌŋkʃn/ n conjunção f

conjur|**e** /'kʌndʒə(r)/ vi fazer truques mágicos □ vt ~ **up** fazer aparecer. ~**or** n mágico m, prestidigitador m

connect /kə'nekt/ vt/i ligar(-se); (of train) fazer ligação. ~**ed** a ligado. be ~**ed with** estar relacionado com

connection /kə'nekʃn/ n relação f; (rail; phone call) ligação f; (electr) contacto m

connoisseur /kɒnə'sɜː(r)/ n conhecedor m, apreciador m

connotation /kɒnə'teɪʃn/ n conotação f

conquer /'kɒŋkə(r)/ vt vencer; (country) conquistar. ~**or** n conquistador m

conquest /'kɒŋkwest/ n conquista f

conscience /'kɒnʃəns/ n consciência f

conscientious /kɒnʃɪ'enʃəs/ a consciencioso

conscious /'kɒnʃəs/ a consciente. ~**ly** adv conscientemente. ~**ness** n consciência f

conscript[1] /kən'skrɪpt/ vt recrutar. ~**ion** /-ʃn/ n serviço m militar obrigatório

conscript[2] /'kɒnskrɪpt/ n recruta m

consecrate /'kɒnsɪkreɪt/ vt consagrar

consecutive /kən'sekjʊtɪv/ a consecutivo, seguido

consensus /kən'sensəs/ n consenso m

consent /kən'sent/ vi consentir (to em) □ n consentimento m

consequence /'kɒnsɪkwəns/ n consequência f, (P) consequência f

consequent /'kɒnsɪkwənt/ a resultante (on, upon de). ~**ly** adv por consequência, (P) consequência, por consequinte

conservation /kɒnsə'veɪʃn/ n conservação f

conservative /kən'sɜːvətɪv/ a conservador; (estimate) moderado. C~ a & n conservador (m)

conservatory /kən'sɜːvətrɪ/ n (greenhouse) estufa f; (house extension) jardim m de inverno

conserve /kən'sɜːv/ vt conservar

consider /kən'sɪdə(r)/ vt considerar; (allow for) levar em consideração. ~**ation** /-'reɪʃn/ n consideração f. ~**ing** prep em vista de, tendo em conta

considerabl|**e** /kən'sɪdərəbl/ a considerável; (much) muito. ~**y** adv consideravelmente

considerate /kən'sɪdərət/ a atencioso, delicado

consign /kən'saɪn/ vt consignar. ~**ment** n consignação f

consist /kən'sɪst/ vi consistir (of, in, em)

consisten|**t** /kən'sɪstənt/ a (unchanging) constante; (not contradictory) coerente. ~ **with** conforme com. ~**cy** n consistência f; (fig) coerência f. ~**tly** adv regularmente

consol|**e** /kən'səʊl/ vt consolar. ~**ation** /kɒnsə'leɪʃn/ n consolação f. ~**ation prize** prémio m de consolação

consolidat|**e** /kən'sɒlɪdeɪt/ vt/i consolidar(-se). ~**ion** /-'deɪʃn/ n consolidação f

consonant /'kɒnsənənt/ n consoante f

consortium /kən'sɔːtɪəm/ n (pl -tia) consórcio m

conspicuous /kən'spɪkjʊəs/ a conspícuo, visível; (striking) notável. make o.s. ~ fazer-se notar, chamar a atenção conspira|cy /kən'spɪrəsɪ/ n conspiração f. ~tor n conspirador m

conspire /kən'spaɪə(r)/ vi conspirar

constable /'kʌnstəbl/ n policia m

constant /'kɒnstənt/ a constante. ~ly adv constantemente

constellation /kɒnstə'leɪʃn/ n constelação f

consternation /kɒnstə'neɪʃn/ n consternação f

constipation /kɒnstɪ'peɪʃn/ n prisão f de ventre

constituency /kən'stɪtjʊənsɪ/ n (pl -cies) circulo m eleitoral

constituent /kən'stɪtjʊənt/ a & n constituinte (m)

constitut|e /'kɒnstɪtjuːt/ vt constituir. ~ion /-'tjuːʃn/ n constituição f. ~ional /-'tjuːʃənl/ a constitucional

constrain /kən'streɪn/ vt constranger

constraint /kən'streɪnt/ n constrangimento m

constrict /kən'strɪkt/ vt constringir, apertar. ~ion /-ʃn/ n constrição f

construct /kən'strʌkt/ vt construir. ~ion /-ʃn/ n construção f. under ~ion em construção

constructive /kən'strʌktɪv/ a construtivo

consul /'kɒnsl/ n cônsul m

consulate /'kɒnsjʊlət/ n consulado m

consult /kən'sʌlt/ vt consultar. ~ation /kɒnsl'teɪʃn/ n consulta f

consultant /kən'sʌltənt/ n consultor m; (med) especialista mf

consume /kən'sjuːm/ vt consumir. ~r /-ə(r)/ n consumidor m

consumption /kən'sʌmpʃn/ n consumo m

contact /'kɒntækt/ n contacto m; (person) relação f. ~ lenses lentes fpl de contacto □ vt contactar

contagious /kən'teɪdʒəs/ a contagioso

contain /kən'teɪn/ vt conter. ~ o.s. conter-se. ~er n recipiente m; (for transport) contentor m

contaminat|e /kən'tæmɪneɪt/ vt contaminar. ~ion /-'neɪʃn/ n contaminação f

contemplat|e /'kɒntempleɪt/ vt contemplar; (intend) ter em vista; (consider) esperar, pensar em. ~ion /-'pleɪʃn/ n contemplação f

contemporary /kən'temprərɪ/ a & n contemporâneo (m)

contempt /kən'tempt/ n desprezo m. ~ible a desprezivel. ~uous /-tʃʊəs/ a desdenhoso

contend /kən'tend/ vt afirmar, sustentar □ vi ~ with lutar contra. ~er n adversário m, contendor m

content¹ /'kɒntent/ a satisfeito, contente □ vt contentar. ~ed a satisfeito,

contente. ~ment n contentamento m, satisfação f

content² /'kɒntent/ n conteúdo m. (table of) ~s índice m

contention /kən'tenʃn/ n disputa f, contenda f; (assertion) argumento m

contest¹ /'kɒntest/ n competição f; (struggle) luta f

contest² /kən'test/ vt contestar; (compete for) disputar. ~ant n concorrente mf

context /'kɒntekst/ n contexto m

continent /'kɒntɪnənt/ n continente m. the C~ a Europa (continental) f. ~al /-'nentl/ a continental; (of mainland Europe) europeu ~al breakfast café m da manhã europeu, (P) pequeno almoço m europeu. ~al quilt edredom m, (P) edredão m

contingen|t /kən'tɪndʒənt/ a & n contingente (m). ~cy n contingência f. ~cy plan plano m de emergência

continual /kən'tɪnjʊəl/ a continual. ~ly adv continuamente

continu|e /kən'tɪnjuː/ vt/i continuar. ~ation /-tɪnjʊ'eɪʃn/ n continuação f.

continuity /kɒntɪ'njuːətɪ/ n continuidade f

continuous /kən'tɪnjʊəs/ a continuo. ~ly adv continuamente

contort /kən'tɔːt/ vt contorcer; (fig) distorcer. ~ion /-ʃn/ n contorção f

contour /'kɒntʊə(r)/ n contorno m

contraband /'kɒntrəbænd/ n contrabando m

contraception /kɒntrə'sepʃn/ n contracepção f

contraceptive /kɒntrə'septɪv/ a & n contraceptivo m

contract¹ /'kɒntrækt/ n contrato m

contract² /kən'trækt/ vt/i contrair (-se); (make a contract) contratar. ~ion /-ʃn/ n contração f, (P) contracção f

contractor /kən'træktə(r)/ n empreiteiro m; (firm) firma f empreiteira de serviços, (P) recrutadora f de mão de obra temporária

contradict /kɒntrə'dɪkt/ vt contradizer. ~ion /-ʃn/ n contradição f. ~ory a contraditório

contraflow /'kɒntrəfləʊ/ n fluxo m em sentido contrário

contrary¹ /'kɒntrərɪ/ a & n (opposite) contrário (m) □ adv ~ to contrariamente a. on the ~ ao ou pelo contrário

contrary² /kən'treərɪ/ a (perverse) do contra, embirrento

contrast¹ /'kɒntrɑːst/ n contraste m

contrast² /kən'trɑːst/ vt/i contrastar. ~ing a contrastante

contraven|e /kɒntrə'viːn/ vt infringir. ~tion /-'venʃn/ n contravenção f

contribut|e /kən'trɪbjuːt/ *vt/i* contribuir (**to** para); (*to newspaper etc*) colaborar (**to** em). **~ion** /kɒntrɪ'bjuːʃn/ *n* contribuição *f*. **~or** /-'trɪbjʊtə(r)/ *n* contribuinte *mf*; (*to newspaper*) colaborador *m*

contrivance /kən'traɪvns/ *n* (*invention*) engenho *m*; (*device*) engenhoca *f*; (*trick*) maquinação *f*

contrive /kən'traɪv/ *vt* imaginar, inventar. **~ to do** conseguir fazer

control /kən'trəʊl/ *vt* (*pt* **controlled**) (*check, restrain*) controlar; (*firm etc*) dirigir □ *n* controle *m*; (*management*) direcção *f*, (*P*) direcção *f*. **~s** (*of car, plane*) comandos *mpl*; (*knobs*) botões *mpl*. **be in ~ of** dirigir. **under ~** sob controle

controversial /kɒntrə'vɜːʃl/ *a* controverso, discutível

controversy /'kɒntrəvɜːsɪ/ *n* controvérsia *f*

convalesce /kɒnvə'les/ *vi* convalescer. **~nce** /-ns/ *n* convalescença *f*. **~nt** /-nt/ *a* & *n* convalescente (*mf*). **~nt home** casa *f* de repouso

convene /kən'viːn/ *vt* convocar □ *vi* reunir-se

convenience /kən'viːnɪəns/ *n* conveniência *f*. **~s** (*appliances*) comodidades *fpl*; (*lavatory*) privada *f*, (*P*) casa *f* de banho. **at your ~** quando (e como) lhe convier. **~ foods** alimentos *mpl* semiprontos

convenient /kən'viːnɪənt/ *a* conveniente. **be ~ for** convir a. **~ly** *adv* sem inconveniente; (*situated*) bem; (*arrive*) a propósito

convent /'kɒnvənt/ *n* convento *m*. **~ school** colégio *m* de freiras

convention /kən'venʃn/ *n* convenção *f*; (*custom*) uso *m*, costume *m*. **~al** *a* convencional

converge /kən'vɜːdʒ/ *vi* convergir

conversant /kən'vɜːsnt/ *a* **be ~ with** conhecer; (*fact*) saber; (*machinery*) estar familiarizado com

conversation /kɒnvə'seɪʃn/ *n* conversa *f*. **~al** *a* de conversa, coloquial

converse[1] /kən'vɜːs/ *vi* conversar

converse[2] /'kɒnvɜːs/ *a* & *n* inverso (*m*). **~ly** /kən'vɜːslɪ/ *adv* ao invés, inversamente

conver|t[1] /kən'vɜːt/ *vt* converter; (*house*) transformar. **~sion** /-ʃn/ *n* conversão *f*; (*house*) transformação *f*. **~tible** /a convertível, conversível □ *n* (*auto*) conversível *m*

convert[2] /'kɒnvɜːt/ *n* convertido *m*, converso *m*

convex /'kɒnveks/ *a* convexo

convey /kən'veɪ/ *vt* transmitir; (*goods*) transportar; (*idea, feeling*) comunicar. **~ance** *n* transporte *m*.

~or belt tapete *m* rolante, correia *f* transportadora

convict[1] /kən'vɪkt/ *vt* declarar culpado. **~ion** /-ʃn/ *n* condenação *f*; (*opinion*) convicção *f*

convict[2] /'kɒnvɪkt/ *n* condenado *m*

convinc|e /kən'vɪns/ *vt* convencer. **~ing** *a* convincente

convoluted /kɒnvə'luːtɪd/ *a* retorcido; (*fig*) complicado; (*bot*) convoluto

convoy /'kɒnvɔɪ/ *n* escolta *f*

convuls|e /kən'vʌls/ *vt* convulsionar; (*fig*) abalar. **be ~ed with laughter** torcer-se de riso. **~ion** /-ʃn/ *n* convulsão *f*

coo /kuː/ *vi* (*pt* **cooed**) arrulhar □ *n* arrulho *m*

cook /kʊk/ *vt/i* cozinhar □ *n* cozinheira *f*, cozinheiro *m*. **~ up** (*colloq*) cozinhar (*fig*), fabricar

cooker /'kʊkə(r)/ *n* fogão *m*

cookery /'kʊkərɪ/ *n* cozinha *f*. **~ book** livro *m* de culinária

cookie /'kʊkɪ/ *n* (*Amer*) biscoito *m*

cool /kuːl/ *a* (**-er, -est**) fresco; (*calm*) calmo; (*unfriendly*) frio □ *n* frescura *f*; (*sl: composure*) sangue-frio *m* □ *vt/i* arrefecer. **~-box** *n* geladeira *f* portátil. **in the ~** no fresco. **~ly** /'kuːllɪ/ *adv* calmamente; (*fig*) friamente. **~ness** *n* frescura *f*; (*fig*) frieza *f*

coop /kuːp/ *n* galinheiro *m* □ *vt* **~ up** engaislar, fechar

co-operat|e /kəʊ'ɒpəreɪt/ *vi* cooperar. **~ion** /-'reɪʃn/ *n* cooperação *f*

cooperative /kəʊ'ɒpərətɪv/ *a* cooperativo □ *n* cooperativa *f*

coordinat|e /kəʊ'ɔːdmeɪt/ *vt* coordenar. **~ion** /-'neɪʃn/ *n* coordenação *f*

cop /kɒp/ *n* (*sl*) porco *m* (*sl*), (*P*) xui *m* (*sl*)

cope /kəʊp/ *vi* aguentar-se, arranjar-se. **~ with** poder com, dar conta de

copious /'kəʊpɪəs/ *a* copioso

copper[1] /'kɒpə(r)/ *n* cobre *m* □ *a* de cobre

copper[2] /'kɒpə(r)/ *n* (*sl*) porco *m* (*sl*), (*P*) xui *m* (*sl*)

coppice /'kɒpɪs/, **copse** /kɒps/ *ns* mata *f* de corte

copulat|e /'kɒpjʊleɪt/ *vi* copular. **~ion** /-'leɪʃn/ *n* cópula *f*

copy /'kɒpɪ/ *n* cópia *f*; (*of book*) exemplar *m*; (*of newspaper*) número *m* □ *vt/i* copiar

copyright /'kɒpɪraɪt/ *n* direitos *mpl* autorais

coral /'kɒrəl/ *n* coral *m*

cord /kɔːd/ *n* cordão *m*; (*electr*) fio *m*

cordial /'kɔːdɪəl/ *a* & *n* cordial (*m*)

cordon /'kɔːdn/ *n* cordão *m* □ *vt* **~ off** fechar (com um cordão de isolamento)

corduroy /'kɔːdərɔɪ/ *n* veludo *m* cotelé

core /kɔː(r)/ n âmago m; (of apple, pear) coração m

cork /kɔːk/ n cortiça f; (for bottle) rolha f □ vt rolhar

corkscrew /'kɔːkskruː/ n sacarolhas m

corn[1] /kɔːn/ n trigo m; (Amer: maize) milho m; (seed) grão m. ~ **on the cob** espiga f de milho

corn[2] /kɔːn/ n (hard skin) calo m

corned /kɔːnd/ a ~ **beef** carne f de vaca enlatada

corner /'kɔːnə(r)/ n canto m; (of street) esquina f; (bend in road) curva f □ vt encurralar; (market) monopolizar □ vi dar uma curva, virar

cornet /'kɔːnɪt/ n (mus) corneta m; (for ice-cream) casquinha f, (P) cone m

cornflakes /'kɔːnfleɪks/ npl cornflakes mpl, cereais mpl

cornflour /'kɔːnflaʊə(r)/ n fécula f de milho, maisena f

Corn|wall /'kɔːnwəl/ n Cornualha f. ~**ish** a da Cornualha

corny /'kɔːnɪ/ a (colloq) batido, (P) estafado

coronary /'kɒrənrɪ/ n ~ **(thrombosis)** infarto m, enfarte m

coronation /kɒrə'neɪʃn/ n coroação f

coroner /'kɒrənə(r)/ n magistrado m que investiga os casos de morte suspeita

corporal[1] /'kɔːpərəl/ n (mil) cabo m

corporal[2] /'kɔːpərəl/ a ~ **punishment** castigo m corporal

corporate /'kɔːpərət/ a colectivo, (P) colectivo; (body) corporativo

corporation /kɔːpə'reɪʃn/ n corporação f; (of town) municipalidade f

corps /kɔː(r)/ n (pl corps /kɔːz/) corpo m

corpse /kɔːps/ n cadáver m

corpuscle /'kɔːpʌsl/ n corpúsculo m

correct /kə'rekt/ a correto, (P) correcto. **the ~ time** a hora certa. **you are ~** você tem razão □ vt corrigir. ~**ion** /-ʃn/ n correção f, (P) correcção f, emenda f

correlat|e /'kɒrəleɪt/ vt/i correlacionar(-se). ~**ion** /-'leɪʃn/ n correlação f

correspond /kɒrɪ'spɒnd/ vi corresponder (to, with, a); (write letters) corresponder-se (with, com). ~**ence** n correspondência f. ~**ent** n correspondente mf. ~**ing** a correspondente

corridor /'kɒrɪdɔː(r)/ n corredor m

corroborate /kə'rɒbəreɪt/ vt corroborar

corro|de /kə'rəʊd/ vt/i corroer(-se). ~**sion** n corrosão f

corrugated /'kɒrəgeɪtɪd/ a corrugado. ~ **cardboard** cartão m canelado. ~ **iron** chapa f ondulada

corrupt /kə'rʌpt/ a corrupto □ vt corromper. ~**ion** /-ʃn/ n corrupção f

corset /'kɔːsɪt/ n espartilho m; (elasticated) cinta f elástica

Corsica /'kɔːsɪkə/ n Córsega f

cosmetic /kɒz'metɪk/ n cosmético m □ a cosmético; (fig) superficial

cosmonaut /'kɒzmənɔːt/ n cosmonauta mf

cosmopolitan /kɒzmə'pɒlɪtən/ a & n cosmopolita (mf)

cosset /'kɒsɪt/ vt (pt cosseted) proteger

cost /kɒst/ vt (pt cost) custar; (pt costed) fixar o preço de □ n custo m. ~**s** (jur) custos mpl. **at all ~s** custe o que custar. **to one's ~** à sua custa. ~ **of living** custo m de vida

costly /'kɒstlɪ/ a (-ier, -iest) a caro; (valuable) precioso

costume /'kɒstjuːm/ n traje m

cos|y /'kəʊzɪ/ a (-ier, -iest) confortável, íntimo □ n abafador m (do bule do chá). ~**iness** n conforto m

cot /kɒt/ n cama f de bebê, berço m

cottage /'kɒtɪdʒ/ n pequena casa f de campo. ~ **cheese** requeijão m, ricota f. ~ **industry** artesanato m. ~ **pie** empada f de carne picada

cotton /'kɒtn/ n algodão m; (thread) fio m, linha f. ~ **wool** algodão m hidrófilo

couch /kaʊtʃ/ n divã m

couchette /kuː'ʃet/ n couchette f

cough /kɒf/ vi tossir □ n tosse f

could /kʊd, kəd/ pt of can[2]

couldn't /'kʊdnt/ = could not

council /'kaʊnsl/ n conselho m. ~ **house** casa f de bairro popular

councillor /'kaʊnsələ(r)/ n vereador m

counsel /'kaʊnsl/ n conselho m; (pl invar) (jur) advogado m. ~**lor** n conselheiro m

count[1] /kaʊnt/ vt/i contar □ n conta f. ~**-down** n (rocket) contagem f regressiva. ~ **on** contar com

count[2] /kaʊnt/ n (nobleman) conde m

counter[1] /'kaʊntə(r)/ n (in shop) balcão m; (in game) ficha f, (P) tento m

counter[2] /'kaʊntə(r)/ adv ~ **to** contrário a; (in the opposite direction) em sentido contrário a □ a oposto □ vt opor; (blow) aparar □ vt ripostar

counter- /'kaʊntə(r)/ pref contra-

counteract /kaʊntə'rækt/ vt neutralizar, frustrar

counter-attack /'kaʊntərətæk/ n contra-ataque m □ vt/i contra-atacar

counterbalance /'kaʊntəbæləns/ n contrapeso m □ vt contrabalançar

counterfeit /'kaʊntəfɪt/ a falsificado, falso □ n falsificação f □ vt falsificar

counterfoil /'kaʊntəfɔɪl/ n talão m, canhoto m

counterpart /'kaʊntəpɑːt/ n equivalente m; (person) homólogo m

counter-productive /'kaʊntəprədʌktɪv/ a contraproducente

countersign /'kaʊntəsaɪn/ vt subscrever documento já assinado; (cheque) contrassinar

countess /'kaʊntɪs/ n condessa f

countless /'kaʊntlɪs/ a sem conta, incontável, inúmero

country /'kʌntrɪ/ n pais m; (homeland) pátria f; (countryside) campo m

countryside /'kʌntrɪsaɪd/ n campo m

county /'kaʊntɪ/ n condado m

coup /kuː/ n ~ (d'état) golpe m (de estado)

couple /'kʌpl/ n par m, casal m □ vt/i unir(-se), ligar(-se); (techn) acoplar. a ~ of um par de

coupon /'kuːpɒn/ n cupão m

courage /'kʌrɪdʒ/ n coragem f. ~ous /kə'reɪdʒəs/ a corajoso

courgette /kʊə'ʒet/ n abobrinha f

courier /'kʊrɪə(r)/ n correio m; (for tourists) guia mf; (for parcels, mail) estafeta m

course /kɔːs/ n curso m; (series) série f; (culin) prato m; (for golf) campo m; (fig) caminho m. in due ~ na altura devida, oportunamente. in the ~ of durante. of ~ está claro, com certeza

court /kɔːt/ n (of monarch) corte f, (courtyard) pátio m; (tennis) court m, quadra f, (P) campo m; (jur) tribunal m □ vt cortejar; (danger) provocar. ~ martial (pl courts martial) conselho m de guerra

courteous /'kɜːtɪəs/ a cortês, delicado

courtesy /'kɜːtəsɪ/ n cortesia f

courtship /'kɔːtʃɪp/ n namoro m, corte f

courtyard /'kɔːtjɑːd/ n pátio m

cousin /'kʌzn/ n primo m. first/second ~ primo m em primeiro/segundo grau

cove /kəʊv/ n angra f, enseada f

covenant /'kʌvənənt/ n convenção f, convénio m; (jur) contrato m; (relig) aliança f

cover /'kʌvə(r)/ vt cobrir □ n cobertura f; (for bed) colcha f; (for book, furniture) capa f; (lid) tampa f; (shelter) abrigo m. ~ charge serviço m. ~ up tapar; (fig) encobrir. ~-up n (fig) encobrimento m. take ~ abrigar-se. under separate ~ em separado. ~ing n cobertura f. ~ing letter carta f (que acompanha um documento)

coverage /'kʌvərɪdʒ/ n (of events) reportagem f, cobertura f

covet /'kʌvɪt/ vt cobiçar

cow /kaʊ/ n vaca f

coward /'kaʊəd/ n covarde mf. ~ly a covarde

cowardice /'kaʊədɪs/ n covardia f

cowboy /'kaʊbɔɪ/ n cowboy m, vaqueiro m

cower /'kaʊə(r)/ vi encolher-se (de medo)

cowshed /'kaʊʃed/ n estábulo m

coy /kɔɪ/ a (-er, -est) (falsamente) tímido

crab /kræb/ n caranguejo m

crack /kræk/ n fenda f; (in glass) rachadura f; (noise) estalo m; (sl: joke) piada f; (drug) crack m □ a (colloq) de élite □ vt/i estalar; (nut) quebrar; (joke) contar; (problem) resolver; (voice) mudar. ~ down on (colloq) cair em cima de, arrochar. get ~ing (colloq) pôr mãos à obra

cracker /'krækə(r)/ n busca-pé m, bomba f de estalo; (culin) bolacha f de água e sal

crackers /'krækəz/ a (sl) desmiolado, maluco

crackle /'krækl/ vi crepitar □ n crepitação f

crackpot /'krækpɒt/ n (sl) desmiolado, maluco

cradle /'kreɪdl/ n berço m □ vt embalar

craft[1] /krɑːft/ n oficio m; (technique) arte f; (cunning) manha f, astúcia f

craft[2] /krɑːft/ n (invar) (boat) embarcação f

craftsman /'krɑːftsmən/ n (pl -men) artífice mf. ~ship n arte f

crafty /'krɑːftɪ/ a (-ier, -iest) manhoso, astucioso

crag /kræg/ n penhasco m. ~gy a escarpado, ingreme

cram /kræm/ vt (pt crammed) ~ (for an exam) decorar, (P) empinar. ~ into/with entulhar com

cramp /kræmp/ n câimbra f □ vt restringir, tolher. ~ed a apertado

crane /kreɪn/ n grua f; (bird) grou m □ vt (neck) esticar

crank[1] /kræŋk/ n (techn) manivela f. ~shaft n (techn) cambota f

crank[2] /kræŋk/ n excêntrico m. ~y a excêntrico

crash /kræʃ/ n acidente m; (noise) estrondo m; (comm) falência f; (financial) colapso m, crash m □ vt/i (fall/strike) cair/bater com estrondo; (two cars) chocar, bater; (comm) abrir falência; (plane) cair □ a (course, programme) intensivo. ~-helmet n capacete m. ~-land vi fazer uma aterrissagem forçada

crate /kreɪt/ n engradado m
crater /'kreɪtə(r)/ n cratera f
crav|e /kreɪv/ vt/i ~e (**for**) ansiar por. ~**ing** n desejo m irresistível, ânsia f
crawl /krɔːl/ vi rastejar; (of baby) engatinhar, (P) andar de gatas; (of car) mover-se lentamente □ n rastejo m; (swimming) crawl m. **be ~ing with** fervilhar de, estar cheio de
crayfish /'kreɪfɪʃ/ n (pl invar) lagostim m
crayon /'kreɪən/ n crayon m, lápis m de pastel
craze /kreɪz/ n moda f, febre f
craz|y /'kreɪzɪ/ a (-ier, -iest) doido, louco (**about** por). ~**iness** n loucura f
creak /kriːk/ n rangido m □ vi ranger
cream /kriːm/ n (milk fat; fig) nata f; (cosmetic; culin) creme m □ a creme invar □ vt desnatar. ~ **cheese** queijo-creme m. ~**y** a cremoso
crease /kriːs/ n vinco m □ vt/i amarrotar(-se)
creat|e /kriː'eɪt/ vt criar. ~**ion** /-ʃn/ n criação f. ~**ive** a criador. ~**or** n criador m
creature /'kriːtʃə(r)/ n criatura f
crèche /kreɪʃ/ n creche f
credentials /krɪ'denʃlz/ npl credenciais fpl; (of competence etc) referências fpl
credib|le /'kredəbl/ a crível, verosímil, (P) verossímil. ~**ility** /-'bɪlətɪ/ n credibilidade f
credit /'kredɪt/ n crédito m; (honour) honra f □ ~**s** (cinema) créditos mpl □ vt (pt **credited**) acreditar em; (comm) creditar. ~ **card** cartão m de crédito. ~ **sb with** atribuir a alg. ~**or** n credor m
creditable /'kredɪtəbl/ a louvável, honroso
credulous /'kredjʊləs/ a crédulo
creed /kriːd/ n credo m
creek /kriːk/ n enseada f estreita. **be up the** ~ (sl) estar frito (sl)
creep /kriːp/ vi (pt **crept**) rastejar; (move stealthily) mover-se furtivamente □ n (sl) cara m nojento. **give sb the** ~**s** dar arrepios a alg. ~**er** n (planta f) trepadeira (f). ~**y** a arrepiante
cremat|e /krɪ'meɪt/ vt cremar. ~**ion** /-ʃn/ n cremação f
crematorium /kremə'tɔːrɪəm/ n (pl -ia) crematório m
crêpe /kreɪp/ n crepe m. ~ **paper** papel m crepom, (P) plissado
crept /krept/ see **creep**
crescent /'kresnt/ n crescente m; (street) rua f em semicírculo
cress /kres/ n agrião m

crest /krest/ n (of bird, hill) crista f; (on coat of arms) timbre m
Crete /kriːt/ n Creta f
crevasse /krɪ'væs/ n fenda f (em geleira)
crevice /'krevɪs/ n racha f, fenda f
crew[1] /kruː/ see **crow**
crew[2] /kruː/ n tripulação f; (gang) bando m. ~-**cut** n corte m à escovinha. ~-**neck** n gola f redonda e um pouco subida
crib[1] /krɪb/ n berço m; (Christmas) presépio m
crib[2] /krɪb/ vt/i (pt **cribbed**) (colloq) colar (sl), (P) cabular (sl) □ n cópia f, plágio m; (translation) burro m (sl)
cricket[1] /'krɪkɪt/ n críquete m. ~**er** n jogador m de críquete
cricket[2] /'krɪkɪt/ n (insect) grilo m
crime /kraɪm/ n crime m; (minor) delito m; (collectively) criminalidade f
criminal /'krɪmɪnl/ a & n criminoso (m)
crimp /krɪmp/ vt preguear; (hair) frisar
crimson /'krɪmzn/ a & n carmesim (m)
cring|e /krɪndʒ/ vi encolher-se. ~**ing** a servil
crinkle /'krɪŋkl/ vt/i enrugar(-se) □ n vinco m, ruga f
cripple /'krɪpl/ n aleijado m, coxo m □ vt estropiar; (fig) paralisar
crisis /'kraɪsɪs/ n (pl **crises** /-siːz/) crise f
crisp /krɪsp/ a (-er, -est) (culin) crocante; (air) fresco; (manners, reply) decidido. ~**s** npl batatas fpl fritas redondas
criterion /kraɪ'tɪərɪən/ n (pl -ia) critério m
critic /'krɪtɪk/ n crítico m. ~**al** a crítico. ~**ally** adv de forma crítica; (ill) gravemente
criticism /'krɪtɪsɪzəm/ n crítica f
criticize /'krɪtɪsaɪz/ vt/i criticar
croak /krəʊk/ n (frog) coaxar m; (raven) crocitar m, crocito m □ vi (frog) coaxar; (raven) crocitar
crochet /'krəʊʃeɪ/ n crochê m □ vt fazer em crochê
crockery /'krɒkərɪ/ n louça f
crocodile /'krɒkədaɪl/ n crocodilo m
crocus /'krəʊkəs/ n (pl -uses /-sɪz/) croco m
crony /'krəʊnɪ/ n camarada mf, amigo m, parceiro m
crook /krʊk/ n (colloq: criminal) vigarista mf; (stick) cajado m
crooked /'krʊkɪd/ a torcido; (winding) tortuoso; (askew) torto; (colloq: dishonest) desonesto. ~**ly** adv de través
crop /krɒp/ n colheita f; (fig) quantidade f; (haircut) corte m rente □ vt (pt

cropped) cortar □ vi ~ up aparecer, surgir

croquet /ˈkrəʊkeɪ/ n croquet m, croqué m

cross /krɒs/ n cruz f □ vt/i cruzar; (cheque) cruzar, (P) barrar; (oppose) contrariar; (of paths) cruzar-se □ a zangado. ~ off or out riscar. ~ o.s. benzer-se. ~ sb's mind passar pela cabeça or pelo espírito de alg, ocorrer a alg. talk at ~ purposes falar sem se entender. ~-country a & adv a corta-mato. ~-examine vt fazer o contra-interrogatório (de testemunhas). ~-eyed a vesgo, estrábico. ~-fire n fogo m cruzado. ~-reference n nota f remissiva. ~-section n corte m transversal; (fig) grupo m or sector m representativo. ~ly adv irritadamente

crossbar /ˈkrɒsbɑː(r)/ n barra f transversal f; (of bicycle) travessão m

crossing /ˈkrɒsɪŋ/ n cruzamento m; (by boat) travessia f; (on road) passagem f

crossroads /ˈkrɒsrəʊdz/ n encruzilhada f, cruzamento m

crossword /ˈkrɒswɜːd/ n palavras fpl cruzadas

crotch /krɒtʃ/ n entrepernas fpl

crotchet /ˈkrɒtʃɪt/ n (mus) semínima f

crouch /kraʊtʃ/ vi agachar-se

crow /krəʊ/ n corvo m □ vi (cock) (pt crew) cantar; (fig) rejubilar-se (over com). as the ~ flies em linha reta, (P) recta

crowbar /ˈkrəʊbɑː(r)/ n alavanca f, pé-de-cabra m

crowd /kraʊd/ n multidão f □ vi afluir □ vt encher. ~ into apinhar-se em. ~ed a cheio, apinhado

crown /kraʊn/ n coroa f; (of hill) topo m, cume m □ vt coroar; (tooth) pôr uma coroa em

crucial /ˈkruːʃl/ a crucial

crucifix /ˈkruːsɪfɪks/ n crucifixo m

crucif|y /ˈkruːsɪfaɪ/ vt crucificar. ~ixion /-ˈfɪkʃn/ n crucificação f

crude /kruːd/ a (-er, -est) (raw) bruto; (rough, vulgar) grosseiro. ~ oil petróleo m bruto

cruel /krʊəl/ a (crueller, cruellest) cruel. ~ty n crueldade f

cruis|e /kruːz/ n cruzeiro m □ vi cruzar; (of tourists) fazer um cruzeiro; (of car) ir a velocidade de cruzeiro. ~er n cruzador m. ~ing speed velocidade f de cruzeiro

crumb /krʌm/ n migalha f, farelo m

crumble /ˈkrʌmbl/ vt/i desfazer(-se); (bread) esmigalhar(-se); (collapse) desmoronar-se

crumple /ˈkrʌmpl/ vt/i amarrotar (-se)

crunch /krʌntʃ/ vt trincar; (under one's feet) fazer ranger

crusade /kruːˈseɪd/ n cruzada f. ~r /-ə(r)/ n cruzado m; (fig) militante mf

crush /krʌʃ/ vt esmagar; (clothes, papers) amassar, amarrotar □ n aperto m. a ~ on (sl) uma paixonite, (P) paixoneta por.

crust /krʌst/ n côdea f, crosta f. ~y a crocante

crutch /krʌtʃ/ n muleta f; (crotch) entrepernas fpl

crux /krʌks/ n (pl cruxes) o ponto crucial

cry /kraɪ/ n grito m □ vi (weep) chorar; (call out) gritar. a far ~ from muito diferente de.

crying /ˈkraɪɪŋ/ a a ~ shame uma grande vergonha

crypt /krɪpt/ n cripta f

cryptic /ˈkrɪptɪk/ a críptico, enigmático

crystal /ˈkrɪstl/ n cristal m. ~lize vt/i cristalizar(-se)

cub /kʌb/ n cria f, filhote m. C~ (Scout) lobito m

Cuba /ˈkjuːbə/ n Cuba f. ~n a & n cubano (m)

cubby-hole /ˈkʌbɪhəʊl/ n cochicho m; (snug place) cantinho m

cub|e /kjuːb/ n cubo m. ~ic a cúbico

cubicle /ˈkjuːbɪkl/ n cubículo m, compartimento m; (at swimming-pool) cabine f

cuckoo /ˈkʊkuː/ n cuco m

cucumber /ˈkjuːkʌmbə(r)/ n pepino m

cuddl|e /ˈkʌdl/ vt/i abraçar com carinho, (nestle) aninhar-se □ n abracinho m, festinha f. ~y a fofo, aconchegante

cudgel /ˈkʌdʒl/ n cacete m, moca f □ vt (pt cudgelled) dar cacetadas em

cue¹ /kjuː/ n (theat) deixa f; (hint) sugestão f, sinal m

cue² /kjuː/ n (billiards) taco m

cuff /kʌf/ n punho m; (blow) sopapo m □ vt dar um sopapo. ~-link n botão m de punho. off the ~ de improviso

cul-de-sac /ˈkʌldəsæk/ n (pl culs-de-sac) beco m sem saída

culinary /ˈkʌlɪnərɪ/ a culinária

cull /kʌl/ vt (select) escolher; (kill) abater seletivamente, (P) selectivamente □ n abate m

culminat|e /ˈkʌlmɪneɪt/ vi ~e in acabar em. ~ion /-ˈneɪʃn/ n auge m, ponto m culminante

culprit /ˈkʌlprɪt/ n culpado m

cult /kʌlt/ n culto m

cultivat|e /ˈkʌltɪveɪt/ vt cultivar. ~ion /-ˈveɪʃn/ n cultivo m, cultivação f

cultural /'kʌltʃərəl/ a cultural

culture /'kʌltʃə(r)/ n cultura f. ∼d a culto

cumbersome /'kʌmbəsəm/ a (un-wieldy) pesado, incómodo, (P) incómodo

cumulative /'kjuːmjʊlətɪv/ a cumulativo

cunning /'kʌnɪŋ/ a astuto, manhoso □ n astúcia f, manha f

cup /kʌp/ n xícara f, (P) chávena f; (prize) taça f. **C**∼ Final Final de Campeonato f

cupboard /'kʌbəd/ n armário m

cupful /'kʌpfʊl/ n xícara f cheia, (P) chávena f (cheia)

curable /'kjʊərəbl/ a curável

curator /kjʊə'reɪtə(r)/ n (museum) conservador m; (jur) curador m

curb /kɜːb/ n freio m □ vt refrear; (price increase etc) sustar

curdle /'kɜːdl/ vt/i coalhar

cure /kjʊə/ vt curar □ n cura f

curfew /'kɜːfjuː/ n toque m de recolher

curio /'kjʊərɪəʊ/ n (pl -os) curiosidade f

curi|ous /'kjʊərɪəs/ a curioso. ∼osity /-'ɒsətɪ/ n curiosidade f

curl /kɜːl/ vt/i encaracolar(-se) □ n caracol m. ∼ **up** enroscar(-se)

curler /'kɜːlə(r)/ n rolo m

curly /'kɜːlɪ/ a (-ier, -iest) encaracolado, crespo

currant /'kʌrənt/ n passa f de Corinto

currency /'kʌrənsɪ/ n moeda f corrente; (general use) circulação f. foreign ∼ moeda f estrangeira

current /'kʌrənt/ a (common) corrente; (event, price, etc) atual, (P) actual □ n corrente f. ∼ **account** conta f corrente. ∼ **affairs** atualidades fpl, (P) actualidades fpl. ∼**ly** adv atualmente, (P) actualmente

curriculum /kə'rɪkjʊləm/ n (pl -la) currículo m, programa m de estudos. ∼ **vitae** n curriculum vitae m

curry[1] /'kʌrɪ/ n caril m

curry[2] /'kʌrɪ/ vt ∼ **favour with** procurar agradar a

curse /kɜːs/ n maldição f, praga f; (bad language) palavrão m □ vt amaldiçoar, praguejar contra □ vi praguejar; (swear) dizer palavrões

cursor /'kɜːsə(r)/ n cursor m

cursory /'kɜːsərɪ/ a apressado, superficial. **a** ∼ **look** uma olhada superficial

curt /kɜːt/ a brusco

curtail /kɜː'teɪl/ vt abreviar; (expenses etc) reduzir

curtain /'kɜːtn/ n cortina f; (theat) pano m

curtsy /'kɜːtsɪ/ n reverência f □ vi fazer uma reverência

curve /kɜːv/ n curva f □ vt/i curvar (-se); (of road) fazer uma curva

cushion /'kʊʃn/ n almofada f □ vt (a blow) amortecer; (fig) proteger

cushy /'kʊʃɪ/ a (-ier, -iest) (colloq) fácil, agradável. ∼ **job** sinecura f, boca f (fig)

custard /'kʌstəd/ n creme m

custodian /kʌ'stəʊdɪən/ n guarda m

custody /'kʌstədɪ/ n (safe keeping) custódia f; (jur) detenção f; (of child) tutela f

custom /'kʌstəm/ n costume m; (comm) freguesia f, clientela f. ∼**ary** a habitual

customer /'kʌstəmə(r)/ n freguês m, cliente mf

customs /'kʌstəmz/ npl alfândega f □ a alfandegário. ∼ **clearance** desembaraço m alfandegário. ∼ **officer** funcionário m da alfândega

cut /kʌt/ vt/i (pt cut, pres p cutting) cortar; (prices etc) reduzir □ n corte m, golpe m; (of clothes, hair) corte m; (piece) pedaço m; (prices etc) redução f, corte m; (sl: share) comissão f, (P) talhada f (sl). ∼ **back** or **down (on)** reduzir. ∼**back** n corte m. ∼ **in** intrometer-se; (auto) cortar. ∼ **off** cortar; (fig) isolar. ∼ **out** recortar; (leave out) suprimir. ∼**-out** n figura f para recortar. ∼**-price** a a preço(s) reduzido(s). ∼ **short** encurtar, (P) atalhar

cute /kjuːt/ a (-er, -est) (colloq: clever) esperto; (attractive) bonito, (P) giro (colloq)

cuticle /'kjuːtɪkl/ n cutícula f

cutlery /'kʌtlərɪ/ n talheres mpl

cutlet /'kʌtlɪt/ n costeleta f

cutting /'kʌtɪŋ/ a cortante □ n (from newspaper) recorte m; (plant) estaca f. ∼ **edge** gume m

CV abbr see curriculum vitae

cyanide /'saɪənaɪd/ n cianeto m

cycl|e /'saɪkl/ n ciclo m; (bicycle) bicicleta f □ vi andar de bicicleta. ∼**ing** n ciclismo m. ∼**ist** n ciclista mf

cyclone /'saɪkləʊn/ n ciclone m

cylind|er /'sɪlɪndə(r)/ n cilindro m. ∼**rical** /-'lɪndrɪkl/ a cilíndrico

cymbals /'sɪmblz/ npl (mus) pratos mpl

cynic /'sɪnɪk/ n cínico m. ∼**al** a cínico. ∼**ism** /-sɪzəm/ n cinismo m

Cypr|us /'saɪprəs/ n Chipre m. ∼**iot** /'sɪprɪət/ a & n cipriota (mf)

cyst /sɪst/ n quisto m

Czech /tʃek/ a & n tcheco (m), (P) checo (m)

D

dab /dæb/ vt (pt **dabbed**) aplicar levemente □ n a ~ of uma aplicaçãozinha de. ~ **sth on** aplicar qq coisa em gestos leves

dabble /'dæbl/ vi ~ **in** interessar-se por, fazer um pouco de (como amador). ~**r** /-ə(r)/ n amador m

dad /dæd/ n (colloq) paizinho m. ~**dy** n (children's use) papai m, (P) papá m. ~**dy-long-legs** n pernilongo m

daffodil /'dæfədɪl/ n narciso m

daft /da:ft/ a (-er, -est) doido, maluco

dagger /'dægə(r)/ n punhal m. at ~**s drawn** prestes a lutar (with com)

daily /'deɪlɪ/ a diário, quotidiano □ adv diariamente, todos os dias □ n (newspaper) diário m; (colloq: charwoman) faxineira f, (P) mulher f a dias

dainty /'deɪntɪ/ a (-ier, -iest) delicado, (pretty, neat) gracioso

dairy /'deərɪ/ n leiteria f. ~ **products** laticínios mpl

daisy /'deɪzɪ/ n margarida f

dam /dæm/ n barragem f, represa f □ vt (pt **dammed**) represar

damag|e /'dæmɪdʒ/ n estrago(s) mpl. ~**es** (jur) perdas fpl e danos mpl □ vt estragar, danificar; (fig) prejudicar. ~**ing** a prejudicial

dame /deɪm/ n (old use) dama f, (Amer sl) mulher f

damn /dæm/ vt (relig) condenar aõ inferno; (swear at) amaldiçoar, maldizer; (fig: condemn) condenar □ int raios!, bolas! □ n **not care a** ~ (colloq) estar pouco ligando (colloq), (P) estar-se marimbando (colloq) □ a (colloq) do diabo, danado □ adv (colloq) muitíssimo. **I'll be** ~**ed if** que um raio me atinja se. ~**ation** /-'neɪ∫n/ n danação f, condenação f. ~**ing** a comprometedor, condenatório

damp /dæmp/ n umidade f, (P) humidade f □ a (-er, -est) úmido, (P) húmido □ vt umedecer, (P) humedecer. ~**en** vt = **damp**. ~**ness** n umidade f, (P) humidade f

dance /da:ns/ vt/i dançar □ n dança f. ~ **hall** sala f de baile. ~**r** /-ə(r)/ n dançarino m; (professional) bailarino m

dandelion /'dændɪlaɪən/ n dente-de-leão m

dandruff /'dændrʌf/ n caspa f

Dane /deɪn/ n dinamarquês m

danger /'deɪndʒə(r)/ n perigo m. **be in** ~ **of** correr o risco de. ~**ous** a perigoso

dangle /'dæŋgl/ vi oscilar, pender □ vt

ter or trazer dependurado; (hold) balançar; (fig: hopes, etc) acenar com

Danish /'deɪnɪ∫/ a dinamarquês □ n (lang) dinamarquês m

dank /dæŋk/ a (-er -est) frio e úmido, (P) húmido

dare /deə(r)/ vt ~ **to do** ousar fazer. ~ **sb to do** desafiar alg a fazer □ n desafio m. **I** ~ **say** creio

daredevil /'deədevl/ n louco m, temerário m

daring /'deərɪŋ/ a audacioso □ n audácia f

dark /da:k/ a (-er, -est) escuro, sombrio; (gloomy) sombrio; (of colour) escuro; (of skin) moreno □ n escuridão f, escuro m; (nightfall) anoitecer m, cair m da noite. ~ **horse** concorrente mf que é uma incógnita. ~**-room** n câmara f escura. **be in the** ~ **about** (fig) ignorar. ~**ness** n escuridão f

darken /'da:kən/ vt/i escurecer

darling /'da:lɪŋ/ a & n querido (m)

darn /da:n/ vt serzir, remendar

dart /da:t/ n dardo m, flecha f. ~**s** (game) jogo m de dardos □ vi lançar-se

dartboard /'da:tbɔ:d/ n alvo m

dash /dæ∫/ vi precipitar-se □ vt arremessar; (hopes) destruir □ n corrida f; (stroke) travessão m; (Morse) traço m. **a** ~ **of** um pouco de. ~ **off** partir a toda a velocidade; (letter) escrever às pressas

dashboard /'dæ∫bɔ:d/ n painel m de instrumentos, quadro m de bordo

data /'deɪtə/ npl dados mpl. ~ **capture** aquisição f de informações, recolha f de dados. ~**base** n base f de dados. ~ **processing** processamento m or tratamento m de dados

date[1] /deɪt/ n data f; (colloq) encontro m marcado □ vt/i datar; (colloq) andar com. **out of** ~ desatualizado, (P) desactualizado. **to** ~ até a data. **up to** ~ (style) moderno; (information etc) em dia. ~**d** a antiquado

date[2] /deɪt/ n (fruit) tâmara f

daub /dɔ:b/ vt borrar, pintar toscamente

daughter /'dɔ:tə(r)/ n filha f. ~**-in-law** n (pl ~**s-in-law**) nora f

daunt /dɔ:nt/ vt assustar, intimidar, desencorajar

dawdle /'dɔ:dl/ vi perder tempo

dawn /dɔ:n/ n madrugada f □ vi madrugar, amanhecer. ~ **on** (fig) fazer-se luz no espírito de, começar a perceber

day /deɪ/ n dia m; (period) época f, tempo m. ~**-dream** n devaneio m □ vi devanear. **the** ~ **before** a véspera

daybreak /'deɪbreɪk/ n romper m do dia, aurora f, amanhecer m

daylight /'deɪlaɪt/ n luz f do dia. ~ **robbery** roubar descaradamente

daytime /'deɪtaɪm/ n dia m, dia m claro

daze /deɪz/ vt aturdir □ n **in a** ~ aturdido

dazzle /'dæzl/ vt deslumbrar; (with headlights) ofuscar

dead /ded/ a morto; (numb) dormente □ adv completamente, de todo □ n **in the** ~ **of the night** a horas mortas, na calada da noite. **the** ~ os mortos. **in the** ~ **centre** bem no meio. **stop** ~ estacar. ~ **beat** a (colloq) morto de cansaço. ~ **end** beco m sem saída. **~-pan** a inexpressivo

deaden /'dedn/ vt (sound, blow) amortecer; (pain) aliviar

deadline /'dedlaɪn/ n prazo m final

deadlock /'dedlɒk/ n impasse m

deadly /'dedlɪ/ a (-ier, -iest) mortal; (weapon) mortífero

deaf /def/ a (-er, -est) surdo. **turn a** ~ **ear** fingir que não ouve. ~ **mute** surdo-mudo m. **~ness** n surdez f

deafen /'defn/ vt ensurdecer. **~ing** a ensurdecedor

deal /di:l/ vt (pt **dealt**) distribuir; (a blow, cards) dar □ vi negociar □ n negócio m; (cards) vez de dar f. **a great** ~ muito (**of** de). ~ **in** negociar em. ~ **with** (person) tratar (com); (affair) tratar de. **~er** n comerciante m; (agent) concessionário m; representante m

dealings /'di:lɪŋz/ npl relações fpl; (comm) negócios mpl

dealt /delt/ see **deal**

dean /di:n/ n decano m

dear /dɪə(r)/ a (-er, -est) (cherished) caro, querido; (expensive) caro □ n amor m □ adv caro □ int **oh** ~! meu Deus! **~ly** adv (very much) muito; (pay) caro

dearth /dɜ:θ/ n escassez f

death /deθ/ n morte f. ~ **certificate** certidão f de óbito. ~ **penalty** pena f de morte. ~ **rate** taxa f de mortalidade. **~-trap** n lugar m perigoso, ratoeira f. **~ly** a de morte, mortal

debase /dɪ'beɪs/ vt degradar

debat|e /dɪ'beɪt/ n debate m □ vt debater. **~able** a discutível

debauchery /dɪ'bɔ:tʃərɪ/ n deboche m, devassidão f

debility /dɪ'bɪlətɪ/ n debilidade f

debit /'debɪt/ n débito m □ vt (pt **debited**) debitar

debris /'deɪbri:/ n destroços mpl

debt /det/ n dívida f. **in** ~ endividado. **~or** n devedor m

debunk /di:'bʌŋk/ vt (colloq) desmitificar

début /'deɪbju:/ n (of actor, play etc) estréia f

decade /'dekeɪd/ n década f

decaden|t /'dekədənt/ a decadente. **~ce** n decadência f

decaffeinated /di:'kæfɪmeɪtɪd/ a sem cafeína

decanter /dɪ'kæntə(r)/ n garrafa f para vinho, de vidro ou cristal

decapitate /dɪ'kæpɪteɪt/ vt decapitar

decay /dɪ'keɪ/ vi apodrecer, estragar-se; (food, fig) deteriorar-se; (building) degradar-se □ n apodrecimento m; (of tooth) cárie f; (fig) declínio m, decadência f

deceased /dɪ'si:st/ a & n falecido (m), defunto (m)

deceit /dɪ'si:t/ n engano m. **~ful** a enganador

deceive /dɪ'si:v/ vt enganar, iludir

December /dɪ'sembə(r)/ n dezembro m

decen|t /'di:snt/ a decente; (colloq: good) (bastante) bom; (colloq: likeable) simpático. **~cy** n decência f

decentralize /di:'sentrəlaɪz/ vt descentralizar

decept|ive /dɪ'septɪv/ a enganador, ilusório. **~ion** /-ʃn/ n engano m

decibel /'desɪbel/ n decibel m

decide /dɪ'saɪd/ vt/i decidir. ~ **on** decidir-se por. ~ **to do** decidir fazer. **~d** /-ɪd/ a decidido; (clear) definido, nítido. **~dly** /-ɪdlɪ/ adv decididamente

decimal /'desɪml/ a decimal □ n (fração f, (P) fracção f) decimal m. ~ **point** vírgula f decimal

decipher /dɪ'saɪfə(r)/ vt decifrar

decision /dɪ'sɪʒn/ n decisão f

decisive /dɪ'saɪsɪv/ a decisivo; (manner) decidido. **~ly** adv decisivamente

deck /dek/ n convés m; (of cards) baralho m. **~-chair** n espreguiçadeira f

declar|e /dɪ'kleə(r)/ vt declarar. **~ation** /deklə'reɪʃn/ n declaração f

decline /dɪ'klaɪn/ vt (refuse) declinar, recusar delicadamente; (gram) declinar □ vi (deteriorate) declinar; (fall) baixar □ n declínio m; (fall) abaixamento m

decode /di:'kəʊd/ vt descodificar

decompos|e /di:kəm'pəʊz/ vt/i decompor(-se). **~ition** /-ɒmpə'zɪʃn/ n decomposição f

décor /'deɪkɔ:(r)/ n decoração f

decorat|e /'dekəreɪt/ vt decorar, enfeitar; (paint) pintar; (paper) pôr papel em. **~ion** /-'reɪʃn/ n decoração f; (medal etc) condecoração f. **~ive** /-ətɪv/ a decorativo

decorum /dɪ'kɔ:rəm/ n decoro m

decoy[1] /'di:kɔɪ/ n chamariz m, engodo m; (trap) armadilha f

decoy² /dɪˈkɔɪ/ vt atrair; apanhar

decrease¹ /diːˈkriːs/ vt/i diminuir

decrease² /diːˈkriːs/ n diminuição f

decree /dɪˈkriː/ n decreto m; (jur) decisão f judicial □ vt decretar

decrepit /dɪˈkrepɪt/ a decrépito

dedicat|e /ˈdedɪkeɪt/ vt dedicar. ~ed a dedicado. ~ion /-ˈkeɪʃn/ n dedicação f; (in book) dedicatória f

deduce /dɪˈdjuːs/ vt deduzir

deduct /dɪˈdʌkt/ vt deduzir; (from pay) descontar

deduction /dɪˈdʌkʃn/ n dedução f; (from pay) desconto m

deed /diːd/ n ato m; (jur) contrato m

deem /diːm/ vt julgar, considerar

deep /diːp/ a (-er, -est) profundo □ adv profundamente. ~-freeze n congelador m □ vt congelar. **take a ~ breath** respirar fundo. ~ly adv profundamente

deepen /ˈdiːpən/ vt/i aprofundar(-se); (mystery, night) adensar-se

deer /dɪə(r)/ n (pl invar) veado m

deface /dɪˈfeɪs/ vt danificar, degradar

defamation /defəˈmeɪʃn/ n difamação f

default /dɪˈfɔːlt/ vi faltar □ n **by** ~ à revelia. **win by** ~ (sport) ganhar por não comparecimento, (P) comparência □ a (comput) default m

defeat /dɪˈfiːt/ vt derrotar; (thwart) malograr □ n derrota f; (of plan, etc) malogro m

defect¹ /ˈdiːfekt/ n defeito m. ~ive /dɪˈfektɪv/ a defeituoso

defect² /dɪˈfekt/ vi desertar. ~ion n defecção m. ~or n trânsfuga mf, dissidente mf; (political) asilado m político

defence /dɪˈfens/ n defesa f. ~less a indefeso

defend /dɪˈfend/ vt defender. ~ant n (jur) réu m, acusado m. ~er n advogado m de defesa, defensor m

defensive /dɪˈfensɪv/ a defensivo □ n **on the** ~ na defensiva f; (person, sport) na retranca f (colloq)

defer /dɪˈfɜː(r)/ vt (pt deferred) adiar, diferir □ vi ~ **to** ceder, deferir

deferen|ce /ˈdefərəns/ n deferência f. ~tial /-ˈrenʃl/ a deferente

defian|t /dɪˈfaɪənt/ n desafio m. **in** ~ **of** sem respeito por. ~t a de desafio. ~tly adv com ar de desafio

deficien|t /dɪˈfɪʃnt/ a deficiente. **be** ~t **in** ter falta de. ~cy n deficiência f

deficit /ˈdefɪsɪt/ n déficit m

define /dɪˈfaɪn/ vt definir

definite /ˈdefɪnɪt/ a definido; (clear) categórico, claro; (certain) certo. ~ly adv decididamente; (clearly) claramente

definition /defɪˈnɪʃn/ n definição f

definitive /dɪˈfɪnətɪv/ a definitivo

deflat|e /dɪˈfleɪt/ vt esvaziar; (person) desemproar, desinchar. ~ion /-ʃn/ n esvaziamento m; (econ) deflação f

deflect /dɪˈflekt/ vt/i desviar(-se)

deform /dɪˈfɔːm/ vt deformar. ~ed a deformado, disforme. ~ity n deformidade f

defraud /dɪˈfrɔːd/ vt defraudar

defrost /diːˈfrɒst/ vt descongelar

deft /deft/ a (-er, -est) hábil

defunct /dɪˈfʌŋkt/ a (law etc) caduco, extinto

defuse /diːˈfjuːz/ vt (a bomb) desativar, (P) desactivar; (a situation) acalmar

defy /dɪˈfaɪ/ vt desafiar; (attempts) resistir a; (the law) desobedecer a; (public opinion) opor-se a

degenerate¹ /dɪˈdʒenəreɪt/ vi degenerar (**into** em)

degrad|e /dɪˈɡreɪd/ vt degradar. ~ation /degrəˈdeɪʃn/ n degradação f

degree /dɪˈɡriː/ n grau m; (univ) diploma m. **to a** ~ ao mais alto grau, muito

dehydrate /diːˈhaɪdreɪt/ vt/i desidratar(-se)

de-ice /diːˈaɪs/ vt descongelar, degelar; (windscreen) tirar o gelo de

deign /deɪn/ vt ~ **to do** dignar-se (a) fazer

deity /ˈdiːɪtɪ/ n divindade f

dejected /dɪˈdʒektɪd/ a abatido

delay /dɪˈleɪ/ vt atrasar; (postpone) retardar □ vi atrasar-se □ n atraso m, demora f

delegate¹ /ˈdelɪɡət/ n delegado m

delegat|e² /ˈdelɪɡeɪt/ vt delegar. ~ion /-ˈɡeɪʃn/ n delegação f

delet|e /dɪˈliːt/ vt riscar. ~ion /-ʃn/ n rasura f

deliberate¹ /dɪˈlɪbərət/ a deliberado; (steps etc) compassado. ~ly adv deliberadamente, de propósito

deliberat|e² /dɪˈlɪbəreɪt/ vt/i deliberar. ~ion /-ˈreɪʃn/ n deliberação f

delica|te /ˈdelɪkət/ a delicado. ~cy n delicadeza f; (food) guloseima f, iguaria f, (P) acepipe m

delicatessen /delɪkəˈtesn/ n (shop) mercearias fpl finas

delicious /dɪˈlɪʃəs/ a delicioso

delight /dɪˈlaɪt/ n grande prazer m, delícia f; (thing) delícia f, encanto m □ vt deliciar □ vi ~ **in** deliciar-se com. ~ed a deliciado, encantado. ~ful a delicioso, encantador

delinquen|t /dɪˈlɪŋkwənt/ a & n delinquente mf; (P) delinquente mf. ~cy n delinquência f, (P) delinquência f

deliri|ous /dɪˈlɪrɪəs/ a delirante. **be** ~ous delirar. ~um /-əm/ n delírio m

deliver /dɪˈlɪvə(r)/ vt entregar;

(*letters*) distribuir; (*free*) libertar; (*med*) fazer o parto. **~ance** *n* libertação *f*. **~y** *n* entrega *f*; (*letters*) distribuição *f*; (*med*) parto *m*

delu|de /dɪˈluːd/ *vt* enganar. **~ de o.s.** ter ilusões. **~sion** /-ʒn/ *n* ilusão *f*

deluge /ˈdeljuːdʒ/ *n* dilúvio *m* □ *vt* inundar

de luxe /dɪˈlʌks/ *a* de luxo

delve /delv/ *vi* **~ into** pesquisar, rebuscar

demand /dɪˈmaːnd/ *vt* exigir; (*ask to be told*) perguntar □ *n* exigência *f*; (*comm*) procura *f*; (*claim*) reivindicação *f*. **in ~** procurado. **~ing** *a* exigente; (*work*) puxado, custoso

demean /dɪˈmiːn/ *vt* **~ o.s.** rebaixar-se

demeanour /dɪˈmiːnə(r)/ *n* comportamento *m*, conduta *f*

demented /dɪˈmentɪd/ *a* louco, demente. **become ~** enlouquecer

demo /ˈdeməʊ/ *n* (*pl* **-os**) (*colloq*) manifestação *f*, (*P*) manif *f*

democracy /dɪˈmɒkrəsɪ/ *n* democracia *f*

democrat /ˈdeməkræt/ *n* democrata *mf*. **~ic** /-ˈkrætɪk/ *a* democrático

demoli|sh /dɪˈmɒlɪʃ/ *vt* demolir. **~tion** /-ˈlɪʃn/ *n* demolição *f*

demon /ˈdiːmən/ *n* demónio *m*

demonstra|te /ˈdemənstreɪt/ *vt* demonstrar □ *vi* (*pol*) fazer uma manifestação, manifestar-se. **~ion** /-ˈstreɪʃn/ *n* demonstração *f*; (*pol*) manifestação *f*. **~or** *n* (*pol*) manifestante *mf*

demonstrative /dɪˈmɒnstrətɪv/ *a* demonstrativo

demoralize /dɪˈmɒrəlaɪz/ *vt* desmoralizar

demote /dɪˈməʊt/ *vt* fazer baixar de posto, rebaixar

demure /dɪˈmjʊə(r)/ *a* recatado, modesto

den /den/ *n* antro *m*, covil *m*; (*room*) cantinho *m*, recanto *m*

denial /dɪˈnaɪəl/ *n* negação *f*; (*refusal*) recusa *f*; (*statement*) desmentido *m*

denigrate /ˈdenɪgreɪt/ *vt* denegrir

denim /ˈdenɪm/ *n* brim *m*. **~s** (*jeans*) blue-jeans *mpl*

Denmark /ˈdenmaːk/ *n* Dinamarca *f*

denomination /dɪˌnɒmɪˈneɪʃn/ *n* denominação *f*; (*relig*) confissão *f*, seita *f*; (*money*) valor *m*

denote /dɪˈnəʊt/ *vt* denotar

denounce /dɪˈnaʊns/ *vt* denunciar

dens|e /dens/ *a* (**-er, -est**) denso; (*colloq: person*) obtuso. **~ely** *adv* (*packed etc*) muito. **~ity** *n* densidade *f*

dent /dent/ *n* mossa *f*, depressão *f* □ *vt* dentear

dental /ˈdentl/ *a* dentário, dental

dentist /ˈdentɪst/ *n* dentista *mf*. **~ry** *n* odontologia *f*

denture /ˈdentʃə(r)/ *n* dentadura *f* (postiça)

denunciation /dɪˌnʌnsɪˈeɪʃn/ *n* denúncia *f*

deny /dɪˈnaɪ/ *vt* negar; (*rumour*) desmentir; (*disown*) renegar; (*refuse*) recusar

deodorant /diːˈəʊdərənt/ *n* & *a* desodorante (*m*), (*P*) desodorizante (*m*)

depart /dɪˈpaːt/ *vi* partir. **~ from** (*deviate*) afastar-se de, desviar-se de

department /dɪˈpaːtmənt/ *n* departamento *m*; (*in shop, office*) secção *f*, (*P*) secção *f*; (*government*) repartição *f*. **~ store** loja *f* de departamentos, (*P*) grande armazém *m*

departure /dɪˈpaːtʃə(r)/ *n* partida *f*. **a ~ from** (*custom, diet etc*) uma mudança de. **a new ~** uma nova orientação

depend /dɪˈpend/ *vi* **~ on** depender de; (*trust*) contar com. **~able** *a* de confiança. **~ence** *n* dependência *f*. **~ent (on)** *a* dependente (de)

dependant /dɪˈpendənt/ *n* dependente *mf*

depict /dɪˈpɪkt/ *vt* descrever; (*in pictures*) representar

deplete /dɪˈpliːt/ *vt* reduzir; (*use up*) esgotar

deplor|e /dɪˈplɔː(r)/ *vt* deplorar. **~able** *a* deplorável

deport /dɪˈpɔːt/ *vt* deportar. **~ation** /diːpɔːˈteɪʃn/ *n* deportação *f*

depose /dɪˈpəʊz/ *vt* depor

deposit /dɪˈpɒzɪt/ *vt* (*pt* **deposited**) depositar □ *n* depósito *m*. **~ account** conta *f* de depósito a prazo. **~or** *n* depositante *mf*

depot /ˈdepəʊ/ *n* (*mil*) depósito *m*; (*buses*) garagem *f*; (*Amer: station*) rodoviária *f*, estação *f* de trem, (*P*) de comboio

deprav|e /dɪˈpreɪv/ *vt* depravar. **~ity** /-ˈprævətɪ/ *n* depravação *f*

depreciat|e /dɪˈpriːʃɪeɪt/ *vt/i* depreciar(-se). **~ion** /-ˈeɪʃn/ *n* depreciação *f*

depress /dɪˈpres/ *vt* deprimir; (*press down*) carregar em. **~ion** /-ʃn/ *n* depressão *f*

deprivation /ˌdeprɪˈveɪʃn/ *n* privação *f*

deprive /dɪˈpraɪv/ *vt* **~ of** privar de. **~d** *a* privado; (*underprivileged*) deserdado (da sorte), destituído; (*child*) carente

depth /depθ/ *n* profundidade *f*. **be out of one's ~** perder pé, (*P*) não ter pé; (*fig*) ficar desnorteado, estar perdido. **in the ~(s) of** no mais fundo de, nas profundezas de

deputation /depjʊ'teɪʃn/ n delegação f

deputy /'depjʊtɪ/ n (pl -ies) delegado m □ a adjunto. ~ chairman vice-presidente m

derail /dɪ'reɪl/ vt descarrilhar. be ~ed descarrilhar. ~ment n descarrilhamento m

deranged /dɪ'reɪndʒd/ a (mind) transtornado, louco

derelict /'derəlɪkt/ a abandonado

deri|de /dɪ'raɪd/ vt escarnecer de. ~sion /-'rɪʒn/ n escárnio m. ~sive a escarninho. ~sory a escarnio; (offer etc) irrisório

derivative /dɪ'rɪvətɪv/ a derivado; (work) pouco original □ n derivado m

deriv|e /dɪ'raɪv/ vt ~e from tirar de □ vi ~e from derivar de. ~ation /derɪ'veɪʃn/ n derivação f

derogatory /dɪ'rɒgətrɪ/ a pejorativo; (remark) depreciativo

derv /dɜːv/ n gasóleo m

descend /dɪ'send/ vt/i descer, descender. be ~ed from descender de. ~ant n descendente mf

descent /dɪ'sent/ n descida f; (lineage) descendência f, origem f

descri|be /dɪs'kraɪb/ vt descrever. ~ption /-'krɪpʃn/ n descrição f. ~ptive /-'krɪptɪv/ a descritivo

desecrat|e /'desɪkreɪt/ vt profanar. ~ion /-'kreɪʃn/ n profanação f

desert¹ /'dezət/ a & n deserto (m). ~ island ilha f deserta

desert² /dɪ'zɜːt/ vt/i desertar. ~ed a abandonado. ~er n desertor m. ~ion /-ʃn/ n deserção f

deserv|e /dɪ'zɜːv/ vt merecer. ~edly /dɪ'zɜːvɪdlɪ/ adv merecidamente, a justo título. ~ing a (person) merecedor; (action) meritório

design /dɪ'zaɪn/ n desenho m; (artistic) design m; (style of dress) modelo m; (pattern) padrão m, motivo m □ vt desenhar; (devise) conceber. ~er n desenhador m; (of dresses) costureiro m; (of machine) inventor m

designat|e /'dezɪgneɪt/ vt designar. ~ion /-'neɪʃn/ n designação f

desir|e /dɪ'zaɪə(r)/ n desejo m □ vt desejar. ~able a desejável, atraente

desk /desk/ n secretária f; (of pupil) carteira f; (in hotel) recepção f; (in bank) caixa f

desolat|e /'desələt/ a desolado. ~ion /-'leɪʃn/ n desolação f

despair /dɪs'peə(r)/ n desespero m □ vi desesperar (of de)

desperate /'despərət/ a desesperado; (criminal) capaz de tudo. be ~ for ter uma vontade doida de. ~ly adv desesperadamente

desperation /despə'reɪʃn/ n desespero m

despicable /dɪ'spɪkəbl/ a desprezível

despise /dɪ'spaɪz/ vt desprezar

despite /dɪ'spaɪt/ prep apesar de, a despeito de, mau grado

despondent /dɪ'spɒndənt/ a desanimado. ~cy n desânimo m

despot /'despɒt/ n déspota mf

dessert /dɪ'zɜːt/ n sobremesa f. ~spoon n colher f de sobremesa

destination /destɪ'neɪʃn/ n destino m, destinação f

destine /'destɪn/ vt destinar

destiny /'destɪnɪ/ n destino m

destitute /'destɪtjuːt/ a destituido, indigente

destr|oy /dɪ'strɔɪ/ vt destruir. ~uction /-'strʌkʃn/ n destruição f. ~uctive a destrutivo, destruidor

detach /dɪ'tætʃ/ vt separar, arrancar. ~able a separável; (lining etc) solto. ~ed a separado; (impartial) imparcial; (unemotional) desprendido. ~ed house casa f sem parede-meia com outra

detachment /dɪ'tætʃmənt/ n separação f; (indifference) desprendimento m; (mil) destacamento m; (impartiality) imparcialidade f

detail /'diːteɪl/ n pormenor m, detalhe m □ vt detalhar; (troops) destacar. ~ed a detalhado

detain /dɪ'teɪn/ vt reter; (in prison) deter. ~ee /diːteɪ'niː/ n detido m

detect /dɪ'tekt/ vt detectar. ~ion /-ʃn/ n detecção f. ~or n detector m

detective /dɪ'tektɪv/ n detective m. ~ story romance m policial

detention /dɪ'tenʃn/ n detenção f. be given a ~ (school) ficar de castigo na escola

deter /dɪ'tɜː(r)/ vt (pt deterred) dissuadir; (hinder) impedir

detergent /dɪ'tɜːdʒənt/ a & n detergente (m)

deteriorat|e /dɪ'tɪərɪəreɪt/ vi deteriorar(-se). ~ion /-'reɪʃn/ n deterioração f

determin|e /dɪ'tɜːmɪn/ vt determinar. ~e to do decidir fazer. ~ation /-'neɪʃn/ n determinação f. ~ed a determinado. ~ed to do decidido a fazer

deterrent /dɪ'terənt/ n dissuasivo m

detest /dɪ'test/ vt detestar. ~able a detestável

detonat|e /'detəneɪt/ vt/i detonar. ~ion /-'neɪʃn/ n detonação f. ~or n espoleta f, detonador m

detour /'diːtʊə(r)/ n desvio m

detract /dɪ'trækt/ vi ~ from depreciar, menosprezar

detriment /'detrɪmənt/ n detrimento m. ~al /-'mentl/ a prejudicial

devalu|e /diːˈvæljuː/ vt desvalorizar. ~**ation** /-ˈeɪʃn/ n desvalorização f

devastat|e /ˈdevəsteɪt/ vi devastar; (fig: overwhelm) arrasar. ~**ing** a devastador; (criticism) de arrasar

develop /dɪˈveləp/ vt/i (pt developed) desenvolver(-se); (get) contrair; (build on) urbanizar; (film) revelar. ~ **into** tornar-se. ~**ing country** país m subdesenvolvido. ~**ment** n desenvolvimento m; (film) revelação f; (of land) urbanização f

deviat|e /ˈdiːvɪeɪt/ vi desviar-se. ~**ion** /-ˈeɪʃn/ n desvio m

device /dɪˈvaɪs/ n dispositivo m; (scheme) processo m. left to one's own ~s entregue a si mesmo

devil /ˈdevl/ n diabo m

devious /ˈdiːvɪəs/ a tortuoso; (fig: means) escuso; (fig: person) pouco franco

devise /dɪˈvaɪz/ vt imaginar, inventar

devoid /dɪˈvɔɪd/ a ~ **of** desprovido de, destituído de

devot|e /dɪˈvəʊt/ vt dedicar, devotar. ~**ed** a dedicado, devotado. ~**ion** /-ʃn/ n devoção f

devotee /devəˈtiː/ n ~ **of** adepto m de, entusiasta mf de

devour /dɪˈvaʊə(r)/ vt devorar

devout /dɪˈvaʊt/ a devota; (prayer) fervoroso

dew /djuː/ n orvalho m

dexter|ity /dekˈsterəti/ n destreza f, jeito m. ~**ous** /ˈdekstrəs/ a destro, hábil

diabet|es /daɪəˈbiːtiːz/ n diabetes f. ~**ic** /-ˈbetɪk/ a & n diabético (m)

diabolical /daɪəˈbɒlɪkl/ a diabólico

diagnose /ˈdaɪəɡnəʊz/ vt diagnosticar

diagnosis /daɪəɡˈnəʊsɪs/ n (pl -oses /-siːz/) diagnóstico m

diagonal /daɪˈæɡənl/ a & n diagonal (f)

diagram /ˈdaɪəɡræm/ n diagrama m, esquema m

dial /ˈdaɪəl/ n mostrador m □ vt (pt dialled) (number) marcar, discar. ~**ling code** código m de discagem. ~**ling tone** sinal m de discar

dialect /ˈdaɪəlekt/ n dialeto m, (P) dialecto m

dialogue /ˈdaɪəlɒɡ/ n diálogo m

diameter /daɪˈæmɪtə(r)/ n diâmetro m

diamond /ˈdaɪəmənd/ n diamante m, brilhante m; (shape) losango m. ~**s** (cards) ouros mpl

diaper /ˈdaɪəpə(r)/ n (Amer) fralda f

diaphragm /ˈdaɪəfræm/ n diafragma m

diarrhoea /daɪəˈrɪə/ n diarréia f, (P) diarreia f

diary /ˈdaɪərɪ/ n agenda f; (record) diário m

dice /daɪs/ n (pl invar) dado m

dictat|e /dɪkˈteɪt/ vt/i ditar. ~**ion** /-ʃn/ n ditado m

dictator /dɪkˈteɪtə(r)/ n ditador m. ~**ship** n ditadura f

diction /ˈdɪkʃn/ n dicção f

dictionary /ˈdɪkʃənrɪ/ n dicionário m

did /dɪd/ see **do**

diddle /ˈdɪdl/ vt (colloq) trapacear, enganar

didn't /ˈdɪdnt/ = **did not**

die /daɪ/ vi (pres p dying) morrer. be dying to estar doido para. ~ **down** diminuir, baixar. ~ **out** desaparecer, extinguir-se

diesel /ˈdiːzl/ n diesel m. ~ **engine** motor m diesel

diet /ˈdaɪət/ n dieta f □ vi fazer dieta, estar de dieta

differ /ˈdɪfə(r)/ vi diferir; (disagree) discordar

differen|t /ˈdɪfrənt/ a diferente. ~**ce** n diferença f; (disagreement) desacordo m. ~**ly** adv diferentemente

differentiate /dɪfəˈrenʃɪeɪt/ vt/i diferençar(-se), diferenciar(-se)

difficult /ˈdɪfɪkəlt/ a difícil. ~**y** n dificuldade f

diffiden|t /ˈdɪfɪdənt/ a acanhado, inseguro. ~**ce** n acanhamento m, insegurança f

diffuse[1] /dɪˈfjuːs/ a difuso

diffus|e[2] /dɪˈfjuːz/ vt difundir. ~**ion** /-ʒn/ n difusão f

dig /dɪɡ/ vt/i (pt dug, pres p digging) cavar; (thrust) espetar □ n (with elbow) cotovelada f; (with finger) cutucada f, (P) espetadela f; (remark) ferroada f; (archaeol) escavação f. ~**s** (colloq) quarto m alugado. ~ **up** desenterrar

digest /dɪˈdʒest/ vt/i digerir. ~**ible** a digerível, digestível. ~**ion** /-ʃn/ n digestão f

digestive /dɪˈdʒestɪv/ a digestivo

digit /ˈdɪdʒɪt/ n dígito m

digital /ˈdɪdʒɪtl/ a digital. ~ **clock** relógio m digital

dignif|y /ˈdɪɡnɪfaɪ/ vt dignificar. ~**ied** a digno

dignitary /ˈdɪɡnɪtərɪ/ n dignitário m

dignity /ˈdɪɡnətɪ/ n dignidade f

digress /daɪˈɡres/ vi digressar, divagar. ~ **from** desviar-se de. ~**ion** /-ʃn/ n digressão f

dike /daɪk/ n dique m

dilapidated /dɪˈlæpɪdeɪtɪd/ a (house) arruinado, degradado; (car) estragado

dilat|e /daɪˈleɪt/ vt/i dilatar(-se). ~**ion** /-ʃn/ n dilatação f

dilemma /dɪˈlemə/ n dilema m

diligen|t /ˈdɪlɪdʒənt/ a diligente, aplicado. ~**ce** n diligência f, aplicação f dilute /dar'lju:t/ vt diluir □ a diluído

dim /dɪm/ a (dimmer, dimmest) (weak) fraco; (dark) sombrio; (indistinct) vago; (colloq: stupid) burro (colloq) □ vt/i (pt dimmed) (light) baixar. ~ly adv (shine) fracamente; (remember) vagamente

dime /daɪm/ n (Amer) moeda f de dez centavos

dimension /dar'menʃn/ n dimensão f

diminish /dɪ'mɪnɪʃ/ vt/i diminuir

diminutive /dɪ'mɪnjʊtɪv/ a diminuto □ n diminutivo m

dimple /'dɪmpl/ n covinha f

din /dɪn/ n barulheira f, (P) chinfrim m

dine /daɪn/ vi jantar. ~r /-ə(r)/ n (person) comensal m; (rail) vagão-restaurante m; (Amer: restaurant) lanchonete f

dinghy /'dɪŋgɪ/ n (pl -ghies) bote m; (inflatable) bote m de borracha, (P) barco m de borracha

dingy /'dɪndʒɪ/ a (-ier, -iest) com ar sujo, esquálido

dining-room /'daɪnɪŋru:m/ n sala f de jantar

dinner /'dɪnə(r)/ n jantar m; (lunch) almoço m. ~-jacket n smoking m

dinosaur /'daɪnəsɔ:(r)/ n dinossauro m

dip /dɪp/ vt/i (pt dipped) mergulhar; (lower) baixar □ n mergulho m; (bathe) banho m rápido, mergulho m; (slope) descida f; (culin) molho m. ~ into (book) folhear. ~ one's headlights baixar para médios

diphtheria /dɪf'θɪərɪə/ n difteria f

diphthong /'dɪfθɒŋ/ n ditongo m

diploma /dɪ'pləʊmə/ n diploma m

diplomacy /dɪ'pləʊməsɪ/ n diplomacia f

diplomat /'dɪpləmæt/ n diplomata mf. ~ic /-'mætɪk/ a diplomático

dire /daɪə(r)/ a (-er, -est) terrível; (need, poverty) extremo

direct /dɪ'rekt/ a direto, (P) directo □ adv diretamente, (P) directamente □ vt dirigir. ~ sb to indicar a alg o caminho para

direction /dɪ'rekʃn/ n direção f, (P) direcção f, sentido m. ~s instruções fpl. ~s for use modo m de emprego

directly /dɪ'rektlɪ/ adv diretamente, (P) directamente; (at once) imediatamente, logo

director /dɪ'rektə(r)/ n diretor m, (P) director m

directory /dɪ'rektərɪ/ n (telephone) ~ lista f telefónica, (P) telefónica

dirt /dɜ:t/ n sujeira f. ~ cheap (colloq) baratíssimo

dirty /'dɜ:tɪ/ a (-ier, -iest) sujo; (word) obsceno □ vt/i sujar(-se). ~ trick golpe m baixo, (P) boa partida f

disability /dɪsə'bɪlətɪ/ n deficiência f

disable /dɪs'eɪbl/ vt incapacitar. ~d a inválido, deficiente

disadvantage /dɪsəd'vɑ:ntɪdʒ/ n desvantagem f

disagree /dɪsə'gri:/ vi discordar (with de). ~ with (food, climate) não fazer bem. ~ment n desacordo m; (quarrel) desintendimento m

disagreeable /dɪsə'gri:əbl/ a desagradável

disappear /dɪsə'pɪə(r)/ vi desaparecer. ~ance n desaparecimento m

disappoint /dɪsə'pɔɪnt/ vt desapontar, decepcionar. ~ment n desapontamento m, decepção f

disapprov|e /dɪsə'pru:v/ vi ~e (of) desaprovar. ~al n desaprovação f

disarm /dɪs'ɑ:m/ vt/i desarmar. ~ament n desarmamento m

disast|er /dɪ'zɑ:stə(r)/ n desastre m. ~rous a desastroso

disband /dɪs'bænd/ vt/i debandar; (troops) dispersar

disbelief /dɪsbɪ'li:f/ n incredulidade f

disc /dɪsk/ n disco m. ~ jockey disc(o) jockey m

discard /dɪs'kɑ:d/ vt pôr de lado, descartar(-se) de; (old clothes etc) desfazer-se de

discern /dɪ'sɜ:n/ vt discernir. ~ible a perceptível. ~ing a perspicaz. ~ment n discernimento m, perspicácia f

discharge[1] /dɪs'tʃɑ:dʒ/ vt descarregar; (dismiss) despedir, mandar embora; (duty) cumprir; (liquid) vazar, (P) deitar; (patient) dar alta a; (prisoner) absolver, pôr em liberdade; (pus) purgar, (P) deitar

discharge[2] /'dɪstʃɑ:dʒ/ n descarga f; (dismissal) despedimento m; (of patient) alta f; (of prisoner) absolvição f; (med) secreção f

disciple /dɪ'saɪpl/ n discípulo m

disciplin|e /'dɪsɪplɪn/ n disciplina f □ vt disciplinar; (punish) castigar. ~ary a disciplinar

disclaim /dɪs'kleɪm/ vt (jur) repudiar; (deny) negar. ~er n desmentido m

disclos|e /dɪs'kləʊz/ vt revelar. ~ure /-ʒə(r)/ n revelação f

disco /'dɪskəʊ/ n (pl -os) (colloq) discoteca f

discolour /dɪs'kʌlə(r)/ vt/i descolorir(-se); (in sunlight) desbotar(-se)

discomfort /dɪs'kʌmfət/ n malestar m; (lack of comfort) desconforto m

disconcert /dɪskən'sɜ:t/ vt desconcertar. ~ing a desconcertante

disconnect /dɪskə'nekt/ vt desligar

discontent /dɪskən'tent/ n descontentamento m. ~ed a descontente

discontinue /dɪskən'tɪnjuː/ vt descontinuar, suspender

discord /'dɪskɔːd/ n discórdia f. ~ant /-'skɔːdənt/ a discordante

discothèque /'dɪskətek/ n discoteca f

discount¹ /'dɪskaʊnt/ n desconto m

discount² /dɪs'kaʊnt/ vt descontar; (disregard) dar o desconto a

discourage /dɪs'kʌrɪdʒ/ vt desencorajar

discourte|ous /dɪs'kɜːtɪəs/ a indelicado. ~sy /-sɪ/ n indelicadeza f

discover /dɪs'kʌvə(r)/ vt descobrir. ~y n descoberta f; (of island etc) descobrimento m

discredit /dɪs'kredɪt/ vt (pt discredited) desacreditar □ n descrédito m

discreet /dɪs'kriːt/ a discreto

discrepancy /dɪ'skrepənsɪ/ n discrepância f

discretion /dɪ'skreʃn/ n discrição f; (prudence) prudência f

discriminat|e /dɪs'krɪmɪneɪt/ vt/i discriminar. ~e against tomar partido contra, fazer discriminação contra. ~ing a discriminador; (having good taste) com discernimento. ~ion /-'neɪʃn/ n discernimento m; (bias) discriminação f

discus /'dɪskəs/ n disco m

discuss /dɪ'skʌs/ vt discutir. ~ion /-ʃn/ n discussão f

disdain /dɪs'deɪn/ n desdém m □ vt desdenhar. ~ful a desdenhoso

disease /dɪ'ziːz/ n doença f. ~d a (plant) atacado por doença; (person, animal) doente

disembark /dɪsɪm'bɑːk/ vt/i desembarcar

disembodied /dɪsɪm'bɒdɪd/ a desencarnado

disenchant /dɪsɪn'tʃɑːnt/ vt desencantar. ~ment n desencantamento m

disengage /dɪsɪn'geɪdʒ/ vt desprender, soltar; (mech) desengatar

disentangle /dɪsɪn'tæŋgl/ vt desembaraçar, desenredar

disfavour /dɪs'feɪvə(r)/ n desfavor m, desgraça f

disfigure /dɪs'fɪgə(r)/ vt desfigurar

disgrace /dɪs'greɪs/ n vergonha f; (disfavour) desgraça f □ vt desonrar. ~ful a vergonhoso

disgruntled /dɪs'grʌntld/ a descontente

disguise /dɪs'gaɪz/ vt disfarçar □ n disfarce m. in ~ disfarçado

disgust /dɪs'gʌst/ n repugnância f □ vt repugnar. ~ing a repugnante

dish /dɪʃ/ n prato m □ vt ~ out (colloq) distribuir. ~ up servir. the ~es (crockery) a louça f

dishcloth /'dɪʃklɒθ/ n pano m de prato

dishearten /dɪs'hɑːtn/ vt desencorajar, desalentar

dishevelled /dɪ'ʃevld/ a desgrenhado

dishonest /dɪs'ɒnɪst/ a desonesto. ~y n desonestidade f

dishonour /dɪs'ɒnə(r)/ n desonra f □ vt desonrar. ~able a desonroso

dishwasher /'dɪʃwɒʃə(r)/ n lavadora f de pratos, (P) máquina f de lavar a louça

disillusion /dɪsɪ'luːʒn/ vt desiludir. ~ment n desilusão f

disinfect /dɪsɪn'fekt/ vt desinfetar, (P) desinfectar. ~ant n desinfetante m, (P) desinfectante m

disinherit /dɪsɪn'herɪt/ vt deserdar

disintegrate /dɪs'ɪntɪgreɪt/ vt/i desintegrar(-se)

disinterested /dɪs'ɪntrəstɪd/ a desinteressado

disjointed /dɪs'dʒɔɪntɪd/ a (talk) descosido, desconexo

disk /dɪsk/ n (comput) disco m; (Amer) = disc. ~ drive unidade f de disco

dislike /dɪs'laɪk/ n aversão f, antipatia f □ vt não gostar de, antipatizar com

dislocat|e /'dɪsləkeɪt/ vt (limb) deslocar. ~ion /-'keɪʃn/ n deslocação f

dislodge /dɪs'lɒdʒ/ vt desalojar

disloyal /dɪs'lɔɪəl/ a desleal. ~ty n deslealdade f

dismal /'dɪzməl/ a tristonho

dismantle /dɪs'mæntl/ vt desmantelar

dismay /dɪs'meɪ/ n consternação f □ vt consternar

dismiss /dɪs'mɪs/ vt despedir; (from mind) afastar, pôr de lado. ~al n despedimento m

dismount /dɪs'maʊnt/ vi desmontar

disobedien|t /dɪsə'biːdɪənt/ a desobediente. ~ce n desobediência f

disobey /dɪsə'beɪ/ vt/i desobedecer (a)

disorder /dɪs'ɔːdə(r)/ n desordem f; (med) perturbações fpl, disfunção f. ~ly a desordenado; (riotous) desordeiro

disorganize /dɪs'ɔːgənaɪz/ vt desorganizar

disorientate /dɪs'ɔːrɪəntet/ vt desorientar

disown /dɪs'əʊn/ vt repudiar

disparaging /dɪ'spærɪdʒɪŋ/ a depreciativo

disparity /dɪ'spærətɪ/ n disparidade f

dispatch /dɪ'spætʃ/ vt despachar □ n despacho m

dispel /dɪ'spel/ vt (pt dispelled) dissipar

dispensary /dɪ'spensərɪ/ n dispensário m, farmácia f

dispense /dɪ'spens/ vt dispensar □ vi

~ with dispensar, passar sem. ~r
/-ə(r)/ n (container) distribuidor m

disperse /dɪ'spɜ:s/ vt/i dispersar
(-se). ~al n dispersão f

dispirited /dɪ'spɪrɪtɪd/ a desanimado

displace /dɪs'pleɪs/ vt deslocar; (take
the place of) substituir. ~d person
deslocado m de guerra

display /dɪ'spleɪ/ vt exibir, mostrar;
(feeling) manifestar, dar mostras de
□ n exposição f; (of computer)
apresentação f visual; (comm) objetos
mpl expostos

displeas|e /dɪs'pli:z/ vt desagradar a.
~ed with descontente com. ~ure
/'pleʒə(r)/ n desagrado m

disposable /dɪ'spəʊzəbl/ a descartável

dispos|e /dɪ'spəʊz/ vt dispor □ vi ~
of desfazer-se de. well ~ed towards
bem disposto para com. ~al n (of
waste) eliminação f. at sb's ~al à
disposição de alg

disposition /dɪspə'zɪʃn/ n disposição
f; (character) índole f

disproportionate /dɪsprə'pɔ:ʃənət/ a
desproporcionado

disprove /dɪs'pru:v/ vt refutar

dispute /dɪ'spju:t/ vt contestar; (fight
for, quarrel) disputar □ n disputa f;
(industrial, pol) conflito m. in ~ em
questão

disqualif|y /dɪs'kwɒlɪfaɪ/ vt tornar
inapto; (sport) desqualificar. ~y from
driving apreender a carteira de
motorista. ~ication /-ɪ'keɪʃn/ n
desqualificação f

disregard /dɪsrɪ'gɑ:d/ vt não fazer
caso de □ n indiferença f (for por)

disrepair /dɪsrɪ'peə(r)/ n mau estado
m, abandono m, degradação f

disreputable /dɪs'repjʊtəbl/ a pouco
recomendável; (in appearance) com
mau aspecto; (in reputation) vergonhoso, de má fama

disrepute /dɪsrɪ'pju:t/ n descrédito m

disrespect /dɪsrɪ'spekt/ n falta f de
respeito. ~ful a desrespeitoso, irreverente

disrupt /dɪs'rʌpt/ vt perturbar;
(plans) transtornar; (break up)
dividir. ~ion /-ʃn/ n perturbação f.
~ive a perturbador

dissatisf|ied /dɪ'sætɪsfaɪd/ a descon-
tente. ~action /dɪsætɪs'fækʃn/ n descontentamento m

dissect /dɪ'sekt/ vt dissecar. ~ion
/-ʃn/ n dissecação f

dissent /dɪ'sent/ vi dissentir, discordar □ n dissensão f, desacordo m

dissertation /dɪsə'teɪʃn/ n dissertação f

disservice /dɪs'sɜ:vɪs/ n do sb a ~
prejudicar alg

dissident /'dɪsɪdənt/ a & n dissidente
(mf)

dissimilar /dɪ'sɪmɪlə(r)/ a diferente

dissipate /'dɪsɪpeɪt/ vt dissipar;
(efforts, time) desperdiçar. ~d a dissoluto

dissociate /dɪ'səʊʃɪeɪt/ vt dissociar,
desassociar

dissolution /dɪsə'lu:ʃn/ n dissolução
f

dissolve /dɪ'zɒlv/ vt/i dissolver(-se)

dissuade /dɪ'sweɪd/ vt dissuadir

distance /'dɪstəns/ n distância f. from
a ~ de longe. in the ~ ao longe, à
distância

distant /'dɪstənt/ a distante; (relative)
afastado

distaste /dɪs'teɪst/ n aversão f. ~ful a
desagradável

distemper /dɪ'stempə(r)/ n pintura f
a têmpera; (animal disease) cinomose
f □ vt pintar a têmpera

distend /dɪ'stend/ vt/i distender(-se)

distil /dɪ'stɪl/ vt (pt distilled) destilar.
~lation /-'leɪʃn/ n destilação f

distillery /dɪ'stɪlərɪ/ n destilaria f

distinct /dɪ'stɪŋkt/ a distinto;
(marked) claro, nítido. ~ion /-ʃn/ n
distinção f. ~ive a distintivo, característico. ~ly adv distintamente;
(markedly) claramente

distinguish /dɪ'stɪŋgwɪʃ/ vt/i distinguir. ~ed a distinto

distort /dɪ'stɔ:t/ vt distorcer; (misrepresent) deturpar. ~ion /-ʃn/ n
distorção f; (misrepresentation) de-
turpação f

distract /dɪ'strækt/ vt distrair. ~ed a
(distraught) desesperado, fora de si.
~ing a enlouquecedor. ~ion /-ʃn/ n
distração f, (P) distracção f

distraught /dɪ'strɔ:t/ a desesperado,
fora de si

distress /dɪ'stres/ n (physical) dor f;
(anguish) aflição f; (poverty) miséria
f; (danger) perigo m □ vt afligir. ~ing
a aflitivo, doloroso

distribut|e /dɪ'strɪbju:t/ vt distribuir.
~ion /-'bju:ʃn/ n distribuição f. ~or
n distribuidor m

district /'dɪstrɪkt/ n região f; (of town)
zona f

distrust /dɪs'trʌst/ n desconfiança f □
vt desconfiar de

disturb /dɪ'stɜ:b/ vt perturbar; (move)
desarrumar; (bother) incomodar.
~ance n (noise, disorder) distúrbio
m. ~ed a perturbado. ~ing a perturbador

disused /dɪs'ju:zd/ a fora de uso, de-
susado, em desuso

ditch /dɪtʃ/ n fosso m □ vt (sl: abandon) abandonar, largar

dither /'dɪðə(r)/ vi hesitar

ditto /'dɪtəʊ/ *adv* idem

div|e /daɪv/ *vi* mergulhar; (*rush*) precipitar-se □ *n* mergulho *m*; (*of plane*) picada *f*; (*sl: place*) espelunca *f*. ~**er** *n* mergulhador *m*. ~**ing-board** *n* prancha *f* de saltos. ~**ing-suit** *n* escafandro *m*

diverge /daɪ'vɜːdʒ/ *vi* divergir

divergent /daɪ'vɜːdʒənt/ *a* divergente

diverse /daɪ'vɜːs/ *a* diverso

diversify /daɪ'vɜːsɪfaɪ/ *vt* diversificar

diversity /daɪ'vɜːsətɪ/ *n* diversidade *f*

diver|t /daɪ'vɜːt/ *vt* desviar; (*entertain*) divertir. ~**sion** /-ʃn/ *n* diversão *f*; (*traffic*) desvio *m*

divide /dɪ'vaɪd/ *vt/i* dividir(-se). ~ **in two** (*branch, river, road*) bifurcar-se

dividend /'dɪvɪdend/ *n* dividendo *m*

divine /dɪ'vaɪn/ *a* divino

divinity /dɪ'vɪnətɪ/ *n* divindade *f*; (*theology*) teologia *f*

division /dɪ'vɪʒn/ *n* divisão *f*

divorce /dɪ'vɔːs/ *n* divórcio *m* □ *vt/i* divorciar(-se) de. ~**d** *a* divorciado

divorcee /dɪvɔː'siː/ *n* divorciado *m*

divulge /daɪ'vʌldʒ/ *vt* divulgar

DIY *abbr see* **do-it-yourself**

dizz|y /'dɪzɪ/ *a* (-ier, -iest) tonto. be *or* feel ~**y** ter tonturas, sentir-se tonto. ~**iness** *n* tontura *f*, vertigem *f*

do /duː/ *vt/i* (3 *sing pres* **does**, *pt* **did**, *pp* **done**) fazer; (*be suitable*) servir; (*be enough*) bastar (a); (*sl: swindle*) enganar, levar (*colloq*). **how ~ you ~?** como vai? **well done** muito bem!, (*P*) bravo!; (*culin*) bem passado. **done for** (*colloq*) liquidado (*colloq*), (*P*) animado (*colloq*) □ *v aux* ~ **you see?** vê?; **I ~ not smoke** não fumo. **don't you?, doesn't he?** *etc* não é? □ *n* (*pl* **dos** *or* **do's**) festa *f*. ~**-it-yourself** *a* faça-você-mesmo. ~ **away with** eliminar, suprimir. ~ **in** (*sl*) matar, liquidar (*colloq*). ~ **out** limpar. ~ **up** (*fasten*) fechar; (*house*) renovar. **I could ~ with a cup of tea** apetecia-me uma xícara de chá. **it could ~ with a wash** precisa de uma lavagem

docile /'dəʊsaɪl/ *a* dócil

dock[1] /dɒk/ *n* doca *f* □ *vt* levar à doca □ *vi* entrar na doca. ~**er** *n* estivador *m*

dock[2] /dɒk/ *n* (*jur*) banco *m* dos réus

dockyard /'dɒkjɑːd/ *n* estaleiro *m*

doctor /'dɒktə(r)/ *n* médico *m*, doutor *m*; (*univ*) doutor *m* □ *vt* (*cat*) capar; (*fig*) adulterar, falsificar

doctorate /'dɒktərət/ *n* doutorado *m*, (*P*) doutoramento *m*

doctrine /'dɒktrɪn/ *n* doutrina *f*

document /'dɒkjʊmənt/ *n* documento *m* □ *vt* documentar. ~**ary** /-'mentrɪ/ *a* documental □ *n* documentário *m*

dodge /dɒdʒ/ *vt/i* esquivar(-se), furtar(-se) a □ *n* (*colloq*) truque *m*

dodgy /'dɒdʒɪ/ *a* (-ier, -iest) (*colloq*) delicado, difícil, embaraçoso

does /dʌz/ *see* **do**

doesn't /'dʌznt/ = **does not**

dog /dɒɡ/ *n* cão *m* □ *vt* (*pt* **dogged**) ir no encalço de, perseguir. ~**-eared** *a* com os cantos dobrados

dogged /'dɒɡɪd/ *a* obstinado, persistente

dogma /'dɒɡmə/ *n* dogma *m*. ~**tic** /-'mætɪk/ *a* dogmático

dogsbody /'dɒɡzbɒdɪ/ *n* (*colloq*) pau-para-toda-obra *m* (*colloq*), factótum *m*

doldrums /'dɒldrəmz/ *npl* **be in the ~** estar com a neura; (*business*) estar parado

dole /dəʊl/ *vt* ~ **out** distribuir □ *n* (*colloq*) auxílio *m* desemprego. **on the ~** (*colloq*) desempregado (titular de auxílio)

doleful /'dəʊlfl/ *a* tristonho, melancólico

doll /dɒl/ *n* boneca *f* □ *vt/i* ~ **up** (*colloq*) embonecar(-se)

dollar /'dɒlə(r)/ *n* dólar *m*

dolphin /'dɒlfɪn/ *n* golfinho *m*

domain /dəʊ'meɪn/ *n* domínio *m*

dome /dəʊm/ *n* cúpula *f*; (*vault*) abóbada *f*

domestic /də'mestɪk/ *a* (*of home, animal, flights*) doméstico; (*trade*) interno; (*news*) nacional. ~**ated** /-keɪtɪd/ *a* (*animal*) domesticado; (*person*) que gosta de trabalhos caseiros

dominant /'dɒmɪnənt/ *a* dominante

dominat|e /'dɒmɪneɪt/ *vt/i* dominar. ~**ion** /-'neɪʃn/ *n* dominação *f*, domínio *m*

domineer /dɒmɪ'nɪə(r)/ *vi* ~ **over** mandar (em), ser autocrático (para com). ~**ing** *a* mandão, autocrático

dominion /də'mɪnjən/ *n* domínio *m*

domino /'dɒmɪnəʊ/ *n* (*pl* -**oes**) dominó *m*

donat|e /dəʊ'neɪt/ *vt* fazer doação de, doar, dar. ~**ion** /-ʃn/ *n* donativo *m*

done /dʌn/ *see* **do**

donkey /'dɒŋkɪ/ *n* burro *m*

donor /'dəʊnə(r)/ *n* (*of blood*) doador *m*, (*P*) dador *m*

don't /dəʊnt/ = **do not**

doodle /'duːdl/ *vi* rabiscar

doom /duːm/ *n* ruína *f*; (*fate*) destino *m*. **be ~ed to** ser/estar condenado a. ~**ed (to failure)** condenado ao fracasso

door /dɔː(r)/ *n* porta *f*

doorman /'dɔːmən/ *n* (*pl* -**men**) porteiro *m*

doormat /'dɔːmæt/ *n* capacho *m*

doorstep /'dɔːstep/ *n* degrau *m* da porta

doorway /ˈdɔːweɪ/ n vão m da porta, (P) entrada f

dope /dəʊp/ n (colloq) droga f; (sl: idiot) imbecil mf □ vt dopar, drogar

dormant /ˈdɔːmənt/ a dormente; (inactive) inativo, (P) inactivo; (latent) latente

dormitory /ˈdɔːmɪtrɪ/ n dormitório m; (Amer univ) residência f

dormouse /ˈdɔːmaʊs/ n (pl -mice) arganaz m

dos|e /dəʊs/ n dose f □ vt medicar. ~age n dosagem f; (on label) posologia f

doss /dɒs/ vi ~ (down) dormir sem conforto. ~-house n pensão f miserável, asilo m noturno, (P) nocturno. ~er n vagabundo m

dot /dɒt/ n ponto m. on the ~ no momento preciso □ vt be ~ted with estar semeado de. ~ted line linha f pontilhada

dote /dəʊt/ vi ~ on ser louco por, adorar

double /ˈdʌbl/ a duplo; (room, bed) de casal □ adv duas vezes mais □ n dobro m. ~s (tennis) dupla f, (P) pares mpl □ vt/i dobrar, duplicar; (fold) dobrar em dois. at the ~ a passo acelerado. ~-bass n contrabaixo m. ~ chin papada f. ~-cross vt enganar. ~-dealing n jogo m duplo. ~-decker n ônibus m, (P) autocarro m de dois andares. ~ Dutch algaraviada f, fala f incompreensível. ~ glazing (janela f de) vidro (m) duplo. **doubly** adv duplamente

doubt /daʊt/ n dúvida f □ vt duvidar de. ~ if or that duvidar que. ~ful a duvidoso; (hesitant) que tem dúvidas. ~less adv sem dúvida, indubitavelmente

dough /dəʊ/ n massa f

doughnut /ˈdəʊnʌt/ n sonho n, (P) bola f de Berlim

dove /dʌv/ n pomba f

dowdy /ˈdaʊdɪ/ a (-ier, -iest) sem graça, sem gosto

down[1] /daʊn/ n (feathers, hair) penugem f

down[2] /daʊn/ adv (to lower place) abaixo, para baixo; (in lower place) em baixo. be ~ (level, price) descer; (sun) estar posto □ prep ~ (+n) (n+) abaixo. ~ the hill/street etc pelo monte/pela rua etc abaixo □ vt (colloq: knock down) jogar abaixo; (colloq: drink) esvaziar. come or go ~ descer. ~-and-out n marginal m. ~-hearted a desencorajado, desanimado. ~-to-earth a terra-a-terra invar. ~ under na Austrália. ~ with abaixo

downcast /ˈdaʊnkaːst/ a abatido, deprimido, desmoralizado

downfall /ˈdaʊnfɔːl/ n queda f, ruína f

downhill /daʊnˈhɪl/ adv go ~ descer; (fig) ir abaixo □ a /ˈdaʊnhɪl/ a descer, descendente

downpour /ˈdaʊnpɔː(r)/ n aguaceiro m forte, (P) chuvada f

downright /ˈdaʊnraɪt/ a franco; (utter) autêntico, verdadeiro □ adv positivamente

downstairs /daʊnˈsteəz/ adv (at/to) em/para baixo, no/para o andar de baixo □ a /ˈdaʊnsteəz/ (flat etc) de baixo, do andar de baixo

downstream /ˈdaʊnstriːm/ adv rio abaixo

downtown /ˈdaʊntaʊn/ a & adv (de, em, para) o centro da cidade. ~ Boston o centro de Boston

downtrodden /ˈdaʊntrɒdn/ a espezinhado, oprimido

downward /ˈdaʊnwəd/ a descendente. ~(s) adv para baixo

dowry /ˈdaʊərɪ/ n dote m

doze /dəʊz/ vi dormitar. ~ off cochilar □ n soneca f, cochilo m

dozen /ˈdʌzn/ n dúzia f. ~s of (colloq) dezenas de, dúzias de

Dr abbr (Doctor) Dr

drab /dræb/ a insípido; (of colour) morto, apagado

draft[1] /draːft/ n rascunho m; (comm) ordem f de pagamento □ vt fazer o rascunho de; (draw up) redigir. the ~ (Amer: mil) recrutamento m

draft[2] /draːft/ n (Amer) = draught

drag /dræg/ vt/i (pt dragged) arrastar(-se); (river) dragar; (pull away) arrancar □ n (colloq: task) chatice f (sl); (colloq: person) estorvo m; (sl: clothes) travesti m

dragon /ˈdrægən/ n dragão m

dragonfly /ˈdrægənflaɪ/ n libélula f

drain /dreɪn/ vt drenar; (vegetables) escorrer; (glass, tank) esvaziar; (use up) esgotar □ vi ~ (off) escoar-se □ n cano m. ~s npl (sewers) esgotos mpl. ~age n drenagem f. ~-(pipe) cano m de esgoto. ~ing-board n escorredouro m

drama /ˈdraːmə/ n arte f dramática; (play, event) drama m. ~tic /drəˈmætɪk/ a dramático. ~tist /ˈdræmətɪst/ n dramaturgo m. ~tize /ˈdræmətaɪz/ vt dramatizar

drank /dræŋk/ see **drink**

drape /dreɪp/ vt ~ round/over dispor (tecido) em pregas à volta de or sobre. ~s npl (Amer) cortinas fpl

drastic /ˈdræstɪk/ a drástico, violento

draught /draːft/ n corrente f de ar; (naut) calado m. ~s (game) (jogo m das) damas fpl. ~ beer chope m, (P) cerveja *f* à caneca, imperial *f* (*colloq*). ~ y a com correntes de ar, ventoso

draughtsman /'drɑːftsmən/ *n* (*pl* -men) desenhista *m*, (*P*) desenhador *m*

draw /drɔː/ *vt* (*pt* drew, *pp* drawn) puxar; (*attract*) atrair; (*picture*) desenhar; (*in lottery*) tirar à sorte; (*line*) traçar; (*open curtains*) abrir; (*close curtains*) fechar □ *vi* desenhar; (*sport*) empatar; (*come*) vir □ *n* (*sport*) empate *m*; (*lottery*) sorteio *m*. ~ back recuar. ~ in (*of days*) diminuir. ~ near aproximar-se. ~ out (*money*) levantar. ~ up deter-se, parar; (*document*) redigir; (*chair*) aproximar, chegar

drawback /'drɔːbæk/ *n* inconveniente *m*, desvantagem *f*

drawer /drɔː(r)/ *n* gaveta *f*

drawing /'drɔːɪŋ/ *n* desenho *m*. ~-board *n* prancheta *f*. ~-pin *n* percevejo *m*

drawl /drɔːl/ *n* fala *f* arrastada

drawn /drɔːn/ *see* draw

dread /dred/ *n* terror *m* □ *vt* temer

dreadful /'dredfl/ *a* medonho, terrível. ~ly *adv* terrivelmente

dream /driːm/ *n* sonho *m* □ *vt/i* (*pt* dreamed *or* dreamt) sonhar (of com) □ *a* (*ideal*) dos seus sonhos. ~ up imaginar. ~er *n* sonhador *m*. ~y *a* sonhador; (*music*) romântico

dreary /'drɪərɪ/ *a* (-ier, -iest) tristonho; (*boring*) aborrecido

dredge /dredʒ/ *n* draga *f* □ *vt/i* dragar. ~r /-ə(r)/ *n* draga *f*; (*for sugar*) polvilhador *m*

dregs /dregz/ *npl* depósito *m*, sedimento *m*; (*fig*) escória *f*

drench /drentʃ/ *vt* encharcar

dress /dres/ *n* vestido *m*; (*clothing*) roupa *f* □ *vt/i* vestir(-se); (*food*) temperar; (*wound*) fazer curativo, (*P*) pensar, (*P*) tratar. ~ rehearsal ensaio *m* geral. ~ up as fantasiar-se de. get ~ed vestir-se

dresser /'dresə(r)/ *n* (*furniture*) guarda-louça *m*

dressing /'dresɪŋ/ *n* (*sauce*) tempero *m*; (*bandage*) curativo *m*, (*P*) penso *m*. ~-gown *n* roupão *m*. ~-room *n* (*sport*) vestiário *m*; (*theat*) camarim *m*. ~-table *n* toucador *m*

dressmak|er /'dresmeɪkə(r)/ *n* costureira *f*, modista *f*. ~ing *n* costura *f*

dressy /'dresɪ/ *a* (-ier, -iest) elegante, chique *invar*

drew /druː/ *see* draw

dribble /'drɪbl/ *vi* pingar; (*person*) babar-se; (*football*) driblar

dried /draɪd/ *a* (*fruit etc*) seco

drier /'draɪə(r)/ *n* secador *m*

drift /drɪft/ *vi* ir à deriva; (*pile up*) amontoar-se □ *n* força *f* da corrente;

(*pile*) monte *m*; (*of events*) rumo *m*; (*meaning*) sentido *m*. ~er *n* pessoa *f* sem rumo

drill /drɪl/ *n* (*tool*) broca *f*; (*training*) exercício *m*, treino *m*; (*routine procedure*) exercícios *mpl* □ *vt* furar, perfurar; (*train*) treinar; (*tooth*) abrir □ *vi* treinar-se

drink /drɪŋk/ *vt/i* (*pt* drank, *pp* drunk) beber □ *n* bebida *f*. a ~ of water um copo de água. ~able *a* potável; (*palatable*) bebível. ~er *n* bebedor *m*. ~ing water água *f* potável

drip /drɪp/ *vi* (*pt* dripped) pingar □ *n* pingar *m*; (*sl: person*) banana *mf* (*colloq*). ~-dry *vt* deixar escorrer □ *a* que não precisa passar

dripping /'drɪpɪŋ/ *n* gordura *f* do assado

drive /draɪv/ *vt* (*pt* drove, *pp* driven /'drɪvn/) empurrar, impelir, levar; (*car, animal*) dirigir, conduzir, (*P*) guiar; (*machine*) acionar, (*P*) accionar □ *vi* dirigir, conduzir, (*P*) guiar □ *n* passeio *m* de carro; (*private road*) entrada *f* para veículos; (*fig*) energia *f*, (*psych*) drive *m*, compulsão *f*, impulso *m*; (*campaign*) campanha *f*. ~ at chegar a. ~ away (*car*) partir. ~ in (*force in*) enterrar. ~-in *n* (*bank, cinema etc*) banco *m*, cinema *m* etc em que se é atendido no carro, drive-in *m*. ~ mad (*fazer*) enlouquecer, pôr fora de si

drivel /'drɪvl/ *n* baboseira *f*, bobagem *f*

driver /'draɪvə(r)/ *n* condutor *m*; (*of taxi, bus*) chofer *m*, motorista *mf*

driving /'draɪvɪŋ/ *n* condução *f*. ~-licence *n* carteira *f* de motorista, (*P*) carta *f* de condução. ~ school autoescola *f*; (*P*) escola *f* de condução. ~ test exame *m* de motorista, (*P*) de condução

drizzle /'drɪzl/ *n* chuvisco *m* □ *vi* chuviscar

drone /drəʊn/ *n* zumbido *m*; (*male bee*) zangão *m* □ *vi* zumbir; (*fig*) falar monotonamente

drool /druːl/ *vi* babar(-se)

droop /druːp/ *vi* pender, curvar-se

drop /drɒp/ *n* gota *f*; (*fall*) queda *f*; (*distance*) altura *f* de queda □ *vt/i* (*pt* dropped) (deixar) cair; (*fall, lower*) baixar. ~ (off) (*person from car*) deixar, largar. ~ a line escrever duas linhas (to a). ~ in passar por (on em casa de). ~ off (*doze*) adormecer. ~ out (*withdraw*) retirar-se; (*of student*) abandonar. ~-out *n* marginal *mf*, marginalizado *m*

droppings /'drɒpɪŋz/ *npl* excrementos *mpl* de animal; (*of birds*) cocô *m* (*colloq*), porcaria *f* (*colloq*)

dross /drɒs/ n escória f; (*refuse*) lixo m

drought /draʊt/ n seca f

drove /drəʊv/ see **drive**

drown /draʊn/ vt/i afogar(-se)

drowsy /'draʊzɪ/ a sonolento. be or feel ~ ter vontade de dormir

drudge /drʌdʒ/ n mouro m de trabalho. ~ry /-ərɪ/ n trabalho m penoso e monótono, estafa f

drug /drʌg/ n droga f; (*med*) medicamento m, remédio m □ vt (*pt* drugged) drogar. ~ addict drogado m, tóxico-dependente m

drugstore /'drʌgstɔː(r)/ n (*Amer*) farmácia f que vende também sorvetes etc

drum /drʌm/ n (*mus*) tambor m; (*for oil*) barril m, tambor m. ~s npl (*mus*) bateria f □ vi (*pt* drummed) tocar tambor; (*with one's fingers*) tamborilar □ vt ~ into sb fazer entrar na cabeça de alg. ~ up (*support*) conseguir obter; (*business*) criar. ~mer /ər/ n tambor m; (*in pop group etc*) baterista m, (P) bateria m

drunk /drʌŋk/ see **drink** □ a embriagado, bêbedo. get ~ embebedar-se, embriagar-se □ n bêbedo m. ~ard n alcoólico m, bêbedo m. ~en a embriagado, bêbedo; (*habitually*) bêbedo

dry /draɪ/ a (drier, driest) seco; (*day*) sem chuva □ vt/i secar. be or feel ~ ter sede. ~-clean vt limpar a seco. ~-cleaner's n (loja de) lavagem f a seco, lavanderia f. ~ up (*dishes*) secar a louça f; (*of supplies*) esgotar-se. ~ness n secura f

dual /'djuːəl/ a duplo. ~ carriageway estrada f dividida por faixa central. ~-purpose a com fim duplo

dub /dʌb/ vt (*pt* dubbed) (*film*) dobrar; (*nickname*) apelidar de

dubious /'djuːbɪəs/ a duvidoso; (*character, compliment*) dúbio. feel ~ about ter dúvidas quanto a

duchess /'dʌtʃɪs/ n duquesa f

duck /dʌk/ n pato m □ vi abaixar-se rapidamente □ vt (*head*) baixar; (*person*) batizar, pregar uma amona em. ~ling n patinho m

duct /dʌkt/ n canal m, tubo m

dud /dʌd/ a (*sl: thing*) que não presta ou não funciona; (*sl: coin*) falso; (*sl: cheque*) sem fundos, (P) careca (*sl*)

due /djuː/ a devido; (*expected*) esperado □ adv ~ east/etc exatamente, (P) exactamente a leste/etc □ n devido m. ~s direitos mpl; (*of club*) cota f. ~ to devido a, por causa de. in ~ course no tempo devido

duel /'djuːəl/ n duelo m

duet /djuː'et/ n dueto m

duffel /'dʌfl/ a ~ bag saco m de lona. ~-coat n casaco m de tecido de lã

dug /dʌg/ see **dig**

duke /djuːk/ n duque m

dull /dʌl/ a (-er, -est) (*boring*) enfadonho; (*colour*) morto; (*mirror*) embaçado; (*weather*) encoberto; (*sound*) surdo; (*stupid*) burro

duly /'djuːlɪ/ adv devidamente; (*in due time*) no tempo devido

dumb /dʌm/ a (-er, -est) mudo; (*colloq: stupid*) bronco, burro

dumbfound /dʌm'faʊnd/ vt pasmar

dummy /'dʌmɪ/ n imitação f, coisa f simulada; (*of tailor*) manequim m; (*of baby*) chupeta f

dump /dʌmp/ vt (*rubbish*) jogar fora; (*put down*) deixar cair; (*colloq: abandon*) largar □ n monte de lixo; (*tip*) lixeira f; (*mil*) depósito m; (*colloq*) buraco m

dunce /dʌns/ n burro m. ~'s cap orelhas fpl de burro

dune /djuːn/ n duna f

dung /dʌŋ/ n esterco m; (*manure*) estrume m

dungarees /dʌŋgə'riːz/ npl macacão m, (P) fato m de macaco

dungeon /'dʌndʒən/ n calabouço m, masmorra f

dupe /djuːp/ vt enganar □ n trouxa m

duplicate[1] /'djuːplɪkət/ n duplicado m □ a idêntico

duplicate[2] /'djuːplɪkeɪt/ vt duplicar, fazer em duplicado; (*on machine*) fotocopiar

duplicity /djuː'plɪsətɪ/ n duplicidade f

durable /'djʊərəbl/ a resistente; (*enduring*) duradouro, durável

duration /djʊ'reɪʃn/ n duração f

duress /djʊ'res/ n under ~ sob coação f, (P) coacção f

during /'djʊərɪŋ/ prep durante

dusk /dʌsk/ n crepúsculo m, anoitecer m

dusky /'dʌskɪ/ a (-ier, -iest) escuro, sombrio

dust /dʌst/ n pó m, poeira f □ vt limpar o pó de; (*sprinkle*) polvilhar. ~-jacket n sobrecapa f de livro

dustbin /'dʌstbɪn/ n lata f do lixo, (P) caixote m

duster /'dʌstə(r)/ n pano m do pó

dustman /'dʌstmən/ n (pl -men) lixeiro m, (P) homem m do lixo

dusty /'dʌstɪ/ a (-ier, -iest) poeirento, empoeirado

Dutch /dʌtʃ/ a holandês □ n (*lang*) holandês m. ~man n holandês m. ~woman n holandesa f. go ~ pagar cada um a sua despesa

dutiful /'djuːtɪfl/ a cumpridor; (*showing respect*) respeitador

dut|y /'dju:tɪ/ n dever m; (tax) impostos mpl. ~ies (of official etc) funções fpl. off ~ de folga. on ~ de serviço. ~y-free a isento de impostos. ~y-free shop free shop m

duvet /'dju:veɪ/ n edredom m, (P) edredão m de penas

dwarf /dwɔːf/ n (pl -fs) anão m

dwell /dwel/ vi (pt dwelt) morar. ~ on alongar-se sobre. ~er n habitante. ~ing n habitação f

dwindle /'dwɪndl/ vi diminuir, reduzir-se

dye /daɪ/ vt (pres p dyeing) tingir □ n tinta f

dying /'daɪɪŋ/ see die

dynamic /daɪ'næmɪk/ a dinâmico

dynamite /'daɪnəmaɪt/ n dinamite f □ vt dinamitar

dynamo /'daɪnəməʊ/ n (pl -os) dínamo m

dynasty /'dɪnəstɪ/ n dinastia f

dysentery /'dɪsəntrɪ/ n disenteria f

dyslex|ia /dɪs'leksɪə/ n dislexia f. ~ic a disléxico

E

each /iːtʃ/ a & pron cada. ~ one cada um. ~ other um ao outro, uns aos outros; they like ~ other gostam um do outro/uns dos outros. know/love/etc ~ other conhecer-se/amar-se/etc

eager /'iːɡə(r)/ a ansioso (to por), desejoso (for de); (supporter) entusiástico. be ~ to ter vontade de. ~ly adv com impaciência, ansiosamente; (keenly) com entusiasmo. ~ness n ansiedade f, desejo m; (keenness) entusiasmo m

eagle /'iːɡl/ n águia f

ear /ɪə(r)/ n ouvido m; (external part) orelha f. ~-drum n tímpano m. ~-ring n brinco m

earache /'ɪəreɪk/ n dor f de ouvidos

earl /ɜːl/ n conde m

early /'ɜːlɪ/ (-ier, -iest) adv cedo □ a primeiro; (hour) matinal; (fruit) temporão; (retirement) antecipado. have an ~ dinner jantar cedo. in ~ summer no princípio do verão

earmark /'ɪəmɑːk/ vt destinar, reservar (for para)

earn /ɜːn/ vt ganhar; (deserve) merecer

earnest /'ɜːnɪst/ a sério. in ~ a sério

earnings /'ɜːnɪŋz/ npl salário m; (profits) ganhos mpl, lucros mpl

earshot /'ɪəʃɒt/ n within ~ ao alcance da voz

earth /ɜːθ/ n terra f □ vt (electr) ligar à terra. why on ~? por que diabo?, por

que cargas d'água? ~ly a terrestre, terreno

earthenware /'ɜːθənweə(r)/ n louça f de barro, faiança f

earthquake /'ɜːθkweɪk/ n tremor m de terra, terremoto m

earthy /'ɜːθɪ/ a terroso, térreo; (coarse) grosseiro

earwig /'ɪəwɪɡ/ n lacrainha f, (P) bicha-cadela f

ease /iːz/ n facilidade f; (comfort) bem-estar m □ vt/i (from pain, anxiety) acalmar(-se); (slow down) afrouxar; (slide) deslizar. at ~ à vontade; (mil) descansar. ill at ~ pouco à vontade. with ~ facilmente. in/out fazer entrar/sair com cuidado

easel /'iːzl/ n cavalete m

east /iːst/ n este m, leste m, pascente m, oriente m. the E~ o Oriente □ a este, (de) leste, oriental □ a/para leste. ~ of para o leste de ~erly a oriental, leste, a/de leste ~ward a, ~ward(s) adv para leste

Easter /'iːstə(r)/ n Páscoa f. ~ egg ovo m de Páscoa

eastern /'iːstən/ a oriental, leste

easy /'iːzɪ/ a (-ier, -iest) fácil; (relaxed) natural, descontraído. take it ~ levar as coisas com calma. ~-chair poltrona f. ~-going a bonacheirão. **easily** adv facilmente

eat /iːt/ vt/i (pt ate, pp eaten) comer. ~ into corroer. ~able a comestível

eaves /iːvz/ npl beiral m

eavesdrop /'iːvzdrɒp/ vi (pt -dropped) escutar por detrás da porta

ebb /eb/ n vazante f, baixa-mar m □ vi vazar; (fig) declinar

EC /iː'siː/ n (abbr of European Community) CE f

eccentric /ɪk'sentrɪk/ a & n excêntrico (m). ~ity /eksen'trɪsətɪ/ n excentricidade f

ecclesiastical /ɪkliːzɪ'æstɪkl/ a eclesiástico

echo /'ekəʊ/ n (pl -oes) eco m □ vt/i (pt echoed, pres p echoing) ecoar; (fig) repetir

eclipse /ɪ'klɪps/ n eclipse m □ vt eclipsar

ecolog|y /iː'kɒlədʒɪ/ n ecologia f. ~ical /iːkə'lɒdʒɪkl/ a ecológico

economic /iːkə'nɒmɪk/ a econômico, (P) económico; (profitable) rentável. ~al a econômico, (P) económico. ~s n economia f política

economist /ɪ'kɒnəmɪst/ n economista mf

econom|y /ɪ'kɒnəmɪ/ n economia f. ~ize vt/i economizar

ecstasy /'ekstəsɪ/ n êxtase m

ecstatic /ɪk'stætɪk/ a extático, extasiado

ecu /'eɪkju:/ n unidade f monetária européia

eczema /'ɛksɪmə/ n eczema m

edge /edʒ/ n borda f, beira f; (of town) periferia f, limite m; (of knife) fio m □ vt debruar □ vi (move) avançar pouco a pouco

edging /'edʒɪŋ/ n borda f, (P) bordadura f

edgy /'edʒɪ/ a irritadiço, nervoso

edible /'edɪbl/ a comestível

edict /'i:dɪkt/ n édito m

edifice /'edɪfɪs/ n edifício m

edit /'edɪt/ vt (pt edited) (newspaper) dirigir; (text) editar

edition /ɪ'dɪʃn/ n edição f

editor /'edɪtə(r)/ n (of newspaper) diretor m, (P) director m, editor m responsável; (of text) organizador m de texto. the ~ (in chief) redator-chefe m, (P) redactor-chefe m. ~ial /edɪ'tɔːrɪəl/ a & n editorial m

educat|e /'edʒʊkeɪt/ vt instruir; (mind, public) educar. ~ed a instruído; educado. ~ion /-'keɪʃn/ n educação f; (schooling) ensino m. ~ional /'keɪʃənl/ a educativo, pedagógico

EEC /i:i:'si:/ n (abbr of European Economic Community) CEE f

eel /i:l/ n enguia f

eerie /'ɪərɪ/ a (-ier, -iest) arrepiante, misterioso

effect /ɪ'fekt/ n efeito m □ vt efetuar, (P) efectuar. come into ~ entrar em vigor. in ~ na realidade. take ~ ter efeito

effective /ɪ'fektɪv/ a eficaz, eficiente; (striking) sensacional; (actual) efetivo, (P) efectivo. ~ly adv (efficiently) eficazmente; (strikingly) de forma sensacional; (actually) efetivamente, (P) efectivamente. ~ness n eficácia f

effeminate /ɪ'femɪnət/ a efeminado, afeminado

effervescent /efə'vesnt/ a efervescente

efficien|t /ɪ'fɪʃnt/ a eficiente, eficaz. ~cy n eficiência f. ~tly adv eficientemente

effigy /'efɪdʒɪ/ n efígie f

effort /'efət/ n esforço m. ~less a fácil, sem esforço

effrontery /ɪ'frʌntərɪ/ n desfaçatez f

effusive /ɪ'fjuːsɪv/ a efusivo, expansivo

e.g. /iː'dʒiː/ abbr por ex

egg[1] /eg/ n ovo m. ~-cup n copinho m para ovo quente, oveiro m. ~-plant n berinjela f

egg[2] /eg/ vt ~ on (colloq) incitar

eggshell /'egʃel/ n casca f de ovo

ego /'egəʊ/ n (pl -os) ego m, eu m. ~ism n egoísmo m. ~ist n egoísta mf. ~tism n egotismo m. ~tist n egotista mf

Egypt /'iːdʒɪpt/ n Egito m. ~ian /ɪ'dʒɪpʃn/ a & n egípcio (m)

eh /eɪ/ int (colloq) hã?

eiderdown /'aɪdədaʊn/ n edredão m, edredom m

eight /eɪt/ a & n oito (m). eighth /eɪtθ/ a & n oitavo (m)

eighteen /eɪ'tiːn/ a & n dezoito (m). ~th a & n décimo-oitavo (m)

eight|y /'eɪtɪ/ a & n oitenta (m). ~ieth a & n octogésimo (m)

either /'aɪðə(r)/ a & pron um e outro; (with negative) nem um nem outro; (each) cada □ adv também não □ conj ~ ... or ou ... ou; (with negative) nem ... nem

ejaculate /ɪ'dʒækjʊleɪt/ vt/i ejacular; (exclaim) exclamar

eject /ɪ'dʒekt/ vt expelir; (expel) expulsar, despejar

elaborate[1] /ɪ'læbərət/ a elaborado, rebuscado, minucioso

elaborate[2] /ɪ'læbəreɪt/ vt elaborar □ vi entrar em pormenores. ~ on estender-se sobre

elapse /ɪ'læps/ vi decorrer

elastic /ɪ'læstɪk/ a & n elástico (m). ~ band elástico m

elat|ed /ɪ'leɪtɪd/ a radiante, exultante. ~ion n exultação f

elbow /'elbəʊ/ n cotovelo m

elder[1] /'eldə(r)/ a mais velho. ~s npl pessoas fpl mais velhas

elder[2] /'eldə(r)/ n (tree) sabugueiro m

elderly /'eldəlɪ/ a idoso. the ~ as pessoas de idade

eldest /'eldɪst/ a & n o mais velho (m)

elect /ɪ'lekt/ vt eleger □ a eleito. ~ion /-kʃn/ n eleição f

electric /ɪ'lektrɪk/ a elétrico, (P) eléctrico. ~al a elétrico, (P) eléctrico

electrician /ɪlek'trɪʃn/ n eletricista m, (P) electricista m

electricity /ɪlek'trɪsətɪ/ n eletricidade f, (P) electricidade f

electrify /ɪ'lektrɪfaɪ/ vt eletrificar, (P) electrificar; (fig: excite) eletrizar, (P) electrizar

electrocute /ɪ'lektrəkjuːt/ vt eletrocutar, (P) electrocutar

electronic /ɪlek'trɒnɪk/ a eletrônico, (P) electrónico. ~s n eletrônica f, (P) electrónica f

elegan|t /'elɪgənt/ a elegante. ~ce n elegância f. ~tly adv elegantemente, com elegância

element /'elɪmənt/ n elemento m; (of heater etc) resistência f. ~ary /-'mentrɪ/ a elementar; (school) primário

elephant /'elɪfənt/ n elefante m

elevat|e /'elɪveɪt/ vt elevar. ~ion /-'veɪʃn/ n elevação f

elevator /'elɪveɪtə(r)/ n (Amer: lift) elevador m, ascensor m

eleven /ɪ'levn/ a & n onze (m). ~th a & n décimo primeiro (m). at the ~th hour à última hora

elf /elf/ n (pl **elves**) elfo m, duende m

elicit /ɪ'lɪsɪt/ vt extrair, obter

eligible /'elɪdʒəbl/ a (for office) idóneo, (P) idóneo (for para); (desirable) aceitável. **be ~ for** (entitled to) ter direito a

eliminat|e /ɪ'lɪmɪneɪt/ vt eliminar. ~ion /-'neɪʃn/ n eliminação f

élite /eɪ'liːt/ n elite f

ellip|se /ɪ'lɪps/ n elipse f. ~tical a elíptico

elm /elm/ n olmo m, ulmeiro m

elocution /elə'kjuːʃn/ n elocução f

elongate /'iːlɒŋɡeɪt/ vt alongar

elope /ɪ'ləʊp/ vi fugir. ~ment n fuga f (de amantes), (P) (de amorosos)

eloquen|t /'eləkwənt/ a eloquente, (P) eloquente. ~ce n eloquência f, (P) eloquência f

else /els/ adv mais. **everybody ~** todos os outros. **nobody ~** mais ninguém. **nothing ~** nada mais. **or ~** ou então, senão. **somewhere ~** noutro lado qualquer. ~**where** adv noutro lado

elude /ɪ'luːd/ vt escapar a; (a question) evadir

elusive /ɪ'luːsɪv/ a (person) esquivo, difícil de apanhar; (answer) evasivo

emaciated /ɪ'meɪʃɪeɪtɪd/ a emaciado, macilento

emancipat|e /ɪ'mænsɪpeɪt/ vt emancipar. ~ion /-'peɪʃn/ n emancipação f

embalm /ɪm'bɑːm/ vt embalsamar

embankment /ɪm'bæŋkmənt/ n (of river) dique m; (of railway) terrapleno m, talude m, (P) aterro m

embargo /ɪm'bɑːɡəʊ/ n (pl -oes) embargo m

embark /ɪm'bɑːk/ vt/i embarcar. ~ **on** (business etc) embarcar em, meter-se em (colloq); (journey) começar

embarrass /ɪm'bærəs/ vt embaraçar, confundir. ~ment n embaraço m, atrapalhação f

embassy /'embəsɪ/ n embaixada f

embellish /ɪm'belɪʃ/ vt embelezar, enfeitar. ~ment n embelezamento m, enfeite m

embezzle /ɪm'bezl/ vt desviar (fundos). ~ment n desfalque m

embitter /ɪm'bɪtə(r)/ vt (person) amargurar; (situation) azedar

emblem /'embləm/ n emblema m

embod|y /ɪm'bɒdɪ/ vt encarnar; (include) incorporar, incluir. ~iment n personificação f

emboss /ɪm'bɒs/ vt (metal) gravar em relevo; (paper) gofrar

embrace /ɪm'breɪs/ vt/i abraçar(-se); (offer, opportunity) acolher □ n abraço m

embroider /ɪm'brɔɪdə(r)/ vt bordar. ~y n bordado m

embryo /'embrɪəʊ/ n (pl -os) embrião m. ~nic /-'ɒnɪk/ a embrionário

emerald /'emərəld/ n esmeralda f

emerge /ɪ'mɜːdʒ/ vi emergir, surgir

emergency /ɪ'mɜːdʒənsɪ/ n emergência f; (urgent case) urgência f. ~ **exit** saída f de emergência. **in an ~** em caso de urgência

emigrant /'emɪɡrənt/ n emigrante mf

emigrat|e /'emɪɡreɪt/ vi emigrar. ~ion /-'ɡreɪʃn/ n emigração f

eminen|t /'emɪnənt/ a eminente. ~tly adv eminentemente

emit /ɪ'mɪt/ vt (pt **emitted**) emitir. ~ssion /-ʃn/ n emissão f

emotion /ɪ'məʊʃn/ n emoção f. ~al a (person, shock) emotivo; (speech, scene) emocionante

emperor /'empərə(r)/ n imperador m

emphasis /'emfəsɪs/ n ênfase f. **lay ~ on** pôr em relevo

emphasize /'emfəsaɪz/ vt enfatizar, sublinhar; (syllable, word) acentuar

emphatic /ɪm'fætɪk/ a enfático; (manner) enérgico. ~ally adv enfaticamente

empire /'empaɪə(r)/ n império m

employ /ɪm'plɔɪ/ vt empregar. ~ee /emplɔɪ'iː/ n empregado m. ~er n patrão m. ~ment n emprego m. ~ment agency agência f de empregos

empower /ɪm'paʊə(r)/ vt autorizar (to do a fazer)

empress /'emprɪs/ n imperatriz f

empt|y /'emptɪ/ a vazio; (promise) falso □ vt/i esvaziar(-se). **on an ~y stomach** com o estômago vazio, em jejum. ~ies npl garrafas fpl vazias. ~iness n vazio m

emulate /'emjʊleɪt/ vt imitar, rivalizar com, emular com

emulsion /ɪ'mʌlʃn/ n emulsão f

enable /ɪ'neɪbl/ vt ~ **sb to** do to do permitir a alg fazer

enact /ɪ'nækt/ vt (jur) decretar; (theat) representar

enamel /ɪ'næml/ n esmalte m □ vt (pt **enamelled**) esmaltar

enamoured /ɪ'næməd/ a ~ **of** enamorado de, apaixonado por

encase /ɪn'keɪs/ vt (enclose) encerrar (in em); (cover) revestir (in de)

enchant /ɪn'tʃɑːnt/ vt encantar. ~ing a encantador. ~ment n encantamento m

encircle /ɪn'sɜːkl/ vt cercar, rodear

enclose /ɪn'kləʊz/ vt (land) cercar; (with letter) enviar incluso/junto. ~d a (space) fechado; (with letter) anexo, incluso, junto enclosure /ɪnˈkləʊʒə(r)/ n cercado m, recinto m; (with letter) documento m anexo

encompass /ɪnˈkʌmpəs/ vt abranger

encore /ɒŋˈkɔː(r)/ int & n bis (m)

encounter /ɪnˈkaʊntə(r)/ vt encontrar, deparar com □ n encontro m

encourage /ɪnˈkʌrɪdʒ/ vt encorajar. ~ment n encorajamento m

encroach /ɪnˈkrəʊtʃ/ vi ~ on (land) invadir; (time) abusar de

encumb|er /ɪnˈkʌmbə(r)/ vt estorvar; (burden) sobrecarregar. ~rance n estorvo m, empecilho m; (burden) ónus m, (P) ônus m, encargo m

encycloped|ia /ɪnsaɪkləˈpiːdɪə/ n enciclopédia f. ~ic a enciclopédico

end /end/ n fim m; (farthest part) extremo m, ponta f □ vt/i acabar, terminar. ~ up (arrive finally) ir parar (in a/em). ~ up doing acabar por fazer. in the ~ por fim. no ~ of (colloq) muito, enorme, imenso. on ~ (upright) em pé; (consecutive) a fio, de seguida

endanger /ɪnˈdeɪndʒə(r)/ vt pôr em perigo

endear|ing /ɪnˈdɪərɪŋ/ a cativante. ~ment n palavra f meiga; (act) carinho m

endeavour /ɪnˈdevə(r)/ n esforço m □ vi esforçar-se (to por)

ending /ˈendɪŋ/ n fim m; (of word) terminação f

endless /ˈendlɪs/ a interminável; (times) sem conta; (patience) infinito

endorse /ɪnˈdɔːs/ vt (document) endossar; (action) aprovar. ~ment n (auto) averbamento m

endow /ɪnˈdaʊ/ vt doar. ~ment n doação f

endur|e /ɪnˈdjʊə(r)/ vt suportar □ vi durar. ~able a suportável. ~ance n resistência f

enemy /ˈenəmɪ/ n & a inimigo (m)

energetic /enəˈdʒetɪk/ a enérgico

energy /ˈenədʒɪ/ n energia f

enforce /ɪnˈfɔːs/ vt aplicar

engage /ɪnˈɡeɪdʒ/ vt (staff) contratar; (mech) engrenar □ vi ~ in envolver-se em, lançar-se em. ~d a noivo; (busy) ocupado. ~ment n noivado m; (undertaking, appointment) compromisso m; (mil) combate m

engender /ɪnˈdʒendə(r)/ vt engendrar, produzir, causar

engine /ˈendʒɪn/ n motor m; (of train) locomotiva f

engineer /endʒɪˈnɪə(r)/ n engenheiro m □ vt engenhar. ~ing n engenharia f

England /ˈɪŋɡlənd/ n Inglaterra f

English /ˈɪŋɡlɪʃ/ a inglês □ n (lang) inglês m. the ~ os ingleses mpl.

~man n inglês m. ~-speaking a de língua inglesa f. ~woman n inglesa f

engrav|e /ɪnˈɡreɪv/ vt gravar. ~ing n gravura f

engrossed /ɪnˈɡrəʊst/ a absorto (in em)

engulf /ɪnˈɡʌlf/ vt engolfar, tragar

enhance /ɪnˈhɑːns/ vt aumentar; (heighten) realçar

enigma /ɪˈnɪɡmə/ n enigma m. ~tic /enɪɡˈmætɪk/ a enigmático

enjoy /ɪnˈdʒɔɪ/ vt gostar de; (benefit from) gozar de. ~ o.s. divertir-se. ~able a agradável. ~ment n prazer m

enlarge /ɪnˈlɑːdʒ/ vt/i aumentar. ~ upon alargar-se sobre. ~ment n ampliação f

enlighten /ɪnˈlaɪtn/ vt esclarecer. ~ment n esclarecimento m, elucidação f

enlist /ɪnˈlɪst/ vt recrutar; (fig) aliciar, granjear □ vi alistar-se

enliven /ɪnˈlaɪvn/ vt animar

enmity /ˈenmɪtɪ/ n inimizade f

enormous /ɪˈnɔːməs/ a enorme

enough /ɪˈnʌf/ a, adv & n bastante (m), suficiente (m) □ int basta!, chega! have ~ of estar farto de

enquir|e /ɪnˈkwaɪə(r)/ vt/i perguntar, indagar. ~e about informar-se de, pedir informações sobre. ~y n pedido m de informações

enrage /ɪnˈreɪdʒ/ vt enfurecer, enraivecer

enrich /ɪnˈrɪtʃ/ vt enriquecer

enrol /ɪnˈrəʊl/ vt/i (pt enrolled) inscrever(-se); (schol) matricular(-se). ~ment n inscrição f; (schol) matrícula f

ensemble /ɒnˈsɒmbl/ n conjunto m

ensign /ˈensən/ n pavilhão m; (officer) guarda-marinha m

ensu|e /ɪnˈsjuː/ vi seguir-se. ~ing a decorrente

ensure /ɪnˈʃʊə(r)/ vt assegurar. ~ that assegurar-se de que

entail /ɪnˈteɪl/ vt acarretar

entangle /ɪnˈtæŋɡl/ vt emaranhar, enredar

enter /ˈentə(r)/ vt (room, club etc) entrar em; (register) registar; (data) entrar com □ vi entrar (into em). ~ for inscrever-se em

enterprise /ˈentəpraɪz/ n empresa f, empreendimento m; (fig) iniciativa f

enterprising /ˈentəpraɪzɪŋ/ a empreendedor

entertain /entəˈteɪn/ vt entreter; (guests) receber; (ideas) alimentar, nutrir. ~er n artista mf. ~ment n entretenimento m; (performance) espetáculo m, (P) espectáculo m

enthral /ɪn'θrɔ:l/ vt (pt **enthralled**) fascinar

enthuse /ɪn'θju:z/ vi ~ over entusiasmar-se por

enthusias|m /ɪn'θju:zɪæzm/ n entusiasmo m. ~t n entusiasta mf. ~tic /-'æstɪk/ a entusiástico. ~tically /-'æstɪkəlɪ/ adv entusiasticamente

entice /ɪn'taɪs/ vt atrair. ~ to do induzir a fazer. ~ment n tentação f, engodo m

entire /ɪn'taɪə(r)/ a inteiro. ~ly adv inteiramente

entirety /ɪn'taɪərətɪ/ n in its ~ por inteiro, na (sua) totalidade

entitle /ɪn'taɪtl/ vt dar direito. ~d a (book) intitulado. be ~d to sth ter direito a alg coisa. ~ment n direito m

entity /'entətɪ/ n entidade f

entrance /'entrəns/ n entrada f (to para); (right to enter) admissão f

entrant /'entrənt/ n (sport) concorrente mf; (in exam) candidato m

entreat /ɪn'tri:t/ vt rogar, suplicar. ~y n rogo m, súplica f

entrench /ɪn'trentʃ/ vt (mil) entrincheirar; (fig) fincar

entrust /ɪn'trʌst/ vt confiar

entry /'entrɪ/ n entrada f; (on list) item m; (in dictionary) verbete m. ~-form ficha f de inscrição, (P) boletim m de inscrição. no ~ entrada proibida

enumerate /ɪ'nju:məreɪt/ vt enumerar

envelop /ɪn'veləp/ vt (pt **enveloped**) envolver

envelope /'envələʊp/ n envelope m, sobrescrito m

enviable /'envɪəbl/ a invejável

envious /'envɪəs/ a invejoso. be ~ of ter inveja de. ~ly adv invejosamente, com inveja

environment /ɪn'vaɪərənmənt/ n meio m; (ecological) meio-ambiente m. ~al /-'mentl/ a do meio; (ecological) do ambiente

envisage /ɪn'vɪzɪdʒ/ vt encarar; (foresee) prever

envoy /'envɔɪ/ n enviado m

envy /'envɪ/ n inveja f □ vt invejar, ter inveja de

enzyme /'enzaɪm/ n enzima f

epic /'epɪk/ n epopéia f □ a épico

epidemic /epɪ'demɪk/ n epidemia f

epilep|sy /'epɪlepsɪ/ n epilepsia f. ~tic /-'leptɪk/ a & n epiléptico (m)

episode /'epɪsəʊd/ n episódio m

epitaph /'epɪta:f/ n epitáfio m

epithet /'epɪθet/ n epíteto m

epitom|e /ɪ'pɪtəmɪ/ n (summary) epítome m; (embodiment) modelo m. ~ize vt (fig) representar, encarnar; (summarize) resumir

epoch /'i:pɒk/ n época f. ~-making a que marca uma época

equal /'i:kwəl/ a & n igual (m) □ vt (pt **equalled**) igualar, ser igual a. ~ to (task) à altura de. ~ity /i:'kwɒlətɪ/ n igualdade f. ~ly adv igualmente; (similarly) de igual modo

equalize /'i:kwəlaɪz/ vt/i igualar; (sport) empatar

equanimity /ekwə'nɪmətɪ/ n equanimidade f, serenidade f

equate /ɪ'kweɪt/ vt equacionar (with com); (treat as equal) equiparar (with a)

equation /ɪ'kweɪʒn/ n equação f

equator /ɪ'kweɪtə(r)/ n equador m. ~ial /ekwə'tɔ:rɪəl/ a equatorial

equilibrium /i:kwɪ'lɪbrɪəm/ n equilíbrio m

equip /ɪ'kwɪp/ vt (pt **equipped**) equipar (with com), munir (with de). ~ment n equipamento m

equitable /'ekwɪtəbl/ a eqüitativo, (P) equitativo

equity /'ekwətɪ/ n eqüidade f, (P) equidade f

equivalent /ɪ'kwɪvələnt/ a & n eqüivalente (m), (P) equivalente m

equivocal /ɪ'kwɪvəkl/ a equívoco

era /'ɪərə/ n era f, época f

eradicate /ɪ'rædɪkeɪt/ vt erradicar, suprimir

erase /ɪ'reɪz/ vt apagar. ~r /-ə(r)/ n borracha f (de apagar)

erect /ɪ'rekt/ a ereto, (P) erecto □ vt erigir. ~ion /-ʃn/ n ereção f, (P) erecção f; (building) construção f, edifício m

erode /ɪ'rəʊd/ vt corroer. ~sion /ɪ'rəʊʒn/ n erosão f

erotic /ɪ'rɒtɪk/ a erótico

err /ɜ:(r)/ vi (pt **erred**) errar

errand /'erənd/ n recado m

erratic /ɪ'rætɪk/ a errático, irregular; (person) variável, imprevisível

erroneous /ɪ'rəʊnɪəs/ a errôneo, (P) errôneo, errado

error /'erə(r)/ n erro m

erudit|e /'eru:daɪt/ a erudito. ~ion /-'dɪʃn/ n erudição f

erupt /ɪ'rʌpt/ vi (war, fire) irromper; (volcano) entrar em erupção. ~ion /-ʃn/ n erupção f

escalat|e /'eskəleɪt/ vt/i intensificar (-se); (of prices) subir em espiral. ~ion /-'leɪʃn/ n escalada f

escalator /'eskəleɪtə(r)/ n escada f rolante

escapade /eskə'peɪd/ n peripécia f

escape /ɪ'skeɪp/ vi escapar-se □ vt escapar a □ n fuga f; (of prisoner) evasão f, fuga f. ~ from sb escapar de alguém. ~ to fugir para. have a lucky or narrow ~ escapar por um triz escapism /ɪˈskeɪpɪzəm/ n escapismo m

escort[1] /ˈeskɔːt/ n escolta f; (of woman) cavalheiro m, acompanhante m

escort[2] /ɪˈskɔːt/ vt escoltar; (accompany) acompanhar

escudo /esˈkjuːdəʊ/ n (pl -os) escudo m

Eskimo /ˈeskɪməʊ/ n (pl -os) esquimó mf

especial /ɪˈspeʃl/ a especial. ~ly adv especialmente

espionage /ˈespɪənɑːʒ/ n espionagem f

espouse /ɪˈspaʊz/ vt (a cause etc) abraçar

espresso /eˈspresəʊ/ n (pl -os) (coffee) expresso m

essay /ˈeseɪ/ n ensaio m; (schol) redação f, (P) redacção f

essence /ˈesns/ n essência f

essential /ɪˈsenʃl/ a essencial □ n the ~s o essencial m. ~ly adv essencialmente

establish /ɪˈstæblɪʃ/ vt estabelecer; (business, state) fundar; (prove) provar, apurar. ~ment n estabelecimento m; (institution) instituição f. the E~ment o Establishment m, a classe f dirigente

estate /ɪˈsteɪt/ n propriedade f; (possessions) bens mpl; (inheritance) herança f. ~ agent agente m imobiliário. (housing) ~ conjunto m habitacional. ~ car perua f

esteem /ɪˈstiːm/ vt estimar □ n estima f

estimate[1] /ˈestɪmət/ n cálculo m, avaliação f; (comm) orçamento m, estimativa f

estimat|e[2] /ˈestɪmeɪt/ vt calcular, estimar. ~ion /-ˈmeɪʃn/ n opinião f

estuary /ˈestʃʊərɪ/ n estuário m

etc abbr = et cetera /ɪtˈsetərə/ etc

etching /ˈetʃɪŋ/ n água-forte f

eternal /ɪˈtɜːnl/ a eterno

eternity /ɪˈtɜːnətɪ/ n eternidade f

ethic /ˈeθɪk/ n ética f. ~s ética f. ~al a ético

ethnic /ˈeθnɪk/ a étnico

etiquette /ˈetɪket/ n etiqueta f

etymology /etɪˈmɒlədʒɪ/ n etimologia f

eulogy /ˈjuːlədʒɪ/ n elogio m

euphemism /ˈjuːfəmɪzəm/ n eufemismo m

euphoria /juːˈfɔːrɪə/ n euforia f

Europe /ˈjʊərəp/ n Europa f. ~an /-ˈpɪən/ a & n europeu (m)

euthanasia /juːθəˈneɪzɪə/ n eutanásia f

evacuat|e /ɪˈvækjʊeɪt/ vt evacuar. ~ion /-ˈeɪʃn/ n evacuação f

evade /ɪˈveɪd/ vt evadir, esquivar-se a

evaluate /ɪˈvæljʊeɪt/ vt avaliar

evangelical /iːvænˈdʒelɪkl/ a evangélico

evaporat|e /ɪˈvæpəreɪt/ vt/i evaporar(-se). ~ed milk leite m evaporado. ~ion /-ˈreɪʃn/ n evaporação f

evasion /ɪˈveɪʒn/ n evasão f

evasive /ɪˈveɪsɪv/ a evasivo

eve /iːv/ n véspera f

even /ˈiːvn/ a regular; (surface) liso, plano; (amounts) igual; (number) par □ vt/i ~ up igualar-se, acertar □ adv mesmo. ~ better ainda melhor. get ~ with ajustar contas com. ~ly adv uniformemente; (amounts) em partes iguais

evening /ˈiːvnɪŋ/ n entardecer m, anoitecer m; (whole evening) serão m. ~ class aula f à noite (para adultos). ~ dress traje m de cerimónia, (P) trajo m de cerimónia or de rigor; (woman's) vestido m de noite

event /ɪˈvent/ n acontecimento m. in the ~ of no caso de. ~ful a movimentado, memorável

eventual /ɪˈventʃʊəl/ a final. ~ity /-ˈælətɪ/ n eventualidade f. ~ly adv por fim; (in future) eventualmente

ever /ˈevə(r)/ adv jamais; (at all times) sempre. do you ~ go? você já foi alguma vez?, vais alguma vez? the best I ~ saw o melhor que já vi. ~ since adv desde então □ prep desde □ conj desde que. ~ so (colloq) muitíssimo, tão. hardly ~ quase nunca

evergreen /ˈevəgriːn/ n sempre-verde f, planta f de folhas persistentes □ a persistente

everlasting /evəˈlɑːstɪŋ/ a eterno

every /ˈevrɪ/ a cada. ~ now and then de vez em quando, volta e meia. ~ one cada um. ~ other day dia sim dia não, de dois em dois dias. ~ three days de três em três dias

everybody /ˈevrɪbɒdɪ/ pron todo mundo, todos

everyday /ˈevrɪdeɪ/ a cotidiano, (P) quotidiano, diário; (common) do dia a dia, vulgar

everyone /ˈevrɪwʌn/ pron todo mundo, todos

everything /ˈevrɪθɪŋ/ pron tudo

everywhere /ˈevrɪweə(r)/ adv (position) em todo lugar, em toda parte; (direction) em todo lugar, a toda parte

evict /ɪˈvɪkt/ vt expulsar, despejar. ~ion /-ʃn/ n despejo m

evidence /ˈevɪdəns/ n evidência f; (proof) prova f; (testimony) testemunho m, depoimento m. ~ of sinal de. give ~ testemunhar. in ~ em evidência

evident /ˈevɪdənt/ a evidente. ~ly adv evidentemente

evil /'i:vl/ a mau □ n mal m

evo|ke /ɪ'vəʊk/ vt evocar. ~cative /ɪ'vɒkətɪv/ a evocativo

evolution /i:və'lu:ʃn/ n evolução f

evolve /ɪ'vɒlv/ vi evolucionar, evoluir □ vt desenvolver, produzir

ex- /eks/ pref ex-

exacerbate /ɪg'zæsəbeɪt/ vt exacerbar

exact /ɪg'zækt/ a exato, (P) exacto □ vt exigir (from de). ~ing a exigente; (task) difícil. ~ly adv exatamente, (P) exactamente

exaggerat|e /ɪg'zædʒəreɪt/ vt/i exagerar. ~ion /-'reɪʃn/ n exagero m

exam /ɪg'zæm/ n (colloq) exame m

examination /ɪgzæmɪ'neɪʃn/ n exame m; (jur) interrogatório m

examine /ɪg'zæmɪn/ vt examinar; (witness etc) interrogar. ~r /-ə(r)/ n examinador m

example /ɪg'za:mpl/ n exemplo m. for ~ por exemplo. make an ~ of castigar para servir de exemplo

exasperat|e /ɪg'zæspəreɪt/ vt exasperar. ~ion /-'reɪʃn/ n exaspero m

excavat|e /'ekskəveɪt/ vt escavar; (uncover) desenterrar. ~ion /-'veɪʃn/ n escavação f

exceed /ɪk'si:d/ vt exceder; (speed limit) ultrapassar, exceder

excel /ɪk'sel/ vi (pt excelled) distinguir-se □ vt superar, ultrapassar

excellen|t /'eksələnt/ a excelente. ~ce excelência f. ~tly adv excelentemente

except /ɪk'sept/ prep exceto, (P) excepto, fora □ vt exceptuar, (P) exceptuar. ~ for a não ser, menos, salvo. ~ing prep à exceção de, (P) à excepção de. ~ion /-ʃn/ n exceção f, (P) excepção f. take ~ion to (object to) achar inaceitável; (be offended by) achar ofensivo

exceptional /ɪk'sepʃənl/ a excepcional. ~ly adv excepcionalmente

excerpt /'eksɜ:pt/ n trecho m, excerto m

excess¹ /ɪk'ses/ n excesso m

excess² /'ekses/ a excedente, em excesso. ~ fare excesso m, suplemento m. ~ luggage excesso m de peso

excessive /ɪk'sesɪv/ a excessivo. ~ly adv excessivamente

exchange /ɪks'tʃeɪndʒ/ vt trocar □ n troca f; (of currency) câmbio m. (telephone) ~ central f telefónica, (P) telefónica. ~ rate taxa f de câmbio

excise /'eksaɪz/ n imposto m (indireto, (P) indirecto)

excit|e /ɪk'saɪt/ vt excitar; (rouse) despertar; (enthuse) entusiasmar. ~able a excitável. ~ed a excitado. get ~ed excitar-se, entusiasmar-se. ~ement n excitação f. ~ing a excitante, emocionante

exclaim /ɪk'skleɪm/ vi exclamar

exclamation /eksklə'meɪʃn/ n exclamação f. ~ mark ponto m de exclamação

exclu|de /ɪk'sklu:d/ vt excluir. ~ding prep excluído, (P) incluindo. ~sion n exclusão f

exclusive /ɪk'sklu:sɪv/ a (rights etc) exclusivo; (club etc) seleto, (P) selecto; (news item) (em) exclusivo. ~ of sem incluir. ~ly adv exclusivamente

excruciating /ɪk'skru:ʃɪeɪtɪŋ/ a excruciante, atroz

excursion /ɪk'skɜ:ʃn/ n excursão f

excus|e¹ /ɪk'skju:z/ vt desculpar. ~e me! desculpe!, com licença! ~e from (exempt) dispensar de. ~able a desculpável

excuse² /ɪk'skju:s/ n desculpa f

ex-directory /eksdɪ'rektərɪ/ a que não vem no anuário, (P) na lista

execute /'eksɪkju:t/ vt executar

execution /eksɪ'kju:ʃn/ n execução f

executive /ɪg'zekjʊtɪv/ a & n executivo (m)

exemplary /ɪg'zemplərɪ/ a exemplar

exemplify /ɪg'zemplɪfaɪ/ vt exemplificar, ilustrar

exempt /ɪg'zempt/ a isento (from de) □ vt dispensar, eximir. ~ion /-ʃn/ n isenção f

exercise /'eksəsaɪz/ n exercício m □ vt (powers, restraint etc) exercer; (dog) levar para passear □ vi fazer exercício. ~ book caderno m

exert /ɪg'zɜ:t/ vt empregar, exercer. ~ o.s. esforçar-se, fazer um esforço. ~ion /-ʃn/ n esforço m

exhaust /ɪg'zɔ:st/ vt esgotar □ n (auto) (tubo de) escape m. ~ed a esgotado, exausto. ~ion /-stʃən/ n esgotamento m, exaustão f

exhaustive /ɪg'zɔ:stɪv/ a exaustivo, completo

exhibit /ɪg'zɪbɪt/ vt exibir, mostrar; (thing, collection) expor □ n objeto m, (P) objecto m exposto

exhibition /eksɪ'bɪʃn/ n exposição f; (act of showing) demonstração f

exhilarat|e /ɪg'zɪləreɪt/ vt regozijar; (invigorate) animar, estimular. ~ion /-'reɪʃn/ n animação f, alegria f

exhort /ɪg'zɔ:t/ vt exortar

exile /'eksaɪl/ n exílio m; (person) exilado m □ vt exilar, desterrar

exist /ɪg'zɪst/ vi existir. ~ence n existência f. be in ~ence existir

exit /'eksɪt/ n saída f

exonerate /ɪg'zɒnəreɪt/ vt exonerar

exorbitant /ɪg'zɔ:bɪtənt/ a exorbitante

exorcize /'eksɔ:saɪz/ vt esconjurar, exorcisar

exotic /ɪg'zɒtɪk/ a exótico

expan|d /ɪk'spænd/ vt/i expandir(-se); (extend) estender(-se), alargar(-se); (gas, liquid, metal) dilatar(-se). ~sion /ɪk'spænʃn/ n expansão f; (extension) alargamento m; (of gas etc) dilatação f

expanse /ɪk'spæns/ n extensão f

expatriate /eks'pætrɪət/ a & n expatriado (m)

expect /ɪk'spekt/ vt esperar; (suppose) crer, supor; (require) contar com, esperar; (baby) esperar. ~ to do contar fazer. ~ation /ekspek'teɪʃn/ n expectativa f

expectan|t /ɪk'spektənt/ a ~t mother gestante f. ~cy n expectativa f

expedient /ɪk'spiːdɪənt/ a oportuno □ n expediente m

expedition /ekspɪ'dɪʃn/ n expedição f

expel /ɪk'spel/ vt (pt expelled) expulsar; (gas, poison etc) expelir

expend /ɪk'spend/ vt despender. ~able a descartável

expenditure /ɪk'spendɪtʃə(r)/ n despesa f, gasto m

expense /ɪk'spens/ n despesa f; (cost) custo m. at sb's ~ à custa de alg. at the ~ of (fig) à custa de

expensive /ɪk'spensɪv/ a caro, dispendioso; (tastes, habits) de luxo

experience /ɪk'spɪərɪəns/ n experiência f □ vt experimentar; (feel) sentir. ~d a experiente

experiment /ɪk'sperɪmənt/ n experiência f □ vi /ɪk'sperɪment/ fazer uma experiência. ~al /-'mentl/ a experimental

expert /'ekspɜːt/ a & n perito (m). ~ly adv com perícia, habilmente

expertise /ekspɜː'tiːz/ n perícia f, competência f

expir|e /ɪk'spaɪə(r)/ vi expirar. ~y n fim m de prazo, expiração f

expl|ain /ɪk'splem/ vt explicar. ~anation /eksplə'neɪʃn/ n explicação f. ~anatory /ɪk'splænətrɪ/ a explicativo

expletive /ɪk'spliːtɪv/ n imprecação f, praga f

explicit /ɪk'splɪsɪt/ a explícito

explo|de /ɪk'spləʊd/ vt/i (fazer) explodir. ~sion /ɪk'spləʊʒn/ n explosão f. ~sive a & n explosivo (m)

exploit[1] /'eksplɔɪt/ n façanha f

exploit[2] /ɪk'splɔɪt/ vt explorar. ~ation /eksplɔɪ'teɪʃn/ n exploração f

exploratory /ɪk'splɒrətrɪ/ a exploratório; (talks) preliminar

explor|e /ɪk'splɔː(r)/ vt explorar; (fig) examinar. ~ation /eksplə'reɪʃn/ n exploração f. ~er n explorador m

exponent /ɪk'spəʊnənt/ n (person) expoente mf; (math) expoente m

export[1] /ɪk'spɔːt/ vt exportar. ~er n exportador m

export[2] /'ekspɔːt/ n exportação f. ~s npl exportações fpl

expos|e /ɪk'spəʊz/ vt expor; (disclose) revelar; (unmask) desmascarar. ~ure /-ʒə(r)/ n exposição f; (cold) frio m

expound /ɪk'spaʊnd/ vt explanar, expor

express[1] /ɪk'spres/ a expresso, categórico □ adv (por) expresso □ n (train) rápido m, expresso m. ~ly adv expressamente

express[2] /ɪk'spres/ vt exprimir. ~ion /-ʃn/ n expressão f. ~ive a expressivo

expulsion /ɪk'spʌlʃn/ n expulsão f

exquisite /'ekskwɪzɪt/ a requintado

extempore /ek'stempərɪ/ adv a improvisado □ adv de improviso, sem preparação prévia

exten|d /ɪk'stend/ vt (stretch) estender; (enlarge) aumentar, ampliar; (prolong) prolongar; (grant) oferecer □ vi (stretch) estender-se; (in time) prolongar-se. ~sion /ɪk'stenʃn/ n (incl phone) extensão f; (of deadline) prorrogação f; (building) anexo m

extensive /ɪk'stensɪv/ a extenso; (damage, study) vasto. ~ly adv muito

extent /ɪk'stent/ n extensão f; (degree) medida f. to some ~ até certo ponto, em certa medida. to such an ~ that a tal ponto que

exterior /ɪk'stɪərɪə(r)/ a & n exterior (m)

exterminat|e /ɪk'stɜːmɪneɪt/ vt exterminar. ~ion /'neɪʃn/ n exterminação f, extermínio m

external /ɪk'stɜːnl/ a externo. ~ly adv exteriormente

extinct /ɪk'stɪŋkt/ a extinto. ~ion /-ʃn/ n extinção f

extinguish /ɪk'stɪŋgwɪʃ/ vt extinguir, apagar. ~er n extintor m

extol /ɪk'stəʊl/ vt (pt extolled) exaltar, elogiar, louvar

extort /ɪk'stɔːt/ vt extorquir (from a). ~ion /-ʃn/ n extorsão f

extortionate /ɪk'stɔːʃənət/ a exorbitante

extra /'ekstrə/ a extra, adicional □ adv extra, excepcionalmente. ~ strong extra-forte □ n extra m; (cine, theat) extra mf, figurante mf. ~ time (football) prorrogação f

extra- /'ekstrə/ pref extra-

extract[1] /ɪk'strækt/ vt extrair; (promise, tooth) arrancar; (fig) obter. ~ion /-ʃn/ n extração f, (P) extracção f; (descent) origem f

extract[2] /'ekstrækt/ n extrato m, (P) extracto m

extradit|e /'ekstrədaɪt/ vt extraditar. ~ion /-'dɪʃn/ n extradição f

extramarital /ekstrə'mærɪtl/ *a* extraconjugal, extramatrimonial

extraordinary /ɪk'strɔːdnrɪ/ *a* extraordinário

extravagan|t /ɪk'strævəgənt/ *a* extravagante; (*wasteful*) esbanjador.~ce *n* extravagância *f*; (*wastefulness*) esbanjamento *m*

extrem|e /ɪk'striːm/ *a & n* extremo (*m*).~ely *adv* extremamente. ~ist *n* extremista *mf*

extremity /ɪk'stremətɪ/ *n* extremidade *f*

extricate /'ekstrɪkeɪt/ *vt* desembaraçar, livrar

extrovert /'ekstrəvɜːt/ *n* extrovertido *m*

exuberan|t /ɪg'zjuːbərənt/ *a* exuberante. ~ce *n* exuberância *f*

exude /ɪg'zjuːd/ *vt* (*charm etc*) destilar, ressumar, (*P*) transpirar

exult /ɪg'zʌlt/ *vi* exultar

eye /aɪ/ *n* olho *m* □ *vt* (*pt* eyed, *pres p* eyeing) olhar. keep an ~ on vigiar. see ~ to ~ concordar inteiramente. ~-opener *n* revelação *f*. ~-shadow *n* sombra *f*

eyeball /'aɪbɔːl/ *n* globo *m* ocular

eyebrow /'aɪbraʊ/ *n* sobrancelha *f*

eyelash /'aɪlæʃ/ *n* pestana *f*

eyelid /'aɪlɪd/ *n* pálpebra *f*

eyesight /'aɪsaɪt/ *n* vista *f*

eyesore /'aɪsɔː(r)/ *n* monstruosidade *f*, horror *m*

eyewitness /'aɪwɪtnɪs/ *n* testemunha *f* ocular

F

fable /'feɪbl/ *n* fábula *f*

fabric /'fæbrɪk/ *n* tecido *m*; (*structure*) edifício *m*

fabricat|e /'fæbrɪkeɪt/ *vt* fabricar; (*invent*) urdir, inventar. ~ion /-'keɪʃn/ *n* fabrico *m*; (*invention*) invenção *f*

fabulous /'fæbjʊləs/ *a* fabuloso

façade /fə'sɑːd/ *n* fachada *f*

face /feɪs/ *n* face *f*, cara *f*, rosto *m*; (*expression*) face *f*; (*grimace*) careta *f*; (*of clock*) mostrador *m* □ *vt* (*look towards*) encarar, (*confront*) enfrentar □ *vi* (*be opposite*) estar de frente para. ~ up to enfrentar. ~ to face cara a cara, frente a frente. in the ~ of em vista de. on the ~ of it a julgar pelas aparências. ~-cloth *n* toalha *f* de rosto, (*P*) toalhete *m* de rosto. ~-lift *n* cirurgia *f* plástica do rosto. ~-pack *n* máscara de beleza *f*

faceless /'feɪslɪs/ *a* (*fig*) anónimo, (*P*) anónimo

facet /'fæsɪt/ *n* faceta *f*

facetious /fə'siːʃəs/ *a* faceto; (*pej*) engraçadinho (*colloq pej*)

facial /'feɪʃl/ *a* facial

facile /'fæsaɪl/ *a* fácil; (*superficial*) superficial

facilitate /fə'sɪlɪteɪt/ *vt* facilitar

facilit|y /fə'sɪlətɪ/ *n* facilidade *f*. ~ies (*means*) facilidades *fpl*; (*installations*) instalações *fpl*

facing /'feɪsɪŋ/ *n* revestimento *m*

facsimile /fæk'sɪmɪlɪ/ *n* fac-símile *m*

fact /fækt/ *n* facto *m*, (*P*) facto *m*. in ~, as a matter of ~ na realidade

faction /'fækʃn/ *n* facção *f*

factor /'fæktə(r)/ *n* fator *m*, (*P*) factor *m*

factory /'fæktərɪ/ *n* fábrica *f*

factual /'fæktʃʊəl/ *a* concreto, real

faculty /'fækltɪ/ *n* faculdade *f*

fad /fæd/ *n* capricho *m*, mania *f*; (*craze*) moda *f*

fade /feɪd/ *vt/i* (*colour*) desbotar; (*sound*) diminuir; (*disappear*) apagar(-se)

fag /fæg/ *n* (*colloq: chore*) estafa *f*; (*sl: cigarette*) cigarro *m*. ~ged *a* estafado

fail /feɪl/ *vt/i* falhar; (*in an examination*) reprovar; (*omit, neglect*) deixar de; (*comm*) falir □ *n* without ~ sem falta

failing /'feɪlɪŋ/ *n* deficiência *f* □ *prep* na falta de, à falta de

failure /'feɪljə(r)/ *n* fracasso *m*, (*P*) falhanço *m*; (*of engine*) falha *f*; (*of electricity*) falta *f*; (*person*) fracassado *m*.

faint /feɪnt/ *a* (-er, -est) (*indistinct*) apagado; (*weak*) fraco; (*giddy*) tonto □ *vi* desmaiar □ *n* desmaio *m*. ~-hearted *a* timido. ~ly *adv* vagamente. ~ness *n* debilidade *f*; (*indistinctness*) apagado *m*

fair[1] /feə(r)/ *n* feira *f*. ~-ground *n* parque *m* de diversões, (*P*) largo *m* de feira

fair[2] /feə(r)/ *a* (-er, -est) (*of hair*) louro; (*weather*) bom; (*moderate quality*) razoável; (*just*) justo. ~ play jogo *m* limpo, fair-play *m*. ~ly *adv* razoavelmente. ~ness *n* justiça *f*

fairy /'feərɪ/ *n* fada *f*. ~-story, ~-tale conto *m* de fadas

faith /feɪθ/ *n* fé *f*; (*religion*) religião *f*; (*loyalty*) lealdade *f*. in good ~ de boa fé, (*P*) à boa fé. ~-healer *n* curandeiro *m*

faithful /'feɪθfl/ *a* fiel. ~ly *adv* fielmente. yours ~ly atenciosamente. ~ness *n* fidelidade *f*

fake /feɪk/ *n* (*thing*) imitação *f*; (*person*) impostor *m* □ *a* falsificado □ *vt* falsificar; (*pretend*) simular, fingir

falcon /'fɔːlkən/ *n* falcão *m*

fall /fɔːl/ *vi* (*pt* fell, *pp* fallen) cair □ *n* queda *f*; (*Amer: autumn*) outono *m*.

~s npl (waterfall) queda-d'água f. **~ back** bater em retirada. **~ back on** recorrer a. **~ behind** atrasar-se (with em). **~ down** or off cair. **~ flat** falhar, não resultar. **~ flat on one's face** estatelar-se. **~ for** (a trick) cair em, deixar-se levar por; (colloq: a person) apaixonar-se por; ficar caído por (colloq). **~ in** (roof) ruir; (mil) alinhar-se, pôr-se em forma. **~ out** brigar, (P) zangar-se (with com). **~out** n poeira f radioactiva, (P) radioactiva. **~ through** (of plans) falhar

fallac|y /ˈfæləsɪ/ n falácia f, engano m. **~ious** /fəˈleɪʃəs/ a errôneo

fallen /ˈfɔːlən/ see **fall**

fallible /ˈfæləbl/ a falível

fallow /ˈfæləʊ/ a (of ground) de pousio; (uncultivated) inculto

false /fɔːls/ a falso. **~ teeth** npl dentes mpl postiços. **~ly** adv falsamente. **~ness** n falsidade f

falsehood /ˈfɔːlshʊd/ n falsidade f, mentira f

falsify /ˈfɔːlsɪfaɪ/ vt (pt -fied) falsificar; (a story) deturpar

falter /ˈfɔːltə(r)/ vi vacilar; (of the voice) hesitar

fame /feɪm/ n fama f. **~d** a afamado

familiar /fəˈmɪlɪə(r)/ a familiar; (intimate) íntimo. **be ~ with** estar familiarizado com

familiarity /fəmɪlɪˈærɪtɪ/ n familiaridade f

familiarize /fəˈmɪlɪəraɪz/ vt familiarizar (with com); (make well known) tornar conhecido

family /ˈfæməlɪ/ n família f. **~ doctor** médico m da família. **~ tree** árvore f genealógica

famine /ˈfæmɪn/ n fome f

famished /ˈfæmɪʃt/ a esfomeado, faminto. **be ~** (colloq) estar morrendo de fome, (P) estar a morrer de fome

famous /ˈfeɪməs/ a famoso

fan[1] /fæn/ n (in the hand) leque m; (mechanical) ventilador m, (P) ventoinha f □ vt (pt fanned) abanar; (a fire; fig) atiçar □ vi **~ out** abrir-se em leque. **~ belt** correia f da ventoinhas

fan[2] /fæn/ n (colloq) fã mf. **~ mail** correio m de fãs

fanatic /fəˈnætɪk/ n fanático m. **~al** a fanático. **~ism** /-sɪzəm/ n fanatismo m

fanciful /ˈfænsɪfl/ a fantasioso, fantasista

fancy /ˈfænsɪ/ n fantasia f; (liking) gosto m □ a extravagante, fantástico; (of buttons etc) de fantasia; (of prices) exorbitante □ vt imaginar; (colloq: like) gostar de; (colloq: want) apetecer. **it took my ~** gostei disso,

(P) deu-me no gosto. **a passing ~** um entusiasmo passageiro. **~ dress** traje m fantasia, (P) trajo m de fantasia

fanfare /ˈfænfeə(r)/ n fanfarra f

fang /fæŋ/ n presa f, dente m canino

fantastic /fænˈtæstɪk/ a fantástico

fantas|y /ˈfæntəsɪ/ n fantasia f. **~ize** vt fantasiar, imaginar

far /fɑː(r)/ adv longe; (much, very) muito □ a distante, longínquo; (end, side) outro. **~ away** ~ **off** ao longe. **as ~ as** (up to) até. **as ~ as I know** tanto quanto saiba. **the F~ East** o Extremo-Oriente m. **~away** a distante, longínquo. **~fetched** a forçado; (unconvincing) pouco plausível. **~reaching** a de grande alcance

farc|e /fɑːs/ n farsa f. **~ical** a de farsa; ridículo

fare /feə(r)/ n preço m da passagem; (in taxi) tarifa f, preço m da corrida; (passenger) passageiro m; (food) comida f □ vi (get on) dar-se

farewell /feəˈwel/ int & n adeus (m)

farm /fɑːm/ n quinta f, fazenda f □ vt cultivar □ vi ser fazendeiro, (P) lavrador. **~ out** (of work) delegar a tarefeiros. **~hand** n trabalhador m rural. **~er** n fazendeiro m, (P) lavrador m. **~ing** n agricultura f, lavoura f

farmhouse /ˈfɑːmhaʊs/ n casa f da fazenda, (P) quinta

farmyard /ˈfɑːmjɑːd/ n quintal m de fazenda m, (P) pátio m de quinta

farth|er /ˈfɑːðə(r)/ adv mais longe □ a mais distante. **~est** adv mais longe □ a o mais distante

fascinat|e /ˈfæsɪneɪt/ vt fascinar. **~ion** /-ˈneɪʃn/ n fascínio m, fascinação f

fascis|t /ˈfæʃɪst/ n fascista mf. **~m** /-zəm/ n fascismo m

fashion /ˈfæʃn/ n moda f; (manner) maneira f □ vt amoldar, (P) moldar. **~able** a na moda, (P) à moda. **~ably** adv na moda, (P) à moda

fast[1] /fɑːst/ a (-er, -est) rápido; (colour) fixo, que não desbota □ adv depressa; (firmly) firmemente. **be ~** (of clock) adiantar-se, estar adiantado. **~ asleep** profundamente adormecido, ferrado no sono. **~ food** n fast-food f

fast[2] /fɑːst/ vi jejuar □ n jejum m

fasten /ˈfɑːsn/ vt/i prender; (door, window) fechar(-se); (seat-belt) apertar. **~er**, **~ing** ns fecho m

fastidious /fəˈstɪdɪəs/ a exigente

fat /fæt/ n gordura f □ a (fatter, fattest) gordo. **~ness** n gordura f

fatal /ˈfeɪtl/ a fatal. **~ injuries** ferimentos mpl mortais. **~ity** /fəˈtælətɪ/ n fatalidade f. **~ly** adv fatalmente, mortalmente

fate /feɪt/ n (destiny) destino m; (one's lot) destino m, sorte f. ~**ful** a fatídico

fated /ˈfeɪtɪd/ a predestinado; (doomed) condenado (to, a)

father /ˈfɑːðə(r)/ n pai m □ vt gerar. ~**-in-law** n (pl ~**s-in-law**) sogro m. ~**ly** a paternal

fathom /ˈfæðəm/ n braça f □ vt ~ (out) (comprehend) compreender

fatigue /fəˈtiːg/ n fadiga f □ vt fatigar

fatten /ˈfætn/ vt/i engordar. ~**ing** a que engorda

fatty /ˈfætɪ/ a (-ier, -iest) gorduroso; (tissue) adiposo

fault /fɔːlt/ n defeito m, falha f; (blame) falta f, culpa f; (geol) falha f. at ~ culpado. it's your ~ é culpa sua. ~**less** a impecável. ~**y** a defeituoso

favour /ˈfeɪvə(r)/ n favor m □ vt favorecer; (prefer) preferir. do sb a ~ fazer um favor a alg. ~**able** a favorável. ~**ably** adv favoravelmente

favourit|e /ˈfeɪvərɪt/ a & n favorito (m). ~**ism** /-ɪzəm/ n favoritismo m

fawn[1] /fɔːn/ n cervo m novo □ a (colour) castanho claro

fawn[2] /fɔːn/ vi ~ on adular, bajular

fax /fæks/ n fax m, fac-simile m □ vt mandar um fax. ~ **machine** fax m

fear /fɪə(r)/ n medo m, receio m, temor m; (likelihood) perigo m □ vt recear, ter medo de. for ~ of/that com medo de/que. ~**ful** a (terrible) medonho; (timid) medroso, receoso. ~**less** a destemido, intrépido

feasib|le /ˈfiːzəbl/ a factível, praticável; (likely) plausível. ~**ility** /-ˈbɪlətɪ/ n possibilidade f; (plausibility) plausibilidade f

feast /fiːst/ n festim m; (relig; fig) festa f □ vt/i festejar; (eat and drink) banquetear-se. ~ **on** regalar-se com

feat /fiːt/ n feito m, façanha f

feather /ˈfeðə(r)/ n pena f, pluma f

feature /ˈfiːtʃə(r)/ n feição f, traço m; (quality) característica f; (film) longa metragem f; (article) artigo m em destaque □ vt representar; (film) ter como protagonista □ vi figurar

February /ˈfebrʊərɪ/ n Fevereiro m

fed /fed/ see **feed** □ a be ~ **up** estar farto (colloq) (with de)

federa|l /ˈfedərəl/ a federal. ~**tion** /-ˈreɪʃn/ n federação f

fee /fiː/ n preço m. ~**(s)** (of doctor, lawyer etc) honorários mpl; (member's subscription) quota f; (univ) (P) propinas fpl. (enrolment/registration) matrícula f school ~**s** mensalidades fpl escolares, (P) mensalidades fpl

feeble /ˈfiːbl/ a (-er, -est) débil, fraco. ~**-minded** a débil mental, (P) deficiente

feed /fiːd/ vt (pt fed) alimentar, dar de comer a; (suckle) alimentar; (supply) alimentar, abastecer □ vi alimentar-se □ n comida f; (breast-feeding) mamada f; (mech) alimentação f

feedback /ˈfiːdbæk/ n reação f, (P) reacção f; (electr) regeneração f

feel /fiːl/ vt (pt felt) sentir; (touch) apalpar, tatear □ vi (tired, lonely etc) sentir-se. ~ **hot/thirsty** ter calor/sede. ~ **as if** ter a impressão (de) que. ~ **like** ter vontade de

feeler /ˈfiːlə(r)/ n antena f

feeling /ˈfiːlɪŋ/ n sentimento m; (physical) sensação f

feet /fiːt/ see **foot**

feign /feɪn/ vt fingir

feline /ˈfiːlaɪn/ a felino

fell[1] /fel/ vt abater, derrubar

fell[2] /fel/ see **fall**

fellow /ˈfeləʊ/ n companheiro m, camarada m; (of society, college) membro m; (colloq) cara m, (P) tipo m (colloq). ~**-traveller** n companheiro m de viagem. ~**-ship** n companheirismo m, camaradagem f; (group) associação f

felt[1] /felt/ n feltro m

felt[2] /felt/ see **feel**

female /ˈfiːmeɪl/ a (animal etc) fêmea f; (voice, sex etc) feminino □ n mulher f; (animal) fêmea f

feminin|e /ˈfemənɪn/ a & n feminino (m). ~**ity** /-ˈnɪnətɪ/ n feminilidade f

feminist /ˈfemɪnɪst/ n feminista mf

fenc|e /fens/ n tapume m, cerca f □ vt cercar □ vi esgrimir. ~**er** n esgrimista mf. ~**ing** n esgrima f; (fences) tapume m

fend /fend/ vi ~ **for o.s.** defender-se, virar-se (colloq), governar-se □ vt ~ **off** defender-se de

fender /ˈfendə(r)/ n guarda-fogo m; (Amer: mudguard) pára-lama m, guarda-lama m, (P) pára-choques m

fennel /ˈfenl/ n (herb) funcho m, erva-doce f

ferment[1] /fəˈment/ vt/i fermentar; (excite) excitar. ~**ation** /fɜːmenˈteɪʃn/ n fermentação f

ferment[2] /ˈfɜːment/ n fermento m; (fig) efervescência f

fern /fɜːn/ n feto m

feroc|ious /fəˈrəʊʃəs/ a feroz. ~**ity** /-ˈrɒsətɪ/ n ferocidade f

ferret /ˈferɪt/ n furão m □ vi (pt ferreted) caçar com furões □ vt ~ **out** desenterrar

ferry /ˈferɪ/ n barco m de travessia, ferry(-boat) m □ vt transportar

fertil|e /ˈfɜːtaɪl/ a fértil, fecundo. ~**ity** /fəˈtɪlətɪ/ n fertilidade f, fecundidade f. ~**ize** /-əlaɪz/ vt fertilizar, fecundar

fertilizer /ˈfɜːtəlaɪzə(r)/ n adubo m, fertilizante m

fervent /'fɜ:vənt/ a fervoroso

fervour /'fɜ:və(r)/ n fervor m, ardor m

fester /'festə(r)/ vt/i infectar; (fig) envenenar

festival /'festɪvl/ n festival m; (relig) festa f

festiv|e /'festɪv/ a festivo. ~e season período m das festas. ~ity /fes'tɪvətɪ/ n festividade f, regozijo m. ~ities festas fpl, festividades fpl

festoon /fe'stu:n/ vt engrinaldar

fetch /fetʃ/ vt (go for) ir buscar; (bring) trazer; (be sold for) vender-se por, render

fetching /'fetʃɪŋ/ a atraente

fête /feit/ n festa f or feira f de caridade ao ar livre □ vt festejar

fetish /'fetɪʃ/ n fetiche m, idolo m; (obsession) mania f

fetter /'fetə(r)/ vt agrilhoar. ~s npl ferros mpl, grilhões mpl, grilhetas fpl

feud /fju:d/ n discórdia f, inimizade f. ~al a feudal

fever /'fi:və(r)/ n febre f. ~ish a febril

few /fju:/ a & n poucos (mpl). ~ books poucos livros. they are ~ são poucos. a ~ a & n alguns (mpl). a good ~, quite a ~ bastantes. ~er a & n menos (de). they were ~er eram menos numerosos. ~est a & n o menor número (de)

fiancé /fɪ'ɒnseɪ/ n noivo m. ~e n noiva f

fiasco /fɪ'æskəʊ/ n (pl -os) fiasco m

fib /fɪb/ n lorota f, cascata f, peta f, (P) mentira f □ vi (pt fibbed) fibbed)

fibre /'faɪbə(r)/ n fibra f

fibreglass /'faɪbəglɑ:s/ n fibra f de vidro

fickle /'fɪkl/ a leviano, inconstante

fiction /'fɪkʃn/ n ficçao f. (works of) ~ romances mpl, obras fpl de ficção. ~al a de ficção, fictício

fictitious /fɪk'tɪʃəs/ a fictício

fiddle /'fɪdl/ n (colloq) violino m; (sl: swindle) trapaça f □ vi (sl) trapacear (sl) □ vt (sl: falsify) falsificar, cozinhar (sl). ~ with (colloq) brincar com, mexer em, (P) estar a brincar com, estar a (re)mexer em. ~r /-ə(r)/ n (colloq) violinista m/f

fidelity /fɪ'delətɪ/ n fidelidade f

fidget /'fɪdʒɪt/ vi (pt fidgeted) estar irrequieto, remexer-se. ~ with remexer em. ~y a irrequieto; (impatient) impaciente

field /fi:ld/ n campo m □ vt/i (cricket) (estar pronto para) apanhar ou interceptar a bola. ~-day n grande dia m. ~-glasses npl binóculo m. F~ Marshal marechal-de-campo m

fieldwork /'fi:ldwɜ:k/ n trabalho m de campo; (mil) fortificação f de campanha

fiend /fi:nd/ n diabo m, demônio m, (P) demónio m. ~ish a diabólico

fierce /fɪəs/ a (-er, -est) feroz; (storm, attack) violento; (heat) intenso, abrasador. ~ness n ferocidade f; (of storm, attack) violência f; (of heat) intensidade f

fiery /'faɪərɪ/ a (-ier, -iest) ardente; (temper, speech) inflamado

fifteen /fɪf'ti:n/ a & n quinze (m). ~th a & n décimo quinto (m)

fifth /fɪfθ/ a & n quinto (m)

fift|y /'fɪftɪ/ a & n cinqüenta (m), (P) cinquenta (m). ~y-~y a meias. ~ieth a & n qüinquagésimo (m), (P) quinquagésimo (m)

fig /fɪg/ n figo m. ~-tree n figueira f

fight /faɪt/ vi (pt fought) lutar, combater □ vt lutar contra, combater □ n luta f; (quarrel, brawl) briga f. ~ over sth lutar por alg coisa. ~ shy of esquivar-se de, fugir de. ~er n lutador m; (mil) combatente mf; (plane) caça m. ~ing n combate m

figment /'fɪgmənt/ n ~ of the imagination fruto m or produto m da imaginação

figurative /'fɪgjərətɪv/ a figurado. ~ly adv em sentido figurado

figure /'fɪgə(r)/ n (number) algarismo m; (diagram, body) figura f. ~s npl (arithmetic) contas fpl, aritmética f □ vt imaginar, supor □ vi (appear) figurar (in em). ~ of speech figura f de retórica. ~ out compreender. ~-head n figura f de proa; (pej: person) testa-de-ferro m, chefe m nominal

filament /'fɪləmənt/ n filamento m

fil|e¹ /faɪl/ n (tool) lixa f, lima f □ vt lixar, limar. ~ings npl limalha f

fil|e² /faɪl/ n fichário m, (P) dossier m; (box, drawer) fichário m, (P) ficheiro m; (comput) arquivo m (line) fila f □ vt arquivar □ vi ~e (past) desfilar, marchar em fila. ~e in/out entrar/ sair em fila. (in) single ~e (em) fila indiana. ~ing cabinet fichário m, (P) ficheiro m

fill /fɪl/ vt/i encher(-se); (vacancy) preencher □ n eat one's ~ comer o que quiser. have one's ~ estar farto. ~ in (form) preencher. ~ out (get fat) engordar. ~ up encher até cima; (auto) encher o tanque

fillet /'fɪlɪt/ n (meat, fish) filé m, (P) filete m □ vt (pt filleted) (meat, fish) cortar em filés, (P) filetes

filling /'fɪlɪŋ/ n recheio m; (of tooth) obturação f, (P) chumbo m. ~ station posto m de gasolina

film /fɪlm/ n filme m □ vt/i filmar. ~ star estrela f or vedete f or (P) vedeta f de cinema, astro m

filter /'fɪltə(r)/ n filtro m □ vt/i filtrar

(-se). ~ **coffee** café m filtro. ~**-tip** n
cigarro m com filtro

filth /fɪlθ/ n imundície f; (fig) obsceni-
dade f. ~**y** a imundo; (fig) obsceno

fin /fɪn/ n barbatana f

final /ˈfaɪnl/ a final; (conclusive) decisivo □ n (sport) final f. ~**s** npl (exams)
finais fpl. ~**ist** n finalista mf. ~**ly**
adv finalmente, por fim; (once and
for all) definitivamente

finale /fɪˈnɑːlɪ/ n final m

finalize /ˈfaɪnəlaɪz/ vt finalizar

financ|e /ˈfaɪnæns/ n finança(s) f (pl)
□ a financeiro □ vt financiar. ~**ier**
/-ˈnænsɪə(r)/ n financeiro m

financial /faɪˈnænʃl/ a financeiro.
~**ly** adv financeiramente

find /faɪnd/ vt (pt **found**) (sth lost)
achar, encontrar; (think) achar; (discover) descobrir; (jur) declarar □ n
achado m. ~ **out** vt apurar, descobrir
□ vi informar-se (about sobre)

fine¹ /faɪn/ n multa f □ vt multar

fine² /faɪn/ a (-er, -est) fino; (splendid)
belo, lindo □ adv (muito) bem; (small)
fino, fininho. ~ **arts** belas artes fpl.
~ **weather** bom tempo. ~**ly** adv lindamente; (cut) finamente, aos bocadinhos

finesse /fɪˈnes/ n finura f, sutileza f

finger /ˈfɪŋɡə(r)/ n dedo m □ vt
apalpar. ~**-mark** n dedada f. ~**-nail**
n unha f

fingerprint /ˈfɪŋɡəprɪnt/ n impressão
f digital

fingertip /ˈfɪŋɡətɪp/ n ponta f do dedo

finicky /ˈfɪnɪkɪ/ a meticuloso, miudi-
nho

finish /ˈfɪnɪʃ/ vt/i acabar, terminar □
n fim m; (of race) chegada f; (on wood,
clothes) acabamento m. ~ **doing** acabar de fazer. ~ **up** vt/i acabar por
fazer. ~ **up in** parar a, acabar em

finite /ˈfaɪnaɪt/ a finito

Fin|land /ˈfɪnlənd/ n Finlândia f. ~**n**
n finlandês m. ~**nish** a & n (lang)
finlandês (m)

fir /fɜː(r)/ n abeto m

fire /ˈfaɪə(r)/ n fogo m; (conflagration)
incêndio m; (heater) aquecedor m □ vt
(bullet, gun, etc) disparar; (dismiss)
despedir; (fig: stimulate) inflamar □
vi atirar, fazer fogo (at sobre). on ~
em chamas. set ~ to pôr fogo em. ~-
alarm n alarme m de incêndio. ~-
brigade bombeiros mpl. ~**-engine** n
carro m de bombeiro, (P) da bomba.
~**-escape** n saída f de incêndio. ~-
extinguisher n extintor m de
incêndio. ~ **station** quartel m dos
bombeiros

firearm /ˈfaɪərɑːm/ n arma f de fogo

fireman /ˈfaɪəmən/ n (pl -men) bombeiro m

fireplace /ˈfaɪəpleɪs/ n chaminé f, lareira f

firewood /ˈfaɪəwʊd/ n lenha f

firework /ˈfaɪəwɜːk/ n fogo m de artifício

firing-squad /ˈfaɪərɪŋskwɒd/ n pelotão m de execução

firm¹ /fɜːm/ n firma f comercial

firm² /fɜːm/ a (-er, -est) firme; (belief)
firme, inabalável. ~**ly** adv firmemente. ~**ness** n firmeza f

first /fɜːst/ a & n primeiro (m); (auto)
primeira (f) □ adv primeiro, em primeiro lugar. **at** ~ a princípio, no
início. ~ **of all** antes de mais nada.
for the ~ **time** pela primeira vez. ~
aid primeiros socorros mpl. ~**-class**
a de primeira classe. ~ **name** nome
de batismo m, (P) baptismo m. ~**-rate**
a excelente. ~**ly** adv primeiramente,
em primeiro lugar

fiscal /ˈfɪskl/ a fiscal

fish /fɪʃ/ n (pl usually invar) peixe m
□ vt/i pescar. ~ **out** (colloq) tirar.
~**ing** n pesca f. **go** ~**ing** ir pescar,
(P) ir à pesca. ~**ing-rod** n vara f de
pescar. ~**y** a de peixe; (fig: dubious)
suspeito

fisherman /ˈfɪʃəmən/ n (pl -men)
pescador m

fishmonger /ˈfɪʃmʌŋɡə(r)/ n dono m/
empregado m de peixaria. ~**'s (shop)**
peixaria f

fission /ˈfɪʃn/ n fissão f, cisão f

fist /fɪst/ n punho m, mão f fechada,
(P) punho m

fit¹ /fɪt/ n acesso m, ataque m; (of gen-
erosity) rasgo m

fit² /fɪt/ a (fitter, fittest) de boa saúde,
em forma, (P) próprio; (good
enough) em condições; (able) capaz □
vt/i (pt fitted) (clothes) assentar, ficar
bem (a); (into space) (match) ajustar
(-se) (a); (install) instalar □ n be a
good ~ assentar bem. be a tight ~
estar justo. ~ **out** equipar. ~**ted carpet** carpete m, (P) alcatifa f. ~**ness** n
saúde f, (P) condição f física

fitful /ˈfɪtfl/ a intermitente

fitment /ˈfɪtmənt/ n móvel m de parede

fitting /ˈfɪtɪŋ/ a apropriado □ n
(clothes) prova f. ~**s** (fixtures) ins-
talações fpl; (fitments) mobiliário m.
~ **room** cabine f

five /faɪv/ a & n cinco (m)

fix /fɪks/ vt fixar; (mend, prepare) arranjar □ n **in a** ~ em apuros, (P)
numa alhada. ~ **sb up with sth** conseguir alg coisa para alguém. ~**ed** a
fixo

fixation /fɪkˈseɪʃn/ n fixação f; (obsession) obsessão f

fixture /ˈfɪkstʃə(r)/ n equipamento m,

instalação f; (sport) (data f marcada para) competição f

fizz /fɪz/ vi efervescer, borbulhar □ n efervescência f. ~y a gasoso

fizzle /ˈfɪzl/ vi ~ out (plan etc) acabar em nada ou (P) em águas de bacalhau (colloq)

flab /flæb/ n (colloq) gordura f, banha f (colloq). ~by a flácido

flabbergasted /ˈflæbəgɑːstɪd/ a (colloq) espantado, pasmado (colloq)

flag[1] /flæg/ n bandeira f □ vt (pt flagged) fazer sinal. ~ down fazer sinal para parar. ~-pole n mastro m (de bandeira)

flag[2] /flæg/ vi (pt flagged) (droop) cair, pender, tombar; (of person) esmorecer

flagrant /ˈfleɪɡrənt/ a flagrante

flagstone /ˈflæɡstəʊn/ n laje f

flair /fleə(r)/ n jeito m, habilidade f

flak|**e** /fleɪk/ n floco m; (paint) lasca f □ vi descamar-se, lascar-se. ~y a (paint) descamado, lascado

flamboyant /flæmˈbɔɪənt/ a flamejante; (showy) flamante, vistoso; (of manner) extravagante

flame /fleɪm/ n chama f, labareda f □ vi flamejar. **burst into** ~**s** incendiar-se

flamingo /fləˈmɪŋɡəʊ/ n (pl -os) flamingo m

flammable /ˈflæməbl/ a inflamável

flan /flæn/ n torta f, (P) tarte f

flank /flæŋk/ n flanco m □ vt flanquear

flannel /ˈflænl/ n flanela f, (for face) toalha f, (P) toalhete m de rosto

flap /flæp/ vi (pt flapped) bater □ vt ~ **its wings** bater as asas □ n (of table, pocket) aba f; (sl: panic) pânico m

flare /fleə(r)/ vi ~ up irromper em chamas; (of war) rebentar; (fig: of person) enfurecer-se □ n chamejar m; (dazzling light) clarão m; (signal) foguete m de sinalização. ~d a (skirt) évasé

flash /flæʃ/ vi brilhar subitamente; (on and off) piscar; (auto) fazer sinal com o pisca-pisca □ vt fazer brilhar; (send) lançar, dardejar; (flaunt) fazer alarde de, ostentar □ n clarão m, lampejo m; (photo) flash m. ~ **past** passar como uma bala, (P) passar como um bólide

flashback /ˈflæʃbæk/ n cena f retrospectiva, flashback m

flashlight /ˈflæʃlaɪt/ n lanterna f eléctrica, (P) eléctrica

flashy /ˈflæʃɪ/ a espalhafatoso, que dá na vista

flask /flɑːsk/ n frasco m; (vacuum flask) garrafa f térmica, (P) garrafa f termos

flat /flæt/ a (flatter, flattest) plano, chato; (tyre) arriado, vazio; (battery) fraco; (refusal) categórico; (fare, rate) fixo; (monotonous) monótono; (mus) bemol; (out of tune) desafinado □ n apartamento m; (mus) bemol m. ~ **out** (drive); (work) a dar tudo por tudo. ~**ly** adv categoricamente

flatter /ˈflætə(r)/ vt lisonjear, adular. ~**er** n lisonjeiro m, adulador m. ~**ing** a lisonjeiro, adulador. ~**y** n lisonja f

flatulence /ˈflætjʊləns/ n flatulência f

flaunt /flɔːnt/ vt/i pavonear(-se), ostentar

flavour /ˈfleɪvə(r)/ n sabor m (of a) □ vt dar sabor a, temperar. ~**ing** n aroma m sintético; (seasoning) tempero m

flaw /flɔː/ n falha f, imperfeição f. ~**ed** a imperfeito. ~**less** a perfeito

flea /fliː/ n pulga f

fled /fled/ see **flee**

fledged /fledʒd/ a **fully-**~ (fig) treinado, experiente

flee /fliː/ vi (pt fled) fugir □ vt fugir de

fleece /fliːs/ n lã f de carneiro, velo m □ vt (fig) esfolar, roubar

fleet /fliːt/ n (of warships) esquadra f; (of merchant ships, vehicles) frota f

fleeting /ˈfliːtɪŋ/ a curto, fugaz

Flemish /ˈflemɪʃ/ a & n (lang) flamengo (m)

flesh /fleʃ/ n carne f; (of fruit) polpa f. ~**y** a carnudo

flew /fluː/ see **fly**[1]

flex[1] /fleks/ vt flexionar

flex[2] /fleks/ n (electr) fio f flexível

flexib|**le** /ˈfleksəbl/ a flexível. ~**ility** /-ˈbɪlətɪ/ n flexibilidade f

flexitime /ˈfleksɪtaɪm/ n horário m flexível

flick /flɪk/ n (light blow) safanão m; (with fingertip) piparote m □ vt dar um safanão em; (with fingertip) dar um piparote a. ~**-knife** n navalha f de ponta e mola. ~ **through** folhear

flicker /ˈflɪkə(r)/ vi vacilar, oscilar, tremular □ n oscilação f, tremular m; (light) luz f oscilante

flier /ˈflaɪə(r)/ n = **flyer**

flies /flaɪz/ npl (of trousers) braguilha f

flight[1] /flaɪt/ n (flying) voo m. ~ **of stairs** lance m, (P) lanço m de escada. ~**-deck** n cabine f, (P) cabina f

flight[2] /flaɪt/ n (fleeing) fuga f. **put to** ~ pôr em fuga. **take** ~ pôr-se em fuga

flimsy /ˈflɪmzɪ/ a (-ier, -iest) (material) fino; (object) frágil; (excuse etc) fraco, esfarrapado

flinch /flɪntʃ/ vi (wince) retrair-se; (draw back) recuar; (hesitate) hesitar

fling /flɪŋ/ vt/i (pt flung) atirar(-se), arremessar(-se); (rush) precipitar(-se)

flint /flɪnt/ n silex m; (for lighter) pedra f

flip /flɪp/ vt (pt flipped) fazer girar com o dedo e o polegar □ n pancadinha f. ~ through folhear

flippant /ˈflɪpənt/ a irreverente, petulante

flipper /ˈflɪpə(r)/ n (of seal) nadadeira f; (of swimmer) pé-de-pato m

flirt /flɜːt/ vt namoriscar, flertar, (P) flartar □ n namorador m, namoradeira f. ~ation /-ˈeɪʃn/ n namorico m, flerte m, (P) flirt m. ~atious a namorador m, namoradeira f

flit /flɪt/ vi (pt flitted) esvoaçar

float /fləʊt/ vt/i (fazer) flutuar; (company) lançar □ n bóia f; (low cart) carro m de alegórico

flock /flɒk/ n (of sheep; congregation) rebanho m; (of birds) bando m; (crowd) multidão □ vi afluir, juntar-se

flog /flɒg/ vt (pt flogged) açoitar; (sl: sell) vender

flood /flʌd/ n inundação f, cheia f; (of tears) dilúvio m □ vt inundar, alagar □ vi estar inundado; (river) transbordar; (fig: people) afluir

floodlight /ˈflʌdlaɪt/ n projetor m, (P) projector m, holofote m □ vt (pt floodlit) iluminar

floor /flɔː(r)/ n chão m, soalho m; (for dancing) pista f; (storey) andar m □ vt assoalhar; (baffle) desconcertar, embatucar

flop /flɒp/ vi (pt flopped) (drop) (deixar-se) cair; (move helplessly) debater-se; (sl: fail) ser um fiasco □ n (sl) fiasco m. ~py a mole, tombado. ~py (disk) disquete m

floral /ˈflɔːrəl/ a floral

florid /ˈflɒrɪd/ a florido

florist /ˈflɒrɪst/ n florista mf

flounce /flaʊns/ n babado m, debrum m

flounder /ˈflaʊndə(r)/ vi esbracejar, debater-se; (fig) meter os pés pelas mãos

flour /ˈflaʊə(r)/ n farinha f. ~y a farinhento

flourish /ˈflʌrɪʃ/ vi florescer, prosperar □ vt brandir □ n (movement) gesto m elegante. ~ing a próspero

flout /flaʊt/ vt escarnecer (de)

flow /fləʊ/ vi correr, fluir; (traffic) mover-se; (hang loosely) flutuar; (gush) jorrar □ n corrente f; (of tide; fig) enchente f. ~ into (of river) desaguar em. ~ chart organograma m, (P) organigrama m

flower /ˈflaʊə(r)/ n flor f □ vi florir, florescer. ~-bed n canteiro m. ~ed a de flores, (P) florido, às flores. ~y a florido

flown /fləʊn/ see fly[2]

flu /fluː/ n (colloq) gripe f

fluctuat|e /ˈflʌktʃʊeɪt/ vi flutuar, oscilar. ~ion /-ˈeɪʃn/ n flutuação f, oscilação f

flue /fluː/ n cano m de chaminé

fluen|t /ˈfluːənt/ a fluente. be ~t (in a language) falar correntemente (uma língua). ~cy n fluência f. ~tly adv fluentemente

fluff /flʌf/ n cotão m; (down) penugem f □ vt (colloq: bungle) estender-se em (sl), executar mal. ~y a penugento, fofo

fluid /ˈfluːɪd/ a & n fluido m

fluke /fluːk/ n bambúrrio (colloq), golpe m de sorte

flung /flʌŋ/ see fling

flunk /flʌŋk/ vt/i (Amer colloq) levar pau (colloq), (P) chumbar (colloq)

fluorescent /flʊəˈresnt/ a fluorescente

fluoride /ˈflʊəraɪd/ n flúor m, fluor m

flurry /ˈflʌrɪ/ n rajada f, rabanada f, lufada f; (fig) atrapalhação f, agitação f

flush[1] /flʌʃ/ vi corar, ruborizar-se □ vt lavar com água, (P) lavar a jorros de água □ n rubor m, vermelhidão f; (fig) excitação f; (of water) jorro m □ a ~ with ao nível de, rente a. ~ the toilet dar descarga

flush[2] /flʌʃ/ vt ~ out desalojar

fluster /ˈflʌstə(r)/ vt atarantar, perturbar, enervar

flute /fluːt/ n flauta f

flutter /ˈflʌtə(r)/ vi esvoaçar; (wings) bater; (heart) palpitar □ vt bater. ~ one's eyelashes pestanejar □ n (of wings) batimento m; (fig) agitação f

flux /flʌks/ n in a state of ~ em mudança f contínua

fly[1] /flaɪ/ n mosca f

fly[2] /flaɪ/ vi (pt flew, pp flown) voar; (passengers) ir de/viajar de avião; (rush) correr □ vt pilotar; (passengers, goods) transportar por avião; (flag) hastear, (P) arvorar □ n (of trousers) braguilha f

flyer /ˈflaɪə(r)/ n aviador m; (Amer: circular) prospecto m

flying /ˈflaɪɪŋ/ a voador. with ~ colours com grande êxito, esplendidamente. ~ saucer disco m voador. ~ start bom arranque m. ~ visit visita f de médico

flyleaf /ˈflaɪliːf/ n (pl -leaves) guarda f, folha f em branco

flyover /ˈflaɪəʊvə(r)/ n viaduto m

foal /fəʊl/ n potro m

foam /fəʊm/ n espuma f □ vi espumar. ~ (rubber) n espuma f de borracha

fob /fɒb/ vt (pt fobbed) ~ off iludir, entreter com artifícios. ~ off on impingir a

focus /ˈfəʊkəs/ n (pl -cuses or -ci /-saɪ/) foco m □ vt/i (pt focused) focar; (fig) concentrar(-se). in ~ focado, em foco. out of ~ desfocado

fodder /ˈfɒdə(r)/ n forragem f

foetus /ˈfiːtəs/ n (pl -tuses) feto m

fog /fɒg/ n nevoeiro m □ vt/i (pt fogged) enevoar(-se). ~-horn n sereia f de nevoeiro. ~gy a enevoado, brumoso. it is ~gy está nevoento

foible /ˈfɔɪbl/ n fraqueza f, ponto m fraco

foil¹ /fɔɪl/ n papel m de alumínio; (fig) contraste m

foil² /fɔɪl/ vt frustrar

foist /fɔɪst/ vt impingir (on a)

fold /fəʊld/ vt/i dobrar(-se); (arms) cruzar; (colloq: fail) falir □ n dobra f. ~er n pasta f; (leaflet) prospecto m (desdobrável). ~ing a dobrável, dobradiço

foliage /ˈfəʊlɪdʒ/ n folhagem f

folk /fəʊk/ n povo m. ~s (family, people) gente f (colloq) □ a folclórico, popular. ~lore n folclore m

follow /ˈfɒləʊ/ vt/i seguir. it ~s that quer dizer que. ~ suit (cards) servir o naipe jogado; (fig) seguir o exemplo, fazer o mesmo. ~ up (letter etc) dar seguimento a. ~er n partidário m, seguidor m. ~ing n partidários mpl □ a seguinte □ prep em seguimento a

folly /ˈfɒlɪ/ n loucura f

fond /fɒnd/ a (-er -est) carinhoso; (hope) caro. be ~ of gostar de, ser amigo de. ~ness n (for people) afeição f; (for thing) gosto m

fondle /ˈfɒndl/ vt acariciar

font /fɒnt/ n pia f batismal, (P) baptismal

food /fuːd/ n alimentação f, comida f; (nutrient) alimento m □ a alimentar. ~ poisoning envenenamento m alimentar

fool /fuːl/ n idiota mf, parvo m □ vt enganar □ vi ~ around andar sem fazer nada

foolhardy /ˈfuːlhaːdɪ/ a imprudente, atrevido

foolish /ˈfuːlɪʃ/ a idiota, parvo. ~ly adv parvamente. ~ness n idiotice f, parvoíce f

foolproof /ˈfuːlpruːf/ a infalível

foot /fʊt/ n (pl feet) (of person, bed, stairs) pé m; (of animal) pata f; (measure) pé m (= 30,48 cm) □ vt ~ the bill pagar a conta. on ~ a pé. on or to one's feet de pé. put one's ~

in it fazer uma gafe. to be under sb's feet atrapalhar alg. ~-bridge n passarela f

football /ˈfʊtbɔːl/ n bola f de futebol; (game) futebol m. ~ pools loteria f esportiva, (P) totobola m. ~er n futebolista mf, jogador m de futebol

foothills /ˈfʊthɪlz/ npl contrafortes mpl

foothold /ˈfʊthəʊld/ n ponto m de apoio

footing /ˈfʊtɪŋ/ n: firm ~ stor. on an equal ~ em pé de igualdade

footlights /ˈfʊtlaɪts/ npl ribalta f

footnote /ˈfʊtnəʊt/ n nota f de rodapé

footpath /ˈfʊtpaːθ/ n (pavement) calçada f, (P) passeio m; (in open country) atalho m, caminho m

footprint /ˈfʊtprɪnt/ n pegada f

footstep /ˈfʊtstep/ n passo m

footwear /ˈfʊtweə(r)/ n calçado m

for /fɔː(r)/; emphatic /fɔː(r)/ prep para; (in favour of; in place of) por; (during) durante □ conj porque, visto que. a liking ~ gosto por. he has been away ~ two years há dois anos que ele está fora. ~ ever para sempre

forage /ˈfɒrɪdʒ/ vi forragear; (rummage) remexer à procura (de) □ n forragem f

forbade /fəˈbæd/ see forbid

forbear /fɔːˈbeə(r)/ vt/i (pt forbore, pp forborne) abster-se (from de). ~ance n paciência f, tolerância f

forbid /fəˈbɪd/ vt (pt forbade, pp forbidden) proibir. you are ~den to smoke você está proibido de fumar, (P) estás proibido de fumar. ~ding a severo, intimidante

force /fɔːs/ n força f □ vt forçar. ~ into fazer entrar à força. ~ on impor a. come into ~ entrar em vigor. the ~s as Forças Armadas. ~d a forçado. ~ful a enérgico

force-feed /ˈfɔːsfiːd/ vt (pt -fed) alimentar à força

forceps /ˈfɔːseps/ n (pl invar) fórceps m

forcibl|e /ˈfɔːsəbl/ a convincente; (done by force) à força. ~y adv à força

ford /fɔːd/ n vau m □ vt passar a vau, vadear

fore /fɔː(r)/ a dianteiro □ n to the ~ em evidência

forearm /ˈfɔːraːm/ n antebraço m

foreboding /fɔːˈbəʊdɪŋ/ n pressentimento m

forecast /ˈfɔːkaːst/ vt (pt forecast) prever □ n previsão f. weather ~ boletim m meteorológico, previsão f do tempo

forecourt /ˈfɔːkɔːt/ n pátio m de entrada; (of garage) área f das bombas de gasolina

forefinger /ˈfɔːfɪŋɡə(r)/ n (dedo) indicador m

forefront /ˈfɔːfrʌnt/ n vanguarda f

foregone /ˈfɔːɡɒn/ a ~ **conclusion** resultado m previsto

foreground /ˈfɔːɡraʊnd/ n primeiro plano m

forehead /ˈfɒrɪd/ n testa f

foreign /ˈfɒrən/ a estrangeiro; (trade) externo; (travel) ao/no estrangeiro. **F~ Office** Ministério m dos Negócios Estrangeiros. ~**er** n estrangeiro m.

foreman /ˈfɔːmən/ n (pl **foremen**) contramestre m; (of jury) primeiro jurado m

foremost /ˈfɔːməʊst/ a principal, primeiro □ adv **first and** ~ antes de mais nada, em primeiro lugar

forename /ˈfɔːneɪm/ n nome m

forensic /fəˈrensɪk/ a forense. ~ **medicine** medicina f legal

forerunner /ˈfɔːrʌnə(r)/ n precursor m

foresee /fɔːˈsiː/ vt (pt -**saw**, pp -**seen**) prever. ~**able** a previsível

foreshadow /fɔːˈʃædəʊ/ vt prefigurar, pressagiar

foresight /ˈfɔːsaɪt/ n previsão f, previdência f

forest /ˈfɒrɪst/ n floresta f

forestall /fɔːˈstɔːl/ vt (do first) antecipar-se a; (prevent) prevenir; (anticipate) antecipar

forestry /ˈfɒrɪstrɪ/ n silvicultura f

foretell /fɔːˈtel/ vt (pt **foretold**) predizer, profetizar

forever /fəˈrevə(r)/ adv (endlessly) constantemente

foreword /ˈfɔːwɜːd/ n prefácio m

forfeit /ˈfɔːfɪt/ n penalidade f, preço m; (in game) prenda f □ vt perder

forgave /fəˈɡeɪv/ see **forgive**

forge¹ /fɔːdʒ/ vi ~ **ahead** tomar a dianteira, avançar

forge² /fɔːdʒ/ n forja f □ vt (metal, friendship) forjar; (counterfeit) falsificar, forjar. ~**r** /-ə(r)/ n falsificador m, forjador m. ~**ry** /-ərɪ/ n falsificação f

forget /fəˈɡet/ vt/i (pt **forgot**, pp **forgotten**) esquecer. ~ **o.s.** portar-se com menos dignidade, esquecer-se de quem é. ~**me-not** n miosótis m. ~**ful** a esquecido. ~**fulness** n esquecimento m

forgive /fəˈɡɪv/ vt (pt **forgave**, pp **forgiven**) perdoar (**sb for sth** alg coisa a alg). ~**ness** n perdão m

forgo /fɔːˈɡəʊ/ vt (pt **forwent**, pp **forgone**) renunciar a

fork /fɔːk/ n garfo m; (for digging etc) forquilha f; (in road) bifurcação f □ vi bifurcar. ~ **out** (sl) desembolsar. ~-**lift truck** empilhadeira f. ~**ed** a bifurcado; (lightning) em zigzag

forlorn /fəˈlɔːn/ a abandonado, desolado

form /fɔːm/ n forma f; (document) impresso m, formulário m; (schol) classe f □ vt/i formar(-se)

formal /ˈfɔːml/ a formal; (dress) de cerimónia, (P) cerimónia. ~**ity** /-ˈmælətɪ/ n formalidade f. ~**ly** adv formalmente

format /ˈfɔːmæt/ n formato m □ vt (pl **formatted**) (disk) formatar

formation /fɔːˈmeɪʃn/ n formação f

former /ˈfɔːmə(r)/ a antigo; (first of two) primeiro. **the** ~ aquele. ~**ly** adv antigamente

formidable /ˈfɔːmɪdəbl/ a formidável, tremendo

formula /ˈfɔːmjʊlə/ n (pl -**ae** /-iː/ or -**as**) fórmula f

formulate /ˈfɔːmjʊleɪt/ vt formular

forsake /fəˈseɪk/ vt (pt **forsook**, pp **forsaken**) abandonar

fort /fɔːt/ n (mil) forte m

forth /fɔːθ/ adv adiante, para a frente. **and so** ~ e assim por diante, etcetera. **go back and** ~ andar de trás para diante.

forthcoming /fɔːθˈkʌmɪŋ/ a que está para vir, próximo; (communicative) comunicativo, receptivo; (book) no prelo

forthright /ˈfɔːθraɪt/ a franco, direto, (P) directo

fortify /ˈfɔːtɪfaɪ/ vt fortificar. ~**ication** /-ɪˈkeɪʃn/ n fortificação f

fortitude /ˈfɔːtɪtjuːd/ n fortitude f, fortaleza f

fortnight /ˈfɔːtnaɪt/ n quinze dias mpl, (P) quinzena f. ~**ly** a quinzenal □ adv de quinze em quinze dias

fortress /ˈfɔːtrɪs/ n fortaleza f

fortuitous /fɔːˈtjuːɪtəs/ a fortuito, acidental

fortunate /ˈfɔːtʃənət/ a feliz, afortunado. **be** ~ ter sorte. ~**ly** adv felizmente

fortune /ˈfɔːtʃən/ n sorte f; (wealth) fortuna f. **have the good** ~ **to** ter a sorte de. ~-**teller** n cartomante mf

forty /ˈfɔːtɪ/ a & n quarenta (m). ~**ieth** a &n quadragésimo (m)

forum /ˈfɔːrəm/ n fórum m, foro m

forward /ˈfɔːwəd/ a (in front) dianteiro; (towards the front) para a frente; (advanced) adiantado; (pert) atrevido □ n (sport) atacante m, (P) avançado m □ adv ~(**s**) para a frente, para diante □ vt (letter) remeter; (goods) expedir; (fig: help) favorecer. **come** ~ apresentar-se. **go** ~ avançar. ~**ness** n adiantamento m; (pertness) atrevimento m

fossil /ˈfɒsl/ a & n fóssil (m)

foster /ˈfɒstə(r)/ vt fomentar; (child)

criar. ~**-child** n filho m adotivo, (P) adoptivo. ~**-mother** n mãe f adotiva, (P) adoptiva

fought /fɔːt/ see **fight**

foul /faʊl/ a (-er, -est) infecto; (language) obsceno; (weather) mau □ n (football) falta f □ vt sujar, emporcalhar. ~**-mouthed** a de linguagem obscena. ~ **play** jogo m desleal; (crime) crime m

found[1] /faʊnd/ see **find**

found[2] /faʊnd/ vt fundar. ~**ation** /-'deɪʃn/ n fundação f; (basis) fundamento m. ~**ations** npl (of building) alicerces mpl

founder[1] /'faʊndə(r)/ n fundador m

founder[2] /'faʊndə(r)/ vi afundar-se

foundry /'faʊndrɪ/ n fundição f

fountain /'faʊntɪn/ n fonte f. ~**-pen** n caneta-tinteiro f, (P) caneta f de tinta permanente

four /fɔː(r)/ a & n quatro (m). ~**fold** a quádruplo □ adv quadruplamente. ~**th** a & n quarto (m)

foursome /'fɔːsəm/ n grupo m de quatro pessoas

fourteen /fɔː'tiːn/ a & n catorze (m). ~**th** a & n décimo quarto (m)

fowl /faʊl/ n ave f de capoeira

fox /fɒks/ n raposa f □ vt (colloq) mistificar, enganar. be ~**ed** ficar perplexo

foyer /'fɔɪeɪ/ n foyer m

fraction /'frækʃn/ n fração f, (P) fracção f; (small bit) bocadinho m, partícula f

fracture /'fræktʃə(r)/ n fratura f, (P) fractura f □ vt/i fraturar(-se), (P) fracturar(-se)

fragile /'frædʒaɪl/ a frágil

fragment /'frægmənt/ n fragmento m. ~**ary** /'frægməntrɪ/ a fragmentário

fragran|**t** /'freɪɡrənt/ a fragrante, perfumado. ~**ce** n fragrância f, perfume m

frail /freɪl/ a (-er, -est) frágil

frame /freɪm/ n (techn; of spectacles) armação f; (of picture) moldura f, (of window) caixilho m; (body) corpo m, (P) estrutura f □ vt colocar a armação em; (picture) emoldurar; (fig) formular; (sl) incriminar falsamente, tramar. ~ **of mind** estado m de espírito

framework /'freɪmwɜːk/ n estrutura f, (context) quadro m, esquema m

France /frɑːns/ n França f

franchise /'fræntʃaɪz/ n (pol) direito m de voto; (comm) concessão f, franchise f

frank[1] /fræŋk/ a franco. ~**ly** adv francamente. ~**ness** n franqueza f

frank[2] /fræŋk/ vt franquear

frantic /'fræntɪk/ a frenético

fraternal /frə'tɜːnl/ a fraternal

fraternize /'frætənaɪz/ vi confraternizar

fraud /frɔːd/ n fraude f; (person) impostor m. ~**ulent** /'frɔːdjʊlənt/ a fraudulento

fraught /frɔːt/ a ~ **with** cheio de

fray[1] /freɪ/ n rixa f

fray[2] /freɪ/ vt/i desfiar(-se), puir, esgarçar(-se)

freak /friːk/ n aberração f, anomalia f □ a anormal. ~ **of nature** aborto m da natureza. ~**ish** a anormal

freckle /'frekl/ n sarda f. ~**d** a sardento

free /friː/ a (freer, freest) livre; (gratis) grátis; (lavish) liberal □ vt (pt freed) libertar (from de); (rid) livrar (of de). ~ **of charge** grátis, de graça. a ~ **hand** carta f branca. ~**lance** a independente, free-lance. ~**-range** a (egg) de galinha criada em galinheiro. ~**ly** adv livremente

freedom /'friːdəm/ n liberdade f

freez|**e** /friːz/ vt/i (pt froze, pp frozen) gelar; (culin; finance) congelar (-se) □ n gelo m; (culin; finance) congelamento m. ~**er** n congelador m. ~**ing** a gélido, glacial. below ~**ing** abaixo de zero

freight /freɪt/ n frete m

French /frentʃ/ a francês □ n (lang) francês m. the ~ os franceses. ~**man** n francês m. ~**-speaking** a francófono. ~ **window** porta f envidraçada. ~**woman** n francesa f

frenz|**y** /'frenzɪ/ n frenesi m. ~**ied** a frenético

frequen|**t**[1] /'friːkwənt/ a freqüente, (P) frequente. ~**cy** n freqüência f, (P) frequência f. ~**tly** adv freqüentemente, (P) frequentemente

frequent[2] /frɪ'kwent/ vt freqüentar, (P) frequentar

fresh /freʃ/ a (-er, -est) fresco; (different, additional) novo; (colloq: cheeky) descarado, atrevido. ~**ly** adv recentemente. ~**ness** n frescura f

freshen /'freʃn/ vt/i refrescar. ~ **up** refrescar-se

fret /fret/ vt/i (pt fretted) ralar(-se). ~**ful** a rabugento

friar /'fraɪə(r)/ n frade m; (before name) frei m

friction /'frɪkʃn/ n fricção f

Friday /'fraɪdɪ/ n sexta-feira f. Good ~ sexta-feira f santa

fridge /frɪdʒ/ n (colloq) geladeira f, (P) frigorífico m

fried /fraɪd/ see **fry** □ a frito

friend /frend/ n amigo m. ~**ship** n amizade f

friendl|**y** /'frendlɪ/ a (-ier, -iest)

amigável, amigo, simpático. ~iness *n* simpatia *f*, gentileza *f*

frieze /fri:z/ *n* friso *m*

frigate /'frɪgət/ *n* fragata *f*

fright /fraɪt/ *n* medo *m*, susto *m*. give sb a ~ pregar um susto em alguém. ~ful *a* medonho, assustador

frighten /'fraɪtn/ *vt* assustar. ~ off afugentar. ~ed *a* assustado. be ~ed (of) ter medo (de)

frigid /'frɪdʒɪd/ *a* frígido. ~ity /-'dʒɪdətɪ/ *n* frigidez *f*, frieza *f*; (*psych*) frigidez *f*

frill /frɪl/ *n* babado *m*, (*P*) folho *m*

fringe /frɪndʒ/ *n* franja *f*; (*of area*) borda *f*; (*of society*) margem *f*. ~ benefits (*work*) regalias *fpl* extras. ~ theatre teatro *m* alternativo, teatro *m* de vanguarda

frisk /frɪsk/ *vi* pular, brincar □ *vt* revistar

fritter¹ /'frɪtə(r)/ *n* bolinho *m* frito, (*P*) frito *m*

fritter² /'frɪtə(r)/ *vt* ~ away desperdiçar

frivol|ous /'frɪvələs/ *a* frívolo. ~ity /-'vɒlətɪ/ *n* frivolidade *f*

fro /frəʊ/ *see* to and fro

frock /frɒk/ *n* vestido *m*

frog /frɒg/ *n* rã *f*

frogman /'frɒgmən/ *n* (*pl* -men) homem-rã *m*

frolic /'frɒlɪk/ *vi* (*pt* frolicked) brincar, fazer travessuras □ *n* brincadeira *f*, travessura *f*

from /frəm/; *emphatic* /frɒm/ *prep* de; (*with time, prices etc*) de, a partir de; (*according to*) por, a julgar por

front /frʌnt/ *n* (*meteo, mil, pol; of car, train*) frente *f*; (*of shirt*) peitilho *m*; (*of building; fig*) fachada *f*; (*promenade*) calçada *f*, à beiramar □ *a* da frente; (*first*) primeiro. in ~ (of) em frente (de). ~ door porta *f* da rua. ~-wheel drive tração *f*, (*P*) tracção *f* dianteira. ~age *n* frontaria *f*. ~al *a* frontal

frontier /'frʌntɪə(r)/ *n* fronteira *f*

frost /frɒst/ *n* gelo *m*, temperatura *f* abaixo de zero; (*on ground, plants etc*) geada *f* □ *vt/i* cobrir(-se) de geada. ~bite *n* queimadura *f* de frio. ~bitten *a* queimado pelo frio. ~ed *a* (*glass*) fosco. ~y *a* glacial

froth /frɒθ/ *n* espuma *f* □ *vi* espumar, fazer espuma. ~y *a* espumoso

frown /fraʊn/ *vi* franzir as sobrancelhas □ *n* franzir *m* de sobrancelhas. ~ on desaprovar

froze, frozen /frəʊz, 'frəʊzn/ *see* freeze

frugal /'fru:gl/ *a* poupado; (*meal*) frugal. ~ly *adv* frugalmente

fruit /fru:t/ *n* fruto *m*; (*collectively*) fruta *f*. ~ machine caçaníqueis *ms/*

pl. ~ salad salada *f* de frutas. ~y *a* que tem gosto *or* cheiro de fruta

fruit|ful /'fru:tfl/ *a* frutífero, produtivo. ~less *n* infrutífero

fruition /fru:'ɪʃn/ *n* come to ~ realizar-se

frustrat|e /frʌ'streɪt/ *vt* frustrar. ~ion /-ʃn/ *n* frustração *f*

fry /fraɪ/ *vt/i* (*pt* fried) fritar. ~ingpan *n* frigideira *f*

fudge /fʌdʒ/ *n* (*culin*) doce *m* de leite, (*P*) doce *m* acaramelado □ *vt/i* ~ (the issue) lançar a confusão

fuel /'fju:əl/ *n* combustível *m*; (*for car*) carburante *m* □ *vt* (*pt* fuelled) abastecer de combustível; (*fig*) atear

fugitive /'fju:dʒətɪv/ *a & n* fugitivo (*m*)

fulfil /fʊl'fɪl/ *vt* (*pt* fulfilled) cumprir, realizar; (*condition*) satisfazer. ~ o.s. realizar-se. ~ling *a* satisfatório. ~ment *n* realização *f*; (*of condition*) satisfação *f*

full /fʊl/ *a* (-er, -est) cheio; (*meal*) completo; (*price*) total, por inteiro; (*skirt*) rodado □ *adv* in ~ integralmente. at ~ speed a toda velocidade. to the ~ ao máximo. be ~ up (*colloq: after eating*) estar cheio (*colloq*). ~ moon lua *f* cheia. ~-scale *a* em grande. ~-size *a* em tamanho natural. ~ stop ponto *m* final. ~-time *a & adv* a tempo integral, fulltime. ~y *adv* completamente

fulsome /'fʊlsəm/ *a* excessivo

fumble /'fʌmbl/ *vi* tatear, (*P*) tactear; (*in the dark*) andar tateando. ~ with estar atrapalhado com, andar às voltas com

fume /fju:m/ *vi* defumar, (*P*) deitar fumo, fumegar; (*with anger*) ferver. ~s *npl* gases *mpl*

fumigate /'fju:mɪgeɪt/ *vt* fumigar

fun /fʌn/ *n* divertimento *m*. for ~ de brincadeira. make ~ of zombar de, fazer troça de. ~-fair *n* parque *m* de diversões, (*P*) feira *f* de diversões, (*P*) feira *f* popular

function /'fʌŋkʃn/ *n* função *f* □ *vi* funcionar. ~al *a* funcional

fund /fʌnd/ *n* fundos *mpl* □ *vt* financiar

fundamental /fʌndə'mentl/ *a* fundamental

funeral /'fju:nərəl/ *n* enterro *m*, funeral *m* □ *a* fúnebre

fungus /'fʌŋgəs/ *n* (*pl* -gi /-gaɪ/) fungo *m*

funnel /'fʌnl/ *n* funil *m*; (*of ship*) chaminé *f*

funn|y /'fʌnɪ/ *a* (-ier, -iest) engraçado, divertido; (*odd*) esquisito. ~ily *adv* comicamente; (*oddly*) estranhamente. ~ily enough por incrível que pareça fur /fɜ:(r)/ n pelo m; (for clothing) pele f; (in kettle) depósito m, crosta f. ~ coat casaco m de pele

furious /'fjʊərɪəs/ a furioso. ~ly adv furiosamente

furnace /'fɜ:nɪs/ n fornalha f

furnish /'fɜ:nɪʃ/ vt mobiliar, (P) mobilar; (supply) prover (with de). ~ings npl mobiliário m e equipamento m

furniture /'fɜ:nɪtʃə(r)/ n mobília f

furrow /'fʌrəʊ/ n sulco m; (wrinkle) ruga f □ vt sulcar; (wrinkle) enrugar

furry /'fɜ:rɪ/ a (-ier, -iest) peludo; (toy) de pelúcia

further /'fɜ:ðə(r)/ a mais distante; (additional) adicional, suplementar □ adv mais longe; (more) mais □ vt promover. ~er education ensino m supletivo, cursos mpl livres, (P) educação f superior. ~est a o mais distante □ adv mais longe

furthermore /fɜ:ðə'mɔ:(r)/ adv além disso

furtive /'fɜ:tɪv/ a furtivo

fury /'fjʊərɪ/ n fúria f, furor m

fuse¹ /fju:z/ vt/i fundir(-se); (fig) amalgamar □ n fusível m. the lights ~d os fusíveis queimaram

fuse² /fju:z/ n (of bomb) espoleta f

fuselage /'fju:zəlɑ:ʒ/ n fuselagem f

fusion /'fju:ʒn/ n fusão f

fuss /fʌs/ n história(s) f(pl), escarcéu m □ vi preocupar-se com ninharias. make a ~ of ligar demasiado para, criar caso com, fazer um espalhafato com. ~y a exigente, complicado

futile /'fju:taɪl/ a fútil

future /'fju:tʃə(r)/ a & n futuro (m). in ~ no futuro, de agora em diante

futuristic /fju:tʃə'rɪstɪk/ a futurista, futurístico

fuzz /fʌz/ n penugem f; (hair) cabelo m frisado

fuzzy /'fʌzɪ/ a (hair) frisado; (photo) pouco nítido, desfocado

G

gab /gæb/ n (colloq) have the gift of the ~ ter o dom da palavra

gabble /'gæbl/ vt/i tagarelar, falar, ler muito depressa □ n tagarelice f, algaravia f

gable /'geɪbl/ n empena f, oitão m

gad /gæd/ vi (pt gadded) ~ about (colloq) badalar

gadget /'gædʒɪt/ n pequeno utensílio m; (fitting) dispositivo m; (device) engenhoca f (colloq)

Gaelic /'geɪlɪk/ n galês m

gaffe /gæf/ n gafe f

gag /gæg/ n mordaça f; (joke) gag m, piada f □ vt (pt gagged) amordaçar

gaiety /'geɪətɪ/ n alegria f

gaily /'geɪlɪ/ adv alegremente

gain /geɪn/ vt ganhar □ vi (of clock) adiantar-se. ~ weight aumentar de peso. ~ on (get closer to) aproximar-se de □ n ganho m; (increase) aumento m. ~ful a lucrativo, proveitoso

gait /geɪt/ n (modo de) andar m

gala /'gɑ:lə/ n gala m; (sport) festival m

galaxy /'gæləksɪ/ n galáxia f

gale /geɪl/ n vento m forte

gall /gɔ:l/ n bílis f; (fig) fel m; (sl: impudence) descaramento m, desplante m, (P) lata f (sl). ~-bladder n vesícula f biliar. ~-stone n cálculo m biliar

gallant /'gælənt/ a galhardo, valente; (chivalrous) galante, cortês. ~ry n galhardia f, valentia f; (chivalry) galanteria f, cortesia f

gallery /'gælərɪ/ n galeria f

galley /'gælɪ/ n (pl -eys) galera f; (ship's kitchen) cozinha f

gallivant /gælɪ'vænt/ vi (colloq) vadiar, (P) andar na paródia

gallon /'gælən/ n galão m (= 4,546 litros; Amer = 3.785 litros)

gallop /'gæləp/ n galope m □ vi (pt galloped) galopar

gallows /'gæləʊz/ npl forca f

galore /gə'lɔ:(r)/ adv à beça, em abundância

galvanize /'gælvənaɪz/ vt galvanizar

gambit /'gæmbɪt/ n gambito m

gamble /'gæmbl/ vt/i jogar □ n jogo (de azar) m; (fig) risco m. ~e on apostar em. ~r n jogador m. ~ing n jogo m (de azar)

game /geɪm/ n jogo m; (football) desafio m; (animals) caça f □ a bravo. ~ for pronto para

gamekeeper /'geɪmki:pə(r)/ n guarda-florestal m

gammon /'gæmən/ n presunto m defumado

gamut /'gæmət/ n gama f

gang /gæŋ/ n bando m, gang m; (of workmen) turma f, (P) grupo m □ vi ~ up ligar-se (on contra)

gangling /'gæŋglɪŋ/ a desengonçado

gangrene /'gæŋgri:n/ n gangrena f

gangster /'gæŋstə(r)/ n gângster m, bandido m

gangway /'gæŋweɪ/ n passagem f; (aisle) coxia f; (on ship) portaló m; (from ship to shore) passadiço m

gaol /dʒeɪl/ n & vt = jail

gap /gæp/ n abertura f, brecha f; (in time) intervalo m; (deficiency) lacuna f

gape /geɪp/ vi ficar boquiaberto or embasbacado. ~ing a escancarado

garage /'gæra:ʒ/ n garagem f; (service station) posto m de gasolina, (P) estação *f* de serviço □ *vt* pôr na garagem

garbage /'ga:bɪdʒ/ *n* lixo *m*. ~ **can** (*Amer*) lata *f* do lixo, (*P*) caixote *m* do lixo

garble /'ga:bl/ *vt* deturpar

garden /'ga:dn/ *n* jardim *m* □ *vi* jardinar. ~**er** *n* jardineiro *m*. ~**ing** *n* jardinagem *f*

gargle /'ga:gl/ *vi* gargarejar □ *n* gargarejo *m*

gargoyle /'ga:gɔɪl/ *n* gárgula *f*

garish /'geərɪʃ/ *a* berrante, espalhafatoso

garland /'ga:lənd/ *n* grinalda *f*

garlic /'ga:lɪk/ *n* alho *m*

garment /'ga:mənt/ *n* peça *f* de vestuário, roupa *f*

garnish /'ga:nɪʃ/ *vt* enfeitar, guarnecer □ *n* guarnição *f*

garrison /'gærɪsn/ *n* guarnição *f* □ *vt* guarnecer

garrulous /'gærələs/ *a* tagarela

garter /'ga:tə(r)/ *n* liga *f*. ~**-belt** *n* (*Amer*) cinta *f* de ligas

gas /gæs/ *n* (*pl* **gases**) gás *m*; (*med*) anestésico *m*; (*Amer colloq: petrol*) gasolina *f* □ *vt* (*pt* **gassed**) asfixiar; (*mil*) gasear □ *vi* (*colloq*) fazer conversa fiada. ~ **fire** aquecedor *m* a gás. ~ **mask** máscara *f* anti-gás. ~ **meter** medidor *m* do gás

gash /gæʃ/ *n* corte *m*, lanho *m* □ *vt* cortar

gasket /'gæskɪt/ *n* junta *f*

gasoline /'gæsəli:n/ *n* (*Amer*) gasolina *f*

gasp /ga:sp/ *vi* arfar, arquejar; (*fig: with rage, surprise*) ficar sem ar □ *n* arquejo *m*

gassy /'gæsɪ/ *a* gasoso; (*full of gas*) cheio de gás

gastric /'gæstrɪk/ *a* gástrico

gastronomy /gæ'strɒnəmɪ/ *n* gastronomia *f*

gate /geɪt/ *n* portão *m*; (*of wood*) cancela *f*; (*barrier*) barreira *f*; (*airport*) porta *f*

gateau /'gætəʊ/ *n* (*pl* ~**x** /-təʊz/) bolo *m* grande com creme

gatecrash /'geɪtkræʃ/ *vt/i* entrar (numa festa) sem convite

gateway /'geɪtweɪ/ *n* (porta de) entrada *f*

gather /'gæðə(r)/ *vt* reunir, juntar; (*pick up, collect*) apanhar; (*amass, pile up*) acumular, juntar; (*conclude*) deduzir; (*cloth*) franzir □ *vi* reunir-se; (*pile up*) acumular-se. ~ **speed** ganhar velocidade. ~**ing** *n* reunião *f*

gaudy /'gɔ:dɪ/ *a* (-ier, -iest) (*bright*) berrante; (*showy*) espalhafatoso

gauge /geɪdʒ/ *n* medida *f* padrão; (*de-*vice) indicador *m*; (*railway*) bitola *f* □ *vt* medir, avaliar

gaunt /gɔ:nt/ *a* emagrecido, macilento; (*grim*) lúgubre, desolado

gauntlet /'gɔ:ntlɪt/ *n* run the ~ of (*fig*) expor-se a. **throw down the** ~ lançar um desafio, (*P*) atirar a luva

gauze /gɔ:z/ *n* gaze *f*

gave /geɪv/ *see* give

gawky /'gɔ:kɪ/ *a* (-ier, -iest) desajeitado

gay /geɪ/ *a* (-er, -est) alegre; (*colloq: homosexual*) homosexual, gay

gaze /geɪz/ *vi* ~ (at) olhar fixamente (para) □ *n* contemplação *f*

gazelle /gə'zel/ *n* gazela *f*

GB *abbr* of Great Britain

gear /gɪə(r)/ *n* equipamento *m*; (*techn*) engrenagem *f*; (*auto*) velocidade *f* □ *vt* equipar; (*adapt*) adaptar. in ~ engrenado. **out of** ~ em ponto morto. ~**-lever** *n* alavanca *f* de mudanças

gearbox /'gɪəbɒks/ *n* caixa *f* de mudança, caixa *f* de transmissão, (*P*) caixa *f* de velocidades

geese /gi:s/ *see* goose

gel /dʒel/ *n* geleia *f*, (*P*) geleia *f*

gelatine /'dʒeləti:n/ *n* gelatina *f*

gelignite /'dʒelɪgnaɪt/ *n* gelignite *f*

gem /dʒem/ *n* gema *f*, pedra *f* preciosa

Gemini /'dʒemɪnaɪ/ *n* (*astr*) Gémeos *mpl*, (*P*) Gémeos *mpl*

gender /'dʒendə(r)/ *n* género *m*, (*P*) género *m*

gene /dʒi:n/ *n* gene *m*

genealogy /dʒi:nɪ'ælədʒɪ/ *n* genealogia *f*

general /'dʒenrəl/ *a* geral □ *n* general *m*. ~ **election** eleições *fpl* legislativas. ~ **practitioner** *n* clínico-geral *m*, (*P*) médico *m* de família. in ~ em geral. ~**ly** *adv* geralmente

generaliz|e /'dʒenrəlaɪz/ *vt/i* generalizar. ~**ation** /-'zeɪʃn/ *n* generalização *f*

generate /'dʒenəreɪt/ *vt* gerar, produzir

generation /dʒenə'reɪʃn/ *n* geração *f*

generator /'dʒenəreɪtə(r)/ *n* gerador *m*

gener|ous /'dʒenərəs/ *a* generoso; (*plentiful*) abundante. ~**osity** /-'rɒsətɪ/ *n* generosidade *f*

genetic /dʒɪ'netɪk/ *a* genético. ~**s** *n* genética *f*

genial /'dʒi:nɪəl/ *a* agradável

genital /'dʒenɪtl/ *a* genital. ~**s** *npl* órgãos *mpl* genitais

genius /'dʒi:nɪəs/ *n* (*pl* -uses) génio *m*, (*P*) génio *m*

genocide /'dʒenəsaɪd/ *n* genocídio *m*

gent /dʒent/ *n* the **G**~**s** (*colloq*) banheiros *mpl* de homens, (*P*) lavabos *mpl* para homens genteel /dʒen'tiːl/ a elegante, fino, refinado

gentl|e /'dʒentl/ a (~er, ~est) brando, suave. ~eness n brandura f, suavidade f. ~y adv brandamente, suavemente

gentleman /'dʒentlmən/ n (pl -men) senhor m; (well-bred) cavalheiro m

genuine /'dʒenjuɪn/ a genuíno, verdadeiro; (belief) sincero

geograph|y /dʒɪ'ɒɡrəfɪ/ n geografia f. ~er n geógrafo m. ~ical /dʒɪə-'ɡræfɪkl/ a geográfico

geolog|y /dʒɪ'ɒlədʒɪ/ n geologia f. ~ical /dʒɪə'lɒdʒɪkl/ a geológico. ~ist n geólogo m

geometr|y /dʒɪ'ɒmətrɪ/ n geometria f. ~ic(al) /dʒɪə'metrɪk(l)/ a geométrico

geranium /dʒə'remɪəm/ n gerânio m

geriatric /dʒerɪ'ætrɪk/ a geriátrico

germ /dʒɜːm/ n germe m, micróbio m

German /'dʒɜːmən/ a & n alemão (m), alemã (f); (lang) alemão (m). ~ measles rubéola f. ~ic /dʒɜ'mænɪk/ a germânico. ~y n Alemanha f

germinate /'dʒɜːmɪneɪt/ vi germinar

gestation /dʒe'steɪʃn/ n gestação f

gesticulate /dʒe'stɪkjʊleɪt/ vi gesticular

gesture /'dʒestʃə(r)/ n gesto m

get /ɡet/ vt (pt got, pres p getting) (have) ter; (receive) receber; (catch) apanhar; (earn, win) ganhar; (fetch) ir buscar; (find) achar; (colloq: understand) entender. ~ sb to do sth fazer com que alguém faça alg coisa □ vi ir, chegar; (become) ficar. ~ married/ready casar-se/aprontar-se. ~ about andar dum lado para o outro. ~ across atravessar. ~ along or by (manage) ir indo. ~ along or on with entender-se com. ~ at (reach) chegar a; (attack) atacar; (imply) insinuar. ~ away ir-se embora; (escape) fugir. ~ back vi voltar □ vt recuperar. ~ by (pass) passar, escapar; (manage) aguentar-se. ~ down descer. ~ in entrar. ~ off vi descer; (leave) partir; (jur) ser absolvido □ vt (remove) tirar. ~ on (succeed) fazer progressos, ir; (be on good terms) dar-se bem. ~ out sair. ~ out of (fig) fugir de. ~ over (illness) restabelecer-se de. ~ round (person) convencer; (rule) contornar. ~ up vi levantar-se □ vt (mount) montar. ~-up n (colloq) apresentação f

getaway /'ɡetəweɪ/ n fuga f

geyser /'ɡiːzə(r)/ n aquecedor m; (geol) géiser m, (P) gêiser m

Ghana /'ɡɑːnə/ n Gana m

ghastly /'ɡɑːstlɪ/ a (-ier, -iest) horrível; (pale) lívido

gherkin /'ɡɜːkɪn/ n pepino m pequeno para conservas, cornichão m

ghetto /'ɡetəʊ/ n (pl -os) gueto m, ghetto m

ghost /ɡəʊst/ n fantasma m, espectro m. ~ly a fantasmagórico, espectral

giant /'dʒaɪənt/ a & n gigante (m)

gibberish /'dʒɪbərɪʃ/ n algaravia f, linguagem f incompreensível

gibe /dʒaɪb/ n zombaria f □ vi ~ (at) zombar (de)

giblets /'dʒɪblɪts/ npl miúdos mpl, miudezas fpl

giddy /'ɡɪdɪ/ a (-ier, -iest) estonteante, vertiginoso. be or feel ~ ter tonturas or vertigens

gift /ɡɪft/ n presente m, dádiva f; (ability) dom m, dote m. ~-wrap vt (pt -wrapped) fazer para embrulho de presente

gifted /'ɡɪftɪd/ a dotado

gig /ɡɪɡ/ n (colloq) show m, sessão f de jazz etc

gigantic /dʒaɪ'ɡæntɪk/ a gigantesco

giggle /'ɡɪɡl/ vi dar risadinhas nervosas □ n risinho m nervoso

gild /ɡɪld/ vt dourar

gills /ɡɪlz/ npl guelras fpl

gilt /ɡɪlt/ a & n dourado (m). ~-edged a de toda a confiança

gimmick /'ɡɪmɪk/ n truque m, artifício m

gin /dʒɪn/ n gin m, genebra f

ginger /'dʒɪndʒə(r)/ n gengibre m □ a louro-avermelhado, ruivo. ~ ale, ~ beer cerveja f de gengibre, (P) ginger ale m

gingerbread /'dʒɪndʒəbred/ n pão m de gengibre

gingerly /'dʒɪndʒəlɪ/ adv cautelosamente

gipsy /'dʒɪpsɪ/ n = gypsy

giraffe /dʒɪ'rɑːf/ n girafa f

girder /'ɡɜːdə(r)/ n trave f, viga f

girdle /'ɡɜːdl/ n cinto m; (corset) cinta f □ vt rodear

girl /ɡɜːl/ n (child) menina f; (young woman) moça f, (P) rapariga f. ~-friend n amiga f; (of boy) namorada f. ~hood n (of child) meninice f; (youth) juventude f

giro /'dʒaɪrəʊ/ n sistema m de transferência de crédito entre bancos; (cheque) cheque m pago pelo governo a desempregados ou doentes

girth /ɡɜːθ/ n circunferência f, perímetro m

gist /dʒɪst/ n essencial m

give /ɡɪv/ vt/i (pt gave, pp given) dar; (bend, yield) ceder. ~ away dar; (secret) revelar, trair. ~ back devolver. ~ in dar-se por vencido, render-se. ~ off emitir. ~ out vt anunciar □ vi esgotar-se. ~ up vt/i desistir (de), renunciar (a). ~ o.s. up entregar-se. ~ way ceder; (traffic) dar prioridade; (collapse) dar de si

given /'gɪvn/ see give □ a dado. ~ name nome m de batismo, (P) baptismo

glacier /'glæsɪə(r)/ n glaciar m, geleira f

glad /glæd/ a contente. ~ly adv com (todo o) prazer

gladden /'glædn/ vt alegrar

glam|our /'glæmə(r)/ n fascinação f, encanto m. ~orize vt tornar fascinante. ~orous a fascinante, sedutor

glance /glɑːns/ n relance m, olhar m □ vi ~ at dar uma olhada a. at first ~ à primeira vista

gland /glænd/ n glândula f

glar|e /gleə(r)/ vi brilhar intensamente, faiscar □ n luz f crua; (fig) olhar m feroz. ~e at olhar ferozmente para. ~ing a brilhante; (obvious) flagrante

glass /glɑːs/ n vidro m; (vessel, its contents) copo m; (mirror) espelho m. ~es óculos mpl. ~y a vitreo

glaze /gleɪz/ vt (door etc) envidraçar; (pottery) vidrar □ n vidrado m

gleam /gliːm/ n raio m de luz frouxa; (fig) vislumbre m □ vi luzir, brilhar

glean /gliːn/ vt catar

glee /gliː/ n alegria f. ~ful a cheio de alegria

glib /glɪb/ a que tem a palavra fácil, verboso. ~ly adv fluentemente, sem hesitação. ~ness n verbosidade f

glide /glaɪd/ vi deslizar; (bird, plane) planar. ~r /-ə(r)/ n planador m

glimmer /'glɪmə(r)/ n luz f trêmula □ vi tremular

glimpse /glɪmps/ n vislumbre m. catch a ~ of entrever, ver de relance

glint /glɪnt/ n brilho m, reflexo m □ vi brilhar, cintilar

glisten /'glɪsn/ vi reluzir

glitter /'glɪtə(r)/ vi luzir, resplandecer □ n esplendor m, cintilação f

gloat /gləʊt/ vi ~ over ter um prazer maligno em, exultar com

global /'gləʊbl/ a global

globe /gləʊb/ n globo m

gloom /gluːm/ n obscuridade f; (fig) tristeza f. ~y a sombrio; (sad) triste; (pessimistic) pessimista

glorif|y /'glɔːrɪfaɪ/ vt glorificar. a ~ied waitress/etc pouco mais que uma garçonete/etc

glorious /'glɔːrɪəs/ a glorioso

glory /'glɔːrɪ/ n glória f; (beauty) esplendor m □ vi ~ in orgulhar-se de

gloss /glɒs/ n brilho m □ a brilhante □ vt ~ over minimizar, encobrir. ~y a brilhante

glossary /'glɒsərɪ/ n (pl -ries) glossário m

glove /glʌv/ n luva f. ~ compartment porta-luvas m. ~d a enluvado

glow /gləʊ/ vi arder; (person) resplandecer; (eyes) brilhar □ n brasa f. ~ing a (fig) entusiástico

glucose /'gluːkəʊs/ n glucose f

glue /gluː/ n cola f □ vt (pres p gluing) colar

glum /glʌm/ a (glummer, glummest) sorumbático; (dejected) abatido

glut /glʌt/ n superabundância f

glutton /'glʌtn/ n glutão m. ~ous a glutão. ~y n gula f

gnarled /nɑːld/ a nodoso

gnash /næʃ/ vt ~ one's teeth ranger os dentes

gnat /næt/ n mosquito m

gnaw /nɔː/ vt/i roer

gnome /nəʊm/ n gnomo m

go /gəʊ/ vi (pt went, pp gone) ir; (leave) ir, ir-se; (mech) andar, funcionar; (become) ficar; (be sold) vender-se; (vanish) ir-se, desaparecer □ n (pl goes) (energy) dinamismo m; (try) tentativa f; (success) sucesso m; (turn) vez f. ~ riding ir andar or montar a cavalo. ~ shopping ir às compras. be ~ing to do ir fazer. ~ ahead ir para diante. ~ away ir-se embora. ~ back voltar atrás (on com). ~ bad estragar-se. ~ by (pass) passar. ~ down descer; (sun) pôr-se; (ship) afundar-se. ~ for ir buscar; (like) gostar de; (sl: attack) atirar-se a, ir-se a (collog). ~ in entrar. ~ in for (exam) apresentar-se a. ~ off ir-se; (explode) rebentar; (sound) soar; (decay) estragar-se. ~ on continuar; (happen) acontecer. ~ out sair; (light) apagar-se. ~ over or through verificar, examinar. ~ round (be enough) chegar. ~ under ir abaixo. ~ up subir. ~ without passar sem. on the ~ em grande atividade, (P) actividade. ~-ahead n luz f verde □ a dinâmico, empreendedor. ~-between n intermediário m. ~-kart n kart m. ~-slow n operação f tartaruga, (P) greve f de zelo

goad /gəʊd/ vt aguilhoar, espicaçar

goal /gəʊl/ n meta f; (area) baliza f; (score) gol m, (P) golo m. ~-post n trave f

goalkeeper /'gəʊlkiːpə(r)/ n goleiro m, (P) guarda-redes m

goat /gəʊt/ n cabra f

gobble /'gɒbl/ vt comer com sofreguidão, devorar

goblet /'gɒblɪt/ n taça f, cálice m

goblin /'gɒblɪn/ n duende m

God /gɒd/ n Deus m. ~-forsaken a miserável, abandonado

god /gɒd/ n deus m. ~-daughter n afilhada f. ~dess n deusa f. ~father n padrinho m. ~ly a devoto. ~mother n madrinha f. ~son n afilhado m

godsend /'gɒdsend/ n achado m, dádiva f do céu

goggles /'gɒglz/ npl óculos mpl de proteção, (P) protecção

going /'gəʊɪŋ/ n it is slow/hard ~ é demorado/difícil □ a (price, rate) corrente, atual, (P) actual. ~s-on npl acontecimentos mpl estranhos

gold /gəʊld/ n ouro m □ a de/em ouro. ~-mine n mina f de ouro

golden /'gəʊldən/ a de ouro; (like gold) dourado; (opportunity) único. ~ wedding bodas fpl de ouro

goldfish /'gəʊldfɪʃ/ n peixe m dourado/vermelho

goldsmith /'gəʊldsmɪθ/ n ourives m inv

golf /gɒlf/ n golfe m. ~ club clube m de golfe, associação f de golfe; (stick) taco m. ~-course n campo m de golfe. ~er n jogador m de golfe

gone /gɒn/ see go □ a ido, passado. ~ six o'clock depois das seis

gong /gɒŋ/ n gongo m

good /gʊd/ a (better, best) bom □ n bem m. as ~ as praticamente. for ~ para sempre. it is no ~ não adianta. it is no ~ shouting/etc não adianta gritar/etc. ~ afternoon int boa(s) tarde(s). ~ evening/night int boa(s) noite(s). G~ Friday Sexta-feira f Santa. ~-looking a bonito. ~ morning int bom dia. ~ name bom nome m

goodbye /gʊd'baɪ/ int & n adeus (m)

goodness /'gʊdnɪs/ n bondade f. my ~ness! meu Deus!

goods /gʊdz/ npl (comm) mercadorias fpl. ~ train trem m de carga, (P) comboio m de mercadorias

goodwill /gʊd'wɪl/ n boa vontade f

goose /guːs/ n (pl geese) ganso m. ~-flesh, ~-pimples ns pele f de galinha

gooseberry /'gʊzbərɪ/ n (fruit) groselha f; (bush) groselheira f

gore¹ /gɔː(r)/ n sangue m coagulado

gore² /gɔː(r)/ vt perfurar

gorge /gɔːdʒ/ n desfiladeiro m, garganta f □ vt ~ o.s. empanturrar-se

gorgeous /'gɔːdʒəs/ a magnífico, maravilhoso

gorilla /gə'rɪlə/ n gorila m

gormless /'gɔːmlɪs/ a (sl) estúpido

gorse /gɔːs/ n giesta f, tojo m, urze f

gory /'gɔːrɪ/ a (-ier, -iest) sangrento

gosh /gɒʃ/ int puxa!, (P) caramba!

gospel /'gɒspl/ n evangelho m

gossip /'gɒsɪp/ n bisbilhotice f, fofoca f; (person) bisbilhoteiro m, fofoqueiro

m □ vi (pt gossiped) bisbilhotar. ~y a bisbilhoteiro, fofoqueiro

got /gɒt/ see get. have ~ ter. have ~ to do ter de or que fazer

Gothic /'gɒθɪk/ a gótico

gouge /gaʊdʒ/ vt ~ out arrancar

gourmet /'gʊəmeɪ/ n gastrónomo m, (P) gastrónomo m, gourmet m

gout /gaʊt/ n gota f

govern /'gʌvn/ vt/i governar. ~ess n preceptora f. ~or n governador m; (of school, hospital etc) diretor m, (P) director m

government /'gʌvənmənt/ n governo m. ~al /-'mentl/ a governamental

gown /gaʊn/ n vestido m; (of judge, teacher) toga f

GP abbr see general practitioner

grab /græb/ vt (pt grabbed) agarrar, apanhar

grace /greɪs/ n graça f □ vt honrar; (adorn) ornar. say ~ dar graças. ~ful a gracioso

gracious /'greɪʃəs/ a gracioso; (kind) amável, afável

grade /greɪd/ n categoria f; (of goods) classe f, qualidade f; (on scale) grau m; (school mark) nota f □ vt classificar

gradient /'greɪdɪənt/ n gradiente m, declive m

gradual /'grædʒʊəl/ a gradual, progressivo. ~ly adv gradualmente

graduate¹ /'grædʒʊət/ n diplomado m, graduado m, licenciado m

graduate² /'grædʒʊeɪt/ vt/i formar (-se). ~ion /-'eɪʃn/ n colação f de grau, (P) formatura f

graffiti /grə'fiːtiː/ npl graffiti mpl

graft /grɑːft/ n (med, bot) enxerto m; (work) batalha f □ vt enxertar; (work) batalhar

grain /greɪn/ n grão m; (collectively) cereais mpl; (in wood) veio m. against the ~ (fig) contra a maneira de ser

gram /græm/ n grama m

grammar /'græmə(r)/ n gramática f. ~atical /grə'mætɪkl/ a gramatical

grand /grænd/ a (-er, -est) grandioso, magnífico; (duke, master) grão. ~ piano piano m de cauda

grandchild /'græntʃaɪld/ n (pl -children) neto m. ~daughter n neta f. ~father n avô m. ~mother n avó f. ~parents npl avós mpl. ~son n neto m

grandeur /'grændʒə(r)/ n grandeza f

grandiose /'grændɪəʊs/ a grandioso

grandstand /'grændstænd/ n tribuna f principal

granite /'grænɪt/ n granito m

grant /grɑːnt/ vt conceder; (a request) ceder a; (admit) admitir (that que) □ n subsídio m; (univ) bolsa f. take for

~ed ter como coisa garantida, contar com

grape /greɪp/ *n* uva *f*

grapefruit /ˈgreɪpfruːt/ *n inv* grapefruit *m*, toronja *f*

graph /grɑːf/ *n* gráfico *m*

graphic /ˈgræfɪk/ *a* gráfico; (*fig*) vívido. ~**s** *npl* (*comput*) gráficos *mpl*

grapple /ˈgræpl/ *vi* ~ **with** estar engalinfado com; (*fig*) estar às voltas com

grasp /grɑːsp/ *vt* agarrar; (*understand*) compreender □ *n* domínio *m*; (*reach*) alcance *m*; (*fig: understanding*) compreensão *f*

grasping /ˈgrɑːspɪŋ/ *a* ganancioso

grass /grɑːs/ *n* erva *f*; (*lawn*) grama *f*, (*P*) relva *f*; (*pasture*) pastagem *f*, (*sl: informer*) delator *m* □ *vt* cobrir com grama; (*sl: betray*) delatar. ~ **roots** (*pol*) bases *fpl*. ~**y** *a* coberto de erva

grasshopper /ˈgrɑːshɒpə(r)/ *n* gafanhoto *m*

grate[1] /greɪt/ *n* (*fireplace*) lareira *f*; (*frame*) grelha *f*

grate[2] /greɪt/ *vt* ralar □ *vi* ranger. ~ **one's teeth** ranger os dentes. ~**r** /-ə(r)/ *n* ralador *m*

grateful /ˈgreɪtfl/ *a* grato, agradecido. ~**ly** *adv* com reconhecimento, com gratidão

gratify /ˈgrætɪfaɪ/ *vt* (*pt* -**fied**) contentar, satisfazer. ~**ing** *a* gratificante

grating /ˈgreɪtɪŋ/ *n* grade *f*

gratis /ˈgrɑːtɪs/ *a* & *adv* grátis (*invar*), de graça

gratitude /ˈgrætɪtjuːd/ *n* gratidão *f*, reconhecimento *m*

gratuitous /grəˈtjuːɪtəs/ *a* gratuito; (*uncalled-for*) sem motivo

gratuity /grəˈtjuːətɪ/ *n* gratificação *f*, gorjeta *f*

grave[1] /greɪv/ *n* cova *f*, sepultura *f*, túmulo *m*

grave[2] /greɪv/ *a* (-**er**, -**est**) grave, sério. ~**ly** *adv* gravemente

grave[3] /grɑːv/ *a* ~ **accent** acento *m* grave

gravel /ˈgrævl/ *n* cascalho *m* miúdo, saibro *m*

gravestone /ˈgreɪvstəʊn/ *n* lápide *f*, campa *f*

graveyard /ˈgreɪvjɑːd/ *n* cemitério *m*

gravity /ˈgrævətɪ/ *n* gravidade *f*

gravy /ˈgreɪvɪ/ *n* molho *m* (de carne)

graze[1] /greɪz/ *vt/i* pastar

graze[2] /greɪz/ *vt* roçar; (*scrape*) esfolar □ *n* esfoladura *f*, (*P*) esfoladela *f*

greas|**e** /griːs/ *n* gordura *f* □ *vt* engordurar; (*culin*) untar; (*mech*) lubrificar. ~**e-proof paper** papel *m* vegetal. ~**y** *a* gorduroso

great /greɪt/ *a* (-**er**, -**est**) grande; (*colloq: splendid*) esplêndido. **G**~ **Brit-** ain Grã-Bretanha *f*. ~**-grandfather** *n* bisavô *m*. ~**-grandmother** *f* bisavó *f*. ~**ly** *adv* grandemente, muito. ~**ness** *n* grandeza *f*

Great Britain /greɪt ˈbrɪtən/ *n* Grã-Bretanha *f*

Greece /griːs/ *n* Grécia *f*

greed /griːd/ *n* cobiça *f*, ganância *f*; (*for food*) gula *f*. ~**y** *a* cobiçoso, ganancioso; (*for food*) guloso

Greek /griːk/ *a* & *n* grego (*m*)

green /griːn/ *a* (-**er**, -**est**) verde □ *n* verde *m*; (*grass*) gramado *m*, (*P*) relvado *m*. ~**s** hortaliças *fpl*. ~ **belt** zona *f* verde, paisagem *f* protegida. ~ **light** luz *f* verde. ~**ery** *n* verdura *f*

greengrocer /ˈgriːngrəʊsə(r)/ *n* quitandeiro *m*, (*P*) vendedor *m* de hortaliças

greenhouse /ˈgriːnhaʊs/ *n* estufa *f*. ~ **effect** efeito estufa

Greenland /ˈgriːnlənd/ *n* Groenlândia *f*

greet /griːt/ *vt* acolher. ~**ing** *n* saudação *f*; (*welcome*) acolhimento *m*. ~**ings** *npl* cumprimentos *mpl*; (*Christmas etc*) votos *mpl*, desejos *mpl*

gregarious /grɪˈgeərɪəs/ *a* gregário; (*person*) sociável

grenade /grɪˈneɪd/ *n* granada *f*

grew /gruː/ *see* **grow**

grey /greɪ/ *a* (-**er**, -**est**) cinzento; (*of hair*) grisalho □ *n* cinzento *m*

greyhound /ˈgreɪhaʊnd/ *n* galgo *m*

grid /grɪd/ *n* (*grating*) gradeamento *m*, grade *f*; (*electr*) rede *f*

grief /griːf/ *n* dor *f*. **come to** ~ acabar mal

grievance /ˈgriːvns/ *n* razão *f* de queixa

grieve /griːv/ *vt* sofrer, afligir □ *vi* sofrer. ~ **for** chorar por

grill /grɪl/ *n* grelha *f*; (*food*) grelhado *m*; (*place*) grill *m* □ *vt* grelhar; (*question*) submeter a interrogatório cerrado, apertar com perguntas □ *vi* grelhar

grille /grɪl/ *n* grade *f*; (*of car*) grelha *f*

grim /grɪm/ *a* (**grimmer**, **grimmest**) sinistro; (*without mercy*) implacável

grimace /grɪˈmeɪs/ *n* careta *f* □ *vi* fazer careta(s)

grim|**e** /graɪm/ *n* sujeira *f*. ~**y** *a* encardido, sujo

grin /grɪn/ *vi* (*pt* **grinned**) sorrir abertamente, dar um sorriso largo □ *n* sorriso *m* aberto

grind /graɪnd/ *vt* (*pt* **ground**) triturar; (*coffee*) moer; (*sharpen*) amolar, afiar. ~ **one's teeth** ranger os dentes. ~ **to a halt** parar freando lentamente

grip /grɪp/ *vt* (*pt* **gripped**) agarrar;

(*interest*) prender □ *n* (*of hands*) aperto *m*; (*control*) controle *m*, domínio *m*. come to ~s with arcar com. ~ping *a* apaixonante

grisly /'grɪzlɪ/ *a* (-ier, -iest) macabro, horrível

gristle /'grɪsl/ *n* cartilagem *f*

grit /grɪt/ *n* areia *f*, grão *m* de areia; (*fig: pluck*) coragem *f*, fortaleza *f* □ *vt* (*pt* gritted) (*road*) jogar areia em; (*teeth*) cerrar

groan /grəʊn/ *vi* gemer □ *n* gemido *m*

grocer /'grəʊsə(r)/ *n* dono/a *m/f* de mercearia. ~ies *npl* artigos *mpl* de mercearia. ~y *n* (*shop*) mercearia *f*

groggy /'grɒgɪ/ *a* (-ier, -iest) grogue, fraco das pernas

groin /grɔɪn/ *n* virilha *f*

groom /grʊːm/ *n* noivo *m*; (*for horses*) moço *m* de estrebaria □ *vt* (*horse*) tratar de; (*fig*) preparar

groove /gruːv/ *n* ranhura *f*; (*for door, window*) calha *f*; (*in record*) estria *f*; (*fig*) rotina *f*

grope /grəʊp/ *vi* tatear. ~ for procurar às cegas

gross /grəʊs/ *a* (-est) (*vulgar*) grosseiro; (*flagrant*) flagrante; (*of error*) crasso; (*of weight, figure etc*) bruto □ *n* (*pl invar*) grosa *f*. ~ly *adv* grosseiramente; (*very*) extremamente

grotesque /grəʊ'tesk/ *a* grotesco

grotty /'grɒtɪ/ *a* (*sl*) sórdido

grouch /graʊtʃ/ *vi* (*colloq*) ralhar. ~y *a* (*colloq*) rabugento

ground¹ /graʊnd/ *n* chão *m*, solo *m*; (*area*) terreno *m*; (*reason*) razão *f*, motivo *m*. ~s jardins *mpl*; (*of coffee*) borra(s) *f* (*pl*) □ *vt/i* (*naut*) encalhar; (*plane*) reter em terra. ~ floor térreo *m*, (*P*) rés-do-chão *m*. ~less *a* infundado, sem fundamento

ground² /graʊnd/ *see* grind

grounding /'graʊndɪŋ/ *n* bases *fpl*, conhecimentos *mpl* básicos

groundsheet /'graʊndʃiːt/ *n* impermeável *m* para o chão

groundwork /'graʊndwɜːk/ *n* trabalhos *mpl* de base *or* preliminares

group /gruːp/ *n* grupo *m* □ *vt/i* agrupar(-se)

grouse¹ /graʊs/ *n* (*pl invar*) galo *m* silvestre

grouse² /graʊs/ *vi* (*colloq: grumble*) resmungar; (*colloq: complain*) queixar-se

grovel /'grɒvl/ *vi* (*pt* grovelled) humilhar-se; (*fig*) rebaixar-se

grow /grəʊ/ *vi* (*pt* grew, *pp* grown) crescer; (*become*) tornar-se □ *vt* cultivar. ~ old envelhecer. ~ up crescer, tornar-se adulto. ~er *n* cultivador *m*, produtor *m*. ~ing *a* crescente

growl /graʊl/ *vi* rosnar □ *n* rosnadela *f*

grown /grəʊn/ *see* grow □ *a* ~ man homem feito. ~-up *a* adulto □ *n* (*increase*) aumento *m*; (*med*) tumor *m*

grub /grʌb/ *n* larva *f*; (*sl: food*) papança *f* (*colloq*) (*B*) bóia (*sl*) *f*, (*P*) alimento *m*

grubby /'grʌbɪ/ *a* (-ier, -iest) sujo, porco

grudge /grʌdʒ/ *vt* dar/reconhecer de má vontade □ *n* má vontade *f*. ~ doing fazer de má vontade. ~ sb sth dar alg a alguém má vontade. have a ~ against ter ressentimento contra. grudgingly *adv* relutantemente

gruelling /'gruːəlɪŋ/ *a* estafante, extenuante

gruesome /'gruːsəm/ *a* macabro

gruff /grʌf/ *a* (-er, -est) carrancudo, rude

grumble /'grʌmbl/ *vi* resmungar (at contra, por)

grumpy /'grʌmpɪ/ *a* (-ier, -iest) malhumorado, rabugento

grunt /grʌnt/ *vi* grunhir □ *n* grunhido *m*

guarantee /gærən'tiː/ *n* garantia *f* □ *vt* garantir

guard /gaːd/ *vt* guardar, proteger □ *vi* ~ against precaver-se contra □ *n* guarda *f*; (*person*) guarda *m*; (*on train*) condutor *m*. ~ian *n* guardião *m*, defensor *m*; (*of orphan*) tutor *m*

guarded /'gaːdɪd/ *a* cauteloso, circunspeto, (*P*) circunspecto

guerrilla /gə'rɪlə/ *n* guerrilheiro *m*, (*P*) guerrilha *m*. ~ warfare guerrilha *f*, guerra *f* de guerrilhas

guess /ges/ *vt/i* adivinhar; (*suppose*) supor □ *n* suposição *f*, conjetura *f*, (*P*) conjectura *f*

guesswork /'gesw3ːk/ *n* suposição *f*, conjetura(s) *f* (*pl*), (*P*) conjectura(s) *f* (*pl*)

guest /gest/ *n* convidado *m*; (*in hotel*) hóspede *mf*. ~-house *n* pensão *f*

guffaw /gə'fɔː/ *n* gargalhada *f* □ *vi* rir à(s) gargalhada(s)

guidance /'gaɪdns/ *n* orientação *f*, direção *f*, (*P*) direcção *f*

guide /gaɪd/ *n* guia *mf* □ *vt* guiar. ~d missile missil *m* guiado; (*remotecontrol*) missil *m* teleguiado. ~-dog *n* cão *m* de cego, cão-guia *m*. ~-lines *npl* diretrizes *fpl*, (*P*) directrizes *fpl*

Guide /gaɪd/ *n* Guia *f*

guidebook /'gaɪdbʊk/ *n* guia *m* (turístico)

guild /gɪld/ *n* corporação *f*

guile /gaɪl/ *n* astúcia *f*, manha *f*

guilt /gɪlt/ *n* culpa *f*. ~y *a* culpado

guinea-pig /ˈɡɪnɪpɪɡ/ *n* cobaia *f*, porquinho-da-India *m*

guitar /ɡɪˈtɑː(r)/ *n* guitarra *f*, violão *m*, (*P*) viola *f*. ~ist *n* guitarrista *mf*, tocador *m* de violão, (*P*) de viola

gulf /ɡʌlf/ *n* golfo *m*; (*hollow*) abismo *m*

gull /ɡʌl/ *n* gaivota *f*

gullible /ˈɡʌləbl/ *a* crédulo

gully /ˈɡʌlɪ/ *n* barranco *m*; (*drain*) sarjeta *f*

gulp /ɡʌlp/ *vt* engolir, devorar □ *vi* engolir em seco □ *n* trago *m*

gum[1] /ɡʌm/ *n* (*anat*) gengiva *f*

gum[2] /ɡʌm/ *n* goma *f*; (*chewing-gum*) chiclete *m*, goma *f* elástica, (*P*) pastilha *f* □ *vt* (*pt* gummed) colar

gumboot /ˈɡʌmbuːt/ *n* bota *f* de borracha

gumption /ˈɡʌmpʃn/ *n* (*colloq*) iniciativa *f* e bom senso *m*, cabeça *f*, juizo *m*

gun /ɡʌn/ *n* (*pistol*) pistola *f*; (*rifle*) espingarda *f*; (*cannon*) canhão *m* □ *vt* (*pt* gunned) ~ down abater a tiro

gunfire /ˈɡʌnfaɪə(r)/ *n* tiroteio *m*

gunman /ˈɡʌnmən/ *n* (*pl* -men) bandido *m* armado

gunpowder /ˈɡʌnpaʊdə(r)/ *n* pólvora *f*

gunshot /ˈɡʌnʃɒt/ *n* tiro *m*

gurgle /ˈɡɜːɡl/ *n* gorgolejo *m* □ *vi* gorgolejar

gush /ɡʌʃ/ *vi* jorrar □ *n* jorro *m*. ~ing *a* efusivo, derretido

gust /ɡʌst/ *n* (*of wind*) rajada *f*; (*of smoke*) nuvem *f*. ~y *a* ventoso

gusto /ˈɡʌstəʊ/ *n* gosto *m*, entusiasmo *m*

gut /ɡʌt/ *n* tripa *f*. ~s (*belly*) barriga *f*; (*colloq: courage*) coragem *f* □ *vt* (*pt* gutted) estripar; (*fish*) limpar; (*fire*) destruir o interior de

gutter /ˈɡʌtə(r)/ *n* calha *f*, caneleta *f*; (*in street*) sarjeta *f*, valeta *f*

guy /ɡaɪ/ *n* (*sl: man*) cara *m*, (*P*) tipo *m* (*colloq*)

guzzle /ˈɡʌzl/ *vt/i* comer/beber com sofreguidão, encher-se (de)

gym /dʒɪm/ *n* (*colloq: gymnasium*) ginásio *m*; (*colloq: gymnastics*) ginástica *f*. ~-slip *n* uniforme *m* escolar

gymnasium /dʒɪmˈneɪzɪəm/ *n* ginásio *m*. ~nast /ˈdʒɪmnæst/ *n* ginasta *mf*. ~nastics /-ˈnæstɪks/ *npl* ginástica *f*

gynaecology /ɡaɪnɪˈkɒlədʒɪ/ *n* ginecologia *f*. ~ist *n* ginecologista *mf*

gypsy /ˈdʒɪpsɪ/ *n* cigano *m*

gyrate /dʒaɪˈreɪt/ *vi* girar

H

haberdashery /ˈhæbədæʃərɪ/ *n* armarinho *m*, (*P*) retrosaria *f*

habit /ˈhæbɪt/ *n* hábito *m*, costume *m*; (*costume*) hábito *m*. be in/get into the ~ of ter/apanhar o hábito de

habitable /ˈhæbɪtəbl/ *a* habitável. ~ation /-ˈteɪʃn/ *n* habitação *f*

habitat /ˈhæbɪtæt/ *n* habitat *m*

habitual /həˈbɪtʃʊəl/ *a* habitual, costumeiro; (*smoker, liar*) inveterado. ~ly *adv* habitualmente

hack[1] /hæk/ *n* (*horse*) cavalo *m* de aluguel; (*writer*) escrevinhador (*pej*) *m*

hack[2] /hæk/ *vt* cortar, despedaçar. ~ to pieces cortar em pedaços

hackneyed /ˈhæknɪd/ *a* banal, batido

had /hæd/ *see* have

haddock /ˈhædək/ *n* *invar* hadoque *m*, eglefim *m*. smoked ~ hadoque *m* fumado

haemorrhage /ˈhemərɪdʒ/ *n* hemorragia *f*

haemorrhoids /ˈhemərɔɪdz/ *npl* hemorróidas *fpl*

haggard /ˈhæɡəd/ *a* desfigurado, com o rosto desfeito, magro e macilento

haggle /ˈhæɡl/ *vi* ~ (over) regatear

hail[1] /heɪl/ *vt* saudar; (*taxi*) fazer sinal para, chamar □ *vi* ~ from vir de

hail[2] /heɪl/ *n* granizo *m*, (*P*) saraiva *f*, (*P*) chuva de pedra *f* □ *vi* chover granizo, (*P*) saraivar

hailstone /ˈheɪlstəʊn/ *n* pedra *f* de granizo

hair /heə(r)/ *n* (*on head*) cabelo(s) *m*(*pl*); (*on body*) pêlos *mpl*; (*single strand*) cabelo *m*; (*of animal*) pêlo *m*. ~do *n* (*colloq*) penteado *m*. ~dryer *n* secador *m* de cabelo. ~-raising *a* horripilante, de pôr os cabelos em pé. ~style *n* estilo *m* de penteado

hairbrush /ˈheəbrʌʃ/ *n* escova *f* para o cabelo

haircut /ˈheəkʌt/ *n* corte *m* de cabelo

hairdresser /ˈheədresə(r)/ *n* cabeleireiro *m*, cabeleireira *f*

hairpin /ˈheəpɪn/ *n* grampo *m*, (*P*) gancho *m* para o cabelo. ~ bend curva *f* techada, quase em W

hairy /ˈheərɪ/ *a* (-ier, -iest) peludo, cabeludo; (*sl: terrifying*) de pôr os cabelos em pé, horripilante

hake /heɪk/ *n* (*pl invar*) abrótea *f*

half /hɑːf/ *n* (*pl* halves /hɑːvz/) metade *f*, meio *m* □ *a* meio □ *adv* ao meio. ~ a dozen meia dúzia. ~ an hour meia hora. ~-caste *n* mestiço *m*. ~-hearted *a* sem grande entusiasmo. ~-term n férias fpl no meio do trimestre. ~-time n meiotempo. ~-way a & adv a meio caminho. ~-wit n idiota mf. go halves dividir as despesas

halibut /'hælɪbət/ n (pl invar) halibute m

hall /hɔ:l/ n sala f; (entrance) vestibulo m, entrada f; (mansion) solar m. ~ of residence residência f de estudantes

hallmark /'hɔ:lma:k/ n (on gold etc) marca f do contraste; (fig) cunho m, selo m

hallo /hə'ləʊ/ int & n (greeting, surprise) olá; (on phone) está

hallow /'hæləʊ/ vt consagrar, santificar

Halloween /hæləʊ'i:n/ n véspera f do Dia de Todos os Santos

hallucination /həlu:sɪ'neɪʃn/ n alucinação f

halo /'heɪləʊ/ n (pl -oes) halo m, auréola f

halt /hɔ:lt/ n parada f, (P) paragem f □ vt deter, fazer parar □ vi fazer alto, parar

halve /ha:v/ vt dividir ao meio; (time etc) reduzir à metade

ham /hæm/ n presunto m

hamburger /'hæmbз:gə(r)/ n hambúrguer m, (P) hamburgo m

hamlet /'hæmlɪt/ n aldeola f, lugarejo m

hammer /'hæmə(r)/ n martelo m □ vt/i martelar; (fig) bater com força

hammock /'hæmək/ n rede f (de dormir)

hamper¹ /'hæmpə(r)/ n cesto m, (P) cabaz m

hamper² /'hæmpə(r)/ vt dificultar, atrapalhar

hamster /'hæmstə(r)/ n hamster m

hand /hænd/ n mão f; (of clock) ponteiro m; (writing) letra f; (worker) trabalhador m; (cards) mão f; (measure) palmo m. (helping) ~ ajuda f, mão f □ vt dar, entregar. at ~ à mão. ~-baggage n bagagem f de mão. ~ in or over entregar. ~ out distribuir. ~-out n impresso m, folheto m; (money) esmola f, donativo m. on the one ~... on the other ~ por um lado ... por outro. out of ~ incontrolável. to ~ à mão

handbag /'hændbæg/ n carteira f, bolsa de mão f, mala de mão f

handbook /'hændbʊk/ n manual m

handbrake /'hændbreɪk/ n freio m de mão, (P) travão m de mão

handcuffs /'hændkʌfs/ npl algemas fpl

handful /'hændfʊl/ n mão-cheia f, punhado m; (a few) punhado m; (diffi-cult task) mão-de-obra f. she's a ~ (colloq) ela é danada

handicap /'hændɪkæp/ n (in competition) handicap m; (disadvantage) desvantagem f □ vt (pt handicapped) prejudicar. ~ped a deficiente. mentally ~ped deficiente mental

handicraft /'hændɪkra:ft/ n artesanato m, trabalho m manual

handiwork /'hændɪwз:k/ n obra f, trabalho m

handkerchief /'hæŋkətʃɪf/ n lenço m

handle /'hændl/ n (of door etc) maçaneta f, puxador m; (of cup etc) asa f; (of implement) cabo m; (of pan etc) alça f, (P) pega f □ vt (touch) manusear, tocar; (operate with hands) manejar; (deal in) negociar em; (deal with) tratar de; (person) lidar com. fly off the ~ (colloq) perder as estribeiras

handlebar /'hændlba:(r)/ n guidão m, (P) guiador m

handmade /'hændmeɪd/ a feito à mão

handshake /'hændʃeɪk/ n aperto m de mão

handsome /'hænsəm/ a bonito; (fig) generoso

handwriting /'hændraɪtɪŋ/ n letra f, caligrafia f

handy /'hændɪ/ a (-ier, -iest) a (convenient, useful) útil, prático; (person) jeitoso; (near) à mão

handyman /'hændɪmæn/ n (pl -men) faz-tudo m

hang /hæŋ/ vt (pt hung) pendurar, suspender; (head) baixar; (pt hanged) (criminal) enforcar □ vi estar dependurado, pender; (criminal) ser enforcado. get the ~ of (colloq) pegar o jeito de, (P) apanhar. ~ about andar por ai. ~ back hesitar. ~-gliding n asa f delta. ~ on (wait) aguardar. ~ on to (hold tightly) agarrar-se a. ~ out (sl: live) morar. ~ up (phone) desligar. ~-up n (sl) complexo m

hangar /'hæŋə(r)/ n hangar m

hanger /'hæŋə(r)/ n (for clothes) cabide m. ~-on n parasita mf

hangover /'hæŋəʊvə(r)/ n (from drinking) ressaca f

hanker /'hæŋkə(r)/ vi ~ after ansiar por, suspirar por

haphazard /hæp'hæzəd/ a ~ ly adv ao acaso, à sorte

happen /'hæpən/ vi acontecer, suceder. he ~s to be out por acaso ele não está. ~ing n acontecimento m

happy /'hæpɪ/ a (-ier, -iest) feliz. be ~y with estar contente com. ~y-go-lucky a despreocupado. ~ily adv com satisfação; (fortunately) felizmente. **she smiled** ~**ily** ela sorriu feliz. ~**iness** n felicidade f

harass /'hærəs/ vt amofinar, atormentar, perseguir. ~**ment** n amofinação f, perseguição f. **sexual** ~**ment** assédio m sexual

harbour /'ha:bə(r)/ n porto m; (shelter) abrigo m □ vt abrigar, dar asilo a; (fig: in the mind) ocultar, obrigar

hard /ha:d/ a (-er, -est) duro; (difficult) difícil □ adv muito, intensamente; (look) fixamente; (pull) com força; (think) a fundo, a sério. ~**back** n livro m encadernado ~**boiled egg** ovo m cozido. ~ **by** muito perto. ~**disk** disco m rígido. ~**headed** a realista, prático. ~ **of hearing** meio surdo. ~ **shoulder** acostamento m, (P) berma f alcatroada. ~ **up** (colloq) sem dinheiro, teso (sl), liso (sl). ~ **water** água f dura

hardboard /'ha:dbɔ:d/ n madeira f compensada, madeira f prensada, (P) tabopan m

harden /'ha:dn/ vt/i endurecer. ~**ed** a (callous) calejado; (robust) enrijado

hardly /'ha:dlɪ/ adv mal, dificilmente, a custo. ~ **ever** quase nunca

hardship /'ha:dʃɪp/ n provação f, adversidade f; (suffering) sofrimento m; (financial) privação f

hardware /'ha:dweə(r)/ n ferragens fpl; (comput) hardware m

hardy /'ha:dɪ/ a (-ier, -iest) resistente

hare /heə(r)/ n lebre f

hark /ha:k/ vi ~ **back to** voltar a, recordar

harm /ha:m/ n mal m □ vt prejudicar, fazer mal a. ~**ful** a prejudicial, nocivo. ~**less** a inofensivo. **out of** ~'**s way** a salvo. **there's no** ~ **in** não há mal em

harmonica /ha:'mɒnɪkə/ n gaita f de boca, (P) beiços

harmon|y /'ha:mənɪ/ n harmonia f. ~**ious** /-'məʊnɪəs/ a harmonioso. ~**ize** vt/i harmonizar(-se)

harness /'ha:nɪs/ n arreios mpl □ vt arrear; (fig: use) aproveitar, utilizar

harp /ha:p/ n harpa f □ vi ~ **on** (about) repisar. ~**ist** n harpista mf

harpoon /ha:'pu:n/ n arpão m

harpsichord /'ha:psɪkɔ:d/ n cravo m

harrowing /'hærəʊɪŋ/ a dilacerante, lancinante

harsh /ha:ʃ/ a (-er, -est) duro, severo; (texture, voice) áspero; (light) cru; (colour) gritante; (climate) rigoroso. ~**ly** adv duramente. ~**ness** n dureza f

harvest /'ha:vɪst/ n colheita f, ceifa f □ vt colher, ceifar

has /hæz/ see **have**

hash /hæʃ/ n picadinho m, carne f cozida; (fig: jumble) bagunça f. **make a** ~ **of** fazer uma bagunça

hashish /'hæʃɪʃ/ n haxixe m

hassle /'hæsl/ n (colloq: quarrel) discussão f; (colloq: struggle) dificuldade f □ vt (colloq) aborrecer

haste /heɪst/ n pressa f. **make** ~ apressar-se

hasten /'heɪsn/ vt/i apressar(-se)

hast|y /'heɪstɪ/ a (-ier, -iest) apressado; (too quick) precipitado. ~**ily** adv às pressas, precipitadamente

hat /hæt/ n chapéu m

hatch[1] /hætʃ/ n (for food) postigo m; (naut) escotilha f

hatch[2] /hætʃ/ vt/i chocar; (a plot etc) tramar, urdir

hatchback /'hætʃbæk/ n carro m de três ou cinco portas

hatchet /'hætʃɪt/ n machadinha f

hate /heɪt/ n ódio m □ vt odiar, detestar. ~**ful** a odioso, detestável

hatred /'heɪtrɪd/ n ódio m

haughty /'hɔ:tɪ/ a (-ier, -iest) altivo, soberbo, arrogante

haul /hɔ:l/ vt arrastar, puxar; (goods) transportar em camião □ n (booty) presa f; (fish caught) apanha f; (distance) percurso m. ~**age** n transporte m de cargas. ~**ier** n (firm) transportadora f rodoviária; (person) fretador m

haunt /hɔ:nt/ vt rondar, freqüentar, (P) frequentar; (ghost) assombrar; (thought) obcecar □ n lugar m favorito. ~**ed house** casa f mal-assombrada

have /hæv/ vt (3 sing pres **has**, pt **had**) ter; (bath etc) tomar; (meal) fazer; (walk) dar □ v aux ter. ~ **done** ter feito. ~ **it out (with)** pôr a coisa em pratos limpos, pedir uma explicação (para). ~ **sth done** mandar fazer alg coisa

haven /'heɪvn/ n porto m; (refuge) refúgio m

haversack /'hævəsæk/ n mochila f

havoc /'hævək/ n estragos mpl. **play** ~ **with** causar estragos em

hawk[1] /hɔ:k/ n falcão m

hawk[2] /hɔ:k/ vt vender de porta em porta. ~**er** n vendedor m ambulante

hawthorn /'hɔ:θɔ:n/ n pilriteiro m, estrepeiro m

hay /heɪ/ n feno m. ~ **fever** febre f do feno

haystack /'heɪstæk/ n palheiro m, (P) meda f de feno

haywire /'heɪwaɪə(r)/ a **go** ~ (colloq) ficar transtornado

hazard /'hæzəd/ n risco m □ vt arriscar. ~ **warning lights** pisca-alerta m. ~**ous** a arriscado

haze /heɪz/ n bruma f, neblina f, cerração f

hazel /'heɪzl/ n aveleira f. ~-nut n avelã f

hazy /'heɪzɪ/ a (-ier, -iest) brumoso, encoberto; (fig: vague) vago

he /hi:/ pron ele □ n macho m

head /hed/ n cabeça f; (chief) chefe m; (of beer) espuma f □ a principal □ vt encabeçar, estar à frente de □ vi ~ for dirigir-se para. ~-dress n toucador m. ~ first de cabeça. ~-on a frontal □ adv de frente. ~s or tails? cara ou coroa? ~ waiter chefe de garçons m, (P) dos criados. ~er n (football) cabeçada f

headache /'hedeɪk/ n dor f de cabeça

heading /'hedɪŋ/ n cabeçalho m, título m; (subject category) rubrica f

headlamp /'hedlæmp/ n farol m

headland /'hedlənd/ n promontório m

headlight /'hedlaɪt/ n farol m

headline /'hedlaɪn/ n título m, cabeçalho m

headlong /'hedlɒŋ/ a de cabeça; (rash) precipitado □ adv de cabeça; (rashly) precipitadamente

head|master /hed'mɑ:stə(r)/ n diretor m, (P) director m. ~mistress n diretora f, (P) directora f

headphone /'hedfəʊn/ n fone m de cabeça, (P) auscultador m

headquarters /hed'kwɔ:təz/ npl sede f; (mil) quartel m general

headrest /'hedrest/ n apoio m para a cabeça

headroom /'hedru:m/ n (auto) espaço m para a cabeça; (bridge) limite m de altura, altura f máxima

headstrong /'hedstrɒŋ/ a teimoso

headway /'hedweɪ/ n progresso m. make ~ fazer progressos

heady /'hedɪ/ a (-ier, -iest) empolgante

heal /hi:l/ vt/i curar(-se), sarar; (wound) cicatrizar

health /helθ/ n saúde f. ~ centre posto m de saúde. ~ foods alimentos mpl naturais. ~y a saudável, sadio

heap /hi:p/ n monte m, pilha f □ vt amontoar, empilhar. ~s of money (colloq) dinheiro aos montes (colloq)

hear /hɪə(r)/ vt/i (pt heard /hɜ:d/) ouvir. ~, hear! apoiado! ~ from ter notícias de. ~ of or about ouvir falar de. I won't ~ of it nem quero ouvir falar nisso. ~ing n ouvido m, audição f; (jur) audiência f. ~ing-aid n aparelho m de audição

hearsay /'hɪəseɪ/ n boato m. it's only ~ é só por ouvir dizer

hearse /hɜ:s/ n carro m funerário

heart /hɑ:t/ n coração m. ~s (cards) copas fpl. at ~ no fundo. by ~ de cor. ~ attack ataque m de coração. ~-beat n pulsação f, batida f. ~-breaking a de cortar o coração. ~-broken a com o coração partido, desfeito. ~-to-heart a com o coração nas mãos. lose ~ perder a coragem, desanimar

heartburn /'hɑ:tbɜ:n/ n azia f

hearten /'hɑ:tn/ vt animar, encorajar

heartfelt /'hɑ:tfelt/ a sincero, sentido

hearth /hɑ:θ/ n lareira f

heartless /'hɑ:tlɪs/ a insensível, desalmado, cruel

heart|y /'hɑ:tɪ/ a (-ier, -iest) caloroso; (meal) abundante. ~ily adv calorosamente; (eat, laugh) com vontade

heat /hi:t/ n calor m; (fig) ardor m; (contest) eliminatória f □ vt/i aquecer. ~stroke n insolação f. ~wave n onda f de calor. ~er n aquecedor m. ~ing n aquecimento m

heated /'hi:tɪd/ a (fig) acalorado, aceso

heathen /'hi:ðn/ n pagão m, pagã f

heather /'heðə(r)/ n urze f

heave /hi:v/ vt/i (lift) içar; (a sigh) soltar; (retch) ter náuseas; (colloq: throw) atirar

heaven /'hevn/ n céu m. ~ly a celestial; (colloq) divino

heav|y /'hevɪ/ a (-ier, -iest) pesado; (blow, rain) forte; (cold, drink) grande; (traffic) intenso. ~ily adv pesadamente; (drink, smoke etc) inveterado

heavyweight /'hevɪweɪt/ n (boxing) peso-pesado m

Hebrew /'hi:bru:/ a hebreu, hebraico □ n (lang) hebreu m

heckle /'hekl/ vt interromper, interpelar

hectic /'hektɪk/ a muito agitado, febril

hedge /hedʒ/ n sebe f □ vt cercar □ vi (in answering) usar de evasivas. ~ one's bets (fig) resguardar-se

hedgehog /'hedʒhɒɡ/ n ouriço-cacheiro m

heed /hi:d/ vt prestar atenção a, escutar □ n pay ~ to prestar atenção a, dar ouvidos a. ~less a ~less of indiferente a, sem prestar atenção a

heel /hi:l/ n calcanhar m; (of shoe) salto m; (sl) canalha m

hefty /'heftɪ/ a (-ier, -iest) robusto e corpulento

height /haɪt/ n altura f; (of mountain, plane) altitude f; (fig) auge m, cúmulo m

heighten /'haɪtn/ vt/i aumentar, elevar(-se)

heir /eə(r)/ n herdeiro m. ~ess n herdeira f

heirloom /'eəlu:m/ n peça f de família, (P) relíquia f de família
held /held/ see hold¹
helicopter /'helɪkɒptə(r)/ n helicóptero m
hell /hel/ n inferno m. for the ~ of it só por gozo. ~-bent a decidido a todo o custo (on a). ~ish a infernal
hello /hə'ləʊ/ int & n = hallo
helm /helm/ n leme m
helmet /'helmɪt/ n capacete m
help /help/ vt/i ajudar □ n ajuda f. home ~ empregada f, faxineira f, (P) mulher f a dias. ~ o.s. to servir-se de. he cannot ~ laughing ele não pode conter o riso. it can't be ~ed não há remédio. ~er n ajudante mf. ~ful a útil; (serviceable) de grande ajuda. ~less a impotente
helping /'helpɪŋ/ n porção f, dose f
hem /hem/ n bainha f □ vt (pt hemmed) fazer a bainha. ~ in cercar, encurralar
hemisphere /'hemɪsfɪə(r)/ n hemisfério m
hemp /hemp/ n cânhamo m
hen /hen/ n galinha f
hence /hens/ adv (from now) a partir desta altura, (for this reason) daí, por isso. a week ~ daqui a uma semana. ~forth adv de agora em diante, doravante
henpecked /'henpekt/ a manietado, (P) dominado pela mulher
her /hɜ:(r)/ pron a (a ela); (after prep) ela. (to) ~ lhe. I know ~ conheço-a □ a seu(s), sua(s) dela
herald /'herəld/ vt anunciar
heraldry /'herəldrɪ/ n heráldica f
herb /hɜ:b/ n erva f culinária or medicinal
herd /hɜ:d/ n manada f; (of pigs) vara f □ vi ~ together juntar-se em rebanho
here /hɪə(r)/ adv aqui □ int tome; aqui está. to/from ~ para aqui/daqui
hereafter /hɪər'a:ftə(r)/ adv de/para o futuro, daqui em diante □ n the ~ a vida de além-túmulo, (P) a vida futura
hereby /hɪə'baɪ/ adv (jur) pelo presente ato ou decreto, etc, (P) pelo presente acto ou decreto, etc
hereditary /hɪ'redɪtrɪ/ a hereditário
heredity /hɪ'redɪtɪ/ n hereditariedade f
here|sy /'herəsɪ/ n heresia f. ~tic n herege mf. ~tical /hɪ'retɪkl/ a herético
heritage /'herɪtɪdʒ/ n herança f, patrimônio m, (P) património m
hermit /'hɜ:mɪt/ n eremita m
hernia /'hɜ:nɪə/ n hérnia f
hero /'hɪərəʊ/ n (pl -oes) herói m
heroic /hɪ'rəʊɪk/ a heróico

heroin /'herəʊɪn/ n heroína f
heroine /'herəʊɪn/ n heroína f
heroism /'herəʊɪzəm/ n heroísmo m
heron /'herən/ n garça f
herring /'herɪŋ/ n arenque m
hers /hɜ:z/ poss pron o(s) seu(s), a(s) sua(s), o(s) dela, a(s) dela. it is ~ é (o) dela or o sua
herself /hɜ:'self/ pron ela mesma; (reflexive) se. by ~ sozinha. for ~ para si mesma. to ~ a/para si mesma. Mary ~ said so foi a própria Maria que o disse
hesitant /'hezɪtənt/ a hesitante
hesitat|e /'hezɪteɪt/ vt hesitar. ~ion /-'teɪʃn/ n hesitação f
heterosexual /hetərəʊ'seksjʊəl/ a & n heterossexual (mf)
hexagon /'heksəgən/ n hexágono m. ~al /-'ægənl/ a hexagonal
hey /heɪ/ int eh, olá
heyday /'heɪdeɪ/ n auge m, apogeu m
hi /haɪ/ int olá, viva
hibernat|e /'haɪbəneɪt/ vi hibernar. ~ion /-'neɪʃn/ n hibernação f
hiccup /'hɪkʌp/ n soluço m □ vi soluçar, estar com soluços
hide¹ /haɪd/ vt/i (pt hid, pp hidden) esconder(-se) (from de). ~-and-seek n (game) esconde-esconde m. ~-out n (colloq) esconderijo m
hide² /haɪd/ n pele f, couro m
hideous /'hɪdɪəs/ a horrendo, medonho
hiding /'haɪdɪŋ/ n (colloq: thrashing) sova f, surra f. go into ~ esconder-se. ~-place n esconderijo m
hierarchy /'haɪəra:kɪ/ n hierarquia f
hi-fi /haɪ'faɪ/ a & n (de) alta fidelidade (f)
high /haɪ/ a (-er, -est) alto; (price, number) elevado; (voice, pitch) agudo □ n alta f □ adv alto. two metres ~ com dois metros de altura. ~ chair cadeira f alta para crianças. ~-handed a autoritário, prepotente. ~-jump salto m em altura. ~-rise building edifício m alto, (P) torre f. ~ school escola f secundária. in the ~ season em plena estação. ~-speed a ultra-rápido. ~-spirited a animado, vivo. ~ spot (sl) ponto m culminante. ~ street rua f principal. ~ tide maré f alta. ~er education ensino m superior
highbrow /'haɪbraʊ/ a & n (colloq) intelectual (m)
highlight /'haɪlaɪt/ n (fig) ponto m alto □ vt salientar, pôr em relevo, realçar
highly /'haɪlɪ/ adv altamente, extremamente. ~-strung a muito sensível, nervoso, tenso. speak ~ of falar bem de

Highness /'haɪnɪs/ n Alteza f

highway /'haɪweɪ/ n estrada f, rodovia f. H~ Code Código m Nacional de Trânsito

hijack /'haɪdʒæk/ vt seqüestrar, (P) sequestrar □ n seqüestro m, (P) sequestro m. ~er n (of plane) pirata m (do ar)

hike /haɪk/ n caminhada no campo f □ vi fazer uma caminhada. ~r /-ə(r)/ n excursionista mf, caminhante mf

hilarious /hɪ'leərɪəs/ a divertido, desopilante

hill /hɪl/ n colina f, monte m; (slope) ladeira f, subida f. ~y a acidentado

hillside /'hɪlsaɪd/ n encosta f, vertente f

hilt /hɪlt/ n punho m. to the ~ completamente, inteiramente

him /hɪm/ pron o (a ele); (after prep) ele. (to) ~ lhe. I know ~ conheço-o

himself /hɪm'self/ pron ele mesmo; (reflexive) se. by ~ sozinho. for ~ para si mesmo. to ~ a/para si mesmo. Peter ~ saw it foi o próprio Pedro que o viu

hind /haɪnd/ a traseiro, posterior

hind|er /'hɪndə(r)/ vt empatar, estorvar; (prevent) impedir. ~rance n estorvo m

hindsight /'haɪndsaɪt/ n with ~ em retrospecto

Hindu /hɪn'du:/ n & a hindu (mf). ~ism /-ɪzəm/ n hinduismo m

hinge /hɪndʒ/ n dobradiça f □ vi ~ on depender de

hint /hɪnt/ n insinuação f, indireta f, (P) indirecta f; (advice) sugestão f, dica f (colloq) □ vt dar a entender, insinuar □ vi ~ at fazer alusão a

hip /hɪp/ n quadril m

hippie /'hɪpɪ/ n hippie mf

hippopotamus /hɪpə'pɒtəməs/ n (pl -muses) hipopótamo m

hire /'haɪə(r)/ vt alugar; (person) contratar □ n aluguel m, (P) aluguer m. ~-purchase n compra f a prestações, (P) crediário m

hirsute /'hɜ:sju:t/ a hirsuto

his /hɪz/ a seu(s), sua(s), dele □ poss pron o(s) seu(s), a(s) sua(s), o(s) dele, a(s) dele. it is ~ é (o) dele or o seu

Hispanic /hɪs'pænɪk/ a hispânico

hiss /hɪs/ n silvo m; (for disapproval) assobio m, vaia f □ vt/i sibilar; (for disapproval) assobiar, vaiar

historian /hɪ'stɔ:rɪən/ n historiador m

histor|y /'hɪstərɪ/ n história f. ~ic(al) /hɪ'stɒrɪk(l)/ a histórico

hit /hɪt/ vt (pt hit, pres p hitting) atingir, bater em; (knock against, collide with) chocar com, ir de encontro a; (strike a target) acertar em; (find) descobrir; (affect) atingir □ vi ~ on dar com □ n pancada f; (fig: success) sucesso m. ~ it off dar-se bem (with com). ~-and-run a (driver) que foge depois do desastre. ~-or-miss a ao acaso

hitch /hɪtʃ/ vt atar, prender; (to a hook) enganchar □ n sacão m; (snag) problema m. ~ a lift, ~-hike viajar de carona, (P) boleia. ~-hiker n o que viaja de carona, boleia. ~ up puxar para cima

hive /haɪv/ n colméia f □ vt ~ off separar e tornar independente

hoard /hɔ:d/ vt juntar, açambarcar □ n provisão f; (of valuables) tesouro m

hoarding /'hɔ:dɪŋ/ n tapume m, outdoor m

hoarse /hɔ:s/ a (-er, -est) rouco. ~ness n rouquidão f

hoax /həʊks/ n (malicious) logro m, embuste m; (humorous) trote m □ vt (malicious) enganar, lograr; passar um trote, pregar uma peça

hob /hɒb/ n placa f de aquecimento (do fogão)

hobble /'hɒbl/ vi coxear □ vt pear

hobby /'hɒbɪ/ n passatempo m favorito. ~-horse n (fig) tópico m favorito

hock /hɒk/ n vinho m branco do Reno

hockey /'hɒkɪ/ n hóquei m

hoe /həʊ/ n enxada f □ vt trabalhar com enxada

hog /hɒg/ n porco m; (greedy person) glutão m □ vt (pt hogged) (colloq) açambarcar

hoist /hɔɪst/ vt içar □ n guindaste m, (P) monta-cargas m

hold¹ /həʊld/ vt (pt held) segurar; (contain) levar; (possess) ter, possuir; (occupy) ocupar; (keep, maintain) conservar, manter; (affirm) manter □ vi (of rope etc) aguentar(-se), (P) aguentar(-se) □ n (influence) domínio m. get ~ of pôr as mãos em; (fig) apanhar. ~ back reter. ~ on (colloq) esperar. ~ on to guardar; (cling to) agarrar-se a. ~ one's breath suster a respiração. ~ one's tongue calar-se. ~ the line não desligar. ~ out resistir. ~ up (support) sustentar; (delay) demorar; (rob) assaltar. ~-up n atraso m; (auto) engarrafamento m; (robbery) assalto m. ~ with aguentar, (P) aguentar. ~er n detentor m; (of post, title etc) titular mf; (for object) suporte m

hold² /həʊld/ n (of ship, plane) porão m

holdall /'həʊldɔ:l/ n saco m de viagem

holding /'həʊldɪŋ/ n (land) propriedade f; (comm) ações fpl, (P) acções fpl, valores mpl, holding m

hole /həʊl/ *n* buraco *m* □ *vt* abrir buraco(s) em, esburacar

holiday /ˈhɒlɪdeɪ/ *n* férias *fpl*; (*day off; public*) feriado *m* □ *vi* passar férias. **~-maker** *n* pessoa *f* em férias; (*in summer*) veranista *mf*, (*P*) veraneante *mf*

holiness /ˈhəʊlɪnɪs/ *n* santidade *f*

Holland /ˈhɒlənd/ *n* Holanda *f*

hollow /ˈhɒləʊ/ *a* oco, vazio; (*fig*) falso; (*cheeks*) fundo; (*sound*) surdo □ *n* (*in the ground*) cavidade *f*; (*in the hand*) cova *f*

holly /ˈhɒlɪ/ *n* azevinho *m*

holster /ˈhəʊlstə(r)/ *n* coldre *m*

holy /ˈhəʊlɪ/ *a* (**-ier, -iest**) santo, sagrado; (*water*) benta. **H~ Ghost, H~ Spirit** Espírito *m* Santo

homage /ˈhɒmɪdʒ/ *n* homenagem *f*. **pay ~ to** prestar homenagem a

home /həʊm/ *n* casa *f*, lar *m*; (*institution*) lar *m*, asilo *m*; (*country*) país *m* natal □ *a* caseiro, doméstico; (*of family*) de família; (*pol*) nacional, interno; (*football match*) em casa □ *adv* (**at**) ~ em casa. **come/go** ~ vir/ir para casa. **make oneself at** ~ não fazer cerimónia, (*P*) cerimónia. **~-made** *a* caseiro. **H~ Office** Ministério *m* do Interior. ~ **town** cidade *f* or terra *f* natal. ~ **truth** dura verdade *f*, verdade(s) *f*(*pl*) amarga(s). **~less** *a* sem casa, desabrigado

homeland /ˈhəʊmlænd/ *n* pátria *f*

homely /ˈhəʊmlɪ/ *a* (**-ier, -iest**) (*simple*) simples; (*Amer: ugly*) sem graça

homesick /ˈhəʊmsɪk/ *a* **be** ~ ter saudades

homeward /ˈhəʊmwəd/ *a* (*journey*) de regresso

homework /ˈhəʊmwɜːk/ *n* trabalho *m* de casa, dever *m* de casa

homicide /ˈhɒmɪsaɪd/ *n* homicídio *m*; (*person*) homicida *mf*

homoeopath|y /ˈhəʊmɪɒpəθɪ/ *n* homeopatia *f*.~**ic** *a* homeopático

homosexual /həʊməˈsekʃʊəl/ *a* & *n* homossexual (*mf*)

honest /ˈɒnɪst/ *a* honesto; (*frank*) franco. ~**ly** *adv* honestamente; (*frankly*) francamente. ~**y** *n* honestidade *f*

honey /ˈhʌnɪ/ *n* mel *m*; (*colloq: darling*) querido *m*, querida *f*, meu bem *m*

honeycomb /ˈhʌnɪkəʊm/ *n* favo *m* de mel

honeymoon /ˈhʌnɪmuːn/ *n* lua de mel *f*

honorary /ˈɒnərərɪ/ *a* honorário

honour /ˈɒnə(r)/ *n* honra *f* □ *vt* honrar. ~**able** *a* honrado, honroso

hood /hʊd/ *n* capuz *m*; (*car roof*) capota *f*, (*P*) tejadilho *m*; (*Amer: bonnet*)

capô *m*, (*P*) capot *m*

hoodwink /ˈhʊdwɪŋk/ *vt* enganar

hoof /huːf/ *n* (*pl* **-fs**) casco *m*

hook /hʊk/ *n* gancho *m*; (*on garment*) colchete *m*; (*for fishing*) anzol *m* □ *vt* enganchar; (*fish*) apanhar, pescar. **off the** ~ livre de dificuldades; (*phone*) desligado

hooked /hʊkt/ *a* **be** ~ **on** (*sl*) ter o vício de, estar viciado em

hookey /ˈhʊkɪ/ *n* **play** ~ (*Amer sl*) fazer gazeta

hooligan /ˈhuːlɪɡən/ *n* desordeiro *m*

hoop /huːp/ *n* arco *m*; (*of cask*) cinta *f*

hooray /huːˈreɪ/ *int* & *n* = **hurrah**

hoot /huːt/ *n* (*of owl*) pio *m* de mocho; (*of horn*) buzinada *f*; (*jeer*) apupo *m* □ *vi* (*of owl*) piar; (*of horn*) buzinar; (*jeer*) apupar. ~**er** *n* buzina *f*; (*of factory*) sereia *f*

Hoover /ˈhuːvə(r)/ *n* aspirador de pó *m*, (*P*) aspirador *m* □ *vt* passar o aspirador

hop[1] /hɒp/ *vi* (*pt* **hopped**) saltar num pé só, (*P*) ao pé coxinho □ *n* salto *m*. ~ **in** (*colloq*) subir, saltar (*colloq*). ~ **it** (*sl*) pôr-se a andar (*colloq*). ~ **out** (*colloq*) descer, saltar (*colloq*)

hop[2] /hɒp/ *n* (*plant*) lúpulo *m*. ~**s** espigas *fpl* de lúpulo

hope /həʊp/ *n* esperança *f* □ *vt/i* esperar. ~ **for** esperar (ter). ~**ful** *a* esperançoso; (*promising*) promissor. **be ~ful (that)** ter esperança (que), confiar (em que). ~**fully** *adv* esperançosamente; (*it is hoped that*) é de esperar que. ~**less** *a* desesperado, sem esperança; (*incompetent*) incapaz

horde /hɔːd/ *n* horda *f*

horizon /həˈraɪzn/ *n* horizonte *m*

horizontal /hɒrɪˈzɒntl/ *a* horizontal

hormone /ˈhɔːməʊn/ *n* hormônio *m*, (*P*) hormona *f*

horn /hɔːn/ *n* chifre *m*, corno *m*; (*of car*) buzina *f*; (*mus*) trompa *f*. ~**y** *a* caloso, calejado

hornet /ˈhɔːnɪt/ *n* vespão *m*

horoscope /ˈhɒrəskəʊp/ *n* horóscopo *m*, (*P*) horoscópio *m*

horrible /ˈhɒrəbl/ *a* horrível, horroroso

horrid /ˈhɒrɪd/ *a* horrível, horripilante

horrific /həˈrɪfɪk/ *a* horrífico

horr|or /ˈhɒrə(r)/ *n* horror *m* □ *a* (*film etc*) de terror. ~**ify** *vt* horrorizar, horripilar

horse /hɔːs/ *n* cavalo *m*. ~**-chestnut** *n* castanha *f* da Índia. ~**-racing** *n* corrida *f* de cavalos, hipismo *m*. ~-**radish** *n* rábano *m*

horseback /ˈhɔːsbæk/ *n* **on** ~ a cavalo

horseplay /'hɔ:spleɪ/ n brincadeira f grosseira, abrutalhada f

horsepower /'hɔ:spaʊə(r)/ n cavalo-vapor m

horseshoe /'hɔ:sʃu:/ n ferradura f

horticultur|e /'hɔ:tɪkʌltʃə(r)/ n horticultura f. ~al /-'kʌltʃərəl/ a horticola

hose /həʊz/ n ~(-pipe) mangueira f □ vt regar com a mangueira

hospice /'hɒspɪs/ n hospício m; (for travellers) hospedaria f

hospit|able /hə'spɪtəbl/ a hospitaleiro. ~ality /-'tælətɪ/ n hospitalidade f

hospital /'hɒspɪtl/ n hospital m

host¹ /həʊst/ n anfitrião m, dono m da casa. ~ess n anfitriã f, dona f da casa

host² /həʊst/ n a ~ of uma multidão de, um grande número de

host³ /həʊst/ n (relig) hóstia f

hostage /'hɒstɪdʒ/ n refém m

hostel /'hɒstl/ n residência f de estudantes etc

hostil|e /'hɒstaɪl/ a hostil. ~ity /hɒ'stɪlətɪ/ n hostilidade f

hot /hɒt/ a (hotter, hottest) quente; (culin) picante. be or feel ~ estar com or ter calor. it is ~ está or faz calor □ vt/i (pt hotted) ~ up (colloq) aquecer. ~ dog cachorro-quente m. ~ line linha direta f, (P) directa esp entre chefes de estado. ~-water bottle saco m de água quente

hotbed /'hɒtbed/ n (fig) foco m

hotchpotch /'hɒtʃpɒtʃ/ n misturada f, (P) salgalhada f

hotel /həʊ'tel/ n hotel m. ~ier /-ɪə(r)/ n hoteleiro m

hound /haʊnd/ n cão m de caça e de corrida, sabujo m □ vt acossar, perseguir

hour /'aʊə(r)/ n hora f. ~ly adv de hora em hora □ a de hora em hora. ~ly pay retribuição f horária. paid ~ly pago por hora

house¹ /haʊs/ n (pl ~s /'haʊzɪz/) n casa f; (pol) câmara f. on the ~ por conta da casa. ~-warming n inauguração f da casa

house² /haʊz/ vt alojar; (store) arrecadar, guardar

houseboat /'haʊsbəʊt/ n casa f flutuante

household /'haʊshəʊld/ n família f, agregado m familiar. ~er n ocupante mf; (owner) proprietário m

housekeep|er /'haʊski:pə(r)/ n governanta f. ~ing n (work) tarefas fpl domésticas

housewife /'haʊswaɪf/ n (pl -wives) dona f de casa

housework /'haʊswɜːk/ n tarefas fpl domésticas

housing /'haʊzɪŋ/ n alojamento m. ~ estate zona f residencial

hovel /'hɒvl/ n casebre m, tugúrio m

hover /'hɒvə(r)/ vi pairar; (linger) deixar-se ficar, demorar-se

hovercraft /'hɒvəkrɑːft/ n invar aerobarco m, hovercraft m

how /haʊ/ adv como. ~ long/old is...? que comprimento/idade tem...? ~ far? a que distância? ~ many? quantos? ~ much? quanto? ~ often? com que frequência, (P) frequência? ~ pretty it is como é lindo. ~ about a walk? e se fôssemos dar uma volta? ~ are you? como vai? ~ do you do? muito prazer! and ~! oh se é!

however /haʊ'evə(r)/ adv de qualquer maneira; (though) contudo, no entanto, todavia. ~ small it may be por menor que seja

howl /haʊl/ n uivo m □ vi uivar

HP abbr see hire-purchase

hp abbr see horsepower

hub /hʌb/ n cubo m da roda; (fig) centro m. ~-cap n calota f, (P) tampão m da roda

hubbub /'hʌbʌb/ n chinfrim m

huddle /'hʌdl/ vt/i apinhar(-se). ~ together aconchegar-se

hue¹ /hju:/ n matiz f, tom m

hue² /hju:/ n ~ and cry clamor m, alarido m

huff /hʌf/ n in a ~ com raiva, zangado

hug /hʌg/ vt (pt hugged) abraçar, apertar nos braços; (keep close to) chegar-se a □ n abraço m

huge /hju:dʒ/ a enorme

hulk /hʌlk/ n casco (esp de navio desmantelado) m. ~ing a (colloq) desajeitadão (colloq)

hull /hʌl/ n (of ship) casco m

hullo /hə'ləʊ/ int & n = hallo

hum /hʌm/ vt/i (pt hummed) cantar com a boca fechada; (of insect, engine) zumbir □ n zumbido m

human /'hju:mən/ a humano □ n ~ (being) ser m humano

humane /hju:'meɪn/ a humano, compassivo

humanitarian /hju:mænɪ'teərɪən/ a humanitário

humanity /hju:'mænətɪ/ n humanidade f

humbl|e /'hʌmbl/ a (-er, -est) humilde □ vt humilhar. ~y adv humildemente

humdrum /'hʌmdrʌm/ a monótono, rotineiro

humid /'hju:mɪd/ a úmido, (P) húmido. ~ity /-'mɪdətɪ/ n umidade f, (P) humidade f

humiliat|e /hju:'mɪlɪeɪt/ vt humilhar. ~ion /-'eɪʃn/ n humilhação f humility /hju:'mɪlətɪ/ n humildade f

humorist /'hju:mərɪst/ n humorista mf

hum|our /'hju:mə(r)/ n humor m □ vt fazer a vontade de. ~orous a humorístico; (person) divertido, espirituoso

hump /hʌmp/ n corcova f; (of the back) corcunda f □ vt corcovar, arquear. the ~ (sl) irritação (colloq)

hunch¹ /hʌntʃ/ vt curvar. ~ed up curvado

hunch² /hʌntʃ/ n (colloq) palpite m

hunchback /'hʌntʃbæk/ n corcunda mf

hundred /'hʌndrəd/ a cem □ n centena f, cento m. ~s of centenas de. ~fold a cêntuplo □ adv cem vezes mais. ~th a & n centésimo (m)

hundredweight /'hʌndrədweɪt/ n quintal m (= 50,8 kg; Amer 45,36 kg)

hung /hʌŋ/ see hang

Hungar|y /'hʌŋgərɪ/ n Hungria f. ~ian /-'geərɪən/ a & n húngaro (m)

hunger /'hʌŋgə(r)/ n fome f □ vi. ~ for ter fome de; (fig) desejar vivamente, ansiar por

hungr|y /'hʌŋgrɪ/ a (ier, -iest) esfomeado, faminto. be ~y ter fome, estar com fome. ~ily adv avidamente

hunk /hʌŋk/ n grande naco m

hunt /hʌnt/ vt/i caçar n caça f. ~ for andar à caça de, andar à procura de. ~er n caçador m. ~ing n caça f, caçada f

hurdle /'hɜ:dl/ n obstáculo m

hurl /hɜ:l/ vt arremessar, lançar com força

hurrah, hurray /hʊ'ra:, hʊ'reɪ/ int & n hurra (m), viva (m)

hurricane /'hʌrɪkən/ n furacão m

hurried /'hʌrɪd/ a apressado. ~ly adv apressadamente, às pressas

hurry /'hʌrɪ/ vt/i apressar(-se), despachar(-se) □ n pressa f. be in a ~ estar com or ter pressa. do sth in a ~ fazer alg coisa às pressas. ~up! ande logo

hurt /hɜ:t/ vt (pt hurt) fazer mal a; (injure, offend) magoar, ferir □ vi doer □ a magoado, ferido □ n mal m; (feelings) mágoa f. ~ful a prejudicial; (remark etc) que magoa

hurtle /'hɜ:tl/ vi despenhar-se; (move rapidly) precipitar-se □ vt arremessar

husband /'hʌzbənd/ n marido m, esposo m

hush /hʌʃ/ vt (fazer) calar. ~! silêncio! □ vi calar-se □ n silêncio m. ~hush a (colloq) muito em segredo. ~ up pôr a ferros, encobrir

husk /hʌsk/ n casca f

husky /'hʌskɪ/ a (-ier, -iest) (hoarse) rouco, enrouquecido; (burly) corpulento □ n cão m esquimó

hustle /'hʌsl/ vt empurrar, dar encontrões a □ n empurrão m. ~ and bustle grande movimento m

hut /hʌt/ n cabana f, barraca f de madeira

hutch /hʌtʃ/ n coelheira f

hyacinth /'haɪəsɪnθ/ n jacinto m

hybrid /'haɪbrɪd/ a & n híbrido (m)

hydrant /'haɪdrənt/ n hidrante m

hydraulic /haɪ'drɔ:lɪk/ a hidráulico

hydroelectric /haɪdrəʊɪ'lektrɪk/ a hidrelétrico, (P) hidroeléctrico

hydrofoil /'haɪdrəʊfɔɪl/ n hydrofoil

hydrogen /'haɪdrədʒən/ n hidrogênio m, (P) hidrogénio m

hyena /haɪ'i:nə/ n hiena f

hygiene /'haɪdʒi:n/ n higiene f

hygienic /haɪ'dʒi:nɪk/ a higiênico, (P) higiénico

hymn /hɪm/ n hino m, cântico m

hyper- /'haɪpə(r)/ pref hiper-

hypermarket /'haɪpəma:kɪt/ n hipermercado m

hyphen /'haɪfn/ n hífen m, traço-de-união m. ~ate vt unir com hífen

hypno|sis /hɪp'nəʊsɪs/ n hipnose f. ~tic /-'nɒtɪk/ a hipnótico

hypnot|ize /'hɪpnətaɪz/ vt hipnotizar. ~ism /-ɪzəm/ n hipnotismo m

hypochondriac /haɪpə'kɒndrɪæk/ n hipocondríaco m

hypocrisy /hɪ'pɒkrəsɪ/ n hipocrisia f

hypocrit|e /'hɪpəkrɪt/ n hipócrita mf. ~ical /-'krɪtɪkl/ a hipócrita

hypodermic /haɪpə'dɜ:mɪk/ a hipodérmico □ n seringa f

hypothe|sis /haɪ'pɒθəsɪs/ n (pl -theses /-si:z/) hipótese f. ~tical /-ə'θetɪkl/ a hipotético

hyster|ia /hɪ'stɪərɪə/ n histeria f. ~ical /hɪ'sterɪkl/ a histérico

I

I /aɪ/ pron eu

Iberian /aɪ'bɪərɪən/ a ibérico □ n íbero m

ice /aɪs/ n gelo m □ vt/i gelar; (cake) cobrir com glacê □ vi. ~ up gelar. ~-box n (Amer) geladeira f, (P) frigorífico m. ~(-cream) n sorvete m, (P) gelado m. ~-cube n cubo m or pedra f de gelo. ~ hockey hóquei m sobre o gelo. ~ lolly picolé m. ~-pack n saco m de gelo. ~-rink n rimque m de patinação, (P) patinagem f no gelo. ~ skating n patinação f, (P) patinagem f no gelo

iceberg /'aɪsbɜ:g/ n iceberg m; (fig) pedaço m de gelo

Iceland /'aɪslənd/ n Islândia f. ~er n islandês m. ~ic /-'lændɪk/ a & n islandês (m)

icicle /'aɪsɪkl/ n pingente m de gelo

icing /'aisiŋ/ n (culin) cobertura f de açúcar, glacê m

icy /'aisi/ a (-ier, -iest) gelado, gélido, glacial; (road) com gelo

idea /ar'dɪə/ n idéia f, (P) ideia f

ideal /ar'dɪəl/ a & n ideal (m). ~ize vt idealizar. ~ly adv idealmente

idealis|t /ar'dɪəlɪst/ n idealista mf. ~m /-zəm/ n idealismo m. ~tic /-'lɪstɪk/ a idealista

identical /ar'dentɪkl/ a idêntico

identif|y /ar'dentɪfaɪ/ vt identificar □ vi ~ with identificar-se com. ~ication /-ɪ'keɪʃn/ n identificação f. (papers) documentos mpl de identificação

identity /ar'dentəti/ n identidade f. ~ card carteira f de identidade

ideolog|y /aɪdɪ'ɒlədʒɪ/ n ideologia f. ~ical a /-ɪ'lɒdʒɪkl/ a ideológico

idiom /'ɪdɪəm/ n idioma m; (phrase) expressão f idiomática. ~atic /-'mætɪk/ a idiomático

idiosyncrasy /ɪdɪə'sɪŋkrəsɪ/ n idiossincrasia f, peculiaridade f

idiot /'ɪdɪət/ n idiota mf. ~ic /-'ɒtɪk/ a idiota

idl|e /'aɪdl/ a (-er, -est) (not active; lazy) ocioso; (unemployed) sem trabalho; (of machines) parado; (fig: useless) inútil □ vt/i (of engine) estar em ponto morto, P estar no ralenti. ~eness n ociosidade f. ~y adv ociosamente

idol /'aɪdl/ n idolo m. ~ize vt idolatrar

idyllic /ɪ'dɪlɪk/ a idílico

i.e. abbr isto é, quer dizer

if /ɪf/ conj se

igloo /'ɪɡluː/ n iglu m

ignite /ɪɡ'naɪt/ vt/i inflamar(-se), acender; (catch fire) pegar fogo; (set fire to) atear fogo a, (P) deitar fogo a

ignition /ɪɡ'nɪʃn/ n (auto) ignição f. ~ (key) chave f de ignição

ignoran|t /'ɪɡnərənt/ a ignorante. ~ce n ignorância f. be ~t of ignorar

ignore /ɪɡ'nɔː(r)/ vt não fazer caso de, passar por cima de; (person in the street etc) fingir não ver

ill /ɪl/ a (sick) doente; (bad) mau □ adv mal □ n mal m. ~-advised a pouco aconselhável. ~ at ease pouco à vontade. ~-bred a mal educado. ~-fated a malfadado. ~-treat vt maltratar. ~ will má vontade f, animosidade f

illegal /ɪ'liːɡl/ a ilegal

illegible /ɪ'ledʒəbl/ a ilegível

illegitima|te /ɪlɪ'dʒɪtɪmət/ a ilegítimo. ~cy n ilegitimidade f

illitera|te /ɪ'lɪtərət/ n analfabeto; (uneducated) iletrado. ~cy n analfabetismo m

illness /'ɪlnɪs/ n doença f

illogical /ɪ'lɒdʒɪkl/ a ilógico

illuminat|e /ɪ'luːmɪneɪt/ vt iluminar; (explain) esclarecer. ~ion /-'neɪʃn/ n iluminação f. ~ions npl luminárias fpl

illusion /ɪ'luːʒn/ n ilusão f

illusory /ɪ'luːsərɪ/ a ilusório

illustra|te /'ɪləstreɪt/ vt ilustrar. ~ion /-'streɪʃn/ n ilustração f. ~ive /-ətɪv/ a ilustrativo

illustrious /ɪ'lʌstrɪəs/ a ilustre

image /'ɪmɪdʒ/ n imagem f. (public) ~ imagem f pública

imaginary /ɪ'mædʒɪnərɪ/ a imaginário

imaginat|ion /ɪmædʒɪ'neɪʃn/ n imaginação f. ~ive /ɪ'mædʒɪnətɪv/ a imaginativo

imagin|e /ɪ'mædʒɪn/ vt imaginar. ~able a imaginável

imbalance /ɪm'bæləns/ n desequilíbrio m

imbecile /'ɪmbəsiːl/ a & n imbecil (mf)

imbue /ɪm'bjuː/ vt imbuir, impregnar

imitat|e /'ɪmɪteɪt/ vt imitar. ~ion /-'teɪʃn/ n imitação f

immaculate /ɪ'mækjʊlət/ a imaculado; (impeccable) impecável

immaterial /ɪmə'tɪərɪəl/ a (of no importance) irrelevante. that's ~ to me para mim tanto faz

immature /ɪmə'tjʊə(r)/ a imaturo

immediate /ɪ'miːdɪət/ a imediato. ~ly adv imediatamente □ conj logo que, assim que

immens|e /ɪ'mens/ a imenso. ~ely adv imensamente. ~ity n imensidade f

immers|e /ɪ'mɜːs/ vt mergulhar, imergir. be ~ed in (fig) estar imerso em. ~ion /-ʃn/ n imersão f. ~ion heater aquecedor m de água elétrico, (P) eléctrico

immigr|ate /'ɪmɪɡreɪt/ vi imigrar. ~ant n & a imigrante (mf), imigrado (m). ~ation /-'ɡreɪʃn/ n imigração f

imminen|t /'ɪmɪnənt/ a iminente. ~ce n iminência f

immobil|e /ɪ'məʊbaɪl/ a imóvel. ~ize /-alaɪz/ vt imobilizar

immoderate /ɪ'mɒdərət/ a imoderado, descomedido

immoral /ɪ'mɒrəl/ a imoral. ~ity /ɪmə'rælɪt/ n imoralidade f

immortal /ɪ'mɔːtl/ a imortal. ~ity /-'tælətɪ/ n imortalidade f. ~ize vt imortalizar

immun|e /ɪ'mjuːn/ a imune, imunizado (from, to contra). ~ity n imunidade f

imp /ɪmp/ n diabrete m

impact /'ɪmpækt/ n impacto m

impair /ɪmˈpeə(r)/ vt deteriorar; (damage) prejudicar

impale /ɪmˈpeɪl/ vt empalar

impart /ɪmˈpɑːt/ vt comunicar, transmitir (to a)

impartial /ɪmˈpɑːʃl/ a imparcial. ∼ity /-ʃɪˈælətɪ/ n imparcialidade f

impassable /ɪmˈpɑːsəbl/ a (road, river) impraticável, intransitável; (barrier etc) intransponível

impasse /ˈæmpɑːs/ n impasse m

impatien|t /ɪmˈpeɪʃənt/ a impaciente. ∼ce n impaciência f. ∼tly adv impacientemente

impeach /ɪmˈpiːtʃ/ vt incriminar, acusar

impeccable /ɪmˈpekəbl/ a impecável

impede /ɪmˈpiːd/ vt impedir, estorvar

impediment /ɪmˈpedɪmənt/ n impedimento m, obstáculo m. (speech) ∼ defeito m (na fala)

impel /ɪmˈpel/ vt (pt impelled) impelir, forçar (to do a fazer)

impending /ɪmˈpendɪŋ/ a iminente

impenetrable /ɪmˈpenɪtrəbl/ a impenetrável

imperative /ɪmˈperətɪv/ a imperativo; (need etc) imperioso □ n imperativo m

imperceptible /ɪmpəˈseptəbl/ a imperceptível

imperfect /ɪmˈpɜːfɪkt/ a imperfeito. ∼ion /-əˈfekʃn/ n imperfeição f

imperial /ɪmˈpɪərɪəl/ a imperial; (of measures) legal (na GB). ∼ism /-lɪzəm/ n imperialismo m

imperious /ɪmˈpɪərɪəs/ a imperioso

impersonal /ɪmˈpɜːsənl/ a impessoal

impersonate /ɪmˈpɜːsəneɪt/ vt fazer-se passar por; (theat) fazer or representar (o papel) de. ∼ion /neɪʃn/ n imitação f

impertinen|t /ɪmˈpɜːtɪnənt/ a impertinente. ∼ce n impertinência f. ∼tly adv com impertinência

impervious /ɪmˈpɜːvɪəs/ a ∼ to (water) impermeável a; (fig) insensível a

impetuous /ɪmˈpetʃʊəs/ a impetuoso

impetus /ˈɪmpɪtəs/ n ímpeto m

impinge /ɪmˈpɪndʒ/ vi ∼ on afetar, P afectar; (encroach) infringir

impish /ˈɪmpɪʃ/ a travesso, malicioso

implacable /ɪmˈplækəbl/ a implacável

implant /ɪmˈplɑːnt/ vt implantar

implement¹ /ˈɪmplɪmənt/ n instrumento m, utensílio m

implement² /ˈɪmplɪment/ vt implementar, executar

implicate /ˈɪmplɪkeɪt/ vt implicar. ∼ion /-ˈkeɪʃn/ n implicação f

implicit /ɪmˈplɪsɪt/ a implícito; (unquestioning) absoluto, incondicional

implore /ɪmˈplɔː(r)/ vt implorar, suplicar, rogar

imply /ɪmˈplaɪ/ vt implicar; (hint) sugerir, dar a entender, insinuar

impolite /ɪmpəˈlaɪt/ a indelicado, incorreto, (P) incorrecto

import¹ /ɪmˈpɔːt/ vt importar. ∼ation /-ˈteɪʃn/ n importação f. ∼er n importador m

import² /ˈɪmpɔːt/ n importação f; (meaning) significado m; (importance) importância f

importan|t /ɪmˈpɔːtnt/ a importante. ∼ce n importância f

impos|e /ɪmˈpəʊz/ vt impôr; (inflict) infligir □ vi ∼e on abusar de. ∼ition /-əˈzɪʃn/ n imposição f, (unfair burden) abuso m

imposing /ɪmˈpəʊzɪŋ/ a imponente

impossib|le /ɪmˈpɒsəbl/ a impossível. ∼ility /-ˈbɪlətɪ/ n impossibilidade f

impostor /ɪmˈpɒstə(r)/ n impostor m

impoten|t /ˈɪmpətənt/ a impotente. ∼ce n impotência f

impound /ɪmˈpaʊnd/ vt apreender, confiscar

impoverish /ɪmˈpɒvərɪʃ/ vt empobrecer

impracticable /ɪmˈpræktɪkəbl/ a impraticável

impractical /ɪmˈpræktɪkl/ a pouco prático

imprecise /ɪmprɪˈsaɪs/ a impreciso

impregnable /ɪmˈpregnəbl/ a inexpugnável; (fig) inabalável, irrefutável

impregnate /ˈɪmpregneɪt/ vt impregnar (with de)

impresario /ɪmprɪˈsɑːrɪəʊ/ n (pl -os) empresário m

impress /ɪmˈpres/ vt impressionar, causar impressão a; (imprint) imprimir. ∼ on s.o. inculcar algo em alguém

impression /ɪmˈpreʃn/ n impressão f. ∼able a impressionável. ∼ist n impressionista mf

impressive /ɪmˈpresɪv/ a impressionante, imponente

imprint¹ /ˈɪmprɪnt/ n impressão f, marca f

imprint² /ɪmˈprɪnt/ vt imprimir

imprison /ɪmˈprɪzn/ vt prender, aprisionar. ∼ment n aprisionamento m, prisão f

improbab|le /ɪmˈprɒbəbl/ a improvável. ∼ility /-ˈbɪlətɪ/ n improbabilidade f

impromptu /ɪmˈprɒmptjuː/ a & adv de improviso □ n impromptu m

improper /ɪmˈprɒpə(r)/ a impróprio; (indecent) indecente, pouco decente; (wrong) incorreto, (P) incorrecto

improve /ɪmˈpruːv/ vt/i melhorar. ∼ on aperfeiçoar. ∼ment n melhoria f;

(*in house etc*) melhoramento *m*; (*in health*) melhoras *fpl*

improvis|e /'ɪmprəvaɪz/ *vt/i* improvisar. **~ce** /-'zeɪʃn/ *n* improvisação *f*

imprudent /ɪm'pru:dnt/ *a* imprudente

impuden|t /'ɪmpjʊdənt/ *a* descarado, insolente. **~ce** *n* descaramento *m*, insolência *f*

impulse /'ɪmpʌls/ *n* impulso *m*

impulsive /ɪm'pʌlsɪv/ *a* impulsivo

impur|e /ɪm'pjʊə(r)/ *a* impuro. **~ity** *n* impureza *f*

in /ɪn/ *prep* em, dentro de □ *adv* dentro; (*at home*) em casa; (*in fashion*) na moda. **~ Lisbon/English** em Lisboa/inglês. **~ winter** no inverno. **~ an hour** (*at end of, within*) numa hora. **~ the rain** na chuva. **~ doing** ao fazer. **~ the evening** à tardinha. **the best ~** o melhor em. **we are ~ for** vamos ter. **~-laws** *npl* (*colloq*) sogros *mpl*. **~-patient** *n* doente *m* internado. **the ~s and outs** meandros *mpl*

inability /ɪnə'bɪlətɪ/ *n* incapacidade *f* (**to do** para fazer)

inaccessible /ɪnæk'sesəbl/ *a* inacessível

inaccura|te /ɪn'ækjərət/ *a* inexato, (*P*) inexacto. **~cy** *n* inexatidão *f*, (*P*) inexactidão *f*, falta *f* de rigor

inaction /ɪn'ækʃn/ *n* inação *f*, (*P*) inacção *f*

inactiv|e /ɪn'æktɪv/ *a* inativo, (*P*) inactivo. **~ity** /-'tɪvətɪ/ *n* inação *f*, (*P*) inacção *f*

inadequa|te /ɪn'ædɪkwət/ *a* inadequado, impróprio; (*insufficient*) insuficiente. **~cy** *n* inadequação *f*, (*insufficiency*) insuficiência *f*

inadmissible /ɪnəd'mɪsəbl/ *a* inadmissível

inadvertently /ɪnəd'vɜ:təntlɪ/ *adv* inadvertidamente; (*unintentionally*) sem querer, sem ser por mal

inadvisable /ɪnəd'vaɪzəbl/ *a* desaconselhável, não aconselhável

inane /ɪ'neɪn/ *a* tolo, oco

inanimate /ɪn'ænɪmət/ *a* inanimado

inappropriate /ɪnə'prəʊprɪət/ *a* impróprio, inadequado

inarticulate /ɪnɑː'tɪkjʊlət/ *a* inarticulado; (*of person*) incapaz de se exprimir claramente

inattentive /ɪnə'tentɪv/ *a* desatento

inaugural /ɪ'nɔːgjərəl/ *a* inaugural

inaugurat|e /ɪ'nɔːgjəreɪt/ *vt* inaugurar. **~ion** /-'reɪʃn/ *n* inauguração *f*

inauspicious /ɪnɔː'spɪʃəs/ *a* pouco auspicioso

inborn /ɪn'bɔːn/ *a* inato

inbred /ɪn'bred/ *a* inato, congénito, (*P*) congénito

incalculable /ɪn'kælkjʊləbl/ *a* incalculável

incapable /ɪn'keɪpəbl/ *a* incapaz

incapacit|y /ɪnkə'pæsətɪ/ *n* incapacidade *f*. **~ate** *vt* incapacitar

incarnat|e /ɪn'kɑːneɪt/ *a* encarnado. **the devil ~e** o diabo em pessoa. **~ion** /-'neɪʃn/ *n* encarnação *f*

incendiary /ɪn'sendɪərɪ/ *a* incendiário □ *n* bomba *f* incendiária

incense[1] /'ɪnsens/ *n* incenso *m*

incense[2] /ɪn'sens/ *vt* exasperar, enfurecer

incentive /ɪn'sentɪv/ *n* incentivo, estímulo

incessant /ɪn'sesənt/ *a* incessante. **~ly** *adv* incessantemente, sem cessar

incest /'ɪnsest/ *n* incesto *m*. **~uous** /ɪn'sestjʊəs/ *a* incestuoso

inch /ɪntʃ/ *n* polegada *f* (= 2.54 *cm*) □ *vt/i* avançar palmo a palmo *or* pouco a pouco. **within an ~ of** a um passo de

incidence /'ɪnsɪdəns/ *n* incidência *f*; (*rate*) percentagem *f*

incident /'ɪnsɪdənt/ *n* incidente *m*

incidental /ɪnsɪ'dentl/ *a* incidental, acessório; (*casual*) acidental; (*expenses*) eventuais; (*music*) de cena, incidental. **~ly** *adv* incidentalmente; (*by the way*) a propósito

incinerat|e /ɪn'sɪnəreɪt/ *vt* incinerar. **~or** *n* incinerador *m*

incision /ɪn'sɪʒn/ *n* incisão *f*

incisive /ɪn'saɪsɪv/ *a* incisivo

incite /ɪn'saɪt/ *vt* incitar, instigar. **~ment** *n* incitamento *m*

inclination /ɪnklɪ'neɪʃn/ *n* inclinação *f*, tendência *f*

incline[1] /ɪn'klaɪn/ *vt/i* inclinar(-se). **be ~d to** inclinar-se para; (*have tendency*) ter tendência para

incline[2] /'ɪnklaɪn/ *n* inclinação *f*, declive *m*

inclu|de /ɪn'kluːd/ *vt* incluir; (*in letter*) enviar junto *or* em anexo. **~ding** *prep* inclusive. **~sion** *n* inclusão *f*

inclusive /ɪn'kluːsɪv/ *a* & *adv* inclusive. **be ~ of** incluir

incognito /ɪnkɒg'niːtəʊ/ *a* & *adv* incógnito

incoherent /ɪnkəʊ'hɪərənt/ *a* incoerente

income /'ɪnkʌm/ *n* rendimento *m*. **~ tax** imposto sobre a renda, (*P*) sobre o rendimento

incoming /'ɪnkʌmɪŋ/ *a* (*tide*) enchente; (*tenant etc*) novo

incomparable /ɪn'kɒmpərəbl/ *a* incomparável

incompatible /ɪnkəm'pætəbl/ *a* incompatível

incompeten|t /ɪn'kɒmpɪtənt/ *a* incompetente. **~ce** *n* incompetência *f*

incomplete /mkəm'pli:t/ a incompleto

incomprehensible /mkɒmprɪ'hensəbl/ a incompreensível

inconceivable /mkən'si:vəbl/ a inconcebível

inconclusive /mkən'klu:sɪv/ a inconcludente

incongruous /m'kɒŋgrʊəs/ a incongruente; (absurd) absurdo

inconsequential /mkɒnsɪ'kwenʃl/ a sem importância

inconsiderate /mkən'sɪdərət/ a impensado, inconsiderado; (lacking in regard) pouco atencioso, sem consideração (pelos sentimentos etc de outrem)

inconsisten|t /mkən'sɪstənt/ a incoerente; (at variance) contraditório. ~t with incompatível com. ~cy n incoerência f. ~cies npl contradições fpl

inconspicuous /mkən'spɪkjʊəs/ a que não dá nas vistas, que não chama a atenção

incontinen|t /m'kɒntmənt/ a incontinente. ~ce n incontinência f

inconvenien|t /mkən'vi:nɪənt/ a conveniente, incómodo. ~ce n inconveniência f; (drawback) inconveniente m □ vt incomodar

incorporate /m'kɔ:pəreɪt/ vt incorporar; (include) incluir

incorrect /mkə'rekt/ a incorrecto, (P) incorreto

incorrigible /m'kɒrɪdʒəbl/ a incorrigível

increas|e[1] /m'kri:s/ vt/i aumentar. ~ing a crescente. ~ingly adv cada vez mais

increase[2] /'mkri:s/ n aumento m. on the ~ aumentando, crescendo

incredible /m'kredəbl/ a incrível

incredulous /m'kredjʊləs/ a incrédulo

increment /'mkrəmənt/ n incremento m, aumento m

incriminat|e /m'krɪmɪneɪt/ vt incriminar. ~ing a comprometedor

incubat|e /'mkjʊbeɪt/ vt incubar. ~ion /-'beɪʃn/ n incubação f. ~or n incubadora f

inculcate /'mkʌlkeɪt/ vt inculcar

incumbent /m'kʌmbənt/ n (pol, relig) titular mf □ a be ~ on incumbir a, caber a

incur /m'kɜ:r/ vt (pt incurred) (displeasure, expense etc) incorrer em; (debts) contrair

incurable /m'kjʊərəbl/ a incurável, que não tem cura

indebted /m'detɪd/ a ~ to s.o. em dívida (para) com alg (for por)

indecen|t /m'di:snt/ a indecente. ~t assault atentado m contra o pudor. ~cy n indecência f

indecision /mdɪ'sɪʒn/ n indecisão f

indecisive /mdɪ'saɪsɪv/ a inconcludente, não decisivo; (hesitating) indeciso

indeed /m'di:d/ adv realmente, deveras, mesmo; (in fact) de fato, (P) facto. very much ~ muitíssimo

indefinite /m'defmət/ a indefinido; (time) indeterminado. ~ly adv indefinidamente

indelible /m'deləbl/ a indelével

indemnify /m'demnɪfaɪ/ vt indenizar, (P) indemnizar (for de); (safeguard) garantir (against contra)

indemnity /m'demnətɪ/ n (legal exemption) isenção f; (compensation) indenização f, (P) indemnização f; (safeguard) garantia f

indent /m'dent/ vt (notch) recortar; (typ) entrar. ~ation /-'teɪʃn/ n recorte m; (typ) entrada f

independen|t /mdɪ'pendənt/ a independente. ~ce n independência f. ~tly adv independentemente

indescribable /mdɪ'skraɪbəbl/ a indescritível

indestructible /mdɪ'strʌktəbl/ a indestrutível

indeterminate /mdɪ'tɜ:mmət/ a indeterminado

index /'mdeks/ n (pl indexes) n (in book) índice m; (in library) catálogo m □ vt indexar. ~ card ficha f (de fichário). ~ finger index m, (dedo) indicador m. ~-linked a ligado ao índice de inflação

India /'mdɪə/ n índia f. ~n a & n (of India) indiano (m); (American) índio (m)

indicat|e /'mdɪkeɪt/ vt indicar. ~ion /-'keɪʃn/ n indicação f. ~or n indicador m; (auto) pisca-pisca m; (board) quadro m

indicative /m'dɪkətɪv/ a & n indicativo (m)

indict /m'daɪt/ vt acusar. ~ment n acusação f

indifferen|t /m'dɪfrənt/ a indiferente; (not good) mediocre. ~ce n indiferença f

indigenous /m'dɪdʒɪnəs/ a indígena, natural, nativo (to de)

indigest|ion /mdɪ'dʒestʃən/ n indigestão f. ~ible /-təbl/ a indigesto

indignant /m'dɪgnənt/ a indignado. ~ation /-'neɪʃn/ n indignação f

indirect /mdɪ'rekt/ a indireto, (P) indirecto. ~ly adv indiretamente, (P) indirectamente

indiscr|eet /mdɪ'skri:t/ a indiscreto; (not wary) imprudente. ~etion

/-'eʃn/ n indiscrição f; (action, remark etc) deslize m

indiscriminate /ɪndɪ'skrɪmɪnət/ a que tem falta de discernimento; (random) indiscriminado. ~ly adv sem discernimento; (at random) indiscriminadamente, ao acaso

indispensable /ɪndɪ'spensəbl/ a indispensável

indispos|ed /ɪndɪ'spəʊzd/ a indisposto. ~ition /-ə'zɪʃn/ n indisposição f

indisputable /ɪndɪ'spjuːtəbl/ a indisputável, incontestável

indistinct /ɪndɪ'stɪŋkt/ a indistinto

indistinguishable /ɪndɪ'stɪŋgwɪʃəbl/ a indistinguível, imperceptível; (identical) indiferenciável

individual /ɪndɪ'vɪdʒʊəl/ a individual □ n indivíduo m. ~ity /-'ælətɪ/ n individualidade f. ~ly adv individualmente

indivisible /ɪndɪ'vɪzəbl/ a indivisível

indoctrinat|e /ɪn'dɒktrɪneɪt/ vt (en) doutrinar. ~ion /-'neɪʃn/ n (en) doutrinação f

indolen|t /'ɪndələnt/ a indolente. ~ce n indolência f

indoor /'ɪndɔː(r)/ a (de) interior, interno; (under cover) coberto; (games) de salão. ~s /ɪn'dɔːz/ adv dentro de casa, no interior

induce /ɪn'djuːs/ vt induzir, levar; (cause) causar, provocar. ~ment n incentivo m, encorajamento m

indulge /ɪn'dʌldʒ/ vt satisfazer; (spoil) fazer a(s) vontade(s) de □ vi ~ in entregar-se a

indulgen|t /ɪn'dʌldʒənt/ a indulgente. ~ce n (leniency) indulgência f; (desire) satisfação f

industrial /ɪn'dʌstrɪəl/ a industrial; (unrest etc) trabalhista; (action) reivindicativo. ~ estate zona f industrial. ~ist n industrial m. ~ized a industrializado

industrious /ɪn'dʌstrɪəs/ a trabalhador, aplicado

industry /'ɪndəstrɪ/ n indústria f; (zeal) aplicação f, diligência f, zelo m

inebriated /ɪ'niːbrɪeɪtɪd/ a embriagado, ébrio

inedible /ɪn'edɪbl/ a não comestível

ineffective /ɪnɪ'fektɪv/ a ineficaz; (person) ineficiente, incapaz

ineffectual /ɪnɪ'fektʃʊəl/ a ineficaz, improfícuo

inefficien|t /ɪnɪ'fɪʃnt/ a ineficiente. ~cy n ineficiência f

ineligible /ɪn'elɪdʒəbl/ a inelegível; (undesirable) indesejável. be ~ for não ter direito a

inept /ɪ'nept/ a inepto

inequality /ɪnɪ'kwɒlətɪ/ n desigualdade f

inert /ɪ'nɜːt/ a inerte. ~ia /-ʃə/ n inércia f

inevitable /ɪn'evɪtəbl/ a inevitável, fatal

inexcusable /ɪnɪk'skjuːzəbl/ a indesculpável, imperdoável

inexhaustible /ɪnɪg'zɔːstəbl/ a inesgotável, inexaurível

inexorable /ɪn'eksərəbl/ a inexorável

inexpensive /ɪnɪk'spensɪv/ a barato, em conta

inexperience /ɪnɪk'spɪərɪəns/ n inexperiência f, falta de experiência f. ~d a inexperiente

inexplicable /ɪn'eksplɪkəbl/ a inexplicável

inextricable /ɪn'ekstrɪkəbl/ a inextricável

infallib|le /ɪn'fæləbl/ a infalível. ~ility /-'bɪlətɪ/ n infalibilidade f

infam|ous /'ɪnfəməs/ a infame. ~y n infâmia f

infan|t /'ɪnfənt/ n bebê m, (P) bebé m; (child) criança f. ~cy n infância f; (babyhood) primeira infância f

infantile /'ɪnfəntaɪl/ a infantil

infantry /'ɪnfəntrɪ/ n infantaria f

infatuat|ed /ɪn'fætʃʊeɪtɪd/ a ~ed with cego or perdido por. ~ion /-'eɪʃn/ n cegueira f, paixão f

infect /ɪn'fekt/ vt infectar. ~ s.o. with contagiar or contaminar alg com. ~ion /-ʃn/ n infecção f, contágio m. ~ious /-ʃəs/ a infeccioso, contagioso

infer /ɪn'fɜː(r)/ vt (pt inferred) inferir, deduzir. ~ence /'ɪnfərəns/ n inferência f

inferior /ɪn'fɪərɪə(r)/ a inferior; (work etc) de qualidade inferior □ n inferior mf; (in rank) subalterno m. ~ity /-'ɒrətɪ/ n inferioridade f

infernal /ɪn'fɜːnl/ a infernal

infertil|e /ɪn'fɜːtaɪl/ a infértil, estéril. ~ity /-ə'tɪlətɪ/ n infertilidade f, esterilidade f

infest /ɪn'fest/ vt infestar (with de). ~ation n infestação f

infidelity /ɪnfɪ'delətɪ/ n infidelidade f

infiltrat|e /'ɪnfɪltreɪt/ vt/i infiltrar (-se). ~ion /-'treɪʃn/ n infiltração f

infinite /'ɪnfɪnət/ a & n infinito (m). ~ly adv infinitamente

infinitesimal /ɪnfɪnɪ'tesɪml/ a infinitesimal, infinitésimo

infinitive /ɪn'fɪnətɪv/ n infinitivo m

infinity /ɪn'fɪnətɪ/ n infinidade f, infinito m

infirm /ɪn'fɜːm/ a débil, fraco. ~ity n (illness) enfermidade f; (weakness) fraqueza f

inflam|e /ɪn'fleɪm/ vt inflamar. ~mable /-'æməbl/ a inflamável. ~mation /-ə'meɪʃn/ n inflamação f inflate /ɪnˈfleɪt/ vt (balloon etc) encher de ar; (prices) causar inflação de

inflation /ɪnˈfleɪʃn/ n inflação f. ~ary a inflacionário

inflection /ɪnˈflekʃn/ n inflexão f; (gram) flexão f, desinência f

inflexible /ɪnˈfleksəbl/ a inflexível

inflict /ɪnˈflɪkt/ vt infligir, impor (on a)

influence /ˈɪnflʊəns/ n influência f □ vt influenciar, influir sobre

influential /ɪnflʊˈenʃl/ a influente

influenza /ɪnflʊˈenzə/ n gripe f

influx /ˈɪnflʌks/ n afluência f, influxo m

inform /ɪnˈfɔːm/ vt informar. ~ against or on denunciar. keep ~ed manter ao corrente or a par. ~ant n informante mf. ~er n delator m, denunciante mf

informal /ɪnˈfɔːml/ a informal; (simple) simples, sem cerimónia, (P) cerimônia; (unofficial) oficioso; (colloquial) familiar; (dress) de passeio, à vontade; (dinner, gathering) intimo. ~ity /-ˈmæləti/ n informalidade f; (simplicity) simplicidade f, (intimacy) intimidade f. ~ly adv informalmente, sem cerimónia, (P) cerimônia, à vontade

information /ɪnfəˈmeɪʃn/ n informação f; (facts, data) informações fpl. ~ technology tecnologia f da informação

informative /ɪnˈfɔːmətɪv/ a informativo

infra-red /ɪnfrəˈred/ a infravermelho

infrequent /ɪnˈfriːkwənt/ a pouco frequente, (P) frequente. ~ly adv raramente

infringe /ɪnˈfrɪndʒ/ vt infringir. ~ on transgredir; (rights) violar. ~ment n infracção f, (P) infracção f; (rights) violação f

infuriate /ɪnˈfjʊərɪeɪt/ vt enfurecer, enraivecer. ~ing a enfurecedor, de enfurecer, de dar raiva

infuse /ɪnˈfjuːz/ vt infundir, incutir; (herbs, tea) pôr de infusão. ~ion /-ʒn/ n infusão f

ingen|ious /ɪnˈdʒiːnɪəs/ a engenhoso, bem pensado. ~uity /-ˈnjuːəti/ n engenho m, habilidade f, imaginação f

ingenuous /ɪnˈdʒenjʊəs/ a cândido, ingênuo, (P) ingênuo

ingot /ˈɪŋɡət/ n barra f, lingote m

ingrained /ɪnˈɡreɪnd/ a arraigado, enraizado; (dirt) entranhado

ingratiate /ɪnˈɡreɪʃɪeɪt/ vt ~ o.s. with insinuar-se junto de, cair nas or ganhar as boas graças de

ingratitude /ɪnˈɡrætɪtjuːd/ n ingratidão f

ingredient /ɪnˈɡriːdɪənt/ n ingrediente m

inhabit /ɪnˈhæbɪt/ vt habitar. ~able a habitável. ~ant n habitante mf

inhale /ɪnˈheɪl/ vt inalar, aspirar. ~r /-ə(r)/ n inalador m

inherent /ɪnˈhɪərənt/ a inerente. ~ly adv inerentemente, em si

inherit /ɪnˈherɪt/ vt herdar (from de). ~ance n herança f

inhibit /ɪnˈhɪbɪt/ vt inibir; (prevent) impedir. be ~ed ser (um) inibido. ~ion /-ˈbɪʃn/ n inibição f

inhospitable /ɪnˈhɒspɪtəbl/ a inóspito; (of person) inospitaleiro, pouco/nada hospitaleiro

inhuman /ɪnˈhjuːmən/ a desumano. ~ity /-ˈmænəti/ n desumanidade f

inhumane /ɪnhjuːˈmeɪn/ a inumano, cruel

inimitable /ɪˈnɪmɪtəbl/ a inimitável

iniquitous /ɪˈnɪkwɪtəs/ a iníquo

initial /ɪˈnɪʃl/ a & n inicial (f) □ vt (pt initialled) assinar com as iniciais, rubricar. ~ly adv inicialmente

initiat|e /ɪˈnɪʃɪeɪt/ vt iniciar (into em); (scheme) lançar. ~ion /-ˈeɪʃn/ n iniciação f; (start) início m

initiative /ɪˈnɪʃətɪv/ n iniciativa f

inject /ɪnˈdʒekt/ vt injetar, (P) injectar; (fig) insuflar. ~ion /-ʃn/ n injeção f, (P) injecção f

injure /ˈɪndʒə(r)/ vt (harm) fazer mal a, prejudicar, lesar; (hurt) ferir

injury /ˈɪndʒərɪ/ n ferimento m, lesão f; (wrong) mal m

injustice /ɪnˈdʒʌstɪs/ n injustiça f

ink /ɪŋk/ n tinta f. ~-well n tinteiro m. ~y a sujo de tinta

inkling /ˈɪŋklɪŋ/ n idéia f, (P) ideia f, suspeita f

inlaid /ɪnˈleɪd/ see inlay [1]

inland /ˈɪnlənd/ a interior □ adv /ɪnˈlænd/ no interior, para o interior. the I~ Revenue o Fisco, a Receita Federal

inlay [1] /ɪnˈleɪ/ vt (pt inlaid) embutir, incrustar

inlay [2] /ˈɪnleɪ/ n incrustação f, obturação f

inlet /ˈɪnlet/ n braço m de mar, enseada f; (techn) admissão f

inmate /ˈɪnmeɪt/ n residente mf; (in hospital) internado m; (in prison) presidiário m

inn /ɪn/ n estalagem f

innards /ˈɪnədz/ npl (colloq) tripas (colloq) fpl

innate /ɪˈneɪt/ a inato

inner /ˈɪnə(r)/ a interior, interno; (fig) íntimo. ~ city n centro m da cidade. ~most a mais profundo, mais íntimo. ~ tube n câmara f de ar

innings /'ɪnɪŋz/ n (cricket) vez f de bater; (pol) período m no poder

innocent /'ɪnəsnt/ a & n inocente (mf). ~ce n inocência f

innocuous /ɪ'nɒkjʊəs/ a inócuo, inofensivo

innovat|e /'ɪnəveɪt/ vi inovar. ~ion /-'veɪʃn/ n inovação f. ~or n inovador m

innuendo /ɪnju:'endəʊ/ n (pl -oes) insinuação f, indireta f, (P) indirecta f

innumerable /ɪ'nju:mərəbl/ a inumerável

inoculat|e /ɪ'nɒkjʊleɪt/ vt inocular. ~ion /-'leɪʃn/ n inoculação f, vacina f

inoffensive /ɪnə'fensɪv/ a inofensivo

inoperative /ɪn'ɒpərətɪv/ a inoperante, ineficaz

inopportune /ɪn'ɒpətjuːn/ a inoportuno

inordinate /ɪ'nɔːdɪnət/ a excessivo, desmedido. ~ly adv excessivamente, desmedidamente

input /'ɪmpʊt/ n (data) dados mpl; (electr: power) energia f; (computer process) entrada f, dados mpl

inquest /'ɪnkwest/ n inquérito m

inquir|e /ɪn'kwaɪə(r)/ vi informar-se □ vt perguntar, indagar, inquirir. ~e about procurar informações sobre, indagar. ~e into inquirir, indagar. ~ing a (look) interrogativo; (mind) inquisitivo. ~y n (question) pergunta f, (jur) inquérito m; (investigation) investigação f

inquisition /ɪnkwɪ'zɪʃn/ n inquisição f

inquisitive /ɪn'kwɪzətɪv/ a curioso, inquisitivo; (prying) intrometido, bisbilhoteiro

insan|e /ɪn'seɪn/ a louco, doido. ~ity /ɪn'sænətɪ/ n loucura f, demência f

insanitary /ɪn'sænɪtrɪ/ a insalubre, anti-higiénico, (P) anti-higiénico

insatiable /ɪn'seɪʃəbl/ a insaciável

inscri|be /ɪn'skraɪb/ vt inscrever; (book) dedicar. ~ption /-ɪpʃn/ n inscrição f; (in book) dedicatória f

inscrutable /ɪn'skruːtəbl/ a impenetrável, misterioso

insect /'ɪnsekt/ n inseto m, (P) insecto m

insecur|e /ɪnsɪ'kjʊə(r)/ a (not firm) inseguro, mal seguro; (unsafe; psych) inseguro. ~ity n insegurança f, falta f de segurança

insensible /ɪn'sensəbl/ a insensível; (unconscious) inconsciente

insensitive /ɪn'sensətɪv/ a insensível

inseparable /ɪn'seprəbl/ a inseparável

insert¹ /ɪn'sɜːt/ vt inserir; (key) meter, colocar; (add) pôr, inserir. ~ion /-ʃn/ n inserção f

insert² /'ɪnsɜːt/ n coisa f inserida

inside /ɪn'saɪd/ n interior m. ~s (colloq) tripas fpl (colloq) □ a interior, interno □ adv no interior, dentro, por dentro □ prep dentro de; (of time) em menos de. ~ out de dentro para fora, do avesso; (thoroughly) por dentro e por fora, a fundo

insidious /ɪn'sɪdɪəs/ a insidioso

insight /'ɪnsaɪt/ n penetração f, perspicácia f; (glimpse) vislumbre m

insignificant /ɪnsɪg'nɪfɪkənt/ a insignificante

insincer|e /ɪnsɪn'sɪə(r)/ a insincero. ~ity /-'serətɪ/ n insinceridade f, falta f de sinceridade

insinuat|e /ɪn'sɪnjʊeɪt/ vt insinuar. ~ion /-'eɪʃn/ n (act) insinuação f; (hint) indireta f, (P) indirecta f, insinuação f

insipid /ɪn'sɪpɪd/ a insípido, sem sabor

insist /ɪn'sɪst/ vt/i ~ (on/that) insistir (em/em que)

insisten|t /ɪn'sɪstənt/ a insistente. ~ce n insistência f. ~tly adv insistentemente

insolen|t /'ɪnsələnt/ a insolente. ~ce n insolência f

insoluble /ɪn'sɒljʊbl/ a insolúvel

insolvent /ɪn'sɒlvənt/ a insolvente

insomnia /ɪn'sɒmnɪə/ n insónia f, (P) insónia f

inspect /ɪn'spekt/ vt inspecionar, (P) inspeccionar, examinar; (tickets) fiscalizar; (passport) controlar; (troops) passar revista a. ~ion /-ʃn/ n inspeção f, (P) inspecção f, exame m; (ticket) fiscalização f; (troops) revista f. ~or n inspetor m, (P) inspector m; (on train) fiscal m

inspir|e /ɪn'spaɪə(r)/ vt inspirar. ~ation /-ə'reɪʃn/ n inspiração f

instability /ɪnstə'bɪlətɪ/ n instabilidade f

install /ɪn'stɔːl/ vt instalar; (heater etc) montar, instalar. ~ation /-ə'leɪʃn/ n instalação f

instalment /ɪn'stɔːlmənt/ n prestação f; (of serial) episódio m

instance /'ɪnstəns/ n exemplo m, caso m. for ~ por exemplo. in the first ~ em primeiro lugar

instant /'ɪnstənt/ a imediato; (food) instantâneo □ n instante m. ~ly adv imediatamente, logo

instantaneous /ɪnstən'teɪnɪəs/ a instantâneo

instead /ɪn'sted/ adv em vez disso, em lugar disso. ~ of em vez de, em lugar de

instigat|e /'ɪnstɪgeɪt/ vt instigar, incitar. ~ion /-'geɪʃn/ n instigação f. ~or n instigador m

instil /ɪnˈstɪl/ vt (pt instilled) instilar, insuflar

instinct /ˈɪnstɪŋkt/ n instinto m. ~ive /ɪnˈstɪŋktɪv/ a instintivo

institut|e /ˈɪnstɪtjuːt/ n instituto m □ vt instituir; (legal proceedings) intentar; (inquiry) ordenar. ~ion /-ˈtjuːʃn/ n instituição f; (school) estabelecimento m de ensino; (hospital) estabelecimento m hospitalar

instruct /ɪnˈstrʌkt/ vt instruir; (order) mandar, ordenar; (a solicitor etc) dar instruções a. ~ s.o. in sth ensinar alg coisa a alguém. ~ion /-ʃn/ n instrução f. ~ions /-ʃnz/ npl instruções fpl, modo m de emprego; (orders) ordens fpl. ~ive a instrutivo. ~or n instrutor m

instrument /ˈɪnstrəmənt/ n instrumento m. ~ panel painel m de instrumentos

instrumental /ɪnstrəˈmentl/ a instrumental. be ~ in ter um papel decisivo em. ~ist n instrumentalista mf

insubordinat|e /ɪnsəˈbɔːdɪnət/ a insubordinado. ~ion /-ˈneɪʃn/ n insubordinação f

insufferable /ɪnˈsʌfrəbl/ a intolerável, insuportável

insufficient /ɪnsəˈfɪʃnt/ a insuficiente

insular /ˈɪnsjʊlə(r)/ a insular; (fig: narrow-minded) bitolado, limitado, (P) tacanho

insulat|e /ˈɪnsjʊleɪt/ vt isolar. ~ing tape fita f isolante. ~ion /-ˈleɪʃn/ n isolamento m

insulin /ˈɪnsjʊlɪn/ n insulina f

insult[1] /ɪnˈsʌlt/ vt insultar, injuriar. ~ing a insultante, injurioso

insult[2] /ˈɪnsʌlt/ n insulto m, injúria f

insur|e /ɪnˈʃʊə(r)/ vt segurar, pôr no seguro; (Amer) = ensure. ~ance n seguro m. ~ance policy apólice f de seguro

insurmountable /ɪnsəˈmaʊntəbl/ a insuperável

intact /ɪnˈtækt/ a intato, (P) intacto

intake /ˈɪnteɪk/ n admissão f; (techn) admissão f, entrada f; (of food) ingestão f

intangible /ɪnˈtændʒəbl/ a intangível

integral /ˈɪntɪɡrəl/ a integral. be an ~ part of ser parte integrante de

integrat|e /ˈɪntɪɡreɪt/ vt/i integrar (-se). ~ed circuit circuito m integrado. ~ion /-ˈɡreɪʃn/ n integração f

integrity /ɪnˈtegrətɪ/ n integridade f

intellect /ˈɪntəlekt/ n intelecto m, inteligência f. ~ual /-ˈlektʃʊəl/ a & n intelectual (mf)

intelligen|t /ɪnˈtelɪdʒənt/ a inteligente. ~ce n inteligência f; (mil) informações fpl. ~tly adv inteligentemente

intelligible /ɪnˈtelɪdʒəbl/ a inteligível

intend /ɪnˈtend/ vt tencionar; (destine) reservar, destinar. ~ed a intencional, propositado

intens|e /ɪnˈtens/ a intenso; (person) emotivo. ~ely adv intensamente; (very) extremamente. ~ity n intensidade f

intensif|y /ɪnˈtensɪfaɪ/ vt intensificar. ~ication /-ˈkeɪʃn/ n intensificação f

intensive /ɪnˈtensɪv/ a intensivo. ~ care tratamento m intensivo

intent /ɪnˈtent/ n intento m, designio m, propósito m □ a atento, concentrado. ~ on absorto em; (intending to) decidido a. ~ly adv atentamente

intention /ɪnˈtenʃn/ n intenção f. ~al a intencional. ~ally adv de propósito

inter /ɪnˈtɜː(r)/ vt (pt interred) enterrar

inter- /ˈɪntə(r)/ pref inter-

interact /ɪntəˈrækt/ vi agir uns sobre os outros. ~ion /-ʃn/ n interação f, (P) interacção f

intercede /ɪntəˈsiːd/ vi interceder

intercept /ɪntəˈsept/ vt interceptar

interchange[1] /ɪntəˈtʃeɪndʒ/ vt permutar, trocar. ~able a permutável

interchange[2] /ˈɪntətʃeɪndʒ/ n permuta f, intercâmbio m; (road junction) trevo m de trânsito, (P) nó m

intercom /ˈɪntəkɒm/ n interfone m, (P) intercomunicador m

interconnected /ɪntəkəˈnektɪd/ a (facts, events etc) ligado, relacionado

intercourse /ˈɪntəkɔːs/ n (sexual) relações fpl sexuais

interest /ˈɪntrəst/ n interesse m; (legal share) título m; (in finance) juro(s) m(pl). rate of ~ taxa f de juros □ vt interessar. ~ed a interessado. be ~ed in interessar-se por. ~ing a interessante

interface /ˈɪntəfeɪs/ n interface f

interfer|e /ɪntəˈfɪə(r)/ vi interferir, intrometer-se (in em); (meddle, hinder) interferir (with com); (tamper) mexer indevidamente (with em). ~ence n interferência f

interim /ˈɪntərɪm/ n in the ~ nesse/neste interim, (P) interim m □ a interino, provisório

interior /ɪnˈtɪərɪə(r)/ a & n interior (m)

interjection /ɪntəˈdʒekʃn/ n interjeição f

interlock /ɪntəˈlɒk/ vt/i entrelaçar; (pieces of puzzle etc) encaixar(-se); (mech: wheels) engrenar, engatar

interloper /ˈɪntələʊpə(r)/ n intruso m

intermarr|iage /ɪntəˈmærɪdʒ/ *n* casamento *m* entre membros de diferentes famílias, raças etc; (*between near relations*) casamento *m* consangüíneo, (*P*) consanguíneo. ~**y** *vi* ligar-se por casamento

intermediary /ɪntəˈmiːdɪərɪ/ *a & n* intermediário (*m*)

intermediate /ɪntəˈmiːdɪət/ *a* intermédio, intermediário

interminable /ɪnˈtɜːmɪnəbl/ *a* interminável, infindável

intermission /ɪntəˈmɪʃn/ *n* intervalo *m*

intermittent /ɪntəˈmɪtnt/ *a* intermitente. ~**ly** *adv* intermitentemente

intern /ɪnˈtɜːn/ *vt* internar. ~**ee** /-ˈniː/ *n* internado *m*. ~**ment** *n* internamento *m*

internal /ɪnˈtɜːnl/ *a* interno, interior. ~**ly** *adv* internamente, interiormente

international /ɪntəˈnæʃnəl/ *a & n* internacional (*mf*)

interpolate /ɪnˈtɜːpəleɪt/ *vt* interpolar

interpret /ɪnˈtɜːprɪt/ *vt/i* interpretar. ~**ation** /-ˈteɪʃn/ *n* interpretação *f*. ~**er** *n* intérprete *mf*

interrelated /ɪntərɪˈleɪtɪd/ *a* inter-relacionado, correlacionado

interrogat|e /ɪnˈterəgeɪt/ *vt* interrogar. ~**ion** /ˈgeɪʃn/ *n* interrogação *f*; (*of police etc*) interrogatório *m*

interrogative /ɪntəˈrɒgətɪv/ *a* interrogativo □ *n* (*pronoun*) pronome *m* interrogativo

interrupt /ɪntəˈrʌpt/ *vt* interromper. ~**ion** /-ʃn/ *n* interrupção *f*

intersect /ɪntəˈsekt/ *vt/i* intersectar (-se); (*roads*) cruzar-se. ~**ion** /-ʃn/ *n* intersecção *f*; (*crossroads*) cruzamento *m*

intersperse /ɪntəˈspɜːs/ *vt* entremear, intercalar; (*scatter*) espalhar

interval /ˈɪntəvl/ *n* intervalo *m*. at ~**s** a intervalos

interven|e /ɪntəˈviːn/ *vi* (*interfere*) intervir; (*of time*) passar-se, decorrer; (*occur*) sobrevir, intervir. ~**tion** /-ˈvenʃn/ *n* intervenção *f*

interview /ˈɪntəvjuː/ *n* entrevista *f* □ *vt* entrevistar. ~**ee** *n* entrevistado *m*. ~**er** *n* entrevistador *m*

intestin|e /ɪnˈtestɪn/ *n* intestino *m*. ~**al** *a* intestinal

intima|te¹ /ˈɪntɪmət/ *a* íntimo; (*detailed*) profundo. ~**cy** *n* intimidade *f*. ~**tely** *adv* intimamente

intimate² /ˈɪntɪmeɪt/ *vt* (*announce*) dar a conhecer, fazer saber; (*imply*) dar a entender

intimidat|e /ɪnˈtɪmɪdeɪt/ *vt* intimidar. ~**ion** /-ˈdeɪʃn/ *n* intimidação *f*

into /ˈɪntə/; *emphatic* /ˈɪntuː/ *prep* para dentro de. divide ~ **three** dividir em tres. ~ **pieces** aos bocados. translate ~ traduzir para

intolerable /ɪnˈtɒlərəbl/ *a* intolerável, insuportável

intoleran|t /ɪnˈtɒlərənt/ *a* intolerante. ~**ce** *n* intolerância *f*

intonation /ɪntəˈneɪʃn/ *n* entonação *f*, entoação *f*, inflexão *f*

intoxicat|ed /ɪnˈtɒksɪkeɪtɪd/ *a* embriagado, etilizado. ~**ion** /-ˈkeɪʃn/ *n* embriaguez *f*

intra- /ɪntrə/ *pref* intra-

intractable /ɪnˈtræktəbl/ *a* intratável, difícil

intransigent /ɪnˈtrænsɪdʒənt/ *a* intransigente

intransitive /ɪnˈtrænsətɪv/ *a* (*verb*) intransitivo

intravenous /ɪntrəˈviːnəs/ *a* intravenoso

intrepid /ɪnˈtrepɪd/ *a* intrépido, arrojado

intrica|te /ˈɪntrɪkət/ *a* intrincado, complexo. ~**cy** *n* complexidade *f*

intrigue /ɪnˈtriːg/ *vt/i* intrigar □ *n* intriga *f*. ~**ing** *a* intrigante, curioso

intrinsic /ɪnˈtrɪnsɪk/ *a* intrínseco. ~**ally** /-klɪ/ *adv* intrinsecamente

introduce /ɪntrəˈdjuːs/ *vt* (*programme, question*) apresentar; (*bring in, insert*) introduzir; (*initiate*) iniciar. ~ **sb to sb** (*person*) apresentar alg a alguém

introduct|ion /ɪntrəˈdʌkʃn/ *n* introdução *f*; (*to person*) apresentação *f*. ~**ory** /-tərɪ/ *a* introdutório, de introdução; (*letter, words*) de apresentação

introspective /ɪntrəˈspektɪv/ *a* introspectivo

introvert /ˈɪntrəvɜːt/ *n & a* introvertido (*m*)

intru|de /ɪnˈtruːd/ *vi* intrometer-se, ser a mais. ~**der** *n* intruso *m*. ~**sion** *n* intrusão *f*. ~**sive** *a* intruso

intuit|ion /ɪntjuːˈɪʃn/ *n* intuição *f*. ~**ive** /ɪnˈtjuːɪtɪv/ *a* intuitivo

inundate /ˈɪnʌndeɪt/ *vt* inundar (with de)

invade /ɪnˈveɪd/ *vt* invadir. ~**r** /-ə(r)/ *n* invasor *m*

invalid¹ /ˈɪnvəlɪd/ *n* inválido *m*

invalid² /ɪnˈvælɪd/ *a* inválido. ~**ate** *vt* invalidar

invaluable /ɪnˈvæljʊəbl/ *a* inestimável

invariabl|e /ɪnˈveərɪəbl/ *a* invariável. ~**y** *adv* invariavelmente

invasion /ɪnˈveɪʒn/ *n* invasão *f*

invective /ɪnˈvektɪv/ *n* invectiva *f*

invent /ɪnˈvent/ vt inventar. ~**ion** n invenção f. ~**ive** a inventivo. ~**or** n inventor m

inventory /ˈɪnvəntrɪ/ n inventário m

inverse /ɪnˈvɜːs/ a & n inverso (m). ~**ly** adv inversamente

inver|t /ɪnˈvɜːt/ vt inverter. ~**ted commas** aspas fpl. ~**sion** n inversão f

invest /ɪnˈvest/ vt investir; (time, effort) dedicar □ vi fazer um investimento. ~ **in** (colloq: buy) gastar dinheiro em. ~**ment** n investimento m. ~**or** n investidor m, financiador m

investigat|e /ɪnˈvestɪgeɪt/ vt investigar. ~**ion** /-ˈgeɪʃn/ n investigação f. **under** ~**ion** em estudo. ~**or** n investigador m

inveterate /ɪnˈvetərət/ a inveterado

invidious /ɪnˈvɪdɪəs/ a antipático, odioso

invigorate /ɪnˈvɪgəreɪt/ vt revigorar; (encourage) estimular

invincible /ɪnˈvɪnsəbl/ a invencível

invisible /ɪnˈvɪzəbl/ a invisível

invit|e /ɪnˈvaɪt/ vt convidar; (bring on) pedir, provocar. ~**ation** /ɪnvɪˈteɪʃn/ n convite m. ~**ing** a (tempting) tentador; (pleasant) acolhedor, convidativo

invoice /ˈɪnvɔɪs/ n fatura f, (P) factura f □ vt faturar, (P) facturar

invoke /ɪnˈvəʊk/ vt invocar

involuntary /ɪnˈvɒləntrɪ/ a involuntário

involve /ɪnˈvɒlv/ vt implicar, envolver. ~**d** a (complex) complicado; (at stake) em jogo; (emotionally) envolvido. ~**d in** implicado em. ~**ment** n envolvimento m, participação f

invulnerable /ɪnˈvʌlnərəbl/ a invulnerável

inward /ˈɪnwəd/ a interior; (thought etc) íntimo. ~(**s**) adv para dentro, para o interior. ~**ly** adv interiormente, intimamente

iodine /ˈaɪədiːn/ n iodo m; (antiseptic) tintura f de iodo

IOU /aɪəʊˈjuː/ n abbr vale m

IQ /aɪˈkjuː/ abbr (intelligence quotient) Q I m

Iran /ɪˈrɑːn/ n Irã m. ~**ian** /ɪˈreɪnɪən/ a & n iraniano (m)

Iraq /ɪˈrɑːk/ n Iraque m. ~**i** a & n iraquiano (m)

irascible /ɪˈræsəbl/ a irascível

irate /aɪˈreɪt/ a irado, enraivecido

Ireland /ˈaɪələnd/ n Irlanda f

iris /ˈaɪərɪs/ n (anat, bot) íris f

Irish /ˈaɪərɪʃ/ a & n (language) irlandês (m). ~**man** n irlandês m. ~**woman** n irlandesa f

irk /ɜːk/ vt aborrecer, ncomodar. ~**some** a aborrecido

iron /ˈaɪən/ n ferro m; (appliance) ferro m de engomar □ a de ferro □ vt passar a ferro. ~ **out** fazer desaparecer; (fig) aplanar, resolver. ~**ing** n do the ~**ing** passar a roupa. ~**ing-board** n tábua f de passar roupa, (P) tábua f de engomar

ironic(al) /aɪˈrɒnɪk(l)/ a irônico, (P) irónico

ironmonger /ˈaɪənmʌŋgə(r)/ n ferreiro m, (P) ferrageiro m. ~'**s** n (shop) loja f de ferragens

irony /ˈaɪərənɪ/ n ironia f

irrational /ɪˈræʃənl/ a irracional; (person) ilógico, que não raciocina

irreconcilable /ɪrekənˈsaɪləbl/ a irreconciliável

irrefutable /ɪrɪˈfjuːtəbl/ a irrefutável

irregular /ɪˈregjʊlə(r)/ a irregular. ~**ity** /-ˈlærətɪ/ n irregularidade f

irrelevant /ɪˈreləvənt/ a irrelevante, que não é pertinente

irreparable /ɪˈrepərəbl/ a irreparável, irremediável

irreplaceable /ɪrɪˈpleɪsəbl/ a insubstituível

irresistible /ɪrɪˈzɪstəbl/ a irresistível

irresolute /ɪˈrezəluːt/ a irresoluto

irrespective /ɪrɪˈspektɪv/ a ~ **of** sem levar em conta, independente de

irresponsible /ɪrɪˈspɒnsəbl/ a irresponsável

irretrievable /ɪrɪˈtriːvəbl/ a irreparável

irreverent /ɪˈrevərənt/ a irreverente

irreversible /ɪrɪˈvɜːsəbl/ a irreversível; (decision) irrevogável

irrigat|e /ˈɪrɪgeɪt/ vt irrigar. ~**ion** /-ˈgeɪʃn/ n irrigação f

irritable /ˈɪrɪtəbl/ a irritável, irascível

irritat|e /ˈɪrɪteɪt/ vt irritar. ~**ion** /-ˈteɪʃn/ n irritação f

is /ɪz/ see be

Islam /ˈɪzlɑːm/ n Islã m. ~**ic** /ɪzˈlæmɪk/ a islâmico

island /ˈaɪlənd/ n ilha f. **traffic** ~ abrigo m de pedestres, (P) placa f de refugio

isolat|e /ˈaɪsəleɪt/ vt isolar. ~**ion** /-ˈleɪʃn/ n isolamento m

Israel /ˈɪzreɪl/ n Israel m. ~**i** /ɪzˈreɪlɪ/ a & n israelense (mf), (P) israelita (mf)

issue /ˈɪʃuː/ n questão f; (outcome) resultado m; (of magazine etc) número m; (of stamps, money etc) emissão f □ vt distribuir, dar; (stamps, money etc) emitir; (orders) dar □ vi ~ **from** sair de. **at** ~ em questão. **take** ~ **with** entrar em discussão com, discutir com

it /ɪt/ *pron* (*subject*) ele, ela; (*object*) o, a; (*non-specific*) isto, isso, aquilo. ~ is cold está *or* faz frio. ~ is the 6th of May hoje é seis de maio. that's ~ é isso. take ~ leva isso. who is ~? quem é?

italic /ɪˈtælɪk/ *a* itálico. ~s *npl* itálico *m*

Ital|y /ˈɪtəlɪ/ *n* Itália *f*. ~ian /ɪˈtæljən/ *a & n* (*person, lang*) italiano (*m*)

itch /ɪtʃ/ coceira *f*, (*P*) comichão *f*; (*fig: desire*) desejo *m* ardente □ *vi* coçar, sentir comichão, comichar. my arm ~es estou com coceira no braço. I am ~ing to estou morto por (*colloq*). ~y *a* que dá coceira

item /ˈaɪtəm/ *n* item *m*, artigo *m*; (*on programme*) número *m*; (*on agenda*) ponto *m*. ~ news ~ notícia *f*. ~ize /-aɪz/ *vt* discriminar, especificar

itinerant /aɪˈtɪnərənt/ *a* itinerante; (*musician, actor*) ambulante

itinerary /aɪˈtɪnərərɪ/ *n* itinerário *m*

its /ɪts/ *a* seu, sua, seus, suas

it's /ɪts/ = **it is, it has**

itself /ɪtˈself/ *pron* ele mesmo, ele próprio, ela mesma, ela própria; (*reflexive*) se; (*after prep*) si mesmo, si próprio, si mesma, si própria. by ~ sozinho, por si

ivory /ˈaɪvərɪ/ *n* marfim *m*

ivy /ˈaɪvɪ/ *n* hera *f*

J

jab /dʒæb/ *vt* (*pt* jabbed) espetar □ *n* espetadela *f*; (*colloq: injection*) picada *f*

jabber /ˈdʒæbə(r)/ *vi* tagarelar; (*indistinctly*) falar confusamente □ *n* tagarelice *f*; (*indistinct speech*) algaravia *f*; (*indistinct voices*) algaraviada *f*

jack /dʒæk/ *n* (*techn*) macaco *m*; (*cards*) valete *m* □ *vt* ~ up levantar com macaco. the Union J~ a bandeira *f* inglesa

jackal /ˈdʒækl/ *n* chacal *m*

jackdaw /ˈdʒækdɔː/ *n* gralha *f*

jacket /ˈdʒækɪt/ *n* casaco (curto) *m*; (*of book*) sobrecapa *f*; (*of potato*) casca *f*

jack-knife /ˈdʒæknaɪf/ *vi* (*lorry*) perder o controle

jackpot /ˈdʒækpɒt/ *n* sorte *f* grande. hit the ~ ganhar a sorte grande

Jacuzzi /dʒəˈkuːziː/ *n* (*P*) jacuzzi *m*, banheira *f* de hidromassagem

jade /dʒeɪd/ *n* (*stone*) jade *m*

jaded /ˈdʒeɪdɪd/ *a* (*tired*) estafado; (*bored*) enfastiado

jagged /ˈdʒægɪd/ *a* recortado, denteado; (*sharp*) pontiagudo

jail /dʒeɪl/ *n* prisão *f* □ *vt* prender,

colocar na cadeia. ~er *n* carcereiro *m*

jam¹ /dʒæm/ *n* geléia *f*, compota *f*

jam² /dʒæm/ *vt/i* (*pt* jammed) (*wedge*) entalar; (*become wedged*) entalar-se; (*crowd*) apinhar(-se); (*mech*) bloquear; (*radio*) provocar interferências em □ *n* (*crush*) aperto *m*; (*traffic*) engarrafamento *m*; (*colloq: difficulty*) apuro *m*, aperto *m*. ~ one's brakes on (*colloq*) pôr o pé no freio, (*P*) no travão subitamente, apertar o freio subitamente. ~-packed *a* (*colloq*) abarrotado (with de)

Jamaica /dʒəˈmeɪkə/ *n* Jamaica *f*

jangle /ˈdʒæŋgl/ *n* som *m* estridente □ *vi* retinir

janitor /ˈdʒænɪtə(r)/ *n* porteiro *m*; (*caretaker*) zelador *m*

January /ˈdʒænjʊərɪ/ *n* Janeiro *m*

Japan /dʒəˈpæn/ *n* Japão *m*. ~ese /dʒæpəˈniːz/ *a* & *n* japonês (*m*)

jar¹ /dʒɑː(r)/ *n* pote *m*. jam-~ *n* frasco *m* de geléia

jar² /dʒɑː(r)/ *vt/i* (*pt* jarred) ressoar, bater ruidosamente (against contra); (*of colours*) destoar; (*disagree*) discorder (with de) □ *n* (*shock*) choque *m*. ~ring *a* dissonante

jargon /ˈdʒɑːgən/ *n* jargão *m*, gíria *f* profissional

jaundice /ˈdʒɔːndɪs/ *n* icterícia *f*. ~d *a* (*fig*) invejoso, despeitado

jaunt /dʒɔːnt/ *n* (*trip*) passeata *f*

jaunty /ˈdʒɔːntɪ/ *a* (-ier, -iest) (*cheerful*) alegre, jovial; (*sprightly*) desenvolto

javelin /ˈdʒævlɪn/ *n* dardo *m*, mandíbula *f*

jaw /dʒɔː/ *n* maxilar *m*, mandíbula *f*

jay /dʒeɪ/ *n* gaio *m*. ~-walker *n* pedestre *m* imprudente, (*P*) peão *m* indisciplinado

jazz /dʒæz/ *n* jazz *m* □ *vt* ~ up animar. ~y *a* (*colloq*) espalhafatoso

jealous /ˈdʒeləs/ *a* ciumento; (*envious*) invejoso. ~y *n* ciúme *m*; (*envy*) inveja *f*

jeans /dʒiːnz/ *npl* (blue-jeans *mpl*, calça *f* de zuarte), (*P*) calças *fpl* de ganga

jeep /dʒiːp/ *n* jipe *m*

jeer /dʒɪə(r)/ *vt/i* ~ at (*laugh*) fazer troça de; (*scorn*) escarnecer de; (*boo*) vaiar □ *n* (*mockery*) troça *f*; (*booing*) vaia *f*

jell /dʒel/ *vi* tomar consistência, gelatinizar-se

jelly /ˈdʒelɪ/ *n* gelatina *f*.

jellyfish /ˈdʒelɪfɪʃ/ *n* água-viva *f*

jeopard|y /ˈdʒepədɪ/ *n* perigo *m*. ~ize *vt* comprometer, pôr em perigo

jerk /dʒɜːk/ *n* solavanco *m*, (*P*) sacão *m*; (*sl: fool*) idiota *mf* □ *vt/i* sacudir; (*move*) mover-se aos solavancos, (*P*) mover(-se) aos sacões. ~y a sacudido

jersey /'dʒɜːzɪ/ n (pl -eys) camisola f, pulóver m, suéter m; (fabric) jérsei m

jest /dʒest/ n gracejo m, graça f □ vi gracejar, brincar

Jesus /'dʒiːzəs/ n Jesus m

jet¹ /dʒet/ n azeviche m. ~-black a negro de azeviche

jet² /dʒet/ n jato m, (P) jacto m; (plane) (avião a) jato m, (P) jacto m. ~ lag cansaço m provocado pela diferença de fuso horário. ~-propelled a de propulsão a jato, (P) jacto

jettison /'dʒetɪsn/ vt alijar; (discard) desfazer-se de; (fig) abandonar

jetty /'dʒetɪ/ n (breakwater) quebra-mar m; (landing-stage) desembarcadouro m, cais m

Jew /dʒuː/ n judeu m

jewel /'dʒuːəl/ n jóia f. ~ler n joalheiro m. ~ler's (shop) joalheria f. ~lery n jóias fpl

Jewish /'dʒuːɪʃ/ a judeu

jib /dʒɪb/ vi (pt jibbed) recusar-se a avançar; (of a horse) empacar. ~ at (fig) opor-se a, ter relutância em □ n (sail) bujarrona f

jig /dʒɪg/ n jiga f

jiggle /'dʒɪgl/ vt (rock) balançar; (jerk) sacolejar

jigsaw /'dʒɪgsɔː/ n ~(-puzzle) puzzle m, quebra-cabeça m, (P) quebra-cabeças m

jilt /dʒɪlt/ vt deixar, abandonar, dar um fora em (colloq), (P) mandar passear (colloq)

jingle /'dʒɪŋgl/ vt/i tilintar, tinir □ n tilintar m, tinido m; (advertising etc) música f de anúncio

jinx /dʒɪŋks/ n (colloq) pessoa f or coisa f azarenta; (fig: spell) azar m

jitter|s /'dʒɪtəz/ npl the ~s (colloq) nervos mpl. ~y /-ərɪ/ a be ~y (colloq) estar nervoso, ter os nervos à flor da pele (colloq)

job /dʒɒb/ n trabalho m; (post) emprego m. have a ~ doing ter dificuldade em fazer. it is a good ~ that felizmente que. ~less a desempregado

jobcentre /'dʒɒbsentə(r)/ n posto m de desemprego

jockey /'dʒɒkɪ/ n (pl -eys) jóquei m

jocular /'dʒɒkjʊlə(r)/ a jocoso, galhofeiro, brincalhão

jog /dʒɒg/ vt (pt jogged) dar um leve empurrão em, tocar em; (memory) refrescar □ vi (sport) fazer jogging. ~ging n jogging m

join /dʒɔɪn/ vt juntar, unir; (become member) fazer-se sócio de, entrar para. ~ sb juntar-se a □ vi (of roads) juntar-se, entroncar-se; (of rivers) confluir □ n junção f, junta f.

~ in vt/i participar (em). ~ up alistar-se

joiner /'dʒɔɪnə(r)/ n marceneiro m

joint /dʒɔɪnt/ a comum, conjunto; (effort) conjunto □ n junta f, junção f; (anat) articulação f; (culin) quarto m; (roast meat) carne f assada; (sl: place) espelunca f. ~ author co-autor m. ~ly adv conjuntamente

joist /dʒɔɪst/ n trave f, barrote m

jok|e /dʒəʊk/ n piada f, gracejo m □ vi gracejar. ~er n brincalhão m; (cards) curinga f de baralho, (P) diabo m. ~ingly adv brincadeira

joll|y /'dʒɒlɪ/ a (-ier, -iest) alegre, bem disposto □ adv (colloq) muito. ~ity n festança f, pândega f

jolt /dʒəʊlt/ vt sacudir, sacolejar □ vi ir aos solavancos □ n solavanco m; (shock) choque m, sobressalto m

jostle /'dʒɒsl/ vt dar um encontrão or encontrões em, empurrar □ vi empurrar, acotovelar-se

jot /dʒɒt/ n (not a) ~ nada □ vt (pt jotted) ~ (down) apontar, tomar nota de. ~ter n (pad) bloco m de notas

journal /'dʒɜːnl/ n diário m; (newspaper) jornal m; (periodical) periódico m, revista f. ~ism n jornalismo m. ~ist n jornalista mf

journey /'dʒɜːnɪ/ n (pl -eys) viagem f; (distance) trajeto m, (P) trajecto m □ vi viajar

jovial /'dʒəʊvɪəl/ a jovial

joy /dʒɔɪ/ n alegria f. ~-ride n passeio m em carro roubado. ~ful, ~ous adjs alegre

jubil|ant /'dʒuːbɪlənt/ a cheio de alegria, jubiloso. ~ation /-'leɪʃn/ n júbilo m, regozijo m

jubilee /'dʒuːbɪliː/ n jubileu m

Judaism /'dʒuːdeɪɪzəm/ n judaísmo m

judder /'dʒʌdə(r)/ vi trepidar, vibrar □ n trepidação f, vibração f

judge /dʒʌdʒ/ n juiz m □ vt julgar. ~ment n (judging) julgamento m, juízo m; (opinion) juízo m; (decision) julgamento m

judic|iary /dʒuːˈdɪʃərɪ/ n magistratura f; (system) judiciário m. ~ial a judiciário

judicious /dʒuːˈdɪʃəs/ a judicioso

judo /'dʒuːdəʊ/ n judô m, (P) judo m

jug /dʒʌg/ n (tall) jarro m; (round) botija f; milk-~ n leiteira f

juggernaut /'dʒʌgənɔːt/ n (lorry) jainanta f, (P) camião m TIR

juggle /'dʒʌgl/ vt/i fazer malabarismos (with com). ~r /-ə(r)/ n malabarista mf

juic|e /dʒuːs/ n suco m, (P) sumo m. ~y a suculento; (colloq: story etc) picante juke-box /'dʒuːkbɒks/ n juke-box m, (P) máquina f de música

July /dʒuː'laɪ/ n julho m

jumble /'dʒʌmbl/ vt misturar □ n mistura f. ~ sale venda f de caridade de objetos usados

jumbo /'dʒʌmbəʊ/ a ~ jet (avião) jumbo m

jump /dʒʌmp/ vt/i saltar; (start) sobressaltar(-se); (of prices etc) subir repentinamente □ n salto m; (start) sobressalto m; (of prices) alta f. ~ at aceitar imediatamente. ~ the gun agir prematuramente. ~ the queue furar a fila. ~ to conclusions tirar conclusões apressadas

jumper /'dʒʌmpə(r)/ n pulôver m, suéter m, (P) camisada f de lã

jumpy /'dʒʌmpɪ/ a nervoso

junction /'dʒʌŋkʃn/ n junção f; (of roads etc) entroncamento m

June /dʒuːn/ n junho m

jungle /'dʒʌŋgl/ n selva f, floresta f

junior /'dʒuːnɪə(r)/ a júnior; (in age) mais novo (to que); (in rank) subalterno; (school) primária □ n o mais novo m; (sport) júnior mf. ~ to (in rank) abaixo de

junk /dʒʌŋk/ n ferro-velho m, velharias fpl; (rubbish) lixo m. ~ food comida f sem valor nutritivo. ~ mail material m impresso, enviado por correio, sem ter sido solicitado. ~ shop loja f de ferro-velho, bricabraque m

junkie /'dʒʌŋkɪ/ n (sl) drogado m

jurisdiction /dʒʊərɪs'dɪkʃn/ n jurisdição f

juror /'dʒʊərə(r)/ n jurado m

jury /'dʒʊərɪ/ n júri m

just /dʒʌst/ a justo □ adv justamente, exatamente, (P) exactamente; (only) só. he has ~ left ele acabou de sair. ~ listen! escuta só! ~ as assim como; (with time) assim que. ~ as tall exatamente tão alto quanto. ~ as well that ainda bem que. ~ before um momento antes (de). ~ly adv com justiça, justamente

justice /'dʒʌstɪs/ n justiça f. J~ of the Peace juiz m de paz

justifiable /'dʒʌstɪfaɪəbl/ a justificável. ~y adv com razão, justificadamente

justify /'dʒʌstɪfaɪ/ vt justificar. ~ication /-ɪ'keɪʃn/ n justificação f

jut /dʒʌt/ vi (pt jutted) ~ out fazer saliência, sobressair

juvenile /'dʒuːvənaɪl/ a (youthful) juvenil; (childish) pueril; (delinquent) jovem; (court) de menores □ n jovem mf

juxtapose /dʒʌksta'pəʊz/ vt justapor

K

kaleidoscope /kə'laɪdəskəʊp/ n caleidoscópio m

kangaroo /kæŋgə'ruː/ n canguru m

karate /kə'rɑːtɪ/ n klaratê m

kebab /kə'bæb/ n churrasquinho m, espetinho m

keel /kiːl/ n quilha f □ vi ~ over virar-se

keen /kiːn/ a (-er, -est) (sharp) agudo; (eager) entusiástico; (of appetite) devorador; (of intelligence) vivo; (of wind) cortante. ~ly adv vivamente; (eagerly) com entusiasmo. ~ness n vivacidade f; (enthusiasm) entusiasmo m

keep /kiːp/ (pt kept) vt guardar; (family) sustentar; (animals) ter, criar; (celebrate) festejar; (conceal) esconder; (delay) demorar; (prevent) impedir (from de); (promise) cumprir; (shop) ter □ vi manter-se, conservar-se; (remain) ficar. ~ (on) continuar (doing fazendo) □ n sustento m; (of castle) torre f de menagem. ~ back vt (withhold) reter □ vi manter-se afastado. ~ in/out impedir de entrar/de sair. ~ up conservar. ~ up (with) acompanhar. ~er n guarda mf

keeping /'kiːpɪŋ/ n guarda f, cuidado m. in ~ with em harmonia com, (P) de harmonia com

keepsake /'kiːpseɪk/ n (thing) lembrança f, recordação f

keg /keg/ n barril m pequeno

kennel /'kenl/ n casota f (de cão). ~s npl canil m

kept /kept/ see keep

kerb /kɜːb/ n meio fio m, (P) borda f do passeio

kernel /'kɜːnl/ n (of nut) miolo m

kerosene /'kerəsiːn/ n (paraffin) querosene m, (P) petróleo m; (aviation fuel) gasolina f

ketchup /'ketʃəp/ n molho m de tomate, ketchup m

kettle /'ketl/ n chaleira f

key /kiː/ n chave f; (of piano etc) tecla f; (mus) clave f □ a chave. ~-ring n chaveiro m, porta-chaves m invar □ vt ~ in digitar, bater. ~ed up tenso

keyboard /'kiːbɔːd/ n teclado m

keyhole /'kiːhəʊl/ n buraco m da fechadura

khaki /'kɑːkɪ/ a & n cáqui (invar m), (P) caqui (invar m)

kick /kɪk/ vt/i dar um pontapé or pontapés (a, em); (ball) chutar (em); (of horse) dar um coice or coices, escoicear □ n pontapé m; (of gun, horse) coice m; (colloq: thrill) excitação f, prazer *m*. ∼-off *n* chute *m* inicial, kick-off *m*. ∼ out (*colloq*) pòr na rua. ∼ up (*colloq: fuss, racket*) fazer

kid /kɪd/ *n* (*goat*) cabrito *m*; (*sl: child*) garoto *m*; (*leather*) pelica *f* □ *vt/i* (*pt* **kidded**) (*colloq*) brincar (com)

kidnap /ˈkɪdnæp/ *vt* (*pt* **kidnapped**) raptar. ∼**ping** *n* rapto *m*

kidney /ˈkɪdnɪ/ *n* rim *m*

kill /kɪl/ *vt* matar; (*fig: put an end to*) acabar com □ *n* matança *f*. ∼**er** *n* assassino *m*. ∼**ing** *n* matança *f*, massacre *m*; (*of game*) caçada *f* □ *a* (*colloq: funny*) de morrer de rir; (*colloq: exhausting*) de morte

killjoy /ˈkɪldʒɔɪ/ *n* desmancha-prazeres *mf*

kiln /kɪln/ *n* forno *m*

kilo /ˈkiːləʊ/ *n* (*pl* -os) quilo *m*

kilogram /ˈkɪləɡræm/ *n* quilograma *m*

kilometre /ˈkɪləmiːtə(r)/ *n* quilómetro *m*, (*P*) quilómetro *m*

kilowatt /ˈkɪləwɒt/ *n* quilowatt *m*, (*P*) quilovate *m*

kilt /kɪlt/ *n* kilt *m*, saiote *m* escocês

kin /kɪn/ *n* família *f*, parentes *mpl*. **next of** ∼ os parentes mais próximos

kind[1] /kaɪnd/ *n* espécie *f*, género *m*, natureza *f*. **in** ∼ em géneros, (*P*) géneros *m*; (*fig: in the same form*) na mesma moeda. ∼ **of** (*colloq: somewhat*) de certo modo, um pouco

kind[2] /kaɪnd/ *a* (-**er**, -**est**) (*good*) bom; (*friendly*) gentil, amável. ∼-**hearted** *a* bom, bondoso. ∼**ness** *n* bondade *f*

kindergarten /ˈkɪndəɡɑːtn/ *n* jardim de infância *m*, (*P*) infantil

kindle /ˈkɪndl/ *vt/i* acender(-se), atear(-se)

kindly /ˈkaɪndlɪ/ *a* (-**ier**, -**iest**) benévolo, bondoso □ *adv* bondosamente, gentilmente, com simpatia. ∼ **wait** tenha a bondade de esperar

kindred /ˈkɪndrɪd/ *a* aparentado; (*fig: connected*) afim. ∼ **spirit** espírito *m* congénere, alma *f* gémea

kinetic /kɪˈnetɪk/ *a* cinético

king /kɪŋ/ *n* rei *m*. ∼-**size(d)** *a* de tamanho grande

kingdom /ˈkɪŋdəm/ *n* reino *m*

kingfisher /ˈkɪŋfɪʃə(r)/ *n* pica-peixe *m*, martim-pescador *m*

kink /kɪŋk/ *n* (*in rope*) volta *f*, nó *m*; (*fig*) perversão *f*. ∼-**y** *a* (*colloq*) excêntrico, pervertido; (*of hair*) encarapinhado

kiosk /ˈkiːɒsk/ *n* quiosque *m*. **telephone** ∼ cabine telefónica, (*P*) telefónica

kip /kɪp/ *n* (*sl*) sono *m* □ *vi* (*pt* **kipped**) (*sl*) dormir

kipper /ˈkɪpə(r)/ *n* arenque *m* defumado

kiss /kɪs/ *n* beijo *m* □ *vt/i* beijar(-se)

kit /kɪt/ *n* equipamento *m*; (*set of tools*) ferramenta *f*; (*for assembly*) kit *m* □ *vt* (*pt* **kitted**) ∼ **out** equipar

kitbag /ˈkɪtbæɡ/ *n* mochila *f* (de soldado etc); saco *m* de viagem

kitchen /ˈkɪtʃɪn/ *n* cozinha *f*. ∼ **garden** horta *f*. ∼ **sink** pia *f*, (*P*) lava-louças *m*

kite /kaɪt/ *n* (*toy*) pipa *f*, (*P*) papagaio *m* de papel

kith /kɪθ/ *n* ∼ **and kin** parentes e amigos *mpl*

kitten /ˈkɪtn/ *n* gatinho *m*

kitty /ˈkɪtɪ/ *n* (*fund*) fundo *m* comum, vaquinha *f*; (*cards*) bolo *m*

knack /næk/ *n* jeito *m*

knapsack /ˈnæpsæk/ *n* mochila *f*

knead /niːd/ *vt* amassar

knee /niː/ *n* joelho *m*

kneecap /ˈniːkæp/ *n* rótula *f*

kneel /niːl/ *vi* (*pt* **knelt**) ∼ (**down**) ajoelhar(-se)

knelt /nelt/ *see* **kneel**

knew /njuː/ *see* **know**

knickers /ˈnɪkəz/ *npl* calcinhas (de senhora) *fpl*

knife /naɪf/ *n* (*pl* **knives**) faca *f* □ *vt* esfaquear, apunhalar

knight /naɪt/ *n* cavaleiro *m*; (*chess*) cavalo *m*. ∼**hood** *n* grau *m* de cavaleiro

knit /nɪt/ *vt* (*pt* **knitted** *or* **knit**) tricotar □ *vi* tricotar, fazer tricô; (*fig: unite*) unir-se; (*of bones*) soldar-se. ∼ **one's brow** franzir as sobrancelhas. ∼**ting** *n* malha *f*, tricô *m*

knitwear /ˈnɪtweə(r)/ *n* roupa *f* de malha, malhas *fpl*

knob /nɒb/ *n* (*of door*) maçaneta *f*; (*of drawer*) puxador *m*; (*of radio, TV etc*) botão *m*; (*of butter*) noz *f*. ∼**bly** *a* nodoso

knock /nɒk/ *vt/i* bater (em); (*sl: criticize*) desancar (em). ∼ **about** *vt* tratar mal □ *vi* (*wander*) andar a esmo. ∼ **down** (*chair, pedestrian*) deitar no chão, derrubar; (*demolish*) jogar abaixo; (*colloq: reduce*) baixar, reduzir; (*at auction*) adjudicar (**to** a). ∼-**down** *a* (*price*) muito baixo. ∼-**kneed** *a* de pernas de tesoura. ∼ **off** *vt* (*colloq: complete quickly*) despachar; (*sl: steal*) roubar □ *vi* (*colloq*) parar de trabalhar, fechar a loja (*colloq*). ∼ **out** pôr fora de combate, eliminar; (*stun*) assombrar. ∼-**out** *n* (*boxing*) nocaute *m*, KO *m*. ∼ **over** entornar. ∼ **up** (*meal etc*) arranjar às pressas. ∼**er** *n* aldrava *f*

knot /nɒt/ *n* nó *m* □ *vt* (*pt* **knotted**) atar com nó, dar nó *or* nós em

knotty /ˈnɒtɪ/ *a* (-**ier**, -**iest**) nodoso, cheio de nós; (*difficult*) complicado, espinhoso

know /nəʊ/ vt/i (pt knew, pp known) saber (that que); (person, place) conhecer □ n in the ~ (colloq) por dentro. ~ about (cars etc) saber sobre, saber de. ~all n sabe-tudo m (colloq). ~-how n know-how m, conhecimentos mpl técnicos, culturais etc. ~ of ter conhecimento de, ter ouvido falar de. ~ingly adv com ar conhecedor; (consciously) conscientemente

knowledge /'nɒlɪdʒ/ n conhecimento m; (learning) saber m. ~able a conhecedor, entendido, versado

known /nəʊn/ see know □ a conhecido

knuckle /'nʌkl/ n nó m dos dedos □ vi ~ under ceder, submeter-se

Koran /kə'rɑːn/ n Alcorão m, Corão m

Korea /kə'rɪə/ n Coréia f

kosher /'kəʊʃə(r)/ a aprovado pela lei judaica; (colloq) como deve ser

kowtow /kaʊ'taʊ/ vi prosternar-se (to diante de); (act obsequiously) bajular

L

lab /læb/ n (colloq) laboratório m

label /'leɪbl/ n (on bottle etc) rótulo m; (on clothes, luggage) etiqueta f □ vt (pt labelled) rotular; etiquetar, pôr etiqueta em

laboratory /lə'bɒrətrɪ/ n laboratório m

laborious /lə'bɔːrɪəs/ a laborioso, trabalhoso

labour /'leɪbə(r)/ n trabalho m, labuta f; (workers) mão-de-obra f □ vi trabalhar; (try hard) esforçar-se □ vt alongar-se sobre, insistir em. in ~ em trabalho de parto. ~ed a (writing) laborioso, sem espontaneidade; (breathing, movement) difícil. ~-saving a que poupa trabalho

Labour /'leɪbə(r)/ n (party) Partido m Trabalhista, os trabalhistas □ a trabalhista

labourer /'leɪbərə(r)/ n trabalhador m; (on farm) trabalhador m rural

labyrinth /'læbərɪnθ/ n labirinto m

lace /leɪs/ n renda f; (of shoe) cordão m de sapato, (P) atacador m □ vt atar; (drink) juntar um pouco (de aguardente, rum etc)

lacerate /'læsəreɪt/ vt lacerar, rasgar

lack /læk/ n falta f □ vt faltar (a), não ter. be ~ing faltar. be ~ing in carecer de

lackadaisical /lækə'deɪzɪkl/ a lânguido, apático, desinteressado

laconic /lə'kɒnɪk/ a lacônico, (P) lacónico

lacquer /'lækə(r)/ n laca f

lad /læd/ n rapaz m, moço m

ladder /'lædə(r)/ n escada de mão f, (P) escadote m; (in stocking) fio m corrido, (P) malha f caida □ vi deixar correr um fio, (P) cair uma malha □ vt fazer malhas em

laden /'leɪdn/ a carregado (with de)

ladle /'leɪdl/ n concha (de sopa) f

lady /'leɪdɪ/ n senhora f; (title) Lady f. ~-in-waiting n dama f de companhia, (P) dama f de honor. young ~ jovem f. ~-like a senhoril, elegante. Ladies n (toilets) toalete m das Senhoras

ladybird /'leɪdɪbɜːd/ n joaninha f

lag[1] /læg/ vi (pt lagged) atrasar-se, ficar para trás □ n atraso m

lag[2] /læg/ vt (pt lagged) (pipes etc) revestir com isolante térmico

lager /'lɑːgə(r)/ n cerveja f leve e clara, "loura" f (sl)

lagoon /lə'guːn/ n lagoa f

laid /leɪd/ see lay[2]

lain /leɪn/ see lie[2]

lair /leə(r)/ n toca f, covil m

laity /'leɪətɪ/ n leigos mpl

lake /leɪk/ n lago m

lamb /læm/ n cordeiro m, carneiro m; (meat) carneiro m

lambswool /'læmzwʊl/ n lã f

lame /leɪm/ a (-er, -est) coxo; (fig: unconvincing) fraco. ~ness n claudicação f, coxeadura f

lament /lə'ment/ n lamento m, lamentação f □ vt/i lamentar(-se) (de). ~able a lamentável

laminated /'læmɪneɪtɪd/ a laminado

lamp /læmp/ n lâmpada f

lamppost /'læmppəʊst/ n poste m (do candeeiro) (de iluminação pública)

lampshade /'læmpʃeɪd/ n abajur m, quebra-luz m

lance /lɑːns/ n lança f □ vt lancetar

lancet /'lɑːnsɪt/ n bisturi m, (P) lanceta f

land /lænd/ n terra f; (country) pais m; (plot) terreno m; (property) terras fpl □ a de terra, terrestre; (policy etc) agrário □ vt/i desembarcar; (aviat) aterrissar, (P) aterrar; (fall) ir parar (on em); (colloq: obtain) arranjar; (a blow) aplicar, mandar. ~-locked a rodeado de terra

landing /'lændɪŋ/ n desembarque m; (aviat) aterrissagem f, (P) aterragem f; (top of stairs) patamar m. ~-stage n cais m flutuante

landlady /'lændleɪdɪ/ n (of rented house) senhoria f, proprietária f; (who lets rooms) dona f da casa; (of boarding-house) dona f da pensão; (of inn etc) proprietária f, estalajadeira f. ~lord n (of rented house) senhorio *m*, proprietário *m*; (*of inn etc*) proprietário *m*, estalajadeiro *m*

landmark /'lændma:k/ *n* (*conspicuous feature*) ponto *m* de referência; (*fig*) marco *m*

landscape /'lændskeɪp/ *n* paisagem *f* □ *vt* projetar, (*P*) projectar paisagisticamente

landslide /'lændslaɪd/ *n* desabamento *m or* desmoronamento *m* de terras; (*fig: pol*) vitória *f* esmagadora

lane /leɪn/ *n* senda *f*, caminho *m*; (*in country*) estrada *f* pequena; (*in town*) viela *f*, ruela *f*; (*of road*) faixa *f*, pista *f*; (*of traffic*) fila *f*; (*aviat*) corredor *m*; (*naut*) rota *f*

language /'læŋgwɪdʒ/ *n* língua *f*; (*speech, style*) linguagem *f*. bad ~ linguagem *f* grosseira. ~ lab laboratório *m* de línguas

languid /'læŋgwɪd/ *a* lânguido

languish /'læŋgwɪʃ/ *vi* elanguescer

lank /læŋk/ *a* (*of hair*) escorrido, liso

lanky /'læŋkɪ/ *a* (*-ier, -iest*) desengonçado, escanifrado

lantern /'læntən/ *n* lanterna *f*

lap[1] /læp/ *n* colo *m*; (*sport*) volta *f* completa. ~-dog *n* cãozinho *m* de estimação

lap[2] /læp/ *vt* ~ up beber lambendo □ *vi* marulhar

lapel /lə'pel/ *n* lapela *f*

lapse /læps/ *vi* decair, degenerar-se; (*expire*) caducar □ *n* lapso *m*; (*jur*) prescrição *f*. ~ into (*thought*) mergulhar em; (*bad habit*) adquirir

larceny /'la:sənɪ/ *n* furto *m*

lard /la:d/ *n* banha de porco *f*

larder /'la:də(r)/ *n* despensa *f*

large /la:dʒ/ *a* (*-er, -est*) grande. at ~ à solta, em liberdade. by and ~ em geral. ~ly *adv* largamente, em grande parte. ~ness *n* grandeza *f*

lark[1] /la:k/ *n* (*bird*) cotovia *f*

lark[2] /la:k/ *n* (*colloq*) pândega *f*, brincadeira *f* □ *vi* ~ about (*colloq*) fazer travessuras, brincar

larva /'la:və/ *n* (*pl* -vae /-vi:/) larva *f*

laryngitis /lærɪn'dʒaɪtɪs/ *n* laringite *f*

larynx /'lærɪŋks/ *n* laringe *f*

lascivious /lə'sɪvɪəs/ *a* lascivo, sensual

laser /'leɪzə(r)/ *n* laser *m*. ~ printer impressora *f* a laser

lash /læʃ/ *vt* chicotear, açoitar; (*rain*) fustigar □ *n* chicote *m*; (*stroke*) chicotada *f*; (*eyelash*) pestana *f*, cílio *m*. ~ out atacar, atirar-se a; (*colloq: spend*) esbanjar dinheiro em algo

lashings /'læʃɪŋz/ *npl* ~ of (*sl*) montes de (*colloq*)

lasso /læ'su:/ *n* (*pl* -os) laço *m* □ *vt* laçar

last[1] /la:st/ *a* último □ *adv* no fim, em

último lugar; (*most recently*) a última vez □ *n* último *m*. at (*long*) ~ por fim, finalmente. ~-minute *a* de última hora. ~ night ontem à noite, a noite passada. the ~ straw a gota d'água. to the ~ até o fim. ~ly *adv* finalmente, em último lugar

last[2] /la:st/ *vt/i* durar, continuar. ~ing *a* duradouro, durável

latch /lætʃ/ *n* trinco *m*

late /leɪt/ *a* (*-er, -est*) atrasado; (*recent*) recente; (*former*) antigo, ex-, anterior; (*hour, fruit etc*) tardio; (*deceased*) falecido □ *adv* tarde. in ~ July no fim de julho. of ~ ultimamente. at the ~st o mais tardar. ~ness *n* atraso *m*

lately /'leɪtlɪ/ *adv* nos últimos tempos, ultimamente

latent /'leɪtnt/ *a* latente

lateral /'lætərəl/ *a* lateral

lathe /leɪð/ *n* torno *m*

lather /'la:ðə(r)/ *n* espuma *f* de sabão □ *vt* ensaboar □ *vi* fazer espuma

Latin /'lætɪn/ *n* (*lang*) latim *m* □ *a* latino. ~ America *n* América *f* Latina. ~ American *a* & *n* latino-americano (*m*)

latitude /'lætɪtju:d/ *n* latitude *f*

latter /'lætə(r)/ *a* último, mais recente □ *n* the ~ este, esta. ~ly *adv* recentemente

lattice /'lætɪs/ *n* treliça *f*, (*P*) gradeamento *m* de ripas

laudable /'lɔ:dəbl/ *a* louvável

laugh /la:f/ *vi* rir (at de). ~ off disfarçar com uma piada □ *n* riso *m*. ~able *a* irrisório, ridículo. ~ing-stock *n* objeto *m*, (*P*) objecto *m* de troça

laughter /'la:ftə(r)/ *n* riso *m*, risada *f*

launch[1] /lɔ:ntʃ/ *vt* lançar □ *n* lançamento *m*. ~ into lançar-se or meter-se em. ~ing pad plataforma *f* de lançamento

launch[2] /lɔ:ntʃ/ *n* (*boat*) lancha *f*

launder /'lɔ:ndə(r)/ *vt* lavar e passar

launderette /lɔ:n'dret/ *n* lavanderia *f* automática

laundry /'lɔ:ndrɪ/ *n* lavanderia *f*; (*clothes*) roupa *f*. do the ~ lavar a roupa

laurel /'lɒrəl/ *n* loureiro *m*, louro *m*

lava /'la:və/ *n* lava *f*

lavatory /'lævətrɪ/ *n* privada *f*, (*P*) retrete *f*; (*room*) toalete *m*, (*P*) lavabo *m*

lavender /'lævəndə(r)/ *n* alfazema *f*, lavanda *f*

lavish /'lævɪʃ/ *a* pródigo; (*plentiful*) copioso, generoso; (*lush*) suntuoso □ *vt* ser pródigoem, encher de. ~ly *adv* prodigamente; copiosamente; suntuosamente

law /lɔ:/ *n* lei *f*; (*profession, study*) direito *m*. ~-abiding *a* cumpridor da lei, respeitador da lei. ~ and order ordem *f* pública. ~-breaker *n* transgressor *m* da lei. ~ful *a* legal, legitimo. ~fully *adv* legalmente. ~less *a* sem lei; (*act*) ilegal; (*person*) rebelde

lawcourt /ˈlɔːkɔːt/ *n* tribunal *m*

lawn /lɔːn/ *n* gramado *m*, (*P*) relvado *m*. ~-mower *n* cortador *m* de grama, (*P*) máquina *f* de cortar a relva

lawsuit /ˈlɔːsuːt/ *n* processo *m*, ação *f*, (*P*) acção *f* judicial

lawyer /ˈlɔːjə(r)/ *n* advogado *m*

lax /læks/ *a* negligente; (*discipline*) frouxo; (*morals*) relaxado. ~ity *n* negligência *f*; (*of discipline*) frouxidão *f*; (*of morals*) relaxamento *m*

laxative /ˈlæksətɪv/ *n* laxante *m*, laxativo *m*

lay¹ /leɪ/ *a* leigo. ~ opinion opinião *f* de um leigo

lay² /leɪ/ *vt* (*pt* laid) pôr, colocar; (*trap*) preparar, pôr; (*eggs, table, siege*) pôr; (*plan*) fazer □ *vi* pôr (ovos). ~ aside pôr de lado. ~ down pousar; (*condition, law, rule*) impor; (*arms*) depor; (*one's life*) oferecer; (*policy*) ditar. ~ hold of agarrar(-se a). ~ off *vt* (*worker*) suspender do trabalho □ *vi* (*colloq*) parar, desistir. ~-off *n* suspensão *f* temporária. ~ on (*gas, water etc*) instalar, ligar; (*entertainment etc*) organizar, providenciar; (*food*) servir. ~ out (*design*) traçar, planejar; (*spread out*) estender, espalhar; (*money*) gastar. ~ up *vt* (*store*) juntar; (*ship, car*) pôr fora de serviço

lay³ /leɪ/ *see* **lie**

layabout /ˈleɪəbaʊt/ *n* (*sl*) vadio *m*

lay-by /ˈleɪbaɪ/ *n* acostamento *m*, (*P*) berma *f*

layer /ˈleɪə(r)/ *n* camada *f*

layman /ˈleɪmən/ *n* (*pl* -men) leigo *m*

layout /ˈleɪaʊt/ *n* disposição *f*; (*typ*) composição *f*

laze /leɪz/ *vi* descansar, vadiar

laz|**y** /ˈleɪzɪ/ *a* (-ier, -iest) preguiçoso. ~iness *n* preguiça *f*. ~y-bones *n* (*colloq*) vadio *m*, vagabundo *m*

lead¹ /liːd/ *vt/i* (*pt* led) conduzir, guiar, levar; (*team etc*) chefiar, liderar; (*life*) levar; (*choir, band etc*) dirigir □ *n* (*distance*) avanço *m*; (*first place*) dianteira *f*; (*clue*) indício *m*, pista *f*; (*leash*) coleira *f*; (*electr*) cabo *m*; (*theatr*) papel *m* principal; (*example*) exemplo *m*. in the ~ na frente. ~ away levar. ~ on (*fig*) encorajar. ~ the way ir na frente. ~ up to conduzir a

lead² /led/ *n* chumbo *m*; (*of pencil*) grafite *f*. ~en *a* de chumbo; (*of colour*) plúmbeo

leader /ˈliːdə(r)/ *n* chefe *m*, líder *m*; (*of country, club, union etc*) dirigente *mf*; (*pol*) líder; (*of orchestra*) regente *mf*, maestro *m*; (*in newspaper*) editorial *m*. ~ship *n* direção *f*, (*P*) direcção *f*, liderança *f*

leading /ˈliːdɪŋ/ *a* principal. ~ article artigo *m* de fundo, editorial *m*

leaf /liːf/ *n* (*pl* leaves) folha *f*; (*flap of table*) aba *f* □ *vi* ~ through folhear. ~y *a* frondoso

leaflet /ˈliːflɪt/ *n* prospecto *m*, folheto *m* informativo

league /liːɡ/ *n* liga *f*; (*sport*) campeonato *m* da Liga. in ~ with de coligação com, em conluio com

leak /liːk/ *n* (*escape*) fuga *f*; (*hole*) buraco *m* □ *vt/i* (*roof, container*) pingar; (*electr gas*) ter um escapamento, (*P*) ter uma fuga; (*naut*) fazer água. ~ (out) (*fig: divulge*) divulgar; (*fig: become known*) transpirar, divulgar-se. ~age *n* vazamento *m*. ~y *a* que tem um vazamento

lean¹ /liːn/ *a* (-er, -est) magro. ~ness *n* magreza *f*

lean² /liːn/ *vt/i* (*pt* leaned *or* leant /lent/) encostar(-se), apoiar-se (on em); (*be slanting*) inclinar(-se). ~ back/forward *or* over inclinar-se para trás/para a frente. ~ on (*colloq*) pressionar. ~ to *n* alpendre *m*

leaning /ˈliːnɪŋ/ *a* inclinado □ *n* inclinação *f*

leap /liːp/ *vt* (*pt* leaped *or* leapt/ lept/) galgar, saltar por cima de □ *vi* saltar □ *n* salto *m*, pulo *m*. ~-frog *n* eixo-badeixo *m*, (*P*) jogo *m* do eixo. ~ year ano *m* bissexto

learn /lɜːn/ *vt/i* (*pt* learned *or* learnt) aprender; (*be told*) vir a saber, ouvir dizer. ~er *n* principiante *mf*, aprendiz *m*

learn|**ed** /ˈlɜːnɪd/ *a* erudito. ~ing *n* saber *m*, erudição *f*

lease /liːs/ *n* arrendamento *m*, aluguel *m*, (*P*) aluguer *m* □ *vt* arrendar, (*P*) alugar

leash /liːʃ/ *n* coleira *f*

least /liːst/ *a* o menor □ *n* o mínimo *m*, o menos *m* □ *adv* o menos. at ~ pelo menos. not in the ~ de maneira alguma

leather /ˈleðə(r)/ *n* couro *m*, cabedal *m*

leave /liːv/ *vt/i* (*pt* left) deixar; (*depart from*) sair/partir (de), ir-se (de) □ *n* licença *f*, permissão *f*. be left (*over*) restar, sobrar. ~ alone deixar em paz, não tocar. ~ out omitir. ~ of absence licença *f*. on ~ (*mil*) de licença. take one's ~ despedir-se (of de)

leavings /ˈliːvɪŋz/ *npl* restos *mpl*

Lebanon /ˈlebənən/ n Líbano m. **~ese** /ˈniːz/ a & n libanês (m)

lecherous /ˈletʃərəs/ a lascivo

lectern /ˈlektən/ n estante f (de coro de igreja)

lecture /ˈlektʃə(r)/ n conferência f; (univ) aula f teórica; (fig) sermão m □ vi dar uma conferência; (univ) dar aula(s) □ vt pregar um sermão a alg (colloq). **~r** /-ə(r)/ n conferente mf; (univ) professor m

led /led/ see lead¹

ledge /ledʒ/ n rebordo m, saliência f; (of window) peitoril m

ledger /ˈledʒə(r)/ n livro-mestre m, razão m

leech /liːtʃ/ n sanguessuga f

leek /liːk/ n alho-poró m, (P) alho-porro m

leer /lɪə(r)/ vi ~ (at) olhar de modo malicioso or manhoso (para) □ n olhar m malicioso or manhoso

leeway /ˈliːweɪ/ n (naut) deriva f; (fig) liberdade f de ação, (P) acção, margem f (colloq)

left¹ /left/ see leave. **~ luggage** (office) depósito m de bagagens. **~overs** npl restos mpl, sobras fpl

left² /left/ a esquerdo; (pol) de esquerda □ n esquerda f □ adv à/para à esquerda. **~-hand** a da esquerda; (position) à esquerda. **~-handed** a canhoto. **~-wing** a (pol) de esquerda

leg /leg/ n perna f; (of table) pé m, perna f; (of journey) etapa f. pull sb's ~ brincar or mexer com alg. stretch one's ~s esticar as pernas. **~-room** n espaço m para as pernas

legacy /ˈlegəsɪ/ n legado m

legal /ˈliːgl/ a legal; (affairs etc) jurídico. **~ adviser** advogado m. **~ity** /liːˈgælətɪ/ n legalidade f. **~ly** adv legalmente

legalize /ˈliːgəlaɪz/ vt legalizar

legend /ˈledʒənd/ n lenda f. **~ary** /ˈledʒəndrɪ/ a lendário

leggings /ˈlegɪŋz/ npl perneiras fpl; (women's) legging m

legible /ˈledʒəbl/ a legível. **~ility** /-ˈbɪlətɪ/ n legibilidade f

legion /ˈliːdʒən/ n legião f

legislat|e /ˈledʒɪsleɪt/ vi legislar. **~ion** /-ˈleɪʃn/ n legislação f

legislat|ive /ˈledʒɪslətɪv/ a legislativo. **~ure** /-ertʃə(r)/ n corpo m legislativo

legitimate /lɪˈdʒɪtɪmət/ a legítimo. **~cy** n legitimidade f

leisure /ˈleʒə(r)/ n lazer m, tempo livre m. at one's ~ ao bel prazer, (P) a seu belo prazer. **~ centre** centro m de lazer. **~ly** a pausado, compassado □ adv sem pressa, devagar

lemon /ˈlemən/ n limão m

lemonade /leməˈneɪd/ n limonada f

lend /lend/ vt (pt lent) emprestar; (contribute) dar. **~ a hand to** (help) ajudar. **~ itself to** prestar-se a. **~er** n pessoa f que empresta. **~ing** n empréstimo m

length /leŋθ/ n comprimento m; (in time) período m; (of cloth) corte m. at ~ extensamente; (at last) por fim, finalmente. **~y** a longo, demorado

lengthen /ˈleŋθən/ vt/i alongar(-se)

lengthways /ˈleŋθweɪz/ adv ao comprido, em comprimento, longitudinalmente

lenien|t /ˈliːnɪənt/ a indulgente, clemente. **~cy** n indulgência f, clemência f

lens /lenz/ n (of spectacles) lente f; (photo) objetiva f, (P) objectiva f

lent /lent/ see lend

Lent /lent/ n Quaresma f

lentil /ˈlentl/ n lentilha f

Leo /ˈliːəʊ/ n (astr) Leão m

leopard /ˈlepəd/ n leopardo m

leotard /ˈliːəʊtɑːd/ n collant(s) m (pl), (P) maillot m de ginástica ou dança

leper /ˈlepə(r)/ n leproso m

leprosy /ˈleprəsɪ/ n lepra f

lesbian /ˈlezbɪən/ a lésbico □ n lésbica f

less /les/ a (in number) menor (than que); (in quantity) menos (than que) □ n, adv & prep menos. **~ and ~** cada vez menos

lessen /ˈlesn/ vt/i diminuir

lesser /ˈlesə(r)/ a menor. to a ~ degree em menor grau

lesson /ˈlesn/ n lição f

let /let/ vt (pt let, pres p letting) deixar, permitir; (lease) alugar, arrendar □ v aux **~'s go** vamos. **~ him do it** que o faça ele. **~ me know** diga-me, avise-me □ n aluguel m, (P) aluguer m. **~ alone** deixar em paz; (not to mention) sem falar em, para não falar em. **~ down** baixar; (deflate) esvaziar; (disappoint) desapontar; (fail to help) deixar na mão. **~-down** n desapontamento m. **~ go** vt/i soltar. **~ in** deixar entrar. **~ o.s. in for** (task, trouble) meter-se em. **~ off** (gun) disparar; (firework) soltar, (P) deitar; (excuse) desculpar. **~ on** (colloq) vt revelar (that que) □ vi descoser-se (colloq), (P) descair-se (colloq). **~ out** deixar sair. **~ through** deixar passar. **~ up** (colloq) abrandar, diminuir. **~-up** n (colloq) pausa f, trégua f

lethal /ˈliːθl/ a fatal, mortal

letharg|y /ˈleθədʒɪ/ n letargia f, apatia f. **~ic** /lɪˈθɑːdʒɪk/ a letárgico, apático

letter /ˈletə(r)/ n (symbol) letra f; (message) carta f. **~-bomb** n carta-bomba f. **~-box** n caixa f do correio. **~ing** n letras fpl lettuce /'letɪs/ n alface f

leukaemia /luːˈkiːmɪə/ n leucemia f

level /'levl/ a plano; (on surface) horizontal; (in height) no mesmo nivel (with que); (spoonful etc) raso □ n nivel m □ vt (pt levelled) nivelar; (gun, missile) apontar; (accusation) dirigir. on the ~ (colloq) franco, sincero. ~ crossing passagem f de nivel. ~-headed a equilibrado, sensato

lever /'liːvə(r)/ n alavanca f □ vt ~ up levantar com alavanca

leverage /'liːvərɪdʒ/ n influência f

levity /'levətɪ/ n frivolidade f, leviandade f

levy /'levɪ/ vt (tax) cobrar □ n imposto m

lewd /luːd/ a (-er, -est) libidinoso, obsceno

liabilit|y /laɪəˈbɪlətɪ/ n responsabilidade f; (colloq handicap) desvantagem f. ~ies dividas fpl

liable /'laɪəbl/ a ~ to do susceptivel, (P) susceptivel de fazer; ~ to (illness etc) susceptivel, (P) susceptivel a; (fine) sujeito a. ~ for responsável por

liaise /lɪˈeɪz/ vi (colloq) servir de intermediário (between entre), fazer a ligação (with com)

liaison /lɪˈeɪzn/ n ligação f

liar /'laɪə(r)/ n mentiroso m

libel /'laɪbl/ n difamação f □ vt (pt libelled) difamar

liberal /'lɪbərəl/ a liberal. ~ly adv liberalmente

Liberal /'lɪbərəl/ a & n liberal (mf)

liberat|e /'lɪbəreɪt/ vt libertar. ~ion /-ˈreɪʃn/ n libertação f; (of women) emancipação f

liberty /'lɪbətɪ/ n liberdade f. at ~ to livre de. take ~ies tomar liberdades

libido /lɪˈbiːdəʊ/ n (pl -os) libido m

Libra /'liːbrə/ n (astr) Balança f, Libra f

librar|y /'laɪbrərɪ/ n biblioteca f. ~ian /-ˈbreərɪən/ n bibliotecário m

Libya /'lɪbɪə/ n Libia f. ~n a & n libio (m)

lice /laɪs/ n see louse

licence /'laɪsns/ n licença f; (for TV) taxa f; (for driving) carteira f, (P) carta f; (behaviour) libertinagem f

license /'laɪsns/ vt dar licença para, autorizar □ n (Amer) = licence. ~ plate placa f do carro, (P) placa f de matricula

licentious /laɪˈsenʃəs/ a licencioso

lichen /'laɪkən/ n liquen m

lick /lɪk/ vt lamber; (sl: defeat) bater (colloq), dar uma surra em (colloq) □ n lambidela f. a ~ of paint uma mão de pintura

lid /lɪd/ n tampa f

lido /'liːdəʊ/ n (pl -os) piscina f pública ao ar livre

lie¹ /laɪ/ n mentira f □ vi (pt lied, pres p lying) mentir. give the ~ to desmentir

lie² /laɪ/ vi (pt lay pp lain, pres p lying) estar deitado; (remain) ficar; (be situated) estar, encontrar-se; (in grave, on ground) jazer. ~ down descansar. ~ in, have a ~-in dormir até tarde. ~ low (colloq: hide) andar escondido

lieu /luː/ n in ~ of em vez de

lieutenant /lefˈtenənt/ n (army) tenente m; (navy) 1° tenente m

life /laɪf/ n (pl lives) vida f. ~ cycle ciclo m vital. ~ expectancy probabilidade f de vida. ~-guard n salvavidas m. ~ insurance seguro m de vida. ~-jacket n colete m salva-vidas. ~-size(d) a (de) tamanho natural invar

lifebelt /'laɪfbelt/ n cinto m salvavidas, (P) cinto m de salvação

lifeboat /'laɪfbəʊt/ n barco m salvavidas

lifebuoy /'laɪfbɔɪ/ n bóia f salva-vidas, (P) bóia f de salvação

lifeless /'laɪflɪs/ a sem vida

lifelike /'laɪflaɪk/ a natural, real; (of portrait) muito parecido

lifelong /'laɪflɒŋ/ a de toda a vida, perpétuo

lifestyle /'laɪfstaɪl/ n estilo m de vida

lifetime /'laɪftaɪm/ n vida f. the chance of a ~ uma oportunidade única

lift /lɪft/ vt/i levantar(-se), erguer(-se); (colloq: steal) roubar, surripiar (colloq); (of fog) levantar, dispersar-se □ n ascensor m, elevador m. give a ~ to dar carona, (P) boleia a (colloq). ~-off n decolagem f, (P) descolagem f

ligament /'lɪgəmənt/ n ligamento m

light¹ /laɪt/ n luz f; (lamp) lâmpada f; (on vehicle) farol m; (spark) lume m □ a claro □ vt (pt lit or lighted) (ignite) acender; (illuminate) iluminar. bring to ~ trazer à luz, revelar. come to ~ vir à luz. ~ up iluminar(-se), acender(-se). ~-year n ano-luz m

light² /laɪt/ a & adv (-er, -est) leve. ~-headed a (dizzy) estonteado, tonto; (frivolous) leviano. ~-hearted a alegre, despreocupado. ~ly adv de leve, levemente, ligeiramente. ~ness n leveza f

lighten¹ /'laɪtn/ vt/i iluminar(-se); (make brighter) clarear

lighten² /'laɪtn/ vt/i (load etc) aligeirar(-se), tornar mais leve

lighter /'laɪtə(r)/ n isqueiro m

lighthouse /'laɪthaʊs/ n farol m

lighting /'laɪtɪŋ/ n iluminação f
lightning /'laɪtnɪŋ/ n relâmpago m; (*thunderbolt*) raio m □ a muito rápido. like ~ como um relâmpago
lightweight /'laɪtweɪt/ a leve
like[1] /laɪk/ a semelhante (a), parecido (com) □ prep como □ conj (*colloq*) como □ n igual a, coisa f parecida. ~-minded a da mesma opinião. the ~s of you gente como você(s).
like[2] /laɪk/ vt gostar (de). ~s npl gostos mpl. I would ~ gostaria (de), queria. if you ~ se quiser. would you ~? gostaria?, queria? ~able a simpático
like|ly /'laɪklɪ/ a (-ier, -iest) provável □ adv provavelmente. he is ~ly to come é provável que ele venha. not ~ly! (*colloq*) nem morto, nem por sonhos. ~lihood n probabilidade f
liken /'laɪkn/ vt comparar (to com)
likeness /'laɪknɪs/ n semelhança f
likewise /'laɪkwaɪz/ adv também; (*in the same way*) da mesma maneira
liking /'laɪkɪŋ/ n gosto m, inclinação f; (*for person*) afeição f. take a ~ to (*thing*) tomar gosto por; (*person*) simpatizar com
lilac /'laɪlək/ n lilás m □ a lilás invar
lily /'lɪlɪ/ n lírio m, lis m. ~ of the valley lírio m do vale
limb /lɪm/ n membro m
limber /'lɪmbə(r)/ vi ~ up fazer exercícios para desenferrujar (*colloq*)
lime[1] /laɪm/ n cal f
lime[2] /laɪm/ n (*fruit*) limão m
lime[3] /laɪm/ n ~(-tree) tília f
limelight /'laɪmlaɪt/ n be in the ~ estar em evidência
limerick /'lɪmərɪk/ n poema m humorístico (*de cinco versos*)
limit /'lɪmɪt/ n limite m □ vt limitar. ~ation /-'teɪʃn/ n limitação f. ~ed company sociedade f anónima, (P) anónima de responsabilidade limitada
limousine /'lɪməziːn/ n limusine f
limp[1] /lɪmp/ vi mancar, coxear □ n have a ~ coxear
limp[2] /lɪmp/ a (-er, -est) mole, frouxo
line[1] /laɪn/ n linha f; (*string*) fio m; (*rope*) corda f; (*row*) fila f; (*of poem*) verso m; (*wrinkle*) ruga f; (*of business*) ramo m; (*of goods*) linha f; (*Amer: queue*) fila f, (P) bicha f □ vt marcar com linhas; (*streets etc*) ladear, enfileirar-se ao longo de. ~d paper papel m pautado. in ~ with de acordo com. ~ up alinhar(-se), enfileirar(-se); (*in queue*) pôr(-se) em fila, (P) bicha. ~-up n (*players*) formação f
line[2] /laɪn/ vt (*garment*) forrar (with de)
lineage /'lɪnɪɪdʒ/ n linhagem f
linear /'lɪnɪə(r)/ a linear

linen /'lɪnɪn/ n (*sheets etc*) roupa f (branca) de cama; (*material*) linho m
liner /'laɪnə(r)/ n navio m de linha regular, (P) paquete m
linesman /'laɪnzmən/ n (*football, tennis*) juiz m de linha
linger /'lɪŋgə(r)/ vi demorar-se, deixar-se ficar; (*of smells etc*) persistir
lingerie /'lænʒərɪ/ n roupa f de baixo (de senhora), lingerie f
linguist /'lɪŋgwɪst/ n língüista mf, (P) linguista mf
linguistic /lɪŋ'gwɪstɪk/ a língüístico, (P) linguístico. ~s n língüística f, (P) linguística f
lining /'laɪnɪŋ/ n forro m
link /lɪŋk/ n laço m; (*of chain; fig*) elo m □ vt unir, ligar; (*relate*) ligar; (*arm*) enfiar. ~ up (*of roads*) juntar-se (with a). ~age n ligação f
lino, linoleum /'laɪnəʊ, lɪ'nəʊlɪəm/ n linóleo m
lint /lɪnt/ n (*med*) curativo m de fibra de algodão; (*fluff*) cotão m
lion /'laɪən/ n leão m. ~ess n leoa f
lip /lɪp/ n lábio m, beiço m; (*edge*) borda f; (*of jug etc*) bico m. ~-read vt/i entender pelos movimentos dos lábios. pay ~-service to fingir pena, admiração etc
lipstick /'lɪpstɪk/ n batom m, (P) báton m
liquefy /'lɪkwɪfaɪ/ vt/i liquefazer(-se)
liqueur /lɪ'kjʊə(r)/ n licor m
liquid /'lɪkwɪd/ n & a líquido (m). ~ize vt liqüidificar, (P) liquidificar. ~izer n liqüidificador m, (P) liquidificador m
liquidat|e /'lɪkwɪdeɪt/ vt liquidar. ~ion /-'deɪʃn/ n liquidação f
liquor /'lɪkə(r)/ n bebida f alcoólica
liquorice /'lɪkərɪs/ n alcaçuz m
Lisbon /'lɪzbən/ n Lisboa f
lisp /lɪsp/ n ceceio m □ vi cecear
list[1] /lɪst/ n lista f □ vt fazer uma lista de; (*enter*) pôr na lista
list[2] /lɪst/ vi (*of ship*) adernar □ n adernamento m
listen /'lɪsn/ vi escutar, prestar atenção. ~ to, ~ in (to) escutar, pôr-se à escuta. ~er n ouvinte mf
listless /'lɪstlɪs/ a sem energia, apático
lit /lɪt/ see light[1]
literal /'lɪtərəl/ a literal. ~ly adv literalmente
litera|te /'lɪtərət/ a alfabetizado. ~cy n alfabetização f, instrução f
literature /'lɪtrətʃə(r)/ n literatura f; (*colloq: leaflets etc*) folhetos mpl
lithe /laɪð/ a ágil, flexível
litigation /lɪtɪ'geɪʃn/ n litígio m
litre /'liːtə(r)/ n litro m
litter /'lɪtə(r)/ n lixo m; (*animals*) ninhada f □ vt cobrir de lixo. ~ed

with coberto de. ~-bin n lata f, (P) caixote m do lixo

little /'lɪtl/ a pequeno; (not much) pouco □ n pouco m □ adv pouco, mal, nem. a ~ um pouco (de). he ~ knows ele mal/nem sabe. ~ by ~ pouco a pouco

liturgy /'lɪtədʒɪ/ n liturgia f

live¹ /laɪv/ a vivo; (wire) eletrizado; (broadcast) em direto, (P) directo, ao vivo

live² /lɪv/ vt/i viver; (reside) habitar, morar, viver. ~ down fazer esquecer. ~ it up cair na farra. ~ on viver de; (continue) continuar a viver. ~ up to mostrar-se à altura de; (fulfil) cumprir

livelihood /'laɪvlɪhʊd/ n modo m de vida

livel|y /'laɪvlɪ/ a (-ier, -iest) vivo, animado. ~iness n vivacidade f, animação f

liven /'laɪvn/ vt/i ~ up animar(-se)

liver /'lɪvə(r)/ n fígado m

livery /'lɪvərɪ/ n libré f

livestock /'laɪvstɒk/ n gado m

livid /'lɪvɪd/ a lívido; (colloq: furious) furioso

living /'lɪvɪŋ/ a vivo □ n vida f; (livelihood) modo de vida m, sustento m. earn or make a ~ ganhar a vida. standard of ~ nível m de vida. ~-room n sala f de estar

lizard /'lɪzəd/ n lagarto m

llama /'lɑːmə/ n lama m

load /ləʊd/ n carga f; (of lorry, ship) carga f, carregamento m; (weight, strain) peso m. ~s of (colloq) montes de (colloq) □ vt carregar. ~ed a (dice) viciado; (sl: rich) cheio da nota

loaf¹ /ləʊf/ n (pl loaves) pão m

loaf² /ləʊf/ vi vadiar. ~er n preguiçoso m, vagabundo m

loan /ləʊn/ n empréstimo m □ vt emprestar. on ~ emprestado

loath /ləʊθ/ a sem vontade de, pouco disposto a, relutante em

loath|e /ləʊð/ vt detestar. ~ing n repugnância f, aversão f. ~some a repugnante

lobby /'lɒbɪ/ n entrada f, vestíbulo m; (pol) lobby m, grupo m de pressão □ vt fazer pressão sobre

lobe /ləʊb/ n lóbulo m

lobster /'lɒbstə(r)/ n lagosta f

local /'ləʊkl/ a local; (shops etc) do bairro □ n pessoa f do lugar; (colloq: pub) taberna f/pub do bairro. ~ government administração f municipal. ~ly adv localmente; (nearby) na vizinhança

locale /ləʊˈkɑːl/ n local m

locality /ləʊˈkælətɪ/ n localidade f; (position) lugar m

localized /'ləʊkəlaɪzd/ a localizado

locat|e /ləʊˈkeɪt/ vt localizar; (situate) situar. ~ion /-ʃn/ n localização f. on ~ion (cinema) em external, (P) no exterior

lock¹ /lɒk/ n (hair) mecha f de cabelo

lock² /lɒk/ n (on door etc) fecho m, fechadura f; (on canal) comporta f □ vt/i fechar à chave; (auto: wheels) imobilizar(-se). ~ in fechar à chave, encerrar. ~ out fechar a porta para, deixar na rua. ~-out n lockout m. ~ up fechar a casa. under ~ and key a sete chaves

locker /'lɒkə(r)/ n compartimento m com chave

locket /'lɒkɪt/ n medalhão m

locksmith /'lɒksmɪθ/ n serralheiro m, chaveiro m

locomotion /ləʊkəˈməʊʃn/ n locomoção f

locomotive /'ləʊkəməʊtɪv/ n locomotiva f

locum /'ləʊkəm/ n (med) substituto m

locust /'ləʊkəst/ n gafanhoto m

lodge /lɒdʒ/ n casa f do guarda numa propriedade; (of porter) portaria f □ vt alojar; (money) depositar. ~ a complaint apresentar uma queixa □ vi estar alojado (with em casa de); (become fixed) alojar-se. ~r /-ə(r)/ n hóspede mf

lodgings /'lɒdʒɪŋz/ n quarto m mobiliado; (flat) apartamento m

loft /lɒft/ n sótão m

lofty /'lɒftɪ/ a (-ier, -iest) elevado; (haughty) altivo

log /lɒg/ n tronco m, toro m. ~ (-book) n (naut) diário m de bordo; (aviat) diário m de vôo. sleep like a ~ dormir como uma pedra □ vt (pt logged) (naut/aviat) lançar no diário de bordo. ~ off acabar de usar. ~ on começar a usar

loggerheads /'lɒgəhedz/ npl at ~ às turras (with com)

logic /'lɒdʒɪk/ a lógico. ~al a lógico. ~ally adv logicamente

logistics /ləˈdʒɪstɪks/ n logística f

logo /'ləʊgəʊ/ n (pl -os) (colloq) emblema m, logotipo m, (P) logótipo m

loin /lɔɪn/ n (culin) lombo m, alcatra f

loiter /'lɔɪtə(r)/ vi andar vagarosamente; (stand about) rondar

loll /lɒl/ vi refestelar-se

lollipop /'lɒlɪpɒp/ n pirulito m, (P) chupa-chupa m. ~y n pirulito m, (P) chupa-chupa m; (sl: money) grana f

London /'lʌndən/ n Londres

lone /ləʊn/ a solitário. ~r /-ə(r)/ n solitário m. ~some a solitário

lonely /'ləʊnlɪ/ a (-ier, -iest) solitário; (person) só, solitário

long[1] /lɒŋ/ a (-er, -est) longo, comprido □ adv muito tempo, longamente. **how ~ is...?** (in size) qual é o comprimento de...? **how ~?** (in time) quanto tempo? **he will not be ~** ele não vai demorar. **a ~ time** muito tempo. **a ~ way** longe. **as** or **so ~ as** contanto que, desde que. **~ ago** há muito tempo. **before ~** (future) daqui a pouco, dentro em pouco; (past) pouco (tempo) depois. **in the ~ run** no fim de contas. **~ before** muito (tempo) antes. **~-distance** a (flight) de longa distância; (phone call) interurbano. **~ face** cara f triste. **~ jump** salto m em distância. **~-playing record** LP m. **~-range** a de longo alcance; (forecast) a longo prazo. **~-sighted** a que enxerga mal à distância. **~-standing** a de longa data. **~-suffering** a com paciência exemplar/de santo. **~-term** a a longo prazo. **~ wave** ondas fpl longas. **~-winded** a prolixo. **so ~!** (colloq) até logo!

long[2] /lɒŋ/ vi **~ for** ansiar por, ter grande desejo de. **~ to** desejar. **~ing** n desejo m ardente

longevity /lɒnˈdʒevətɪ/ n longevidade f, vida f longa

longhand /ˈlɒŋhænd/ n escrita f à mão

longitude /ˈlɒŋdʒɪtjuːd/ n longitude f

loo /luː/ n (colloq) banheiro m, (P) casa f de banho

look /lʊk/ vt/i olhar; (seem) parecer □ n olhar m; (appearance) ar m, aspecto m. **(good) ~s** beleza f. **~ after** tomar conta de, olhar por. **~ at** olhar para. **~ down on** desprezar. **~ for** procurar. **~ forward to** aguardar com impaciência. **~ in on** visitar. **~ into** examinar, investigar. **~ like** parecer-se com, ter ar de. **~ on** (as spectator) ver, assistir; (regard as) considerar. **~ out** ter cautela. **~ out for** procurar; (watch) estar à espreita de. **~-out** n (mil) posto m de observação; (watcher) vigia m. **~ round** olhar em redor. **~ up** (word) procurar; (visit) ir ver. **~ up to** respeitar

loom[1] /luːm/ n tear m

loom[2] /luːm/ vi surgir indistintamente; (fig) ameaçar

loony /ˈluːnɪ/ n & a (sl) maluco (m), doido (m)

loop /luːp/ n laçada f; (curve) volta f, arco m; (aviat) loop m □ vt dar uma laçada

loophole /ˈluːphəʊl/ n (in rule) saída f, furo m

loose /luːs/ a (-er, -est) (knot etc) frouxo; (page etc) solto; (clothes) folgado; (not packed) a granel; (inexact) vago; (morals) dissoluto, imoral. **at a ~ end** sem saber o que fazer, sem ocupação definida. **break ~** soltarse. **~ly** adv sem apertar; (roughly) vagamente

loosen /ˈluːsn/ vt (slacken) soltar, desapertar; (untie) desfazer, desatar

loot /luːt/ n saque m □ vt pilhar, saquear. **~er** n assaltante mf. **~ing** n pilhagem f, saque m

lop /lɒp/ vt (pt lopped) **~ off** cortar, podar

lop-sided /lɒpˈsaɪdɪd/ a torto, inclinado para um lado

lord /lɔːd/ n senhor m; (title) lord m. **the L~** o Senhor. **the L~'s Prayer** o Pai-Nosso. **(good) L~!** meu Deus! **~ly** a magnífico, nobre; (haughty) altivo, arrogante

lorry /ˈlɒrɪ/ n camião m, caminhão m

lose /luːz/ vt/i (pt lost) perder. **get lost** perder-se. **get lost** (sl) vai passear! (colloq). **~r** /-ə(r)/ n perdedor m

loss /lɒs/ n perda f. **be at a ~** estar perplexo. **at a ~ for words** sem saber o que dizer

lost /lɒst/ see lose □ a perdido. **~ property** objetos mpl, (P) objectos mpl perdidos (e achados)

lot[1] /lɒt/ n sorte f; (at auction, land) lote m. **draw ~s** tirar à sorte

lot[2] /lɒt/ n **the ~** tudo; (people) todos mpl. **a ~ (of), ~s (of)** (colloq) uma porção (de) (colloq). **quite a ~ (of)** (colloq) uma boa porção (de) (colloq)

lotion /ˈləʊʃn/ n loção f

lottery /ˈlɒtərɪ/ n loteria f, (P) lotaria f

loud /laʊd/ a (-er, -est) alto, barulhento, ruidoso; (of colours) berrante □ adv alto. **~hailer** n megafone m. **out ~** em voz alta. **~ly** adv alto

loudspeaker /laʊdˈspiːkə(r)/ n altofalante m

lounge /laʊndʒ/ vi recostar-se preguiçosamente □ n sala f, salão m

louse /laʊs/ n (pl lice) piolho m

lousy /ˈlaʊzɪ/ a (-ier, -iest) piolhento; (sl: very bad) péssimo

lout /laʊt/ n pessoa f grosseira, arruaceiro m

lovable /ˈlʌvəbl/ a amoroso, adorável

love /lʌv/ n amor m; (tennis) zero m, nada m □ vt amar, gostar apaixonadamente por; (like greatly) gostar muito de. **in ~** apaixonado (with por). **~ affair** aventura f amorosa. **she sends you her ~** ela lhe manda lembranças

lovely /ˈlʌvlɪ/ a (-ier, -iest) lindo; (colloq: delightful) encantador, delicioso

lover /ˈlʌvə(r)/ n namorado m, apaixonado m; (illicit) amante m; (devotee) admirador m, apreciador m

lovesick /ˈlʌvsɪk/ a perdido de amor

loving /ˈlʌvɪŋ/ a amoroso, terno, extremoso

low /ləʊ/ a (-er, -est) baixo □ adv baixo □ n baixa f; (low pressure) área de baixa pressão f. ~cut a decotado. ~-down a baixo, reles □ n (colloq) a verdade autêntica, (P) a verdade nua e crua. ~-fat a de baixo teor de gordura. ~-key a (fig) moderado, discreto

lower /ˈləʊə(r)/ a & adv see low □ vt baixar. ~ o.s. (re)baixar-se (to a)

lowlands /ˈləʊləndz/ npl planície(s) f (pl)

lowly /ˈləʊlɪ/ a (-ier, -iest) humilde, modesto

loyal /ˈlɔɪəl/ a leal. ~ly adv lealmente. ~ty n lealdade f

lozenge /ˈlɒzɪndʒ/ n (shape) losango m; (tablet) pastilha f

LP abbr see long-playing record

lubric|ate /ˈluːbrɪkeɪt/ vt lubrificar. ~ant n lubrificante m. ~ation /-ˈkeɪ/ n lubrificação f

lucid /ˈluːsɪd/ a lúcido. ~ity /luːˈsɪdətɪ/ n lucidez f

luck /lʌk/ n sorte f. bad ~ pouca sorte f. for ~ para dar sorte. good ~!

luck|y /ˈlʌkɪ/ a (-ier, -iest) sortudo, com sorte; (event etc) feliz; (number etc) que dá sorte. ~ily adv felizmente

lucrative /ˈluːkrətɪv/ a lucrativo, rentável

ludicrous /ˈluːdɪkrəs/ a ridículo, absurdo

lug /lʌg/ vt (pt lugged) arrastar

luggage /ˈlʌgɪdʒ/ n bagagem f. ~-rack n porta-bagagem m. ~-van n furgão m

lukewarm /ˈluːkwɔːm/ a morno; (fig) sem entusiasmo, indiferente

lull /lʌl/ vt (send to sleep) embalar; (suspicions) acalmar □ n calmaria f, (P) acalmia f

lullaby /ˈlʌləbaɪ/ n canção f de embalar

lumbago /lʌmˈbeɪgəʊ/ n lumbago m

lumber /ˈlʌmbə(r)/ n trastes mpl velhos; (wood) madeira f cortada □ vt ~ sb with

luminous /ˈluːmɪnəs/ a luminoso

lump /lʌmp/ n bocado m; (swelling) caroço m; (in the throat) nó m; (in liquid) grumo m; (of sugar) torrão m □ vt ~ together amontoar, juntar indiscriminadamente. ~ sum quantia f total; (payment) pagamento m de uma vez. ~y a grumoso, encaroçado

lunacy /ˈluːnəsɪ/ n loucura f

lunar /ˈluːnə(r)/ a lunar

lunatic /ˈluːnətɪk/ n lunático m. ~ asylum manicómio m, (P) manicómio m

lunch /lʌntʃ/ n almoço m □ vi almoçar. ~-time n hora f do almoço

luncheon /ˈlʌntʃən/ n (formal) almoço m. ~ meat carne f enlatada, (P) 'merenda' f. ~ voucher senha f de almoço

lung /lʌŋ/ n pulmão m

lunge /lʌndʒ/ n mergulho m, movimento m súbito para a frente; (thrust) arremetida f □ vi mergulhar, arremessar-se (at para cima de, contra)

lurch¹ /lɜːtʃ/ leave sb in the ~ deixar alg em apuros

lurch² /lɜːtʃ/ vi ir aos ziguezagues, dar guinadas; (stagger) cambalear

lure /lʊə(r)/ vt atrair, tentar □ n chamariz m, engodo f □ n cha- a atracção f do mar

lurid /ˈlʊərɪd/ a berrante; (fig: sensational) sensacional; (fig: shocking) horrífico

lurk /lɜːk/ vi esconder-se à espreita; (prowl) rondar; (be latent) estar latente

luscious /ˈlʌʃəs/ a apetitoso; (voluptuous) desejável

lush /lʌʃ/ a viçoso, luxuriante

Lusitanian /luːsɪˈteɪnɪən/ a & n lusitano (m)

lust /lʌst/ n luxúria f, sensualidade f; (fig) cobiça f, desejo m ardente □ vi ~ after cobiçar, desejar ardentemente. ~ful a sensual

lustre /ˈlʌstə(r)/ n lustre m; (fig) prestígio m

lusty /ˈlʌstɪ/ a (-ier, -iest) robusto, vigoroso

lute /luːt/ n alaúde m

Luxembourg /ˈlʌksəmbɜːg/ n Luxemburgo m

luxuriant /lʌgˈʒʊərɪənt/ a luxuriante

luxurious /lʌgˈʒʊərɪəs/ a luxuoso

luxury /ˈlʌkʃərɪ/ n luxo m □ a de luxo

lying /ˈlaɪŋ/ see lie¹, lie²

lynch /lɪntʃ/ vt linchar

lynx /lɪŋks/ n lince m

lyre /ˈlaɪə(r)/ n lira f

lyric /ˈlɪrɪk/ a lírico. ~s npl (mus) letra f. ~al a lírico

M

MA abbr see Master of Arts

mac /mæk/ n (colloq) impermeável m, gabardine f

macabre /məˈkɑːbrə/ a macabro

macaroni /mækəˈrəʊnɪ/ n macarrão m

macaroon /mækəˈruːn/ n bolinho m seco de amêndoa ralada

mace¹ /meɪs/ n (staff) maça f

mace² /meɪs/ n (spice) macis m

machination /mækɪ'neɪʃn/ n maquinação f

machine /mə'ʃi:n/ n máquina f □ vt fazer à máquina; (sewing) coser à máquina. ~-gun n metralhadora f. ~-readable a em linguagem de máquina. ~ tool máquina-ferramenta f

machinery /mə'ʃi:nərɪ/ n maquinaria f; (working parts; fig) mecanismo m

machinist /mə'ʃi:nɪst/ n maquinista m

macho /'mætʃəʊ/ a machista

mackerel /'mækrəl/ n (pl invar) cavala f

mackintosh /'mækɪntɒʃ/ n impermeável m, gabardine f

mad /mæd/ a (madder, maddest) doido, louco; (dog) raivoso; (colloq: angry) furioso (colloq). be ~ about ser doido por. like ~ como (um) doido. ~ly adv loucamente; (frantically) enlouquecidamente. ~ness n loucura f

Madagascar /mædə'gæskə(r)/ n Madagáscar m

madam /'mædəm/ n senhora f. no, ~ não senhora

madden /'mædn/ vt endoidecer, enlouquecer. it's ~ing é de enlouquecer

made /meɪd/ see make. ~ to measure feito sob medida

Madeira /mə'dɪərə/ n Madeira f; (wine) Madeira m

madman /'mædmən/ n (pl -men) doido m

madrigal /'mædrɪgl/ n madrigal m

Mafia /'mæfɪə/ n Máfia f

magazine /mægə'zi:n/ n revista f, magazine m; (of gun) carregador m

magenta /mə'dʒentə/ a & n magenta (m), carmin (m)

maggot /'mægət/ n larva f. ~y a bichento

Magi /'meɪdʒaɪ/ npl the ~ os Reis mpl Magos

magic /'mædʒɪk/ n magia f □ a mágico. ~al a mágico

magician /mə'dʒɪʃn/ n (conjuror) prestidigitador m; (wizard) feiticeiro m

magistrate /'mædʒɪstreɪt/ n magistrado m

magnanim|ous /mæg'nænɪməs/ a magnânimo. ~ity /-ə'nɪmətɪ/ n magnanimidade f

magnate /'mægneɪt/ n magnata m

magnet /'mægnɪt/ n imã m, (P) íman m. ~ic /-'netɪk/ a magnético. ~ism /-ɪzəm/ n magnetismo m. ~ize vt magnetizar

magnificen|t /mæg'nɪfɪsnt/ a magnífico. ~ce n magnificência f

magnif|y /'mægnɪfaɪ/ vt aumentar; (sound) ampliar, amplificar. ~ication /-ɪ'keɪʃn/ n aumento m, ampliação f. ~ying glass lupa f

magnitude /'mægnɪtju:d/ n magnitude f

magpie /'mægpaɪ/ n pega f

mahogany /mə'hɒgənɪ/ n mogno m

maid /meɪd/ n criada f, empregada f. old ~ solteirona f

maiden /'meɪdn/ n (old use) donzela f □ a (aunt) solteira; (speech, voyage) inaugural. ~ name nome m de solteira

mail¹ /meɪl/ n correio m; (letters) correio m, correspondência f □ a postal □ vt postar, pôr no correio; (send by mail) mandar pelo correio. ~-bag n mala f postal. ~-box n (Amer) caixa f do correio. ~ing-list n lista f de endereços. ~ order n encomenda f por correspondência, (P) por correio

mail² /meɪl/ n (armour) cota f de malha

mailman /'meɪlmæn/ n (pl -men) (Amer) carteiro m

maim /meɪm/ vt mutilar, aleijar

main¹ /meɪn/ a principal □ n in the ~ em geral, essencialmente. ~ road estrada f principal. ~ly adv principalmente, sobretudo

main² /meɪn/ n (water/gas) ~ cano m de água/gás. the ~s (electr) a rede f elétrica

mainland /'meɪnlənd/ n continente m

mainstay /'meɪnsteɪ/ n (fig) esteio m

mainstream /'meɪnstri:m/ n tendência f dominante, linha f principal

maintain /meɪn'teɪn/ vt manter, sustentar; (rights) defender, manter

maintenance /'meɪntənəns/ n (care, continuation) manutenção f; (allowance) pensão f

maisonette /meɪzə'net/ n dúplex m

maize /meɪz/ n milho m

majestic /mə'dʒestɪk/ a majestoso. ~ally adv majestosamente

majesty /'mædʒəstɪ/ n majestade f

major /'meɪdʒə(r)/ a maior; (very important) de vulto □ n major m □ vi ~ in (Amer: univ) especializar-se em. ~ road estrada f principal

Majorca /mə'dʒɔ:kə/ n Maiorca f

majority /mə'dʒɒrətɪ/ n maioria f; (age) maioridade f □ a maioritário, (P) maioritário. the ~ of people a maioria or a maior parte das pessoas

make /meɪk/ vt/i (pt made) fazer; (decision) tomar; (destination) chegar a; (cause to) fazer (+ inf) or (com) que (+ subj). you ~ me angry você me aborrece □ n (brand) marca f. on the ~ (sl) oportunista. be made of ser feito de. ~ o.s. at home estar à vontade/

como em sua casa. ~ it chegar; (*succeed*) triunfar. I ~ it two o'clock são duas pelo meu relógio. ~ as if to fazer *ou* fingir que. ~-believe *a* fingido □ *n* fantasia *f*. ~-do *vi* arranjar-se com, contentar-se com. ~ for dirigir-se para; (*contribute to*) ajudar a. ~ good *vi* triunfar □ *vt* compensar; (*repair*) reparar. ~ off fugir (with com). ~ out avistar, distinguir; (*understand*) entender; (*claim*) pretender; (*a cheque*) passar, emitir. ~ over ceder, transferir. ~ up *vt* fazer, compor; (*story*) inventar; (*deficit*) suprir □ *vi* fazer as pazes. ~ up (one's face)maquilar-se, (P) maquilhar-se. ~-up *n* maquilagem *f*, (P) maquilhagem *f*; (*of object*) composição *f*; (*psych*) maneira *f* de ser, natureza *f*. ~ up for compensar. ~ up one's mind decidir-se

maker /'meɪkə(r)/ *n* fabricante *mf*

makeshift /'meɪkʃɪft/ *n* solução *f* temporária □ *a* provisório

making /'meɪkɪŋ/ *n* be the ~ offazer, ser a causa do sucesso de. in the ~ em formação. he has the ~s of ele tem as qualidades essenciais de

maladjusted /mælə'dʒʌstɪd/ *a* desajustado, inadaptado

maladministration /mælədmɪnɪ'streɪʃn/ *n* mau governo *m*, má gestão *f*

malaise /mæ'leɪz/ *n* mal-estar *m*

malaria /mə'leərɪə/ *n* malária *f*

Malay /mə'leɪ/ *a* & *n* malaio (*m*). ~sia /-ʒə/ *n* Malásia *f*

male /meɪl/ *a* (*voice, sex*) masculino; (*biol, techn*) macho □ *n* (*human*) homem *m*, indivíduo *m* do sexo masculino; (*arrival*) macho *m*

malevolen|t /mə'levələnt/ *a* malévolo. ~ce *n* malevolência *f*, má vontade *f*

malformation /mælfɔ:'meɪʃn/ *n* malformação *f*, deformidade *f*. ~ed *a* deformado

malfunction /mæl'fʌŋkʃn/ *n* mau funcionamento *m* □ *vi* funcionar mal

malice /'mælɪs/ *n* maldade *f*, malícia *f*. bear sb ~ guardar rancor a alg

malicious /mə'lɪʃəs/ *a* maldoso, malicioso. ~ly *adv* maldosamente, maliciosamente

malign /mə'laɪn/ *vt* caluniar, difamar

malignan|t /mə'lɪgnənt/ *a* (*tumour*) maligno; (*malevolent*) malévolo. ~cy *n* malignidade *f*; malevolência *f*

malinger /mə'lɪŋgə(r)/ *vi* fingir-se doente. ~er *n* pessoa *f* que se finge doente

mallet /'mælɪt/ *n* maço *m*

malnutrition /mælnju:'trɪʃn/ *n* desnutrição *f*, subalimentação *f*

malpractice /mæl'præktɪs/ *n* abuso *m*; (*incompetence*) incompetência *f* profissional, negligência *f*

malt /mɔ:lt/ *n* malte *m*

Malt|a /'mɔ:ltə/ *n* Malta *f*. ~ese /-'ti:z/ *a* & *n* maltês (*m*)

maltreat /mæl'tri:t/ *vt* maltratar. ~ment *n* mau(s) trato(s) *m* (*pl*)

mammal /'mæml/ *n* mamífero *m*

mammoth /'mæməθ/ *n* mamute *m* □ *a* gigantesco, colossal

man /mæn/ *n* (*pl* men) homem *m*; (*in sports team*) jogador *m*; (*chess*) peça *f* □ *vt* (*pt* manned) prover de pessoal; (*mil*) guarnecer; (*naut*) guarnecer, equipar, tripular; (*be on duty at*) estar de serviço em. ~ in the street *o* homem da rua. ~-hour *n* hora *f* de trabalho per capita, homem-hora *f*. ~-hunt *n* caça *f* ao homem. ~-made *a* artificial. to man *de* homem para homem

manage /'mænɪdʒ/ *vt* (*household*) governar; (*tool*) manejar; (*boat, affair, crowd*) manobrar; (*shop*) dirigir, gerir. I could ~ another drink (*colloq*) até que tomaria mais um drinque (*colloq*) □ *vi* arranjar-se. ~ to do conseguir fazer. ~able *a* manejável; (*easily controlled*) controlável. ~ment *n* gerência *f*, direção *f*, (P) direcção *f*. managing director diretor *m*, (P) director *m* geral

manager /'mænɪdʒə(r)/ *n* diretor *m*, (P) director *m*; (*of bank, shop*) gerente *m*; (*of actor*) empresário *m*; (*sport*) treinador *m*. ~ess /-'res/ *n* diretora *f*, (P) directora *f*; gerente *f*. ~ial /-'dʒɪərɪəl/*a* diretivo, (P) directivo, administrativo. ~ial staff gestores *mpl*

mandarin /'mændərɪn/ *n* mandarim *m*. ~ (orange) mandarina *f*, tangerina *f*

mandate /'mændeɪt/ *n* mandato *m*

mandatory /'mændətrɪ/ *a* obrigatório

mane /meɪn/ *n* crina *f*; (*of lion*) juba *f*

mangle[1] /'mæŋgl/ *n* calandra *f* □ *vt* espremer (com a calandra)

mangle[2] /'mæŋgl/ *vt* (*mutilate*) mutilar, estropiar

mango /'mæŋgəʊ/ *n* (*pl* -oes) manga *f*

manhandle /'mænhændl/ *vt* mover à força de braço; (*treat roughly*) tratar com brutalidade

manhole /'mænhəʊl/ *n* poço *m* de inspeção, (P) inspecção

manhood /'mænhʊd/ *n* idade adulta *f*; (*quality*) virilidade *f*

mania /'meɪnɪə/ *n* mania *f*. ~c /-ɪæk/ *n* maníaco *m*

manicur|e /'mænɪkjʊə(r)/ *n* manicure *f* □ *vt* fazer. ~ist *n* manicure *m*

manifest /'mænɪfest/ a manifes to □ vt manifestar. **~ation** /-'steɪʃn/ n manifestação f

manifesto /mænɪ'festəʊ/ n (pl -os) manifesto m

manipulat|e /mə'nɪpjʊleɪt/ vt manipular. **~ion** /-'leɪʃn/ n manipulação f

mankind /mæn'kaɪnd/ n humanidade f, gênero m, (P) género m humano

manly /'mænlɪ/ a viril, másculo

manner /'mænə(r)/ n maneira f, modo m; (attitude) modo(s) m (pl); (kind) espécie f. **~s** maneiras fpl. **bad ~s** má-criação f, falta f de educação. **good ~s** (boa) educação f. **~ed** a afetado.

mannerism /'mænərɪzəm/ n maneirismo m

manoeuvre /mə'nuːvə(r)/ n manobra f □ vt/i manobrar

manor /'mænə(r)/ n solar m

manpower /'mænpaʊə(r)/ n mão-de-obra f

mansion /'mænʃn/ n mansão f

manslaughter /'mænslɔːtə(r)/ n homicídio m involuntário

mantelpiece /'mæntlpiːs/ n (shelf) consolo m da lareira, (P) prateleira f da chaminé

manual /'mænjʊəl/ a manual □ n manual m

manufacture /mænjʊ'fæktʃə(r)/ vt fabricar □ n fabrico m, fabricação f. **~r** /-ə(r)/ n fabricante mf

manure /mə'njʊə(r)/ n estrume m

manuscript /'mænjʊskrɪpt/ n manuscrito m

many /'menɪ/ a (more, most) muitos □ n muitos; (many people) muita gente f. **a great ~** muitíssimos. **~ a man/tear/etc** muitos homens/muitas lágrimas/etc. **you may take as ~ as you want** você pode levar quantos quiser. **~ of us/them/you** muitos de nós/deles/de vocês. **how ~?** quantos? **one too ~** um a mais

map /mæp/ n mapa m □ vt (pt mapped) fazer mapa de. **~ out** planear em pormenor; (route) traçar

maple /'meɪpl/ n bordo m

mar /mɑː(r)/ vt (pt marred) estragar; (beauty) desfigurar

marathon /'mærəθən/ n maratona f

marble /'mɑːbl/ n mármore m; (for game) bola f de gude, (P) berlinde m

March /mɑːtʃ/ n março m

march /mɑːtʃ/ vi marchar □ vt **~ off** fazer marchar, conduzir à força. **he was ~ed off to prison** fizeram-no marchar para a prisão □ n marcha f. **~-past** n desfile m em revista militar

mare /meə(r)/ n égua f

margarine /mɑːdʒə'riːn/ n margarina f

margin /'mɑːdʒɪn/ n margem f. **~al** a marginal. **~al seat** (pol) lugar m ganho com pequena maioria. **~ally** adv por uma pequena margem, muito pouco

marigold /'mærɪɡəʊld/ n cravo-de-defunto m, (P) malmequer m

marijuana /mærɪ'wɑːnə/ n maconha f

marina /mə'riːnə/ n marina f

marinade /mærɪ'neɪd/ n vinha d'alho, escalabeche m □ vt pôr na vinha d'alho

marine /mə'riːn/ a marinho; (of ship, trade etc) marítimo □ n (shipping) marinha f; (sailor) fuzileiro m naval

marionette /mærɪə'net/ n fantoche m, marionete f

marital /'mærɪtl/ a marital, conjugal, matrimonial. **~ status** estado m civil

maritime /'mærɪtaɪm/ a marítimo

mark¹ /mɑːk/ n (currency) marco m

mark² /mɑːk/ n marca f; (trace) marca f, sinal m; (stain) mancha f; (schol) nota f; (target) alvo m □ vt marcar; (exam etc) marcar, classificar. **~ out** marcar. **~ out for** escolher para, designar para. **~ time** marcar passo. **make one's ~** ganhar nome. **~er** n marcador m. **~ing** n marcas fpl, marcação f

marked /mɑːkt/ a marcado. **~ly** /-ɪdlɪ/ adv manifestamente, visivelmente

market /'mɑːkɪt/ n mercado m □ vt vender; (launch) comercializar, lançar. **~ garden** horta f de legumes para a venda. **~-place** n mercado m. **~ research** pesquisa f de mercado. **on the ~** à venda. **~ing** n marketing m

marksman /'mɑːksmən/ n (pl -men) atirador m especial

marmalade /'mɑːməleɪd/ n compota f de laranja

maroon /mə'ruːn/ a & n bordô (m), (P) bordeaux (m)

marooned /mə'ruːnd/ a abandonado em ilha, costa deserta etc; (fig: stranded) encalhado (fig)

marquee /mɑː'kiː/ n barraca f ou tenda f grande; (Amer: awning) toldo m

marriage /'mærɪdʒ/ n casamento m, matrimônio m, (P) matrimónio m. **~ certificate** certidão f de casamento. **~able** a casadouro

marrow /'mærəʊ/ n (of bone) tutano m, medula f, (vegetable) abóbora f. **chilled to the ~** gelado até os ossos

marr|y /'mærɪ/ vt casar(-se) com; (give or unite in marriage) casar □ vi casar-se. **~ied** a casado; (life) de casado, conjugal. **get ~ied** casar-se

Mars /mɑːz/ n Marte m

marsh /maːʃ/ n pântano m. ~y a pantanoso

marshal /ˈmaːʃl/ n (mil) marechal m; (steward) mestre m de cerimónias, (P) cerimónias □ vt (pt **marshalled**) dispor em ordem, ordenar; (usher) conduzir, escoltar

marshmallow /maːʃˈmæləu/ n marshmallow m

martial /ˈmaːʃl/ a marcial. ~ **law** lei f marcial

martyr /ˈmaːtə(r)/ n mártir mf □ vt martirizar. ~**dom** n martírio m

marvel /ˈmaːvl/ n maravilha f, prodígio m □ vi (pt **marvelled**) (feel wonder) maravilhar-se (**at** com); (be astonished) pasmar (**at** com)

marvellous /ˈmaːvələs/ a maravilhoso

Marxis|t /ˈmaːksɪst/ a & n marxista (mf). ~**m** /-zəm/ n marxismo m

marzipan /ˈmaːzɪpæn/ n maçapão m

mascara /mæˈskaːrə/ n rímel m

mascot /ˈmæskət/ n mascote f

masculin|e /ˈmæskjulɪn/ a masculino □ n masculino m. ~**ity** /-ˈlɪnətɪ/ n masculinidade f

mash /mæʃ/ n (pulp) papa f □ n esmagar. ~**ed potatoes** purê m de batata(s)

mask /maːsk/ n máscara f □ vt mascarar

masochis|t /ˈmæsəkɪst/ n masoquista mf. ~**m** /-zəm/ n masoquismo m

mason /ˈmeɪsn/ n maçom m; (building) pedreiro m. ~**ry** n maçonaria f; (building) alvenaria f

Mason /ˈmeɪsn/ n Maçónico m, (P) Maçónico m. ~**ic** /məˈsɒnɪk/ a Maçónico, (P) Maçónico

masquerade /mæːskəˈreɪd/ n mascarada f □ vi ~ **as** mascarar-se de, disfarçar-se de

mass[1] /mæs/ n (relig) missa f

mass[2] /mæs/ n massa f; (heap) montão m □ vt/i aglomerar(-se), reunir(-se) em massa. ~**-produce** vt produzir em série. **the** ~**es** as massas, a grande massa

massacre /ˈmæsəkə(r)/ n massacre m □ vt massacrar

massage /ˈmæsaːʒ/ n massagem f □ vt massagear, fazer massagens em, (P) dar massagens a

masseu|r /mæˈsɜː(r)/ n massagista m. ~**se** /mæˈsɜːz/ n massagista f

massive /ˈmæsɪv/ a (heavy) maciço; (huge) enorme

mast /maːst/ n mastro m; (for radio etc) antena f

master /ˈmaːstə(r)/ n (in school) professor m, mestre m; (expert) mestre m; (boss) patrão m; (owner) dono m. **M**~ (boy) menino m □ vt dominar. ~**-key**

n chave-mestra f. ~**-mind** n (of scheme etc) cérebro m □ vt planejar, dirigir. **M**~ **of Arts**/etc Licenciado m em Letras/etc. ~**-stroke** n golpe m de mestre. ~**y** n domínio m (over sobre); (knowledge) conhecimento m; (skill) perícia f

masterly /ˈmaːstəlɪ/ a magistral

masterpiece /ˈmaːstəpiːs/ n obra-prima f

masturbat|e /ˈmæstəbeɪt/ vi masturbar-se. ~**ion** /-ˈbeɪʃn/ n masturbação f

mat /mæt/ n tapete m pequeno; (at door) capacho m. (**table-**)~ n (of cloth) paninho m de mesa; (for hot dishes) descanso m para pratos

match[1] /mætʃ/ n fósforo m

match[2] /mætʃ/ n (contest) competição f, torneio m; (game) partida f; (equal) par m, parceiro m, igual mf; (fig: marriage) casamento m; (marriage partner) partido m □ vt/i (set against) contrapôr (**against** a); (equal) igualar; (go with) condizer; (be alike) ir com, emparceirar com. **her shoes** ~**ed her bag** os sapatos dela combinavam com a bolsa. ~**ing** a condizente, a condizer

matchbox /ˈmætʃbɒks/ n caixa f de fósforos

mat|e[1] /meɪt/ n companheiro m, camarada mf; (of birds, animals) macho m, fêmea f; (assistant) ajudante mf □ vt/i acasalar(-se) (**with** com). ~**ing season** n época f de cio

mate[2] /meɪt/ n (chess) mate m, xeque-mate m

material /məˈtɪərɪəl/ n material m; (fabric) tecido m; (equipment) apetrechos mpl □ a material; (significant) importante

materialis|m /məˈtɪərɪəlɪzəm/ n materialismo m. ~**tic** /-ˈlɪstɪk/ a materialista

materialize /məˈtɪərɪəlaɪz/ vi realizar-se, concretizar-se; (appear) aparecer

maternal /məˈtɜːnl/ a maternal

maternity /məˈtɜːnətɪ/ n maternidade f □ a (clothes) de grávida. ~ **hospital** maternidade f. ~ **leave** licença f de maternidade

mathematic|s /mæθəˈmætɪks/ n matemática f. ~**al** a matemático. ~**ian** /-əˈtɪʃn/ n matemático m.

maths /mæθs/ n (colloq) matemática f

matinée /ˈmætɪneɪ/ n matinê f, (P) matinée f

matrimon|y /ˈmætrɪmənɪ/ n matrimónio m, (P) matrimónio m. ~**ial** /-ˈməunɪəl/ a matrimonial, conjugal

matrix /ˈmeɪtrɪks/ n (pl **matrices** /-siːz/) matriz f

matron /'meɪtrən/ *n* matrona *f*; (*in school*) inspetora *f*; (*former use: senior nursing officer*) enfermeira-chefe *f*. ~**ly** *a* respeitável, muito digno

matt /mæt/ *a* fosco, sem brilho

matted /'mætɪd/ *a* emaranhado

matter /'mætə(r)/ *n* (*substance*) matéria *f*; (*affair*) assunto *m*, caso *m*, questão *f*; (*pus*) pus *m* □ *vi* importar. **as a ~ of fact** na verdade. **it does not ~** não importa. ~**-of-fact** *a* prosaico, terra-a-terra. **no ~ what happens** não importa o que acontecer. **what is the ~**? o que é que há? **what is the ~ with you**? o que é que você tem?

mattress /'mætrɪs/ *n* colchão *m*

mature /mə'tʃʊə(r)/ *a* maduro, amadurecido □ *vt/i* amadurecer; (*comm*) vencer-se. ~**ity** *n* madureza *f*, maturidade *f*; (*comm*) vencimento *m*

maul /mɔːl/ *vt* maltratar, atacar

Mauritius /mə'rɪʃəs/ *n* Ilha *f* Maurícia

mausoleum /mɔːsə'lɪəm/ *n* mausoléu *m*

mauve /məʊv/ *a & n* lilás (*m*)

maxim /'mæksɪm/ *n* máxima *f*

maximum /'mæksɪməm/ *a & n* (*pl* -ima) máximo (*m*). ~**ize** *vt* aumentar ao máximo, maximizar

may /meɪ/ *v aux* (*pt* **might**) poder. **he ~/might come** talvez venha/viesse. **you might have** podia ter. **you ~ leave** pode ir. ~ **I smoke**? posso fumar?, dá licença que eu fume? ~ **he be happy** que ele esteja feliz. **I ~ or might as well go** talvez seja *or* fosse melhor eu ir

May /meɪ/ *n* maio *n*. ~ **Day** o primeiro de maio

maybe /'meɪbi:/ *adv* talvez

mayhem /'meɪhem/ *n* (*disorder*) distúrbios *mpl* violentos; (*havoc*) estragos *mpl*

mayonnaise /meɪə'neɪz/ *n* maionese *f*

mayor /meə(r)/ *n* prefeito *m*. ~**ess** *n* prefeita *f*; (*mayor's wife*) mulher *f* do prefeito

maze /meɪz/ *n* labirinto *m*

me /mi:/ *pron* me; (*after prep*) mim. **with ~** comigo. **he knows ~** ele me conhece. **it's ~** sou eu

meadow /'medəʊ/ *n* prado *m*, campina *f*

meagre /'miːgə(r)/ *a* (*thin*) magro; (*scanty*) escasso

meal¹ /mi:l/ *n* refeição *f*

meal² /mi:l/ *n* (*grain*) farinha *f* grossa

mean¹ /mi:n/ *a* (-**er**, -**est**) mesquinho; (*unkind*) mau. ~**ness** *n* mesquinhez *f*

mean² /mi:n/ *a* médio □ *n* média *f*. **Greenwich ~ time** tempo *m* médio de Greenwich

mean³ /mi:n/ *vt* (*pt* **meant**) (*intend*) tencionar *or* ter (a) intenção (**to** de); (*signify*) querer dizer, significar; (*entail*) dar em resultado, resultar provavelmente em; (*refer to*) referir-se a. **be meant for** destinar-se a. **I didn't ~ it** desculpe, foi sem querer. **he ~s what he says** ele está falando sério

meander /mɪ'ændə(r)/ *vi* serpentear; (*wander*) perambular

meaning /'miːnɪŋ/ *n* sentido *m*, significado *m*. ~**ful** *a* significativo. ~**less** *a* sem sentido

means /mi:nz/ *n* meio/s (*m*)(*pl*) □ *npl* meios *mpl* pecuniários, recursos *mpl*. **by all ~** com certeza. **by ~ of** por meio de, através de. **by no ~** de modo nenhum

meant /ment/ *see* **mean³**

meantime /'miːntaɪm/ *adv* (**in the**) ~**time** entretanto. ~**while** /-waɪl/ *adv* entretanto

measles /'miːzlz/ *n* sarampo *m*. **German ~** rubéola *f*

measly /'miːzlɪ/ *a* (*sl*) miserável, ínfimo

measurable /'meʒərəbl/ *a* mensurável

measure /'meʒə(r)/ *n* medida *f* □ *vt/i* medir. **made to ~** feito sob medida. ~ **up to** mostrar-se à altura de. ~**d** *a* medido, calculado. ~**ment** *n* medida *f*

meat /mi:t/ *n* carne *f*. ~**y** *a* carnudo; (*fig: substantial*) substancial

mechanic /mɪ'kænɪk/ *n* mecânico *m*

mechanical /mɪ'kænɪkl/ *a* mecânico. ~**s** *n* mecânica *f*; *npl* mecanismo *m*

mechanism /'mekənɪzəm/ *n* mecanismo *m*. ~**ize** *vt* mecanizar

medal /'medl/ *n* medalha *f*. ~**list** *n* condecorado *m*. **be a gold ~list** ser medalha de ouro

medallion /mɪ'dælɪən/ *n* medalhão *m*

meddle /'medl/ *vi* (*interfere*) imiscuir-se, intrometer-se (**in** em); (*tinker*) mexer (**with** em). ~**some** *a* intrometido, abelhudo

media /'miːdɪə/ *see* **medium** □ *npl* **the ~** a média, os meios de comunicação social *or* de massa

mediate /'miːdɪeɪt/ *vi* servir de intermediário, mediar. ~**ion** /-'eɪʃn/ *n* mediação *f*. ~**or** *n* mediador *m*, intermediário *m*

medical /'medɪkl/ *a* médico □ *n* (*colloq: examination*) exame *m* médico

medicated /'medɪkeɪtɪd/ *a* medicinal. ~**ion** /-'keɪʃn/ *n* medicamentação *f*

medicinal /mɪ'dɪsɪnl/ *a* medicinal

medicine /'medsn/ *n* medicina *f*; (*substance*) remédio *m*, medicamento *m*

medieval /medɪ'iːvl/ *a* medieval

mediocre /miːdɪ'əʊkə(r)/ *a* medíocre. ~**ity** /-'ɒkrətɪ/ *n* mediocridade *f*

meditat|e /'mediteit/ *vt/i* meditar. ~**ion** /-'teiʃn/ *n* meditação *f*

Mediterranean /meditə'reiniən/ *a* mediterrâneo □ *n* the ~ o Mediterrâneo

medium /'mi:diəm/ *n* (*pl* media) meio *m*; (*pl* mediums) (*person*) médium *mf* □ *a* médio. ~ **wave** (*radio*) onda *f* média. the happy ~ o meio-termo

medley /'medli/ *n* (*pl* -eys) miscelânea *f*

meek /mi:k/ *a* (-er, -est) manso, submisso, sofrido

meet /mi:t/ *vt* (*pt* met) encontrar; (*intentionally*) encontrar-se com, ir ter com; (*at station etc*) ir esperar, ir buscar; (*make the acquaintance of*) conhecer; (*conform with*) ir ao encontro de, satisfazer; (*opponent, obligation etc*) fazer face a; (*bill, expenses*) pagar □ *vi* encontrar-se; (*get acquainted*) familiarizar-se; (*in session*) reunir-se. ~ **with** encontrar; (*accident, misfortune*) sofrer, ter

meeting /'mi:tɪŋ/ *n* reunião *f*, encontro *m*; (*between two people*) encontro *m*. ~**-place** *n* ponto *m* de encontro

megalomania /megaləu'meiniə/ *n* megalomania *f*, mania *f* de grandezas

megaphone /'megafəun/ *n* megafone *m*, porta-voz *m*

melancholy /'melənkɒli/ *n* melancolia *f* □ *a* melancólico

mellow /'meləu/ *a* (-er, -est) (*fruit, person*) amadurecido, maduro; (*sound, colour*) quente, suave □ *vt/i* amadurecer; (*soften*) suavizar

melodious /mɪ'ləudiəs/ *a* melodioso

melodrama /'meladra:mə/ *n* melodrama *m*. ~**tic** /-ə'mætik/ *a* melodramático

melod|y /'meladi/ *n* melodia *f*. ~**ic** /mɪ'lɒdɪk/ *a* melódico

melon /'melən/ *n* melão *m*

melt /melt/ *vt/i* (*metals*) fundir(-se); (*butter, snow etc*) derreter (-se), (*fade away*) desvanecer (-se). ~**ing-pot** *n* cadinho *m*

member /'membə(r)/ *n* membro *m*; (*of club etc*) sócio *m*. M~ **of Parliament** deputado *m*. ~**ship** *n* qualidade *f* de sócio; (*members*) número *m* de sócios; (*fee*) cota *f*. ~**ship card** carteira *f*, (*P*) cartão *m* de sócio

membrane /'membrein/ *n* membrana *f*

memento /mɪ'mentəu/ *n* (*pl* -oes) lembrança *f*, recordação *f*

memo /'meməu/ *n* (*pl* -os) (*colloq*) nota *f*, apontamento *m*, lembrete *m*

memoir /'memwa:(r)/ *n* (*record, essay*) memória *f*, memorial *m*; ~**s** *npl* (*autobiography*) memórias *fpl*

memorable /'memərəbl/ *a* memorável

memorandum /memə'rændəm/ *n* (*pl* -da *or* -dums) nota *f*, lembrete *m*; (*diplomatic*) memorando *m*

memorial /mɪ'mɔ:riəl/ *n* monumento *m* comemorativo □ *a* comemorativo

memorize /'meməraɪz/ *vt* decorar, memorizar, aprender de cor

memory /'meməri/ *n* memória *f*. from ~ de memória, de cor. in ~ of em memória de

men /men/ *see* man

menac|e /'menəs/ *n* ameaça *f*; (*nuisance*) praga *f*, chaga *f* □ *vt* ameaçar. ~**ingly** *adv* ameaçadoramente, de modo ameaçador

menagerie /mɪ'nædʒəri/ *n* coleção *f*, (*P*) colecção *f* de animais ferozes em jaulas

mend /mend/ *vt* consertar, reparar; (*darn*) remendar □ *n* conserto *m*; (*darn*) remendo *m*. ~ **one's ways** corrigir-se, emendar-se. on the ~ melhorando

menial /'mi:niəl/ *a* humilde

meningitis /menin'dʒaɪtɪs/ *n* meningite *f*

menopause /'menəpɔ:z/ *n* menopausa *f*

menstruation /menstru'eiʃn/ *n* menstruação *f*

mental /'mentl/ *a* mental; (*hospital*) de doentes mentais, psiquiátrico

mentality /men'tæləti/ *n* mentalidade *f*

mention /'menʃn/ *vt* mencionar □ *n* menção *f*. don't ~ it! não tem de quê, de nada

menu /'menju:/ *n* (*pl* -us) menu *m*, (*P*) ementa *f*

mercenary /'mɜ:snəri/ *a* & *n* mercenário (*m*)

merchandise /'mɜ:tʃəndaɪz/ *n* mercadorias *fpl* □ *vt/i* negociar

merchant /'mɜ:tʃənt/ *n* mercador *m* □ *a* (*ship, navy*) mercante. ~ **bank** banco *m* comercial

merciful /'mɜ:sɪfl/ *a* misericordioso

merciless /'mɜ:sɪlɪs/ *a* impiedoso, sem dó

mercury /'mɜ:kjʊri/ *n* mercúrio *m*

mercy /'mɜ:sɪ/ *n* piedade *f*, misericórdia *f*. at the ~ of à mercê de

mere /mɪə(r)/ *a* mero, simples. ~**ly** *adv* meramente, simplesmente, apenas

merge /mɜ:dʒ/ *vt/i* fundir(-se), amalgamar(-se); (*comm: companies*) fundir(-se). ~**r** /-ə(r)/ *n* fusão *f*

meringue /mə'ræŋ/ *n* merengue *m*, suspiro *m*

merit /'merit/ *n* mérito *m* □ *vt* (*pt* merited) merecer

mermaid /'mɜ:meɪd/ n sereia f
merriment /'merɪmənt/ n divertimento m, alegria f, folguedo m
merry /'merɪ/ a (**-ier, -iest**) alegre, divertido. ~ **Christmas** Feliz Natal. ~**-go-round** n carrossel m. ~**making** n festa f, divertimento m. **merrily** adv alegremente
mesh /meʃ/ n malha f. ~**es** npl (network; fig) malhas fpl.
mesmerize /'mezmraɪz/ vt hipnotizar
mess /mes/ n (disorder) desordem f, trapalhada f; (trouble) embrulhada f, trapalhada f; (dirt) porcaria f; (mil: place) cantina f; (mil: food) rancho m □ vt ~ **up** (make untidy) desarrumar; (make dirty) sujar; (confuse) atrapalhar, estragar □ vi ~ **about** perder tempo; (behave foolishly) fazer asneiras. ~ **about with** (tinker with) entreter-se com, andar às voltas com. **make a** ~ **of** estragar
message /'mesɪdʒ/ n mensagem f; (informal) recado m
messenger /'mesɪndʒə(r)/ n mensageiro m
Messiah /mɪ'saɪə/ n Messias m
messy /'mesɪ/ a (**-ier, -iest**) desarrumado, bagunçado; (dirty) sujo, porco
met /met/ see **meet**
metabolism /mɪ'tæbəlɪzm/ n metabolismo m
metal /'metl/ n metal m □ a de metal. ~**lic** /mɪ'tælɪk/ a metálico; (paint, colour) metalizado
metamorphosis /metə'mɔ:fəsɪs/ n (pl **-phoses** /-si:z/) metamorfose f
metaphor /'metəfə(r)/ n metáfora f. ~**ical** /-'fɒrɪkl/ a metafórico
meteor /'mi:tɪə(r)/ n meteoro m
meteorolog|y /mi:tɪə'rɒlədʒɪ/ n meteorologia f. ~**ical** /-ə'lɒdʒɪkl/ a meteorológico
meter[1] /'mi:tə(r)/ n contador m
meter[2] /'mi:tə(r)/ n (Amer) = **metre**
method /'meθəd/ n método m
methodical /mɪ'θɒdɪkl/ a metódico
Methodist /'meθədɪst/ n metodista mf
methylated /'meθɪleɪtɪd/ a ~ **spirit** álcool m metílico
meticulous /mɪ'tɪkjʊləs/ a meticuloso
metre /'mi:tə(r)/ n metro m
metric /'metrɪk/ a métrico. ~**ation** /-'keɪʃn/ n conversão f para o sistema métrico
metropol|is /mə'trɒpəlɪs/ n metrópole f. ~**itan** /metrə'pɒlɪtən/ a metropolitano
mettle /'metl/ n têmpera f, caráter m, (P) carácter m; (spirit) brio m
mew /mju:/ n miado m □ vi miar
Mexic|o /'meksɪkəʊ/ n México m. ~**an** a & n mexicano (m)

miaow /mi:'aʊ/ n & vi = **mew**
mice /maɪs/ see **mouse**
mickey /'mɪkɪ/ n **take the** ~ **out of** (sl) fazer troça de, gozar (colloq)
micro- /'maɪkrəʊ/ pref micro-
microbe /'maɪkrəʊb/ n micróbio m
microchip /'maɪkrəʊtʃɪp/ n microchip m
microcomputer /'maɪkrəʊkəmpju:tə(r)/ n microcomputador m
microfilm /'maɪkrəʊfɪlm/ n microfilme m
microlight /'maɪkrəʊlaɪt/ n (aviat) ultraleve m
microphone /'maɪkrəfəʊn/ n microfone m
microprocessor /maɪkrəʊ'prəʊsesə(r)/ n microprocessador m
microscop|e /'maɪkrəskəʊp/ n microscópio m. ~**ic** /'skɒpɪk/ a microscópico
microwave /'maɪkrəʊweɪv/ n microonda f. ~ **oven** forno m de microondas
mid /mɪd/ a meio. **in** ~**-air** no ar, em pleno vôo. **in** ~**-March** em meados de março
midday /mɪd'deɪ/ n meio-dia m
middle /'mɪdl/ a médio, meio; (quality) médio, mediano □ n meio m. **in the** ~ **of** no meio de. ~**-aged** a de meia idade. **M**~ **Ages** Idade f Média. ~ **class** classe f média. ~**-class** a burguês. **M**~ **East** Médio Oriente m. ~ **name** segundo nome m
middleman /'mɪdlmæn/ n (pl **-men**) intermediário m
midge /mɪdʒ/ n mosquito m
midget /'mɪdʒɪt/ n anão m □ a minúsculo
Midlands /'mɪdləndz/ npl região f do centro da Inglaterra
midnight /'mɪdnaɪt/ n meia-noite f
midriff /'mɪdrɪf/ n diafragma m; (abdomen) ventre m
midst /mɪdst/ n **in the** ~ **of** no meio de
midsummer /mɪd'sʌmə(r)/ n pleno verão m; (solstice) solstício m do verão
midway /mɪd'weɪ/ adv a meio caminho
midwife /'mɪdwaɪf/ n (pl **-wives**) parteira f
might[1] /maɪt/ n potência f; (strength) força f. ~**y** a poderoso; (fig: great) imenso □ adv (colloq) muito
might[2] /maɪt/ see **may**
migraine /'mi:greɪn/ n enxaqueca f
migrant /'maɪɡrənt/ a migratório □ n (person) migrante mf, emigrante mf
migrat|e /maɪ'ɡreɪt/ vi migrar. ~**ion** /-ʃn/ n migração f
mike /maɪk/ n (colloq) microfone m

mild /maɪld/ a (**-er, -est**) brando, manso; (*illness, taste*) leve; (*climate*) temperado; (*weather*) ameno. **~ly** adv brandamente, mansamente. **to put it ~ly** para não dizer coisa pior. **~ness** n brandura f

mildew /ˈmɪldjuː/ n bolor m, mofo m; (*in plants*) míldio m

mile /maɪl/ n milha f (= 1.6 km). **~s too big/etc** (*colloq*) grande demais. **~age** n (*loosely*) quilometragem f

milestone /ˈmaɪlstəʊn/ n marco m miliário; (*fig*) data f or acontecimento m importante

militant /ˈmɪlɪtənt/ a & n militante (mf)

military /ˈmɪlɪtrɪ/ a militar

militate /ˈmɪlɪteɪt/ vi militar. **~ against** militar contra

milk /mɪlk/ n leite m □ a (*product*) lácteo □ vt ordenhar; (*fig: exploit*) explorar. **~-shake** n milk-shake m, leite m batido. **~y** a (*like milk*) leitoso; (*tea etc*) com muito leite. **M~ Way** Via f Láctea

milkman /ˈmɪlkmən/ n (pl **-men**) leiteiro m

mill /mɪl/ n moinho m; (*factory*) fábrica f □ vt moer □ vi **~ around** aglomerar-se; (*crowd*) apinhar-se, (P) agitar-se. **~er** n moleiro m. **pepper-~** n moedor m de pimenta

millennium /mɪˈlenɪəm/ n (pl **-iums** or **-ia**) milénio m, (P) milénio m

millet /ˈmɪlɪt/ n painço m, milhete m

milli- /ˈmɪlɪ/ pref mili-

milligram /ˈmɪlɪgræm/ n miligrama m

millilitre /ˈmɪlɪliːtə(r)/ n mililitro m

millimetre /ˈmɪlɪmiːtə(r)/ n milímetro m

million /ˈmɪljən/ n milhão m. **a ~ pounds** um milhão de libras. **~aire** /-ˈneə(r)/ n milionário m

millstone /ˈmɪlstəʊn/ n mó f. **a ~ round one's neck** um peso nos ombros

mime /maɪm/ n mímica f; (*actor*) mímico m □ vt/i exprimir por mímica, mimar

mimic /ˈmɪmɪk/ vt (pt **mimicked**) imitar □ n imitador m, parodiante mf. **~ry** n imitação f

mince /mɪns/ vt picar □ n carne f moída, (P) carne f picada. **~-pie** n pastel m recheado com massa de passas, amêndoas, especiarias etc. **~r** n máquina f de moer

mincemeat /ˈmɪnsmiːt/ n massa f de passas, amêndoas, especiarias etc usada para recheio. **make ~ of** (*colloq*) arrasar, aniquilar

mind n espírito m, mente f; (*intellect*) intelecto m; (*sanity*) razão f □ vt (*look*

after) tomar conta de, tratar de; (*heed*) prestar atenção a; (*object to*) importar-se com, incomodar-se com. **do you ~ if I smoke?** você se incomoda que eu fume? **do you ~ helping me?** quer fazer o favor de me ajudar? **never ~** não se importe, não tem importância. **to be out of one's ~** estar fora de si, louco. **have a good ~ to** estar disposto a. **make up one's ~** decidir-se. **presence of ~** presença f de espírito. **to my ~** a meu ver. **~ful of** atento a, consciente de. **~less** a insensato

minder /ˈmaɪndə(r)/ n pessoa f que toma conta mf; (*bodyguard*) guarda-costa mf, (P) guarda-costas mf

mine¹ /maɪn/ poss pron o(s) meu(s), a(s) minha(s). **it is ~** é (o) meu or (a) minha

min|e² /maɪn/ n mina f □ vt escavar, explorar; (*extract*) extrair; (*mil*) minar. **~er** n mineiro m. **~ing** n exploração f mineira □ a mineiro

minefield /ˈmaɪnfiːld/ n campo m minado

mineral /ˈmɪnərəl/ n mineral m; (*soft drink*) bebida f gasosa. **~ water** água f mineral

minesweeper /ˈmaɪnswiːpə(r)/ n caça-minas m

mingle /ˈmɪŋgl/ vt/i misturar(-se) (**with** com)

mingy /ˈmɪndʒɪ/ a (**-ier, -iest**) (*colloq*) sovina, unha(s)-de-fome (*colloq*)

mini- /ˈmɪnɪ/ pref mini-

miniature /ˈmɪnɪtʃə(r)/ n miniatura f □ a miniatural

minibus /ˈmɪnɪbʌs/ n (*public*) microónibus m, (P) autocarro m pequeno

minim /ˈmɪnɪm/ n (*mus*) mínima f

minim|um /ˈmɪnɪməm/ a & n (pl **-ma**) mínimo (m). **~al** a mínimo. **~ize** vt minimizar, dar pouca importância a

miniskirt /ˈmɪnɪskɜːt/ n minissaia f

minist|er /ˈmɪnɪstə(r)/ n ministro m; (*relig*) pastor m. **~erial** /-ˈstɪərɪəl/ a ministerial. **~ry** n ministério m

mink /mɪŋk/ n (*fur*) marta f, visão m

minor /ˈmaɪnə(r)/ a & n menor (mf)

minority /maɪˈnɒrətɪ/ n minoria f □ a minoritário

mint¹ /mɪnt/ n **the M~** a Casa da Moeda. **a ~** uma fortuna □ vt cunhar. **in ~ condition** em perfeito estado, como novo, impecável

mint² /mɪnt/ n (*plant*) hortelã f; (*sweet*) pastilha f de hortelã

minus /ˈmaɪnəs/ prep menos; (*colloq: without*) sem □ n menos m

minute¹ /ˈmɪnɪt/ n minuto m. **~s** (*of meeting*) ata f, (P) acta f

minute² /marˈnjuːt/ a diminuto, minúsculo; (*detailed*) minucioso

mirac|le /ˈmɪrəkl/ n milagre m. ~**ulous** /mɪˈrækjʊləs/ a milagroso, miraculoso

mirage /ˈmɪraːʒ/ n miragem f

mire /maɪə(r)/ n lodo m, lama f

mirror /ˈmɪrə(r)/ n espelho m; (*in car*) retrovisor m □ vt refletir, (P) reflectir, espelhar

mirth /mɜːθ/ n alegria f, hilaridade f

misadventure /mɪsədˈventʃə(r)/ n desgraça f. death by ~ morte f acidental

misanthropist /mɪsˈænθrəpɪst/ n misantropo m

misapprehension /mɪsæprɪˈhenʃn/ n mal-entendido m

misbehav|e /mɪsbɪˈheɪv/ vi portar-se mal, proceder mal. ~**iour** /-ˈheɪvɪə(r)/ n mau comportamento m, má conduta f

miscalculat|e /mɪsˈkælkjʊleɪt/ vi calcular mal, enganar-se. ~**ion** /-ˈleɪʃn/ n erro m de cálculo

miscarr|y /mɪsˈkærɪ/ vi abortar, ter um aborto; (*fail*) falhar, malograrse. ~**iage** /-ɪdʒ/ n aborto m. ~**iage of justice** erro m judiciário

miscellaneous /mɪsəˈleɪnɪəs/ a variado, diverso

mischief /ˈmɪstʃɪf/ n (*of children*) diabrura f, travessura f; (*harm*) mal m, dano m. get **into** ~ fazer disparates. make ~ criar or semear discórdias

mischievous /ˈmɪstʃɪvəs/ a endiabrado, travesso

misconception /mɪskənˈsepʃn/ n idéia f errada, falso conceito m

misconduct /mɪsˈkɒndʌkt/ n conduta f imprópria

misconstrue /mɪskənˈstruː/ vt interpretar mal

misdeed /mɪsˈdiːd/ n má ação f, (P) acção f, (*crime*) crime m

misdemeanour /mɪsdɪˈmiːnə(r)/ n delito m

miser /ˈmaɪzə(r)/ n avarento m, sovina mf. ~**ly** a avarento, sovina

miserable /ˈmɪzrəbl/ a infeliz; (*wretched, mean*) desgraçado, miserável

misery /ˈmɪzərɪ/ n infelicidade f

misfire /mɪsˈfaɪə(r)/ vi (*plan, gun, engine*) falhar

misfit /ˈmɪsfɪt/ n inadaptado m

misfortune /mɪsˈfɔːtʃən/ n desgraça f, infelicidade f, pouca sorte f

misgiving(s) /mɪsˈgɪvɪŋ(z)/ n(pl) dúvida(s) f(pl), receio(s) m(pl)

misguided /mɪsˈgaɪdɪd/ a (*mistaken*) desencaminhado; (*misled*) mal aconselhado, enganado

mishap /ˈmɪshæp/ n contratempo, desastre m

misinform /mɪsɪnˈfɔːm/ vt informar mal

misinterpret /mɪsɪnˈtɜːprɪt/ vt interpretar mal

misjudge /mɪsˈdʒʌdʒ/ vt julgar mal

mislay /mɪsˈleɪ/ vt (*pt* mislaid) perder, extraviar

mislead /mɪsˈliːd/ vt (*pt* misled) induzir em erro, enganar. ~**ing** a enganador

mismanage /mɪsˈmænɪdʒ/ vt dirigir mal. ~**ment** n má gestão f, desgoverno m

misnomer /mɪsˈnəʊmə(r)/ n termo m impróprio

misogynist /mɪˈsɒdʒɪnɪst/ n misógino m

misprint /ˈmɪsprɪnt/ n erro m tipográfico

mispronounce /mɪsprəˈnaʊns/ vt pronunciar mal

misquote /mɪsˈkwəʊt/ vt citar incorretamente

misread /mɪsˈriːd/ vt (*pt* misread /-ˈred/) ler or interpretar mal

misrepresent /mɪsreprɪˈzent/ vt deturpar, desvirtuar

miss /mɪs/ vt/i (*chance, bus etc*) perder; (*target*) errar, falhar; (*notice the loss of*) dar pela falta de; (*regret the absence of*) sentir a falta de, ter saudades de. he ~**es** her/Portugal/*etc* ele sente a falta *or* tem saudades dela/de Portugal/*etc* □ n falha f. it was a near ~ foi *or* escapou por um triz. ~ **out** omitir. ~ **the point** não compreender

Miss /mɪs/ n (*pl* Misses) Senhorita f, (P) Senhora f

misshapen /mɪsˈʃeɪpn/ a disforme

missile /ˈmɪsaɪl/ n míssil m; (*object thrown*) projétil m, (P) projéctil m

missing /ˈmɪsɪŋ/ a que falta; (*lost*) perdido; (*person*) desaparecido. a book with a page ~ um livro com uma página a menos

mission /ˈmɪʃn/ n missão f

missionary /ˈmɪʃənrɪ/ n missionário m

misspell /mɪsˈspel/ vt (*pt* misspelt *or* misspelled) escrever mal

mist /mɪst/ n neblina f, névoa f, bruma f; (*fig*) névoa f □ vt/i enevoar(-se); (*window*) embaçar(-se)

mistake /mɪˈsteɪk/ n engano m, erro m □ vt (*pt* mistook, *pp* mistaken) compreender mal; (*choose wrongly*) enganar-se em. ~ **for** confundir com, tomar por. ~**n** /-ən/ a errado. be ~**n** enganar-se. ~**nly** /-ənlɪ/ adv por engano

mistletoe /ˈmɪsltəʊ/ n visco m

mistreat /mɪsˈtriːt/ vt maltratar. ~**ment** n mau trato m mistress /ˈmɪstrɪs/ n senhora f, dona f; (teacher) professora f; (lover) amante f

mistrust /mɪsˈtrʌst/ vt desconfiar de, duvidar de □ n desconfiança f

misty /ˈmɪstɪ/ a (-ier, -iest) enevoado, brumoso; (window) embaçado; (indistinct) indistinto

misunderstand /mɪsʌndəˈstænd/ vt (pt -stood) compreender mal. ~ing n mal-entendido m

misuse¹ /mɪsˈjuːz/ vt empregar mal; (power etc) abusar de

misuse² /mɪsˈjuːs/ n mau uso m; (abuse) abuso m; (of funds) desvio m

mitigat|e /ˈmɪtɪɡeɪt/ vt atenuar, mitigar. ~ing circumstances circunstâncias fpl atenuantes

mitten /ˈmɪtn/ n luva f com uma única divisão entre o polegar e os dedos

mix /mɪks/ vt/i misturar(-se) □ n mistura f. ~ up misturar bem; (fig: confuse) confundir. ~-up n trapalhada f, confusão f. ~ with associar-se com. ~er n (culin) batedeira f

mixed /mɪkst/ a (school etc) misto; (assorted) sortido. be ~ up (colloq) estar confuso

mixture /ˈmɪkstʃə(r)/ n mistura f. cough ~ xarope m para a tosse

moan /məʊn/ n gemido m □ vi gemer; (complain) queixar-se, lastimar-se (about). ~er n pessoa f lamurienta

moat /məʊt/ n fosso m

mob /mɒb/ n multidão f; (tumultuous) turba f; (sl: gang) bando m □ vt (pt mobbed) cercar, assediar

mobil|e /ˈməʊbaɪl/ a móvel. ~e home caravana f, trailer m. ~ity /-ˈbɪlətɪ/ n mobilidade f

mobiliz|e /ˈməʊbɪlaɪz/ vt/i mobilizar. ~ation /-ˈzeɪʃn/ n mobilização f

moccasin /ˈmɒkəsɪn/ n mocassim m

mock /mɒk/ vt/i zombar de, gozar □ a falso. ~-up n modelo m, maqueta f

mockery /ˈmɒkərɪ/ n troça f, gozação f. a ~ of uma gozação de

mode /məʊd/ n modo m; (fashion) moda f

model /ˈmɒdl/ n modelo m □ a modelo; (exemplary) exemplar; (toy) em miniatura □ vt (pt modelled) modelar; (clothes) apresentar □ vi ser or trabalhar como modelo

modem /ˈməʊdem/ n modem m

moderate¹ /ˈmɒdərət/ a & n moderado (m). ~ly adv moderadamente. ~ly good sofrível

moderat|e² /ˈmɒdəreɪt/ vt/i moderar (-se). ~ion /-ˈreɪʃn/ n moderação f. in ~ion com moderação

modern /ˈmɒdn/ a moderno. ~ languages línguas fpl vivas. ~ize vt modernizar

modest /ˈmɒdɪst/ a modesto. ~y n modéstia f. ~ly adv modestamente

modicum /ˈmɒdɪkəm/ n a ~ of um pouco de

modif|y /ˈmɒdɪfaɪ/ vt modificar. ~ication /-ɪˈkeɪʃn/ n modificação f

modulat|e /ˈmɒdjʊleɪt/ vt/i modular. ~ion /-ˈleɪʃn/ n modulação f

module /ˈmɒdjuːl/ n módulo m

mohair /ˈməʊheə(r)/ n mohair m

moist /mɔɪst/ a (-er, -est) úmido, (P) húmido. ~ure /ˈmɔɪstʃə(r)/ n umidade f, (P) humidade f. ~urizer /-tʃəraɪzə(r)/ n creme m hidratante

moisten /ˈmɔɪsn/ vt/i umedecer, (P) humedecer

molasses /məˈlæsɪz/ n melaço m

mole¹ /məʊl/ n (on skin) sinal na pele m

mole² /məʊl/ n (animal) toupeira f

molecule /ˈmɒlɪkjuːl/ n molécula f

molest /məˈlest/ vt meter-se com, molestar

mollusc /ˈmɒləsk/ n molusco m

mollycoddle /ˈmɒlɪkɒdl/ vt mimar

molten /ˈməʊltən/ a fundido

moment /ˈməʊmənt/ n momento m

momentar|y /ˈməʊməntrɪ/ a momentâneo. ~ily /ˈməʊməntrəlɪ/ adv momentaneamente

momentous /məˈmentəs/ a grave, importante

momentum /məˈmentəm/ n ímpeto m, velocidade f adquirida

Monaco /ˈmɒnəkəʊ/ n Mónaco m

monarch /ˈmɒnək/ n monarca mf. ~y n monarquia f

monast|ery /ˈmɒnəstrɪ/ n mosteiro m, convento m. ~ic /məˈnæstɪk/ a monástico

Monday /ˈmʌndɪ/ n segunda-feira f

monetary /ˈmʌnɪtrɪ/ a monetário

money /ˈmʌnɪ/ n dinheiro m. ~-box n cofre m. ~-lender n agiota mf. ~ order vale m postal

mongrel /ˈmʌŋɡrəl/ n (cão) vira-lata m, (P) rafeiro m

monitor /ˈmɒnɪtə(r)/ n chefe m de turma; (techn) monitor m □ vt controlar; (a broadcast) monitorar (a transmissão)

monk /mʌŋk/ n monge m, frade m

monkey /ˈmʌŋkɪ/ n (pl -eys) macaco m. ~-nut n amendoim m. ~-wrench n chave f inglesa

mono /ˈmɒnəʊ/ n (pl -os) gravação f mono □ a mono invar

monocle /ˈmɒnəkl/ n monóculo m

monogram /ˈmɒnəɡræm/ n monograma m

monologue /ˈmɒnəlɒɡ/ n monólogo m

monopol|y /məˈnɒpəlɪ/ n monopólio m. ~ize vt monopolizar

monosyllab|le /ˈmɒnəsɪləbl/ n

monossilabo *m.* **~ic** /-'læbɪk/ *a* monossilábico

monotone /'mɒnətəʊn/ *n* tom *m* uniforme

monoton|ous /mə'nɒtənəs/ *a* monótono. **~y** *n* monotonia *f*

monsoon /mɒn'suːn/ *n* monção *f*

monst|er /'mɒnstə(r)/ *n* monstro *m*. **~rous** *a* monstruoso

monstrosity /mɒn'strɒsətɪ/ *n* monstruosidade *f*

month /mʌnθ/ *n* mês *m*

monthly /'mʌnθlɪ/ *a* mensal □ *adv* mensalmente □ *n* (*periodical*) revista *f* mensal

monument /'mɒnjʊmənt/ *n* monumento *m*. **~al** /-'mentl/ *a* monumental

moo /muː/ *n* mugido *m* □ *vi* mugir

mood /muːd/ *n* humor *m*, disposição *f*. **in a good/bad ~** de bom/mau humor. **~y** *a* de humor instável; (*sullen*) carrancudo

moon /muːn/ *n* lua *f*

moon\light /'muːnlaɪt/ *n* luar *m*. **~lit** *a* iluminado pela lua, enluarado

moonlighting /'muːnlaɪtɪŋ/ *n* (*colloq*) segundo emprego *m*, esp à noite

moor[1] /mʊə(r)/ *n* charneca *f*

moor[2] /mʊə(r)/ *vt* amarrar, atracar. **~ings** *npl* amarras *fpl*; (*place*) amarradouro *m*, fundeadouro *m*

moose /muːs/ *n* (*pl invar*) alce *m*

moot /muːt/ *a* discutível □ *vt* levantar

mop /mɒp/ *n* esfregão *m* □ *vt* (*pt* mopped) **~ (up)** limpar. **~ of hair** trunfa *f*

mope /məʊp/ *vi* estar *or* andar abatido e triste

moped /'məʊped/ *n* (bicicleta) motorizada *f*

moral /'mɒrəl/ *a* moral □ *n* moral *f*. **~s** moral *f*, bons costumes *mpl*. **~ize** *vi* moralizar. **~ly** *adv* moralmente

morale /mə'rɑːl/ *n* moral *m*

morality /mə'rælətɪ/ *n* moralidade *f*

morass /mə'ræs/ *n* pântano *m*

morbid /'mɔːbɪd/ *a* mórbido

more /mɔː(r)/ *a & adv* mais (**than** (do) que) □ *n* mais *m*. (**some**) **~ tea/pens**/*etc* mais chá/canetas/*etc*. **there is no ~ bread** não há mais pão. **~ or less** mais ou menos

moreover /mɔː'rəʊvə(r)/ *adv* além disso, de mais a mais

morgue /mɔːg/ *n* morgue *f*, necrotério *m*

moribund /'mɒrɪbʌnd/ *a* moribundo, agonizante

morning /'mɔːnɪŋ/ *n* manhã *f*. **in the ~** de manhã

Morocc|o /mə'rɒkəʊ/ *n* Marrocos *m*. **~an** *a & n* marroquino (*m*)

moron /'mɔːrɒn/ *n* idiota *mf*

morose /mə'rəʊs/ *a* taciturno e insociável, carrancudo

morphine /'mɔːfiːn/ *n* morfina *f*

Morse /mɔːs/ *n* **(code)** (alfabeto) Morse *m*

morsel /'mɔːsl/ *n* bocado *m* (esp de comida)

mortal /'mɔːtl/ *a & n* mortal (*mf*). **~ity** /mɔː'tælətɪ/ *n* mortalidade *f*

mortar /'mɔːtə(r)/ *n* argamassa *f*; (*bowl*) almofariz *m*; (*mil*) morteiro *m*

mortgage /'mɔːgɪdʒ/ *n* hipoteca *f* □ *vt* hipotecar

mortify /'mɔːtɪfaɪ/ *vt* mortificar

mortuary /'mɔːtʃərɪ/ *n* casa *f* mortuária

mosaic /məʊ'zeɪɪk/ *n* mosaico *m*

Moscow /'mɒskəʊ/ *n* Moscou *m*, (*P*) Moscovo *m*

mosque /mɒsk/ *n* mesquita *f*

mosquito /mə'skiːtəʊ/ *n* (*pl* -oes) mosquito *m*

moss /mɒs/ *n* musgo *m*. **~y** *a* musgoso

most /məʊst/ *a* o mais, o maior; (*majority*) a maioria de, a maior parte de □ *n* mais *m*; (*majority*) a maioria, a maior parte, o máximo □ *adv* o mais; (*very*) muito. **at ~** no máximo. **for the ~ part** na maior parte, na grande maioria. **make the ~ of** aproveitar ao máximo, tirar o melhor partido de. **~ly** *adv* sobretudo

motel /məʊ'tel/ *n* motel *m*

moth /mɒθ/ *n* mariposa *f*, (*P*) borboleta *f* nocturna. (**clothes-**)**~** *n* traça *f*. **~-ball** *n* bola *f* de naftalina. **~-eaten** *a* roído por traças

mother /'mʌðə(r)/ *n* mãe *f* □ *vt* tratar como a um filho. **~hood** *n* maternidade *f*. **~-in-law** *n* (*pl* **~s-in-law**) sogra *f*. **~-of-pearl** *n* madrepérola *f*. **M~'s Day** o Dia das Mães. **~-to-be** *n* futura mãe *f*. **~ly** *a* maternal

motif /məʊ'tiːf/ *n* tema *m*

motion /'məʊʃn/ *n* movimento *m*; (*proposal*) moção *f* □ *vt*/*i* **~ (to) sb to** fazer sinal a alg para. **~less** *a* imóvel

motivat|e /'məʊtɪveɪt/ *vt* motivar. **~ion** /-'veɪʃn/ *n* motivação *f*

motive /'məʊtɪv/ *n* motivo *m*

motor /'məʊtə(r)/ *n* motor *m*; (*car*) automóvel *m* □ *a* (*anat*) motor; (*boat*) a motor □ *vi* ir de automóvel. **~ bike** (*colloq*) moto *f* (*colloq*). **~ car** carro *m*. **~ cycle** motocicleta *f*. **~ cyclist** *n* motociclista *mf*. **~ vehicle** veículo *m* automóvel. **~ing** *n* automobilismo *m*. **~ized** *a* motorizado

motorist /'məʊtərɪst/ *n* motorista *mf*, automobilista *mf*

motorway /'məʊtəweɪ/ *n* autoestrada *f*

mottled /'mɒtld/ a sarapintado, pintalgado

motto /'mɒtəʊ/ n (pl -oes) divisa f, lema m

mould[1] /məʊld/ n (container) forma f, molde m; (culin) forma f □ vt moldar. ~ing n (archit) moldura f

mould[2] /məʊld/ n (fungi) bolor m, mofo m. ~y a bolorento

moult /məʊlt/ vi estar na muda

mound /maʊnd/ n monte m de terra or de pedras; (small hill) monticulo m

mount /maʊnt/ vt/i montar □ n (support) suporte m; (for gem etc) engaste m. ~ up aumentar, subir

mountain /'maʊntɪn/ n montanha f. ~ bike mountain bike f. ~ous a montanhoso

mountaineer /maʊntɪ'nɪə(r)/ n alpinista mf. ~ing n alpinismo m

mourn /mɔːn/ vt/i ~ (for) chorar (a morte de). ~ (over) sofrer (por). ~er n pessoa f que acompanha o enterro. ~ing n luto m. in ~ing de luto

mournful /'mɔːnfl/ a triste; (sorrowful) pesaroso

mouse /maʊs/ n (pl mice) camundongo m

mousetrap /'maʊstræp/ n ratoeira f

mousse /muːs/ n mousse f

moustache /mə'stɑːʃ/ n bigode m

mouth[1] /maʊθ/ n boca f. ~-organ n gaita f de boca, (P) beiços

mouth[2] /maʊð/ vt/i declamar; (silently) articular sem som

mouthful /'maʊθfʊl/ n bocado m

mouthpiece /'maʊθpiːs/ n (mus) bocal m, boquilha f; (fig: person) porta-voz mf

mouthwash /'maʊθwɒʃ/ n liquido m para bochecho

movable /'muːvəbl/ a móvel

move /muːv/ vt/i mover(-se), mexer (-se), deslocar(-se); (emotionally) comover; (incite) convencer, levar a; (act) agir; (propose) propor; (depart) ir, partir; (go forward) avançar. ~ (out) mudar-se, sair □ n movimento m; (in game) jogada f; (player's turn) vez f; (house change) mudança f. ~ back recuar. ~ forward avançar. ~ in mudar-se para. ~ on! circulem! ~ over, please chegue-se para lá, por favor. on the ~ em marcha

movement /'muːvmənt/ n movimento m

movie /'muːvɪ/ n (Amer) filme m. the ~s o cinema

moving /'muːvɪŋ/ a (touching) comovente; (movable) móvil; (in motion) em movimento

mow /məʊ/ vt (pp mowed or mown) ceifar; (lawn) cortar a grama, (P) relva. ~ down ceifar. ~er n (for lawn) máquina f de cortar a grama, (P) relva

MP abbr see Member of Parliament

Mr /'mɪstə(r)/ n (pl Messrs) Senhor m. ~ Smith o Sr Smith

Mrs /'mɪsɪz/ n Senhora f. ~ Smith a Sra Smith. Mr and ~ Smith o Sr Smith e a mulher

Ms /mɪz/ n Senhora D f

much /mʌtʃ/ (more, most) a, adv & n muito (m). very ~ muito, muitíssimo. you may have as ~ as you need você pode levar o que precisar. ~ of it muito or grande parte dele. so ~ the better/worse tanto melhor/pior. how ~? quanto? not ~ não muito. too ~ demasiado, demais. he's not ~ of a gardener não é lá grande jardineiro

muck /mʌk/ n estrume m; (colloq: dirt) porcaria f □ vi ~ about (sl) entreter-se, perder tempo. ~ in (sl) ajudar, dar uma mão □ vt ~ up (sl) estragar. ~y a sujo

mucus /'mjuːkəs/ n muco m

mud /mʌd/ n lama f. ~dy a lamacento, enlameado

muddle /'mʌdl/ vt baralhar, atrapalhar, confundir □ vi ~ through sair-se bem, desenrascar-se (sl) □ n desordem f; (mix-up) confusão f, trapalhada f

mudguard /'mʌdgɑːd/ n para-lama m

muff /mʌf/ n (for hands) regalo m

muffle /'mʌfl/ vt abafar. ~ (up) agasalhar(-se). ~d sounds sons mpl abafados. ~r /-ə(r)/ n cachecol m

mug /mʌg/ n caneca f; (sl: face) cara f; (sl: fool) trouxa mf (colloq) □ vt (pt mugged) assaltar, agredir. ~ger n assaltante mf. ~ging n assalto m

muggy /'mʌgɪ/ a abafado

mule /mjuːl/ n mulo m; (female) mula f

mull /mʌl/ vt ~ over ruminar; (fig) matutar em

multi- /'mʌltɪ/ pref mult(i)-

multicoloured /'mʌltɪkʌləd/ a multicolor

multinational /mʌltɪ'næʃnəl/ a & n multinacional (f)

multiple /'mʌltɪpl/ a & n múltiplo (m)

multiply /'mʌltɪplaɪ/ vt/i multiplicar(-se). ~ication /-ɪ'keɪʃn/ n multiplicação f

multi-storey /mʌltɪ'stɔːrɪ/ a (car park) com vários níveis

multitude /'mʌltɪtjuːd/ n multidão f

mum[1] /mʌm/ a keep ~ (colloq) ficar calado

mum[2] /mʌm/ (B) mamãe f (colloq) n (colloq) (P) mamã

mumble /'mʌmbl/ vt/i resmungar, resmonear

mummy¹ /'mʌmɪ/ n (body) múmia f

mummy² /'mʌmɪ/ n (esp child's lang) mamã (B) mamãe f (colloq) mãezinha f (colloq), (P)

mumps /mʌmps/ n parotidite f, papeira f

munch /mʌntʃ/ vt mastigar

mundane /mʌn'deɪn/ a banal; (worldly) mundano

municipal /mju:'nɪsɪpl/ a municipal. ~ity /-'pælətɪ/ n municipalidade f

munitions /mju:'nɪʃnz/ npl munições fpl

mural /'mjʊərəl/ a & n mural (m)

murder /'mɜːdə(r)/ n assassínio m, assassinato m □ vt assassinar. ~er n assassino m, assassina f. ~ous a assassino, sanguinário; (of weapon) mortífero

murky /'mɜːkɪ/ a (-ier, -iest) escuro, sombrio

murmur /'mɜːmə(r)/ n murmúrio m □ vt/i murmurar

muscle /'mʌsl/ n músculo m □ vi ~ in (colloq) impor-se, intrometer-se

muscular /'mʌskjʊlə(r)/ a muscular; (brawny) musculoso

muse /mju:z/ vi meditar, cismar

museum /mju:'zɪəm/ n museu m

mush /mʌʃ/ n papa f de farinha de milho. ~y a mole; (sentimental) piegas inv

mushroom /'mʌʃrʊm/ n cogumelo m □ vi pulular, multiplicar-se com rapidez

music /'mju:zɪk/ n música f. ~al a musical □ n (show) comédia f musical, musical m. ~al box n caixa f de música. ~-stand n estante f de música

musician /mju:'zɪʃn/ n músico m

musk /mʌsk/ n almíscar m

Muslim /'mʊzlɪm/ a & n muçulmano (m)

muslin /'mʌzlɪn/ n musselina f

mussel /'mʌsl/ n mexilhão m

must /mʌst/ v aux dever. you ~ go é necessário que você parta. he ~ be old ele deve ser velho. I ~ have done it eu devo tê-lo feito □ n be a ~ (colloq) ser imprescindível

mustard /'mʌstəd/ n mostarda f

muster /'mʌstə(r)/ vt/i juntar(-se), reunir(-se). pass ~ ser aceitável

musty /'mʌstɪ/ a (-ier, -iest) mofado, bolorento

mutation /mju:'teɪʃn/ n mutação f

mute /mju:t/ a & n mudo (m)

muted /'mju:tɪd/ a (sound) em surdina; (colour) suave

mutilat|e /'mju:tɪleɪt/ vt mutilar. ~ion /-'leɪʃn/ n mutilação f

mutin|y /'mju:tɪnɪ/ n motim f □ vi amotinar-se. ~ous a amotinado

mutter /'mʌtə(r)/ vt/i resmungar

mutton /'mʌtn/ n (carne de) carneiro m

mutual /'mju:tʃʊəl/ a mútuo; (colloq: common) comum. ~ly adv mutuamente

muzzle /'mʌzl/ n focinho m; (device) focinheira f; (of gun) boca f □ vt amordaçar; (dog) pôr focinheira em

my /maɪ/ a meu(s), minha(s)

myself /maɪ'self/ pron eu mesmo, eu próprio; (reflexive) me; (after prep) mim (próprio, mesmo). by ~ sozinho

mysterious /mɪ'stɪərɪəs/ a misterioso

mystery /'mɪstərɪ/ n mistério m

mystic /'mɪstɪk/ a & n místico (m). ~al a místico. ~ism /-sɪzəm/ n misticismo m

mystify /'mɪstɪfaɪ/ vt deixar perplexo

mystique /mɪ'sti:k/ n mística f

myth /mɪθ/ n mito m. ~ical a mítico

mytholog|y /mɪ'θɒlədʒɪ/ n mitologia f. ~ical /mɪθə'lɒdʒɪkl/ a mitológico

N

nab /næb/ vt (pt nabbed) (sl) apanhar em flagrante, apanhar com a boca na botija (colloq), pilhar

nag /næg/ vt/i (pt nagged) implicar (com), criticar constantemente; (pester) apoquentar

nagging /'nægɪŋ/ a implicante; (pain) constante, contínuo

nail /neɪl/ n prego m; (of finger, toe) unha f □ vt pregar. ~-brush n escova f de unhas. ~-file n lixa f de unhas. ~ polish esmalte m, (P) verniz m para as unhas. hit the ~ on the head acertar em cheio. on the ~ sem demora

naïve /naɪ'i:v/ a ingênuo, (P) ingénuo

naked /'neɪkɪd/ a nu. to the ~ eye a olho nu, à vista desarmada ~ness f nudez f

name /neɪm/ n nome m; (fig) reputação f, fama f □ vt (mention; appoint) nomear; (give a name to) chamar, dar o nome de; (a date) marcar. be ~d after ter o nome de. ~less a sem nome, anônimo, (P) anónimo

namely /'neɪmlɪ/ adv a saber

namesake /'neɪmseɪk/ n homônimo m (P) homónimo m

nanny /'nænɪ/ n ama f, babá f

nap¹ /næp/ n soneca f □ vi (pt napped) dormitar, tirar um cochilo. catch ~ping apanhar desprevenido

nap² /næp/ n (of material) felpa f

nape /neɪp/ n nuca f

napkin /'næpkɪn/ n guardanapo m; (for baby) fralda f

nappy /'næpɪ/ n fralda f. ∼-**rash** n assadura f

narcotic /na:'kɒtɪk/ a & n narcótico (m)

narrat|e /nə'reɪt/ vt narrar. ∼**ion** /-ʃn/ n narrativa f. ∼**or** n narrador m

narrative /'nærətɪv/ n narrativa f □ a narrativo

narrow /'nærəʊ/ a (-er, -est) estreito; (fig) restrito □ vt/i estreitar(-se); (limit) limitar(-se). ∼**ly** adv (only just) por pouco; (closely, carefully) de perto, com cuidado. ∼-**minded**·a bitolado, de visão limitada. ∼**ness** n estreiteza f

nasal /'neɪzl/ a nasal

nast|y /'na:stɪ/ a (-ier, -iest) (malicious, of weather) mau; (unpleasant) desagradável, intragável; (rude) grosseiro. ∼**ily** adv maldosamente; (unpleasantly) desagradavelmente. ∼**iness** n (malice) maldade f; (rudeness) grosseria f

nation /'neɪʃn/ n nação f. ∼-**wide** a em todo o país, em escala or a nível nacional

national /'næʃnəl/ a nacional □ n natural mf. ∼ **anthem** hino m nacional. ∼**ism** n nacionalismo m. ∼**ize** vt nacionalizar. ∼**ly** adv em escala nacional

nationality /næʃə'nælətɪ/ n nacionalidade f

native /'neɪtɪv/ n natural mf, nativo m □ a nativo; (country) natal; (inborn) inato. be a ∼ of ser natural de. ∼ **language** lingua f materna. ∼ **speaker of Portuguese** pessoa f de língua portuguesa, falante m nativo de Português

Nativity /nə'tɪvətɪ/ n the ∼ a Natividade f

natter /'nætə(r)/ vi fazer conversa fiada, falar à toa, tagarelar

natural /'nætʃrəl/ a natural. ∼ **history** história f natural. ∼**ist** n naturalista mf. ∼**ly** adv naturalmente; (by nature) por natureza

naturaliz|e /'nætʃrəlaɪz/ vt/i naturalizar(-se); (animal, plant) aclimatar(-se). ∼**ation** /-'zeɪʃn/ n naturalização f

nature /'neɪtʃə(r)/ n natureza f; (kind) género m, (P) gênero m; (of person) índole f

naughty /'nɔ:tɪ/ a (-ier, -iest) (child) levado; (indecent) picante

nause|a /'nɔ:sɪə/ n náusea f. ∼**ate** /'nɔ:sɪeɪt/ vt nausear. ∼**ating**, ∼**ous** a nauseabundo, repugnante

nautical /'nɔ:tɪkl/ a náutico. ∼ **mile** milha f marítima

naval /'neɪvl/ a naval; (officer) de marinha

nave /neɪv/ n nave f

navel /'neɪvl/ n umbigo m

navigable /'nævɪɡəbl/ a navegável

navigat|e /'nævɪɡeɪt/ vt (sea etc) navegar; (ship) pilotar □ vi navegar. ∼**ion** /-'ɡeɪʃn/ n navegação f. ∼**or** n navegador m

navy /'neɪvɪ/ n marinha f de guerra. ∼ (**blue**) azul-marinho m invar

near /nɪə(r)/ adv perto, quaze □ prep perto de □ a próximo □ vt aproximarse, chegar-se a. **draw** ∼ aproximar(-se) (**to de**). ∼ **by** adv perto, próximo. **N**∼ **East** Oriente m Próximo. ∼ **to** perto de. ∼**ness** n proximidade f

nearby /'nɪəbaɪ/ a & adv próximo, perto

nearly /'nɪəlɪ/ adv quase, por pouco. **not** ∼ **as pretty/etc as** longe de ser tão bonita/etc como

neat /ni:t/ a (-er, -est) (bem) cuidado; (room) bem arrumado; (spirits) puro, sem gelo. ∼**ly** adv (with care) com cuidado; (cleverly) habilmente. ∼**ness** n aspecto m cuidado

nebulous /'nebjʊləs/ a nebuloso; (vague) vago, confuso

necessar|y /'nesəsərɪ/ a necessário. ∼**ily** adv necessariamente

necessitate /nɪ'sesɪteɪt/ vt exigir, obrigar a, tornar necessário

necessity /nɪ'sesətɪ/ n necessidade f; (thing) coisa f indispensável, artigo m de primeira necessidade

neck /nek/ n pescoço m; (of dress) gola f. ∼ **and neck** emparelhados

necklace /'neklɪs/ n colar m

neckline /'neklaɪn/ n decote m

nectarine /'nektərɪn/ n pêssego m

née /neɪ/ a em solteira **Ann Jones** ∼ **Drewe** Ann Jones cujo nome de solteira era Drewe

need /ni:d/ n necessidade f □ vt precisar de, necessitar de. **you** ∼ **not come** não temde or não precisa vir. ∼**less** a inútil, desnecessário. ∼**lessly** adv inutilmente, sem necessidade

needle /'ni:dl/ n agulha f □ vt (colloq: provoke) provocar

needlework /'ni:dlwɜ:k/ n costura f; (embroidery) bordado m

needy /'ni:dɪ/ a (-ier, -iest) necessitado, carenciado

negation /nɪ'ɡeɪʃn/ n negação f

negative /'neɡətɪv/ a negativo □ n negativa f, negação f; (photo) negativo m. **in the** ∼ (answer) na negativa; (gram) na forma negativa. ∼**ly** adv negativamente

neglect /nɪ'ɡlekt/ vt descuidar; (opportunity) desprezar; (family) não cuidar de, abandonar; (duty) não cumprir □ n falta f de cuidado(s), descuido m. (**state of**) ∼ abandono *m.* ~ **to** (*omit to*) esquecer-se de. ~**ful** *a* negligente

negligen|t /'neglɪdʒənt/ *a* negligente. ~**ce** *n* negligência *f,* desleixo *m*

negligible /'neglɪdʒəbl/ *a* insignificante, ínfimo

negotiable /nɪ'gəʊʃəbl/ *a* negociável

negotiat|e /nɪ'gəʊʃɪeɪt/ *vt/i* negociar; (*obstacle*) transpor; (*difficulty*) vencer. ~**ion** /-'sɪeɪʃn/ *n* negociação *f.* ~**or** *n* negociador *m*

Negro /'niːɡrəʊ/ *a* & *n* (*pl* ~**oes**) negro (*m*), preto (*m*)

neigh /neɪ/ *n* relincho *m* □ *vi* relinchar

neighbour /'neɪbə(r)/ *n* vizinho *m.* ~**hood** *n* vizinhança *f.* ~**ing** *a* vizinho. ~**ly** *a* de boa vizinhança

neither /'naɪðə(r)/ *a* & *pron* nenhum(a) (de duas *ou* duas), nem um nem outro, nem uma nem outra □ *adv* tampouco, também não □ *conj* nem. ~ **big nor small** nem grande nem pequeno. ~ **am I** nem eu

neon /'niːɒn/ *n* néon *m* □ *a* (*lamp etc*) de néon

nephew /'nevjuː/ *n* sobrinho *m*

nerve /nɜːv/ *n* nervo *m;* (*fig: courage*) coragem *f;* (*colloq: impudence*) descaramento *m,* (*P*) lata *f* (*colloq*). **get on sb's nerves** irritar, dar nos nervos de alg. ~**-racking** *a* de arrasar os nervos, enervante

nervous /'nɜːvəs/ *a* nervoso. **be** *or* **feel** ~ (*afraid*) ter receio/um certo medo. ~ **breakdown** esgotamento *m* nervoso. ~**ly** *adv* nervosamente. ~**ness** *n* nervosismo *m;* (*fear*) receio *m*

nest /nest/ *n* ninho *m* □ *vi* aninhar-se, fazer *or* ter ninho. ~**-egg** *n* pé-de-meia *m*

nestle /'nesl/ *vi* aninhar-se

net[1] /net/ *n* rede *f* □ *vt* (*pt* **netted**) apanhar na rede. ~**ting** *n* rede *f.* **wire** ~**ting** rede *f* de arame

net[2] /net/ *a* (*weight etc*) líquido

Netherlands /'neðələndz/ *npl* **the** ~ os Países Baixos

nettle /'netl/ *n* urtiga *f*

network /'netwɜːk/ *n* rede *f,* cadeia *f*

neuro|sis /njʊə'rəʊsɪs/ *n* (*pl* -**oses** /-siːz/) neurose *f.* ~**tic** /-'rɒtɪk/ *a* & *n* neurótico *m*

neuter /'njuːtə(r)/ *a* & *n* neutro (*m*) □ *vt* castrar, capar

neutral /'njuːtrəl/ *a* neutro. ~ (**gear**) ponto *m* morto. ~**ity** /-'trælətɪ/ *n* neutralidade *f*

never /'nevə(r)/ *adv* nunca; (*colloq: not*) não. **he** ~ **refuses** ele nunca recusa. **I** ~ **saw him** (*colloq*) nunca o vi. ~ **mind** não faz mal, deixe por lá. ~**-ending** *a* interminável

nevertheless /nevəðə'les/ *adv* & *conj* contudo, no entanto

new /njuː/ *a* (-**er,** -**est**) novo. ~**-born** *a* recém-nascido. ~ **moon** lua *f* nova. ~ **year** ano *m* novo. **N**~ **Year's Day** dia *m* de Ano Novo. **N**~ **Year's Eve** véspera *f* de Ano Novo. **N**~ **Zealand** Nova Zelândia *f.* **N**~ **Zealander** neozelandês *m.* ~**ness** *n* novidade *f*

newcomer /'njuːkʌmə(r)/ *n* recém-chegado *m,* (*P*) recém-vindo *m*

newfangled /njuː'fæŋgld/ *a* (*pej*) moderno

newly /'njuːlɪ/ *adv* há pouco, recentemente. ~**-weds** *npl* recém-casados *mpl*

news /njuːz/ *n* notícia(s) *f(pl)*; (*radio*) noticiário *m,* notícias *fpl;* (*TV*) telejornal *m.* ~**-caster,** ~**-reader** *n* locutor *m.* ~**-flash** *n* notícia *f* de última hora

newsagent /'njuːzeɪdʒənt/ *n* jornaleiro *m*

newsletter /'njuːzletə(r)/ *n* boletim *m* informativo

newspaper /'njuːzpeɪpə(r)/ *n* jornal *m*

newsreel /'njuːzriːl/ *n* atualidades *fpl,* (*P*) actualidades *fpl*

newt /njuːt/ *n* tritão *m*

next /nekst/ *a* próximo; (*adjoining*) pegado, ao lado, contíguo; (*following*) seguinte □ *adv* a seguir □ *n* seguinte *mf.* ~**-door** *a* do lado. ~ **of kin** parente *m* mais próximo. ~ **to** ao lado de. ~ **to nothing** quase nada

nib /nɪb/ *n* bico *m,* (*P*) aparo *m*

nibble /'nɪbl/ *vt* mordiscar, dar dentadinhas em

nice /naɪs/ *a* (-**er,** -**est**) agradável, bom; (*kind*) simpático, gentil; (*pretty*) bonito; (*respectable*) bem educado, correto, (*P*) correcto; (*subtle*) fino, subtil. ~**ly** *adv* agradavelmente; (*well*) bem

nicety /'naɪsətɪ/ *n* sutileza *f,* (*P*) subtileza *f*

niche /nɪtʃ/ *n* nicho *m;* (*fig*) bom lugar *m*

nick /nɪk/ *n* corte *m,* chanfradura *f;* (*sl: prison*) cadeia *f* □ *vt* dar um corte em; (*sl: steal*) roubar, limpar (*colloq*); (*sl: arrest*) apanhar, pôr a mão em (*colloq*). **in good** ~ (*colloq*) em boa forma, em bom estado. **in the** ~ **of time** mesmo a tempo

nickel /'nɪkl/ *n* níquel *m;* (*Amer*) moeda *f* de cinco cêntimos

nickname /'nɪkneɪm/ *n* apelido *m,* (*P*) alcunha *f;* (*short form*) diminutivo *m* □ *vt* apelidar de

nicotine /'nɪkətiːn/ *n* nicotina *f*

niece /niːs/ *n* sobrinha *f*

Nigeria /naɪ'dʒɪərɪə/ *n* Nigéria *f.* ~**n** *a* & *n* nigeriano (*m*)

niggardly /'nɪgədlɪ/ a miserável
night /naɪt/ n noite f □ a de noite, noturno, (P) nocturno. **at** ~ à/de noite. **by** ~ de noite. ~-**cap** n (drink) bebida f na hora de deitar. ~-**club** n boate f, (P) boîte f. ~-**dress**, ~-**gown** ns camisola f de dormir, (P) camisa f de noite. ~-**life** n vida f noturna, (P) nocturna. ~-**school** n escola f noturna, (P) nocturna. ~-**time** n noite f. ~-**watchman** n guarda-noturno m, (P) guarda-nocturno m
nightfall /'naɪtfɔːl/ n anoitecer m
nightingale /'naɪtɪŋgeɪl/ n rouxinol m
nightly /'naɪtlɪ/ a noturno, (P) nocturno □ adv de noite, à noite, todas as noites
nightmare /'naɪtmeə(r)/ n pesadelo m
nil /nɪl/ n nada m; (sport) zero m □ a nulo
nimble /'nɪmbl/ a (-er, -est) ágil, ligeiro
nin|e /naɪn/ a & n nove (m). ~**th** a & n nono (m)
nineteen /naɪn'tiːn/ a & n dezenove (m), (P) dezanove (m). ~**th** a & n décimo nono (m)
ninet|y /'naɪntɪ/ a & n noventa (m). ~**ieth** a & n nonagésimo (m)
nip /nɪp/ vt/i (pt **nipped**) apertar, beliscar; (colloq: rush) ir correndo, ir num pulo (colloq) □ n aperto m, beliscão m; (drink) gole m, trago m. **a ~ in the air** um frio cortante. ~ **in the bud** cortar pela raiz
nipple /'nɪpl/ n mamilo m
nippy /'nɪpɪ/ a (-ier, -iest) (colloq: quick) rápido; (colloq: chilly) cortante
nitrogen /'naɪtrədʒən/ n azoto m, nitrogénio m, (P) nitrogénio m
nitwit /'nɪtwɪt/ n (colloq) imbecil m
no /nəʊ/ a nenhum □ adv não □ n (pl **noes**) não m. ~ **entry** entrada f proibida. ~ **money/time/**etc. nenhum dinheiro/tempo/etc. ~ **man's land** terra f de ninguém. ~ **one** = **nobody**. ~ **smoking** é proibido fumar. ~ **way!** (colloq) de modo nenhum!
nob|le /'nəʊbl/ a (-er, -est) nobre. ~**ility** /-'bɪlətɪ/ n nobreza f
nobleman /'nəʊblmən/ n (pl -men) nobre m, fidalgo m
nobody /'nəʊbɒdɪ/ pron ninguém □ n nulidade f. **he knows** ~ ele não conhece ninguém. ~ **is there** não tem ninguém lá
nocturnal /nɒk'tɜːnl/ a noturno, (P) nocturno
nod /nɒd/ vt/i (pt **nodded**) ~ (**one's head**) acenar (com) a cabeça; ~ (**off**) cabecear □ n aceno m com a cabeça

(para dizer que sim or para cumprimentar)
noise /nɔɪz/ n ruido m, barulho m. ~**less** a silencioso
nois|y /'nɔɪzɪ/ a (-ier, -iest) ruidoso, barulhento. ~**ily** adv ruidosamente
nomad /'nəʊmæd/ n nómade mf, (P) nómade mf. ~**ic** /-'mædɪk/ a nómade, (P) nómade
nominal /'nɒmɪnl/ a nominal; (fee, sum) simbólico
nominat|e /'nɒmɪneɪt/ vt (appoint) nomear; (put forward) propor. ~**ion** /-'neɪʃn/ n nomeação f
non- /nɒn/ pref não, sem, in-, a-, anti-, des-. ~-**skid** a antiderrapante. ~-**stick** a não-aderente
nonchalant /'nɒnʃələnt/ a indiferente, desinteressado
non-commissioned /nɒnkə'mɪʃnd/ a ~ **officer** sargento m, cabo m
non-committal /nɒnkə'mɪtl/ a evasivo
nondescript /'nɒndɪskrɪpt/ a insignificante, mediocre, indefinível
none /nʌn/ pron (person) nenhum, ninguém; (thing) nenhum, nada. ~ **of us** nenhum de nós. **I have** ~ não tenho nenhum. ~ **of that!** nada disso! □ adv ~ **too** não muito. **he is** ~ **the happier** nem por isso ele é mais feliz. ~ **the less** contudo, no entanto, apesar disso
nonentity /nɒ'nentətɪ/ n nulidade f, zero m à esquerda, João Ninguém m
non-existent /nɒnɪg'zɪstənt/ a inexistente
nonplussed /nɒn'plʌst/ a perplexo, pasmado
nonsens|e /'nɒnsns/ n absurdo m, disparate m. ~**ical** /-'sensɪkl/ a absurdo, disparatado
non-smoker /nɒn'sməʊkə(r)/ n não-fumante m, (P) não-fumador m
non-stop /nɒn'stɒp/ a ininterrupto, continuo; (train) direto, (P) directo; (flight) sem escala □ adv sem parar
noodles /'nuːdlz/ npl talharim m, (P) macaronete m
nook /nʊk/ n (re)canto m
noon /nuːn/ n meio-dia m
noose /nuːs/ n laço m corrediço
nor /nɔː(r)/ conj & adv nem, também não. ~ **do I** nem eu
norm /nɔːm/ n norma f
normal /'nɔːml/ a & n normal (m). **above/below** ~ acima/abaixo do normal. ~**ity** /nɔː'mælətɪ/ n normalidade f. ~**ly** adv normalmente
north /nɔːθ/ n norte m □ a norte, do norte; (of country, people etc) setentrional □ adv a, ao, para o norte. **N~ America** América f do Norte. **N~ American** a & n norte-americano

(m). ~-**east** n nordeste m. ~**erly** /'nɔːðəlɪ/ a do norte. ~**ward** a ao norte. ~**ward(s)** adv para o norte. ~-**west** n noroeste m

northern /'nɔːðən/ a do norte
Norw|ay /'nɔːweɪ/ n Noruega f. ~**egian** /nɔː'wiːdʒən/ a & n norueguês (m)
nose /nəʊz/ n nariz m; (of animal) focinho m □ vi ~ **about** farejar. **pay through the** ~ pagar um preço exorbitante
nosebleed /'nəʊzbliːd/ n hemorragia f nasal or pelo nariz
nosedive /'nəʊzdaɪv/ n vôo m picado
nostalg|ia /nɒ'stældʒə/ n nostalgia f. ~**ic** a nostálgico
nostril /'nɒstrəl/ n narina f; (of horse) venta f (usually pl)
nosy /'nəʊzɪ/ a (-ier, -iest) (colloq) bisbilhoteiro
not /nɒt/ adv não. ~ **at all** nada, de modo nenhum; (reply to thanks) de nada. **he is** ~ **at all bored** ele não está nem um pouco entediado. ~ **yet** ainda não. **I suppose** ~ creio que não
notable /'nəʊtəbl/ a notável □ n notabilidade f
notably /'nəʊtəblɪ/ adv notavelmente; (particularly) especialmente
notch /nɒtʃ/ n corte m em V □ vt marcar (com cortes). ~ **up** (score etc) marcar
note /nəʊt/ n nota f; (banknote) nota (de banco) f; (short letter) bilhete m □ vt notar
notebook /'nəʊtbʊk/ n livrinho m de notas, (P) bloco-notas m
noted /'nəʊtɪd/ a conhecido, famoso
notepaper /'nəʊtpeɪpə(r)/ n papel m de carta
noteworthy /'nəʊtwɜːðɪ/ a notável
nothing /'nʌθɪŋ/ n nada m; (person) nulidade f, zero m □ adv nada, de modo algum or nenhum, de maneira alguma or nenhuma. **he eats** ~ ele não come nada. ~ **big/etc** nada (de grande/etc. ~ **else** nada mais. ~ **much** pouca coisa. **for** ~ (free) de graça; (in vain) em vão
notice /'nəʊtɪs/ n anúncio m, notícia f; (in street, on wall) letreiro m; (warning) aviso m; (attention) atenção f. (advance) ~ pré-aviso m □ vt notar, reparar. **at short** ~ num prazo curto. **a week's** ~ o prazo de uma semana. ~-**board** n quadro m para afixar anúncios etc. **hand in one's** ~ pedir demissão. **take** ~ reparar (of em). **take no** ~ não fazer caso (of de)
noticeab|le /'nəʊtɪsəbl/ a visível. ~**y** adv visivelmente
notif|y /'nəʊtɪfaɪ/ vt participar, notificar. ~**ication** /-ɪ'keɪʃn/ n participação f, notificação f
notion /'nəʊʃn/ n noção f
notor|ious /nəʊ'tɔːrɪəs/ a notório. ~**iety** /-ə'raɪətɪ/ n fama f
notwithstanding /nɒtwɪθ'stændɪŋ/ prep apesar de, não obstante □ adv mesmo assim, ainda assim □ conj embora, conquanto, apesar de que
nougat /'nuːgaː/ n nugá m, torrone m
nought /nɔːt/ n zero m
noun /naʊn/ n substantivo m, nome m
nourish /'nʌrɪʃ/ vt alimentar, nutrir. ~**ing** a alimentício, nutritivo. ~**ment** n alimento m, sustento m
novel /'nɒvl/ n romance m □ a novo, original. ~**ist** n romancista mf. ~**ty** n novidade f
November /nəʊ'vembə(r)/ n novembro m
novice /'nɒvɪs/ n (beginner) noviço m, novato m; (relig) noviço m
now /naʊ/ adv agora □ conj ~ (**that**) agora que. **by** ~ a estas horas, por esta altura. ~ **from** ~ **on** de agora em diante. ~ **and again**, ~ **and then** de vez em quando. **right** ~ já
nowadays /'naʊədeɪz/ adv hoje em dia, presentemente, atualmente, (P) actualmente
nowhere /'nəʊweə(r)/ adv (position) em lugar nenhum, em lado nenhum; (direction) a lado nenhum, a parte alguma or nenhuma
nozzle /'nɒzl/ n bico m, bocal m; (of hose) agulheta f
nuance /'njuːɑːns/ n nuance f, matiz m
nuclear /'njuːklɪə(r)/ a nuclear
nucleus /'njuːklɪəs/ n (pl -lei /-lɪaɪ/) núcleo m
nud|e /njuːd/ a & n nu (m). **in the** ~e nu. ~**ity** n nudez f
nudge /nʌdʒ/ vt tocar com o cotovelo, cutucar □ n ligeira cotovelada f, cutucada f
nudis|t /'njuːdɪst/ n nudista mf. ~**m** /-zəm/ n nudismo m
nuisance /'njuːsns/ n aborrecimento m, chatice f (sl); (person) chato m (sl)
null /nʌl/ a nulo. ~ **and void** (jur) irrito e nulo. ~**ify** vt anular, invalidar
numb /nʌm/ a entorpecido, dormente □ vt entorpecer, adormecer
number /'nʌmbə(r)/ n número m; (numeral) algarismo m □ vt numerar; (amount to) ser em número de; (count) contar, incluir. ~-**plate** n chapa (do carro) f
numeral /'njuːmərəl/ n número m, algarismo m
numerate /'njuːmərət/ a que tem conhecimentos básicos de matemática

numerical /njuːˈmerɪkl/ a numérico

numerous /ˈnjuːmərəs/ a numeroso

nun /nʌn/ n freira f, religiosa f

nurse /nɜːs/ n enfermeira f, enfermeiro m; (nanny) ama(-seca) f, babá f □ vt cuidar de, tratar de; (hopes etc) alimentar, acalentar. ~ing n enfermagem f. ~ing home clínica f de repouso

nursery /ˈnɜːsərɪ/ n quarto m de crianças; (for plants) viveiro m. (day) ~ creche f. ~ rhyme poema m or canção f infantil. ~ school jardim m de infância

nurture /ˈnɜːtʃə(r)/ vt educar

nut /nʌt/ n (bot) noz f; (techn) porca f de parafuso

nutcrackers /ˈnʌtkrækəz/ npl quebra-nozes m invar

nutmeg /ˈnʌtmeg/ n noz-moscada f

nutrient /ˈnjuːtrɪənt/ n substância f nutritiva, nutriente m

nutrition /njuːˈtrɪʃn/ n nutrição f. ~ious a nutritivo

nutshell /ˈnʌtʃel/ n casca f de noz. in a ~ em poucas palavras

nuzzle /ˈnʌzl/ vt esfregar com o focinho

nylon /ˈnaɪlɒn/ n nylon m. ~s meias fpl de nylon

O

oaf /əʊf/ n (pl oafs) imbecil m, idiota m

oak /əʊk/ n carvalho m

OAP abbr see old-age pensioner

oar /ɔː(r)/ n remo m

oasis /əʊˈeɪsɪs/ n (pl oases /-siːz/) oásis m

oath /əʊθ/ n juramento m; (swearword) praga f

oatmeal /ˈəʊtmiːl/ n farinha f de aveia; (porridge) papa f de aveia

oats /əʊts/ npl aveia f

obedien|t /əˈbiːdɪənt/ a obediente. ~ce n obediência f. ~tly adv obedientemente

obes|e /əʊˈbiːs/ a obeso. ~ity n obesidade f

obey /əˈbeɪ/ vt/i obedecer (a)

obituary /əˈbɪtʃʊərɪ/ n necrológio m, (P) necrologia f

object¹ /ˈɒbdʒɪkt/ n objeto m, (P) objecto m; (aim) objetivo m, (P) objectivo m; (gram) complemento m

object² /əbˈdʒekt/ vt/i objetar, (P) objectar (que). ~ to opor-se a, discordar de. ~ion /-ʃn/ n objeção f, (P) objecção f

objectionable /əbˈdʒekʃnəbl/ a censurável; (unpleasant) desagradável

objective /əbˈdʒektɪv/ a objetivo, (P)

objectivo. ~ity /-ˈtɪvətɪ/ n objetividade f, (P) objectividade f

obligation /ɒblɪˈɡeɪʃn/ n obrigação f. be under an ~ to sb dever favores a alg

obligatory /əˈblɪɡətrɪ/ a obrigatório

oblig|e /əˈblaɪdʒ/ vt obrigar; (do a favour) fazer um favor a, obsequiar. ~ed a obrigado (to a). ~ed to sb em dívida (para) com alg. ~ing a prestável, amável. ~ingly adv amavelmente

oblique /əˈbliːk/ a oblíquo

obliterat|e /əˈblɪtəreɪt/ vt obliterar. ~ion /-ˈreɪʃn/ n obliteração f

oblivion /əˈblɪvɪən/ n esquecimento m

oblivious /əˈblɪvɪəs/ a esquecido, sem consciência (of/to de)

oblong /ˈɒblɒŋ/ a oblongo □ n retângulo m, (P) rectângulo m

obnoxious /əbˈnɒkʃəs/ a ofensivo, detestável

oboe /ˈəʊbəʊ/ n oboé m

obscen|e /əbˈsiːn/ a obsceno. ~ity /-ˈenətɪ/ n obscenidade f

obscur|e /əbˈskjʊə(r)/ a obscuro □ vt obscurecer; (conceal) encobrir. ~ity n obscuridade f

obsequious /əbˈsiːkwɪəs/ a demasiado obsequioso, subserviente

observan|t /əbˈzɜːvənt/ a observador. ~ce n observância f, cumprimento m

observatory /əbˈzɜːvətrɪ/ n observatório m

observ|e /əbˈzɜːv/ vt observar. ~ation /ˌɒbzəˈveɪʃn/ n observação f. keep under ~ation vigiar. ~er n observador m

obsess /əbˈses/ vt obcecar. ~ion /-ʃn/ n obsessão f. ~ive a obsessivo

obsolete /ˈɒbsəliːt/ a obsoleto, antiguado

obstacle /ˈɒbstəkl/ n obstáculo m

obstetric|s /əbˈstetrɪks/ n obstetrícia f. ~ian /ˌɒbstɪˈtrɪʃn/ n obstetra mf

obstina|te /ˈɒbstɪnət/ a obstinado. ~cy n obstinação f

obstruct /əbˈstrʌkt/ vt obstruir, bloquear; (hinder) estorvar, obstruir. ~ion /-ʃn/ n obstrução f; (thing) obstáculo m

obtain /əbˈteɪn/ vt obter □ vi prevalecer, estar em vigor. ~able a que se pode obter

obtrusive /əbˈtruːsɪv/ a importuno; (thing) demasiadamente em evidência, que dá muito na vista (colloq)

obvious /ˈɒbvɪəs/ a óbvio, evidente. ~ly adv obviamente

occasion /əˈkeɪʒn/ n ocasião f; (event) acontecimento m □ vt ocasionar. on ~ de vez em quando, ocasionalmente

occasional /əˈkeɪʒənl/ a ocasional.

~ly *adv* de vez em quando, ocasionalmente

occult /ɒ'kʌlt/ *a* oculto

occupation /ɒkjʊ'peɪʃn/ *n* ocupação *f*.
~al *a* profissional; (*therapy*) ocupa-
cional

occup|**y** /'ɒkjʊpaɪ/ *vt* ocupar. ~ant,
~ier *ns* ocupante *mf*

occur /ə'kɜ:(r)/ *vi* (*pt* **occurred**) ocorrer, acontecer, dar-se; (*arise*) apresentar-se, aparecer. ~ **to sb** ocorrer a alg

occurrence /ə'kʌrəns/ *n* acontecimento *m*, ocorrência *f*

ocean /'əʊʃn/ *n* oceano *m*

o'clock /ə'klɒk/ *adv* **it is one** ~ é
uma hora. **it is six** ~ são seis horas

octagon /'ɒktəgən/ *n* octógono *m*.
~al *a* /-'tægənl/ *a* octogonal

octave /'ɒktɪv/ *n* oitava *f*

October /ɒk'təʊbə(r)/ *n* outubro *m*

octopus /'ɒktəpəs/ *n* (*pl* -**puses**) polvo
m

odd /ɒd/ *a* (-**er**, -**est**) estranho, singular; (*number*) ímpar; (*left over*) de sobra; (*not of set*) desemparelhado;
(*occasional*) ocasional. ~ **jobs** (*paid*)
biscates *mpl*; (*in garden etc*) trabalhos
mpl diversos. ~ **twenty** ~ vinte e
tantos. ~**ity** *n* singularidade *f*;
(*thing*) curiosidade *f*. ~**ly** *adv* de
modo estranho

oddment /'ɒdmənt/ *n* resto *m*, artigo
m avulso

odds /ɒdz/ *npl* probabilidades *fpl*; (*in
betting*) ganhos *mpl* líquidos. **at** ~
em desacordo; (*quarrelling*) de mal,
brigado. **it makes no** ~ não faz
diferença. ~ **and ends** artigos *mpl*
avulsos, coisas *fpl* pequenas

odious /'əʊdɪəs/ *a* odioso

odour /'əʊdə(r)/ *n* odor *m*. ~**less** *a*
inodoro

of /əv/; *emphatic* /ɒv/ *prep* de. **a
friend** ~ **mine** um amigo meu. **the
fifth** ~ **June** (no dia) cinco de junho.
take six ~ **them** leve seis deles

off /ɒf/ *adv* embora, fora; (*switched
off*) apagado, desligado; (*taken off*)
tirado, desligado; (*cancelled*) cancela-
do; (*food*) estragado □ *prep* (fora) de;
(*distant from*) a alguma distância de.
be ~ (*depart*) ir-se embora, partir. **be
well** ~ ser abastado. **be better**/
worse ~ estar em melhor/pior
situação. **a day** ~ um dia de folga.
20% ~ redução de 20%. **on the** ~
chance that no caso de. ~ **colour**
indisposto, adoentado. ~**licence** *n*
loja *f* de bebidas alcoólicas. ~**load**
vt descarregar. ~**putting** *a*
desconcertante. ~**stage** *adv* fora de
cena. ~**white** *a* branco-sujo

offal /'ɒfl/ *n* miudezas *fpl*, fressura *f*

offence /ə'fens/ *n* (*feeling*) ofensa *f*;

(*crime*) delito *m*, transgressão *f*. **give**
~ **to** ofender. **take** ~ ofender-se (**at**
com)

offend /ə'fend/ *vt* ofender. **be** ~**ed**
ofender-se (**at** com). ~**er** *n* delinquente *mf*, (P) delinquente *mf*

offensive /ə'fensɪv/ *a* ofensivo; (*disgusting*) repugnante □ *n* ofensiva *f*

offer /'ɒfə(r)/ *vt* (*pt* **offered**) oferecer
□ *n* oferta *f*. **on** ~ em promoção.
~**ing** *n* oferenda *f*

offhand /ɒf'hænd/ *a* espontâneo;
(*curt*) seco □ *adv* de improviso, sem
pensar

office /'ɒfɪs/ *n* escritório *m*; (*post*) cargo *m*; (*branch*) filial *f*. ~ **hours**
fpl de expediente. **in** ~ no poder. **take**
~ assumir o cargo

officer /'ɒfɪsə(r)/ *n* oficial *m*; (*policeman*) agente *m*

official /ə'fɪʃl/ *a* oficial □ *n* funcionário *m*. ~**ly** *adv* oficialmente

officiate /ə'fɪʃɪeɪt/ *vi* (*relig*) oficiar. ~
as presidir, exercer as funções de

officious /ə'fɪʃəs/ *a* intrometido

offing /'ɒfɪŋ/ *n* **in the** ~ (*fig*) em
perspectiva

offset /'ɒfset/ *vt* (*pt* -**set**, *pres p* -**setting**) compensar, contrabalançar

offshoot /'ɒfʃuːt/ *n* rebento *m*; (*fig*)
efeito *m* secundário

offshore /'ɒfʃɔ:(r)/ *a* ao largo da costa

offside /ɒf'saɪd/ *a* & *adv* offside, em
impedimento, (P) fora de jogo

offspring /'ɒfsprɪŋ/ *n* (*pl* invar)
descendência *f*, prole *f*

often /'ɒfn/ *adv* muitas vezes, frequentemente, (P) frequentemente.
every so ~ de vez em quando. **how**
~? quantas vezes?

oh /əʊ/ *int* oh, ah

oil /ɔɪl/ *n* óleo *m*; (*petroleum*) petróleo
m □ *vt* lubrificar. ~**painting** *n* pintura *f* a óleo. ~ **rig** plataforma *f* de
poço de petróleo. ~ **well** poço *m* de
petróleo. ~**y** *a* oleoso; (*food*) gorduroso

oilfield /'ɔɪlfiːld/ *n* campo *m* petrolífero

oilskins /'ɔɪlskɪnz/ *npl* roupa *f* de
oleado

ointment /'ɔɪntmənt/ *n* pomada *f*

OK /əʊ'keɪ/ *a* & *adv* (*colloq*) (está)
bem, (está) certo, (está) legal

old /əʊld/ *a* (-**er**, -**est**) velho; (*person*)
velho, idoso; (*former*) antigo. **how** ~
is he? que idade tem ele? **he is eight
years** ~ ele tem oito anos (de idade).
of ~ (d)antes, antigamente. ~ **age**
velhice *f*. ~**age pensioner** reformado *m*, aposentado *m*, pessoa *f* de terceira idade. ~ **boy** antigo aluno *m*.
~**fashioned** *a* fora de moda. ~ **girl**
antiga aluna *f*. ~ **maid** solteirona *f*.

~ **man** homem *m* idoso, velho *m*. ~-**time** *a* antigo. ~ **woman** mulher *f* idosa, velha *f*

olive /'ɒlɪv/ *n* azeitona *f* □ *a* de azeitona. ~ **oil** azeite *m*

Olympic /ə'lɪmpɪk/ *a* olímpico. ~**s** *npl* Olimpíadas *fpl*. ~ **Games** Jogos *mpl* Olímpicos

omelette /'ɒmlɪt/ *n* omelete *f*

omen /'əʊmən/ *n* agouro *m*, presságio *m*

ominous /'ɒmɪnəs/ *a* agourento; (*fig: threatening*) ameaçador

omi|t /ə'mɪt/ *vt* (*pt* **omitted**) omitir. ~**ssion** /-ʃn/ *n* omissão *f*

on /ɒn/ *prep* sobre, em cima de, de, em □ *adv* para diante, para a frente; (*switched on*) aceso, ligado; (*tap on*) aberto; (*machine*) em funcionamento; (*put on*) posto; (*happening*) em curso. ~ **arrival** na chegada, ao chegar. ~ **foot** *etc* a pé *etc*. ~ **doing** ao fazer. ~ **time** na hora, dentro do horário. ~ **Tuesday** na terça-feira. ~ **Tuesdays** às terças-feiras. **walk**/*etc* ~ continuar a andar/*etc*. **be** ~ **at** (*film, TV*) estar levando *or* passando. ~ **and off** de vez em quando. ~ **and** ~ sem parar

once /wʌns/ *adv* uma vez; (*formerly*) noutro(s) tempo(s) □ *conj* uma vez que, desde que. **all at** ~ de repente; (*simultaneously*) todos ao mesmo tempo. **just this** ~ só esta vez. ~ **(and) for all** duma vez para sempre. ~ **upon a time** era uma vez. ~-**over** *n* (*colloq*) vista *f* de olhos

oncoming /'ɒnkʌmɪŋ/ *a* que se aproxima, próximo. **the** ~ **traffic** o trânsito que vem do sentido oposto, (*P*) no sentido contrário

one /wʌn/ *a* um(a); (*sole*) único □ *n* um(a) *mf* □ *pron* um(a) *mf*; (*impersonal*) se. ~ **by** ~ um a um. **a big red**/*etc* ~ um grande/vermelho/*etc*. **this**/**that** ~ este/esse. ~ **another** um ao outro, uns aos outros. ~-**sided** *a* parcial. ~-**way** *a* (*street*) mão única; (*ticket*) simples

oneself /wʌn'self/ *pron* si, si mesmo/próprio; (*reflexive*) se. **by** ~ sozinho

onion /'ʌnɪən/ *n* cebola *f*

onlooker /'ɒnlʊkə(r)/ *n* espectador *m*, circunstante *mf*

only /'əʊnlɪ/ *a* único □ *adv* apenas, só, somente □ *conj* só que. **an** ~ **child** um filho único. **he** ~ **has six** ele só tem seis. **not** ~ ... **but also** não só ... mas também. ~ **too** muito, mais que

onset /'ɒnset/ *n* começo *m*; (*attack*) ataque *m*

onslaught /'ɒnslɔ:t/ *n* ataque *m* violento, assalto *m*

onward(s) /'ɒnwəd(z)/ *adv* para a frente/diante

ooze /u:z/ *vt/i* escorrer, verter

opal /'əʊpl/ *n* opala *f*

opaque /əʊ'peɪk/ *a* opaco, tosco

open /'əʊpən/ *a* aberto; (*view*) aberto, amplo; (*free to all*) aberto ao público; (*attempt*) aberto □ *vt/i* abrir(-se); (*of shop, play*) abrir. **in the** ~ **air** ao ar livre. **keep** ~ **house** receber muito, abrir a porta para todos. ~ **on to** dar para. ~ **out** *or* **up** abrir(-se). ~-**heart** *a* (*of surgery*) de coração aberto. ~-**minded** *a* imparcial. ~-**plan** *a* sem divisórias. ~ **secret** segredo *m* de polichinelo. ~ **sea** mar *m* alto. ~**ness** *n* abertura *f*; (*frankness*) franqueza *f*

opener /'əʊpənə(r)/ *n* (*tins*) abridor *m* de latas; (*bottles*) saca-rolhas *m invar*

opening /'əʊpənɪŋ/ *n* abertura *f*; (*beginning*) começo *m*; (*opportunity*) oportunidade *f*; (*job*) vaga *f*

openly /'əʊpənlɪ/ *adv* abertamente

opera /'ɒprə/ *n* ópera *f*. ~-**glasses** *npl* binóculo (de teatro) *m*, (*P*) binóculos *mpl*. ~**tic** /ɒpə'rætɪk/ *a* de ópera

operat|e /'ɒpəreɪt/ *vt/i* operar; (*techn*) (pôr a) funcionar. ~**e on** (*med*) operar. ~**ing-theatre** *n* (*med*) anfiteatro *m*, sala *f* de operações. ~**ion** /-'reɪʃn/ *n* operação *f*. **in** ~**ion** em vigor; (*techn*) em funcionamento. ~**ional** /-'reɪʃənl/ *a* operacional. ~**or** *n* operador *m*; (*telephonist*) telefonista *mf*

operative /'ɒpərətɪv/ *a* (*surgical*) operatório; (*law etc*) em vigor

opinion /ə'pɪnɪən/ *n* opinião *f*, parecer *m*. **in my** ~ a meu ver. ~ **poll** *n* sondagem (de opinião) *f*. ~**ated** /-eɪtɪd/ *a* dogmático

opium /'əʊpɪəm/ *n* ópio *m*

Oporto /ə'pɔːtəʊ/ *n* Porto *m*

opponent /ə'pəʊnənt/ *n* adversário *m*, antagonista *mf*, oponente *mf*

opportune /'ɒpətjuːn/ *a* oportuno

opportunity /ɒpə'tjuːnətɪ/ *n* oportunidade *f*

oppos|e /ə'pəʊz/ *vt* opor-se a. ~**ed to** oposto a. ~**ing** *a* oposto

opposite /'ɒpəzɪt/ *a* & *n* oposto (*m*), contrário (*m*) □ *adv* em frente □ *prep* ~ **(to)** em frente de

opposition /ɒpə'zɪʃn/ *n* oposição *f*

oppress /ə'pres/ *vt* oprimir. ~**ion** /-ʃn/ *n* opressão *f*. ~**ive** *a* opressivo. ~**or** *n* opressor *m*

opt /ɒpt/ *vi* ~ **for** optar por. ~ **out** recusar-se a participar (**of** de). ~ **to do** escolher fazer

optical /'ɒptɪkl/ *a* óptico. ~ **illusion** ilusão *f* óptica

optician /ɒp'tɪʃn/ *n* oculista *mf*

optimis|t /'ɒptɪmɪst/ n otimista mf. (P) optimista mf. ~m /-zəm/ n otimismo m, (P) optimismo m. ~tic /-'mɪstɪk/ a otimista, (P) optimista. ~tically /-'mɪstɪklɪ/ adv com otimismo, (P) optimismo

optimum /'ɒptɪməm/ a & n (pl -ima) ótimo (m), (P) óptimo (m)

option /'ɒpʃn/ n escolha f, opção f. have no ~ (but) não ter outro remédio (senão)

optional /'ɒpʃənl/ a opcional, facultativo

opulen|t /'ɒpjʊlənt/ a opulento. ~ce n opulência f

or /ɔ:(r)/ conj ou; (with negative) nem. ~ else senão

oracle /'ɒrəkl/ n oráculo m

oral /'ɔ:rəl/ a oral

orange /'ɒrɪndʒ/ n laranja f; (colour) laranja m, cor f de laranja □ a de laranja; (colour) alaranjado, cor de laranja

orator /'ɒrətə(r)/ n orador m. ~y n oratória f

orbit /'ɔ:bɪt/ n órbita f □ vt (pt orbited) gravitar em torno de

orchard /'ɔ:tʃəd/ n pomar m

orchestra /'ɔ:kɪstrə/ n orquestra f. ~l /-'kestrəl/ a orquestral

orchestrate /'ɔ:kɪstreɪt/ vt orquestrar

orchid /'ɔ:kɪd/ n orquídea f

ordain /ɔ:'deɪn/ vt decretar; (relig) ordenar

ordeal /ɔ:'di:l/ n prova f, provação f

order /'ɔ:də(r)/ n ordem f, (comm) encomenda f, pedido m □ vt ordenar; (goods etc) encomendar. in ~ that para que. in ~ to para

orderly /'ɔ:dəlɪ/ a ordenado, em ordem; (not unruly) ordeiro □ n (mil) ordenança f; (med) servente m de hospital

ordinary /'ɔ:dɪnrɪ/ a normal, ordinário, vulgar. out of the ~ fora do comum

ordination /ɔ:dɪ'neɪʃn/ n (relig) ordenação f

ore /ɔ:(r)/ n minério m

organ /'ɔ:gən/ n órgão m. ~ist n organista mf

organic /ɔ:'gænɪk/ a orgânico

organism /'ɔ:gənɪzəm/ n organismo m

organiz|e /'ɔ:gənaɪz/ vt organizar. ~ation /-'zeɪʃn/ n organização f. ~er n organizador m

orgasm /'ɔ:gæzəm/ n orgasmo m

orgy /'ɔ:dʒɪ/ n orgia f

Orient /'ɔ:rɪənt/ n the ~ o Oriente m. ~al /-'entl/ a & n oriental (mf)

orientat|e /'ɔ:rɪənteɪt/ vt orientar. ~ion /-'teɪʃn/ n orientação f

orifice /'ɒrɪfɪs/ n orifício m

origin /'ɒrɪdʒɪn/ n origem f

original /ə'rɪdʒənl/ a original; (not copied) original. ~ity /-'nælətɪ/ n originalidade f. ~ly adv originalmente; (in the beginning) originariamente

originat|e /ə'rɪdʒəneɪt/ vt/i originar (-se). ~e from provir de. ~or n iniciador m, criador m, autor m

ornament /'ɔ:nəmənt/ n ornamento m; (object) peça f decorativa. ~al /-'mentl/ a ornamental. ~ation /-en'teɪʃn/ n ornamentação f

ornate /ɔ:'neɪt/ a florido, floreado

ornitholog|y /ɔ:nɪ'θɒlədʒɪ/ n ornitologia f. ~ist n ornitólogo m

orphan /'ɔ:fn/ n órfã(o) f(m) □ vt deixar órfão. ~age n orfanato m

orthodox /'ɔ:θədɒks/ a ortodoxo

orthopaedic /ɔ:θə'pi:dɪk/ a ortopédico

oscillate /'ɒsɪleɪt/ vi oscilar, vacilar

ostensibl|e /ɒs'tensəbl/ a aparente, pretenso. ~y adv aparentemente, pretensamente

ostentati|on /ɒsten'teɪʃn/ n ostentação f. ~ous /-'teɪʃəs/ a ostentoso, ostensivo

osteopath /'ɒstɪəpæθ/ n osteopata mf

ostracize /'ɒstrəsaɪz/ vt pôr de lado, marginalizar

ostrich /'ɒstrɪtʃ/ n avestruz mf

other /'ʌðə(r)/ a, n & pron outro (m) □ adv ~ than diferente de, senão. (some) ~s outros. the ~ day no outro dia. the ~ one o outro

otherwise /'ʌðəwaɪz/ adv de outro modo □ conj senão, caso contrário

otter /'ɒtə(r)/ n lontra f

ouch /aʊtʃ/ int ai!, ui!

ought /ɔ:t/ v aux (pt ought) dever. you ~ to stay você devia ficar. he ~ to succeed ele deve vencer. I ~ to have done it eu devia tê-lo feito

ounce /aʊns/ n onça f (= 28,35g)

our /'aʊə(r)/ a nosso(s), nossa(s)

ours /'aʊəz/ poss pron o(s) nosso(s), a(s) nossa(s)

ourselves /aʊə'selvz/ pron nós mesmos/próprios; (reflexive) nos. by ~ sozinhos

oust /aʊst/ vt expulsar, obrigar a sair

out /aʊt/ adv fora; (of light, fire) apagado; (in blossom) aberto, desabrochado; (of tide) baixo. be ~ não estar em casa, estar fora (de casa); (wrong) enganar-se. be ~ to estar resolvido a. run/etc ~ sair correndo/etc. ~-and-~ a completo, rematado. ~ of fora de; (without) sem. ~ of pity/etc por pena/etc. made ~ of feito de or em. take ~ of tirar de. 5 ~ of 6 5 (de) entre 6. ~ of date fora de moda; (not valid) fora do prazo. ~ of doors ao ar livre. ~ of one's mind doido. ~ of

order quebrado. **~ of place** deslocado. **~ of the way** afastado. **~-patient** n doente mf de consulta externa

outboard /'aʊtbɔːd/ a **~ motor** motor m de popa

outbreak /'aʊtbreɪk/ n (of flu etc) surto m, epidemia f; (of war) deflagração f

outburst /'aʊtbɜːst/ n explosão f

outcast /'aʊtkɑːst/ n pária m

outcome /'aʊtkʌm/ n resultado m

outcry /'aʊtkraɪ/ n clamor m; (protest) protesto m

outdated /aʊt'deɪtɪd/ a fora da moda, ultrapassado

outdo /aʊt'duː/ vt (pt -did, pp -done) ultrapassar, superar

outdoor /'aʊtdɔː(r)/ a ao ar livre. **~s** /-'dɔːz/ adv fora de casa, ao ar livre

outer /'aʊtə(r)/ a exterior. **~ space** espaço (cósmico) m

outfit /'aʊtfɪt/ n equipamento m; (clothes) roupa f

outgoing /'aʊtgəʊɪŋ/ a que vai sair; (of minister etc) demissionário; (fig) sociável. **~s** npl despesas fpl

outgrow /aʊt'grəʊ/ vt (pt -grew, pp -grown) crescer mais do que; (clothes) já não caber em

outhouse /'aʊthaʊs/ n anexo m, dependência f

outing /'aʊtɪŋ/ n saída f, passeio m

outlandish /aʊt'lændɪʃ/ a exótico, estranho

outlaw /'aʊtlɔː/ n fora-da-lei mf, bandido m □ vt banir, proscrever

outlay /'aʊtleɪ/ n despesa(s) f(pl)

outlet /'aʊtlet/ n saída f, escoadouro m; (for goods) mercado m, saída f; (for feelings) escape m, vazão m; (electr) tomada f

outline /'aʊtlaɪn/ n contorno m; (summary) plano m geral, esquema m, esboço m □ vt contornar; (summarize) descrever em linhas gerais

outlive /aʊt'lɪv/ vt sobreviver a

outlook /'aʊtlʊk/ n (view) vista f; (mental attitude) visão f; (future prospects) perspectiva(s) f(pl)

outlying /'aʊtlaɪɪŋ/ a afastado, remoto

outnumber /aʊt'nʌmbə(r)/ vt ultrapassar em número

outpost /'aʊtpəʊst/ n posto m avançado

output /'aʊtpʊt/ n rendimento m; (of computer) saída f, output m

outrage /'aʊtreɪdʒ/ n atrocidade f, crime m; (scandal) escândalo m □ vt ultrajar

outrageous /aʊt'reɪdʒəs/ a (shocking) escandaloso; (very cruel) atroz

outright /'aʊtraɪt/ adv completamente; (at once) imediatamente;

(frankly) abertamente □ a completo; (refusal) claro

outset /'aʊtset/ n início m, começo m, princípio m

outside[1] /aʊt'saɪd/ n exterior m □ adv (lá) (por) fora □ prep (para) fora de, além de; (in front of) diante de. **at the ~** no máximo

outside[2] /'aʊtsaɪd/ a exterior

outsider /aʊt'saɪdə(r)/ n estranho m; (in race) cavalo m com poucas probabilidades, azarão m

outsize /'aʊtsaɪz/ a tamanho extra invar

outskirts /'aʊtskɜːts/ npl arredores mpl, subúrbios mpl

outspoken /aʊt'spəʊkn/ a franco

outstanding /aʊt'stændɪŋ/ a saliente, proeminente; (debt) por saldar; (very good) notável, destacado

outstretched /aʊt'stretʃt/ a (arm) estendido, esticado

outstrip /aʊt'strɪp/ vt (pt -stripped) ultrapassar, passar à frente de

outward /'aʊtwəd/ a para o exterior; (sign etc) exterior; (journey) de ida. **~ly** adv exteriormente. **~s** adv para o exterior

outwit /aʊt'wɪt/ vt (pt -witted) ser mais esperto que, enganar

oval /'əʊvl/ n & a oval (m)

ovary /'əʊvəri/ n ovário m

ovation /əʊ'veɪʃn/ n ovação f

oven /'ʌvn/ n forno m

over /'əʊvə(r)/ prep sobre, acima de, por cima de; (across) de para o/do outro lado de; (during) durante, em; (more than) mais de □ adv por cima; (too) demais, demasiadamente; (ended) acabado. **the film is ~** o filme já acabou. **jump/etc ~** saltar/ etc por cima. **he has some ~** ele tem uns de sobra. **all ~ the country** em/ por todo o país. **all ~ the table** por toda a mesa. **~ and above** (besides, in addition to) (para) além de. **~ and ~** repetidas vezes. **~ there** ali, lá, acolá

over- /'əʊvə(r)/ pref sobre-, super-; (excessively) demais, demasiado

overall[1] /'əʊvərɔːl/ n bata f. **~s** macacão m, (P) fato-macaco m

overall[2] /'əʊvərɔːl/ a global; (length etc) total □ adv globalmente

overawe /əʊvər'ɔː/ vt intimidar

overbalance /əʊvə'bæləns/ vt/i (fazer) perder o equilíbrio

overbearing /əʊvə'beərɪŋ/ a autoritário, despótico; (arrogant) arrogante

overboard /'əʊvəbɔːd/ adv (pela) borda fora

overcast /əʊvə'kɑːst/ a encoberto, nublado

overcharge /əʊvə'tʃɑːdʒ/ vt **~ sb (for)** cobrar demais a alg (por)

overcoat /ˈəʊvəkəʊt/ n casacão m; (for men) sobretudo m

overcome /əʊvəˈkʌm/ vt (pt -came, pp -come) superar, vencer. ~ by sucumbindo a, dominado or vencido por

overcrowded /əʊvəˈkraʊdɪd/ a apinhado, superlotado; (country) superpovoado

overdo /əʊvəˈduː/ vt (pt -did, pp -done) exagerar, levar longe demais. ~ne (culin) cozinhado demais

overdose /ˈəʊvədəʊs/ n dose f excessiva

overdraft /ˈəʊvədrɑːft/ n saldo m negativo

overdraw /əʊvəˈdrɔː/ vt (pt -drew, pp -drawn) sacar a descoberto

overdue /əʊvəˈdjuː/ a em atraso, atrasado; (belated) tardio

overestimate /əʊvərˈestɪmeɪt/ vt sobreestimar, atribuir valor excessivo a

overexpose /əʊvərɪkˈspəʊz/ vt expor demais

overflow[1] /əʊvəˈfləʊ/ vt/i extravasar, transbordar (with de)

overflow[2] /ˈəʊvəfləʊ/ n (outlet) descarga f; (excess) excesso m

overgrown /əʊvəˈɡrəʊn/ a que cresceu demais; (garden etc) invadido pela vegetação

overhang /əʊvəˈhæŋ/ vt (pt -hung) estar sobranceiro a, pairar sobre □ vi projetar-se, (P) projectar-se para fora □ n saliência f

overhaul[1] /əʊvəˈhɔːl/ vt fazer uma revisão em

overhaul[2] /ˈəʊvəhɔːl/ n revisão f

overhead[1] /əʊvəˈhed/ adv em or por cima, ao or no alto

overhead[2] /ˈəʊvəhed/ a aéreo. ~s npl despesas fpl gerais

overhear /əʊvəˈhɪə(r)/ vt (pt -heard) (eavesdrop) ouvir sem conhecimento do falante; (hear by chance) ouvir por acaso

overjoyed /əʊvəˈdʒɔɪd/ a radiante, felicíssimo

overlap /əʊvəˈlæp/ vt/i (pt -lapped) sobrepor(-se) parcialmente; (fig) coincidir

overleaf /əʊvəˈliːf/ adv no verso

overload /əʊvəˈləʊd/ vt sobrecarregar

overlook /əʊvəˈlʊk/ vt deixar passar; (of window) dar para; (of building) dominar

overnight /əʊvəˈnaɪt/ adv durante a noite; (fig) dum dia para o outro □ a (train) da noite; (stay, journey, etc) noite, noturno; (fig) súbito

overpass /əʊvəˈpɑːs/ n passagem f superior

overpay /əʊvəˈpeɪ/ vt (pt -paid) pagar em excesso

overpower /əʊvəˈpaʊə(r)/ vt dominar, subjugar; (fig) esmagar. ~ing a esmagador; (heat) sufocante, insuportável

overpriced /əʊvəˈpraɪst/ a muito caro

overrate /əʊvəˈreɪt/ vt sobreestimar, exagerar o valor de

overrid|e /əʊvəˈraɪd/ vt (pt -rode, pp -ridden) prevalecer sobre, passar por cima de. ~ing a primordial, preponderante; (importance) maior

overripe /ˈəʊvəraɪp/ a demasiado maduro

overrule /əʊvəˈruːl/ vt anular, rejeitar; (claim) indeferir

overrun /əʊvəˈrʌn/ vt (pt -ran, pp -run, pres p -running) invadir; (a limit) exceder, ultrapassar

overseas /əʊvəˈsiːz/ a ultramarino; (abroad) estrangeiro □ adv no ultramar, no estrangeiro

oversee /əʊvəˈsiː/ vt (pt -saw pp -seen) supervisionar. ~r /ˈəʊvəsɪə(r)/ n capataz m

overshadow /əʊvəˈʃædəʊ/ vt (fig) eclipsar, ofuscar

oversight /ˈəʊvəsaɪt/ n lapso m

oversleep /əʊvəˈsliːp/ vi (pt -slept) acordar tarde, dormir demais

overt /ˈəʊvɜːt/ a manifesto, claro, patente

overtake /əʊvəˈteɪk/ vt/i (pt -took, pp -taken) ultrapassar

overthrow /əʊvəˈθrəʊ/ vt (pt -threw, pp -thrown) derrubar □ n /ˈəʊvəθrəʊ/ (pol) derrubada f

overtime /ˈəʊvətaɪm/ n horas fpl extras

overtones /ˈəʊvətəʊnz/ npl (fig) tom m, implicação f

overture /ˈəʊvətʃʊə(r)/ n (mus) abertura f; (fig) proposta f, abordagem f

overturn /əʊvəˈtɜːn/ vt/i virar(-se); (car, plane) capotar, virar-se

overweight /əʊvəˈweɪt/ a be ~ ter excesso de peso

overwhelm /əʊvəˈwelm/ vt oprimir; (defeat) esmagar; (amaze) assoberbar. ~ing a esmagador; (urge) irresistível

overwork /əʊvəˈwɜːk/ vt/i sobrecarregar(-se) com trabalho □ n excesso m de trabalho

overwrought /əʊvəˈrɔːt/ a muito agitado, superexcitado

ow|e /əʊ/ vt dever. ~ing a devido. ~ing to devido a

owl /aʊl/ n coruja f

own[1] /əʊn/ a próprio. **a house**/etc **of one's** ~ uma casa/etc própria. **get one's** ~ **back** (collog) ir à forra, (P) desforrar-se, (P) aguentar-se. **on one's** ~ sozinho

own² /əʊn/ *vt* possuir. ~ **up (to)** (*colloq*) confessar. ~**er** *n* proprietário *m*, dono *m*. ~**ership** *n* posse *f*, propriedade *f*

ox /ɒks/ *n* (*pl* **oxen**) boi *m*

oxygen /ˈɒksɪdʒən/ *n* oxigénio *m*, (*P*) oxigénio *m*

oyster /ˈɔɪstə(r)/ *n* ostra *f*

ozone /ˈəʊzəʊn/ *n* ozónio *m*, (*P*) ozono *m*. ~ **layer** camada *f* de ozónio, (*P*) ozono *m*

P

pace /peɪs/ *n* passo *m*; (*fig*) ritmo *m* □ *vt* percorrer passo a passo □ *vi* ~ **up and down** andar de um lado para o outro. **keep** ~ **with** acompanhar, manter-se a par de

pacemaker /ˈpeɪsmeɪkə(r)/ *n* (*med*) marcapasso *m*, (*P*) pacemaker *m*

Pacific /pəˈsɪfɪk/ *a* pacífico □ *n* ~ (**Ocean**) (Oceano) Pacífico *m*

pacifist /ˈpæsɪfɪst/ *n* pacifista *mf*

pacify /ˈpæsɪfaɪ/ *vt* pacificar, apaziguar

pack /pæk/ *n* pacote *m*; (*mil*) mochila *f*; (*of hounds*) matilha *f*; (*of lies*) porção *f*; (*of cards*) baralho *m* □ *vt* empacotar; (*suitcase*) fazer; (*box, room*) encher; (*press down*) atulhar, encher até não caber mais □ *vi* fazer as malas. ~ **into** (*cram*) apinhar em, comprimir em. **send** ~**ing** pôr a andar, mandar passear. ~**ed** *a* apinhado. ~**ed lunch** merenda *f*

package /ˈpækɪdʒ/ *n* pacote *m*, embrulho *m* □ *vt* embalar. ~ **deal** pacote *m* de propostas. ~ **holiday** pacote *m* turístico, (*P*) viagem *f* organizada

packet /ˈpækɪt/ *n* pacote *m*; (*of cigarettes*) maço *m*

pact /pækt/ *n* pacto *m*

pad /pæd/ *n* (*in clothing*) chumaço *m*; (*for writing*) bloco *m* de papel/de notas; (*for ink*) almofada *f* de carimbo *f*. (**launching**) ~ rampa *f* de lançamento □ *vt* (*pt* **padded**) enchumaçar, acolchoar; (*fig: essay etc*) encher linguiça. ~**ding** *n* chumaço *m*; (*fig*) linguiça *f*

paddle¹ /ˈpædl/ *n* remo *m* de canoa. ~-**steamer** *n* vapor *m* movido a rodas

paddle² /ˈpædl/ *vi* chapinhar, molhar os pés. ~**ing pool** piscina *f* de plástico para crianças

paddock /ˈpædək/ *n* cercado *m*; (*at racecourse*) paddock *m*

padlock /ˈpædlɒk/ *n* cadeado *m* □ *vt* fechar com cadeado

paediatrician /piːdɪəˈtrɪʃn/ *n* pediatra *mf*

pagan /ˈpeɪgən/ *a* & *n* pagão (*m*), pagã (*f*)

page¹ /peɪdʒ/ *n* (*of book etc*) página *f*

page² /peɪdʒ/ *vt* mandar chamar

pageant /ˈpædʒənt/ *n* espetáculo *m*, (*P*) espectáculo *m* (histórico); (*procession*) cortejo *m*. ~**ry** *n* pompa *f*

pagoda /pəˈgəʊdə/ *n* pagode *m*

paid /peɪd/ *see* **pay** □ *a* **put** ~ **to** (*colloq: end*) pôr fim a

pail /peɪl/ *n* balde *m*

pain /peɪn/ *n* dor *f*. ~**s** esforços *mpl* □ *vt* magoar. **be in** ~ sofrer, ter dores. ~-**killer** *n* analgésico *m*. **take** ~**s to** esforçar-se por. ~**ful** *a* doloroso; (*grievous, laborious*) penoso. ~**less** *a* sem dor, indolor

painstaking /ˈpeɪnzteɪkɪŋ/ *a* cuidadoso, esmerado, meticuloso

paint /peɪnt/ *n* tinta *f*. ~**s** (*in box*) tintas *fpl* □ *vt/i* pintar. ~**er** *n* pintor *m*. ~**ing** *n* pintura *f*

paintbrush /ˈpeɪntbrʌʃ/ *n* pincel *m*

pair /peə(r)/ *n* par *m*. **a** ~ **of scissors** uma tesoura. **a** ~ **of trousers** um par de calças. **in** ~**s** aos pares □ *vi* ~ **off** formar pares

Pakistan /pɑːkɪˈstɑːn/ *n* Paquistão *m*. ~**i** *a* & *n* paquistanês (*m*)

pal /pæl/ *n* (*colloq*) colega *mf*, amigo *m*

palace /ˈpælɪs/ *n* palácio *m*

palat|e /ˈpælət/ *n* palato *m*. ~**able** *a* saboroso, gostoso; (*fig*) agradável

palatial /pəˈleɪʃl/ *a* suntuoso, (*P*) sumptuoso

pale /peɪl/ *a* (**-er**, **-est**) pálido; (*colour*) claro □ *vi* empalidecer. ~**ness** *n* palidez *f*

Palestin|e /ˈpæləstaɪn/ *n* Palestina *f*. ~**ian** /-ˈstɪnɪən/ *a* & *n* palestino (*m*)

palette /ˈpælɪt/ *n* paleta *f*. ~-**knife** *n* espátula *f*

pall /pɔːl/ *vi* tornar-se enfadonho, perder o interesse (**on** para)

pallid /ˈpælɪd/ *a* pálido

palm /pɑːm/ *n* (*of hand*) palma *f*; (*tree*) palmeira *f* □ *vt* impingir (**on** a). **P**~ **Sunday** Domingo *m* de Ramos

palpable /ˈpælpəbl/ *a* palpável

palpitat|e /ˈpælpɪteɪt/ *vi* palpitar. ~**ion** /-ˈteɪʃn/ *n* palpitação *f*

paltry /ˈpɔːltrɪ/ *a* (**-ier**, **-iest**) irrisório

pamper /ˈpæmpə(r)/ *vt* mimar, paparicar

pamphlet /ˈpæmflɪt/ *n* panfleto *m*, folheto *m*

pan /pæn/ *n* panela *f*; (*for frying*) frigideira *f* □ *vt* (*pt* **panned**) (*colloq*) criticar severamente

panacea /pænəˈsɪə/ *n* panaceia *f*

panache /pæˈnæʃ/ *n* brio *m*, estilo *m*, panache *m*

pancake /ˈpænkeɪk/ *n* crepe *m*, panqueca *f*

pancreas /'pæŋkrɪəs/ *n* páncreas *m*

panda /'pændə/ *n* panda *m*

pandemonium /pændɪ'məonɪəm/ *n* pandemónio *m*, (P) pandemónio *m*, caos *m*

pander /'pændə(r)/ *vi* ~ to prestar-se a servir, ir ao encontro de, fazer concessões a

pane /peɪn/ *n* vidraça *f*

panel /'pænl/ *n* painel *m*; (*jury*) júri *m*; (*speakers*) convidados *mpl*. (*instrument*) ~ painel *m* de instrumentos, (P) de bordo. ~led *a* apainelado. ~ling *n* apainelamento *m*. ~list *n* convidado *m*

pang /pæŋ/ *n* pontada *f*, dor *f* aguda e súbita. ~s (*of hunger*) ataques *mpl* de fome. ~s of conscience remorsos *mpl*

panic /'pænɪk/ *n* pânico *m* □ *vt/i* (*pt* panicked) desorientar(-se), (fazer) entrar em pânico. ~-stricken *a* tomado de pânico

panoram|a /pænə'rɑːmə/ *n* panorama *m*. ~ic /-'ræmɪk/ *a* panorâmico

pansy /'pænzɪ/ *n* amor-perfeito *m*

pant /pænt/ *vi* ofegar, arquejar

panther /'pænθə(r)/ *n* pantera *f*

panties /'pæntɪz/ *npl* (*colloq*) calcinhas *fpl*

pantomime /'pæntəmaɪm/ *n* pantomima *f*

pantry /'pæntrɪ/ *n* despensa *f*

pants /pænts/ *npl* (*colloq: underwear*) cuecas *fpl*; (*colloq: trousers*) calças *fpl*

papal /'peɪpl/ *a* papal

paper /'peɪpə(r)/ *n* papel *m*; (*newspaper*) jornal *m*; (*exam*) prova *f* escrita; (*essay*) comunicação *f*. ~s *npl* (*for identification*) documentos *mpl* □ *vt* forrar com papel. on ~ por escrito. ~-clip *n* clipe *m*

paperback /'peɪpəbæk/ *a* & *n* ~ (book) livro *m* de capa mole

paperweight /'peɪpəweɪt/ *n* pesa-papéis *m invar*, (P) pisa-papéis *m invar*

paperwork /'peɪpəwɜːk/ *n* trabalho *m* de secretária; (*pej*) papelada *f*

paprika /'pæprɪkə/ *n* páprica *f*, pimentão *m* doce

par /pɑː(r)/ *n* be below ~ estar abaixo do padrão desejado. on a ~ with em igualdade com

parable /'pærəbl/ *n* parábola *f*

parachut|e /'pærəʃuːt/ *n* pára-quedas *m invar* □ *vi* descer de pára-quedas. ~ist *n* pára-quedista *m/f*

parade /pə'reɪd/ *n* (*mil*) parada *f* militar; (*procession*) procissão *f* □ *vi* desfilar □ *vt* alardear, exibir

paradise /'pærədaɪs/ *n* paraíso *m*

paradox /'pærədɒks/ *n* paradoxo *m*. ~ical /-'dɒksɪkl/ *a* paradoxal

paraffin /'pærəfɪn/ *n* querosene *m*, (P) petróleo *m*

paragon /'pærəgən/ *n* modelo *m* de perfeição

paragraph /'pærəgrɑːf/ *n* parágrafo *m*

parallel /'pærəlel/ *a* & *n* paralelo (*m*) □ *vt* (*pt* parelleled) comparar(-se) a

paralyse /'pærəlaɪz/ *vt* paralisar

paraly|sis /pə'ræləsɪs/ *n* paralisia *f*. ~tic /-'lɪtɪk/ *a* & *n* paralítico (*m*)

parameter /pə'ræmɪtə(r)/ *n* parâmetro *m*

paramount /'pærəmaʊnt/ *a* supremo, primordial

parapet /'pærəpɪt/ *n* parapeito *m*

paraphernalia /pærəfə'neɪlɪə/ *n* equipamento *m*, tralha *f* (*colloq*)

paraphrase /'pærəfreɪz/ *n* paráfrase *f* □ *vt* parafrasear

paraplegic /pærə'pliːdʒɪk/ *n* paraplégico *m*

parasite /'pærəsaɪt/ *n* parasita *mf*

parasol /'pærəsɒl/ *n* sombrinha *f*; (*on table*) pára-sol *m*, guarda-sol *m*

parcel /'pɑːsl/ *n* embrulho *m*; (*for post*) encomenda *f*

parch /pɑːtʃ/ *vt* ressecar. be ~ed estar com muita sede

parchment /'pɑːtʃmənt/ *n* pergaminho *m*

pardon /'pɑːdn/ *n* perdão *m*; (*jur*) perdão *m*, indulto *m* □ *vt* (*pt* pardoned) perdoar. I beg your ~ perdão, desculpe. (I beg your) ~? como?

pare /peə(r)/ *vt* aparar, cortar; (*peel*) descascar

parent /'peərənt/ *n* pai *m*, mãe *f*. ~s *npl* pais *mpl*. ~al /pə'rentl/ *a* dos pais, paterno, materno

parenthesis /pə'renθəsɪs/ *n* (*pl* -theses) /-siːz/ parêntese *m*, parêntesis *m*

Paris /'pærɪs/ *n* Paris *m*

parish /'pærɪʃ/ *n* paróquia *f*; (*municipal*) freguesia *f*. ~ioner /pə-'rɪʃənə(r)/ *n* paroquiano *m*

parity /'pærətɪ/ *n* paridade *f*

park /pɑːk/ *n* parque *m* □ *vt* estacionar. ~ing *n* estacionamento *m*. no ~ing estacionamento proibido. ~ing-meter *n* parquímetro *m*

parliament /'pɑːləmənt/ *n* parlamento *m*, assembleia *f*. ~ary /-'mentrɪ/ *a* parlamentar

parochial /pə'rəʊkɪəl/ *a* paroquial; (*fig*) provinciano, tacanho

parody /'pærədɪ/ *n* paródia *f* □ *vt* parodiar

parole /pə'rəʊl/ *n* on ~ em liberdade condicional □ *vt* pôr em liberdade condicional

parquet /'pɑːkeɪ/ *n* parquê *m*, parquete *m*

parrot /'pærət/ n papagaio m

parry /'pærɪ/ vt (a)parar □ n parada f

parsimonious /pɑ:sɪ'məʊnɪəs/ a parco; (mean) avarento

parsley /'pɑ:slɪ/ n salsa f

parsnip /'pɑ:snɪp/ n cherovia f, pastinaga f

parson /'pɑ:sn/ n pároco m, pastor m

part /pɑ:t/ n parte f; (of serial) episódio m; (of machine) peça f; (theatre) papel m; (side in dispute) partido m □ a parcial □ adv em parte □ vt/i separar (-se) (from de). in ~ em parte. on the ~ of da parte de. ~ exchange n troca f parcial. ~ of speech categoria f gramatical. ~time a & adv a tempo parcial, part-time. take ~ in tomar parte em. these ~s estas partes

partial /'pɑ:ʃl/ a (incomplete, biased) parcial. be ~ to gostar de. ~ity /-ɪ'ælətɪ/ n parcialidade f; (liking) predileção f, (P) predilecção f (for por). ~ly adv parcialmente

particip|ate /pɑ:'tɪsɪpeɪt/ vi participar (in em). ~ant n /-ənt/ participante mf. ~ation /-'peɪʃn/ n participação f

participle /'pɑ:tɪsɪpl/ n particípio m

particle /'pɑ:tɪkl/ n partícula f; (of dust) grão m; (fig) mínimo m

particular /pə'tɪkjʊlə(r)/ a especial, particular; (fussy) exigente; (careful) escrupuloso. ~s npl pormenores mpl. in ~ adv em especial, particularmente. ~ly adv particularmente

parting /'pɑ:tɪŋ/ n separação f; (in hair) risca f □ a de despedida

partisan /pɑ:tɪ'zæn/ n partidário m; (mil) guerrilheiro m

partition /pɑ:'tɪʃn/ n (of room) tabique m, divisória f; (pol: division) partilha f, divisão f □ vt dividir, repartir. ~ off dividir por meio de tabique

partly /'pɑ:tlɪ/ adv em parte

partner /'pɑ:tnə(r)/ n sócio m; (cards, sport) parceiro m; (dancing) par m. ~ship n associação f; (comm) sociedade f

partridge /'pɑ:trɪdʒ/ n perdiz f

party /'pɑ:tɪ/ n festa f, reunião f; (group) grupo m; (pol) partido m; (jur) parte f. ~ line (telephone) linha f coletiva, (P) colectiva

pass /pɑ:s/ vt/i (pt passed) passar; (overtake) ultrapassar; (exam) passar; (approve) aprovar. (law) aprovar. ~ (by) passar por □ n (permit, sport) passe m; (geog) desfiladeiro m, garganta f; (in exam) aprovação f. make a ~ at (colloq) atirar-se para (colloq). ~ away falecer. ~ out or round distribuir. ~ out (colloq: faint) perder os sentidos, desmaiar. ~ over (disre-

gard, overlook) passar por cima de. ~ up (colloq: forgo) deixar perder

passable /'pɑ:səbl/ a passável; (road) transitável

passage /'pæsɪdʒ/ n (voyage) travessia f; (corridor) corredor m, passagem f

passenger /'pæsɪndʒə(r)/ n passageiro m

passer-by /pɑ:sə'baɪ/ n (pl passers-by) transeunte mf

passion /'pæʃn/ n paixão f. ~ate a apaixonado, exaltado

passive /'pæsɪv/ a passivo. ~ness n passividade f

Passover /'pɑ:səʊvə(r)/ n Páscoa f dos judeus

passport /'pɑ:spɔ:t/ n passaporte m

password /'pɑ:swɜ:d/ n senha f

past /pɑ:st/ a passado m; (former) antigo □ n passado m □ prep para além de; (in time) mais de; (in front of) diante de □ adv em frente. be ~ it já não ser capaz. it's five ~ eleven são onze e cinco. these ~ months estes últimos meses

pasta /'pæstə/ n prato m de massa(s)

paste /peɪst/ n cola f; (culin) massa(s) f(pl); (dough) massa f; (jewellery) strass m □ vt colar

pastel /'pæstl/ n pastel m □ a pastel invar

pasteurize /'pæstʃəraɪz/ vt pasteurizar

pastille /'pæstɪl/ n pastilha f

pastime /'pɑ:staɪm/ n passatempo m

pastoral /'pɑ:stərəl/ a & n pastoral (f)

pastry /'peɪstrɪ/ n massa f de (pastelaria); (tart) pastel m

pasture /'pɑ:stʃə(r)/ n pastagem f

pasty¹ /'pæstɪ/ n empadinha f

pasty² /'peɪstɪ/ a pastoso

pat /pæt/ vt (pt patted) (hit gently) dar pancadinhas em; (caress) fazer festinhas a □ n pancadinha f; (caress) festinha f □ adv a propósito; (readily) prontamente □ a preparado, pronto

patch /pætʃ/ n remendo m; (over eye) tapa-ôlho m; (spot) mancha f; (small area) pedaço m; (of vegetables) canteiro m, (P) leira f □ vt ~ up remendar. ~ up a quarrel fazer as pazes. bad ~ mau bocado m. not be a ~ on não chegar aos pés de. ~work n obra f de retalhos. ~y a desigual

pâté /'pæteɪ/ n paté m

patent /'peɪtnt/ a & n patente (f) □ vt patentear. ~ leather verniz m, polimento m. ~ly adv claramente

paternal /pə'tɜ:nl/ a paternal; (relative) paterno

paternity /pə'tɜ:nətɪ/ n paternidade f

path /pɑːθ/ n (pl -s /pɑːðz/) caminho m, trilha f; (in park) aléia f; (of rocket) trajetória f, (P) trajectória f

pathetic /pəˈθetɪk/ a patético; (colloq: contemptible) desgraçado (colloq)

patholog|y /pəˈθɒlədʒɪ/ n patologia f. ~ist n patologista mf

pathos /ˈpeɪθɒs/ n patos m, patético m

patience /ˈpeɪʃns/ n paciência f

patient /ˈpeɪʃnt/ a paciente □ n doente mf, paciente mf. ~ly adv pacientemente

patio /ˈpætɪəʊ/ n (pl -os) pátio m

patriot /ˈpætrɪət/ n patriota mf. ~ic /-ˈɒtɪk/ a patriótico. ~ism /-ɪzəm/ n patriotismo m

patrol /pəˈtrəʊl/ n patrulha f □ vt/i patrulhar. ~ car carro m de patrulha

patron /ˈpeɪtrən/ n (of the arts etc) patrocinador m, protetor m, (P) protector m; (of charity) benfeitor m; (customer) freguês m, cliente mf. ~ saint padroeiro m, patrono m

patron|age /ˈpætrənɪdʒ/ n freguesia f, clientela f; (support) patrocinio m. ~ize vt ser cliente de; (support) patrocinar; (condescend) tratar com ares de superioridade

patter[1] /ˈpætə(r)/ n (of rain) tamborilar m, rufo m. ~ of steps som m leve de passos miúdos, corridinha f leve

patter[2] /ˈpætə(r)/ n (of class, profession) giria f, jargão m; (chatter) conversa f fiada

pattern /ˈpætn/ n padrão m; (for sewing) molde m; (example) modelo m

paunch /pɔːntʃ/ n pança f

pause /pɔːz/ n pausa f □ vi pausar, fazer (uma) pausa

pav|e /peɪv/ vt pavimentar. ~e the way preparar o caminho (for para). ~ing-stone n paralelepipedo m, laje f

pavement /ˈpeɪvmənt/ n passeio m

pavilion /pəˈvɪlɪən/ n pavilhão m

paw /pɔː/ n pata f □ vt dar patadas em; (horse) escarvar; (colloq: person) pôr as patas em cima de

pawn[1] /pɔːn/ n (chess) peão m; (fig) joguete m

pawn[2] /pɔːn/ vt empenhar. ~-shop casa f de penhores, prego m (colloq)

pawnbroker /ˈpɔːnbrəʊkə(r)/ n penhorista mf, dono m de casa de penhores, agiota mf

pay /peɪ/ vt/i (pt paid) pagar; (interest) render; (visit, compliment) fazer □ n pagamento m; (wages) vencimento m, ordenado m, salário m. in the ~ of em pagamento de. ~ attention prestar atenção. ~ back restituir. ~ for pagar. ~ homage prestar homenagem. ~ in depositar. ~-slip n contracheque m, (P) folha f de pagamento

payable /ˈpeɪəbl/ a pagável

payment /ˈpeɪmənt/ n pagamento m; (fig: reward) recompensa f

payroll /ˈpeɪrəʊl/ n folha f de pagamentos. be on the ~ fazer parte da folha de pagamento de uma firma

pea /piː/ n ervilha f

peace /piːs/ n paz f. disturb the ~ perturbar a ordem pública. ~able a pacífico

peaceful /ˈpiːsfl/ a pacífico; (calm) calmo, sereno

peacemaker /ˈpiːsmeɪkə(r)/ n mediador m, pacificador m

peach /piːtʃ/ n pêssego m

peacock /ˈpiːkɒk/ n pavão m

peak /piːk/ n pico m, cume m, cimo m; (of cap) pala f; (maximum) máximo m. ~ hours horas fpl de ponta; (electr) horas fpl de carga máxima. ~ed cap boné m de pala

peaky /ˈpiːkɪ/ a com ar doentio

peal /piːl/ n (of bells) repique m; (of laughter) gargalhada f, risada f

peanut /ˈpiːnʌt/ n amendoim m. ~s (sl: small sum) uma bagatela f

pear /peə(r)/ n pera f

pearl /pɜːl/ n pérola f. ~y a nacarado

peasant /ˈpeznt/ n camponês m, aldeão m

peat /piːt/ n turfa f

pebble /ˈpebl/ n seixo m, calhau m

peck /pek/ vt/i bicar; (attack) dar bicadas (em) □ n bicada f; (colloq: kiss) beijo m seco. ~ing order hierarquia f, ordem f de importância

peckish /ˈpekɪʃ/ a be ~ (colloq) ter vontade de comer

peculiar /pɪˈkjuːlɪə(r)/ a bizarro, singular; (special) peculiar (to a), característico (to de). ~ity /-ˈærətɪ/ n singularidade f; (feature) peculiaridade f

pedal /ˈpedl/ n pedal m □ vi (pt pedalled) pedalar

pedantic /prˈdæntɪk/ a pedante

peddle /ˈpedl/ vt vender de porta em porta; (drugs) fazer tráfico de

pedestal /ˈpedɪstl/ n pedestal m

pedestrian /prˈdestrɪən/ n pedestre mf, (P) peão m □ a pedestre; (fig) prosaico. ~ crossing faixa f para pedestres, (P) passadeira f

pedigree /ˈpedɪgriː/ n estirpe f, linhagem f; (of animal) raça f □ a de raça

pedlar /ˈpedlə(r)/ n vendedor m ambulante

peek /piːk/ vi espreitar □ n espreitadela f

peel /piːl/ n casca f □ vt descascar □ vi (skin) pelar; (paint) escamar-se, descascar; (wallpaper) descolar-se. ~ings npl cascas fpl

peep /piːp/ vi espreitar □ n espreitadela f. ~-hole n vigia f; (in door) olho m mágico

peer[1] /pɪə(r)/ vi ~ at/into (searchingly) perscrutar; (with difficulty) esforçar-se por ver

peer[2] /pɪə(r)/ n (equal, noble) par m. ~age n pariato m

peeved /pi:vd/ a (sl) irritado, chateado (sl)

peevish /'pi:vɪʃ/ a irritável

peg /peg/ n cavilha f; (for washing) pregador m de roupa, (P) mola f; (for coats etc) cabide m; (for tent) estaca f □ vt (pt pegged) prender com estacas. off the ~ prêt-à-porter

pejorative /pɪ'dʒɒrətɪv/ a pejorativo

pelican /'pelɪkən/ n pelicano m. ~ crossing passagem f com sinais manobrados pelos pedestres

pellet /'pelɪt/ n bolinha f; (for gun) grão m de chumbo

pelt[1] /pelt/ n pele f

pelt[2] /pelt/ vt bombardear (with com) □ vi chover a cântaros; (run fast) correr em disparada

pelvis /'pelvɪs/ n (anat) pélvis m, bacia f

pen[1] /pen/ n (enclosure) cercado m. play-~ n cercado m, (P) pargue m □ vt (pt penned) encurralar

pen[2] /pen/ n caneta f □ vt (pt penned) escrever. ~-friend n correspondente mf. ~-name n pseudónimo m, (P) pseudónimo m

penal /'pi:nl/ a penal. ~ize vt impôr uma penalidadea; (sport) penalizar

penalty /'penltɪ/ n pena f; (fine) multa f; (sport) penalidade f. ~ kick pênalti m, (P) grande penalidade f

penance /'penəns/ n penitência f

pence /pens/ see penny

pencil /'pensl/ n lápis m □ vt (pt pencilled) escrever or desenhar a lápis. ~-sharpener n apontador m, (P) apara-lápis m invar

pendant /'pendənt/ n berloque m

pending /'pendɪŋ/ a pendente □ prep (during) durante; (until) até

pendulum /'pendjʊləm/ n pêndulo m

penetrat|**e** /'penɪtreɪt/ vt/i penetrar (em). ~ing a penetrante. ~ion /-'treɪʃn/ n penetração f

penguin /'peŋgwɪn/ n pinguim m, (P) pinguim m

penicillin /penɪ'sɪlɪn/ n penicilina f

peninsula /pə'nɪnsjʊlə/ n peninsula f

penis /'pi:nɪs/ n pénis m, (P) pénis m

peniten|**t** /'penɪtənt/ a & n penitente (mf). ~ce n /-əns/ contrição f, penitência f

penitentiary /penɪ'tenʃərɪ/ n (Amer) penitenciária f, cadeia f

penknife /'pennaɪf/ n (pl -knives) canivete m

penniless /'penɪlɪs/ a sem vintém, sem um tostão

penny /'penɪ/ n (pl pennies or pence) péni m, (P) péni m; (fig) centavo m, vintém m

pension /'penʃn/ n pensão f; (in retirement) aposentadoria f, (P) reforma f □ vt ~ off reformar, aposentar. ~er (old-age) ~er reformado m

pensive /'pensɪv/ a pensativo

Pentecost /'pentɪkɒst/ n Pentecostes m

penthouse /'penthaʊs/ n cobertura f, (P) apartamento de luxo (no último andar)

pent-up /'pentʌp/ a reprimido

penultimate /pen'ʌltɪmət/ a penúltimo

people /'pi:pl/ npl pessoas fpl □ n gente f, povo m □ vt povoar. the Portuguese ~ os portugueses mpl. ~ say dizem, diz-se

pep /pep/ n vigor m □ vt ~ up animar. ~ talk discurso m de encorajamento

pepper /'pepə(r)/ n pimenta f; (vegetable) pimentão m, (P) pimento m □ vt apimentar. ~y a apimentado, picante

peppermint /'pepəmɪnt/ n hortelã-pimenta f; (sweet) bala f, (P) pastilha f de hortelã-pimenta

per /pɜ:(r)/ prep por. ~ annum por ano. ~ cent por cento. ~ kilo/etc o quilo/etc

perceive /pə'si:v/ vt perceber; (notice) aperceber-se de

percentage /pə'sentɪdʒ/ n percentagem f

perceptible /pə'septəbl/ a perceptível

percept|**ion** /pə'sepʃn/ n percepção f. ~ive /-tɪv/ a perceptivo, penetrante, perspicaz

perch[1] /pɜ:tʃ/ n poleiro m □ vi empoleirar-se, pousar

perch[2] /pɜ:tʃ/ n (fish) perca f

percolat|**e** /'pɜ:kəleɪt/ vt/i filtrar(-se), passar. ~or n máquina f de café com filtro, cafeteira f

percussion /pə'kʌʃn/ n percussão f

peremptory /pə'remptərɪ/ a peremptório, decisivo

perennial /pə'renɪəl/ a perene; (plant) perene

perfect[1] /'pɜ:fɪkt/ a perfeito. ~ly adv perfeitamente

perfect[2] /pə'fekt/ vt aperfeiçoar. ~ion /-ʃn/ n perfeição f. ~ionist n perfeccionista mf

perforat|**e** /'pɜ:fəreɪt/ vt perfurar. ~ion /-'reɪʃn/ n perfuração f; (line of holes) pontilhado m, picotado m

perform /pə'fɔ:m/ vt (a task; mus) executar; (a function; theat) desempenhar □ vi representar; (function) funcionar. ~ance n (of task; mus) execução f; (of function; theat) desempenho m; (of car) performance f, comportamento m, rendimento m; (colloq: fuss) drama m, cena f. ~er n artista mf

perfume /'pɜ:fju:m/ n perfume m

perfunctory /pə'fʌŋktərɪ/ a superficial, negligente

perhaps /pə'hæps/ adv talvez

peril /'perəl/ n perigo m. ~ous a perigoso

perimeter /pə'rɪmɪtə(r)/ n perímetro m

period /'pɪərɪəd/ n período m, época f; (era) época f; (lesson) hora f de aula, período m letivo, (P) lectivo; (med) período m; (full stop) ponto (final) m □ a (of novel) de costumes; (of furniture) de estilo. ~ic /-'ɒdɪk/ a periódico. ~ical /-'ɒdɪkl/ n periódico m. ~ically /-'ɒdɪklɪ/ adv periodicamente

peripher|y /pə'rɪfərɪ/ n periferia f. ~al a periférico; (fig) marginal, à margem

perish /'perɪʃ/ vi morrer, perecer; (rot) estragar-se, deteriorar-se. ~able a (of goods) deteriorável

perjur|e /'pɜ:dʒə(r)/ vpr ~e o.s. jurar falso, perjurar. ~y n perjúrio m

perk[1] /pɜ:k/ vt/i ~ up (colloq) arrebitar(-se). ~y a (colloq) vivo, animado

perk[2] /pɜ:k/ n (colloq) regalia f, extra m

perm /pɜ:m/ n permanente f □ vt have one's hair ~ed fazer uma permanente

permanen|t /'pɜ:mənənt/ a permanente. ~ce n permanência f. ~tly adv permanentemente, a título permanente

permeable /'pɜ:mɪəbl/ a permeável

permeate /'pɜ:mɪeɪt/ vt/i permear, penetrar

permissible /pə'mɪsəbl/ a permissível, admissível

permission /pə'mɪʃn/ n permissão f, licença f

permissive /pə'mɪsɪv/ a permissivo. ~ society sociedade f permissiva. ~ness n permissividade f

permit[1] /pə'mɪt/ vt (pt permitted) permitir, consentir (sb to a alguém que)

permit[2] /'pɜ:mɪt/ n licença f; (pass) passe m

permutation /pɜ:mju:'teɪʃn/ n permutação f

pernicious /pə'nɪʃəs/ a pernicioso, prejudicial

perpendicular /pɜ:pən'dɪkjʊlə(r)/ a & n perpendicular (f)

perpetrat|e /'pɜ:pɪtreɪt/ vt perpetrar. ~or n autor m

perpetual /pə'petʃʊəl/ a perpétuo

perpetuate /pə'petʃʊeɪt/ vt perpetuar

perplex /pə'pleks/ vt deixar perplexo. ~ed a perplexo. ~ing a confuso. ~ity n perplexidade f

persecut|e /'pɜ:sɪkju:t/ vt perseguir. ~ion /-'kju:ʃn/ n perseguição f

persever|e /pɜ:sɪ'vɪə(r)/ vi perseverar. ~ance n perseverança f

Persian /'pɜ:ʃn/ a & n (lang) persa (m)

persist /pə'sɪst/ vi persistir (in doing em fazer). ~ence n persistência f. ~ent a persistente; (obstinate) teimoso; (continual) contínuo, constante. ~ently adv persistentemente

person /'pɜ:sn/ n pessoa f. in ~ em pessoa

personal /'pɜ:sənl/ a pessoal; (secretary) particular. ~ stereo estéreo m pessoal. ~ly adv pessoalmente

personality /pɜ:sə'nælətɪ/ n personalidade f; (on TV) vedete f

personify /pə'sɒnɪfaɪ/ vt personificar

personnel /pɜ:sə'nel/ n pessoal m

perspective /pə'spektɪv/ n perspectiva f

perspir|e /pə'spaɪə(r)/ vi transpirar. ~ation /-ə'reɪʃn/ n transpiração f

persua|de /pə'sweɪd/ vt persuadir (to a). ~sion /-'sweɪʒn/ n persuasão f; (belief) crença f, convicção f. ~sive /-'sweɪsɪv/ a persuasivo

pert /pɜ:t/ a (saucy) atrevido, descarado; (lively) vivo

pertain /pə'teɪn/ vi ~ to pertencer a; (be relevant) ser pertinente a, (P) ser próprio de

pertinent /'pɜ:tɪnənt/ a pertinente

perturb /pə'tɜ:b/ vt perturbar, transtornar

Peru /pə'ru:/ n Peru m. ~vian a & n peruano (m), (P) peruviano (m)

peruse /pə'ru:z/ vt ler com atenção

perva|de /pə'veɪd/ vt espalhar-se por, invadir. ~sive a penetrante

pervers|e /pə'vɜ:s/ a que insiste no erro; (wicked) perverso; (wayward) caprichoso. ~ity n obstinação f; (wickedness) perversidade f; (waywardness) capricho m, birra f

pervert[1] /pə'vɜ:t/ vt perverter. ~sion n perversão f

pervert[2] /'pɜ:vɜ:t/ n pervertido m

peseta /pə'seɪtə/ n peseta f

pessimis|t /'pesɪmɪst/ n pessimista mf. ~m /-zəm/ n pessimismo m. ~tic /-'mɪstɪk/ a pessimista

pest /pest/ n inseto m, (P) insecto m nocivo; (animal) animal m daninho; (person) peste f

pester /'pestə(r)/ vt incomodar (colloq)

pesticide /'pestɪsaɪd/ n pesticida m

pet /pet/ n animal m de estimação; (*favourite*) preferido m, querido m □ a (*rabbit etc*) de estimação □ vt (pt petted) acariciar. ~ **name** nome m usado em família

petal /'petl/ n pétala f

peter /'pi:tə(r)/ vi ~ **out** extinguir-se, acabar pouco a pouco, morrer (*fig*)

petition /pɪ'tɪʃn/ n petição f □ vt requerer

petrify /'petrɪfaɪ/ vt petrificar

petrol /'petrəl/ n gasolina f. ~ **pump** bomba f de gasolina. ~ **station** posto m de gasolina. ~ **tank** tanque m de gasolina

petroleum /pɪ'trəʊlɪəm/ n petróleo m

petticoat /'petɪkəʊt/ n combinação f, anágua f

petty /'petɪ/ a (-ier, -iest) pequeno, insignificante; (*mean*) mesquinho. ~ **cash** fundo m para pequenas despesas, caixa f pequena

petulan|t /'petjʊlənt/ a irritável. ~**ce** n irritabilidade f

pew /pju:/ n banco (de igreja) m

pewter /'pju:tə(r)/ n estanho m

phallic /'fælɪk/ a fálico

phantom /'fæntəm/ n fantasma m

pharmaceutical /fa:mə'sju:tɪkl/ a farmacêutico

pharmac|y /'fa:məsɪ/ n farmácia f. ~**ist** n farmacêutico m

phase /feɪz/ n fase f □ vt ~ **in/out** introduzir/retirar progressivamente

PhD abbr of Doctor of Philosophy n doutorado m

pheasant /'feznt/ n faisão m

phenomen|on /fɪ'nɒmɪnən/ n (pl -ena) fenómeno m, (P) fenómeno m. ~**al** a fenomenal

philanthrop|ist /fɪ'lænθrəpɪst/ n filantropo m. ~**ic** /-ən'θrɒpɪk/ a filantrópico

Philippines /'fɪlɪpi:nz/ npl the ~ as Filipinas fpl

philistine /'fɪlɪstam/ n filisteu m

philosoph|y /fɪ'lɒsəfɪ/ n filosofia f. ~**er** n filósofo m. ~**ical** /-ə'sɒfɪkl/ a filosófico

phlegm /flem/ n (*med*) catarro m, fleuma f

phobia /'fəʊbɪə/ n fobia f

phone /fəʊn/ n (*colloq*) telefone m □ vt/i (*colloq*) telefonar (para). on the ~ no telefone. ~ **back** voltar a telefonar, ligar de volta. ~ **book** lista f telefónica, (P) telefónica. ~ **box** cabine f telefónica, (P) telefónica. ~ **call** chamada f, telefonema m. ~**-in** n programa m de rádio ou tv com participação dos ouvintes

phonecard /'fəʊnka:d/ n cartão m para uso em telefone público

phonetic /fə'netɪk/ a fonético. ~**s** n fonética f

phoney /'fəʊnɪ/ a (-ier, -iest) (*sl*) falso, fingido □ n (*sl: person*) fingido m; (*sl: thing*) falso m, (P) falsificação f

phosphate /'fɒsfeɪt/ n fosfato m

phosphorus /'fɒsfərəs/ n fósforo m

photo /'fəʊtəʊ/ n (pl -os) (*colloq*) retrato m, foto f

photocop|y /'fəʊtəʊkɒpɪ/ n fotocópia f □ vt fotocopiar. ~**ier** n fotocopiadora f

photogenic /fəʊtəʊ'dʒenɪk/ a fotogénico, (P) fotogénico

photograph /'fəʊtəgra:f/ n fotografia f □ vt fotografar. ~**er** /fə'tɒgrəfə(r)/ n fotógrafo m. ~**ic** /-'græfɪk/ a fotográfico. ~**y** /fə'tɒgrəfɪ/ n fotografia f

phrase /freɪz/ n expressão f, frase f; (*gram*) locução f, frase f elíptica □ vt exprimir. ~**-book** n livro m de expressões idiomáticas

physical /'fɪzɪkl/ a físico

physician /fɪ'zɪʃn/ n médico m

physicist /'fɪzɪsɪst/ n físico m

physics /'fɪzɪks/ n física f

physiology /fɪzɪ'ɒlədʒɪ/ n fisiologia f

physiotherap|y /fɪzɪəʊ'θerəpɪ/ n fisioterapia f. ~**ist** n fisioterapeuta mf

physique /fɪ'zi:k/ n físico m

pian|o /pɪ'ænəʊ/ n (pl -os) piano m. ~**ist** /'pɪənɪst/ n pianista mf

pick[1] /pɪk/ n (*tool*) picareta f

pick[2] /pɪk/ vt escolher; (*flowers, fruit etc*) colher; (*lock*) forçar; (*teeth*) palitar □ n escolha f; (*best*) o/a melhor. ~ **a quarrel with** puxar uma briga com. ~ **holes in an argument** descobrir os pontos fracos dum argumento. ~ **sb's pocket** bater a carteira de alg. ~ **off** tirar, arrancar. ~ **on** implicar com. ~ **out** escolher; (*identify*) identificar, reconhecer. ~ **up** vt apanhar; (*speed*) ganhar. **take one's** ~ escolher livremente

pickaxe /'pɪkæks/ n picareta f

picket /'pɪkɪt/ n piquete m; (*single striker*) grevista mf de piquete □ vt (pt picketed) colocar um piquete em □ vi fazer piquete

pickings /'pɪkɪŋz/ npl restos mpl

pickle /'pɪkl/ n vinagre m. ~**s** picles mpl, (P) pickles mpl □ vt conservar em vinagre. **in a** ~ (*colloq*) numa encrenca (*colloq*)

pickpocket /'pɪkpɒkɪt/ n batedor m de carteiras, (P) carteirista m

picnic /'pɪknɪk/ n piquenique m □ vi (pt picnicked) piquenicar, (P) fazer um piquenique

pictorial /pɪk'tɔ:rɪəl/ a ilustrado

picture /'pɪktʃə(r)/ n imagem f; (*illustration*) estampa f, ilustração f; (*painting*) quadro m, pintura f;

(*photo*) fotografia *f*, retrato *m*; (*drawing*) desenho *m*; (*fig*) descrição *f*, quadro *m* □ *vt* imaginar; (*describe*) pintar, descrever. the ~s o cinema

picturesque /pɪktʃə'resk/ *a* pitoresco

pidgin /'pɪdʒɪn/ *a* ~ **English** inglês *m* estropiado

pie /paɪ/ *n* torta *f*, (P) tarte *f*, (of meat) empada *f*

piece /pi:s/ *n* pedaço *m*, bocado *m*; (of machine, in game) peça *f*; (of currency) moeda *f* □ *vt* ~ **together** juntar, montar. **a** ~ **of advice/furniture/** *etc* um conselho/um móvel/*etc*. ~-**work** *n* trabalho *m* por, (P) a peça *or* por, (P) a tarefa. **take to** ~**s** desmontar

piecemeal /'pi:smi:l/ *a* aos poucos, pouco a pouco

pier /pɪə(r)/ *n* molhe *m*

pierc|**e** /pɪəs/ *vt* furar, penetrar. ~**ing** *a* penetrante; (of scream, pain) lancinante

piety /'paɪətɪ/ *n* piedade *f*, devoção *f*

pig /pɪg/ *n* porco *m*. ~-**headed** *a* cabeçudo, teimoso

pigeon /'pɪdʒɪn/ *n* pombo *m*. ~-**hole** *n* escaninho *m*

piggy /'pɪgɪ/ *a* como um porco. ~-**back** *adv* nas costas. ~ **bank** cofre *m* de criança

pigment /'pɪgmənt/ *n* pigmento *m*. ~**ation** /-'teɪʃn/ *n* pigmentação *f*

pigsty /'pɪgstaɪ/ *n* pocilga *f*, chiqueiro *m*

pigtail /'pɪgteɪl/ *n* trança *f*

pike /paɪk/ *n* (*pl invar*) (*fish*) lúcio *m*

pilchard /'pɪltʃəd/ *n* peixe *m* pequeno da família do arenque, sardinha *f* européia

pile /paɪl/ *n* pilha *f*; (of carpet) pêlo *m* □ *vt/i* amontoar(-se), empilhar(-se) (**into**). **a** ~ **of** (*colloq*) um monte de (*colloq*). ~ **up** acumular(-se). ~-**up** *n* choque *m* em cadeia

piles /paɪlz/ *npl* hemorróidas *fpl*

pilfer /'pɪlfə(r)/ *vt* furtar. ~**age** *n* furto *m* (de coisas pequenas *or* em pequenas quantidades)

pilgrim /'pɪlgrɪm/ *n* peregrino *m*, romeiro *m*. ~**age** *n* peregrinação *f*, romaria *f*

pill /pɪl/ *n* pílula *f*, comprimido *m*

pillage /'pɪlɪdʒ/ *n* pilhagem *f*, saque *m* □ *vt* pilhar, saquear

pillar /'pɪlə(r)/ *n* pilar *m*. ~-**box** *n* marco *m* do correio

pillion /'pɪlɪən/ *n* assento *m* traseiro de motorizada. **ride** ~ ir no assento de trás

pillow /'pɪləʊ/ *n* travesseiro *m*

pillowcase /'pɪləʊkeɪs/ *n* fronha *f*

pilot /'paɪlət/ *n* piloto *m* □ *vt* (*pt* **piloted**) pilotar. ~-**light** *n* piloto *m*;

(*electr*) lâmpada *f* testemunho; (*gas*) piloto *m*

pimento /pɪ'mentəʊ/ *n* (*pl* -os) pimentão *m* vermelho

pimple /'pɪmpl/ *n* borbulha *f*, espinha *f*

pin /pɪn/ *n* alfinete *m*; (*techn*) cavilha *f* □ *vt* (*pt* **pinned**) pregar *or* prender com alfinete(s); (hold down) prender, segurar. **have** ~**s and needles** estar com cãibra. ~ **sb down** (*fig*) obrigar alg a definir-se, apertar alg (*fig*). ~-**point** *vt* localizar com precisão. ~-**stripe** *a* de listras finas. ~ **up** pregar. ~-**up** *n* (*colloq*) pin-up *f*

pinafore /'pɪnəfɔ:(r)/ *n* avental *m*. ~ **dress** veste *f*

pincers /'pɪnsəz/ *npl* (tool) torquês *f*, (P) alicate *m*; (med) pinça *f*; (zool) pinça(s) *f(pl)*, tenaz(es) *f(pl)*

pinch /pɪntʃ/ *vt* apertar; (*sl: steal*) surripiar (*colloq*) □ *n* aperto *m*; (tweak) beliscão *m*; (small amount) pitada *f*. **at a** ~ em caso de necessidade

pine[1] /paɪn/ *n* (tree) pinheiro *m*; (wood) pinho *m*

pine[2] /paɪn/ *vi* ~ **away** definhar, consumir-se. ~ **for** suspirar por

pineapple /'paɪnæpl/ *n* abacaxi *m*, (P) ananás *m*

ping-pong /'pɪŋpɒŋ/ *n* pingue-pongue *m*

pink /pɪŋk/ *a* & *n* rosa (*m*)

pinnacle /'pɪnəkl/ *n* pináculo *m*

pint /paɪnt/ *n* quartilho *m* (= *0,57l*; *Amer* = *0,47l*)

pioneer /paɪə'nɪə(r)/ *n* pioneiro *m* □ *vt* ser o pioneiro em, preparar o caminho para

pious /'paɪəs/ *a* piedoso, devoto

pip /pɪp/ *n* (seed) pevide *f*

pipe /paɪp/ *n* cano *m*, tubo *m*; (of smoker) cachimbo *m* □ *vt* encanar, canalizar. ~ **down** calar a boca

pipeline /'paɪplaɪn/ *n* (for oil) oleoduto *m*; (for gas) gaseoduto *m*, (P) gasoduto *m*. **in the** ~ (fig) encaminhado

piping /'paɪpɪŋ/ *n* tubagem *f*. ~ **hot** muito quente

piquant /'pi:kənt/ *a* picante

pira|**te** /'paɪərət/ *n* pirata *m*. ~**cy** *n* pirataria *f*

Pisces /'paɪsi:z/ *n* (astr) Peixe *m*, (P) Pisces *m*

pistol /'pɪstl/ *n* pistola *f*

piston /'pɪstən/ *n* êmbolo *m*, pistão *m*

pit /pɪt/ *n* (hole) cova *f*, fosso *m*; (mine) poço *m*; (quarry) pedreira *f* □ *vt* (*pt* **pitted**) picar, esburacar; (*fig*) opor. ~ **o.s. against** (*struggle*) medir-se com

pitch[1] /pɪtʃ/ *n* breu *m*. ~-**black** *a* escuro como breu

pitch² /pɪtʃ/ vt (throw) lançar; (tent) armar □ vi cair □ n (slope) declive m; (of sound) som m; (of voice) altura f, (sport) campo m

pitchfork /'pɪtʃfɔːk/ n forcado m

pitfall /'pɪtfɔːl/ n (fig) cilada f, perigo m inesperado

pith /pɪθ/ n (of orange) parte f branca da casca, mesocarpo m; (fig: essential part) cerne m, âmago m

pithy /'pɪθɪ/ a (-ier, -iest) preciso, conciso

piti|ful /'pɪtɪfl/ a lastimoso; (contemptible) miserável. ~less a impiedoso

pittance /'pɪtns/ n salário m miserável, miséria f

pity /'pɪtɪ/ n dó m, pena f, piedade f □ vt compadecer-se de. it's a ~ é uma pena. take ~ on ter pena de. what a ~! que pena!

pivot /'pɪvət/ n eixo m □ vt (pt pivoted) girar em torno de

placard /'plækɑːd/ n (poster) cartaz m

placate /plə'keɪt/ vt apaziguar, aplacar

place /pleɪs/ n lugar m, sítio m; (house) casa f; (seat, rank etc) lugar m □ vt colocar, pôr. ~ an order fazer uma encomenda. at/to my ~ em a or na minha casa. ~-mat n pano m de mesa individual, (P) napperon m à americana

placid /'plæsɪd/ a plácido

plagiar|ize /'pleɪdʒəraɪz/ vt plagiar. ~ism n plágio m

plague /pleɪg/ n peste f; (of insects) praga f □ vt atormentar, atazanar

plaice /pleɪs/ n (pl invar) solha f

plain /pleɪn/ a (-er, -est) claro, (candid) franco; (simple) simples; (not pretty) sem beleza; (not patterned) liso □ adv com franqueza □ n planície f. in ~ clothes à paisana. ~ly adv claramente; (candidly) francamente

plaintiff /'pleɪntɪf/ n queixoso m

plaintive /'pleɪntɪv/ a queixoso

plait /plæt/ vt entrançar □ n trança f

plan /plæn/ n plano m, projeto m, (P) projecto m; (of a house, city etc) plano m, planta f □ vt (pt planned) planear, planejar □ vi fazer planos. ~ to do ter a intenção de fazer

plane¹ /pleɪn/ n (level) plano m; (aeroplane) avião m □ a plano

plane² /pleɪn/ n (tool) plaina f □ vt aplainar

planet /'plænɪt/ n planeta m

plank /plæŋk/ n prancha f

planning /'plænɪŋ/ n planeamento m, planejamento m. ~ permission permissão f para construir

plant /plɑːnt/ n planta f; (techn) aparelhagem f; (factory) fábrica f □ vt

plantar. ~ a bomb colocar uma bomba. ~ation /plæn'teɪʃn/ n plantação f

plaque /plɑːk/ n placa f; (on teeth) tártaro m, pedra f

plaster /'plɑːstə(r)/ n reboco m; (adhesive) esparadrapo m, band-aid m □ vt rebocar; (cover) cobrir (with com, de). in ~ engessado. ~ of Paris gesso m. ~er n rebocador m, caiador m

plastic /'plæstɪk/ a plástico □ n plástica f. ~ surgery cirurgia f plástica

plate /pleɪt/ n prato m; (in book) gravura f □ vt revestir de metal

plateau /'plætəʊ/ n (pl -eaux /-əʊz/) planalto m, plató m

platform /'plætfɔːm/ n estrado m; (for speaking) tribuna f; (rail) plataforma f, cais m; (fig) programa m de partido político. ~ ticket bilhete m de gare

platinum /'plætɪnəm/ n platina f

platitude /'plætɪtjuːd/ n banalidade f, lugar-comum m

platonic /plə'tɒnɪk/ a platónico, (P) platónico

plausible /'plɔːzəbl/ a plausível; (person) convincente

play /pleɪ/ vt/i (for amusement) brincar; (instrument) tocar; (cards, game) jogar; (opponent) jogar contra; (match) disputar □ n jogo m; (theatre) peça f; (movement) folga f, margem f. ~ down minimizar. ~ on (take advantage of) aproveitar-se de. ~ safe jogar pelo seguro (a). ~ up (colloq) dar problemas (a). ~-group n jardim m de infância, (P) jardim m infantil. ~-pen n cercado m para crianças

playboy /'pleɪbɔɪ/ n play-boy m

player /'pleɪə(r)/ n jogador m; (theat) artista mf; (mus) artista mf, executante mf, instrumentista mf

playful /'pleɪfl/ a brincalhão m

playground /'pleɪgraʊnd/ n pátio m de recreio

playing /'pleɪɪŋ/ n atuação f, (P) actuação f. ~-card n carta f de jogar. ~-field n campo m de jogos

playwright /'pleɪraɪt/ n dramaturgo m

plc abbr (of public limited company) SARL

plea /pliː/ n súplica f; (reason) pretexto m, desculpa f; (jur) alegação f da defesa

plead /pliːd/ vt/i pleitear; (as excuse) alegar. ~ guilty confessar-se culpado. ~ with implorar a

pleasant /'pleznt/ a agradável

pleas|e /pliːz/ vt/i agradar (a), dar prazer (a) □ adv por favor, (P) se faz favor. they ~e themselves, they do as they ~e eles fazem como bem entendem. ~ed *a* contente, satisfeito (with com). ~ing *a* agradável

pleasur|e /'pleʒə(r)/ *n* prazer *m*. ~able *a* agradável

pleat /pliːt/ *n* prega *f* □ *vt* preguear

pledge /pledʒ/ *n* penhor *m*, garantia *f*; (*fig*) promessa *f* □ *vt* prometer; (*pawn*) empenhar

plentiful /'plentɪfl/ *a* abundante

plenty /'plentɪ/ *n* abundância *f*, fartura *f*. ~ (of) muito (de); (*enough*) bastante (de)

pliable /'plaɪəbl/ *a* flexível

pliers /'plaɪəz/ *npl* alicate *m*

plight /plaɪt/ *n* triste situação *f*

plimsoll /'plɪmsəl/ *n* alpargata *f*, tênis *m*, (P) ténis *m*

plinth /plɪnθ/ *n* plinto *m*

plod /plɒd/ *vi* (*pt* **plodded**) caminhar lentamente, (*work*) trabalhar, marrar (*sl*). ~der *n* trabalhador *m* lento mas perseverante. ~ding *a* lento

plonk /plɒŋk/ *n* (*sl*) vinho *m* ordinário, (P) carrascão *m*

plot /plɒt/ *n* complô *m*, conspiração *f*; (*of novel etc*) trama *f*; (*of land*) lote *m* □ *vt/i* (*pt* **plotted**) conspirar; (*mark out*) traçar

plough /plaʊ/ *n* arado *m* □ *vt/i* arar. ~ back reinvestir. ~ into colidir. ~ through abrir caminho por

ploy /plɔɪ/ *n* (*colloq*) estratagema *m*

pluck /plʌk/ *vt* apanhar; (*bird*) depenar; (*eyebrows*) depilar; (*mus*) tanger □ *n* coragem *f*. ~ up courage ganhar coragem. ~y *a* corajoso

plug /plʌg/ *n* tampão *m*, (*electr*) tomada *f*, (P) ficha *f* □ *vt* (*pt* **plugged**) tapar um tampão; (*colloq: publicize*) fazer grande propaganda de □ *vi* ~ away (*colloq*) trabalhar com afinco. ~ in (*electr*) ligar. ~-hole *n* buraco *m* do cano

plum /plʌm/ *n* ameixa *f*

plumb /plʌm/ *adv* exatamente, (P) exactamente, mesmo □ *vt* sondar. ~-line *n* fio *m* de prumo

plumb|er /'plʌmə(r)/ *n* bombeiro *m*, encanador *m*, (P) canalizador *m*. ~ing *n* encanamento *m*, (P) canalização *f*

plummet /'plʌmɪt/ *vi* (*pt* **plummeted**) despencar

plump /plʌmp/ *a* (-er, -est) rechonchudo, roliço □ *vi* ~ for optar por. ~ness *n* gordura *f*

plunder /'plʌndə(r)/ *vt* pilhar, saquear □ *n* pilhagem *f*, saque *m*; (*goods*) despojo *m*

plunge /plʌndʒ/ *vt/i* mergulhar, atirar(-se), afundar(-se) □ *n* mergulho *m*. take the ~ (*fig*) decidir-se, dar o salto *f* (*fig*)

plunger /'plʌndʒə(r)/ *n* (*of pump*)

êmbolo *m*, pistão *m*; (*for sink etc*) desentupidor *m*

pluperfect /pluː'pɜːfɪkt/ *n* mais-que-perfeito *m*

plural /'plʊərəl/ *a* plural; (*noun*) no plural □ *n* plural *m*

plus /plʌs/ *prep* mais □ *a* positivo □ *n* sinal +; (*fig*) qualidade *f* positiva

plush /plʌʃ/ *n* pelúcia *f* □ *a* de pelúcia, (*colloq*) de luxo

ply /plaɪ/ *vt* (*tool*) manejar; (*trade*) exercer □ *vi* (*ship*, *bus*) fazer carreira entre dois lugares. ~ sb with drink encher alguém de bebidas

plywood /'plaɪwʊd/ *n* madeira *f* compensada

p.m. /piː'em/ *adv* da tarde, da noite

pneumatic /njuː'mætɪk/ *a* pneumático. ~ drill broca *f* pneumática

pneumonia /njuː'məʊnɪə/ *n* pneumonia *f*

PO *abbr see* Post Office

poach /pəʊtʃ/ *vt/i* (*steal*) caçar/pescar em propriedade alheia; (*culin*) fazer poché, (P) escalfar. ~ed eggs ovos *mpl* pochés, (P) ovos *mpl* escalfados

pocket /'pɒkɪt/ *n* bolso *m*, algibeira *f* □ *a* de algibeira □ *vt* meter no bolso. ~-book *n* (*notebook*) livro *m* de apontamentos; (*Amer: handbag*) carteira *f*. ~-money *n* (*monthly*) mesada *f*; (*weekly*) semanada *f*, dinheiro *m* para pequenas despesas

pod /pɒd/ *n* vagem *f*

poem /'pəʊɪm/ *n* poema *m*

poet /'pəʊɪt/ *n* poeta *m*, poetisa *f*. ~ic /-'etɪk/ *a* poético

poetry /'pəʊɪtrɪ/ *n* poesia *f*

poignant /'pɔɪnjənt/ *a* pungente, doloroso

point /pɔɪnt/ *n* ponto *m*; (*tip*) ponta *f*; (*decimal point*) vírgula *f*; (*meaning*) sentido *m*, razão *m*; (*electr*) tomada *f*. ~s (*rail*) agulhas *fpl* □ *vt/i* (*aim*) apontar (at para); (*show*) apontar, indicar (at/to para). on the ~ of prestes a, quase a. ~-blank *a* & *adv* à queima-roupa; (*fig*) categórico. ~ of view ponto *m* de vista. ~ out apontar, fazer ver. that is a good ~ (*remark*) é uma boa observação. to the ~ a propósito. what is the ~? de que adianta?

pointed /'pɔɪntɪd/ *a* ponteagudo; (*of remark*) intencional, contundente

pointer /'pɔɪntə(r)/ *n* ponteiro *m*; (*colloq: hint*) sugestão *f*

pointless /'pɔɪntlɪs/ *a* inútil, sem sentido

poise /pɔɪz/ *n* equilíbrio *m*; (*carriage*) porte *m*, (*fig: self-possession*) presença *f*, segurança *f*. ~d *a* equilibrado; (*person*) seguro de si

poison /'pɔɪzn/ n veneno m, peçonha f □ vt envenenar. blood-~ing n envenenamento m do sangue. food-~ing n intoxicação f alimentar. ~ous a venenoso

poke /pəʊk/ vt/i espetar; (with elbow) acotovelar; (fire) atiçar □ n espetadela f; (with elbow) cotovelada f. ~ about esgaravatar, remexer, procurar. ~ fun at fazer troça/pouco de. ~ out (head) enfiar

poker[1] /'pəʊkə(r)/ n atiçador m

poker[2] /'pəʊkə(r)/ n (cards) póquer m, (P) póquer m

poky /'pəʊkɪ/ a (-ier, -iest) acanhado, apertado

Poland /'pəʊlənd/ n Polónia f, (P) Polónia f

polar /'pəʊlə(r)/ a polar. ~ bear urso m branco

polarize /'pəʊləraɪz/ vt polarizar

pole[1] /pəʊl/ n vara f; (for flag) mastro m; (post) poste m

pole[2] /pəʊl/ n (geog) pólo m

Pole /pəʊl/ n polaco m

polemic /pə'lemɪk/ n polémica f, (P) polémica f

police /pə'liːs/ n policia f □ vt policiar. ~ state estado m policial. ~ station distrito m, delegacia f, (P) esquadra f de policia

police|man /pə'liːsmən/ n (pl -men) policial m, (P) policia m, guarda m, agente m de policia. ~-woman (pl -women) n policia f feminina, (P) mulher-policia f

policy[1] /'pɒlɪsɪ/ n (plan of action) politica f

policy[2] /'pɒlɪsɪ/ n (insurance) apólice f de seguro

polio /'pəʊlɪəʊ/ n polio f

polish /'pɒlɪʃ/ vt polir, dar lustro em; (shoes) engraxar; (floor) encerar □ n (for shoes) graxa f; (for floor) cera f; (for nails) esmalte m, (P) verniz m; (shine) polimento m; (fig) requinte m. ~ off acabar (rapidamente). ~ up (language) aperfeiçoar. ~ed a requintado, elegante

Polish /'pəʊlɪʃ/ a & n polonés (m), (P) polaco (m)

polite /pə'laɪt/ a polido, educado, delicado. ~ly adv delicadamente. ~ness n delicadeza f, cortesia f

political /pə'lɪtɪkl/ a político

politician /pɒlɪ'tɪʃn/ n político m

politics /'pɒlətɪks/ n política f

polka /'pɒlkə/ n polca f. ~ dots bolas fpl

poll /pəʊl/ n votação f; (survey) sondagem f, pesquisa f □ vt (votes) obter. go to the ~s votar, ir às urnas. ~ing-booth n cabine f de voto

pollen /'pɒlən/ n pólen m

pollut|e /pə'luːt/ vt poluir. ~ion /-ʃn/ n poluição f

polo /'pəʊləʊ/ n pólo m. ~ neck gola f rolê

polyester /pɒlɪ'estə/ n poliéster m

polytechnic /pɒlɪ'teknɪk/ n politécnica f

polythene /'pɒlɪθiːn/ n politeno m. ~ bag n saco m de plástico

pomegranate /'pɒmɪgrænɪt/ n romã f

pomp /pɒmp/ n pompa f

pompon /'pɒmpɒn/ n pompom m

pomp|ous /'pɒmpəs/ a pomposo. ~osity /-'pɒsətɪ/ n imponência f

pond /pɒnd/ n lagoa f, lago m; (artificial) tanque m, lago m

ponder /'pɒndə(r)/ vt/i ponderar, meditar (over sobre)

pong /pɒŋ/ n (sl) pivete m □ vi (sl) cheirar mal, tresandar

pony /'pəʊnɪ/ n pónei m, (P) pónei m. ~-tail n rabo m de cavalo. ~-trekking n passeio m de pónei, (P) pónei

poodle /'puːdl/ n cão m de água, caniche m

pool[1] /puːl/ n (puddle) charco m, poça f; (for swimming) piscina f

pool[2] /puːl/ n (fund) fundo m comum; (econ, comm) pool m; (game) forma f de bilhar. ~s loteca f, (P) totobola m □ vt pôr num fundo comum

poor /pʊə(r)/ a (-er, -est) pobre; (not good) mediocre. ~ly adv mal □ a doente

pop[1] /pɒp/ n estalido m, ruido m seco □ vt/i (pt popped) dar um estalido, estalar; (of cork) saltar. ~ in/out/off entrar/sair/ir-se embora. ~ up aparecer de repente, saltar

pop[2] /pɒp/ n música f pop □ a pop invar

popcorn /'pɒpkɔːn/ n pipoca f

pope /pəʊp/ n papa m

poplar /'pɒplə(r)/ n choupo m, álamo m

poppy /'pɒpɪ/ n papoula f

popular /'pɒpjʊlə(r)/ a popular; (in fashion) em voga, na moda. be ~ with ser popular entre. ~ity /-'lærətɪ/ n popularidade f. ~ize vt popularizar, vulgarizar

populat|e /'pɒpjʊleɪt/ vt povoar. ~ion /-'leɪʃn/ n população f

populous /'pɒpjʊləs/ a populoso

porcelain /'pɔːslɪn/ n porcelana f

porch /pɔːtʃ/ n alpendre m; (Amer) varanda f

porcupine /'pɔːkjʊpaɪn/ n porco-espinho m

pore[1] /pɔː(r)/ n poro m

pore[2] /pɔː(r)/ vi ~ over examinar, estudar

pork /pɔːk/ n carne f de porco

pornograph|y /pɔːˈnɒɡrəfɪ/ n pornografia f. ~**ic** /-əˈɡræfɪk/ a pornográfico

porous /ˈpɔːrəs/ a poroso

porpoise /ˈpɔːpəs/ n toninha f, (P) golfinho m

porridge /ˈpɒrɪdʒ/ n (papa f de) flocos mpl de aveia

port[1] /pɔːt/ n (harbour) porto m

port[2] /pɔːt/ n (wine) (vinho do) Porto m

portable /ˈpɔːtəbl/ a portátil

porter[1] /ˈpɔːtə(r)/ n (carrier) carregador m

porter[2] /ˈpɔːtə(r)/ n (doorkeeper) porteiro m

portfolio /pɔːtˈfəʊlɪəʊ/ n (pl -os) (case, post) pasta f; (securities) carteira f de investimentos

porthole /ˈpɔːthəʊl/ n vigia f

portion /ˈpɔːʃn/ n (share, helping) porção f; (part) parte f

portly /ˈpɔːtlɪ/ a (-ier, -iest) corpulento e digno

portrait /ˈpɔːtrɪt/ n retrato m

portray /pɔːˈtreɪ/ vt retratar, pintar; (fig) descrever. ~**al** n retrato m

Portug|al /ˈpɔːtjʊɡl/ n Portugal m. ~**uese** /-ˈɡiːz/ a & n invar português (m)

pose /pəʊz/ vt/i (fazer) posar; (question) fazer □ n pose f, postura f. ~ **as** fazer-se passar por

poser /ˈpəʊzə(r)/ n quebra-cabeças m

posh /pɒʃ/ a (sl) chique invar

position /pəˈzɪʃn/ n posição f; (job) lugar m, colocação f; (state) situação f □ vt colocar

positive /ˈpɒzətɪv/ a positivo; (definite) categórico, definitivo; (colloq: downright) autêntico. **she's ~ that** ela tem certeza que. ~**ly** adv positivamente; (absolutely) completamente

possess /pəˈzes/ vt possuir. ~**ion** /-ʃn/ n posse f; (thing possessed) possessão f. ~**or** n possuidor m

possessive /pəˈzesɪv/ a possessivo

possib|le /ˈpɒsəbl/ a possível. ~**ility** /-ˈbɪlətɪ/ n possibilidade f

possibly /ˈpɒsəblɪ/ adv possivelmente, talvez. **if I ~ can** se me for possível. **I cannot ~ leave** estou impossibilitado de partir

post[1] /pəʊst/ n (pole) poste m □ vt (notice) afixar, pregar

post[2] /pəʊst/ n (station, job) posto m □ vt colocar; (appoint) colocar

post[3] /pəʊst/ n (mail) correio m □ vt postal □ vt mandar pelo correio. **keep** ~**ed** manter informado. ~**-code** n código m postal. **P~ Office** agência f dos correios, (P) estação f dos correios; (corporation) Departamento m dos Correios e Telégrafos, (P) Correios, Telégrafos e Telefones mpl (CTT)

post- /pəʊst/ pref pós-

postage /ˈpəʊstɪdʒ/ n porte m

postal /ˈpəʊstl/ a postal. ~ **order** vale m postal

postcard /ˈpəʊstkaːd/ n cartão-postal m, (P) (bilhete) postal m

poster /ˈpəʊstə(r)/ n cartaz m

posterity /pɒˈsterətɪ/ n posteridade f

postgraduate /pəʊstˈɡrædʒʊət/ n pós-graduado m

posthumous /ˈpɒstjʊməs/ a póstumo. ~**ly** adv a titulo póstumo

postman /ˈpəʊstmən/ n (pl -men) carteiro m

postmark /ˈpəʊstmaːk/ n carimbo m do correio

post-mortem /pəʊstˈmɔːtəm/ n autópsia f

postpone /pəˈspəʊn/ vt adiar. ~**ment** n adiamento m

postscript /ˈpəʊsskrɪpt/ n post scriptum m

postulate /ˈpɒstjʊleɪt/ vt postular

posture /ˈpɒstʃə(r)/ n postura f, posição f □ vi posar

post-war /ˈpəʊstwɔː(r)/ a de após-guerra

posy /ˈpəʊzɪ/ n raminho m de flores

pot /pɒt/ n pote m; (for cooking) panela f; (for plants) vaso m; (sl: marijuana) maconha f □ vt (pt potted) ~ (up) plantar em vaso. **go to ~** (sl: business) arruinar, degringolar (colloq); (sl: person) estar arruinado or liquidado. ~**-belly** n pança f, barriga f. **take ~ luck** aceitar o que houver. **take a ~-shot** dar um tiro de perto (at em); (at random) dar um tiro a esmo (at em)

potato /pəˈteɪtəʊ/ n (pl -oes) batata f

poten|t /ˈpəʊtnt/ a potente, poderoso; (drink) forte. ~**cy** n potência f

potential /pəˈtenʃl/ a & n potencial (m). ~**ly** adv potencialmente

pothol|e /ˈpɒthəʊl/ n caverna f, caldeirão m; (in road) buraco m. ~**ing** n espeleologia f

potion /ˈpəʊʃn/ n poção f

potted /ˈpɒtɪd/ a (of plant) de vaso; (preserved) de conserva

potter[1] /ˈpɒtə(r)/ n oleiro m, ceramista mf. ~**y** n olaria f, cerâmica f

potter[2] /ˈpɒtə(r)/ vi entreter-se com isto ou aquilo

potty[1] /ˈpɒtɪ/ a (-ier, -iest) (sl) doido, pirado (sl), (P) chanfrado (colloq)

potty[2] /ˈpɒtɪ/ n (-ties) (colloq) penico m de criança

pouch /paʊtʃ/ n bolsa f; (for tobacco) tabaqueira f

poultice /ˈpəʊltɪs/ n cataplasma f

poultry /'pəʊltrɪ/ n aves fpl domésticas

pounce /paʊns/ vi atirar-se (on sobre, para cima de) □ n salto m

pound¹ /paʊnd/ n (weight) libra f (= 453 g); (money) libra f

pound² /paʊnd/ n (for dogs) canil municipal m; (for cars) parque de viaturas rebocadas m

pound³ /paʊnd/ vt/i (crush) esmagar, pisar; (of heart) bater com força; (bombard) bombardear; (on piano etc) martelar

pour /pɔ:(r)/ vt deitar □ vi correr; (rain) chover torrencialmente. ~ in/out (of people) afluir/sair em massa. ~ off or out esvaziar, vazar. ~ing rain chuva f torrencial

pout /paʊt/ vt/i ~ (one's lips) (sulk) fazer beicinho; (in annoyance) ficar de trombas □ n beicinho m

poverty /'pɒvətɪ/ n pobreza f, miséria f. ~-stricken a pobre

powder /'paʊdə(r)/ n pó m; (for face) pó-de-arroz m □ vt polvilhar; (face) empoar. ~ed a em pó. ~-room n toalete m, toucador m. ~y a como pó

power /'paʊə(r)/ n poder m; (maths, mech) potência f; (energy) energia f; (electr) corrente f. ~ cut corte m de energia, blecaute m. ~ station central f eléctrica, (P) eléctrica. ~ed by movido a; (jet etc) de propulsão. ~ful a poderoso; (mech) potente. ~less a impotente

practicable /'præktɪkəbl/ a viável

practical /'præktɪkl/ a prático. ~ joke brincadeira f de mau gosto

practically /'præktɪklɪ/ adv praticamente

practice /'præktɪs/ n prática f; (of law etc) exercício m; (sport) treino m; (clients) clientela f. in ~ (in fact) na prática; (well-trained) em forma. out of ~ destreinado, sem prática. put into ~ pôr em prática

practise /'præktɪs/ vt/i (skill, sport) praticar, exercitar-se em; (profession) exercer; (put into practice) pôr em prática. ~ed a experimentado, experiente. ~ing a (Catholic etc) praticante

practitioner /præk'tɪʃənə(r)/ n praticante mf. general ~ médico m de clínica geral or de família

pragmatic /præg'mætɪk/ a pragmático

prairie /'preərɪ/ n pradaria f

praise /preɪz/ vt louvar, elogiar □ n elogio(s) m(pl), louvor(es) m(pl)

praiseworthy /'preɪzwɜ:ðɪ/ a louvável, digno de louvor

pram /præm/ n carrinho m de bebê, (P) bebé

prance /prɑ:ns/ vi (of horse) curvetear, empinar-se; (of person) pavonear-se

prank /præŋk/ n brincadeira f de mau gosto

prattle /'prætl/ vi tagarelar

prawn /prɔ:n/ n camarão m grande, (P) gamba f

pray /preɪ/ vi rezar, orar

prayer /preə(r)/ n oração f. the Lord's P~ o Padre-Nosso. ~-book n missal m

pre- /pri:/ pref pré-

preach /pri:tʃ/ vt/i pregar (at, to a). ~er n pregador m

preamble /pri:'æmbl/ n preâmbulo m

prearrange /pri:ə'reɪndʒ/ vt combinar or arranjar de antemão

precarious /prɪ'keərɪəs/ a precário; (of position) instável, inseguro

precaution /prɪ'kɔ:ʃn/ n precaução f. ~ary a de precaução

preced|e /prɪ'si:d/ vt preceder. ~ing a precedente

precedent /'presɪdənt/ n precedente m

precinct /'pri:sɪŋkt/ n precinto m; (Amer: district) circunscrição f. (pedestrian) ~ área f de pedestres, (P) zona f para pedres

precious /'preʃəs/ a precioso

precipice /'presɪpɪs/ n precipício m

precipitat|e /prɪ'sɪpɪteɪt/ vt precipitar □ a /-ɪtət/ precipitado. ~ion /-'teɪʃn/ n precipitação f

precis|e /prɪ'saɪs/ a preciso; (careful) meticuloso. ~ely adv precisamente. ~ion /-'sɪʒn/ n precisão f

preclude /prɪ'klu:d/ vt evitar, excluir, impedir

precocious /prɪ'kəʊʃəs/ a precoce

preconc|eived /pri:kən'si:vd/ a pre-concebido. ~eption /pri:kən'sepʃn/ n idéia f preconcebida

precursor /pri:'kɜ:sə(r)/ n precursor m

predator /'predətə(r)/ n animal m de rapina, predador m. ~y a predatório

predecessor /'pri:dɪsesə(r)/ n predecessor m

predicament /prɪ'dɪkəmənt/ n situação f difícil

predict /prɪ'dɪkt/ vt predizer, prognosticar. ~able a previsível. ~ion /-ʃn/ n predição f, prognóstico m

predominant /prɪ'dɒmɪnənt/ a predominante, preponderante. ~ly adv predominantemente, preponderantemente

predominate /prɪ'dɒmɪneɪt/ vi predominar

pre-eminent /pri:'emɪnənt/ a preeminente, superior

pre-empt /pri:'empt/ vt adquirir por

preempção. ~ive *a* antecipado; (*mil*) preventivo

preen /priːn/ *vt* alisar. ~ **o.s.** enfeitar-se

prefab /ˈpriːfæb/ *n* (*colloq*) casa *f* pré-fabricada. ~**ricated** /-ˈfæbrɪkeɪtɪd/ *a* pré-fabricado

preface /ˈprefɪs/ *n* prefácio *m*

prefect /ˈpriːfekt/ *n* aluno *m* autorizado a disciplinar outros; (*official*) prefeito *m*

prefer /prɪˈfɜː(r)/ *vt* (*pt* **preferred**) preferir. ~**able** /ˈprefrəbl/ *a* preferível

preferen|ce /ˈprefrəns/ *n* preferência *f*. ~**tial** /-əˈrenʃl/ *a* preferencial, privilegiado

prefix /ˈpriːfɪks/ *n* (*pl* -**ixes**) prefixo *m*

pregnan|t /ˈpregnənt/ *a* (*woman*) grávida; (*animal*) prenhe. ~**cy** *n* gravidez *f*

prehistoric /priːhɪˈstɒrɪk/ *a* pré-histórico

prejudice /ˈpredʒʊdɪs/ *n* preconceito *m*, idéia *f* preconcebida, prejuizo *m*; (*harm*) prejuizo *m* □ *vt* influenciar. ~**d** *a* com preconceitos

preliminar|y /prɪˈlɪmɪnərɪ/ *a* preliminar. ~**ies** *npl* preliminares *mpl*, preâmbulos *mpl*

prelude /ˈpreljuːd/ *n* prelúdio *m*

premarital /priːˈmærɪtl/ *a* antes do casamento, pré-marital

premature /ˈpremətjʊə(r)/ *a* prematuro

premeditated /priːˈmedɪteɪtɪd/ *a* premeditado

premier /ˈpremɪə(r)/ *a* primeiro *m* □ *n* (*pol*) primeiro-ministro *m*

premises /ˈpremɪsɪz/ *npl* local *m*, edificio *m*. **on the** ~ neste estabelecimento, no local

premium /ˈpriːmɪəm/ *n* prêmio *m*, (*P*) prémio *m*. **at a** ~ a peso de ouro

premonition /priːməˈnɪʃn/ *n* pressentimento *m*

preoccup|ation /priːɒkjʊˈpeɪʃn/ *n* preocupação *f*. ~**ied** /-ˈɒkjʊpaɪd/ *a* preocupado

preparation /prepəˈreɪʃn/ *n* preparação *f*. ~**s** preparativos *mpl*

preparatory /prɪˈpærətrɪ/ *a* preparatório. ~ **school** escola *f* primária particular

prepare /prɪˈpeə(r)/ *vt/i* preparar(-se) (**for** para). ~**d to** pronto a, preparado para

preposition /prepəˈzɪʃn/ *n* preposição *f*

preposterous /prɪˈpɒstərəs/ *a* absurdo, disparatado, ridiculo

prerequisite /priːˈrekwɪzɪt/ *n* condição *f* prévia

prerogative /prɪˈrɒgətɪv/ *n* prerrogativa *f*

Presbyterian /prezbɪˈtɪərɪən/ *a & n* presbiteriano (*m*)

prescri|be /prɪˈskraɪb/ *vt* prescrever; (*med*) receitar, prescrever. ~**ption** /-ɪpʃn/ *n* prescrição *f*; (*med*) receita *f*

presence /ˈprezns/ *n* presença *f*. ~ **of mind** presença *f* de espirito

present[1] /ˈpreznt/ *a & n* presente (*mf*). **at** ~ no momento, presentemente

present[2] /ˈpreznt/ *n* (*gift*) presente *m*

present[3] /prɪˈzent/ *vt* apresentar; (*film etc*) dar. ~ **sb with** oferecer a alg. ~**able** *a* apresentável. ~**ation** /prezn'teɪʃn/ *n* apresentação *f*. ~**er** *n* apresentador *m*

presently /ˈprezntlɪ/ *adv* dentro em pouco, daqui a pouco; (*Amer: now*) neste momento

preservative /prɪˈzɜːvətɪv/ *n* preservativo *m*

preserv|e /prɪˈzɜːv/ *vt* preservar; (*maintain; culin*) conservar □ *n* reserva *f*; (*fig*) área *f*, terreno *m*; (*jam*) compota *f*. ~**ation** /prezəˈveɪʃn/ *n* conservação *f*

preside /prɪˈzaɪd/ *vi* presidir (**over** a)

presiden|t /ˈprezɪdənt/ *n* presidente *mf*. ~**cy** *n* presidência *f*. ~**tial** /-ˈdenʃl/ *a* presidencial

press /pres/ *vt/i* carregar (**on** em); (*squeeze*) espremer; (*urge*) pressionar; (*iron*) passar a ferro □ *n* imprensa *f*; (*mech*) prensa *f*; (*for wine*) lagar *m*. **be** ~**ed for** estar apertado com falta de. ~ **on (with)** continuar (com), prosseguir (com). ~ **conference** entrevista *f* coletiva. ~-**stud** *n* mola *f*, botão *m* de pressão

pressing /ˈpresɪŋ/ *a* premente, urgente

pressure /ˈpreʃə(r)/ *n* pressão *f* □ *vt* fazer pressão sobre. ~-**cooker** *n* panela *f* de pressão. ~ **group** grupo *m* de pressão

pressurize /ˈpreʃəraɪz/ *vt* pressionar, fazer pressão sobre

prestige /preˈstiːʒ/ *n* prestigio *m*

prestigious /preˈstɪdʒəs/ *a* prestigioso

presumably /prɪˈzjuːməblɪ/ *adv* provavelmente

presum|e /prɪˈzjuːm/ *vt* presumir. ~**e to** tomar a liberdade de, atrever-se a. ~**ption** /-ˈzʌmpʃn/ *n* presunção *f*

presumptuous /prɪˈzʌmptʃʊəs/ *a* presunçoso

pretence /prɪˈtens/ *n* fingimento *m*; (*claim*) pretensão *f*; (*pretext*) desculpa *f*, pretexto *m*

pretend /prɪˈtend/ *vt/i* fingir (**to do** fazer). ~ **to** (*lay claim to*) ter pretensões a, ser pretendente a; (*profess to have*) pretender ter

pretentious /prɪˈtenʃəs/ a pretencioso

pretext /ˈpriːtekst/ n pretexto m

pretty /ˈprɪtɪ/ a (-ier, -iest) bonito, lindo □ adv bastante

prevail /prɪˈveɪl/ vi prevalecer. ~ on sb to convencer alguéma. ~ing a dominante

prevalen|t /ˈprevələnt/ a geral, dominante. ~ce n frequência f

prevent /prɪˈvent/ vt impedir (from doing de fazer). ~able a que se pode evitar, evitável. ~ion /-ʃn/ n prevenção f. ~ive a preventivo

preview /ˈpriːvjuː/ n pré-estréia f, (P) ante-estreia f

previous /ˈpriːvɪəs/ a precedente, anterior. ~ to antes de. ~ly adv antes, anteriormente

pre-war /priːˈwɔː(r)/ a do pré-guerra, (P) de antes da guerra

prey /preɪ/ n presa f □ vi ~ on dar caça a; (worry) preocupar, atormentar. bird of ~ ave f de rapina, predador m

price /praɪs/ n preço m □ vt marcar o preço de. ~less a inestimável; (colloq: amusing) impagável

prick /prɪk/ vt picar, furar □ n picada f. ~ up one's ears arrebitar a(s) orelha(s)

prickl|e /ˈprɪkl/ n pico m, espinho m; (sensation) picada f. ~y a espinhoso, que pica; (person) irritável

pride /praɪd/ n orgulho m □ vpr ~ o.s. on orgulhar-se de

priest /priːst/ n padre m, sacerdote m. ~hood n sacerdócio m; (clergy) clero m

prim /prɪm/ a (primmer, primmest) formal, cheio de nove-horas; (prudish) pudico

primary /ˈpraɪmərɪ/ a primário; (chief, first) primeiro. ~ school escola f primária

prime[1] /praɪm/ a primeiro, principal; (first-rate) de primeira qualidade. P~ Minister Primeiro-Ministro m. ~ number número m primo

prime[2] /praɪm/ vt aprontar, aprestar; (with facts) preparar; (surface) preparar, aparelhar. ~r /-ə(r)/ n (paint) aparelho m

primeval /praɪˈmiːvl/ a primitivo

primitive /ˈprɪmɪtɪv/ a primitivo

primrose /ˈprɪmrəʊz/ n primavera f, prímula f

prince /prɪns/ n príncipe m

princess /prɪnˈses/ n princesa f

principal /ˈprɪnsəpl/ a principal □ n (schol) diretor m, (P) director m. ~ly adv principalmente

principle /ˈprɪnsəpl/ n princípio m. in/on ~ em/por princípio

print /prɪnt/ vt imprimir; (write) escrever em letra de imprensa □ n marca f, impressão f; (letters) letra f de imprensa; (photo) prova (fotográfica) f; (engraving) gravura f. out of ~ esgotado. ~-out n cópia f impressa. ~ed matter impressos mpl

print|er /ˈprɪntə(r)/ n tipógrafo m; (comput) impressora f. ~ing n impressão f, tipografia f

prior /ˈpraɪə(r)/ a anterior, precedente. ~ to antes de

priority /praɪˈɒrətɪ/ n prioridade f

prise /praɪz/ vt forçar (com alavanca). ~ open arrombar

prison /ˈprɪzn/ n prisão f. ~er n prisioneiro m

pristine /ˈprɪstiːn/ a primitivo; (condition) perfeito, como novo

privacy /ˈprɪvəsɪ/ n privacidade f, intimidade f; (solitude) isolamento m

private /ˈpraɪvət/ a privado; (confidential) confidencial; (lesson, life, house etc) particular; (ceremony) íntimo □ n soldado m raso. in ~ em particular; (of ceremony) na intimidade. ~ly adv particularmente; (inwardly) no fundo, interiormente

privet /ˈprɪvɪt/ n (bot) alfena f, ligustro m

privilege /ˈprɪvəlɪdʒ/ n privilégio m. ~d a privilegiado. be ~d to ter o privilégio de

prize /praɪz/ n prémio m, (P) prémio m □ a premiado; (fool etc) perfeito □ vt ter em grande apreço, apreciar muito. ~-giving n distribuição f de prémios, (P) prémios. ~-winner n premiado m, vencedor m

pro[1] /prəʊ/ n the ~s and cons os prós e os contras

pro- /prəʊ/ pref (acting for) pro-; (favouring) pró-

probab|le /ˈprɒbəbl/ a provável. ~ility /-ˈbɪlətɪ/ n probabilidade f. ~ly adv provavelmente

probation /prəˈbeɪʃn/ n (testing) estágio m, tirocínio m; (jur) liberdade f condicional. ~ary a probatório

probe /prəʊb/ n (med) sonda f; (fig: investigation) inquérito m □ vt/i ~ (into) sondar, investigar

problem /ˈprɒbləm/ n problema m □ a difícil. ~atic /-ˈmætɪk/ a problemático

procedure /prəˈsiːdʒə(r)/ n procedimento m, processo m, norma f

proceed /prəˈsiːd/ vi prosseguir, ir para diante, avançar. ~ to do passar a fazer. ~ with sth continuar or avançar com alguma coisa. ~ing n procedimento m

proceedings /prəˈsiːdɪŋz/ npl (jur) processo m; (report) ata f, (P) acta f

proceeds /'prəʊsiːdz/ *npl* produto *m*, luco *m*, proventos *mpl*

process /'prəʊses/ *n* processo *m* □ *vt* tratar; (*photo*) revelar. **in ~** em curso. **in the ~ of doing** sendo feito

procession /prə'seʃn/ *n* procissão *f*, cortejo *m*

procl|aim /prə'kleɪm/ *vt* proclamar. **~amation** /prɒklə'meɪʃn/ *n* proclamação *f*

procure /prə'kjʊə(r)/ *vt* obter

prod /prɒd/ *vt/i* (*pt* prodded) (*push*) empurrar; (*poke*) espetar; (*fig: urge*) incitar □ *n* espetadela *f*; (*fig*) incitamento *m*

prodigal /'prɒdɪgl/ *a* pródigo

prodigious /prə'dɪdʒəs/ *a* prodigioso

prodigy /'prɒdɪdʒɪ/ *n* prodígio *m*

produc|e[1] /prə'djuːs/ *vt/i* produzir; (*bring out*) tirar, extrair; (*show*) apresentar, mostrar; (*cause*) causar, provocar; (*theat*) pôr em cena. **~er** *n* produtor *m*. **~tion** /-'dʌkʃn/ *n* produção *f*; (*theat*) encenação *f*

produce[2] /'prɒdjuːs/ *n* produtos (agrícolas) *mpl*

product /'prɒdʌkt/ *n* produto *m*

productiv|e /prə'dʌktɪv/ *a* produtivo. **~ity** /prɒdʌk'tɪvətɪ/ *n* produtividade *f*

profan|e /prə'feɪn/ *a* profano; (*blasphemous*) blasfemo. **~ity** /-'fænətɪ/ *n* profanidade *f*

profess /prə'fes/ *vt* professar. **~ to do** alegar fazer

profession /prə'feʃn/ *n* profissão *f*. **~al** *a* profissional; (*well done*) de profissional; (*person*) que exerce uma profissão liberal □ *n* profissional *mf*

professor /prə'fesə(r)/ *n* professor (universitário) *m*

proficien|t /prə'fɪʃnt/ *a* proficiente, competente. **~cy** *n* proficiência *f*, competência *f*

profile /'prəʊfaɪl/ *n* perfil *m*

profit /'prɒfɪt/ *n* proveito *m*; (*money*) lucro *m* □ *vi* (*pt* profited) **~ by** aproveitar-se de; **~ from** tirar proveito de. **~able** *a* proveitoso; (*of business*) lucrativo, rentável

profound /prə'faʊnd/ *a* profundo. **~ly** *adv* profundamente

profus|e /prə'fjuːs/ *a* profuso. **~ely** *adv* profusamente, em abundância. **~ion** /-ʒn/ *n* profusão *f*

program /'prəʊgræm/ *n* (*computer*) **~** programa *m* □ *vt* (*pt* programmed) programar. **~mer** *n* programador *m*

programme /'prəʊgræm/ *n* programa *m*

progress[1] /'prəʊgres/ *n* progresso *m*. **in ~** em curso, em andamento

progress[2] /prə'gres/ *vi* progredir. **~ion** /-ʃn/ *n* progressão *f*

progressive /prə'gresɪv/ *a* progressivo; (*reforming*) progressista. **~ly** *adv* progressivamente

prohibit /prə'hɪbɪt/ *vt* proibir (**sb from doing** alg de fazer)

project[1] /prə'dʒekt/ *vt* projetar, (P) projectar □ *vi* ressaltar, sobressair. **~ion** /-ʃn/ *n* projeção *f*, (P) projecção *f*; (*protruding*) saliência *f*, ressalto *m*

project[2] /'prɒdʒekt/ *n* projeto *m*, (P) projecto *m*

projectile /prə'dʒektaɪl/ *n* projétil *m*, (P) projéctil *m*

projector /prə'dʒektə(r)/ *n* projetor *m*, (P) projector *m*

proletari|at /prəʊlɪ'teərɪət/ *n* proletariado *m*. **~an** *a* & *n* proletário (*m*)

proliferat|e /prə'lɪfəreɪt/ *vi* proliferar. **~ion** /-'reɪʃn/ *n* proliferação *f*

prolific /prə'lɪfɪk/ *a* prolífico

prologue /'prəʊlɒg/ *n* prólogo *m*

prolong /prə'lɒŋ/ *vt* prolongar

promenade /prɒmə'nɑːd/ *n* passeio *m* □ *vt/i* passear

prominen|t /'prɒmɪnənt/ *a* (*projecting; important*) proeminente; (*conspicuous*) bem à vista, conspícuo. **~ce** *n* proeminência *f*. **~tly** *adv* bem à vista

promiscu|ous /prə'mɪskjʊəs/ *a* promíscuo, de costumes livres. **~ity** /prɒmɪs'kjuːətɪ/ *n* promiscuidade *f*, liberdade *f* de costumes

promis|e /'prɒmɪs/ *n* promessa *f* □ *vt/i* prometer. **~ing** *a* prometedor, promissor

promot|e /prə'məʊt/ *vt* promover. **~ion** /-'məʊʃn/ *n* promoção *f*

prompt /prɒmpt/ *a* pronto, rápido, imediato; (*punctual*) pontual □ *adv* **em ponto** □ *vt* levar; (*theat*) soprar, servir de ponto para. **~er** *n* ponto *m*. **~ly** *adv* prontamente; pontualmente. **~ness** *n* prontidão *f*

prone /prəʊn/ *a* deitado de bruços. **~ to** propenso a

prong /prɒŋ/ *n* (*of fork*) dente *m*

pronoun /'prəʊnaʊn/ *n* pronome *m*

pron|ounce /prə'naʊns/ *vt* pronunciar; (*declare*) declarar. **~ounced** *a* pronunciado. **~ouncement** *n* declaração *f*. **~unciation** /-ʌnsɪ'eɪʃn/ *n* pronúncia *f*

proof /pruːf/ *n* prova *f*; (*of liquor*) teor *m* alcoólico, graduação *f* □ *a* **~ against** à prova de

prop[1] /prɒp/ *n* suporte *m*; (*lit & fig*) apoio *m*, esteio *m* □ *vt* (*pt* propped) sustentar, suportar. **~ against** apoiar contra

prop² /prɒp/ n (colloq: theat) acessório m, (P) adereço m

propaganda /propə'gændə/ n propaganda f

propagat|e /'propəgeɪt/ vt/i propagar(-se). ~ion /-'geɪʃn/ n propagação f

propel /prə'pel/ vt (pt propelled) propulsionar, impelir

propeller /prə'pelə(r)/ n hélice f

proper /'propə(r)/ a correto, (P) correcto; (seemly) conveniente; (real) propriamente dito; (colloq: thorough) belo. ~ noun substantivo m próprio. ~ly adv corretamente, (P) correctamente; (rightly) com razão, acertadamente; (accurately) propriamente

property /'propətɪ/ n (house) imóvel m; (land, quality) propriedade f; (possessions) bens mpl

prophecy /'profəsɪ/ n profecia f

prophesy /'profəsaɪ/ vt/i profetizar. ~ that predizer que

prophet /'profɪt/ n profeta m. ~ic /prə'fetɪk/ a profético

proportion /prə'pɔ:ʃn/ n proporção f. ~al, ~ate adjs proporcional

proposal /prə'pəʊzl/ n proposta f; (of marriage) pedido m de casamento

propos|e /prə'pəʊz/ vt propor □ vi pedir em casamento. ~e to do propor-se fazer. ~ition /propə'zɪʃn/ n proposição f; (colloq: matter) caso m, questão f

propound /prə'paʊnd/ vt propor

proprietor /prə'praɪətə(r)/ n proprietário m

propriety /prə'praɪətɪ/ n propriedade f, correção f, (P) correcção f

propulsion /prə'pʌlʃn/ n propulsão f

prosaic /prə'zeɪɪk/ a prosaico

prose /prəʊz/ n prosa f

prosecut|e /'prosɪkju:t/ vt (jur) processar. ~ion /-'kju:ʃn/ n (jur) acusação f

prospect¹ /'prospekt/ n perspectiva f

prospect² /prə'spekt/ vt/i pesquisar, prospectar

prospective /prə'spektɪv/ a futuro; (possible) provável

prosper /'prospə(r)/ vi prosperar

prosper|ous /'prospərəs/ a próspero. ~ity /-'sperətɪ/ n prosperidade f

prostitut|e /'prostɪtju:t/ n prostituta f. ~ion /-'tju:ʃn/ n prostituição f

prostrate /'prostreɪt/ a prostrado

protect /prə'tekt/ vt proteger. ~ion /-ʃn/ n proteção f, (P) protecção f. ~ive a protetor, (P) protector. ~or n protetor m, (P) protector m

protégé /'protɪʒeɪ/ n protegido m. ~e n protegida f

protein /'prəʊti:n/ n proteína f

protest¹ /'prəʊtest/ n protesto m

protest² /prə'test/ vt/i protestar. ~er n (pol) manifestante mf

Protestant /'protɪstənt/ a & n protestante (mf). ~ism /-ɪzəm/ n protestantismo m

protocol /'prəʊtəkɒl/ n protocolo m

prototype /'prəʊtətaɪp/ n protótipo m

protract /prə'trækt/ vt prolongar, arrastar

protru|de /prə'tru:d/ vi sobressair, sair do alinhamento. ~ing a saliente

proud /praʊd/ a (er, -est) orgulhoso. ~ly adv orgulhosamente

prove /pru:v/ vt provar, demonstrar □ vi ~ (to be) easy/etc verificar-se ser fácil/etc. ~ o.s. dar provas de si. ~n /-n/ a provado

proverb /'prɒvɜ:b/ n provérbio m. ~ial /prə'vɜ:bɪəl/ a proverbial

provid|e /prə'vaɪd/ vt prover, munir (sb with sth alg de alguma coisa) □ vi ~ for providenciar para; (person) prover de, cuidar de; (allow for) levar em conta. ~ed, ~ing (that) conj desde que, contanto que

providence /'prɒvɪdəns/ n providência f

province /'prɒvɪns/ n província f; (fig) competência f

provincial /prə'vɪnʃl/ a provincial; (rustic) provinciano

provision /prə'vɪʒn/ n provisão f; (stipulation) disposição f. ~s (pl food) provisões fpl

provisional /prə'vɪʒənl/ a provisório. ~ly adv provisoriamente

proviso /prə'vaɪzəʊ/ n (pl -os) condição f

provo|ke /prə'vəʊk/ vt provocar. ~cation /prɒvə'keɪʃn/ n provocação f. ~cative /-'vɒkətɪv/ a provocante

prowess /'praʊɪs/ n proeza f, façanha f

prowl /praʊl/ vi rondar □ n be on the ~ andar à espreita. ~er n pessoa f que anda à espreita

proximity /prɒk'sɪmətɪ/ n proximidade f

proxy /'prɒksɪ/ n by ~ por procuração

prude /pru:d/ n puritano m, pudico m

pruden|t /'pru:dnt/ a prudente. ~ce n prudência f

prune¹ /pru:n/ n ameixa f seca

prune² /pru:n/ vt podar

pry /praɪ/ vi bisbilhotar. ~ into meter o nariz em, intrometer-se em

psalm /sa:m/ n salmo m

pseudo- /'sju:dəʊ/ pref pseudo-

pseudonym /'sju:dənɪm/ n pseudónimo m, (P) pseudónimo m

psychiatr|y /saɪ'kaɪətrɪ/ n psiquiatria f. ~ic /-ɪ'ætrɪk/ a psiquiátrico. ~ist n psiquiatra mf

psychic /'saɪkɪk/ a psíquico; (person) com capacidade de telepatia

psychoanalys|e /saɪkəʊ'ænəlaɪz/ vt psicanalisar. ~t /-ɪst/ n psicanalista mf

psychoanalysis /saɪkəʊə'næləsɪs/ n psicanálise f

psycholog|y /saɪ'kɒlədʒɪ/ n psicologia f. ~ical /-ə'lɒdʒɪkl/ a psicológico. ~ist n psicólogo m

psychopath /'saɪkəʊpæθ/ n psicopata mf

pub /pʌb/ n pub m

puberty /'pjuːbətɪ/ n puberdade f

public /'pʌblɪk/ a público; (holiday) feriado. in ~ em público. ~ house pub m. ~ relations relações fpl públicas. ~ school escola f particular; (Amer) escola f oficial. ~-spirited a de espírito cívico, patriótico. ~ly adv publicamente

publication /pʌblɪ'keɪʃn/ n publicação f

publicity /pʌ'blɪsətɪ/ n publicidade f

publicize /'pʌblɪsaɪz/ vt fazer publicidade de

publish /'pʌblɪʃ/ vt publicar. ~er n editor m. ~ing n publicação f. ~ing house editora f

pucker /'pʌkə(r)/ vt/i franzir

pudding /'pʊdɪŋ/ n pudim m; (dessert) doce m

puddle /'pʌdl/ n poça f de água, charco m

puerile /'pjʊəraɪl/ a pueril

puff /pʌf/ n baforada f □ vt/i lançar baforadas; (breathe hard) arquejar, ofegar. ~ at (cigar etc) dar baforadas em. ~ out (swell) inchar(-se). ~-pastry n massa f folhada

puffy /'pʌfɪ/ a inchado

pugnacious /pʌg'neɪʃəs/ a belicoso, combativo

pull /pʊl/ vt/i puxar; (muscle) distender □ n puxão m; (fig: influence) influência f, empenho m. give a ~ dar um puxão. ~ a face fazer uma careta. ~ one's weight (fig) fazer a sua quota-parte. ~ sb's leg brincar com alguém, meter-se com alguém. ~ away or out (auto) arrancar. ~ down puxar para baixo; (building) demolir. ~ in (auto) encostar-se. ~ off tirar; (fig) sair-se bem em, conseguir alcançar. ~ out partir; (extract) arrancar, tirar. ~ through sair-se bem. ~ o.s. together recompor-se, refazer-se. ~ up puxar para cima; (uproot) arrancar; (auto) parar

pulley /'pʊlɪ/ n roldana f

pullover /'pʊləʊvə(r)/ n pulôver m

pulp /pʌlp/ n polpa f; (for paper) pasta f de papel

pulpit /'pʊlpɪt/ n púlpito m

pulsat|e /pʌl'seɪt/ vi pulsar, bater, palpitar. ~ion /-'seɪʃn/ n pulsação f

pulse /pʌls/ n pulso m. feel sb's ~ tirar o pulso de alguém

pulverize /'pʌlvəraɪz/ vt (grind, defeat) pulverizar

pummel /'pʌml/ vt (pt pummelled) esmurrar

pump[1] /pʌmp/ n bomba f □ vt/i bombear; (person) arrancar or extrair informações de. ~ up encher com bomba

pump[2] /pʌmp/ n (shoe) sapato m

pumpkin /'pʌmpkɪn/ n abóbora f

pun /pʌn/ n trocadilho m, jogo m de palavras

punch[1] /pʌntʃ/ vt esmurrar, dar um murro or soco; (perforate) furar, perfurar; (a hole) fazer □ n murro m, soco m; (device) furador m. ~-line n remate m. ~-up n (colloq) pancadaria f

punch[2] /pʌntʃ/ n (drink) ponche m

punctual /'pʌŋktʃʊəl/ a pontual. ~ity /-'ælətɪ/ n pontualidade f

punctuat|e /'pʌŋktʃʊeɪt/ vt pontuar. ~ion /-'eɪʃn/ n pontuação f

puncture /'pʌŋktʃə(r)/ n (in tyre) furo m □ vt/i furar

pundit /'pʌndɪt/ n autoridade f, sumidade f

pungent /'pʌndʒənt/ a acre, pungente

punish /'pʌnɪʃ/ vt punir, castigar. ~able a punível. ~ment n punição f, castigo m

punitive /'pjuːnɪtɪv/ a (expedition, measure etc) punitivo; (taxation etc) penalizador

punt /pʌnt/ n (boat) chalana f

punter /'pʌntə(r)/ n (gambler) jogador m; (colloq: customer) freguês m

puny /'pjuːnɪ/ a (-ier, -iest) fraco, débil

pup(py) /'pʌp(ɪ)/ n cachorro m, cachorrinho m

pupil /'pjuːpl/ n aluno m; (of eye) pupila f

puppet /'pʌpɪt/ n (lit & fig) fantoche m, marionete f

purchase /'pɜːtʃəs/ vt comprar (from sb de alg) □ n compra f. ~r /-ə(r)/ n comprador m

pur|e /'pjʊə(r)/ a (-er, -est) puro. ~ely adv puramente. ~ity n pureza f

purgatory /'pɜːgətrɪ/ n purgatório m

purge /pɜːdʒ/ vt purgar; (pol) sanear □ n (med) purgante m; (pol) saneamento m

purif|y /'pjʊərɪfaɪ/ vt purificar. ~ication /-ɪ'keɪʃn/ n purificação f

puritan /'pjʊərɪtən/ n puritano m. ~ical /-'tænɪkl/ a puritano

purple /'pɜːpl/ a roxo, purpúreo □ n roxo m, púrpura f

purport /pə'pɔ:t/ vt dizer-se, (P) dar a entender. ~ to be pretender ser
purpose /'pɜ:pəs/ n propósito m; (determination) firmeza f. on ~ de propósito. to no ~ em vão. ~-built a construído especialmente.
purposely /'pɜ:pəslɪ/ adv de propósito, propositadamente
purr /pɜ:r/ n ronrom m □ vi ronronar
purse /pɜ:s/ n carteira f; (Amer) bolsa f □ vt franzir
pursue /pə'sju:/ vt perseguir; (go on with) prosseguir; (engage in) entregar-se a, dedicar-se a. ~r /-ə(r)/ n perseguidor m
pursuit /pə'sju:t/ n perseguição f; (fig) atividade f, (P) actividade f
pus /pʌs/ n pus m
push /pʊʃ/ vt/i empurrar; (button) apertar; (thrust) enfiar; (colloq: recommend) insistir □ n empurrão m; (effort) esforço m; (drive) energia f. be ~ed for (time etc) estar com pouco. be ~ing thirty/etc (colloq) estar beirando os trinta/etc. give the ~ to (sl) dar o fora em alguém. ~ s.o. around fazer alguém de bobo. ~ back repelir. ~-chair n carrinho m (de criança). ~er n fornecedor m (de droga). ~ off (sl) dar o fora. ~ on continuar. ~-over n canja f, coisa f fácil. ~ up (lift) levantar; (prices) forçar o aumento de. ~-up n (Amer) flexão f. ~y a (colloq) agressivo, furão
put /pʊt/ vt/i (pt put, pres p putting) colocar, pôr; (question) fazer. ~ the damage at a million estimar os danos em um milhão. I'd ~ it at a thousand eu diria mil. ~ sth tactfully dizer alg coisa com tato. ~ across comunicar. ~ away guardar. ~ back repor; (delay) retardar, atrasar. ~ by pôr de lado. ~ down pôr em lugar baixo; (write) anotar; (pay) pagar; (suppress) sufocar, reprimir. ~ forward (plan) submeter. ~ in (insert) introduzir; (fix) instalar; (submit) submeter. ~ in for fazer um pedido, candidatar-se. ~ off (postpone) adiar; (disconcert) desanimar; (displease) desagradar. ~ s.o. off sth tirar o gosto de alguém por alg coisa. ~ on (clothes) pôr; (radio) ligar; (light) acender; (speed, weight) ganhar; (accent) adotar. ~ out pôr para fora; (stretch) esticar; (extinguish) extinguir, apagar; (disconcert) desconcertar; (inconvenience) incomodar. ~ up levantar; (building) erguer, construir; (notice) colocar; (price) aumentar; (guest) hospedar; (offer) oferecer. ~-up job embuste m. ~ up with suportar

putrefy /'pju:trɪfaɪ/ vi putrefazer-se, apodrecer
putty /'pʌtɪ/ n massa de vidraceiro f, betume m
puzzl|e /'pʌzl/ n puzzle m, quebra-cabeça m □ vt deixar perplexo, intrigar □ vi quebrar a cabeça. ~ing a intrigante
pygmy /'pɪgmɪ/ n pigmeu m
pyjamas /pə'dʒɑ:məz/ npl pijama m
pylon /'paɪlən/ n poste m
pyramid /'pɪrəmɪd/ n pirâmide f
python /'paɪθn/ n piton m

Q

quack¹ /kwæk/ n (of duck) grasnido m □ vi grasnar
quack² /kwæk/ n charlatão m
quadrangle /'kwɒdræŋgl/ n quadrângulo m; (of college) pátio m quadrangular
quadruped /'kwɒdruped/ n quadrúpede m
quadruple /'kwɒdrʊpl/ a & n quádruplo (m) □ vt/i /kwɒ'dru:pl/ quadruplicar. ~ts /-plɪts/ npl quadrigémeos mpl, (P) quadrigémeos mpl
quagmire /'kwægmaɪə(r)/ n pântano m, lamaçal m
quail /kweɪl/ n codorniz f
quaint /kweɪnt/ a (-er, -est) pitoresco; (whimsical) estranho, bizarro
quake /kweɪk/ vi tremer □ n (colloq) tremor m de terra
Quaker /'kweɪkə(r)/ n quaker mf, quacre m
qualification /kwɒlɪfɪ'keɪʃn/ n qualificação f; (accomplishment) habilitação f; (diploma) diploma m, título m; (condition) requisito m, condição f; (fig) restrição f, reserva f
qualif|y /'kwɒlɪfaɪ/ vt qualificar; (fig: moderate) atenuar, moderar; (fig: limit) pôr ressalvas or restrições a □ vi (fig: be entitled to) ter os requisitos (for sport); (sport) classificar-se. he ~ied as a vet ele formou-se em veterinária. ~ied a formado; (able) qualificado, habilitado; (moderated) atenuado; (limited) limitado
quality /'kwɒlətɪ/ n qualidade f
qualm /kwɑ:m/ n escrúpulo m
quandary /'kwɒndərɪ/ n dilema m
quantity /'kwɒntətɪ/ n quantidade f
quarantine /'kwɒrəntiːn/ n quarentena f
quarrel /'kwɒrəl/ n zanga f, questão f, discussão f □ vi (pt quarrelled) zangar-se, questionar, discutir. ~some a conflituoso, brigão
quarry¹ /'kwɒrɪ/ n (prey) presa f, caça f

quarry[2] /'kwɒrɪ/ n (*excavation*) pedreira f

quarter /'kwɔːtə(r)/ n quarto m; (*of year*) trimestre m; (*Amer: coin*) quarto m de dólar, 25 cêntimos mpl; (*district*) bairro m, quarteirão m. ~s (*lodgings*) alojamento m, residência f; (*mil*) quartel m □ vt dividir em quarto; (*mil*) aquartelar. from all ~s de todos os lados. ~ of an hour quarto m de hora. (a) ~ past six seis e quinze. (a) ~ to seven quinze para as sete. ~-final n (*sport*) quarta f de final. ~ly a trimestral □ adv trimestralmente

quartet /kwɔː'tet/ n quarteto m

quartz /kwɔːts/ n quartzo m □ a (*watch etc*) de quartzo

quash /kwɒʃ/ vt reprimir; (*jur*) revogar

quaver /'kweɪvə(r)/ vi tremer, tremular □ n (*mus*) colcheia f

quay /kiː/ n cais m

queasy /'kwiːzɪ/ a delicado. feel ~ estar enjoado

queen /kwiːn/ n rainha f; (*cards*) dama f

queer /kwɪə(r)/ a (-er, -est) estranho; (*slightly ill*) indisposto; (*sl: homosexual*) bicha, maricas (*sl*); (*dubious*) suspeito □ n (*sl*) bicha m, maricas m (*sl*)

quell /kwel/ vt reprimir, abafar, sufocar

quench /kwentʃ/ vt (*fire, flame*) apagar; (*thirst*) matar, saciar

query /'kwɪərɪ/ n questão f □ vt pôr em dúvida

quest /kwest/ n busca f, procura f. in ~ of em demanda de

question /'kwestʃən/ n pergunta f, interrogação f; (*problem, affair*) questão f □ vt perguntar, interrogar; (*doubt*) pôr em dúvida or em causa. in ~ em questão or em causa. out of the ~ fora de toda a questão. there's no ~ of nem pensar em. without ~ sem dúvida. ~ mark ponto m de interrogação. ~able a discutível

questionnaire /kwestʃə'neə(r)/ n questionário m

queue /kjuː/ n fila f, (P) bicha f □ vi (*pres p queuing*) fazer fila, (P) fazer bicha

quibble /'kwɪbl/ vi tergiversar, usar de evasivas; (*raise petty objections*) discutir por coisas insignificantes

quick /kwɪk/ a (-er, -est) rápido □ adv depressa. be ~ despachar-se. have a ~ temper exaltar-se facilmente. ~ly adv rapidamente, depressa. ~ness n rapidez f

quicken /'kwɪkən/ vt/i apressar(-se)

quicksand /'kwɪksænd/ n areia f movediça

quid /kwɪd/ n invar (*sl*) libra f

quiet /'kwaɪət/ a (-er, -est) quieto, sossegado, tranquilo □ n quietude f, sossego m, tranquilidade f. keep ~ calar-se. on the ~ às escondidas, na calada. ~ly adv sossegadamente, silenciosamente. ~ness n sossego m, tranquilidade f, calma f

quieten /'kwaɪətn/ vt/i sossegar, acalmar(-se)

quilt /kwɪlt/ n coberta f acolchoada. (*continental*) ~ edredão m de penas □ vt acolchoar

quince /kwɪns/ n marmelo m

quintet /kwɪn'tet/ n quinteto m

quintuplets /kwɪn'tjuːplɪts/ npl quíntuplos mpl

quip /kwɪp/ n piada f □ vt contar piadas

quirk /kwɜːk/ n mania f, singularidade f

quit /kwɪt/ vt (*pt quitted*) deixar □ vi ir-se embora; (*resign*) demitir-se. ~ doing (*Amer*) parar de fazer

quite /kwaɪt/ adv completamente, absolutamente; (*rather*) bastante. ~ (so)! isso mesmo!, exatamente! ~ a few bastante, alguns/algumas. ~ a lot bastante

quiver /'kwɪvə(r)/ vi tremer, estremecer □ n tremor m, estremecimento m

quiz /kwɪz/ n (*pl quizzes*) teste m; (*game*) concurso m □ vt (*pt quizzed*) interrogar

quizzical /'kwɪzɪkl/ a zombeteiro

quorum /'kwɔːrəm/ n quorum m

quota /'kwəʊtə/ n cota f, quota f

quotation /kwəʊ'teɪʃn/ n citação f; (*estimate*) orçamento m. ~ marks aspas fpl

quote /kwəʊt/ vt citar; (*estimate*) fazer um orçamento □ n (*colloq: passage*) citação f; (*colloq: estimate*) orçamento m

R

rabbi /'ræbaɪ/ n rabino m

rabbit /'ræbɪt/ n coelho m

rabble /'ræbl/ n turba f. the ~ a ralé, a gentalha, o povinho

rabid /'ræbɪd/ a (*fig*) fanático, ferrenho; (*dog*) raivoso

rabies /'reɪbiːz/ n raiva f

race[1] /reɪs/ n corrida f □ vt (*horse*) fazer correr □ vi correr, dar uma corrida; (*rush*) ir em grande or a toda (a) velocidade. ~-track n pista f

race[2] /reɪs/ n (*group*) raça f □ a racial

racecourse /'reɪskɔːs/ n hipódromo m

racehorse /'reɪshɔːs/ n cavalo m de corrida

racial /'reɪʃl/ a racial

racing /'reɪsɪŋ/ n corridas fpl. ~ car carro m de corridas

racis|t /'reɪsɪst/ a & n racista (mf). ~m /-zəm/ n racismo m

rack¹ /ræk/ n (for luggage) porta-bagagem m, bagageiro m; (for plates) escorredor m de prato □ vt ~ one's brains dar tratos à imaginação

rack² /ræk/ n go to ~ and ruin arruinar-se; (of buildings etc) cair em ruínas

racket¹ /'rækɪt/ n (sport) raquete f, (P) raqueta f

racket² /'rækɪt/ n (din) barulheira f; (swindle) roubalheira f; (sl: business) negociata f (colloq)

racy /'reɪsɪ/ a (-ier, -iest) vivo, vigoroso

radar /'reɪdɑː(r)/ n radar m □ a de radar

radian|t /'reɪdɪənt/ a radiante. ~ce n brilho m

radiator /'reɪdɪeɪtə(r)/ n radiador m

radical /'rædɪkl/ a & n radical (m)

radio /'reɪdɪəʊ/ n (pl -os) rádio f; set (aparelho de) rádio m □ vt transmitir pelo rádio. ~ station estação f de rádio, emissora f

radioactiv|e /'reɪdɪəʊ'æktɪv/ a radioativo, (P) radioactivo. ~ity /'tɪvətɪ/ n radioatividade f, (P) radioactividade f

radiograph|er /'reɪdɪ'ɒɡrəfə(r)/ n radiologista mf. ~y n radiografia f

radish /'rædɪʃ/ n rabanete m

radius /'reɪdɪəs/ n (pl -dii /-dɪaɪ/) raio m

raffle /'ræfl/ n rifa f □ vt rifar

raft /rɑːft/ n jangada f

rafter /'rɑːftə(r)/ n trave f, viga f

rag¹ /ræɡ/ n farrapo m; (for wiping) trapo m; (pej: newspaper) jornaleco m. ~s npl farrapos mpl, andrajos mpl. in ~s maltrapilho. ~ doll boneca f de trapos

rag² /ræɡ/ vt (pt ragged) zombar de

rage /reɪdʒ/ n raiva f, fúria f □ vi estar furioso; (of storm) rugir; (of battle) estar acesa. be all the ~ (colloq) fazer furor, estar na moda (colloq)

ragged /'ræɡɪd/ a (clothes, person) esfarrapado, roto; (edge) esfiapado, esgarçado

raid /reɪd/ n (mil) ataque m; (by police) batida f; (by criminals) assalto m □ vt fazer um ataque or uma batida or um assalto. ~er n atacante m, assaltante m

rail /reɪl/ n (of stairs) corrimão m; (of ship) amurada f; (on balcony) parapeito m; (for train) trilho m; (for cur-tain) varão m. by ~ por estrada, (P) caminho de ferro

railings /'reɪlɪŋz/ npl grade f

railroad /'reɪlrəʊd/ n (Amer) = railway

railway /'reɪlweɪ/ n estrada f, (P) caminho m de ferro. ~ line linha f do trem. ~ station estação f ferroviária, (P) estação f de caminho de ferro

rain /reɪn/ n chuva f □ vi chover. ~ forest floresta f tropical. ~storm n tempestade f com chuva. ~water n água f da chuva

rainbow /'reɪnbəʊ/ n arco-íris m

raincoat /'reɪnkəʊt/ n impermeável m

raindrop /'reɪndrɒp/ n pingo m de chuva

rainfall /'reɪnfɔːl/ n precipitação f, pluviosidade f

rainy /'reɪnɪ/ a (-ier, -iest) chuvoso

raise /reɪz/ vt levantar, erguer; (breed) criar; (voice) levantar; (question) fazer; (price etc) aumentar, subir; (funds) angariar; (loan) obter □ n (Amer) aumento m

raisin /'reɪzn/ n passa f

rake /reɪk/ n ancinho m □ vt juntar, alisar com ancinho; (search) revolver, remexer. ~ in (money) ganhar a rodos. ~-off n (colloq) percentagem f (colloq). ~ up desenterrar, ressuscitar

rally /'rælɪ/ vt/i reunir(-se); (reassemble) reagrupar(-se), reorganizar(-se); (health) restabelecer(-se); (strength) recuperar as forças □ n (recovery) recuperação f; (meeting) comício m, assembléia f; (auto) rally m, rali m

ram /ræm/ n (sheep) carneiro m □ vt (pt rammed) (beat down) calcar; (push) meter à força; (crash into) bater contra

rambl|e /'ræmbl/ n caminhada f, perambulação f □ vi perambular, vaguear. ~e on divagar. ~er n caminhante mf; (plant) trepadeira f. ~ing a (speech) desconexo

ramp /ræmp/ n rampa f

rampage /'ræmpeɪdʒ/ vi causar distúrbios violentos

rampant /'ræmpənt/ a be ~ vicejar, florescer; (diseases etc) grassar

rampart /'ræmpɑːt/ n baluarte m; (fig) defesa f

ramshackle /'ræmʃækl/ a (car) desconjuntado; (house) caindo aos pedaços

ran /ræn/ see run

ranch /rɑːntʃ/ n rancho m, estância f. ~er n rancheiro m

rancid /'rænsɪd/ a rançoso

rancour /'ræŋkə(r)/ n rancor m

random /'rændəm/ a feito, tirado etc ao acaso □ n at ~ ao acaso, a esmo, aleatoriamente

randy /'rændɪ/ a (-ier, -iest) lascivo, sensual

rang /ræŋ/ see ring

range /reɪndʒ/ n (distance) alcance m; (scope) âmbito m; (variety) gama f, variedade f; (stove) fogão m; (of voice) registo m, (P) registo m; (of temperature) variação f □ vt dispor, ordenar □ vi estender-se; (vary) variar. ~ of mountains cordilheira f, serra f. ~r n guarda m florestal

rank¹ /ræŋk/ n fila f, fileira f; (mil) posto m; (social position) classe f, categoria f □ vt/i ~ among contar(-se) entre. the ~ and file a massa

rank² /ræŋk/ a (-er, -est) (plants) luxuriante; (smell) fétido; (out-and-out) total

ransack /'rænsæk/ vt (search) espionar, revistar, remexer; (pillage) pilhar, saquear

ransom /'rænsəm/ n resgate m □ vt resgatar. hold to ~ prender como refém

rant /rænt/ vi usar linguagem bombástica

rap /ræp/ n pancadinha f seca □ vt/i (pt rapped) bater, dar uma pancada seca em

rape /reɪp/ vt violar, estuprar □ n violação f, estupro m

rapid /'ræpɪd/ a rápido. ~ity /rə-'pɪdətɪ/ n rapidez f

rapids /'ræpɪdz/ npl rápidos mpl

rapist /'reɪpɪst/ n violador m, estuprador m

rapport /ræ'pɔ:(r)/ n bom relacionamento m

rapt /ræpt/ a absorto. ~ in mergulhado em

raptur|e /'ræptʃə(r)/ n êxtase m. ~ous a extático; (welcome etc) entusiástico

rar|e¹ /reə(r)/ a (-er, -est) raro. ~ely adv raramente, raras vezes. ~ity n raridade f

rare² /reə(r)/ a (-er, -est) (culin) mal passado

rarefied /'reərɪfaɪd/ a rarefeito; (refined) requintado

raring /'reərɪŋ/ a ~ to (colloq) impaciente por, louco por (colloq)

rascal /'ra:skl/ n (dishonest) patife m; (mischievous) maroto m

rash¹ /ræʃ/ n erupção f cutânea, irritação f na pele (colloq)

rash² /ræʃ/ a (-er, -est) imprudente, precipitado. ~ly adv imprudentemente, precipitadamente

rasher /'ræʃə(r)/ n fatia f (de presunto or de bacon)

rasp /ra:sp/ n lixa f grossa, (P) lima f grossa

raspberry /'ra:zbrɪ/ n framboesa f

rasping /'ra:spɪŋ/ a áspero

rat /ræt/ n rato m, (P) ratazana f. ~ race (fig) luta renhida para vencer na vida, arrivismo m

rate /reɪt/ n (ratio) razão f; (speed) velocidade f; (price) tarifa f; (of exchange) (taxa m de) câmbio m; (of interest) taxa f. ~s (taxes) impostos mpl municipais, taxas fpl □ vt avaliar; (fig: consider) considerar. at any ~ de qualquer modo, pelo menos. at the ~ of à razão de. at this ~ desse jeito, desse modo

ratepayer /'reɪtpeɪə(r)/ n contribuinte mf

rather /'ra:ðə(r)/ adv (by preference) antes; (fairly) muito, bastante; (a little) um pouco. I would ~ go preferia ir

ratif|y /'rætɪfaɪ/ vt ratificar. ~ication /-ɪ'keɪʃn/ n ratificação f

rating /'reɪtɪŋ/ n (comm) rating m, (P) valor m; (sailor) praça f, marinheiro m; (radio, TV) índice m de audiência

ratio /'reɪʃɪəʊ/ n (pl -os) proporção f

ration /'ræʃn/ n ração f □ vt racionar

rational /'ræʃnəl/ a racional; (person) sensato, razoável. ~ize vt racionalizar

rattle /'rætl/ vt/i matraquear; (of door, window) bater; (of bottles) chocalhar; (colloq) agitar, mexer com os nervos de □ n (baby's toy) guizo m, chocalho m; (of football fan) matraca f; (sound) matraquear m, chocalhar m. ~ off despejar (colloq)

rattlesnake /'rætlsneɪk/ n cobra f cascavel

raucous /'rɔ:kəs/ a áspero, rouco

ravage /'rævɪdʒ/ vt devastar, causar estragos a. ~s npl devastação f, estragos mpl

rave /reɪv/ vi delirar; (in anger) urrar. ~ about delirar (de entusiasmo) com

raven /'reɪvn/ n corvo m

ravenous /'rævənəs/ a esfomeado; (greedy) voraz

ravine /rə'vi:n/ n ravina f, barranco m

raving /'reɪvɪŋ/ a ~ lunatic doido m varrido □ adv ~ mad loucamente

ravish /'rævɪʃ/ vt (rape) violar; (enrapture) arrebatar, encantar. ~ing a arrebatador, encantador

raw /rɔ:/ a (-er, -est) cru; (not processed) bruto; (wound) em carne viva; (weather) frio e úmido, (P) húmido; (immature) inexperiente, verde. ~ deal tratamento m injusto. ~ material matéria-prima f

ray /reɪ/ n raio m

raze /reɪz/ vt arrasar

razor /'reɪzə(r)/ n navalha f de barba. **~-blade** n lâmina f de barbear

re /ri:/ prep a respeito de, em referência a, relativo a

re- /ri/ pref re-

reach /ri:tʃ/ vt chegar a atingir; (contact) contatar; (pass) passar □ vi estender-se, chegar □ n alcance m. out of ~ fora de alcance. ~ for estender a mão para agarrar. within ~ of ao alcance de; (close to) próximo de

react /rɪ'ækt/ vi reagir

reaction /rɪ'ækʃn/ n reação f, (P) reacção f. ~ary a & n reacionário (m), (P) reaccionário (m)

reactor /rɪ'æktə(r)/ n reator m, (P) reactor m

read /ri:d/ vt/i (pt read /red/) ler; (fig: interpret) interpretar; (study) estudar; (of instrument) marcar, indicar □ n (colloq) leitura f. ~ about ler um artigo sobre. ~ out ler em voz alta. ~able a agradável or fácil de ler; (legible) legível. ~er n leitor m; (book) livro m de leitura. ~ing n leitura f; (of instrument) registro m, (P) registo m

readily /'redɪlɪ/ adv de boa vontade, prontamente; (easily) facilmente

readiness /'redɪnɪs/ n prontidão f. in ~ pronto (for para)

readjust /ri:ə'dʒʌst/ vt reajustar □ vi readaptar-se

ready /'redɪ/ a (-ier, -iest) pronto □ n at the ~ pronto para disparar. ~-made a pronto. ~ money dinheiro m vivo, (P) dinheiro m de contado, pagamento m à vista. ~-to-wear a prêt-à-porter

real /rɪəl/ a real, verdadeiro; (genuine) autêntico □ adv (Amer: colloq) realmente. ~ estate bens mpl imobiliários

realis|t /'rɪəlɪst/ n realista mf. ~m /-zəm/ n realismo m. ~tic /'lɪstɪk/ a realista. ~tically /'lɪstɪkəlɪ/ adv realisticamente

reality /rɪ'ælətɪ/ n realidade f

realiz|e /'rɪəlaɪz/ vt dar-se conta de, aperceber-se de, perceber; (fulfil; turn into cash) realizar. ~ation /-'zeɪʃn/ n consciência f, noção f; (fulfilment) realização f

really /'rɪəlɪ/ adv realmente, na verdade

realm /relm/ n reino m; (fig) domínio m, esfera f

reap /ri:p/ vt (cut) ceifar; (gather; fig) colher

reappear /ri:ə'pɪə(r)/ vi reaparecer. ~ance n reaparição f

rear[1] /rɪə(r)/ n traseira f, retaguarda f □ a traseiro, de trás, posterior. bring up the ~ ir na retaguarda, fechar a marcha. ~-view mirror espelho m retrovisor

rear[2] /rɪə(r)/ vt levantar, erguer; (children, cattle) criar □ vi (of horse etc) empinar-se. ~ one's head levantar a cabeça

rearrange /ri:ə'reɪndʒ/ vt arranjar doutro modo, reorganizar

reason /'ri:zn/ n razão f □ vt/i raciocinar, argumentar. ~ with sb procurar convencer alguém. within ~ razoável. ~ing n raciocínio m

reasonable /'ri:znəbl/ a razoável

reassur|e /ri:ə'ʃuə(r)/ vt tranquilizar, sossegar. ~ance n garantia f. ~ing a animador, reconfortante

rebate /'ri:beɪt/ n (refund) reembolso m; (discount) desconto m, abatimento m

rebel[1] /'rebl/ n rebelde mf

rebel[2] /rɪ'bel/ vi (pt rebelled) rebelar-se, revoltar-se, sublevar-se. ~lion n rebelião f, revolta f. ~lious a rebelde

rebound[1] /rɪ'baʊnd/ vi repercutir, ressoar; (fig: backfire) recair (on sobre)

rebound[2] /'ri:baʊnd/ n ricochete m

rebuff /rɪ'bʌf/ vt receber mal, repelir (colloq) □ n rejeição f

rebuild /ri:'bɪld/ vt (pt rebuilt) reconstruir

rebuke /rɪ'bju:k/ vt repreender □ n repreenda f

recall /rɪ'kɔ:l/ vt chamar, mandar regressar; (remember) lembrar-se de □ n (summons) ordem f de regresso

recant /rɪ'kænt/ vi retratar-se, (P) retractar-se

recap /'ri:kæp/ vt/i (pt recapped) (colloq) recapitular □ n recapitulação f

recapitulat|e /ri:kə'pɪtʃʊleɪt/ vt/i recapitular. ~ion /-'leɪʃn/ n recapitulação f

reced|e /rɪ'si:d/ vi recuar, retroceder. his hair is ~ing ele está ficando com entradas. ~ing a (forehead, chin) recuado, voltado para dentro

receipt /rɪ'si:t/ n recibo m; (receiving) recepção f. ~s (comm) receitas fpl

receive /rɪ'si:v/ vt receber. ~r /-ə(r)/ n (of stolen goods) receptador m; (phone) fone m, (P) auscultador m; (radio/TV) receptor m. (official) ~r síndico m de massa falida

recent /'ri:snt/ a recente. ~ly adv recentemente

receptacle /rɪ'septəkl/ n recipiente m, receptáculo m

reception /rɪ'sepʃn/ n recepção f; (welcome) acolhimento m. ~ist n recepcionista mf

receptive /rɪ'septɪv/ a receptivo

recess /rɪ'ses/ n recesso m; (of legisla-

ture) recesso *m*; (*Amer: school*) recreio *m*

recession /rɪ'seʃn/ *n* recessão *f*, depressão *f*

recharge /ri:'tʃɑ:dʒ/ *vt* tornar a carregar, recarregar

recipe /'resəpɪ/ *n* (*culin*) receita *f*

recipient /rɪ'sɪpɪənt/ *n* recipiente *mf*; (*of letter*) destinatário *m*

reciprocal /rɪ'sɪprəkl/ *a* recíproco

reciprocate /rɪ'sɪprəkeɪt/ *vt/i* reciprocar(-se), retribuir, fazer o mesmo

recital /rɪ'saɪtl/ *n* (*music etc*) recital *m*

recite /rɪ'saɪt/ *vt* recitar; (*list*) enumerar

reckless /'reklɪs/ *a* inconsciente, imprudente, estouvado

reckon /'rekən/ *vt/i* calcular; (*judge*) considerar; (*think*) supor, pensar. ~ on contar com, depender de. ~ with contar com, levar em conta. ~ing *n* conta(s) *f* (*pl*)

reclaim /rɪ'kleɪm/ *vt* (*demand*) reclamar; (*land*) recuperar

reclin|**e** /rɪ'klaɪn/ *vt/i* reclinar(-se). ~ing *a* (*person*) reclinado; (*chair*) reclinável

recluse /rɪ'klu:s/ *n* solitário *m*, recluso *m*

recognition /rekəg'nɪʃn/ *n* reconhecimento *m*. **beyond** ~ irreconhecível. **gain** ~ ganhar nome, ser reconhecido

recogniz|**e** /'rekəgnaɪz/ *vt* reconhecer. ~able /'rekəgnaɪzəbl/ *a* reconhecível

recoil /rɪ'kɔɪl/ *vi* recuar; (*gun*) dar coice □ *n* recuo *m*; (*gun*) coice *m*. ~ **from doing** recusar-se a fazer

recollect /rekə'lekt/ *vt* recordar-se de. ~ion /-ʃn/ *n* recordação *f*

recommend /rekə'mend/ *vt* recomendar. ~ation /-'deɪʃn/ *n* recomendação *f*

recompense /'rekəmpens/ *vt* recompensar □ *n* recompensa *f*

reconcil|**e** /'rekənsaɪl/ *vt* (*people*) reconciliar; (*facts*) conciliar. ~**e o.s. to** resignar-se a, conformar-se com. ~iation /-sɪlɪ'eɪʃn/ *n* reconciliação *f*

reconnaissance /rɪ'kɒnɪsns/ *n* reconhecimento *m*

reconnoitre /rekə'nɔɪtə(r)/ *vt/i* (*pres p* -tring) (*mil*) reconhecer, fazer um reconhecimento (de)

reconsider /ri:kən'sɪdə(r)/ *vt* reconsiderar

reconstruct /ri:kən'strʌkt/ *vt* reconstruir. ~ion /-ʃn/ *n* reconstrução *f*

record[1] /rɪ'kɔ:d/ *vt* registar; (*disc, tape etc*) gravar. ~ **that** referir/relatar que. ~ing *n* (*disc, tape etc*) gravação *f*

record[2] /'rekɔ:d/ *n* (*register*) registro *m*, (*P*) registo *m*; (*mention*) menção *f*, nota *f*; (*file*) arquivo *m*; (*mus*) disco

m; (*sport*) record(e) *m* □ *a* record(e) *invar*. **have a (criminal)** ~ ter cadastro. **off the** ~ (*unofficial*) oficioso; (*secret*) confidencial. ~-player *n* toca-discos *m invar*, (*P*) gira-discos *m invar*

recorder /rɪ'kɔ:də(r)/ *n* (*mus*) flauta *f* de ponta; (*techn*) instrumento *m* registrador

recount /rɪ'kaʊnt/ *vt* narrar em pormenor, relatar

re-count /'ri:kaʊnt/ *n* (*pol*) nova contagem *f*

recoup /rɪ'ku:p/ *vt* compensar; (*recover*) recuperar

recourse /rɪ'kɔ:s/ *n* recurso *m*. **have** ~ **to** recorrer a

recover /rɪ'kʌvə(r)/ *vt* recuperar □ *vi* restabelecer-se. ~y *n* recuperação *f*; (*health*) recuperação *f*, restabelecimento *m*

recreation /rekrɪ'eɪʃn/ *n* recreação *f*, recreio *m*; (*pastime*) passatempo *m*. ~al *a* recreativo

recrimination /rɪkrɪmɪ'neɪʃn/ *n* recriminação *f*

recruit /rɪ'kru:t/ *n* recruta *m* □ *vt* recrutar. ~ment *n* recrutamento *m*

rectangl|**e** /'rektæŋgl/ *n* retângulo *m*, (*P*) rectângulo *m*. ~ular /-'tæŋgjʊlə(r)/ *a* retangular, (*P*) rectangular

rectify /'rektɪfaɪ/ *vt* retificar, (*P*) rectificar

recuperat|**e** /rɪ'kju:pəreɪt/ *vt/i* recuperar(-se)

recur /rɪ'kɜ:(r)/ *vi* (*pt* recurred) repetir-se; (*come back*) voltar (**to** a)

recurren|**t** /rɪ'kʌrənt/ *a* frequente, (*P*) frequente, repetido, periódico. ~ce *n* repetição *f*

recycle /ri:'saɪkl/ *vt* reciclar

red /red/ *a* (**redder, reddest**) encarnado, vermelho; (*hair*) ruivo □ *n* encarnado *m*, vermelho *m*. **in the** ~ em déficit. ~ **carpet** (*fig*) recepção *f* solene, tratamento *m* de favor. **R~ Cross** Cruz *f* Vermelha. ~-**handed** *a* em flagrante (delito), com a boca na botija (*colloq*). ~ **herring** (*fig*) pista *f* falsa. ~-**hot** *a* escaldante, incandescente. ~ **light** luz *f* vermelha. ~ **tape** (*fig*) papelada *f*, burocracia *f*. ~ **wine** vinho *m* tinto

redden /'redn/ *vt/i* avermelhar(-se); (*blush*) corar, ruborizar-se

redecorate /ri:'dekəreɪt/ *vt* decorar/pintar de novo

red|**eem** /rɪ'di:m/ *vt* (*sins etc*) redimir; (*sth pawned*) tirar do prego (*colloq*); (*voucher etc*) resgatar. ~**emption** /rɪ'dempʃn/ *n* resgate *m*; (*of honour*) salvação *f*

redirect /ri:daɪ'rekt/ *vt* (*letter*) reendereçar

redness /'redns/ *n* vermelhidão *f*, cor *f* vermelha

redo /riː'duː/ *vt* (*pt* -did, *pp* -done) refazer

redress /rɪ'dres/ *vt* reparar; (*set right*) remediar, emendar. ~ the balance restabelecer o equilíbrio □ *n* reparação *f*

reduc|e /rɪ'djuːs/ *vt* reduzir; (*temperature etc*) baixar. ~tion /rɪ'dʌkʃən/ *n* redução *f*

redundan|t /rɪ'dʌndənt/ *a* redundante, supérfluo; (*worker*) desempregado. be made ~t ficar desempregado. ~cy *n* demissão *f* por excesso de pessoal

reed /riːd/ *n* cana *f*, junco *m*; (*mus*) palheta *f*

reef /riːf/ *n* recife *m*

reek /riːk/ *n* mau cheiro *m* □ *vi* cheirar mal, tresandar. he ~s of wine ele está com cheiro de vinho

reel /riːl/ *n* carretel *m*; (*spool*) bobina *f* □ *vi* cambalear, vacilar □ *vt* ~ off recitar (*colloq*)

refectory /rɪ'fektərɪ/ *n* refeitório *m*

refer /rɪ'fɜː(r)/ *vt/i* (*pt* referred) ~ to referir-se a; (*concern*) aplicar-se a, dizer respeito a; (*consult*) consultar; (*direct*) remeter a

referee /refə'riː/ *n* árbitro *m*; (*for job*) pessoa *f* que dá referências □ *vt* (*pt* refereed) arbitrar

reference /'refrəns/ *n* referência *f*; (*testimonial*) referências *fpl*. in ~ or with ~ to com referência a. ~ book livro *m* de consulta

referendum /refə'rendəm/ *n* (*pl* -dums *or* -da) referendo *m*, plebiscito *m*

refill[1] /riː'fɪl/ *vt* encher de novo; (*pen etc*) pôr carga nova em

refill[2] /'riːfɪl/ *n* (*pen etc*) carga *f* nova, (*P*) recarga *f*

refine /rɪ'faɪn/ *vt* refinar. ~d *a* refinado; (*taste, manners etc*) requintado. ~ment *n* (*taste, manners etc*) refinamento *m*, requinte *m*; (*tech*) refinação *f*. ~ry /-ərɪ/ *n* refinaria *f*

reflect /rɪ'flekt/ *vt/i* refletir, (*P*) reflectir (on/upon em). ~ion /-ʃn/ *n* reflexão *f*; (*image*) reflexo *m*. ~or *n* refletor *m*, (*P*) reflector *m*

reflective /rɪ'flektɪv/ *a* refletor, (*P*) reflector; (*thoughtful*) refletido, (*P*) reflectido, ponderado

reflex /'riːfleks/ *a & n* reflexo (*m*)

reflexive /rɪ'fleksɪv/ *a* (*gram*) reflexivo, (*P*) reflexo

reform /rɪ'fɔːm/ *vt/i* reformar(-se) □ *n* reforma *f*. ~er *n* reformador *m*

refract /rɪ'frækt/ *vt* refratar, (*P*) refractar

refrain[1] /rɪ'freɪn/ *n* refrão *m*, estribilho *m*

refrain[2] /rɪ'freɪn/ *vi* abster-se (from de)

refresh /rɪ'freʃ/ *vt* refrescar; (*of rest etc*) restaurar. ~ one's memory avivar *or* refrescar a memória. ~ing *a* refrescante; (*of rest etc*) reparador. ~ments *npl* refeição *f* leve; (*drinks*) refrescos *mpl*

refresher /rɪ'freʃə(r)/ *n* ~ course curso *m* de reciclagem

refrigerat|e /rɪ'frɪdʒəreɪt/ *vt* refrigerar. ~or *n* frigorífico *m*, refrigerador *m*, geladeira *f*

refuel /riː'fjuːəl/ *vt/i* (*pt* refuelled) reabastecer(-se) (de combustível)

refuge /'refjuːdʒ/ *n* refúgio *m*, asilo *m*. take ~ refugiar-se

refugee /refjʊ'dʒiː/ *n* refugiado *m*

refund[1] /rɪ'fʌnd/ *vt* reembolsar

refund[2] /'riːfʌnd/ *n* reembolso *m*

refus|e[1] /rɪ'fjuːz/ *vt/i* recusar(-se). ~al *n* recusa *f*. first ~al preferência *f*, primeira opção *f*

refuse[2] /'refjuːs/ *n* refugo *m*, lixo *m*. ~-collector *n* lixeiro *m*, (*P*) homem *m* do lixo

refute /rɪ'fjuːt/ *vt* refutar

regain /rɪ'geɪn/ *vt* recobrar, recuperar

regal /'riːgl/ *a* real, régio

regalia /rɪ'geɪlɪə/ *npl* insígnias *fpl*

regard /rɪ'gɑːd/ *vt* considerar; (*gaze*) olhar □ *n* consideração *f*, estima *f*; (*gaze*) olhar *m*. ~s cumprimentos *mpl*, (*less formally*) lembranças *fpl*, saudações *fpl*. as ~s, ~ing *prep* no que diz respeito a, quanto a. ~less *adv* apesar de tudo. ~less of apesar de

regatta /rɪ'gætə/ *n* regata *f*

regenerate /rɪ'dʒenəreɪt/ *vt* regenerar

regen|t /'riːdʒənt/ *n* regente *mf*. ~cy *n* regência *f*

regime /reɪ'ʒiːm/ *n* regime *m*

regiment /'redʒɪmənt/ *n* regimento *m*. ~al /-'mentl/ *a* de regimento, regimental. ~ation /-en'teɪʃn/ *n* arregimentação *f*, disciplina *f* excessiva

region /'riːdʒən/ *n* região *f*. in the ~ of por volta de. ~al *a* regional

regist|er /'redʒɪstə(r)/ *n* registro *m*, (*P*) registo *m* □ *vt* (*record*) anotar; (*notice*) fixar, registar, prestar atenção a; (*birth, letter*) registar, (*P*) registar; (*vehicle*) registar; (*emotions etc*) exprimir □ *vi* inscrever-se. ~er office registro *m*, (*P*) registo *m*. ~ration /-'streɪʃn/ *n* registro *m*, (*P*) registo *m*; (*for course*) inscrição *f*, matrícula *f*. ~ration (number) número *m* de placa

registrar /redʒɪ'strɑː(r)/ *n* oficial *m* do registro, (*P*) registo civil; (*univ*) secretário *m*

regret /rɪ'gret/ n pena f, pesar m; (*repentance*) remorso m. **I have no ~s** não estou arrependido □ vt (*pt regretted*) lamentar, sentir (to do fazer); (*feel repentance*) arrepender-se de, lamentar. com pena, pesarosamente. **~fully** adv com pena, pesarosamente. **~table** a lamentável. **~tably** adv infelizmente

regular /'regjʊlə(r)/ a regular; (*usual*) normal; (*colloq: thorough*) perfeito, verdadeiro, autêntico □ n (*colloq: client*) cliente mf habitual. **~ity** /-'lærətɪ/ n regularidade f. **~ly** adv regularmente

regulat|e /'regjʊleɪt/ vt regular. **~ion** /-'leɪʃn/ n regulação f; (*rule*) regulamento m, regra f

rehabilitat|e /ri:ə'bɪlɪteɪt/ vt reabilitar. **~ion** /-'teɪʃn/ n reabilitação f

rehash[1] /ri:'hæʃ/ vt apresentar sob nova forma, (P) cozinhar (*colloq*)

rehash[2] /'ri:hæʃ/ n (*fig*) apanhado m, (P) cozinhado m (*colloq*)

rehears|e /rɪ'hɜ:s/ vt ensaiar. **~al** n ensaio m. **dress ~al** ensaio m geral

reign /reɪn/ n reinado m □ vi reinar (over em)

reimburse /ri:ɪm'bɜ:s/ vt reembolsar. **~ment** n reembolso m

rein /reɪn/ n rédea f

reincarnation /ri:ɪnkɑ:'neɪʃn/ n reencarnação f

reindeer /'reɪndɪə(r)/ n invar rena f

reinforce /ri:ɪn'fɔ:s/ vt reforçar. **~ment** n reforço m. **~ments** reforços mpl. **~d concrete** concreto m armado, (P) cimento m or betão m armado

reinstate /ri:ɪn'steɪt/ vt reintegrar

reiterate /ri:'ɪtəreɪt/ vt reiterar

reject[1] /rɪ'dʒekt/ vt rejeitar. **~ion** /-ʃn/ n rejeição f

reject[2] /'ri:dʒekt/ n (artigo de) refugo m

rejoic|e /rɪ'dʒɔɪs/ vi regozijar-se (at/over com). **~ing** n regozijo m

rejuvenate /ri:'dʒu:vəneɪt/ vt rejuvenescer

relapse /rɪ'læps/ n recaída f □ vi recair

relate /rɪ'leɪt/ vt relatar; (*associate*) relacionar □ vi **~ to** ter relação com, dizer respeito a; (*get on with*) entender-se com. **~d** a aparentado; (*ideas etc*) afim, reinado m

relation /rɪ'leɪʃn/ n relação f; (*person*) parente mf. **~ship** n parentesco m; (*link*) relação f; (*affair*) ligação f

relative /'relətɪv/ n parente mf □ a relativo. **~ly** adv relativamente

relax /rɪ'læks/ vt/i relaxar(-se); (*fig*) descontrair(-se). **~ation** /ri:læk-'seɪʃn/ n relaxamento m; (*fig*) descontração f, (P) descontracção f;

(*recreation*) distração f, (P) distracção f **~ing** a relaxante

relay[1] /'ri:leɪ/ n turma f, (P) turno m. **~ race** corrida f de revezamento, (P) estafetas

relay[2] /rɪ'leɪ/ vt (*message*) retransmitir

release /rɪ'li:s/ vt libertar, soltar; (*mech*) desengatar, soltar; (*bomb, film, record*) lançar; (*news*) dar, publicar; (*gas, smoke*) soltar □ n libertação f; (*mech*) desengate m; (*bomb, film, record*) lançamento m; (*news*) publicação f; (*gas, smoke*) emissão f. **new ~** estréia f

relegate /'relɪgeɪt/ vt relegar

relent /rɪ'lent/ vi ceder. **~less** a implacável, inexorável, inflexível

relevan|t /'reləvənt/ a relevante, pertinente, a propósito. **be ~ to** ter a ver com. **~ce** n pertinência f, relevância f

reliab|le /rɪ'laɪəbl/ a de confiança, com que se pode contar; (*source etc*) fidedigno; (*machine etc*) seguro, confiável. **~ility** /-'bɪlətɪ/ n confiabilidade f

reliance /rɪ'laɪəns/ n (*dependence*) segurança f; (*trust*) confiança f, fé f (on em)

relic /'relɪk/ n relíquia f. **~s** vestígios mpl, ruinas fpl

relief /rɪ'li:f/ n alívio m; (*assistance*) auxílio m, assistência f, (*outline, design*) relevo m. **~ road** estrada f alternativa

relieve /rɪ'li:v/ vt aliviar; (*help*) socorrer; (*take over from*) revezar, substituir; (*mil*) render

religion /rɪ'lɪdʒən/ n religião f

religious /rɪ'lɪdʒəs/ a religioso

relinquish /rɪ'lɪŋkwɪʃ/ vt abandonar, renunciar a

relish /'relɪʃ/ n prazer m, gosto m; (*culin*) molho m condimentado □ vt saborear, apreciar, gostar de

relocate /ri:ləʊ'keɪt/ vt/i transferir (-se), mudar(-se)

reluctan|t /rɪ'lʌktənt/ a relutante (to em), pouco inclinado (to a). **~ce** n relutância f. **~tly** adv a contragosto, relutantemente

rely /rɪ'laɪ/ vi **~ on** contar com; (*depend*) depender de

remain /rɪ'meɪn/ vi ficar, permanecer. **~s** npl restos mpl; (*ruins*) ruínas fpl. **~ing** a restante

remainder /rɪ'meɪndə(r)/ n restante m, remanescente m

remand /rɪ'mɑ:nd/ vt reconduzir à prisão para detenção provisória □ n **on ~** sob prisão preventiva

remark /rɪ'mɑ:k/ n observação f, comentário m □ vt observar, comentar □ *vi* ~ **on** fazer observações *or* comentários sobre. ~**able** *a* notável

remarr|y /riːˈmærɪ/ *vt/i* tornar a casar(-se) (com). ~**iage** *n* novo casamento *m*

remed|y /ˈremədɪ/ *n* remédio *m* □ *vt* remediar. ~**ial** /rɪˈmiːdɪəl/ *a* (*med*) corretivo, (*P*) correctivo

remember /rɪˈmembə(r)/ *vt* lembrar-se de, recordar-se de. ~**rance** *n* lembrança *f*, recordação *f*

remind /rɪˈmaɪnd/ *vt* (fazer) lembrar (sb of sth alg coisa a alguém). ~ **sb to do** lembrar a alguém que faça. ~**er** *n* o que serve para fazer lembrar; (*note*) lembrete *m*

reminisce /remɪˈnɪs/ *vi* (re)lembrar (coisas passadas). ~**nces** *npl* reminiscências *fpl*

reminiscent /remɪˈnɪsnt/ *a* ~ **of** que faz lembrar, evocativo de

remiss /rɪˈmɪs/ *a* negligente, descuidado

remission /rɪˈmɪʃn/ *n* remissão *f*; (*jur*) comutação *f* (de pena)

remit /rɪˈmɪt/ *vt* (*pt* **remitted**) (*money*) remeter. ~**tance** *n* remessa *f* (de dinheiro)

remnant /ˈremnənt/ *n* resto *m*; (*trace*) vestígio *m*; (*of cloth*) retalho *m*

remorse /rɪˈmɔːs/ *n* remorso *m*. ~**ful** *a* arrependido, com remorsos. ~**less** *a* implacável

remote /rɪˈməʊt/ *a* remoto, distante; (*person*) distante; (*slight*) vago, leve. ~ **control** comando *m* à distância, telecomando *m*. ~**ly** *adv* de longe; vagamente

remov|e /rɪˈmuːv/ *vt* tirar, remover; (*lead away*) levar; (*dismiss*) demitir; (*get rid of*) eliminar. ~**al** *n* remoção *f*; (*dismissal*) demissão *f*; (*from house*) mudança *f*

remunerat|e /rɪˈmjuːnəreɪt/ *vt* remunerar. ~**ion** /-ˈreɪʃn/ *n* remuneração *f*

rename /riːˈneɪm/ *vt* rebatizar, (*P*) rebaptizar

render /ˈrendə(r)/ *vt* retribuir; (*services*) prestar; (*mus*) interpretar; (*translate*) traduzir. ~**ing** *n* (*mus*) interpretação *f*; (*plaster*) reboco *m*

renegade /ˈrenɪgeɪd/ *n* renegado *m*

renew /rɪˈnjuː/ *vt* renovar; (*resume*) retomar. ~**able** *a* renovável. ~**al** *n* renovação *f*; (*resumption*) reatamento *m*

renounce /rɪˈnaʊns/ *vt* renunciar a; (*disown*) renegar, repudiar

renovat|e /ˈrenəveɪt/ *vt* renovar. ~**ion** /-ˈveɪʃn/ *n* renovação *f*

renown /rɪˈnaʊn/ *n* renome *m*. ~**ed** *a* conceituado, célebre, de renome

rent /rent/ *n* aluguel *m*, (*P*) aluguer *m*, renda *f* □ *vt* alugar, arrendar. ~**al** *n* (*charge*) aluguel *m*, (*P*) aluguer *m*, renda *f*; (*act of renting*) aluguel *m*, (*P*) aluguer *m*

renunciation /rɪnʌnsɪˈeɪʃn/ *n* renúncia *f*

reopen /riːˈəʊpən/ *vt/i* reabrir(-se). ~**ing** *n* reabertura *f*

reorganize /riːˈɔːgənaɪz/ *vt/i* reorganizar(-se)

rep /rep/ *n* (*colloq*) vendedor *m*, caixeiro-viajante *m*

repair /rɪˈpeə(r)/ *vt* reparar, consertar □ *n* reparo *m*, conserto *m*. **in good** ~ em bom estado (de conservação)

repartee /repaːˈtiː/ *n* resposta *f* pronta e espirituosa

repatriat|e /riːˈpætrɪeɪt/ *vt* repatriar. ~**ion** /-ˈeɪʃn/ *n* repatriamento *m*

repay /riːˈpeɪ/ *vt* (*pt* **repaid**) pagar, devolver, reembolsar; (*reward*) recompensar. ~**ment** *n* pagamento *m*, reembolso *m*

repeal /rɪˈpiːl/ *vt* revogar □ *n* revogação *f*

repeat /rɪˈpiːt/ *vt/i* repetir(-se) □ *n* repetição *f*; (*broadcast*) retransmissão *f*. ~**edly** *adv* repetidas vezes, repetidamente

repel /rɪˈpel/ *vt* (*pt* **repelled**) repelir. ~**lent** *a* & *n* repelente (*m*)

repent /rɪˈpent/ *vi* arrepender-se (**of** de). ~**ance** *n* arrependimento *m*. ~**ant** *a* arrependido

repercussion /riːpəˈkʌʃn/ *n* repercussão *f*

repertoire /ˈrepətwɑː(r)/ *n* repertório *m*

repertory /ˈrepətrɪ/ *n* repertório *m*

repetit|ion /repɪˈtɪʃn/ *n* repetição *f*. ~**ious** /-ˈtɪʃəs/, ~**ive** /rɪˈpetətɪv/ *a* repetitivo

replace /rɪˈpleɪs/ *vt* colocar no mesmo lugar, repor; (*take the place of*) substituir. ~**ment** *n* reposição *f*; (*substitution*) substituição *f*; (*person*) substituto *m*

replenish /rɪˈplenɪʃ/ *vt* voltar a encher, reabastecer; (*renew*) renovar

replica /ˈreplɪkə/ *n* réplica *f*, cópia *f*, reprodução *f*

reply /rɪˈplaɪ/ *vt/i* responder, replicar □ *n* resposta *f*, réplica *f*

report /rɪˈpɔːt/ *vt* relatar; (*notify*) informar; (*denounce*) denunciar, apresentar queixa de □ *vi* fazer um relatório. ~ **(on)** (*news item*) fazer uma reportagem (sobre). ~ **to** (*go*) apresentar-se a □ *n* (*in newspapers*) reportagem *f*; (*of company, doctor*) relatório *m*; (*schol*) boletim *m* escolar; (*sound*) detonação *f*; (*rumour*) rumores *mpl*. ~**edly** *adv* segundo consta. ~**er** *n* repórter *m* repose /rɪ'pəʊz/ n repouso m

repossess /riːpə'zes/ vt reapossar-se de, retomar de

represent /reprɪ'zent/ vt representar. ~ation /-'teɪʃn/ n representação f

representative /reprɪ'zentətɪv/ a representativo □ n representante m

repress /rɪ'pres/ vt reprimir. ~ion /-ʃn/ n repressão f. ~ive a repressivo, repressivo

reprieve /rɪ'priːv/ n suspensão f temporária; (temporary relief) tréguas fpl □ vt suspender temporariamente; (fig) dar tréguas a

reprimand /'reprɪmɑːnd/ vt repreender □ n repreensão f, reprimenda f

reprint /'riːprɪnt/ n reimpressão f, reedição f □ vt /riː'prɪnt/

reprisals /rɪ'praɪzlz/ npl represálias fpl

reproach /rɪ'prəʊtʃ/ vt censurar, repreender (sb for sth alguém por alg coisa, alg coisa a alguém) □ n censura f. above ~ irrepreensível. ~ful a repreensivo, reprovador. ~fully adv reprovadoramente

reproduce /riːprə'djuːs/ vt/i reproduzir(-se). ~tion /-'dʌkʃn/ n reprodução f. ~tive /-'dʌktɪv/ a reprodutivo, reprodutor

reptile /'reptaɪl/ n réptil m

republic /rɪ'pʌblɪk/ n república f. ~an a & n republicano (m)

repudiate /rɪ'pjuːdɪeɪt/ vt repudiar, rejeitar

repugnan|t /rɪ'pʌgnənt/ a repugnante. ~ce n repugnância f

repuls|e /rɪ'pʌls/ vt repelir, repulsar. ~ion /-ʃn/ n repulsa f. ~ive a repulsivo, repelente, repugnante

reputable /'repjʊtəbl/ a respeitado, honrado; (firm, make etc) de renome, conceituado

reputation /repjʊ'teɪʃn/ n reputação f

repute /rɪ'pjuːt/ n reputação f. ~d /-ɪd/ a suposto, putativo. ~d to be tido como, tido na conta de. ~dly /-ɪdlɪ/ adv segundo consta, com fama de

request /rɪ'kwest/ n pedido m □ vt pedir, solicitar (of, from a)

requiem /'rekwɪəm/ n réquiem m; (mass) missa f de réquiem

require /rɪ'kwaɪə(r)/ vt requerer. ~d a requerido; (needed) necessário, preciso. ~ment n (fig) requisito m; (need) necessidade f, (demand) exigência f

requisite /'rekwɪzɪt/ a necessário □ n coisa necessária f, requisito m. ~s (for travel etc) artigos mpl

requisition /rekwɪ'zɪʃn/ n requisição f □ vt requisitar

resale /'riːseɪl/ n revenda f

rescue /'reskjuː/ vt salvar, socorrer (from de) □ n salvamento m, (help) socorro m, ajuda f. ~r /-ə(r)/ n salvador m

research /rɪ'sɜːtʃ/ n pesquisa f, investigação f □ vt/i pesquisar, fazer investigação (into sobre). ~er n investigador m

resembl|e /rɪ'zembl/ vt assemelhar-se a, parecer-se com. ~ance n semelhança f, similaridade f (to com)

resent /rɪ'zent/ vt ressentir(-se de), ficar ressentido com. ~ful a ressentido. ~ment n ressentimento m

reservation /rezə'veɪʃn/ n (booking) reserva f; (Amer) reserva f (de índios)

reserve /rɪ'zɜːv/ vt reservar □ n reserva f; (sport) suplente mf. in ~ de reserva. ~d a reservado

reservoir /'rezəvwɑː(r)/ n (lake, supply etc) reservatório m; (container) depósito m

reshape /riː'ʃeɪp/ vt remodelar

reshuffle /riː'ʃʌfl/ vt (pol) remodelar □ n (pol) reforma f (do Ministério)

reside /rɪ'zaɪd/ vi residir

residen|t /'rezɪdənt/ a residente □ n morador m, habitante mf; (foreigner) residente mf; (in hotel) hóspede mf. ~ce n residência f; (of students) residência f, lar m. ~ce permit visto m de residência

residential /rezɪ'denʃl/ a residencial

residue /'rezɪdjuː/ n resíduo m

resign /rɪ'zaɪn/ vt (post) demitir-se. ~ o.s. to resignar-se a □ vi demitir-se de. ~ation /rezɪg'neɪʃn/ n resignação f; (from job) demissão f. ~ed a resignado

resilien|t /rɪ'zɪlɪənt/ a (springy) elástico; (person) resistente. ~ce n elasticidade f; (of person) resistência f

resin /'rezɪn/ n resina f

resist /rɪ'zɪst/ vt/i resistir (a). ~ance n resistência f. ~ant a resistente

resolut|e /'rezəluːt/ a resoluto. ~ion /-'luːʃn/ n resolução f

resolve /rɪ'zɒlv/ vt resolver. ~ to do resolver fazer □ n resolução f. ~d a (resolute) resoluto; (decided) resolvido (to a)

resonan|t /'rezənənt/ a ressonante. ~ce n ressonância f

resort /rɪ'zɔːt/ vi ~ to recorrer a, valer-se de □ n recurso m; (place) estância f, local m turístico. as a last ~ em último recurso. seaside ~ praia f, balneário m, (P) estância f balnear

resound /rɪ'zaʊnd/ vi reboar, ressoar (with com). ~ing a ressoante; (fig) retumbante

resource /rɪ'sɔːs/ n recurso m. ~s recursos mpl, riquezas fpl. ~ful a expedito, engenhoso, desembaraçado. ~fulness *n* expediente *m*, engenho *m*

respect /rɪˈspekt/ *n* respeito *m* □ *vt* respeitar. with ~ to a respeito de, com respeito a, relativamente a. ~ful *a* respeitoso

respectab|le /rɪˈspektəbl/ *a* respeitável; (*passable*) passável, aceitável. ~ility /-ˈbɪlətɪ/ *n* res-peitabilidade *f*

respective /rɪˈspektɪv/ *a* respectivo. ~ly *adv* respectivamente

respiration /respəˈreɪʃn/ *n* respiração *f*

respite /ˈrespaɪt/ *n* pausa *f*, trégua *f*, folga *f*

respond /rɪˈspɒnd/ *vi* responder (to a); (*react*) reagir (to a)

response /rɪˈspɒns/ *n* resposta *f*; (*reaction*) reação *f*, (P) reacção *f*

responsib|le /rɪˈspɒnsəbl/ *a* responsável; (*job*) de responsabilidade. ~ility /-ˈbɪlətɪ/ *n* responsabilidade *f*

responsive /rɪˈspɒnsɪv/ *a* receptivo, que reage bem. ~ to sensível a

rest¹ /rest/ *vt/i* descansar, repousar; (*lean*) apoiar(-se) □ *n* descanso *m*, repouso *m*; (*support*) suporte *m*. ~-room (*Amer*) banheiro *m*, (P) toaletes *mpl*

rest² /rest/ *vi* (*remain*) ficar □ *n* (*remainder*) resto *m* (of de). the ~ (of the) (*others*) os outros. it ~s with him cabe a ele

restaurant /ˈrestrɒnt/ *n* restaurante *m*

restful /ˈrestfl/ *a* sossegado, repousante, tranquilo, (P) tranquilo

restitution /restɪˈtjuːʃn/ *n* restituição *f*, (*for injury*) indenização *f*, (P) indemnização *f*

restless /ˈrestlɪs/ *a* agitado, desassossegado

restor|e /rɪˈstɔː(r)/ *vt* restaurar; (*give back*) restituir, devolver. ~ation /restəˈreɪʃn/ *n* restauração *f*

restrain /rɪˈstreɪn/ *vt* conter, reprimir. ~ o.s. controlar-se. ~ sb from impedir alguém de. ~ed *a* comedido, reservado. ~t *n* controle *m*; (*moderation*) moderação *f*, comedimento *m*

restrict /rɪˈstrɪkt/ *vt* restringir, limitar. ~ion /-ʃn/ *n* restrição *f*. ~ive *a* restritivo

result /rɪˈzʌlt/ *n* resultado *m* □ *vi* resultar (from de). ~ in resultar em

resume /rɪˈzjuːm/ *vt/i* reatar, retomar; (*work, travel*) recomeçar. ~ption /rɪˈzʌmpʃn/ *n* reatamento *m*, retomada *f*; (*of work*) recomeço *m*

résumé /ˈrezjuːmeɪ/ *n* resumo *m*

resurgence /rɪˈsɜːdʒəns/ *n* reaparecimento *m*, ressurgimento *m*

resurrect /rezəˈrekt/ *vt* ressuscitar. ~ion /-ʃn/ *n* ressurreição *f*

resuscitat|e /rɪˈsʌsɪteɪt/ *vt* ressuscitar, reanimar. ~ion /-ˈteɪʃn/ *n* reanimação *f*

retail /ˈriːteɪl/ *n* retalho *m* □ *a* & *adv* a retalho □ *vt/i* vender(-se) a retalho. ~er *n* retalhista *mf*

retain /rɪˈteɪn/ *vt* reter; (*keep*) conservar, guardar

retaliat|e /rɪˈtælɪeɪt/ *vi* retaliar, exercer represálias, desforrar-se. ~ion /-ˈeɪʃn/ *n* retaliação *f*, represália *f*, desforra *f*

retarded /rɪˈtɑːdɪd/ *a* retardado, atrasado

retch /retʃ/ *vi* fazer esforço para vomitar, estar com ânsias de vômito

retention /rɪˈtenʃn/ *n* retenção *f*

retentive /rɪˈtentɪv/ *a* retentivo. ~ memory boa memória *f*

reticen|t /ˈretɪsnt/ *a* reticente. ~ce *n* reticência *f*

retina /ˈretɪnə/ *n* retina *f*

retinue /ˈretɪnjuː/ *n* séquito *m*, comitiva *f*

retire /rɪˈtaɪə(r)/ *vi* reformar-se, aposentar-se; (*withdraw*) retirar-se; (*go to bed*) ir deitar-se □ *vt* reformar, aposentar. ~d *a* reformado, aposentado. ~ment *n* reforma *f*, aposentadoria *f*, (P) aposentação *f*

retiring /rɪˈtaɪərɪŋ/ *a* reservado, retraído

retort /rɪˈtɔːt/ *vt/i* retrucar, retorquir □ *n* réplica *f*

retrace /riːˈtreɪs/ *vt* ~ one's steps refazer o mesmo caminho; (*fig*) recordar, recapitular

retract /rɪˈtrækt/ *vt/i* retratar(-se); (*wheels*) recolher; (*claws*) encolher, recolher

retreat /rɪˈtriːt/ *vi* retirar-se; (*mil*) retirar, bater em retirada □ *n* retirada *f*; (*seclusion*) retiro *m*

retrial /riːˈtraɪəl/ *n* novo julgamento *m*

retribution /retrɪˈbjuːʃn/ *n* castigo (merecido) *m*; (*vengeance*) vingança *f*

retriev|e /rɪˈtriːv/ *vt* ir buscar; (*rescue*) salvar; (*recover*) recuperar; (*put right*) reparar. ~al *n* recuperação *f*. information ~al (*comput*) acesso à informação. ~er *n* (*dog*) perdigueiro *m*, (P) cobrador *m*

retrograde /ˈretrəɡreɪd/ *a* retrógrado □ *vt* retroceder, recuar

retrospect /ˈretrəspekt/ *n* in ~ em retrospecto, (P) retrospectivamente. ~ive /-ˈspektɪv/ *a* retrospectivo; (*of law, payment*) retroativo, (P) retroactivo

return /rɪˈtɜːn/ *vi* voltar, regressar, retornar (to, a) □ *vt* devolver; (*compli-*

ment, visit) retribuir; (*put back*) pôr de volta □ *n* volta *f*, regresso *m*, retorno *m*; (*profit*) lucro *m*, rendimento *m*; (*restitution*) devolução *f*. ~ **in** ~ **for** em troca de. ~ **journey** viagem *f* de volta. ~ **match** (*sport*) desafio *m* de desforra. ~ **ticket** bilhete *m* de ida e volta. **many happy** ~**s (of the day)** muitos parabéns

reunion /riːˈjuːnɪən/ *n* reunião *f*

reunite /riːjuːˈnaɪt/ *vt* reunir

rev /rev/ *n* (*colloq: auto*) rotação *f* □ *vt/i* (*pt* **revved**) ~ **(up)** (*colloq: auto*) acelerar (o motor)

reveal /rɪˈviːl/ *vt* revelar; (*display*) expor. ~**ing** *a* revelador

revel /ˈrevl/ *vi* (*pt* **revelled**) divertir-se. ~ **in** deleitar-se com. ~**ry** *n* festas *fpl*, festejos *mpl*

revelation /revəˈleɪʃn/ *n* revelação *f*

revenge /rɪˈvendʒ/ *n* vingança *f*; (*sport*) desforra *f* □ *vt* vingar

revenue /ˈrevənjuː/ *n* receita *f*, rendimento *m*. **Inland R**~ Fisco *m*

reverberate /rɪˈvɜːbəreɪt/ *vi* ecoar, repercutir

revere /rɪˈvɪə(r)/ *vt* reverenciar, venerar

reverend /ˈrevərənd/ *a* reverendo. **R**~ Reverendo

reverent /ˈrevərənt/ *a* reverente. ~**ce** *n* reverência *f*, veneração *f*

reverse /rɪˈvɜːs/ *a* contrário, inverso □ *n* contrário *m*; (*back*) reverso *m*; (*gear*) marcha *f* à ré, (*P*) atrás □ *vt* virar ao contrário; (*order*) inverter; (*turn inside out*) virar do avesso; (*decision*) anular □ *vi* (*auto*) fazer marcha à ré, (*P*) atrás. ~**al** *n* inversão *f*, mudança *f* em sentido contrário; (*of view etc*) mudança *f*

revert /rɪˈvɜːt/ *vi* ~ **to** reverter a

review /rɪˈvjuː/ *n* (*inspection; magazine*) revista *f*; (*of a situation*) revisão *f*; (*critique*) crítica *f* □ *vt* revistar, passar revista em; (*situation*) rever; (*book, film etc*) fazer a crítica de. ~**er** *n* crítico *m*

revis|e /rɪˈvaɪz/ *vt* rever; (*amend*) corrigir. ~**ion** /-ɪʒn/ *n* revisão *f*; (*amendment*) correção *f*

reviv|e /rɪˈvaɪv/ *vt/i* ressuscitar, reavivar; (*play*) reapresentar; (*person*) reanimar(-se). ~**al** *n* reflorescimento *m*, renascimento *m*

revoke /rɪˈvəʊk/ *vt* revogar, anular, invalidar

revolt /rɪˈvəʊlt/ *vt/i* revoltar(-se) □ *n* revolta *f*

revolting /rɪˈvəʊltɪŋ/ *a* (*disgusting*) repugnante

revolution /revəˈluːʃn/ *n* revolução *f*. ~**ary** *a* & *n* revolucionário (*m*). ~**ize** *vt* revolucionar

revolv|e /rɪˈvɒlv/ *vi* girar. ~**ing door** porta *f* giratória

revolver /rɪˈvɒlvə(r)/ *n* revólver *m*

revulsion /rɪˈvʌlʃn/ *n* repugnância *f*, repulsa *f*

reward /rɪˈwɔːd/ *n* prêmio *m*, (*P*) prémio *m*; (*for criminal, for lost/stolen property*) recompensa *f* □ *vt* recompensar. ~**ing** *a* compensador; (*task etc*) gratificante

rewind /riːˈwaɪnd/ *vt* (*pt* **rewound**) rebobinar

rewrite /riːˈraɪt/ *vt* (*pt* **rewrote**, *pp* **rewritten**) reescrever

rhetoric /ˈretərɪk/ *n* retórica *f*. ~**al** /rɪˈtɒrɪkl/ *a* retórico; (*question*) pro forma

rheumati|c /ruːˈmætɪk/ *a* reumático. ~**sm** /ˈruːmətɪzm/ *n* reumatismo *m*

rhinoceros /raɪˈnɒsərəs/ *n* (*pl* -oses) rinoceronte *m*

rhubarb /ˈruːbɑːb/ *n* ruibarbo *m*

rhyme /raɪm/ *n* rima *f*; (*poem*) versos *mpl* □ *vt/i* (fazer) rimar

rhythm /ˈrɪðəm/ *n* ritmo *m*. ~**ic(al)** /ˈrɪðmɪk(l)/ *a* rítmico, compassado

rib /rɪb/ *n* costela *f*

ribbon /ˈrɪbən/ *n* fita *f*. **in** ~**s** em tiras

rice /raɪs/ *n* arroz *m*

rich /rɪtʃ/ *a* (-**er**, -**est**) rico; (*food*) rico em açúcar e gordura. ~**es** *npl* riquezas *fpl*. ~**ly** *adv* ricamente. ~**ness** *n* riqueza *f*

rickety /ˈrɪkətɪ/ *a* (*shaky*) desconjuntado

ricochet /ˈrɪkəʃeɪ/ *n* ricochete *m* □ *vi* (*pt* **ricocheted** /-ʃeɪd/) fazer ricochete, ricochetear

rid /rɪd/ *vt* (*pt* **rid**, *pres p* **ridding**) desembaraçar (*of* de). **get** ~ **of** desembaraçar-se de, livrar-se de

riddance /ˈrɪdns/ *n* **good** ~! que alívio!, vai com Deus!

ridden /ˈrɪdn/ *see* **ride**

riddle[1] /ˈrɪdl/ *n* enigma *m*; (*puzzle*) charada *f*

riddle[2] /ˈrɪdl/ *vt* ~ **with** crivar de

ride /raɪd/ *vi* (*pt* **rode**, *pp* **ridden**) andar de bicicleta, a cavalo, de carro □ *vt* (*horse*) montar; (*bicycle*) andar de; (*distance*) percorrer □ *n* passeio *m* or volta *f* (de carro, a cavalo etc); (*distance*) percurso *m*. ~**r** /-ə(r)/ *n* cavaleiro *m*, amazona *f*; (*cyclist*) ciclista *mf*; (*in document*) aditamento *m*

ridge /rɪdʒ/ *n* aresta *f*; (*of hill*) cume *m*

ridicule /ˈrɪdɪkjuːl/ *n* ridículo *m* □ *vt* ridicularizar

ridiculous /rɪˈdɪkjʊləs/ *a* ridículo

riding /ˈraɪdɪŋ/ *n* equitação *f*

rife /raɪf/ *a* **be** ~ estar espalhado; (*of illness*) grassar. ~ **with** cheio de

riff-raff /'rɪfræf/ *n* gentinha *f*, povinho *m*, ralé *f*

rifle /'raɪfl/ *n* espingarda *f* □ *vt* revistar e roubar, saquear

rift /rɪft/ *n* fenda *f*, brecha *f*; (*fig: dissension*) desacordo *m*, desavença *f*, desentendimento *m*

rig¹ /rɪg/ *vt* (*pt* **rigged**) equipar □ *n* (*for oil*) plataforma *f* de poço de petróleo. ~ **out** enfarpelar (*colloq*). ~**out** (*colloq*) roupa *f*, farpela *f* (*colloq*). ~ **up** arranjar

rig² /rɪg/ *vt* (*pt* **rigged**) (*pej*) manipular. ~**ged** *a* (*election*) fraudulento

right /raɪt/ *a* (*correct, moral*) certo, correto, (*P*) correcto; (*fair*) justo; (*not left*) direito; (*suitable*) certo, próprio □ *n* (*entitlement*) direito *m*; (*not left*) direita *f*; (*not evil*) o bem □ *vt* (*a wrong*) reparar; (*sth fallen*) endireitar □ *adv* (*not left*) à direita; (*directly*) direito; (*exactly*) mesmo, bem; (*completely*) completamente. **be** ~ (*person*) ter razão (**to** em). **be in the** ~ ter razão. **on the** ~ à direita. **put** ~ acertar, corrigir. ~ **of way** (*auto*) prioridade *f*. ~ **angle** *n* ângulo reto *m*, (*P*) recto. ~ **away** logo, imediatamente. ~**hand** *a* à *ou* de direita. ~**handed** *a* (*person*) destro. ~**wing** *a* (*pol*) de direita

righteous /'raɪtʃəs/ *a* justo, virtuoso

rightful /'raɪtfl/ *a* legítimo. ~**ly** *adv* legitimamente, legalmente

rightly /'raɪtlɪ/ *adv* devidamente, corretamente, (*P*) correctamente; (*with reason*) justificadamente

rigid /'rɪdʒɪd/ *a* rígido. ~**ity** /rɪ-'dʒɪdətɪ/ *n* rigidez *f*

rigmarole /'rɪgmərəʊl/ *n* (*speech: procedure*) embrulhada *f*

rig|our /'rɪgə(r)/ *n* rigor *m*. ~**orous** *a* rigoroso

rile /raɪl/ *vt* (*colloq*) irritar, exasperar

rim /rɪm/ *n* borda *f*; (*of wheel*) aro *m*

rind /raɪnd/ *n* (*on cheese, fruit*) casca *f*; (*on bacon*) pele *f*

ring¹ /rɪŋ/ *n* (*on finger*) anel *m*; (*for napkin, key etc*) argola *f*; (*circle*) roda *f*, círculo *m*; (*boxing*) ringue *m*; (*arena*) arena *f*; (*of people*) quadrilha *f* □ *vt* rodear, cercar. ~ **road** *n* estrada *f* periférica *or* perimetral

ring² /rɪŋ/ *vt/i* (*pt* **rang**, *pp* **rung**) tocar; (*of words etc*) soar □ *n* toque *m*; (*colloq: phone call*) telefonadela *f* (*colloq*). ~ **the bell** tocar a campainha. ~ **back** telefonar de volta. ~ **off** desligar. ~ **up** telefonar (a)

ringleader /'rɪŋliːdə(r)/ *n* cabeça *m*, cérebro *m*

rink /rɪŋk/ *n* rinque *m* de patinação

rinse /rɪns/ *vt* passar uma água, enxaguar □ *n* enxaguadura *f*, (*P*) enxaguadela *f*; (*hair tint*) rinsagem *f*

riot /'raɪət/ *n* distúrbio *m*, motim *m*; (*of colours*) festival *m* □ *vi* fazer distúrbios *or* motins. **run** ~ desenfrear-se, descontrolar-se; (*of plants*) crescer em matagal. ~**er** *n* desordeiro *m*

riotous /'raɪətəs/ *a* desenfreado, turbulento, desordeiro

rip /rɪp/ *vt/i* (*pt* **ripped**) rasgar(-se) □ *n* rasgão *m*. ~ **off** (*sl: defraud*) defraudar, enrolar (*sl*). ~**off** *n* (*sl*) roubalheira *f* (*colloq*)

ripe /raɪp/ *a* (**-er, -est**) maduro. ~**ness** *n* madureza *f*, (*P*) amadurecimento *m*

ripen /'raɪpən/ *vt/i* amadurecer

ripple /'rɪpl/ *n* ondulação *f* leve; (*sound*) murmúrio *m* □ *vt/i* encrespar(-se), agitar(-se), ondular

rise /raɪz/ *vi* (*pt* **rose**, *pp* **risen**) subir, elevar-se; (*stand up*) erguer-se, levantar-se; (*rebel*) sublevar-se; (*sun*) nascer; (*curtain, prices*) subir □ *n* (*increase*) aumento *m*; (*slope*) subida *f*, ladeira *f*; (*origin*) origem *f*. **give** ~ **to** originar, causar, dar origem a. ~**r** /-ə(r)/ *n* **early** ~**r** madrugador *m*

rising /'raɪzɪŋ/ *n* (*revolt*) insurreição *f* □ *a* (*sun*) nascente

risk /rɪsk/ *n* risco *m* □ *vt* arriscar. **at** ~ em risco, em perigo. **at one's own** ~ por sua conta e risco. ~ **doing** (*venture*) arriscar-se a fazer. ~**y** *a* arriscado

risqué /'riːskeɪ/ *a* picante

rite /raɪt/ *n* rito *m*. **last** ~**s** últimos sacramentos *mpl*

ritual /'rɪtʃʊəl/ *a* & *n* ritual (*m*)

rival /'raɪvl/ *n* & *a* rival (*mf*), (*fig*) concorrente (*mf*), competidor (*m*) □ *vt* (*pt* **rivalled**) rivalizar com. ~**ry** *n* rivalidade *f*

river /'rɪvə(r)/ *n* rio *m* □ *a* fluvial

rivet /'rɪvɪt/ *n* rebite *m* □ *vt* (*pt* **riveted**) rebitar; (*fig*) prender, cravar. ~**ing** *a* fascinante

road /rəʊd/ *n* estrada *f*; (*in town*) rua *f*; (*small; fig*) caminho *m*. ~**block** *n* barricada *f*. ~**map** *n* mapa *m* das estradas. ~ **sign** *n* sinal *m*, placa *f* de sinalização. ~ **tax** imposto *m* de circulação. ~**works** *npl* obras *fpl*

roadside /'rəʊdsaɪd/ *n* beira *f* da estrada

roadway /'rəʊdweɪ/ *n* pista *f* de rolamento, (*P*) rodagem *f*

roadworthy /'rəʊdwɜːðɪ/ *a* em condições de ser utilizado na rua/estrada

roam /rəʊm/ *vi* errar, andar sem destino □ *vt* percorrer

roar /rɔː(r)/ *n* berro *m*, rugido *m*; (*of thunder*) ribombo *m*, troar *m*; (*of sea*, *wind*) bramido *m* □ *vt/i* berrar, rugir; (*of lion*) rugir; (*of thunder*) ribombar, troar; (*of sea, wind*) bramir. ~ **with laughter** rir às gargalhadas

roaring /'rɔːrɪŋ/ *a* (*trade*) florescente; (*success*) enorme; (*fire*) com grandes chamas

roast /rəʊst/ *vt/i* assar □ *a* & *n* assado (*m*)

rob /rɒb/ *vt* (*pt* **robbed**) roubar (sb of sth alg coisa de alguém); (*bank*) assaltar; (*deprive*) privar (of de). ~**ber** *n* ladrão *m*; ~**bery** *n* roubo *m*; (*of bank*) assalto *m*

robe /rəʊb/ *n* veste *f* comprida e solta; (*dressing-gown*) robe *m*. ~**s** *npl* (*of judge etc*) toga *f*

robin /'rɒbɪn/ *n* papo-roxo *m*, (*P*) pintarroxo *m*

robot /'rəʊbɒt/ *n* robô *m*, (*P*) robot *m*, autómato *m*, (*P*) autómato *m*

robust /rəʊ'bʌst/ *a* robusto

rock[1] /rɒk/ *n* rocha *f*; (*boulder*) penhasco *m*, rochedo *m*; (*sweet*) pirulito *m*, (*P*) chupa-chupa *m* comprido. **on the** ~**s** (*colloq: of marriage*) em crise; (*colloq: of drinks*) com gelo. ~-**bottom** *n* ponto *m* mais baixo □ *a* (*of prices*) baixíssimo (*colloq*)

rock[2] /rɒk/ *vt/i* balouçar(-se); (*shake*) abanar, sacudir; (*child*) embalar □ *n* (*mus*) rock *m*. ~**ing-chair** *n* cadeira *f* de balanço, (*P*) cadeira *f* de baloiço. ~**ing-horse** *n* cavalo *m* de balanço, (*P*) cavalo *m* de baloiço

rocket /'rɒkɪt/ *n* foguete *m*

rocky /'rɒkɪ/ *a* (-**ier**, -**iest**) (*ground*) pedregoso; (*hill*) rochoso; (*colloq: unsteady*) instável; (*colloq: shaky*) tremido (*colloq*)

rod /rɒd/ *n* vara *f*, vareta *f*; (*mech*) haste *f*; (*for curtains*) bastão *m*; (*P*) varão *m*; (*for fishing*) vara (de pescar) *f*

rode /rəʊd/ *see* **ride**

rodent /'rəʊdnt/ *n* roedor *m*

rodeo /rəʊ'deɪəʊ/ *n* (*pl* -**os**) rode(i)o *m*

roe /rəʊ/ *n* ova(s) *f* (*pl*) de peixe

rogue /rəʊg/ *n* (*dishonest*) patife *m*, velhaco *m*; (*mischievous*) brincalhão *m*

role /rəʊl/ *n* papel *m*

roll /rəʊl/ *vt/i* (fazer) rolar; (*into ball or cylinder*) enrolar(-se) □ *n* rolo *m*; (*list*) rol *m*, lista *f*; (*bread*) pãozinho *m*; (*of ship*) balanço *m*; (*of drum*) rufar *m*; (*of thunder*) ribombo *m*. **be** ~**ing in money** (*colloq*) nadar em dinheiro (*colloq*). ~ **over** (*turn over*) virar-se ao contrário. ~ **up** *vi* (*colloq*) aparecer □ *vt* (*sleeves*) arregaçar; (*umbrella*) fechar. ~-**call** *n* chamada *f*. ~**ing-pin** *n* rolo *m* de pastel

roller /'rəʊlə(r)/ *n* cilindro *m*; (*wave*) vagalhão *m*; (*for hair*) rolo *m*. ~-**blind** *n* estore *m*. ~-**coaster** *n* montanha *f* russa. ~-**skate** *n* patim *m* de rodas

rolling /'rəʊlɪŋ/ *a* ondulante

Roman /'rəʊmən/ *a* & *n* romano (*m*). **R~ Catholic** *a* & *n* católico (*m*). ~ **numerals** algarismos *mpl* romanos

romance /rəʊ'mæns/ *n* (*love affair*) romance *m*; (*fig*) poesia *f*

Romania /rʊ'meɪnɪə/ *n* Roménia *f*, (*P*) Roménia *f*. ~**n** *a* & *n* romeno (*m*)

romantic /rəʊ'mæntɪk/ *a* romântico. ~**ally** *adv* romànticamente. ~**ism** *n* romantismo *m*. ~**ize** *vi* fazer romance □ *vt* romantizar

romp /rɒmp/ *vi* brincar animadamente □ *n* brincadeira *f* animada. ~**ers** *npl* macacão *m* de bebé, (*P*) fato *m* de bebé

roof /ruːf/ *n* (*pl* **roofs**) telhado *m*; (*of car*) teto *m*, (*P*) capota *f*; (*of mouth*) palato *m*, céu *m* da boca □ *vt* cobrir com telhado. **hit the** ~ (*colloq*) ficar furioso. ~**ing** *n* material *m* para telhados. ~-**rack** *n* porta-bagagem *m*. ~-**top** *n* cimo *m* do telhado

rook[1] /rʊk/ *n* (*bird*) gralha *f*

rook[2] /rʊk/ *n* (*chess*) torre *f*

room /ruːm/ *n* quarto *m*, divisão *f*; (*bedroom*) quarto *m* de dormir; (*large hall*) sala *f*; (*space*) espaço *m*, lugar *m*. ~**s** (*lodgings*) apartamento *m*, cómodos *mpl*. ~-**mate** *n* companheiro *m* de quarto. ~**y** *a* espaçoso; (*clothes*) amplo, largo

roost /ruːst/ *n* poleiro *m* □ *vi* empoleirar-se. ~**er** *n* (*Amer*) galo *m*

root[1] /ruːt/ *n* raiz *f*; (*fig*) origem *f* □ *vt/i* enraizar(-se), radicar(-se). ~ **out** extirpar, erradicar. **take** ~ criar raízes. ~**less** *a* sem raízes, desenraizado

root[2] /ruːt/ *vi* ~ **about** revolver, remexer. ~ **for** (*Amer sl*) torcer por

rope /rəʊp/ *n* corda *f* □ *vt* atar. **know the** ~**s** estar por dentro (do assunto). ~ **in** convencer a participar de

rosary /'rəʊzərɪ/ *n* rosário *m*

rose[1] /rəʊz/ *n* rosa *f*; (*nozzle*) ralo *m* (de regador). ~-**bush** *n* roseira *f*

rose[2] /rəʊz/ *see* **rise**

rosé /'rəʊzeɪ/ *n* rosé *m*

rosette /rəʊ'zet/ *n* roseta *f*

rosewood /'rəʊzwʊd/ *n* pau-rosa *m*

roster /'rɒstə(r)/ *n* lista (de serviço) *f*, escala *f* de serviço)

rostrum /'rɒstrəm/ *n* tribuna *f*; (*for conductor*) estrado *m*; (*sport*) podium *m*

rosy /'rəʊzɪ/ *a* (-**ier**, -**iest**) rosado; (*fig*) risonho

rot /rɒt/ *vt/i* (*pt* **rotted**) apodrecer □ *n*

putrefação f, podridão f; (sl: nonsense) disparate m, asneiras fpl

rota /'rəʊtə/ n escala f de serviço

rotary /'rəʊtərɪ/ a rotativo, giratório

rotat|e /rəʊ'teɪt/ vt/i (fazer) girar, (fazer) revolver; (change round) alternar. ~ing a rotativo. ~ion /-ʃn/ n rotação f

rote /rəʊt/ n by ~ de cor, maquinalmente

rotten /'rɒtn/ a podre; (corrupt) corrupto; (colloq: bad) mau, ruim. ~ eggs ovos mpl podres. feel ~ (ill) não se sentir nada bem

rotund /rəʊ'tʌnd/ a rotundo, redondo

rough /rʌf/ a (-er, -est) rude; (to touch) áspero, rugoso; (of ground) acidentado, irregular; (violent) violento; (of sea) agitado, encapelado; (of weather) tempestuoso; (not perfect) tosco, rudimentar; (of estimate etc) aproximado □ n (ruffian) rufia m, desordeiro m □ adv (live) ao relento; (play) bruto □ vt ~ it viver de modo primitivo, não ter onde morar (colloq). ~ out fazer um esboço preliminar de. ~-and-ready a grosseiro mas eficiente. ~ paper rascunho m, borrão m. ~ly adv asperamente, rudemente; (approximately) aproximadamente. ~ness n rudeza f, aspereza f; (violence) brutalidade f

roughage /'rʌfɪdʒ/ n alimentos mpl fibrosos

roulette /ru:'let/ n roleta f

round /raʊnd/ a (-er, -est) redondo □ n (circle) círculo m, (slice) fatia f; (postman's) entrega f; (patrol) ronda f; (of drinks) rodada f; (competition) partida f, rodada f; (boxing) round m; (of talks) ciclo m, série f □ prep & adv em volta (de), em torno de □ vt arredondar; (cape, corner) dobrar, virar. come ~ (into consciousness) voltar a si. go or come ~ to (a friend etc) dar um pulo na casa de. ~ about (nearby) por aí; (fig) mais ou menos. ~ of applause salva f de palmas. ~ off terminar. ~-shouldered a curvado. ~ the clock noite e dia sem parar. ~ trip viagem f de ida e volta. ~ up (gather) juntar; (a figure) arredondar. ~-up n (of cattle) rodeio m; (of suspects) captura f

roundabout /'raʊndəbaʊt/ n carrossel m; (for traffic) rotatória f, (P) rotunda f □ a indireto, (P) indirecto

rous|e /raʊz/ vt acordar, despertar. be ~ed (angry) exaltar-se, inflamar-se, ser provocado. ~ing a (speech) inflamado, exaltado; (music) vibrante; (cheers) frenético

rout /raʊt/ n derrota f; (retreat) debandada f □ vt derrotar; (cause to retreat) pôr em debandada

route /ru:t/ n percurso m, itinerário m; (naut, aviat) rota f

routine /ru:'ti:n/ n rotina f; (theat) número m □ a de rotina, rotineiro. daily ~ rotina f diária

rov|e /rəʊv/ vt/i errar (por), vaguear (em/por). ~ing a (life) errante

row¹ /rəʊ/ n fila f, fileira f; (in knitting) carreira f. in a ~ (consecutive) em fila

row² /rəʊ/ vt/i remar. ~ing n remo m. ~ing-boat n barco m a remo

row³ /raʊ/ n (colloq: noise) barulho m, bagunça f, banzé m (colloq); (colloq: quarrel) discussão f, briga f. ~ (with) vi (colloq) brigar (com), discutir (com)

rowdy /'raʊdɪ/ a (-ier, -iest) desordeiro

royal /'rɔɪəl/ a real

royalty /'rɔɪəltɪ/ n família real f; (payment) direitos mpl (de autor, de patente, etc)

rub /rʌb/ vt/i (pt rubbed) esfregar; (with ointment etc) esfregar, friccionar □ n esfrega f; (with ointment etc) fricção f. ~ it in repisar/insistir em. ~ off on comunicar-se a, transmitir-se a. ~ out (with rubber) apagar

rubber /'rʌbə(r)/ n borracha f. ~-band elástico m. ~-stamp carimbo m. ~-stamp vt aprovar sem questionar. ~y a semelhante à borracha

rubbish /'rʌbɪʃ/ n (refuse) lixo m; (nonsense) disparates mpl. ~-dump n lixeira f. ~y a sem valor

rubble /'rʌbl/ n entulho m

ruby /'ru:bɪ/ n rubi m

rucksack /'rʌksæk/ n mochila f

rudder /'rʌdə(r)/ n leme m

ruddy /'rʌdɪ/ a (-ier, -iest) avermelhado; (of cheeks) corado, vermelho; (sl: damned) maldito (colloq)

rude /ru:d/ a (-er, -est) mal-educado, malcriado, grosseiro. ~ly adv grosseiramente, malcriadamente. ~ness n má-educação f, má-criação f, grosseria f

rudiment /'ru:dɪmənt/ n rudimento m. ~ary /-'mentrɪ/ a rudimentar

rueful /'ru:fl/ a contrito, pesaroso

ruffian /'rʌfɪən/ n desordeiro m

ruffle /'rʌfl/ vt (feathers) eriçar; (hair) despentear; (clothes) amarrotar; (fig) perturbar □ n (frill) franzido m, (P) folho m

rug /rʌg/ n tapete m; (covering) manta f

rugged /'rʌgɪd/ a rude, irregular; (coast, landscape) acidentado; (character) forte; (features) marcado

ruin /'ru:ın/ n ruina f □ vt arruinar; (fig) estragar. **~ous** a desastroso

rule /ru:l/ n regra f; (regulation) regulamento m; (pol) governo m □ vt governar; (master) dominar; (jur) decretar; (decide) decidir □ vi governar. **as a ~** regra geral, por via de regra. **~ out** excluir. **~d paper** papel m pautado. **~r** /-ə(r)/ n (sovereign) soberano m; (leader) governante m; (measure) régua f

ruling /'ru:lıŋ/ a (class) dirigente; (pol) no poder □ n decisão f

rum /rʌm/ n rum m

rumble /'rʌmbl/ vi ribombar, ressoar; (of stomach) roncar □ n ribombo m, estrondo m

rummage /'rʌmıdʒ/ vt revistar, remexer

rumour /'ru:mə(r)/ n boato m, rumor m □ vt it is **~ed that** corre o boato de que, consta que

rump /rʌmp/ n (of horse etc) garupa f; (of fowl) mitra f. **~ steak** n bife m de alcatra

run /rʌn/ vi (pt ran, pp run, pres p **running**) correr; (flow) correr; (pass) passar; (function) andar, funcionar; (melt) derreter, pingar; (bus etc) circular; (play) estar em cartaz; (colour) desbotar; (in election) candidatar-se (for a) □ vt (manage) dirigir, gerir; (a risk) correr; (a race) disputar em; (water) deixar correr; (a car) ter, manter □ n corrida f; (journey) passeio m, ida f; (rush) corrida f, correria f; (in cricket) ponto m. **be on the ~** estar foragido. **have the ~ of** ter à sua disposição. **in the long ~** a longo prazo. **~ across** encontrar por acaso, dar com. **~ away** fugir. **~ down** descer correndo; (of vehicle) atropelar; (belittle) dizer mal de, denegrir. **be ~ down** estar exausto. **~ in** (engine) ligar. **~ into** (meet) encontrar por acaso; (hit) bater em, ir de encontro a. **~ off** vt (copies) tirar; (water) deixar correr □ vi fugir. **~-of-the-mill** a vulgar. **~ out** esgotar-se; (lease) expirar. **I ran out of sugar** o açúcar acabou. **~ over** (of vehicle) atropelar. **~ up** deixar acumular. **the ~-up to** o período que precede

runaway /'rʌnəweɪ/ n fugitivo m □ a fugitivo; (horse) desembestado; (vehicle) desgovernado; (success) grande

rung¹ /rʌŋ/ n (of ladder) degrace m

rung² /rʌŋ/ see **ring**²

runner /'rʌnə(r)/ n (person) corredor m; (carpet) passadeira f. **~ bean** feijão m verde. **~-up** n segundo classificado m

running /'rʌnıŋ/ n corrida f; (functioning) funcionamento m □ a consecutivo, seguido; (water) corrente. **be in the ~** (competitor) ter probabilidades de êxito. **four days ~** quatro dias seguidos or a fio. **~ commentary** reportagem f, comentário m

runny /'rʌnı/ a derretido

runway /'rʌnweɪ/ n pista f de decolagem, (P) descolagem

rupture /'rʌptʃə(r)/ n ruptura f; (med) hérnia f □ vt/i romper(-se), rebentar

rural /'rʊərəl/ a rural

ruse /ru:z/ n ardil m, estratagema m, manha f

rush¹ /rʌʃ/ n (plant) junco m

rush² /rʌʃ/ vi (move) precipitar-se, (be in a hurry) apressar-se □ vt fazer, mandar etc a toda a pressa; (person) pressionar; (mil) tomar de assalto □ n tropel m; (haste) pressa f. **in a ~** às pressas. **~ hour** rush m, (P) hora f de ponta

rusk /rʌsk/ n bolacha f, biscoito m

russet /'rʌsıt/ a castanho avermelhado □ n maçã f reineta

Russia /'rʌʃə/ n Rússia f. **~n** a & n russo (m)

rust /rʌst/ n (on iron, plants) ferrugem f □ vt/i enferrujar(-se). **~-proof** a inoxidável. **~y** a ferrugento, enferrujado; (fig) enferrujado

rustic /'rʌstık/ a rústico

rustle /'rʌsl/ vt/i restolhar, (fazer) farfalhar; (Amer: steal) roubar. **~ up** (colloq: food etc) arranjar

rut /rʌt/ n sulco m; (fig) rotina f. **in a ~** numa vida rotineira

ruthless /'ru:θlıs/ a implacável

rye /raı/ n centeio m

S

sabbath /'sæbəθ/ n (Jewish) sábado m; (Christian) domingo m

sabbatical /sə'bætıkl/ n (univ) período m de licença

sabot|age /'sæbətɑ:ʒ/ n sabotagem f □ vt sabotar. **~eur** /-'tɜ:(r)/ n sabotador m

sachet /'sæʃeɪ/ n saché m

sack /sæk/ n saco m, saca f □ vt (colloq) despedir. **get the ~** (colloq) ser despedido

sacrament /'sækrəmənt/ n sacramento m

sacred /'seɪkrıd/ a sagrado

sacrifice /'sækrıfaıs/ n sacrifício m; (fig) sacrifício m □ vt sacrificar

sacrileg|e /'sækrılıdʒ/ n sacrilégio m. **~ious** /-'lıdʒəs/ a sacrílego

sad /sæd/ a (sadder, saddest) (person) triste; (story, news) triste. **~ly**

adv tristemente; (*unfortunately*) infelizmente. ~ness *n* tristeza *f*

sadden /'sædn/ *vt* entristecer

saddle /'sædl/ *n* sela *f* □ *vt* (*horse*) selar. ~ sb with sobrecarregar alguém com

sadis|m /'seɪdɪzəm/ *n* sadismo *m*. ~t /-ɪst/ *n* sádico *m*. ~tic /sə'dɪstɪk/ *a* sádico

safe /seɪf/ *a* (-er, -est) (*not dangerous*) seguro; (*out of danger*) fora de perigo; (*reliable*) confiável. ~ from salvo de risco de □ *n* cofre *m*, caixa-forte *f*. ~ and sound são e salvo. ~ conduct salvo-conduto *m*. ~ keeping custódia *f*, proteção *f*. to be on the ~ side por via das dúvidas. ~ly *adv* (*arrive etc*) em segurança; (*keep*) seguro

safeguard /'seɪfɡɑːd/ *n* salvaguarda *f* □ *vt* salvaguardar

safety /'seɪftɪ/ *n* segurança *f*. ~-belt *n* cinto *m* de segurança. ~-pin *n* alfinete *m* de fralda. ~-valve *n* válvula *f* de segurança

sag /sæɡ/ *vi* (*pt* sagged) afrouxar

saga /'sɑːɡə/ *n* saga *f*

sage[1] /seɪdʒ/ *n* (*herb*) salva *f*

sage[2] /seɪdʒ/ *a* sensato, prudente □ *n* sábio *m*

Sagittarius /sædʒɪ'teərɪəs/ *n* (*astrol*) Sagitário *m*

said /sed/ *see* say

sail /seɪl/ *n* vela *f*; (*trip*) viagem *f* em barco à vela □ *vi* navegar; (*leave*) partir; (*sport*) velejar □ *vt* navegar. ~ing *n* navegação *f* à vela. ~ing-boat *n* barco *m* à vela

sailor /'seɪlə(r)/ *n* marinheiro *m*

saint /seɪnt/ *n* santo *m*. ~ly *a* santo, santificado

sake /seɪk/ *n* for the ~ of em consideração a. for my/your/its own ~ por mim/por isso

salad /'sæləd/ *n* salada *f*. ~ dressing *n* molho *m* para salada

salary /'sælərɪ/ *n* salário *m*

sale /seɪl/ *n* venda *f*; (*at reduced prices*) liquidação *f*. for ~ "vende-se". on ~ à venda. ~s assistant, (*Amer*) ~s clerk vendedor *m*. ~s department departamento *m* de vendas

sales|man /'seɪlzmən/ *n* (*pl* -men) (*in shop*) vendedor *m*; (*traveller*) caixeiro-viajante *m*. ~woman *n* (*pl* -women) (*in shop*) vendedora *f*; (*traveller*) caixeira-viajante *f*

saline /'seɪlaɪn/ *a* salino □ *n* salina *f*

saliva /sə'laɪvə/ *n* saliva *f*

sallow /'sæləʊ/ *a* (-er, -est) amarelado

salmon /'sæmən/ *n* (*pl invar*) salmão *m*

saloon /sə'luːn/ *n* (*on ship*) salão *m*; (*bar*) botequim *m*. ~ (car) sedã *m*

salt /sɔːlt/ *n* sal *m* □ *a* salgado □ *vt* (*season*) salgar; (*cure*) pôr em salmoura. ~-cellar *n* saleiro *m*. ~ water água *f* salgada, água *f* do mar. ~y *a* salgado

salutary /'sæljʊtrɪ/ *a* salutar

salute /sə'luːt/ *n* saudação *f* □ *vt*/*i* saudar

salvage /'sælvɪdʒ/ *n* (*naut*) salvamento *m*; (*of waste*) reciclagem *f* □ *vt* salvar

salvation /sæl'veɪʃn/ *n* salvação *f*

same /seɪm/ *a* mesmo (as que) □ *pron* the ~ o mesmo □ *adv* the ~ o mesmo. all the ~ (*nevertheless*) mesmo assim, apesar de tudo. at the ~ time (*at once*) ao mesmo tempo

sample /'sɑːmpl/ *n* amostra *f* □ *vt* experimentar, provar

sanatorium /sænə'tɔːrɪəm/ *n* (*pl* -iums) sanatório *m*

sanctify /'sæŋktɪfaɪ/ *vt* santificar

sanctimonious /sæŋktɪ'məʊnɪəs/ *a* santarrão, carola

sanction /'sæŋkʃn/ *n* (*approval*) aprovação *f*; (*penalty*) pena *f*, sanção *f* □ *vt* sancionar

sanctity /'sæŋktɪtɪ/ *n* santidade *f*

sanctuary /'sæŋktʃʊərɪ/ *n* (*relig*) santuário *m*; (*refuge*) refúgio *m*; (*for animals*) reserva *f*

sand /sænd/ *n* areia *f*; (*beach*) praia *f* □ *vt* (*with sandpaper*) lixar

sandal /'sændl/ *n* sandália *f*

sandbag /'sændbæɡ/ *n* saco *m* de areia

sandbank /'sændbæŋk/ *n* banco *m* de areia

sandcastle /'sændkɑːsl/ *n* castelo *m* de areia

sandpaper /'sændpeɪpə(r)/ *n* lixa *f* □ *vt* lixar

sandpit /'sændpɪt/ *n* caixa *f* de areia

sandwich /'sænwɪdʒ/ *n* sanduíche *m*, (*P*) sandes *f invar* □ *vt* ~ed between encaixado entre. ~ course curso *m* profissionalizante envolvendo estudo teórico e estágio em local de trabalho

sandy /'sændɪ/ *a* (-ier, iest) arenoso; (*beach*) arenoso; (*hair*) ruivo

sane /seɪn/ *a* (-er, -est) (*not mad*) são *m*; (*sensible*) sensato, ajuizado

sang /sæŋ/ *see* sing

sanitary /'sænɪtrɪ/ *a* sanitário; (*system*) sanitário. ~ towel, (*Amer*) ~ napkin toalha *f* absorvente

sanitation /sænɪ'teɪʃn/ *n* condições *fpl* sanitárias, saneamento *m*

sanity /'sænɪtɪ/ *n* sanidade *f*

sank /sæŋk/ *see* sink

Santa Claus /'sæntəklɔːz/ *n* Papai Noel *m*

sap /sæp/ *n* seiva *f* □ *vt* (*pt* sapped) esgotar, minar

sapphire /'sæfaɪə(r)/ n safira f
sarcas|m /'sɑːrkæzəm/ n sarcasmo m.
~tic /sɑːˈkæstɪk/ a sarcástico
sardine /sɑːˈdiːn/ n sardinha f
sardonic /sɑːˈdɒnɪk/ a sardónico
sash /sæʃ/ n (around waist) cinto m;
(over shoulder) faixa f. ~window n
janela f de guilhotina
sat /sæt/ see sit
satanic /səˈtænɪk/ a satânico
satchel /'sætʃl/ n sacola f
satellite /'sætəlaɪt/ n satélite m. ~
dish antena f de satélite. ~ television televisão f via satélite
satin /'sætɪn/ n cetim m
satir|e /'sætaɪə(r)/ n sátira f. ~ical
/səˈtɪrɪkl/ a satirical. ~ist
/n satirista mf. ~ize vt satirizar
satisfaction /sætɪsˈfækʃn/ n satisfação f. ~ory /fæktərɪ/ a satisfatório
satisfy /'sætɪsfaɪ/ vt satisfazer; (convince) convencer; (fulfil) atender.
~ing a satisfatório
saturat|e /'sætʃəreɪt/ vt saturar; (fig)
~ed (wet) encharcado; (fat)
saturado. ~ion /'reɪʃn/ n saturação f
Saturday /'sætədɪ/ n sábado m
sauce /sɔːs/ n molho m; (colloq: cheek)
atrevimento m
saucepan /'sɔːspən/ n panela f, (P)
caçarola f
saucer /'sɔːsə(r)/ n pires m invar
saucy /'sɔːsɪ/ a (-ier, -iest) picante
Saudi Arabia /saʊdɪəˈreɪbɪə/ n
Arábia f Saudita
sauna /'sɔːnə/ n sauna f
saunter /'sɔːntə(r)/ vi perambular
sausage /'sɒsɪdʒ/ n salsicha f,
linguiça f; (precooked) salsicha f
savage /'sævɪdʒ/ a (wild) selvagem;
(fierce) cruel; (brutal) brutal □ n selvagem mf □ vt atacar ferozmente.
~ry n selvageria f, ferocidade f
sav|e /seɪv/ vt (rescue) salvar; (keep)
guardar; (collect) colecionar; (money)
economizar; (time) ganhar; (prevent)
evitar, impedir (from de) □ n (sport)
salvamento m □ prep salvo, exceto.
~er n poupador m. ~ing n economia f, poupança f. ~ings npl econo-
mias fpl
saviour /'seɪvɪə(r)/ n salvador m
savour /'seɪvə(r)/ n sabor m □ vt
saborear. ~y a (tasty) saboroso; (not
sweet) salgado
saw¹ /sɔː/ see see¹
saw² /sɔː/ n serra f □ vt (pt sawed, pp
sawn or sawed) serrar
sawdust /'sɔːdʌst/ n serragem f
saxophone /'sæksəfəʊn/ n saxofone
m
say /seɪ/ vt/i (pt said /sed/) □ n have
a ~ (in) opinar sobre alg coisa. have

one's ~ exprimir sua opinião. I ~!
olhe! or escute! ~ing n ditado m,
provérbio m
scab /skæb/ n casca f, crosta f; (colloq:
blackleg) fura-greve mf invar
scaffold /'skæfəʊld/ n cadafalso m,
andaime m. ~ing /-əldɪŋ/ n andaime
m
scald /skɔːld/ vt escaldar, queimar □ n
escaldadura f
scale¹ /skeɪl/ n (of fish etc) escama f
scale² /skeɪl/ n (ratio, size) escala f;
(mus) escala f; (of salaries, charges)
tabela f. on a small/large/etc ~
numa pequena/grande/etc escala □
vt (climb) escalar. ~ down reduzir
scales /skeɪlz/ npl (for weighing)
balança f
scallop /'skɒləp/ n (culin) concha f de
vieira; (shape) concha f de vieira
scalp /skælp/ n couro m cabeludo □ vt
escalpar
scalpel /'skælpl/ n bisturi m
scamper /'skæmpə(r)/ vi sair correndo
scampi /'skæmpɪ/ npl camarões mpl
fritos
scan /skæn/ vt (pt scanned) (intently)
perscrutar, esquadrinhar; (quickly)
passar os olhos em; (med) examinar;
(radar) explorar □ n (med) exame m
scandal /'skændl/ n (disgrace)
escândalo m; (gossip) fofoca f. ~ous
a escandaloso
Scandinavia /skændɪˈneɪvɪə/ n
Escandinávia f. ~n a & n escandinavo (m)
scanty /'skæntɪ/ a (-ier, -iest) escasso;
(clothing) sumário
scapegoat /'skeɪpgəʊt/ n bode m expiatório
scar /skɑː(r)/ n cicatriz f □ vt (pt
scarred) marcar; (fig) deixar marcas
scarc|e /skeəs/ a (-er, -est) escasso,
raro. make o.s. ~e (colloq) sumir,
dar o fora (colloq). ~ely adv mal,
apenas. ~ity n escassez f
scare /skeə(r)/ vt assustar, apavorar.
be ~d estar com medo (of de) □ n
pavor m, pânico m. bomb ~ pânico
m causado por suspeita de bomba
num local
scarecrow /'skeəkrəʊ/ n espantalho
m
scarf /skɑːf/ n (pl scarves) (oblong)
cachecol m; (square) lenço m de cabelo
scarlet /'skɑːlət/ a escarlate m
scary /'skeərɪ/ a (-ier, -iest) (colloq)
assustador, apavorante
scathing /'skeɪðɪŋ/ a mordaz
scatter /'skætə(r)/ vt (strew) espalhar;
(disperse) dispersar □ vi espalhar-se
scavenge /'skævɪndʒ/ vi procurar

comida *etc* no lixo. ~r /-ə(r)/ *n* (*person*) que procura comida *etc* no lixo; (*animal*) que se alimenta de carniça

scenario /sɪ'nɑːrɪəʊ/ *n* (*pl* -os) sinopse *f*, resumo *m* detalhado

scene /siːn/ *n* cena *f*; (*of event*) cenário *m*; (*sight*) vista *f*, panorama *m*. behind the ~s nos bastidores. make a ~ fazer um escândalo

scenery /'siːnərɪ/ *n* cenário *m*, paisagem *f*; (*theat*) cenário *m*

scenic /'siːnɪk/ *a* pitoresco, cénico

scent /sent/ *n* (*perfume*) perfume *m*, fragância *f*; (*trail*) rastro *m*, pista *f* □ *vt* (*discern*) sentir. ~ed *a* perfumado

sceptic /'skeptɪk/ *n* cético *m*. ~al *a* cético. ~ism /-sɪzəm/ *n* ceticismo *m*

schedule /'ʃedjuːl/ *n* programa *m*; (*timetable*) horário *m* □ *vt* marcar, programar. **according to** ~ conforme planejado. **behind** ~ atrasado. **on** ~ (*train*) na hora; (*work*) em dia. ~d *flight n* vôo *m* regular

scheme /skiːm/ *n* esquema *m*; (*plan of work*) plano *m*; (*plot*) conspiração *f*, maquinação *f* □ *vi* planejar, (*P*) planear; (*pej*) intrigar, maquinar, tramar

schism /'sɪzəm/ *n* cisma *m*

schizophreni|**a** /skɪtsəʊ'friːnɪə/ *n* esquizofrenia *f*. ~c /-'frenɪk/ *a* esquizofrénico, (*P*) esquizofrénico

scholar /'skɒlə(r)/ *n* erudito *m*, estudioso *m*, escolar *m*. ~ly *a* erudito. ~ship *n* erudição *f*, saber *m*; (*grant*) bolsa *f* de estudo

school /skuːl/ *n* escola *f*; (*of university*) escola *f*, faculdade *f* □ *a* (*age, year, holidays*) escolar □ *vt* ensinar; (*train*) treinar, adestrar. ~ing *n* instrução *f*; (*attendance*) escolaridade *f*

school|**boy** /'skuːlbɔɪ/ *n* aluno *m*. ~**girl** *n* aluna *f*

school|**master** /'skuːlmɑːstə(r)/, ~**mistress**, ~**teacher** *ns* professor *m*, professora *f*

schooner /'skuːnə(r)/ *n* escuna *f*; (*glass*) copo *m* alto

sciatica /sar'ætɪkə/ *n* ciática *f*

scien|**ce** /'saɪəns/ *n* ciência *f*. ~ce fiction ficção *f* científica. ~tific /-'tɪfɪk/ *a* científico

scientist /'saɪəntɪst/ *n* cientista *mf*

scintillate /'sɪntɪleɪt/ *vi* cintilar; (*fig: person*) brilhar

scissors /'sɪzəz/ *npl* (pair of) ~ tesoura *f*

scoff[1] /skɒf/ *vi* ~ at zombar de, (*P*) troçar de

scoff[2] /skɒf/ *vt* (*sl: eat*) devorar, tragar

scold /skəʊld/ *vt* ralhar com. ~ing *n* repreensão *f*, (*P*) descompostura *f*

scone /skɒn/ *n* (*culin*) scone *m*, bolinho *m* para o chá

scoop /skuːp/ *n* (*for grain, sugar etc*) pá *f*; (*ladle*) concha *f*; (*news*) furo *m* □ *vt* ~ out (*hollow out*) esvaziar, tirar com concha or pá. ~ up (*lift*) apanhar

scoot /skuːt/ *vi* (*colloq*) fugir, mandar-se (*colloq*), (*P*) pôr-se a milhas (*colloq*)

scooter /'skuːtə(r)/ *n* (*child's*) patinete *f*, (*P*) trotinete *m*; (*motor cycle*) motoreta *f*, lambreta *f*

scope /skəʊp/ *n* âmbito *m*; (*fig: opportunity*) oportunidade *f*

scorch /skɔːtʃ/ *vt/i* chamuscar(-se), queimar de leve. ~ing *a* (*colloq*) escaldante, abrasador

score /skɔː(r)/ *n* (*sport*) contagem *f*, escore *m*; (*mus*) partitura *f* □ *vt* marcar com corte(s), riscar; (*a goal*) marcar; (*mus*) orquestrar □ *vi* marcar pontos; (*keep score*) fazer a contagem; (*football*) marcar um gol, (*P*) golo. a ~ (of) (*twenty*) uma vintena (de), vinte. ~s muitos, dezenas. **on that** ~ nesse respeito, quanto a isso. ~**board** *n* marcador *m*. ~**r** /-ə(r)/ *n* (*score-keeper*) marcador *m*; (*of goals*) autor *m*

scorn /skɔːn/ *n* desprezo *m* □ *vt* desprezar. ~**ful** *a* desdenhoso, escarninho. ~**fully** *adv* com desdém, desdenhosamente

Scorpio /'skɔːpɪəʊ/ *n* (*astr*) Escorpião *m*

scorpion /'skɔːpɪən/ *n* escorpião *m*

Scot /skɒt/ *n*, ~**tish** *a* escocês (*m*)

Scotch /skɒtʃ/ *a* escocês □ *n* uísque *m*

scotch /skɒtʃ/ *vt* pôr fim a, frustrar

scot-free /skɒt'friː/ *a* impune □ *adv* impunemente

Scotland /'skɒtlənd/ *n* Escócia *f*

Scots /skɒts/ *a* escocês. ~**man** *n* escocês *m*. ~**woman** *n* escocesa *f*

scoundrel /'skaʊndrəl/ *n* patife *m*, canalha *m*

scour[1] /'skaʊə(r)/ *vt* (*clean*) esfregar, arear. ~**er** *n* esfregão *m* de palha de aço *or* de nylon

scour[2] /'skaʊə(r)/ *vt* (*search*) percorrer, esquadrinhar

scourge /skɜːdʒ/ *n* açoite *m*; (*fig*) flagelo *m*

scout /skaʊt/ *n* (*mil*) explorador *m* □ *vi* ~ about (for) andar à procura de

Scout /skaʊt/ *n* escoteiro *m*, (*P*) escuteiro *m*. ~**ing** *n* escotismo *m*, (*P*) escutismo *m*

scowl /skaʊl/ *n* carranca *f*, ar *m* carrancudo □ *vi* fazer um ar carrancudo

scraggy /'skrægɪ/ *a* (-ier, -iest) descarnado, ossudo

scramble /'skræmbl/ *vi* trepar; (*crawl*) avançar de rastros, rastejar, arrastar-se □ *vt* (*eggs*) mexer □ *n* luta *f*, confusão *f*

scrap[1] /skræp/ *n* bocadinho *m*. ~s

npl restos *mpl* □ *vt* (*pt* scrapped) jogar fora, (*P*) deitar fora; (*plan etc*) abandonar, pôr de lado. ~-book *n* álbum *m* de recortes. ~ heap monte *m* de ferro-velho. ~-iron *n* ferro *m* velho, sucata *f*. ~ merchant sucateiro *m*. ~-paper *n* papel *m* de rascunho. ~py *a* fragmentário

scrap² /skræp/ *n* (*colloq: fight*) briga *f*, pancadaria *f* (*colloq*), rixa *f*

scrape /skreɪp/ *vt* raspar; (*graze*) esfolar, arranhar □ *vi* (*graze, rub*) roçar □ *n* (*act of scraping*) raspagem *f*; (*mark*) raspão *m*, esfoladura *f*; (*fig*) encrenca *f*, maus lençóis *mpl*. ~ through escapar pela tangente, (*P*) à tangente; (*exam*) passar pela tangente, (*P*) à tangente. ~ together conseguir juntar. ~r /-ə(r)/ *n* raspadeira *f*

scratch /skrætʃ/ *vt/i* arranhar(-se); (*a line*) riscar; (*to relieve itching*) coçar(-se) □ *n* arranhão *m*; (*line*) risco *m*; (*wound with claw, nail*) unhada *f*. start from ~ começar do princípio. up to ~ à altura, ao nível requerido

scrawl /skrɔːl/ *n* rabisco *m*, garrancho *m*, garatuja *f* □ *vt/i* rabiscar, fazer garranchos, garatujar

scrawny /skrɔːni/ *a* (-ier, -iest) descarnado, ossudo, magricela

scream /skriːm/ *vt/i* gritar □ *n* grito *m* (agudo)

screech /skriːtʃ/ *vi* guinchar, gritar; (*of brakes*) chiar, guinchar □ *n* guincho *m*, grito *m* agudo

screen /skriːn/ *n* écran *m*, tela *f*; (*folding*) biombo *m*; (*fig: protection*) manto *m* (*fig*), capa *f* (*fig*) □ *vt* resguardar, tapar; (*film*) passar; (*candidates etc*) fazer a triagem de. ~ing *n* (*med*) exame *m* médico

screw /skruː/ *n* parafuso *m* □ *vt* aparafusar, atarraxar. ~ up (*eyes, face*) franzir; (*sl: ruin*) estragar. ~ up one's courage cobrar coragem

screwdriver /skruːdraɪvə(r)/ *n* chave *f* de parafusos *or* de fenda

scribble /skrɪbl/ *vt/i* rabiscar, garatujar □ *n* rabisco *m*, garatuja *f*

script /skrɪpt/ *n* escrita *f*; (*of film*) roteiro *m*, (*P*) guião *m*. ~-writer *n* (*film*) roteirista *m*, (*P*) autor *m* do guião

Scriptures /skrɪptʃəz/ *npl* the ~ a Sagrada Escritura

scroll /skrəʊl/ *n* rolo *m* (de papel ou pergaminho); (*archit*) voluta *f* □ *vt/i* (*comput*) passar na tela

scrounge /skraʊndʒ/ *vt* (*colloq: cadge*) filar (*sl*), (*P*) cravar (*sl*) □ *vi* (*beg*) parasitar, viver às custas de alguém. ~r /-ə(r)/ *n* parasita *mf*, filão *m* (*sl*), (*P*) crava *mf* (*sl*)

scrub¹ /skrʌb/ *n* (*land*) mato *m*

scrub² /skrʌb/ *vt/i* (*pt* scrubbed) esfregar, lavar com escova e sabão; (*colloq: cancel*) cancelar □ *n* esfrega *f*

scruff /skrʌf/ *n* by the ~ of the neck pelo cangote, (*P*) pelo cachaço

scruffy /skrʌfɪ/ *a* (-ier, -iest) desmazelado, deselixado, mal ajambrado (*colloq*)

scrum /skrʌm/ *n* rixa *f*; (*Rugby*) placagem *f*

scruple /skruːpl/ *n* escrúpulo *m*

scrupulous /skruːpjʊləs/ *a* escrupuloso. ~ly *adv* escrupulosamente. ~ly clean impecavelmente limpo

scrutin|y /skruːtɪnɪ/ *n* averiguação *f*, escrutínio *m*. ~ize *vt* examinar em detalhes

scuff /skʌf/ *vt* (*scrape*) esfolar, safar □ *n* esfoladura *f*

scuffle /skʌfl/ *n* tumulto *m*, briga *f*

sculpt /skʌlpt/ *vt/i* esculpir. ~or *n* escultor *m*. ~ure /-tʃə(r)/ *n* escultura *f* □ *vt/i* esculpir

scum /skʌm/ *n* (*on liquid*) espuma *f*; (*pej: people*) gentinha *f*, escumalha *f*, ralé *f*

scurf /skɜːf/ *n* películas *fpl*; (*dandruff*) caspa *f*

scurrilous /skʌrɪləs/ *a* injurioso, insultuoso

scurry /skʌrɪ/ *vi* dar corridinhas; (*hurry*) apressar-se. ~ off escapulir-se

scurvy /skɜːvɪ/ *n* escorbuto *m*

scuttle¹ /skʌtl/ *n* (*bucket, box*) balde *m* para carvão

scuttle² /skʌtl/ *vt* (*ship*) afundar abrindo rombos *or* as torneiras de fundo

scuttle³ /skʌtl/ *vi* ~ away *or* off fugir, escapulir-se

scythe /saɪð/ *n* gadanha *f*, foice *f* grande

sea /siː/ *n* mar *m* □ *a* do mar, marinho, marítimo. at ~ no alto mar, ao largo. all at ~ desnorteado. by ~ por mar. ~-bird *ave f* marinha. ~-green *a* verde-mar. ~ horse cavalo-marinho *m*, hipocampo *m*. ~ level nível *m* do mar. ~ lion leão-marinho *m*. ~ shell concha *f*. ~-shore *n* litoral *m*; (*beach*) praia *f*. ~ water água *f* do mar

seaboard /siːbɔːd/ *n* litoral *m*, costa *f*

seafarer /siːfeərə(r)/ *n* marinheiro *m*, navegante *m*

seafood /siːfuːd/ *n* marisco(s) *m* (*pl*)

seagull /siːgʌl/ *n* gaivota *f*

seal¹ /siːl/ *n* (*animal*) foca *f*

seal² /siːl/ *n* selo *m*, sinete *m* □ *vt* selar; (*with wax*) lacrar. ~ing-wax *n* lacre *m*. ~ off (*area*) vedar

seam /siːm/ *n* (*in cloth etc*) costura *f*; (*of mineral*) veio *m*, filão *m*. ~less *a* sem costura

seaman /'si:mən/ n (pl -men) marinheiro m, marítimo m

seamy /'si:mɪ/ a ~ **side** lado m (do) avesso; (fig) lado m sórdido

seance /'seɪɑːns/ n sessão f espírita

seaplane /'si:pleɪn/ n hidroavião m

seaport /'si:pɔ:t/ n porto m de mar

search /sɜ:tʃ/ vt/i revistar, dar busca (a); (one's heart, conscience etc) examinar □ n revista f, busca f; (quest) procura f, busca f; (official) inquérito m. **in ~ of** à procura de. ~ **for** procurar. **~-party** n equipe f de busca. **~-warrant** n mandado m de busca. **~ing** a (of look) penetrante; (of test etc) minucioso

searchlight /'sɜ:tʃlaɪt/ n holofote m

seasick /'si:sɪk/ a enjoado. **~ness** n enjôo m, P enjoo m

seaside /'si:saɪd/ n costa f, praia f, beira-mar f. ~ **resort** n balneário m, praia f

season /'si:zn/ n (of year) estação f; (proper time) época f; (cricket, football etc) temporada f □ vt temperar; (wood) secar. **in ~** na época. **~able** a próprio da estação. **~al** a sazonal. **~ed** a (of people) experimentado. **~ing** n tempero m. **~-ticket** n (train etc) passe m; (theatre etc) assinatura f

seat /si:t/ n assento m; (place) lugar m; (of bicycle) selim m; (of chair) assento m; (of trousers) fundilho m □ vt sentar; (have seats for) ter lugares sentados para. **be ~ed, take a ~** sentar-se. ~ **of learning** centro m de cultura. **~-belt** n cinto m de segurança

seaweed /'si:wi:d/ n alga f marinha

seaworthy /'si:wɜ:ðɪ/ a navegável, em condições de navegabilidade

secateurs /'sekətɜ:z/ npl tesoura f de poda

seclu|de /sɪ'klu:d/ vt isolar. **~ded** a isolado, retirado. **~sion** /sɪ'klu:ʒn/ n isolamento m

second[1] /'sekənd/ a segundo □ n segundo m; (in duel) testemunha f. ~ **(gear)** (auto) segunda f (velocidade). **the ~ of April** dois de Abril. **~s** (goods) artigos mpl de segunda or de refugo □ adv (in race etc) em segundo lugar □ vt secundar. **~-best** a escolhido em segundo lugar. **~-class** a de segunda classe. **~-hand** a de segunda mão □ n (on clock) ponteiro m dos segundos. **~-rate** a medíocre, de segunda ordem. ~ **thoughts** dúvidas fpl. **on ~ thoughts** pensando melhor. **~ly** adv segundo, em segundo lugar

second[2] /sɪ'kɒnd/ vt (transfer) destacar (**to** para)

secondary /'sekəndrɪ/ a secundário. ~ **school** escola f secundária

secrecy /'si:krəsɪ/ n segredo m

secret /'si:krɪt/ a secreto □ n segredo m. **in ~** em segredo. ~ **agent** n agente mf secreto. **~ly** adv em segredo, secretamente

secretar|y /'sekrətrɪ/ n secretário m, secretária f. **S~y of State** ministro m de Estado, (P) Secretário m de Estado; (Amer) ministro m dos Negócios Estrangeiros. **~ial** /-'teərɪəl/ a (work, course etc) de secretária

secret|e /sɪ'kri:t/ vt segregar; (hide) esconder. **~ion** /-ʃn/ n secreção f

secretive /'si:krətɪv/ a misterioso, reservado

sect /sekt/ n seita f. **~arian** /-'teərɪən/ a sectário

section /'sekʃn/ n seção f, (P) secção f; (of country, community etc) setor m, (P) sector m; (district of town) zona f

sector /'sektə(r)/ n setor m, (P) sector m

secular /'sekjʊlə(r)/ a secular, leigo, P laico; (art, music etc) profano

secure /sɪ'kjʊə(r)/ a seguro, em segurança; (firm) seguro, sólido; (in mind) tranqüilo, P tranquilo □ vt prender bem or com segurança; (obtain) conseguir, arranjar; (ensure) assegurar; (windows, doors) fechar bem. **~ly** adv solidamente; (safely) em segurança

securit|y /sɪ'kjʊərətɪ/ n segurança f. (for loan) fiança f, caução f. **~ies** npl (finance) títulos mpl

sedate /sɪ'deɪt/ a sereno, comedido □ vt tratar com sedativos

sedation /sɪ'deɪʃn/ n (med) sedação f. **under ~** sob o efeito de sedativos

sedative /'sedətɪv/ n (med) sedativo m

sedentary /'sedntrɪ/ a sedentário

sediment /'sedɪmənt/ n sedimento m, depósito m

seduce /sɪ'dju:s/ vt seduzir

seduct|ion /sɪ'dʌkʃn/ n sedução f. **~ive** /-tɪv/ a sedutor, aliciante

see[1] /si:/ vt/i (pt saw, pp seen) ver; (escort) acompanhar. ~ **about** or **to** tratar de, encarregar-se de. ~ **off** vt (wave goodbye) ir despedir-se de; (chase) ~ **through** (task) levar a cabo; (not be deceived by) não se deixar enganar por. ~ **(to it) that** assegurar que, tratar de fazer com que. **~ing that** visto que, uma vez que. ~ **you later!** (colloq) até logo! (colloq)

see[2] /si:/ n sé f, bispado m

seed /si:d/ n semente f; (fig: origin) germe(n) m; (tennis) cabeça f de série; (pip) caroço m. **go to ~** produzir sementes; (fig) desmazelar-se (colloq).

~**ling** *n* planta *f* brotada a partir da semente

seedy /'si:dɪ/ *a* (-**ier**, -**iest**) (com um ar) gasto, surrado; (*colloq: unwell*) abatido, deprimido, em baixo astral (*colloq*)

seek /si:k/ *vt* (*pt* **sought**) procurar; (*help etc*) pedir

seem /si:m/ *vi* parecer. ~**ingly** *adv* aparentemente, ao que parece

seemly /'si:mlɪ/ *adv* decente, conveniente, próprio

seen /si:n/ *see* **see**[1]

seep /si:p/ *vi* (*ooze*) filtrar-se; (*trickle*) pingar, escorrer, passar. ~**age** *n* infiltração *f*

see-saw /'si:sɔ:/ *n* gangorra *f*, (*P*) balanço *m*

seethe /si:ð/ *vi* ~ **with** (*anger*) ferver de; (*people*) fervilhar de

segment /'segmənt/ *n* segmento *m*; (*of orange*) gomo *m*

segregat|e /'segrɪgeɪt/ *vt* segregar, separar. ~**ion** /-'geɪʃn/ *n* segregação *f*

seize /si:z/ *vt* agarrar, (*P*) deitar a mão a, apanhar; (*take possession by force*) apoderar-se de; (*by law*) apreender, confiscar, (*P*) apresar □ *vi* ~ **on** (*opportunity*) aproveitar. ~ **up** (*engine etc*) grimpar, emperrar. **be** ~**d with** (*fear, illness*) ter um ataque de

seizure /'si:ʒə(r)/ *n* (*med*) ataque *m*, crise *f*; (*law*) apreensão *f*, captura *f*

seldom /'seldəm/ *adv* raras vezes, raramente, raro

select /sɪ'lekt/ *vt* escolher, selecionar, (*P*) seleccionar □ *a* seleto, (*P*) selecto. ~**ion** /-ʃn/ *n* seleção *f*, (*P*) selecção *f*; (*comm*) sortido *m*

selective /sɪ'lektɪv/ *a* seletivo, (*P*) selectivo

self /self/ *n* (*pl* **selves**) **the** ~ o eu, o ego

self- /self/ *pref* ~**-assurance** *n* segurança *f*. ~**-assured** *a* seguro de si. ~**-catering** *a* em que os hóspedes têm facilidades de cozinhar. ~**-centred** *a* egocêntrico. ~**-confidence** *n* autoconfiança, confiança *f* em si mesmo. ~**-confident** *a* que tem confiança em si mesmo. ~**-conscious** *a* inibido, constrangido. ~**-contained** *a* independente. ~**-control** *n* autodomínio *m*. ~**-controlled** *a* senhor de si. ~**-defence** *n* legítima defesa *f*. ~**-denial** *n* abnegação *f*. ~**-employed** *a* autónomo. ~**-esteem** *n* amor *m* próprio. ~**-evident** *a* evidente. ~**-indulgent** *a* que não resiste a tentações; (*for ease*) comodista. ~**-interest** *n* interesse *m* pessoal. ~**-portrait** *n* auto-retrato *m*. ~**-possessed** *a* senhor de si. ~**-reliant** *a* independente, seguro de si.

~**-respect** *n* amor *m* próprio. ~**-righteous** *a* que se tem em boa conta. ~**-sacrifice** *n* abnegação *f*, sacrifício *m*. ~**-satisfied** *a* cheio de si, convencido (*colloq*). ~**-seeking** *a* egoísta. ~**-service** *a* auto-serviço, self-service. ~**-styled** *a* pretenso. ~**-sufficient** *a* auto-suficiente. ~**-willed** *a* voluntarioso

selfish /'selfɪʃ/ *a* egoísta; (*motive*) interesseiro. ~**ness** *n* egoismo *m*

selfless /'selflɪs/ *a* desinteressado

sell /sel/ *vt/i* (*pt* **sold**) vender(-se). ~**-by date** ~ **off** liquidar. **be sold out** estar esgotado. ~**-out** *n* (*show*) sucesso *m*; (*colloq: betrayal*) traição *f*. ~**er** *n* vendedor *m*

Sellotape /'seləteɪp/ *n* fita *f* adesiva, (*P*) fitacola *f*

semantic /sɪ'mæntɪk/ *a* semântico. ~**s** *n* semântica *f*

semblance /'sembləns/ *n* aparência *f*

semen /'si:mən/ *n* sémen *m*, (*P*) sémen *m*, esperma *m*

semester /sɪ'mestə(r)/ *n* (*Amer: univ*) semestre *m*

semi- /'semɪ/ *pref* semi-, meio

semibreve /'semɪbri:v/ *n* (*mus*) semibreve *f*

semicirc|le /'semɪsɜ:kl/ *n* semicírculo *m*. ~**ular** /-sɜ:kjələ(r)/ *a* semicircular

semicolon /semɪ'kəʊlən/ *n* ponto-e-vírgula *m*

semi-detached /semɪdɪ'tætʃt/ *a* ~ **house** casa *f* geminada

semifinal /semɪ'faɪnl/ *n* semifinal *f*, (*P*) meiafinal *f*

seminar /'semɪnɑ:(r)/ *n* seminário *m*

semiquaver /'semɪkweɪvə(r)/ *n* (*mus*) semicolcheia *f*

Semit|e /'si:maɪt/ *a* & *n* semita (*mf*). ~**ic** /sɪ'mɪtɪk/ *a* & *n* (*lang*) semítico (*m*)

semitone /'semɪtəʊn/ *n* (*mus*) semitom *m*

semolina /semə'li:nə/ *n* sêmola *f*, (*P*) sémola *f*, semolina *f*

senat|e /'senɪt/ *n* senado *m*. ~**or** /-ətə(r)/ *n* senador *m*

send /send/ *vt/i* (*pt* **sent**) enviar, mandar. ~ **back** devolver. ~ **for** (*person*) chamar, mandar vir; (*help*) pedir. ~ (*away or off*) **for** encomendar, mandar vir (por carta). ~**-off** *n* despedida *f*, bota-fora *m*. ~ **up** (*colloq*) parodiar. ~**er** *n* expedidor *m*, remetente *m*

senil|e /'si:naɪl/ *a* senil. ~**ity** /sɪ'nɪlətɪ/ *n* senilidade *f*

senior /'si:nɪə(r)/ *a* mais velho, mais idoso (**to** que); (*in rank*) superior; (*in service*) mais antigo; (*after surname*) sênior, (*P*) sénior □ *n* pessoa *f* mais velha; (*schol*) finalista *mf*. ~ **citizen**

pessoa *f* de idade *or* da terceira idade.
~**ity** /-'prətɪ/ *n* (*in age*) idade *f*; (*in service*) antiguidade *f*
sensation /sen'seɪʃn/ *n* sensação *f*.
~**al** *a* sensacional. ~**alism** *n* sensacionalismo *m*
sense /sens/ *n* sentido *m*; (*wisdom*) bom senso *m*; (*sensation*) sensação *f*; (*mental impression*) sentimento *m*. ~**s** (*sanity*) razão *f* □ *vt* pressentir. **make** ~ fazer sentido. **make** ~ **of** compreender. ~**less** *a* disparatado, sem sentido; (*med*) sem sentidos, inconsciente
sensible /'sensəbl/ *a* sensato, razoável; (*clothes*) prático
sensitiv|**e** /'sensɪtɪv/ *a* sensível (**to** a); (*touchy*) susceptível. ~**ity** /-'tɪvətɪ/ *n* sensibilidade *f*
sensory /'sensərɪ/ *a* sensorial
sensual /'senʃʊəl/ *a* sensual. ~**ity** /-'ælətɪ/ *n* sensualidade *f*
sensuous /'senʃʊəs/ *a* sensual
sent /sent/ *see* **send**
sentence /'sentəns/ *n* frase *f*; (*jur: decision*) sentença *f*; (*punishment*) pena *f* □ *vt* ~ **to** condenar a
sentiment /'sentɪmənt/ *n* sentimento *m*; (*opinion*) modo *m* de ver
sentimental /sentɪ'mentl/ *a* sentimental. ~**ity** /-men'tælətɪ/ *n* sentimentalidade *f*, sentimentalismo *m*. ~ **value** valor *m* estimativo
sentry /'sentrɪ/ *n* sentinela *f*
separable /'sepərəbl/ *a* separável
separate[1] /'seprət/ *a* separado, diferente. ~**s** *npl* (*clothes*) conjuntos *mpl*. ~**ly** *adv* separadamente, em separado
separat|**e**[2] /'sepəreɪt/ *vt/i* separar (-se). ~**ion** /-'reɪʃn/ *n* separação *f*
September /sep'tembə(r)/ *n* setembro *m*
septic /'septɪk/ *a* séptico, infectado
sequel /'si:kwəl/ *n* resultado *m*, sequela *f*, (*P*) sequela *f*; (*of novel, film*) continuação *f*
sequence /'si:kwəns/ *n* sequência *f*, (*P*) sequência *f*
sequin /'si:kwɪn/ *n* lantejoula *f*
serenade /serə'neɪd/ *n* serenata *f* □ *vt* fazer uma serenata para
seren|**e** /sɪ'ri:n/ *a* sereno. ~**ity** /-'enətɪ/ *n* serenidade *f*
sergeant /'sɑ:dʒənt/ *n* sargento *m*
serial /'sɪərɪəl/ *n* folhetim *m* □ *a* (*number*) de série. ~**ize** /-laɪz/ *vt* publicar em folhetim
series /'sɪərɪ:z/ *n invar* série *f*
serious /'sɪərɪəs/ *a* sério; (*very bad, critical*) grave, sério. ~**ly** *adv* seriamente, gravemente, a sério. **take** ~**ly** levar a sério. ~**ness** *n* seriedade *f*, gravidade *f*

sermon /'sɜ:mən/ *n* sermão *m*
serpent /'sɜ:pənt/ *n* serpente *f*
serrated /sɪ'reɪtɪd/ *a* (*edge*) serr(e)ado, com serrilha
serum /'sɪərəm/ *n* (*pl* -**a**) soro *m*
servant /'sɜ:vənt/ *n* criado *m*, criada *f*, empregado *m*, empregada *f*
serv|**e** /sɜ:v/ *vt/i* servir; (*a sentence*) cumprir; (*jur: a writ*) entregar; (*mil*) servir, prestar serviço; (*apprenticeship*) fazer □ *n* (*tennis*) saque *m*, (*P*) serviço *m*. ~**e as/to** servir de/para. ~**e its purpose** servir para o que é (*colloq*), servir os seus fins. **it** ~**es you/him** *etc* **right** é bem feito. ~**ing** *n* (*portion*) dose *f*, porção *f*
service /'sɜ:vɪs/ *n* serviço *m*; (*relig*) culto *m*; (*tennis*) saque *m*, (*P*) serviço *m*; (*maintenance*) revisão *f*. ~**s** (*mil*) forças *fpl* armadas □ *vt* (*car etc*) fazer a revisão de. **of** ~ **to** útil a, de utilidade a. ~ **area** área *f* de serviço. ~ **charge** serviço *m*. ~ **station** posto *m* de gasolina
serviceable /'sɜ:vɪsəbl/ *a* (*of use, usable*) útil, prático; (*durable*) resistente; (*of person*) prestável
serviceman /'sɜ:vɪsmən/ *n* (*pl* -**men**) militar *m*
serviette /sɜ:vɪ'et/ *n* guardanapo *m*
servile /'sɜ:vaɪl/ *a* servil
session /'seʃn/ *n* sessão *f*; (*univ*) ano *m* académico, (*P*) académico; (*Amer: univ*) semestre *m*. **in** ~ (*sitting*) em sessão, reunidos
set /set/ *vt* (*pt* **set**, *pres p* **setting**) pôr, colocar; (*put down*) pousar; (*limit etc*) fixar; (*watch, clock*) regular; (*example*) dar; (*exam, task*) marcar; (*in plaster*) engessar □ *vi* (*of sun*) pôr-se; (*of jelly*) endurecer, solidificar(-se) □ *n* (*of people*) círculo *m*, roda *f*; (*of books*) coleção *f*, (*P*) colecção *f*; (*of tools, chairs etc*) jogo *m*; (*TV, radio*) aparelho *m*; (*hair*) mise *f*; (*theat*) cenário *m*; (*tennis*) partida *f*, set *m* □ *a* fixo; (*habit*) inveterado; (*jelly*) duro, sólido; (*book*) do programa, (*P*) adoptado; (*meal*) a preço fixo. **be** ~ **on** estar decidido a fazer. ~ **about** *or* **to** começar a, pôr-se a. ~ **back** (*plans etc*) atrasar; (*sl: cost*) custar. ~**back** *n* revés *m*, contratempo *m*, atraso *m* de vida (*colloq*). ~ **fire** to atear fogo a, (*P*) deitar fogo a. ~ **free** pôr em liberdade. ~ **in** (*rain etc*) pegar. ~ **off** *or* **out** partir, começar a viajar. ~ **off** (*mechanism*) pôr para funcionar, (*P*) pôr a funcionar; (*bomb*) explodir; (*by contrast*) realçar. ~ **out** (*state*) expor; (*arrange*) dispor. ~ **sail** partir, içar as velas. ~ **square** esquadro *m*. ~ **the table** pôr a mesa. ~ **theory** teoria *f* de conjuntos. ~**-to** *n* briga *f*.

~ up (*establish*) fundar, estabelecer.
~-up *n* (*system*) sistema *m*, organização *f*; (*situation*) situação *f*
settee /se'ti:/ *n* sofá *m*
setting /'setɪŋ/ *n* (*framework*) quadro *m*; (*of jewel*) engaste *m*; (*typ*) composição *f*; (*mus*) arranjo *m* musical
settle /'setl/ *vt* (*arrange*) resolver; (*date*) marcar; (*nerves*) acalmar; (*doubts*) esclarecer; (*new country*) colonizar, povoar; (*bill*) pagar □ *vi* assentar; (*in country*) estabelecer-se; (*in house, chair etc*) instalar-se; (*weather*) estabilizar-se. **~ down** acalmar-se; (*become orderly*) assentar; (*sit, rest*) instalar-se. **~ for** aceitar. **~ up (with)** fazer contas (com). **~up (with)** fazer contas (com). **~r** /-ə(r)/ *n* colono *m*, colonizador *m*
settlement /'setlmənt/ *n* (*agreement*) acordo *m*; (*payment*) pagamento *m*; (*colony*) colónia *f*; (*P*) colónia *f*; (*colonization*) colonização *f*
seven /'sevn/ *a* & *n* sete (*m*). **~th** *a* & *n* sétimo (*m*)
seventeen /sevn'ti:n/ *a* & *n* dezessete (*m*), (*P*) dezassete (*m*). **~th** *a* & *n* décimo sétimo (*m*)
sevent|**y** /'sevntɪ/ *a* & *n* setenta (*m*). **~ieth** *a* & *n* septuagésimo (*m*)
sever /'sevə(r)/ *vt* cortar. **~ance** *n* corte *m*
several /'sevrəl/ *a* & *pron* vários, diversos
sever|**e** /sɪ'vɪə(r)/ *a* (**-er**, **-est**) severo; (*pain*) forte, violento; (*illness*) grave; (*winter*) rigoroso. **~ely** *adv* severamente; (*seriously*) gravemente. **~ity** /sɪ'verɪtɪ/ *n* severidade *f*; (*seriousness*) gravidade *f*
sew /səʊ/ *vt/i* (*pt* **sewed**, *pp* **sewn** *or* **sewed**) coser, costurar. **~ing** *n* costura *f*. **~ing-machine** *n* máquina *f* de costura
sewage /'sju:ɪdʒ/ *n* efluentes *mpl* dos esgotos, detritos *mpl*
sewer /'sju:ə(r)/ *n* cano *m* de esgoto
sewn /səʊn/ *see* **sew**
sex /seks/ *n* sexo *m* □ *a* sexual. **have ~** ter relações. **~ maniac** tarado *m* sexual, **~v** *a* sexy *invar*, que tem sex-appeal
sexist /'seksɪst/ *a* & *n* sexista *mf*
sexual /'sekʃʊəl/ *a* sexual. **~ harassment** assédio *m* sexual. **~ intercourse** relações *fpl* sexuais. **~ity** /'ælətɪ/ *n* sexualidade *f*
shabb|**y** /'ʃæbɪ/ *a* (**-ier**, **-iest**) (*clothes, object*) gasto, surrado; (*person*) maltrapilho, mal vestido; (*mean*) miserável. **~ily** *adv* miseravelmente
shack /ʃæk/ *n* cabana *f*, barraca *f*
shackles /'ʃæklz/ *npl* grilhões *mpl*, algemas *fpl*

shade /ʃeɪd/ *n* sombra *f*; (*of colour*) tom *m*, matiz *m*; (*of opinion*) matiz *m*; (*for lamp*) abat-jour *m*, quebra-luz *m*; (*Amer: blind*) estore *m* □ *vt* resguardar da luz; (*darken*) sombrear. **a ~ bigger**/*etc* ligeiramente maior/*etc*. **in the ~** à sombra
shadow /'ʃædəʊ/ *n* sombra *f* □ *vt* cobrir de sombra; (*follow*) seguir, vigiar. **S~ Cabinet** gabinete *m* formado pelo partido da oposição. **~y** *a* ensombrado, sombreado; (*fig*) vago, indistinto
shady /'ʃeɪdɪ/ *a* (**-ier**, **-iest**) sombreiro, (*P*) que dá sombra; (*in shade*) à sombra; (*fig: dubious*) suspeito, duvidoso
shaft /ʃɑ:ft/ *n* (*of arrow, spear*) haste *f*; (*axle*) eixo *m*, veio *m*; (*of mine, lift*) poço *m*; (*of light*) raio *m*
shaggy /'ʃægɪ/ *a* (**-ier**, **-iest**) (*beard*) hirsuto; (*hair*) desgrenhado; (*animal*) peludo, felpudo
shake /ʃeɪk/ *vt* (*pt* **shook**, *pp* **shaken**) abanar, sacudir; (*belief, house etc*) abalar □ *vi* estremecer, tremer □ *n* (*violent*) abanão *m*, safanão *m*; (*light*) sacudidela *f*. **~ hands with** apertar a mão de. **~ off** (*get rid of*) sacudir, livrar-se de. **~ one's head** (*to say no*) fazer que não com a cabeça. **~ up** agitar. **~-up** *n* (*upheaval*) reviravolta *f*
shaky /'ʃeɪkɪ/ *a* (**-ier**, **-iest**) (*hand, voice*) trémulo, (*P*) trémulo; (*unsteady, unsafe*) pouco firme, inseguro; (*weak*) fraco
shall /ʃæl/; *unstressed* /ʃəl/ *v aux* I/**we ~ do** (*future*) farei/faremos. I/**you/he ~ do** (*command*) eu hei de/você há de/tu hás de/ele há de fazer
shallot /ʃə'lɒt/ *n* cebolinha *f*, (*P*) chalota *f*
shallow /'ʃæləʊ/ *a* (**-er**, **-est**) pouco fundo, raso; (*fig*) superficial
sham /ʃæm/ *n* fingimento *m*; (*jewel etc*) imitação *f*; (*person*) impostor *m*, fingido *m* □ *a* fingido; (*false*) falso □ *vt* (*pt* **shammed**) fingir
shambles /'ʃæmblz/ *npl* (*colloq: mess*) balbúrdia *f*, trapalhada *f*
shame /ʃeɪm/ *n* vergonha *f* □ *vt* (fazer) envergonhar. **it's a ~** é uma pena. **what a ~!** que pena! **~ful** *a* vergonhoso. **~less** *a* sem vergonha, descarado; (*immodest*) despudorado, desavergonhado
shamefaced /'ʃeɪmfeɪst/ *a* envergonhado
shampoo /ʃæm'pu:/ *n* xampu *m*, (*P*) champô *m*, shampoo *m* □ *vt* lavar com xampu, (*P*) champô *or* shampoo
shan't /ʃɑ:nt/ = **shall not**
shanty /'ʃæntɪ/ *n* barraca *f*. **~ town** favela *f*, (*P*) bairro(s) *m*(*pl*) da lata

shape /ʃeɪp/ n forma f □ vt moldar □ vi ~ **(up)** andar bem, fazer progressos. **take** ~ concretizar-se, avançar. ~**less** a informe, sem forma; (of body) deselegante, disforme

shapely /ʃeɪplɪ/ a (-ier, -iest) (leg, person) bem feito, elegante

share /ʃeə(r)/ n parte f, porção f; (comm) ação f, (P) acção f □ vt/i partilhar (with com, in de)

shareholder /ʃeəhəʊldə(r)/ n acionista mf, (P) accionista mf

shark /ʃɑːk/ n tubarão m

sharp /ʃɑːp/ a (-er, -est) (knife, pencil etc) afiado; (pin, point etc) pontiagudo, aguçado; (words, reply) áspero; (of bend) fechado; (acute) agudo; (sudden) brusco; (dishonest) pouco honesto; (well-defined) nítido; (brisk) rápido, vigoroso; (clever) vivo □ adv (stop) de repente □ n (mus) sustenido m. **six o'clock** ~ seis horas em ponto. ~**ly** adv (harshly) rispidamente; (suddenly) de repente

sharpen /ʃɑːpən/ vt aguçar; (pencil) fazer a ponta de, (P) afiar; (knife etc) afiar, amolar. ~**er** n afiadeira f; (for pencil) apontador m, (P) apára-lápis m, (P) afia-lápis m

shatter /ʃætə(r)/ vt/i despedaçar (-se), esmigalhar(-se); (hopes) destruir(-se); (nerves) abalar(-se). ~**ed** a (upset) passado; (exhausted) estourado (collog)

shav|e /ʃeɪv/ vt/i barbear(-se), fazer a barba (de) □ n **have a** ~**e** barbear-se. **have a close** ~**e** (fig) escapar por um triz. ~**en** a raspado, barbeado. ~**er** n aparelho m de barbear, (P) máquina f de barbear. ~**ing-brush** n pincel m para a barba. ~**ing-cream** n creme m de barbear

shaving /ʃeɪvɪŋ/ n apara f

shawl /ʃɔːl/ n xale m, (P) xaile m

she /ʃiː/ pron ela □ n fêmea f

sheaf /ʃiːf/ n (pl sheaves) feixe m; (of papers) maço m, molho m

shear /ʃɪə(r)/ vt (pp **shorn** or **sheared**) (sheep etc) tosquiar

shears /ʃɪəz/ npl tesoura f para jardim

sheath /ʃiːθ/ n (pl ~**s** /ʃiːðz/) bainha f; (condom) preservativo m, camisade-Vénus f

sheathe /ʃiːð/ vt embainhar

shed¹ /ʃed/ n (hut) casinhola f; (for cows) estábulo m

shed² /ʃed/ vt (pt **shed**, pres p **shedding**) perder, deixar cair; (spread) espalhar; (blood, tears) deitar, derramar. ~ **light on** lançar luz sobre

sheen /ʃiːn/ n brilho m, lustre m

sheep /ʃiːp/ n (pl invar) carneiro m, ovelha f. ~**-dog** n cão m de pastor

sheepish /ʃiːpɪʃ/ a encabulado. ~**ly** adv com um ar encabulado

sheepskin /ʃiːpskɪn/ n pele f de carneiro; (leather) carneira f

sheer /ʃɪə(r)/ a mero, simples; (steep) íngreme, a pique; (fabric) diáfano, transparente □ adv a pique, verticalmente

sheet /ʃiːt/ n lençol m; (of glass, metal) chapa f, placa f; (of paper) folha f

sheikh /ʃeɪk/ n xeque m, sheik m

shelf /ʃelf/ n (pl shelves) prateleira f

shell /ʃel/ n (of egg, nut etc) casca f; (of mollusc) concha f; (of ship, tortoise) casco m; (of building) estrutura f, armação f; (of explosive) cartucho m □ vt descascar; (mil) bombardear

shellfish /ʃelfɪʃ/ n (pl invar) crustáceo m; (as food) marisco m

shelter /ʃeltə(r)/ n abrigo m, refúgio m □ vt abrigar; (protect) proteger; (harbour) dar asilo a □ vi abrigar-se, refugiar-se. ~**ed** a (life etc) protegido; (spot) abrigado

shelve /ʃelv/ vt pôr em prateleiras; (fit with shelves) pôr prateleiras em; (fig) engavetar, pôr de lado

shelving /ʃelvɪŋ/ n (shelves) prateleiras fpl

shepherd /ʃepəd/ n pastor m □ vt guiar. ~**'s pie** empadão m de batata e carne moída

sheriff /ʃerɪf/ n xerife m

sherry /ʃerɪ/ n Xerez m

shield /ʃiːld/ n (armour, heraldry) escudo m; (screen) anteparo m □ vt proteger (from contra, de)

shift /ʃɪft/ vt/i mudar de posição, deslocar(-se); (exchange, alter) mudar de □ n mudança f, (workers; work) turno m. **make** ~ arranjar-se

shiftless /ʃɪftlɪs/ a (lazy) molengão, preguiçoso

shifty /ʃɪftɪ/ a (-ier, -iest) velhaco, duvidoso

shimmer /ʃɪmə(r)/ vi luzir suavemente □ n luzir m

shin /ʃɪn/ n perna f. ~**-bone** n tibia f, canela f. ~**-pad** n (football) caneleira f

shin|e /ʃaɪn/ vt/i (pt **shone**) (fazer) brilhar, (fazer) reluzir; (shoes) engraxar □ n lustro m. ~**e a torch (on)** iluminar com uma lanterna de mão. **the sun is** ~**ing** faz sol

shingle /ʃɪŋgl/ n (pebbles) seixos mpl

shingles /ʃɪŋglz/ npl med zona f, herpes-zóster f

shiny /ʃaɪnɪ/ a (-ier, -iest) brilhante; (of coat, trousers) lustroso

ship /ʃɪp/ n barco m, navio m □ vt (pt **shipped**) transportar; (send) mandar por via marítima; (load) embarcar. ~**ment** n (goods) carregamento m;

(*shipping*) embarque *m*. ~**ping** *n* navegação *f*; (*ships*) navios *mpl*

shipbuilding /'ʃɪpbɪldɪŋ/ *n* construção *f* naval

shipshape /'ʃɪpʃeɪp/ *adv & a* em (perfeita) ordem, impecável

shipwreck /'ʃɪprek/ *n* naufrágio *m*. ~**ed** *a* naufragado. be ~**ed** naufragar

shipyard /'ʃɪpjɑːd/ *n* estaleiro *m*

shirk /ʃɜːk/ *vt* fugir a, furtar-se a, (*P*) baldar-se a (*sl*). ~**er** *n* parasita *mf*

shirt /ʃɜːt/ *n* camisa *f*; (*of woman*) blusa *f*. in ~-**sleeves** em mangas de camisa

shiver /'ʃɪvə(r)/ *vi* arrepiar-se, tiritar □ *n* arrepio *m*

shoal /ʃəʊl/ *n* (*of fish*) cardume *m*

shock /ʃɒk/ *n* choque *m*, embate *m*; (*electr*) choque *m* elétrico, (*P*) eléctrico; (*med*) choque *m* □ *a* de choque □ *vt* chocar. ~ **absorber** (*mech*) amortecedor *m*. ~**ing** *a* chocante; (*colloq: very bad*) horrível

shod /ʃɒd/ *see* **shoe**

shodd|y /'ʃɒdɪ/ *a* (-ier, -iest) mal feito, ordinário, de má qualidade. ~**ily** *adv* mal

shoe /ʃuː/ *n* sapato *m*; (*footwear*) calçado *m*; (*horse*) ferradura *f*; (*brake*) sapata *f*, (*P*) calço *m* (de travão) □ *vt* (*pt* shod, *pres p* shoeing) (*horse*) ferrar. ~ **polish** *n* pomada *f*, (*P*) graxa *f* para sapatos. ~-**shop** *n* sapataria *f*. on a ~-**string** (*colloq*) com/por muito pouco dinheiro, na pindaíba (*colloq*)

shoehorn /'ʃuːhɔːn/ *n* calçadeira *f*

shoelace /'ʃuːleɪs/ *n* cordão *m* de sapato, (*P*) atacador *m*

shoemaker /'ʃuːmeɪkə(r)/ *n* sapateiro *m*

shone /ʃɒn/ *see* **shine**

shoo /ʃuː/ *vt* enxotar □ *int* xô

shook /ʃʊk/ *see* **shake**

shoot /ʃuːt/ *vt* (*pt* shot) (*gun*) disparar; (*glance, missile*) lançar; (*kill*) matar a tiro; (*wound*) ferir a tiro; (*execute*) executar, fuzilar, (*hunt*) caçar; (*film*) filmar, rodar □ *vi* atirar (at contra, sobre); (*bot*) rebentar; (*football*) rematar □ *n* (*bot*) rebento *m*. ~ **down** abater (a tiro). ~ **in/out** (*rush*) entrar/sair correndo *or* disparado. ~ **up** (*spurt*) jorrar; (*grow quickly*) crescer a olhos vistos, dar um pulo; (*prices*) subir em disparada. ~**ing** *n* (*shots*) tiroteio *m*. ~**ing-range** *n* carreira *f* de tiro. ~**ing star** estrela *f* cadente

shop /ʃɒp/ *n* loja *f*; (*workshop*) oficina *f* □ *vi* (*pt* shopped) fazer compras. ~ **around** procurar, ver o que há. ~

assistant empregado *m*, caixeiro *m*; vendedor *m*. ~-**floor** *n* (*workers*) trabalhadores *mpl*. ~-**per** *n* comprador *m*. ~-**soiled**, (*Amer*) ~-**worn** *adjs* enxovalhado. ~ **steward** delegado *m* sindical. ~ **window** vitrina *f*, (*P*) montra *f*. **talk** ~ falar de coisas profissionais

shopkeeper /'ʃɒpkiːpə(r)/ *n* lojista *mf*, comerciante *mf*

shoplift|er /'ʃɒplɪftə(r)/ *n* gatuno *m* de lojas. ~**ing** *n* furto *m* em lojas

shopping /'ʃɒpɪŋ/ *n* (*goods*) compras *fpl*. go ~ ir às compras. ~ **bag** sacola *f* de compras. ~ **centre** centro *m* comercial

shore /ʃɔː(r)/ *n* (*of sea*) praia *f*, costa *f*; (*of lake*) margem *f*

shorn /ʃɔːn/ *see* **shear** □ *a* tosquiado. ~ **of** despojado de

short /ʃɔːt/ *a* (-er, -est) curto; (*person*) baixo; (*brief*) breve, curto; (*curt*) seco, brusco. be ~ **of** (*lack*) ter falta de □ *adv* (*abruptly*) bruscamente, de repente. cut ~ abreviar; (*interrupt*) interromper □ *n* (*electr*) curto-circuito *m*; (*film*) curta-metragem *f*, short *m*. ~**s** (*trousers*) calção *m*, (*P*) calções *mpl*, short *m*, (*P*) shorts *mpl*. a ~ **time** pouco tempo. he is called Tom for ~ o diminutivo dele é Tom. in ~ em suma. ~-**change** *vt* (*cheat*) enganar. ~ **circuit** circuito *m*, curto-circuito *m* -**circuit** *vt/i* (*electr*) fazer *or* dar um curto-circuito (em). ~ **cut** atalho *m*. ~-**handed** *a* com falta de pessoal. ~ **list** pré-seleção *f*, (*P*) selecção *f*. ~-**lived** *a* de pouca duração. ~-**sighted** *a* míope, (*P*) curto de vista. ~-**tempered** *a* irritadiço. ~ **story** conto *m*. ~ **wave** (*radio*) onda(s) *f*(*pl*) curta/s

shortage /'ʃɔːtɪdʒ/ *n* falta *f*, escassez *f*

shortbread /'ʃɔːtbred/ *n* shortbread *m*, biscoito *m* de massa amanteigada

shortcoming /'ʃɔːtkʌmɪŋ/ *n* falha *f*, imperfeição *f*

shorten /'ʃɔːtn/ *vt/i* encurtar(-se), abreviar(-se), diminuir

shorthand /'ʃɔːthænd/ *n* estenografia *f*. ~ **typist** estenodactilógrafa *f*

shortly /'ʃɔːtlɪ/ *adv* (*soon*) em breve, dentro em pouco

shot /ʃɒt/ *see* **shoot** □ *n* (*firing, bullet*) tiro *m*; (*person*) atirador *m*; (*pellets*) chumbo *m*; (*photograph*) fotografia *f*; (*injection*) injeção *f*, (*P*) injecção *f*; (*in golf, billiards*) tacada *f*. **go like a** ~ ir disparado. **have a** ~ (**at sth**) experimentar (fazer alg coisa). ~-**gun** *n* espingarda *f*, caçadeira *f*

should /ʃʊd/; *unstressed* /ʃəd/ *v aux* **you** ~ **help me** você devia me ajudar. **I** ~ **have stayed** devia ter

ficado. I ~ like to gostaria de or gostava de. if he ~ come se ele vier
shoulder /ˈʃəʊldə(r)/ n ombro m □ vt (responsibility) tomar, assumir; (burden) carregar, arcar com. ~-blade n (anat) omoplata f. ~-pad n enchimento m de ombro, ombreira f
shout /ʃaʊt/ n grito m, brado m; (very loud) berro m □ vt/i gritar (at com); (very loudly) berrar (at com). ~ down fazer calar com gritos. ~ing n gritaria f, berraria f
shove /ʃʌv/ n empurrão m □ vt/i empurrar; (colloq: put) meter, enfiar. ~ off (colloq: depart) começar a andar (colloq), dar o fora (colloq), (P) cavar (colloq)
shovel /ˈʃʌvl/ n pá f; (machine) escavadora f □ vt (pt shovelled) remover com pá
show /ʃəʊ/ vt (pt showed, pp shown) mostrar; (of dial, needle) marcar; (put on display) expor; (film) dar, passar □ vi ver-se, aparecer, estar à vista □ n mostra f, demonstração f, manifestação f; (ostentation) alarde m, espalhafato m; (exhibition) mostra f, exposição f; (theatre, cinema) espetáculo m, (P) espectáculo m, show m. for ~ para fazer vista. on ~ exposto, em exposição. ~-down n confrontação f. ~-jumping n concurso m hípico. ~ in mandar entrar. ~ off vt exibir, ostentar □ vi exibir-se, querer fazer figura. ~-off n exibicionista mf. ~ out acompanhar à porta. ~-piece n peça f digna de se expor. ~ up ser claramente visível, ver-se bem; (colloq: arrive) aparecer. ~ing n (performance) atuação f, performance f; (cinema) exibição f
shower /ˈʃaʊə(r)/ n (of rain) aguaceiro m, chuvarada f; (of blows etc) saraivada f; (in bathroom) chuveiro m, ducha f, (P) duche m □ vt ~ with cumular de, encher de □ vi tomar um banho de chuveiro or uma ducha, (P) um duche. ~y a chuvoso
showerproof /ˈʃaʊəpruːf/ a impermeável
shown /ʃəʊn/ see show
showroom /ˈʃəʊrʊm/ n espaço m de exposição, show-room m; (for cars) stand m
showy /ˈʃəʊɪ/ a (-ier, -iest) vistoso; (too bright) berrante; (pej) espalhafatoso
shrank /ʃræŋk/ see shrink
shred /ʃred/ n tira f, retalho m, farrapo m; (fig) mínimo m, sombra f □ vt (pt shredded) reduzir a tiras, estraçalhar; (culin) desfiar. ~der n trituradora f; (for paper) fragmentadora f
shrewd /ʃruːd/ a (-er, -est) astucioso,

fino, perspicaz. ~ness n astúcia f, perspicácia f
shriek /ʃriːk/ n grito m agudo, guincho m □ vt/i gritar, guinchar
shrift /ʃrɪft/ n give sb short ~ tratar alguém com brusquidão, despachar alguém sem mais cerimónias, (P) cerimónias
shrill /ʃrɪl/ a estridente, agudo
shrimp /ʃrɪmp/ n camarão m
shrine /ʃraɪn/ n (place) santuário m; (tomb) túmulo m; (casket) relicário m
shrink /ʃrɪŋk/ vt/i (pt shrank, pp shrunk) encolher; (recoil) encolher-se. ~ from esquivar-se a, fugir a (+ inf)/de (+ noun), retrair-se de. ~age n encolhimento m; (comm) contração f
shrivel /ˈʃrɪvl/ vt/i (pt shrivelled) encarquilhar(-se)
shroud /ʃraʊd/ n mortalha f □ vt (veil) encobrir, envolver
Shrove /ʃrəʊv/ n ~ Tuesday Terça-feira f gorda or de Carnaval
shrub /ʃrʌb/ n arbusto m. ~bery n arbustos mpl
shrug /ʃrʌg/ vt (pt shrugged) ~ one's shoulders encolher os ombros □ n encolher m de ombros. ~ off não dar importância a
shrunk /ʃrʌŋk/ see shrink. ~en a encolhido; (person) mirrado, chupado
shudder /ˈʃʌdə(r)/ vi arrepiar-se, estremecer, tremer □ n arrepio m, tremor m, estremecimento m. I ~ to think tremo só de pensar
shuffle /ˈʃʌfl/ vt (feet) arrastar; (cards) embaralhar □ vi arrastar os pés □ n marcha f arrastada
shun /ʃʌn/ vt (pt shunned) evitar, fugir de
shunt /ʃʌnt/ vt/i (train) mudar de linha, manobrar
shut /ʃʌt/ vt (pt shut, pres p shutting) fechar □ vi fechar-se; (shop, bank etc) encerrar, fechar. ~ down or up fechar. ~-down n encerramento m. ~ in or up trancar. ~ up vi (colloq: stop talking) calar-se □ vt (colloq: silence) mandar calar. ~ up! (colloq) cale-se!, cala a boca!
shutter /ˈʃʌtə(r)/ n taipais mpl, (P) portada f de madeira; (of laths) persiana f; (in shop) taipais mpl; (photo) obturador m
shuttle /ˈʃʌtl/ n (of spaceship) ônibus m espacial. ~ service (plane) ponte f aérea; (bus) navete f
shuttlecock /ˈʃʌtlkɒk/ n volante m
shy /ʃaɪ/ a (-er, -est) tímido, acanhado, envergonhado □ vi (horse) espantar-se (at com); (fig) assustar-se (at or away from com). ~ness n timidez f, acanhamento m, vergonha f

Siamese /saɪə'mi:z/ a & n siamês (m). ~ **cat** gato m siamês

Sicily /'sɪsɪlɪ/ n Sicília f

sick /sɪk/ a doente; (humour) negro. **be** ~ (vomit) vomitar. **be** ~ **of** estar farto de. **feel** ~ estar enjoado. ~**bay** n enfermaria f. ~**leave** n licença f por doença ~**room** n quarto m de doente

sicken /'sɪkn/ vt (distress) desesperar; (disgust) repugnar □ vi **be** ~**ing for flu** etc começar a pegar uma gripe (colloq)

sickle /'sɪkl/ n foice f

sickly /'sɪklɪ/ a (-ier, -iest) (person) doentio, achacado; (smell) enjoativo; (pale) pálido

sickness /'sɪknɪs/ n doença f; (vomiting) náusea f, vómito m; (of child) enjôo m

side /saɪd/ n lado m; (of road, river) beira f; (of hill) encosta f; (sport) equipe f, (P) equipa f □ a lateral □ vi ~ **with** tomar o partido de. **on the** ~ (extra) nas horas vagas; (secretly) pela calada. ~ **by** ~ lado a lado. ~**car** n sidecar m. ~**effect** n efeito m secundário. ~**show** n espetáculo m, (P) espectáculo m suplementar. ~**step** vt (pt -**stepped**) evitar. ~**track** vt (fazer) desviar dum propósito

sideboard /'saɪdbɔ:d/ n aparador m

sideburns /'saɪdbɜ:nz/ npl suíças fpl, costeletas fpl, (P) patilhas fpl

sidelight /'saɪdlaɪt/ n (auto) luz f lateral, (P) farolim m

sideline /'saɪdlaɪn/ n atividade f, (P) actividade f secundária; (sport) linha f lateral

sidelong /'saɪdlɒŋ/ adv & a de lado

sidewalk /'saɪdwɔ:k/ n (Amer) passeio m

sideways /'saɪdweɪz/ adv & a de lado

siding /'saɪdɪŋ/ n desvio m, ramal m

sidle /'saɪdl/ vi ~ **up (to)** avançar furtivamente (para), chegar-se furtivamente (a)

siege /si:dʒ/ n cerco m

siesta /sɪ'estə/ n sesta f

sieve /sɪv/ n peneira f; (for liquids) coador m □ vt peneirar; (liquids) passar, coar

sift /sɪft/ vt peneirar; (sprinkle) polvilhar. ~ **through** examinar minuciosamente, esquadrinhar

sigh /saɪ/ n suspiro m □ vt/i suspirar

sight /saɪt/ n vista f; (scene) cena f; (on gun) mira f □ vt avistar, ver, divisar. **at** or **on** ~ à vista. **catch** ~ **of** avistar. **in** ~ à vista, visível. **lose** ~ **of** perder de vista. **out of** ~ longe dos olhos

sightsee|**ing** /'saɪtsi:ɪŋ/ n visita f, turismo m. **go** ~**ing** visitar lugares turísticos. ~**r** /'saɪtsi:ə(r)/ n turista mf

sign /saɪn/ n sinal m; (symbol) signo m □ vt (in writing) assinar □ vi (make a sign) fazer sinal. ~ **on** or **up** (worker) assinar contrato. ~**board** n tabuleta f. ~ **language** n mímica f

signal /'sɪgnəl/ n sinal m □ vi (pt **signalled**) fazer signal □ vt comunicar (por sinais); (person) fazer sinal para. ~**box** n cabine f de sinalização

signature /'sɪgnətʃə(r)/ n assinatura f. ~ **tune** indicativo m musical

signet-ring /'sɪgnɪtrɪŋ/ n anel m de sinete

significan|**t** /sɪg'nɪfɪkənt/ a importante; (meaningful) significativo. ~**ce** n importância f; (meaning) significado m. ~**tly** adv (much) sensivelmente

signify /'sɪgnɪfaɪ/ vt significar

signpost /'saɪnpəʊst/ n poste m de sinalização □ vt sinalizar

silence /'saɪləns/ n silêncio m □ vt silenciar, calar. ~**r** /-ə(r)/ n (on gun) silenciador m; (on car) silencioso m

silent /'saɪlənt/ a silencioso; (not speaking) calado; (film) mudo. ~**ly** adv silenciosamente

silhouette /sɪlu'et/ n silhueta f □ vt **be** ~**d against** estar em silhueta contra

silicon /'sɪlɪkən/ n silicone m. ~ **chip** circuito m integrado

silk /sɪlk/ n seda f. ~**en**, ~**y** adjs sedoso

sill /sɪl/ n (of window) parapeito m; (of door) soleira f, limiar m

sill|**y** /'sɪlɪ/ a (-ier, -iest) tolo, idiota. ~**iness** n tolice f, idiotice f

silo /'saɪləʊ/ n (pl -os) silo m

silt /sɪlt/ n aluvião m, sedimento m

silver /'sɪlvə(r)/ n prata f; (silverware) prataria f, pratas fpl □ a de prata. ~ **paper** papel m prateado. ~ **wedding** bodas fpl de prata. ~**y** a prateado; (sound) argentino

silversmith /'sɪlvəsmɪθ/ n ourives m

silverware /'sɪlvəweə(r)/ n prataria f, pratas fpl

similar /'sɪmɪlə(r)/ a ~ **(to)** semelhante (a), parecido (com). ~**ity** /-ə'lærətɪ/ n semelhança f. ~**ly** adv de igual modo, analogamente

simile /'sɪmɪlɪ/ n símile m, comparação f

simmer /'sɪmə(r)/ vt/i cozinhar em fogo brando; (fig: smoulder) ferver, fremir; ~ **down** acalmar(-se)

simpl|**e** /'sɪmpl/ a (-er, -est) simples. ~**e-minded** a simples; (feeble-minded) pobre de espírito, tolo. ~**icity** /-'plɪsətɪ/ n simplicidade f.

~**y** *adv* simplesmente; (*absolutely*) absolutamente, simplesmente

simpleton /'simpltən/ *n* simplório *m*

simplif|y /'simplifai/ *vt* simplificar. ~**ication** /-i'keiʃn/ *n* simplificação *f*

simulat|e /'simjʊleit/ *vt* simular, imitar. ~**ion** /-'leiʃn/ *n* simulação *f*, imitação *f*

simultaneous /siml'teiniəs/ *a* simultâneo, concomitante. ~**ly** *adv* simultaneamente

sin /sin/ *n* pecado *m* □ *vi* (*pt* sinned) pecar

since /sins/ *prep* desde □ *adv* desde então □ *conj* desde que; (*because*) uma vez que, visto que. ~ **then** desde então

sincer|e /sin'siə(r)/ *a* sincero. ~**ely** *adv* sinceramente. ~**ity** /-'serəti/ *n* sinceridade *f*

sinew /'sinju:/ *n* (*anat*) tendão *m*. ~**s** músculos *mpl*. ~**y** *a* forte, musculoso

sinful /'sinfl/ *a* (*wicked*) pecaminoso; (*shocking*) escandaloso

sing /siŋ/ *vt/i* (*pt* sang, *pp* sung) cantar. ~**er** *n* cantor *m*

singe /sindʒ/ *vt* (*pres p* singeing) chamuscar

single /'siŋgl/ *a* único, só; (*unmarried*) solteiro; (*bed*) de solteiro; (*room*) individual; (*ticket*) de ida, simples □ *n* (*ticket*) bilhete *m* de ida *or* simples; (*record*) disco *m* de 45 r.p.m. ~**s** (*tennis*) singulares *mpl* □ *vt* ~ **out** escolher. **in** ~ **file** em fila indiana. ~-**handed** *a* sem ajuda, sozinho. ~-**minded** *a* decidido, aferrado à sua idéia, tenaz. ~ **parent** pai *m* solteiro, mãe *f* solteira. **singly** *adv* um a um, um por um

singsong /'siŋsɒŋ/ *n* **have a** ~ cantar em coro □ *a* (*voice*) monótono, monocórdico

singular /'siŋgjʊlə(r)/ *n* singular *m* □ *a* (*uncommon; gram*) singular; (*noun*) no singular. ~**ly** *adv* singularmente

sinister /'sinistə(r)/ *a* sinistro

sink /siŋk/ *vt* (*pt* sank, *pp* sunk) (*ship*) afundar, ir a pique; (*well*) abrir; (*invest money*) empatar; (*lose money*) enterrar □ *vi* afundar-se; (*of ground*) ceder; (*of voice*) baixar □ *n* pia *f*, (P) lava-louça *m*. ~ **in** (*fig*) ficar gravado, entrar (*colloq*). ~ **or swim** ou vai ou racha

sinner /'sinə(r)/ *n* pecador *m*

sinuous /'sinjʊəs/ *a* sinuoso

sinus /'sainəs/ *n* (*pl* -es) (*anat*) seio (nasal) *m*. ~**itis** /sainə'saitis/ *n* sinusite *f*

sip /sip/ *n* gole *m* □ *vt* (*pt* sipped) beberricar, beber aos golinhos

siphon /'saifn/ *n* sifão *m* □ *vt* ~ **off** extrair por meio de sifão

sir /sɜ:(r)/ *n* senhor *m*. **S~** (*title*) Sir *m*. **Dear S~** Exmo Senhor. **excuse me,** ~ desculpe, senhor. **no,** ~ não, senhor

siren /'saiərən/ *n* sereia *f*, sirene *f*

sirloin /'sɜ:lɔin/ *n* lombo *m* de vaca

sissy /'sisi/ *n* maricas *m*

sister /'sistə(r)/ *n* irmã *f*, freira *f*; (*nurse*) enfermeira-chefe *f*. ~-**in-law** (*pl* ~**s-in-law**) cunhada *f*. ~**ly** *a* fraterno, fraternal

sit /sit/ *vt/i* (*pt* sat, *pres p* sitting) sentar(-se); (*of committee etc*) reunir-se. ~ **for an exam** fazer um exame, prestar uma prova. **be** ~**ting** estar sentado. ~ **around** não fazer nada. ~ **down** sentar-se. ~-**in** *n* ocupação *f*. ~**ting** *n* reunião *f*, sessão *f*; (*in restaurant*) serviço *m*. ~**ting-room** *n* sala *f* de estar. ~ **up** endireitar-se na cadeira; (*not go to bed*) passar a noite acordado

site /sait/ *n* local *m*. (**building**) ~ terreno *m* para construção, lote *m* □ *vt* localizar, situar

situat|e /'sitʃʊeit/ *vt* situar. **be** ~**ed** estar situado. ~**ion** /-'eiʃn/ *n* (*position, condition*) situação *f*; (*job*) emprego *m*, colocação *f*

six /siks/ *a* & *n* seis (*m*). ~**th** *a* & *n* sexto (*m*)

sixteen /sik'sti:n/ *a* & *n* dezesseis *m*, (P) dezasseis (*m*). ~**th** *a* & *n* décimo sexto (*m*)

sixt|y /'siksti/ *a* & *n* sessenta (*m*). ~**ieth** *a* & *n* sexagésimo (*m*)

size /saiz/ *n* tamanho *m*; (*of person, garment*) tamanho *m*, medida *f*; (*of shoes*) número *m*; (*extent*) grandeza *f* □ *vt* ~ **up** calcular o tamanho de; (*colloq: judge*) formar um juízo sobre, avaliar. ~**able** *a* bastante grande, considerável

sizzle /'sizl/ *vi* chiar, rechinar

skate[1] /skeit/ *n* (*pl invar*) (*fish*) (ar)raia *f*

skat|e[2] /skeit/ *n* patim *m* □ *vi* patinar. ~**er** *n* patinador *m*. ~**ing** *n* patinação *f*. ~**ing-rink** *n* rinque *m* de patinação

skateboard /'skeitbɔ:d/ *n* skate *m*

skelet|on /'skelitən/ *n* esqueleto *m*; (*framework*) armação *f*. ~**on crew** *or* **staff** pessoal *m* reduzido. ~**on key** chave *f* mestra. ~**al** *a* esquelético

sketch /sketʃ/ *n* esboço *m*, croqui(s) *m*; (*theat*) sketch *m*, peça *f* curta e humorística; (*outline*) idéia *f* geral, esboço *m* □ *vt* esboçar, delinear □ *vi* fazer esboços. ~-**book** *n* caderno *m* de desenho

sketchy /'sketʃi/ *a* (-**ier**, -**iest**) incompleto, esboçado

skewer /'skjʊə(r)/ *n* espeto *m*

ski /ski:/ *n* (*pl* -**s**) esqui *m* □ *vi* (*pt* **ski'd** *or* **skied**, *pres p* **skiing**) esquiar; (*go skiing*) fazer esqui. ~**er** *n* esquiador *m*. ~**ing** *n* esqui *m*

skid /skɪd/ *vi* (*pt* **skidded**) derrapar, patinar □ *n* derrapagem *f*

skilful /'skɪlfl/ *a* hábil, habilidoso. ~**ly** *adv* habilmente, com perícia

skill /skɪl/ *n* habilidade *f*, jeito *m*; (*craft*) arte *f*. ~**s** aptidões *fpl. a* hábil, habilidoso; (*worker*) especializado

skim /skɪm/ *vt* (*pt* **skimmed**) tirar a espuma de; (*milk*) desnatar, tirar a nata de; (*pass or glide over*) deslizar sobre, roçar □ *vi* ~ **through** ler por alto, passar os olhos por. ~**med milk** leite *m* desnatado

skimp /skɪmp/ *vt/i* (*use too little*) poupar em □ *vi* ser poupado

skimpy /'skɪmpɪ/ *a* (-**ier**, -**iest**) (*clothes*) sumário; (*meal*) escasso, racionado (*fig*)

skin /skɪn/ *n* (*of person, animal*) pele *f*; (*of fruit*) casca *f* □ *vt* (*pt* **skinned**) (*animal*) esfolar, tirar a pele de; (*fruit*) descascar. ~-**diving** *n* mergulho *m*, caça *f* submarina

skinny /'skɪnɪ/ *a* (-**ier**, -**iest**) magricela, escanzelado

skint /skɪnt/ *a* (*sl*) sem dinheiro, na última lona (*sl*), (*P*) nas lonas

skip[1] /skɪp/ *vi* (*pt* **skipped**) saltar, pular; (*jump about*) saltitar; (*with rope*) pular corda □ *vt* (*page*) saltar; (*class*) faltar a □ *n* salto *m*. ~**ping rope** *n* corda *f* de pular

skip[2] /skɪp/ *n* (*container*) container *m* grande para entulho

skipper /'skɪpə(r)/ *n* capitão *m*

skirmish /'skɜ:mɪʃ/ *n* escaramuça *f*

skirt /skɜ:t/ *n* saia *f* □ *vt* contornar, ladear. ~**ing-board** *n* rodapé *m*

skit /skɪt/ *n* (*theat*) paródia *f*, sketch *m* satírico

skittle /'skɪtl/ *n* pino *m*. ~**s** *npl* boliche *m*, (*P*) jogo *m* de laranjinha

skive /skaɪv/ *vi* (*sl*) eximir-se de um dever, evitar trabalhar (*sl*)

skulk /skʌlk/ *vi* (*move*) rondar furtivamente; (*hide*) esconder-se

skull /skʌl/ *n* caveira *f*, crânio *m*

skunk /skʌŋk/ *n* (*animal*) gambá *m*

sky /skaɪ/ *n* céu *m*. ~-**blue** *a & n* azul-celeste (*m*)

skylight /'skaɪlaɪt/ *n* clarabóia *f*

skyscraper /'skaɪskreɪpə(r)/ *n* arranha-céus *m invar*

slab /slæb/ *n* (*of marble*) placa *f*; (*of paving-stone*) laje *f*; (*of metal*) chapa *f*; (*of cake*) fatia *f* grossa

slack /slæk/ *a* (-**er**, -**est**) (*rope*) bambo, frouxo; (*person*) descuidado, negligente; (*business*) parado, fraco; (*period, season*) morto □ *n* **the** ~ (*in rope*) a parte bamba □ *vt/i* (*be lazy*) estar com preguiça, fazer cera (*fig*)

slacken /'slækən/ *vt/i* (*speed, activity etc*) afrouxar, abrandar

slacks /slæks/ *npl* calças *fpl*

slag /slæg/ *n* escória *f*

slain /sleɪn/ *see* **slay**

slam /slæm/ *vt* (*pt* **slammed**) bater violentamente com; (*throw*) atirar; (*sl: criticize*) criticar, malhar □ *vi* (*door etc*) bater violentamente □ *n* (*noise*) bater *m*, pancada *f*

slander /'slɑ:ndə(r)/ *n* calúnia *f*, difamação *f* □ *vt* caluniar, difamar. ~**ous** *a* calunioso, difamatório

slang /slæŋ/ *n* calão *m*, gíria *f*. ~**y** *a* de calão

slant /slɑ:nt/ *vt/i* inclinar(-se); (*news*) apresentar de forma tendenciosa □ *n* inclinação *f*; (*bias*) tendência *f*; (*point of view*) ângulo *m*. **be** ~**ing** ser/estar inclinado *or* em declive

slap /slæp/ *vt* (*pt* **slapped**) (*strike*) bater, dar uma palmada em; (*on face*) esbofetear, dar uma bofetada em; (*put forcefully*) atirar com □ *n* palmada *f*, bofetada *f* □ *adv* em cheio. ~-**up** *a* (*sl: excellent*) excelente

slapdash /'slæpdæʃ/ *a* descuidado; (*impetuous*) precipitado

slapstick /'slæpstɪk/ *n* farsa *f* com palhaçadas

slash /slæʃ/ *vt* (*cut*) retalhar, dar golpes em; (*sever*) cortar; (*a garment*) golpear; (*fig: reduce*) reduzir drasticamente, fazer um corte radical em □ *n* corte *m*, golpe *m*

slat /slæt/ *n* (*in blind*) ripa *f*, (*P*) lâmina *f*

slate /sleɪt/ *n* ardósia *f* □ *vt* (*colloq: criticize*) criticar severamente

slaughter /'slɔ:tə(r)/ *vt* chacinar, massacrar; (*animals*) abater □ *n* chacina *f*, massacre *m*, mortandade *f*; (*animals*) abate *m*

slaughterhouse /'slɔ:təhaʊs/ *n* matadouro *m*

slave /sleɪv/ *n* escravo *m* □ *vi* mourejar, trabalhar como um escravo. ~-**driver** *n* (*fig*) o que obriga os outros a trabalharem como escravos, condutor *m* de escravos. ~**ry** /-ərɪ/ *n* escravatura *f*

slavish /'sleɪvɪʃ/ *a* servil

slay /sleɪ/ *vt* (*pt* **slew**, *pp* **slain**) matar

sleazy /'sli:zɪ/ *a* (-**ier**, -**iest**) (*colloq*) esquálido, sórdido

sledge /sledʒ/ *n* trenó *m*. ~-**hammer** *n* martelo *m* de forja, marreta *f*

sleek /sli:k/ *a* (-**er**, -**est**) liso, macio e lustroso

sleep /sli:p/ *n* sono *m* □ *vi* (*pt* **slept**) dormir □ *vt* ter lugar para, alojar. **go**

to ~ ir dormir; adormecer. **put to ~**
(*kill*) mandar matar. ~ **around** ser
promíscuo. **~er** *n* aquele que dorme;
(*rail: beam*) dormente *m*; (*berth*)
couchette *f*. **~ing-bag** *n* saco *m*
de dormir. **~ing-car** *n* carro-
dormitório *m*, carruagemcama *f*, (P)
vagon-lit *m*. **~less** *a* insone; (*night*)
em claro, insone. **~-walker** *n*
sonâmbulo *m*
sleep|y /'sli:pɪ/ *a* (-ier, -iest) sono-
lento. **be ~y** ter *or* estar com sono.
~ily *adv* meio dormindo
sleet /sli:t/ *n* geada *f* miúda □ *vi* cair
geada miúda
sleeve /sli:v/ *n* manga *f*; (*of record*)
capa *f*. **up one's ~** de reserva,
escondido. **~less** *a* sem mangas
sleigh /sleɪ/ *n* trenó *m*
sleight /slaɪt/ *n* ~ **of hand** pres-
tidigitação *f*, passe *m* de mágica
slender /'slendə(r)/ *a* esguio, esbelto;
(*fig: scanty*) escasso. **~ness** *n* aspecto
m esguio, esbelteza *f*, elegância *f*;
(*scantiness*) escassez *f*
slept /slept/ *see* **sleep**
sleuth /slu:θ/ *n* (*colloq*) detective *m*
slew[1] /slu:/ *vi* (*turn*) virar-se
slew[2] /slu:/ *see* **slay**
slice /slaɪs/ *n* fatia *f* □ *vt* cortar em
fatias; (*golf, tennis*) cortar
slick /slɪk/ *a* (*slippery*) escorregadio;
(*cunning*) astuto, habilidoso; (*unctuous*) melífluo □ *n* (*oil*) ~ mancha *f*
de óleo
slid|e /slaɪd/ *vt/i* (*pt* **slid**) escorregar,
deslizar □ *n* escorregadela *f*, escorregão *m*; (*in playground*) escorrega *m*; (*for hair*) prendedor *m*, (P)
travessa *f*; (*photo*) diapositivo *m*, slide
m. **~e-rule** *n* régua *f* de cálculo.
~ing *a* (*door, panel*) corrediço, de
correr. **~ing scale** escala *f* móvel
slight /slaɪt/ *a* (-er, -est) (*slender,
frail*) delgado, franzino; (*inconsider-
able*) leve, ligeiro □ *vt* desconsiderar,
desfeitear □ *n* desconsideração *f*, desfeita *f*. **the ~est** *a* o/a menor. **not
in the ~est** em absoluto. **~ly** *adv* ligeiramente, um pouco
slim /slɪm/ *a* (**slimmer, slimmest**)
magro, esbelto; (*chance*) pequeno, remoto □ *vi* (*pt* **slimmed**) emagrecer.
~ness *n* magreza *f*, esbelteza *f*
slim|e /slaɪm/ *n* lodo *m*. **~y** *a* lodoso;
(*slippery*) escorregadio; (*fig: servile*)
servil, bajulador
sling /slɪŋ/ *n* (*weapon*) funda *f*; (*for
arm*) tipóia *f* □ *vt* (*pt* **slung**) atirar,
lançar
slip /slɪp/ *vt/i* (*pt* **slipped**) escorregar;
(*move quietly*) mover-se de mansinho
□ *n* escorregadela *f*, escorregão *m*;
(*mistake*) engano *m*, lapso *m*; (*petti-*

coat) combinação *f*; (*of paper*) tira *f*
de papel. **give the ~ to** livrar-se de,
escapar(-se) de. **~ away** esgueirar-se.
~ by passar sem se dar conta, passar
despercebido. **~-cover** *n* (*Amer*) capa
f para móveis. **~ into** (*go*) entrar de
mansinho, enfiar-se em; (*clothes*)
enfiar. **~ of the tongue** lapso *m*.
~ped disc disco *m* deslocado. **~-
road** *n* acesso *m* à autoestrada. **~
sb's mind** passar pela cabeça de
alguém. **~ up** (*colloq*) cometer uma
gafe. **~-up** *n* (*colloq*) gafe *f*
slipper /'slɪpə(r)/ *n* chinelo *m*
slippery /'slɪpərɪ/ *a* escorregadio;
(*fig: person*) que não é de confiança,
sem escrúpulos
slipshod /'slɪpʃɒd/ *a* (*person*) desleixado, desmazelado; (*work*) feito sem
cuidado, desleixado
slit /slɪt/ *n* fenda *f*; (*cut*) corte *m*; (*tear*)
rasgão *m* □ *vt* (*pt* **slit**, *pres p* **slitting**)
fender; (*cut*) fazer um corte em, cortar
slither /'slɪðə(r)/ *vi* escorregar, resvalar
sliver /'slɪvə(r)/ *n* (*of cheese etc*) fatia *f*;
(*splinter*) lasca *f*
slobber /'slɒbə(r)/ *vi* babar-se
slog /slɒg/ *vt* (*pt* **slogged**) (*hit*) bater
com força □ *vi* (*walk*) caminhar com
passos pesados e firmes; (*work*) trabalhar duro □ *n* (*work*) trabalheira *f*;
(*walk, effort*) estafa *f*
slogan /'sləʊgən/ *n* slogan *m*, lema *m*,
palavra *f* de ordem
slop /slɒp/ *vt/i* (*pt* **slopped**) transbordar, entornar. **~s** *npl* (*dirty water*)
água(s) *f*(*pl*) suja(s); (*liquid refuse*)
despejos *mpl*
slop|e /sləʊp/ *vt/i* inclinar(-se), for-
mar declive □ *n* (*of mountain*) encosta
f; (*of street*) rampa *f*, ladeira *f*. **~ing** *a*
inclinado, em declive
sloppy /'slɒpɪ/ *a* (-ier, -iest) (*ground*)
molhado, com poças de água; (*food*)
aguado, (*clothes*) desleixado; (*work*)
descuidado, feito de qualquer jeito *or*
maneira (*colloq*); (*person*) desmazelado; (*maudlin*) piegas
slosh /slɒʃ/ *vt* entornar; (*colloq:
splash*) esparrinhar; (*sl: hit*) bater
em, dar (uma) sova em □ *vi* chapinhar
slot /slɒt/ *n* ranhura *f*; (*in timetable*)
horário *m*; (*TV*) espaço *m*; (*aviat*) slot
m □ *vt/i* (*pt* **slotted**) enfiar(-se), me-
ter(-se), encaixar (-se). **~-machine** *n*
(*for stamps, tickets etc*) distribuidor
m automático; (*for gambling*) caçaníqueis *m*, (P) slot machine *f*
sloth /sləʊθ/ *n* preguiça *f*, indolência
f; (*zool*) preguiça *f*
slouch /slaʊtʃ/ *vi* (*stand, move*) andar
com as costas curvadas; (*sit*) sentar
em má postura

slovenly /ˈslʌvnlɪ/ a desmazelado, desleixado

slow /sləʊ/ a (-er, -est) lento, vagaroso □ adv devagar, lentamente □ vt/i ~ (**up** or **down**) diminuir a velocidade, afrouxar; (auto) desacelerar. **be** ~ (clock etc) atrasar-se, estar atrasado. **in** ~ **motion** em câmara lenta. ~**ly** adv devagar, lentamente, vagarosamente

slow|coach /ˈsləʊkəʊtʃ/, (Amer) ~**poke** ns lesma m/f, (P) pastelão m (fig)

sludge /slʌdʒ/ n lama f, lodo m

slug /slʌg/ n lesma f

sluggish /ˈslʌgɪʃ/ a (slow) lento, moroso; (lazy) indolente, preguiçoso

sluice /sluːs/ n (gate) comporta f; (channel) canal m □ vt lavar com jorros de água

slum /slʌm/ n favela f, (P) bairro m da lata; (building) cortiço m

slumber /ˈslʌmbə(r)/ n sono m □ vi dormir

slump /slʌmp/ n (in prices) baixa f, descida f; (in demand) quebra f na procura; (econ) depressão f □ vi (fall limply) cair, afundar-se; (of price) baixar bruscamente

slung /slʌŋ/ see **sling**

slur /slɜː(r)/ vt/i (pt **slurred**) (speech) pronunciar indistintamente, mastigar □ n (in speech) som m indistinto; (discredit) nódoa f, estigma m

slush /slʌʃ/ n (snow) neve f meio derretida. ~ **fund** (comm) fundo m para subornos. ~**y** a (road) coberto de neve derretida, lamacento

slut /slʌt/ n (dirty woman) porca f, desmazelada f; (immoral woman) desavergonhada f

sly /slaɪ/ a (**slyer, slyest**) (crafty) manhoso; (secretive) sonso □ n **on the** ~ na calada. ~**ly** adv (craftily) astutamente; (secretively) sonsamente

smack[1] /smæk/ n palmada f, (on face) bofetada f □ vt dar uma palmada or tapa em; (on the face) esbofetear, dar uma bofetada em □ adv (colloq) em cheio, direto

smack[2] /smæk/ vi ~ **of sth** cheirar a alg coisa

small /smɔːl/ a (-er, -est) pequeno □ n ~ **of the back** zona f dos rins □ adv (cut etc) em pedaços pequenos, aos bocadinhos. ~ **change** trocado m, dinheiro m miúdo. ~ **talk** conversa f fiada, bate-papo m. ~**ness** n pequenez f

smallholding /ˈsmɔːlhəʊldɪŋ/ n pequena propriedade f

smallpox /ˈsmɔːlpɒks/ n variola f

smarmy /ˈsmɑːmɪ/ a (-ier, -iest) (colloq) bajulador, puxa-saco (colloq)

smart /smɑːt/ a (-er, -est) elegante;

(clever) esperto, vivo; (brisk) rápido □ vi (sting) arder, picar. ~**ly** adv elegantemente, com elegância; (cleverly) com esperteza, vivamente; (briskly) rapidamente. ~**ness** n elegância f

smarten /ˈsmɑːtn/ vt/i ~ (**up**) arranjar, dar um ar mais cuidado a. ~ (**o.s.**) **up** embelezar-se, arrumar-se, (P) pôr-se elegante/bonito; (tidy) arranjar-se

smash /smæʃ/ vt/i (to pieces) despedaçar(-se), espatifar(-se) (colloq); (a record) quebrar; (opponent) esmagar; (ruin) (fazer) falir; (of vehicle) espatifar(-se) □ n (noise) estrondo m; (blow) pancada f forte, golpe m; (collision) colisão f; (tennis) smash m

smashing /ˈsmæʃɪŋ/ a (colloq) formidável, estupendo (colloq)

smattering /ˈsmætərɪŋ/ n leves noções fpl

smear /smɪə(r)/ vt (stain; discredit) manchar; (coat) untar, besuntar □ n mancha f, nódoa f; (med) esfregaço m

smell /smel/ n cheiro m, odor m; (sense) cheiro m, olfato m, (P) olfacto m □ vt/i (pt **smelt** or **smelled**) ~ (**of**) cheirar (a). ~**y** a malcheiroso

smelt[1] /smelt/ see **smell**

smelt[2] /smelt/ vt (ore) fundir

smile /smaɪl/ n sorriso m □ vi sorrir. ~**ing** a sorridente, risonho

smirk /smɜːk/ n sorriso m falso or afetado, (P) afectado

smithereens /smɪðəˈriːnz/ npl **to** or **in** ~ em pedaços mpl

smock /smɒk/ n guarda-pó m

smog /smɒg/ n mistura f de nevoeiro e fumaça, smog m

smoke /sməʊk/ n fumo m, fumaça f □ vt fumar; (bacon etc) fumar, defumar □ vi fumar, fumegar. ~-**screen** n (lit & fig) cortina f de fumaça. ~-**less** a (fuel) sem fumo. ~**r** /-ə(r)/ n (person) fumante mf, (P) fumador m. **smoky** a (air) enfumaçado, fumacento

smooth /smuːð/ a (-er, -est) liso; (soft) macio; (movement) regular, suave; (manners) lisonjeiro, conciliador, suave □ vt alisar. ~ **out** (fig) aplanar, remover. ~**ly** adv suavemente, facilmente

smother /ˈsmʌðə(r)/ vt (stifle) abafar, sufocar; (cover, overwhelm) cobrir (**with** de); (suppress) abafar, reprimir

smoulder /ˈsməʊldə(r)/ vi (lit & fig) arder, abrasar-se

smudge /smʌdʒ/ n mancha f, borrão m □ vt/i sujar(-se), manchar(-se), borrar(-se)

smug /smʌg/ a (**smugger, smuggest**) presunçoso, convencido (colloq). ~**ly** adv presunçosamente. ~**ness** n presunção f

smuggl|e /'smʌgl/ vt contrabandear, fazer contrabando de. ~**er** n contrabandista mf. ~**ing** n contrabando m

smut /smʌt/ n fuligem f. ~**ty** a cheio de fuligem; (colloq: obscene) indecente, sujo (colloq)

snack /snæk/ n refeição f ligeira. ~**bar** n lanchonete f, (P) snack(-bar)

snag /snæg/ n (obstacle) obstáculo m; (drawback) problema m, contra m; (in cloth) rasgão m; (in stocking) fio m puxado

snail /sneɪl/ n caracol m. at a ~'s pace em passo de tartaruga

snake /sneɪk/ n serpente f, cobra f

snap /snæp/ vt/i (pt snapped) (whip, fingers) (fazer) estalar; (break) estalar(-se), partir(-se) com um estalo, rebentar; (say) dizer irritadamente □ n estalo m; (photo) instantâneo m (Amer: fastener) mola f □ a súbito, repentino; (speak angrily) retrucar asperamente. ~ **at** (bite) abocanhar, tentar morder; (speak angrily) retrucar asperamente. ~ **up** (buy) comprar rapidamente

snappish /'snæpɪʃ/ a irritadiço

snappy /'snæpɪ/ a (-ier, -iest) (colloq) vivo, animado. make it ~ (colloq) vai rápido!, apresse-se! (colloq)

snapshot /'snæpʃɒt/ n instantâneo m

snare /sneə(r)/ n laço m, cilada f, armadilha f

snarl /snɑːl/ vi rosnar □ n rosnadela f

snatch /snætʃ/ vt (grab) agarrar, apanhar; (steal) roubar. ~ **from** sb arrancar de alguém □ n (theft) roubo m; (bit) bocado m, pedaço m

sneak /sniːk/ vi (slink) esgueirar-se furtivamente; (sl: tell tales) fazer queixa, delatar □ vt (sl: steal) rapinar (colloq) □ n (sl) dedo-duro m, queixinhas mf (sl). ~**ing** a secreto. ~**y** a sonso

sneer /snɪə(r)/ n sorriso m de desdém □ vi sorrir desdenhosamente

sneeze /sniːz/ n espirro m □ vi espirrar

snide /snaɪd/ a (colloq) sarcástico

sniff /snɪf/ vi fungar □ vt/i ~ (at) (smell) cheirar; (dog) farejar. ~ **at** (fig: in contempt) desprezar □ n fungadela f

snigger /'snɪgə(r)/ n riso m abafado □ vi rir dissimuladamente

snip /snɪp/ vt (pt snipped) cortar com tesoura □ n pedaço m, retalho m; (sl: bargain) pechincha f

snipe /snaɪp/ vi dar tiros de emboscada. ~**r** /-ə(r)/ n franco-atirador m

snivel /'snɪvl/ vi (pt snivelled) choramingar, lamuriar-se

snob /snɒb/ n esnobe mf, (P) snob mf. ~**bery** n esnobismo m, (P) snobismo m. ~**bish** a esnobe, (P) snob

snooker /'snuːkə(r)/ n snooker m, sinuca f

snoop /snuːp/ vi (colloq) bisbilhotar, meter o nariz em toda a parte. ~ **on** espiar, espionar. ~**er** n bisbilhoteiro m

snooty /'snuːtɪ/ a (-ier, -iest) (colloq) convencido, arrogante (colloq)

snooze /snuːz/ n (colloq) soneca f (colloq) □ vi (colloq) tirar uma soneca

snore /snɔː(r)/ n ronco m □ vi roncar

snorkel /'snɔːkl/ n tubo m de respiração, snorkel m

snort /snɔːt/ n resfôlego m , bufido m □ vi resfolegar, bufar

snout /snaʊt/ n focinho m

snow /snəʊ/ n neve f □ vi nevar. be ~**ed under** (fig: be overwhelmed) estar sobrecarregado (of). ~**-bound** a bloqueado pela neve. ~**-drift** n banco m de neve. ~**-plough** n limpa-neve m. ~**y** a nevado, coberto de neve

snowball /'snəʊbɔːl/ n bola f de neve □ vi atirar bolas de neve (em); (fig) acumular-se, ir num crescendo, aumentar rapidamente

snowdrop /'snəʊdrɒp/ n (bot) furaneve m

snowfall /'snəʊfɔːl/ n nevada f, (P) nevão m

snowflake /'snəʊfleɪk/ n floco m de neve

snowman /'snəʊmæn/ n (pl -men) boneco m de neve

snub /snʌb/ vt (pt snubbed) desdenhar, tratar com desdém □ n desdém m

snuff¹ /snʌf/ n rapé m

snuff² /snʌf/ vt ~ **out** (candles, hopes etc) apagar, extinguir

snuffle /'snʌfl/ vi fungar

snug /snʌg/ a (snugger, snuggest) (cosy) aconchegado; (close-fitting) justo

snuggle /'snʌgl/ vt/i (nestle) aninhar-se, aconchegar-se; (cuddle) aconchegar

so /səʊ/ adv tão, de tal modo; (thus) assim, deste modo □ conj por isso, portanto, por consequente. ~ **am I** eu também. ~ **does he** ele também. **that is** ~ é isso. **I think** ~ acho que sim. **five or** ~ uns cinco. ~ **as to** de modo a. ~ **far** até agora, até aqui. ~ **long!** (colloq) até já! (colloq). ~ **many** tantos. ~ **much** tanto. ~ **that** para que, de modo que. ~**-and-**~ fulano m. ~**-called** a pretenso, soidisant. ~**-so** a & adv assim assim, mais ou menos

soak /səʊk/ vt/i molhar(-se), ensopar(-se), encharcar(-se), (P) pôr de molho. ~ **in** or **up** vt absorver, embeber. ~ **through** repassar. ~**ing** a ensopado, encharcado

soap /səʊp/ n sabão m.　(toilet) ~ sabonete m □ vt ensaboar. ~ **opera** (radio) novela f radiofónica, (P) radiofónica; (TV) telenovela f. ~ **flakes** flocos mpl de sabão. ~ **powder** sabão m em pó. ~y a ensaboado

soar /sɔ:(r)/ vi voar alto; (go high) elevar-se; (hover) pairar

sob /sɒb/ n soluço m □ vi (pt sobbed) soluçar

sober /'səʊbə(r)/ a (not drunk, calm, of colour) sóbrio; (serious) sério, grave □ vt/i ~ **up** (fazer) ficar sóbrio, (fazer) curar a bebedeira (colloq)

soccer /'sɒkə(r)/ n (colloq) futebol m

sociable /'səʊʃəbl/ a sociável

social /'səʊʃl/ a social; (sociable) sociável; (gathering, life) de sociedade □ n reunião f social. ~**ly** adv socialmente; (meet) em sociedade. ~ **security** previdência f social, (P for old age) pensão f. ~ **worker** assistente mf social

socialis|t /'səʊʃəlɪst/ n socialista mf. ~**m** /-zəm/ n socialismo m

socialize /'səʊʃəlaɪz/ vi socializar-se, reunir-se em sociedade. ~ **with** freqüentar, (P) frequentar, conviver com

society /sə'saɪətɪ/ n sociedade f

sociolog|y /səʊsɪ'ɒlədʒɪ/ n sociologia f. ~**ical** /-ə'lɒdʒɪkl/ a sociológico. ~**ist** n sociólogo m

sock[1] /sɒk/ n meia f curta; (men's) meia f (curta), (P) peúga f; (women's) soquete f

sock[2] /sɒk/ vt (sl: hit) esmurrar, dar um murro em (colloq)

socket /'sɒkɪt/ n cavidade f; (for lamp) suporte m; (electr) tomada f; (of tooth) alvéolo m

soda /'səʊdə/ n soda f. **baking** ~ (culin) bicarbonato m de soda. ~ (-**water**) água f gasosa, soda f limonada, (P) água f gaseificada

sodden /'sɒdn/ a ensopado, empapado

sodium /'səʊdɪəm/ n sódio m

sofa /'səʊfə/ n sofá m

soft /sɒft/ a (-**er**, -**est**) (not hard, feeble) mole; (not rough, not firm) macio; (gentle, not loud, not bright) suave; (tender-hearted) sensível; (fruit) sem caroço; (wood) de coníferas; (drink) não alcoólico. ~-**boiled** a (egg) quente. ~ **spot** (fig) fraco m. ~**ly** adv docemente. ~**ness** n moleza f; (to touch) maciez f; (gentleness) suavidade f, brandura f

soften /'sɒfn/ vt/i amaciar, amolecer; (tone down, lessen) abrandar

software /'sɒftweə(r)/ n software m

soggy /'sɒgɪ/ a (-**ier**, -**iest**) ensopado, empapado

soil[1] /sɔɪl/ n solo m, terra f

soil[2] /sɔɪl/ vt/i sujar(-se). ~**ed** a sujo

solace /'sɒlɪs/ n consolo m; (relief) alívio m

solar /'səʊlə(r)/ a solar

sold /səʊld/ see **sell** □ a ~ **out** esgotado

solder /'səʊldə(r)/ n solda f □ vt soldar

soldier /'səʊldʒə(r)/ n soldado m □ vi ~ **on** (colloq) perseverar com afinco, batalhar (colloq)

sole[1] /səʊl/ n (of foot) planta f, sola f do pé; (of shoe) sola f

sole[2] /səʊl/ n (fish) solha f

sole[3] /səʊl/ a único. ~**ly** adv unicamente

solemn /'sɒləm/ a solene. ~**ity** /sə'lemnətɪ/ n solenidade f. ~**ly** adv solenemente

solicit /sə'lɪsɪt/ vt (seek) solicitar □ vi (of prostitute) aproximar-se de homens na rua

solicitor /sə'lɪsɪtə(r)/ n advogado m

solicitous /sə'lɪsɪtəs/ a solícito

solid /'sɒlɪd/ a sólido; (not hollow) maciço, cheio, compacto; (gold etc) maciço; (meal) substancial □ n sólido m. ~**s** (food) alimentos mpl sólidos. ~**ity** /sə'lɪdətɪ/ n solidez f. ~**ly** adv solidamente

solidarity /sɒlɪ'dærətɪ/ n solidariedade f

solidify /sə'lɪdɪfaɪ/ vt/i solidificar(-se)

soliloquy /sə'lɪləkwɪ/ n monólogo m, solilóquio m

solitary /'sɒlɪtrɪ/ a solitário, só; (only one) um único. ~ **confinement** prisão f celular, solitária f

solitude /'sɒlɪtju:d/ n solidão f

solo /'səʊləʊ/ n (pl -**os**) solo m □ a solo. ~ **flight** vôo m solo. ~**ist** n solista mf

soluble /'sɒljʊbl/ a solúvel

solution /sə'lu:ʃn/ n solução f

solve /sɒlv/ vt resolver, solucionar. ~**able** a resolúvel, solúvel

solvent /'sɒlvənt/ a (dis)solvente; (comm) solvente □ n (dis)solvente m

sombre /'sɒmbə(r)/ a sombrio

some /sʌm/ a (quantity) algum(a); (number) alguns, algumas, uns, umas; (unspecified, some or other) um(a)... qualquer, uns... quaisquer, umas... quaisquer; (a little) um pouco de, algum; (a certain) um certo; (contrasted with others) uns, umas, alguns, algumas, certos, certas □ pron uns, umas, algum(a), alguns, algumas; (a little) um pouco, algum □ adv (approximately) uns, umas. **will you have** ~ **coffee/**etc? você quer café/etc? ~ **day** algum dia. ~ **of my friends** alguns dos meus amigos. ~ **people say...** algumas pessoas dizem... ~ **time ago** algum tempo atrás

somebody /'sʌmbədɪ/ *pron* alguém □ *n* be a ~ ser alguém

somehow /'sʌmhaʊ/ *adv* (*in some way*) de algum modo, de alguma maneira; (*for some reason*) por alguma razão

someone /'sʌmwʌn/ *pron* & *n* = **somebody**

somersault /'sʌməsɔ:lt/ *n* cambalhota *f*; (*in the air*) salto *m* mortal □ *vi* dar uma cambalhota/um salto mortal

something /'sʌmθɪŋ/ *pron* & *n* uma/alguma/qualquer coisa *f*, algo. ~ **good**/*etc* uma coisa boa/*etc*, qualquer coisa de bom/*etc*. ~ **like** um pouco como

sometime /'sʌmtaɪm/ *adv* a certa altura, um dia □ *a* (*former*) antigo. ~ **last summer** a certa altura no verão passado. **I'll go** ~ hei de ir um dia

sometimes /'sʌmtaɪmz/ *adv* às vezes, de vez em quando

somewhat /'sʌmwɒt/ *adv* um pouco, um tanto (ou quanto)

somewhere /'sʌmweə(r)/ *adv* (*position*) em algum lugar; (*direction*) para algum lugar

son /sʌn/ *n* filho *m*. ~**-in-law** *n* (*pl* ~**s-in-law**) genro *m*

sonar /'səʊna:(r)/ *n* sonar *m*

sonata /sə'na:tə/ *n* (*mus*) sonata *f*

song /sɒŋ/ *n* canção *f*. ~**-bird** *n* ave *f* canora

sonic /'sɒnɪk/ *a* ~ **boom** estrondo *m* sónico, (*P*) sónico

sonnet /'sɒnɪt/ *n* soneto *m*

soon /su:n/ *adv* (-**er**, -**est**) em breve, dentro em pouco, daqui a pouco; (*early*) cedo. **as** ~ **as possible** o mais rápido possível. **I would** ~**er stay** preferia ficar. ~ **after** pouco depois. ~**er or later** mais cedo ou mais tarde

soot /sʊt/ *n* fuligem *f*. ~**y** *a* coberto de fuligem

sooth|e /su:ð/ *vt* acalmar, suavizar; (*pain*) aliviar. ~**ing** *a* (*remedy*) calmante, suavizante; (*words*) confortante

sophisticated /sə'fɪstɪkeɪtɪd/ *a* sofisticado, refinado, requintado; (*machine etc*) sofisticado

soporific /sɒpə'rɪfɪk/ *a* soporífico

sopping /'sɒpɪŋ/ *a* encharcado, ensopado

soppy /'sɒpɪ/ *a* (-**ier**, -**iest**) (*colloq: sentimental*) piegas; (*colloq: silly*) bobo

soprano /sə'pra:nəʊ/ *n* (*pl* ~**s**) & *adj* soprano (*mf*)

sorbet /'sɔ:beɪ/ *n* (*water-ice*) sorvete *m* feito sem leite

sorcerer /'sɔ:sərə(r)/ *n* feiticeiro *m*

sordid /'sɔ:dɪd/ *a* sórdido

sore /sɔ:(r)/ *a* (-**er**, -**est**) dolorido; (*vexed*) aborrecido (**at, with** com) □ *n* ferida *f*. **have a** ~ **throat** ter a garganta inflamada, ter dores de garganta

sorely /'sɔ:lɪ/ *adv* fortemente, seriamente

sorrow /'sɒrəʊ/ *n* dor *f*, mágoa *f*, pesar *m*. ~**ful** *a* pesaroso, triste

sorry /'sɒrɪ/ *a* (-**ier**, -**iest**) (*state, sight etc*) triste. **be** ~ **to/that** (*regretful*) sentir muito/que, lamentar que; **be** ~ **about/for** (*repentant*) ter pena de, estar arrependido de. **feel** ~ **for** ter pena de. ~**!** desculpe!, perdão!

sort /sɔ:t/ *n* género *m*, (*P*) género *m*, espécie *f*, qualidade *f*. ~ **of** (*colloq*) uma espécie de (*colloq, pej*). **out of** ~**s** indisposto □ *vt* separar por grupos; (*tidy*) arrumar. ~ **out** (*problem*) resolver; (*arrange, separate*) separar, distribuir

soufflé /'su:fleɪ/ *n* (*culin*) suflê *m*, (*P*) soufflé *m*

sought /sɔ:t/ *see* **seek**

soul /səʊl/ *n* alma *f*. **the life and** ~ **of** (*fig*) a alma *f* de (*fig*)

soulful /'səʊlfl/ *a* emotivo, expressivo, cheio de sentimento

sound[1] /saʊnd/ *n* som *m*, barulho *m*, ruído *m* □ *vt/i* soar; (*seem*) dar a impressão de, parecer (**as if** que). ~ **a horn** tocar uma buzina, buzinar. ~ **barrier** barreira *f* de som. ~ **like** parecer ser, soar como. ~**-proof** *a* à prova de som □ *vt* fazer o isolamento sonoro de, isolar. ~**-track** *n* (*of film*) trilha *f* sonora, (*P*) banda *f* sonora

sound[2] /saʊnd/ *a* (-**er**, -**est**) (*healthy*) saudável, sadio; (*sensible*) sensato, acertado; (*secure*) firme, sólido. ~ **asleep** profundamente adormecido. ~**ly** *adv* solidamente

sound[3] /saʊnd/ *vt* (*test*) sondar; (*med; views*) auscultar

soup /su:p/ *n* sopa *f*

sour /'saʊə(r)/ *a* (-**er**, -**est**) azedo □ *vt/i* azedar, envinagrar

source /sɔ:s/ *n* fonte *f*; (*of river*) nascente *f*

souse /saʊs/ *vt* (*throw water on*) atirar água em cima de; (*pickle*) pôr em vinagre; (*salt*) pôr em salmoura

south /saʊθ/ *n* sul *m* □ *a* a sul, do sul; (*of country, people etc*) meridional □ *adv* a, ao/para o sul. **S~ Africa/ America** África *f*/ América *f* do Sul. **S~ African/American** *a* & *n* sul-africano (*m*)/sul-americano (*m*). ~**-east** *n* sudeste *m*. ~**erly** /'sʌðəlɪ/ *a* do sul, meridional. ~**ward** *a* ao sul. ~**ward(s)** *adv* para o sul. ~**-west** *n* sudoeste *m*

southern /'sʌðən/ *a* do sul, meridional, austral

souvenir /suːvəˈnɪə(r)/ n recordação f, lembrança f

sovereign /ˈsɒvrɪn/ n & a soberano (m). ~**ty** n soberania f

Soviet /ˈsəʊvɪət/ a soviético. **the S~ Union** a União Soviética

sow[1] /səʊ/ vt (pt sowed, pp sowed or sown) semear

sow[2] /saʊ/ n (zool) porca f

soy /sɔɪ/ n ~ **sauce** molho m de soja

soya /ˈsɔɪə/ n soja f. ~-**bean** semente f de soja

spa /spɑː/ n termas fpl

space /speɪs/ n espaço m; (room) lugar m; (period) espaço m, período m □ a (research etc) espacial □ vt ~ **out** espaçar

space|craft /ˈspeɪskrɑːft/ n (pl invar), ~**ship** n nave espacial

spacious /ˈspeɪʃəs/ a espaçoso

spade /speɪd/ n (gardener's) pá f de ferro; (child's) pá f. ~**s** (cards) espadas fpl

spadework /ˈspeɪdwɜːk/ n (fig) trabalho m preliminar

spaghetti /spəˈgetɪ/ n esparguete m, (P) esparguete m

Spain /speɪn/ n Espanha f

span[1] /spæn/ n (of arch) vão m; (of wings) envergadura f; (of time) espaço m, duração f; (measure) palmo m □ vt (pt spanned) (extend across) transpor; (measure) medir em palmos; (in time) abarcar, abranger, estender-se por

span[2] /spæn/ see **spick**

Spaniard /ˈspænɪəd/ n espanhol m

Spanish /ˈspænɪʃ/ a espanhol □ n (lang) espanhol m

spaniel /ˈspænɪəl/ n spaniel m, epagneul m

spank /spæŋk/ vt dar palmadas or chineladas no. ~**ing** n (with hand) palmada f; (with slipper) chinelada f

spanner /ˈspænə(r)/ n (tool) chave f de porcas; (adjustable) chave f inglesa

spar /spɑː(r)/ vi (pt sparred) jogar boxe, esp para treino; (fig: argue) discutir

spare /speə(r)/ vt (not hurt; use with restraint) poupar; (do without) dispensar, ceder □ a (in reserve) de reserva, de sobra; (tyre) sobressalente; (bed) extra; (room) de hóspedes □ n (part) sobressalente m. ~ **time** horas fpl vagas. **have an hour to ~** dispor de uma hora. **have no time to ~** não ter tempo a perder

sparing /ˈspeərɪŋ/ a poupado. **be ~ of** poupar em, ser poupado com. ~**ly** adv frugalmente

spark /spɑːk/ n centelha f, faísca f □ vt lançar faíscas. ~ **off** (initiate) desencadear, provocar. ~**(ing)-plug** n vela f de ignição

sparkle /ˈspɑːkl/ vi cintilar, brilhar □ n brilho m, cintilação f

sparkling /ˈspɑːklɪŋ/ a (wine) espumante

sparrow /ˈspærəʊ/ n pardal m

sparse /spɑːs/ a raro; (hair) ralo. ~**ly** adv (furnished etc) escassamente

spasm /ˈspæzəm/ n (of muscle) espasmo m; (of coughing, anger etc) ataque m, acesso m

spasmodic /spæzˈmɒdɪk/ a espasmódico; (at irregular intervals) intermitente

spastic /ˈspæstɪk/ n deficiente mf motor

spat /spæt/ see **spit**[1]

spate /speɪt/ n (in river) enxurrada f, cheia f. **a ~ of** (letters etc) uma avalanche de

spatter /ˈspætə(r)/ vt salpicar (**with** de, com)

spawn /spɔːn/ n ovas fpl □ vi desovar □ vt gerar em quantidade

speak /spiːk/ vt/i (pt spoke, pp spoken) falar (to/with sb about sth com alguém de/sobre alg coisa); (say) dizer. ~ **out/up** falar abertamente; (louder) falar mais alto. ~ **one's mind** dizer o que se pensa. **so to ~** por assim dizer. **English/Portuguese spoken** fala-se português/inglês

speaker /ˈspiːkə(r)/ n (in public) orador m; (loudspeaker) alto-falante m; (of a language) pessoa f de língua nativa

spear /spɪə(r)/ n lança f

spearhead /ˈspɪəhed/ n ponta f de lança □ vt (lead) estar à frente de, encabeçar

special /ˈspeʃl/ a especial. ~**ity** /-rˈælətɪ/ n especialidade f. ~**ly** adv especialmente. ~**ty** n especialidade f

specialist /ˈspeʃəlɪst/ n especialista mf

specialize /ˈspeʃəlaɪz/ vi especializar-se (**in** em). ~**d** a especializado

species /ˈspiːʃiːz/ n (pl invar) espécie f

specific /spəˈsɪfɪk/ a específico. ~**ally** adv especificamente, explicitamente

specif|y /ˈspesɪfaɪ/ vt especificar. ~**ication** /-rˈkeɪʃn/ n especificação f. ~**ications** npl (of work etc) caderno m de encargos

specimen /ˈspesɪmɪn/ n espécime(n) m, amostra f

speck /spek/ n (stain) mancha f pequena; (dot) pontinho m, pinta f; (particle) grão m

speckled /ˈspekld/ a salpicado, manchado

specs /speks/ *npl* (*colloq*) óculos *mpl*

spectacle /'spektəkl/ *n* espetáculo *m*, (P) espectáculo *m*. **(pair of)** ~**s** (par *m* de) óculos *mpl*

spectacular /spek'tækjʊlə(r)/ *a* espetacular, (P) espectacular

spectator /spek'teitə(r)/ *n* espectador *m*

spectre /'spektə(r)/ *n* espectro *m*, fantasma *m*

spectrum /'spektrəm/ *n* (*pl* **-tra**) espectro *m*; (*of ideas etc*) faixa *f*, gama *f*, leque *m*

speculat|e /'spekjʊleit/ *vi* especular, fazer especulações *or* conjeturas, (P) conjeturas (**about** sobre); (*comm*) especular, fazer especulação (**in** em). ~**ion** /-'leiʃn/ *n* especulação *f*, conjetura *f*, (P) conjectura *f*; (*comm*) especulação *f*. ~**or** *n* especulador *m*

speech /spi:tʃ/ *n* (*faculty*) fala *f*; (*diction*) elocução *f*; (*dialect*) falar *m*; (*address*) discurso *m*. ~**less** *a* mudo, sem fala (**with** com, de)

speed /spi:d/ *n* velocidade *f*, rapidez *f* □ *vt/i* (*pt* **sped**) (*move*) ir depressa *or* a grande velocidade; (*send*) despedir, mandar; (*pt* **speeded**) (*drive too fast*) ultrapassar o limite de velocidade. ~ **limit** limite *m* de velocidade. ~ **up** acelerar(-se). ~**ing** *n* excesso *m* de velocidade

speedometer /spi:'dɒmitə(r)/ *n* velocímetro *m*, (P) conta-quilómetros *m* *inv*

speed|y /'spi:di/ *a* (**-ier, -iest**) rápido; (*prompt*) pronto. ~**ily** *adv* rapidamente; (*promptly*) prontamente

spell[1] /spel/ *n* (*magic*) sortilégio *m*

spell[2] /spel/ *vt/i* (*pt* **spelled** *or* **spelt**) escrever; (*fig: mean*) ter como resultado. ~ **out** soletrar; (*fig: explain*) explicar claramente. ~**ing** *n* ortografia *f*

spell[3] /spel/ *n* (*short period*) período *m* curto, breve espaço *m* de tempo; (*turn*) turno *m*

spend /spend/ *vt* (*pt* **spent**) (*money, energy*) gastar (**on** em); (*time, holiday*) passar. ~**er** *n* gastador *m*

spendthrift /'spendθrift/ *n* perdulário *m*, esbanjador *m*

spent /spent/ *see* **spend** □ *a* (*used*) gasto

sperm /spɜːm/ *n* (*pl* **sperms** *or* **sperm**) (*semen*) esperma *m*, sémen *m*, (P) sémen *m*; (*cell*) espermatozóide *m*

spew /spju:/ *vt/i* vomitar, lançar

sphere /sfiə(r)/ *n* esfera *f*

spherical /'sferikl/ *a* esférico

spic|e /spais/ *n* especiaria *f*, condimento *m*; (*fig*) picante *m* □ *vt* condimentar. ~**y** *a* condimentado; (*fig*) picante

spick /spik/ *a* ~ **and span** novo em folha, impecável

spider /'spaidə(r)/ *n* aranha *f*

spik|e /spaik/ *n* (*of metal etc*) bico *m*, espigão *m*, ponta *f*. ~**y** *a* guarnecido de bicos *or* pontas

spill /spil/ *vt/i* (*pt* **spilled** *or* **spilt**) derramar(-se), entornar(-se), espalhar(-se). ~ **over** transbordar, extravasar

spin /spin/ *vt/i* (*pt* **spun**, *pres p* **spinning**) (*wool, cotton*) fiar; (*web*) tecer; (*turn*) (fazer) girar, (fazer) rodopiar. ~ **out** (*money, story*) fazer durar; (*time*) (fazer) parar □ *n* volta *f*; (*aviat*) parafuso *m*. **go for a** ~ dar uma volta *or* um giro. ~**-drier** *n* centrifugadora *f* para a roupa, secadora *f*. ~**ning-wheel** *n* roda *f* de fiar. ~**-off** *n* bónus *m*, (P) bónus *m* inesperado; (*by-product*) derivado *m*

spinach /'spinidʒ/ *n* (*plant*) espinafre *m*; (*as food*) espinafres *mpl*

spinal /'spainl/ *a* vertebral. ~ **cord** espina *f* dorsal

spindl|e /'spindl/ *n* roca *f*, fuso *m*; (*mech*) eixo *m*. ~**y** *a* alto e magro; (*of plant*) espigado

spine /spain/ *n* espinha *f*, coluna *f* vertebral; (*prickle*) espinho *m*, pico *m*; (*of book*) lombada *f*

spineless /'spainlis/ *a* (*fig: cowardly*) covarde, sem fibra (*fig*)

spinster /'spinstə(r)/ *n* solteira *f*; (*pej*) solteirona *f*

spiral /'spaiərəl/ *a* (em) espiral; (*staircase*) em caracol □ *n* espiral *f* □ *vi* (*pt* **spiralled**) subir em espiral

spire /spaiə(r)/ *n* agulha *f*, flecha *f*

spirit /'spirit/ *n* espírito *m*; (*boldness*) coragem *f*, brio *m*. ~**s** (*morale*) moral *m*; (*drink*) bebidas *fpl* alcoólicas, (P) bebidas *fpl* espirituosas. **in high** ~**s** alegre □ *vt* ~ **away** dar sumiço em, arrebatar. ~**-level** *n* nível *m* de bolha de ar

spirited /'spiritid/ *a* fogoso; (*attack, defence*) vigoroso, enérgico

spiritual /'spiritʃʊəl/ *a* espiritual

spiritualism /'spiritʃʊəlizəm/ *n* espiritismo *m*

spit[1] /spit/ *vt/i* (*pt* **spat** *or* **spit**, *pres p* **spitting**) cuspir; (*of rain*) chuviscar; (*of cat*) bufar □ *n* cuspe *m*, (P) cuspo *m*. **the** ~**ting image of** o retrato vivo de, a cara chapada de (*colloq*)

spit[2] /spit/ *n* (*for meat*) espeto *m*; (*of land*) restinga *f*, (P) língua *f* de terra

spite /spait/ *n* má vontade *f*, rancor *m*, rancor □ *vt* aborrecer, mortificar. **in** ~ **of** a despeito de, apesar de. ~**ful** *a* rancoroso, maldoso. ~**fully** *adv* rancorosamente, maldosamente

spittle /'spɪtl/ n cuspe m, (P) cuspo m, saliva f

splash /splæʃ/ vt salpicar, respingar □ vi esparrinhar, esparramar-se. ~ (about) chapinhar □ n (act, mark) salpico m; (sound) chape m; (of colour) mancha f. **make a ~** (striking display) fazer um vistão, causar furor

spleen /spli:n/ n (anat) baço m. **vent one's ~ on sb** descarregar a neura em alguém (colloq)

splendid /'splendɪd/ a esplêndido, magnífico; (excellent) estupendo (colloq), ótimo, (P) óptimo

splendour /'splendə(r)/ n esplendor m

splint /splɪnt/ n (med) tala f

splinter /'splɪntə(r)/ n lasca f, estilhaço m; (under the skin) farpa f, lasca f □ vi estilhaçar-se, lascar-se. **~ group** grupo m dissidente

split /splɪt/ vt/i (pt split, pres p splitting) rachar, fender(-se); (divide, share) dividir; (tear) romper(-se) □ n racha f, fenda f; (share) quinhão m, parte f; (pol) cisão f. **~ on** (sl: inform on) denunciar. **~ one's sides** rebentar de risa. **~ up** (of couple) separar-se. **a ~ second** uma fração de segundo. **~ting headache** dor f de cabeça forte

splurge /splɜ:dʒ/ n (colloq) espalhafato m, estardalhaço m □ vi (colloq: spend) gastar os tubos, (P) gastar à doida (colloq)

spool /spu:l/ n (of sewing machine) bobina f; (for cotton thread) carretel m, carrinho m; (naut; fishing) carretel m

splutter /'splʌtə(r)/ vi falar cuspindo; (engine) cuspir; (fat) crepitar

spoil /spɔɪl/ vt (pt spoilt or spoiled) estragar; (pamper) mimar □ n ~(s) (plunder) despojo(s) m(pl), espólios mpl. **~-sport** n desmancha-prazeres mf invar. **~t** a (pampered) mimado, estragado com mimos

spoke¹ /spəʊk/ n raio m

spoke², **spoken** /spəʊk, 'spəʊkən/ see **speak**

spokes|man /'spəʊksmən/ n (pl -men) **~woman** n (pl -women) porta-voz mf

sponge /spʌndʒ/ n esponja f □ vt (clean) lavar com esponja; (wipe) limpar com esponja □ vi. **~ on** (colloq: cadge) viver à custa de. **~ bag** bolsa f de toalete. **~ cake** pão-de-ló m. **~r** /-ə(r)/ n parasita mf (colloq) (sl). **spongy** a esponjoso

sponsor /'spɒnsə(r)/ n patrocinador m; (for membership) (sócio) proponente m □ vt patrocinar; (for membership) propor. **~ship** n patrocínio m

spontaneous /spɒn'teɪnɪəs/ a espontâneo

spoof /spu:f/ n (colloq) paródia f

spooky /'spu:kɪ/ a (-ier, -iest) (colloq) fantasmagórico, que dá arrepios

spool /spu:l/ n (of sewing machine) bobina f; (for thread, line) carretel m, (P) carrinho m

spoon /spu:n/ n colher f. **~-feed** vt (pt -fed) alimentar de colher; (fig: help) dar na bandeja para (fig). **~ful** n (pl ~fuls) colherada f

sporadic /spə'rædɪk/ a esporádico, acidental

sport /spɔ:t/ n esporte m, (P) desporto m. **(good) ~** (sl: person) gente f fina, (P) bom tipo m (colloq), (P) tipo m bestial □ vt (display) exibir, ostentar. **~s car/coat** carro m/casaco m esporte, (P) de desporto. **~y** a (colloq) esportivo, (P) desportivo

sporting /'spɔ:tɪŋ/ a esportivo, (P) desportivo. **a ~ chance** uma certa possibilidade de sucesso, uma boa chance

sports|man /'spɔ:tsmən/ n (pl -men) **~woman** (pl -women) desportista mf. **~manship** n (spirit) espírito m esportivo, (P) desportivo; (activity) esportismo m, (P) desportismo m

spot /spɒt/ n (mark, stain) mancha f; (in pattern) pinta f, bola f; (drop) gota f; (place) lugar m, ponto m; (pimple) borbulha f, espinha f; (TV) spot m televisivo □ vt (pt spotted) manchar; (colloq: detect) descobrir, detectar (colloq). **be in a ~** (colloq) estar numa encrenca (colloq), (P) estar metido numa alhada (colloq). **on the ~** no local; (there and then) ali mesmo, logo ali. **~-on** a (colloq) certo. **~ check** inspeção f, (P) inspecção f de surpresa; (of cars) fiscalização f de surpresa. **~ted** a manchado; (with dots) de pintas, de bolas; (animal) malhado. **~ty** a (with pimples) com borbulhas

spotless /'spɒtlɪs/ a impecável, imaculado

spotlight /'spɒtlaɪt/ n foco m; (cine, theat) refletor m, holofote m

spouse /spaʊz/ n cônjuge mf, esposo m

spout /spaʊt/ n (of vessel) bico m; (of liquid) esguicho m, jorro m; (pipe) cano m □ vi jorrar, esguichar. **up the ~** (sl: ruined) liquidado (sl)

sprain /spreɪn/ n entorse f, mau jeito m □ vt torcer, dar um mau jeito a

sprang /spræŋ/ see **spring**

sprawl /sprɔ:l/ vi (sit) estirar-se, esparramar-se; (fall) estatelar-se; (town) estender-se, espraiar-se

spray¹ /spreɪ/ n (of flowers) raminho m, ramalhete m

spray² /spreɪ/ n (water) borrifo m, salpico m; (from sea) borrifo m de espuma; (device) bomba f, aerossol m; (for perfume) vaporizador m, atomizador m □ vt aspergir, borrifar, pulverizar; (with insecticide) pulverizar. **~-gun** n (for paint) pistola f

spread /spred/ vt/i (pt **spread**) (extend, stretch) estender(-se); (news, fear, illness etc) espalhar(-se), alastrar(-se), propagar(-se); (butter etc) passar; (wings) abrir □ n (expanse) expansão f, extensão f; (spreading) propagação f; (paste) pasta f para passar pão; (colloq: meal) banquete m. **~-eagled** a de braços e pernas abertos. **~sheet** n (comput) folha f de cálculo

spree /spriː/ n **go on a ~** (colloq) cair na farra

sprig /sprɪg/ n raminho m

sprightly /'spraɪtlɪ/ a (-ier, -iest) vivo, animado

spring /sprɪŋ/ vi (pt **sprang**, pp **sprung**) (arise) nascer; (jump) saltar, pular □ vt (produce suddenly) sair-se com; (a surprise) fazer (**on sb** a alguém) □ n salto m, pulo m; (device) mola f; (season) primavera f; (of water) fonte f, nascente f. **~ from** vir de, originar, provir de. **~-clean** vt fazer limpeza geral. **~ onion** cebolinha f. **~ up** surgir

springboard /'sprɪŋbɔːd/ n trampolim m

springtime /'sprɪŋtaɪm/ n primavera f

springy /'sprɪŋɪ/ a (-ier -iest) elástico

sprinkle /'sprɪŋkl/ vt (with liquid) borrifar, salpicar; (with salt, flour) polvilhar (**with** de). **~ sand/etc** espalhar areia/etc. **~r** /-ə(r)/ n (in garden) regador m; (for fires) sprinkler m

sprinkling /'sprɪŋklɪŋ/ n (amount) pequena quantidade f; (number) pequeno número m

sprint /sprɪnt/ n (sport) corrida f de pequena distância, sprint m □ vi correr em sprint or a toda a velocidade; (sport) correr

sprout /spraʊt/ vt/i brotar, germinar; (put forth) brotar (on plant etc) broto m. (**Brussels**) **~s** couves f de Bruxelas

spruce /spruːs/ a bem arrumado □ vt **~ o.s. up** arrumar(-se)

sprung /sprʌŋ/ see **spring** □ a (mattress etc) de molas

spry /spraɪ/ a (**spryer, spryest**) vivo, ativo, (P) activo; (nimble) ágil

spud /spʌd/ n (sl) batata f

spun /spʌn/ see **spin**

spur /spɜː(r)/ n (of rider) espora f; (fig: stimulus) aguilhão m; (fig)

espora f (fig) □ vt (pt **spurred**) esporear, picar com esporas; (fig: incite) aguilhoar, esporear. **on the ~ of the moment** impulsivamente

spurious /'spjʊərɪəs/ a falso, espúrio

spurn /spɜːn/ vt desdenhar, desprezar, rejeitar

spurt /spɜːt/ vi jorrar, esguichar; (fig: accelerate) acelerar subitamente, dar um arranco súbito □ n jorro m, esguicho m; (of energy, speed) arranco m, surto m

spy /spaɪ/ n espião m □ vt (make out) avistar, descortinar □ vi ~ (**on**) espiar, espionar. **~ out** descobrir. **~ing** n espionagem f

squabble /'skwɒbl/ vi discutir, brigar □ n briga f, disputa f

squad /skwɒd/ n (mil) pelotão m; (team) equipe f, (P) equipa f. **firing ~** pelotão m de fuzilamento. **flying ~** brigada f móvel

squadron /'skwɒdrən/ n (mil) esquadrão m; (aviat) esquadrilha f; (naut) esquadra f

squalid /'skwɒlɪd/ a esquálido, sórdido. **~or** n sordidez f

squall /skwɔːl/ n borrasca f

squander /'skwɒndə(r)/ vt desperdiçar

square /skweə(r)/ n quadrado m; (in town) largo m, praça f, (T-square) régua-tê f; (set-square) esquadro m □ a (of shape) quadrado; (metre, mile etc) quadrado; (honest) direito, honesto, (of meal) abundante, substancial. (**all**) **~** (quits) quite(s) □ vt (math) elevar ao quadrado; (settle) acertar □ vi (agree) concordar. **go back to ~ one** recomeçar tudo do princípio, voltar à estaca zero. **~ brackets** parênteses mpl retos, (P) rectos. **~ up to** enfrentar. **~ly** adv diretamente, (P) directamente; (fairly) honestamente

squash /skwɒʃ/ vt (crush) esmagar; (squeeze) espremer; (crowd) comprimir, apertar □ n (game) squash m; (Amer: marrow) abóbora f. **lemon ~** limonada f. **orange ~** laranjada f. **~y** a mole

squat /skwɒt/ vi (pt **squatted**) acocorar-se, agachar-se; (be a squatter) ser ocupante ilegal □ a (dumpy) atarracado. **~ter** n ocupante mf ilegal de casa vazia, posseiro m

squawk /skwɔːk/ n grasnido m, crocito m □ vi grasnar, crocitar

squeak /skwiːk/ n guincho m, chio m; (of door, shoes etc) rangido m □ vi guinchar, chiar; (of door, shoes etc) ranger. **~y** a (shoe etc) que range; (voice) esganiçado

squeal /skwiːl/ vi dar gritos agudos,

guinchar □ n grito m agudo, guincho m. ~ (on) (sl: inform on) delatar, (P) denunciar

squeamish /'skwi:mɪʃ/ a (nauseated) que enjoa à toa

squeeze /skwi:z/ vt (lemon, sponge etc) espremer; (hand, arm) apertar; (extract) arrancar, extorquir (from de) □ vi (force one's way) passar à força, meter-se por □ n aperto m, apertão m; (hug) abraço m; (comm) restrições fpl de crédito

squelch /skweltʃ/ vi chapinhar or fazer chape-chape na lama

squid /skwɪd/ n lula f

squiggle /'skwɪgl/ n rabisco m, floreado m

squint /skwɪnt/ vi ser estrábico or vesgo; (with half-shut eyes) franzir os olhos □ n (med) estrabismo m

squirm /skwɜ:m/ vi (re)torcer-se, contorcer-se

squirrel /'skwɪrəl/ n esquilo m

squirt /skwɜ:t/ vt/i esguichar □ n esguicho m

stab /stæb/ vt (pt stabbed) apunhalar; (knife) esfaquear □ n punhalada f; (with knife) facada f; (of pain) pontada f; (colloq: attempt) tentativa f

stabilize /'steɪbəlaɪz/ vt estabilizar

stab|le¹ /'steɪbl/ a (-er, -est) estável. ~ility /stə'bɪlətɪ/ n estabilidade f

stable² /'steɪbl/ n cavalariça f, estrebaria f. ~-boy n moço m de estrebaria

stack /stæk/ n pilha f, montão m; (of hay etc) meda f □ vt (up) empilhar, amontoar

stadium /'steɪdɪəm/ n estádio m

staff /stɑ:f/ n pessoal m; (in school) professores mpl; (mil) estado-maior m; (stick) bordão m, cajado m; (mus) (pl staves) pauta f □ vt prover de pessoal

stag /stæg/ n veado (macho) m, cervo m. ~-party n (colloq) reunião f masculina; (before wedding) despedida f de solteiro

stage /steɪdʒ/ n (theatre) palco m; (phase) fase f, ponto m; (platform in hall) estrado m □ vt encenar, pôr em cena; (fig: organize) organizar. go on the ~ seguir a carreira teatral, ir para o teatro (colloq). ~ door entrada f dos artistas. ~-fright n nervosismo m

stagger /'stægə(r)/ vi vacilar, cambalear □ vt (shock) atordoar, chocar; (holidays etc) escalonar. ~ing a atordoador, chocante

stagnant /'stægnənt/ a estagnado, parado

stagnat|e /stæg'neɪt/ vi estagnar. ~ion /-ʃn/ n estagnação f

staid /steɪd/ a sério, sensato, estável

stain /steɪn/ vt manchar, pôr nódoa em; (colour) tingir, dar cor a □ n mancha f, nódoa f; (colouring) corante m. ~ed glass window vitral m. ~less steel aço m inoxidável

stair /steə(r)/ n degrau m. ~s escada(s) f(pl)

stair|case /'steəkeɪs/, ~way /-weɪ/ ns escada(s) f(pl), escadaria f

stake /steɪk/ n (post) estaca f, poste m; (wager) parada f, aposta f □ vt (area) demarcar, delimitar; (wager) jogar, apostar. at ~ em jogo. have a ~ in ter interesse em. ~ a claim to reivindicar

stale /steɪl/ a (-er, -est) estragado, velho; (bread) duro, mofado; (smell) rançoso; (air) viciado; (news) velho

stalemate /'steɪlmeɪt/ n (chess) empate m; (fig: deadlock) impasse m, beco-sem-saída m

stalk¹ /stɔ:k/ n (of plant) caule m

stalk² /stɔ:k/ vi andar com ar empertigado □ vt (prey) perseguir furtivamente, tocaiar

stall /stɔ:l/ n (in stable) baia f; (in market) tenda f, barraca f. ~s (theat) poltronas fpl de orquestra; (cinema) plateia f, (P) plateia f □ vt/i (auto) enguiçar, (P) ir abaixo. ~ (for time) ganhar tempo

stalwart /'stɔ:lwət/ a forte, rijo; (supporter) fiel

stamina /'stæmɪnə/ n resistência f

stammer /'stæmə(r)/ vt/i gaguejar □ n gagueira f, (P) gaguez f

stamp /stæmp/ vt/i ~ (one's foot) bater com o pé (no chão), pisar com força □ vt estampar; (letter) estampilhar, selar; (with rubber stamp) carimbar. ~ out (fire, rebellion etc) esmagar; (disease) erradicar □ n estampa f; (for postage) selo m; (fig: mark) cunho m. (rubber) ~ carimbo m. ~-collecting n filatelia f

stampede /stæm'pi:d/ n (scattering) debandada f; (of horses, cattle etc) tresma/hada f, debandada f; (fig: rush) corrida f □ vt/i (fazer) debandar; (horses, cattle etc) tresmalhar

stance /stæns/ n posição f, postura f

stand /stænd/ vi (pt stood) estar em pé; (keep upright position) ficar em pé; (rise) levantar-se; (be situated) encontrar-se, ficar, situar-se; (pol) candidatar-se (for por) □ vt pôr (de pé), colocar; (tolerate) suportar, agüentar, (P) agüentar □ n posição f; (support) apoio m; (mil) resistência f; (at fair) stand m, pavilhão m; (in street) quiosque m; (for spectators) arquibancada f, (P) bancada f; (Amer: witness-box) banco m das testemunhas. ~ a

chance ter uma possibilidade. ~
back recuar. ~ **by** or **around** estar
parado sem fazer nada. ~ **by** (be
ready) estar a postos; (promise, person) manter-se fiel a. ~ **down** desistir, retirar-se. ~ **for** representar,
simbolizar; (colloq: tolerate) aturar.
~ **in for** substituir. ~ **out** (be conspicuous) sobressair. ~ **still** estar/ficar imóvel. ~ **still!** não se mexa!,
quieto! ~ **to reason** ser lógico. ~
up levantar-se, pôr-se em or de pé. ~
up for defender, apoiar. ~ **up to**
enfrentar. ~**-by** a (for emergency) de
reserva; (ticket) de stand-by □ n (at
airport) stand-by m. **on** ~**-by** (mil)
de prontidão; (med) de plantão. ~**-in**
n substituto m, suplente mf. ~**-offish**
a (colloq: aloof) reservado, distante

standard /'stændəd/ n norma f,
padrão m; (level) nível m; (flag) estandarte m, bandeira f. ~**s** (morals)
princípios mpl □ a regulamentar;
(average) standard, normal. ~ **lamp**
abajur m de pé. ~ **of living** padrão m
de vida, (P) nível m de vida

standardize /'stændədaɪz/ vt padronizar

standing /'stændɪŋ/ a em pé, de pé
invar; (army, committee etc) permanente □ n posição f; (reputation)
prestígio m; (duration) duração f. ~
order (at bank) ordem f permanente.
~**-room** n lugares mpl em pé

standpoint /'stændpɔɪnt/ n ponto m
de vista

standstill /'stændstɪl/ n paralisação f.
at a ~ parado, paralisado. **bring/
come to a** ~ (fazer) parar, paralisar(-se), imobilizar (-se)

stank /stæŋk/ see **stink**

staple[1] /'steɪpl/ n (for paper) grampo
m, (P) agrafo m □ vt (paper) grampear, (P) agrafar. ~**r** /-ə(r)/ n grampeador m, (P) agrafador m

staple[2] /'steɪpl/ a principal, básico □ n
(comm) artigo m básico

star /stɑ:(r)/ n estrela f; (cinema) estrela f, vedete f; (celebrity) celebridade
f □ vt (pt **starred**) (of film) ter no
papel principal, (P) ter como actor
principal □ vi ~ **in** ser a vedete or
ter o papel principal em. ~**dom** n
celebridade f, estrelato m

starch /stɑ:tʃ/ n amido m, fécula f;
(for clothes) goma f □ vt pôr em goma,
engomar. ~**y** a (of food) farináceo,
feculento; (fig: of person) rígido, formal

stare /steə(r)/ vi ~ **at** olhar fixamente
□ n olhar m fixo

starfish /'stɑ:fɪʃ/ n (pl invar) estrela-do-mar f

stark /stɑ:k/ a (-er, -est) (desolate) ári-

do, desolado; (severe) austero, severo;
(utter) completo, rematado; (fact etc)
brutal □ adv completamente. ~
naked nu em pêlo, (P) em pelota
(colloq)

starling /'stɑ:lɪŋ/ n estorninho m

starlit /'stɑ:lɪt/ a estrelado

starry /'stɑ:rɪ/ a estrelado. ~**-eyed** a
(colloq) sonhador, idealista

start /stɑ:t/ vt/i começar; (machine)
ligar, pôr em andamento; (fashion
etc) lançar; (leave) partir; (cause) causar, provocar; (jump) sobressaltar-se,
estremecer; (of car) arrancar, partir □
n começo m, início m; (of race) largada f, partida f; (lead) avanço m;
(jump) sobressalto m, estremecimento m. **by fits and** ~**s** aosarrancos,
intermitentemente. **for a** ~ para
começar. **give sb a** ~ sobressaltar alguém, pregar um susto a alguém. ~**er**
n (auto) arranque m; (competitor) corredor m; (culin) entrada f. ~**ing-
point** n ponto m de partida

startl|e /'stɑ:tl/ vt (make jump) sobressaltar, pregar um susto a; (shock)
alarmar, chocar. ~**ing** a alarmante;
(surprising) surpreendente

starv|e /stɑ:v/ vi (die) morrer de fome;
(die) morrer de fome. **be** ~**ing** (colloq:
very hungry) ter muita fome, morrer
de fome (colloq) □ vt fazer passar fome
a; (deprive) privar. ~**ation** /-'veɪʃn/ n
fome f

stash /stæʃ/ vt (sl) guardar, esconder,
enfurnar (colloq)

state /steɪt/ n estado m, condição f;
(pomp) pompa f, gala f; (pol) Estado
m □ a de Estado, do Estado; (school)
público; (visit etc) oficial □ vt afirmar
(that que); (views) exprimir; (fix)
marcar, fixar. **in a** ~ muito abalado

stateless /'steɪtlɪs/ a apátrida

stately /'steɪtlɪ/ a (-ier, -iest)
majestoso. ~ **home** solar m, palácio
m

statement /'steɪtmənt/ n declaração f;
(of account) extrato m, (P) extracto m
de conta

statesman /'steɪtsmən/ n (pl -men)
homem m de estado, estadista m

static /'stætɪk/ a estático □ n (radio,
TV) estática f, interferência f

station /'steɪʃn/ n (position) posto m;
(rail, bus, radio) estação f; (rank)
condição f, posição f social □ vt
colocar. ~**-wagon** n perua f, (P) carrinha f. ~**ed at** or **in** (mil) estacionado em

stationary /'steɪʃnrɪ/ a estacionário,
parado, imóvel; (vehicle) estacionado,
parado

stationer /'steɪʃənə(r)/ n dono m de

papelaria. ~'s **shop** papelaria f. ~y n artigos mpl de papelaria; (writing-paper) papel m de carta

statistic /stə'tɪstɪk/ n dado m estatístico. ~s n (as a science) estatística f. ~al a estatístico

statue /'stætʃu:/ n estátua f

stature /'stætʃə(r)/ n estatura f

status /'steɪtəs/ n (pl -uses) situação f, posição f, categoria f; (prestige) prestígio m, importância f, status m. ~ **quo** status quo m. ~ **symbol** símbolo m de status

statut|e /'stætʃu:t/ n estatuto m, lei f. ~**ory** /-ʊtrɪ/ a estatutário, regulamentar; (holiday) legal

staunch /stɔ:ntʃ/ a (-er, -est) (friend) fiel, leal

stave /steɪv/ n (mus) pauta f □ vt ~ **off** (keep off) conjurar, evitar; (delay) adiar

stay /steɪ/ vi estar, ficar, permanecer; (dwell temporarily) ficar, alojar-se, hospedar-se; (spend time) demorar-se □ vt (hunger) enganar □ n estada f, visita f, permanência f. ~ **behind** ficar para trás. ~ **in** ficar em casa. ~ **put** (colloq) não se mexer (colloq). ~ **up** (late) deitar-se tarde. ~**ing-power** n resistência f

stead /sted/ n in my/your/etc ~ no meu/teu/etc lugar. **stand in good** ~ ser muito útil

steadfast /'stedfɑ:st/ a firme, constante

stead|y /'stedɪ/ a (-ier, -iest) (stable) estável, firme, seguro; (regular) regular, constante; (hand, voice) firme □ vt firmar, fixar, estabilizar; (calm) acalmar. **go** ~y **with** (colloq) namorar. ~**ily** adv firmemente; (regularly) regularmente, de modo constante

steak /steɪk/ n bife m

steal /sti:l/ vt/i (pt stole, pp stolen) roubar (from sb de alguém). ~ **away/in**/etc sair/entrar/etc furtivamente, esgueirar-se. ~ **the show** pôr os outros na sombra

stealth /stelθ/ n by ~ furtivamente, na calada, às escondidas. ~y a furtivo

steam /sti:m/ n vapor m de água; (on window) condensação f □ vt (cook) cozinhar a vapor. ~ **up** (window) embaciar. □ vi soltar vapor, fumegar; (move) avançar. ~**-engine** n máquina f a vapor; (locomotive) locomotiva f a vapor. ~ **iron** ferro m a vapor. ~**y** a (heat) úmido, (P) húmido

steamer /'sti:mə(r)/ n (ship) (barco a) vapor m; (culin) utensílio m para cozinhar a vapor

steamroller /'sti:mrəʊlə(r)/ n cilindro m a vapor, rolo m compressor

steel /sti:l/ n aço m □ a de aço □ vpr ~ o.s. endurecer-se, fortalecer-se. ~ **industry** siderurgia f

steep[1] /sti:p/ vt (soak) mergulhar, pôr de molho; (permeate) passar, impregnar. ~**ed in** (fig: vice, misery etc) mergulhado em; (fig: knowledge, wisdom etc) impregnado de, repassado de

steep[2] /sti:p/ a (-er, -est) íngreme, escarpado; (colloq) exagerado, exorbitante. **rise** ~**ly** (slope) subir a pique; (price) disparar

steeple /'sti:pl/ n campanário m, torre f

steeplechase /'sti:pltʃeɪs/ n (race) corrida f de obstáculos

steer /stɪə(r)/ vt/i guiar, conduzir, dirigir; (ship) governar; (fig) guiar, orientar. ~ **clear of** evitar passar perto de. ~**ing** n (auto) direção f, (P) direcção f. ~**ing-wheel** n (auto) volante m

stem[1] /stem/ n caule m, haste f; (of glass) pé m; (of pipe) boquilha f; (of word) radical m □ vi (pt stemmed) ~ **from** provir de, vir de

stem[2] /stem/ vt (pt stemmed) (check) conter; (stop) estancar

stench /stentʃ/ n mau cheiro m, fedor m

stencil /'stensl/ n estêncil m, (P) stencil m □ vt (pt stencilled) (document) policopiar

step /step/ vi (pt stepped) ir andar □ vt ~ **up** aumentar □ n passo m, passada f; (of stair, train) degrau m; (action) medida f, passo m. ~**s** (ladder) escada f. **in** ~ no mesmo passo, a passo certo; (fig) em conformidade (with com). ~ **down** (resign) demitir-se. ~ **in** (intervene) intervir. ~**ladder** n escada f portátil. ~**ping-stone** n (fig: means to an end) ponte f, trampolim m

stepbrother /'stepbrʌðə(r)/ n meio-irmão m. ~**daughter** n nora f, (P) enteada f. ~**father** n padrasto m. ~**mother** n madrasta f. ~**sister** n meio-irmã f. ~**son** n genro m, (P) enteado m

stereo /'sterɪəʊ/ n (pl -os) estéreo m; (record-player etc) equipamento m or sistema m estéreo □ a estéreo invar. ~**phonic** /-ə'fɒnɪk/ a estereofônico, (P) estereofónico

stereotype /'sterɪətaɪp/ n estereótipo m. ~**d** a estereotipado

steril|e /'steraɪl/ a estéril. ~**ity** /stə'rɪlətɪ/ n esterilidade f

steriliz|e /'steraɪlaɪz/ vt esterilizar. ~**ation** /-'zeɪʃn/ n esterilização f

sterling /'stɜ:lɪŋ/ n libra f esterlina □ a esterlino; (silver) de lei; (fig) excelente, de (primeira) qualidade

stern¹ /stɜːn/ a (-er, -est) severo

stern² /stɜːn/ n (of ship) popa f, ré f

stethoscope /ˈsteθəskəʊp/ n estetoscópio m

stew /stjuː/ vt/i estufar, guisar; (fruit) cozer □ n ensopado m. ~ed fruit compota f

steward /ˈstjuəd/ n (of club etc) ecónomo m, (P) ecónomo m, administrador m; (on ship etc) camareiro m (de bordo), (P) criado m (de bordo). ~ess /-ˈdes/ n aeromoça f, (P) hospedeira f

stick¹ /stɪk/ n pau m; (for walking) bengala f; (of celery) talo m

stick² /stɪk/ vt (pt stuck) (glue) colar; (thrust) cravar, espetar; (colloq: put) enfiar, meter; (sl: endure) agüentar, (P) aguentar, aturar, suportar □ vi (adhere) colar, aderir; (remain) ficar enfiado or metido; (be jammed) emperrar, ficar engatado. ~ in one's mind ficar na memória. be stuck with sb/sth (colloq) não conseguir descartar-se de alguém/alg coisa (colloq). ~ out vt (head) esticar; (tongue etc) mostrar □ vi (protrude) sobressair. ~ to (promise) ser fiel a. ~-up n (sl) assalto m à mão armada. ~ up for (colloq) tomar o partido de, defender. ~ing-plaster n esparadrapo m, (P) adesivo m

sticker /ˈstɪkə(r)/ n adesivo m, etiqueta f (adesiva)

stickler /ˈstɪklə(r)/ n be a ~ for fazer grande questão de, insistir em

sticky /ˈstɪkɪ/ a (-ier, -iest) pegajoso; (label, tape) adesivo; (weather) abafado, mormacento

stiff /stɪf/ a (-er, -est) teso, hirto, rigido; (limb, joint; hard) duro; (unbending) inflexível; (price) elevado, puxado (colloq); (penalty) severo; (drink) forte; (manner) reservado, formal. be bored/scared ~ (colloq) estar muito aborrecido/com muito medo (colloq). ~ neck torcicolo m. ~ness n rigidez f

stiffen /ˈstɪfn/ vt/i (harden) endurecer; (limb, joint) emperrar

stifl|e /ˈstaɪfl/ vt/i abafar, sufocar. ~ing a sufocante

stigma /ˈstɪɡmə/ n estigma m. ~tize vt estigmatizar

stile /staɪl/ n degrau m para passar por cima de cerca

stiletto /stɪˈletəʊ/ n (pl -os) estilete m. ~ heel n salto m alto fino

still¹ /stɪl/ a imóvel, quieto; (quiet) sossegado □ n silêncio m, sossego m □ adv ainda; (nevertheless) apesar disso, apesar de tudo. keep ~! fique quieto!, não se mexa! ~ life natureza f morta. ~ness n calma f

still² /stɪl/ n (apparatus) alambique m

stillborn /ˈstɪlbɔːn/ a natimorto, (P) nado-morto

stilted /ˈstɪltɪd/ a afetado, (P) afectado

stilts /stɪlts/ npl pernas de pau fpl, (P) andas fpl

stimul|ate /ˈstɪmjʊleɪt/ vt estimular. ~ant n estimulante m. ~ating a estimulante. ~ation /-ˈleɪʃn/ n estimulação f

stimulus /ˈstɪmjʊləs/ n (pl -li /-laɪ/) (spur) estímulo m

sting /stɪŋ/ n picada f; (organ) ferrão m □ vt (pt stung) picar □ vi picar, arder. ~ing nettle urtiga f

stingy /ˈstɪndʒɪ/ a (-ier, -iest) pão-duro m, sovina (with com)

stink /stɪŋk/ n fedor m, catinga f, mau cheiro m □ vi (pt stank or stunk, pp stunk) ~ (of) cheirar (a), tresandar (a) □ vt ~ out (room etc) empestar. ~ing a malcheiroso. ~ing rich (sl) podre de rico (colloq)

stinker /ˈstɪŋkə(r)/ n (sl: person) cara m horroroso (colloq); (sl: sth difficult) osso m duro de moer

stint /stɪnt/ vi ~ on poupar em, apertar em □ n (work) tarefa f, parte f, quinhão m

stipulate /ˈstɪpjʊleɪt/ vt estipular. ~ion /-ˈleɪʃn/ n condição f, estipulação f

stir /stɜː(r)/ vt/i (pt stirred) (move) mexer(-se), mover(-se); (excite) excitar; (a liquid) mexer □ n agitação f, rebuliço m. ~ up (trouble etc) provocar, fomentar. ~ring a excitante

stirrup /ˈstɪrəp/ n estribo m

stitch /stɪtʃ/ n (in sewing; meat) ponto m; (in knitting) malha f, ponto m; (pain) pontada f □ vt coser. in ~es (colloq) às gargalhadas (colloq)

stoat /stəʊt/ n arminho m

stock /stɒk/ n (comm) estoque m, (P) stock m, provisão f; (finance) valores mpl, fundos mpl; (family) família f, estirpe f; (culin) caldo m; (flower) goivo m □ a (goods) corrente, comum; (hackneyed) estereotipado □ vt (shop etc) abastecer, fornecer; (sell) vender □ vi ~ up with abastecer-se de. in ~ em estoque. out of ~ esgotado. take ~ (fig) fazer um balanço. ~-car n stock-car m. ~-cube n cubo m de caldo. ~ market Bolsa f (de Valores). ~-still a, adv imóvel. ~-taking n (comm) inventário m

stockbroker /ˈstɒkbrəʊkə(r)/ n corretor m da Bolsa

stocking /ˈstɒkɪŋ/ n meia f

stockist /ˈstɒkɪst/ n armazenista m

stockpile /ˈstɒkpaɪl/ n reservas fpl □ vt acumular reservas de, estocar

stocky /ˈstɒkɪ/ a (-ier, -iest) atarracado

stodg|e /stɒdʒ/ n (colloq) comida f pesada (colloq). **~y** a (of food, book) pesado, maçudo

stoic /'stəʊɪk/ n estóico m. **~al** a estoico. **~ism** /-sɪzəm/ n estoicismo m

stoke /stəʊk/ vt (boiler, fire) alimentar, carregar

stole[1] /stəʊl/ n (garment) estola m

stole[2], **stolen** /stəʊl, 'stəʊlən/ see steal

stomach /'stʌmək/ n (abdomen) barriga f, ventre m □ vt (put up with) aturar. **~-ache** n dor f de estômago; (abdomen) dores fpl de barriga

ston|e /stəʊn/ n pedra f; (pebble) seixo m; (in fruit) caroço m; (weight) 6,348 kg; (med) cálculo m, pedra f □ vt apedrejar; (fruit) tirar o caroço de. **with-in a ~e's throw (of)** muito perto (de). **~e-cold** gelado. **~e-deaf** totalmente surdo. **~ed** a (colloq: drunk) bêbado m (colloq); (colloq: drugged) drogado. **~y** a pedregoso. **~y-broke** a (sl) duro, liso (sl)

stonemason /'stəʊnmeɪsn/ n pedreiro m

stood /stʊd/ see stand

stooge /stuːdʒ/ n (colloq: actor) ajudante mf; (colloq: puppet) antoche m, (P) comparsa mf, parceiro m

stool /stuːl/ n banco m, tamborete m

stoop /stuːp/ vi (bend) curvar-se, baixar-se; (condescend) condescender, dignar-se. **~ to sth** rebaixar-se para (fazer) alg coisa □ n walk with a **~** andar curvado

stop /stɒp/ vt/i (pt stopped) parar; (prevent) impedir (from de); (hole, leak etc) tapar, vedar; (pain, noise etc) parar; (colloq: stay) ficar □ n (of bus) parada f, (P) paragem f; (full stop) ponto m final. **put a ~ to** pôr fim a. **~ it!** acabe logo com isso! **~-over** n (break in journey) parada f, (P) paragem f; (port of call) escala f. **~press** n notícia f de última hora. **~-watch** n cronómetro m, (P) cronómetro m

stopgap /'stɒpgæp/ n substituto m provisório, tapa-buracos mpl (colloq) □ a temporário

stoppage /'stɒpɪdʒ/ n parada f, (P) paragem f; (of work) paralisação f de trabalho; (of pay) suspensão f

stopper /'stɒpə(r)/ n rolha f, tampa f

storage /'stɔːrɪdʒ/ n (of goods, food etc) armazenagem f, armazenamento m. **in cold ~** em frigorífico

store /stɔː(r)/ n reserva f, provisão f; (warehouse) armazém m, entreposto m; (shop) grande armazém m; (Amer) loja f; (in computer) memória f □ vt (for future) pôr de reserva, juntar, fazer provisão de; (in warehouse)

armazenar. **be in ~** estar guardado. **have in ~ for** reservar para. **set ~ by** dar valor a. **~-room** n depósito m, almotarifado m, (P) armazém m

storey /'stɔːrɪ/ n (pl -eys) andar m

stork /stɔːk/ n cegonha f

storm /stɔːm/ n tempestade f □ vt tomar de assalto □ vi enfurecer-se. **a ~ in a teacup** uma tempestade num copo de água. **~y** a tempestuoso

story /'stɔːrɪ/ n estória f, (P) história f; (in press) artigo m, matéria f; (Amer: storey) andar m; (colloq: lie) cascata f, (P) peta f. **~-teller** n contador m de estórias, (P) histórias

stout /staʊt/ a (-er, -est) (fat) gordo, corpulento; (strong, thick) resistente, sólido, grosso; (brave) resoluto □ n cerveja f preta forte

stove /stəʊv/ n (for cooking) fogão m (de cozinha)

stow /stəʊ/ vt **~ (away)** (put away) guardar, arrumar; (hide) esconder □ vi **~ away** viajar clandestinamente

stowaway /'stəʊəweɪ/ n passageiro m clandestino

straddle /'strædl/ vt (sit) escarranchar-se em, montar; (stand) pôr-se de pernas abertas sobre

straggle /'strægl/ vi (lag behind) desgarrar-se, ficar para trás; (spread) estender-se desordenadamente. **~r** /-ə(r)/ n retardatário m

straight /streɪt/ a (-er, -est) direito; (tidy) em ordem; (frank) franco, direto, (P) directo; (of hair) liso; (of drink) puro □ adv (in straight line) reto; (directly) direto, direto, (P) directo, diretamente, (P) directamente □ n linha f reta, (P) recta. **~ ahead** or **on** (sempre) em frente. **~ away** logo, imediatamente. **go ~** viver honestamente. **keep a ~ face** não se desmanchar, manter um ar sério

straighten /'streɪtn/ vt endireitar; (tidy) arrumar, pôr em ordem

straightforward /streɪt'fɔːwəd/ a franco, sincero; (easy) simples

strain[1] /streɪn/ n (breed) raça f; (streak) tendência f, veia f

strain[2] /streɪn/ vt (rope) esticar, puxar; (tire) cansar; (filter) filtrar, passar; (vegetables, tea etc) coar; (med) distender, torcer; (fig) forçar, pôr à prova □ vi esforçar-se □ n tensão f; (fig: effort) esforço m; (med) distensão f. **~s** (music) melodias fpl. **~ one's ears** apurar o ouvido. **~ed** a forçado; (relations) tenso. **~er** n coador m, (P) passador m

strait /streɪt/ n estreito m. **~s** estreito m; (fig) apuros mpl, dificuldades fpl. **~-jacket** n camisa-de-força f. **~-laced** a severo, puritano

strand /strænd/ n (*thread*) fio m; (*lock of hair*) mecha f, madeixa f

stranded /'strændɪd/ a (*person*) em dificuldades, deixado para trás, abandonado

strange /streɪndʒ/ a (-er, -est) estranho. ~ly adv estranhamente. ~ness n estranheza f

stranger /'streɪndʒə(r)/ n estranho m, desconhecido m

strangle /'stræŋgl/ vt estrangular, sufocar

stranglehold /'stræŋglhəʊld/ n have a ~ on ter domínio sobre

strangulation /stræŋgjʊ'leɪʃn/ n estrangulamento m

strap /stræp/ n (*of leather etc*) correia f; (*of dress*) alça f; (*of watch*) pulseira f com correia □ vt (pt strapped) prender com correia

strapping /'stræpɪŋ/ a robusto, grande

strata /'streɪtə/ see stratum

stratagem /'strætədʒəm/ n estratagema m

strategic /strə'tiːdʒɪk/ a estratégico; (*of weapons*) de longo alcance

strategy /'strætədʒɪ/ n estratégia f

stratum /'strɑːtəm/ n (pl strata) estrato m, camada f

straw /strɔː/ n palha f; (*for drinking*) canudo m, (P) palhinha f. the last ~ a última gota f

strawberry /'strɔːbrɪ/ n (*fruit*) morango m; (*plant*) morangueiro m

stray /streɪ/ vi (*deviate from path etc*) extraviar-se, desencaminhar-se, afastar-se (from de); (*lose one's way*) perder-se; (*wander*) vagar, errar □ a perdido, extraviado; (*isolated*) isolado, raro, esporádico □ n animal m perdido or vadio

streak /striːk/ n risca f, lista f; (*strain*) veia f; (*period*) período m. ~ of lightning relâmpago m □ vt listrar, riscar □ vi ir como um raio. ~er n (colloq) pessoa f que corre nua em lugares públicos. ~y a listrado, riscado. ~y bacon toucinho m entremeado com gordura

stream /striːm/ n riacho m, córrego m, regato m; (*current*) corrente f; (*fig: flow*) jorro m, torrente f; (*schol*) nível m, grupo m □ vi correr; (*of banner, hair*) flutuar; (*sweat*) escorrer, pingar

streamer /'striːmə(r)/ n (*of paper*) serpentina f; (*flag*) flâmula f, bandeirola f

streamline /'striːmlaɪn/ vt dar forma aerodinâmica a; (*fig*) racionalizar. ~d a (*shape*) aerodinâmico

street /striːt/ n rua f. the man in the ~ (*fig*) o homem da rua. ~ lamp poste m de iluminação

streetcar /'striːtkɑː(r)/ n (*Amer*) bonde m, (P) carro m eléctrico

strength /streŋθ/ n força f; (*of wall*) solidez f; (*of fabric etc*) resistência f. on the ~ of à base de, em virtude de

strengthen /'streŋθn/ vt fortificar, fortalecer, reforçar

strenuous /'strenjʊəs/ a enérgico; (*arduous*) árduo, estrênuo, (P) estrênuo; (*tiring*) fatigante, esgotante. ~ly adv esforçadamente, energicamente

stress /stres/ n acento m; (*pressure*) pressão f, tensão f; (*med*) stress m □ vt acentuar, sublinhar; (*sound*) acentuar. ~ful a estressante

stretch /stretʃ/ vt (*pull taut*) esticar; (*arm, leg, neck*) estender, esticar; (*clothes*) alargar; (*truth*) forçar, torcer □ vi estender-se; (*after sleep etc*) espreguiçar-se; (*of clothes*) alargar-se □ n extensão f, trecho m; (*period*) período m; (*of road*) troço m □ a (*of fabric*) com elasticidade. at a ~ sem parar. ~ one's legs esticar as pernas

stretcher /'stretʃə(r)/ n maca f, padiola f. ~-bearer n padioleiro m, (P) maqueiro m

strew /struː/ vt (pt strewed, pp strewed or strewn) (*scatter*) espalhar; (*cover*) juncar, cobrir

stricken /'strɪkən/ a ~ with atacado or acometido de

strict /strɪkt/ a (-er, -est) estrito, rigoroso. ~ly adv estritamente. ~ly speaking a rigor. ~ness n severidade f, rigor m

stride /straɪd/ vi (pt strode, pp stridden) caminhar a passos largos □ n passada f. make great ~s (*fig*) fazer grandes progressos. take sth in one's ~ fazer alg coisa sem problemas

strident /'straɪdnt/ a estridente

strife /straɪf/ n conflito m, dissensão f, luta f

strike /straɪk/ vt (pt struck) bater (em); (*blow*) dar; (*match*) riscar, acender; (*gold etc*) descobrir; (*of clock*) soar, dar, bater (horas); (*of lightning*) atingir □ vi fazer greve; (*attack*) atacar □ n (*of workers*) greve f; (*mil*) ataque m; (*find*) descoberta f. on ~ em greve. ~ a bargain fechar negócio. ~ off or out riscar. ~ up (*mus*) começar a tocar; (*friendship*) travar

striker /'straɪkə(r)/ n grevista mf

striking /'straɪkɪŋ/ a notável, impressionante; (*attractive*) atraente

string /strɪŋ/ n corda f, fio m; (*of violin, racket etc*) corda f; (*of pearls*) fio m; (*of onions, garlic*) réstia f; (*of lies etc*) série f; (*row*) fila f □ vt (pt strung) (*thread*) enfiar. pull ~s usar pistolão, (P) puxar os cordelinhos. ~ out espaçar-se. ~ed a (instrument) de cordas. ~y a filamentoso, fibroso; (meat) com nervos

stringent /'strɪndʒənt/ a rigoroso, estrito

strip¹ /strɪp/ vt/i (pt stripped) (undress) despir/-se); (machine) desmontar; (deprive) despojar, privar. ~per n artista mf de striptease; (solvent) removedor m

strip² /strɪp/ n tira f; (of land) faixa f. ~ **comic** ~ história f em quadrinhos, (P) banda f desenhada. ~ **light** tubo m de luz fluorescente

stripe /straɪp/ n risca f, lista f, barra f. ~d a listado, com listras

strive /straɪv/ vi (pt strove, pp striven) esforçar-se (to por)

strode¹ /strəʊd/ see stride

stroke¹ /strəʊk/ n golpe m; (of pen) penada f, (P) traço m; (in swimming) braçada f; (in rowing) remada f; (med) ataque m, congestão f. ~ **of genius** rasgo m de genialidade. ~ **of luck** golpe m de sorte

stroke² /strəʊk/ vt (with hand) acariciar, fazer festas em

stroll /strəʊl/ vi passear, dar uma volta □ n volta f, (P) giro m. ~ **in**/etc entrar/etc tranquilamente

strong /strɒŋ/ a (-er, -est) forte; (shoes, fabric etc) resistente. **be a hundred**/etc ~ ser em número de cem/etc. ~**-box** n cofre-forte m. ~ **language** linguagem f grosseira, palavrões mpl. ~**-minded** a resoluto, firme. ~**-room** n casa-forte f. ~**ly** adv (greatly) fortemente, grandemente; (with energy) com força; (deeply) profundamente

stronghold /'strɒŋhəʊld/ n fortaleza f, (fig) baluarte m, bastião m

strove /strəʊv/ see strive

struck /strʌk/ see strike □ a ~ **on** (sl) apaixonado por

structur|**e** /'strʌktʃə(r)/ n estrutura f; (of building etc) edifício m, construção f. ~**al** a estrutural, de estrutura, de construção

struggle /'strʌgl/ vi (to get free) debater-se; (contend) lutar; (strive) esforçar-se (to, for por) □ n luta f; (effort) esforço m. **have a** ~ **to** ter dificuldade em. **to one's feet** levantar-se a custo

strum /strʌm/ vt (pt strummed) (banjo etc) dedilhar

strung /strʌŋ/ see string

strut /strʌt/ n (support) suporte m, escora f □ vi (pt strutted) (walk) pavonear-se

stub /stʌb/ n (of pencil, cigarette) ponta f; (of tree) cepo m, toco m; (counterfoil) talão m, canhoto m □ vt (pt

stubbed) ~ **one's toe** dar uma topada. ~ **out** esmagar

stubble /'stʌbl/ n (on chin) barba f por fazer; (of crop) restolho m

stubborn /'stʌbən/ a teimoso, obstinado. ~**ly** adv obstinadamente, teimosamente. ~**ness** n teimosia f, obstinação f

stubby /'stʌbɪ/ a (-ier, -iest) (finger) curto e grosso; (person) atarracado

stuck /stʌk/ see stick² □ a emperrado. ~**-up** a (colloq: snobbish) convencido, esnobe

stud¹ /stʌd/ n tacha f; (for collar) botão m de colarinho □ vt (pt studded) enfeitar com tachas. ~**ded with** salpicado de

stud² /stʌd/ n (horses) haras m. ~ **(-farm)** n coudelaria f. ~**(-horse)** n garanhão m

student /'stju:dnt/ n (univ) estudante mf, aluno m; (schol) aluno m □ a (life, residence) universitário

studied /'stʌdɪd/ a estudado

studio /'stju:dɪəʊ/ n (pl -os) estúdio m. ~ **flat** estúdio m

studious /'stju:dɪəs/ a (person) estudioso; (deliberate) estudado. ~**ly** adv (carefully) cuidadosamente

study /'stʌdɪ/ n estudo m; (office) escritório m □ vt/i estudar

stuff /stʌf/ n substância f, matéria f; (sl: things) coisa(s) f (pl) □ vt encher; (animal) empalhar; (cram) apinhar, encher ao máximo; (culin) rechear; (block up) entupir; (put) enfiar, meter. ~**ing** n enchimento m; (culin) recheio m

stuffy /'stʌfɪ/ a (-ier, -iest) abafado, mal arejado; (dull) enfadonho

stumbl|**e** /'stʌmbl/ vi tropeçar. ~**e across** or **on** dar com, encontrar por acaso, topar com. ~**ing-block** n obstáculo m

stump /stʌmp/ n (of tree) cepo m, toco m; (of limb) coto m; (of pencil, cigar) ponta f

stumped /stʌmpt/ a (colloq: baffled) atrapalhado, perplexo

stun /stʌn/ vt (pt stunned) aturdir, estontear

stung /stʌŋ/ see sting

stunk /stʌŋk/ see stink

stunning /'stʌnɪŋ/ a atordoador; (colloq: delightful) fantástico, sensacional

stunt¹ /stʌnt/ vt (growth) atrofiar. ~**ed** a atrofiado

stunt² /stʌnt/ n (feat) façanha f, proeza f; (trick) truque m; (aviat) acrobacia f aérea. ~ **man** n dublê m, (P) duplo m

stupefy /'stju:pɪfaɪ/ vt estupefazer, (P) estupeficar

stupendous /stju:'pendəs/ a estupendo, assombroso, prodigioso

stupid /'stju:pɪd/ a estúpido, obtuso. ~ity /-'pɪdətɪ/ n estupidez f. ~ly adv estupidamente

stupor /'stju:pə(r)/ n estupor m, torpor m

sturdy /'stɜ:dɪ/ a (-ier, -iest) robusto, vigoroso, forte

stutter /'stʌtə(r)/ vi gaguejar □ n gagueira f, (P) gaguez f

sty /staɪ/ n (pigsty) pocilga f, chiqueiro m

stye /staɪ/ n (on eye) terçol m, terçolho m

styl|e /staɪl/ n estilo m; (fashion) moda f; (kind) género m, (P) gênero m, tipo m; (pattern) feitio m, modelo m □ vt (design) desenhar, criar. in ~e (live) em grande estilo; (do things) com classe. ~e sb's hair fazer um penteado em alguém. ~ist n (of hair) cabeleireiro m

stylish /'staɪlɪʃ/ a elegante, na moda

stylized /'staɪlaɪzd/ a estilizado

stylus /'staɪləs/ n (pl -uses) (of record-player) agulha f, safira f

suave /swɑ:v/ a polido, de fala mansa, (P) melifluo

sub- /sʌb/ pref sub-

subconscious /sʌb'kɒnʃəs/ a & n subconsciente (m)

subcontract /sʌbkən'trækt/ vt dar de subempreitada

subdivide /sʌbdɪ'vaɪd/ vt subdividir

subdue /səb'dju:/ vt (enemy, feeling) dominar, subjugar; (sound, voice) abrandar. ~d a (weak) submisso; (quiet) recolhido; (light) velado

subject[1] /'sʌbdʒɪkt/ a (state etc) dominado □ n sujeito m; (schol, univ) disciplina f, matéria f; (citizen) súdito m. ~-matter n conteúdo m, tema m, assunto m. ~ to sujeito a

subject[2] /səb'dʒekt/ vt submeter. ~ion /-kʃn/ n submissão f

subjective /sʌb'dʒektɪv/ a subjetivo, (P) subjectivo

subjunctive /səb'dʒʌŋktɪv/ a & n subjuntivo (m), (P) conjuntivo (m)

sublime /sə'blaɪm/ a sublime

submarine /sʌbmə'ri:n/ n submarino m

submerge /səb'mɜ:dʒ/ vt submergir □ vi submergir, mergulhar

submissive /səb'mɪsɪv/ a submisso

submit /səb'mɪt/ vt/i (pt submitted) submeter(-se) (to a); (jur: argue) alegar. ~ssion /-'mɪʃn/ n submissão f

subnormal /sʌb'nɔ:ml/ a subnormal; (temperature) abaixo do normal

subordinate[1] /sə'bɔ:dɪnət/ a subordinado, subalterno; (gram) subordinado □ n subordinado m, subalterno m

subordinate[2] /sə'bɔ:dɪneɪt/ vt subordinar (to a)

subpoena /səb'pi:nə/ n (pl -as) (jur) citação f, intimação f

subscribe /səb'skraɪb/ vt/i subscrever, contribuir (to para). ~ to (theory, opinion) subscrever, aceitar; (newspaper) assinar. ~r /-ə(r)/ n subscritor m, assinante m

subscription /səb'skrɪpʃn/ n subscrição f; (to newspaper) assinatura f

subsequent /'sʌbsɪkwənt/ a subsequente, (P) subsequente, posterior. ~ly adv subsequentemente, a seguir, posteriormente

subservient /səb'sɜ:vɪənt/ a servil, subserviente

subside /səb'saɪd/ vi (flood, noise etc) baixar; (land) ceder, afundar; (wind, storm, excitement) abrandar. ~nce /-əns/ n (of land) afundamento m

subsidiary /səb'sɪdɪərɪ/ a subsidiário □ n (comm) filial f, sucursal f

subsid|y /'sʌbsədɪ/ n subsidio m, subvenção f. ~ize /-ɪdaɪz/ vt subsidiar, subvencionar

subsist /səb'sɪst/ vi subsistir. ~ on viver de. ~ence n subsistência f. ~ence allowance ajudas fpl de custo

substance /'sʌbstəns/ n substância f

substandard /sʌb'stændəd/ a de qualidade inferior

substantial /səb'stænʃl/ a substancial. ~ly adv substancialmente

substantiate /səb'stænʃɪeɪt/ vt comprovar, fundamentar

substitut|e /'sʌbstɪtju:t/ n (person) substituto m, suplente mf (for de); (thing) substituto m (for de) □ vt substituir (for por). ~ion /'tju:ʃn/ n substituição f

subterfuge /'sʌbtəfju:dʒ/ n subterfúgio m

subtitle /'sʌbtaɪtl/ n subtítulo m

subtle /'sʌtl/ a (-er, -est) sutil, (P) subtil. ~ty n sutileza f, (P) subtileza f

subtotal /'sʌbtəʊtl/ n soma f parcial

subtract /səb'trækt/ vt subtrair, diminuir. ~ion /-kʃn/ n subtração f, diminuição f

suburb /'sʌbɜ:b/ n subúrbio m, arredores mpl. ~an /sə'bɜ:bən/ a dos subúrbios, suburbano. ~ia /sə'bɜ:bɪə/ n (pej) os arredores

subvert /səb'vɜ:t/ vt subverter. ~sion /-ʃn/ n subversão f. ~sive /-sɪv/ a subversivo

subway /'sʌbweɪ/ n passagem f subterrânea; (Amer: underground) metropolitano m

succeed /sək'si:d/ vi ser bem sucedido, ter êxito. ~ in doing sth conseguir fazer alg coisa □ vt (follow) suceder a. ~ing a seguinte, sucessivo

success /sək'ses/ *n* sucesso *m*, êxito *m*
succession /sək'seʃn/ *n* sucessão *f*; *(series)* série *f*. **in ~** seguidos, consecutivos
successive /sək'sesɪv/ *a* sucessivo, consecutivo
successor /sək'sesə(r)/ *n* sucessor *m*
succinct /sək'sɪŋkt/ *a* sucinto
succulent /'sʌkjʊlənt/ *a* suculento
succumb /sə'kʌm/ *vi* sucumbir
such /sʌtʃ/ *a & pron* tal, semelhante, assim; *(so much)* tanto □ *adv* tanto. **~ a book/etc** um tal livro/*etc* or um livro/*etc* assim. **~ books/etc** tais livros/*etc* or livros/*etc* assim. **~ courage/etc** tanta coragem/*etc*. **~ a big house** uma casa tão grande. **as ~** como tal. **~ as** como, tal como. **there's no ~ thing** uma coisa dessa não existe. **~-and-such** *a & pron* tal e tal
suck /sʌk/ *vt* chupar; *(breast)* mamar. **~ in** or **up** *(absorb)* absorver, aspirar; *(engulf)* tragar. **~ up to** puxar o saco a *(colloq)*. **~ one's thumb** chupar o dedo. **~er** *n* *(sl: greenhorn)* trouxa *mf (colloq)*; *(bot)* broto *m*
suckle /'sʌkl/ *vt* amamentar, dar de mamar a
suction /'sʌkʃn/ *n* sucção *f*
sudden /'sʌdn/ *a* súbito, repentino. **all of a ~** de repente, de súbito. **~ly** *adv* subitamente, repentinamente. **~ness** *n* subitaneidade *f*, brusquidão *f*
suds /sʌdz/ *npl* espuma *f* de sabão; *(soapy water)* água *f* de sabão
sue /suː/ *vt (pres p* suing*)* processar
suede /sweɪd/ *n* camurça *f*
suet /'suːɪt/ *n* sebo *m*
suffer /'sʌfə(r)/ *vt/i* sofrer; *(tolerate)* tolerar, suportar. **~er** *n* sofredor *m*, o que sofre; *(patient)* doente *mf*, vítima *f*. **~ing** *n* sofrimento *m*
suffice /sə'faɪs/ *vi* bastar, chegar, ser suficiente
sufficien|t /sə'fɪʃnt/ *a* suficiente, bastante. **~cy** *n* suficiência *f*, quantidade *f* suficiente. **~tly** *adv* suficientemente
suffix /'sʌfɪks/ *n* sufixo *m*
suffocat|e /'sʌfəkeɪt/ *vt/i* sufocar. **~ion** /-'keɪʃn/ *n* sufocação *f*, asfixia *f*. **~ing** *a* sufocante, asfixiante
sugar /'ʃʊgə(r)/ *n* açúcar *m* □ *vt* adoçar, pôr açúcar em. **~-bowl** *n* açucareiro *m*. **~-lump** *n* torrão *m* de açúcar, *(P)* quadradinho *m* de açúcar. **brown ~** açúcar *m* preto, *(P)* açúcar *m* amarelo. **~y** *a* açucarado; *(fig: too sweet)* delico-doce
suggest /sə'dʒest/ *vt* sugerir. **~ion** /-tʃn/ *n* sugestão *f*. **~ive** *a* sugestivo; *(improper)* brejeiro, picante. **be ~ive of** sugerir, fazer lembrar

suicid|e /'suːɪsaɪd/ *n* suicídio *m*. **commit ~e** suicidar-se. **~al** /-'saɪdl/ *a* suicida
suit /suːt/ *n* terno *m*, *(P)* fato *m*; *(woman's)* costume *m*, *(P)* saia-casaco *m*; *(cards)* naipe *m* □ *vt* convir a; *(of garment, style)* ficar bem em; *(adapt)* adaptar. **follow ~** *(fig)* seguir o exemplo. **~ability** *n* *(of action)* conveniência *f*, oportunidade *f*; *(of candidate)* aptidão *f*. **~able** *a* conveniente, apropriado *(for* para*)*. **~ably** *adv* convenientemente. **~ed** *a* **be ~ed to** ser feito para, servir para. **be well ~ed** *(matched)* combinar-se bem; *(of people)* ser o ideal
suitcase /'suːtkeɪs/ *n* mala *f* de viagem*)*
suite /swiːt/ *n* *(of rooms; mus)* suite *f*, *(P)* suite *f*; *(of furniture)* mobília *f*
suitor /'suːtə(r)/ *n* pretendente *m*
sulk /sʌlk/ *vi* amuar, ficar emburrado. **~y** *a* amuado, emburrado *(collog)*
sullen /'sʌlən/ *a* carrancudo
sulphur /'sʌlfə(r)/ *n* enxofre *m*. **~ic** /-'fjʊərɪk/ *a* **~ic acid** ácido *m* sulfúrico
sultan /'sʌltən/ *n* sultão *m*
sultana /sʌl'tɑːnə/ *n* *(fruit)* passa *f* branca, *(P)* sultana *f*
sultry /'sʌltrɪ/ *a* (**-ier, -iest**) abafado, opressivo; *(fig)* sensual
sum /sʌm/ *n* soma *f*; *(amount of money)* soma *f*, quantia *f*, importância *f*; *(in arithmetic)* conta *f* □ *vt* *(pt* summed*)* somar. **~ up** recapitular, resumir; *(assess)* avaliar, medir
summar|y /'sʌmərɪ/ *n* sumário *m*, resumo *m* □ *a* sumário. **~ize** *vt* resumir
summer /'sʌmə(r)/ *n* verão *m*, estio *m* □ *a* de verão. **~-time** *n* verão *m*, época *f* de verão. **~y** *a* estival, próprio de verão
summit /'sʌmɪt/ *n* cume *m*, cimo *m*. **~ conference** *(pol)* conferência *f* de cúpula, *(P)* reunião *f* de cimeira
summon /'sʌmən/ *vt* mandar chamar; *(to meeting)* convocar. **~ up** *(strength, courage etc)* chamar a si, fazer apelo a
summons /'sʌmənz/ *n* *(jur)* citação *f*, intimação *f* □ *vt* citar, intimar
sump /sʌmp/ *n* *(auto)* cárter *m*
sumptuous /'sʌmptʃʊəs/ *a* suntuoso, *(P)* sumptuoso, luxuoso
sun /sʌn/ *n* sol *m* □ *vt* *(pt* sunned*)* **~ o.s.** aquecer-se ao sol. **~-glasses** *npl* óculos *mpl* de sol. **~-roof** *n* teto *m* solar. **~-tan** *n* bronzeado *m*. **~-tanned** *a* bronzeado. **~-tan oil** *n* óleo *m* de bronzear
sunbathe /'sʌnbeɪð/ *vi* tomar um banho de sol

sunburn /'sʌnbɜːn/ n queimadura f de sol. ~t a queimado pelo sol

Sunday /'sʌndɪ/ n domingo m. ~ school catecismo m

sundial /'sʌndaɪəl/ n relógio m de sol

sundown /'sʌndaʊn/ n = sunset

sundr|y /'sʌndrɪ/ a vários, diversos. ~ies npl artigos mpl diversos. all and ~y todo o mundo

sunflower /'sʌnflaʊə(r)/ n girassol m

sung /sʌŋ/ see sing

sunk /sʌŋk/ see sink

sunken /'sʌŋkən/ a (ship etc) afundado; (eyes) fundo

sunlight /'sʌnlaɪt/ n luz f do sol, sol m

sunny /'sʌnɪ/ a (-ier, -iest) (room, day etc) ensolarado

sunrise /'sʌnraɪz/ n nascer m do sol

sunset /'sʌnset/ n pôr m do sol

sunshade /'sʌnʃeɪd/ n (awning) toldo m; (parasol) pára-sol m, (P) guarda-sol m

sunshine /'sʌnʃaɪn/ n sol m, luz f do sol

sunstroke /'sʌnstrəʊk/ n (med) insolação f

super /'suːpə(r)/ a (colloq: excellent) formidável

superb /suːˈpɜːb/ a soberbo, esplêndido

supercilious /suːpəˈsɪlɪəs/ a (haughty) altivo; (disdainful) desdenhoso

superficial /suːpəˈfɪʃl/ a superficial. ~ity /-ˈræləti/ n superficialidade f. ~ly adv superficialmente

superfluous /suːˈpɜːflʊəs/ a supérfluo

superhuman /suːpəˈhjuːmən/ a sobre-humano

superimpose /suːpərɪmˈpəʊz/ vt sobrepor (on a)

superintendent /suːpərɪnˈtendənt/ n superintendente m; (of police) comissário m, chefe m de policia

superior /suːˈpɪərɪə(r)/ a & n superior (m). ~ity /-ˈɒrətɪ/ n superioridade f

superlative /suːˈpɜːlətɪv/ a supremo, superlativo □ n (gram) superlativo m

supermarket /'suːpəmɑːkɪt/ n supermercado m

supernatural /suːpəˈnætʃrəl/ a sobrenatural

superpower /'suːpəpaʊə(r)/ n superpotência f

supersede /suːpəˈsiːd/ vt suplantar, substituir

supersonic /suːpəˈsɒnɪk/ a supersónico, (P) supersónico

superstiti|on /suːpəˈstɪʃn/ n superstição f. ~ous a /-ˈstɪʃəs/ supersticioso

superstore /'suːpəstɔː(r)/ n hipermercado m

supertanker /'suːpətæŋkə(r)/ n superpetroleiro m

supervis|e /'suːpəvaɪz/ vt supervisar, fiscalizar. ~ion /-ˈvɪʒn/ n supervisão f. ~or n supervisor m; (shop) chefe mf de seção; (firm) chefe mf de serviço. ~ory /'suːpəvaɪzərɪ/ a de supervisão

supper /'sʌpə(r)/ n jantar m; (late at night) ceia f

supple /'sʌpl/ a flexível, maleável

supplement¹ /'sʌplɪmənt/ n suplemento m. ~ary /-ˈmentrɪ/ a suplementar

supplement² /'sʌplɪment/ vt suplementar

supplier /səˈplaɪə(r)/ n fornecedor m

suppl|y /səˈplaɪ/ vt suprir, prover; (comm) fornecer, abastecer □ n provisão f; (of goods, gas etc) fornecimento m, abastecimento m □ a (teacher) substituto. ~ies (food) víveres mpl; (mil) suprimentos mpl. ~y and demand oferta e procura

support /səˈpɔːt/ vt (hold up, endure) suportar; (provide for) sustentar, suster; (back) apoiar, patrocinar; (sport) torcer por □ n apoio m; (techn) suporte m. ~er n partidário m; (sport) torcedor m

suppos|e /səˈpəʊz/ vt/i supor. ~e that supondo que, na hipótese de que. ~ed a suposto. he's ~ed to do ele deve fazer; (believed to) consta que ele faz. ~edly /-ɪdlɪ/ adv segundo dizem; (probably) supostamente, em principio. ~ing conj se. ~ition /sʌpəˈzɪʃn/ n suposição f

suppress /səˈpres/ vt (put an end to) suprimir; (restrain) conter, reprimir; (stifle) abafar, sufocar; (psych) recalcar. ~ion /-ʃn/ n supressão f; (restraint) repressão f; (psych) recalque m, (P) recalcamento m

suprem|e /suːˈpriːm/ a supremo. ~acy /-eməsɪ/ n supremacia f

surcharge /'sɜːtʃɑːdʒ/ n sobretaxa f; (on stamp) sobrecarga f

sure /ʃʊə(r)/ a (-er, -est) seguro, certo □ adv (colloq: certainly) deveras, não há dúvida que, de certeza. be ~ about or of ter a certeza de. be ~ to (not fail) não deixar de. he is ~ to find out ele vai descobrir com certeza. make ~ assegurar. ~ly adv com certeza, certamente

surety /'ʃʊərətɪ/ n (person) fiador m; (thing) garantia f

surf /sɜːf/ n (waves) ressaca f, rebentação f. ~er n surfista mf. ~ing n surfe m, (P) surf m, jacaré-na-praia m

surface /'sɜːfɪs/ n superficie f □ a superficial □ vt/i revestir; (rise, become known) emergir. ~ mail via f maritima

surfboard /'sɜːfbɔːd/ n prancha f de surfe, (P) surf

surfeit /'sɜːfɪt/ n excesso m (**of** de)

surge /sɜːdʒ/ vi (waves) ondular, enca-pelar-se; (move forward) avançar □ n (wave) onda f, vaga f; (motion) arre-metida f

surgeon /'sɜːdʒən/ n cirurgião m

surg|ery /'sɜːdʒərɪ/ n cirurgia f; (of-fice) consultório m; (session) consulta f; (consulting hours) horas fpl de consulta. ~**ical** a cirúrgico

surly /'sɜːlɪ/ a (-ier, -iest) carrancudo, trombudo

surmise /sə'maɪz/ vt imaginar, supor, calcular □ n conjetura f, (P) conjec-tura f; hipótese f

surmount /sə'maʊnt/ vt sobrepujar, vencer, (P) superar

surname /'sɜːneɪm/ n sobrenome m, (P) apelido m

surpass /sə'pɑːs/ vt superar, ultrapas-sar, exceder

surplus /'sɜːpləs/ n excedente m, ex-cesso m; (finance) saldo m positivo □ a excedente, em excesso

surpris|e /sə'praɪz/ n surpresa f □ vt surpreender. ~**ed** a surpreendido, admirado (**at** com). ~**ing** a sur-preendente. ~**ingly** adv surpreen-dentemente

surrender /sə'rendə(r)/ vi render-se □ vt (hand over; mil) entregar □ n (mil) rendição f; (of rights) renúncia f

surreptitious /ˌsʌrep'tɪʃəs/ a sub-reptício, furtivo

surrogate /'sʌrəgeɪt/ n delegado m. ~ **mother** mãe f de aluguel, (P) alu-guer

surround /sə'raʊnd/ vt rodear, cer-car; (mil etc) cercar. ~**ing** a circun-dante, vizinho. ~**ings** npl arredores mpl; (setting) meio m, ambiente m

surveillance /sɜː'veɪləns/ n vigilân-cia f

survey[1] /sə'veɪ/ vt (landscape etc) ob-servar; (review) passar em revista; (inquire about) pesquisar; (land) fa-zer o levantamento de; (building) vis-toriar, inspecionar, (P) inspeccionar. ~**or** n (of buildings) fiscal m, (P) (of land) agrimensor m

survey[2] /'sɜːveɪ/ n (inspection) vistor-ia f, inspeção f, (P) inspecção f; (gen-eral view) panorâmica f; (inquiry) pesquisa f

survival /sə'vaɪvl/ n sobrevivência f; (relic) relíquia f, vestígio m

surviv|e /sə'vaɪv/ vt/i sobreviver (a). ~**or** n sobrevivente mf

susceptib|le /sə'septəbl/ a (prone) susceptível (**to** a); (sensitive, impres-sionable) susceptível, sensível. ~**ility** /-'bɪlətɪ/ n susceptibilidade f

suspect[1] /sə'spekt/ vt suspeitar; (doubt, distrust) desconfiar de, suspei-tar de

suspect[2] /'sʌspekt/ a & n suspeito (m)

suspen|d /sə'spend/ vt (hang, stop) suspender; (from duty etc) sus-pender. ~**ded sentence** suspensão f da pena. ~**sion** n suspensão f. ~**sion bridge** ponte f suspensa or pênsil

suspender /sə'spendə(r)/ n (presilha de) liga f. ~ **belt** n cintaliga f, (P) cinta f de ligas. ~**s** (Amer: braces) suspensórios mpl

suspense /sə'spens/ n ansiedade f, in-certeza f; (in book etc) suspense m, tensão f

suspicion /sə'spɪʃn/ n suspeita f; (dis-trust) desconfiança f; (trace) vestígio m, (P) traço m

suspicious /sə'spɪʃəs/ a desconfiado; (causing suspicion) suspeito. **be** ~ **of** desconfiar de. ~**ly** adv de modo suspeito

sustain /sə'stem/ vt (support) suster, sustentar; (suffer) sofrer; (keep up) sustentar; (jur: uphold) sancionar; (interest, effort) manter. ~**ed effort** esforço m contínuo

sustenance /'sʌstməns/ n (food) ali-mento m, sustento m

swagger /'swægə(r)/ vi pavonear-se, andar com arrogância

swallow[1] /'swɒləʊ/ vt/i engolir. ~ **up** (absorb, engulf) devorar, tragar

swallow[2] /'swɒləʊ/ n (bird) andori-nha f

swam /swæm/ see **swim**

swamp /swɒmp/ n pântano m, brejo m □ vt (flood, overwhelm) inundar, submergir. ~**y** a pantanoso

swan /swɒn/ n cisne m

swank /swæŋk/ vi (colloq: show off) gabar-se, mostrar-se (colloq)

swap /swɒp/ vt/i (pt **swapped**) (col-loq) trocar (**for** por) □ n (colloq) troca f

swarm /swɔːm/ n (of insects, people) enxame m □ vi formigar. ~ **into** or **round** invadir

swarthy /'swɔːðɪ/ a (-ier, -iest) more-no, trigueiro

swat /swɒt/ vt (pt **swatted**) (fly etc) esmagar, esborrachar

sway /sweɪ/ vt/i oscilar, balançar(-se); (influence) mover, influenciar □ n oscilação f, balanceio m; (rule) domínio m, poder m

swear /sweə(r)/ vt/i (pt **swore**, pp **sworn**) jurar; (curse) praguejar, rogar pragas (**at** contra). ~ **by** jurar por; (colloq: recommend) ter grande fé em. ~-**word** n palavrão m

sweat /swet/ n suor m □ vi suar. ~**y** a suado

sweater /ˈswetə(r)/ n suéter m, (P) camisola f

sweatshirt /ˈswetʃɜːt/ n suéter m de malha or algodão

swede /swiːd/ n couve-nabo f

Swed|e /swiːd/ n sueco m. ~**en** n Suécia f. ~**ish** a & n sueco (m)

sweep /swiːp/ vt/i (pt swept) varrer; (go majestically) avançar majestosamente; (carry away) arrastar; (chimney) limpar □ n (with broom) varredela f; (curve) curva f; (movement) gesto m largo. (chimney-)~ limpa-chaminés m. ~**ing** a (gesture) largo; (action) de grande alcance. ~**ing statement** generalização f fácil

sweet /swiːt/ a (-er, -est) doce; (colloq: charming) doce, gracinha; (colloq: pleasant) agradável □ n doce m. ~**corn** milho m. ~ **pea** ervilha-de-cheiro f. ~ **shop** confeitaria f. **have a** ~ **tooth** gostar de doce. ~**ly** adv docemente. ~**ness** n doçura f

sweeten /ˈswiːtn/ vt adoçar; (fig: mitigate) suavizar. ~**er** n (for tea, coffee) adoçante m (artificial); (colloq: bribe) agrado m

sweetheart /ˈswiːthaːt/ n namorado m, namorada f; (term of endearment) querido m, querida f, amor m

swell /swel/ vt/i (pt swelled, pp swollen or swelled) (expand) inchar; (increase) aumentar □ n (of sea) ondulação f □ a (colloq: excellent) excelente; (colloq : smart) chique. ~**ing** n (med) inchação f, inchaço m

swelter /ˈsweltə(r)/ vi fazer um calor abrasador; (person) abafar (com calor)

swept /swept/ see **sweep**

swerve /swɜːv/ vi desviar-se, dar uma guinada

swift /swɪft/ a (-er, -est) rápido, veloz. ~**ly** adv rapidamente. ~**ness** n rapidez f

swig /swɪg/ vt (pt swigged) (colloq: drink) emborcar, beber em longos tragos □ n (colloq) trago m, gole m

swill /swɪl/ vt passar por água □ n (pig-food) lavagem f, (P) lavadura f

swim /swɪm/ vi (pt swam, pp swum, pres p swimming) nadar; (room, head) rodar □ vt atravessar a nado; (distance) nadar □ n banho m. ~**mer** n nadador m. ~**ming** n natação f. ~**ming-bath**, ~**ming-pool** ns piscina f. ~**ming-cap** n touca f de banho. ~**ming-costume**, ~-**suit** ns maiô m, (P) fato m de banho. ~**ming-trunks** npl calção m de banho

swindle /ˈswɪndl/ vt trapacear, fraudar, (P) vigarizar □ n vigarice f. ~**r** /-ə(r)/ n vigarista mf

swine /swaɪn/ npl (pigs) porcos mpl □

n (pl invar) (colloq: person) animal m, canalha m (colloq)

swing /swɪŋ/ vt/i (pt swung) balançar(-se); (turn round) girar □ n (seat) balanço m; (of opinion) reviravolta f; (mus) swing m; (rhythm) ritmo m. **in full** ~ no máximo, em plena atividade, (P) actividade. ~**round** (of person) virar-se. ~-**bridge**/**door** n ponte f/porta f giratória

swipe /swaɪp/ vt (colloq: hit) bater em, dar uma pancada em (colloq); (colloq: steal) afanar, roubar (colloq) □ n (colloq: hit) pancada f (colloq)

swirl /swɜːl/ vi rodopiar, redemoinhar □ n turbilhão m, redemoinho m

swish /swɪʃ/ vt/i sibilar, zunir, (fazer) cortar o ar; (with brushing sound) roçar □ a (colloq) chique

Swiss /swɪs/ a & n suíço (m)

switch /swɪtʃ/ n interruptor m; (change) mudança f □ vt (transfer) transferir; (exchange) trocar □ vi desviar-se. ~ **off** desligar

switchboard /ˈswɪtʃbɔːd/ n (telephone) PBX m, mesa f telefônica

Switzerland /ˈswɪtsələnd/ n Suíça f

swivel /ˈswɪvl/ vt/i (pt swivelled) (fazer) girar. ~ **chair** cadeira f giratória

swollen /ˈswəʊlən/ see **swell** □ a inchado

swoop /swuːp/ vi (bird) lançar-se, cair (**down on** sobre); (police) dar uma batida policial, (P) rusga

sword /sɔːd/ n espada f

swore /swɔː(r)/ see **swear**

sworn /swɔːn/ see **swear** □ a (enemy) jurado, declarado; (ally) fiel

swot /swɒt/ vt/i (pt swotted) (colloq: study) estudar muito, (P) marrar (sl) □ n (colloq) estudante m muito aplicado, (P) marrão m (sl)

swum /swʌm/ see **swim**

swung /swʌŋ/ see **swing**

sycamore /ˈsɪkəmɔː(r)/ n (maple) sicômoro m, (P) sicómoro m; (Amer: plane) plátano m

syllable /ˈsɪləbl/ n sílaba f

syllabus /ˈsɪləbəs/ n (pl -uses) programa m

symbol /ˈsɪmbl/ n símbolo m. ~**ic(al)** /-ˈbɒlɪk(l)/ a simbólico. ~**ism** n simbolismo m

symbolize /ˈsɪmbəlaɪz/ vt simbolizar

symmetr|y /ˈsɪmətrɪ/ n simetria f. ~**ical** /sɪˈmetrɪkl/ a simétrico

sympathize /ˈsɪmpəθaɪz/ vi ~ **with** ter pena de, condoer-se de; (fig) compartilhar os sentimentos de. ~**r** n simpatizante mf

sympathy /ˈsɪmpəθɪ/ n (pity) pena f, compaixão f; (solidarity) solidariedade f; (condolences) pêsames mpl, condolências fpl. **be in** ~**y with** estar

de acordo com. ~etic /-ˈθetɪk/ a compreensivo, simpático; (likeable) simpático; (showing pity) compassivo. ~etically /-ˈθetɪklɪ/ adv compassivamente; (fig) compreensivamente
symphon|y /ˈsɪmfənɪ/ n sinfonia f □ a sinfónico, (P) sinfónico. ~ic /-ˈfɒnɪk/ a sinfónico, (P) sinfónico
symptom /ˈsɪmptəm/ n sintoma m. ~atic /-ˈmætɪk/ a sintomático (of de)
synagogue /ˈsɪnəgɒg/ n sinagoga f
synchronize /ˈsɪŋkrənaɪz/ vt sincronizar
syndicate /ˈsɪndɪkət/ n sindicato m
syndrome /ˈsɪndrəʊm/ n (med) síndrome m, (P) síndroma m
synonym /ˈsɪnənɪm/ n sinónimo m, (P) sinónimo m. ~ous /sɪˈnɒnɪməs/ a sinónimo, (P) sinónimo (with de)
synopsis /sɪˈnɒpsɪs/ n (pl -opses /-siːz/) sinopse f, resumo m
syntax /ˈsɪntæks/ n sintaxe f
synthesis /ˈsɪnθəsɪs/ n (pl -theses /-siːz/) síntese f
synthetic /sɪnˈθetɪk/ a sintético
syphilis /ˈsɪfɪlɪs/ n sífilis f
Syria /ˈsɪrɪə/ n Síria f. ~n a & n sírio (m)
syringe /sɪˈrɪndʒ/ n seringa f □ vt seringar
syrup /ˈsɪrəp/ n (liquid) xarope m; (treacle) calda f de açúcar. ~y a (fig) melado, enjoativo
system /ˈsɪstəm/ n sistema m; (body) organismo m; (order) método m. ~atic /sɪstəˈmætɪk/ a sistemático

T

tab /tæb/ n (flap) lingueta f; (for fastening, hanging) aba f; (label) etiqueta f; (loop) argola f; (Amer colloq: bill) conta f. **keep ~s on** (colloq) vigiar
table /ˈteɪbl/ n mesa f; (list) tabela f, lista f □ vt (submit) apresentar; (postpone) adiar. **at ~** à mesa. **lay** or **set the ~** pôr a mesa. **~ of contents** índice m (das matérias). **turn the ~s** inverter as posições. **~-cloth** n toalha de mesa f. **~-mat** n descanso m. **~ tennis** pingue-pongue m
tablespoon /ˈteɪblspuːn/ n colher f grande de sopa. **~ful** n (pl **~fuls**) colher f de sopa cheia
tablet /ˈtæblɪt/ n (of stone) lápide f, placa f; (drug) comprimido m
tabloid /ˈtæblɔɪd/ n tablóide m. **~ journalism** (pej) jornalismo m sensacionalista, imprensa f marron
taboo /təˈbuː/ n & a tabu (m)
tacit /ˈtæsɪt/ a tácito
taciturn /ˈtæsɪtɜːn/ a taciturno
tack /tæk/ n (nail) tacha f; (stitch)

ponto m de alinhavo; (naut) amura f; (fig: course of action) rumo m □ vt (nail) pregar com tachas; (stitch) alinhavar □ vi (naut) bordejar. **~ on** (add) acrescentar, juntar
tackle /ˈtækl/ n equipamento m, apetrechos mpl; (sport) placagem f □ vt (problem etc) atacar; (sport) placar; (a thief etc) agarrar-se a
tacky /ˈtækɪ/ a (-ier, -iest) peganhento, pegajoso
tact /tækt/ n tacto m, (P) tacto m. **~ful** a cheio de tato, (P) tacto, diplomático. **~fully** adv com tato, (P) tacto. **~less** a sem tato, (P) tacto. **~lessly** adv sem tato, (P) tacto
tactic /ˈtæktɪk/ n (expedient) tática f, (P) táctica f. **~s** n(pl) (procedure) tática f, (P) táctica f. **~al** a tático, (P) táctico
tadpole /ˈtædpəʊl/ n girino m
tag /tæg/ n (label) etiqueta f; (on shoelace) agulheta f; (phrase) chavão m, cliché m □ vi (pt tagged) etiquetar; (add) juntar □ vi **~ along** (colloq) andar atrás, seguir
Tagus /ˈteɪgəs/ n Tejo m
tail /teɪl/ n cauda f, rabo m; (of shirt) fralda f. **~s!** (tossing coin) coroa! □ vt (follow) seguir, vigiar □ vi **~ away** or **off** diminuir, baixar. **~-back** n (traffic) fila f, (P) bicha f. **~-end** n parte f traseira, cauda f. **~-light** n (auto) farolete m traseiro, (P) farolim m da rectaguarda
tailor /ˈteɪlə(r)/ n alfaiate m □ vt (garment) fazer; (fig: adapt) adaptar. **~made** a feito sob medida, (P) por medida. **~-made for** (fig) feito para, talhado para
tainted /ˈteɪntɪd/ a (infected) contaminado; (decayed) estragado; (fig) manchado
take /teɪk/ vt/i (pt **took**, pp **taken**) (get hold of) agarrar em, pegar em; (capture) tomar; (a seat, a drink; train, bus etc) tomar; (carry) levar (to a, para); (contain, escort) levar; (tolerate) suportar, agüentar, (P) aguentar; (choice, exam) fazer; (photo) tirar; (require) exigir. **be ~n by** or **with** ficar encantado com. **be ~n ill** adoecer. **it ~s time** leva tempo para. **~ after** parecer-se a. **~-away** n (meal) comida f para levar, take-away m; (shop) loja f que só vende comida para ser consumida em outro lugar. **~ away** levar. **~ away from** sb/sth tirar de alguém/de alg coisa. **~ back** aceitar de volta; (return) devolver; (accompany) acompanhar; (statement) retirar, retratar. **~ down** (object) tirar para baixo; (notes) tirar, tomar. **~ in** (garment) meter para

dentro; (*include*) incluir; (*cheat*) enganar, levar (*colloq*); (*grasp*) compreender; (*receive*) receber. ~ **it that** supor que. ~ **off** *vt* (*remove*) tirar; (*mimic*) imitar, arremedar □ *vi* (*aviat*) descolar, levantar vôo. ~ **off** *n* imitação *f*; (*aviat*) decolagem *f*, (*P*) descolagem *f*. ~ **on** (*task*) encarregar-se de; (*staff*) admitir, contratar. ~ **out** tirar; (*on an outing*) levar para sair. ~ **over** *vt* tomar conta de, assumir a direção, (*P*) direcção de □ *vi* tomar o poder. ~ **over from** (*relieve*) render, substituir; (*succeed*) suceder a. ~ **over** *n* (*pol*) tomada *f* de poder; (*comm*) take-over *m*. ~ **part** participar *or* tomar parte (*in* em). ~ **place** ocorrer, suceder. ~ **sides** tomar partido. ~ **sides with** tomar o partido de. ~ **to** gostar de, simpatizar com; (*activity*) tomar gosto por, entregar-se a. ~ **up** (*object*) apanhar, pegar em; (*hobby*) dedicar-se a; (*occupy*) ocupar, tomar

takings /ˈteɪkɪŋz/ *npl* receita *f*

talcum /ˈtælkəm/ *n* talco *m*. ~ **powder** pó *m* talco

tale /teɪl/ *n* conto *m*, história *f*

talent /ˈtælənt/ *n* talento *m*. ~**ed** *a* talentoso, bem dotado

talk /tɔːk/ *vt/i* falar; (*chat*) conversar □ *n* conversa *f*; (*mode of speech*) fala *f*; (*lecture*) palestra *f*. **small** ~ conversa *f* banal. ~ **into doing** convencer a fazer. ~ **nonsense** dizer disparates. ~ **over** discutir. ~ **shop** falar de assuntos profissionais. ~ **to o.s.** falar sozinho, falar com os seus botões. **there's** ~ **of** fala-se de. ~**er** *n* conversador *m*. ~**ing-to** *n* (*colloq*) descompostura *f*

talkative /ˈtɔːkətɪv/ *a* falador, conversador, tagarela

tall /tɔːl/ *a* (-**er**, -**est**) alto. ~ **story** (*colloq*) história *f* do arco-da-velha

tallboy /ˈtɔːlbɔɪ/ *n* cómoda *f*, (*P*) cómoda *f* alta

tally /ˈtælɪ/ *vi* corresponder (**with** a), conferir (**with** com)

tambourine /tæmbəˈriːn/ *n* tamborim *m*, pandeiro *m*

tame /teɪm/ *a* (-**er**, -**est**) manso; (*domesticated*) domesticado; (*dull*) insípido □ *vt* amansar, domesticar

tamper /ˈtæmpə(r)/ *vi* ~ **with** mexer indevidamente em; (*text*) alterar

tampon /ˈtæmpən/ *n* (*med*) tampão *m*; (*sanitary towel*) toalha *f* higiénica

tan /tæn/ *vt/i* (*pt* **tanned**) queimar, bronzear; (*hide*) curtir □ *n* bronzeado *m* □ *a* castanho amarelado

tandem /ˈtændəm/ *n* (*bicycle*) tandem *m*. **in** ~ em tandem, um atrás do outro

tang /tæŋ/ *n* (*taste*) sabor *m* or gosto

m característico; (*smell*) cheiro *m* característico

tangent /ˈtændʒənt/ *n* tangente *f*

tangerine /tændʒəˈriːn/ *n* tangerina *f*

tangible /ˈtændʒəbl/ *a* tangível

tangle /ˈtæŋgl/ *vt* emaranhar, enredar □ *n* emaranhado *m*. **become** ~**d** emaranhar-se, enredar-se

tank /tæŋk/ *n* tanque *m*, reservatório *m*; (*for petrol*) tanque *m*, (*P*) depósito *m*; (*for fish*) aquário *m*; (*mil*) tanque *m*

tankard /ˈtæŋkəd/ *n* caneca *f* grande

tanker /ˈtæŋkə(r)/ *n* carro-tanque *m*, camião-cisterna *m*; (*ship*) petroleiro *m*

tantalize /ˈtæntəlaɪz/ *vt* atormentar, tantalizar. ~**ing** *a* tentador

tantamount /ˈtæntəmaʊnt/ *a* **be** ~ **to** equivaler a

tantrum /ˈtæntrəm/ *n* chilique *m*, ataque *m* de mau génio, (*P*) génio, birra *f*

tap /tæp/ *n* (*for water etc*) torneira *f* □ *vt* (*pt* **tapped**) (*resources*) explorar; (*telephone*) gram-pear. **on** ~ (*colloq: available*) disponível

tap /tæp/ *vt/i* (*pt* **tapped**) bater levemente. ~-**dance** *n* sapateado *m*

tape /teɪp/ *n* (*for dressmaking*) fita *f*; (*sticky*) fita adesiva. (**magnetic**) ~ fita *f* (magnética) □ *vt* (*tie*) atar, prender; (*stick*) colar; (*record*) gravar. ~-**measure** *n* fita *f* métrica. ~-**recorder** *n* gravador *m*

taper /ˈteɪpə(r)/ *n* vela *f* comprida e fina □ *vt/i* ~ (**off**) estreitar(-se), afilar(-se). ~**ed** ~**ing** *adjs* (*fingers etc*) afilado; (*trousers*) afunilado

tapestry /ˈtæpɪstrɪ/ *n* tapeçaria *f*

tapioca /tæpɪˈəʊkə/ *n* tapioca *f*

tar /tɑː(r)/ *n* alcatrão *m* □ *vt* (*pt* **tarred**) alcatroar

target /ˈtɑːgɪt/ *n* alvo *m* □ *vt* ter como alvo

tariff /ˈtærɪf/ *n* tarifa *f*; (*on import*) direitos *mpl* aduaneiros

Tarmac /ˈtɑːmæk/ *n* macadame (alcatroado) *m*; (*runway*) pista *f*

tarnish /ˈtɑːnɪʃ/ *vt/i* (fazer) perder o brilho; (*stain*) manchar

tarpaulin /tɑːˈpɔːlɪn/ *n* lona *f* impermeável (alcatroada *or* encerada)

tart /tɑːt/ *a* (-**er**, -**est**) ácido, (*fig: cutting*) mordaz, azedo

tart /tɑːt/ *n* (*culin*) torta *f* de fruta, (*P*) tarte *f*; (*sl: prostitute*) prostituta *f*, mulher *f* da vida (*sl*) □ *vt* ~ **up** (*colloq*) embonecar(-se)

tartan /ˈtɑːtn/ *n* tecido *m* escocês □ *a* escocês

tartar /ˈtɑːtə(r)/ *n* (*on teeth*) tártaro *m*, (*P*) pedra *f*. ~ **sauce** molho *m* tártaro

task /tɑːsk/ *n* tarefa *f*, trabalho *m*.

take to ~ repreender, censurar. ~ **force** (*mil*) força-tarefa *f*

tassel /'tæsl/ *n* borla *f*

taste /teɪst/ *n* gosto *m*; (*fig: sample*) amostra *f* □ *vt* (*eat, enjoy*) saborear; (*try*) provar; (*perceive taste of*) sentir o gosto de □ *vi* ~ **of** or **like** ter o sabor de. **have a** ~ **of** (*experience*) provar. ~**ful***a* de bom gosto. ~**fully***adv* com bom gosto. ~**less***a* insípido, insosso; (*fig: not in good taste*) sem gosto; (*fig: in bad taste*) de mau gosto

tasty /'teɪstɪ/ *a* (-**ier**, -**iest**) saboroso, gostoso

tat /tæt/ *see* **tit**[^1]

tatter|s /'tætəz/ *npl* farrapos *mpl*. ~**ed** /-əd/ *a* esfarrapado

tattoo[^1] /tə'tuː/ *vt* tatuar □ *n* tatuagem *f*

tatty /'tætɪ/ *a* (-**ier**, -**iest**) (*colloq*) enxovalhado, em mau estado

taught /tɔːt/ *see* **teach**

taunt /tɔːnt/ *vt* escarnecer de, zombar de □ *n* escárnio *m*. ~**ing** *adv* escarninho

Taurus /'tɔːrəs/ *n* (*astr*) Touro *m*, (*P*) Taurus *m*

taut /tɔːt/ *a* esticado, retesado; (*fig: of nerves*) tenso

tawdry /'tɔːdrɪ/ *a* (-**ier**, -**iest**) espalhafatoso e ordinário

tawny /'tɔːnɪ/ *a* fulvo

tax /tæks/ *n* taxa *f*, imposto *m*; (*on income*) imposto *m* de renda, (*P*) sobre o rendimento □ *vt* taxar, lançar impostos sobre; tributar; (*fig: put to test*) pôr à prova. ~-**collector** *n* cobrador *m* de impostos. ~-**free** *a* isento de imposto. ~ **relief** isenção *f* de imposto. ~ **return** declaração *f* do imposto de renda, (*P*) sobre o rendimento. ~ **year** ano *m* fiscal. ~**able** *a* tributável, passível de imposto. ~**ation** /-'seɪʃn/ *n* impostos *mpl*, tributação *f*. ~**ing** *a* penoso, difícil

taxi /'tæksɪ/ *n* (*pl* -**is**) táxi *m* □ *vi* (*pt* **taxied** *pres p* **taxiing**) (*aviat*) rolar na pista, taxiar. ~-**cab** *n* táxi *m*. ~-**driver** *n* motorista *mf* de táxi. ~-**rank** (*Amer*) ~ **stand** ponto *m* de táxis, (*P*) praça *f* de táxis

taxpayer /'tækspeɪə(r)/ *n* contribuinte *mf*

tea /tiː/ *n* chá *m*. **high** ~ refeição *f* leve à noite. ~-**bag** *n* saquinho *m* de chá. ~-**break** *n* intervalo *m* para o chá. ~-**cosy** *n* abafador *m* de chá. ~-**leaf** *n* folha *f* de chá. ~-**set** *n* serviço *m* de chá. ~-**shop** *n* salão *m* or casa *f* de chá. ~-**time** *n* hora *f* do chá. ~-**towel** *n* pano *m* de prato

teach /tiːtʃ/ *vt* (*pt* **taught**) ensinar, lecionar, (*P*) leccionar (**sb sth** alg coisa a alguém) □ *vi* ensinar, ser professor. ~**er** *n* professor *m*. ~**ing** *n* ensino *m*; (*doctrines*) ensinamento(s) *m* (*pl*) □ *a* pedagógico, de ensino; (*staff*) docente

teacup /'tiːkʌp/ *n* xícara *f* de chá, (*P*) chávena *f*

teak /tiːk/ *n* teca *f*

team /tiːm/ *n* equipe *f*, (*P*) equipa *f*; (*of oxen*) junta *f*; (*of horses*) parelha *f* □ *vi* ~ **up** juntar-se, associar-se (**with** a). ~-**work** *n* trabalho *m* de equipe, (*P*) equipa

teapot /'tiːpɒt/ *n* bule *m*

tear[^1] /teə(r)/ *vt/i* (*pt* **tore** *pp* **torn**) rasgar(-se); (*snatch*) arrancar, puxar; (*rush*) lançar-se, ir numa correria; (*fig*) dividir □ *n* rasgão *m*. ~ **o.s. away** arrancar-se (**from** de)

tear[^2] /tɪə(r)/ *n* lágrima *f*. ~-**gas** *n* gases *mpl* lacrimogênios, (*P*) lacrimogénios

tearful /'tɪəfl/ *a* lacrimoso, choroso. ~**ly** *adv* choroso, com (as) lágrimas nos olhos

tease /tiːz/ *vt* implicar; (*make fun of*) caçoar de

teaspoon /'tiːspuːn/ *n* colher *f* de chá. ~**ful** *n* (*pl* -**fuls**) colher *f* de chá cheia

teat /tiːt/ *n* (*of bottle*) bico *m*; (*of animal*) teta *f*

technical /'teknɪkl/ *a* técnico. ~**ity** /-'kælətɪ/ *n* questão *f* de ordem técnica. ~**ly** *adv* tecnicamente

technician /tek'nɪʃn/ *n* técnico *m*

technique /tek'niːk/ *n* técnica *f*

technolog|y /tek'nɒlədʒɪ/ *n* tecnologia *f*. ~**ical** /-ə'lɒdʒɪkl/ *a* tecnológico

teddy /'tedɪ/ *a* ~ (-**bear**) ursinho *m* de pelúcia, (*P*) peluche

tedious /'tiːdɪəs/ *a* maçante

tedium /'tiːdɪəm/ *n* tédio *m*

tee /tiː/ *n* (*golf*) tee *m*

teem[^1] /tiːm/ *vi* ~ (**with**) (*swarm*) pulular (de), fervilhar (de), abundar (em)

teem[^2] /tiːm/ *vi* ~ (**with rain**) chover torrencialmente

teenage /'tiːneɪdʒ/ *a* juvenil, de/para adolescente. ~**r** /-ə(r)/ *n* jovem *mf*, adolescente *mf*

teens /tiːnz/ *npl* na adolescência, entre os 13 e os 19 anos

teeter /'tiːtə(r)/ *vi* cambalear, vacilar

teeth /tiːθ/ *see* **tooth**

teeth|e /tiːð/ *vi* começar a ter dentes. ~**ing troubles** (*fig*) problemas *mpl* iniciais

teetotaller /tiː'təʊtlə(r)/ *n* abstêmio *m*, (*P*) abstémio *m*

telecommunications /telɪkəmjuːnɪ-'keɪʃnz/ *npl* telecomunicações *fpl*

telegram /'telɪgræm/ *n* telegrama *m*

telegraph /'telɪgrɑːf/ *n* telégrafo *m* □

a telegráfico. ~**ic** /-'græfɪk/ *a* telegráfico

telepath|y /tɪ'lepəθɪ/ *n* telepatia *f*. ~**ic** /telɪ'pæθɪk/ *a* telepático

telephone /'telɪfəʊn/ *n* telefone *m* □ *vt* (*person*) telefonar a; (*message*) telefonar □ *vi* telefonar. ~ **book** lista *f* telefônica, (P) telefónica, guia *m* telefônico, (P) telefónico. ~ **box**, ~ **booth** cabine *f* telefônica, (P) telefónica. ~ **call** chamada *f*. ~ **directory** lista *f* telefônica, (P) telefónica, guia *m* telefônico, (P) telefónico. ~ **number** número *m* de telefone

telephonist /tɪ'lefənɪst/ *n* (*in exchange*) telefonista *mf*

telephoto /telɪ'fəʊtəʊ/ *n* ~ **lens** teleobjetiva *f*, (P) teleobjectiva *f*

telescop|e /'telɪskəʊp/ *n* telescópio *m* □ *vt/i* encaixar(-se). ~**ic** /-'skɒpɪk/ *a* telescópico

teletext /'telɪtekst/ *n* teletexto *m*

televise /'telɪvaɪz/ *vt* televisionar

television /'telɪvɪʒn/ *n* televisão *f*. ~ **set** aparelho *m* de televisão, (P) televisor *m*

telex /'teleks/ *n* telex *m* □ *vt* transmitir por telex, telexar

tell /tel/ *vt* (*pt* **told**) dizer (*sb sth* algo coisa a alguém); (*story*) contar; (*distinguish*) distinguir, diferençar □ *vi* (*know*) ver-se, saber. **I told you so** bem lhe disse. ~ **of** falar de. ~ **off** (*colloq: scold*) ralhar, dar uma bronca em. ~ **on** (*have effect on*) afetar, (P) afectar; (*colloq: inform on*) fazer queixa de (*colloq*). ~**-tale** *n* mexeriqueiro *m*, fofoqueiro *m* □ *a* (*revealing*) revelador. **tales** mexericar, fofocar

telly /'telɪ/ *n* (*colloq*) TV *f* (*colloq*)

temp /temp/ *n* (*colloq*) empregado *m* temporário

temper /'tempə(r)/ *n* humor *m*, disposição *f*; (*anger*) mau humor *m* □ *vt* temperar. **keep/lose one's** ~ manter a calma/perder a calma *or* a cabeça, zangar-se

temperament /'temprəmənt/ *n* temperamento *m*. ~**al** /-'mentl/ *a* caprichoso

temperance /'tempərəns/ *n* (*in drinking*) moderação *f*, sobriedade *f*

temperate /'tempərət/ *a* moderado, comedido; (*climate*) temperado

temperature /'temprətʃə(r)/ *n* temperatura *f*. **have a** ~ estar com *or* ter febre

tempest /'tempɪst/ *n* tempestade *f*, temporal *m*

tempestuous /tem'pestʃʊəs/ *a* tempestuoso

template /'templ(e)ɪt/ *n* molde *m*

temple[1] /'templ/ *n* templo *m*

temple[2] /'templ/ *n* (*anat*) têmpora *f*, fonte *f*

tempo /'tempəʊ/ *n* (*pl* -**os**) (*mus*) tempo *m*; (*pace*) ritmo *m*

temporar|y /'temprərɪ/ *a* temporário, provisório. ~**ily** *adv* temporariamente, provisoriamente

tempt /tempt/ *vt* tentar. ~ **sb to do** dar a alguém vontade de fazer, tentar alguém a fazer. ~**ation** /-'teɪʃn/ *n* tentação *f*. ~**ing** *a* tentador

ten /ten/ *a* & *n* dez (*m*)

tenac|ious /tɪ'neɪʃəs/ *a* tenaz. ~**ity** /-'æsətɪ/ *n* tenacidade *f*

tenant /'tenənt/ *n* inquilino *m*, locatário *m*

tend[1] /tend/ *vt* tomar conta de, cuidar de

tend[2] /tend/ *vi* ~ **to** (*be apt to*) tender a, ter tendência para

tendency /'tendənsɪ/ *n* tendência *f*

tender[1] /'tendə(r)/ *a* (*soft, delicate*) terno; (*sore, painful*) sensível, dolorido; (*loving*) terno, meigo. ~**-hearted** *a* compassivo. ~**ly** *adv* (*lovingly*) ternamente, meigamente; (*delicately*) delicadamente. ~**ness** *n* (*love*) ternura *f*, meiguice *f*

tender[2] /'tendə(r)/ *vt* (*money*) oferecer; (*apologies, resignation*) apresentar □ *vi* ~ (**for**) apresentar orçamento (para) □ *n* (*comm*) orçamento *m*. **legal** ~ (*money*) moeda *f* corrente

tendon /'tendən/ *n* tendão *m*

tenement /'tenəmənt/ *n* prédio *m* de apartamentos de renda moderada; (*Amer: slum*) prédio *m* pobre

tenet /'tenɪt/ *n* princípio *m*, dogma *m*

tennis /'tenɪs/ *n* tênis *m*, (P) ténis *m*. ~ **court** quadra *f* de tênis, (P) court *m* de ténis

tenor /'tenə(r)/ *n* (*meaning*) teor *m*; (*mus*) tenor *m*

tense[1] /tens/ *n* (*gram*) tempo *m*

tense[2] /tens/ *a* (-**er**, -**est**) tenso □ *vt* (*muscles*) retesar

tension /'tenʃn/ *n* tensão *f*

tent /tent/ *n* tenda *f*, barraca *f*. ~**-peg** *n* estaca *f*

tentacle /'tentəkl/ *n* tentáculo *m*

tentative /'tentətɪv/ *a* provisório; (*hesitant*) hesitante. ~**ly** *adv* tentativamente, a título experimental; (*hesitantly*) hesitantemente

tenterhooks /'tentəhʊks/ *npl* **on** ~ em suspense

tenth /tenθ/ *a* & *n* décimo (*m*)

tenuous /'tenjʊəs/ *a* tênue, (P) ténue

tepid /'tepɪd/ *a* tépido, morno

term /tɜːm/ *n* (*word*) termo *m*; (*limit*) prazo *m*, termo *m*; (*schol etc*) período *m*, trimestre *m*; (*Amer*) semestre *m*; (*of imprisonment*) (duração) pena *f*. ~**s** (*conditions*) condições *fpl* □ *vt* designar, denominar, chamar. **on good/**

bad ~s de boas/más relações. **not on
speaking** ~s de relações cortadas.
come to ~s with chegar a um acordo
com; (*become resigned to*) resignar-se
a. ~ **of office** (*pol*) mandato *m*

terminal /'tɜːmɪnl/ *a* terminal, final;
(*illness*) fatal, mortal □ *n* (*oil, computer*) terminal *m*; (*rail*) estação *f*
terminal; (*electr*) borne *m*. **(air)** ~
terminal *m* (de avião)

terminat|e /'tɜːmɪneɪt/ *vt* terminar,
pôr termo a □ *vi* terminar. ~**ion**
/-'neɪʃn/ *n* término *m*, (*P*) terminação *f*, termo *m*

terminology /tɜːmɪ'nɒlədʒɪ/ *n* termi-
nologia *f*

terminus /'tɜːmənəs/ *n* (*pl* -**ni** /-naɪ/)
(*rail, coach*) estação *f* terminal

terrace /'terəs/ *n* terraço *m*; (*in culti-
vation*) socalco *m*; (*houses*) casas *fpl*
em fileira continua, lance *m* de
casas. **the** ~**s** (*sport*) arquibancada
f. ~**d house** casa *f* ladeada por outras
casas

terrain /te'reɪn/ *n* terreno *m*

terribl|e /'terəbl/ *a* terrível. ~**y** *adv*
terrivelmente; (*colloq: very*) extremamente, espantosamente

terrific /tə'rɪfɪk/ *a* terrífico, tremendo; (*colloq: excellent; great*) tremendo.
~**ally** *adv* (*colloq: very*) tremenda-
mente (*colloq*); (*colloq: very well*) lindamente, maravilhosamente

terrif|y /'terɪfaɪ/ *vt* aterrar, ater-
rorizar. **be** ~**ied of** ter pavor de

territorial /terɪ'tɔːrɪəl/ *a* territorial

territory /'terɪtərɪ/ *n* território *m*

terror /'terə(r)/ *n* terror *m*, pavor *m*

terroris|t /'terərɪst/ *n* terrorista *mf*.
~**m** /-zəm/ *n* terrorismo *m*

terrorize /'terəraɪz/ *vt* aterrorizar,
aterrar

terse /tɜːs/ *a* conciso, lapidar; (*curt*)
lacónico, (*P*) lacónico

test /test/ *n* teste *m*, exame *m*, prova *f*;
(*schol*) prova *f*, teste *m*; (*of goods*) controle *m*; (*of machine etc*) ensaio *m*; (*of
strength*) prova *f* □ *vt* examinar;
(*check*) controlar; (*try*) ensaiar;
(*pupil*) interrogar. **put to the** ~ pôr
à prova. ~ **match** jogo *m* internacional. ~-**tube** *n* proveta *f*. ~-**tube
baby** bebê *m* de proveta

testament /'testəmənt/ *n* testamento
m. **Old/New T**~ Antigo/Novo Testamento *m*

testicle /'testɪkl/ *n* testículo *m*

testify /'testɪfaɪ/ *vt/i* testificar, testemunhar, depôr

testimonial /testɪ'məʊnɪəl/ *n* carta *f*
de recomendação

testimony /'testɪmənɪ/ *n* testemunho
m

tetanus /'tetənəs/ *n* tétano *m*

tether /'teðə(r)/ *vt* prender com corda
□ *n* **be at the end of one's** ~ não
poder mais, estar nas últimas

text /tekst/ *n* texto *m*

textbook /'tekstbʊk/ *n* compêndio *m*,
manual *m*, livro *m* de texto

textile /'tekstaɪl/ *n* & *a* têxtil (*m*)

texture /'tekstʃə(r)/ *n* (*of fabric*) tex-
tura *f*; (*of paper*) grão *m*

Thai /taɪ/ *a* & *n* tailandês (*m*). ~**land**
n Tailândia *f*

Thames /temz/ *n* Tâmisa *m*

than /ðæn/; *unstressed* /ðən/ *conj* que,
do que; (*with numbers*) de. **more/less**
~ **ten** mais/menos de dez

thank /θæŋk/ *vt* agradecer. ~ **you!**
obrigado! ~**s!** (*colloq*) (*P*) obrigadinho! (*colloq*). ~**s** *npl* agradecimentos
mpl. ~**s to** graças a. **T**~**sgiving
(Day)** (*Amer*) Dia *m* de Ação, (*P*) Acção de Graças

thankful /'θæŋkfl/ *a* grato, agradecido, reconhecido (**for** por). ~**ly** *adv*
com gratidão; (*happily*) felizmente

thankless /'θæŋklɪs/ *a* ingrato, mal
agradecido

that /ðæt/; *unstressed* /ðət/ *a* & *pron*
(*pl* **those**) esse/essa, esses/essas;
(*more distant*) aquele/aquela, aqueles
/aquelas; (*neuter*) isso *invar*; (*more
distant*) aquilo *invar* □ *adv* tão, tanto,
de tal modo □ *rel pron* que □ *conj* que.
~ **boy** esse/aquele rapaz. **what is** ~?
o que é isso? **who is** ~? quem é? **is** ~
you? é você? **give me** ~ **(one)** dá-me
esse. ~ **is (to say)** isto é, quer dizer.
after ~ depois disso. **the day** ~ o dia
em que. ~ **much** tanto assim, tanto
como isto

thatch /θætʃ/ *n* colmo *m*. ~**ed** *a* de
colmo. ~**ed cottage** casa *f* com telhado de colmo

thaw /θɔː/ *vt/i* derreter(-se), degelar;
(*food*) descongelar □ *n* degelo *m*, der-
retimento *m*

the /*before vowel* ðɪ/, *before consonant*
ðə/, *stressed* ðiː/ *a* o, a (*pl* os, as). **of**
~, **from** ~ do, da (*pl* dos, das). **at** ~,
to ~ ao, à (*pl* aos, às), para o/a/os/
as. **in** ~ no, na (*pl* nos, nas). **by** ~
hour a cada hora □ *adv* **all** ~ **better**
tanto melhor. ~ **more...** ~ **more...**
quanto mais... tanto mais...

theatre /'θɪətə(r)/ *n* teatro *m*

theatrical /θɪ'ætrɪkl/ *a* teatral

theft /θeft/ *n* roubo *m*

their /ðeə(r)/ *a* deles, delas, seu

theirs /ðeəz/ *poss pron* o(s) seu(s), a(s)
sua(s), o(s) deles, a(s) delas. **it is** ~ é
(o) deles/delas *or* o seu

them /ðem/; *unstressed* /ðəm/ *pron* os,
as; (*after prep*) eles, elas. **(to)** ~ lhes

theme /θiːm/ *n* tema *m*

themselves /ðəm'selvz/ *pron* eles

mesmos/próprios, elas mesmas/próprias; (*reflexive*) se; (*after prep*) si (mesmos, próprios). **by ~** sozinhos. **with ~** consigo

then /ðen/ *adv* (*at that time*) então, nessa altura; (*next*) depois, em seguida; (*in that case*) então, nesse caso; (*therefore*) então, portanto, por conseguinte □ *a* (de) então. **from ~** on desde então

theolog|y /θɪˈɒlədʒɪ/ *n* teologia *f*. **~ian** /θɪəˈlɒdʒən/ *n* teólogo *m*

theorem /ˈθɪərəm/ *n* teorema *m*

theor|y /ˈθɪərɪ/ *n* teoria *f*. **~etical** /ˈretɪkl/ *a* teórico

therapeutic /θerəˈpjuːtɪk/ *a* terapêutico

therap|y /ˈθerəpɪ/ *n* terapia *f*. **~ist** *n* terapeuta *mf*

there /ðeə(r)/ *adv* aí, ali, lá; (*over there*) lá, acolá □ *int* (*triumphant*) pronto, viu! lá está; (*consoling*) vamos lá. **he goes ~** ele vai aí *or* lá. **~ he goes** aí vai ele. **~ is, ~ are** há. **~ you are** (*giving*) toma. **~ and then** logo ali. **~abouts** *adv* por aí. **~after** *adv* daí em diante, depois disso. **~by** *adv* desse modo

therefore /ˈðeəfɔː(r)/ *adv* por isso, portanto, por conseguinte

thermal /ˈθɜːml/ *a* térmico

thermometer /θəˈmɒmɪtə(r)/ *n* termómetro *m*, (*P*) termômetro *m*

Thermos /ˈθɜːməs/ *n* garrafa *f* térmica, (*P*) termo *m*

thermostat /ˈθɜːməstæt/ *n* termostato *m*

thesaurus /θɪˈsɔːrəs/ *n* (*pl* -ri /-raɪ/) dicionário *m* de sinónimos, (*P*) sinónimos

these /ðiːz/ *see* **this**

thesis /ˈθiːsɪs/ *n* (*pl* **theses** /-siːz/) tese *f*

they /ðeɪ/ *pron* eles, elas. **~ say (that)...** diz-se *or* dizem que...

thick /θɪk/ *a* (**-er, -est**) espesso, grosso; (*colloq: stupid*) estúpido □ *adv* = **thickly** □ *n* **in the ~ of** no meio de. **~-skinned** *a* insensível. **~ly** *adv* espessamente; (*spread*) em camada espessa. **~ness** *n* espessura *f*, grossura *f*

thicken /ˈθɪkən/ *vt/i* engrossar, espessar(-se). **the plot ~s** o enredo complica-se

thickset /θɪkˈset/ *a* (*person*) atarracado

thief /θiːf/ *n* (*pl* **thieves** /θiːvz/) ladrão *m*, gatuno *m*

thigh /θaɪ/ *n* coxa *f*

thimble /ˈθɪmbl/ *n* dedal *m*

thin /θɪn/ *a* (**thinner, thinnest**) (*slender*) estreito, fino, delgado; (*lean, not plump*) magro; (*sparse*) ralo, escasso;

(*flimsy*) leve, fino; (*soup*) aguado; (*hair*) ralo □ *adv* = **thinly** □ *vt/i* (*pt* **thinned**) (*of liquid*) diluir(-se); (*of fog etc*) dissipar(-se); (*of hair*) rarear. **~out** (*in quantity*) diminuir, reduzir; (*seedlings etc*) desbastar. **~ly** *adv* (*sparsely*) esparsamente. **~ness** *n* (*of board, wire etc*) finura *f*; (*of person*) magreza *f*

thing /θɪŋ/ *n* coisa *f*. **~s** (*belongings*) pertences *mpl*. **the best ~ is to** o melhor é. **for one ~** em primeiro lugar. **just the ~** exatamente o que era preciso. **poor ~** coitado

think /θɪŋk/ *vt/i* (*pt* **thought**) pensar (*about, of* em); (*carefully*) refletir, (*P*) reflectir (*about, of* em). **I ~ so** eu acho que sim. **~ better of it** (*change one's mind*) pensar melhor. **~ nothing of** achar natural. **~ of** (*hold opinion of*) pensar de, achar de. **~ over** pensar bem em. **~-tank** *n* comissão *f* de peritos. **~ up** inventar. **~er** *n* pensador *m*

third /θɜːd/ *a* terceiro □ *n* terceiro *m*; (*fraction*) terço *m*. **~-party insurance** seguro *m* contra terceiros. **~-rate** *a* inferior, medíocre. **T~ World** Terceiro Mundo *m*. **~ly** *adv* em terceiro lugar

thirst /θɜːst/ *n* sede *f*. **~y** *a* sequioso, sedento. **be ~y** estar com *or* ter sede. **~ily** *adv* sofregamente

thirteen /θɜːˈtiːn/ *a & n* treze (*m*). **~th** *a & n* décimo terceiro (*m*)

thirt|y /ˈθɜːtɪ/ *a & n* trinta (*m*). **~ieth** *a & n* trigésimo (*m*)

this /ðɪs/ *a & pron* (*pl* **these**) este, esta □ *pron* isto *invar*. **~ one** este, esta. **these ones** estes, estas. **~ boy** este rapaz. **~ is** isto é. **after ~** depois disto. **like ~** assim. **~ is the man** este é o homem. **~ far** até aqui. **~ morning** esta manhã. **~ Wednesday** esta quarta-feira

thistle /ˈθɪsl/ *n* cardo *m*

thorn /θɔːn/ *n* espinho *m*, pico *m*. **~y** *a* espinhoso; (*fig*) bicudo, espinhoso

thorough /ˈθʌrə/ *a* a consciencioso; (*deep*) completo, profundo; (*cleaning, washing*) a fundo. **~ly** *adv* (*clean, study etc*) completo, a fundo, (*very*) perfeitamente, muito bem

thoroughbred /ˈθʌrəbred/ *n* (*horse etc*) puro-sangue *m invar*

thoroughfare /ˈθʌrəfeə(r)/ *n* artéria *f*. **no ~** passagem *f* proibida

those /ðəʊz/ *see* **that**

though /ðəʊ/ *conj* se bem que, embora, conquanto □ *adv* (*colloq*) contudo, no entanto

thought /θɔːt/ *see* **think** □ *n* pensamento *m*; idéia *f*. **on second ~s** pensando bem

thoughtful /ˈθɔːtfl/ a pensativo; (*considerate*) atencioso, solícito. ~ly adv pensativamente; (*considerately*) com consideração, atenciosamente

thoughtless /ˈθɔːtlɪs/ a irrefletido, (P) irreflectido; (*inconsiderate*) pouco atencioso. ~ly adv sem pensar; (*inconsiderately*) sem consideração

thousand /ˈθaʊznd/ a & n mil(m).~s of milhares de. ~th a & n milésimo (m)

thrash /θræʃ/ vt surrar, espancar; (*defeat*) dar uma surra or sova em. ~ about debater-se. ~ out debater a fundo, discutir bem

thread /θred/ n fio m; (*for sewing*) linha f de coser; (*of screw*) rosca f □ vt enfiar. ~ one's way abrir caminho, furar

threadbare /ˈθredbeə(r)/ a puído, surrado

threat /θret/ n ameaça f

threaten /ˈθretn/ vt/i ameaçar. ~ingly adv com ar ameaçador, ameaçadoramente

three /θriː/ a & n três (m)

thresh /θreʃ/ vt (*corn etc*) malhar, debulhar

threshold /ˈθreʃəʊld/ n limiar m, soleira f; (fig) limiar m

threw /θruː/ see **throw**

thrift /θrɪft/ n economia f, poupança f. ~y a económico, (P) económico, poupado

thrill /θrɪl/ n arrepio m de emoção, frêmito m, (P) frémito m □ vt excitar(-se), emocionar(-se), (fazer) vibrar. ~ed a estar/ficar encantado. ~ing a excitante, emocionante

thriller /ˈθrɪlə(r)/ n livro m or filme m de suspense

thriv|e /θraɪv/ vi (pt **thrived** or **throve**, pp **thrived** or **thriven**) prosperar, florescer; (*grow strong*) crescer, dar-se bem (on com). ~ing a próspero

throat /θrəʊt/ n garganta f. **have a sore ~** ter dores de garganta

throb /θrɒb/ vi (pt **throbbed**) (*wound, head*) latejar; (*heart*) palpitar, bater; (*engine; fig*) vibrar, trepidar □ n (*of pain*) latejo m, espasmo m; (*of heart*) palpitação f, batida f; (*of engine*) vibração f, trepidação f. ~bing a (*pain*) latejante

throes /θrəʊz/ npl **in the ~ of** (fig) às voltas com, no meio de

thrombosis /θrɒmˈbəʊsɪs/ n trombose f

throne /θrəʊn/ n trono m

throng /θrɒŋ/ n multidão f □ vt/i apinhar(-se); (*arrive*) afluir

throttle /ˈθrɒtl/ n (*auto*) válvula-borboleta f, estrangulador m, acelerador m de mão □ vt estrangular

through /θruː/ prep através de, por; (*during*) durante; (*by means or way of, out of*) por; (*by reason of*) por, por causa de □ adv através; (*entirely*) completamente, até o fim □ a (*train, traffic etc*) direto, (P) directo. **be ~** ter acabado (with com); (*telephone*) estar ligado. **come** or **go ~** (*cross, pierce*) atravessar. **get ~** (*exam*) passar. **be wet ~** estar ensopado or encharcado

throughout /θruːˈaʊt/ prep durante, por todo. ~ **the country** por todo o país afora. ~ **the day** durante todo a dia, pelo dia afora □ adv completamente; (*place*) por toda a parte; (*time*) durante todo o tempo

throw /θrəʊ/ vt (pt **threw**, pp **thrown**) atirar, jogar, lançar; (*colloq: baffle*) desconcertar □ n lançamento m; (*of dice*) lance m. ~ **a party** (*colloq*) dar uma festa. ~ **away** jogar fora, (P) deitar fora. ~ **off** (*get rid of*) livrar-se de. ~ **out** (*person*) expulsar; (*reject*) rejeitar. ~ **up** (*one's arms*) levantar; (*resign from*) abandonar; (*colloq: vomit*) vomitar

thrush /θrʌʃ/ n (*bird*) tordo m

thrust /θrʌst/ vt (pt **thrust**) arremeter, empurrar, impelir □ n empurrão m, arremetida f. ~ **into** (*put*) enfiar em, mergulhar em. ~ **upon** (*force on*) impor a

thud /θʌd/ n som m surdo, baque m

thug /θʌg/ n bandido m, facínora m, malfeitor m

thumb /θʌm/ n polegar m □ vt (*book*) manusear. ~ **a lift** pedir carona, (P) boleia. **under sb's ~** completamente dominado por alguém. ~-**index** n índice m de dedo

thumbtack /ˈθʌmtæk/ n (*Amer*) percevejo m

thump /θʌmp/ vt/i bater (em), dar pancadas (em); (*with fists*) dar murros (em); (*piano*) martelar (em); (*of heart*) bater com força □ n pancada f; (*thud*) baque m. ~**ing** a (*colloq*) enorme

thunder /ˈθʌndə(r)/ n trovão m, trovoada f; (*loud noise*) estrondo m □ vi (*weather, person*) trovejar. ~ **past** passar como um raio. ~**y** a (*weather*) tempestuoso

thunderbolt /ˈθʌndəbəʊlt/ n raio m e ribombo m de trovão; (fig) raio m fulminante (fig)

thunderstorm /ˈθʌndəstɔːm/ n tempestade f com trovoadas, temporal m

Thursday /ˈθɜːzdɪ/ n quinta-feira f

thus /ðʌs/ adv assim, desta maneira. ~ **far** até aqui

thwart /θwɔːt/ vt frustrar, contrariar

thyme /taɪm/ n tomilho m

tiara /tɪˈɑːrə/ n tiara f, diadema m

tic /tɪk/ n tique m

tick¹ /tɪk/ n (sound) tique-taque m; (mark) sinal m; (colloq: moment) instantinho m □ vi fazer tique-taque □ vt ~ (off) marcar com sinal (V). ~ off (colloq: scold) dar uma bronca em (colloq). ~ over (engine, factory) funcionar em marcha lenta, (P) no "ralenti"

tick² /tɪk/ n (insect) carrapato m

ticket /'tɪkɪt/ n bilhete m; (label) etiqueta f; (for traffic offence) aviso m de multa. ~-collector n (railway) guarda m. ~-office n bilheteira f

tickle /'tɪkl/ vt fazer cócegas; (fig: amuse) divertir □ n cócegas fpl, comichão m

ticklish /'tɪklɪʃ/ a coceguento, sensível a cócegas; (fig) delicado, melindroso

tidal /'taɪdl/ a de marés, que tem marés. ~ wave onda f gigantesca; (fig) onda f de sentimento popular

tiddly-winks /'tɪdlɪwɪŋks/ n (game) jogo m da pulga

tide /taɪd/ n maré f; (of events) marcha f, curso m. high ~ maré f cheia, preia-mar f. low ~ maré f baixa, baixa-mar f □ vt ~ over (help temporarily) agüentar, (P) aguentar

tid|y /'taɪdɪ/ a (-ier, -iest) (room) arrumado; (appearance, work) asseado, cuidado; (methodical) bem ordenado; (colloq: amount) belo (colloq) □ vt ~ arrumar, arranjar. ~ily adv com cuidado. ~iness n arrumação f, ordem f

tie /taɪ/ vt (pres p tying) atar, amarrar, prender; (link) ligar, vincular; (a knot) dar, fazer □ vi (sport) empatar □ n fio m, cordel m; (necktie) gravata f; (link) laço m, vínculo m; (sport) empate m. ~ in with estar ligado com, relacionar-se com. ~ up amarrar, atar; (animal) prender; (money) imobilizar; (occupy) ocupar

tier /tɪə(r)/ n cada fila f, camada f, prateleira f etc colocada em cima de outra; (in stadium) bancada f; (of cake) andar m; (of society) camada f

tiff /tɪf/ n arrufo m

tiger /'taɪgə(r)/ n tigre m

tight /taɪt/ a (-er, -est) (clothes) apertado, justo; (rope) esticado, tenso; (control) rigoroso; (knot, schedule, lid) apertado; (colloq: drunk) embriagado (colloq) □ adv = tightly. be in a ~ corner (fig) estar em apuros or num aperto, (P) estar entalado (colloq). ~-fisted a sovina, pão-duro, (P) agarrado (colloq). ~ly adv bem; (squeeze) com força

tighten /'taɪtn/ vt/i (rope) esticar; (bolt, control) apertar. ~ up on apertar o cinto

tightrope /'taɪtrəʊp/ n corda f (de acrobacias). ~ walker funâmbulo m

tights /taɪts/ npl collants mpl, meias-colant fpl

tile /taɪl/ n (on wall, floor) ladrilho m, azulejo m; (on roof) telha f □ vt ladrilhar, pôr azulejos em; (roof) telhar, cobrir com telhas

till¹ /tɪl/ vt (land) cultivar

till² /tɪl/ prep & conj = until

till³ /tɪl/ n caixa (registadora) f

tilt /tɪlt/ vt/i inclinar(-se), pender □ n (slope) inclinação f. (at) full ~ a toda a velocidade

timber /'tɪmbə(r)/ n madeira f (de construção); (trees) árvores fpl

time /taɪm/ n tempo m; (moment) momento m; (epoch) época f, tempo m; (by clock) horas fpl; (occasion) vez f; (rhythm) compasso m. ~s (multiplying) vezes □ vt escolher a hora para; (measure) marcar o tempo; (sport) cronometrar; (regulate) acertar. at ~s às vezes. for the ~ being por agora, por enquanto. from ~ to ~ de vez em quando. have a good ~ divertir-se. have no ~ for não ter paciência para. in no ~ num instante. in ~ a tempo; (eventually) com o tempo. in two days ~ daqui a dois dias. on ~ na hora, (P) a horas. take your ~ não se apresse. what's the ~? que horas são? ~ bomb bomba-relógio f. ~-limit n prazo m. ~ off tempo m livre. ~-sharing n time-sharing n ~ zone fuso m horário

timeless /'taɪmlɪs/ a intemporal; (unending) eterno

timely /'taɪmlɪ/ a oportuno

timer /'taɪmə(r)/ n (techn) relógio m; (with sand) ampulheta f

timetable /'taɪmteɪbl/ n horário m

timid /'tɪmɪd/ a tímido; (fearful) assustadiço, medroso. ~ly adv timidamente

timing /'taɪmɪŋ/ n (measuring) cronometragem f; (of artist) ritmo m; (moment) cálculo m do tempo, timing m. good/bad ~ (moment) momento m bem/mal escolhido

tin /tɪn/ n estanho m; (container) lata f □ vt (pt tinned) estanhar; (food) enlatar. ~ foil papel m de alumínio. ~-opener n abridor m de latas, (P) abre-latas m. ~ plate lata f, folha(-de-Flandes) f. ~ned foods conservas fpl. ~ny a (sound) metálico

tinge /tɪndʒ/ vt ~ (with) tingir (de); (fig) dar um toque (de) □ n tom m, matiz m; (fig) toque m

tingle /'tɪŋgl/ vi (sting) arder; (prickle) picar □ n ardor m; (prickle) picadela f

tinker /'tɪŋkə(r)/ n latoeiro m ambulante □ vi ~ (**with**) mexer (em), tentar consertar

tinkle /'tɪŋkl/ n tinido m, tilintar m □ vt/i tilintar

tinsel /'tɪnsl/ n fio m prateado/dourado, enfeites mpl metálicos de Natal; (fig) falso brilho m, ouropel m

tint /tɪnt/ n tom m, matiz m, (for hair) tintura f, tinta f □ vt tingir, colorir

tiny /'taɪnɪ/ a (**-ier, -iest**) minúsculo, pequenino

tip [1] /tɪp/ n ponta f. (**have sth**) **on the ~ of one's tongue** ter alg coisa na ponta de língua

tip [2] /tɪp/ vt/i (pt **tipped**) (tilt) inclinar(-se); (overturn) virar(-se); (pour) colocar; (empty) despejar(-se) □ n (money) gorjeta f; (of advice) sugestão f, dica f (colloq); (for rubbish) lixeira f. ~ **off** avisar, prevenir. ~**-off** n (warning) aviso m; (information) informação f

tipsy /'tɪpsɪ/ a ligeiramente embriagado, alegre, tocado

tiptoe /'tɪptəʊ/ n **on** ~ na ponta dos pés

tir|**e** [1] /'taɪə(r)/ vt/i cansar(-se) **of** etc. ~**less** a incansável, infatigável. ~**ing** a fatigante, cansativo

tire [2] /'taɪə(r)/ n (Amer) pneu m

tired /'taɪəd/ a cansado, fatigado. ~ **of** (sick of) farto de. ~ **out** morto de cansaço

tiresome /'taɪəsəm/ a maçador, aborrecido, chato (sl)

tissue /'tɪʃu:/ n tecido m; (handkerchief) lenço m de papel. ~**-paper** n papel m de seda

tit [1] /tɪt/ n (bird) chapim m, canário-da-terra m

tit [2] /tɪt/ n **give** ~ **for tat** pagar na mesma moeda

titbit /'tɪtbɪt/ n petisco m

titillate /'tɪtɪleɪt/ vt excitar, titilar, (P) dar gozo a

title /'taɪtl/ n título m. ~**-deed** n título m de propriedade. ~**-page** n página f de rosto, (P) frontispício m. ~**-role** n papel m principal

titter /'tɪtə(r)/ vi rir com riso abafado

to /tu:/; (unstressed /tə/ prep a, para; (as far as) até; (towards) para; (of attitude) para (com) □ adv **push** or **pull** ~ (close) fechar. ~ **Portugal** (for a short time) a Portugal; (to stay) para Portugal. **the baker's** para o padeiro, (P) ao padeiro. ~ **do**/**sit**/ etc (infinitive) fazer/sentar-se/etc; (expressing purpose) para fazer/para se sentar/etc. **it's ten** ~ **six** são dez para as seis, faltam dez para as seis. ~ **and fro** andar de um lado para outro. **husband**/etc~-**be** n futuro marido

m/etc. ~-**do** n (fuss) agitação f, alvoroço m

toad /təʊd/ n sapo m

toadstool /'təʊdstu:l/ n cogumelo m venenoso

toady /'təʊdɪ/ n lambe-botas mf, puxa-saco m □ vi puxar saco

toast /təʊst/ n fatia f de pão torrado, torrada f; (drink) brinde m, saúde f □ vt (bread) torrar; (drink to) brindar, beber à saúde de. ~**er** n torradeira f

tobacco /tə'bækəʊ/ n tabaco m

tobacconist /tə'bækənɪst/ n vendedor m de tabaco, homem m da tabacaria (colloq). ~'**s shop** tabacaria f

toboggan /tə'bɒgən/ n tobogã m, (P) toboggan m

today /tə'deɪ/ n & adv hoje (m)

toddler /'tɒdlə(r)/ n criança f que está aprendendo a andar

toe /təʊ/ n dedo m do pé; (of shoe, stocking) biqueira f □ vt ~ **the line** andar na linha. **on one's** ~**s** alerta, vigilante. ~-**hold** n apoio (precário) m. ~**nail** n unha f do dedo do pé

toffee /'tɒfɪ/ n puxa-puxa m, (P) caramelo m. ~-**apple** n maçã f caramelizada

together /tə'geðə(r)/ adv junto, juntamente, juntos; (at the same time) ao mesmo tempo. ~ **with** juntamente com. ~**ness** n camaradagem f, companheirismo m

toil /tɔɪl/ vi labutar □ n labuta f, labor m

toilet /'tɔɪlɪt/ n banheiro m, (P) casa f de banho; (grooming) toalete f. ~-**paper** n papel m higiênico, (P) higiénico. ~-**roll** n rolo m de papel higiênico, (P) higiénico. ~ **water** água-de-colônia f

toiletries /'tɔɪlɪtrɪz/ npl artigos mpl de toalete

token /'təʊkən/ n sinal m, prova f; (voucher) cheque m; (coin) ficha f □ a simbólico

told /təʊld/ see **tell** □ a **all** ~ (all in all) ao todo

tolerab|**le** /'tɒlərəbl/ a tolerável; (not bad) sofrível, razoável. ~**y** adv (work, play) razoavelmente

toleran|**t** /'tɒlərənt/ a tolerante **of** para com). ~**ce** n tolerância f. ~**tly** adv com tolerância

tolerate /'tɒləreɪt/ vt tolerar

toll [1] /təʊl/ n pedágio m, (P) portagem f. **death** ~ número m de mortos. **take its** ~ (of age) fazer sentir o seu peso

toll [2] /təʊl/ vt/i (of bell) dobrar

tomato /tə'mɑ:təʊ/ n (pl -**oes**) tomate m

tomb /tu:m/ n túmulo m, sepultura f

tomboy /'tɒmbɔɪ/ n menina f levada (E masculinizada), (P) maria-rapaz f

tombstone /'tu:mstəʊn/ n lápide f, pedra f tumular

tome /təʊm/ n tomo m, volume m

tomfoolery /tɒm'fu:ləri/ n disparates mpl, imbecilidades fpl

tomorrow /tə'mɒrəʊ/ n & adv amanhã (m). ~ **morning/night** amanhã de manhã/à noite

ton /tʌn/ n tonelada f (= 1016 kg). **(metric)** n tonelada f (= 1000 kg). ~**s of** (colloq) montes de (colloq), (P) carradas de (colloq)

tone /təʊn/ n tom m; (of radio, telephone etc) sinal m; (colour) tom m, tonalidade f; (med) tonicidade f □ vt ~ **down** atenuar □ vi ~ **in** combinar-se, harmonizar-se (with com). ~ **up** (muscles) tonificar. ~**-deaf** a sem ouvido musical

tongs /tɒŋz/ n tenaz f; (for sugar) pinça f; (for hair) pinça f

tongue /tʌŋ/ n língua f. ~**-in-cheek** a & adv sem ser a sério, com ironia. ~**-tied** a calado. ~**-twister** n trava-língua

tonic /'tɒnɪk/ n (med) tónico m, (P) tónico m; (mus) tónica f, (P) tónica f □ a tónico, (P) tónico

tonight /tə'naɪt/ adv & n hoje à noite, logo à noite, esta noite (f)

tonne /tʌn/ n (metric) tonelada f

tonsil /'tɒnsl/ n amígdala f

tonsillitis /tɒnsɪ'laɪtɪs/ n amigdalite f

too /tu:/ adv demasiado, demais; (also) também, igualmente; (colloq: very) muito. ~ **many** a demais, de masiados. ~ **much** a & adv demais, demasiado

took /tʊk/ see **take**

tool /tu:l/ n (carpenter's, plumber's etc) ferramenta f; (gardener's) utensílio m; (fig: person) joguete m. ~**-bag** n saco m de ferramenta

toot /tu:t/ n toque m de buzina □ vt/i ~ **(the horn)** buzinar, tocar a buzina

tooth /tu:θ/ n (pl **teeth**) dente m. ~**less** a desdentado

toothache /'tu:θeɪk/ n dor f de dentes

toothbrush /'tu:θbrʌʃ/ n escova f de dentes

toothpaste /'tu:θpeɪst/ n pasta f de dentes, dentifrício m

toothpick /'tu:θpɪk/ n palito m

top¹ /tɒp/ n (highest point; upper part) alto m, cimo m, topo m; (of hill; fig) cume m; (upper surface) cimo m, topo m; (surface of table) tampo m; (lid) tampa f; (of bottle) rolha f; (of list) cabeça f □ a (shelf etc) de cima, superior; (in rank) primeiro; (best) melhor; (distinguished) eminente; (maximum) máximo □ vt (pt **topped**) (exceed) ultrapassar, ir acima de. **from** ~ **to bottom** de alto a baixo. **on** ~ **of** em

cima de; (fig) além de. **on** ~ **of that** ainda por cima. ~ **gear** (auto) a velocidade mais alta. ~ **hat** chapéu m alto. ~**-heavy** a mais pesado na parte de cima. ~ **secret** ultra-secreto. ~ **up** encher. ~**ped with** a coberto de

top² /tɒp/ n (toy) pião m. **sleep like a** ~ dormir como uma pedra

topic /'tɒpɪk/ n tópico m, assunto m

topical /'tɒpɪkl/ a da atualidade, (P) actualidade, corrente

topless /'tɒplɪs/ a com o peito nu, topless

topple /'tɒpl/ vt/i (fazer) desabar, (fazer) tombar, (fazer) cair

torch /tɔːtʃ/ n (electric) lanterna f elétrica, (P) eléctrica; (flaming) archote m, facho m

tore /tɔː(r)/ see **tear**¹

torment¹ /'tɔːment/ n tormento m

torment² /tɔː'ment/ vt atormentar, torturar; (annoy) aborrecer, chatear

torn /tɔːn/ see **tear**¹

tornado /tɔː'neɪdəʊ/ n (pl **-oes**) tornado m

torpedo /tɔː'piːdəʊ/ n (pl **-oes**) torpedo m □ vt torpedear

torrent /'tɒrənt/ n torrente f. ~**ial** /tə'renʃl/ a torrencial

torrid /'tɒrɪd/ a (climate etc) tórrido; (fig) intenso, ardente

torso /'tɔːsəʊ/ n (pl **-os**) torso m

tortoise /'tɔːtəs/ n tartaruga f

tortoiseshell /'tɔːtəsʃel/ n (for ornaments etc) tartaruga f

tortuous /'tɔːtʃʊəs/ a (of path etc) que dá muitas voltas, sinuoso; (fig) tortuoso, retorcido

torture /'tɔːtʃə(r)/ n tortura f, suplício m □ vt torturar. ~**r** /-ə(r)/ n carrasco m, algoz m, torturador m

Tory /'tɔːrɪ/ a & n (colloq) conservador (m), (P) tóri (m)

toss /tɒs/ vt atirar, jogar, (P) deitar; (shake) agitar, sacudir □ vi agitar-se, debater-se. ~ **a coin**, ~ **up** tirar cara ou coroa

tot¹ /tɒt/ n criancinha f; (colloq: glass) copinho m

tot² /tɒt/ vt/i (pt **totted**) ~ **up** (colloq) somar

total /'təʊtl/ a & n total (m) □ vt (pt **totalled**) (find total of) totalizar; (amount to) elevar-se a, montar a. ~**ity** /-'tæləti/ n totalidade f. ~**ly** adv totalmente

totalitarian /təʊtælɪ'teərɪən/ a totalitário

totter /'tɒtə(r)/ vi cambalear, andar aos tombos; (of tower etc) oscilar

touch /tʌtʃ/ vt/i tocar; (of ends, gardens etc) tocar-se; (tamper with) mexer em; (affect) comover □ n (sense) tato m, (P) tacto m; (contact) toque m; (of *colour*) toque *m*, retoque *m*. **a ~ of** (*small amount*) um pouco de. **get in ~ with** entrar em contato, (*P*) contacto com. **lose ~** perder contato, (*P*) contacto. **~ down** (*aviat*) aterrissar, (*P*) aterrar. **~ off** disparar; (*cause*) dar início a, desencadear. **~ on** (*mention*) tocar em. **~ up** retocar. **~-and-go** *a* (*risky*) arriscado; (*uncertain*) duvidoso, incerto. **~-line** *n* linha *f* lateral

touching /'tʌtʃɪŋ/ *a* comovente, comovedor

touchy /'tʌtʃɪ/ *a* melindroso, suscetível, (*P*) susceptível, que se ofende facilmente

tough /tʌf/ *a* (**-er, -est**) (*hard, difficult; relentless*) duro; (*strong*) forte, resistente □ *n* **~ (guy)** valentão *m*, durão *m* (*colloq*). **~ luck!** (*colloq*) pouca sorte! **~ness** *n* dureza *f*; (*strength*) força *f*, resistência *f*

toughen /'tʌfn/ *vt/i* (*person*) endurecer; (*strengthen*) reforçar

tour /tʊə(r)/ *n* viagem *f*, (*visit*) visita *f*; (*by team etc*) tournée *f* □ *vt* visitar.**on ~** em tournée

tourism /'tʊərɪzəm/ *n* turismo *m*

tourist /'tʊərɪst/ *n* turista *mf* □ *a* turístico. **~ office** agência *f* de turismo

tournament /'tʊənəmənt/ *n* torneio *m*

tousle /'taʊzl/ *vt* despentear, esguedelhar

tout /taʊt/ *vi* angariar clientes (**for** para) □ *vt* (*try to sell*) tentar revender □ *n* (*hotel etc*) angariador *m*; (*ticket*) cambista *m*, (*P*) revendedor *m*

tow /təʊ/ *vt* rebocar □ *n* reboque *m*. **on ~** a reboque. **~ away** (*vehicle*) rebocar. **~-path** *n* caminho *m* de sirga. **~-rope** *n* cabo *m* de reboque

toward(s) /tə'wɔːd(z)/ *prep* para, em direção, (*P*) direcção a, na direção, (*P*) direcção de; (*of attitude*) para com; (*time*) por volta de

towel /'taʊəl/ *n* toalha *f*; (*tea towel*) pano *m* de prato □ *vt* (*pt* **towelled**) esfregar com a toalha. **~-rail** *n* toalheiro *m*. **~ling** *n* atoalhado *m*, (*P*) pano *m* turco

tower /'taʊə(r)/ *n* torre *f* □ *vi* **~ above** dominar. **~ block** prédio *m* alto. **~ing** *a* muito alto; (*fig: of rage etc*) violento

town /taʊn/ *n* cidade *f*. **go to ~** (*colloq*) perder a cabeça (*colloq*). **~ council** município *m*. **~ hall** câmara *f* municipal.**~ planning** urbanização *f*

toxic /'tɒksɪk/ *a* tóxico

toy /tɔɪ/ *n* brinquedo *m* □ *vi* **~ with** (*object*) brincar com; (*idea*) considerar, cogitar

trace /treɪs/ *n* traço *m*, rastro *m*, sinal *m*; (*small quantity*) traço *m*, vestígio *m* □ *vt* seguir ao encontrar a pista de; (*draw*) traçar; (*with tracing-paper*) decalcar

tracing /'treɪsɪŋ/ *n* decalque *m*, desenho *m*.**~-paper** *n* papel *m* vegetal

track /træk/ *n* (*of person etc*) rastro *m*, pista *f*; (*race-track, of tape*) pista *f*; (*record*) faixa *f*; (*path*) trilho *m*, carreiro *m*; (*rail*) via *f* □ *vt* seguir a pista or a trajetória, (*P*) trajectória de. **keep ~ of** manter-se em contato com; (*keep oneself informed*) seguir. **~ down** (*find*) encontrar, descobrir; (*hunt*) seguir a pista de. **~ suit** conjunto *m* de jogging, (*P*) fato *m* de treino

tract /trækt/ *n* (*land*) extensão *f*, (*anat*) aparelho *m*

tractor /'træktə(r)/ *n* trator *m*, (*P*) tractor *m*

trade /treɪd/ *n* comércio *m*; (*job*) ofício *m*, profissão *f*; (*swap*) troca *f* □ *vt/i* comerciar (em), negociar (em) □ *vt* (*swap*) trocar. **~ in** (*used article*) trocar.**~-in** *n* troca *f*.**~ mark** marca *f* de fábrica. **~ on** (*exploit*) tirar partido de, abusar de. **~ union** sindicato *m*.**~r** /-ə(r)/ *n* negociante *mf*, comerciante *mf*

tradesman /'treɪdzmən/ *n* (*pl* **-men**) comerciante *m*

trading /'treɪdɪŋ/ *n* comércio *m*. **~ estate** zona *f* industrial

tradition /trə'dɪʃn/ *n* tradição *f*.**~al** *a* tradicional

traffic /'træfɪk/ *n* (*trade*) tráfego *m*, tráfico *m*; (*on road*) trânsito *m*, tráfego *m*; (*aviat*) tráfego *m* □ *vi* (*pt* **trafficked**) traficar (**in** em). **~ circle** (*Amer*) giratória *f*, (*P*) rotunda *f*. **~ island** ilha *f* de pedestres, (*P*) refúgio *m* para peões. **~ jam** engarrafamento *m*.**~-lights** *npl* sinal *m* luminoso, (*P*) semáforo *m*.**~ warden** guarda *mf* de trânsito.**~ker** *n* traficante *mf*

tragedy /'trædʒədɪ/ *n* tragédia *f*

tragic /'trædʒɪk/ *a* trágico

trail /treɪl/ *vt/i* arrastar(-se), rastejar; (*of plant, on ground*) rastejar; (*of plant, over wall*) trepar; (*track*) seguir □ *n* (*of powder, smoke etc*) esteira *f*, rastro *m*, (*P*) rasto *m*; (*track*) pista *f*; (*beaten path*) trilho *m*

trailer /'treɪlə(r)/ *n* reboque *m*; (*Amer: caravan*) reboque *m*, caravana *f*, trailer *m*; (*film*) trailer *m*, apresentação *f* de filme

train /treɪn/ *n* (*rail*) trem *m*, (*P*) comboio *m*; (*procession*) fila *f*; (*of dress*) cauda *f*; (*retinue*) comitiva *f* □ *vt* (*instruct, develop*) educar, formar, treinar; (*plant*) guiar; (*sportsman, animal*) treinar; (*aim*) assestar, apon-

tar □ *vi* estudar, treinar-se. ~ed *a*
(*skilled*) qualificado; (*doctor etc*)
diplomado. ~er *n* (*sport*) treinador
m; (*shoe*) tênis *m*.~ing *n* treino *m*
trainee /treɪ'ni:/ *n* estagiário *m*
trait /tret(t)/ *n* traço *m*, característica *f*
traitor /'treɪtə(r)/ *n* traidor *m*
tram /træm/ *n* bonde *m*, (*P*) (carro)
eléctrico *m*
tramp /træmp/ *vi* marchar (com passo pesado) □ *vt* percorrer, palmilhar □
n som *m* de passos pesados; (*vagrant*)
vagabundo *m*, andarilho *m*; (*hike*)
longa caminhada *f*
trample /'træmpl/ *vt/i* ~ (on) pisar
com força; (*fig*) menosprezar
trampoline /'træmpəli:n/ *n* (lona *f*
usada como) trampolim *m*
trance /tra:ns/ *n* (*hypnotic*) transe *m*;
(*ecstasy*) êxtase *m*, arrebatamento *m*;
(*med*) estupor *m*
tranquil /'træŋkwɪl/ *a* tranqüilo, (*P*)
tranquilo, sossegado.~lity /-'kwɪlətɪ/
n tranqüilidade *f*, (*P*) tranquilidade *f*,
sossego *m*
tranquillizer /'træŋkwɪlaɪzə(r)/ *n*
(*drug*) tranqüilizante *m*, (*P*) tranqui-
lizante *m*, calmante *m*
transact /træn'zækt/ *vt* (*business*) fazer, efetuar, (*P*) efectuar. ~ion /-kʃn/
n transação *f*, (*P*) transacção *f*
transcend /træn'send/ *vt* trans-
cender. ~ent *a* transcendente
transcri|be /træn'skraɪb/ *vt* trans-
crever. ~pt, ~ption /-ɪpʃn/ *ns*
transcrição *f*
transfer [1] /træns'fɜ:(r)/ *vt* (*pt* trans-
ferred) transferir; (*power, property*)
transmitir □ *vi* mudar, ser transferi-
do; (*change planes etc*) fazer transferência. ~ the charges (*telephone*)
ligar a cobrar
transfer [2] /'trænsfɜ:(r)/ *n* transferência *f*, (*of power, property*)
transmissão *f*; (*image*) decalcomania *f*
transfigure /træns'fɪgə(r)/ *vt* trans-
figurar
transform /træns'fɔ:m/ *vt* transfor-
mar. ~ation /-ə'meɪʃn/ *n* trans-
formação *f*. ~er *n* (*electr*) transfor-
mador *m*
transfusion /træns'fju:ʒn/ *n* (*of
blood*) transfusão *f*
transient /'trænzɪənt/ *a* transitório,
transiente, efêmero, (*P*) efémero, passageiro
transistor /træn'zɪstə(r)/ *n* (*device,
radio*) transistor *m*
transit /'trænsɪt/ *n* tránsito *m*. in ~
em tránsito
transition /træn'zɪʃn/ *n* transição *f*.
~al *a* transitório
transitive /'trænsɪtɪv/ *a* transitivo
transitory /'trænsɪtərɪ/ *a* transitório

translat|e /trænz'leɪt/ *vt* traduzir.
~ion /-ʃn/ *n* tradução *f*.~or *n* tradu-
tor *m*
translucent /trænz'lu:snt/ *a* translúcido
transmi|t /trænz'mɪt/ *vt* (*pt* trans-
mitted) transmitir. ~ssion *n*
transmissão *f*.~tter *n* transmissor *m*
transparen|t /trænz'pærənt/ *a* transpa-
rente. ~cy *n* transparência *f*;
(*photo*) diapositivo *m*
transpire /træn'spaɪə(r)/ *vi* (*secret
etc*) transpirar; (*happen*) suceder,
acontecer
transplant [1] /træns'pla:nt/ *vt* trans-
plantar
transplant [2] /'trænspla:nt/ *n* (*med*)
transplantação *f*, transplante *m*
transport [1] /træn'spɔ:t/ *vt* (*carry, delight*) transportar. ~ation /'teɪʃn/ *n*
transporte *m*
transport [2] /'trænspɔ:t/ *n* (*of goods,
delight etc*) transporte *m*
transpose /træn'spəʊz/ *vt* transpor
transverse /'trænzvɜ:s/ *a* transversal
transvestite /trænz'vestaɪt/ *n* travesti *mf*
trap /træp/ *n* armadilha *f*, ratoeira *f*,
cilada *f* □ *vt* (*pt* trapped) apanhar na
armadilha; (*cut off*) prender,
bloquear.~per *n* caçador *m* de armadilha (esp de peles)
trapdoor /træp'dɔ:(r)/ *n* alçapão *m*
trapeze /trə'pi:z/ *n* trapézio *m*
trash /træʃ/ *n* (*worthless stuff*) porcaria *f*; (*refuse*) lixo *m*; (*nonsense*) disparates *mpl*.~ can *n* (*Amer*) lata *f* do
lixo, (*P*) caixote *m* do lixo.~y *a* que
não vale nada, porcaria
trauma /'trɔ:mə/ *n* trauma *m*, trau-
matismo *m*.~tic /-'mætɪk/ *a* traumá-
tico
travel /'trævl/ *vi* (*pt* travelled) viajar; (*of vehicle, bullet, sound*) ir □ *vt*
percorrer □ *n* viagem *f*. ~ agent
agente *mf* de viagem.~ler *n* viajante
mf. ~ler's cheque cheque *m* de
viagem. ~ling *n* viagem *f*, viagens
fpl, viajar
travesty /'trævəstɪ/ *n* paródia *f*, caricatura *f*
trawler /'trɔ:lə(r)/ *n* traineira *f*, (*P*)
arrastão *m*
tray /treɪ/ *n* tabuleiro *m*, bandeja *f*
treacherous /'tretʃərəs/ *a* traiçoeiro
treachery /'tretʃərɪ/ *n* traição *f*,
perfídia *f*, deslealdade *f*
treacle /'tri:kl/ *n* melaço *m*
tread /tred/ *vt/i* (*pt* trod, *pp* trodden)
(*step*) pisar; (*walk*) andar, caminhar;
(*walk along*) seguir □ *n* passo *m*, maneira *f* de andar; (*of tyre*) trilho *m*.~
sth into (*carpet*) esmigalhar alg coisa sobre/em

treason /'tri:zn/ n traição f
treasure /'treʒə(r)/ n tesouro m □ vt ter o maior apreço por; (store) guardar bem guardado.~r n tesoureiro m
treasury /'treʒərɪ/ n (building) tesouraria f; (department) Ministério m das Finanças or da Fazenda; (fig) tesouro m
treat /tri:t/ vt/i tratar □ n (pleasure) prazer m, regalo m; (present) mimo m, gentileza f.~ sb to sth convidar alguém para alg coisa
treatise /'tri:tɪz/ n tratado m
treatment /'tri:tmənt/ n tratamento m
treaty /'tri:tɪ/ n (pact) tratado m
treble /'trebl/ a triplo □ vt/i triplicar □ n (mus: voice) soprano m.~y adv triplamente
tree /tri:/ n árvore f
trek /trek/ n viagem f penosa; (walk) caminhada f □ vi (pt trekked) viajar penosamente; (walk) caminhar
trellis /'trelɪs/ n grade f para trepadeiras, treliça f
tremble /'trembl/ vi tremer
tremendous /trɪ'mendəs/ a (fearful, huge) tremendo; (colloq: excellent) fantástico, formidável
tremor /'tremə(r)/ n tremor m, estremecimento m. (earth) ~ abalo (sísmico) m, tremor m de terra
trench /trentʃ/ n fossa f, vala f; (mil) trincheira f
trend /trend/ n tendência f; (fashion) moda f.~y a (colloq) na última moda, (P) na berra (colloq)
trepidation /trepɪ'deɪʃn/ n (fear) receio m, apreensão f
trespass /'trespəs/ vi entrar ilegalmente (on em). no ~ing entrada f proibida.~er n intruso m
trestle /'tresl/ n cavalete m, armação f de mesa. ~-table n mesa f de cavaletes
trial /'traɪəl/ n (jur) julgamento m, processo m; (test) ensaio m, experiência f, prova f; (ordeal) provação f. on ~ em julgamento. ~ and error tentativas fpl
triang|le /'traɪæŋgl/ n triângulo m. ~ular /-'æŋgjʊlə(r)/ a triangular
trib|e /traɪb/ n tribo f.~al a tribal
tribulation /trɪbjʊ'leɪʃn/ n tribulação f
tribunal /traɪ'bju:nl/ n tribunal m
tributary /'trɪbjʊtərɪ/ n afluente m, tributário m
tribute /'trɪbju:t/ n tributo m. pay ~ to prestar homenagem a, render tributo a
trick /trɪk/ n truque m; (prank) partida f; (habit) jeito m □ vt enganar. do the ~ (colloq: work) dar resultado

trickery /'trɪkərɪ/ n trapaça f
trickle /'trɪkl/ vi pingar, gotejar, escorrer (□ n fio m de água etc; (fig: small number) punhado m
tricky /'trɪkɪ/ a (crafty) manhoso; (problem) delicado, complicado
tricycle /'traɪsɪkl/ n triciclo m
trifle /'traɪfl/ n ninharia f, bagatela f; (sweet) sobremesa f feita de pão-de-ló e frutas e creme □ vi~ with brincar com. a ~ um pouquinho, (P) um poucochinho
trifling /'traɪflɪŋ/ a insignificante
trigger /'trɪgə(r)/ n (of gun) gatilho m □ vt ~ (off) (initiate) desencadear, despoletar
trill /trɪl/ n trinado m, gorjeio m
trilogy /'trɪlədʒɪ/ n trilogia f
trim /trɪm/ a (trimmer, trimmest) bem arranjado, bem cuidado; (figure) elegante, esbelto □ vt (pt trimmed) (cut) aparar; (sails) orientar, marear; (ornament) enfeitar, guarnecer (with com) □ n (cut) aparadela f, corte m leve; (decoration) enfeite m; (on car) acabamento(s) m(pl), estofado m. in ~ em ordem; (fit) em boa forma. ~ming(s) n(pl) (dress) enfeite m; (culin) guarnição f, acompanhamento m
Trinity /'trɪnətɪ/ n the (Holy) ~ a Santíssima Trindade
trinket /'trɪŋkɪt/ n bugiganga f; (jewel) bijuteria f, berloque m
trio /'tri:əʊ/ n (pl-os) trio m
trip /trɪp/ vi (pt tripped) (stumble) tropeçar, dar um passo em falso; (go or dance lightly) andar/dançar com passos leves □ vt~ (up) fazer tropeçar, passar uma rasteira a □ n (journey) viagem f; (outing) passeio m, excursão f; (stumble) tropeção m, passo m em falso
tripe /traɪp/ n (food) dobrada f, tripas fpl; (colloq: nonsense) disparates mpl
triple /'trɪpl/ a triplo, tríplice □ vt/i triplicar. ~ts /-plɪts/ npl trigémeos mpl, (P) trigémeos mpl
triplicate /'trɪplɪkət/ n in ~ em triplicata
tripod /'traɪpɒd/ n tripé m
trite /traɪt/ a banal, corriqueiro
triumph /'traɪəmf/ n triunfo m □ vi triunfar (over sobre); (exult) exultar, rejubilar-se. ~al /-'ʌmfl/ a triunfal. ~ant /-'ʌmfənt/ a triunfante. ~antly /-'ʌmfəntlɪ/ adv em triunfo, triunfantemente
trivial /'trɪvɪəl/ a insignificante
trod, trodden /trɒd, 'trɒdn/ see tread
trolley /'trɒlɪ/ n carrinho m. (tea-)~ carrinho m de chá
trombone /trɒm'bəʊn/ n (mus) trombone m
troop /tru:p/ n bando m, grupo m.~s

(*mil*) tropas *fpl* □ *vi* ~ **in/out**entrar/ sair em bando *or* grupo. ~**ing the colour** saudação da bandeira. ~**er** *n* soldado *m* de cavalaria

trophy /'trəʊfɪ/ *n* troféu *m*

tropic /'trɒpɪk/ *n* trópico *m*. ~**s** trópicos *mpl*. ~**al** *a* tropical

trot /trɒt/ *n* trote *m* □ *vi* (*pt* **trotted**) trotar; (*of person*) correr em passos curtos, ir num *or* a trote (*colloq*). **on the** ~ (*colloq*) a seguir, a fio. ~ **out** (*colloq: produce*) exibir; (*colloq: state*) desfiar

trouble /'trʌbl/ *n* (*difficulty*) dificuldade(s) *f(pl)*, problema(s) *m(pl)*; (*distress*) desgosto(s) *m(pl)*, aborrecimento(s) *m(pl)*; (*pains, effort*) cuidado *m*, trabalho *m*, maçada *f*; (*inconvenience*) transtorno *m*, incómodo *m*, (*P*) incómodo *m*; (*med*) doença *f*. ~**(s)** (*unrest*) agitação *f*, conflito(s) *m(pl)* □ *vt/i* (*bother*) incomodar(-se), (*P*) maçar(-se); (*worry*) preocupar(-se); (*agitate*) perturbar. **be in** ~ estar em apuros, estar em dificuldades. **get into** ~ meter-se em encrenca/apuros. **it is not worth the** ~ não vale a pena. ~**-maker** *n* desordeiro *m*, provocador *m*. ~**-shooter** *n* mediador *m*, negociador *m*. ~**d** *a* agitado, perturbado; (*of sleep*) agitado; (*of water*) turvo

troublesome /'trʌblsəm/ *a* problemático, importuno, (*P*) maçador

trough /trɒf/ *n* (*drinking*) bebedouro *m*; (*feeding*) comedouro *m*. ~ (**of low pressure**) depressão *f*, linha *f* de baixa pressão

trounce /traʊns/ *vt* (*defeat*) esmagar; (*thrash*) espancar

troupe /truːp/ *n* (*theat*) companhia *f*, troupe *f*

trousers /'traʊzəz/ *npl* calça *f*, (*P*) calças *fpl*. **short** ~ calções *mpl*

trousseau /'truːsəʊ/ *n* (*pl* ~**s** /-əʊz/) (*of bride*) enxoval *m* de noiva

trout /traʊt/ *n* (*pl invar*) truta *f*

trowel /'traʊəl/ *n* (*garden*) colher *f* de jardineiro; (*for mortar*) trolha *f*

truant /t/'truːənt/ *n* absenteísta *mf*, (*P*) absentista *mf*; (*schol*) gazeteiro *m*. **play** ~**t** fazer gazeta. ~**cy** *n* absenteísmo *m*, (*P*) absentismo *m*

truce /truːs/ *n* trégua(s) *f(pl)*, armistício *m*

truck /trʌk/ *n* (*lorry*) camião *m*; (*barrow*) carro *m* de bagageiro; (*wagon*) vagão *m* aberto. ~**-driver** *n* motorista *mf* de camião, (*P*) camionista *mf*

truculent /'trʌkjʊlənt/ *a* agressivo, brigão

trudge /trʌdʒ/ *vi* caminhar com dificuldade, caminhar a custo, arrastar-se

true /truː/ *a* (-**er**, -**est**) verdadeiro; (*accurate*) exato, (*P*) exacto; (*faithful*) fiel. **come** ~ (*happen*) realizar-se, concretizar-se. **it is** ~ é verdade

truffle /'trʌfl/ *n* trufa *f*

truism /'truːɪzəm/ *n* truísmo *m*, verdade *f* evidente, (*P*) verdade *f* do Amigo Banana (*colloq*)

truly /'truːlɪ/ *adv* verdadeiramente; (*faithfully*) fielmente; (*truthfully*) sinceramente

trump /trʌmp/ *n* trunfo *m* □ *vt* jogar trunfo, trunfar. ~ **up** forjar, inventar. ~ **card** carta *f* de trunfo; (*colloq: valuable resource*) trunfo *m*

trumpet /'trʌmpɪt/ *n* trombeta *f*

truncheon /'trʌntʃən/ *n* cassetete *m*, (*P*) cassetête *f*

trundle /'trʌndl/ *vt/i* (fazer) rolar ruidosamente/pesadamente

trunk /trʌŋk/ *n* (*of tree, body*) tronco *m*; (*of elephant*) tromba *f*; (*box*) mala *f* grande; (*Amer, auto*) mala *f*. ~**s** (*for swimming*) calção *m* de banho. ~ **call** *n* chamada *f* interurbana. ~ **road** *n* estrada *f* nacional

truss /trʌs/ *n* (*med*) funda *f* □ *vt* atar, amarrar

trust /trʌst/ *n* confiança *f*; (*association*) truste *m*, (*P*) trust *m*, consórcio *m*; (*foundation*) fundação *f*; (*responsibility*) responsabilidade *f*; (*jur*) fideicomisso *m* □ *vt* (*rely on*) ter confiança em, confiar em; (*hope*) esperar □ *vi* ~ **in** *or* **to** confiar em. **in** ~ em fideicomisso. **on** ~ (*without proof*) sem verificação prévia; (*on credit*) a crédito. ~ **sb with** confiar em alguém. ~**ed** *a* (*friend etc*) de confiança, seguro. ~**ful**, ~**ing** *adjs* confiante. ~**y** *a* fiel

trustee /trʌs'tiː/ *n* administrador *m*; (*jur*) fideicomissário *m*

trustworthy /'trʌstwɜːðɪ/ *a* (digno) de confiança

truth /truːθ/ *n* (*pl* ~**s** /truːðz/) verdade *f*. ~**ful** *a* (*account etc*) verídico; (*person*) verdadeiro, que fala verdade. ~**fully** *adv* sinceramente

try /traɪ/ *vt/i* (*pt* **tried**) tentar, experimentar; (*be a strain on*) cansar, pôr à prova; (*jur*) julgar □ *n* (*attempt*) tentativa *f*, experiência *f*; (*Rugby*) ensaio *m*. ~ **for** (*post, scholarship*) candidatar-se a; (*record*) tentar alcançar. ~ **on** (*clothes*) provar. ~ **out** experimentar. ~ **to do** tentar fazer. ~**ing** *a* difícil

tsar /zɑː(r)/ *n* czar *m*

T-shirt /'tiːʃɜːt/ *n* T-shirt *f*, camiseta *f* de algodão de mangas curtas

tub /tʌb/ *n* selha *f*; (*colloq: bath*) tina *f*, banheira *f*

tuba /'tjuːbə/ *n* (*mus*) tuba *f*

tubby /'tʌbɪ/ a (-ier, -iest) baixote e gorducho

tub|e /tjuːb/ n tubo m; (colloq: railway) metrô m. **inner ~e** câmara f de ar. **~ing** n tubos mpl, tubagem f

tuber /'tjuːbə(r)/ n tubérculo m

tuberculosis /tjuːbɜːkjʊ'ləʊsɪs/ n tuberculose f

tubular /'tjuːbjʊlə(r)/ a tubular

tuck /tʌk/ n (fold) prega f cosida; (for shortening or ornament) refego m □ vt/i fazer pregas; (put) guardar, meter, enfiar; (hide) esconder. **~ in** or **into** (colloq: eat) atacar. **~ in** (shirt) meter nas fraldas para dentro; (blanket) prender em; (person) cobrir bem, aconchegar. **~-shop** (schol) loja f de balas, (P) pastelaria f (junto à escola)

Tuesday /'tjuːzdɪ/ n terça-feira f

tuft /tʌft/ n tufo m

tug /tʌɡ/ vt/i (pt tugged) puxar com força; (vessel) rebocar □ n (boat) rebocador m; (pull) puxão m. **~ of war** cabo-de-guerra m, (P) jogo m da guerra

tuition /tjuː'ɪʃn/ n ensino m

tulip /'tjuːlɪp/ n tulipa f

tumble /'tʌmbl/ vi tombar, baquear, dar um trambolhão □ n tombo m, trambolhão m. **~-drier** n máquina f de secar (roupa)

tumbledown /'tʌmbldaʊn/ a em ruínas

tumbler /'tʌmblə(r)/ n copo m

tummy /'tʌmɪ/ n (colloq: stomach) estômago m; (colloq: abdomen) barriga f. **~-ache** (colloq) dor f de barriga/de estômago

tumour /'tjuːmə(r)/ n tumor m

tumult /'tjuːmʌlt/ n tumulto m. **~uous** /'mʌltʃʊəs/ a tumultuado, barulhento, agitado

tuna /'tjuːnə/ n (pl invar) atum m

tune /tjuːn/ n melodia f □ vt (engine) regular; (piano etc) afinar □ vi ~ **in** (to) (radio, TV) ligar (em), (P) sintonizar. **~ up** afinar. **be in/out of ~** (instrument) estar afinado/desafinado; (singer) cantar afinado/desafinado. **~ful** a melodioso, harmonioso. **~r** n afinador m; (radio) sintonizador m

tunic /'tjuːnɪk/ n túnica f

Tunisia /tjuː'nɪzɪə/ n Tunísia f. **~n** a & n tunisiano (m), (P) tunisino (m)

tunnel /'tʌnl/ n túnel m □ vi (pt tunnelled) abrir um túnel (into em)

turban /'tɜːbən/ n turbante m

turbine /'tɜːbaɪn/ n turbina f

turbo- /'tɜːbəʊ/ pref turbo-

turbot /'tɜːbət/ n rodovalho m

turbulen|t /'tɜːbjʊlənt/ a turbulento. **~ce** n turbulência f

tureen /tə'riːn/ n terrina f

turf /tɜːf/ n (pl **turfs** or **turves**) gramado m, (P) relva f, relvado m □ vt ~ **out** (colloq) jogar fora, (P) deitar fora. **the ~** (racing) turfe m, hipismo m. **~ accountant** corretor m de apostas

turgid /'tɜːdʒɪd/ a (speech, style) pomposo, empolado

Turk /tɜːk/ n turco m. **~ey** n Turquia f. **~ish** a turco m □ n (lang) turco m

turkey /'tɜːkɪ/ n peru m

turmoil /'tɜːmɔɪl/ n agitação f, confusão f, desordem f. **in ~** em ebulição

turn /tɜːn/ vt/i virar(-se), voltar(-se), girar; (change) transformar(-se) (into em); (become) ficar, tornar-se; (corner) virar, dobrar; (page) virar, voltar □ n volta f; (in road) curva f, (of mind, events) mudança f; (occasion, opportunity) vez f; (colloq) ataque m, crise f; (colloq: shock) susto m. **do a good ~** prestar (um) serviço. **in ~** por sua vez, sucessivamente. **speak out of ~** dizer o que não se deve, cometer uma indiscrição. **take ~s** revezar-se. **~ of the century** virada f do século. **~ against** vi virar-se or voltar-se contra. **~ away** vi virar-se or voltar-se para o outro lado □ vt (avert) desviar; (reject) recusar; (send back) mandar embora. **~ back** vi (return) devolver; (vehicle) dar meia volta, voltar para trás □ vt (fold) dobrar para trás. **~ down** recusar; (fold) dobrar para baixo; (reduce) baixar. **~ in** (hand in) entregar; (colloq: go to bed) deitar-se. **~ off** (light etc) apagar; (tap) fechar; (road) virar (para rua transversal). **~ on** (light etc) acender, ligar; (tap) abrir. **~ out** vt (light) apagar; (empty) esvaziar, despejar; (pocket) virar do avesso; (produce) produzir □ vi (transpire) vir a saber-se, descobrir-se; (colloq: come) aparecer. **~ round** virar-se, voltar-se. **~ up** vi aparecer, chegar; (be found) aparecer □ vt (find) desenterrar; (increase) aumentar; (collar) levantar. **~-out** n assistência f. **~-up** n (of trousers) dobra f

turning /'tɜːnɪŋ/ n rua f transversal; (corner) esquina f. **~-point** n momento m decisivo

turnip /'tɜːnɪp/ n nabo m

turnover /'tɜːnəʊvə(r)/ n (pie, tart) pastel m, empada f; (money) faturamento m, (P) facturação f; (of staff) rotatividade f

turnpike /'tɜːnpaɪk/ n (Amer) auto-estrada f com pedágio, (P) portagem f

turnstile /'tɜːnstaɪl/ n (gate) torniquete m, borboleta f

turntable /'tɜːnteɪbl/ n (for record) prato m do toca-disco, (P) giradiscos; (record-player) toca-disco m, (P) giradiscos m

turpentine /'tɜːpəntaɪn/ n terebentina f, aguarrás m

turquoise /'tɜːkwɔːz/ a turquesa invar

turret /'tʌrɪt/ n torreão m, torrinha f

turtle /'tɜːtl/ n tartaruga-do-mar f. ~-**neck** a de gola alta

tusk /tʌsk/ n (tooth) presa f; (elephant's) defesa f, dente m

tussle /'tʌsl/ n luta f, briga f

tutor /'tjuːtə(r)/ n professor m particular; (univ) professor m universitário

tutorial /tjuː'tɔːrɪəl/ n (univ) seminário m

TV /tiː'viː/ n tevê f

twaddle /'twɒdl/ n disparates mpl

twang /twæŋ/ n (mus) som m duma corda esticada; (in voice) nasalação f □ vt/i (mus) (fazer) vibrar, dedilhar

tweet /twiːt/ n pio m, pipilo m □ vi pipilar

tweezers /'twiːzəz/ npl pinça f

twel|ve /twelv/ a & n doze (m). ~(o'clock)doze horas. ~**fth** a & n décimo segundo (m). **T~fth Night** véspera f de Reis

twent|y /'twentɪ/ a & n vinte (m). ~**ieth** a & n vigésimo (m)

twice /twaɪs/ adv duas vezes

twiddle /'twɪdl/ vt/i ~ (with)(fiddle with) torcer, brincar (com). ~ one's thumbsgirar os polegares

twig /twɪg/ n galho m, graveto m

twilight /'twaɪlaɪt/ n crepúsculo m □ a crepuscular

twin /twɪn/ n & a gêmeo (m), (P) gémeo (m) □ vt (pt **twinned** (pair) emparelhar, emparceirar. ~ **beds**par m de camas de solteiro. ~**ning**n emparelhamento m

twine /twaɪn/ n guita f, cordel m □ vt/i (weave together) entrançar; (wind) enroscar(-se)

twinge /twɪndʒ/ n dor f aguda e súbita, pontada f, (fig) pontada f, (P) ferroada f

twinkle /'twɪŋkl/ vi cintilar, brilhar □ n cintilação f, brilho m

twirl /twɜːl/ vt/i (fazer) girar; (moustache) torcer

twist /twɪst/ vt torcer; (weave together) entrançar; (roll) enrolar; (distort) torcer, deturpar □ vi (rope etc) torcer-se, enrolar-se; (road) dar voltas or curvas, serpentear □ n (act of twisting) torcedura f, (P) torcedela f, (of rope) nó m; (of events) reviravolta f. ~ **sb's arm**(fig) forçar alguém

twit /twɪt/ n (colloq) idiota mf

twitch /twɪtʃ/ vt/i contrair(-se) □ n (tic) tique m; (jerk) puxão m

two /tuː/ a & n dois (m). in **or** of ~ minds indeciso. put ~ and ~ together tirar conclusões. ~-faced a de duas caras, hipócrita. ~-piece n (garment) duas-peças m invar. ~-seater n (car) carro m de dois lugares. ~-waya (of road) mão dupla

twosome /'tuːsəm/ n par m

tycoon /taɪ'kuːn/ n magnata m

tying /'taɪɪŋ/ see **tie**

type /taɪp/ n (example, print) tipo m; (kind) tipo m, gênero m, (P) género m; (colloq: person) cara m, (P) tipo m (colloq) □ vt/i (write) bater à máquina, datilografar, (P) dactilografar

typescript /'taɪpskrɪpt/ n texto m datilografado, (P) dactilografado

typewrit|er /'taɪpraɪtə(r)/ n máquina f de escrever. ~**ten** /-ɪtn/ a batido à máquina, datilografado, (P) dactilografado

typhoid /'taɪfɔɪd/ n ~ **(fever)**febre f tifóide

typhoon /taɪ'fuːn/ n tufão m

typical /'tɪpɪkl/ a típico. ~**ly**adv tipicamente

typify /'tɪpɪfaɪ/ vt ser o (protó)tipo de, tipificar

typing /'taɪpɪŋ/ n datilografia f, (P) dactilografia f

typist /'taɪpɪst/ n datilógrafa f, (P) dactilógrafa f

tyrann|y /'tɪrənɪ/ n tirania f. ~**ical** /tɪ'rænɪkl/ a tirânico

tyrant /'taɪərənt/ n tirano m

tyre /'taɪə(r)/ n pneu m

U

ubiquitous /juː'bɪkwɪtəs/ a ubíquo, onipresente

udder /'ʌdər/ n úbere m

UFO /'juːfəʊ/ n OVNI m

ugl|y /'ʌglɪ/ a (-ier -iest) feio. ~**iness** n feiúra f, (P) fealdade f

UKabbr see **United Kingdom**

ulcer /'ʌlsə(r)/ n úlcera f

ulterior /ʌl'tɪərɪə(r)/ a ulterior. ~ **motive** razão f inconfessada, segundas intenções fpl

ultimate /'ʌltɪmət/ a último, derradeiro; (definitive) definitivo; (maximum) supremo; (basic) fundamental. ~**ly**adv finalmente

ultimatum /ʌltɪ'meɪtəm/ n (pl -ums) ultimato m

ultra- /'ʌltrə/ pref ultra-, super-

ultraviolet /ʌltrə'vaɪələt/ a ultravioleta

umbilical /ʌm'bɪlɪkl/ a ~ **cord**cordão m umbilical

umbrage /'ʌmbrɪdʒ/ n take ~ (at sth) ofender-se or melindrar-se (com alg coisa)

umbrella /ʌm'brelə/ n guardachuva m

umpire /'ʌmpaɪə(r)/ n (sport) árbitro m □ vt arbitrar

umpteen /'ʌmpti:n/ a (sl) sem conta, montes de (colloq). **for the ~th time** (sl) pela centésima or enésima vez

UN abbr (United Nations) ONU f

un- /ʌn/ pref não, pouco

unable /ʌn'eɪbl/ a **be ~ to do** ser incapaz de/não poder fazer

unabridged /ʌnə'brɪdʒd/ a (text) integral

unacceptable /ʌnək'septəbl/ a inaceitável, inadmissível

unaccompanied /ʌnə'kʌmpənɪd/ a só, desacompanhado

unaccountable /ʌnə'kaʊntəbl/ a (strange) inexplicável; (not responsible) que não tem que dar contas

unaccustomed /ʌnə'kʌstəmd/ a desacostumado. **~ to** não acostumado or não habituado a

unadulterated /ʌnə'dʌltəreɪtɪd/ a (pure, sheer) puro

unaided /ʌn'eɪdɪd/ a sem ajuda, sozinho, por si só

unanim|ous /ju:'nænɪməs/ a unânime. **~ity** /-ə'nænəti/ n unanimidade f. **~ously** adv unânimemente, por unanimidade

unarmed /ʌn'ɑ:md/ a desarmado, indefeso

unashamed /ʌnə'ʃeɪmd/ a desavergonhado, sem vergonha. **~ly** /-ɪdlɪ/ adv sem vergonha

unassuming /ʌnə'sju:mɪŋ/ a modesto, despretencioso

unattached /ʌnə'tætʃt/ a (person) livre

unattainable /ʌnə'teɪnəbl/ a inacessível

unattended /ʌnə'tendɪd/ a (person) desacompanhado; (car, luggage) abandonado

unattractive /ʌnə'træktɪv/ a sem atrativos, (P) atractivos; (offer) de pouco interesse

unauthorized /ʌn'ɔ:θəraɪzd/ a não-autorizado, sem autorização

unavoidabl|e /ʌnə'vɔɪdəbl/ a inevitável. **~y** adv inevitavelmente

unaware /ʌnə'weə(r)/ a **be ~ of** desconhecer, ignorar, não ter consciência de. **~s** /-eəz/ adv (unexpectedly) inesperadamente. **catch sb ~s** apanhar alguém desprevenido

unbalanced /ʌn'bælənst/ a (mind, person) desequilibrado

unbearable /ʌn'beərəbl/ a insuportável

unbeat|able /ʌn'bi:təbl/ a imbatível. **~en** a não vencido, invicto; (unsurpassed) insuperado

unbeknown(st) /ʌnbɪ'nəʊn(st)/ a ~ **to** (colloq) sem o conhecimento de

unbelievable /ʌnbɪ'li:vəbl/ a inacreditável, incrível

unbend /ʌn'bend/ vi (pt unbent) (relax) descontrair. **~ing** a inflexível

unbiased /ʌn'baɪəst/ a imparcial

unblock /ʌn'blɒk/ vt desbloquear, desobstruir; (pipe) desentupir

unborn /ʌn'bɔ:n/ a por nascer; (future) vindouro, futuro

unbounded /ʌn'baʊndɪd/ a ilimitado

unbreakable /ʌn'breɪkəbl/ a inquebrável

unbridled /ʌn'braɪdld/ a desequilibrado, (P) desenfreado

unbroken /ʌn'brəʊkən/ a (intact) intato, (P) intacto, inteiro; (continuous) ininterrupto

unburden /ʌn'bɜ:dn/ vpr ~ **o.s.** (open one's heart) desabafar (**to** com)

unbutton /ʌn'bʌtn/ vt desabotoar

uncalled-for /ʌn'kɔ:ldfɔ:(r)/ a injustificável, gratuito

uncanny /ʌn'kænɪ/ a (-ier -iest) estranho, misterioso

unceasing /ʌn'si:sɪŋ/ a incessante

unceremonious /ʌnserɪ'məʊnɪəs/ a sem cerimónia, (P) cerimónia, brusco

uncertain /ʌn'sɜ:tn/ a incerto. **~ whether** não saber ao certo se, estar indeciso quanto a. **~ty** n incerteza f

unchang|ed /ʌn'tʃeɪndʒd/ a inalterado, sem modificação. **~ing** a inalterável, imutável

uncivilized /ʌn'sɪvɪlaɪzd/ a não civilizado, bárbaro

uncle /'ʌŋkl/ n tio m

uncomfortable /ʌn'kʌmfətəbl/ a (thing) desconfortável, incómodo, (P) incómodo; (unpleasant) desagradável. **feel** or **be ~** (uneasy) sentir-se or estar pouco à vontade

uncommon /ʌn'kɒmən/ a pouco vulgar, invulgar, fora do comum. **~ly** adv invulgarmente, excepcionalmente

uncompromising /ʌn'kɒmprəmaɪzɪŋ/ a intransigente

unconcerned /ʌnkən'sɜ:nd/ a (indifferent) indiferente (**by** a)

unconditional /ʌnkən'dɪʃənl/ a incondicional

unconscious /ʌn'kɒnʃəs/ a inconsciente (**of** de). **~ly** adv inconscientemente. **~ness** n inconsciência f

unconventional /ʌnkən'venʃənl/ a não convencional, fora do comum

uncooperative /ʌnkəʊ'ɒpərətɪv/ a

(*person*) pouco cooperativo, do contra (*colloq*)

uncork /ʌnˈkɔːk/ *vt* desarrolhar, tirar a rolha de

uncouth /ʌnˈkuːθ/ *a* rude, grosseiro

uncover /ʌnˈkʌvə(r)/ *vt* descobrir, revelar

unctuous /ˈʌŋktʃʊəs/ *a* untuoso, gorduroso; (*fig*) melífluo

undecided /ʌndɪˈsaɪdɪd/ *a* (*irresolute*) indeciso; (*not settled*) por decidir, pendente

undeniable /ʌndɪˈnaɪəbl/ *a* inegável, incontestável

under /ˈʌndə(r)/ *prep* debaixo de, sob; (*less than*) com menos de; (*according to*) conforme, segundo □ *adv* por baixo, debaixo. ~ age menor de idade. ~ way em preparo

under- /ˈʌndə(r)/ *pref* sub-

undercarriage /ˈʌndəkærɪdʒ/ *n* (*aviat*) trem *m* de aterrissagem, (*P*) trem *m* de aterragem

underclothes /ˈʌndəkləʊðz/ *npl see* **underwear**

undercoat /ˈʌndəkəʊt/ *n* (*of paint*) primeira mão *f*, (*P*) primeira demão *f*

undercover /ʌndəˈkʌvə(r)/ *a* (*agent, operation*) secreto

undercurrent /ˈʌndəkʌrənt/ *n* corrente *f* subterrânea; (*fig*) filão *m* (*fig*), tendência *f* oculta

undercut /ˈʌndəkʌt/ *vt* (*pt* undercut, *pres p* undercutting) (*comm*) vender a preços mais baixos que

underdeveloped /ʌndədɪˈveləpt/ *a* atrofiado; (*country*) subdesenvolvido

underdog /ˈʌndədɒg/ *n* desprotegido *m*, o mais fraco (*colloq*)

underdone /ˈʌndədʌn/ *a* (*of meat*) mal passado

underestimate /ʌndərˈestɪmeɪt/ *vt* subestimar, não dar o devido valor a

underfed /ʌndəˈfed/ *a* subalimentado, subnutrido

underfoot /ʌndəˈfʊt/ *adv* debaixo dos pés; (*on the ground*) no chão

undergo /ʌndəˈgəʊ/ *vt* (*pt* -went, *pp* -gone) (*be subjected to*) sofrer; (*treatment*) ser submetido a

undergraduate /ʌndəˈgrædʒʊət/ *n* estudante *mf* universitário

underground[1] /ʌndəˈgraʊnd/ *adv* debaixo da terra; (*fig: secretly*) clandestinamente

underground[2] /ˈʌndəgraʊnd/ *a* subterrâneo; (*fig: secret*) clandestino □ *n* (*rail*) metro(politano) *m*

undergrowth /ˈʌndəgrəʊθ/ *n* mato *m*

underhand /ˈʌndəhænd/ *a* (*deceitful*) sonso, dissimulado

underlie /ʌndəˈlaɪ/ *vt* (*pt* -lay, *pp* -lain, *pres p* -lying) estar por baixo de. ~lying *a* subjacente

underline /ʌndəˈlaɪn/ *vt* sublinhar

undermine /ʌndəˈmaɪn/ *vt* minar, solapar

underneath /ʌndəˈniːθ/ *prep* sob, debaixo de, por baixo de □ *adv* abaixo, em baixo, por baixo

underpaid /ʌndəˈpeɪd/ *a* mal pago

underpants /ˈʌndəpænts/ *npl* (*man's*) cuecas *fpl*

underpass /ˈʌndəpɑːs/ *n* (*for cars, people*) passagem *f* inferior

underprivileged /ʌndəˈprɪvɪlɪdʒd/ *a* desfavorecido

underrate /ʌndəˈreɪt/ *vt* subestimar, depreciar

underside /ˈʌndəsaɪd/ *n* lado *m* inferior, base *f*

underskirt /ˈʌndəskɜːt/ *n* anágua *f*

understand /ʌndəˈstænd/ *vt/i* (*pt* -stood) compreender, entender. ~able *a* compreensível. ~ing *a* compreensivo □ *n* compreensão *f*; (*agreement*) acordo *m*, entendimento *m*

understatement /ˈʌndəsteɪtmənt/ *n* versão *f* atenuada da verdade, litotes *f*

understudy /ˈʌndəstʌdɪ/ *n* substituto *m*

undertake /ʌndəˈteɪk/ *vt* (*pt* -took, *pp* -taken) empreender; (*responsibility*) assumir. ~e to encarregar-se de. ~ing *n* (*task*) empreendimento *m*; (*promise*) compromisso *m*

undertaker /ˈʌndəteɪkə(r)/ *n* agente *m* funerário, papa-defuntos *m* (*colloq*)

undertone /ˈʌndətəʊn/ *n* in an ~ a meia voz

undervalue /ʌndəˈvæljuː/ *vt* avaliar por baixo, subestimar

underwater /ʌndəˈwɔːtə(r)/ *a* submarino □ *adv* debaixo de água

underwear /ˈʌndəweə(r)/ *n* roupa *f* interior *or* de baixo

underweight /ˈʌndəweɪt/ *a* be ~ estar com o peso abaixo do normal, ter peso a menos

underwent /ʌndəˈwent/ *see* **undergo**

underworld /ˈʌndəwɜːld/ *n* (*of crime*) submundo *m*, bas-fonds *mpl*

underwriter /ˈʌndəraɪtə(r)/ *n* segurador *m*; (*marine*) ressegurador *m*

undeserved /ʌndɪˈzɜːvd/ *a* imerecido, injusto

undesirable /ʌndɪˈzaɪərəbl/ *a* indesejável, inconveniente

undies /ˈʌndɪz/ *npl* (*colloq*) roupa *f* de baixo *or* interior

undignified /ʌnˈdɪgnɪfaɪd/ *a* pouco digno, sem dignidade

undisputed /ʌndɪˈspjuːtɪd/ *a* incontestado

undo /ʌnˈduː/ *vt* (*pt* -did, *pp* -done /dʌn/) desfazer; (*knot*) desfazer, desatar; (*coat, button*) abrir. leave ~ne não fazer, deixar por fazer. ∼ing n desgraça f, ruína f

undoubted /ʌnˈdaʊtɪd/ a indubitável. ∼ly adv indubitavelmente

undress /ʌnˈdres/ vt/i despir(-se). get ∼ed despir-se

undu|e /ʌnˈdjuː/ a excessivo, indevido. ∼ly adv excessivamente, indevidamente

undulate /ˈʌndjʊleɪt/ vi ondular

undying /ʌnˈdaɪɪŋ/ a eterno, perene

unearth /ʌnˈɜːθ/ vt desenterrar; (fig) descobrir

unearthly /ʌnˈɜːθlɪ/ a sobrenatural, misterioso. ∼ hour (colloq) hora f absurda or inconveniente

uneasy /ʌnˈiːzɪ/ a (ill at ease) pouco à vontade; (worried) preocupado

uneconomic /ʌniːkəˈnɒmɪk/ a antieconômico. ∼al a antieconômico

uneducated /ʌnˈedʒʊkeɪtɪd/ a (person) inculto, sem instrução

unemploy|ed /ʌnɪmˈplɔɪd/ a desempregado. ∼ment n desemprego m. ∼ment benefit auxílio-desemprego m

unending /ʌnˈendɪŋ/ a interminável, sem fim

unequal /ʌnˈiːkwəl/ a desigual. ∼led a sem igual, igualalável

unequivocal /ʌnɪˈkwɪvəkl/ a inequívoco, claro

uneven /ʌnˈiːvn/ a desigual, irregular

unexpected /ʌnɪkˈspektɪd/ a inesperado. ∼ly a inesperadamente

unfair /ʌnˈfeə(r)/ a injusto (to com). ∼ness n injustiça f

unfaithful /ʌnˈfeɪθfl/ a infiel

unfamiliar /ʌnfəˈmɪlɪə(r)/ a estranho, desconhecido. be ∼ with desconhecer, não conhecer, não estar familiarizado com

unfashionable /ʌnˈfæʃənəbl/ a fora de moda

unfasten /ʌnˈfɑːsn/ vt (knot) desatar, soltar; (button) abrir

unfavourable /ʌnˈfeɪvərəbl/ a desfavorável

unfeeling /ʌnˈfiːlɪŋ/ a insensível

unfinished /ʌnˈfɪnɪʃt/ a incompleto, inacabado

unfit /ʌnˈfɪt/ a sem preparo físico, fora de forma; (unsuitable) impróprio (for para)

unfold /ʌnˈfəʊld/ vt desdobrar; (expose) expor, revelar □ vi desenrolar-se

unforeseen /ʌnfɔːˈsiːn/ a imprevisto, inesperado

unforgettable /ʌnfəˈgetəbl/ a inesquecível

unforgivable /ʌnfəˈgɪvəbl/ a imperdoável, indesculpável

unfortunate /ʌnˈfɔːtʃənət/ a (unlucky) infeliz; (regrettable) lamen-

tável. it was very ∼ that foi uma pena que ∼ly adv infelizmente

unfounded /ʌnˈfaʊndɪd/ a (rumour etc) infundado, sem fundamento

unfriendly /ʌnˈfrendlɪ/ a pouco amável, antipático, frio

unfurnished /ʌnˈfɜːnɪʃt/ a sem mobília

ungainly /ʌnˈgeɪnlɪ/ a desajeitado, desgracioso

ungodly /ʌnˈgɒdlɪ/ a ímpio. ∼ hour (colloq) hora f absurda, às altas horas (colloq)

ungrateful /ʌnˈgreɪtfl/ a ingrato

unhapp|y /ʌnˈhæpɪ/ a (-ier, -iest) infeliz, triste; (not pleased) descontente, pouco contente (with com). ∼ily adv infelizmente. ∼iness n infelicidade f, tristeza f

unharmed /ʌnˈhɑːmd/ a incólume, são e salvo, ileso

unhealthy /ʌnˈhelθɪ/ a (-ier, -iest) (climate etc) doentio, insalubre; (person) adoentado, com pouca saúde

unheard-of /ʌnˈhɜːdɒv/ a inaudito, sem precedentes

unhinge /ʌnˈhɪndʒ/ vt (person, mind) desequilibrar

unholy /ʌnˈhəʊlɪ/ a (-ier, -iest) (person, act etc) ímpio; (colloq: great) incrível, espantoso

unhook /ʌnˈhʊk/ vt desenganchar; (dress) desapertar

unhoped /ʌnˈhəʊpt/ a ∼ for inesperado

unhurt /ʌnˈhɜːt/ a ileso, incólume

unicorn /ˈjuːnɪkɔːn/ n unicórnio m

uniform /ˈjuːnɪfɔːm/ n uniforme m □ a uniforme, sempre igual. ∼ity /ˈfɔːmətɪ/ n uniformidade f. ∼ly adv uniformemente

unif|y /ˈjuːnɪfaɪ/ vt unificar. ∼ication /-ɪˈkeɪʃn/ n unificação f

unilateral /juːnɪˈlætrəl/ a unilateral

unimaginable /ʌnɪˈmædʒɪnəbl/ a inimaginável

unimportant /ʌnɪmˈpɔːtnt/ a sem importância, insignificante

uninhabited /ʌnɪnˈhæbɪtɪd/ a desabitado

unintentional /ʌnɪnˈtenʃənl/ a involuntário, não propositado

uninterest|ed /ʌnˈɪntrəstɪd/ a desinteressado (in em), indiferente (in a). ∼ing a desinteressante, sem interesse

union /ˈjuːnɪən/ n união f; (trade union) sindicato m. ∼ist n sindicalista mf; (pol) unionista mf. U∼ Jack bandeira f britânica

unique /juːˈniːk/ a único, sem igual

unisex /ˈjuːnɪseks/ a unisexo

unison /ˈjuːnɪsn/ n in ∼ em uníssono

unit /'ju:nɪt/ n unidade f; (of furniture) peça f, unidade f, (P) módulo m

unite /ju:'naɪt/ vt/i unir(-se). U~d Kingdom n Reino m Unido. U~d Nations (Organization) n Organização f das Nações Unidas. U~ States (of America) Estados mpl Unidos (da América)

unity /'ju:nətɪ/ n unidade f; (fig: harmony) união f

universal /ju:nɪ'vɜ:sl/ a universal

universe /'ju:nɪvɜ:s/ n universo m

university /ju:nɪ'vɜ:sətɪ/ n universidade f □ a universitário; (student, teacher) universitário, da universidade

unjust /ʌn'dʒʌst/ a injusto

unkempt /ʌn'kempt/ a desmazelado, desleixado; (of hair) despenteado, desgrenhado

unkind /ʌn'kaɪnd/ a desagradável, duro. ~ly adv mal

unknowingly /ʌn'nəʊɪŋlɪ/ adv sem saber, inconscientemente

unknown /ʌn'nəʊn/ a desconhecido □ n the ~ o desconhecido

unleaded /ʌn'ledɪd/ a sem chumbo

unless /ʌn'les/ conj a não ser que, a menos que, salvo se, se não

unlike /ʌn'laɪk/ a diferente □ prep ao contrário de

unlikely /ʌn'laɪklɪ/ a improvável

unlimited /ʌn'lɪmɪtɪd/ a ilimitado

unload /ʌn'ləʊd/ vt descarregar

unlock /ʌn'lɒk/ vt abrir (com chave)

unlucky /ʌn'lʌkɪ/ a (-ier, -iest) infeliz, sem sorte; (number) que dá azar. be ~y ter pouca sorte. ~ily adv infelizmente

unmarried /ʌn'mærɪd/ a solteiro, celibatário

unmask /ʌn'mɑːsk/ vt desmascarar

unmistakable /ʌnmɪs'teɪkəbl/ a (voice etc) inconfundível; (clear) claro, inequívoco

unmitigated /ʌn'mɪtɪgeɪtɪd/ a (absolute) completo, absoluto

unmoved /ʌn'muːvd/ a impassível; (indifferent) indiferente (by a), insensível (by a)

unnatural /ʌn'nætʃrəl/ a que não é natural; (wicked) desnaturado

unnecessary /ʌn'nesəsərɪ/ a desnecessário; (superfluous) supérfluo, dispensável

unnerve /ʌn'nɜːv/ vt desencorajar, desmoralizar, intimidar

unnoticed /ʌn'nəʊtɪst/ a go ~ passar despercebido

unobtrusive /ʌnəb'truːsɪv/ a discreto

unofficial /ʌnə'fɪʃl/ a oficioso, que não é oficial; (strike) ilegal, inautorizado

unorthodox /ʌn'ɔːθədɒks/ a pouco ortodoxo, não ortodoxo

unpack /ʌn'pæk/ vt (suitcase etc) desfazer; (contents) desembalar, desempacotar □ vi desfazer a mala

unpaid /ʌn'peɪd/ a não remunerado; (bill) a pagar

unpalatable /ʌn'pælətəbl/ a (food, fact etc) desagradável, intragável

unparalleled /ʌn'pærəleld/ a sem paralelo, incomparável

unpleasant /ʌn'pleznt/ a desagradável (to com); (person) antipático

unplug /ʌn'plʌg/ vt (pt -plugged) (electr) desligar a tomada, (P) tirar a ficha da tomada

unpopular /ʌn'pɒpjʊlə(r)/ a impopular

unprecedented /ʌn'presɪdentɪd/ a sem precedentes, inaudito, nunca visto

unpredictable /ʌnprə'dɪktəbl/ a imprevisível

unprepared /ʌnprɪ'peəd/ a sem preparação, improvisado; (person) desprevenido

unpretentious /ʌnprɪ'tenʃəs/ a despretencioso, sem pretensões

unprincipled /ʌn'prɪnsəpld/ a sem princípios, sem escrúpulos

unprofessional /ʌnprə'feʃənl/ a (work) de amador; (conduct) sem consciência profissional

unprofitable /ʌn'prɒfɪtəbl/ a não lucrativo

unqualified /ʌn'kwɒlɪfaɪd/ a sem habilitações; (success etc) total, absoluto. be ~ to não estar habilitado para

unquestionable /ʌn'kwestʃənəbl/ a incontestável, indiscutível

unravel /ʌn'rævl/ vt (pt unravelled) desenredar, desemaranhar; (knitting) desmanchar

unreal /ʌn'rɪəl/ a irreal

unreasonable /ʌn'riːznəbl/ a pouco razoável, disparatado; (excessive) excessivo

unrecognizable /ʌn'rekəgnaɪzəbl/ a irreconhecível

unrelated /ʌnrɪ'leɪtɪd/ a (facts) desconexo, sem relação (to com); (people) não aparentado (to com)

unreliable /ʌnrɪ'laɪəbl/ a que não é de confiança

unremitting /ʌnrɪ'mɪtɪŋ/ a incessante, infatigável

unreservedly /ʌnrɪ'zɜːvɪdlɪ/ adv sem reservas

unrest /ʌn'rest/ n agitação f, distúrbios mpl

unrivalled /ʌn'raɪvld/ a sem igual, incomparável

unroll /ʌn'rəʊl/ vt desenrolar

unruffled /ʌn'rʌfld/ a calmo, tranquilo, imperturbável

unruly /ʌn'ruːlɪ/ a indisciplinado, turbulento

unsafe /ʌnˈseɪf/ a (*dangerous*) que não é seguro, perigoso; (*person*) em perigo

unsaid /ʌnˈsed/ a leave ~ não mencionar, não dizer, deixar algo por dizer

unsatisfactory /ʌnsætɪsˈfæktərɪ/ a insatisfatório, pouco satisfatório

unsavoury /ʌnˈseɪvərɪ/ a desagradável, repugnante

unscathed /ʌnˈskeɪðd/ a ileso, incólume

unscrew /ʌnˈskruː/ vt desenroscar, desparafusar

unscrupulous /ʌnˈskruːpjʊləs/ a sem escrúpulos, pouco escrupuloso, sem consciência

unseemly /ʌnˈsiːmlɪ/ a inconveniente, indecoroso, impróprio

unsettle /ʌnˈsetl/ vt perturbar, agitar. ~d a perturbado; (*weather*) instável, variável; (*bill*) não saldado

unshakeable /ʌnˈʃeɪkəbl/ a (*person, belief etc*) inabalável

unshaven /ʌnˈʃeɪvn/ a com a barba por fazer, por barbear

unsightly /ʌnˈsaɪtlɪ/ a feio

unskilled /ʌnˈskɪld/ a inexperiente; (*work, worker*) não especializado; (*labour*) mão-de-obra f não especializada

unsociable /ʌnˈsəʊʃəbl/ a insociável, misantropo

unsophisticated /ʌnsəˈfɪstɪkeɪtɪd/ a insofisticado, simples

unsound /ʌnˈsaʊnd/ a pouco sólido. of ~ mind (*jur*) não estar em plena posse das suas faculdades mentais (*jur*)

unspeakable /ʌnˈspiːkəbl/ a indescritível; (*bad*) inqualificável

unspecified /ʌnˈspesɪfaɪd/ a não especificado, indeterminado

unstable /ʌnˈsteɪbl/ a instável

unsteady /ʌnˈstedɪ/ a (*step*) vacilante, incerto; (*ladder*) instável; (*hand*) pouco firme

unstuck /ʌnˈstʌk/ a (*not stuck*) descolado. come ~ (*colloq: fail*) falhar

unsuccessful /ʌnsəkˈsesfl/ a (*candidate*) mal sucedido; (*attempt*) malogrado, fracassado. be ~ não ter êxito. ~ly adv em vão

unsuit|able /ʌnˈs(j)uːtəbl/ a impróprio, pouco apropriado, inadequado (for para). ~ed a inadequado (to para)

unsure /ʌnˈʃʊə(r)/ a incerto

unsuspecting /ʌnsəˈspektɪŋ/ a sem desconfiar de nada, insuspeitado

untangle /ʌnˈtæŋgl/ vt desemaranhar, desenredar

unthinkable /ʌnˈθɪŋkəbl/ a impensável, inconcebível

untid|y /ʌnˈtaɪdɪ/ a (-ier, -iest) (*room, desk etc*) desarrumado; (*appearance*) desleixado, desmazelado; (*hair*) despenteado. ~ily adv sem cuidado. ~iness n desordem f; (*of appearance*) desmazelo m

untie /ʌnˈtaɪ/ vt (*knot, parcel*) desatar, desfazer; (*person*) desamarrar

until /ənˈtɪl/ prep até. not ~ não antes de □ conj até

untimely /ʌnˈtaɪmlɪ/ a inoportuno, intempestivo; (*death*) prematuro

untold /ʌnˈtəʊld/ a incalculável

untoward /ʌntəˈwɔːd/ a inconveniente, desagradável

untrue /ʌnˈtruː/ a falso

unused[1] /ʌnˈjuːzd/ a (*new*) novo, por usar; (*not in use*) não utilizado

unused[2] /ʌnˈjuːst/ a ~ to não habituado, não acostumado a

unusual /ʌnˈjuːʒʊəl/ a insólito, fora do comum. ~ly adv excepcionalmente

unveil /ʌnˈveɪl/ vt descobrir; (*statue, portrait etc*) desvelar

unwanted /ʌnˈwɒntɪd/ a (*useless*) que já não serve; (*child*) indesejado

unwarranted /ʌnˈwɒrəntɪd/ a injustificado

unwelcome /ʌnˈwelkəm/ a desagradável; (*guest*) indesejável

unwell /ʌnˈwel/ a indisposto

unwieldy /ʌnˈwiːldɪ/ a difícil de manejar, pouco jeitoso

unwilling /ʌnˈwɪlɪŋ/ a relutante (to em), pouco disposto (to a)

unwind /ʌnˈwaɪnd/ vt/i (*pt unwound* /ʌnˈwaʊnd/) desenrolar(-se); (*colloq: relax*) descontrair(-se)

unwise /ʌnˈwaɪz/ a imprudente, insensato

unwittingly /ʌnˈwɪtɪŋlɪ/ adv sem querer

unworthy /ʌnˈwɜːðɪ/ a indigno

unwrap /ʌnˈræp/ vt (*pt unwrapped*) desembrulhar, abrir, desfazer

unwritten /ʌnˈrɪtn/ a (*agreement*) verbal, tácito

up /ʌp/ adv (*to higher place*) cima, para cima, para cima, (*in higher place*) em cima, no alto; (*out of bed*) acordado, de pé; (*up and dressed*) pronto; (*finished*) acabado; (*sun*) alto □ prep no cimo de, em cima de, no alto de. ~ the street/river/etc pela rua/pelo rio/etc acima □ vt (*pt upped*) (*increase*) aumentar. be ~ against defrontar, enfrentar. be ~ in (*colloq*) saber. be ~ to (*do*) estar fazendo; (*plot*) estar tramando; (*task*) estar à altura de. feel ~ to doing (*able*) sentir-se capaz de fazer. it is ~ to you depende de você. come or go ~ subir. have ~s and downs (*fig*) ter (os seus) altos e baixos. **walk ~ and down** andar dum lado para o outro *or* para a frente e para trás. **~-and-coming** *a* prom"etedor. **~-market** *a* requintado, fino

upbringing /'ʌpbrɪŋɪŋ/ *n* educação *f*

update /ʌp'deɪt/ *vt* atualizar, (*P*) actualizar

upheaval /ʌp'hiːvl/ *n* pandemónio *m*, (*P*) pandemónio *m*, revolução *f* (*fig*); (*social, political*) convulsão *f*

uphill /'ʌphɪl/ *a* ladeira acima, ascendente; (*fig: difficult*) árduo □ *adv* /ʌp'hɪl/ **go ~** subir

uphold /ʌp'həʊld/ *vt* (*pt* **upheld**) sustentar, manter, apoiar

upholster /ʌp'həʊlstə(r)/ *vt* estofar. **~y** *n* estofados *mpl*, (*P*) estofo(s) *m* (*pl*)

upkeep /'ʌpkiːp/ *n* manutenção *f*

upon /ə'pɒn/ *prep* sobre

upper /'ʌpə(r)/ *a* superior □ *n* (*of shoe*) gáspea *f*. **have the ~ hand** estar por cima, estar em posição de superioridade. **~ class** aristocracia *f*. **~most** *a* (*highest*) o mais alto, superior

upright /'ʌpraɪt/ *a* vertical; (*honourable*) honesto, honrado, (*P*) recto

uprising /'ʌpraɪzɪŋ/ *n* insurreição *f*, sublevação *f*, levantamento *m*

uproar /'ʌprɔː(r)/ *n* tumulto *m*, alvoroço *m*

uproot /ʌp'ruːt/ *vt* desenraizar; (*fig*) erradicar, desarraigar

upset[1] /ʌp'set/ *vt* (*pt* **upset**, *pres p* **upsetting**) (*overturn*) entornar, virar; (*plan*) contrariar, transtornar; (*stomach*) desarranjar; (*person*) contrariar, transtornar, incomodar □ *a* aborrecido

upset[2] /'ʌpset/ *n* transtorno *m*; (*of stomach*) indisposição *f*; (*distress*) choque *m*

upshot /'ʌpʃɒt/ *n* resultado *m*

upside-down /ʌpsaɪd'daʊn/ *adv* (*lit & fig*) ao contrário, de pernas para o ar

upstairs /ʌp'steəz/ *adv* (*at/to*) em/para cima, no/para o andar de cima □ *a* /'ʌpsteəz/ (*flat etc*) de cima, do andar de cima

upstart /'ʌpstɑːt/ *n* arrivista *mf*

upstream /ʌp'striːm/ *adv* rio acima, contra a corrente

upsurge /'ʌpsɜːdʒ/ *n* recrudescência *f*, recrudescimento *m*; (*of anger*) acesso *m*, ataque *m*

uptake /'ʌpteɪk/ *n* **be quick on the ~** pegar rapidamente as coisas; (*fig*) ser de compreensão rápida, ser vivo

up-to-date /ʌptə'deɪt/ *a* moderno, atualizado, (*P*) actualizado

upturn /'ʌptɜːn/ *n* melhoria *f*

upward /'ʌpwəd/ *a* ascendente, voltado para cima. **~s** *adv* para cima

uranium /jʊ'reɪnɪəm/ *n* urânio *m*

urban /'ɜːbən/ *a* urbano

urbane /ɜː'beɪn/ *a* delicado, cortês, urbano

urge /ɜːdʒ/ *vt* aconselhar vivamente (**to** a) □ *n* (*strong desire*) grande vontade *f*. **~ on** (*impel*) incitar

urgen|t /'ɜːdʒənt/ *a* urgente. **be ~t** urgir. **~cy** *n* urgência *f*

urinal /jʊə'raɪnl/ *n* urinol *m*

urin|e /'jʊərɪn/ *n* urina *f*. **~ate** *vi* urinar

urn /ɜːn/ *n* urna *f*; (*for tea, coffee*) espécie *f* de samovar

us /ʌs/; *unstressed* /əs/ *pron* nos; (*after preps*) nós. **with ~** conosco. **he knows ~** ele nos conhece

US *abbr* United States

USA *abbr* United States of America

usable /'juːzəbl/ *a* utilizável

usage /'juːzɪdʒ/ *n* uso *m*

use[1] /juːz/ *vt* usar, utilizar, servir-se de; (*exploit*) servir-se de; (*consume*) gastar, usar, consumir. **~ up** esgotar, consumir. **~r** /-ə(r)/ *n* usuário *m*, (*P*) utente *mf*. **~r-friendly** *a* fácil de usar

use[2] /juːs/ *n* uso *m*, emprego *m*. **in ~** em uso. **it is no ~ shouting**/*etc* não serve de nada *or* não adianta gritar/*etc*. **make ~ of** servir-se de. **of ~** útil

used[1] /juːzd/ *a* (*second-hand*) usado

used[2] /juːst/ *pt* **he ~ to** ele costumava, ele tinha *or* tinha o costume *or* hábito □ *a* **~ to** acostumado a, habituado a

use|ful /'juːsfl/ *a* útil. **~less** *a* inútil; (*person*) incompetente

usher /'ʌʃə(r)/ *n* vagalume *m*, (*P*) arrumador *m* □ *vt* **~ in** mandar entrar. **~ette** *n* vagalume *m*, (*P*) arrumadora *f*

usual /'juːʒʊəl/ *a* usual, habitual, normal. **as ~** como de costume, como habitualmente. **at the ~ time** na hora de costume, (*P*) à(s) hora(s) de costume. **~ly** *adv* habitualmente, normalmente

USSR *abbr* URSS

usurp /juː'zɜːp/ *vt* usurpar

utensil /juː'tensl/ *n* utensílio *m*

uterus /'juːtərəs/ *n* útero *m*

utilitarian /juːtɪlɪ'teərɪən/ *a* utilitário

utility /juː'tɪlətɪ/ *n* utilidade *f*. **(public)** serviço *m* público. **~ room** área *f* de serviço (para as máquinas de lavar a roupa e a louça)

utilize /'juːtɪlaɪz/ *vt* utilizar

utmost /'ʌtməʊst/ *a* (*furthest, most intense*) extremo. **the ~ care**/*etc* (*greatest*) o maior cuidado/*etc* □ *n* **do one's ~** fazer todo o possível

utter[1] /'ʌtə(r)/ a completo, absoluto. ~ly adv completamente

utter[2] /'ʌtə(r)/ vt proferir; (sigh, shout) dar. ~ance n expressão f

U-turn /'ju:tɜ:n/ n retorno m

V

vacan|t /'veɪkənt/ a (post, room, look) vago; (mind) vazio; (seat, space, time) desocupado, livre. ~cy n (post) vaga f; (room in hotel) quarto m

vacate /və'keɪt/ vt vagar, deixar vago

vacation /və'keɪʃn/ n férias fpl

vaccinat|e /'væksɪneɪt/ vt vacinar. ~ion /-'neɪʃn/ n vacinação f

vaccine /'væksi:n/ n vacina f

vacuum /'vækjʊəm/ n (pl -cuums or -cua) vácuo m, vazio m. ~ flask garrafa f térmica, (P) termo(s) m. ~ cleaner aspirador m de pó

vagina /və'dʒaɪnə/ n vagina f

vagrant /'veɪgrənt/ n vadio m, vagabundo m

vague /veɪg/ a (-er, -est) vago; (outline) impreciso. be ~ about ser vago acerca de, não precisar. ~ly adv vagamente

vain /veɪn/ a (-er, -est) (conceited) vaidoso; (useless) vão, inútil; (fruitless) infrutífero. in ~ em vão. ~ly adv em vão

valentine /'væləntaɪn/ n (card) cartão m do dia de São Valentim

valet /'vælɪt, 'væleɪ/ n (manservant) criado m de quarto; (of hotel) camareiro m □ vt (car) lavar e limpar o interior

valiant /'væliənt/ a corajoso, valente

valid /'vælɪd/ a válido. ~ity /və'lɪdətɪ/ n validade f

validate /'vælɪdeɪt/ vt validar, confirmar, ratificar

valley /'vælɪ/ n vale m

valuable /'væljʊəbl/ a (object) valioso, de valor; (help, time etc) precioso. ~s npl objetos mpl, (P) objectos mpl de valor

valuation /vælju'eɪʃn/ n avaliação f

value /'vælju:/ n valor m □ vt avaliar; (cherish) dar valor a. ~ added tax imposto m de valor adicional, (P) acrescentado. ~r /-ə(r)/ n avaliador m

valve /vælv/ n (anat, techn, of car tyre) válvula f; (of bicycle tyre) pipo m; (of radio) lâmpada f, válvula f

vampire /'væmpaɪə(r)/ n vampiro m

van /væn/ n (large) camião m; (small) camioneta f, comercial m; (milkman's, baker's etc) camionete f; (rail) bagageiro m, (P) furgão m

vandal /'vændl/ n vândalo m. ~ism /-əlɪzəm/ n vandalismo m

vandalize /'vændəlaɪz/ vt destruir, estragar

vanguard /'vænga:d/ n vanguarda f

vanilla /və'nɪlə/ n baunilha f

vanish /'vænɪʃ/ vi desaparecer, sumir-se, desvanecer-se

vanity /'vænətɪ/ n vaidade f. ~ case bolsa f de maquilhagem

vantage-point /'va:ntɪdʒpɔɪnt/ n (bom) ponto m de observação

vapour /'veɪpə(r)/ n vapor m; (mist) bruma f

vari|able /'veərɪəbl/ a variável. ~ation /-'eɪʃn/ n variação f. ~ed /-ɪd/ a variado

variance /'veərɪəns/ n at ~ em desacordo (with com)

variant /'veərɪənt/ a diverso, diferente □ n variante f

varicose /'værɪkəʊs/ a ~ veins varizes fpl

variety /və'raɪətɪ/ n variedade f; (entertainment) variedades fpl

various /'veərɪəs/ a vários, diversos, variados

varnish /'va:nɪʃ/ n verniz m □ vt envernizar; (nails) pintar

vary /'veərɪ/ vt/i variar. ~ing a variado

vase /va:z/ n vaso m, jarra f

vast /va:st/ a vasto, imenso. ~ly adv imensamente, infinitamente. ~ness n vastidão f, imensidão f, imensidade f

vat /væt/ n tonel m, dorna f, cuba f

VAT /vi:'eɪ'ti:, væt/ abbr ICM m, (P) IVA m

vault[1] /vɔ:lt/ n (roof) abóbada f; (in bank) casa-forte f; (tomb) cripta f; (cellar) adega f

vault[2] /vɔ:lt/ vt/i saltar □ n salto m

vaunt /vɔ:nt/ vt/i gabar(-se), ufanar (-se) (de), vangloriar(-se)

VD abbr see venereal disease

VDU abbr see visual display unit

veal /vi:l/ n (meat) vitela f

veer /vɪə(r)/ vi virar, mudar de direção, (P) direcção

vegan /'vi:gən/ a & n vegetariano (m) estrito

vegetable /'vedʒtəbl/ n hortaliça f, legume m □ a vegetal

vegetarian /vedʒɪ'teərɪən/ a & n vegetariano (m)

vegetate /'vedʒɪteɪt/ vi vegetar

vegetation /vedʒɪ'teɪʃn/ n vegetação f

vehement /'vi:əmənt/ a veemente. ~ly adv veementemente

vehicle /'vi:ɪkl/ n veículo m

veil /veɪl/ n véu m □ vt velar, cobrir com véu; (fig) esconder, disfarçar

vein /veɪn/ n (in body; mood) veia f; (in rock) veio m, filão m; (of leaf) nervura f

velocity /vɪˈlɒsətɪ/ n velocidade f
velvet /ˈvelvɪt/ n veludo m. ~y a aveludado
vendetta /venˈdetə/ n vendeta f
vending-machine /ˈvendɪŋməʃiːn/ n vendedora f automática, (P) máquina f de distribuição
vendor /ˈvendə(r)/ n vendedor m. **street** ~ vendedor m ambulante
veneer /vəˈnɪə(r)/ n folheado m; (fig) fachada f, máscara f
venerable /ˈvenərəbl/ a venerável
venereal /vəˈnɪərɪəl/ a venéreo. ~ **disease** doença f venérea
venetian /vəˈniːʃn/ a ~ **blinds** persiana f
Venezuela /venɪzˈweɪlə/ n Venezuela f. ~**n** a & n venezuelano (m)
vengeance /ˈvendʒəns/ n vingança. **with a** ~ furiosamente, em excesso, com mais força do que se pretende
venison /ˈvenɪzn/ n carne f de veado
venom /ˈvenəm/ n veneno m. ~**ous** /ˈvenəməs/ a venenoso
vent[1] /vent/ n (in coat) abertura f
vent[2] /vent/ n (hole) orifício m, abertura f; (for air) respiradouro m □ vt (anger) descarregar (**on** para cima de). **give** ~ **to** (fig) desabafar, dar vazão a
ventilat|e /ˈventɪleɪt/ vt ventilar. ~**ion** /-ˈleɪʃn/ n ventilação f. ~**or** n ventilador m
ventriloquist /venˈtrɪləkwɪst/ n ventríloquo m
venture /ˈventʃə(r)/ n empreendimento m arriscado, aventura f □ vt/i arriscar(-se)
venue /ˈvenjuː/ n porto m de encontro
veranda /vəˈrændə/ n varanda f
verb /vɜːb/ n verbo m
verbal /ˈvɜːbl/ a verbal; (literal) literal
verbatim /vɜːˈbeɪtɪm/ adv literalmente, palavra por palavra
verbose /vɜːˈbəʊs/ a palavroso, prolixo
verdict /ˈvɜːdɪkt/ n veredicto m; (opinion) opinião f
verge /vɜːdʒ/ n beira f, borda f □ vi ~ **on** estar à beira de. **on the** ~ **of doing** prestes a fazer
verify /ˈverɪfaɪ/ vt verificar
veritable /ˈverɪtəbl/ a autêntico, verdadeiro
vermicelli /vɜːmɪˈselɪ/ n aletria f
vermin /ˈvɜːmɪn/ n animais mpl nocivos; (lice, fleas etc) parasitas mpl
vermouth /ˈvɜːməθ/ n vermute m
vernacular /vəˈnækjʊlə(r)/ n vernáculo m; (dialect) dialeto m, (P) dialecto m
versatile /ˈvɜːsətaɪl/ a versátil; (tool) que serve para vários fins. ~**ity** /-ˈtɪlətɪ/ n versatilidade f

verse /vɜːs/ n (poetry) verso m, poesia f; (stanza) estrofe f; (of Bible) versículo m
versed /vɜːst/ a ~ **in** versado em, conhecedor de
version /ˈvɜːʃn/ n versão f
versus /ˈvɜːsəs/ prep contra
vertebra /ˈvɜːtɪbrə/ n (pl-brae /-briː/) vértebra f
vertical /ˈvɜːtɪkl/ a vertical. ~**ly** adv verticalmente
vertigo /ˈvɜːtɪɡəʊ/ n vertigem f
verve /vɜːv/ n verve f, vivacidade f
very /ˈverɪ/ adv muito □ a (actual) mesmo, próprio; (exact) preciso, exato, (P) exacto. **the** ~ **day**/etc o próprio or o mesmo dia/etc. **at the** ~ **end** mesmo or precisamente no fim. **the** ~ **first**/**best**/etc (emph) o primeiro/melhor/etc de todos. ~ **much** muito. ~ **well** muito bem
vessel /ˈvesl/ n vaso m
vest[1] /vest/ n corpete m, (P) camisola f interior; (Amer: waistcoat) colete m
vest[2] /vest/ vt conferir (**in** a). ~**ed interests** interesses mpl
vestige /ˈvestɪdʒ/ n vestígio m
vestry /ˈvestrɪ/ n sacristia f
vet /vet/ n (colloq) veterinário m □ vt (pt **vetted**) (candidate etc) examinar atentamente, estudar
veteran /ˈvetərən/ n veterano m. (**war**) ~ veterano m de guerra
veterinary /ˈvetərɪnərɪ/ a veterinário. ~ **surgeon** veterinário m
veto /ˈviːtəʊ/ n (pl-**oes**) veto m; (right) direito m de veto □ vt vetar, opor o veto a
vex /veks/ vt aborrecer, irritar, contrariar. ~**ed question** questão f muito debatida, assunto m controverso
via /ˈvaɪə/ prep por, via
viable /ˈvaɪəbl/ a viável. ~**ility** /-ˈbɪlətɪ/ n viabilidade f
viaduct /ˈvaɪədʌkt/ n viaduto m
vibrant /ˈvaɪbrənt/ a vibrante
vibrat|e /vaɪˈbreɪt/ vt/i (fazer) vibrar. ~**ion** /-ʃn/ n vibração f
vicar /ˈvɪkə(r)/ n (Anglican) pastor m; (Catholic) vigário m, pároco m. ~**age** n presbitério m
vicarious /vɪˈkeərɪəs/ a vivido indiretamente, (P) indirectamente
vice[1] /vaɪs/ n (depravity) vício m
vice[2] /vaɪs/ n (techn) torno m
vice- /vaɪs/ pref vice-. ~**chairman** vice-presidente m. ~**chancellor** n vice-chanceler m; (univ) reitor m. ~**consul** n vice-cônsul m. ~**president** n vice-presidente mf
vice versa /ˈvaɪsɪˈvɜːsə/ adv vice-versa
vicinity /vɪˈsɪnətɪ/ n vizinhança f,

cercania(s) *fpl*, arredores *mpl*. **in the ~ of** nos arredores de

vicious /'vɪʃəs/ *a* (*spiteful*) mau, maldoso; (*violent*) brutal, feroz. **~ circle** circulo *m* vicioso. **~ly** *adv* maldosamente; (*violently*) brutalmente, ferozmente

victim /'vɪktɪm/ *n* vitima *f*

victimiz|e /'vɪktɪmaɪz/ *vt* perseguir. **~ation** /-'zeɪʃn/ *n* perseguição *f*

victor /'vɪktə(r)/ *n* vencedor *m*

victor|y /'vɪktərɪ/ *n* vitória *f*. **~ious** /-'tɔːrɪəs/ *a* vitorioso

video /'vɪdɪəʊ/ *a* video □ *n* (*pl* -os) (*colloq*) video □ *vt* (*record*) gravar em video. **~ cassette** video-cassete *f*. **~ recorder** videocassete *m*

vie /vaɪ/ *vi* (*pres p* vying) rivalizar, competir (**with** com)

view /vjuː/ *n* vista *f* □ *vt* ver; (*examine*) examinar; (*consider*) considerar, ver; (*a house*) visitar, ver. **in my ~** a meu ver, na minha opinião. **in ~ of** em vista de, em atenção a. **on ~** em exposição, à mostra; (*open to the public*) aberto ao público. **with a ~ to** com a intenção de, com o fim de. **~er** *n* (*TV*) telespectador *m*; (*for slides*) visor *m*

viewfinder /'vjuːfaɪndə(r)/ *n* visor *m*

viewpoint /'vjuːpɔɪnt/ *n* ponto *m* de vista

vigil /'vɪdʒɪl/ *n* vigília *f*; (*over corpse*) velório *m*; (*relig*) vigília *f*

vigilan|t /'vɪdʒɪlənt/ *a* vigilante. **~ce** *n* vigilância *f*. **~te** /vɪdʒɪ'læntɪ/ *n* vigilante *m*

vig|our /'vɪgə(r)/ *n* vigor *m*. **~orous** /'vɪgərəs/ *a* vigoroso

vile /vaɪl/ *a* (*base*) infame, vil; (*colloq: bad*) horroroso, péssimo

vilify /'vɪlɪfaɪ/ *vt* difamar

villa /'vɪlə/ *n* vivenda *f*, vila *f*; (*country residence*) casa *f* de campo

village /'vɪlɪdʒ/ *n* aldeia *f*, povoado *m*. **~r** *n* aldeão *m*, aldeã *f*

villain /'vɪlən/ *n* patife *m*, mau-caráter *m*. **~y** *n* infâmia *f*, vilania *f*

vindicat|e /'vɪndɪkeɪt/ *vt* vindicar, justificar. **~ion** /-'keɪʃn/ *n* justificação *f*

vindictive /vɪn'dɪktɪv/ *a* vingativo

vine /vaɪn/ *n* (*plant*) vinha *f*

vinegar /'vɪnɪɡə(r)/ *n* vinagre *m*

vineyard /'vɪnjəd/ *n* vinha *f*, vinhedo *m*

vintage /'vɪntɪdʒ/ *n* (*year*) ano *m* de colheita de qualidade excepcional □ *a* (*wine*) de colheita excepcional e de um determinado ano; (*car*) de museu (*colloq*), fabricado entre 1917 e 1930

vinyl /'vaɪnɪl/ *n* vinil *m*

viola /vɪ'əʊlə/ *n* (*mus*) viola *f*, violeta *f*

violat|e /'vaɪəleɪt/ *vt* violar. **~ion** /-'leɪʃn/ *n* violação *f*

violen|t /'vaɪələnt/ *a* violento. **~ce** *n* violência *f*. **~tly** *adv* violentamente, com violência

violet /'vaɪələt/ *n* (*bot*) violeta *f*; (*colour*) violeta *m* □ *a* violeta

violin /vaɪə'lɪn/ *n* violino *m*. **~ist** *n* violinista *mf*

VIP /viː'aɪpiː/ *abbr* (*very important person*) VIP *m*, personalidade *f* importante

viper /'vaɪpə(r)/ *n* vibora *f*

virgin /'vɜːdʒɪn/ *a & n* virgem (*f*)

virgin /'vɜːdʒɪnətɪ/ *n* virgindade *f*

Virgo /'vɜːɡəʊ/ *n* (*astr*) Virgem *f*, (*P*) virgo *m*

viril|e /'vɪraɪl/ *a* viril, varonil. **~ity** /vɪ'rɪlətɪ/ *n* virilidade *f*

virtual /'vɜːtʃʊəl/ *a* que é na prática embora não em teoria, verdadeiro. **a ~ failure/etc** praticamente um fracasso/etc. **~ly** *adv* praticamente

virtue /'vɜːtʃuː/ *n* (*goodness, chastity*) virtude *f*; (*merit*) mérito *m*. **by or in ~ of** por or em virtude de

virtuos|o /vɜːtʃʊ'əʊsəʊ/ *n* (*pl* -si /-siː/) virtuoso *m*, virtuose *mf*. **~ity** /-'ɒsətɪ/ *n* virtuosidade *f*, virtuosismo *m*

virtuous /'vɜːtʃʊəs/ *a* virtuoso

virulen|t /'vɪrʊlənt/ *a* virulento. **~ce** /-ləns/ *n* virulência *f*

virus /'vaɪərəs/ *n* (*pl* -es) virus *m*; (*colloq: disease*) virose *f*

visa /'viːzə/ *n* visto *m*

viscount /'vaɪkaʊnt/ *n* visconde *m*. **~ess** /-ɪs/ *n* viscondessa *f*

viscous /'vɪskəs/ *a* viscoso

vise /vaɪs/ *n* (*Amer: vice*) torno *m*

visib|le /'vɪzəbl/ *a* visível. **~ility** /-'bɪlətɪ/ *n* visibilidade *f*. **~ly** *adv* visivelmente

vision /'vɪʒn/ *n* (*dream, insight*) visão *f*; (*seeing, sight*) vista *f*, visão *f*

visionary /'vɪʒənərɪ/ *a* visionário; (*plan, scheme etc*) fantasista, quimérico □ *n* visionário *m*

visit /'vɪzɪt/ *vt* (*pt* visited) (*person*) visitar, fazer uma visita a; (*place*) visitar □ *vi* estar de visita □ *n* (*tour, call*) visita *f*; (*stay*) estada *f*, visita *f*. **~or** *n* visitante *mf*; (*guest*) visita *f*

visor /'vaɪzə(r)/ *n* viseira *f*; (*in vehicle*) visor *m*

vista /'vɪstə/ *n* vista *f*, panorama *m*

visual /'vɪʒʊəl/ *a* visual. **~ display unit** terminal *m* de vídeo. **~ly** *adv* visualmente

visualize /'vɪʒʊəlaɪz/ *vt* visualizar; (*foresee*) imaginar, prever

vital /'vaɪtl/ *a* vital. **~ statistics** estatística *fpl* demográficas; (*colloq: woman*) medidas *fpl*

vitality /vaɪ'tælətɪ/ *n* vitalidade *f*

vitamin /'vɪtəmɪn/ *n* vitamina *f*

vivac|ious /vɪ'veɪʃəs/ *a* cheio de vida,

vivo, animado. ~ity /-'væsəti/ n vivacidade f, animação f

vivid /'vivid/ a vívido; (imagination) vivo. ~ly adv vividamente

vivisection /vivi'sekʃn/ n vivissecção f

vixen /'viksn/ n raposa f fêmea

vocabulary /və'kæbjʊləri/ n vocabulário m

vocal /'vəʊkl/ a vocal; (fig: person) eloqüente, (P) eloquente. ~ cords cordas fpl vocais. ~ist n vocalista mf

vocation /və'keiʃn/ n vocação f; (trade) profissão f. ~al a vocacional, profissional

vociferous /və'sifərəs/ a vociferante

vodka /'vɒdkə/ n vodka m

vogue /vəʊg/ n voga f, moda f, popularidade f. in ~ em voga, na moda

voice /vɔis/ n voz f □ vt (express) exprimir

void /vɔid/ a vazio; (jur) nulo, sem validade □ n vácuo m, vazio m. make ~ anular, invalidar. ~ of sem, destituído de

volatile /'vɒlətail/ a (substance) volátil; (fig: changeable) instável

volcano /vɒl'keməʊ/ n (pl -oes) vulcão m. ~ic /-ænik/ a vulcânico

volition /və'liʃn/ n of one's own ~ de sua própria vontade

volley /'vɒli/ n (of blows etc) saraivada f, (of gunfire) salva f; (tennis) voleio m. ~ball n voleibol m, vôlei m

volt /vəʊlt/ n volt m. ~age n voltagem f

voluble /'vɒljʊbl/ a falante, loquaz

volume /'vɒljuːm/ n (book, sound) volume m; (capacity) capacidade f

voluntary /'vɒləntəri/ a voluntário; (unpaid) não-remunerado. ~ily /-trəli/ adv voluntariamente

volunteer /vɒlən'tiə(r)/ n voluntário m □ vi oferecer-se (to do para fazer); (mil) alistar-se como voluntário □ vt oferecer espontaneamente

voluptuous /və'lʌptʃʊəs/ a voluptuoso, sensual

vomit /'vɒmit/ vt/i (pt vomited) vomitar □ n vómito m, (P) vômito m

voodoo /'vuːduː/ n vodu m

voracious /və'reiʃəs/ a voraz. ~ously adv vorazmente. ~ty /və-'ræsəti/ n voracidade f

vote /vəʊt/ n voto m, (right) direito m de voto □ vt/i votar. ~er n eleitor m. ~ing n votação f; (poll) escrutínio m

vouch /vaʊtʃ/ vi ~ for responder por, garantir

voucher /'vaʊtʃə(r)/ n (for meal, transport) vale m; (receipt) comprovante m

vow /vaʊ/ n voto m □ vt (loyalty etc) jurar (to a). ~ to do jurar fazer

vowel /'vaʊəl/ n vogal f

voyage /'vɔiidʒ/ n viagem (por mar) f. ~r /-ə(r)/ n viajante m

vulgar /'vʌlgə(r)/ a ordinário, grosseiro; (in common use) vulgar. ~ity /-'gærəti/ n (behaviour) grosseria f, vulgaridade f

vulnerab|le /'vʌlnərəbl/ a vulnerável. ~ility /-'biləti/ n vulnerabilidade f

vulture /'vʌltʃə(r)/ n abutre m, urubu m

vying /'vaiiŋ/ see vie

W

wad /wɒd/ n bucha f, tampão m; (bundle) maço m, rolo m

wadding /'wɒdiŋ/ n enchimento m

waddle /'wɒdl/ vi bambolear-se, rebolar-se, gingar

wade /weid/ vi ~ through (fig) avançar a custo por; (mud, water) patinhar em

wafer /'weifə(r)/ n (biscuit) bolacha f de baunilha; (relig) hóstia f

waffle[1] /'wɒfl/ n (colloq: talk) lengalenga f, papo m, conversa f; (colloq: writing) □ vi (colloq) escrever muito sem dizer nada de importante

waffle[2] /'wɒfl/ n (culin) waffle m

waft /wɒft/ vi flutuar □ vt espalhar, levar suavemente

wag /wæg/ vt/i (pt wagged) abanar, agitar, sacudir

wage[1] /weidʒ/ vt (campaign, war) fazer

wage[2] /weidʒ/ n ~(s) (weekly, daily) salário m, ordenado m. ~-claim n pedido m de aumento de salário. ~-earner n trabalhador m assalariado. ~-freeze n congelamento m de salários

wager /'weidʒə(r)/ n (bet) aposta f □ vt apostar (that que)

waggle /'wægl/ vt/i abanar, agitar, sacudir

wagon /'wægən/ n (horse-drawn) carroça f; (rail) vagão m de mercadorias

waif /weif/ n criança f abandonada

wail /weil/ vi lamentar-se, gemer lamentosamente □ n lamentação f, gemido m lamentoso

waist /weist/ n cintura f. ~line n cintura f

waistcoat /'weiskəʊt/ n colete m

wait /weit/ vt/i esperar □ n espera f. ~ for esperar. ~ on servir. lie in ~ (for) estar escondido à espera (de), armar uma emboscada (para). keep sb ~ing fazer alguém esperar. ~ing-list n lista *f* de espera. **~ing-room** *n* sala *f* de espera

wait|er /ˈweɪtə(r)/ *n* garçon *m*, (P) criado *m* (de mesa). **~ress** *n* garçonete *f*, (P) criada *f* (de mesa)

waive /weɪv/ *vt* renunciar a, desistir de

wake¹ /weɪk/ *vt/i* (*pt* **woke**, *pp* **woken**) ~ (**up**) acordar, despertar □ *n* (*before burial*) velório *m*

wake² /weɪk/ *n* (*ship*) esteira (de espuma) *f*. **in the ~ of** (*following*) atrás de, em seguida a

waken /ˈweɪkən/ *vt/i* acordar, despertar

Wales /weɪlz/ *n* País *m* de Gales

walk /wɔːk/ *vi* andar, caminhar; (*not ride*) ir a pé; (*stroll*) passear □ *vt* (*streets*) andar por, percorrer; (*distance*) andar, fazer a pé, percorrer; (*dog*) levar para) passear □ *n* (*stroll*) passeio *m*, volta *f*; (*excursion*) caminhada *f*; (*gait*) passo *m*, maneira *f* de andar; (*pace*) passo *m*; (*path*) caminho *m*. **it's a 5-minute ~** são 5 minutos a pé. ~ **of life** meio *m*, condição *f* social. ~ **out** (*go away*) sair; (*go on strike*) fazer greve. ~ **out on** abandonar. **~-over** *n* vitória *f* fácil

walker /ˈwɔːkə(r)/ *n* caminhante *mf*

walkie-talkie /wɔːkɪˈtɔːkɪ/ *n* walkie-talkie *m*

walking /ˈwɔːkɪŋ/ *n* andar (a pé) *m*, marcha (a pé) *f* □ *a* (*colloq: dictionary*) vivo. **~-stick** *n* bengala *f*

Walkman /ˈwɔːkmæn/ *n* walkman *m*

wall /wɔːl/ *n* parede *f*; (*around land*) muro *m*; (*of castle, town, fig*) muralha *f*; (*of stomach etc*) paredes *f* (*pl*) □ *vt* (*city*) fortificar; (*property*) murar. **go to the ~** sucumbir, falir; (*firm*) ir à falência. **up the ~** (*colloq*) fora de si

wallet /ˈwɒlɪt/ *n* carteira *f*

wallflower /ˈwɔːlflaʊə(r)/ *n* (*bot*) goivo *m*. **be a ~** (*fig*) tomar chá de cadeira, (P) levar banho de cadeira

wallop /ˈwɒləp/ *vt* (*pt* **walloped**) (*sl*) espancar (*colloq*) □ *n* (*sl*) pancada *f* forte

wallow /ˈwɒləʊ/ *vi* (*in mud*) chafurdar, atolar-se; (*fig*) regozijar-se

wallpaper /ˈwɔːlpeɪpə(r)/ *n* papel *m* de parede □ *vt* forrar com papel de parede

walnut /ˈwɔːlnʌt/ *n* (*nut*) noz *f*; (*tree*) nogueira *f*

walrus /ˈwɔːlrəs/ *n* morsa *f*

waltz /wɔːls/ *n* valsa *f* □ *vi* valsar

wan /wɒn/ *a* pálido

wand /wɒnd/ *n* (*magic*) varinha *f* mágica *or* de condão

wander /ˈwɒndə(r)/ *vi* andar ao acaso, vagar, errar; (*river*) serpentear; (*mind, speech*) divagar; (*stray*) extra-

viar-se. **~er** *n* vagabundo *m*, andarilho *m*. **~ing** *a* errante

wane /weɪn/ *vi* diminuir, minguar; (*decline*) declinar □ *n* **on the ~** em declínio; (*moon*) no quarto minguante

wangle /ˈwæŋgl/ *vt* (*colloq*) conseguir algo através de pistolão

want /wɒnt/ *vt* querer □ (**to do** fazer); (*need*) precisar (de); (*ask for*) exigir, requerer □ *vi* ~ **for** ter falta de □ *n* (*need*) necessidade *f*, precisão *f*; (*desire*) desejo *m*; (*lack*) falta *f*, carência *f*. **for ~ of** por falta de. **I ~ you to go** eu quero que você vá. **~ed** *a* (*criminal*) procurado pela polícia; (*in ad*) precisa(m)-se

wanting /ˈwɒntɪŋ/ *a* falho, falto (**in** de). **be found ~** não estar à altura

wanton /ˈwɒntən/ *a* (*playful*) travesso, brincalhão; (*cruelty, destruction etc*) gratuito; (*woman*) despudorado

war /wɔː(r)/ *n* guerra *f*. **at ~** em guerra. **on the ~-path** em pé de guerra

warble /ˈwɔːbl/ *vt/i* gorjear

ward /wɔːd/ *n* (*in hospital*) enfermaria *f*; (*jur: minor*) pupilo *m*; (*pol*) círculo *m* eleitoral □ *vt* ~ **off** (*a blow*) aparar; (*anger*) desviar; (*danger*) prevenir, evitar

warden /ˈwɔːdn/ *n* (*of institution*) diretor *m*, (P) director *m*; (*of park*) guarda *m*

warder /ˈwɔːdə(r)/ *n* guarda (de prisão) *m*, carcereiro *m*

wardrobe /ˈwɔːdrəʊb/ *n* (*place*) armário *m*, guarda-roupa *m*, (P) guarda-fato *m*, (P) roupeiro *m*; (*clothes*) guarda-roupa *m*

warehouse /ˈweəhaʊs/ *n* (*pl* **-s** /-haʊzɪz/) armazém *m*, depósito *m* de mercadorias

wares /weəz/ *npl* (*goods*) mercadorias *fpl*, artigos *mpl*

warfare /ˈwɔːfeə(r)/ *n* guerra *f*

warhead /ˈwɔːhed/ *n* ogiva (de combate) *f*

warlike /ˈwɔːlaɪk/ *a* marcial, guerreiro; (*bellicose*) belicoso

warm /wɔːm/ *a* (**-er, -est**) quente; (*hearty*) caloroso, cordial. **be** *or* **feel ~** ter calor *or* ter *or* sentir calor □ *vt/i* ~ (**up**) aquecer(-se). **~-hearted** *a* afetuoso, (P) afectuoso, com calor humano. **~ly** *adv* (*heartily*) calorosamente. **wrap up ~ly** agasalhar-se bem. **~th** *n* calor *m*

warn /wɔːn/ *vt* avisar, prevenir. ~ **sb off sth** (*advise against*) pôr alguém de prevenção *or* de pé atrás com alg coisa; (*forbid*) proibir alg coisa a alguém. **~ing** *n* aviso *m*. **~ing light** lâmpada *f* de advertência. **without ~ing** sem aviso, sem prevenir

warp /wɔ:p/ vt/i (wood etc) empenar; (fig: pervert) torcer, deformar, desvirtuar. ~ed a (fig) deturpado, pervertido

warrant /'wɒrənt/ n autorização f; (for arrest) mandato (de captura) m; (comm) título m de crédito, warrant m □ vt justificar; (guarantee) garantir

warranty /'wɒrənti/ n garantia f

warring /'wɔ:rɪŋ/ a em guerra; (rival) contrário, antagónico, (P) antagónico

warrior /'wɒrɪə(r)/ n guerreiro m

warship /'wɔ:ʃɪp/ n navio m de guerra

wart /wɔ:t/ n verruga f

wartime /'wɔ:taɪm/ n in ~ em tempo de guerra

wary /'weərɪ/ a (-ier, -iest) cauteloso, prudente

was /wɒz/; unstressed /wəz/ see be

wash /wɒʃ/ vt/i lavar(-se); (flow over) molhar, inundar □ n lavagem f; (dirty clothes) roupa f para lavar; (of ship) esteira f; (of paint) fina camada f de tinta. have a ~ lavar-se. ~-basin n pia f, (P) lavatório m. ~-cloth n (Amer: face-cloth) toalha f de rosto. ~ one's hands of lavar as mãos de. ~ out (cup etc) lavar; (stain) tirar lavando. ~-out n (sl) fiasco m. ~-room n (Amer) banheiro m, (P) casa f de banho. ~ up lavar a louça; (Amer: wash oneself) lavar-se. ~able a lavável. ~ing n (dirty) roupa f suja; (clean) roupa f lavada. ~ing-machine n máquina f de lavar roupa. ~ing-powder n detergente m em pó. ~ing-up n lavagem f da louça

washed-out /wɒʃt'aʊt/ a (faded) desbotado; (exhausted) exausto

washer /'wɒʃə(r)/ n (machine) máquina f de lavar roupa, louça f, (P) loiça f; (ring) anilha f

wasp /wɒsp/ n vespa f

wastage /'weɪstɪdʒ/ n desperdício m, perda f. natural ~ desgaste m natural

waste /weɪst/ vt desperdiçar, esbanjar; (time) perder □ vi ~ away consumir-se □ a (useless) inútil; (material) de refugo □ n desperdício m, perda f; (of time) perda f; (rubbish) lixo m. lay ~ assolar, devastar. ~ (land) (desolate) região f desolada, ermo m; (unused) (terreno) baldio m. ~-disposal unit triturador m de lixo. ~ paper papéis mpl velhos. ~-paper basket cesto m de papéis

wasteful /'weɪstfl/ a dispendioso; (person) esbanjador, gastador, perdulário

watch /wɒtʃ/ vt/i ver bem, olhar com atenção, observar; (game, TV) ver; (guard, spy on) vigiar; (be careful about) tomar cuidado com □ n vigia f, vigilância f; (naut) quarto m; (for telling time) relógio m. ~-dog n cão m de guarda. ~ out (look out) estar à espreita (for de); (take care) acautelar-se. ~-strap n correia f, pulseira f do relógio. ~-tower n torre f de observação. ~ful a atento, vigilante

watchmaker /'wɒtʃmeɪkə(r)/ n relojoeiro m

watchman /'wɒtʃmən/ n (pl -men) (of building) guarda m. (night-)~ guarda-noturno m

watchword /'wɒtʃwɜ:d/ n lema m, divisa f

water /'wɔ:tə(r)/ n água f □ vt regar □ vi (of eyes) lacrimejar, chorar. ~ down juntar água a, diluir; (milk, wine) aguar, batizar, (P) baptizar (colloq); (fig: tone down) suavizar. ~-closet n WC m, banheiro m, (P) lavabos mpl. ~-colour n aquarela f. ~-ice n sorvete m. ~-lily n nenúfar m. ~-main n cano m principal da rede. ~-melon n melancia f. ~-pistol n pistola f de água. ~ polo pólo m aquático. ~-skiing n esqui m aquático. ~-wheel n roda f hidráulica

watercress /'wɔ:təkres/ n agrião m

waterfall /'wɔ:təfɔ:l/ n queda f de água, cascata f

watering-can /'wɔ:tərɪŋkæn/ n regador m

waterlogged /'wɔ:təlɒgd/ a saturado de água; (land) empapado, alagado; (vessel) inundado, alagado

watermark /'wɔ:təmɑ:k/ n (in paper) marca-d'água f, filigrana f

waterproof /'wɔ:təpru:f/ a impermeável; (watch) à prova d'água

watershed /'wɔ:təʃed/ n (fig) momento m decisivo; (in affairs) ponto m crítico

watertight /'wɔ:tətaɪt/ a à prova d'água, hermético; (fig: argument etc) inequívoco, irrefutável

waterway /'wɔ:təweɪ/ n via f navegável

waterworks /'wɔ:təwɜ:ks/ n (place) estação f hidráulica

watery /'wɔ:tərɪ/ a (colour) pálido; (eyes) lacrimoso; (soup) aguado; (tea) fraco

watt /wɒt/ n watt m

wave /weɪv/ n onda f; (in hair; radio) onda f; (sign) aceno m □ vt acenar com; (sword) brandir; (hair) ondular □ vi acenar (com a mão); (hair etc) ondular; (flag) tremular. ~band n faixa f de onda. ~e goodbye dizer adeus. ~elength n comprimento m de onda. ~y a ondulado

waver /'weɪvə(r)/ *vi* vacilar; (*hesitate*) hesitar

wax¹ /wæks/ *n* cera *f* □ *vt* encerar; (*car*) polir. ~**en**, ~**y** *adjs* de cera

wax² /wæks/ *vi* (*of moon*) aumentar, crescer

waxwork /'wækswɜːk/ *n* (*dummy*) figura *f* de cera. ~**s** *npl* (*exhibition*) museu *m* de figuras de cera

way /weɪ/ *n* (*road, path*) caminho *m*, estrada *f*, rua *f* (**to** para); (*distance*) percurso *m*; (*direction*) (P) direção *f*; (*manner*) modo *m*, maneira *f*; (*means*) meios *mpl*; (*respect*) respeito *m*. ~**s** (*habits*) costumes *mpl* □ *adv* (*colloq*) consideravelmente, de longe. **be in the** ~ atrapalhar. **be on one's** ~ **the** ~ estar a caminho. **by the** ~ a propósito. **by** ~ **of** por, via, através. **get one's own** ~ conseguir o que quer. **give** ~ (*yield*) ceder; (*collapse*) desabar; (*auto*) dar a preferência. **in a** ~ de certo modo. **make one's** ~ ir. **that** ~ dessa maneira. **this** ~ desta maneira. ~ **in** entrada *f*. ~ **out** saída *f*. ~**out** *a* (*colloq*) excêntrico

waylay /weɪ'leɪ/ *vt* (*pt* -**laid**) (*assail*) armar uma cilada para; (*stop*) interceptar

wayward /'weɪwəd/ *a* (*wilful*) teimoso; (*perverse*) caprichoso, difícil

WC /dʌb(ə)ljuːˈsiː/ *n* WC *m*, banheiro *m*, (P) casa *f* de banho

we /wiː/ *pron* nós

weak /wiːk/ *a* (-**er**, -**est**) fraco; (*delicate*) frágil. ~**en** *vt/i* enfraquecer; (*give way*) fraquejar. ~**ly** *adv* fracamente. ~**ness** *n* fraqueza *f*; (*fault*) ponto *m* fraco. **a** ~**ness for** (*liking*) um fraco por

weakling /'wiːklɪŋ/ *n* fraco *m f*

wealth /welθ/ *n* riqueza *f*; (*riches, resources*) riquezas *fpl*; (*quantity*) abundância *f*

wealthy /'welθɪ/ *a* (-**ier**, -**iest**) rico

wean /wiːn/ *vt* (*baby*) desmamar; (*from habit etc*) desabituar

weapon /'wepən/ *n* arma *f*

wear /weə(r)/ *vt* (*pt* **wore** *pp* **worn**) (*have on*) usar, trazer; (*put on*) pôr; (*expression*) ter; (*damage*) gastar. ~ **black/red/***etc* vestir-se de preto/vermelho/*etc* □ *vi* (*last*) durar; (*become old, damaged etc*) gastar-se □ *n* (*use*) uso *m*; (*deterioration*) gasto *m*, uso *m*; (*endurance*) resistência *f*; (*clothing*) roupa *f*. ~ **and tear** desgaste *m*. ~ **down** gastar; (*person*) extenuar. ~ **off** passar. ~ **on** (*time*) passar lentamente. ~ **out** gastar; (*tire*) cansar, esgotar

wear|**y** /'wɪərɪ/ *a* (-**ier**, -**iest**) fatigado, cansado; (*tiring*) fatigante, cansativo □ *vi* ~**y of** cansar-se de. ~**ily** *adv* com

lassidão, cansadamente. ~**iness** *n* fadiga *f*, cansaço *m*

weasel /'wiːzl/ *n* doninha *f*

weather /'weðə(r)/ *n* tempo *m* □ *a* meteorológico □ *vt* (*survive*) agüentar, (P) aguentar, resistir a. **under the** ~ (*colloq: ill*) indisposto, achacado. ~-**beaten** *a* curtido pelo tempo. ~-**forecast** *n* boletim *m* meteorológico. ~-**vane** *n* cata-vento *m*

weathercock /'weðəkɒk/ *n* (*lit & fig*) cata-vento *m*

weav|**e**¹ /wiːv/ *vt* (*pt* **wove** *pp* **woven**) (*cloth etc*) tecer; (*plot*) urdir, criar □ *n* (*style*) tipo *m* de tecido. ~**er** /-ə(r)/ *n* tecelão *m*, tecelã *f*. ~**ing** *n* tecelagem *f*

weave² /wiːv/ *vi* (*move*) serpear; (*through traffic, obstacles*) ziguezaguear

web /web/ *n* (*of spider*) teia *f*; (*fabric*) tecido *m*; (*on foot*) membrana *f* interdigital. ~**bed** *a* (*foot*) palmado. ~-**bing** *n* (*in chair*) tira *f* de tecido forte. ~-**footed** *a* palmípede

wed /wed/ *vt/i* (*pt* **wedded**) casar(-se)

wedding /'wedɪŋ/ *n* casamento *m*. ~-**cake** *n* bolo *m* de noiva. ~-**ring** *n* aliança (de casamento) *f*

wedge /wedʒ/ *n* calço *m*, cunha *f*; (*cake*) fatia *f*; (*of lemon*) quarto *m*; (*under wheel etc*) calço *m*, cunha *f* □ *vt* calçar; (*push*) meter or enfiar à força; (*pack in*) entalar

Wednesday /'wenzdɪ/ *n* quartafeira *f*

weed /wiːd/ *n* erva *f* daninha □ *vt/i* arrancar as ervas, capinar. ~-**killer** *n* herbicida *m*. ~ **out** suprimir, arrancar. ~-**y** *a* (*fig: person*) fraco

week /wiːk/ *n* semana *f*. **a** ~ **today/tomorrow** de hoje/de amanhã a oito dias. ~-**ly** *a* semanal □ *a & n* (*periodical*) (jornal) semanário (*m*) □ *adv* semanalmente, toda as semanas

weekday /'wiːkdeɪ/ *n* dia *m* de semana

weekend /'wiːkend/ *n* fim-de-semana *m*

weep /wiːp/ *vt/i* (*pt* **wept**) chorar (**for sb** por alguém). ~**ing willow** (*salgueiro*)chorão *m*

weigh /weɪ/ *vt/i* pesar. ~ **anchor** levantar âncora *or* ferro, zarpar. ~ **down** (*weight*) sobrecarregar; (*bend*) envergar; (*fig*) acabrunhar. ~ **up** (*colloq: examine*) pesar

weight /weɪt/ *n* peso *m*. **lose** ~ emagrecer. **put on** ~ engordar. ~**less** *a* imponderável. ~-**lifter** *n* halterofilista *m*. ~-**lifting** *n* halterofilia *f*. ~**y** *a* pesado; (*subject etc*) de peso; (*influential*) influente

weighting /'weɪtɪŋ/ *n* suplemento *m* salarial

weir /wɪə(r)/ *n* represa *f*, açude *m*

weird /wɪəd/ *a* (-er, -est) misterioso; (*strange*) estranho, bizarro

welcom|e /'welkəm/ *a* agradável; (*timely*) oportuno □ *int* (seja) benvindo! □ *n* acolhimento *m* □ *vt* acolher, receber; (*as greeting*) dar as boas vindas a. **be ~e** ser bem-vindo. **you're ~e!** (*after thank you*) não tem de quê!, de nada! **~e to do** livre para fazer. **~ing** *a* acolhedor

weld /weld/ *vt* soldar □ *n* solda *f*. **~er** *n* soldador *m*. **~ing** *n* soldagem *f*, soldadura *f*

welfare /'welfeə(r)/ *n* bem-estar *m*; (*aid*) assistência *f*, previdência *f* social. **W~ State** Estado-Providência *m*

well[1] /wel/ *n* (*for water, oil*) poço *m*; (*of stairs*) vão *m*; (*of lift*) poço *m*

well[2] /wel/ *adv* (**better, best**) bem □ *a* bem (*invar*) □ *int* bem! **as ~** também. **we may as ~** go é melhor irnos andando. **as ~ as** tão bem como; (*in addition*) assim como. **be ~** (*healthy*) ir or passar bem. **do ~** (*succeed*) sair-se bem, ser bem sucedido. **very ~** muito bem. □ **done!** bravo!, muito bem! **~-behaved** *a* bem comportado, educado. **~-being** *n* bem-estar *m*. **~-bred** *a* (bem) educado. **~-done** *a* (*of meat*) bem passado. **~-dressed** *a* bem vestido. **~-heeled** *a* (*colloq: wealthy*) rico. **~-informed** *a* versado, bem informado. **~-known** *a* (bem-)conhecido. **~-meaning** *a* bem intencionado. **~-off** *a* rico, próspero. **~-read** *a* instruído. **~-spoken** *a* bem-falante. **~-timed** *a* oportuno. **~-to-do** *a* rico. **~-wisher** *n* admirador *m*, simpatizante *mf*

wellington /'welɪŋtən/ *n* (*boot*) bota *f* alta de borracha

Welsh /welʃ/ *a* galês □ *n* (*lang*) galês *m*. **~man** *n* galês *m*. **~woman** *n* galesa *f*

wend /wend/ *vt* **~ one's way** dirigir-se, seguir o seu caminho

went /went/ *see* **go**

wept /wept/ *see* **weep**

were /wɜː(r)/; *unstressed* /wə(r)/ *see* **be**

west /west/ *n* oeste *m*. **the W~** (*pol*) o Oeste, o Ocidente □ *a* ocidental, do oeste □ *adv* ao oeste, para o oeste. **W~ Indian** *a* & *n* antilhano (*m*). **the W~ Indies** as Antilhas. **~erly** *a* ocidental, oeste. **~ward** *a* para o oeste. **~ward(s)** *adv* para o oeste

western /'westən/ *a* ocidental, do oeste; (*pol*) ocidental □ *n* (*film*) filme *m* de cowboys, bangue-bangue *m*

westernize /'westənaɪz/ *vt* ocidentalizar

wet /wet/ *a* (**wetter, wettest**) molhado; (*of weather*) chuvoso, de chuva; (*colloq: person*) fraco. **get ~** molhar-se □ *vt* (*pt* wetted) molhar. **~ blanket** (*colloq*) desmancha-prazeres *mf invar* (*colloq*). **~ paint** pintado de fresco. **~ suit** roupa *f* de mergulho

whack /wæk/ *vt* (*colloq*) bater em □ *n* (*colloq*) pancada *f*. **~ed** *a* (*colloq*) morto de cansaço, rebentado (*colloq*). **~ing** *a* (*sl*) enorme, de todo o tamanho

whale /weɪl/ *n* baleia *f*

wharf /wɔːf/ *n* (*pl* **wharfs**) cais *m*

what /wɒt/ *a* (*interr, excl*) que. **~ time is it?** que horas são? **~ an idea!** que idéia! □ *pron* (*interr*) (o) quê, como, o que, qual, quais; (*object*) o que; (*after prep*) que; (*that which*) o que, aquilo que. **~?** (o) quê?, como? **~ is it?** o que é? **~ is your address?** qual é o seu endereço? **~ is your name?** como se chama? **~ can you see?** o que é que você pode ver? **this is ~** I write with é com isto que escrevo. **that's ~** I need é disso que eu preciso. **do ~** you want faça o que *or* aquilo que quiser. **~ about me/him/***etc*? e eu/ele/*etc*? **~ about doing sth?** e se fizéssemos alg coisa? **~ for?** para quê?

whatever /wɒt'evə(r)/ *a* **~ book/***etc* qualquer livro/*etc* que seja □ *pron* (*no matter what*) qualquer que seja; (*anything that*) o que quer que, tudo o que. **nothing ~** absolutamente nada. **~ happens** aconteça o que acontecer. **do ~** you like faça o que quiser

whatsoever /wɒtsəʊ'evə(r)/ *a* & *pron* = **whatever**

wheat /wiːt/ *n* trigo *m*

wheedle /'wiːdl/ *vt* convencer, persuadir, levar a

wheel /wiːl/ *n* roda *f* □ *vt* empurrar □ *vi* rodar, rolar. **at the ~** (*of vehicle*) ao volante; (*helm*) ao leme

wheelbarrow /'wiːlbærəʊ/ *n* carrinho *m* de mão

wheelchair /'wiːltʃeə(r)/ *n* cadeira *f* de rodas

wheeze /wiːz/ *vi* respirar ruidosamente □ *n* respiração *f* difícil

when /wen/ *adv, conj* & *pron* quando. **the day/moment ~** o dia/momento em que

whenever /wen'evə(r)/ *conj* & *adv* (*at whatever time*) quando quer que, quando; (*every time that*) (de) cada vez que, sempre que

where /weə(r)/ *adv, conj* & *pron* onde, aonde; (*in which place*) onde, em que; (*whereas*) enquanto que, ao passo que. **~ is he going?** aonde é que ele vai? **~abouts** *adv* onde □ *n* paradeiro *m*.

~**by** *adv* pelo que. ~**upon** *adv* após o que, depois do que

whereas /weər'æz/ *conj* enquanto que, ao passo que

wherever /weər'evə(r)/ *conj* & *adv* onde quer que. ~ **can it be?** onde pode estar?

whet /wet/ *vt* (*pt* **whetted**) (*appetite, desire*) aguçar, despertar

whether /'weðə(r)/ *conj* se. **not know** ~ não saber se. ~ **I go or not** caso eu vá ou não

which /wɪtʃ/ *interr a & pron* qual, que ~ **bag is yours?** qual das malas é a sua? ~ **is your coat?** qual é o seu casaco? **do you know** ~ **he's taken?** sabe qual/quais é que ele levou? □ *rel pron* que, o qual; (*referring to whole sentence*) o que; (*after prep*) que, o qual, cujo. **at** ~ em qual/que. **from** ~ do qual/que. **of** ~ do qual/de que. **to** ~ para o qual/o que

whichever /wɪtʃ'evə(r)/ *a* ~ **book/ etc** qualquer livro/*etc* que seja, seja que livro/*etc* for. **take** ~ **book you wish** leve o livro que quiser □ *pron* qualquer, quaisquer

whiff /wɪf/ *n* (*of fresh air*) sopro *m*, lufada *f*; (*smell*) baforada *f*

while /waɪl/ *n* (espaço de) tempo *m*, momento *m*. **once in a** ~ de vez em quando □ *conj* (*when*) enquanto; (*although*) embora; (*whereas*) enquanto que □ *vt* ~ **away** (*time*) passar

whim /wɪm/ *n* capricho *m*

whimper /'wɪmpə(r)/ *vi* gemer; (*baby*) choramingar □ *n* gemido *m*; (*baby*) choro *m*

whimsical /'wɪmzɪkl/ *a* (*person*) caprichoso; (*odd*) bizarro

whine /waɪn/ *vi* lamuriar-se, queixar-se; (*dog*) ganir □ *n* lamúria *f*, queixume *m*; (*dog*) ganido *m*

whip /wɪp/ *n* chicote *m* □ *vt* (*pt* **whipped**) chicotear; (*culin*) bater □ *vi* (*move*) ir a toda a pressa. ~-**round** *n* (*colloq*) coleta *f*, vaquinha *f*. ~ **up** excitar; (*cause*) provocar; (*colloq: meal*) preparar rapidamente. ~**ped cream** creme *m* chantilly

whirl /wɜːl/ *vt/i* (fazer) rodopiar, girar □ *n* rodopio *m*

whirlpool /'wɜːlpuːl/ *n* redemoinho *m*

whirlwind /'wɜːlwɪnd/ *n* redemoinho *m* de vento, turbilhão *m*

whirr /wɜː(r)/ *vi* zunir, zumbir

whisk /wɪsk/ *vt/i* (*snatch*) levar/tirar bruscamente; (*culin*) bater; (*flies*) sacudir □ *n* (*culin*) batedeira *f*. ~ **away** (*brush away*) sacudir

whisker /'wɪskə(r)/ *n* fio *m* de barba. ~**s** *npl* (*of animal*) bigode *m*; (*beard*) barba *f*; (*sideboards*) suiças *fpl*

whisky /'wɪskɪ/ *n* uísque *m*

whisper /'wɪspə(r)/ *vt/i* sussurrar, murmurar; (*of stream, leaves*) sussurrar □ *n* sussurro *m*, murmúrio *m*. **in a** ~ baixinho, em voz baixa

whist /wɪst/ *n* uíste *m*, (*P*) whist *m*

whistle /'wɪsl/ *n* assobio *m*; (*instrument*) apito *m* □ *vt/i* assobiar; (*with instrument*) apitar

Whit /wɪt/ *a* ~ **Sunday** domingo *m* de Pentecostes

white /waɪt/ *a* (*-er, -est*) branco, alvo; (*pale*) pálido □ *n* (*colour; of eyes; person*) branco *m*; (*of egg*) clara (do ovo) *f*. **go** ~ (*turn pale*) empalidecer; (*of hair*) branquear, embranquecer. ~ **coffee** café *m* com leite. ~-**collar worker** empregado *m* de escritório. ~ **elephant** (*fig*) trambolho *m*, elefante *m* branco. ~ **lie** mentirinha *f*. ~**ness** *n* brancura *f*, alvura *f*

whiten /'waɪtn/ *vt/i* branquear

whitewash /'waɪtwɒʃ/ *n* cal *f*; (*fig*) encobrimento *m* □ *vt* caiar; (*fig*) encobrir

Whitsun /'wɪtsn/ *n* Pentecostes *m*

whittle /'wɪtl/ *vt* ~ **down** aparar, cortar aparas; (*fig*) reduzir gradualmente

whiz /wɪz/ *vi* (*pt* **whizzed**) (*through air*) zunir, sibilar; (*rush*) passar a toda a velocidade. ~-**kid** *n* (*colloq*) prodígio *m*

who /huː/ *interr pron* quem □ *rel pron* que, o(a) qual, os(as) quais

whoever /huː'evə(r)/ *pron* (*no matter who*) quem quer que, seja quem for; (*the one who*) aquele que

whole /həʊl/ *a* inteiro, todo; (*not broken*) intacto. **the** ~ **house**/*etc* toda a casa/*etc* □ *n* totalidade *f*; (*unit*) todo *m*. **as a** ~ no conjunto, como um todo. **on the** ~ de um modo geral. ~-**hearted** *a* de todo o coração; (*person*) dedicado. ~-**heartedly** *adv* sem reservas, sinceramente

wholefood /'həʊlfuːd/ *n* comida *f* integral

wholemeal /'həʊlmiːl/ *a* ~ **bread** pão *m* integral

wholesale /'həʊlseɪl/ *n* venda *f* por grosso *or* por atacado □ *a* (*firm*) por grosso, por atacado; (*fig*) sistemático, em massa □ *adv* (*in large quantities*) por atacado; (*fig*) em massa, em grande escala. ~**r** /-ə(r)/ *n* grossista *mf*, atacadista *mf*

wholesome /'həʊlsəm/ *a* sadio, saudável

wholewheat /'həʊlwiːt/ *a* = **wholemeal**

wholly /'həʊlɪ/ *adv* inteiramente, completamente

whom /huːm/ *interr pron* quem □ *rel*

pron (*that*) que; (*after prep*) quem, que, o qual

whooping cough /'hu:pɪŋkɒf/ *n* coqueluche *f*

whore /hɔ:(r)/ *n* prostituta *f*

whose /hu:z/ *rel pron* & *a* cujo, de quem □ *interr pron* de quem. ∼ **hat is this?**. ∼ **is this hat?** de quem é este chapéu? ∼ **son are you?** de quem é que o senhor é filho?

why /waɪ/ *adv* porque, por que motivo, por que razão, porquê. **she doesn't know** ∼ **he's here** ela não sabe porque or por que motivo ele estáaqui. **she doesn't know** ∼ ela não sabe porquê. **do you know** ∼? você sabe porquê? □ *int* (*protest*) ora, ora essa; (*discovery*) oh. ∼ **yes/** *etc*

wick /wɪk/ *n* torcida *f*, mecha *f*, pavio *m*

wicked /'wɪkɪd/ *a* mau, malvado; (*mischievous, spiteful*) maldoso. ∼**ly** *adv* maldosamente. ∼**ness** *n* maldade *f*, malvadeza *f*

wicker /'wɪkə(r)/ *n* verga *f*, vime *m*. ∼**-work** *n* trabalho *m* de verga or de vime

wicket /'wɪkɪt/ *n* (*cricket*) arco *m*

wide /waɪd/ *a* (**-er, -est**) largo; (*extensive*) vasto, grande, extenso. **two metres** ∼ com dois metros de largura □ *adv* longe; (*fully*) completamente. **open** ∼ (*door, window*) abrir(-se) de par em par, escancarar(-se); (*mouth*) abrir bem. ∼ **awake** desperto, acordado. **far and** ∼ por toda a parte. ∼**ly** *adv* largamente; (*travel, spread*) muito; (*generally*) geralmente; (*extremely*) extremamente

widen /'waɪdn/ *vt/i* alargar(-se)

widespread /'waɪdspred/ *a* muito espalhado, difundido

widow /'wɪdəʊ/ *n* viúva *f*. ∼**ed** *a* (*man*) viúvo; (*woman*) viúva. **be** ∼**ed** enviuvar, ficar viúvo or viúva. ∼**er** *n* viúvo *m*. ∼**hood** *n* viuvez *f*

width /wɪdθ/ *n* largura *f*

wield /wi:ld/ *vt* (*axe etc*) manejar; (*fig: power*) exercer

wife /waɪf/ *n* (*pl* **wives**) mulher *f*, esposa *f*

wig /wɪg/ *n* cabeleira (postiça) *f*; (*judge's etc*) peruca *f*

wiggle /'wɪgl/ *vt/i* remexer(-se), retorcer(-se), mexer(-se) dum lado para outro

wild /waɪld/ *a* (**-er, -est**) selvagem; (*of plant*) silvestre; (*mad*) louco; (*enraged*) furioso, violento □ *adv* a esmo; (*without control*) à solta. ∼**s** *npl* regiões *fpl* selvagens. ∼**-goose chase** falsa pista *f*, tentativa *f* inútil. ∼**ly**

adv violentamente; (*madly*) loucamente

wildcat /'waɪldkæt/ *a* ∼ **strike** greve *f* ilegal

wilderness /'wɪldənɪs/ *n* deserto *m*

wildlife /'waɪldlaɪf/ *n* animais *mpl* selvagens

wile /waɪl/ *n* artimanha *f*; (*cunning*) astúcia *f*, manha *f*

wilful /'wɪlfl/ *a* (*person*) voluntarioso; (*act*) intencional, proposital

will[1] /wɪl/ *v aux* **you** ∼ **sing/he** ∼ **do/***etc* tu cantarás/ele fará/*etc*. (*1st person: future expressing will or intention*) **I** ∼ **sing/we** ∼ **do/***etc* eu cantarei/nós faremos/*etc*. ∼ **you have a cup of coffee?** quer tomar um cafézinho? ∼ **you shut the door?** quer fazer o favor de fechar a porta?

will[2] /wɪl/ *n* vontade *f*; (*document*) testamento *m*. **at** ∼ à vontade, quando or como se quiser □ *vt* (*wish*) querer; (*bequeath*) deixar em testamento. ∼**-power** *n* força *f* de vontade

willing /'wɪlɪŋ/ *a* pronto, de boa vontade. ∼ **to** disposto a. ∼**ly** *adv* (*with pleasure*) de boa vontade, de bom grado; (*not forced*) voluntariamente. ∼**ness** *n* boa vontade *f*, disposição *f* (**to do** em fazer)

willow /'wɪləʊ/ *n* salgueiro *m*

willy-nilly /wɪlɪ'nɪlɪ/ *adv* de bom ou de mau grado, quer queira ou não

wilt /wɪlt/ *vi* murchar, definhar

wily /'waɪlɪ/ *a* (**-ier, -iest**) manhoso, matreiro

win /wɪn/ *vt/i* (*pt* **won**, *pres p* **winning**) ganhar □ *n* vitória *f*. ∼ **over** *vt* convencer, conquistar

wince /wɪns/ *vi* estremecer, contrair-se. **without** ∼**ing** sem pestanejar

winch /wɪntʃ/ *n* guincho *m* □ *vt* içar com guincho

wind[1] /wɪnd/ *n* vento *m*; (*breath*) fôlego *m*; (*flatulence*) gases *mpl*. **get** ∼ **of** (*fig*) ouvir rumor de. **put the** ∼ **up** (*sl*) assustar. **in the** ∼ no ar. ∼ **instrument** (*mus*) instrumento *m* de sopro. ∼**-swept** *a* varrido pelo vento

wind[2] /waɪnd/ *vt/i* (*pt* **wound**) enrolar(-se); (*wrap*) envolver, pôr em volta; (*of path, river*) serpentear. ∼ (**up**) (*clock etc*) dar corda em. ∼ **up** (*end*) terminar, acabar; (*fig: speech etc*) concluir; (*firm*) liquidar. **he'll** ∼ **up in jail** (*colloq*) ele vai acabar na cadeia. ∼**ing** *a* (*path*) sinuoso; (*staircase*) em caracol

windfall /'wɪndfɔ:l/ *n* fruta *f* caída; (*fig: money*) sorte *f* grande

windmill /'wɪndmɪl/ *n* moinho *m* de vento

window /'wɪndəʊ/ *n* janela *f*; (*of shop*) vitrine *f*, (*P*) montra *f*; (*counter*) guiché *m*, (P) guichet *m*. ~-**box** *n* jardineira *f*, (P) floreira *f*. ~-**cleaner** *n* limpador *m* de janelas. ~-**dressing** *n* decoração *f* de vitrines; (*fig*) apresentação *f* cuidadosa. ~-**ledge** *n* peitoril *m*. ~-**pane** *n* vidro *m*, vidraça *f*. **go** ~-**shopping** ir ver vitrines. ~-**sill** *n* peitoril *m*

windpipe /'wɪndpaɪp/ *n* traqueia *f*, (P) traqueia *f*

windscreen /'wɪndskriːn/ *n* pára-brisa *m*, (P) pára-brisas *m invar*. ~-**wiper** *n* -waɪpə(r)/ *n* limpador *m* de pára-brisa

windshield /'wɪndʃiːld/ *n* (*Amer*) = **windscreen**

windsurfer /'wɪndsɜːfə(r)/ *n* surfista *mf*. ~**ing** *n* surfe *m*

windy /'wɪndɪ/ *a* (**-ier, -iest**) ventoso. **it is very** ~ está ventando muito

wine /waɪn/ *n* vinho *m*. ~-**bar** bar *m* para degustação de vinhos. ~-**cellar** *n* adega *f*, cave *f*. ~-**grower** *n* vinicultor *m*. ~-**growing** *n* vinicultura *f*. ~-**list** *n* lista *f* de vinhos. ~-**tasting** *n* prova *f* or degustação *f* de vinhos. ~-**waiter** garçon *m*

wineglass /'waɪnglɑːs/ *n* copo *m* de vinho; (*with stem*) cálice *m*

wing /wɪŋ/ *n* asa *f*; (*mil*) flanco *m*; (*archit*) ala *f*; (*auto*) pára-lamas *m invar*, (P) guarda-lamas *m invar*. ~**s** (*theat*) bastidores *mpl*. **under sb's** ~ debaixo das asas de alguém. ~**ed** *a* alado

wink /wɪŋk/ *vi* piscar o olho; (*light, star*) cintilar, piscar □ *n* piscadela *f*. **not sleep a** ~ não pregar olho

winner /'wɪnə(r)/ *n* vencedor *m*

winning /'wɪnɪŋ/ *see* **win** □ *a* vencedor, vitorioso; (*number*) premiado; (*smile*) encantador, atraente. ~-**post** *n* meta *f*, poste de chegada *f*. ~**s** *npl* ganhos *mpl*

wint|er /'wɪntə(r)/ *n* inverno *m* □ *vi* hibernar. ~**ry** *a* de inverno, invernoso; (*smile*) glacial

wipe /waɪp/ *vt* limpar; (*dry*) enxugar, limpar □ *n* limpadela *f*. ~ **off** limpar. ~ **out** (*destroy*) aniquilar, limpar (*colloq*); (*cancel*) cancelar. ~ **up** enxugar

wir|e /'waɪə(r)/ *n* arame *m*; (*electr: telegram*) telegrama *m*. (**electric**) ~**e** fio elétrico *m*, (P) eléctrico □ *vt* (*a house*) montar a instalação elétrica em; (*colloq: telegraph*) telegrafar. ~**e netting** rede *f* de arame. ~**ing** *n* (*electr*) instalação *f* elétrica, (P) eléctrica

wireless /'waɪəlɪs/ *n* rádio *f*, (*set*) rádio *m*

wiry /'waɪərɪ/ *a* (**-ier, -iest**) magro e rijo

wisdom /'wɪzdəm/ *n* sagacidade *f*, sabedoria *f*; (*common sense*) bom senso

m, sensatez *f*. ~ **tooth** dente *m* (do) siso

wise /waɪz/ *a* (**-er, -est**) (*person*) sábio, avisado, sensato; (*look*) entendedor. ~ **guy** (*colloq*) sabichão *m* (*colloq*), sabetudo *m* (*colloq*). **none the** ~**r** sem entender nada. ~**ly** *adv* sensatamente

wisecrack /'waɪzkræk/ *n* (*colloq*) (boa) piada *f*

wish /wɪʃ/ *n* (*desire, aspiration*) desejo *m*, vontade *f*; (*request*) pedido *m*; (*greeting*) desejo *m*, voto *m*. **I have no** ~ **to go** não tenho nenhum desejo *or* nenhuma vontade de ir □ *vt* (*desire, bid*) desejar; (*want*) apetecer, ter vontade de, desejar (**to do** fazer) □ *vi* ~ **for** desejar. ~ **sb well** desejar felicidades a alguém. **I don't** ~ **to go** não me apetece ir, não tenho vontade de ir, não desejo ir. **I** ~ **he'd leave** eu gostaria que ele partisse. **with best** ~**es** (*formal: in letter*) com os melhores cumprimentos, com saudações cordiais; (*on greeting card*) com desejos *or* votos (**for** de)

wishful /'wɪʃfl/ *a* ~ **thinking** sonhar acordado

wishy-washy /'wɪʃɪwɒʃɪ/ *a* sem expressão, fraco, inexpressivo

wisp /wɪsp/ *n* (*of hair*) pequena mecha *f*; (*of smoke*) fio *m*

wistful /'wɪstfl/ *a* melancólico, saudoso

wit /wɪt/ *n* inteligência *f*; (*humour*) presença *f* de espírito, humor *m*; (*person*) senso *m* de humor. **be at one's** ~**'s** *or* ~**s' end** não saber o que fazer. **keep one's** ~**s about one** estar alerta. **live by one's** ~**s** ganhar a vida de maneira suspeita. **scared out of one's** ~**s** apavorado

witch /wɪtʃ/ *n* feiticeira *f*, bruxa *f*. ~**craft** *n* feitiçaria *f*, bruxaria *f*, magia *f*

with /wɪð/ *prep* com; (*having*) de; (*because of*) de; (*at the house of*) em casa de. **the man** ~ **the beard** o homem de barbas. **fill/etc** ~ encher/etc de. **laughing/shaking/etc** ~ a rir/a tremer/etc de. **I'm not** ~ **you** (*colloq*) não estou compreendendo-o

withdraw /wɪð'drɔː/ *vt/i* (*pt* **withdrew**, *pp* **withdrawn**) retirar (-se); (*money*) tirar. ~**al** *n* retirada *f*; (*med*) estado *m* de privação. ~**n** *a* (*person*) retraído, fechado

wither /'wɪðə(r)/ *vt/i* murchar, secar. ~**ed** *a* (*person*) mirrado. ~**ing** *a* (*fig: scornful*) desdenhoso

withhold /wɪð'həʊld/ *vt* (*pt* **withheld**) negar, recusar; (*retain*) reter; (*conceal, not tell*) esconder (**from** de)

within /wɪ'ðɪn/ *prep* & *adv* dentro (de), por dentro de(m); (*in distances*) a menos de. **~ a month** (*before*) dentro de um mês. **~ sight** à vista

without /wɪ'ðaʊt/ *prep* sem. **~ fail** sem falta. **go ~ saying** não ser preciso dizer

withstand /wɪð'stænd/ *vt* (*pt* **withstood**) resistir a, opor-se a

witness /'wɪtnɪs/ *n* testemunha *f*; (*evidence*) testemunho *m* □ *vt* testemunhar, presenciar; (*document*) assinar como testemunha. **bear ~ to** testemunhar, dar testemunho de. **~box** *n* banco *m* das testemunhas

witticism /'wɪtɪsɪzəm/ *n* dito *m* espirituoso

witty /'wɪtɪ/ *a* (**-ier, -iest**) espirituoso

wives /waɪvz/ *see* **wife**

wizard /'wɪzəd/ *n* feiticeiro *m*; (*fig: genius*) gênio *m*, (*P*) génio *m*

wizened /'wɪznd/ *a* encarquilhado

wobbl|e /'wɒbl/ *vi* (*of jelly, voice, hand*) tremer; (*stagger*) cambalear, vacilar; (*of table, chair*) balançar. **~y** *a* (*trembling*) trêmulo; (*staggering*) cambaleante, vacilante; (*table, chair*) pouco firme

woe /wəʊ/ *n* dor *f*, infortúnio *m*

woke, woken /wəʊk, 'wəʊkən/ *see* **wake**[1]

wolf /wʊlf/ *n* (*pl* **wolves** /wʊlvz/) lobo *m* □ *vt* (*food*) devorar. **cry ~** dar alarme falso. **~-whistle** *n* assobio *m* de admiração

woman /'wʊmən/ *n* (*pl* **women**) mulher *f*. **~hood** *n* as mulheres, o sexo feminino; (*maturity*) maturidade *f*. **~ly** *a* feminino

womb /wuːm/ *n* seio *m*, ventre *m*; (*med*) útero *m*; (*fig*) seio *m*

women /'wɪmɪn/ *see* **woman**. **~'s movement** movimento *m* feminista

won /wʌn/ *see* **win**

wonder /'wʌndə(r)/ *n* admiração *f*; (*thing*) maravilha *f* □ *vt* perguntar-se a si mesmo (**if** se) □ *vi* admirar-se (**at** de, com), ficar admirado, espantar-se (**at** com); (*reflect*) pensar (**about** em). **it is no ~** não admira (**that** que)

wonderful /'wʌndəfl/ *a* maravilhoso. **~ly** *adv* maravilhosamente. **it works ~ly** funciona às mil maravilhas

won't /wəʊnt/ = **will not**

wood /wʊd/ *n* madeira *f*, pau *m*; (*for burning*) lenha *f*. **~(s)** *n* (*pl*) (*area*) bosque *m*, mata *f*, floresta *f*. **~ed** *a* arborizado. **~en** *a* de ou em madeira, de pau; (*fig: stiff*) rígido; (*fig: inexpressive*) inexpressivo, de pau

woodcut /'wʊdkʌt/ *n* gravura *f* em madeira

woodland /'wʊdlənd/ *n* região *f* arborizada, bosque *m*, mata *f*

woodlouse /'wʊdlaʊs/ *n* (*pl* **-lice** /laɪs/) baratinha *f*, tatuzinho *m*

woodpecker /'wʊdpekə(r)/ *n* (*bird*) pica-pau *m*

woodwind /'wʊdwɪnd/ *n* (*mus*) instrumentos *mpl* de sopro de madeira

woodwork /'wʊdwɜːk/ *n* (*of building*) madeiramento *m*; (*carpentry*) carpintaria *f*

woodworm /'wʊdwɜːm/ *n* caruncho *m*

woody /'wʊdɪ/ *a* (*wooded*) arborizado; (*like wood*) lenhoso

wool /wʊl/ *n* lã *f*. **~len** *a* de lã. **~lens** *npl* roupas *fpl* de lã. **~ly** *a* de lã; (*vague*) confuso □ *n* (*colloq: garment*) roupa *f* de lã

word /wɜːd/ *n* palavra *f*; (*news*) notícia(s) *f*(*pl*); (*promise*) palavra *f* □ *vt* exprimir, formular. **by ~ of mouth** de viva voz. **have a ~ with** dizer duas palavras a. **in other ~s** em outras palavras. **~-perfect** *a* que sabe de cor seu papel, a lição etc. **~ processor** processador *m* de textos. **~ing** *n* termos *mpl*, redação *f*, (*P*) redacção *f*. **~y** *a* prolixo

wore /wɔː(r)/ *see* **wear**

work /wɜːk/ *n* trabalho *m*; (*product, book etc*) obra *f*; (*building etc*) obras *fpl*. **at ~** no trabalho. **out of ~** desempregado. **~s** *npl* (*techn*) mecanismo *m*; (*factory*) fábrica *f* □ *vt/i* (*of person*) trabalhar; (*techn*) fazer funcionar, (fazer) andar; (*of drug etc*) agir, fazer efeito; (*farm, mine*) explorar; (*land*) lavrar. **~ sb** (*make work*) fazer alguém trabalhar. **~ in** introduzir, inserir. **~ loose** soltar-se. **~ off** (*get rid of*) descarregar. **~ out** *vt* (*solve*) resolver; (*calculate*) calcular; (*devise*) planejar □ *vi* (*succeed*) resultar; (*sport*) treinar-se. **~-station** *n* estação *f* de trabalho. **~-to-rule** *n* greve *f* de zelo. **~ up** *vt* criar □ *vi* (*to climax*) ir num crescendo. **~ed up** (*person*) enervado, transtornado, agitado

workable /'wɜːkəbl/ *a* viável, praticável

workaholic /wɜːkə'hɒlɪk/ *n* **be a ~** (*colloq*) trabalhar como um possesso (*colloq*)

worker /'wɜːkə(r)/ *n* trabalhador *m*, trabalhadora *f*; (*factory*) operário *m*

working /'wɜːkɪŋ/ *a* (*day, clothes, hypothesis, lunch etc*) de trabalho. **the ~ class(es)** a classe operária, a(s) classe(s) trabalhadora(s), o proletariado. **~-class** *a* operário, trabalhador. **~ mother** mãe *f* que trabalha. **~ party** comissão *f* consultiva, de estudo *etc*. **~s** *npl* mecanismo *m*. **in ~ order** em condições de funcionamento

workman /'wɜːkmən/ *n* (*pl* **-men**)

trabalhador *m*; (*factory*) operário *m*.
~ship *n* trabalho *m*, execução *f*, mão-de-obra *f*; (*skill*) arte *f*, habilidade *f*
workshop /'wɜːkʃɒp/ *n* oficina *f*
world /wɜːld/ *n* mundo *m* □ *a* mundial. **a ~ of** muito(s), grande quantidade de, um mundo de. **~-wide** *a* mundial, universal
worldly /'wɜːldlɪ/ *a* terreno; (*devoted to the affairs of life*) mundano. ~-**goods** bens *mpl* materiais. **~-wise** *a* com experiência do mundo
worm /wɜːm/ *n* verme *m*; (*earthworm*) minhoca *f* □ *vt* **~ one's way into** insinuar-se, introduzir-se, enfiar-se. **~-eaten** *a* (*wood*) carunchoso; (*fruit*) bichado, bichoso
worn /wɔːn/ *see* **wear** □ *a* usado. **~-out** *a* (*thing*) completamente gasto; (*person*) esgotado
worr|**y** /'wʌrɪ/ *vt/i* preocupar(-se) □ *n* preocupação *f*. **don't ~y** fique descansado, não se preocupe. **~ied** *a* preocupado. **~ying** *a* preocupante, inquietante
worse /wɜːs/ *a & adv* pior □ *n* pior *m*. **get ~** piorar. **from bad to ~** de mal a pior. **~ luck** pouca sorte, pena
worsen /'wɜːsn/ *vt/i* piorar
worship /'wɜːʃɪp/ *n* (*reverence*) reverência *f*, veneração *f*; (*religious*) culto *m* □ *vt* (*pt* **worshipped**) adorar, venerar □ *vi* fazer as suas devoções, praticar o culto. **~per** *n* (*in church*) fiel *m*. **Your/His W~** Vossa/Sua Excelência *f*
worst /wɜːst/ *a & n* pior □ *n* (*o/a*) pior (*mf*) □ *adv* pior. **if the ~ comes to the ~** se o pior acontecer, na pior das hipóteses. **do one's ~** fazer todo o mal que se quiser. **get the ~ of it** ficar a perder. **the ~** (*thing*) **that** o pior que
worth /wɜːθ/ *a* **be ~** valer; (*deserving*) merecer □ *n* valor *m*, mérito *m*. **ten pounds ~ of** dez libras de. **it's ~ it**, **it's ~ while** vale a pena. **it's not ~ my while** não vale a pena. **it's ~ waiting**/*etc* vale a pena esperar/*etc*. **for all one's ~** (*colloq*) dando todo por tudo. **~less** *a* sem valor
worthwhile /'wɜːθwaɪl/ *a* que vale a pena; (*cause*) louvável, meritório
worthy /'wɜːðɪ/ *a* (**-ier**, **-iest**) (*deserving*) digno, merecedor (**of** de); (*laudable*) meritório, louvável □ *n* (*person*) pessoa *f* ilustre
would /wʊd/; *unstressed* /wəd/ *v aux* **he ~ do/you ~ sing**/*etc* (*conditional tense*) ele faria/você cantaria/*etc*. **he ~ have done** ele teria feito. **she ~ come every day** (*used to*) ela vinha/ou costumava vir aqui todos os dias. **~ you please come here?** chegue aqui

por favor. **~ you like some tea?** você quer um chazinho? **he ~n't go** (*refused to*) ele não queria ir. **~-be author/doctor**/*etc* aspirante *a* autor/médico/*etc*
wound[1] /wuːnd/ *n* ferida *f* □ *vt* ferir. **the ~ed** os feridos *mpl*
wound[2] /waʊnd/ *see* **wind**[2]
wove, **woven** /wəʊv, 'wəʊvn/ *see* **weave**
wrangle /'ræŋgl/ *vi* disputar, discutir, brigar □ *n* disputa *f*, discussão *f*, briga *f*
wrap /ræp/ *vt* (*pt* **wrapped**) ~ (**up**) embrulhar (**in** em); (*in cotton wool*, *mystery etc*) envolver (**in** em) □ *vi* ~ **up** (*dress warmly*) abrigar-se bem, agasalhar-se bem □ *n* xale *m*. **~ped up in** (*engrossed*) absorto em, mergulhado em. **~per** *n* (*of sweet*) papel *m*; (*of book*) capa *f* de papel. **~ing** *n* embalagem *f*
wrath /rɒθ/ *n* ira *f*. **~ful** *a* irado
wreak /riːk/ *vt* ~ **havoc** (*of storm etc*) fazer estragos
wreath /riːθ/ *n* (*pl* -**s** /-ðz/) (*of flowers*, *leaves*) coroa *f*, grinalda *f*
wreck /rek/ *n* (*sinking*) naufrágio *m*; (*ship*) navio *m* naufragado; restos *mpl* de navio; (*remains*) destroços *mpl*; (*vehicle*) veículo *m* destroçado □ *vt* destruir; (*ship*) fazer naufragar, afundar; (*fig*: *hope*) acabar. **be a nervous ~** estar com os nervos arrasados. **~age** *n* (*pieces*) destroços *mpl*
wren /ren/ *n* (*bird*) carriça *f*
wrench /rentʃ/ *vt* (*pull*) puxar; (*twist*) torcer; (*snatch*) arrancar (**from** a) □ *n* (*pull*) puxão *m*; (*of ankle*, *wrist*) torcedura *f*; (*tool*) chave *f* inglesa; (*fig*) dor *f* de separação
wrest /rest/ *vt* arrancar (**from** a)
wrestl|**e** /'resl/ *vi* lutar, debater-se (**with** com *or* contra). **~er** *n* lutador *m*. **~ing** *n* luta *f*
wretch /retʃ/ *n* desgraçado *m*, miserável *mf*; (*rascal*) miserável *mf*
wretched /'retʃɪd/ *a* (*pitiful*, *poor*) miserável; (*bad*) horrível, desgraçado
wriggle /'rɪgl/ *vt/i* remexer(-se), contorcer-se
wring /rɪŋ/ *vt* (*pt* **wrung**) (*twist*; *clothes*) torcer. **~ out of** (*obtain from*) arrancar a. **~ing wet** encharcado; (*of person*) encharcado até os ossos
wrinkle /'rɪŋkl/ *n* (*on skin*) ruga *f*; (*crease*) prega *f* □ *vt/i* enrugar(-se)
wrist /rɪst/ *n* pulso *m*. **~-watch** *n* relógio *m* de pulso
writ /rɪt/ *n* (*jur*) mandado *m* judicial
write /raɪt/ *vt/i* (*pt* **wrote**, *pp* **written**) escrever. **~ back** responder. **~ down** escrever, tomar nota de. **~ off** (*debt*) dar por liquidado; (*vehicle*) des-

tinar à sucata. ~**-off** n perda f total.
~ **out** (in full) escrever por extenso.
~ **up** (from notes) redigir. ~**-up** n
relato m; (review) crítica f
writer /'raɪtə(r)/ n escritor m, autor
m
writhe /raɪð/ vi contorcer(-se)
writing /'raɪtɪŋ/ n escrita f. ~**(s)**
(works) escritos mpl, obras fpl. **in** ~
por escrito. ~**-paper** n papel m de
carta
written /'rɪtn/ see **write**
wrong /rɒŋ/ a (incorrect, mistaken)
mal, errado; (unfair) injusto; (wicked)
mau; (amiss) que não está bem; (mus:
note) falso; (clock) que não está certo
□ adv mal □ n mal m; (injustice)
injustiça f □ vt (be unfair to) ser injusto com; (do a wrong to) fazer mal a.
what's ~? qual é o problema? **what's**
~ **with it?** (amiss) o que é que não
vai bem?; (morally) que mal há nisso?, que mal tem? **he's in the** ~ (his
fault) ele não tem razão. **go** ~ (err)
desencaminhar-se; (fail) ir mal;
(vehicle) quebrar. ~**ly** adv mal;
(blame etc) sem razão, injustamente
wrongful /'rɒŋfl/ a injusto, ilegal
wrote /rəʊt/ see **write**
wrought /rɔːt/ a ~ **iron** ferro m
forjado. ~**-up** a excitado
wrung /rʌŋ/ see **wring**
wry /raɪ/ a (**wryer wryest**) torto;
(smile) forçado. ~ **face** careta f

X

Xerox /'zɪərɒks/ n fotocópia f, xerox
m □ vt fotocopiar, xerocar, tirar um
xerox de
Xmas /'krɪsməs/ n Christmas
X-ray /'eksreɪ/ n raio X m; (photograph) radiografia f □ vt radiografar.
have an ~ tirar uma radiografia
xylophone /'zaɪləfəʊn/ n xilofone m

Y

yacht /jɒt/ n iate m. ~**ing** n iatismo
m, andar m de iate; (racing) regata f
de iate
yank /jæŋk/ vt (colloq) puxar bruscamente □ n (colloq) puxão m
Yank /jæŋk/ n (collog) ianque mf
yap /jæp/ vi (pt **yapped**) latir
yard¹ /jɑːd/ n (measure) jarda f (=
0,9144 m). ~**age** n medida f em jardas
yard² /jɑːd/ n (of house) pátio m;
(Amer: garden) jardim m; (for storage) depósito m
yardstick /'jɑːdstɪk/ n jarda f; (fig)
bitola f, craveira f

yarn /jɑːn/ n (thread) fio m; (colloq:
tale) longa história f
yawn /jɔːn/ vi bocejar; (be wide open)
abrir-se, escancarar-se □ n bocejo m.
~**ing** a escancarado
year /jɪə(r)/ n ano m. **school/tax** ~
ano m escolar/fiscal. **be ten/** etc ~**s**
old ter dez/etc anos de idade. ~**book**
n anuário m. ~**ly** a anual □ adv
anualmente
yearn /jɜːn/ vi ~ **for, to** desejar, ansiar por, suspirar por. ~**ing** n desejo
m, anseio m (**for** de)
yeast /jiːst/ n levedura f
yell /jel/ vt/i gritar, berrar □ n grito
m, berro m
yellow /'jeləʊ/ a amarelo; (colloq: cowardly) covarde, poltrão □ n amarelo m
yelp /jelp/ n (of dog etc) ganido m □ vi
ganir
yen /jen/ n (colloq: yearning) grande
vontade f (**for** de)
yes /jes/ adv & n sim (m). ~**-man** n
(colloq) lambe-botas m invar, puxa-
saco m
yesterday /'jestədɪ/ n & adv ontem
(m). ~ **morning/afternoon/even-
ing** ontem de manhã/à tarde/à
noite. **the day before** ~ anteontem.
~ **week** há oito dias, há uma semana
yet /jet/ adv ainda; (already) já □ conj
contudo, no entanto. **as** ~ até agora,
por enquanto. **his best book** ~ o seu
melhor livro até agora
yew /juː/ n teixo m
Yiddish /'jɪdɪʃ/ n idiche m
yield /jiːld/ vt (produce) produzir, dar;
(profit) render; (surrender) entregar □
vi (give way) ceder □ n produção f;
(comm) rendimento m
yoga /'jəʊgə/ n ioga f
yoghurt /'jɒgət/ n iogurte m
yoke /jəʊk/ n jugo m, canga f; (of garment) pala f □ vt jungir; (unite) unir,
ligar
yokel /'jəʊkl/ n caipira m, labrego m
yolk /jəʊk/ n gema (de ovo) f
yonder /'jɒndə(r)/ adv acolá, além
you /juː/ pron (familiar) tu, você (pl
vocês); (polite) vós, o(s) senhor(es),
a(s) senhora(s); (object: familiar) te,
lhe (pl vocês); (polite) o(s), a(s), lhes,
vós, o(s) senhor(es), a(s) senhora(s);
(after prep) ti, si, você (pl vocês); (polite) vós, o senhor, a senhora (pl os
senhores, as senhoras); (indefinite)
se; (after prep) si, você. **with** ~ (familiar) contigo, consigo, com você (pl
com vocês); (polite) com o senhor/a
senhora (pl convosco, com os senho-
res/as senhoras). **I know** ~ (familiar) eu te conheço, eu o/a
conheço (pl eu os/as conheço); (polite) eu vos conheço, conheço o

senhor/a senhora (*pl* conheço os senhores/as senhoras). ~ **can see the sea** você pode ver o mar

young /jʌŋ/ *a* (**-er**, **-est**) jovem, novo, moço □ *n* (*people*) jovens *mpl*, a juventude *f*, a mocidade *f*; (*of animals*) crias *fpl*, filhotes *mpl*

youngster /'jʌŋstə(r)/ *n* jovem *mf*, moço *m*, rapaz *m*

your /jɔː(r)/ *a* (*familiar*) teu, tua, seu, sua (*pl* teus, tuas, seus, suas); (*polite*) vosso, vossa, do senhor, da senhora (*pl* vossos, vossas, dos senhores, das senhoras)

yours /jɔːz/ *poss pron* (*familiar*) o teu, a tua, o seu, a sua (*pl* os teus, as tuas, os seus, as suas); (*polite*) o vosso, a vossa, o/a do senhor, o/a da senhora (*pl* os vossos, as vossas; os/as do(s) senhor(es), os/as da(s) senhora(s)). **a book of** ~ um livro seu. ~ **sincerely/faithfully** atenciosamente, com os cumprimentos de

yourself /jɔː'self/ (*pl* **-selves** /-'selvz/) *pron* (*familiar*) tu mesmo/a, você mesmo/a (*pl* vocês mesmos/as); (*polite*) vós mesmo/a, o senhor mesmo, a senhora mesma (*pl* vós mesmos/as, os senhores mesmos, as senhoras mesmas); (*reflexive: familiar*) te, a ti mesmo/a, se, a si mesmo/a (*pl* a vocês mesmos/as); (*polite*) ao senhor mesmo, à senhora mesma (*pl* aos senhores mesmos, às senhoras mesmas); (*after prep: familiar*) ti mesmo/a, si mesmo/a, você mesmo/a (*pl* vocês mesmos/as); (*after prep: polite*) vós mesmo/a, o senhor mesmo, a senhora mesma (*pl* vós mesmos/as, os senhores mesmos, as senhoras mesmas). **with** ~ (*familiar*) contigo mesmo/a, consigo mesmo/a, com você (*pl* com vocês); (*polite*) convosco, com o senhor, com a senhora (*pl* com os senhores, com as senhoras). **by** ~ sozinho

youth /juːθ/ *n* (*pl* **-s** /-ðz/) mocidade *f*, juventude *f*; (*young man*) jovem *m*, moço *m*. ~ **club** centro *m* de jovens.

~ **hostel** albergue *m* da juventude.
~**ful** *a* juvenil, jovem

yo-yo /'jəʊjəʊ/ *n* (*pl* **-os**) ioiô *m*

Yugoslav /'juːɡəslɑːv/ *a & n* iogoslavo (*m*), (*P*) jugoslavo (*m*). ~**ia** /-'slɑːvɪə/ *n* Iogoslávia *f*, (*P*) Jugoslávia *f*

Z

zany /'zeɪnɪ/ *a* (**-ier**, **-iest**) tolo, bobo

zeal /ziːl/ *n* zelo *m*

zealous /'zeləs/ *a* zeloso. ~**ly** *adv* zelosamente

zebra /'zebrə, 'ziːbrə/ *n* zebra *f*. ~ **crossing** faixa *f* para pedestres, (*P*) passagem *f* para peões

zenith /'zenɪθ/ *n* zênite *m*, (*P*) zénite *m*, auge *m*

zero /'zɪərəʊ/ *n* (*pl* **-os**) zero *m*. ~ **hour** a hora H. **below** ~ abaixo de zero

zest /zest/ *n* (*gusto*) entusiasmo *m*; (*fig: spice*) sabor *m* especial; (*lemon or orange peel*) casca *f* de limão/laranja ralada

zigzag /'zɪɡzæɡ/ *n* ziguezague *m* □ *a & adv* em ziguezague □ *vi* (*pt* **zig-zagged**) ziguezaguear

zinc /zɪŋk/ *n* zinco *m*

zip /zɪp/ *n* (*vigour*) energia *f*, alma *f*. ~(**-fastener**) fecho *m* ecler □ *vt* (*pt* **zipped**) fechar o fecho eclerde □ *vi* ir a toda a velocidade. **Z**~ **code** (*Amer*) CEP de endereçamento postal *m*, (*P*) código *m* postal

zipper /'zɪpə(r)/ *n* = **zip(-fastener)**

zodiac /'zəʊdɪæk/ *n* zodiaco *m*

zombie /'zɒmbɪ/ *n* zumbi *m*; (*colloq*) zumbi *m*, (*P*) autómato *m*

zone /zəʊn/ *n* zona *f*

zoo /zuː/ *n* jardim *m* zoológico

zoolog|y /zəʊ'ɒlədʒɪ/ *n* zoologia *f*. ~**ical** /-ə'lɒdʒɪkl/ *a* zoológico. ~**ist** *n* zoólogo *m*

zoom /zuːm/ *vi* (*rush*) sair roando □ ~ **lens** zum *m*, zoom *m*. ~ **off** *or* **past** passar zunindo

zucchini /zuː'kiːnɪ/ *n* (*pl invar*) (*Amer*) courgette *f*

Portuguese Verbs · Verbos portugueses

Introduction
Portuguese verbs can be divided into three categories: regular verbs, those with spelling peculiarities determined by their sound and irregular verbs.

Regular verbs
in -ar (*e.g.* comprar)
Present: compr|o, ~as, ~a, ~amos, ~ais, ~am
Future: comprar|ei, ~ás, ~á, ~emos, ~eis, ~ão
Imperfect: compr|ava, ~avas, ~ava, ~ávamos, ~áveis, ~avam
Preterite: compr|ei, ~aste, ~ou, ~amos (P:~ámos), ~astes, ~aram
Pluperfect: compr|ara, ~aras, ~ara, ~áramos, ~áreis, ~aram
Present subjunctive: compr|e, ~es, ~e, ~emos, ~eis, ~em
Imperfect subjunctive: compr|asse, ~asses, ~asse, ~ássemos, ~ásseis, ~assem
Future subjunctive: compr|ar, ~ares, ~ar, ~armos, ~ardes, ~arem
Conditional: comprar|ia, ~ias, ~ia, ~íamos, ~íeis, ~iam
Personal infinitive: comprar, ~es, ~, ~mos, ~des, ~em
Present participle: comprando
Past participle: comprado
Imperative: compra, comprai

in ~er (*e.g.* bater)
Present: bat|o, ~es, ~e, ~emos, ~eis, ~em
Future: bater|ei, ~ás, ~á, ~emos, ~eis, ~ão
Imperfect: bat|ia, ~ias, ~ia, ~íamos, ~íeis, ~iam
Preterite: bat|i, ~este, ~eu, ~emos, ~estes, ~eram
Pluperfect: bat|era, ~eras, ~era, ~êramos, ~êreis, ~eram
Present subjunctive: bat|a, ~as, ~a, ~amos ais, ~am
Imperfect subjunctive: bat|esse, ~esses, ~esse, ~êssemos, ~êsseis, ~essem
Future subjunctive: bat|er, ~eres, ~er, ~ermos, ~erdes, ~erem
Conditional: bater|ia, ~ias, ~ia, ~íamos, ~íeis, ~iam
Personal infinitive: bater, ~es, ~, ~mos, ~des, ~em
Present participle: batendo
Past participle: batido
Imperative: bate, batei

in ~ir (*e.g.* admitir)
Present: admit|o, ~es, ~e, ~imos, ~is, ~em

Future: admitir|ei, ~ás, ~á, ~emos, ~eis, ~ão
Imperfect: admit|ia, ~ias, ~ia, ~íamos, ~íeis, ~iam
Preterite: admit|i, ~iste, ~iu, ~imos, ~istes, ~iram
Pluperfect: admit|ira, ~iras, ~ira, ~iramos, ~íreis, ~iram
Present subjunctive: admit|a, ~as, ~a, ~amos, ~ais, ~am
Imperfect subjunctive: admit|isse, ~isses, ~isse, ~íssemos, ~ísseis, ~issem
Future subjunctive: admit|ir, ~ires, ~ir, ~irmos, ~irdes, ~irem
Conditional: admitir|ia, ~ias, ~ia, ~íamos, ~íeis, ~iam
Personal infinitive: admitir, ~es, ~, ~mos, ~des, ~em
Present participle: admitindo
Past participle: admitido
Imperative: admite, admiti

Regular verbs with spelling changes:

-ar verbs:
in -car (*e.g.* ficar)
Preterite: fiquei, ficaste, ficou, ficamos (P: ficámos), ficais, ficam
Present subjunctive: fique, fiques, fique, fiquemos, fiqueis, fiquem

in -çar (*e.g.* abraçar)
Preterite: abracei, abraçaste, abraçou, abraçamos (P: abraçámos), abraçastes, abraçaram
Present subjunctive: abrace, abraces, abrace, abracemos, abraceis, abracem

in -ear (*e.g.* passear)
Present: passeio, passeias, passeia, passeamos, passeais, passeiam
Present subjunctive: passeie, passeies, passeie, passeemos, passeeis, passeiem
Imperative: passeia, passeai

in -gar (*e.g.* apagar)
Preterite: apaguei, apagaste, apagou, apagamos (P: apagámos), apagastes, apagaram
Present subjunctive: apague, apagues, apague, apaguemos, apagueis, apaguem

in -oar (*e.g.* voar)
Present: vôo (P: voo), voas, voa, voamos, voais, voam

averiguar
Preterite: averigüei (*P*: averiguei), averiguaste, averiguou, averiguamos (*P*: averiguámos), averiguastes, averiguaram
Present subjunctive: averigúe, averigúes, averigúe, averiguemos (*P*: averigúemos), averigueis (*P*: averigúeis), averigúem

enxaguar
Present: enxáguo, enxáguas, enxágua, enxaguamos, enxaguais, enxáguam
Preterite: enxagüei (*P*: enxaguei), enxaguaste, enxaguou, enxaguamos (*P*: enxaguámos), enxaguastes, enxaguaram
Present subjunctive: enxagúe, enxágües, enxágüe, enxagüemos, enxágüeis, enxágüem (*P*: enxágue, enxágues, enxágue, enxaguemos, enxagueis, enxáguem)
Similarly: aguar, desaguar

saudar
Present: saúdo, saúdas, saúda, saudamos, saudais, saúdam
Present subjunctive: saúde, saúdes, saúde, saudemos, saudeis, saúdem
Imperative: saúda, saudai

-er verbs:
in -cer (*e.g.* tecer)
Present: teço, teces, tece, tecemos, teceis, tecem
Present subjunctive: teça, teças, teça, teçamos, teçais, teçam

in -ger (*e.g.* proteger)
Present: protejo, proteges, protege, protegemos, protegeis, protegem
Present subjunctive: proteja, protejas, proteja, protejamos, protejais, protejam

in -guer (*e.g.* erguer)
Present: ergo, ergues, ergue, erguemos, ergueis, erguem
Present subjunctive: erga, ergas, erga, ergamos, ergais, ergam

in -oer (*e.g.* roer)
Present: rôo (*P*: roo), róis, rói, roemos, roeis, roem
Imperfect: roia, roías, roía, roíamos, roieis, roíam
Preterite: roi, roeste, roeu, roemos, roestes, roeram
Past participle: roído
Imperative: rói, roei

-ir verbs:
in -ir with -e- in stem (*e.g.* vestir)
Present: visto, vestes, veste, vestimos, vestis, vestem

Present subjunctive: vista, vistas, vista, vistamos, vistais, vistam
Similarly: mentir, preferir, refletir, repetir, seguir, sentir, servir

in -ir with -o- in stem (*e.g.* dormir)
Present: durmo, dormes, dorme, dormimos, dormis, dormem
Present subjunctive: durma, durmas, durma, durmamos, durmais, durmam
Similarly: cobrir, descobrir, tossir

in -ir with -u- in the stem (*e.g.* subir)
Present: subo, sobes, sobe, subimos, subis, sobem
Similarly: consumir, cuspir, fugir, sacudir, sumir

in -air (*e.g.* sair)
Present: saio, sais, sai, saímos, saís, saem
Imperfect: saía, saías, saía, saíamos, saieis, saíam
Preterite: sai, saíste, saiu, saímos, saístes, sairam
Pluperfect: saira, sairas, saira, sairamos, saireis, sairam
Present subjunctive: saia, saias, saia, saiamos, saiais, saiam
Imperfect subjunctive: saísse, saísses, saísse, saíssemos, saísseis, saíssem
Future subjunctive: sair, saires, sair, sairmos, sairdes, sairem
Personal infinitive: sair, saires, sair, sairmos, sairdes, sairem
Present participle: saindo
Past participle: saido
Imperative: sai, sai

in -gir (*e.g.* dirigir)
Present: dirijo, diriges, dirige, dirigimos, dirigis, dirigem
Present subjunctive: dirija, dirijas, dirija, dirijamos, dirijais, dirijam

in -guir (*e.g.* distinguir)
Present: distingo, distingues, distingue, distinguimos, distinguis, distinguem
Present subjunctive: distinga, distingas, distinga, distingamos, distingais, distingam

in -uir (*e.g.* atribuir)
Present: atribuo, atribuis, atribui, atribuimos, atribuis, atribuem
Imperfect: atribuía, atribuías, atribuía, atribuíamos, atribuíeis, atribuíam
Preterite: atribui, atribuiste, atribuiu, atribuimos, atribuístes, atribuiram
Pluperfect: atribuira, atribuiras, atribuira, atribuíramos, atribuíreis, atribuiram

Present subjunctive: atribua, atribuas, atribua, atribuamos, atribuais, atribuam

Imperfect subjunctive: atribuísse, atribuísses, atribuísse, atribuíssemos, atribuísseis, atribuíssem

Future subjunctive: atribuir, atribuíres, atribuir, atribuirmos, atribuirdes, atribuírem

Personal infinitive: atribuir, atribuíres, atribuir, atribuirmos, atribuirdes, atribuírem

Present participle: atribuindo

Past participle: atribuído

Imperative: atribui, atribuí

proibir

Present: proíbo, proíbes, proíbe, proíbimos, proíbis, proíbem

Present subjunctive: proíba, proíbas, proíba, proibamos, proibais, proíbam

Imperative: proíbe, proibi

Similarly: coibir

reunir

Present: reúno, reúnes, reúne, reunimos, reunis, reúnem

Present subjunctive: reúna, reúnas, reúna, reunamos, reunais, reúnam

Imperative: reúne, reuni

in -struir (*e.g.* construir) - like atribuir except:

Present: construo, constrói/construis, constrói/construi, construímos, construis, constroem/construem

Imperative: constrói/construi, construi

in -duzir (*e.g.* produzir)

Present: produzo, produzes, produz, produzimos, produzis, produzem

Imperative: produz(e), produzi

Similarly: luzir, reluzir

Irregular verbs

caber

Present: caibo, cabes, cabe, cabemos, cabeis, cabem

Preterite: coube, coubeste, coube, coubemos, coubestes, couberam

Pluperfect: coubera, couberas, coubera, coubéramos, coubéreis, couberam

Present subjunctive: caiba, caibas, caiba, caibamos, caibais, caibam

Imperfect subjunctive: coubesse, coubesses, coubesse, coubéssemos, coubésseis, coubessem

Future subjunctive: couber, couberes, couber, coubermos, couberdes, couberem

dar

Present: dou, dás, dá, damos, dais, dão

Preterite: dei, deste, deu, demos, destes, deram

Pluperfect: dera, deras, dera, déramos, déreis, deram

Present subjunctive: dê, dês, dê, demos, deis, dêem

Imperfect subjunctive: desse, desses, desse, déssemos, désseis, dessem

Future subjunctive: der, deres, der, dermos, derdes, derem

Imperative: dá, dai

dizer

Present: digo, dizes, diz, dizemos, dizeis, dizem

Future: direi, dirás, dirá, diremos, direis, dirão

Preterite: disse, disseste, disse, dissemos, dissestes, disseram

Pluperfect: dissera, disseras, dissera, disséramos, disséreis, disseram

Present subjunctive: diga, digas, diga, digamos, digais, digam

Imperfect subjunctive: dissesse, dissesses, dissesse, disséssemos, dissésseis, dissessem

Future subjunctive: disser, disseres, disser, dissermos, disserdes, disserem

Conditional: diria, dirias, diria, diríamos, diríeis, diriam

Present participle: dizendo

Past participle: dito

Imperative: diz, dizei

estar

Present: estou, estás, está, estamos, estais, estão

Preterite: estive, estiveste, esteve, estivemos, estivestes, estiveram

Pluperfect: estivera, estiveras, estivera, estivéramos, estivéreis, estiveram

Present subjunctive: esteja, estejas, esteja, estejamos, estejais, estejam

Imperfect subjunctive: estivesse, estivesses, estivesse, estivéssemos, estivésseis, estivessem

Future subjunctive: estiver, estiveres, estiver, estivermos, estiverdes, estiverem

Imperative: está, estai

fazer

Present: faço, fazes, faz, fazemos, fazeis, fazem

Future: farei, farás, fará, faremos, fareis, farão

Preterite: fiz, fizeste, fez, fizemos, fizestes, fizeram

Pluperfect: fizera, fizeras, fizera, fizéramos, fizéreis, fizeram

Present subjunctive: faça, faças, faça, façamos, façais, façam
Imperfect subjunctive: fizesse, fizesses, fizesse, fizéssemos, fizésseis, fizessem
Future subjunctive: fizer, fizeres, fizer, fizermos, fizerdes, fizerem
Conditional: faria, farias, faria, faríamos, faríeis, fariam
Present participle: fazendo
Past participle: feito
Imperative: faz(e), fazei

frigir
Present: frijo, freges, frege, frigimos, frigis, fregem
Present subjunctive: frija, frijas, frija, frijamos, frijais, frijam
Imperative: frege, frigi

ir
Present: vou, vais, vai, vamos, ides, vão
Imperfect: ia, ias, ia, íamos, íeis, iam
Preterite: fui, foste, foi, fomos, fostes, foram
Pluperfect: fora, foras, fora, fôramos, fôreis, foram
Present subjunctive: vá, vás, vá, vamos, vades, vão
Imperfect subjunctive: fosse, fosses, fosse, fôssemos, fôsseis, fossem
Future subjunctive: for, fores, for, formos, fordes, forem
Present participle: indo
Past participle: ido
Imperative: vai, ide

haver
Present: hei, hás, há, hemos/havemos, haveis/heis, hão
Preterite: houve, houveste, houve, houvemos, houvestes, houveram
Pluperfect: houvera, houveras, houvera, houvéramos, houvéreis, houveram
Present subjunctive: haja, hajas, haja, hajamos, hajais, hajam
Imperfect subjunctive: houvesse, houvesses, houvesse, houvéssemos, houvésseis, houvessem
Future subjunctive: houver, houveres, houver, houvermos, houverdes, houverem
Imperative: há, havei

ler
Present: leio, lês, lê, lemos, ledes, lêem
Imperfect: lia, lias, lia, liamos, líeis, liam
Preterite: li, leste, leu, lemos, lestes, leram
Pluperfect: lera, leras, lera, lêramos, lêreis, leram

Present subjunctive: leia, leias, leia, leiamos, leiais, leiam
Imperfect subjunctive: lesse, lesses, lesse, lêssemos, lêsseis, lessem
Future subjunctive: ler, leres, ler, lermos, lerdes, lerem
Present participle: lendo
Past participle: lido
Imperative: lê, lede
Similarly: crer

odiar
Present: odeio, odeias, odeia, odiamos, odiais, odeiam
Present subjunctive: odeie, odeies, odeie, odiemos, odieis, odeiem
Imperative: odeia, odiai
Similarly: incendiar

ouvir
Present: ouço (*P also*: oiça), ouves, ouve, ouvimos, ouvis, ouvem
Present subjunctive: ouça, ouças, ouça, ouçamos, ouçais, ouçam (*P also*: oiça, oiças, oiça, oiçamos, oiçais, oiçam)

pedir
Present: peço, pedes, pede, pedimos, pedis, pedem
Present subjunctive: peça, peças, peça, peçamos, peçais, peçam
Similarly: despedir, impedir, medir

perder
Present: perco, perdes, perde, perdemos, perdeis, perdem
Present subjunctive: perca, percas, perca, percamos, percais, percam

poder
Present: posso, podes, pode, podemos, podeis, podem
Preterite: pude, pudeste, pôde, pudemos, pudestes, puderam
Pluperfect: pudera, puderas, pudera, pudéramos, pudéreis, puderam
Present subjunctive: possa, possas, possa, possamos, possais, possam
Imperfect subjunctive: pudesse, pudesses, pudesse, pudéssemos, pudésseis, pudessem
Future subjunctive: puder, puderes, puder, pudermos, puderdes, puderem

polir
Present: pulo, pules, pule, polimos, polis, pulem
Present subjunctive: pula, pulas, pula, pulamos, pulais, pulam
Imperative: pule, poli

pôr
Present: ponho, pões, põe, pomos, pondes, põem

Future: porei, porás, porá, poremos, poreis, porão
Imperfect: punha, punhas, punha, púnhamos, púnheis, punham
Preterite: pus, puseste, pôs, pusemos, pusestes, puseram
Pluperfect: pusera, puseras, pusera, puséramos, puséreis, puseram
Present subjunctive: ponha, ponhas, ponha, ponhamos, ponhais, ponham
Imperfect subjunctive: pusesse, pusesses, pusesse, puséssemos, pusésseis, pusessem
Future subjunctive: puser, puseres, puser, pusermos, puserdes, puserem
Conditional: poria, porias, poria, poríamos, poríeis, poriam
Present participle: pondo
Past participle: posto
Imperative: põe, ponde
Similarly: compor, depor, dispor, opor, supor etc

prover
Present: provejo, provês, provê, provemos, provedes, provêem
Present subjunctive: proveja, provejas, proveja, provejamos, provejais, provejam
Imperative: provê, provede

querer
Present: quero, queres, quer, queremos, quereis, querem
Preterite: quis, quiseste, quis, quisemos, quisestes, quiseram
Pluperfect: quisera, quiseras, quisera, quiséramos, quiséreis, quiseram
Present subjunctive: queira, queiras, queira, queiramos, queirais, queiram
Imperfect subjunctive: quisesse, quisesses, quisesse, quiséssemos, quisésseis, quisessem
Future subjunctive: quiser, quiseres, quiser, quisermos, quiserdes, quiserem
Imperative: quer, querei

requerer
Present: requeiro, requeres, requer, requeremos, requereis, requerem
Present subjunctive: requeira, requeiras, requeira, requeiramos, requeirais, requeiram
Imperative: requer, requerei

rir
Present: rio, ris, ri, rimos, rides, riem
Present subjunctive: ria, rias, ria, riamos, riais, riam
Imperative: ri, ride
Similarly: sorrir

saber
Present: sei, sabes, sabe, sabemos, sabeis, sabem
Preterite: soube, soubeste, soube, soubemos, soubestes, souberam
Pluperfect: soubera, souberas, soubera, soubéramos, soubéreis, souberam
Present subjunctive: saiba, saibas, saiba, saibamos, saibais, saibam
Imperfect subjunctive: soubesse, soubesses, soubesse, soubéssemos, soubésseis, soubessem
Future subjunctive: souber, souberes, souber, soubermos, souberdes, souberem
Imperative: sabe, sabei

ser
Present: sou, és, é, somos, sois, são
Imperfect: era, eras, era, éramos, éreis, eram
Preterite: fui, foste, foi, fomos, fostes, foram
Pluperfect: fora, foras, fora, fôramos, fôreis, foram
Present subjunctive: seja, sejas, seja, sejamos, sejais, sejam
Imperfect subjunctive: fosse, fosses, fosse, fôssemos, fôsseis, fossem
Future subjunctive: for, fores, for, formos, fordes, forem
Present participle: sendo
Past participle: sido
Imperative: sê, sede

ter
Present: tenho, tens, tem, temos, tendes, têm
Imperfect: tinha, tinhas, tinha, tinhamos, tinheis, tinham
Preterite: tive, tiveste, teve, tivemos, tivestes, tiveram
Pluperfect: tivera, tiveras, tivera, tivéramos, tivéreis, tiveram
Present subjunctive: tenha, tenhas, tenha, tenhamos, tenhais, tenham
Imperfect subjunctive: tivesse, tivesses, tivesse, tivéssemos, tivésseis, tivessem
Future subjunctive: tiver, tiveres, tiver, tivermos, tiverdes, tiverem
Present participle: tendo
Past participle: tido
Imperative: tem, tende

trazer
Present: trago, trazes, traz, trazemos, trazeis, trazem
Future: trarei, trarás, trará, traremos, trareis, trarão
Preterite: trouxe, trouxeste, trouxe, trouxemos, trouxestes, trouxeram

Pluperfect: trouxera, trouxeras, trouxera, trouxéramos, trouxéreis, trouxeram

Present subjunctive: traga, tragas, traga, tragamos, tragais, tragam

Imperfect subjunctive: trouxesse, trouxesses, trouxesse, trouxéssemos, trouxésseis, trouxessem

Future subjunctive: trouxer, trouxeres, trouxer, trouxermos, trouxerdes, trouxerem

Conditional: traria, trarias, traria, trariamos, trarieis, trariam

Imperative: traze, trazei

valer

Present: valho, vales, vale, valemos, valeis, valem

Present subjunctive: valha, valhas, valha, valhamos, valhais, valham

ver

Present: vejo, vês, vê, vemos, vedes, vêem

Imperfect: via, vias, via, viamos, vieis, viam

Preterite: vi, viste, viu, vimos, vistes, viram

Pluperfect: vira, viras, vira, viramos, vireis, viram

Present subjunctive: veja, vejas, veja, vejamos, vejais, vejam

Imperfect subjunctive: visse, visses, visse, vissemos, visseis, vissem

Future subjunctive: vir, vires, vir, virmos, virdes, virem

Present participle: vendo

Past participle: visto

Imperative: vê, vede

vir

Present: venho, vens, vem, vimos, vindes, vêm

Imperfect: vinha, vinhas, vinha, vinhamos, vinheis, vinham

Preterite: vim, vieste, veio, viemos, viestes, vieram

Pluperfect: viera, vieras, viera, viéramos, viéreis, vieram

Present subjunctive: venha, venhas, venha, venhamos, venhais, venham

Imperfect subjunctive: viesse, viesses, viesse, viéssemos, viésseis, viessem

Future subjunctive: vier, vieres, vier, viermos, vierdes, vierem

Present participle: vindo

Past participle: vindo

Imperative: vem, vinde